MANAGEMENT

Randall B. Dunham
University of Wisconsin–Madison

Jon L. Pierce
University of Minnesota–Duluth

SCOTT, FORESMAN AND COMPANY
Glenview, Illinois   London, England

To the people who make life worth managing: Susanne, Greg, and Elizabeth
R.B.D.

To four beautiful people: Tanya, Eric, Sarah, and Candy—family and friends
J.L.P.

Literary and photo credits begin on page C1, constituting a legal extension of the copyright page.

Library of Congress Cataloging-in-Publication Data

Dunham, Randall B.
  Management/Randall B. Dunham, Jon L. Pierce.
    p.   cm.
  Bibliography
  Includes index.
  ISBN 0-673-39801-3
  1. Management.   I. Pierce, Jon L. (Jon Lepley)   II. Title.
HD31.D839 1989   88-29678
658.4—dc19   CIP

1 2 3 4 5 6 - VHJ - 93 92 91 90 89 88

Preface

During the relatively uncomplicated 1950s, 1960s, and even early 1970s, many organizations and their managers flourished despite often haphazard approaches to managing. In the 1980s, the environments in which organizations operate grew vastly more complex and competitive. Widespread mergers and acquisitions became commonplace. International competition threatened the existence of many organizations. Today, mistakes seem to be magnified by the turbulence surrounding organizations. Muddling through, or "winging it," is now likely to result in a manager's—if not an organization's—ultimate decline.

Significant criticism that was leveled at American organizations during the 1980s focused on lack of innovation, failure to develop organizational human resources, poor product quality, and stunted productivity. Organizational leaders, such as Carl Icahn, T. Boone Pickens, and H. Ross Perot, attributed many of these problems to poor management. Managerial carelessness from the preceding decades, they argued, not only blunted many organizations' competitive edge but dimmed the esteem they once held in the eyes of the world.

The 1990s mark a turning point for American organizations and their managers. Many are beginning to recognize the need for a new style of management and a new breed of manager. Managers question their own purpose, their organization's structure, and their leaders' strategies. They also acknowledge the importance of organizational culture. Organization leaders smart enough to respond to these issues have initiated significant efforts to professionalize their management practices.

Organizations must take care, however, to be certain that their efforts are well directed. Studies of American organizations have indicated that the speed with which managers were promoted in American organizations during the 1950s, 1960s, and 1970s was often influenced by the amount of time managers spent socializing and politicking with outsiders. Organizations that employ today's rising stars should heed recent studies indicating that managers who contribute the most to an organization's effectiveness (and, therefore, success) are those who are expert at planning, organizing, directing, and controlling. The message from the research is the same as that from Icahn, Pickens, and Perot. Organizations must encourage, nurture, and reward these productive activities rather than the more glamorous social and political activities of the fast-tracking, suave—but less effective—managers or be prepared to wither and die.

This book reveals the aspects of the management process that you must learn to become an effective manager. In our discussion, we have kept in mind the decades-old dilemma of whether to consider management a science or an art. We believe that effective management is both a science and an art. It requires both the skillful *and* the passionate application of scientific knowledge about organizations. Indeed, the words *systematic* and *intuition* appear repeatedly throughout the information, which is designed both to develop the knowledge and skills required for effective management and to stimulate the analytical thinking required to determine when and how to use such knowledge and skills.

We do not believe that there is a single and universally applicable road to organizational effectiveness. We do, however, believe that our book can help you become proficient at thinking about, diagnosing, and reacting to organizational events.

Learning about and practicing management should be stimulating, challenging, and enjoyable. By increasing your knowledge, you increase your potential as a manager. We want you to enter into the learning process wholeheartedly; therefore, we have incorporated a variety of features into this book and the accompanying supplements to communicate information about management, to stimulate your interest in the material, and to encourage you to look forward to using this information in your own management career.

Organization of the Book

This book is divided into six parts, each of which examines one component of the management field. At the beginning of each part, we present a profile of a manager who has found a unique way to claim success.

Part 1 explores the management process and the managers who engage in it. This part introduces the four functions that define the job of management: planning, organizing, directing, and controlling. It also examines the external and internal environments in which organizations either thrive or fail. This part looks at how managers behave in organizations and how knowledge about management and the practice of managing have evolved into their current states.

Part 2 deals with the first major management function—planning. It explores the critical aspects of planning, such as decision making, and describes managers' planning activities. This part also presents the tools and techniques that help managers plan more effectively. Part 2 also discusses the ways in which managers develop both the short-term and the long-term strategic plans they need to guide their organization to success.

Part 3 concerns the second major management function—organizing. It describes how managers put together the building blocks of an organization—it focuses on the ways in which managers structure and design organizations and how they assign authority.

Part 4 deals with the third major management function—directing. It shows how important people are to an organization. Understanding people and the ways in which they interact helps managers motivate, lead, and effectively utilize this valuable organizational human resource.

Part 5 examines the controlling function, concentrating on organizational effectiveness. It explores the ways in which managers can measure and enhance organizational effectiveness through controlling organizations—often by developing and changing them as necessary.

Part 6 looks at special topics that are important to contemporary managers. It discusses the systems used to manage the information an organization needs to operate effectively. Part 6 also examines the planning, organizing, directing, and controlling functions that produce goods and services. This part also explores a topic of growing importance—international management. The next topic in this part—entrepreneurship and intrapreneurship—deals with individuals who create new organizational opportunities and unique methods of achieving success. The final topic in this part attempts to help you manage the careers of organization members more effectively and to help you plan and develop your own career.

Chapter Contents and Special Features

Each chapter begins with an outline of its major topics and a list of learning objectives and ends with a summary of key terms, a set of issues for review and discussion, and a list of suggested readings. Chapters 1 through 20 also end with a case study that describes an organizational problem situation for you to analyze and resolve using information from the chapter. Between these openings and closings you will encounter a management text enhanced by special features to make these facts come alive. The following are a few samples from these features and some of the issues they present.

Learning Objectives

The objectives indicate areas of special importance to help you read each chapter effectively. By the time you have completed each chapter, you should be able to review and respond easily to its learning objectives. The following are a few of the approximately 200 objectives that appear in the book:

- Identify four tactics that managers can use to increase their power over the task environment. (Chapter 2)
- Discuss steps managers can take to encourage ethical behavior in organizations. (Chapter 4)
- Discuss the reasons for strategic planning in both small and not-for-profit organizations. (Chapter 9)
- Describe how people use and abuse power. (Chapter 15)
- Identify the five primary reasons change does and should occur in organizations. (Chapter 20)

A Closer Look

Chapters 1 through 20 each contains two special features, entitled "A Closer Look," that describe real-world events relating to text material. Each Closer Look allows you to see how a real organization has handled a managerial issue discussed in the chapter. Here are summarized excerpts from two of the forty Closer Looks:

- *The Coming of the Network Organizations:* A new corporate look is emerging. Recently, a company called Ocean Pacific Sunwear generated $15 million in sales with only 67 employees; Electronic Arts, a software firm, $20 million in revenues with 75 employees; and Lewis Galoob Toys Inc., over $58 million in sales with just 115 employees. None of these organizations had even a single employee involved in the manufacturing of products. So how could these companies perform that way? By using the newest corporate structure . . . (Chapter 12)

- *The High Cost of Terminating Employees:* What does singer Diana Ross have in common with insurance broker Larry W. Buck? Both have been embroiled in an increasingly common type of lawsuit brought by people involving terminated employment. Larry Buck felt that he was fired from his job without warning. When he found it difficult to get another job in the insurance industry, he decided to hire a private investigator to find out why. The case went all the way to the U.S. Supreme Court, and his former employers were forced to pay $605,000 in lost wages, and other damages, plus a $1.3 million penalty. So, how can organizations terminate employees without being sued? The answer lies . . . (Chapter 17)

Interviews

Each chapter in the first five parts presents an interview with a person uniquely qualified to answer questions often asked by management students. Here are summarized excerpts from two of those twenty question-and-answer sessions:

- *Steven B. Fink* (author of the book *Crisis Management: Planning for the Inevitable*): In a survey of Fortune 500 CEOs, 89 percent agreed that a crisis in business is as inevitable as death and taxes, but fully 50 percent admitted that they or their companies did not have a written crisis-management plan in place. The best way to plan for a crisis is . . . (Chapter 6)

- *Phyllis A. Mason* (professor at Baruch College): Strategic planning, like anything else, can be done well or badly. It has certainly been demonstrated that organizations that plan well—such as IBM and General Electric—have reaped benefits from that planning. Organizations that are only interested in paying lip service to strategic planning probably . . . (Chapter 9)

In Review

A brief summary of the major issues discussed in each chapter helps organize the material and places it in context.

Key Terms

At the end of each chapter is a list of important terms. After reading the chapter, you should be able to scan the list and quickly define each key term. If you are unsure of the meaning of any term, check its definition in the glossary of approximately 700 terms at the end of the book. The lists include such crucial management terms as *boundary spanning* (Chapter 2), *organizational culture* (Chapter 3), *strategic management* (Chapter 9), *self-designing organization* (Chapter 12), *motivation* (Chapter 14), *communication channels* (Chapter 15), and *sociotechnical changes* (Chapter 20).

Issues for Review and Discussion

After you have read each chapter and have studied its features, you should look at the end-of-chapter issues for review and discussion, which are designed to help you assess your mastery of the material. The following are a few samples of the approximately 200 discussion questions and exercises that appear in the book:

- What is the relationship between planning and decision making? (Chapter 6)
- Identify the assets and liabilities associated with group decision making. (Chapter 7)
- Use PERT (Program Evaluation and Review Technique) to outline a plan for writing a term paper. (Chapter 8)
- Define influence, authority, and power and explain why organizations must manage each. (Chapter 11)
- Explain why the goal "I'm going to do my best" is not effective for motivating high performance. (Chapter 14)
- What are substitutes for leadership? What are neutralizers? Give an example of each. (Chapter 16)
- What are some of the negative (dysfunctional) features associated with organizational control features? (Chapter 19)

Suggested Readings

The end of each chapter also provides a list of suggested readings from a wide variety of sources, including books (such as *Organizational Culture and Leadership, Coffin Nails and Corporate Strategies*, and *Thriving on Chaos*), academic journals, business publications (such as *Business Week, The Wall Street Journal*, and *Fortune*), and articles from the popular press. Some are the original sources used in a particularly important part of the chapter; others expand on a critical issue raised in the text. Sometimes a suggested reading provides an organizational application of concepts explored in the chapter. We have chosen these readings to help you explore issues of interest and to give you an overview of the material being read by contemporary managers.

Cases

At the end of each of the first twenty chapters, you will find a case about one of a group of organizations as diverse as Hammond General Hospital, AgBanCorporation, Xerox Corporation, and the River City Library. Each case informs you about an organization and asks you to apply the knowledge you have acquired from reading the chapter. The following is a summarized excerpt from a case involving Central South Music Sales:

> *Central South Music Sales, Inc., (CSM) was formed in 1970 by Randy Davidson, Chuck Adams, and J. P. Bennett, all former employees of a recently failed record distributor. Armed with their knowledge of good customers and warehouse operations, they established CSM as a "one stop" record distributor handling a full line of all record labels. Sales were made directly to smaller record stores that were either too small to buy directly from the labels' branch distribution warehouses or who found it more convenient to deal with one source for all of their records. By 1980, the company had twenty-three stores. CSM stocked over 50,000 titles in all available formats. (Chapter 2)*

This case then provides additional information about the company—including its growth, status, and current subsidiaries—and concludes with a brief series of questions that draws on what you have learned from the chapter.

Instructional Materials

No contemporary approach to teaching is complete unless it incorporates rapidly developing modern technology. We have assembled a total package that capitalizes on these new technologies to bring teachers and students the most stimulating and rewarding learning experience possible. We believe that just as there is no one best way to manage an organization, there is no one best way to manage a course about managing organizations; thus, these additional instructional materials offer teachers and students a vast array of choices. This section briefly describes the many options available for testing, grading, and recordkeeping; for class design, planning, and teaching; for computerized learning; and for student-directed study.

Testing, Grading, and Recordkeeping

A printed test bank to accompany the text contains approximately 100 assorted multiple-choice, true/false, completion, matching, and essay questions for each chapter. All of these questions are also available in computerized format, enabling teachers to select, edit, and even create additional items (if desired) for easy construction of personalized tests. Additional computerized tools—grades, including routines for scheduling classes, keeping grades, and determining final grades—are also available.

These resources are designed both to facilitate effective class management and to reduce the amount of time required for administrative chores.

Instructor's Resource Manual (IRM)

Recognizing that these additional instructional materials comprise a large and varied package with many potential uses, we have created the *Instructor's Resource Manual* to help teachers and students use the package without being overwhelmed by it. No ordinary instructor's manual, our IRM is a complete class design, planning, and teaching aid. It suggests a variety of teaching strategies, including alternative combinations of materials and syllabi for both quarter and semester schedules.

The IRM is complete and detailed; it provides an outline and overview of each text chapter and answers to all learning objectives and issues for review and discussion. The IRM also presents questions to stimulate discussion of the Closer Looks that appear in each chapter, and it offers suggested answers. The manual also answers the case study questions in text Chapters 1–20, and it provides additional questions and answers for each case. An additional case, with questions and suggested answers, is also presented for Chapters 1–20 in the IRM. For Chapters 21–25, the IRM contains two cases per chapter, with questions and suggested answers.

We are particularly proud of the manual's unique items. There are two original experiential exercises per chapter, which enliven the book's material in a personal and interesting fashion. Four essays on high-interest topics can be used as the bases of lectures or can be copied and distributed in class.

Color Acetates

A set of approximately 150 full-color acetates is available to adopters of *Management*. Some of these are reprints of important tables and artwork from the book; others have been created to further enrich the classroom experience.

Computerized Teaching Tools

We have developed three innovative computerized packages to enhance the management course. Together, these three tools provide previously unavailable opportunities for learning about the realities of management. Instructions and suggestions for classroom use of these computerized teaching aids are contained in the IRM.

Computer-Assisted Review and Tutorial (CART) CART modules are designed to help you evaluate your mastery of the text material. Chapter by chapter, CARTs lead you through multiple-choice, true/false, and completion questions about key issues. When you answer a question correctly, your response is reinforced. When you answer incorrectly, you are given a tutorial that briefly explains the issue and, when necessary, guides you to the specific part of the text that covers that issue.

Self-assessments   You are likely to learn better when you have a personal interest in the material you are studying. You also learn better when you receive immediate feedback. Our self-assessment exercises provide both. After answering a series of questions about such issues as job satisfaction, leadership style, stress, and receptivity to change, you are immediately given an on-screen image and a computer printout of your personal profile and its comparison to national and class norms. As noted in the IRM, the printed profiles are readily integrated into classroom discussion.

Computerized Information Retrieval System (CIRS)   Many students are stimulated by their management courses and wish to pursue issues from them in greater depth. An extremely easy-to-use database, the CIRS allows you to gather reference and abstract information from recent key management journals. Identifying an article on a topic and obtaining a summary of its content is as simple as typing your topic of interest. Retrieval on-screen or in printed form is quick and efficient.

New teaching technologies take a lot of time to develop and can be difficult to use. We have spent our time developing state-of-the-art technologies that will not intimidate you. Best of all, the instructional materials described to this point are provided to adopters free of charge, because we are committed to improving the quality of management education and want to make available every tool possible to those who are also committed to this end.

Compatible Resources

Four additional resources are available for purchase from Scott, Foresman. One of these is the *Student's Resource Manual* designed specifically for this book. Others were developed by people with whom we have collaborated.

Student's Resource Manual   More than just a "study guide," the *Student's Resource Manual* provides pretests and posttests, along with an answer key, for each chapter. "Concepts-at-a-Glance" and other techniques help you master key material, with an emphasis on making the process enjoyable. For example, rather than just providing drill in rote recall, crossword puzzles help make key terms familiar.

A Management Simulation   Developed by Charles S. (Steve) White, University of Tennessee at Chattanooga, this decision-making game illustrates the complexities of managing a real organization. In this easy-to-use computerized simulation, students run a computer printer company (Allison Industries) in competition with other computer printer companies. The challenge is to gather and evaluate data and make decisions (as individuals or as part of a team). Success or failure depends on the management decisions that are made.

Interactive Cases in Management   Dennis Moberg and Dave Caldwell, Santa Clara University, have developed a wonderful set of computerized interactive cases that allow users to play the role of manager within an organization. As day-to-day decisions are made, the cases unfold quickly and realistically, illustrating the impact of various management strategies. These interactive cases concentrate on intraorganizational events. They reveal that once decisions are made, their implications can be significant and long-lasting.

Managerial Reality: Balancing Techniques, Practice, and Values   This book, by Peter J. Frost and Vance F. Mitchell of the University of British Columbia and Walter R. Nord of Washington University, presents a realistic view of the balancing act required of contemporary managers, making clear that technique alone is not enough for organizational success. The strength of this book is that it stimulates serious, meaningful thought about the delicate issues that managers face.

Acknowledgments

Substantial contributions to the design, development, and preparation of this book were made by a wide range of people. We have listened, and we have learned from each of them.

The basic design of this book and its accompanying resource materials was influenced substantially by 200 teachers of management courses who responded in detail to a survey concerning the design of the course and teaching tools. To these colleagues, we extend our heartfelt thanks. They helped us identify topics of special interest to contemporary managers, which we address in the last five chapters. Four of these chapters were prepared by specialists, and we are grateful to them: Thomas Duff of the University of Minnesota-Duluth, management information systems (MIS); Peter J. Billington of Northeastern University, operations management; Heidi Vernon-Wortzel of Northeastern University, international management; and Ann Cope in consultation with Gene Dalton of Brigham Young University, careers.

To help students analyze the complexities of managing today's organizations from a variety of perspectives, we interviewed a group of important organizational experts. We thank them for these interviews, all of which appear in the book.

We recognize the importance of cases for a management text, and Philip C. Fisher of the University of South Dakota provided the expertise needed to locate and refine them for each chapter of the book and the *Instructor's Resource Manual*. We enjoyed working with Phil and greatly appreciate his dedication. We also are grateful to the Midwest Society for Case Research (MSCR), which gave Phil substantial assistance in supplying cases for Chapters 3, 4, 7, 8, 9, 15, and 17, as well as many that appear in the IRM. We would also like to thank the many authors of the cases used in the book.

Each chapter in this book has gone through a number of versions. We especially appreciate the efforts of six reviewers who went beyond the call of duty, each reviewing chapters in several stages: Karen A. Brown, Seattle University; Lee G. Caldwell, University of Utah; David A. Cowan, Notre Dame University; David B. Greenberger, The Ohio State University; Robert F. Pethia, Western Kentucky University; and Roger Volkema, George Mason University. We also thank the following people, who each reviewed portions of the text:

Daniel Baugher	*Pace University*
William D. Biggs	*Beaver College*
Allen Bluedorn	*University of Missouri*
Kenneth J. Buck	*Oregon State University*
Jane Burman-Holtom	*University of Oklahoma*
Thomas M. Calero	*Illinois Institute of Technology*
David J. Cherrington	*Brigham Young University*
Raymond Cook	*University of Texas, Austin*
Philip C. Fisher	*University of South Dakota*
Donald G. Gardner	*University of Colorado*
Roger Griffeth	*Louisiana State University*
Joyce Henson	*St. Peters College*
Russ Holloman	*Augusta College*
William Holstein	*SUNY at Albany*
Bruce H. Johnson	*Gustavus Adolphus College*
Ki Hee Kim	*William Peterson College*
Andrew Luzi	*University of Oklahoma*
Joseph W. McGuire	*University of California, Irvine*
Gus Manoochehri	*California State University, Fullerton*
Lyman W. Porter	*University of California, Irvine*
Samuel Rabinowitz	*Rutgers University, Camden*
Joseph C. Schabacker	*Arizona State University*
Paul L. Wilkens	*Florida State University*
Charles R. Williams	*Oklahoma State University*

We would like to thank individuals and organizations for contributing to the teaching package, which, although not contained within the pages of this textbook, is linked closely to its use: Boeing Computer Services for the program Scholar/Teach, which was used to develop and present the computer-assisted review and tutorial modules; AskSam Systems for the database program used in the computerized information and retrieval system; Jean A. Grube, University of Wisconsin, for the modules for the CARTs; Lillian Huang, with consultation from David Dickens, University of Wisconsin, for the programming for the computerized self-assessments created for this text; Cynthia Lengnick-Hall, University of Minnesota-Duluth, for the test bank and contributions to the *Instructor's Resource*

Manual; and Loren Kuzuhara, University of Wisconsin, for the IRM. We cannot overstate the importance of their contributions.

A number of individuals at Scott, Foresman were instrumental in the creation and development of this project. Acquisitions editor Alexander Greene convinced us that this teaching package was needed and persuaded us to create it. James R. Sitlington, Jr., editorial vice-president, kept the project moving and shared our vision for a quality, innovative package. Shelley E. Roth and Jane Steinmann, developmental editors, provided the professional touch needed to refine our reader-friendly package. Project editor Debra DeBord made sure we had the right words in the right places, and design manager Debbie Costello created the book's design. Marketing manager Mary Jo Kovach worked with us throughout the development of the book to assure that we were attuned to the needs of the marketplace. To all of these people, we are greatly indebted.

Manuscript preparation and secretarial help was provided at the University of Minnesota-Duluth by Susan E. Morgan, Connie J. Johnson, and Jean A. Jacobson. These services were offered at the University of Wisconsin by Jean Trager and Susan M. Kasper. Thanks for the help.

In closing, we would like to express our sincere gratitude to Randi K. Huntsman, who assisted in the preparation of this package from beginning to end. Without her help, this book would never have happened. Her help in writing, coordinating, and producing these materials was invaluable.

R.B.D.
J.L.P.

Contents

PART 5   *Controlling*   640

5.9

CHAPTER 18   *Organizational Effectiveness*   644

CHAPTER 19   *Control Methods and Their Effects*   678

CHAPTER 20 *Organizational Change and Development* 714

PART 1

An Introduction to Management

Jack Welch

"Hero or villian? Corporate rejuvenator or destructive wheeler-dealer?"[1] Jack Welch, the top executive at General Electric, is described as a tyrant as well as a man who has established a strong esprit de corps among the top management group. He has been called "Mad Jack"; many current and former employees refer to him as "Neutron Jack," since he has eliminated nearly a quarter of all the jobs at GE.[2] Perceived as a tough guy, managing by fear and intimidation, Welch has lost the dedication of thousands of people, and yet he has been branded as a financial wizard and put into the same league as the J. P. Morgans of the American business world.[3]

Jack Welch rose to the top position at GE in 1981. Since that time he has taken a number of large and bold steps in an effort to change the organization. GE has trimmed its payroll by more than 100,000. Layers in GE's hierarchy have been removed, and middle managers who are not trained in tomorrow's technology continually fall by the wayside. Many of the corporation's less-profitable operations have been sold, there have been bold experiments with factory automation, and resources have been shifted from stodgy manufacturing to high technology and fast-growing services. GE has moved out of a number of long-standing business domains, such as television, and into investment banking, broadcasting, and high-tech manufacturing. Not only has Welch changed GE's corporate strategy, he has revamped the organization's structure, realigned GE's corporate culture, and watched corporate revenues grow by 48 percent.

Accompanying the change in GE's business units, Welch has worked at making GE less bureaucratic. He has delegated authority, pushing it to lower levels; he has made the organization's structure wider and flatter by eliminating levels in the hierarchy; and he has adopted an informal and rigorous management style. In order to achieve integration among the organization's many business units, Welch has attempted to develop a team-oriented corporate culture. Camraderie and communication are emphasized, almost to the extreme.

> *He has been branded as a financial wizard. . . .*

Today GE's internal environment has been characterized as aggressive, argumentative, confrontational, tough, and iconoclastic. This is a far cry from GE's long-time history of being formal and gentlemanly. GE's internal environment used to be stable; today it is aggressively and boldly on the move. Whether or not it is moving in the right direction is open to debate. Some believe that instead of getting larger and larger, GE should become a "smaller, more focused, nimbler entity."[5]

During the 1950s, GE was one of the leaders in moving toward profit centers. Today Welch deals directly with the heads of GE's profit centers, limiting his involvement in the management of their operations to strategic and important personnel issues. It appears to be Welch's belief that the business unit directors should be left alone to run their divisions. He wants his managers to feel as though they own their operations, and therefore he encourages them to operate as entrepreneurs instead of seeing themselves as being on someone's payroll.[6] As long as they meet their financial targets, he does not intervene and heads do not roll. Since becoming CEO, he has installed eleven new managers at GE's fourteen business units.

A new breed of managers appears to stand at the core of Welch's GE management system. The development of a team system characterized by communication, candor, and trust seems to be critical. A measured amount of turmoil is seen as desirable, since turmoil is intended to challenge the organization and its management team, keeping them finely honed and on the winning edge. Strong performers are pushed to become stronger; the term *winaholics* is being used to characterize Welch's management team.[7]

Much of Welch's management philosophy appears to be built on the utilization of the organization's human resources. His vision suggests that an organization that is tightly controlled stifles individuality. Welch's management style calls for opening up the organization. He encourages people to take initiative and push themselves to develop better skills and to achieve. He pushes people hard, expects accomplishment and high performance, and shows little patience for those who do not measure up.

Welch has spent his entire career at GE. After receiving a Ph.D. in chemical engineering at the University of Illinois, he went to work in GE's plastics business. At age forty-five, he became GE's youngest CEO. His goal for GE is to make it number one or number two in every business in which it is engaged. He wants GE "to become the most competitive business enterprise in the world," and to be the most valuable corporation in terms of market capitalization.[8] Toward this end, Welch has changed the emphasis of the company and is continually in the process of buying and selling businesses. GE is in such businesses as aircraft engines, major appliances, medical systems, plastics, investment banking, and broadcasting.

In Welch's estimation, a good manager is a person with a vision and the ability to articulate that vision to the entire business unit while listening through shared discussion. A good manager is someone who can "relentlessly drive implementation of that vision to a successful conclusion."[9] The successful manager who is going to survive as a part of Welch's team must be a self-starter, a visionary, and an orchestrator of others. The challenge for Welch is to be able to develop the organizational climate in which such independent managers can be melded into a strong top-management team.

Four times a year, the fourteen business leaders, the heads of corporate staff, and the CEO meet and discuss their business plans. It is a time for everyone to be an active participant. Challenging, criticizing, and offering constructive suggestions to further each business plan is the norm. It is through this type of confrontation, turmoil, tension, and conflict that Welch believes GE will find its advantage.[10]

While it has been claimed that Welch has built a strong team at the top, this strength may not have filtered down through the lower levels of the management hierarchy. In fact, disenchantment and dissatisfaction appear to be commonplace. Stress is leading to the burnout of many of GE's employees. According to Welch, he wants employees to see GE as a place where they will find a challenge, as a place where a worker who seeks an opportunity to develop his or her skills will find it. That is what Welch's management philosophy has to offer. It is a work environment that is clearly not designed for everyone, "yet GE can be enormously exciting for those in the right place or attuned to the Welch mentality."[11]

1. Mitchell and Dobrzynski, 92.
2. Petre, Elliott, and Perry.
3. Mitchell and Dobrzynski.
4. Mitchell and Dobrzynski.
5. Mitchell and Dobrzynski, 94.
6. Petre, Elliott, and Perry.
7. Mitchell and Dobrzynski.
8. Mitchell and Dobrzynski, 94.
9. Mitchell and Dobrzynski, 96.
10. *Ibid.*
11. Petre, Elliott, and Perry.

Source: P. Petre with M. A. Elliott and N. J. Perry (7 July 1986), What Welch has wrought at GE, *Fortune*, 43–47; R. Mitchell with J. H. Dobrzynski (14 December 1987), Jack Welch: How good a manager? *Business Week*, 92–96, 98, 102–3.

The Nature of Management

Student Learning Objectives

After reading this chapter, you should be able to:

1. Define management and what managers do.
2. Understand the characteristics of organizations.
3. Distinguish between the sociological and process perspectives on management.
4. Discuss some of the categories of managers.
5. Identify variations in the ways managers execute the management process.
6. Specify the skills that managers need.
7. Give six reasons organizations need managers.
8. Distinguish between management as a process and management as a set of roles.

*T*hink for a moment about the organizations you have belonged to. Think about the types of management systems you have seen. You probably have seen more systems than you realize—at your high school, at the places where you have held jobs, at your place of worship, at your parents' places of work, at your college, and probably at many other places. Did you always understand why these organizations were managed as they were? Did you ever say to yourself, "There must be a better way to run an organization?" In the pages of this book, you will explore management. You will examine the philosophies and practices that guide managers. You will gain insights into *what* works and *why*. Knowledge, understanding, and a systematic approach are the keys to effective management. You will come to understand better the organizational experiences that you have already had, and you will become better prepared to meet the challenge when you are asked to manage.

Management and Organizations

Management in U.S. organizations has received a lot of criticism over the years. Productivity problems, deteriorating plants and machinery, lost ground in research and development, lack of competitive responsiveness at home and abroad, and increases in worker discontent have become symbolic of many of our nation's organizations. Carl Icahn, of Trans World Airlines, for example, has charged that the crises facing U.S. corporations are largely the result of "bad management."[1] In fact, poor management is often cited as a major reason for organizational failure. There are, however, many effective organizations in our society from which one can learn. Effective organizations—be they a local high school, a fast-food restaurant, or a giant international corporation—are characterized by effective communication, strong leadership, appropriate organizational design, productive participation, systematic planning, high-quality decision making, and competent human resource management.

Managers are organization members whose primary responsibilities are to plan, organize, direct, and control organizational resources.

What Management Is

The study of organizational management is relatively young. Consequently, there is no universally accepted language, set of symbols, or theoretical underpinning that managers can use to analyze, understand, explain, or make predictions about the management of organizations. This lack of consensus becomes apparent as soon as one tries to define management. Nearly every manager and writer about management has a favorite way to define the process. Perhaps the best reaction to this diversity is to take it as grist for the mill, to treat the many definitions as a useful variety that add to a manager's stock of knowledge. There is a variety of approaches to the effective management of organizations.

In general, **management** can be defined as the process of planning, organizing, directing, and controlling organizational resources (human, financial, physical, and informational) in the pursuit of organizational goals. **Managers** are organization members who are assigned the primary responsibility of carrying out the management process. As you will discover, there can be many levels of management and many activities that managers must plan for, organize, direct, and control. Among these are the production (operations), marketing, human resource, finance, and accounting functions of an organization (see Chapter 3).

The Nature of Organizations

Fifty years ago, Chester Barnard, the noted expert on management as a science, defined an **organization** as "a system of consciously coordinated activities of two or more persons."[2] This definition is still viable today. An organization is held together by the purposes and goals that its members share. It may own buildings and equipment, but these do not define its nature. An organization is a social system, characterized by relatively enduring interaction patterns that link people to people and people to work as they pursue organizational goals.[3] Take away the interaction patterns in a hospital that link nurses with doctors, doctors with technicians, medical staff members with administrators, and all of these people with the patients they care for, and the essence of the hospital as a health care delivery system vanishes. The buildings and equipment remain, but the organization is gone.

Organizations differ in both degree of permanence and complexity.[4] Each organization also has a distinct structure, goals, norms, boundaries, and internal systems. Each also has a relatively enduring pattern of interaction among those within the organization, an external environment and relationships to it, and a social order. Communities, societies, social movements, families, friendship groups, governmental bodies, and charitable foundations are all organizations. Work organizations are systems that import resources from outside of the organization, convert them into a product or service, and export the results.

Most people use the term *organization* to refer to a legal or registered entity. In this book, organization may bring to mind such corporations as Sears, CBS, and General Motors or such governmental bodies as the Environmental Protection Agency, Congress, or city hall. You may also think of such organizations as the United Way or other charities, police or

FIGURE 1.1   The Work Organization
as an Import-Export System

Imported Resources   The Work Organization   Exported Goods
and Services

fire departments, or school systems. All of these are organizations, but such large, readily identifiable organizations often contain other organizations.

Sometimes it is easy to spot an organization within an organization. Tenneco, for example, is a conglomerate that is actually a collection of individual companies, such as Tenneco Oil Company, Tenneco Realty, Tennessee-American Water Company, Tennessee Apparel Corporation, Tennessee Book Company, Tennessee Fabricating Company, Tennessee Eastman Company, and Tennessee Armature and Electric Company. In many cases, the presence of organizations within organizations is somewhat less formal than Tenneco's serving as the umbrella for other legal or registered organizations. The internal legal division and the accounting department of Tenneco Oil, for example, are complete organizations just as real as Tenneco itself, even though they are less visible to an outside observer. Each has distinct interaction patterns that link people to people and people to work and members who share goals. Each also transforms resources into goods and services.

This book offers information about the management of all organizations, obvious or subtle, large or small. Whether it is a manufacturing organization or a governmental agency, a freestanding corporation or a tiny organization embedded in another, every organization must be managed through planning, organizing, directing, and controlling.

The Management Process

In the previous section, management was defined as a series of processes. The process (or activity) perspective focuses on the *actions* taken by managers. There is also a useful approach, known as the sociological perspective, that defines management according to the *social positions* of organization members.

FIGURE 1.2   *An Organizational Chart*

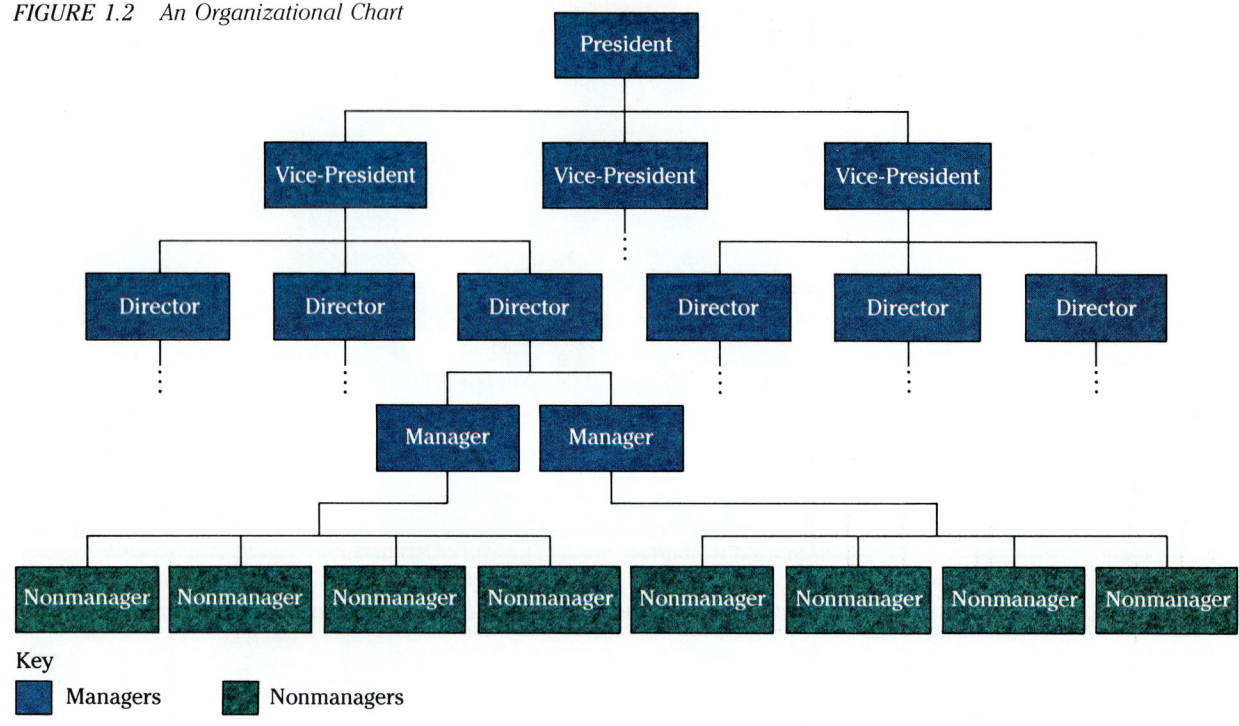

The Sociological Perspective

For many, the word *management* creates an image of a certain *group of individuals* in an organization. From this point of view, there are two kinds of organization members: managers and everybody else. The **sociological perspective,** thus, defines management as the group of organization members that occupies the social position responsible for making sure that an organization achieves its mission (its "reason for being"). As you might expect, these people are called *managers.* The second group of organization members—"everybody else"—consists of workers, employees, laborers, troops, support staff, and technical analysts—*nonmanagers.* An **organizational chart,** such as that shown in Figure 1.2, is a schematic drawing of the positions within an organization. It can be used to distinguish among these social positions. Notice that, in Figure 1.2, the management group spans several different levels and units (departments, sections, and divisions) in the organizational **hierarchy** (that is, its managerial levels of authority and responsibility).

Other factors also distinguish managers from nonmanagers. Managers generally control more power, influence, rewards, status, and responsibility than do nonmanagers. The two groups also have different organizational roles to fill. Managers are often hired, fired, promoted, and demoted according to whether their organization achieves its objectives: sells enough airline tickets, earns enough profits, serves enough hamburgers, and so on. Managers' primary responsibilities are to design, to pursue, and to achieve organizational objectives by working with and through the nonmanagers. Nonmanagers are usually hired to perform specific technical tasks, such as operating machinery, maintaining clerical records, flipping hamburgers, teaching courses, or performing surgery. Their rewards usually are closely tied to how well they apply their technical skills.

The Process Perspective

One of the oldest and most widely adopted definitions of management is the "art of getting things done through people."[5] Mary Parker Follett, a pioneer in the study of management, described it as an activity concerned with the orchestration of people, work, and systems in the pursuit of organizational goals. The way in which managers accomplish this is the basis for the **process perspective.** This book adopts the process perspective to examine the roles, activities, and processes that managers engage in as they plan, organize, direct, and control their organization.

Managing an organization from the process perspective is like conducting a symphony orchestra. An orchestra's overall organizational goal is to play each piece of music flawlessly. The conductor is the orchestra's manager, coaxing the best performance possible from symphony members and coordinating all of the various sections. The conductor's management role is very different from the technical role of individual flutists, clarinetists, violinists, and other musicians. Without the musicians, there would be no orchestra, but without the conductor, the musicians could not coordinate their playing into a harmonious performance. It is the role of every manager to orchestrate organizational effectiveness through the management process.

In 1916, French industrialist Henri Fayol described a "functional approach to management" and suggested that all managers perform similar activities. Whether they are top-level or low-level managers, whether their organization is as small as a hair stylist's shop or as large as the U.S. government, whether they manage a manufacturing organization or health care institution, whether they are in accounting or marketing, all managers must execute a universal set of management processes (see Figure 1.3).[6] Fayol's universal set of management functions included planning, organizing, commanding, coordinating, and controlling.[7]

After Fayol, several theorists, such as Chester Barnard, Ralph C. Davis, and Lyndall Urwick, revised the idea of universal management functions (see Table 1.1).[8] The result is a useful process definition that is popular today. It modifies Fayol's categories into four universal management

TABLE 1.1   *The Range of Managerial Activities*

Planning	Representing	Staffing
Organizing	Activating	Motivating
Commanding	Administering	Innovating
Coordinating	Investigating	Decision making
Controlling	Communicating	Evaluating
Directing	Securing efforts	
Leading	Formulating purposes	

functions: planning, organizing (which includes Fayol's coordinating activities), directing (which includes Fayol's commanding activities), and controlling.

The **planning** function involves establishing organizational goals and defining the methods by which they are to be attained. The **organizing** function involves designing, structuring, and coordinating the components of an organization to meet organizational goals. The **directing** function involves managing interpersonal activities, leading and motivating employees so that they will effectively and efficiently accomplish the tasks necessary to realize organizational goals. The **controlling** function involves monitoring both the behavior of organization members and the effectiveness of the organization itself, determining whether plans are achieving organizational goals, and taking corrective actions as needed. Parts 2 through 5 of this text explore each of the four managerial functions in detail. As shown in Figure 1.4, managers use all four functions when applying an organization's resources to achieve its goals.

The Reality

The process and sociological perspectives on management are useful, but they are only viewpoints, not reality, and there often are differences between theory and practice. Consider the definition of management as a set of activities. Does that make you a manager any time you are engaged in planning, organizing, directing, or controlling? Possibly, yet most people sense a basic difference between managerial and nonmanagerial

FIGURE 1.3   *The Universalism of Management*

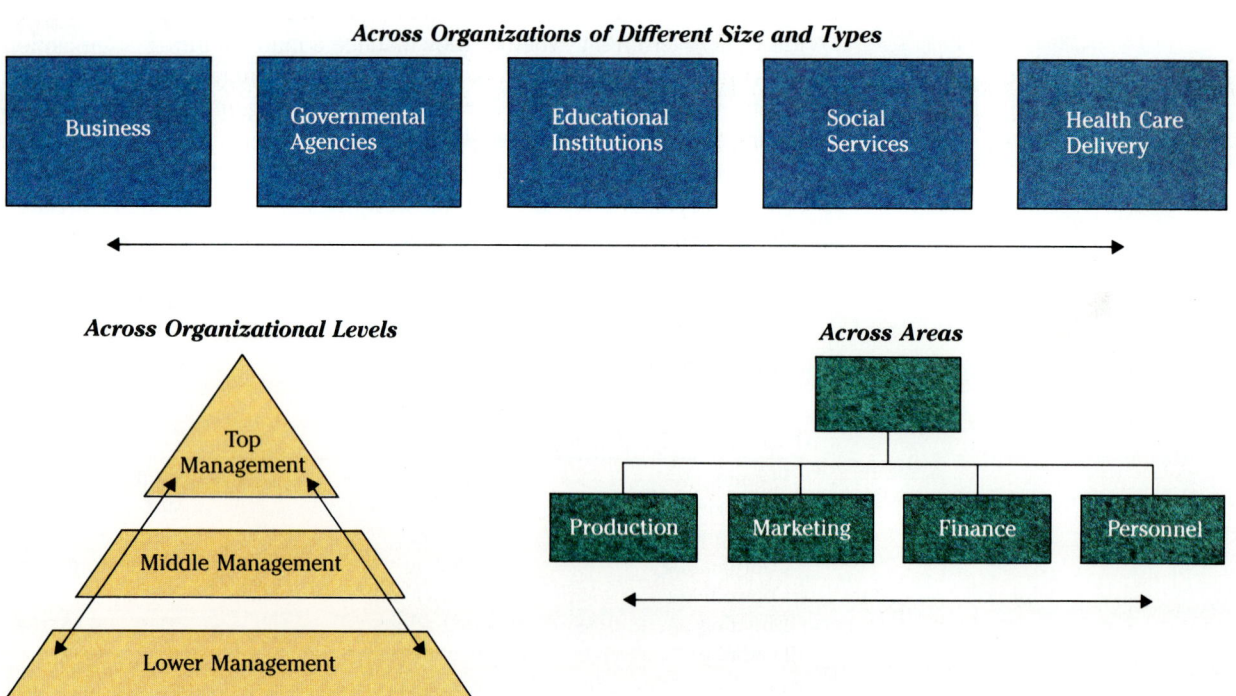

FIGURE 1.4   *The Managerial Process*

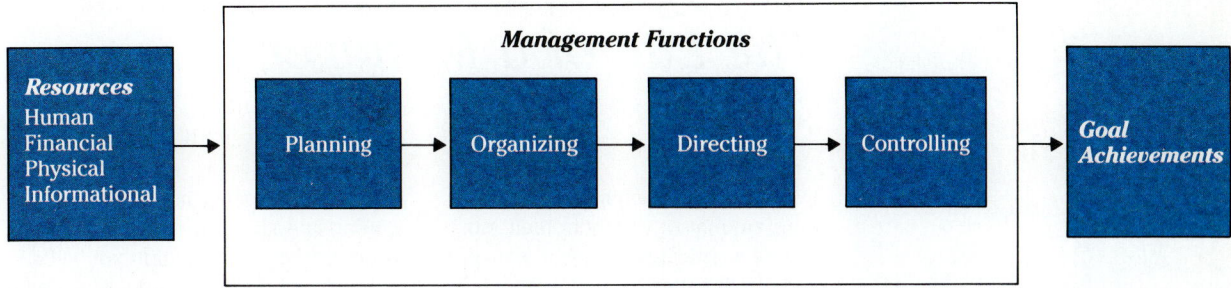

Source: Adapted from G. Terry (1972), *Principles of management*, Homewood, IL: Irwin, 4.

organization members and between managerial and nonmanagerial work. This is due primarily to a *division of labor* that managers create by assigning activities to individuals and to groups in organizations. Managers have traditionally assigned different kinds of tasks to the two social positions. Nonmanagers usually are assigned technical tasks, such as operating machines, sweeping floors, and removing tonsils. Managers are assigned the broader tasks of planning, organizing, directing, and controlling the individuals, resources, and work of the nonmanagerial group.

There are exceptions to the absolute division of labor just described, however. The distinctions between managers and nonmanagers may be clearer in theory than in practice. For example, many organizations today expect nonmanagers to participate in making certain decisions that traditionally were the responsibility of managers. With participative management, for example, a team of workers might decide on the amount of supplies to order, the number of units it can produce, and the particular team members who will do the work—tasks traditionally performed by managers. The recent implementation of worker-management participation teams at such organizations as General Foods has transferred many planning and control responsibilities to nonmanagers; thus, participative management and the delegation of responsibility (both of which are discussed fully in later chapters) tend to blur the distinction between the two social positions that are so crisp in theory. Ultimately, however, an organization contains a management group with the primary responsibility for planning, organizing, directing, and controlling its activities.

Are all managers actually involved in all four sets of management functions? Yes, although rarely in a controlled and systematic fashion.[9] A manager tends to navigate through his or her days by following a sequence of planning (identifying goals), organizing (designing the systems needed to meet goals), directing (energizing the systems through people), and controlling (measuring results against the plan).[10] This sequence, however, does not mean that managers plan on Monday, organize on Tuesday, direct on Wednesday, and control on Thursday; rather, a manager's day is a sea of scheduled and unscheduled events, opportunities, and crises through which he or she navigates by using the four functions. Even for the highest-level managers, half of their activities last less than nine minutes. Only 10 percent of their activities exceed one hour.[11] (See ''A Closer Look: Managerial Work.'')

A CLOSER LOOK

Managerial Work: The Life of a Manager

Most of this book is organized around the four managerial functions of planning, organizing, directing, and controlling, and techniques that managers can use to carry out those functions; however, real life is seldom as organized and systematic. What is the life of a manager really like? People at the Center for Creative Leadership in Greensboro, North Carolina, have examined the daily routines of managers.[1] You might be interested in what the future holds in store if you become a manager.

For one thing, you can expect to work long hours. Most managers work at least fifty hours a week; some put in as many as ninety. If you are like most managers, you will spend most of this time working inside your own organization. Despite the importance of outside factors—such as customers, competitors, and suppliers—most managers spend little time interacting directly with these groups. They spend over 95 percent of their time inside the walls of their own workplace.

Expect not to be bored, especially if you become a first-level manager. There will be plenty to keep you busy. First-level managers perform from 200 to 450 separate activities in a single eight-hour day. The work is not repeti-

tive. Most managers find a tremendous amount of variety in their job. During a typical workday, a manager completes paperwork, makes and takes phone calls, attends scheduled and unscheduled meetings, conducts inspection tours and visits at the workplace, has personal contact with many people, and addresses a wide range of work-related issues.

This level of activity will not allow you much time for contemplation. First-level managers encounter a new demand on their time almost every minute of the workday; therefore, most of their activities tend to be of very short duration. Trivial and important matters are often interspersed, and you will be expected to isolate and handle problems in rapid-fire order. Although this pace gives most managers little time to reflect or plan systematically, you should try to reserve some time for these activities. As you will see later in this book, one of the factors that distinguishes effective from ineffective managers is how well they reflect on their work and systematically plan their actions.

Handle problems
in rapid-fire order.

Most managers do most of their work orally, not in writing. The managers studied by the Center for Creative Leadership conducted between 28 and 80 percent of their work orally. Managers need to be able to communicate well with their superiors, subordinates, and peers. You can expect to exchange a lot of information. Information is the soul of a manager's

job. You will spend much of your day getting and giving information. If you do not get the information you need, you will not make good decisions or plans. If you do not give information to the people who need it, your activities will be in vain.

Exchange a lot
of information.

The reality of what a manager's life is actually like is not necessarily what it should be like. The reality, from a manager's perspective, also is not necessarily what others see. If you were to ask the managers who were observed in the Center's study how many hours they spend at work, how often they are interrupted, how much time they spend working inside their organization, or other aspects about how they spend their time, their answers would not match those of observers. Managers usually do not know how much time they devote to specific activities, and that is a problem. If managers do not know how they spend their day, how can they modify it to become more effective?

These *descriptions* of a typical managerial day are, therefore, not *prescriptions*. The reality is that a manager's day is hectic; however, managers must attack the management process more systematically in order to improve effectiveness.

1. M. W. McCall, Jr., A. M. Morrison, and R. L. Hannan (1978), *Studies of managerial work: Results and methods* (Technical Report No. 9), Greensboro, NC: Center for Creative Leadership.

FIGURE 1.5   The Management
Process Under Pressure

*When you are up to your ears in alligators, it's hard to remember that your
objective was to drain the swamp.*

Types of Managers

Now that you have an idea of what the management process is,
consider the roles of managers themselves. It is possible to classify
managers by the nature of the position they hold. This section will review
some of the major categories of managers. The next section will identify
how these differences affect a manager's job.

Zones of Responsibility

An organization can be viewed as a cake with three distinct layers, or
zones of responsibility: the institutional zone, the managerial zone, and
the technical core (see Figure 1.6).[12] Managers can be classified according to the zones in which they operate.

The Institutional Zone   Managers in the **institutional zone** are
primarily responsible for two aspects of an organization's external (outside) environment (see Chapter 2 for a detailed discussion of the
components of an organization's external environment). First, they must
establish their organization's importance to the external community by
letting people outside of it and in other organizations know about its role
and significance. The institutional zone is where Lee Iacocca has been
operating for years with his public appearances promoting Chrysler as an
organization "Born in America."

Second, managers in the institutional zone are responsible for identifying the needs of the external environment and for finding ways for their

organization to satisfy those needs (for example, providing goods and services). It was strong management in the institutional zone which saved *The New York Times* from probable failure in the early 1980s. Three *Times* institutional zone managers reversed the newspaper's trend of decreasing profits and slow growth by plotting and pursuing an aggressive strategy that included a series of acquisitions. The resulting success of the Times Corporation showed that the three managers had successfully read the needs of the external environment and positioned the company to capitalize on them. In general, institutional zone managers fashion long-term strategies, plans, and objectives for the organization as a whole.

The Technical Core   Managers in the **technical core** have direct responsibility for producing and delivering an organization's goods and services. They manage the day-to-day activities of an organization. One set of technical core managers at *The New York Times*, for example, oversees the people who operate the printing presses. Another set of technical core managers oversees delivery of newspapers to distributors.

The Managerial Zone   Sandwiched between the institutional zone and the technical core is the **managerial zone.** Here, managers create and manage systems to coordinate and integrate the various parts of the technical core. For example, they coordinate the work of those who produce the *Times* with the work of those who deliver it. They also

FIGURE 1.6   Zones of Organizational Responsibility

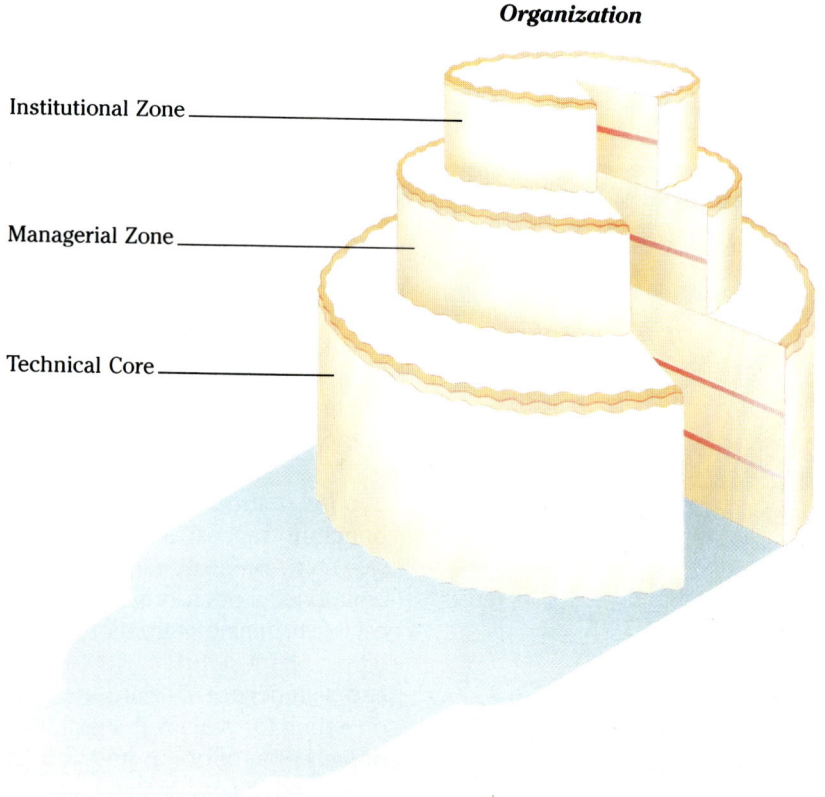

Institutional Zone

Managerial Zone

Technical Core

Organization

Staff managers usually wield influence based on personal skill and knowledge.

develop the specific operating strategies for implementing the overall plans and objectives set forth by upper-level managers. In general, managers in the managerial zone are responsible for translating the vision of the institutional zone managers into the realities of the technical core.

Line-Staff Distinctions

Another helpful way to classify managers is according to their direct involvement in producing an organization's goods or services—that is, whether they perform line or staff duties. **Line managers** have a *direct* responsibility for producing the service or product line of an organization. At Goodyear Rubber Company, for example, the department supervisor in charge of a tire molding department is a line manager. Every manager who links the tire molding department supervisor with the company president is a line manager. Line managers are usually given a considerable amount of command-type authority—they are able to tell subordinates what to do and how to do it.

It is the job of **staff managers** to *support* line managers, but staff managers are not directly involved in the production of goods or services. Staff managers, who can be found in any of the zones of responsibility, usually are not given command-type authority but must wield influence based on their personal skill and knowledge. For example, a staff manager in the legal department at Dairycraft, Inc., a manufacturer of stainless steel products for the dairy industry, does not manage the production or sale of stainless steel containers; rather, the staff manager supervises the lawyers, who advise the line managers, who establish contractual relationships with suppliers, customers, and employees. The legal staff manager cannot *order* a line manager to sign or reject a purchasing contract. The staff manager can only use personal legal knowledge to help line managers decide whether the contract is a good one. Line managers are responsible for the decisions made and actions taken; staff managers are responsible for the quality of the advice that they give to line managers. Chapter 11 discusses line-staff authority in more detail.

Hierarchical Distinctions

Managers are also classified by their positions in an organization's hierarchy. The lowest level of managers consists of **first-level managers.** They are involved primarily with managing an organization's technical core and are the only managers who direct nonmanagerial organization members. First-level managers often have such titles as "unit manager" or "department manager." Those who manage first-level managers are referred to as second-level managers. Next come third-level managers, and so on, up to the top level of management.

People often describe managers' general positions in a hierarchy as lower, middle, and upper-level. "I'm in middle management at MCI," says a regional sales manager. "She's an upper-level manager at Federated Department Stores." These terms are a bit vague, because there is no definite rule about where the levels begin and end. Despite this lack of specificity, the terms are widely used to identify a manager's general location in the organizational hierarchy. Middle-level managers often have such titles as "division head" or "plant manager." Upper-level managers may be called "general manager," "director," "vice-president," or "president."

The traditional roles of upper, middle, and lower managers are undergoing change in many organizations. Much of the work traditionally performed by some lower-level managers is being given to nonmanagers through participative management programs, autonomous work groups, and computerized decision-making and control programs (see Chapter 10 for alternative approaches to organizing jobs). Lower-level managers are likely to become managers of human relations and to represent the organization to "outsiders" (a role historically reserved for upper-level managers).[13] These roles are shifting as those lower in the organizational hierarchy become more capable and willing, and as organizations change in attempts to become more efficient and effective.

Functional Areas

Managers also are classified according to their area of specialized activity (also known as the organizational function served). They are the organization's **functional managers.** "I'm in accounting," says one manager. "I've been transferred from marketing to production," says another. Functional areas should not be confused with the general management functions of planning, organizing, directing, and controlling. Instead, specialized functional areas describe the specific set of activities that a manager oversees. While these vary somewhat depending on the industry, it is common for organizations to have operations (production), marketing, finance, accounting, and human resource functions.

Functional managers oversee a specific set of organizational activities, such as human resource functions.

Organizational Type Distinctions

As you might expect, the sector of the economy (for example, government, education, or health care) in which an organization operates also influences the nature of a manager's job and, often, the titles used to designate the manager's position. The managers who oversaw the acquisition, development, production, and marketing of this textbook have particular titles in the publishing industry. James Levy is the senior vice-president and general manager of Scott, Foresman's college division. James Sitlington is the editorial vice-president who manages the editorial work on the business and economics books published by Scott, Foresman. John Beasley is the editorial vice-president and director of editorial services, who managed the actual production of this book. Carl Tyson is the vice-president of sales and marketing, who manages sales of the book. In a different industry, however, the titles for managers at similar levels might be quite different. At American Family Insurance, for example, James Eldridge is the vice-president of claims, Al Hunter is the vice-president of underwriting, and Nancy Johnson is the vice-president of corporate research. A head nurse in a hospital can be the counterpart of a foreman or forewoman in a manufacturing shop. The dean of an engineering school may be doing work on a level comparable to that of a manufacturing organization's division head.

Each set of categories for classifying a particular manager's job has merit. To classify a manager's job thoroughly, however, requires the use of several of these categories. Carl Tyson's job at Scott, Foresman, for example, can be described as an upper-level, line, marketing manager's job in the publishing industry. Donald Hawk, executive vice-president and manager of the administration department for Texas Commerce Bancshares, holds a job best described as an upper-level, staff, organization development and planning job in the financial industry. These systems for categorizing managers' jobs are useful for describing where a manager operates in an industry. They are also important because the specific nature of managers' jobs varies substantially among categories.

Variations in the Management Job

Definitions of management that focus on its universal aspects show that managing involves the same basic functions in any management setting. It flies in the face of common sense, however, to say that all managers engage in exactly the same behaviors and activities as they conduct these functions.[14] Managers at Edina High School and managers at General Foods, for example, plan, organize, direct, and control their organization's operations. In one case, however, the focus is on the education of children. In the other, the focus is on the manufacture and distribution of food products. In addition to differences in content issues or problems dealt with, management jobs differ fundamentally in four areas: (1) the time frame they must consider, (2) the way managers allocate their time among the functions, (3) the organizational responsibility for which they are accountable, and (4) the skills needed to perform effectively.

Time Perspectives

The unit supervisor of a company is concerned with production for the next six weeks. As one moves from lower to higher management levels in an organization, the time frame that a manager deals with often shifts from the here-and-now to the distant future (see Figure 1.7). Lower-level managers are concerned with delivering current services and meeting current production schedules. Upper-level managers, at least in some of

FIGURE 1.7   Time Perspective Differences Among Management Levels

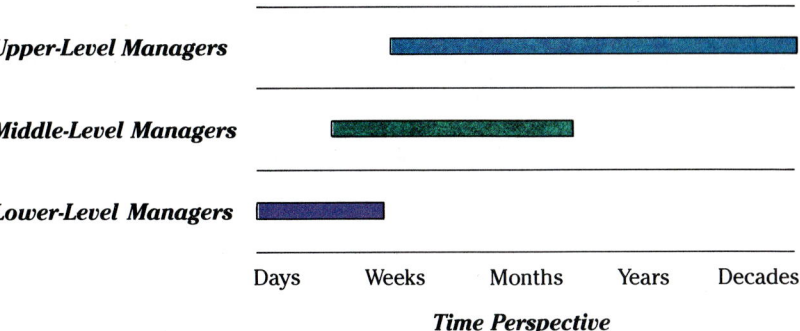

FIGURE 1.8   *The Distribution of Managers' Time Among Job Levels*

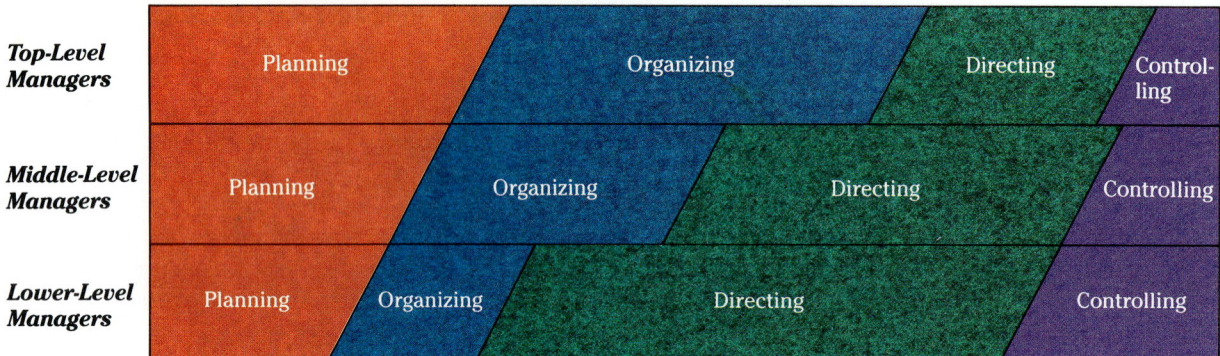

Proportion of Time

the more progressive U.S. firms, regularly work with issues that will have impact five to fifteen years in the future. As John W. Teets, chairman of the board of Greyhound Corporation, sees it, "Management's job is to see the company not as it is . . . but as it can become."[15] Institutional-level managers plan, organize, direct, and control an organization's future; managers in the technical core carry out the same activities but focus on delivering today's services and meeting current production schedules.

Perspectives on time can also vary by industry. Managers in the aerospace industry, for example, must look many years into the future. Managers in the fashion industry may only have to look ahead to the next season. It is unfortunate that managers often adopt time perspectives that are too short. Many organizations have lost their competitive edge by concentrating on quarterly profits at the expense of long-term needs.

Time Allocation Differences

One of the biggest variations among managers is in how much time they devote to each of the four functions: planning, organizing, directing, and controlling. The amount of time managers spend performing each function varies from zone to zone, from line to staff, across hierarchical levels, from area to area, and across industry. Level and functional area make the biggest difference. Upper-level managers, for example, typically spend more of their time planning and organizing than they do directing or controlling. Lower-level managers usually spend less time planning and organizing and more time directing and controlling.

Researchers at the University of Minnesota systematically examined the day-to-day activities of managers from different levels of each of thirteen organizations.[16] They found that, whereas lower-level managers spend an average of only 15 percent of their time in planning, upper-level managers spend almost twice as much. They also found that lower-level managers spend more than half of their time on directing activities, but upper-level managers use less than a fourth of their time on such activities. Figure 1.8 illustrates how managers at these different levels tend to distribute their time. Similar patterns exist across zones of responsibility.

As previously noted, the functional area in which a manager works also affects his or her allocation of time.[17] Figure 1.9 shows this allocation for middle-level managers. As you can see, production, marketing, and financial managers spend the largest percentage of their time controlling, but human resource managers spend the least amount of their time controlling. Instead, they devote more of their time to planning.

Organizational Responsibility Differences

The way that managers plan, organize, direct, and control also varies according to their organizational responsibilities. The zone for which managers are accountable influences the management process and the scope of their responsibilities. For example, top-level managers deal with institutional-level responsibilities. The strategic plans they devise encompass their entire organization. First-level managers, on the other hand, usually concentrate on an organizational subsystem, such as a department. For example, the director of a hospital's trauma unit plans for activities within the unit, whereas the hospital's administrator manages operations for the entire hospital.

Skill Differences

Managers also vary in the skills that they need and the degree to which they use each skill. For example, the manager who is responsible for planning the strategies to keep the aerospace industry competitive in the world arena needs a different mixture of skills from the manager who trains the astronauts or the manager who assembles the rocket booster engines. Daniel Katz, a psychology professor at the University of Michigan,

FIGURE 1.9   *Distribution of Managers' Time Among Functional Areas*

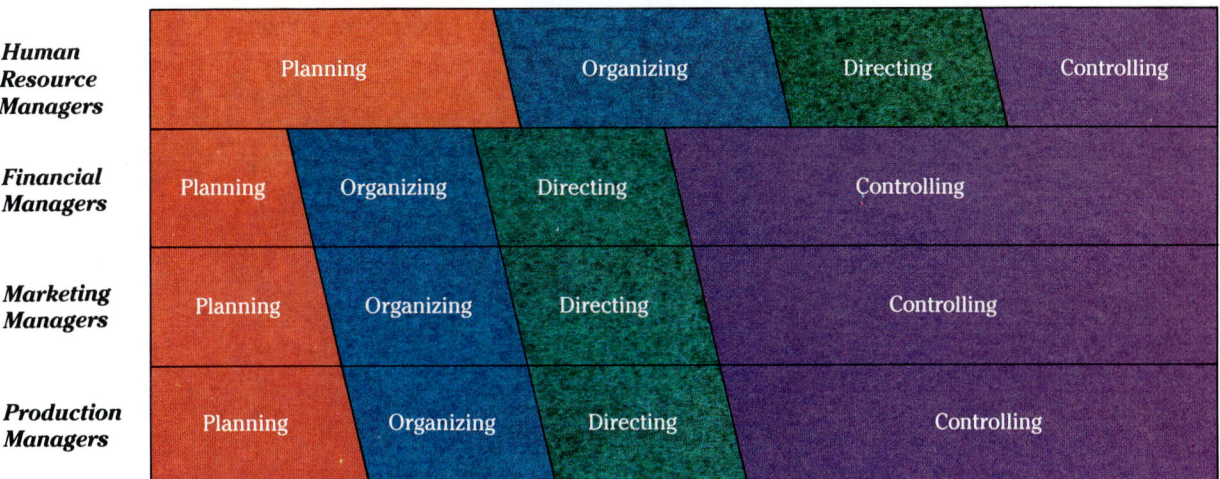

Proportion of Time

Source: Based on data from J. Horne and T. Lupton (1965), The work activities of middle managers: An exploratory study, *Journal of Management Studies, 2,* 14–33.

FIGURE 1.10   *Required Skills for Successful Management*

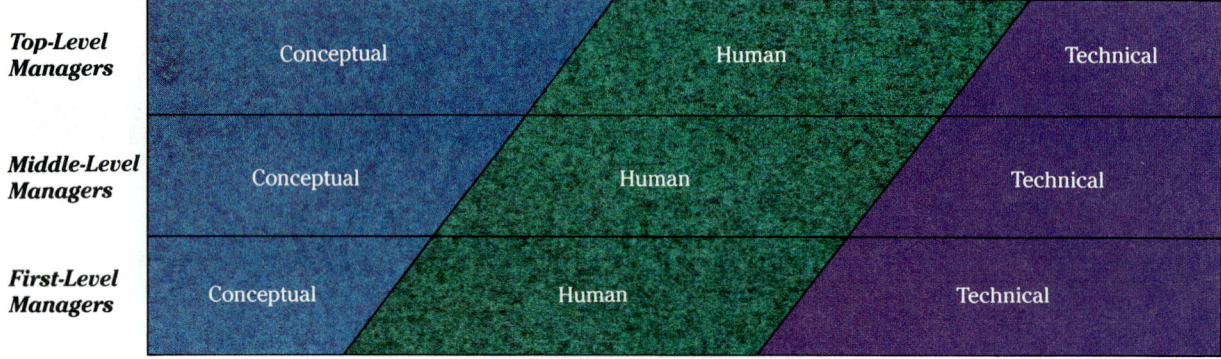

Amount of Skill Required

Source: Based on data from D. Katz (September-October 1974), Skills of an effective administrator, *Harvard Business Review*, 90-102.

examined the skills managers use and placed them into three categories: conceptual, human, and technical.[18] All managers must have these skills to be effective, but the type and amount required varies from level to level and from organization to organization (see Figure 1.10).

A manager with **technical skills** understands and can use the tools, procedures, and techniques needed to perform a given task. Computer operators, diesel mechanics, artists, and dentists all need technical skills. Managers at lower levels, particularly in the technical core, usually need considerable technical skill to understand how the various components of their unit work. The relative importance of technical skills to managerial performance decreases for managers at higher levels in an organization.

Human, or **interpersonal, skills** are an individual's ability to work with and understand others, to lead, to motivate, to manage conflict, and to build group effort. Human skills are important to managers at all levels. Upper-level managers, particularly those from the institutional zone, must use these skills to deal effectively with groups outside of the organization and with other managers. A hospital administrator or the head of a hospital's board of directors must deal with community groups to build new facilities and must test opinions about controversial new treatments or procedures, for example. Middle-level managers need human skills to manage individuals from a wide range of technical areas and to interact productively with upper-level managers. The head of the surgery department, for example, must be able to help attract talented people to join the hospital. First-level managers must use human skills to challenge, to motivate, and to coordinate the work of the nonmanagerial subordinates who produce an organization's goods and services. A dietician manager must see that nutritious, tasty meals are prepared and served to patients with special needs.

Good **conceptual skills** allow people to see, to diagnose, and to understand concepts at an abstract level of analysis. Although everyone needs conceptual skills, their relative importance generally decreases from top to middle to first-level management. This is because upper-level managers often deal with abstract ideas, and lower-level managers spend

more time dealing with observable objects and processes. Because managers in the institutional zone devote a large portion of their time to planning, they draw on conceptual skills to think in terms of relative tendencies, probabilities, patterns, and connections. Conceptual skills provide upper-level managers with the ability to anticipate changes or to estimate the value of corporate strategies. (See "A Closer Look: Management in the 1990s.")

Managerial Roles

This section focuses on two questions: "Why do organizations need managers?" and "How do managers spend their time?" The work of Henry Mintzberg provides a useful insight into both of these questions.

Why Organizations Need Managers

Organizations are tools created to achieve a set of objectives. Boswell Hospital in Phoenix, Arizona, was created to deliver high-quality health care. Hanover College in Hanover, Indiana, was created to provide a sound liberal arts education. The Miller Brewing Company, with plants in Milwaukee, Wisconsin, and other areas, was created to make a profit by manufacturing and selling beer. Every organization has a technical set of tasks that must be performed to convert its mission into reality. It is the job of managers to define an organization's goals, to determine how to achieve them, and to make them happen. There are six reasons organizations need managers:

1. Managers ensure that an organization serves its basic purpose—the efficient production of specific goods or services.
2. Managers design and maintain the stability of an organization's operations.

A CLOSER LOOK

Management in the 1990s: The Times, They Are A'Changin'

Traditionally, the route to the top of corporate America has been through managing in blue chip industrial companies, but that route is likely to change. The Bureau of Labor Statistics (BLS), for example, estimates that by 1995 almost three quarters of all jobs in the United States will be in the service sector (including transportation, communication, trade, finance, real estate, and government), and some estimates raise that figure to 88 percent by the year 2000.[1] BLS projects that many of the new jobs will be in such areas as business services (for example, management consulting, public relations, and advertising), professional services (such as law, accounting, and engineering), maintenance and repair services for the highly technological equipment found in the workplace today, and financial services (particularly general financial management).

There is another change that will affect managers' futures, however. Middle-management positions are becoming an endangered species. For one thing, upper-level managers are being asked to do much of the analysis work previously done by their middle-level subordinates. For another

thing, lower-level managers are being asked to become more active and to make many of the day-to-day decisions formerly made by middle-level managers. Computers and new communications technology have taken over many information-handling chores, and private contractors are being given legal, accounting, and other chores previously handled by an organization's middle-level managers. The result is that thousands of middle-level management positions are simply disappearing.

Middle managers will be expected to use their technical skills much later in their careers than once was the case. By drumming up new business, servicing clients, and continuing to add to profits rather than merely overseeing administration, many middle managers "will find their jobs riskier and more demanding, but also more purposeful and rewarding, than those of the old bureaucratic middle managers."[2]

In the 1990s, the fastest route to the top for managers may be through ". . . marketing, sales and then moving into general management. . . . [A]dmiration for the number crunchers has diminished."[3] People on their way should try to avoid mergers and reorganizations, organizations in slowly rather than rapidly expanding industries, and bosses who feel threatened by their approach. They probably also should get a graduate degree as well as a B.S. or a B.A. Perhaps most importantly, they must develop an "absolute, total dedication to being the boss."[4]

Middle management disappearing . . . .

Those who succeed to top management can expect to be paid well for their work. As of the late 1980s, the average annual base salary for a top executive was $215,000, plus another 85 percent in bonuses. Increases in pay for top managers have outpaced inflation and are expected to continue to do so, but there is every indication that, more and more, managers will have to *earn* their pay. So, keep your technical skills sharp and prepare to add value to your organization.

1. Based on P. Nulty (2 February 1987), How managers will manage, *Fortune*, 47.
2. Nulty, 48.
3. What makes top executives run? [An interview with Lester Korn, founder and chair of Korn/Ferry International, a large executive search firm] (14 April 1986), *U.S. News & World Report*, 52.
4. *Ibid.*

Every organization needs managers to convert its mission into reality.

3. Managers choose the strategies needed to keep an organization adapting in a controlled way to its changing environment.
4. Managers ensure that an organization serves the ends of the people who control it.
5. Managers are the key informational link between an organization and its environment.
6. As formal authorities, managers are responsible for the operation of an organization's status system and serve as symbols of the organization in ceremonial activities.[19]

Every organization needs managers. For example, imagine that Melissa Lerner wants to turn her love of cooking into a business. Melissa becomes a manager on several levels: (1) an upper-level manager when she plans whether to specialize in all desserts or just pastries and whether to sell to area restaurants or on consignment to local grocery stores, (2) a middle-level manager when she must decide how much and what kinds of supplies to purchase and where to obtain them, and (3) a first-level manager when she directs the actual cooking.

How Managers Spend Their Time

Managers must fill many roles as they carry out the four management functions (see Table 1.2). Mintzberg grouped these roles into three categories: interpersonal, informational, and decisional.[20] Managers have formal authority, which gives rise to the three interpersonal roles that they perform. Managers receive and transmit information, thereby defining the informational roles. The information that managers receive, coupled with their formal authority position, create their decisional roles.

Interpersonal Roles Managers fill several **interpersonal roles** because of their position in their organization:

- As a *figurehead,* a manager is a symbol of the organization. Managers sign legal documents and participate in events, such as ground-breaking ceremonies or the opening of a new branch office.
- As a *leader,* a manager uses power, coordination techniques, and motivation tools to integrate the needs of individual subordinate organization members with the needs of the organization in the pursuit of organizational objectives.

TABLE 1.2 *Major Managerial Roles*

Interpersonal Roles	Informational Roles	Decisional Roles
Figurehead	Monitor	Entrepreneur
Leader	Disseminator	Disturbance handler
Liaison	Spokesperson	Resource allocator
		Negotiator

Source: Based on H. Mintzberg (1973), *The nature of managerial work,* Englewood Cliffs, NJ: Prentice-Hall.

- As a *liaison,* a manager develops and cultivates relationships with individuals and groups outside of his or her area of direct responsibility. A supervisor, for example, may develop a network with other supervisors, a middle manager with other middle managers, and a chief executive officer (CEO) with other CEOs. The liaison role is important for the exchange of information and for the coordination of the many components of an organization.

Informational Roles   In **informational roles,** managers collect and disperse knowledge, thus becoming an important nerve center for an organization:

- As a *monitor,* a manager collects information about the organization and its environment from all available sources, including subordinates, peers, superiors, and liaison contacts.
- As a *disseminator,* a manager transmits information collected through the monitor role to subordinates in the organization. This can involve both factual information ("We must fill an order for 1000 widgets by Thursday") and value information ("The director of marketing wants us to be more aware of and responsive to our customers' needs").
- As a *spokesperson,* a manager transmits information about the organization (such as its policies or plans) to individuals and groups outside of the organization.

Decisional Roles   The third major role that managers must play is a **decisional,** or **strategy-making, role:**

- As an *entrepreneur,* a manager identifies opportunities for and threats to an organization and initiates changes to capitalize on these. For

Managers fill interpersonal, informational, and decisional roles.

Walter Kiechel III

Walter Kiechel III is a writer and editor at *Fortune* magazine.

1. In your opinion, what are some of the most important factors that characterize good managers?

Because a manager, by definition, is someone who gets things done through other people, a good manager has to have interpersonal skills. He or she has to be able to listen to other people, hear what they're saying, and pay attention to what is heard. Managers also have to have some capacity for change and for personal growth, so curiosity is very important. Some pundits are saying that in fifteen or twenty years, the top manager in organizations will be the one who is the best learner. In fact, that may already be true. Managers must also have certain conceptual skills, a way of thinking about problems. There are a lot of managers who aren't particularly creative, but their ability to put together evidence and reach decisions based on insufficient or inadequate information sets them apart from other people. It also helps immeasurably if a manager has a good sense of humor!

2. What are some of the most common mistakes managers make?

Neglecting the human side of the job in efforts to be rational, calculating machines. The media through which managers work aren't numbers, reports, or computer screen displays, but *people*. Dealing with people means taking into account their feelings and acknowledging your own. Managers who take the view that business should be work, not fun, have an awfully long, "unfun" life ahead of them. Confusing the appearance of something with the underlying reality is another common mistake. Managers should strive to look past a glossy, glitzy presentation to examine the substance of the ideas or facts it contained, for example. Similarly, a person can work seventy hours a week but only produce thirty-five hours worth of product. Companies that are well managed don't place too heavy an emphasis on appearance.

Probably the biggest mistake managers can make is failing to pay enough attention to the communications they give and receive in their organization. If I were to set up a mutual fund, I would select stocks for it from those companies that have the best internal communications—not just from the top down but, even more importantly, from the bottom up.

3. What significant changes do you expect to occur in the manager's job during the coming decade?

I think a number of things are going to happen. I believe that we are going to have to change the central model that has characterized managing—the hierarchy that specifies a boss, then a subboss, and so on down the line. Future organizations will probably be comprised of relatively independent professionals, something on the order of today's management consulting firms or groups of physicians who practice together.

We have made progress in modifying the top-down, "do it my way" model that emerged after World War II by using participatory management that asked people doing a job how it should be done. The ideal for the year 2000 is the concept of self-management. This model holds that the person who knows best what it takes to motivate him- or herself is that person. Likewise, the person who knows best how to do a job is the person who performs it. A manager's job will be to give workers all of the resources and tools they need to do their job—and then get out of their way so they can do it. This means that good interpersonal skills—the ability to work with people rather than merely give them orders—will become even more important (and more complicated).

Another change managers are going to have to make is to become less provincial in their point of view. The globalization of business has become astonishing, but how many American managers speak a second language, particularly one as difficult as Japanese? You cannot know how the competition's mind works if you don't know its language.

4. What advice do you have for a college student who hopes to become a manager?

While you're in an educational environment, attempt to learn everything that you can—not just about business, because you'll have ample time and opportunity to do that, but about liberal arts and sciences in general. The kind of curiosity and thoughtfulness that can arise from these studies really is important. A broadly based education can help you develop a lasting set of ideas that will carry you through your career. It helps you build a foundation that will enable you to maintain a kind of independence from the organization you manage.

example, Susan Wilcox-Garner, the manager of a photo processing lab, might identify the development of electronic (filmless) photography as a threat to her film-based processing business. When she decides to offer electronic processing to customers, she is turning the threat into an opportunity to beat her competitors to the punch. As an entrepreneur, a manager is the designer and initiator of controlled change.

■ As a *disturbance handler*, a manager reacts to and attempts to resolve day-to-day crises involving conflicts between individuals, problems with other organizations, and any other threats to the orderly conduct of business. Susan, for example, has been receiving complaints from customers about an employee whom Susan likes and trusts. She might decide to reassign the employee from the front counter to the processing lab, where her skills are needed and where she will get along well with co-workers. As a disturbance handler, a manager reacts to situations forced on him or her.

■ As a *resource allocator*, a manager schedules his or her own time; programs the work of subordinates; and controls decisions involving

FIGURE 1.11   Managerial Roles and the Functions of Management

Through each of the major managerial roles, managers accomplish the four management functions of planning, organizing, directing, and controlling. The leadership role, for example, gives managers the authority they need to execute directing activities. The informational role provides leaders with the information they need to make decisions as resource allocators and negotiators.

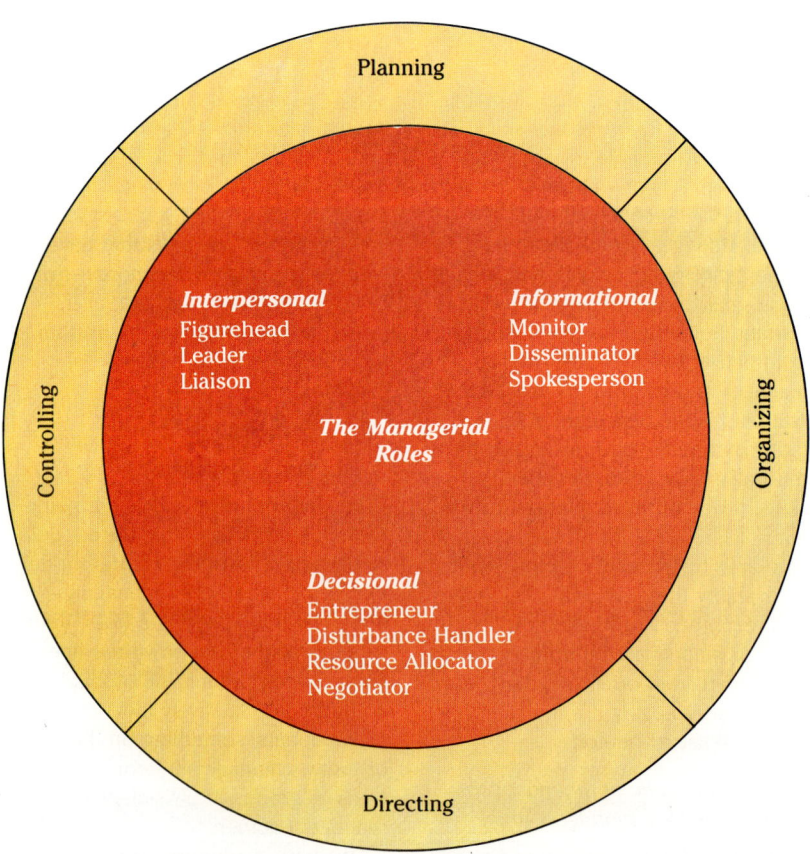

the allocation of other resources, such as money, supplies, and equipment. This is what Susan does when she decides to order a new one-hour photo processing machine for her lab.

- As a *negotiator,* a manager attempts to obtain beneficial solutions for the organization in nonroutine situations, such as arranging a contract with a supplier or customer, reaching an agreement with a regulatory agency, or receiving a tax break from the state government in exchange for building a new plant in that state. Susan, for example, had to negotiate with the local zoning board for permission to install an animated sign outside of her store.

Although neither the functional nor the role approach provides complete insight into many aspects of a manager's daily routine (such as how long each activity should last or the optimum frequency of interruptions), the role-oriented approach and the process perspective add up to a comprehensive and useful way of looking at the nature of management (see Figure 1.11). The four process functions

> . . . *still represent the most useful way of conceptualizing the manager's job. . . . The classical functions provide clear and discrete methods of classifying the thousands of different activities that managers carry out and the techniques they use in terms of the functions they perform for the achievement of organizational goals.*[21]

It is in part through the interpersonal, informational, and decisional roles that managers execute the planning, organizing, directing, and controlling functions; therefore, managers can and should integrate the role-oriented approach with the traditional four-function process perspective. The roles identified by Mintzberg encompass the majority of responsibilities assigned to managers, but the interpersonal, informational, and decisional roles will help managers execute the four functions of management only if managers fulfill them in a systematic fashion that meets their organization's needs.

The Nature of Management in Review

There are at least two perspectives on and many definitions of management. This book uses a definition based on the process perspective. It views management as a combination of the processes of planning, organizing, directing, and controlling resources in pursuit of organizational goals. These four processes are put into effect by managers. All managers plan, organize, direct, and control, so this set of functions can be considered universal, yet the specific ways in which managers apply the four functions vary with the type of management position held.

Management positions vary according to zone, line or staff, hierarchical level, functional area, and organizational type. There are three zones of responsibility in an organization: the institutional zone (whose managers oversee the entire organization), the managerial zone (whose managers create the systems necessary to enact the plans developed in the institutional zone), and the technical core (whose managers supervise the people who produce the organization's goods and services). Line managers oversee the workers who produce an organization's goods and services, and staff managers counsel and advise line managers. Distinctions within an organization's hierarchy result in upper-level, middle-level, and first-level managers. Functional managers oversee specific areas of a company, such as marketing, production, and finance. Managers can also be classified according to the industry in which their organization operates.

Differences among types of managers produce differences in time perspectives, in the allocation of time among the four functions, and in the profile of skills needed for effective management. For example, upper-level managers deal with the long term as they plan their organization's future; they allocate a great deal of their time to planning; and they rely on conceptual skills to develop an organization's strategy. Lower-level managers often deal with daily time frames and production schedules, allocate much of their time to directing and controlling functions, and need good technical skills.

In carrying out the four major management functions, managers play three roles. To fill interpersonal roles, managers are required to be figureheads, leaders, and liaisons. To fill informational roles, managers become monitors, disseminators, and spokespeople. To fill decisional roles, managers act as entrepreneurs, disturbance handlers, resource allocators, and negotiators.

The planning, organizing, directing, and controlling functions and the activities that managers perform as they apply these functions to their organizations are discussed in detail throughout this book.

Notes

1. C. Icahn (27 October 1986), What ails corporate America—and what should be done, *Business Week,* 101.
2. C. I. Barnard (1938), *The functions of the executive,* Cambridge, MA: Harvard University Press, 73.
3. A. K. Rice (1958), *Productivity and social organization: The Ahmedabad experiment,* London: Tavistock.
4. J. E. Haas and T. E. Drabek (1973), *Complex organizations: A sociological perspective,* New York: Macmillan.
5. M. P. Follett (1949), *Freedom and coordination: Lectures in business organization,* London: Pitman.
6. H. Fayol (1949), *General and industrial management,* C. Storrs, trans., London: Sir Isaac Pitman and Sons, Ltd. (Original work published in 1916).
7. Fayol, 1916/1949.
8. Barnard, 1938; R. C. Davis (1951), *The fundamentals of top management,* New York: Harper; L. F. Urwick (1943), *The elements of administration,* New York: Harper & Row; J. B. Miner (1973), *The management process: Theory, research, and practice,* New York: Macmillan.

9. M. W. McCall, Jr., A. M. Morrison, and R. L. Hannan (1978), *Studies of managerial work: Results and methods* (Technical Report No. 9), Greensboro, NC: Center for Creative Leadership.

10. R. A. Mackenzie (November-December 1969), The management process in 3-D, *Harvard Business Review*, 87.

11. H. Mintzberg (July-August 1975), The manager's job: Folklore and fact, *Harvard Business Review*, 49–61.

12. T. Parsons (1960), *Structure and process in modern society*, Chicago: Free Press; C. Perrow (1967), A framework for the comparative analyses of organizations, *American Sociological Review*, 32, 194–208.

13. S. Kerr, K. D. Hill, and L. Broedling (1986), The first-line supervisor: Phasing out or here to stay? *Academy of Management Review*, 11, 103–17.

14. W. W. Torrow and P. R. Pinto (1976), The development of a managerial job taxonomy: A system for describing, classifying, and evaluating executive positions, *Journal of Applied Psychology*, 61, 410–18; W. Whitely (1985), Managerial work behavior: An integration of results from two major approaches, *Academy of Management Journal*, 28, 358.

15. John W. Teets, chairman of the Board for Greyhound Corp., in an advertisement (31 March 1986), *Fortune*, 46.

16. T. A. Mahoney, T. H. Jerdee, and S. J. Carroll, Jr. (1963), *Development of managerial performance: A research approach*, Cincinnati: South-Western; T. A. Mahoney, T. H. Jerdee, and S. J. Carroll, Jr. (1965), The jobs of management, *Industrial Relations*, 4, 97–110.

17. J. Horne and T. Lupton (1965), The work activities of middle managers: An exploratory study, *Journal of Management Studies*, 2, 14–33.

18. D. Katz (September-October 1974), Skills of an effective administrator, *Harvard Business Review*, 90–102.

19. H. Mintzberg (1980), *The nature of managerial work*, Englewood Cliffs, NJ: Prentice-Hall, 94–96.

20. This discussion is based on Mintzberg, 1980.

21. S. J. Carroll and D. J. Gillen (1987), Are the classical management functions useful in describing managerial work? *Academy of Management Review*, 12, 48.

Key Terms

management
managers
organization
sociological perspective
organizational chart
hierarchy
process perspective
planning
organizing
directing
controlling
institutional zone
technical core

managerial zone
line managers
staff managers
hierarchy
first-level managers
functional managers
technical skills
human (interpersonal) skills
conceptual skills
interpersonal roles
informational roles
decisional (strategy-making) roles

Issues for Review and Discussion

1. Describe the management process.
2. Describe the characteristics of an organization.
3. List and define the four managerial functions and explain how they are interrelated.
4. Explain the concept of universalism of management.
5. Explain several systems by which you could classify all of the managers from one large corporation.
6. Name the three managerial zones in an organization and describe what managers do in each.
7. Identify three types of skills needed by effective managers and relate their importance to the managers' levels in the hierarchy.
8. Identify and discuss at least two reasons organizations need managers.
9. Name three managerial roles and the duties that managers perform in each.

Suggested Readings

Drucker, P. F. (1954). *The practice of management.* New York: Harper & Brothers, 3–5.

Fayol, H. (1949). *General and industrial management.* C. Storrs, trans. London: Sir Isaac Pitman and Sons, Ltd. (Original work published in 1916), 3–6.

Heller, R. E. (1988). A review of *Iacocca: An autobiography.* In Pierce, J. L. and Newstrom, J. W., eds. *The manager's bookshelf: A mosaic of contemporary views.* New York: Harper & Row, 145–49.

Iacocca, L., with Novak, W. (1984). *Iacocca: An autobiography.* New York: Bantam.

Luthans, F. (1988). Successful vs. effective real managers. *Academy of Management Executive*, 2, 127–32.

Katz, R. L. (January/February 1955). Skills of an effective administrator. *Harvard Business Review*, 33–42.

Kerr, S., Hill, K. D., and Broedling, L. (1986). The first-line supervisor: Phasing out or here to stay? *Academy of Management Review*, 11, 103–17.

Mintzberg, H. (July/August 1975). The manager's job: Folklore and fact. *Harvard Business Review*, 49–61.

Mintzberg, H. (1971). Managerial work: Analysis from observation. *Management Science*, 18 (2), B97–B110.

Peters, T. and Austin, N. (1985). *A passion for excellence: The leadership difference.* New York: Random House.

CASE *A Conversation with Socrates*

Seeing Nicomachides, one day, coming from the assembly for the election of magistrates, Socrates asked him, "Who have been chosen generals, Nicomachides?"

"Are not the Athenians the same as ever, Socrates?" he replied; "for they have not chosen me, who am worn out with serving from the time I was first elected, both as captain and centurion, and with having received so many wounds from the enemy (he then drew aside his robe and showed the scars of the wounds) but have elected Antisthenes, who has never served in the heavy-armed infantry, nor done anything remarkable in the cavalry, and who indeed knows nothing, but how to get money."

"Is it not good, however, to know this," said Socrates, "since he will then be able to get necessaries for the troops?"

"But merchants," replied Nicomachides, "are able to collect money; and yet would not, on that account be capable of leading an army."

"Antisthenes, however," continued Socrates, "is given to emulation, a quality necessary in a general. Do you not know that whenever he has been chorus manager he has gained superiority in all his choruses?"

"But, by Jupiter," rejoined Nicomachides, "there is nothing similar in managing a chorus and an army."

"Yet Antisthenes," said Socrates, "though neither skilled in music nor teaching a chorus, was able to find out the best masters in these departments."

"In the Army, accordingly," exclaimed Nicomachides, "he will find others to range his troops for him, and others to fight for him!"

"Well then," rejoined Socrates, "if he finds out and selects the best men in military affairs, as he has done in the conduct of his choruses, he will probably attain superiority in this respect also."

"Do you say then, Socrates," he said, "that it is in the power of the same man to manage a chorus well, and to manage an army well?"

"I say," said Socrates, "that over whatever a man may preside, he will if he knows what he needs, and is able to provide it, be a good president, whether he have the direction of a chorus, a family, a city, or an army."

"By Jupiter, Socrates," cried Nicomachides, "I should never have expected to hear from you that good managers of a family would also be good generals."

"Come then," proceeded Socrates, "let us consider what are the duties of each of them, that we may understand whether they are the same, or are in any respect different."

"By all means," he said.

"Is it not, then, the duty of both," asked Socrates, "to render those under their command obedient and submissive to them?"

"Unquestionably."

"Is it not also the duty of both to appoint fitting persons to fulfill the various duties?"

"That is also unquestionable."

"To punish the bad, and to honor the good too, belongs, I think, to each of them."

"Undoubtedly."

"And is it not honorable in both to render those under them well disposed towards them?"

"That also is certain."

"And do you think it for the interest of both to gain for themselves allies and auxiliaries or not?"

"Certainly; but what, I ask, will skill managing a household avail if it be necessary to fight?"

"It will doubtless, in that case, be of the greatest avail," said Socrates; "for a good manager of a house, knowing that nothing is so advantageous or profitable and prejudicial as to get the better of your enemies when you contend with them, nothing so unprofitable and prejudicial as to be defeated, will zealously seek and provide everything that may conduce to victory, will carefully watch and guard against whatever tends to defeat, will vigorously engage if he sees that his force is likely to conquer, and, what is not the least important point, will cautiously avoid engaging if he finds himself insufficiently prepared."

"Do not, therefore, Nicomachides," he added, "despise men skillful in managing a household; for the conduct of private affairs differs from that of public concerns only in magnitude; in other respects they are similar; but what is most to be observed, is, that neither of them are managed without men; and that private matters are not managed by one species of men, and public matters by another; for those who conduct public business make use of men not at all differing in nature from those whom the managers of private affairs employ; and those who know how to employ them, conduct either private or public affairs judiciously, while those who do not know, will err in the management of both."

Questions

1. What is Socrates' (470?–399 B.C.) main point?
2. Of what level of management is Socrates speaking?
3. What management roles and functions does he identify? How do these compare with the traditional process views? with Henry Mintzberg's views?
4. What else does this dialogue tell us about management in Greece in the fifth century B.C.?

From Xenophon (n.d.), *Memorabilia and Oeconomicus*, E. C. Marchant, trans., The Loeb Classical Library ed., Cambridge: Harvard University Press, 186–87.

CHAPTER 2

Management and the External Environment

Student Learning Objectives

After reading this chapter, you should be able to:

1. Identify and discuss key aspects of the general external environment.

2. Identify and discuss aspects of the task environment.

3. Identify the major problems that confront managers as a result of the relationship between an organization and its external environment.

4. Identify four tactics that managers can use to increase their power over the task environment.

5. Understand the importance of the boundary-spanning function.

6. Explain how differences in environmental stability and segmentation influence managerial planning and decision making.

7. Explain the difference between open and closed management systems.

*M*anagement does not exist in isolation. Like any system, it exists within a larger environment. Threats of being bought by a major competitor, strikes by suppliers, legislation requiring an increase in corporate taxes, and public pressures for greater organizational contributions to community projects are not unusual events for organizations. The common ingredient in these events is the commanding of managers' attention by forces outside the organization.

Every organization exists in an environment that extends beyond its formal boundaries. This **external environment** represents a set of conditions, circumstances, and influences that surround and affect the functioning of an organization. CBS, for example, found Ted Turner to be part of its external environment several years ago when he attempted an unfriendly takeover. Several banks (particularly in Texas) faced serious economic problems when the price of oil went from $60 a barrel to under $20. In response to public pressure, Coca-Cola reintroduced its original-formula soft drink after a disappointing attempt to introduce "new" Coke. All of these are examples of how the external environment touches an organization.

As they carry out their roles, managers are affected by the external environment; therefore, to understand management, you must understand the nature of this environment. Effective organizations develop management systems that harmonize with the characteristics of their external environment.

The External Environment

The legal/political system is part of an organization's external environment.

The external environment, by definition, lies outside of the formal boundaries of an organization. This environment is made up of many different individuals (for example, customers, members of other organizations, local citizens), organizations (suppliers, civic groups, labor unions), and government bodies (regulatory agencies, legislators, local officials). It includes those people who are capable of influencing an organization and its management system, as well as those who might be affected by the organization's actions. For most organizations, the external environment is large, diverse, and complex. As a result, organization scholars have partitioned it into two sections. The **general environment** refers to the general and overall environment within which an organization operates. The **task environment** is the more specific and immediate environment in which an organization conducts its business. Every organization must cope with both facets of its external environment.

Consider for a moment the general and task environments of Embassy Suites, a hotel chain specializing in "all-suite" accommodations. It built a hotel in Schaumburg, Illinois, to capitalize on the potential market offered by O'Hare Airport and a number of nearby national corporate headquarters. The general business environment of the entire country is relevant to the managers of Embassy Suites. The general business recession of the early 1980s, for example, reduced the amount of optional overnight travel and the willingness of many corporations to pay for suites.

The task environment for Embassy Suites includes not only the local hotel, restaurant, and bar market, but also weekend hotel business. Managers at the Schaumburg hotel must be concerned about the potential lack of weekend business customers, although many residents in the Schaumburg area have fairly substantial incomes and could define a potential weekend market for the Embassy Suites (which offers a pool, sauna, steam room, free breakfast, and free cocktail hour). Even these relatively affluent individuals are not willing to pay $100 a night for a weekend room, but at $59 a night, local residents might reserve rooms and spend substantial amounts in the bar and restaurant. The success of this hotel, therefore, depends on management being aware of and coping effectively with both the general and task environments.

The General Environment

The general environment of an organization includes its social and cultural context, the economic system surrounding the organization, the legal and political atmosphere, the technology from which knowledge and tools for reaching goals are derived, and the international climate. Managers in different general environments often adopt different management systems.[1] For example, the management group for a major manufacturer of computer systems in Minneapolis, Minnesota, is less likely to feel the need for lifetime commitment to employment than would its Japanese counterpart.

Not only is any organization affected by pressure from the general environment, but organizational activity also affects the environment. One way in which an organization can affect the general environment is by influencing its local task environment. Consider the impact on the environment of the following organizational decisions announced in 1987. IBM closed a distribution center in Greencastle, Indiana, leaving the city without its major employer. Chrysler announced a $200 million investment to be made in the Kenosha, Wisconsin, AMC plant it acquired. This action was expected to add thousands of jobs to a beleaguered community. The company then changed its mind and, in 1988, announced the closing of the plant. Instead of adding jobs, the company's action would devastate the community's employment base. Figure 2.1 illustrates the major components of an organization's general environment.

The Sociocultural Domain The sociocultural domain consists of the values, customs, mores, and demographic characteristics (ages, education levels, mobility patterns, and the like) of the people within a society. A century ago, E. B. Taylor defined culture as "that complex whole which includes knowledge, belief, art, morals, law, custom and any other capabilities and habits acquired by a person as a member of society."[2]

Organizations have a special place within cultures. As French sociologist Michael Crozier has argued, "organizational systems are cultural answers to the problems encountered by human beings in achieving their collective ends."[3] Because most organizations are created to serve the needs of members of a society, it is easy to see how the values, customs,

FIGURE 2.1   *An Organization and the General Environment*

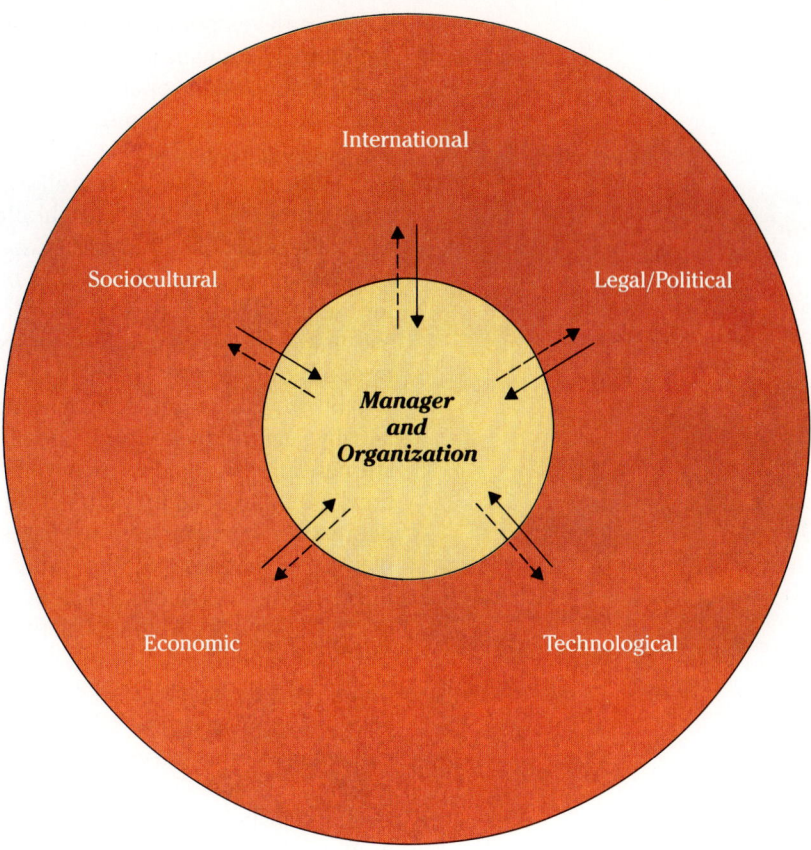

and social mores of that society can influence an organization and its management systems. Organizations are manifestations of social and cultural forces.

The values brought to an organization by its members stem from their social and cultural roots. Societal mores, for example, dictate what is acceptable and unacceptable organizational behavior. For example, traditional Japanese employees are willing to make a lifelong commitment to one organization and trust that organization to treat them fairly. The demographic patterns of a society also influence people's expectations of organizations. For example, demographic patterns influence expectations of organizations' social obligations, such as health care for retirees in populations where early retirement is common and life expectancy is long. Managers, as leaders and organizational decision makers, must be alert to social and cultural forces, because their actions will be driven by, affected by, and evaluated by the society.

The Economic Domain   Although organizations may be strongly influenced by the sociocultural domain, the fulfillment of these needs requires resources (for example, land, labor, and capital). Whenever people enter a relationship that involves the transfer of land, labor, capital, goods, and services, rules emerge to govern these transactions. As societies develop and countries are created, these rules take the form of increasingly formalized economic systems.

All organizations operate in at least one type of economic system—for example, socialist, communist, or capitalist. Each system has its own standards and institutions governing economic activity. In the United States, the capitalistic system allows free enterprise and the possession of private property, both of which affect the nature of managers' decisions and organizational activities. Capitalism's respect for private property provides citizens with the right to own labor, land, and capital. Its respect for the institution of free (private) enterprise provides owners the right to use that land, labor, and capital as they wish, as long as the rights and freedom of others are not violated.

Not only does the dominant economic system affect organizational activity, but the economic health of the external environment also strongly affects organizations. Both for-profit and not-for-profit organizations are influenced by such economic conditions as inflation, recession, depression, interest rates, and rates of international exchange. For example, partly because of the growing national deficit, state universities throughout the United States face declining budgets. As a result, they must cut back on the programs they offer, the research they sponsor, the student financial aid they provide, and the library facilities they support.

The private sector also must respond to pressure from the general environment. During the oil embargo of the 1970s, for example, American car manufacturers stepped up the design and production of smaller, more gas-efficient cars. They did so to meet public demand and to comply with federal legislation requiring minimum guaranteed mileage ratings. When fuel supplies became plentiful again during the mid-1980s, the government extended the deadline for meeting the conditions set forth in the legislation (leaving the one auto manufacturer who had met the conditions crying foul). It is not enough for managers to understand how the economic environment has influenced their organizations in the past. They must anticipate future effects and trends and manage accordingly.

The Technological Domain   *Technology* is the means by which an organization converts its inputs (such as raw materials, unfinished goods, energy) into outputs (products or services). The technological domain includes the knowledge, processes, means, systems, hardware, and software available to an organization for this transformation process. In the past few decades, for example, optic fibers have facilitated communications, robots have revolutionized manufacturing, computers have processed enormous amounts of information, and lasers have assisted surgeons.

Educational organizations have changed enormously as personal computers have become available to students and teachers. These and other technological advances have had major effects on the management of organizations. Imagine how the management of utilities would change if technology allowed the cost of solar-generated electricity to drop below that of coal, oil, water, and nuclear-generated power. Management must constantly monitor the technological domain for emerging developments and their possible effects on organizational activities.

The Legal/Political Domain   The sociocultural system establishes the spirit and sets the tone for acceptable and unacceptable organizational behavior. Many social values then are translated into laws designed to control and influence members of the society. The laws are made by legislators and interpreted by the courts, which are expected to apply "the will of the people"; thus, the legal and political systems are inextricably linked. This legal/political system allocates power among various groups in the society and settles disputes as they arise. The system also develops, administers, and enforces the law. Societies use their legal and political systems to ensure compliance with the values of the society and to maintain the existence of the society and its shared values and beliefs.[4] To achieve these ends, the legal/political system controls members of society and social institutions. If necessary, physical force can be used to accomplish this control.[5]

Within any society, a certain political ideology prevails at a particular time. Sometimes the ideology is toward the liberal end of the spectrum, sometimes the conservative end. Organizations and managers operate, of course, within this ideological climate. Political ideology affects organizations in many ways, including a governing body's enforcement or nonenforcement of selected laws, its tendency to multiply or subtract regulations that affect business, and its support for particular levels of taxes and interest rates. Political ideology strongly influences the economic atmosphere.

The legal/political environment generally plays a major role in establishing a probusiness or antibusiness mood within the general society. The "pro-big-business" attitude brought to Washington by the Reagan administration in the 1980s resulted in the deregulation of a number of industries and stimulated a wide range of organizational mergers. This attitude—located within a political ideology at the conservative end of the spectrum—made possible organizational decisions unlikely under

Technological advances in the use of robotics have revolutionized the manufacturing industry.

An increase in international interaction has meant stiff competition for American automobile manufacturers.

other, more liberal administrations. The 1986–87 merger of Texas Air, Eastern, Frontier, and People Express, for example, probably would not have occurred during earlier, less "pro-big-business" administrations.

In sum, the legal and political components of the environment strongly affect organizational behavior and, therefore, must be a target of managers' attention. Managers must monitor not only the laws that govern organizational activity but also the shifts in ideology among the major groups that make up the legal/political domain—the Supreme Court and elected judges, the Justice Department, the Congress, and other elected officials—that control the legal/political system.

The International Domain For a variety of reasons, an increasing number of organizations are interacting with the organizations and cultures of other countries. Among these reasons are limited domestic resources, the availability of international currency, the search for new markets, and increasingly more vigorous competition. The American automobile industry faces stiff competition from Japanese and German automobile producers. Even local liquor stores are influenced by international factors, such as the weather conditions in the Bordeaux region of France. By entering the international domain, organizations encounter economic systems and political ideologies different from their own.

More and more organizations are being influenced by international activities, such as the rise and fall in the value of the dollar and other currencies, the cost of foreign labor, international terrorism, restrictions on the flow of capital, trade barriers, and coups d'etat. Organizations that conduct business in foreign countries employ people with different languages and cultural backgrounds and are owned or managed by people from a number of different countries (see "A Closer Look: International Investment"). Thus, managers must consider the realities of the international domain as they make decisions.

The Task Environment

An organization's task environment is the means through which the general environment exercises its most immediate influences on an organization's management. The sociocultural domain describes the general values and mores of a society, but the people of a society are the actual customers of an organization. They exert direct influence on organizational operations and form part of the task environment. Manag-

FIGURE 2.2 *The Relationship Between Task and General Environments*

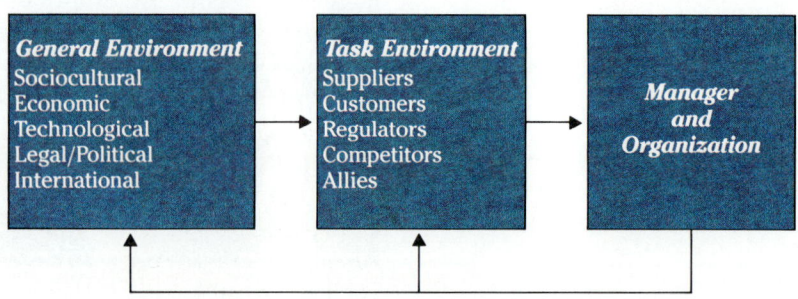

A CLOSER LOOK

International Investment: Europe Buys Back a Piece of the New World

In the eighteenth century, the United States of America claimed independence from its European master. Today Great Britain, joined by countries such as France, West Germany, and Sweden, are regaining some of their control over the former colonies. Today's weapons may seem less destructive, but they are much more powerful than those used two centuries ago. The pounds, francs, marks, and kroners aimed at the United States have more often than not hit their targets.

In 1987, over $10 billion worth of U.S. corporate assets were acquired through British takeovers alone. French interests assumed more than $1 billion of American holdings. According to *Business Week,* "A new, swashbuckling style of raider capital-ism is in vogue across Europe. The economic recovery on the Continent has produced scores of cash-rich companies with too few investment opportunities. . . ."[1]

It is not surprising that U.S. corporations are attractive to European investors. Many of these excellent corporations have outstanding promise as established profit makers. Add to this the fact that the value of the U.S. dollar relative to its European counterparts has been suppressed by at least 20 percent during recent years, and it is easy to understand what makes these companies appear to be major bargains.

Should U.S. businesses go to war?

Should U.S. businesses go to war? Only if they want to bite the hand that feeds them. As noted by Jean-Jacques P. Netter of the French brokerage house Nivard Flornoy & Cie, "A few years ago the U.S. economy seemed so invulnerable, . . . Now it's the healthy Europeans saving ailing industrial America. It's bizarre."[2]

Much of the money coming from Europe originated here as expenditures on European imports. Perhaps the returning money will ease the huge and chronic trade imbalance.

Is it just the Europeans who are "buying American?" Clearly not. The Japanese have a penchant for American real estate. Tokyo's Shuwa Corporation now owns the Arco Plaza in Los Angeles and paid $625 million for it in cash. The luxury Hyatt Regency Waikiki Hotel belongs to Azabu Jidosha Corporation, a Japanese business that considered the $245 million price tag reasonable. Japanese investment in U.S. real estate is encouraged by the very low interest rates available to investors in Japan and the limited real estate investment opportunities in their homeland. In 1987 alone, the Japanese spent $12.7 billion acquiring real estate in Phoenix, Seattle, San Diego, and other U.S. cities. Put quite simply, American real estate is too good a deal for the Japanese to resist.

1. F. J. Comes, R. A. Melcher, J. Kapstein, and E. Weiner (27 October 1986), Europe goes on a shopping spree in the states, *Business Week,* 54.

2. Comes, et al., 55.

---

ers should focus managerial strategies primarily on current and potential customers rather than on the general beliefs, values, and mores of society as a whole. Figure 2.2 depicts the relationship between the two environments (general and task) and an organization.

Whereas the general environment affects the operations of an organization, the effects of the task environment usually are more immediate. For instance, of particular concern to David Lavold, owner and operator of Lavold's Car Company in Monona, Wisconsin, are laws pertaining to the

FIGURE 2.3 *Lavold's Car Company's External Environment*

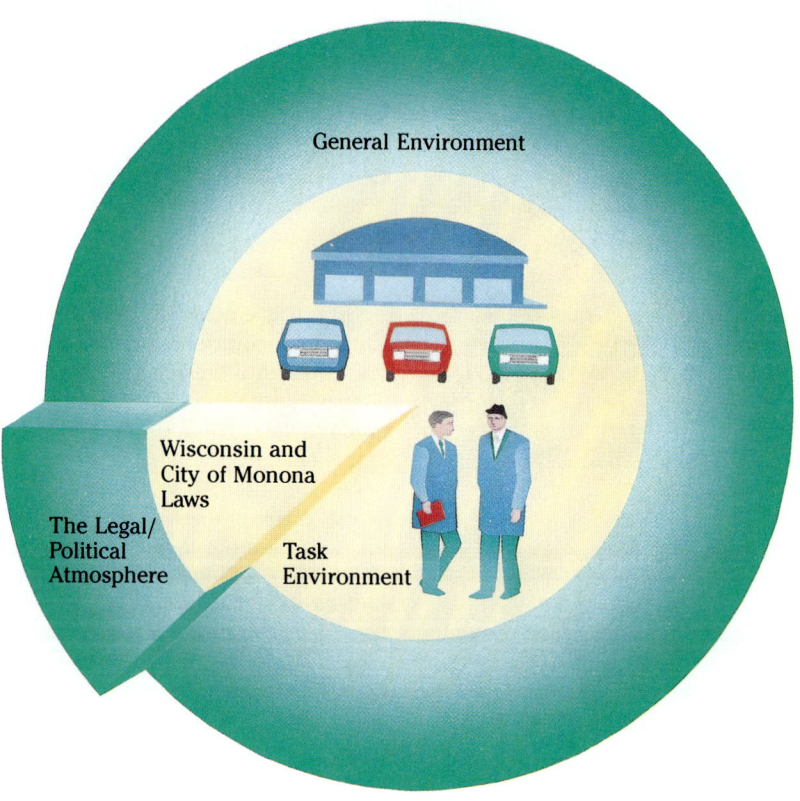

General Environment

Wisconsin and City of Monona Laws

The Legal/ Political Atmosphere

Task Environment

sale of used cars in Wisconsin.[6] In particular, the state's "lemon" law is important to him. This law provides car buyers with certain rights should a car purchased from Lavold's plague them with repeated problems. Lavold is bound by these regulations even if he sells a car in good faith which turns out to be a "lemon." The laws of Wisconsin and the city of Monona are part of the legal/political atmosphere, but they are also part of this automobile dealer's task environment.

Sociologists William R. Dill and James D. Thompson have used the term *task environment* to identify four important components of the external environment.[7] These critical four components are:

1. Suppliers—providers of materials, labor, capital, equipment, and work space

2. Customers/markets—including distributors and users

3. Regulatory and influence groups—for example, government agencies, unions, and professional associations (Originally Dill and Thompson dealt only with regulatory groups. Here, unions, professional associations, and outside influence groups have been added to this category.)

4. Competitors—for both markets and resources

A fifth component of the task environment includes *allies* (such as partners in joint ventures).[8] This section will examine each of these in detail.

Suppliers Organizations require a vast supply of resources—capital, people, raw materials, information—to carry out their objectives. These resources come from an organization's suppliers, one component of the task environment. To obtain adequate resources, managers must monitor the activities of and interact with the suppliers of these various resources.

1. *Capital*. The old saying "It takes money to make money" could just as easily be "It costs money to get money." Capital is an essential resource. Managers' decisions at all levels in an organization are influenced by the availability and cost of capital. Suppliers of capital include industrial and corporate investors, banks, and insurance companies. The availability of capital and the cost associated with borrowing can exert a major influence on managers' activities.

2. *Human resources*. Organizations, as social systems, rely heavily on human resources. Human resources are another essential component of the task environment. The size and characteristics (such as age, mobility, education, and training) of the external environment's human

FIGURE 2.4   *The Task Environment*

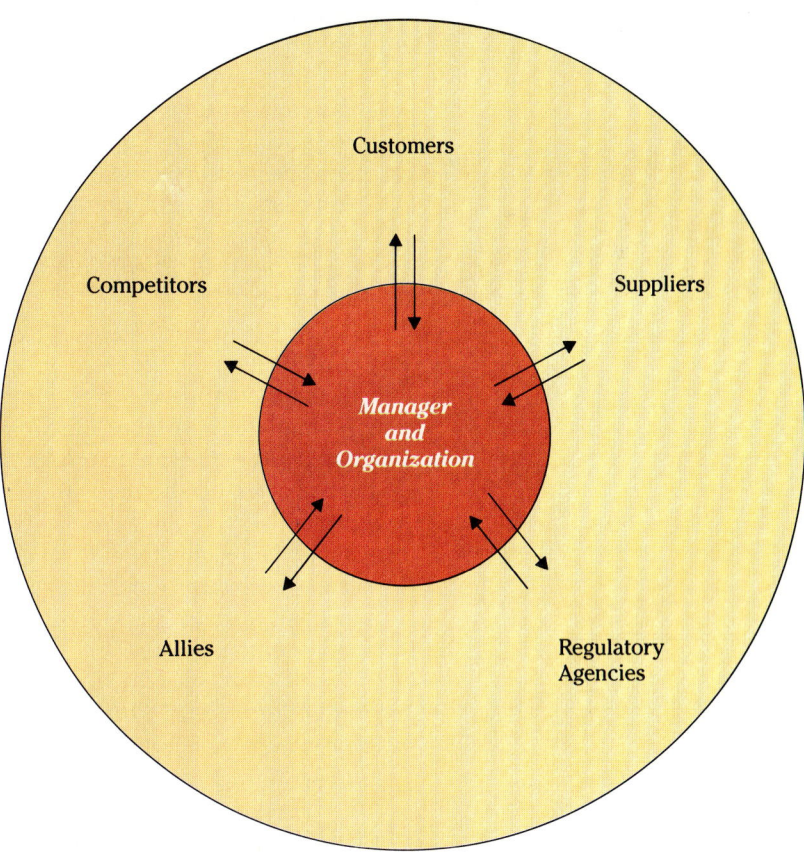

resource pool strongly affect an organization and its operations. For example, in searching for a new plant location, Endotronics, a Minnesota-based cell research laboratory, paid particular attention to the targeted communities' ability to offer an adequate supply of employees who could be trained in medical technology.

3. *Raw materials.* To produce goods and services, many organizations require natural resources and raw materials. For example, Potlatch's decision on where to locate a particle board manufacturing plant was influenced by the availability of trees. Similarly, the quality, quantity, and cost of coal encouraged the Salt River Utility Company to turn to nuclear resources for energy production.

4. *Information.* Some people do not regard information as a resource, but organizations have a tremendous need for a wide range of information. Management must, for example, keep informed of technological developments, market changes, economic developments, and other environmental events with the potential to influence organizational effectiveness.

Organizations fill their needs for information in many ways. They get information through organization members who are in contact with information-providing sources. An organization's scientists, for example, attend professional conferences. Managers often develop a network of relationships outside of their organization. Through these relationships, they gain access to information that they can bring back to the organization.

Some information is obtained from formal information-providing systems. An organization may use a market research firm, for example, to provide specific market information. Economic consulting agencies provide local, regional, state, national, and international economic forecasts. In addition, publications (such as *Hospitals, California Management Review, The Academy of Management Executive, Fortune,* and *The Wall Street Journal*) also offer important information for managers.

Customers/Markets   A second major component of the task environment is composed of customers and markets. Organizations survive by importing the resources that they need from their environment and returning to it a desirable product or service. The part of the environment that wants (or can be made to want) a particular product or service is the *market.* Every organization serves one or more markets: educational institutions teach students; hospitals treat patients; accounting firms balance hospitals' books; tire manufacturers sell to automobile manufacturers and owners. Thus, an organization's customers may be individuals or other organizations.

Regulatory and Influence Groups   Several components in the task environment can influence the policies and practices of management formally through the legislative system and informally through the pressures brought to bear by special interest groups. Local, regional, state, and national government agencies, for example, are formally responsible for controlling and regulating many organizational policies and practices.

Government agencies regulate many organizational practices in an effort to protect the interests of society at large.

Labor unions, professional associations, and interest groups also have a significant effect on the behavior of organizations.

1. *Government*. Organizational sociologists Peter M. Blau and W. Richard Scott treat government agencies as "commonwealth organizations" that exist to serve the needs of the larger society.[9] Agencies such as the Federal Commerce Commission and the Environmental Protection Agency play a major role in defining what organizations may or may not do. The Food and Drug Administration's information and labeling laws, the Occupational Safety and Health Agency's regulations, and the U.S. Commerce Department's import and export restrictions are just some of the regulations that affect managerial decision making.

2. *Unions*. Federal legislation has given labor unions a number of rights that influence their interactions with organizations. The National Labor Relations Act of 1935, for example, required organizations to recognize and bargain with a union if that union was legally established as a representative of the organization's employees. As a result, labor unions have a position of formal power. Managers, therefore, must know what these rights are so that organizational decisions and practices do not produce unwanted conflict. (See "A Closer Look: Influence Groups.")

3. *Professional associations*. Many members of organizations are also members of professional associations, such as the American Society for Personnel Administration, the American Medical Association, the American Federation of Teachers, and the American Society for Mechanical Engineers. Not only do association members exchange ideas and information, which they bring back to their own organizations, but they also propose policies and even laws governing the general and task environments. The American Medical Association, for example, sets policy on whether doctors may advertise and recommends laws on health-related issues. In addition, many professional associations have developed a code of ethics to govern their respective professions, and these also affect the task environment.

A CLOSER LOOK

Influence Groups: When the Union Owns the Company

In late 1985, the United Auto Workers (UAW) voluntarily agreed to compensation cutbacks of $2 per hour for 900 of its members working at the Exide Corporation in Horsham, Pennsylvania. In 1986, the union agreed to cutbacks of $2.63 per hour for its members working at the Wallace Barnes Steel Company in Bristol, Connecticut. What has gotten into the UAW? Why would they take such unusual steps? The answer lies in union concerns with the current merger mania running rampant in the United States.

According to *Business Week*, "For years, organized labor has watched helplessly as takeovers and leveraged buyouts thinned its ranks."[1] Now unions are fighting back. At Exide, the $2-per-hour compensation concession was exchanged for a profit-sharing plan and a contract provision that workers would get their concessions back if the company were ever sold. At Wallace Barnes Steel, the concessions were in exchange for an agreement that workers would be repaid not only if the company were sold but even if it were closed. These agreements can give the union tremendous power if a merger or buyout is proposed. If the union supports such a

deal, it can agree to forego the repayment of concessions. If it does not support the deal, it has the right to demand repayment should the deal go through. In many cases, the magnitude of repayments would make any would-be buyer think twice about the soundness of the investment.[2]

Some unions have even made direct attempts recently to thwart merger negotiations. In 1986, Texas Air Corporation tried to buy Eastern Airlines. Recognizing that Texas Air tended to pay employees lower wages than Eastern, the four unions representing Eastern employees made their own bid to buy the company. In 1987, the unions representing Pan American World Airways attempted to buy 37 percent of company stock by using compensation concessions.

When the Soo Line Corporation put its Lake States Transportation Division up for sale in 1987, unions representing 800 employees offered to buy. The steelworkers' union has already coordinated employee buyouts of a steel mill equipment plant in Ohio and of two Republic Steel Corporation

shops and had plans to gain control over Sharon Steel Corporation in exchange for large wage concessions.

What does all of this mean for businesses, for unions, and for employees? Right now it means that unions have found a powerful new way to influence merger and buyout decisions. In the long term, however, it may mean much more. Traditionally, being a member of a union has meant that an employee could influence compensation and working conditions, but when employees (or their unions) also own part of the company, they have a right to influence any business decisions. In the future, expect to see more union representatives sitting on company boards of directors and more attention paid to the wishes of employee-owners.

---

1. Z. Schiller (23 March 1987), Merger phobia has unions wheeling and dealing, *Business Week*, 118.
2. Recently the parent company of Wallace Barnes Steel sold the steel company. The owner bought the company and the burden of repayment.

4. *Interest groups*. Like professional associations, interest groups, such as Greenpeace and the National Organization for Women, are neither governmentally created nor sanctioned. Although they do not exercise a legally based form of influence over organizations, they can have a considerable influence on organizational policy and practice. Interest groups rely heavily on their ability to use the media and to persuade the general public in their attempts to influence organizational activities. The Sierra Club and other environmental protection groups, for example, wielded considerable influence over a number of legislative decisions regarding the dumping of iron ore residue into Lake Superior by Reserve Mining.

Competitors   Because the supply of resources in the external environment is limited, organizations must compete for their share of the supply. Competitors thus are another significant component of the task environment. SONY, Panasonic, RCA, and Fisher compete for consumer dollars, for example. The Big Eight accounting firms compete to hire the most qualified accountants and to get the best clients. With varying degrees of intensity, most organizations engage in attempts to attract consumers to their organizations and away from other organizations that provide similar goods and services.

Allies   Allies are the individuals and organizations with whom an organization develops interdependent relationships and shares things important to both parties. Allies, thus, are the fifth major component of the task environment. Allies may, for example, combine resources to start a joint venture that one organization does not want to undertake alone. This situation arose when Minnesota Power and Pentair joined forces to establish a new paper manufacturing firm (Lake Superior Paper Industries). Thus, the task environment for many organizations includes other, cooperating organizations. Dealing with allies requires organizations to develop and maintain good working relationships with allies to serve their common interests.

The relationships between organizations and their task environments are dynamic. Much as the task environment influences an organization, an organization attempts to control and influence the task environment. Most managers would agree that it is better to study and manage the external environment than to allow it to control an organization.

The Organization-Environment Power Relationship

As you have seen, the external environment is one context within which managers must operate. Managers must understand this environment so that they can guide an organization appropriately toward its goals. As an organization and environment interact, managers confront two kinds of problems: uncertainty and interdependence.

James D. Thompson has contributed substantially to an understanding of the role of external environments and has developed strategies for managing these environments.

The Problems of Uncertainty and Interdependence

Inevitably, managers and their organizations interact with the external environment, but under most circumstances, managers can neither control nor predict everything that will happen in this interaction. As a consequence, managers are faced with varying amounts of *environmental uncertainty*. This is the source of one kind of problem for managers.

A second kind of problem for managers arises as a natural part of doing business as managers develop a variety of exchange relationships with others, such as suppliers, customers, and allies. Through purchases and sales, a form of *interdependence* between two organizations doing business begins to develop. For example, Northwest Outlet (a retailer) is dependent on the Hudson Bay Company, a manufacturer of wool blankets and clothing, to supply them with the much-sought-after Hudson Bay wool blankets.

Uncertainty and organizational interdependence represent two forces that often constrain managers' activities. Unless managed effectively, these forces can interfere with the attainment of organizational goals. A number of strategies that can help managers minimize the power of the task environment over the organization have been identified and will be discussed in the next section.

Managing Uncertainty and Interdependence

It has been argued by many managers and scholars alike that managers should attempt to manage the amount of power that the external environment exercises over the operations of their organization. In fact, organizational sociologist James D. Thompson contended that managers should actively pursue strategies that would give them power over their external environment. An organization has power over its external environment if it can satisfy the needs of the environment. It also has power if it can act without regard for the actions of members of its task environment. To the extent that managers can manage uncertainty and environmental dependency, they gain power over their external environment and greater control over their organizational operations.

Thompson offered two possible sets of strategies for managers to deal with the problems of uncertainty and interdependence.[10] The first represents attempts to manage the boundary that separates an organization from its environment. This approach is aimed at minimizing the degree to which environmental forces are allowed to penetrate an organization and affect its daily operations. Effective managers frequently engage in strategies aimed at sealing off their organization off from the environment's control and influence. Although it is unrealistic to believe that an organization can completely isolate itself from environmental influences, it is reasonable for managers to engage in strategies that insulate it from erratic and potentially damaging environmental demands. The following are four strategies for minimizing these disruptions.

1. **Buffering.** Organizations can buffer themselves by stockpiling resources or warehousing outputs. For example, Goodyear may stockpile lampblack for the manufacture of tires and then warehouse

Claudia Conlon Appleby

Claudia Conlon Appleby apprenticed on Broadway as a press agent and currently directs public relations at Sterling Vineyards in the Napa Valley of California.

1. How is the management of your organization influenced by public opinion and values?

The public has a love-hate relationship with beverage alcohol products. At present wine is seen as a friend to food and an enemy to drivers, and this affects our marketing strategy. I find it more useful to follow public sentiment rather than challenge it. For example, several years ago we might have had a television producer film a segment of visitors tasting wine in the Sterling tasting room. Now, we refrain from shots of people drinking and tell the wine story differently. The media are always intrigued by the winemaking process, but their avoidance of portraying wine as something one drinks is on the rise. Do public values influence that decision? Very definitely.

2. How is the management of your organization influenced by the fact that you are competing in a market traditionally dominated by Europeans?

The wine industry in this country is influenced by the European tradition in many ways—positively in the sense that hundreds of years of European PR have positioned wine as a desirable and affordable luxury, and negatively in the sense that Americans, because of their cultural naiveté, are intimidated by fine wines. The quality of the product and its availability ultimately forge the bottom line in the

---

"Capitalize on features . . . that are unique."

---

public's awareness. Americans, to their credit, have an unending appetite for the new, the well made, and the delicious; therefore, as professionals with tremendous pride in our product, we tend to view the European influence as waning and our own influence as ascending.

3. How is the management of your organization influenced by governmental relations?

The BATF (Bureau of Alcohol, Tobacco, and Firearms) regulates our industry with a firm hand. Wine labels and contents are rigorously monitored. Recent legislation on drunk driving has also had an enormous impact on the public's perception of beverage alcohol products; the company in turn has spent millions in advertising to sensitize the public in developing responsible, moderate drinking patterns.

4. What can management of your organization do to distinguish your wines from those of Napa Valley competitors?

Based on the assumption that our competition also grows or buys excellent fruit, uses state-of-the-art equipment, and runs attractive tasting rooms, our marketing strategy seeks to capitalize on features of our winery that are unique. The beautiful location; hilltop winery; aerial tram; sit-down tasting; self-guided tour experience; and restrained, delicate wine all tell a story of excellence in a given style. Telling and reinforcing that story through our point-of-sale sales approach, tour and tasting, label copy, newsletter, logo, and advertising are all part of an integrated plan.

---

finished tires to avoid potential shortages and to be ready for unexpected demands. These buffering techniques enable an organization to maintain operations when there are shortages of raw resources and when there are peaks and valleys in demand for the organization's products. In essence, through buffering, an organization absorbs environmental fluctuations much as the shock absorbers in a car stabilize its ride over bumps and potholes.

Buffering allows an organization to operate smoothly during environmental fluctuations.

2. **Smoothing.** Through the process of smoothing, or leveling, managers attempt to influence the behavior of the environment. During low demand periods, organizations may offer inducements, such as price reductions, to encourage consumers to buy their products and services. During peak periods, they may charge a premium rate, thereby discouraging excessive demand. Smoothing explains why snow tires are cheaper during the summer and air conditioners are less expensive during the winter.

3. **Anticipating and adapting.** Under some circumstances, managers can anticipate changes in environmental conditions and adapt appropriately. With information gleaned from forecasting activities, managers can help their organizations adapt internally to anticipated environmental demands. Bars and restaurants in popular summer vacation areas, for example, anticipate the tourist season and increase their supplies of liquor, food, and employees.

4. **Rationing.** "When buffering, leveling, and forecasting do not protect their technical cores from environmental fluctuations, organizations . . . [may] resort to rationing."[11] Rationing establishes a set of priorities for using an organization's resources. Many organizations, under conditions of economic decline, ration the existing work across the current workforce instead of laying off some people and keeping the remaining employees working full time. In this way, they reduce the total number of hours worked by each employee.[12]

These strategies for insulating organizations from environmental stresses can go a long way toward protecting organizations, but there is a second set of strategies that affects an organization's relationship with the external environment. These strategies allow managers to gain control over aspects of the external environment, thereby reducing the level of uncertainty and dependency. There are several strategies that an organization can use to reduce its dependency on the environment and thereby increase its power over that environment.

1. **Prestige.** If an organization can develop a favorable image among members of its task environment, and if it can make forming relationships with it "the thing to do," the organization gains power over members of its task environment.

2. **Contracting.** The creation of an agreement between an organization and a member of its task environment represents a cooperative strategy. When an organization enters into a contract with another organization—for example, to purchase its raw materials for the next year—the contract reduces uncertainty about purchases and sales for both organizations. The effect of contracting is to reduce uncertainty about the behavior of a member of the environment by formally agreeing on how the organization and the contractor will behave.

3. **Co-opting.** Co-opting is the process of absorbing part of the task environment into an organization. For example, an organization may place someone from a major lending institution on its board of directors. As a result of this act of absorption, the organization is likely to gain an element of support for its actions.[13]

4. **Coalescing.** Coalescing refers to merging or joining into a venture with a member of the task environment. A coalition is formed, and those involved in the coalition become allies. A merger combines all resources of both organizations. In a joint venture, however, only those resources relevant to the common activity are combined. In 1987, IBM and Microsoft formed a coalition of this type to develop jointly spreadsheet software for IBM's PS/2 microcomputers.

Stanford University management professor Jeffrey Pfeffer has identified several other tactics that managers can use to reduce uncertainty and interdependence.[14]

1. **Selective recruitment** of key employees. By hiring knowledgeable individuals from key organizations in the external environment, managers can bring into their fold people with information and knowledge about the operations and policies of competitors. In this way, they reduce interdependence and uncertainty. This is exactly what Digital Equipment Corporation (DEC) does each time it hires a former IBM employee.

2. **Regulation.** Organizations can encourage and support various forms of control by regulatory agencies. Regulations often affect the interdependence of organizations and the level of uncertainty. In the late 1980s, for example, automobile manufacturers in the United States encouraged the government to restrict the number of cars imported from Japan. The direct result of this regulation was to reduce competition for U.S. car makers, allowing them to charge higher prices than they could otherwise command.

3. Engaging in **political activity.** Managers may become involved in political processes not only to influence regulations but also to exercise political power in other ways that favorably affect the organization. For example, many university administrators have used government officials to secure funds for university projects. Columbia Univer-

sity built a new chemistry laboratory with funds from the Department of Energy, Rochester Institute of Technology received money from the Defense Nuclear Agency for its Center for Microelectronic Engineering, and Northeastern University got money for a library through the Air Force's electronics research fund.[15]

Managers, thus, have a wide variety of tactics by which they can reduce the uncertainty and power of the external environment. Chapter 9 will discuss specific strategies available to managers for fitting their organizations into the task environment.

Linking Environments and Organizations

It is often difficult to determine where an organization ends and its environment begins. If someone asked you how large your college is, you would probably refer to the number of students who are enrolled, but are the students part of the organization or part of the external environment? If asked to describe the size of your hair stylist's shop, would you refer to the number of stylists who work there or to the number of customers? Although the external environment is defined as being separate and distinct from an organization, it is seldom easy to identify the exact location of the boundary between the two. In fact, many organizations (such as prisons, hospitals, and universities) attempt to encompass various aspects of the environment within their boundaries. Many of the tactics described in the previous section help them accomplish this goal. When an organization buys its key suppliers, co-opts a board member, hires an important employee away from a competitor, or shapes the laws and regulations that govern its business, it assimilates part of its external environment. In such cases, although an organization and its environment are separate, they have an interdependent relationship.

The Boundary-Spanning Process

Boundary spanners link their organization to its external environment.

Many of the tactics described earlier for reducing uncertainty and managing interdependence are ways that organizations span their boundaries with the external environment. Because organizations exist within and depend on their external environments, managers need to link their organization carefully to the external environment. The **boundary-spanning process** is one means through which organizations conduct transactions with their external environment. At General Mills, for example, when the market research department brings information into the organization about customer preferences, it performs a boundary-spanning activity. **Boundary roles** are the positions that link an organization to its external environment. Sales representatives, market researchers, and organizational lobbyists hold boundary roles. **Boundary spanners** are the individuals who fill these roles. A boundary spanner operates both within and outside of an organization, as when a manager acts as a liaison between the organization and the external environment. The various roles played by managers—figureheads and spokespeople—enable them to span the boundaries between the organization and the environment.[16]

As you have learned, individuals other than managers can perform the role of organizational boundary spanners. Purchasing agents, salespeople, lawyers, technological specialists, and lobbyists often link an organization to its suppliers, customers, regulatory bodies, and informational resources. Although some positions are created specifically to serve the boundary-spanning function, many individuals are informal carriers of information across organizational boundaries. A waiter, for example, might learn about an especially good wine from customers and suggest to the wine steward that it be included in the restaurant's wine selection. In the reciprocal relationship between an organization and its external environment, the external environment influences decisions made by managers, and managers engage in a variety of tactics to influence the external environment.

Environmental Stability and Segmentation

James Thompson has suggested that two characteristics of an organization's task environment significantly influence the behavior of effective managers: the degree of environmental change and the degree of environmental segmentation.[17]

Environmental change reflects the degree to which an organization's task environment is stable (undergoing few and slow changes) or shifting (undergoing frequent and rapid changes). During the late 1970s, for example, domestic airlines operated within a fairly stable environment. Although fuel prices continued to rise, they did not rise nearly so fast as they had soon after the oil embargo of the early 1970s. During the 1980s, however, the U.S. government deregulated the airlines, which caused numerous and frequent changes in flight schedules, airfares, and even airline ownership. Competition for new routes intensified, as did competition for new passengers, whom the airlines tried to attract with low fares. Clearly, this previously stable environment changed rapidly.

Environmental segmentation describes the similarities and differences among components of the task environment and the demands that

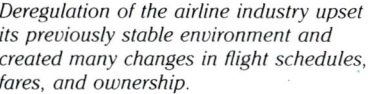

Deregulation of the airline industry upset its previously stable environment and created many changes in flight schedules, fares, and ownership.

they place on an organization. In other words, it describes whether the characteristics of an organization's suppliers, customers, competitors, and regulatory agencies are very different or little different from one another in their demands on the organization. A **homogeneous task environment** is characterized by very little segmentation. That is, components of the task environment place similar demands on an organization. For example, nearly all of the customers at the Badger Tap, a student bar near the University of Wisconsin, place essentially the same demands on the organization. Most of the bar's suppliers and its competitors also place similar demands. Because of the similarity of their demands, these segments of the Badger Tap's task environment can be regarded as homogeneous. Conversely, a **heterogeneous task environment** is highly segmented or differentiated. For example, IBM developed its personal computer line to target part of a highly segmented market. Computer customers include groups with very different demands. Some want word processors, some graphics capabilities, some spreadsheets, and some scholarly capabilities. The computer needs of the Pentagon, the college student, and the business executive differ greatly.

The stability and segmentation of the task environment combine to define the four environmental conditions that managers encounter: (1) stable and homogeneous, (2) stable and heterogeneous, (3) shifting and homogeneous, or (4) shifting and heterogeneous (see Figure 2.5). The challenge is to design an organization/management system that can handle the conditions presented by its task environment.

Stable and Homogeneous Environments   When the environment of an organization is stable and homogeneous, managers face a relatively low level of uncertainty. Under these conditions, management can develop rules, regulations, and standard operating procedures to guide internal operations and interactions with the external environment. The structure of an organization can be simple, with clearly defined areas of authority, responsibility, information systems, and division of labor. This is what the U.S. car industry was like prior to the invasion of foreign car manufacturers.

FIGURE 2.5   *Environmental Conditions*

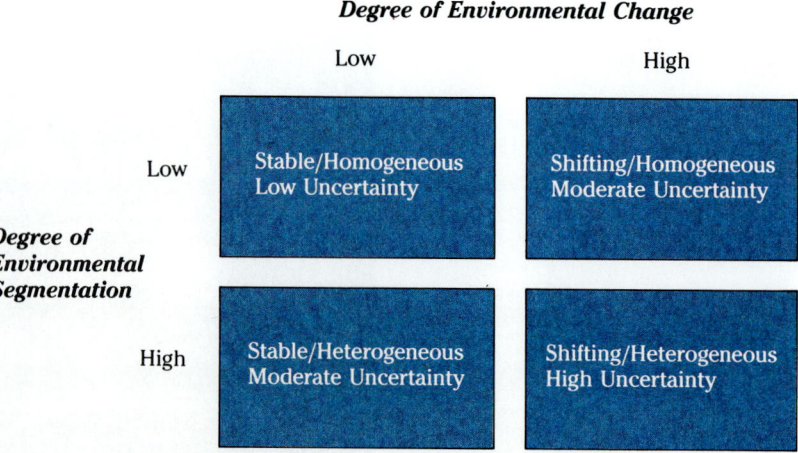

Source: J. D. Thompson (1967), *Organizations in action*, New York: McGraw-Hill, 72.

Stable and Heterogeneous Environments   A stable external environment with a number of highly differentiated components presents managers with a moderate level of uncertainty. Under these conditions of moderate uncertainty, managers must collect information from the external environment and bring it into their organization so that it can be used to influence organizational activity. In addition, information from the organization must be carried back to the segmented environment so that the organization can influence its external environment.

These demands on management result in the creation of specialized subsystems (jobs, departments, divisions) within an organization, each of which is responsible for dealing with a component of the external environment. As these specialized roles are created, the internal structure of an organization becomes more complex. For example, if a major regional automobile distributor extends its market to include institutional buyers as well as private citizens, it may have to create a special sales office to handle institutional sales. With two different sales units, managers have a structurally more complex organization to manage.

The primary demands facing managers in a heterogeneous environment are to monitor and respond to the environment, while maintaining internal integration and coordination of their organization's activities. The heterogeneity of the environment brings about a more complex structure and places greater demands on the planning, organizing, and control systems than does a homogeneous environment, but the external environment's stability still permits management to govern internal activities by relying on rules, regulations, and standard operating procedures.

Shifting and Homogeneous Environments   Managers in shifting and homogeneous environments also face moderate levels of uncertainty, yet this degree of change places different demands on managers from those that arise from a stable environment. Consequently, managers' responses to these demands should also differ.

When an organization's environment changes rapidly, creating standard routines for handling activities becomes increasingly difficult. Critical environmental clues let a manager know when and how to act. Organizational boundaries must remain open so that information flows quickly from the environment into the organization and to the appropriate point for action. Some organizations keep their boundaries open by developing a number of specialized boundary-spanning positions to monitor the environment and by collecting, interpreting, and channeling information into the organization. This is the role played by the market research group of the Wilson Sporting Goods company that monitors consumer preferences. It is this information which helped identify the need for colored golf and tennis balls. The number of boundary-spanning units depends on the degree of environmental segmentation.

Many organizations in shifting and homogeneous environments hire people with high levels of specialization, education, and professionalism. These people are placed in key positions and given substantial authority for making organizational decisions. The simplicity of the environment enables an organization to limit the number of specialized divisions that deal with these environmental components. The changeableness of the environment, however, requires a more professional workforce, few programmed operating procedures, and the sharing of decision-making authority. In recent years, the banking industry has faced such conditions. The more progressive banks have responded by allowing key officers great latitude and flexibility in dealing with clients.

Shifting and Heterogeneous Environments When the environment is shifting and filled with heterogeneous segments, managers face the highest degree of uncertainty. This is currently the case in the cable television industry, where market demands are changing rapidly, and a variety of distinct viewing groups exist. City, state, and federal regulations are relevant. Competition is increasing between cable companies and traditional broadcast stations, as well as with the videotape and satellite TV industries. At the same time, technology is changing rapidly. The task environment is made up of many highly differentiated suppliers, customers, competitors, and regulatory bodies, all of which place a variety of demands on organizations. In addition, these demands undergo rapid change. Customers may want modifications made to a product or service; at the same time, suppliers may change the nature of the materials they are capable of delivering. Meanwhile, legislators, courts, and regulatory agencies may rewrite the laws and regulations that govern the manufacture or sale of products and services. Many of the organizations operating in this industry are facing a shifting and heterogeneous task environment.

In a shifting and heterogeneous environment, each of management's boundary-spanning systems must be attuned to its special segment of the external environment. In addition, managers must create internal communication and authority systems for processing incoming information so that their organization can effectively respond to environmental conditions. Ricoh, a manufacturer of copy machines, faces an environment which has undergone rapid technological changes. It also must compete not only with other manufacturers of copying machines, such as Savin, but also with huge corporations, such as IBM and Xerox. With the increasingly blurred distinction among copy machines, printers, and telefax systems, Ricoh faces an increasingly heterogeneous environment, as well as one in which advancements in technology are undergoing extremely rapid changes. Ricoh must know which direction consumer preferences are heading and what changes in technology are likely. Ideally, these challenges should result in the creation of a flexible organization with a highly decentralized authority structure. The organization should be structurally complex but not too bureaucratic in design or function.

In sum, the challenge that faces all managers is to design an organization/management system that can handle the conditions presented by the task environment. Task environments vary according to the degree of environmental change, segmentation, and uncertainty. A manager's approach to organizing should be different under each of the four combinations of environmental conditions.

Environmental Studies

Empirical research studies provide evidence that an organization's external task environment strongly affects its organizational and management systems. Results from two such studies will be discussed in this section.

One of the first major empirical studies to concentrate on the relationship between organizations and their environments was conducted by British researchers Tom Burns and George Stalker.[18] They examined the relationships among environmental conditions, management practice, and organizational design in twenty manufacturing firms in England and Scotland. The study, which has had tremendous impact on the science of management, focused on the rate of environmental change in the firms' scientific technology and product markets. Results identified two different systems of management practice. One system was labeled *organic*, the other *mechanistic* (see Table 2.1).

An **organic system** is characterized by

- A flexible structure that can change when confronted with different kinds of task demands
- Loosely defined tasks to be performed by employees
- Consultative-type organizational communications (as opposed to a commanding type of relationship)
- Authority that flows more from knowledge centers (individuals, groups, or specialized departments) and the nature of relationships than from strict hierarchical positions

In contrast, a **mechanistic system** of management is characterized by

- Clear definition and relative stability of tasks and responsibility
- Vesting of authority in position and its arrangement according to hierarchical level
- Communications in the form of a downward flow of instructions issued as commands

Burns and Stalker argued that organic and mechanistic management systems are appropriate for different kinds of environmental conditions. Dynamic environments, in which uncertainty is high and unique problems and events often arise, require an organic system. The mechanistic system is more compatible with stable environmental conditions. Rather than

TABLE 2.1   *Mechanistic and Organic Management Systems*

	Mechanistic	*Organic*
Structure	Rigid	Flexible
Tasks	Well defined, stable, standardized	Dynamic, loosely defined
Change	Resistant	Receptive
Authority source	From hierarchy and position	From knowledge and expertise
Control	Hierarchy	From self and peers
Communication direction	Command-type and downward	Consultative-type, up, down, horizontal, and diagonal
Communication content	Instructions and decisions issued by superiors	Information and advice

Source: T. Burns and G. Stalker (1961), *The management of innovation*, London: Tavistock.

proposing that one system of management is superior to the other, the researchers suggested that the nature of an organization's task environment plays a major role in determining the type of system that an organization should use.

A second study of the relationship between organizations and their environments was conducted by Harvard University researchers Paul Lawrence and Jay Lorsch.[19] In their field studies, they found that effective organizations operating in highly uncertain environments had management systems different from effective organizations operating in relatively stable environments. Specifically, firms that operated in highly uncertain environments had more differentiated or segmented management systems than did those that operated in highly certain environments. Firms in highly certain environments had internal divisions, such as departments, that operated with similar goals, time frames, interpersonal coordination, and structures. Firms in highly uncertain environments had internal divisions that differed from one another in all of these respects.

When structures, goals, and temporal and interpersonal orientations were dissimilar, managers in the studies found it more difficult to coordinate and control organizational activities. Lawrence and Lorsch found that managers of effective organizations in highly uncertain environments achieved successful integration of their organizational units by using personal and informal integrating mechanisms. Managers operating in more certain environments achieved integration through rules, policies, and standard operating procedures. Lawrence and Lorsch concluded their reports by noting that effective organizations develop designs and management systems to fit the environment in which they operate.

The work of Thompson, Burns and Stalker, and Lawrence and Lorsch leads to a number of observations. First, there appears to be a relationship between characteristics of the task environment and the type of management systems that an organization develops. To be effective, an organization must obtain the best possible fit between the environment and its management system(s). Second, organizations create different management systems to deal with the different amounts of uncertainty that managers face in performing their jobs. Organic management systems appear appropriate for high levels of environmental change and segmentation, mechanistic systems for more stable environments and lower levels of uncertainty.

Management Theory and the Environment

One way to characterize the different approaches that managers take to their external environments is by the *open* and *closed* systems philosophies.

Closed Systems   Years ago, classical management theorists proposed that organizations are rational systems that can be designed according to a specific set of laws. They asserted that organizations will be efficient if managers properly define the nature of the work, standardize work procedures, assign an appropriate division of labor, group tasks into departments, and specify appropriate authority and responsibility relationships. These primary forces, they said, are internal to the system and arise from the nature of the work itself. Thus, according to this

FIGURE 2.6   Open and Closed Systems Management

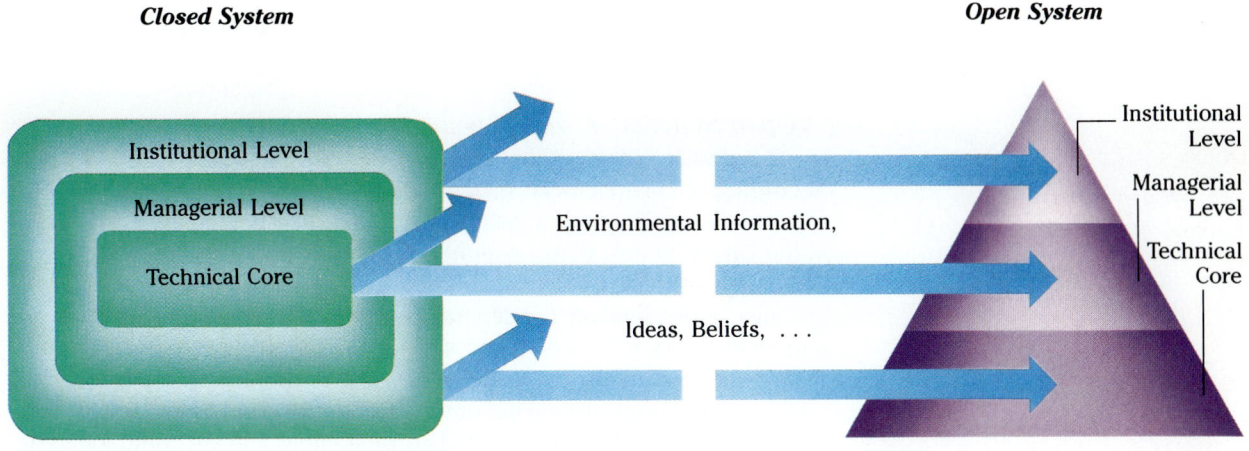

perspective, an organization could be designed appropriately if managers paid attention to the relationships among these parts of the system. Much as an engineer designs a bridge according to the principles of physics, followers of classical management theories believed managers can design an organization by adhering to the principles of organization.

In contrast, behavioral management theorists believe that the forces defining an effective management system are to be found in the nature of individuals and groups. They reason that management systems must be designed to accommodate workers' social and self-fulfillment needs. Both the classical and behavioral management theories concentrate on the inner workings of organizations in an effort to achieve order, consistency, efficiency, and predictability. They consider that a manager working in such a system does not have to pay particular attention to the external environment. In fact, neither classical nor behavioral management theories include the environment in their models.

From both the classical and behavioral perspectives, managers look only within an organization to improve productivity and efficiency. The organization is considered a **closed system** that operates as though it were in a world by itself. As Figure 2.6 shows, the walls of a closed system are thick. They block out ideas, information, and external environmental forces. Whatever environmental uncertainty penetrates the walls of an organization is absorbed at the institutional and managerial levels. Operations in the organization's technical core are not disrupted. The American automobile industry's refusal to believe in the shift to small and fuel-efficient cars is a classic example of a closed system at work. The goals of those within a closed system are to eliminate or control the uncertainty that originates in the external environment so that the management process is as easy and predictable as possible.

Although no organization can close itself off absolutely from external forces, managers can design a system that minimizes the uncertainty, pressures, information, and ideas of outside influences. For example, if managers assign all boundary-spanning activities to people at the institutional level of their organization, such as to a president or Chief Executive Officer, the effects of external forces on the technical core and the managerial zone are minimized. In addition, if managers at the institutional level adopt a closed-systems perspective, they further reduce the intrusion of the external environment into their organization's internal affairs.

Open Systems   A second perspective of an organization in relation to its external environment is the **open system** (review Figure 2.6). According to this perspective, an organization is a system that interacts with and depends on other systems. Consider the situation faced by banks in the United States. Banks cannot survive unless people and companies make deposits, take out loans, and purchase other banking services. They are also dependent on the federal government, which sets the cost of underlying money, as well as on state and federal regulations governing their bank charters.

". . . [O]rganizations are not autonomous entities; instead, the best laid plans of managers have unintended consequences and are conditioned or upset by other social units—other complex organizations or publics—on whom the organization is dependent."[20] An organization's survival depends on its ability to mesh with the larger environment. Open-systems advocates believe that this meshing allows organization members to deal effectively with the influences in the external environment. To cope with the external environment's inevitable intrusion and uncertainty, organizations must create management systems different from those found within a closed system. Rather than designing systems to ignore the external environment, they must design systems sensitive and responsive to the environment.

Managers who view their organization as an open system, therefore, face a major challenge. They must play an active role as organizational boundary spanners. They must carry information outward to influence the external environment and simultaneously serve as conduits through which external environmental factors can influence internal organizational operations. Such managers meet the public, talk to the press, and actively lobby regulatory and legislative bodies. Henry Mintzberg has noted that in all three critical managerial roles—interpersonal, informational, and decisional—effective managers are used to dealing with environments external to their organization.[21] To do so effectively requires at least a small degree of openness in management systems.

The open systems model suggests that an organization should create a number of open windows to let ideas, beliefs, information, and pressures from the environment influence the organization at each of its three levels—institutional, managerial, and technical core. As was noted in Chapter 1, changes that face organizations in society mean that the jobs of first-level managers increasingly will become externally oriented.[22] The institutional zone of management becomes more and more important as organizations become more dependent on coalitions with other organizations, as regulation of business expands and society increases its level of expectations for social responsibility by organizations. Effective organizations will have to become more open to environmental information, allowing it to flow in at each hierarchical level and permitting organizations to influence the environment at each level as well.

Management and the External Environment in Review

In the ordinary course of events, organizations interact with their external environments in a dynamic relationship. Managers try to control forces within the external environment, and, concurrently, the external environment exerts pressures on the organization. This external environment is large and complex, and it contains both general and task components. The general components include the culture in which the organization operates, the economic climate, the technological domain, and the legal/political atmosphere. The task component includes an organization's suppliers, customers, competitors, a number of regulatory and influence groups, and allies.

Through interaction with the external environment, managers face varying degrees of uncertainty and change, as well as various degrees of dependency on members of the task environment. Managers adopt a variety of tactics as they attempt to increase their power over the external environment and manage this uncertainty and interdependence. Ways to deal effectively with the external environment are discussed in more detail in later chapters.

Organizations exist, not in isolation, but within a broader external reality. Appropriate boundary-spanning activities help organization members exchange the information and knowledge necessary to deal effectively with the external environment. Boundary spanning identifies the techniques for dealing effectively and appropriately with the nature of the environment in which an organization operates.

Research has shown that management systems are and should be influenced by the external environment. Organic systems are better fitted to dynamic environments with high levels of uncertainty. Mechanistic systems, on the other hand, fit better when the external environment is quite stable. Although rules, policies, and standardized procedures may be effective in the absence of environmental uncertainty, more personal and informal procedures are preferable under conditions of high uncertainty. Classical management theorists suggested closed systems to isolate organizations from their environments. Contemporary environments require open systems if an organization is to survive. The most effective organizations are sensitive and responsive to their external environment.

Notes

1. J. Child (1981), Culture, contingency and capitalism in the cross-national study of organizations, in L. L. Cummings and Barry M. Staw, eds., *Research in organizational behavior*, Greenwich, CT: JAI Press, 303–56; M. Crozier (1973), Cultural determinants of organizational behavior, in A. R. Negandhi, ed., *Modern organizational theory*, Kent, OH: Kent State University Press, 219–28.
2. E. B. Taylor (1871), *Primitive culture*, London: Murray, 71.

3. M. Crozier (1972), The relationship between micro and macro sociology, *Human Relations*, 25, 239–51.

4. A. Ranney (1971), *The governing of men*, New York: Holt, Rinehart and Winston.

5. R. N. Osborn, J. G. Hunt, and L. R. Lauch (1980), *Organization theory: An integrated approach*, New York: John Wiley & Sons, 150.

6. Personal communication, 1987.

7. W. R. Dill (1958), Environment as an influence on managerial autonomy, *Administrative Science Quarterly*, 2, 409–43; J. D. Thompson (1967), *Organizations in action*, New York: McGraw-Hill.

8. P. E. Connor (1980), *Organizations: Theory and design*, Chicago: Science Research Associates.

9. P. M. Blau and W. R. Scott (1962), *Formal organizations*, San Francisco: Chandler.

10. Thompson, 1967.

11. Thompson, 23.

12. Thompson, 18–24.

13. Thompson, 26–36.

14. J. Pfeffer (1976), Beyond management and the worker: The institutional function of management, *Academy of Management Review*, 1, 36–46.

15. Lobbying 101: Colleges discover the pork barrel (27 October 1986), *Business Week*, 116, 118.

16. H. Mintzberg (1973), *The nature of managerial work*, Englewood Cliffs, NJ: Prentice-Hall.

17. Thompson, 1967.

18. T. Burns and G. M. Stalker (1961), *The management of innovation*, London: Tavistock.

19. P. R. Lawrence and J. W. Lorsch (1969), *Organization and environment*, Homewood, IL: Richard D. Irwin.

20. Connor, 1980, 15.

21. Mintzberg, 1973.

22. S. Kerr, K. D. Hill, and L. Broedling (1986), The first-line supervisor: Phasing out or here to stay? *Academy of Management Review*, 11, 103–17.

Key Terms

external environment
general environment
task environment
buffering
smoothing
anticipating and adapting
rationing
prestige
contracting
co-opting
coalescing
selective recruitment
regulation

political activity
boundary-spanning process
boundary roles
boundary spanners
environmental change
environmental segmentation
homogeneous task environment
heterogeneous task environment
organic system
mechanistic system
closed system
open system

Issues for Review and Discussion

1. Identify and briefly discuss each component of the general external environment.
2. What is an organization's task environment? Name the five components of the task environment.
3. What is the relationship between the general and task environments? What is their relationship with an organization?
4. What are the four tactics that help managers seal an organization from environmental forces?
5. Pfeffer identified a set of strategies that has been adopted by managers to manage the level of environmentally induced uncertainty and interdependence. Identify and briefly discuss each of these strategies.
6. Who acts as an organizational boundary spanner?
7. Explain why it is important for organizations to have boundary spanners.
8. Discuss why management planning and decision making should be different under conditions of low stability and high segmentation from conditions of high stability and low segmentation.
9. What is the difference between closed and open management systems?

Suggested Readings

Arogyaswamy, B. and Byles, C. M. (1987). Organizational culture: Internal and external fits. *Journal of Management,* 13, 4, 647–59.

Burns, T. and Stalker, G. M. (1961). Mechanistic and organic systems. In Burns, T. and Stalker G. M. *The management of innovation.* London: Tavistock Publications, 119–25.

Child, J. (1981). Culture, contingency and capitalism in the cross-national study of organizations. In Cummings, L. L. and Staw, B. M., eds. *Research in organizational behavior.* Greenwich, CT: JAI Press, 303–56.

Jurkovich, R. (1974). A core typology of organizational environments. *Administrative Science Quarterly,* 19, 380–94.

Lawrence, P. R. and Lorsch, J. W. (1967). Environmental demands and organizational states. Chapter four in Lawrence, P. R. and Lorsch, J. W. *Organization and environment: Managing differentiation and integration.* Boston: Division of Research, Harvard Business School.

Naisbitt, J. (1982). *Megatrends: Ten new directions transforming our lives.* New York: Warner Books; Chamberlain, P. C. (1988). A review of *Megatrends: Ten new directions transforming our lives.* In Pierce, J. L. and Newstrom, J. W., eds. *The manager's bookshelf: A mosaic of contemporary views.* New York: Harper & Row, 207–11.

Wilson, I. H. (Winter 1978). Business management and the winds of change. *Journal of Contemporary Business,* 45–54.

Zald, M. N. (1981). Political economy: A framework for comparative analysis. In Zey-Farrell, M. and Aiken, M., eds. *Complex organizations: Critical perspectives.* Glenview, IL: Scott, Foresman, 237–62.

CASE *Central South Music Sales, Inc.*

By Geoffrey P. Hull of Middle State Tennessee University

Central South Music Sales, Inc., (CSM) was formed in 1970 by Randy Davidson, Chuck Adams, and J. P. Bennett, all former employees of a recently failed record distributor. Davidson and Adams were former sales representatives, and Bennett had managed the company's warehouse. Armed with their knowledge of good customers and warehouse operations, they established CSM as a "one stop" record distributor handling a full line of all record labels. Sales were made directly to smaller record stores that were either too small to buy directly from the labels' branch distribution warehouses or who found it more convenient to deal with one source for all of their records.

The three had not planned retail operations initially, but with an out-side investor, Randy Davidson formed the KAR Corporation to operate a record store, The Sound Shop, in Clarksville, Tennessee, that same year. This first shop grew to five as Davidson's corporation opened two more stores in Kentucky and acquired two more when CSM took over a small record store chain, Record Central, which was heavily in debt, much of it owed to CSM.

These five retail stores became profitable, and, in 1975, CSM opened its first corporately owned Sound Shop. By 1980, the company had twenty-three stores in operation and had grown to employ 50 employees working for the distribution operation and 100 employees working in the retail stores. A chart of the corporation's divisions is shown in Figure 2A. The warehouse operations included the general wholesale operations, the rack division, the one stop division, and central media.

General Wholesale Operations

Warehouse operations were located in a 27,000-square-foot building in Nashville, Tennessee. They serviced over 650 accounts located throughout the Southeast. Accounts were divided among six order takers who contacted them by telephone. (About one third of the division's sales were to the company-owned stores.) CSM's competitive advantage was that all orders were shipped on the same day they were placed. For most of their customers, this meant receiving their records the day after placing an order.

To provide this service, CSM stocked over 50,000 titles in all available formats—LPs, tapes, and so on. Product specialists at the warehouse were responsible for all buying.

Central South Rack, Inc. The rack jobbing division was also operated out of the Nashville warehouse.

FIGURE 2A *Divisional Chart*

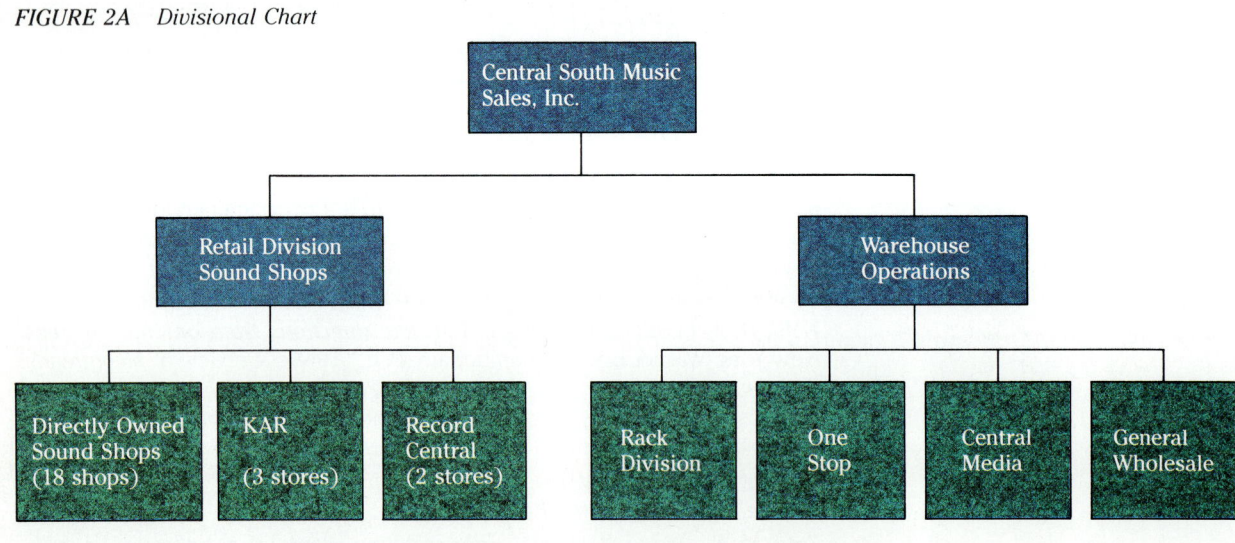

This division supplied complete record service to stores that had small record departments. The records were priced at the warehouse and placed in the store's racks by CSM route sales persons. They also were responsible for the appearance of the racks, the removal of damaged records, and the ordering of records. CSM serviced eighty rack locations, mostly Gibson Discount Stores in Mississippi, Tennessee, Kentucky, and Indiana.

Central South One Stop, Inc.

CSM's one stop division provided single records for juke box operators. CSM employees actually programmed the juke boxes. All the customers had to do was replace the designated records with new ones and insert new title strips, also provided by CSM. The one stop operation accounted for about 2 percent of CSM's total sales.

Central Media, Inc.

Central Media, Inc., was an in-house advertising agency. It created print and radio advertising and special promotional items, such as point-of-purchase signs, for the Sound Shops and for CSM customers. The agency received a 15-percent commission on all advertising placed. Record companies paid for the advertising, as was usual in this industry.

Retail Operations

The first Sound Shop stores were located in small college towns, but this approach gave way to locating them in shopping malls that contained a Sears or J. C. Penney store. In this way, CSM made use of the market research capabilities of these chains to locate their stores. In order to obtain space in desirable new malls, a record chain must have a good reputation with the mall developer. This reputation is based on having successful operations in existing malls owned by, or familiar to, the developer. CSM was able to get desirable locations by becoming the record store preferred by two major mall developers in the region. This gave CSM the first chance to locate in new malls opened by these developers.

Sound Shops were designed around two key factors, merchandise and service. The merchandise concept was to overwhelm the customer with a large selection of recordings of all types. Stores were given a uniform appearance through design characteristics and the use of common fixtures constructed by the company. All signs were also printed at CSM. Service was provided by staffing the stores with an average of five employees.

Store managers typically were recruited out of college and first assigned to work in the warehouse and learn the company's internal operations. Employees judged to have management promise were then assigned to stores as assistant managers. If successful, the assistant manager would then be assigned to manage one of the smaller stores. Managers were given considerable freedom to run their stores as if they were their own and reported to district managers, who supervised five or six stores.

CSM provided store managers with a monthly operating expense report and a quarterly net profit report. In these reports, each store was compared with chain averages and with its results in the previous period. While CSM had no required profit ratios, it used certain warning signals, such as sales per square foot or total costs of operations as a percentage of sales.

By the early '80s, the future appeared to be very bright for CSM. The company was growing at about 3 stores per year and expected that rate to increase with a goal of reaching 100 stores by 1990. The company planned to limit its operations to southeastern locations within 1000 miles of Nashville. This limitation was based on the belief that the Southeast economy would grow faster than that of most regions in the nation and on the company's inability to provide fast shipment to Sound Shops and CSM customers located more than 1000 miles from the Nashville warehouse.

Questions

1. Identify the key external environments for CSM's warehouse division and for its retail operations.

2. Identify boundary-spanning tasks for each of CSM's divisions.

3. In what ways does CSM appear to be a closed system? An open system?

4. What aspects of the external environment would CSM have to consider before deciding whether to add videotape sales and rentals to its business?

5. Discuss the pros and cons of CSM's limiting its operations to within 1000 miles of Nashville.

Management and the Internal Environment

Student Learning Objectives

After reading this chapter, you should be able to:

1. Identify the major sources of structure that define the internal environment.

2. Discuss the managerial processes that play major roles in shaping the internal environment.

3. Define organizational culture and explain why it is important.

4. Define organizational climate and identify the forces that shape it.

5. Specify and describe the five organizational functions.

6. Understand the importance of integrating the five organizational functions effectively.

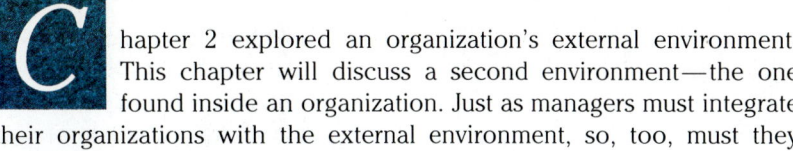

C hapter 2 explored an organization's external environment. This chapter will discuss a second environment—the one found inside an organization. Just as managers must integrate their organizations with the external environment, so, too, must they manage and coordinate the internal environment.

Components of the Internal Environment

The **internal environment** of an organization consists of a wide range of factors within its formal boundaries. The internal environment includes the jobs that people perform, as well as the work units, departments, divisions, and other structures in which they perform those jobs; the technologies people use to produce products and deliver services; the processes that managers use to guide workers; and, of course, the people who do the work—both managers and nonmanagers —together with their values and beliefs. These factors combine to form the climate of an organization. It is this climate that people "feel" when they perceive an organization as being, for example, cold and uncaring. The many aspects of the internal environment are addressed by organizational functions that managers execute in the areas of operations, marketing, accounting, finance, and human resources to promote an organization's efficiency and effectiveness.

Structures

Volvo's Kalmar plant uses a team approach for building cars rather than the traditional assembly line method. The results are better cars and happier workers.

Several structural features of an organization define its internal environment. Three salient sources of structure that have been identified by researchers are the design of jobs, the structural arrangement of an organization's work units (such as its departments), and the technology used within these units.[1] Managers make decisions about how these sources of structure are to be arranged and maintain that structure, while directing the internal activities of their organization. An organization's functioning and its management needs vary greatly, according to the structure of these components of the internal environment.

Job Design Part of a manager's responsibility is to divide the work that needs to be done into tasks and then to assemble these tasks into jobs. The way these tasks are assembled to form a job is known as **job design,** and managers can design the same job differently in different organizations. Consider, for example, the assembly of automobile engines. In the traditional American manufacturing process, employees stand along a conveyor belt. Their job is to add one or more parts to each engine as it passes by them. The time elapsed between the beginning and the completion of the task is short. The nature of the task is simple, permitting a quick, efficient execution of the assigned work. This short-cycle task is repeated many times an hour as engine blocks move down the assembly line from employee to employee. Contrast this American design with the way engines are assembled at the Volvo plant in Kalmar,

Sweden.[2] Swedish employees work together in teams to assemble an entire engine block. Each job consists of several tasks of varying complexity and duration. As a manager, you will have to make decisions on how to design jobs appropriately for your subordinates.

Since the late 1950s, managers and organizational scientists have tried to understand the effects of various job designs. They have focused on the following criteria and their effect on employees' attitudes, motivation, and behavior:

1. How many different skills and abilities are required of a worker while performing a particular job?
2. How much of the finished product does a worker make? Does the worker create a whole and identifiable piece of work from beginning to end?
3. Does the performance of the job's activities influence the quality of life or work of others?
4. Can a worker exercise discretion in the scheduling of work and in determining work procedures?
5. Does a worker receive feedback from the work itself about the consequences of the work?
6. Does the work permit learning and the development of new skills and abilities?

When analyzed in terms of these criteria, the job of engine assembly at an American plant would be considered simple and routine. The skill level demanded is low; a worker completes only a small part of the final product, such as putting butterfly valves in carburetors; the job has little direct, identifiable influence on others; the worker exercises little personal discretion; there is practically no feedback about task performance from the job itself; and the work provides few opportunities for learning new skills and abilities. By the same criteria, a Volvo employee's job in the Kalmar plant is more complex and less routine.

The complex issue of job design is discussed in more detail in Chapter 10. In this chapter, the focus is on job design as part of the structure of the internal environment. The design of employees' jobs has been found to be a major influence on employees' work-related motivation, attitudes, and behaviors.[3] Managers must be attuned to the issue of job design because its consequences are so important. They must redesign jobs as necessary to incorporate new technologies or to improve performance.

Work Unit and Organizational Structure Just as job design specifies the manner in which tasks are assigned to individual jobs, managers use **work unit design** to group jobs into structures usually consisting of a relatively small number of employees. In **organization design,** top-level managers combine work units into larger collections, such as departments and divisions. Thus, work unit and organizational structures depict the "arena in which organizational action takes place."[4] One aspect of this structure can be drawn on an organizational chart, such as the number of levels in an organization's hierarchy and its major organizational divisions (see Figure 3.1).

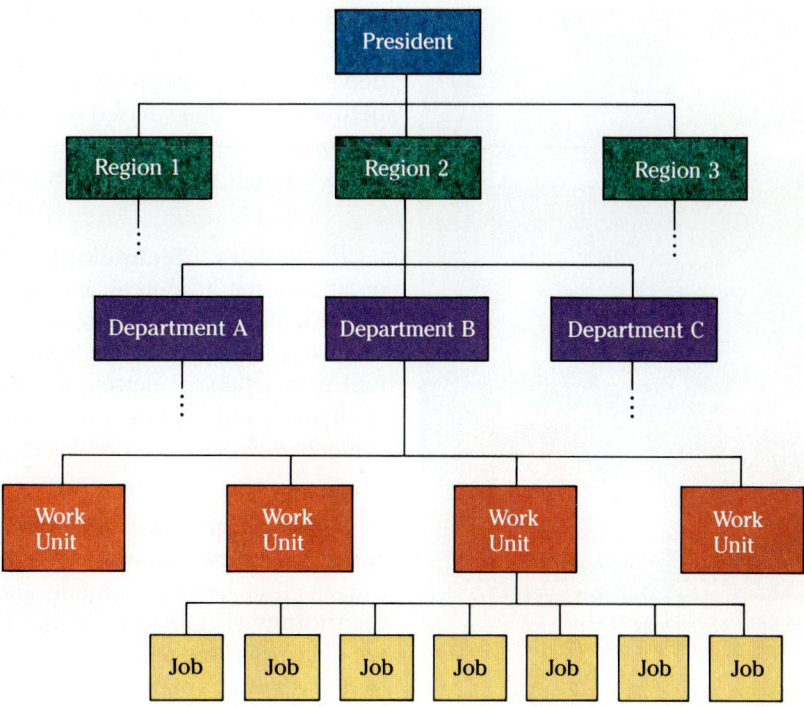

FIGURE 3.1 *Organizational Chart: Job Training Program*

Source: R. L. Daft, K. D. Skivington, and M. P. Sharfman (1986), *Instructor's manual for organization theory and design*, St. Paul, MN: West, 225.

A second aspect of an organization's structure concerns the interaction patterns that link people to people and people to work. These patterns may be hierarchical, with influence flowing down from one position to another. They can also be reciprocal, in which influence flows back and forth from one person to another. An organization's interaction pattern reveals its authority structure. Organizations with hierarchical patterns place people in superior positions to command subordinates. If the decision were made to reduce staff in the parts and service division of Ford Motor Company, for example, a regional manager would inform the district manager of top management's decision. The district manager would tell the service operations manager, who would decide how to make the reductions and inform the field service managers. The field service managers supervise the service zone managers, who are the employees that would be redistricted, transferred, or laid off, depending on the service operations manager's decision.

In organizations with reciprocal patterns, authority is shared in give-and-take relationships between superiors and subordinates. Reciprocal patterns are often found in professional companies, such as law offices, where general partners consult with junior partners regarding client case load and projected administrative expenses.

These two radically different approaches correspond to the mechanistic and organic structures described in Chapter 2. The bureaucratic

Routine technology is characterized by high levels of automation and a well-developed body of knowledge to direct the transformation of resources into products or services.

structure of a mechanistic organization provides detailed rules and standard operating procedures to govern interactions between people and between people and their work. An organic structure lets authority flow between individuals based on their expertise and the nature of their task. The organic structure emphasizes teamwork and rarely sets work procedures through written policies.

Technology **Technology** refers to the processes that transform organizational resources into a product or service. For example, an author's personal computer, a carpenter's hammer, and a surgeon's scalpel are elements of technology; however, technology need not be a tool or mechanical device. A psychologist's counseling and therapeutic techniques and a professor's method of transferring information to help students become better-educated people are also forms of technology.

Routine and Nonroutine Technology Technologies may be categorized in a variety of ways. One particularly helpful categorization makes a distinction between routine and nonroutine technology.[5] A **routine technology** is characterized by (1) standard operating procedure (SOP), (2) rigid workflow patterns,* (3) high levels of automation, (4) standardized production (that is, the production of many similar objects), (5) little variability in the nature and character of the raw materials (objects, information, or people) worked on, and (6) a well-developed body of knowledge to direct the transformation process. The way that the Internal Revenue Service processes tax returns and the conveyor belt technology used to assemble automobiles are routine technologies. **Nonroutine technology,** on the other hand, is marked by (1) flexible work flow patterns, (2) low levels of automation, (3) a more customized product, (4) great variation in the nature and character of the materials worked on, and (5) a developing body of knowledge to guide the transformation of raw materials. Nonroutine technologies are used by various "think tanks," such as the Brookings Institute; such research laboratories as MEDTRONICS, a biomedical firm working on a cure for AIDS and the next generation of artificial hearts; and psychiatric counselors.

Technology strongly affects many facets of an organization, including job design; social system structure; managerial control and coordination processes; and the behaviors, attitudes, and motivation of employees. For example, following World War II, middle management positions grew rapidly as organizations had to process large amounts of information. Today, however, as computers process information, the number of middle management positions in many organizations is being reduced.[6] Because of technology's importance in an organization's internal environment, managers must decide what types of technology to use and manage their relationship with other facets of the organization.

*The term *workflow pattern* refers to the path that raw materials follow as they go through an organization's transformation process. The path can be highly fixed (rigid) in that it follows a specified route from one work station to the next. The assembly line in the manufacture of automobiles is a fixed work flow pattern. The path can also be flexible, as in the selection of courses that a student takes toward a college degree.

Processes

Organization and management scholars refer to certain organizational activities as *organizational processes*. Coordinating, decision making, and communicating are three of the most common organizational processes and are especially important in a discussion of the internal environment.

Coordinating The people, jobs, departments, levels, and other components of an organization must be coordinated. Part of a manager's task in dealing with the internal environment is to achieve this integration through the **coordinating process.** This chapter will discuss two basic approaches to the coordinating process: personal and impersonal.

Managers who use the **personal mode** of integration deal directly with the people whose activities they coordinate through direct relationships with peers, subordinates, and superiors; group meetings; informal contact between two individuals; and special integrating positions by which one individual serves as the integrator of two or more highly interdependent individuals or organizational units. Compared to impersonal coordination, personal coordination generally is quicker, more satisfying for those involved, capable of handling complex issues, and well suited to unique and nonprogrammed events.

The second approach to the coordinating process is the **impersonal mode,** in which managers assign rules, policies, and standard operating procedures to the individuals and activities that need to be integrated. Much like drawing up blueprints for a house, managers create plans of action, in which schedules and connections among necessary activities are planned. Compared to the personal mode, this approach requires less person-to-person contact and lets managers coordinate the work of larger groups, because it frees them from having to tell each worker how a particular task should be performed. The impersonal mode appears to work well for routine tasks and under conditions where change occurs infrequently. It permits the development of an efficient routine for people

FIGURE 3.2   *An Impersonal Mode of Integration*

How to Wash Windows

Equipment

Stepladder	Pail of Warm Water	Paper Towels
Treated Dustcloth	Sponge	Ammonia or Cleaning Agent
Putty Knife	Squeegee (One-Bladed)	

Frequency

As Needed

Procedure

1. Politely ask whoever is in the room to remove any nearby equipment that might be damaged. If it cannot be moved at this time, offer to come back later.

2. Put your ladder under the window to see if you can reach the top pane easily when standing on the third step from the top or lower.

3. Dust off frames and sills with your dustcloth.

4. Pour half a cup of ammonia into a pail of warm water.

5. Dip your sponge in the cleaning solution and squeeze it out enough so it doesn't drip; otherwise it will spot varnish on the sill or frame.

Source: *Custodial methods at the University of Minnesota* (1975), 47.

to follow, but it may offend people who enjoy dealing with others in the performance of their jobs. A routine of this nature appears in Figure 3.2. It is taken from a custodial handbook at the University of Minnesota and specifies in writing how all janitors shall perform a specific aspect of work so that it is coordinated across the entire university.

Decision Making   **Decision making** is the process through which a course of action is chosen. In some organizations, managerial and nonmanagerial personnel are encouraged or even required to participate in decision making. In other organizations, decisions are made only at high levels and often behind closed doors. The style of decision making within an organization, thus, may be open, as in the first instance, or closed, as in the second. Decision-making style has been tied to employee satisfaction, commitment to the organization, work motivation, goal acceptance, and performance.[7] Chapter 7 will discuss decision making in detail; however, as you read about the internal environment in this chapter, note that the way in which decision making is handled affects a number of dimensions of organizational effectiveness, as well as an organization's internal climate.

Communicating   **Communicating** is the process of transmitting information to organizational members. Some organizations deliver formal communications through written messages, or memos. Some communicate verbally, either face to face or in group settings. In some organizations, communicating is a downward flow of information: bosses tell their subordinates, who tell their subordinates, and so on. In other organiza-

A CLOSER LOOK

Organizational Culture: Recognizing and Imposing a Corporate Culture

Pericles, the father of Athens' Golden Age, made a speech in 431 B.C. outlining his picture of an ideal society. The focus of his speech was that the success of Athens was based on the values and beliefs that the Athenians shared.[1] Pericles' ages-old management tool, organizational culture, is now the latest corporate buzzword.

There are many times that an appropriate culture has helped an organization prosper, but it does not guarantee success in all cases, as anthropologist Peter C. Reynolds discovered when he worked for a company he calls Falcon Computer.[2] An apparently successful company in the Silicon Valley, Falcon Computer expanded rapidly from less than 50 to over 250 employees. Reynolds was on hand for this growth; he was still there when the company permanently closed its doors following a loss of over 32 million dollars. Although there are many reasons the company failed, much of the blame rests with Falcon's attempts to create a new culture and impose it on the organization. In the process, its executives created a description of an "ideal" culture that differed so much from what employees knew to be true that it became a source of bitter amusement.

For example, according to the formal "values document" that purported to state the corporate culture at Falcon, management encouraged ". . . open, direct person-to-person communication as part of our daily routine,"[3] yet the document itself was created secretly by top managers, without input from middle managers, and distributed through the formal chain of command to employees only after it had been adopted. Another aspect of the corporate culture as set forth in the values document was ". . . to do it right the first time. We intend to deliver defect-free products and services to our customers on time. . . ."[4] Flaws were so common, however, that employees joked about Falcon's ". . . zero-defect program: Don't test the product and you'll find zero defects."[5]

Falcon Computer hired a management consulting firm to help the company define a corporate culture, conducted numerous meetings to discuss the concept, and spent a lot of money developing the values document to guide it. All of this was in vain,

though, because the company's actual practices belied its false image. According to Reynolds, an important lesson to be learned from Falcon is that, although it might seem desirable for an organization to try to promote a prevailing pervasive corporate culture,

. . . it makes more sense to accept cultural diversity as a fact of life and ask instead how it facilitates or impedes the larger goals of the organization. . . . Corporate culture is not an ideological gimmick to be imposed from above by management or management consulting firms but a stubborn fact of human social organization that can scuttle the best of corporate plans if not taken into account.[6]

1. J. K. Clemens (13 October 1986), A lesson from 431 B.C., *Fortune*, 161, 164.

2. P. C. Reynolds (March 1987), Imposing a corporate culture, *Psychology Today*, 33, 34, 36, 38.

3. Reynolds, 34.

4. *Ibid.*

5. Reynolds, 36.

6. Reynolds, 38.

tions, communication is relatively unrestricted; it flows downward, upward, diagonally, and horizontally.

The style of communication used by managers strongly influences their organization's internal environment. Employees who receive information almost exclusively in written form, for example, may perceive their work environments as being closed and impersonal. Written communication also makes it difficult for message senders to see if their ideas have been received as intended; written communications leave recipients unable to seek explanations and clarification easily.

Managers use the coordinating, decision-making, and communication processes to guide people within their organization's structure. The ways in which organization members respond to this guidance will influence the organization's effectiveness.

People and Their Beliefs

Of course, the most carefully structured organization and smoothly applied managerial processes would be useless without people in place to use them. A critical component of an organization's internal environment, thus, is its social system, which includes organizational members and the values and beliefs that they share. This section will take a closer look at an organization's people and the culture that results from their combined values and beliefs.

Management and Formal Leaders   In any organization, there are people who manage and people who are managed. Many organizations have a dominant key manager, whose decisions and control systems influence the character of his or her organization's internal environment. The environment created by a supervisor who is obsessed with task performance, for example, differs dramatically from the environment created by a supervisor who is relaxed, sociable, warm, and supportive of subordinates' needs. H. Ross Perot, founder of Electronic Data Systems Corporation, and Chrysler's Lee Iacocca have obviously shaped the nature of their organization's internal environments. Sometimes the key manager's role is held instead by a dominant management group or powerful organizational coalition, such as the "Holy Trinity," the name given three powerful editors at *The New York Times*.[8]

The values, beliefs, and demographic characteristics (such as age, experience, education, and social class) of key upper-echelon managers affect an organization, the strategies it pursues, the demands on its employees, and its overall effectiveness.[9] For example, Donald Hambrick of Columbia University and Phyllis Mason of Hofstra University have noted that "firms with young managers will be more inclined to pursue risky strategies than will firms with older managers." They also have hypothesized that significant organizational power brokers, such as dominant coalitions, are more likely to emphasize growth and a search for new domains if they have a marketing background. Those from production tend to emphasize improving work methods and developing new technologies.[10]

Once an organizational culture has been established, it becomes highly resistant to change.

The idea that demographic and personality characteristics of managers and leadership groups make a difference to an organization is not new. In 1835, economist Samuel P. Newman wrote that a good manager possesses foresight, perseverance, and constancy of purpose.[11] The idea that successful leadership is characterized by certain personality traits was still going strong in the 1940s.[12] Since then, theory and research have made clear that an organization's environment is significantly affected by the styles that its managers and leaders adopt.

Nonmanagerial Employees Like managerial employees, nonmanagerial employees also differ from one another according to demographic characteristics and patterns of personality, attitude, motivation, and behavior. They also vary according to the groups that they join. Organizations offer many opportunities for both formal and informal group membership in structured work groups, committees, social networks, and cliques. Both group and individual differences influence an organization's internal environment. A work environment containing employees with strong achievement motivation and a strong work ethic, for example, is likely to be more production oriented than a work environment in which employees have strong affiliation needs and a strong leisure ethic. As the profile of individuals and groups within an organization changes, so does the nature of the internal environment. Being sensitive and responsive to these environmental factors is a major challenge for managers.

Organizational Culture Understanding an organization's culture is crucial for managers because, once an organizational culture has been established, it becomes relatively stable and is highly resistant to change. Attempts to introduce new suggestions may be countered with remarks such as ''Things aren't done that way around here.'' When asked why not, employees often have no logical explanation. Instead, they seem to rely on tradition or a mystical organizational embodiment of values.[13]

This unseen presence, called **organizational culture,** can be considered

> *a pattern of basic assumptions—invented, discovered, or developed by a given group as it learns to cope with its problems of external adaptation and internal integration—that has worked well enough to be considered valid and, therefore, to be taught to new members as the correct way to perceive, think, and feel in relation to those problems.[14]*

This combination of shared beliefs, values, perceptions, language, and reactions to situations is a critical part of an organization's internal environment. The survival of an organization may depend on its culture.

> *Thomas Watson of IBM, Harley Procter of Procter & Gamble, and General Johnson of Johnson & Johnson believed that strong culture brought success. . . . These builders saw their role as creating an environment . . . —a culture—in their companies in which employees could be secure and thereby do the work necessary to make the business a success.[15]*

Some believe that a strong culture is almost always a driving force behind a successful business.[16] Consultants from McKinsey & Company observed that companies that do best over the long run are those whose employees have strong beliefs. Strong cultures sometimes are reflected in an organization's slogans:

- "IBM means service."
- "Progress is our most important product."(GE)
- "Better things for better living through chemistry." (DuPont)

Thomas Peters and Robert Waterman, Jr., authors of *In Search of Excellence,* suggest that organizations such as IBM, Disney, 3M, and McDonald's can attribute much of their effectiveness to the strong corporate culture that permeates their internal environments.[17] Believing that culture has been an important ingredient in their success, managers of McDonald's and other organizations are concerned about whether they will be able to transport their organizational culture into such markets as the Soviet Union.[18] Other researchers have observed that corporate culture influences the strategies that organizations choose to pursue and their effectiveness in doing so.[19] Consider the words of Thomas Watson of IBM:

Of the top twenty-five industrial corporations in the United States in 1900, only two remain in that select company today. One retains its original identity; the other is a merger of seven corporations on that original list. Two of those twenty-five failed. Three others merged and dropped behind. The remaining twelve have continued in business, but each has fallen substantially in its standing.

Figures like these help to remind us that corporations are expendable and that success—at best—is an impermanent achievement which can always slip out of hand.

One may speculate at length as to the cause of the decline or fall of a corporation. Technology, changing tastes, changing fashions, all play a part. But the fact remains that some companies manage to flourish while others in the very same industry may falter or fail. Normally we ascribe these differences to such things as business competence, market judgment, and the quality of leadership in a corporation. Each one of these is a vital factor. No one can dispute their importance. But I question whether they in themselves are decisive. . . .

This, then, is my thesis: I firmly believe that any organization, in order to survive and achieve success, must have a sound set of beliefs on which it premises all its policies and actions.

Next, I believe that the most important single factor in corporate success is faithful adherence to those beliefs.

And finally, I believe that if an organization is to meet the challenges of a changing world, it must be prepared to change everything about itself except those beliefs as it moves through corporate life.

In other words, the basic philosophy, spirit, and drive of an organization have far more to do with its relative achievements than do technological or economic resources, organizational structure, innovation, and timing. All these things weigh heavily in success. But

A CLOSER LOOK

Organizational Culture: The Need for Change at General Motors

General Motors clearly has a strong corporate culture, but the giant it created has bogged down under its own size. Its huge bureaucracy—as many as fourteen levels of management—discourages risk taking; decision making is slowed by the processes and procedures managers follow to avoid making mistakes. Emphasis on short-term results has led to and supported long-term shortsightedness. Innovation and creativity are seldom encouraged and often discouraged. Today, GM chair, Roger Smith, is fighting hard to change that culture so that the giant can survive.

Emphasis on short-term results has led to . . . long-term shortsightedness.

One initiative in this war was GM's acquisition of Electronic Data Systems (EDS), the brainchild of outspoken H. Ross Perot, to coordinate, organize, and redirect the handling of information in the GM organization. Asked for his perspective on the GM culture he encountered during his efforts to contribute to a turnaround, Perot replied:

The first EDSer to see a snake kills it. At GM, first thing you do is organize a committee on snakes. Then you bring in a consultant who knows a lot about snakes. Third thing you do is talk about it for a year.[1]

Perot and his EDS staff were not alone in their shock at the new culture they found after the acquisition. GM attempted to allow EDS to operate independently, but existing GM employees who were transferred to EDS protested the strict EDS culture that included a rigid dress code, prohibitions against drinking during the working day, and requirements for employees' signatures on codes of conduct and employment contracts. Where GM often followed traditions, EDS refused to allow ceremony to stand in the way of getting the job done. After making Perot a director following the acquisition, GM eventually bought him out in a megamillion dollar deal. His opinion: "GM is moving neither fast nor effectively enough to reverse its slide."[2]

After taking EDS into the fold with decidedly mixed results, GM acquired Hughes Aircraft Company primarily for its expertise with advanced technologies. Having learned from his EDS experiences, though, GM Chairman Roger Smith has handled the Hughes acquisition differently. According to Donald J. Atwood, a GM executive vice-president, "Hughes has a culture we don't want to disturb and a technology we want to tap," so Smith ". . . has protected both units from culture shock by turning them into independent subsidiaries."[3]

In addition to the infusion of new technologies and resources, Smith has tried decentralizing GM by streamlining its hierarchy and permitting workers at much lower levels in the organization to make significant decisions. He is working on encouraging and rewarding creativity and innovation, allowing employees to take risks—and possibly fail. The acquisitions of EDS and Hughes have provided needed new expertise and fresh perspectives on GM's old problems, and both are contributing to the improved automation of the organization and enhanced efficiency; however, it is clear that ". . . the entrenched GM organization remains dominant even after the reshuffling. . . ."[4]

Acquisitions have provided needed new expertise.

Over the years, GM's culture contributed substantially to its success, but in recent years, it has hindered the organization's effectiveness. How well has Smith succeeded at changing the culture at GM? The final results are still to come. It is clear, however, that Smith must continue his campaign to change the GM culture if the organization is to succeed in the future.

1. T. Mason, R. Mitchell, W. J. Hampton, and M. Frons (6 October 1986), Ross Perot's crusade, *Business Week*, 61.
2. Mason, et al., 60.
3. D. E. Whiteside (7 April 1986), Roger Smith's campaign to change the GM culture, *Business Week*, 84.
4. W. J. Hampton and J. R. Norman (16 March 1987), *Business Week*, 110.

FIGURE 3.3   The Internal
Environment and Organizational
Climate

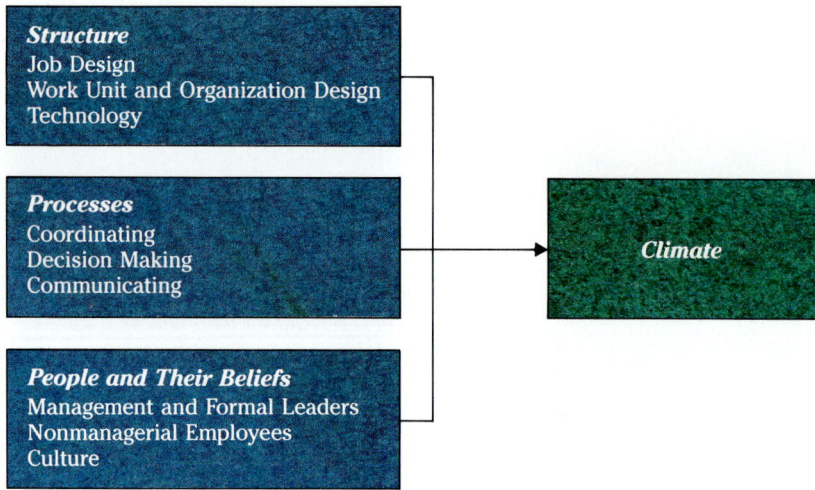

they are, I think, transcended by how strongly the people in the organization believe in its basic precepts and how faithfully they carry them out.[20]

Climate

Much as the physical climate of an area is composed of such factors as temperature, humidity, and precipitation, an **organizational climate** is composed of such factors as structure, processes, and culture (see Figure 3.3). This climate is the prevailing organizational condition and reflects an organization's overall character or tone.[21] Prior to the court-ordered breakup of AT&T, comedienne Lily Tomlin played a telephone operator who would answer a customer's complaint with "We don't care. We don't have to. We're the telephone company"—a succinct characterization of a company's climate, or "personality."

The climate within an organization is a function of both its internal environment and its reactions to the external environment. You have seen that variations in job design, organization and work unit structures, technologies, managerial processes, and employees create a wide range of environments. The organizational climate affects and is affected by employees' attitudes, motivation, and work-related behaviors. For example, the extent to which employees are willing to perform above and beyond the call of duty is likely to result from the type of climate within their organization.

The challenge for managers is to be aware of the climate that they produce with their managerial style. They cannot forget that an organization is a social system. An organization's level of innovation, the quality of its performance, and the way that its workers react to management are largely the result of its employees' attitudes. These attitudes are influenced to a certain degree by an organization's climate, and the climate is shaped largely by management.

Ted E. Smith

Ted E. Smith is vice-president of human resources at Lake Superior Paper Industries and has seventeen years of experience in human resource management and organizational design and development. His career has focused on the design and start-up of new plants using team-based, sociotechnical principles.

1. What do you see as the biggest challenge facing managers as they attempt to manage the environment inside an organization?

Managing productivity and human resources within a changing technological environment is our biggest challenge. Technological changes are introducing severe changes in the kinds and meaning of work; in the meaning of efficiency or productivity; and in the differentiation of white-collar, blue-collar, and professional work. The trend of technical design is evermore in the direction of "high technology." High-technology, or automated, systems alter the relationship between people and machines or machine systems; therefore, such systems change the nature and meaning of work. What emerges is a sociotechnical system based on the principles of team participation in controlling the automated technical systems.

2. Why is it important for managers to deal concurrently with the social and technical sides of their organizations?

Sociotechnical systems stress that both the technical and social systems are essential parts of a successful operation and that neither can be designed independently of the other. Maximizing the overall effectiveness of operations requires joint design of the distinctly different technical and social systems. This is particularly necessary in the application of high technology, where closer and more crucial interdependence exists between the two systems; thus, there are two major reasons for designing sociotechnical systems. First, when training people in the control of new equipment, we can eliminate prospective inappropriate behaviors that were required to operate the original equipment. Second, we provide for the design of operational means by which work and the manner in which the organization functions can be adjusted to meet individual and group needs and expectations.

3. Is it possible for a manager to achieve a balance between the social and technical sides of an organization? What are some ways this might be accomplished?

Yes. What we have learned from the design of new organizations is that the most effective way to achieve such a balance is through a sociotechnical system (STS). Only through the STS joint-design approach can the high-commitment, balanced organization be created. During the last ten years, methods of doing joint-design STS have been developed and successfully applied in the design and redesign of the chemical plants, paper mills, synthetic fiber plants, computer plants, and food-manufacturing plants

of such companies as Shell Canada; Mead Corporation; Zilog, Inc.; CPC International, Inc.; Continental Can Company; and International Paper. STS plants perform better than others in their companies. They have lower costs, higher product quality, fewer grievances, lower turnover, and more satisfied workforces.

4. Organizational culture is big news these days. Is this just a fad, or is this an important and enduring organizational issue?

Organizational culture is a system of shared values and beliefs. This system interacts with staff, corporate structures, and control systems to produce behavioral norms. Organizational culture is not a fad. It is driven by the need to equip the organization with the knowledge to operate in the real world of the 1980s and beyond.

"Organizational culture is not a fad."

---

5. Why is it important for a manager/organization to take the time to nurture the culture of an organization? How is this done?

We must nurture our culture to create an environment in which people can realize their full potential as individuals and, collectively, as an organization. If the primary goal of the culture-change process is to maximize individual and organizational excellence, it follows that the primary consequence of individual and organizational excellence is competitive excellence in the marketplace. It then follows that the consequence of competitive excellence is the effective development and implementation of strategy or the ability to react to, anticipate, or lead the marketplace.

Management and the Organizational Functions

Managers oversee the performance of many different types of activities within organizations. To coordinate these activities, managers frequently group them according to the organizational function they serve. These functions include operations, accounting, finance, marketing, and human resource management. This section concentrates on the internal environment represented by these functions. As you read, you should realize that each of the three managerial roles (interpersonal, informational, and decisional) is carried out for each organizational function. Planning, organizing, directing, and controlling activities must be performed for each organizational function as well (see Figure 3.4).

Operations Management

Every organization provides a product or service. **Operations management** applies planning, organizing, directing, and controlling activities to that part of an organization in charge of making this product. (When referring to operations management, the term *product* is used to include both goods and services.) Universities, for example, create and disseminate knowledge, so operations management in this case requires the building and operating of efficient systems—researchers, teachers, classes, classrooms, laboratories, and so forth—to develop and deliver information to student consumers. Oscar Mayer makes and sells meat products, so operations management for this organization oversees systems for the acquisition of animals, slaughtering, packaging, and shipping their foods. Every organization—public or private, for-profit or not-for-profit, manufacturing or service—requires efficient and effective management of this production function. Operations managers try to accomplish this by using systems and activities to control production.

Operating Systems **Operating systems** consist of the processes and activities needed to transform inputs, such as information and raw materials, into goods and services for delivery to consumers in the task environment (see Figure 3.5). In a law office, the operating system

FIGURE 3.4 Managerial and Organizational Functions

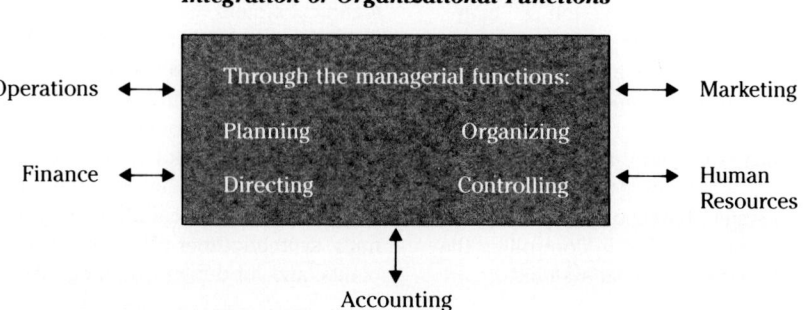

FIGURE 3.5   *An Organization's Operating System*

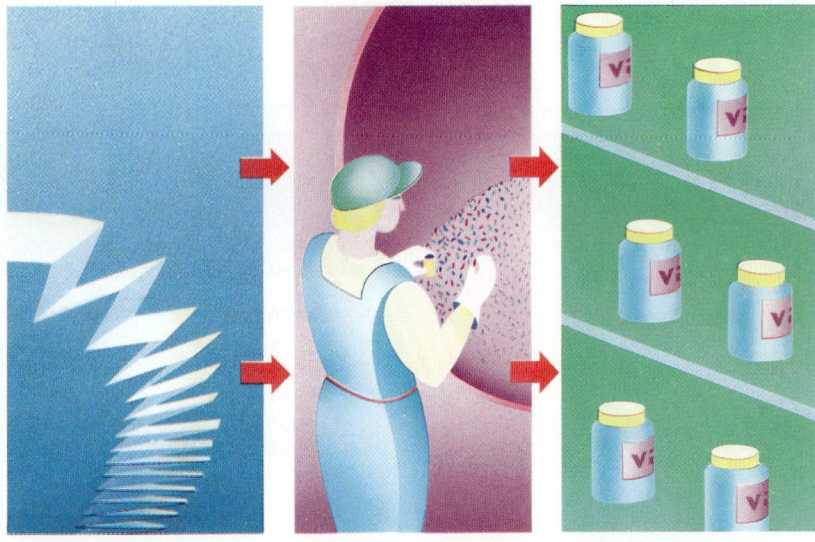

**Inputs from the
Task Environment**   **Conversion or
Transformation System**   **Outputs to the
Task Environment**

includes the lawyers, law clerks, microcomputers, photocopy machines, secretarial support, and other processes necessary to finalize divorces, mortgage houses, and settle estates. At Ford Motor Company, the operating system includes the people and robots who work on the assembly line, the conveyor belts and the auto parts that ride on them, the welding and soldering equipment used to join the parts, and the processes required to send cars to dealerships. Because the operating systems of most organizations use the largest portion of its human, financial, and informational resources, managers must integrate these systems as effectively as possible with all of the other organizational functions.

A major part of an organization's operating system consists of the technologies that transform inputs into outputs, such as students into graduates or raw pork into hot dogs. Technologies vary from department to department within organizations and between organizations. The knowledge, tools, techniques, and processes used in the automated bottling operation at a soft drink plant are vastly different from those needed to guide a doctor through the successful delivery of a baby. Organizations are frequently classified as either having manufacturing or service-oriented operating systems according to the type of technology that dominates their technical core (see Figure 3.6). Universities are service oriented; food industry corporations such as Oscar Mayer are manufacturing oriented.

There are two major elements characterizing the technology of operating systems in service organizations:

1. *Simultaneous production and consumption*—employees in an organization's technical core generally interact with customers while a product is being delivered. A professor, for example, usually interacts directly with students receiving his or her lecture. Manufacturing organizations, on the other hand, generally separate customers

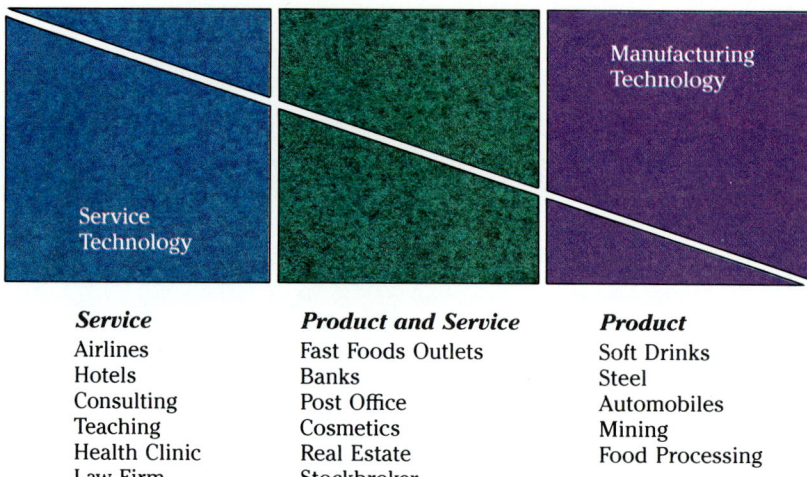

FIGURE 3.6 *Examples of Service vs. Manufacturing Technology*

The left side of the figure identifies organizations characterized by a service technology, and the right side identifies organizations characterized by a manufacturing technology. Those in the middle use a mix of the two.

Service	*Product and Service*	*Product*
Airlines	Fast Foods Outlets	Soft Drinks
Hotels	Banks	Steel
Consulting	Post Office	Automobiles
Teaching	Cosmetics	Mining
Health Clinic	Real Estate	Food Processing
Law Firm	Stockbroker	

Source: R. L. Daft (1986), *Organization theory and design*, 2nd ed., St. Paul, MN: West, 143.

from technical employees. Sausage stuffers at Oscar Mayer do not interact with customers who will buy and eat the sausages.

2. *Intangibility*—a service is generally abstract in nature, and its output is frequently intangible, unable to be stockpiled in anticipation of consumer demand. The good health to which a doctor restores a patient cannot be created in advance and handed over to the next sick person who walks into the clinic. In contrast, manufacturing organizations create physical products that can be produced at one point in time and sold at another.[22] For example, a vineyard produces wines that are stored for years before being bottled and sold. Even after being purchased, the wine may end up on a buyer's shelf to await a special occasion rather than being served immediately.[23]

A number of elements characterize the technology of operating systems in manufacturing organizations. The following are three of these features:

1. *Automation of equipment*—the extent to which the transformation process is performed by machines instead of by human beings. For example, robots, guided by a central computer, have replaced humans and now stand beside some of Chrysler's conveyor belts, welding auto parts that pass by.

2. *Workflow rigidity*—the degree to which the knowledge, skills, and equipment used in the transformation process are adaptable from one task to another, and the degree to which there is a fixed and rigid path through the transformation process. Optic surgical procedures, such as those done at the Institute of Eye Microsurgery in Moscow, are performed along an assembly line in an example of relatively high levels of workflow rigidity.

3. *Specificity of evaluation*—the degree to which workflow activity can be measured using precise, quantitative means. For example, the

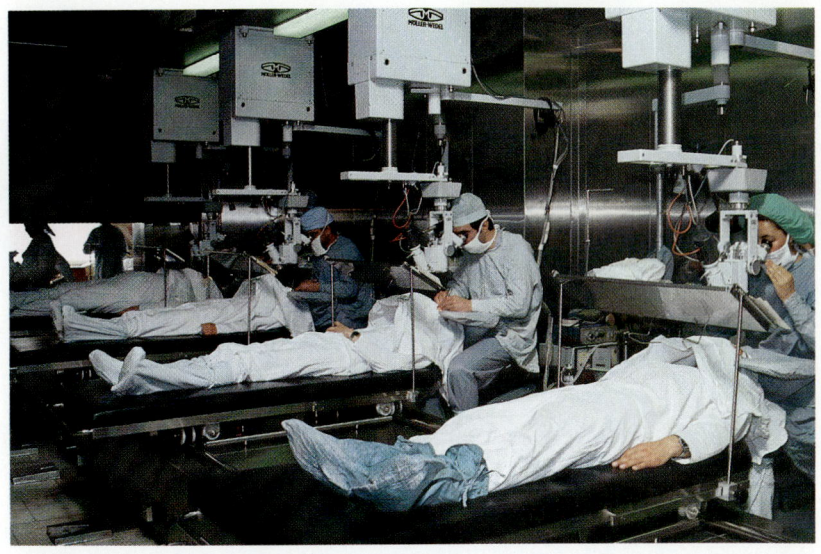

Optic surgical procedures, such as those done at the Institute of Eye Microsurgery in Moscow, are performed along an assembly line in an example of relatively high levels of workflow rigidity.

number of sausages produced in a shift at Oscar Mayer can be weighed and counted, but a professor's effectiveness cannot be evaluated merely by counting the number of lectures he or she presents in a semester.[24]

In addition to characterizing operating systems according to their technology, there is a second approach that classifies them by workflow type. Production systems can be placed along a continuum ranging from continuous to unit workflows (see Figure 3.7). Organizations with continuous workflows include fast-food restaurants, breweries, paper mills, automobile manufacturers, and sewage and water treatment plants. Organizations with a continuous workflow or large-batch and mass-production technologies deal in standardized products. One can of 10W/30 Mobil motor oil is the same as the next; every Oreo cookie tastes the same as the first. Although some characteristics may differ slightly—there are blue Ford Escorts and white Ford Escorts—a major feature of these types of operating systems is that they produce either a continuous product flow or else large batches of a particular item before switching to a slightly different product. A large-batch clothing manufacturer, for example, cuts 8500 gray, size 38, corduroy sport coats before switching to cut 6300 blue, size 40, blazers.

On the other end of the continuum are organizations whose operating systems use a unit, or small-batch, workflow. This type of workflow is intermittent and used by organizations that often deal in specialized goods and services for one customer at a time, such as dentists, hair stylists, and advertising agencies. These organizations cannot take advantage of the economies of scale associated with large-volume production, where an increase in size results in an increase in efficiency. Small-scale standardization is possible when a small number of similar products can be delivered to a small set of customers with similar demands. This kind of standardization is possible in group therapy, Chinese cooking classes, and the like.

FIGURE 3.7
Workflow Operating
Systems

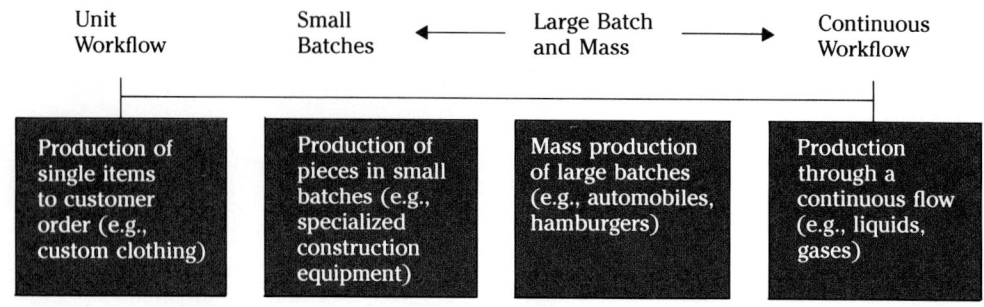

Clearly, different types of operating systems present different manageri-al challenges. Operations managers overseeing service-oriented technologies face challenges their counterparts in manufacturing do not. Likewise, the planning and work scheduling demands involved in preparing to bottle 300 cases of a new Cabernet wine are not the same as those necessary to produce a year of management courses at a university. Regardless of the operating system being used, however, all operations managers must carry out certain activities for the operations management function to be complete.

Operations Activities   In addition to tending an organization's operating system, operations managers must perform six basic activities:

1. *Design and development.* Managers must make sure that products are designed to meet the specifications determined to satisfy market demand. To identify these specifications, managers should operate an organization that is open enough to the external environment so that these requirements can be identified through market research and appropriately channeled to those in charge of product design. The organization must then be able to persuade customers to buy its product.

An increasing number of organizations use **computer-aided design (CAD) systems** to help engineers design and draft products. CAD systems frequently accompany **computer-aided manufacturing (CAM) systems,** in which computers monitor and steer products through various stages of the production process.

2. *Determination of location, workflow layout, and work methods.* The location, workflow layout, and work methods of an organization's operating system strongly influence its efficiency and effectiveness. *Location,* of course, refers to where the organization's operating system is situated. Managers must consider where the organization's potential workforce will come from as they examine regions, communities, and specific sites. A poor location can create unnecessary costs and delays in doing business. For example, a national newspaper such as *The Wall Street Journal* should not be printed and distributed solely from New York City. Doing so would increase shipping costs and delay delivery. Instead, the content of the *Journal* can be transmitted by satellite to a large number of regional printing plants for printing and distribution.

Workflow layout describes the placement of people, machines, and tools to achieve orderly and efficient production. Managers dealing with layout decisions strive to minimize investment in equipment, to reduce production time, and to use space effectively.[25] This is why tellers are generally located in one area as opposed to being spread throughout a bank's various departments.

Work methods are the means by which goods and services are developed. Managers must identify the most effective way to do a particular job from among the various job design and technology options available. For example, the design of the cockpit for the Boeing 757 airplane took into consideration the need for quick and efficient presentation and processing of information by those flying the plane.

3. *Production planning.* In production planning, managers identify the demand characteristics that are associated with various product designs. For example, the surge in microwave oven sales has been accompanied by a demand for "instant" foods to be cooked in them. Product designs have to include microwave-safe containers, account for ease and speed of preparation, and give customers the flavor and texture they want. French fries have to crunch; pizzas can't be soggy. Based on this product demand information, managers create a production plan (see Chapter 7 for a detailed discussion of the planning process and Chapter 8 for an examination of planning and decision-making tools that can help managers in this stage of operations management).

4. *Purchasing and acquisitions management.* Purchasing managers oversee the acquisition of raw materials, services, equipment, semifinished goods, and the subcomponents necessary to produce and deliver an organization's goods and services. *Materials management* refers to planning and controlling the purchases that affect an organization's input inventories, which consist of the raw materials, subcomponents, and semifinished goods that will enter the organization's operating system.

5. *Inventory management.* Organizations carry three types of inventories: (1) the input inventories just described; (2) transformation inventories, also known as *work in process*, which are the materials that have entered the operating system but have not yet completed the transformation cycle; and (3) finished goods. In a Volvo plant, for example, managers buy windows from an automotive glass manufacturer as part of the input inventory, the Volvo cars moving through the assembly process are part of the transformation inventory, and the completed Volvo sedans ready to ship to car dealers are the finished goods inventory.

Clearly, both short- and long-term organizational efficiency and effectiveness are affected by managers' skills in inventory management. The expenses associated with inventories that are too large or too small can be crucial. Effective inventory management makes work more efficient, smooths production runs, and allows an organization to respond to market demands in a timely fashion.

6. *Quality control.* The quality of a product determines its value to consumers and how well it performs the function for which it was designed.[26] A product's quality is an expression of a standard and the

An increasing number of organizations use computer-aided design systems to help engineers design products.

Quality control ensures that products conform to standards of functionality, reliability, esthetics, and safety.

degree of conformity to that standard in terms of functionality, reliability, durability, esthetics, and safety. Quality ought to be incorporated into a product at each step of the transformation process, but many organizations in the United States control quality primarily by inspecting the finished product and then blowing the whistle if problems are found. The Japanese operate from a different philosophy. **Total quality control (TQC)** represents the Japanese belief that any errors should be caught and corrected at the source, that is, where the work is performed and within the production process.[27] Under this system, the responsibility for quality control does not lie with a distinct department; every employee is a quality control inspector.

Operations management clearly requires managers to apply management techniques to their organization's production function. An understanding of an organization's operating system must be supported by skillful execution of the six basic activities that send the product from its initial design through the operating system, to end up with a finished product.

Marketing Management

If operations managers do their job correctly, their organization can efficiently complete a product for consumers to buy. What makes a company think that people would want to buy its product in the first place? How will people know about the product, and where will they go to find it? **Marketing** is the activity that identifies consumer wants and needs in order for an organization to convert them into tangible products and services and deliver them to consumers through effective distribution, promotion, and pricing.[28] **Marketing management,** therefore, applies the management process to satisfying the needs and wants of an organization's customers through its goods and services.

To achieve these goals, marketing managers gather and use the best information available to deploy their organization's physical, financial, and human resources in the most effective and efficient manner (see Figure 3.8).[29] They then develop plans in such areas as personal selling, advertising, pricing, sales, and distribution. When market researchers at Procter & Gamble, for example, found that two-income families with infants would be willing to pay for diapers that were thinner and kept babies drier longer, research and development staffs were instructed to come up with new absorbent materials and elastic designs. Finance departments directed money toward such development. Marketing managers targeted Wichita, Kansas, for a trial of the new product in October 1984 and bombarded consumers there with commercials, advertisements, and discount coupons announcing its arrival. After a successful trial run, managers distributed the diapers nationwide in February 1986. The results were immediately impressive.

Just as the purpose of the operations function is to create a product, the purpose of the marketing function is to create **utilities,** or reasons for consumers to want the product. *Time utility* refers to the value consumers

FIGURE 3.8   *The System of Marketing Management*
Market knowledge and objectives balanced with corporate objectives help define an organization's marketing strategy.

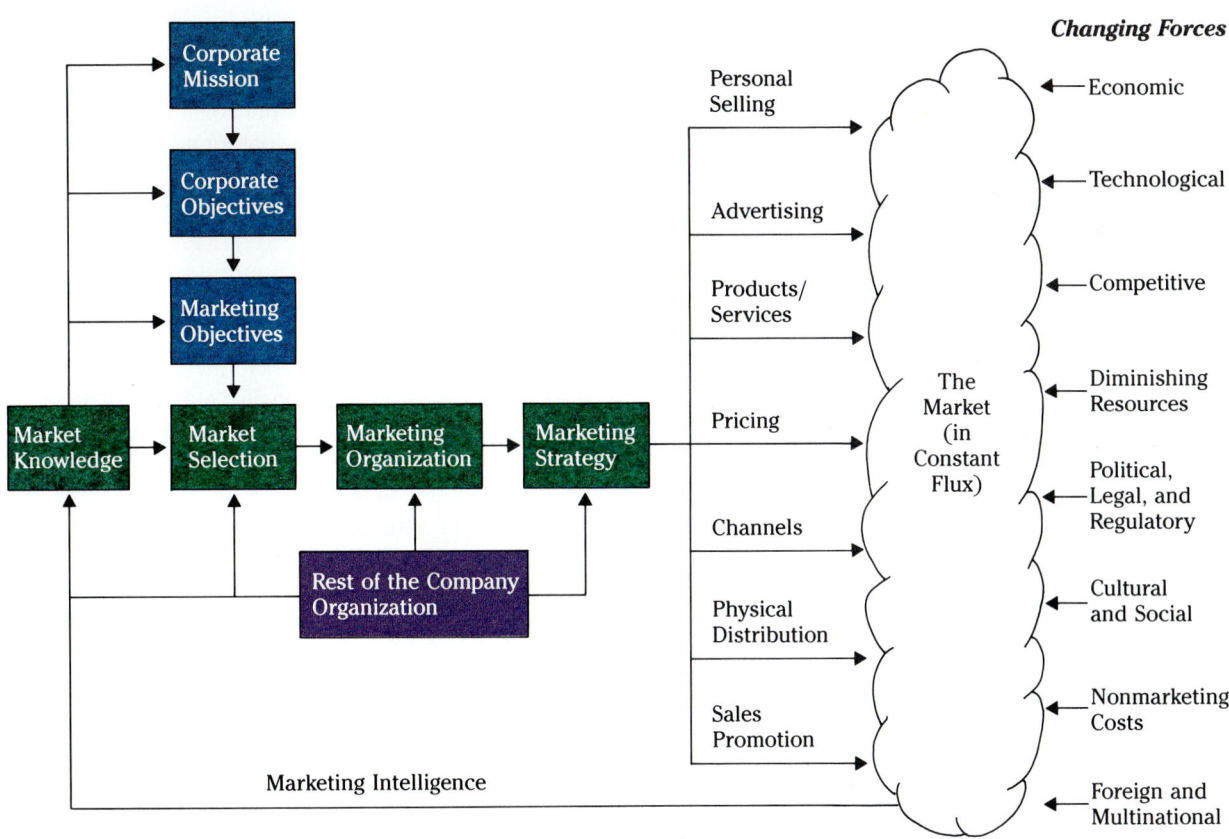

Source: R. W. Haas and T. R. Wotruba (1983), *Marketing management: Concepts, practice and cases,* Plano, TX: Business Publications, 6.

assign a product because it is available when they want it. The manager who is considering buying a new suit to wear to the grand opening of a branch office is not likely to choose that suit unless his tailor can guarantee that necessary alterations will be completed on time. *Place utility* refers to the value that a good or service has because it is available where a consumer wants it. Lynn Butler, a busy account executive, might choose Mark Weber's Television Repair Service over a competitor because Weber's will send someone to her home to fix the set instead of demanding that she bring it into the service department for repairs. *Possession utility* refers to the value derived from owning something. Thus, marketers use information from the external environment to shape a product to meet customer demand, thereby encouraging people to want to own the product.

How can an organization encourage consumers to want its product? The marketing function creates time, place, and possession utilities through line and service functions. Line and service functions are complementary, and organizations need both to be efficient.

Line Functions **Line functions** include four marketing activities that are directly involved in preparing or delivering a product. The first line function, often associated with production, is *purchasing.* Before managers purchase something, they must first use market research results to identify a need, find a product that will satisfy that need, select a supplier, and negotiate with the supplier to transfer the title. The second line function is *selling,* and it consists of several stages. Selling frequently starts through the communication process of advertising, in which managers try to create a demand by letting potential consumers know that a product is available. It ends with a negotiation for the exchange of title—in other words, when the buyer agrees to hand over the money and walk away with the product. This exchange gives the purchaser possession utility.

The remaining two line functions create time and place utility. *Transportation* creates both time and place utility by moving products when they are needed to the place where they are needed. Airline transportation, for example, makes it possible for Candace Holmes, the owner and operator of a small gourmet restaurant on Wisconsin's Madeline Island, to serve fresh Pacific salmon, New England lobster, and Gulf shrimp on a regular basis. *Storage* also creates both time and place utility by letting organizations store products in times of abundance for a time of scarcity, and to move them from places of abundance to places of scarcity. Farm silos and cooperative grain elevators enable farmers to store grain until they can sell it under favorable market conditions. Through transportation and storage, organizations can make products available to customers when and where they are demanded.

Service Functions There are three **service functions,** so called because they support the line functions managers use to create the primary utilities. The first service function, using *market information,* enables managers to learn about the market for a good or a service by using the knowledge derived from research about the market. Managers

Managers make purchases based on the results of market research.

can use market information in a number of ways, which include locating a potential customer base, identifying its needs, and estimating its size. Marketing people use this information when they construct advertising programs to stimulate market demand for an organization's products. Market information also describes the nature of the competition.

The second service function is *financing*. Managers use the financing activity to acquire and distribute the financial resources that an organization needs to obtain goods and services. It also may support the sales activity by providing funds, often through charge accounts, to customers who need to borrow to complete their transaction. Some organizations develop a separate finance entity, such as the General Motors Acceptance Corporation (GMAC), which lends money to people so that they can afford to buy GM cars.

Standardization and grading represent the third service function. This activity facilitates an organization's marketing function by providing consumers with uniform criteria by which to evaluate products. Eggs, for example, are packaged according to size, quality, and color. Standardization and grading are especially helpful when customers cannot inspect a product before it is purchased or when meaningful inspection is prevented either by the product's design or by consumers' lack of knowledge. By enhancing consumers' confidence in producers and products, standardization and grading enhance the marketing function.

Marketing managers must see to it that these line and service functions are executed successfully. An even greater challenge is to execute marketing activities successfully at the same time as they are integrated with finance, production, and the other organizational activities. As always, this requires detailed planning, organizing, directing, and controlling.

Accounting Management

Accounting is the process of recording, classifying, summarizing, and reporting the financial transactions between an organization and its customers, creditors, suppliers, partners in joint ventures, employees, and government agencies. Nonmanagerial personnel, known as *accountants*, perform the accounting activity for organizations. **Accounting management** plans, organizes, directs, and controls the successful execution of these activities. In addition, it is the responsibility of accounting managers to organize financial information for use in other phases of organizational planning and control (for example, production planning and control, human resource planning and control).

An organization's accounting system is designed to answer three basic questions:

1. How is the organization doing compared to what it set out to do and compared to what other organizations are doing?
2. Which problem should the organization look into?
3. Of the several ways of doing a job, which is the best?[30]

To answer the first question, the accounting system provides *scorekeeping*, data accumulated so that people within and outside the organization can

Accountants and their managers provide information that is vital to an organization's planning and evaluating processes.

evaluate its performance. To answer the second question, the accounting system provides *attention directing*, information reported and interpreted in such a way that managers are shown where to concentrate on operating problems, imperfections, inefficiencies, and opportunities. To answer the third question, the accounting system provides *problem solving*, information assembled to help managers make decisions and solve problems.

As you can see, accountants and their managers provide information that is vital to an organization's planning and evaluating processes. The accounting function also provides information to other *stakeholder groups*, those who are directly affected by an organization's actions. Owners, creditors, suppliers, and government agencies are stakeholders who have a use for and a right to certain financial records of an organization at various times. The accounting function must organize this information so that it serves the needs of stakeholders as well as of managers.

Financial Management

Financial management is a staff function that applies the management process to an organization's financial assets. Although the importance of financial management activities varies from organization to organization, there are four primary financial functions:

1. *Planning*—preparing operating budgets and a master financial plan
2. *Acquiring* money—from sales, accounts receivable, notes, borrowing, long-term assets, stocks and bonds, and so on, and monitoring and planning for its use
3. *Distributing* money—regulating its flow to various stakeholders
4. *Evaluating*—assessing the use of an organization's assets

Financial managers use many quantitative measures to evaluate an organization's financial status across time. For example, they calculate financial rates of return on investments. Financial managers interpret these figures for the total management group so that they can be used for organizational planning and control.

Human Resource Management

Human resource management is the managerial function that tries to match an organization's needs and the skills and abilities of its employees. It attempts to motivate these employees by offering rewards that meet their needs, wants, and expectations.[31] To accomplish this, human resource managers must engage in such activities as staffing, training and development, compensation, and labor relations. If done well, the results will be employees who are attracted to and stay with an organization, who attend work and perform acceptably, and who are satisfied with their jobs (see Figure 3.9). This extremely important organizational function is examined more fully in Chapter 17.

Several activities performed by human resource managers help managers throughout an organization. These include individual and job analysis,

FIGURE 3.9   The Human Resource Management System

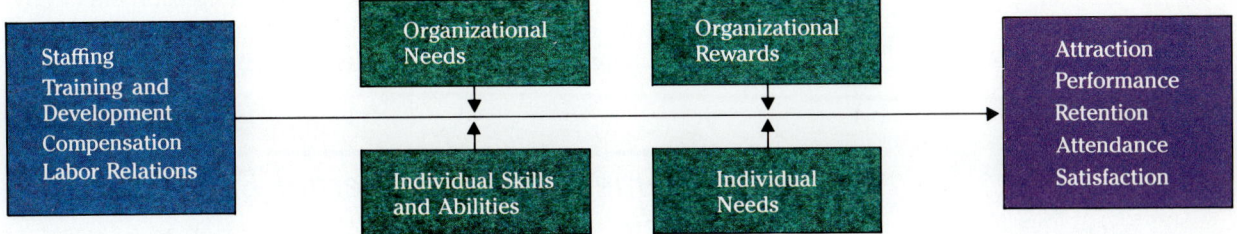

Source: Modified from H. G. Heneman III, D. P. Schwab, J. A. Fossum, and L. D. Dyer (1983), *Personnel/human resource management,* Homewood, IL: Irwin, 8.

outcome assessment, and personnel planning.[32] Some of these directly affect the match between individual and job:

- *External staffing*—identifies and brings new employees into the organization
- *Internal staffing and development*—identifies and moves current employees to different jobs or units within the organization; also expels employees from the organization into the external environment
- *Compensation*—administers direct compensation, such as wages and salaries, as well as indirect compensation, such as vacations, pensions, and insurance
- *Labor relations*—deals with unions through contract negotiation, contract administration, and grievance resolution activities
- *Work environment*—copes with a variety of issues related to the working environment that affect the human side of an organization, such as job design and work schedules

As social systems, organizations achieve their objectives through the people working in them. Organizational success, therefore, depends to a large extent on how well these human resources are managed.

Integration of the Organizational Functions

For an organization to be effective, information from each of its subsystems must flow freely from one to another. Otherwise, the organization cannot operate as a unified whole and respond to changes from within and outside of its boundaries. The organization's production function, for example, cannot successfully be managed or make viable organizational contributions unless its managers receive information from marketing about the demand for the product and support from finance to make the product.

Each of the functional areas discussed in this chapter represents a critical organizational resource. As you will discover in Chapter 9 on strategic management, organizations use these resources in designing an overall plan of attack. They then develop a supporting strategic plan for each functional area to make sure that their activities achieve the goals and strategies of the total organization.

The internal environment, then, presents two challenges to managers. The first challenge is to manage each organizational function effectively. The second is to integrate these functions so that they promote an organization's strategic position in its external environment.

Management and the Internal Environment in Review

This chapter has explored the second environment in which managers operate. This internal environment consists of a number of different factors including environmental structure, organizational processes, people and their beliefs, and organizational climate. These environmental factors affect the decisions made and actions taken by management groups. A manager who attempts to implement a new procedure that runs counter to existing organizational norms, for example, will probably encounter strong resistance. The internal environment also represents a target of managerial attention. In the interest of organizational efficiency and effectiveness, managers must manage the many facets of this environment.

This chapter also has described several organizational functions. A major challenge facing managers as they attempt to deal with the internal management of organizations is to manage each of these functions— operations, marketing, accounting, finance, and human resources— effectively while simultaneously managing their interrelationships. The marketing department, for example, need not bother to design an advertising campaign for a new product if the production department cannot build it.

Chapters 2 and 3 have demonstrated that managers do not operate in isolation. Managers practice inside organizations, and organizations conduct business under pressure from both the external and internal environments.

Notes

1. J. L. Pierce, R. B. Dunham, and L. L. Cummings (1984), Sources of environmental structuring and participant responses, *Organizational Behavior and Human Performance*, 33, 214–42.
2. P. G. Gyllenhammar (1977), *People at work*, Reading, MA: Addison-Wesley.
3. J. R. Hackman and G. R. Oldham (1980), *Work redesign*, Reading, MA: Addison-Wesley; R. W. Griffin (1982), *Task design: An integrative approach*, Glenview, IL: Scott, Foresman.
4. R. H. Hall (1987), *Organizations: Structure, processes, and outcomes*, Englewood Cliffs, NJ: Prentice-Hall, 56.
5. C. W. Perrow (1967), A framework for the comparative analysis of organizations, *American Sociological Review*, 32, 194–208.
6. A new era for management (25 April 1983), *Business Week*, 50–53.

7. J. L. Pierce and R. B. Dunham (1987), Organizational commitment: Pre-employment propensity and initial work experiences, *Journal of Management,* 13, 163–78; Pierce, Dunham, and Cummings, 1984, 214–42; J. Hage (1965), An axiomatic theory of organizations, *Administrative Science Quarterly,* 10, 289–320.

8. The best of times at the New York Times (28 April 1986), *Business Week,* 46–48.

9. D. C. Hambrick and P. A. Mason (1984), Upper echelons: The organization as a reflection of its top managers, *Academy of Management Review,* 9, 193–206; R. J. House (1977), A 1976 theory of charismatic leadership, in J. G. Hunt and L. L. Larson, eds., *Leadership: The cutting edge,* Carbondale, IL: Southern Illinois University Press.

10. Hambrick and Mason, 1984, 198–99.

11. S. P. Newman (1835), *Elements of political economy,* Andover, MA: Gould and Newman, 283.

12. R. M. Stogdill (1948), Personal factors associated with leadership: A survey of the literature, *Journal of Psychology,* 25, 35–71.

13. P. Selznick (1957), *Leadership in administration,* Evanston, IL: Row, Peterson.

14. E. H. Schein (1985), *Organizational culture and leadership,* San Francisco: Jossey-Bass, 9.

15. T. E. Deal and A. A. Kennedy (1982), *Corporate cultures: The rites and rituals of corporate life,* Reading, MA: Addison-Wesley, 5.

16. *Ibid;* J. J. Sherwood (1988), Creating work cultures with competitive advantage, *Organizational Dynamics,* 16, 4–27.

17. R. H. Waterman, Jr. (1982), *In search of excellence: Lessons from America's best-run companies,* New York: Harper & Row.

18. McWorld?: McDonald's can make a big mac anywhere, but duplicating its culture abroad won't be so easy (13 October 1986), *Business Week,* 78–82, 86.

19. D. R. Denison (1984), Bringing corporate culture to the bottom line, *Organizational Dynamics,* 13, 5–22; H. Schwartz and S. M. Davis (1981), Matching corporate culture and business strategy, *Organizational Dynamics,* 10, 30–48.

20. T. J. Watson, Jr. (1963), *A business and its beliefs: The ideas that helped build IBM,* New York: McGraw-Hill, 3–6.

21. W. H. Glick (1985), Conceptualizing and measuring organizational and psychological climate: Pitfalls in multilevel research, *Academy of Management Review,* 10, 601–16.

22. R. L. Daft (1986), *Organization theory and design,* St. Paul: West, 142.

23. D. J. Hickson, D. S. Pugh, and D. C. Pheysey (1969), Operations technology and organization structure: An empirical reappraisal, *Administrative Science Quarterly,* 14, 378–97; D. Pugh, D. Hickson, and C. Turner (1968), Dimensions of organization structure, *Administrative Science Quarterly,* 8, 289–315; P. K. Mills and N. Margulies (1980), Toward a core typology of service organizations, *Academy of Management Review,* 5, 255–65; P. K. Mills and D. J. Moberg (1982), Perspectives on the technology of service operations, *Academy of Management Review,* 7, 467–78; F. M. Hull and P. D. Collins (1987), High technology batch production systems: Woodward's missing type, *Academy of Management Journal,* 4, 786–97.

24. Hickson, et al., 1969; Daft, 1986, 140.

25. R. L. Francis and J. A. White (1974), *Facility layout and location: An analytical approach,* Englewood Cliffs, NJ: Prentice-Hall, 33–34.
26. H. E. Fearon, W. A. Ruch, P. G. Decker, R. R. Reck, V. C. Reuter, and C. D. Wieters (1979), *Fundamentals of production/operations management,* St. Paul, MN: West, 140.
27. R. J. Schonberger (1982), *Japanese manufacturing techniques: Nine hidden lessons in simplicity,* New York: The Free Press, 35.
28. R. W. Haas and T. R. Wotruba (1983), *Marketing management: Concepts, practices and cases,* Plano, TX: Business Publications, 4–5.
29. Haas and Wotruba, 11.
30. C. T. Horngren (1984), *Introduction to management accounting,* Englewood Cliffs, NJ: Prentice-Hall.
31. H. G. Heneman III, D. P. Schwab, J. A. Fossum, and L. A. Dyer (1986), *Personnel/human resource management,* 3rd ed., Homewood, IL: Irwin.
32. Heneman, et al., 10–15.

Key Terms

internal environment
job design
work unit design
organizational design
technology
routine technology
nonroutine technology
coordinating process
personal mode
impersonal mode
decision making
communicating
organizational culture
organizational climate
operations management

operating systems
computer-aided design (CAD) systems
computer-aided manufacturing (CAM) systems
total quality control (TQC)
marketing
marketing management
utilities
line functions
service functions
accounting management
financial management
human resource management

Issues for Review and Discussion

1. Identify and briefly discuss each component of the internal environment.
2. Name the three major sources of environmental structure and discuss the role played by each.
3. Discuss the concept of organizational culture and its importance to management.
4. What is an organization's climate and how is it formed?
5. Which major organizational functions take place in the internal environment?
6. Briefly discuss the operations, marketing, and finance functions of organizations.
7. How are open and closed management systems related to the relationships among the major organizational functions?

Suggested Readings

Changing a corporate culture (14 May 1984). *Business Week*, 130–33, 137–38.

Deal, T. E. and Kennedy, A. A. (1982). *Corporate cultures: The rites and rituals of corporate life*. Reading, MA: Addison-Wesley; Marx, R. (1988). In Pierce, J. L. and Newstrom, J. W., eds. *The manager's bookshelf: A mosaic of contemporary views*. New York: Harper & Row, 46–56.

Hambrick, D. C. and Mason, P. A. (1984). Upper echelons: The organization as a reflection of its top managers. *Academy of Management Review*, 9, 193–206.

Kilman, R. H., Saxton, M. J., Serpa, R., and Associates (1986). *Gaining control of the corporate culture*. San Francisco: Jossey-Bass.

Murrin, T. J. (1988). Building a quality culture at Westinghouse. In Kilman, R. H., Saxton, M. J., Serpa, R., and Associates, eds. *Corporate transformation: Revitalizing organizations for a competitive world*. San Francisco: Jossey-Bass, 451–69.

Perrow, C. (April 1967). A framework for the comparative analysis of organizations. *American Sociological Review*, 194–208.

Peters, T. and Austin, N. (1985). *A passion for excellence: The leadership difference*. New York: Random House.

Schein, E. H. (Winter 1984). Coming to a new awareness of organizational culture. *Sloan Management Review*, 3–16.

Sherwood, J. J. (1988). Creating work cultures with competitive advantage. *Organizational Dynamics*, 16, 4–27.

CASE *Hammond General Hospital*

By Cyril C. Ling and David
Skeehan of the University of
Wisconsin-Whitewater

Dave Smith came to Hammond General Hospital in October 1985 to become director of food service. Mr. Smith was employed by Master Host Company, a large national food service corporation which had just been awarded the management contract for the department. Prior to this time, the hospital had always operated its own food service. The previous director had been employed by the hospital in that capacity for twenty-eight years and was also a registered dietician (R.D.).

Dave recalled his reception at Hammond. "Prior to assuming official control of the department, I spent a week there just getting to know the people and learning their system. I immediately met resistance from the acting director, Pat Stone, R.D. Ms. Stone felt she should have been promoted and that an outside food service company was not needed. She had been acting director for six months and before that had been the assistant director for ten years. Further resistance was quickly made obvious by the entire dietician staff, who all felt that the director should be an R.D. There was also a concern among the nursing staff at the hospital that a man had taken a position that had traditionally been held by a woman."

"After encountering nothing but resistance wherever I went, I made an appointment to see the assistant administrator to whom I reported at the hospital. His name was John Block, and he had only been at Hammond General for one month himself. In fact, his first assignment was to hire an outside company to run the food service and then approve me as director. On hearing my problems, John smiled and said, 'That's nothing, I understand the entire city is upset that a big company has taken over the department; the hospital's Board of Directors is having second thoughts, and the president of the hospital is not comfortable with my selection of you as director.'"

The very next day John was admitted to Hammond as a patient for emergency surgery and would be away from work for two months. "I was virtually alone to succeed or fail," Dave said.

The Industry

In 1985, approximately 15 percent of all hospital food service departments were contracted. It was a very young and growing industry. "My company has about fifty such contracts making them about fourth as far as size in the industry is concerned," Dave related.

The usual procedure is for a contractor to supply a director and assistant director and provide such support systems as recipes, production systems, and accounting procedures. The company charges hospitals for the salaries and benefits for the management team and a fee for service. The director reports to a hospital administrator as well as to the company's district manager.

The Hospital Food Service Department

Hammond General Hospital is a 334-bed general hospital located in a Midwestern town of 45,000 and serves a county-wide population of approximately 140,000. The hospital is one of the largest employers in the city. The administrative team is young and aggressive but feels a genuine obligation to provide a pleasant, positive work environment.

The food service department has forty full-time and twenty-five part-time employees. Dave Smith and his assistant, Doris Horn, are the only two staff members employed by Master Host. The department has three sections:

Clinical staff: Headed by the chief dietician, Cynthia Thomas, R.D. It consists of three clinical dieticians and four diet clerks.

Operations: Headed by the Master Host assistant manager, Doris Horn, R.D. Her responsibilities include food production, sanitation, the patient trayline, and the employee cafeteria. Three supervisors report to her, one each for mornings and afternoons and a relief supervisor.

Catering and special projects: Pat Stone, R.D., is in charge of catering all events and is responsible for coordinating many of the new changes that would come with the management change.

John Block had given several reasons for contracting with the Master Host Company to run the department.

1. The department was considered to be overstaffed by ten full-time employees or their equivalent.

2. The food and supply costs were excessive in comparison to industry standards.

3. Department morale was at an all-time low. Its employees had supported a recent unsuccessful attempt to unionize all hourly employees in the hospital.

4. The medical staff was unhappy with the quality of patient food.

5. The hospital employees were unhappy with the quality of the cafeteria food.

6. Overtime pay in the department was the highest in the hospital.

7. Performance evaluations had not

been taken seriously for several years.

8. Ordering of food lacked systematic procedures and was not well related to dietary planning or cost estimates.

Block summed it all by saying, "The department was run last year the same way it was run twenty-eight years ago. There have been no new systems, improvements, or changes in management philosophy for more than a quarter of a century."

Comments from supervisors and employees gave a more detailed picture of the situation in the food service department. Sally Manley, the morning supervisor, said, "We are supervisors in name only; we make no decisions, take no disciplinary actions, are not involved in performance appraisals, and are not involved in interviewing any new hires. If we do discipline someone, it is usually overturned."

Jane Harper, the afternoon supervisor, said, "The morning shift does everything wrong. There is no procedure that we do the same as them. People that cross shifts don't know what to do. When we ask management for a decision as to what to do, they say, 'do whatever will work for you.' Also, we have no authority to discipline, so no one pays any attention to us."

Shelia Rafferty, the relief supervisor, reported, "This place is a zoo. No one knows what they're supposed to do. There is no direction and no management whatsoever. The employees do what they please and nobody does anything about it."

Millie Park, head cook, said, "I have been here for twenty years and this place gets worse every year. No one in there (the office) ever comes out here. I'll bet they don't even know what's on the menu today. They order food and don't even take inventory; they do it sitting on their butts. I'll bet there is $30,000 in outdated food in the basement. Also, no one else can cook; they pay dishwashers as much as cooks, so we have two cooks who can't even read a recipe if we had some, which we don't."

Pat Baker, a cook, said, "We never have enough food to cook what is on the menu. We are always running out and then we get blamed. We can't cook what we don't have. Also, everyone else in the other departments thinks everyone in the kitchen is a stupid jerk, when they (management) are the only stupid ones."

Lora Lee Butram, a cafeteria cashier, explained, "We run out of food halfway through lunch. No one in the kitchen knows what is going on. Everyone in the hospital thinks everyone in this department is an idiot."

James Wilson, a janitor, said, "They want us to clean the kitchen. I don't even have a good broom or a mop. Half the time, I don't even have soap to use on the floor. How can I clean the kitchen?"

Hospital employees from other departments were even more critical. Ed Norton of maintenance said, "They should close food service and have McDonald's deliver. No one in that department can do anything right."

Allie Crow, head nurse, said, "The patients don't get what they ordered. Their trays are late and incomplete, and the food is cold. If a patient has a problem, we can't get a dietician to come visit them."

Noreen Watson, a housekeeper, said, "We are supposed to clean the cafeteria at night. Food service is supposed to clean it during the day. They don't. It is a mess, and no one can do anything about it."

Ralph Mason, director of personnel, added, "I think there are a lot of good people in food service. I think they care, but they need help and a lot of it."

On the first official day of the management contract, Dave Smith met with his assistant, Doris Horn. Her comments were, "Let's bomb this place and go home. It's hopeless! Look at what we face:

1. No one wants us here.
2. Our budget is unrealistic. It is based on having people that can walk and chew gum at the same time.
3. The former assistant director thinks she should be the director and hates you for taking her job.
4. The chief dietician is 100 pounds overweight (great example, eh?) and she is afraid of her dieticians who don't want to leave their desks.
5. There are no systems of any kind.
6. The place is filthy.
7. The whole hospital hates this department.
8. The supervisors can't manage people and don't.
9. Administration thinks we will have the best food service department in a year because our salesman said we would.

Why did I take this stupid job?"

Dave's reply was, "We will fix the department the same way you would eat an elephant, one bite at a time. Let's get them all (managers, dieticians, and supervisors) in here and start right now."

Questions

1. Why do you think this situation developed as it did?
2. Identify the key aspects of the organizational culture and climate of the food service department.
3. What would you do if you were Dave Smith and Doris Horn?

CHAPTER 4

Social Responsibility and Managerial Ethics

Student Learning Objectives

After reading this chapter, you should be able to:

1. Define social responsibility and trace its historical development, including the two principles on which contemporary attitudes toward corporate social responsibility are based.

2. Name and discuss three levels of commitment to social responsibility.

3. Compare and contrast two divergent views on corporate social responsibility.

4. Discuss the relationship between social responsibility and the law.

5. Define and distinguish ethics from social responsibility.

6. Understand individuals' and organizations' responsibility for ethical behavior and list sources of unethical behavior.

7. Identify utilitarian and formalistic ethics and discuss how they affect decision making.

8. Discuss steps managers can take to encourage ethical behavior in organizations.

A manager's primary responsibility is, of course, organizational effectiveness. Most of this book, in fact, is devoted to describing how managers can meet this responsibility. Managers have an equally pressing responsibility to behave ethically, however, and to honor social values when pursuing effectiveness goals. Some managers and their organizations do a good job of this. Control Data Corporation, for example, has built plants in Minneapolis, St. Paul, and Washington, DC, to provide jobs and develop an economic base for inner-city residents of poor urban areas. Control Data also has undertaken numerous vocational training programs for the handicapped, launched Rural Ventures Corporation to encourage small businesses and to help small farms in rural areas, and created City Venture Corporation to contribute to urban revitalization projects.

Other organizations and their members do not do as well. Financial wizard Ivan Boesky was sentenced to prison and fined $100,000 for profiting unfairly from information that others did not have. Metropolitan Edison, the operator of Pennsylvania's Three Mile Island nuclear plant, withheld information and lied to the public immediately following the nuclear disaster at that plant.[1] E. F. Hutton, a giant financial services organization, pleaded guilty to 2000 counts of mail and wire fraud. One Stop Motor Parts, Inc., was accused of obtaining bid information by bribing employees at the Defense Industrial Supply Center.

Each of these examples shows something about the ethics and socially responsible—or irresponsible—behavior of managers and organizations. They also show something of the relationships between organizations and various groups in their environments who have an interest in the decisions and actions made by organization members. This chapter looks at the external and internal environments discussed in Chapters 2 and 3 from a different perspective. Contemporary managers must examine the way they respond to matters posed by these environments. A manager today must ask: "What is socially responsible behavior?" "What is ethical behavior?" and "What is the responsibility of management in dealing with each of these issues?"

Control Data Corporation has built plants in poor urban areas to provide jobs for inner-city residents.

The Nature of Social Responsibility

Many members of society argue strongly that managers must consider the impact of their decisions and actions on society as a whole and must assume responsibility for their activities. They argue that managers should take steps to protect and improve the welfare of society. In short, managers must evaluate their decisions and actions, not just from the perspective of organizational effectiveness, but also from the perspective of social welfare.[2]

All managers must obey the law, but social responsibility goes beyond the requirements of law. **Social responsibility** is an organization's obligation to engage in activities that protect and contribute to the welfare of society.[3] Although there are several specific definitions and interpretations of social responsibility, an organization's social responsibilities are always shaped by its culture and the historical period in which the organization operates.[4] Just as a society's values, norms, and mores change over time, so does the definition of socially responsible behavior.

The appropriate nature of an organization's social responsibility is a matter of intense debate. At one extreme are those who strongly believe that organizations are in business solely to produce goods and services that societies want—be they atomic weapons, legal advice, or life-saving drugs—and that they are entitled to make a profit in return. For these people, social responsibility is simply not an issue. At the other extreme are those who believe that organizations should be allowed to do business only if they help solve social problems, do no harm, and put some of the profits they earn back to work for society. This disagreement is not one that lends itself to quick and easy resolution.

A Historical Perspective

At the start of the twentieth century, there were few corporate acts of charity. Instead, wealthy businesspeople gave as individuals from their personal wealth to charitable causes. How, then, did commitment to social responsibility evolve? Two principles provided the foundation for contemporary views on social responsibility.[5] The first of these, the *principle of charity,* is rooted in biblical tradition and suggests that those who have plenty should give to those who do not. Under the influence of this principle, individuals in the business community increasingly decided to use some of their corporate power and wealth for the social good. For example, steel magnate Andrew Carnegie put much of his great wealth to work for education. Henry Ford adopted a paternalistic style of management and made recreational and health programs available to Ford employees. Over time, an increasing number of business leaders adopted and spread the idea that business has a responsibility to society beyond simply providing necessary goods and services.[6]

A second principle that shaped corporate social responsibility is the *principle of stewardship.* This principle asserts that organizations have an obligation to see that the public's interests are served by corporate actions and the way in which profits are spent. Because corporations control vast resources, because they are powerful, and because this power and wealth come from their operations within society, they have an obligation to serve society's needs. In this way, managers and corporations become the stewards, or trustees, for society.[7] Under the influence of this principle, the popular press, Congress, and other factions started to attack many large and powerful organizations whose attitudes they perceived to be both anticompetitive and antisocial. Antitrust laws and other legislation began to place constraints on the actions of organizations.[8] In general, there was a shift in the public perception of a corporation's place within and obligations to society.

When management professors Robert Hay and Edward Gray examined changes in attitudes toward social responsibility throughout much of business history, they found that managers have long been influenced by the concept of social responsibility. They also found that the influence of social responsibility has steadily increased for both managers and other members of society in recent years.[9] Attitudes about what is and is not considered socially responsible behavior also have changed substantially over time.[10]

Steel magnate Andrew Carnegie embodied the principle of charity by putting much of his wealth to work for education (left). At the same time, many segments of society—including President Theodore Roosevelt—attempted to ensure that corporate "giants" upheld the principle of stewardship (right).

Phase One: Profit-Maximizing Management During the period of economic scarcity in the nineteenth and early part of the twentieth century, most American business managers felt they had one primary responsibility to society. They were to underwrite the country's economic growth and oversee the accumulation of wealth. Business managers could pursue, almost single-mindedly, the objective of maximizing profits. Neither the principle of charity nor the principle of stewardship played an influential role in shaping corporate social responsibility during this period, as managers essentially felt that what was good for business was good for the country. This strong business ethos was shattered, however, by the Great Depression of the 1930s.

Phase Two: Trusteeship Management After the Great Depression, the number of privately held American corporations began to decline. No longer accountable only to a single owner, organizations had to respond to the demands of both internal and external groups, such as stockholders, customers, suppliers, and creditors. Consequently, organizations had to shift their orientation to social responsibility, and the result was the emergence of trusteeship management, in which it was the job of corporate managers to maintain an equitable balance among the competing interests of all groups with a stake in the organization. Pressure from these groups led to the use of some of the corporate economic wealth to meet social needs.

Phase Three: Quality-of-Life Management In the 1960s, a new set of national priorities began to develop, and the pressure on managers to behave in socially responsible ways intensified. Such issues as poverty, pollution, and deteriorating inner cities raised widespread concern about the quality of life in the United States. The consensus was that managers had to do more than achieve narrow economic goals. They should

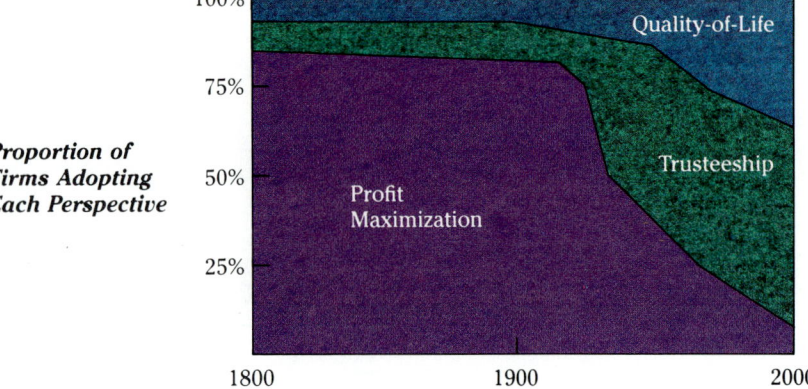

FIGURE 4.1   *A Historical Perspective on Social Responsibility*

Proportion of Firms Adopting Each Perspective

manage the quality of life by helping develop solutions for society's ills. The principles of charity and stewardship were firmly in place. (See Figure 4.1.)

As orientations toward social responsibility shifted, so did managers' orientations toward the relationship among economics, technology, politics, the environment, and esthetics. For example, during the era of profit maximization, managers downplayed the importance of the federal government in business and expected government to allow the dynamics of the unfettered market to regulate business activity. During the trusteeship period, managers grudgingly allowed that government had a necessary role to play but still looked on government with scorn. As the orientation shifted toward the quality-of-life approach, managers increasingly looked on government as a partner—for better or for worse—in helping them solve social problems.[11] Table 4.1 presents other managerial values in the three eras discussed in this section.

Social Responsibility and Organizational Stakeholders

The internal and external groups that emerged during the trustee management period have grown in strength and size. Today, every manager must be aware of the needs of stockholders; customers; suppliers; creditors; and all the men and women, managers and nonmanagers, who work full- or part-time for an organization. Figure 4.2 shows the variety of individuals and groups who are organizational stakeholders.

The large number of stakeholder groups complicates management's social responsibility. An organization should be responsive to everyone; but there are many groups, each with its own particular set of needs, and these needs may well conflict. How, for example, can an organization meet the needs and interests of its investors while it meets its community's needs for money to build a new library?

This is only one of the challenges managers face when considering socially responsible behavior. Not only does an organization have a large number of constituent groups, often with conflicting sets of demands, but the set of needs of any particular group may be large. For example, an

TABLE 4.1   *Comparison of Managerial Values*

Profit Maximization Management	Trusteeship Management	Quality-of-Life Management
	Economic Values	
1. Raw self-interest	1. Self-interest 2. Contributor's interest	1. Enlightened self-interest 2. Contributors' interests 3. Society's interests
What's good for me is good for my country.	What's good for GM is good for our country.	What is good for society is good for our company.
Profit maximizer	Profit satisficer	Profit is necessary, but . . .
Money and wealth are most important.	Money is important, but so are people.	People are more important than money.
Let the buyer beware. (*caveat emptor*)	Let us not cheat the customer.	Let the seller beware. (*caveat venditor*)
Labor is a commodity to be bought and sold	Labor has certain rights, which must be recognized.	Employee dignity has to be satisfied.
Accountability of management is to the owners.	Accountability of management is to the owners, customers, employees, suppliers, and other contributors.	Accountability of management is to the owners, contributors, and society.
	Technology Values	
Technology is very important.	Technology is important but so are people.	People are more important than technology.
	Social Values	
Employee personal problems must be left at home.	We recognize that employees have needs beyond their economic needs.	We hire the whole person.
I am a rugged individualist, and I will manage my business as I please.	I am an individualist, but I recognize the value of group participation.	Group participation is fundamental to our success.
Minority groups are inferior to whites. They must be treated accordingly.	Minority groups have their place in society, and their place is inferior to mine.	Minority group members are people as you and I are.
	Political Values	
That government is best which governs least.	Government is a necessary evil.	Business and government must cooperate to solve society's problems.
	Environmental Values	
The natural environment controls the destiny of humankind.	Human beings can control and manipulate the environment.	We must preserve the environment in order to lead a quality life.
	Esthetic Values	
Esthetic values? What are they?	Esthetic values are okay, but not for us.	We must preserve our esthetic values, and we will do our part.

Source: R. Hay and E. Gray (1974), Social responsibilities of business managers, *Academy of Management Journal*, 17, 142.

FIGURE 4.2 *Organizational Stakeholders*

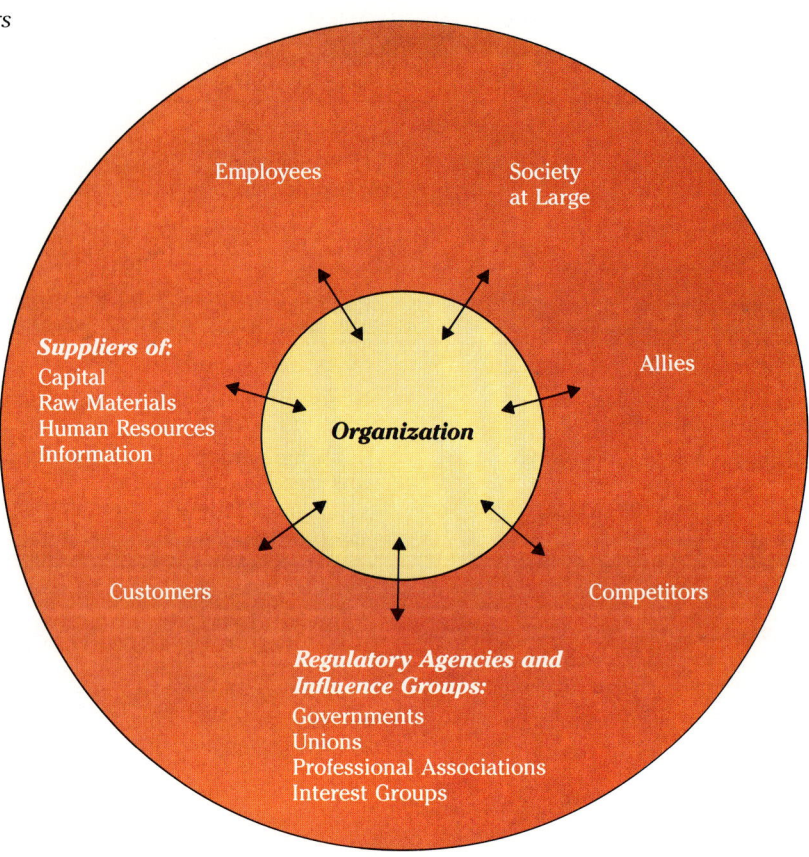

organization has many areas of responsibility to its customers. Some of these include product reliability (the responsibility to provide a product that does what it is supposed to do), product promotion (the responsibility to make honest claims about the nature of the product), and product safety (the responsibility to protect the user of a product from harm and danger). Responsibility to investors also spreads into a number of different areas. These include providing truthful information about an organization's financial status and past use of capital, as well as prudently using current capital for organizational activities.

An organization also faces the problem of defining its areas of responsibility to society at large. For one thing, the nature of an organization's social responsibility changes as social and cultural norms and mores change. Today, for example, many organizations are asked to demonstrate social responsibility in such areas as ecology, employment of minority groups, community development, and organizational involvement in political affairs (such as divestment in South Africa). Organizations also are expected to demonstrate social responsibility toward women, older people, and the handicapped. In an attempt to identify social needs, to learn the needs of their stakeholders, and ultimately to begin meeting some of those needs, many organizations take a hard look at their level of social responsibility.

FIGURE 4.3   *The Social Audit*

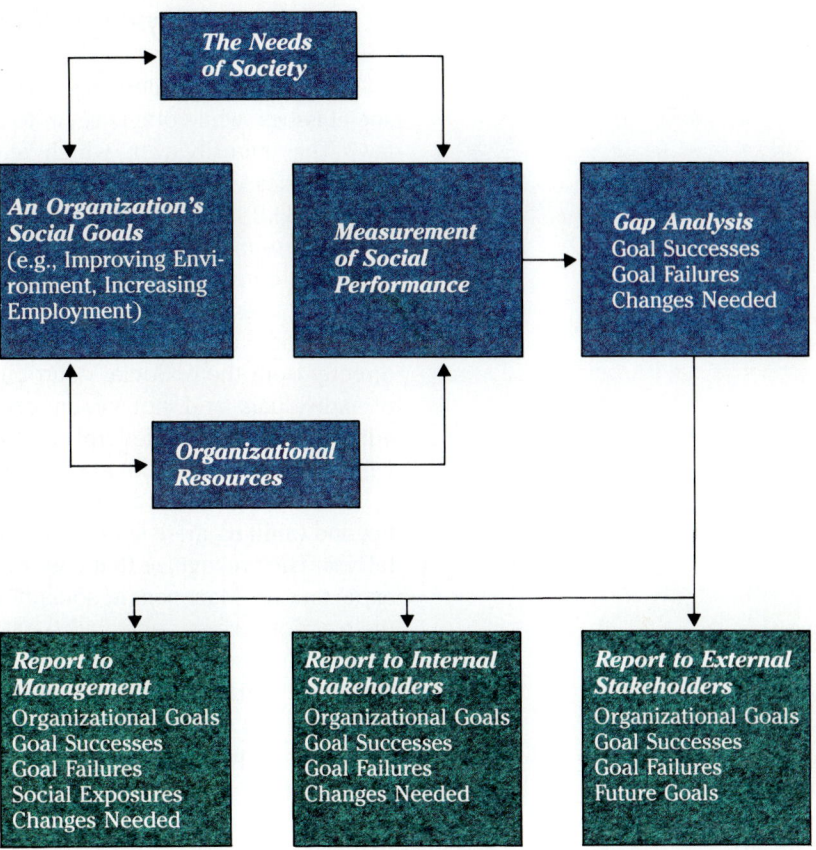

The Social Audit   Many organizations perform a formal social audit to identify and communicate issues of public interest to both internal and external stakeholders. A **social audit** is a detailed examination and evaluation of an organization's social performance.[12] Figure 4.3 illustrates the audit process followed by some organizations. A thorough social audit involves sophisticated strategic planning and evaluation (see Chapter 9). In the United States, social audits are voluntary, and few organizations go to such lengths today. Many aspects of the process are pursued more aggressively by organizations in other countries, including Germany, France, Norway, and Spain, where social audits are mandated by law.

The majority of the top 500 corporations in the United States include information about their social performance in their annual reports. Some also prepare a special report that details their activities that are of interest to the general public. In 1976, for example, the National Aeronautics and Space Administration issued a report called "Spinoff 1976" that detailed the many ways in which technology developed by NASA has been applied to nonaerospace uses. General Motors regularly prepares a public interest report that outlines the areas included in its social audit. Inspection of its table of contents (see Table 4.2) shows GM's involvement in such issues as alternative fuel and power development, automotive safety design, activities in South Africa, programs for minorities and women, and environmental concerns.[13]

Levels and Types of Social Commitment

What makes managers in some organizations respond so vigorously to social issues, while others seem to do only what they are forced to do by law? The intensity with which managers involve their organization in social issues varies according to the principles that motivate them (see Figure 4.4).[14] At the lowest level of social commitment are the organizations whose managers adhere to the principle of *social obligation*. These managers confine their responses to social issues to those mandated by prevailing laws and the operation of the economic system. They engage in philanthropic acts only when they believe their organization will benefit directly from them. Social contributions are viewed as the responsibility of individuals and not of an organization. Such organizations might adhere to the letter of federal and local environmental protection laws, yet willingly allow pollution when no legal punishment is likely.

At a middle level of commitment are organizations whose managers go beyond fulfilling mere social obligations and pursue their social responsibilities. They recognize that laws often change more slowly than society's expectations. Managers in socially responsible organizations try to make their actions keep pace with—rather than lag behind—social norms, values, and expectations of performance.[15] Frequently seen as "good corporate citizens," socially responsible organizations are willing to assume a broader responsibility than that prescribed only by law and economic requirements. For example, these organizations are likely to take steps to reduce pollution if they consider certain levels to be

TABLE 4.2   Table of Contents: GM Public Interest Report

Source: *1986 General Motors public interest report* (15 March 1986).

FIGURE 4.4 *Levels of Social Commitment*

Social Obligation	Social Responsibility	Social Responsiveness
Low	*Levels of Social Commitment*	*High*
Reactive	Prescriptive	Proactive
Proscriptive	Does more than required by law	Anticipates and prevents problems
Adheres to legal requirements	Does more than required by economic considerations	Searches for socially responsible acts
Adheres to economic considerations	Avoids public stands on issues	Takes public stands on issues

dangerous, even if these levels are acceptable by legal standards. They are also likely to loan employees to United Way campaigns and to financially support worthy causes.

At the highest level of social commitment are organizations whose managers are *socially responsive.* Managers in socially responsive organizations communicate and interact with external groups to anticipate social issues and to prevent problems, as well as to correct problems after the fact. Organizations in this category, for example, take the lead in adopting new technologies to protect the environment. When IBM planned massive automation at their Lexington typewriter plant, they evaluated the effects this might have on the local labor market and the economy. They then implemented corrective action before the problems could occur.

How do organizations in the United States perform when they are rated on these criteria? Although many organizations are still driven by the principle of social obligation, since the 1950s many organizations have demonstrated a growing social consciousness. More and more have adopted attitudes of social responsibility and social responsiveness.[16]

Integrating Dimensions of Social Responsibility

Given the large number of stakeholders, their often-conflicting sets of demands, and the sometimes large set of needs of any particular group, how can managers keep track of their organization's current level of social commitment and plan for the future? The social audit discussed earlier in this section is one method, but you've already learned that many organizations do not engage in such a systematic approach. There is another way to integrate the components of corporate social responsibility, and that is to envision them as a three-dimensional cube (see Figure 4.5).[17]

Each side of the cube represents an area in which organizations have an obligation to society. Lying along Dimension I are categories of social responsibilities:

1. **Economic responsibilities** to produce goods and services to be sold at a profit
2. **Legal responsibilities** to obey society's laws and regulations while fulfilling economic responsibilities
3. **Ethical responsibilities** to meet society's expectations for conscientious and proper behavior, even when these expectations are not reflected in the letter of laws and regulations

FIGURE 4.5   The Organizational Social Performance Model

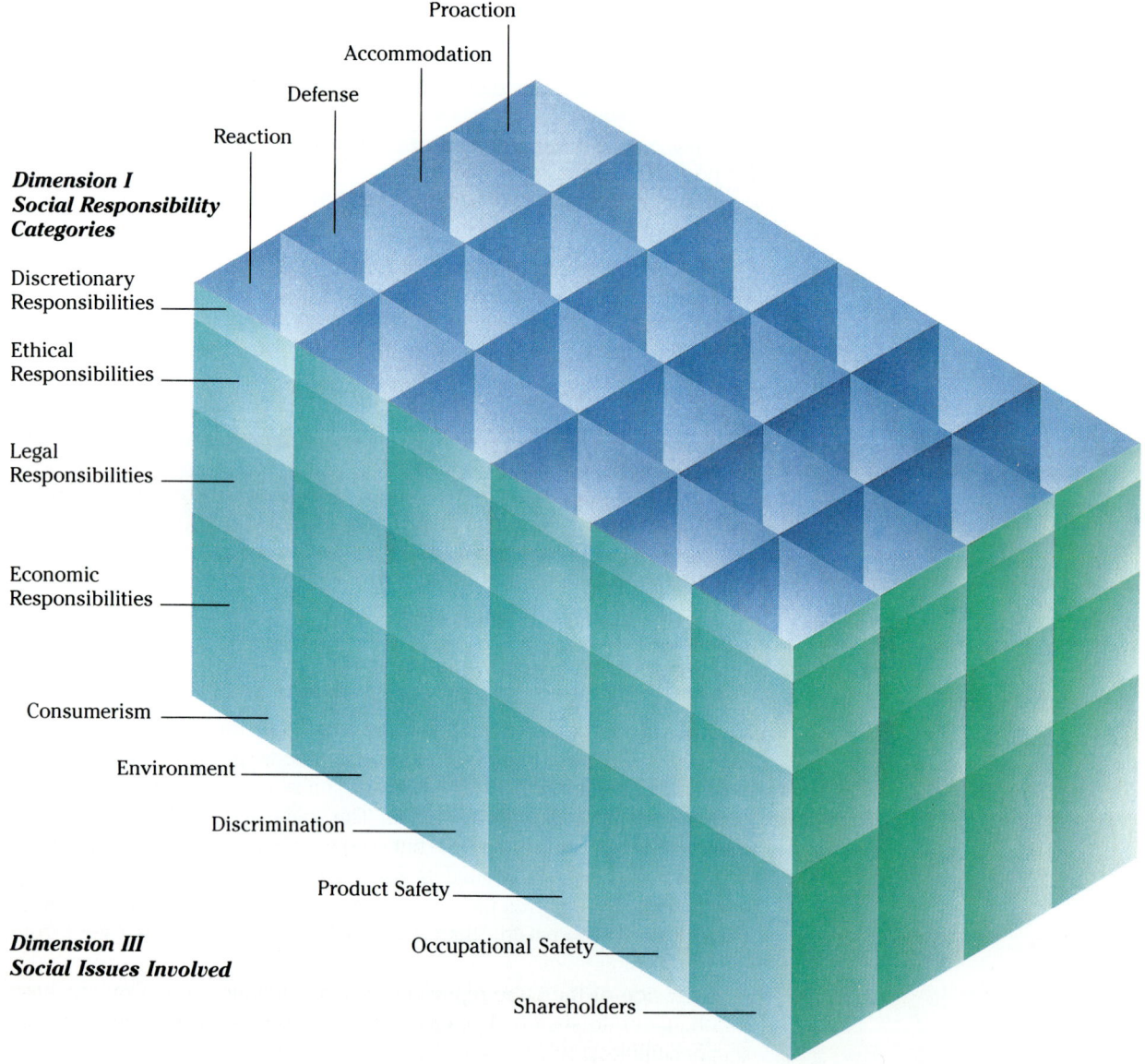

Source: A. B. Carroll (1979), A three-dimensional conceptual model of corporate performance, *Academy of Management Review*, 4, 503.

TABLE 4.3 *Degree to Which U.S. Business Community Supports Socially Responsible Activities Over Time: CEOs and Business School Deans*

Corporate Support For:	Was Five Years Ago		Is Now		Will Be in Five Years	
	CEO	Dean	CEO	Dean	CEO	Dean
Higher education	49.1%	20.5%	65.6%	29.9%	72.2%	50.8%
Ethical practice codes	48.7	12.8	70.8	35.0	74.8	47.4
Minority hiring and training	34.5	21.6	52.6	33.3	63.2	27.8
Charitable and philanthropic	28.4	23.7	56.0	27.1	71.1	33.7
Pollution control	24.6	6.0	31.6	14.4	39.3	18.8
Quality of work life program	22.6	11.2	47.8	28.4	75.7	61.6
Building and ground beautification	22.3	13.7	33.0	18.5	36.7	25.6
Environmental protection laws	20.2	3.5	26.1	8.1	31.5	18.2
Community renewal and revitalization	18.9	9.3	30.4	16.1	43.1	22.0
Arts and cultural	17.2	20.9	32.8	28.9	51.3	36.9
Handicap hiring and training	13.9	4.6	28.1	14.2	42.3	16.1
Minority business	11.7	7.2	17.0	8.6	22.9	8.9
Political action committee	11.3	18.4	40.0	41.8	60.7	54.6
Consumer protection laws	10.4	6.5	15.7	9.5	20.5	13.0
Executive loan to governments	9.3	10.0	14.8	11.6	22.9	19.1

All numbers represent the percentage of respondents indicating considerable or extensive support for an activity.

Source: R. Ford and F McLaughlin (1984), Perceptions of socially responsible activities and attitudes: A comparison of business school deans and corporate chief executives, *Academy of Management Journal*, 27, 672.

4. **Discretionary responsibilities** to carry out voluntary acts, even if failing to do so would not be judged unethical. Making philanthropic contributions and providing day care for employees' children fall into this category.

Along Dimension II of the cube are the philosophies that govern an organization's response to social issues:

1. **Reaction philosophies** to address social issues because the organization is compelled to do so by outside forces, such as legal, regulatory, or social pressures
2. **Defense philosophies** to address social issues to avoid being compelled to by outside forces
3. **Accommodation philosophies** to address social issues because they exist, even if demands to do so are not likely
4. **Proaction philosophies** to anticipate and address social issues before society in general recognizes the issues as important

Along Dimension III of this model are the general types of social issues demanding an organization's response. These general categories include consumerism, concern for the environment, (non)discrimination, product safety, occupational safety, and shareholders. The relative importance of specific issues varies by historical era, industry, and community. Table 4.3, for example, shows how the relative importance of fifteen specific social issues has changed over time.

Managers can use the model in Figure 4.5 to analyze current social issues facing their organization and to plan future action. A manager begins by identifying each specific social issue confronting the organization and selecting the general category along Dimension III into which it fits. Each issue is then classified on Dimension II based on the philosophy driving the response that the organization has made to that issue to date. Finally, managers classify the responses along Dimension I to show their economic, legal, ethical, or discretionary nature. As new social issues emerge, managers can add them to the cube, assess their organization's social responsibilities, and look at the philosophies that have guided the organization in the past to anticipate its responses for these new issues.

Diverging Views on Social Responsibility

Not everyone agrees that contemporary organizations should be driven by the principles of charity and stewardship. Proponents of corporate social responsibility have suggested that firms that take a major role in tackling social issues are good investment risks and will eventually be more profitable than less socially responsive firms. Current research, however, does not show a simple relationship between social responsibility and profitability.[18] As a consequence, the profitability claim cannot legitimately be used to argue either for or against corporate social responsibility, but other arguments can be made on both sides.

Arguments for and Against Social Responsibility

Those who argue in favor of organizations acting in socially responsible ways have offered these reasons:

- The assumption of social responsibility balances corporate power with corporate responsibilities.
- The voluntary assumption of social responsibility discourages the creation and imposition of government regulations.
- Social initiatives taken by organizations tend to promote goodwill, public favor, and corporate trust, and these may contribute to the long-run success of the organizations.
- Socially responsible acts enhance an organization's image and business in general.
- Socially responsible acts help society deal with its problems, changing needs, and expectations.
- Acts of social responsibility by organizations help correct the social problems (such as air and water pollution) that the organizations create.
- Organizations often possess the resources (such as money and expertise) needed to tackle social problems.
- Organizations, as members of society, have a moral obligation to help society deal with its problems and to contribute to its welfare.[19]

Sociologists have suggested that, because society has many needs, an organization can be categorized according to: (1) the needs it fulfills and (2) the benefits that society derives from the organization's existence.[20] Critics of corporate social responsibility have, in essence, used the

The chemical industry has one of the best safety records of all American industries; however, a toxic gas leak at a Bhopal, India, plant forced Union Carbide to reassure the public that it has acted in a socially responsible manner.

sociologists' analysis to propose that each type of organization in society should specialize. According to this way of thinking, corporations are a particular type of organization that exists to provide goods and services and to earn profits. Curing society's social ills, thus, becomes the responsibility of other organizations, including governmental and charitable organizations. The major arguments against corporate social responsibility include:

- The costs of socially responsible behavior lower a corporation's operating efficiency and, therefore, weaken its ability to offer goods and services at the lowest possible competitive cost.
- The costs of socially responsible behavior may not be borne by the competition, so a socially responsible firm may penalize itself.
- The costs of socially responsible behavior are often passed along in the form of lower dividends to stockholders, lower wages for employees, or higher prices for consumers.
- Accepting social responsibility sends mixed signals about an organization's goals to both organization and community members. Organization members may have difficulty meeting goals if they do not know whether their primary mission is to make a profit or to act responsibly. Community members may develop unrealistic expectations that the organization is unable to fulfill. For example, expecting an organization to keep a plant open to protect jobs in the community even when the plant becomes unprofitable may be asking too much of the organization.
- By assuming social responsibilities, corporations would only become more powerful, and many already exercise too much power over society.
- Individuals in the business community are trained in such areas as marketing, finance, and manufacturing, not in how to deal with social problems.
- When corporations, as opposed to individuals, act to solve social problems, no one can really be held accountable. Responsibility should reside with individuals, not with institutions.[21]

As you can see, people have used several arguments for and against corporate social responsibility. The result has been the emergence of two distinct sides to the social responsibility debate.

Side One: An Argument Against   Economist Milton Friedman of the University of Chicago has argued that managers should not be required to earn profits for business owners while simultaneously trying to enhance societal welfare.[22] According to Friedman, these two goals are basically incompatible and will lead to the demise of business as we now know it. Friedman also has suggested that forcing organizations to engage in socially responsible behavior may actually be unethical, because it requires managers to spend money that really belongs to other individuals, which otherwise would be given back to stakeholders in the form of higher dividends, wages, and the like.

According to Keith Davis, organizations have a responsibility to return a certain value to society. Some organizations did so by sponsoring participants in the Hands Across America campaign in 1986.

Side Two: An Argument in Favor   Keith Davis, professor emeritus at Arizona State University, provides another perspective on corporate social responsibility.[23] To Davis, organizations are members of society. Because they take resources from society for their own use, they have a responsibility to return to society a value for those resources. Society should be able to determine the nature of the value to be returned and to expect organizations to assist in solving social problems.

Davis maintains that business was unprepared during the 1950s and 1960s to deal with its social responsibility and that the public was also unprepared for its role in the exchange process. By the mid-1970s, though, the debate over business and its involvement in the social arena had evolved to the point that a set of guidelines for socially responsible behavior by business could be identified:

■ *Proposition One: Social responsibility arises from social power.* If an organization has power in an area, it bears social responsibility for its actions in that area. Organizations, for example, wield enormous power in determining employment. Because minority employment is a crucial social issue and businesses are primary employers, organizations are responsible for helping society address the issue of minority employment.

■ *Proposition Two: An open system.* To know what society needs, organizations must absorb information from society. To meet those needs, an organization must broadcast information to society. A socially responsible organization should be willing to disclose its activities to the public in the form of social audits conducted along the same lines as accounting audits. These social audits should measure, monitor, and evaluate the social objectives and programs of the organization.

■ *Proposition Three: Calculation of social costs.* The social costs and benefits of activities, products, and services should be thoroughly considered and calculated so that organizations can decide whether to proceed with them. Traditionally, organizations have examined the technical feasibility and profitability of a venture before proceeding. Now a third factor, the *social effect,* considers the impact a proposed action will have on society. For example, if an organization plans to build a replacement plant in Indiana, its managers should consider the social effects that will occur when the older facility is closed in Illinois.

■ *Proposition Four: The user pays.* The social costs of activities, products, and services should be included in their price so that users pay for the social effects of their consumption. In other words, a fair consumer price for a product or service would include social costs in addition to the traditional costs of production. If water, for example, is inadvertently polluted as an organization produces its product, the user of that product should pay an additional price for developing ways to clean the water. Weyerhaeuser, for example, plants trees to replace those they cut to make lumber. Under this proposition, consumers would pay more, at least in the short term, for wood products.

■ *Proposition Five: Social responsibilities as citizens.* According to Davis, improving society increases economic activity. Because business will eventually receive increased profits because of this increased activity, it is obligated to share in solving social problems; thus, business has a responsibility for improving education—even though business has not directly caused educational problems—because business will benefit from improvements in education.[24]

Where Corporate America Stands Today

Given the many arguments both for and against corporate involvement in addressing the needs of society, it seems appropriate to ask, "Where does corporate America stand today?" Included in the Academy of Management's recent publication celebrating 100 years of modern management is an article on the evolution of social issues in management.[25] This article presents and discusses the social issues growth curve shown in Figure 4.6. According to the author, the gestation and innovation phase of the 1950s and 1960s was a time when people in the United States became increasingly conscious of the wide-scale importance of large

FIGURE 4.6   The Growth of Attention to Social Issues

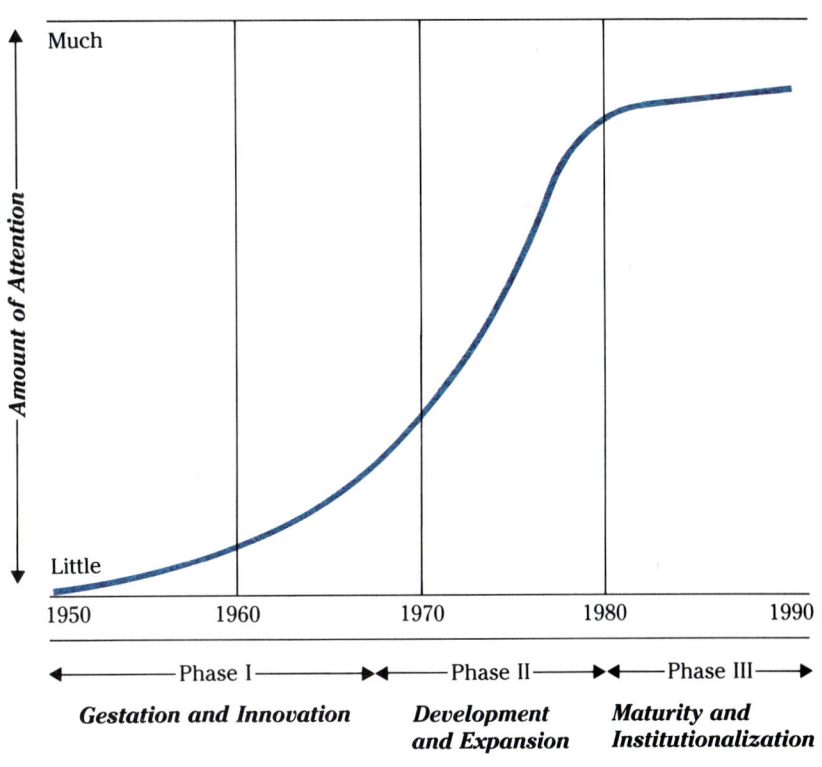

Source: L. E. Preston (1986), Social issues in management: An evolutionary perspective, in D. A. Wren and J. A. Pearce, eds., *Papers dedicated to the development of modern management,* Chicago: Academy of Management, 52.

TABLE 4.4   *Agreement with Statements for Corporate Acceptance*
of Social Responsibility

Statements	Total % of Agree Strongly and Mildly Agree	
	CEOs	Deans
Responsible corporate behavior can be in the best economic interest of the stockholders.	92.2%	90.1%
Efficient production of goods and servies is no longer the only thing society expects from business.	88.8	92.1
Long-run success of business depends on its ability to understand that it is part of a larger society and to behave accordingly.	87.0	86.1
Involvement by business in improving its community's quality of life will also improve long run profitability.	78.4	75.7
A business that wishes to capture a favorable public image will have to show that it is socially responsible.	77.6	76.2
Social problems, such as pollution control, sometimes can be solved in ways that produce profits from the problem solution.	71.9	75.6
If business is more socially responsible, it will discourage additional regulation of the economic system by government.	70.7	68.3
If business delays dealing with social problems now, it may find itself increasingly occupied with bigger social issues later such that it will be unable to perform its primary business tasks.	55.2	57.4
The idea of social responsibility is needed to balance corporate power and discourage irresponsible behavior.	36.5	55.0
Other social institutions have failed in solving social problems so business should try.	27.8	32.3
Since businesses have such a substantial amount of society's managerial and financial resources, they should be expected to solve social problems.	16.6	31.8

Source: R. Ford and F. McLaughlin (1984), Perceptions of socially responsible activities and attitudes: A comparison of business school deans and corporate chief executives, *Academy of Management Journal*, 27, 670.

organizations for society. Managers became aware of the need to be socially responsive. During the development and expansion phase of the 1970s, organizations began to formally act on this awareness. Corporate social reports started to appear, and social audits became more common. Finally, today's maturity and institutionalization phase is one in which "many of the changes that were anticipated in the Sixties and Seventies have in fact taken place. . . ."[26]

In another survey, Robert Ford and Frank McLaughlin surveyed 116 chief executive officers (CEOs) and 203 college business school deans (see Tables 4.4 and 4.5). The subjects' responses to questions suggest that many consider it important for today's corporations to take an active role in solving social problems.[27] The study also shows that both CEOs and business school deans believe that business support of corporate involvement in addressing social problems has increased.

TABLE 4.5 *Disagreement with Statements Against Corporate Acceptance of Social Responsibility*

Statements	Total % of Mildly Disagree and Disagree Strongly	
	CEOs	Deans
Business already has too much social power and should not engage in social activities that might give it more.	77.0%	73.1%
If business does become socially involved, it will create so much friction among dissident parties that it will be unable to perform its economic mission.	69.3	77.2
A firm that ignores social responsibility can obtain a competitive advantage over a firm that does not.	69.3	44.1
Involvement in socially responsible activities threatens business by diverting time and money away from its primary business purpose.	68.1	60.9
It is unwise to allow business to participate in social activities where there is no direct way to hold it accountable for its actions.	67.6	67.0
Business is most socially responsive when it attends strictly to its economic interests and leaves social activites to social institutions.	64.7	57.4
Business leaders are trained to manage economic institutions and not to work effectively on social issues.	60.5	49.5
Business will become uncompetitive if it commits many economic resources to social responsibility.	49.1	47.3
If social programs add to business costs it will make business uncompetitive in international trade.	44.7	33.8
Business will participate more actively in social responsibility in prosperous economic times than in recession.	24.6	9.0
Consumers and the general public will bear the costs of business social involvement because businesses will pass these costs along through their pricing structure.	15.8	5.0

Source: R. Ford and F. McLaughlin (1984), Perceptions of socially responsible activities and attitudes: A comparison of business school deans and corporate chief executives, *Academy of Management Journal*, 27, 671.

Legality and Social Responsibility

Organizations can adopt any of a number of strategies to deal with issues of social responsibility. One way to define these strategies is along the dimensions of legality and responsibility.[28]

A Categorizing Strategy

The approaches to social responsibility can be broken down into four distinct categories: illegal and irresponsible, illegal and responsible, irresponsible and legal, and legal and responsible.

Illegal and Irresponsible Some organizations behave illegally and irresponsibly. For example, an investigation was launched in early 1988 to examine claims that some companies were taking advantage of the catastrophic Pennsylvania Ashland Petroleum tank collapse by dumping their own toxic wastes into the already polluted Monongahela River. Dumping this type of material into the river is prohibited by law, and it is clearly irresponsible to contaminate the water. Another organization may decide not to install equipment to control air pollution in one of its plants in the hope that it will not get caught or because it can afford to pay the fine. Today, an illegal and irresponsible strategy is highly risky and may be fatal to an organization, because a broad spectrum of society will no longer tolerate such behavior.

Legal and Irresponsible   Some organizations can operate without violating a single law but still not act in a socially responsible manner. For example, beer companies produce commercials that appeal to underage drinkers; casinos sometimes make special offers that encourage people to trade their Social Security checks for gambling chips; and some organizations manufacture handguns, which repeatedly are used by criminals. All of these organizations are acting within the limits of the law. All, it can be argued, endanger the well-being of society.

Illegal and Responsible   Some organizations follow strategies that are socially conscious and responsible but that violate the letter of the law. An organization might, for example, create a program to train "underprivileged children," only to find itself violating a minimum wage law. Another example of a social consciousness entangled in a legal issue arose when American Telephone and Telegraph Company was found guilty of discriminating against women. Thereafter, the company undertook an affirmative action program to improve working conditions for women only to have a group of male workers sue for discrimination.

Legal and Responsible   Finally, some organizations obey the law and, at the same time, engage in socially responsible behavior. For example, the Minneapolis-based Dayton organization gives a percentage of its profits to charity, an act that is both legal and highly socially responsible. The IBM Corporation loans executives to teach for a year at colleges with large minority populations. These and other organizations believe that it is possible to play by the rules, turn a profit, and still be a good corporate citizen.

The Role of a Corporate Board

What role should a board of directors play in seeing that an organization meets its legal and social responsibilities? It has been argued that most corporate boards of directors have done an inadequate job of monitoring the social responsibility of managerial decisions and behaviors. As Harold Geneen, past president of International Telephone and Telegraph, commented, "The boards of directors of U.S. industry include numerous first-rate people doing what amounts to a second-rate job."[29] Others have argued that the design of a board restricts the independence of its members and basically renders them ineffective in their monitoring role.[30]

A CLOSER LOOK

Social Responsibility: The Wine Industry

Side by side in an issue of *The Wine Spectator* were two stories. The first story bore the headline "Cancer Study Recommended" and described a proposed study to investigate whether urethane in wine and other alcoholic beverages causes cancer in humans. The U.S. Food and Drug Administration believes that urethane, a natural by-product of fermentation, exists in "minute amounts in some wines, brandies, beers, distilled spirits and liqueurs."[1] The study would cost more than $1 million and would include laboratory tests to determine whether the small doses of urethane in some wines can lead to cancer.

The second article bore the headline "Mondavi Strikes Back at Critics." It said that Napa Valley vintner Robert Mondavi was embarking on a "personal mission to 'educate ourselves and the world' about wine's beneficial qualities" and to show that wine is a healthy product.[2] Mondavi has undertaken this campaign because he feels that the wine industry is not doing enough to counter accusations such as those expressed by health and consumer activists in California. These critics are urging wine producers to put warning labels on their bottles stating, for example, the health risks to pregnant women if they drink wine.

To Robert Mondavi, wine is a food and an "essential part of the gracious way of living," a message he believes should be taken to the public.[3] The San Francisco-based Wine Institute, however, does not want to make sweeping claims that wine is healthful, apparently fearing that such claims might legitimize lawsuits from individuals who claim that they were misled and subsequently became injured or ill as a result of drinking wine. Given the Wine Institute's unwillingness to combat these claims more aggressively, Mondavi has launched his own educational campaign. He plans to involve "priests, rabbis, philosophers, physicians, artists and poets and others to expound on the contributions wine has made to civilization."[4]

These two stories from *The Wine Spectator* emphasize the type of dilemma often faced by organizations. It can be argued that, if urethane is present in wine and can cause cancer, a socially responsible organization would want to know this and take steps to eliminate the hazard, but a fiscally responsible organization does not want to decrease its earnings. A vote to support the study is probably a vote to reduce profitability, because the public is likely to reduce wine consumption if they think that there is even a chance that the claim is true. People tend to believe that "if it is serious enough to study, it must be a problem."

What about Mondavi's plans? Is there anything wrong with educating the public? Many argue that wine does indeed have beneficial qualities; however, is it socially responsible behavior to present only positive information about a product without mentioning the hazards? Is it possible to promote wine as a product in a socially responsible manner? The wine industry is not the first, nor will it be the last, business to experience the frustrations of balancing profitability and social responsibility.

1. B. Giliberti (31 January 1988), Cancer study recommended, *The Wine Spectator*, 8.
2. L. Bauman (31 January 1988), Mondavi strikes back at critics, *The Wine Spectator*, 8.
3. *Ibid.*
4. *Ibid.*

One solution might lie in inviting people outside an organization to become board members.[31] Outsiders give a board a broader base of power and knowledge and enable it to become more independent and, therefore, better able to monitor objectively the decisions and actions taken by management.[32] In spite of these potential advantages, over 75 percent of large U.S. firms in the 1980s allowed their chief executive officer to chair their board of directors as well.[33] This situation presents certain dangers.[34]

On the one hand, a CEO is supposed to make strategic decisions for an organization. On the other hand, a board of directors is supposed to sit in judgment of management. For one person to assume both roles raises serious questions about conflicts of interest. In an effort to reduce the number of illegal and irresponsible acts committed by corporations, critics have argued that boards should be made up of men and women who are not members of management.

Although the arguments for outsiders sitting on boards are strong, the existing (although limited) evidence shows no significant relationship between the number of insiders on boards and corporate involvement in illegal acts.[35] Perhaps insiders are simply more effective at concealing illegal activities. At any rate, it still appears likely that responsible behavior is encouraged by outside members who feel free to ask hard questions without worrying that it will affect their jobs or working relationships.

In sum, to act in a socially responsible way requires managers to consider the effect of their decisions on the well-being of society; thus, managers must ask themselves what their actions do *to* society and what their actions do *for* society. When similar considerations are made at a personal level, managers must rely on their ethics to help them choose an appropriate course of action.

The Nature of Managerial Ethics

Ethics is the set of standards and code of conduct that define what is right, wrong, and just in human actions. Managers' decisions and actions affect the health, safety, morale, and behavior of all organization members. For example, at General Motors, massive plant closings followed large pay increases for high-level executives. In another example, flawed decision making led to the death of the entire crew of the spaceshuttle *Challenger*.

Unfortunately, ethical issues often do not fall neatly into categories of right and wrong. Attempts to do what is ethical can be complex, revealing that there are varying degrees of rightness and wrongness. Suppose, for example, that two students each missed passing their management course by only five points. The first student wants the professor to adjust his grade in exchange for sexual favors. The second student wants the professor to adjust the grade because her spouse died during the semester and she received passing grades on all exams except the one that she took the day after the funeral. Most people would agree that the professor who agrees to adjust the first student's grade is acting unethically. The second student's case is not so clear-cut.

Of course, behaving ethically involves more than just performing individual acts of helping others and behaving honestly. Ethics arise in all issues associated with human relationships. For managers, ethical issues surface in numerous interactions with an organization's external and internal stakeholders.

Ethical considerations, like considerations of social responsibility, are influenced by existing social values, norms, and mores. The two are also similar in that both revolve around concerns for the well-being of others;

however, ethical considerations differ from those of social responsibility in certain ways. Ethical judgments are based on personal values that have been learned over a number of years. They usually are involved in situations that do not influence society as a whole. Frequently, in fact, ethical judgments affect only one person, the people in a manager's organization, or an organization's stakeholders, rather than society as a whole. Ethics usually involve one person's judgment and behavior; social responsibility usually involves those of entire organizations. In short, ethics are primarily a personal issue; social responsibility is more an organizational issue.

Sources of Ethics

People in all societies create standards and codes of conduct to govern their dealings with one another, but not all societies define right, wrong, and just in terms of the same behaviors. In the United States, for example, kickbacks to purchasing agents are generally considered unethical. In some countries, however, kickbacks are an accepted business custom. According to sociologist Talcott Parsons, all societies need to maintain patterns of stability and continuity to pass on their culture from one generation to the next.[36] This need is fulfilled by religious, educational, and cultural organizations, as well as by the family unit. Organizations and families teach social values and norms through the process of **socialization.** Through this process, people develop beliefs about what is right, wrong, and just. Through the socialization process, new members of society adopt at least some of the values, norms, and mores of that society and develop a definition of ethical conduct.

Managerial Ethics

Managerial ethics are not fundamentally different from other ethics; usually they are only a matter of applying personal ethics within the context of the management of organizations. What are a manager's ethical responsibilities? Managers are responsible for the decisions and actions they take on their own initiative. They also are ethically responsible for actions that they take at the direction of another. In other words, managers are not relieved of ethical responsibility just because their boss "ordered" them to behave unethically. A manager who must choose whether to behave unethically or lose his or her job faces a painful decision, but the ethical choice is to lose the job. (If you are placed in a situation in which you must either cheat on an exam or fail a course, you are behaving unethically if you cheat, regardless of the consequences.)

Managers also are ethically responsible for the behavior of subordinates who are following their instructions. If managers tell subordinates to behave in a manner that the managers consider unethical, the managers are responsible for the subordinates' unethical behavior. Managers are equally responsible if they instruct subordinates to behave in a manner that the subordinates consider unethical. Managers are even ethically responsible when they fail to act, if their inaction allows unethical behavior to occur. Just as you are behaving unethically as a student if you are aware of another student's cheating but do nothing to prevent it,

Through socialization, new members of society adopt at least some of the values, norms, and mores of that society and develop a definition of ethical conduct.

A CLOSER LOOK

Ethics: How Much Are Those Ethics in the Window?

You have probably figured out by now that money cannot buy love. The question today in business schools around the country seems to be, "Can money buy ethics?" At least one influential businessperson seems to think so. John Shad, the former chair of the Securities and Exchange Commission, recently turned over $20 million of his own funds to Harvard and spearheaded the raising of an additional $10 million from other Harvard alumni. The purpose of the gift, according to Shad, was to teach students that ethics pay.

Clearly, Shad is very interested in improving the ethical behavior of students who represent future businesspeople. After all, $20 million is greater than the annual operating budget of almost every graduate

school of business in the United States. With it and the additional $10 million, Harvard intends to develop better business ethics through faculty research, teaching improvement grants, and increased opportunities for students to explore the impact of ethical issues. Will this be enough? The school has stated that it will not require students to study ethics and has recently denied tenure to its two MBA ethics teachers. Will Shad's gift achieve its purpose if Harvard cannot convince its tenured faculty to take the issue of ethics seriously and incorporate it into their courses?

Can money buy ethics?

What are other schools doing that don't have $30 million to spend on teaching ethics? Whatever they want to do, apparently. In a recent survey, 89 percent of all accredited business schools reported that they teach ethics. Some—about one fifth—have created separate, freestanding courses. The rest attempt to integrate the teaching of ethics into existing classes. Most of those that do have separate ethics courses offer them as

electives. Unfortunately, elective ethics classes traditionally have not been very popular among students unless they are considered an easy *A*. It may be that the only students who choose the elective are those students who least need ethical development. Lastly, there is tremendous variation in intensity of the training and the quality of the training. Often, a case approach is used that may make students *aware* of ethical considerations as they discuss and debate the issues posed but may not *change* ethical values. Many schools seem to concentrate on teaching students what is "right." As *Newsweek* concluded, "Even in today's complex world, knowing what's right is comparatively easy. It's doing what's right that's hard."[1]

The real question is if business school courses—whether elective or mandatory, freestanding or intermixed—can change the ethics of students. Unfortunately, there is little conclusive evidence of such an effect; however, the search for ways to monitor ethics must continue if tomorrow's businesspeople are to consider ethics as more than just an option.

1. T. Noah (25 May 1987), The business ethics debate, *Newsweek*, 36.

---

managers are behaving unethically if they do not take steps to stop the unethical behavior of a subordinate, peer, or superior.

Managers also are responsible for the behavior of any group to which they belong. If not prevented, a diffusion of responsibility can occur in groups as individual members rationalize that they are not responsible for the behavior of others in the group. Although individual managers cannot always control the behavior of a group, they are as ethically responsible for the group's behavior as they are for their personal behavior. A discussion of how groups work and how to manage them effectively is contained in Chapter 13.

An Organization's Responsibility

The foregoing discussion makes it sound as if managers are ethically responsible for everything that happens inside organizations. In fact, some people argue that the "real role of the chief executive is to manage the values of the organization."[37] Top managers, with their key organizational roles and formal authority, can and should infuse a sense of moral reasoning and ethically guided decisions and behavior into their organization's culture. By being good role models, by reinforcing ethical behavior and punishing unethical behavior, and by making explicit what ethical conduct is, top managers help ensure that the expectation of ethical behavior, as well as ethical behavior itself, permeates the organizational culture.[38] In fact, research has shown that unethical behavior can be reduced through steps as simple as issuing organizational statements that support ethical behavior.

Of course, top management is not exclusively responsible for instilling and enacting ethical behavior. Every organization member carries the values, norms, and mores of society into the organization. With this goes responsibility for his or her personal conduct; therefore, the responsibility for moral reasoning and ethical conduct falls on each member. With this in mind, some organizations encourage their members to report unethical behavior. The term **whistleblowing** refers to a member's disclosure that someone within the organization has engaged in an illegal, immoral, unethical, or illegitimate act.[39] Traditionally, whistleblowing has been discouraged both by group norms and by company practice, but today more and more organizations are actively encouraging such action, because it is the responsible thing to do, and because

> . . . *if bad news isn't dealt with inhouse, public whistleblowing by employees can generate disastrous headlines*, 60 Minutes *specials, inquiries by state and federal regulatory agencies, congressional investigations, and multimillion-dollar class-action lawsuits.*[40]

In order to persuade employees to blow the whistle inside an organization rather than to the press or to regulatory agencies, many organizations have set up systems to handle internal complaints. When surveyed about corporate ethics, in fact, over 70 percent of U.S. corporations responding said that they had written codes of conduct, and over 35 percent had formal training programs encouraging ethical behavior.[41] Some companies, such as General Dynamics, have an ombudsperson, whose job includes soliciting and dealing with whistleblowing in-house.

Ethical and Unethical Managerial Behavior

Managers should behave ethically, but do they? Consider the following observations:

- A study reported in *Fortune* showed that 117 (11 percent) of 1043 major corporations have been involved in blatant illegalities.[42]
- In another study, *Fortune* 500 executives in finance, operations, and marketing overwhelmingly admitted to compromising their personal values in order to succeed.[43]

- A *Wall Street Journal* survey reported that four out of ten executives said they were asked to behave in unethical ways on the job.[44]

- After studying the changing nature of business ethics, researchers noted that there is growing cynicism regarding the ethical conduct of managers. An executive commonly "observes generally accepted practices which he or she feels are unethical."[45]

- Although the vast majority of managers believe that managers should apply ethics to business practices, many report that they simply do not live up to these standards. Nearly two thirds indicate that generally accepted unethical practices were being conducted within their industries, and this represented an increase over the degree of unethical practices in the early 1960s.[46]

Such observations of widespread illegality, unethical behavior, and cynicism have led two students of managerial values to conclude that it is important to keep a "continual vigilance . . . focusing attention on values and ethical behavior."[47]

Influences on Unethical Behavior

Why do managers choose to behave unethically? Sometimes managers behave unethically simply because they do not take the time to think about the implications of their behavior. Managers are commonly overworked and highly stressed. Under these conditions, people sometimes do things they later regret. There are other reasons that managers sometimes behave unethically. Some of these have been documented in a systematic examination that showed that managers' personality characteristics can influence unethical behavior.[48] (Personality characteristics are discussed further in Chapter 13.) Persons most likely to behave unethically are those who believe that: the ends justify the means; things that happen are due to luck or chance, not to their actions; and economic and political values are of great importance. It has also been shown that people placed in competitive situations are more likely than others to behave unethically.

As shown in Figure 4.7, among the most powerful determinants of ethical or unethical behavior are rewards and punishment. People who receive rewards for unethical behavior (such as receiving a pay increase for providing a kickback to a customer) are much more likely to behave unethically than those who are not rewarded for unethical behavior. The use of punishment for unethical behavior, however, can lead to higher levels of ethical behavior, even when rewards for unethical behavior are also present. Rewards and punishment probably influence the ethics of behavior both because rewards increase the likelihood that behavior will be repeated and punishment decreases the likelihood of repetition (more on this idea appears in Chapter 14) and because they call attention to the potentially unethical behavior.

Three parallel studies, one conducted in 1961, another in 1977, and the third in 1984, focused on factors that were believed to influence unethical behavior. In each of these investigations, the behavior of one's superiors was identified as the strongest influence on a manager to make ethical or

FIGURE 4.7   The Impact
of Rewards and Punishment
on Unethical Behavior

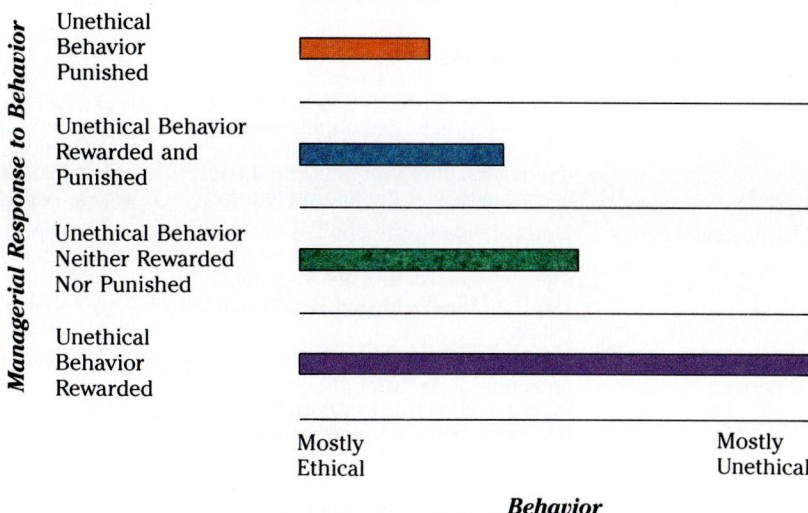

Source: W. H. Hegarty and H. P. Sims, Jr. (1979), Organizational philosophy, policies, and objectives related to unethical decision behavior: A laboratory experiment, *Journal of Applied Psychology*, 64, 331–38.

unethical decisions. Among the other major influences were the behavior of one's peers in an organization, the general ethical practices of one's industry or profession, and formal organizational policy on ethics (or the lack thereof).[49]

Ethical Standards and a Manager's Dilemma

No independent set of standards exists for ethical behavior in organizations. Ethics for organizations are based on the ethics of the society within which the organizations exist. The societal standards that guide ethical behavior should be used to guide the decisions and actions of managers who operate within society. When managers confront an ethically difficult decision, they should consider how each of these standards applies to their situation and should try to incorporate the most relevant ones within their moral reasoning. It is hoped that this kind of analysis will guide managers in making ethical decisions.[50]

The roles of three of these ethical standards in managers' decision making have been studied.[51] Decision makers guided by *utilitarian theories* focus on the results of particular actions. They evaluate an anticipated course of action by concentrating on the social consequences that the act is likely to produce. Managers operating according to a utilitarian theory, for example, might create a training program for minority employees so that the Equal Employment Opportunity offices will leave the organization alone. Another ethical standard deals with *rights*. Decision makers who apply this standard are concerned with respecting the rights to which people in the United States are entitled, such as the right of free consent, the right to privacy, the right to freedom of conscience, the right to free speech, and the right to due process. Managers operating under a rights

TABLE 4.6   *Five Major Ethical Systems*

	Nature of the Ethical Belief	Problems in the Ethical System
Eternal Law	Moral standards are given in an Eternal Law, which is revealed in Scripture or apparent in nature and then interpreted by religious leaders or humanist philosophers; the belief is that everyone should act in accordance with the interpretation.	There are multiple interpretations of the Law, but no method to choose among them beyond human rationality, and human rationality needs an absolute principle or value as the basis for choice.
Utilitarian Theory	Moral standards are applied to the outcome of an action or decision; the principle is that everyone should act to generate the greatest benefits for the largest number of people.	Immoral acts can be justified if they provide substantial benefits for the majority, even at an unbearable cost or harm to the minority; an additional principle or value is needed to balance the benefit-cost equation.
Universalist Theory	Moral standards are applied to the intent of an action or decision; the principle is that everyone should act to ensure that similar decisions would be reached by others, given similar circumstances.	Immoral acts can be justified by persons who are prone to self-deception or self-importance, and there is no scale to judge between "wills"; an additional principle or value is needed to refine the Categorical Imperative concept.
Distributive Justice	Moral standards are based on the primacy of a single value, which is justice. Everyone should act to ensure a more equitable distribution of benefits, for this promotes individual self-respect, which is essential for social cooperation.	The primacy of the value of justice is dependent on acceptance of the proposition that an equitable distribution of benefits ensures social cooperation.
Personal Liberty	Moral standards are based on the primacy of a single value, which is liberty. Everyone should act to ensure greater freedom of choice, for this promotes market exchange, which is essential for social productivity.	The primacy of the value of liberty is dependent on acceptance of the proposition that a market system of exchange ensures social productivity.

Source: L. Hosmer (1987), *The ethics of management*, Homewood, IL: Irwin, 106.

theory would not prohibit organizational members from speaking in favor of a gay rights bill or participating in a racially mixed marriage. The third ethical standard studied is based on the *theory of justice*. Managers who apply this standard emphasize engaging in acts that are fair and impartial. Managers operating under a theory of justice might create an affirmative action program, not because they are required to, but because it is a fair response to past discrimination. See Table 4.6 for an analysis of several ethical standards.

The suggestion that managers should consider the social consequences, the rights of others, and other ethical standards when making decisions sounds reasonable; however, doing so will not prevent managers from encountering ethical dilemmas from time to time. Consider, for example, the dilemma posed by new scientific developments. In one recent case, the Environmental Protection Agency caused public controversy by announcing that it was going to allow BioTechnica International, Inc., to test genetically altered organisms on a Wisconsin farm.[52] The dilemma is whether the potential benefit to the human race is greater than the cost and risks associated with releasing genetically altered organisms into the environment. Should the decision be made in favor of a new technology or in favor of minimizing health and safety risks?

San Diego State University management professor F. Neil Brady has used a model of the two-headed Roman god Janus to illustrate the

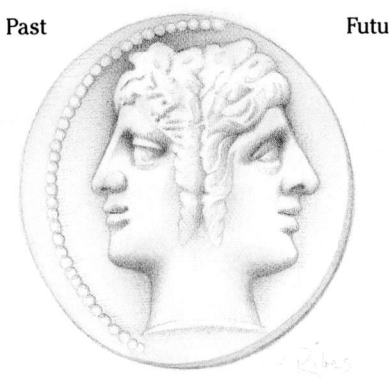

FIGURE 4.8   A Janus-Headed Model of the Ethical Process

Past   Future

dilemma that managers often face as they attempt to balance ethical and social responsibility considerations with other factors that influence decisions.[53] Janus, the god of gates and entryways, has one head facing forward and a second facing backward. The forward-looking face represents the utilitarian ethic which, as you saw, is future oriented, anticipating opportunities and results. According to this ethic, today's decisions are designed to do things that are proper and socially responsive to future social needs and conditions. The other face of Janus looks back at a formalistic ethic concerned with maintaining the cultural heritage established by tradition, language, and law. According to this ethic, today's decisions are designed to do things that will conform to and preserve the cultural heritage (see Figure 4.8).

Many managerial ethical dilemmas arise from the need to make ethical decisions while simultaneously dealing with utilitarian and formalistic issues. Managerial decision making in the utilitarian ethic is future oriented. It seeks innovations, encourages new practices, improves techniques, and promotes organizational change as ways to meet organizational goals and the changing needs of the external environment. Decision making in the formalistic ethic is concerned with preserving current definitions of right and just, maintaining tradition, and perpetuating the heritage of an organization and of society. In the Biotechnica case mentioned earlier, a utilitarian ethic would favor the new technology and permit the release of the organisms. A formalistic ethic, however, would favor minimizing potential risks to people and the environment. Managers must continually reconcile new practices with accumulated wisdom that has shaped current behavior and thought.[54]

Encouraging Ethical Behavior

What guides managers as they cope with ethical decisions and the dilemmas they may pose? Linda Klebe Trevino, from Pennsylvania State University, has developed a model that suggests that individuals' standards of right and wrong are not the sole determinant of their decisions.[55] Instead, these beliefs interact with other individual characteristics (such as locus of control) and situational forces (such as an organization's rewards and punishments and its culture). All of these factors shape the ethics of decisions and the behavior that results from them. This interactive process is illustrated in Figure 4.9. It shows how people can choose to engage in acts they consider unethical when the culture of an organization and its prevailing reward structure overwhelm personal belief systems.

Organizations can encourage ethical behavior by considering both long- and short-term factors.[56] For the long term, managers should develop their organization's culture so that it supports the learning—and, if necessary, relearning—of personal values that promote ethical behavior. For example, when decisions are made, managers should explicitly and publicly explain the ethical factors that accompany each alternative considered. Managers also should nurture an organizational culture that supports and values ethical behavior. This can be done, for example, by encouraging organization members to display signs of ethical values through whistleblowing.

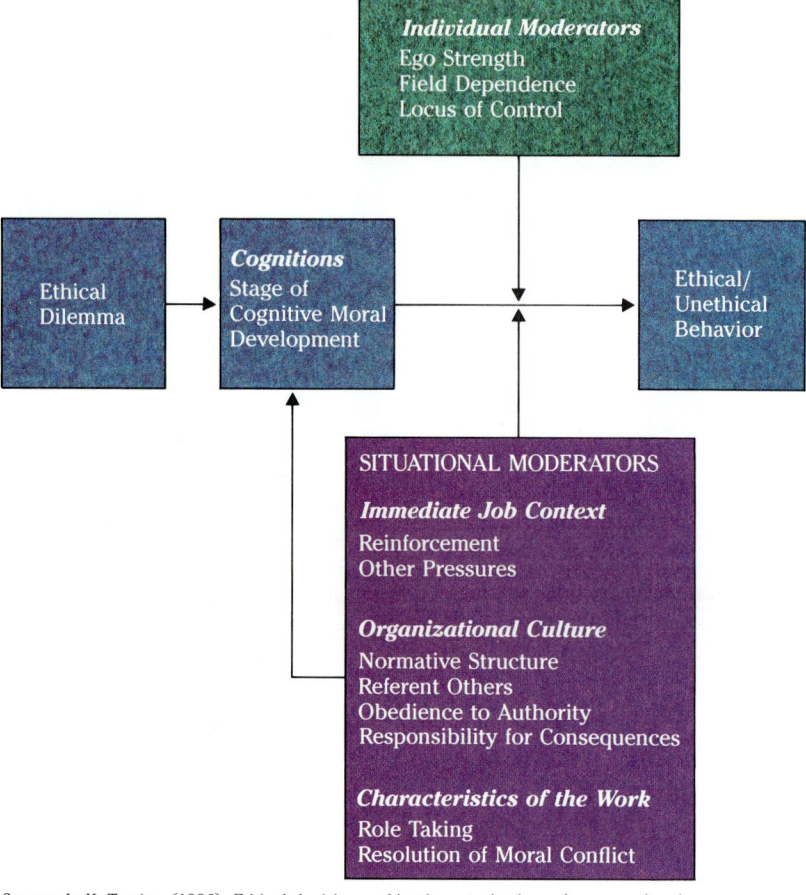

FIGURE 4.9 *The Interactionist Model of Ethical Decision Making in Organizations*

Individual Moderators
Ego Strength
Field Dependence
Locus of Control

Cognitions
Stage of Cognitive Moral Development

Ethical Dilemma

Ethical/ Unethical Behavior

SITUATIONAL MODERATORS

Immediate Job Context
Reinforcement
Other Pressures

Organizational Culture
Normative Structure
Referent Others
Obedience to Authority
Responsibility for Consequences

Characteristics of the Work
Role Taking
Resolution of Moral Conflict

Source: L. K. Trevino (1986), Ethical decision making in organizations: A person-situation interactionist model, *Academy of Management Review*, 11, 603.

To encourage ethical standards in the short term, managers can:

- Consider the personality characteristics of people applying to join the organization (see Chapter 13). Either avoid personalities that are prone to unethical behavior or make sure that policies block unethical tendencies.

- Make public statements that ethical behavior is important and expected.

- Develop organizational policies that specify ethical objectives.

- Provide rewards for ethical behavior and avoid providing rewards for unethical behavior.

- Punish unethical behavior and avoid punishing ethical behavior.

- When placing members into competitive situations, be sensitive to the potential for unethical behavior and take appropriate steps to avoid it.[57]

- Remember that when decisions require moral judgment, group decision making generally results in higher levels of moral reasoning than does individual decision making.[58]

Mary Ann Von Glinow

Mary Ann Von Glinow is an Associate Professor of Management and Organization at the University of Southern California's Graduate School of Business Administration. Dr. Von Glinow has authored and coauthored two books and numerous articles dealing with the management of high technology and professional employees, international technology transfer, and cross-cultural comparisons of human resource management.

1. Many recent articles in both the business and popular press detail unethical behavior by managers. Do you feel that unethical behavior by managers is increasing?

I don't think unethical behavior by managers is increasing. I think what's happening now is that there is an increased awareness in the marketplace of unethical kinds of activities. As a result, we're starting to see more corporate responses that try to deal with some of these kinds of issues. There has been, for example, widespread development of codes of ethics, or codes of conduct, and some statements of values in business organizations. There has also been a lot of open discussion among a variety of corporate executives about the issues of ethics and how to deal with them.

It is perhaps this increasing discussion and the number of different types of programs that currently exist out there today that give the illusion that unethical behavior by managers is increasing.

2. Does unethical behavior by managers promote unethical behavior by the people who work for them?

I think subordinates are very tuned to what managers suggest or say they want from their subordinates. In rare cases, there is some whistleblowing activity when managers behave unethically. It is more likely, however, that subordinates who fear for their jobs or who are keen in progressing up the organization ladder may commit or fall prone to an unethical behavior if they have an unethical manager. This is why organizations wanting to promote employees' awareness of ethical violations and ethical issues have to start at the top. To become known as an organization that is concerned about ethics, the organization's leader or CEO has to give a strong message that communicates that type of commitment. This might be done by way of policy statements, directive speeches, attention in the company newsletter paid to ethical concerns or values, and so on.

3. Are you aware of any organizations that have formal programs designed to teach ethics?

Boeing, Champion International, Chemical Bank, General Mills, Arthur Andersen, GTE, General Dynamics, Hewlett-Packard, Johnson & Johnson, and Xerox, to name a few. When the individual at the top of an organization demonstrates that ethical behavior is important, it gets translated into formal programs designed not only to teach ethics but to sensitize employees with respect to values and ethical concerns within the company. Organizations with a formal program, such as DANA Corporation, sometimes spell out all details very precisely. Other, more informal approaches outline appropriate employee conduct and appropriate ethical behavior for the entire organization in a series of general statements.

The areas covered in both formal and informal programs vary across industry and with respect to the topics that they cover. These programs deal with ethical concerns ranging from product safety and quality topics, health and safety issues, conflict of interest concerns, and general employment practices. Also popular are programs involving financial reporting, supplier relationships, and fairness in selling and marketing practices.

4. Does asking members to follow a formal code of ethics really reduce unethical behavior? If so, how?

It depends on how specifically some of these issues are presented. In many of the companies just discussed, there were a series of key incidents that triggered attention to ethical concerns or ethical codes of conduct. To an extent, the documents that have emerged as a result of those critical incidents do, in fact, promote ethical behavior. At least, those companies that were mentioned have so reported in the business roundtable. Generally speaking, however, codes are not enough and must be accompanied by an ongoing process of implementation. A process of implementation differs somewhat from a formal code of ethics in that it tends to be more specific, concentrating on two main objectives: ensuring compliance with company standards of conduct and linking a corporate culture that values ethics with survival and profitability in a highly competitive world.

Implications for Managers

The guidelines for promoting ethical behavior discussed in this chapter are just that—suggestions that may be used to encourage ethical behavior. No one can tell you which one or how many of these guidelines you should adopt. Any decision you make that involves ethics is likely to be based on values you have already learned and experiences you have already had. Rest assured, as a manager you *will* be asked to make decisions that involve ethics. Some of these decisions will affect only you. Others will affect subordinates, superiors, or even the organization. What, for example, will you do when you encounter organizational policies and practices that you consider inappropriate? Are you willing to blow the whistle on those policies and practices? Are you willing to take a personal stand and perhaps put your own career at risk if necessary?

Ethics are not clear-cut. Although there are many behaviors that are clearly ethical or unethical, the vast majority of decisions managers must make concern issues that fall into "gray" areas. When others cannot agree on whether a particular behavior is ethical, your personal values and the cultural values of an organization come into play. Think about the nature of ethics and the various guidelines discussed in this chapter. Then let your behavior reflect your values.

Many organizations are becoming increasingly active in addressing such social concerns as the need for reforestation.

Social Responsibility and Managerial Ethics in Review

Organizations at the start of the twentieth century were concerned mostly with making profits and leaving the well-being of others up to individual acts of charity. After the Great Depression, however, people began to demand that organizations share some of their profits to improve society. Today, all managers must be aware of what society expects from their organizations and whether their actions will meet expectations.

This is not an easy task. There are many external and internal stakeholders, and one group's needs may conflict with another's. Also complicating the situation is the fact that the social issues that are considered important change as society changes. Many organizations try to specify current social issues and their response to them through a social audit. The level of commitment found in an organization's response is determined largely by the principles it follows and ranges from performing only those socially responsible acts that are imposed by laws and regulations to initiating policies and programs that try to anticipate and react to social issues before they become problems. Managers can determine how responsive their organization is by placing its social responsibilities, the philosophies guiding its responses to social issues, and the issues themselves along the three dimensions of a cube. Managers can also use the cube as a planning tool to predict their organization's response to new social issues as they emerge.

There are many arguments for and against corporate social responsibility. These arguments have been encapsulated into two points of view. Those who believe that organizations should not be concerned about social responsibility base many of their arguments on the costs involved and whether organizations should shoulder those costs on behalf of society. Those who are in favor of corporate social responsibility feel that organizations benefit from society and, therefore, have an obligation to improve it. Although there is no universal agreement, surveys and other reports indicate that many organizations are, in fact, becoming increasingly active in addressing social concerns.

An organization's response to social issues can be classified according to its relationship with the law. Organizations who behave illegally and irresponsibly flout the law and public opinion. Some organizations obey the letter of the law but not the spirit. Other organizations break the law in the midst of their attempts to act responsibly. A fourth category of organizations manages to adhere to laws and regulations and still respond to society's needs. One way to promote an organization's adherence to the law and attention to social issues is to put its board of directors in charge of monitoring decisions and behaviors. This charge is best met if the board includes members from outside as well as inside the organization.

The societal values, norms, and mores that shape an organization's social responsibility considerations also influence the ethics of individuals. Every society has a set of standards to guide the behavior of its citizens, although acceptable codes of conduct for one society may be judged more harshly by another. Like social responsibility considerations, ethical considerations address the well-being of others, but on a smaller scale. These personal values are learned through one's family, religious, educational, and cultural experiences.

A manager's personal ethics become managerial ethics when applied to situations in organizations. Managers bear a tremendous ethical responsibility for the actions they take, for the actions other take at their behest, and even for the results of their failure to act. They also bear the responsibility for encouraging others to act ethically. Although many people might behave unethically under certain conditions, there are steps managers can take to promote ethical behavior, including developing an organizational culture and organizational policies and practices that reflect a high ethical standard for both managers and nonmanagers.

Notes

1. L. Wolfson (3 January 1988), Helping business handle crises, interview with Steven B. Fink, president of Lexicon Communications Corp., *Wisconsin State Journal*, 8.
2. K. Davis and R. L. Blomstrom (1971), *Business society and environment: Social power and social response*, New York: McGraw-Hill.
3. K. Davis and W. C. Frederick (1984), *Business and society: Management, public policy, and ethics*, 5th ed., New York: McGraw-Hill.
4. D. Votaw and S. P. Sethi (1973), *The corporate dilemma: Traditional values versus contemporary problems*, Englewood Cliffs, NJ: Prentice-Hall; S. P. Sethi (1975), Dimensions of corporate social performance: An analytical framework, *California Management Review*, 17(3), 58–64.
5. W. C. Frederick, K. Davis, and J. E. Post (1988), *Business and society: Corporate strategy, public policy, ethics*, New York: McGraw-Hill.

6. M. Heald (1970), *The social responsibilities of business: Company and community, 1900–1960,* Cleveland: Case-Western Reserve Press.

7. Frederick, Davis, and Post, 1988.

8. *Ibid.*

9. P. L. Berger (September/October 1981), New attack on the legitimacy of business, *Harvard Business Review,* 82–89.

10. R. Hay and E. Gray (1974), Social responsibilities of business managers, *Academy of Management Journal,* 17, 135–143.

11. Hay and Gray, 1974, 142.

12. A discussion of the social audit can be found in R. A. Bauer and D. H. Fenn, Jr. (1972), *The corporate social audit,* New York: Russell Sage.

13. General Motors Corporation (1986), *1986 General Motors Public Interest Report,* Detroit, MI: Author, i.

14. Sethi, 1975, 63.

15. Sethi, 1975, 62.

16. Frederick, Davis, and Post, 1988, 32.

17. A. B. Carroll (1979), A three-dimensional conceptual model of corporate performance, *Academy of Management Review,* 4, 497–505.

18. K. E. Aupperle, A. B. Carroll, and J. D. Hatfield (1985), An empirical examination of the relationship between corporate social responsibility and profitability, *Academy of Management Journal,* 28, 446–63.

19. Frederick, Davis, and Post, 1988, 36–39.

20. T. Parsons (1960), *Structure and process in modern society,* Glencoe, IL: Free Press; P. M. Blau and W. R. Scott (1962), *Formal organizations: A comparative approach,* San Francisco: Chandler Publishing Company.

21. Frederick, Davis, and Post, 1988, 39–43.

22. M. Friedman (September 1970), The social responsibility of business is to increase profits, *The New York Times Magazine,* 33, 122–26; M. Friedman (April, 1971), Does business have social responsibility? *Bank Administration,* 13–14.

23. K. Davis (1973), The case for and against business assumption of social responsibility, *Academy of Management Journal,* 16, 312–22.

24. K. Davis (June 1975), Five propositions for social responsibility, *Business Horizons,* 19–24.

25. L. E. Preston (1986), Social issues in management: An evolutionary perspective, in D. A. Wren and J. A. Pearce II, eds., *Papers dedicated to the development of modern management,* 52–57.

26. Preston, 1986, 56.

27. R. Ford and F. McLaughlin (1984), Perceptions of socially responsible activities and attitudes: A comparison of business school deans and corporate chief executives, *Academy of Management Journal,* 27, 666–74.

28. D. Dalton and R. Cosier (May-June 1982), The four faces of social responsibility, *Business Horizons,* 19–27.

29. H. Geneen (1984), *Managing,* New York: Doubleday & Co., 258.

30. P. F. Drucker (1973), *Management: Tasks, responsibilities, practices,* New York: Harper & Row; H. Mintzberg (1983), *Power in and around organizations,* Englewood Cliffs, NJ: Prentice-Hall.

31. D. J. Dunn (16 March 1987), Directors aren't doing their jobs, *Fortune,* 17–19.

32. I. F. Kesner, B. Victor, and B. T. Lamont (1986), Board composition and the commission of illegal acts: An investigation of Fortune 500 Companies, *Academy of Management Journal,* 29, 789–99.

33. Korn/Ferry International (1981), *Board of directors: Eighth annual study*, Los Angeles: Author.

34. Geneen, 1984.

35. Kesner, Victor, and Lamont, 1986.

36. Parsons, 1960.

37. T. J. Peters and R. H. Waterman, Jr. (1982), *Lessons from America's best run corporations*, New York: Harper & Row, 26.

38. J. G. Longenecker (1985), Management priorities and management ethics, *Journal of Business Ethics*, 4, 65–70.

39. M. P. Miceli and J. P. Near (1984), The relationship among beliefs, organizational position, and whistle-blowing status: A discriminant analysis, *Academy of Management Journal*, 27, 687–705.

40. M. Brody (24 November 1986), Listen to your whistleblower, *Fortune*, 77.

41. A. L. Otten (14 July 1986), Ethics on the job: Companies alert employees to potential dilemmas, *The Wall Street Journal*, 17.

42. I. Ross (December 1980), How lawless are big companies? *Fortune*, 57–63.

43. D. J. Lincoln, M. M. Pressley, and T. Little (1982), Ethical beliefs and personal values of top level executives, *Journal of Business Research*, 10, 475–87.

44. R. Ricklees (31 October–3 November 1983), Ethics in America, *The Wall Street Journal*, 33.

45. S. N. Brenner and E. A. Molander (January/February 1977), Is the ethics of business changing? *Harvard Business Review*, 64.

46. Brenner and Mollander, 1977, 57–71.

47. B. Z. Posner and W. H. Schmidt (1984), Values and the American manager: An update, *California Management Review*, 26(3), 202.

48. W. H. Hegarty and H. P. Sims, Jr. (1978), Some determinants of unethical decision behavior: An experiment, *Journal of Applied Psychology*, 63, 451–57; W. H. Hegarty and H. P. Sims, Jr. (1979), Organizational philosophy, policies, and objectives related to unethical decision behavior: A laboratory experiment, *Journal of Applied Psychology*, 64, 331–38.

49. Posner and Schmidt, 1984, 202–16; Brenner and Mollander, 1977; R. Baumhart (July/August 1961), How ethical are businessmen? *Harvard Business Review*, 6–12, 16, 19, 156–76.

50. L. Hosmer (1987), *The ethics of management*, Homewood, IL: Irwin, 107–9.

51. D. J. Fritzsche and H. Becker (1984), Linking management behavior to ethical philosophy: An empirical investigation, *Academy of Management Journal*, 27, 166–75.

52. J. Wilke (7 May 1987), BioTechnica to get OK to test genetically-altered bacteria, *Boston Globe*, 61.

53. F. N. Brady (1985), A Janus-Headed model of ethical theory: Looking two ways at business/society issues, *Academy of Management Review*, 10, 568–76.

54. Brady, 1985, 570.

55. L. K. Trevino (1986), Ethical decision making in organizations: A person-situation interactionist model, *Academy of Management Review*, 11, 601–17.

56. R. B. Dunham (1984), *Organizational behavior: People and processes in management*, Homewood, IL: Irwin.

57. Dunham, 1984, 495.

58. M. L. Nichols and V. E. Day (1982), A comparison of moral reasoning of groups and individuals on the "defining issues test," *Academy of Management Journal*, 25, 201–8.

Key Terms

social responsibility
social audit
economic responsibilities
legal responsibilities
ethical responsibilities
discretionary responsibilities
reaction philosophies

defense philosophies
accommodation philosophies
proaction philosophies
ethics
socialization
whistleblowing

Issues for Review and Discussion

1. Define both ethics and social responsibility. How are they alike? How do they differ?
2. Discuss the managerial values associated with profit maximizing management, trusteeship management, and quality-of-life management.
3. Identify and discuss the two principles guiding contemporary acts of social responsibility.
4. What are the major points of disagreement between Milton Friedman and Keith Davis on corporate social responsibility?
5. Discuss the distinction among social obligation, social responsibility, and social responsiveness.
6. List several sources of unethical managerial behaviors.
7. Discuss the steps that managers can take to encourage ethical behavior by all organization members.
8. Describe the ethical dilemma symbolized by the two heads of the Roman god Janus.

Suggested Readings

Carroll, A. B. (1984). *Social responsibility of management*. Chicago: Science Research Associates, Inc.

Dierkes, M. and Antal, A. B. (1986). Whither corporate social reporting: Is it time to legislate? *California Management Review*, 28, 106–21.

Marx, T. G. (1985). *Business & society: Economic, moral, and political foundations*. Englewood Cliffs, NJ: Prentice-Hall.

Miles, R. H. (1987). *Managing the corporate social environment: A grounded theory*. Englewood Cliffs, NJ: Prentice-Hall.

Preston, L. E. (1986). Social issues in management: An evolutionary perspective. In Wren, D. A. and Pearce, J. A., II, eds. *Papers dedicated to the development of modern management*. Chicago: Academy of Management, 52–57.

CASE *Frank Pearson and the Allied Research Corporation*

By David B. Thompson and
Michael J. DiNoto of the
University of Idaho

Dr. Frank Pearson was an associate director of medical research for the Allied Research Corporation, where he supervised a research team assigned to develop therapeutic drugs. The team's duties included establishing procedures to test drugs for effectiveness, safety, and marketability. Dr. Pearson was the only physician on the research team and had been employed by Allied since 1980.

In the spring of 1985, the team was engaged in the development of loperamide, a liquid drug for treatment of diarrhea in infants, children, and the elderly. The proposed formula contained forty-four times the concentration of saccharin permitted by the Federal Drug Administration (FDA) in twelve ounces of a soft drink. Accordingly, the team agreed that the formula was unsuitable for use and suspended work on the project.

In March of 1986, Allied's Marketing Division issued a directive to resume the research and development of loperamide. The company intended to file an investigational new drug application with the FDA, to continue laboratory studies on loperamide, and to complete the formula. In Dr. Pearson's professional judgment, however, there was no justification for seeking permission from the FDA to continue to develop the drug because of the heated controversy over the safety of saccharin. He made his position clear to the other team members. The team, however, decided to continue the research despite Dr. Pearson's objections.

Dr. Pearson met with his supervisor, Dr. Antonucci. During the meeting, Dr. Pearson stated that, in his professional opinion, the decision to pursue the development of loperamide was medically unsound. He also told Dr. Antonucci that he believed continuing his work on the loperamide research would violate his Hippocratic oath, a generally accepted standard of medical ethics. The risk, he said, that saccharin might be harmful should prevent testing the formula on children or the elderly, especially when an alternative formula might soon be available.

Dr. Antonucci responded that the company had no intention of testing the formula on any human subjects unless and until the FDA gave its approval. He assured Dr. Pearson that all proper procedures would be scrupulously observed in the development and testing of the drug. He also emphasized the differences between the development and testing phases of research projects in general and suggested that continuing to do research would, in his opinion, violate no law or professional code of ethics. He also stressed the need to work constructively with the marketing division.

At the end of the meeting, Dr. Pearson remained unpersuaded, and Dr. Antonucci asked him to choose another research project. He assured Dr. Pearson that the request would be honored and that no salary adjustment would be made. Dr. Pearson responded that, even so, he interpreted this offer as a demotion.

Later in the day, Dr. Pearson submitted his letter of resignation to Dr. Antonucci. It said, in part, "Upon learning that you believe that I have not 'acted as a Director' and have displayed inadequacies as to my inability to relate to the marketing division and that I am now—or soon will be—demoted, I find it impossible to continue my employment at Allied." Dr. Antonucci accepted the resignation without comment.

Questions

1. What are the ethical issues in this case?

2. If the FDA had given permission to test the drug, would that permission make the testing ethical? Explain.

3. What alternatives were open to Dr. Antonucci? Which should he have taken?

4. Was Dr. Antonucci correct in dealing with Dr. Pearson as he did?

CHAPTER 5

Schools of Management Thought: Approaches to Managing

Student Learning Objectives

After reading this chapter, you should be able to:

1. Identify the early management pioneers, their views of organizations, and their contributions to the classical theory of management.

2. Understand the major elements of Taylor's approach to scientific management.

3. Explain the significance of the Hawthorne studies.

4. Discuss the emergence of the human relations movement and describe how it views workers in organizations.

5. Identify the major contributors to the behavioral theory of management, their views of organizations, and their contributions to the management literature.

6. Explain the systems theory perspective of managing organizations.

7. Identify and describe three contemporary perspectives of management.

8. Compare the management schools of thought and their contributions and limitations.

9. Understand the difference between the science of management and the art of management.

*I*t would be extremely difficult for managers to memorize every possible action to take for every possible management situation; therefore, managers and management scientists develop theories that can be used to clarify and organize information. Although these theories do not provide all of the answers managers need, they offer guidance that managers can use as they develop answers to specific management problems.

Each theory offers a different approach to management, and managerial styles differ depending on which theory a manager follows. As you will recall from the discussion on the internal environment in Chapter 3, the style managers use when performing such functions as coordinating, decision-making, and communicating greatly influences the climate of their organization. Differences in organizational climates can be explained by the fact that managers do not have the same beliefs, opinions, and theories on what management is and on how organizations ought to be managed. An understanding of different philosophies of management helps explain why one manager's approach is different from another's. This chapter explores the major theoretical "schools of management thought" that guide managers.

The Classical School

Managers have needed efficient planning, organizing, staffing, decision-making, and control systems since ancient times, but long ago there was no centralized source of assistance. There were no books or journals about management, no professional management societies, and no schools to which a manager could turn. Through trial and error in managing families, tribes, armies, commercial organizations, and political units, people accumulated knowledge about organizations and management. Although history provided some insight into managerial practice, the Industrial Revolution in the 1700s and early 1800s stimulated sustained systematic efforts to understand organizations and their management. These efforts resulted in the emergence of well-defined schools of management thought on how to approach the practice of management as well as a body of management literature, professional management associations, and schools to create and disseminate knowledge about management and organization managers.

The **classical school** of management thought and practice emerged during the late 1800s and early 1900s as managers struggled with organizational complexities brought on by the Industrial Revolution. Organizations were growing larger and more complex, their technologies more sophisticated. These new organizations demanded that managers control inventory and production, schedule and coordinate work, integrate diverse work systems, and manage human resources. There was little information, however, to guide these managers on how to perform such activities. The ideas and experiences of earlier managers, economists, political thinkers, and philosophers had not been organized, recorded, or directed toward enhancing organizational management. It was not until the 1800s and early 1900s that a new breed of industrial managers, most

The Academy of Management considers May 26, 1896, to be the beginning of management as a formal discipline. It was on this date that Henry Towne called for both management research and education at a meeting of the American Society of Mechanical Engineers.

In the early 1900s, managers struggled with organizational complexities brought on by the Industrial Revolution.

of whom had engineering backgrounds, consciously set out to develop "principles" of organizational management and, thus, to find practical solutions to the problems facing managers.

Classical management theorists proposed that there was "one best way" to manage a complex industrial organization. Their theories focused primarily on the idea that norms of *economic rationality* controlled the behavior of and decisions made by managers and individual employees. In other words, the theorists assumed that people make logical, rational decisions when trying to maximize personal returns from a work experience. Their theories of management were driven by their belief that rational, logical behavior should focus on making economic sense.

The classical school of management thought emerged from the almost simultaneous occurrence of the scientific management movement in the United States; Henri Fayol's work in France on classical administrative theory; and the work of German sociologist Max Weber, who developed a model of the bureaucratic organization. The classical school actually consists of two approaches to management: scientific management and classical organization theory.

The Scientific Management Movement

Scientific management refers to "that kind of management which conducts a business or affairs by standards established by facts or truths gained through systematic observation, experiment, or reasoning."[1] Promoters of the scientific management movement tried to increase labor efficiency primarily by managing the work of employees in an organization's technical core (on the "shop floor"). The scientific management approach produced several stars of management theory and practice, who used experiments and systematic observation to develop effective management techniques.

Charles Babbage Charles Babbage (1792–1871) was one early contributor to the scientific management movement. He argued that

Charles Babbage advocated division of labor as a way of lowering costs and boosting productivity.

Frederick W. Taylor is considered to be the "father of scientific management."

organizations could realize greater profit if employees specialized in performing a specific set of job activities. Along with classical economist Adam Smith, Babbage advocated a division of labor and the design of jobs so that each employee performed only a small set of simple tasks. Managers were to train workers to perform each of these small tasks as efficiently as possible and were to offer incentives for executing them quickly and effectively. Babbage believed that managers should conduct time studies to determine how long it should take to perform each task and noted that "if the observer stands with his watch in his hand before a person heading a pin, the workman will almost certainly increase his speed."[2] Managers could then use such time study information to establish standards for expected performance levels and to reward employees with bonuses based on the degree to which they exceeded those standards.

Frederick W. Taylor The best known of the scientific management theorists was Frederick W. Taylor (1856–1915). Taylor's contributions built on the work of Babbage and others to propel the scientific management movement forward during the late 1800s and early 1900s. Taylor, an engineer and consultant, observed firsthand what he considered to be inexcusable work methods at such organizations as Midvale Steel, Simonds Rolling Machine, and Bethlehem Steel. At that time, industries were plagued by an inadequate supply of skilled labor. Taylor maintained that organizations were using available employees ineffectively and that managers needed to act decisively to increase labor efficiency.

In the steel industry, Taylor observed and documented many factors that contributed to low production rates and inefficiency.[3] Workers often brought their own tools to the workplace, and these often were poorly designed for the work to be done. Job training typically was haphazard, and workers themselves often determined machine speed and workpace. Hiring frequently occurred on a "first-come, first-hired" basis rather than on individuals' skills and abilities. Managers worked side by side with laborers, often ignoring such management responsibilities as planning and organizing work. As a result, inadequately trained employees were repeatedly left in charge of planning, decision making, scheduling, and controlling shop-floor activities.

Taylor severely criticized managers for failing to manage effectively and for allowing workers to determine their own methods and pace. He believed that managers should develop and implement the "science" of work—the underlying laws, or principles, that govern various work activities. Laborers could function effectively by following these scientific principles.

Taylor applied his belief in the scientific approach to management to the task of handling pig iron, a basic task in the steel industry. He observed inefficiencies and wasted energy in the methods used to carry 92-pound pieces of iron from the fabrication site to railroad cars. He was convinced that, using scientific principles, he could identify the "one best way" to pick up a 92-pound piece of pig iron, hold it, walk with it, and lay it down. Through time-and-motion studies and fatigue studies, Taylor identified a "science" of pig iron handling. This science enabled an average laborer to increase the amount of pig iron handled from 12-1/2 tons to 48 tons a day.

By using the same approach, Taylor created "sciences" of shoveling coal, iron ore, and ash. He developed shovels with scoops tailored to the particular substance being shoveled and capable of handling the load that he determined "ideal." Taylor called for managers to develop a science of all jobs in an organization's technical core. An example of the level of fine detail Taylor expected is found in the science he identified for handling the shovel:

Press the forearm hard against the upper part of the right leg just below the thigh, . . . take the end of the shovel in your right hand, . . . and when you push the shovel into the pile, instead of using the muscular effort of your arms which is tiresome . . . throw the weight of your body on the shovel. . . . [4]

Taylor's scientific management approach was rooted in a classical perspective of economics. According to this perspective, both managers and employees are economically motivated. Managers want to increase profits, and employees want to increase their personal economic gains. Taylor saw this mutual interest as linking management and workers, so they could work together to satisfy their needs. Instead, the competing demands of management and labor for larger portions of a fixed economic pie were a primary cause of industrial conflict. Taylor felt that the solution was to increase the size of the pie by raising organizational productivity and efficiency through scientific management; thus, if employees complied with the prescriptions of scientific management, they and managers alike would receive portions from an increasingly larger financial pie. Taylor thought that rational, economically motivated employees would see the financial benefits from scientific management and would be willing to listen and comply with these prescriptions:

1. *Develop the science of work* using time, motion, and fatigue studies to identify the one best way to perform a job and the level at which it can be performed.
2. *Adhere absolutely to work standards,* not allowing the daily production rate identified through the science of work to be changed by the arbitrary whim of either manager or employee.
3. *Select, place, and train workers scientifically,* assigning workers to the most interesting and profitable tasks for which they are suited.
4. *Apply a financial incentive system* that encourages workers to perform efficiently and effectively by tying pay to output: low production leads to low pay, high production to high pay.
5. *Use specialized functional supervision* by a number of expert managers to oversee workers on the different aspects of their work rather than by one general manager who supervises an entire department. (Taylor referred to this as "functional foremanship." This text will refer to it as *functional supervision.*)
6. *Keep labor-management relations friendly,* because a cooperative alliance between employee and employer helps ensure the willing application of the scientific principles of work. [5]

Although Taylor's scientific management presented many technical mechanisms, one of the furthest-reaching aspects of his work was its new

FIGURE 5.1   *Functional Supervision*

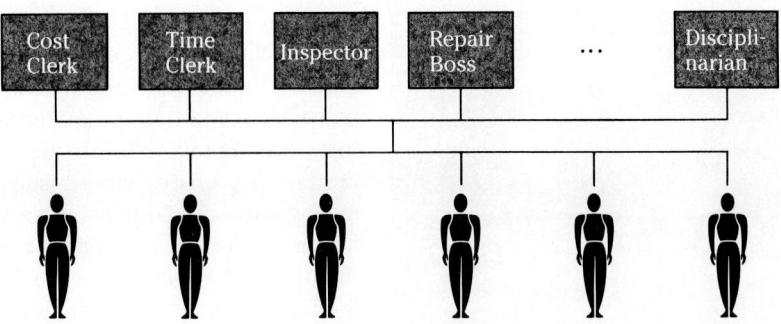

philosophical approach to managing work and people. To be successful, Taylor stated, the scientific management approach would require a mental revolution on the part of both labor and management. Employees and managers would have to understand the scientific management principles and work together in harmony, accepting new work roles and new methods. Only through this mental revolution would labor and management achieve both higher wages and increased output.

The Gilbreths   Frank and Lillian Gilbreth, a husband and wife team, also were pioneers in the scientific management movement. Frank Bunker Gilbreth (1868–1924) focused on improving work methods to enhance productivity and efficiency. With her background in psychology and management, Lillian Moller Gilbreth (1878–1972) viewed scientific management as a technique to help workers reach their full potential.

The Gilbreths developed a scheme to classify the motions used in the performance of a job. A motion was referred to as a *therblig*, a play on their name spelled backwards. Their classifications included such motions as grasping, holding, and moving. The motion scheme documented the relationship between types and frequencies of motion and worker fatigue, demonstrating that unnecessary motions wasted energy. By separating appropriate from inappropriate motions, the Gilbreths helped make more of a worker's energy available for job performance.

Frank Gilbreth carefully studied and improved methods used for bricklaying. He observed that different bricklayers used different procedures and was amazed that one of the oldest crafts in the world had never been standardized. Even on relatively casual inspection, bricklaying seemed full of inefficiency. Convinced that bricklayers' efficiency could be improved substantially, Gilbreth analyzed motion pictures of bricklaying and discovered that the process typically used 18 distinct movements. He timed the various activities, explored fatigue factors, and proposed an alternative procedure that reduced the number of movements from 18 to 5. He designed a special scaffold that positioned bricks, mud, and the bricklayer at appropriate levels and created a formula for making a consistent, uniform mud mixture. He also divided the bricklaying job into parts. One worker delivered bricks and mud. Another worker only laid brick. Gilbreth's prescriptions increased the average output of individual bricklayers from 120 to 250 bricks an hour.

Frank and Lillian Gilbreth were pioneers in the scientific management movement.

Lillian Gilbreth's Ph.D. thesis at Brown University was entitled "The Psychology of Management" and was published in 1914. She pioneered modern human resource management, especially the scientific selection, placement, and training of employees, and became president of Gilbreth, Inc., after Frank Gilbreth died in 1924. She later joined the faculty of Purdue University, where she became the first female professor of management. In addition to serving Presidents Hoover, Roosevelt, Eisenhower, Kennedy, and Johnson in the areas of aging and rehabilitation of the physically handicapped, Lillian Gilbreth held faculty appointments at the University of Wisconsin, Rutgers University, New Jersey University, and Newark College of Engineering; received twenty honorary degrees; and was named an honorary member of the American Society of Mechanical Engineers.

Together, the Gilbreths were interested in developing individual workers through training programs, improved work environments, and a healthy psychological outlook. They were so convinced of the benefits of such efforts that they even applied their management principles to raising their twelve children, as described in the book and movie *Cheaper by the Dozen*.

Henry Gantt Henry Gantt (1861–1919), an associate of Taylor's at Midvale, Simonds, and Bethlehem Steel, added two techniques to scientific management: the Gantt chart and a minimum-wage-based incentive system.

In an attempt to increase managers' control over planning, designing, and monitoring work activities, Gantt developed the *Gantt chart*, which is still in use today. Managers use the Gantt chart to summarize work activities and identify those that should be performed simultaneously or sequentially. As illustrated in Figure 5.2, for a Lil'America Builders remodeling job, plans must be drawn before any other activity can commence, but rough electrical work and the ordering of cabinets can occur concurrently. Wallboard installation can overlap a bit with final electrical work, but cabinets cannot be installed before wallboard installation has been completed. In addition to assisting with work scheduling, the Gantt chart can be used as a work-monitoring tool. Managers can record on the chart the amount of time it actually took to complete a task and can compare it to the amount of time originally planned for completion.

Henry Gantt created the Gantt Chart to aid production and control.

Gantt promoted the idea that employees should receive a minimum daily wage whether or not they achieved their specified daily work objectives. He also recommended that employees receive monetary incentives in the form of bonuses for work above and beyond the expected standard. Furthermore, Gantt proposed bonuses for supervisors whose subordinates reached their daily standard and additional bonuses if all workers reached their goals, because he felt that this would encourage supervisors to manage subordinates effectively.

Classical Organization Theory

Whereas scientific management focuses on an organization's technical core, *classical organization theory* concentrates on the management of an entire organization. Contributors to classical organization theory were

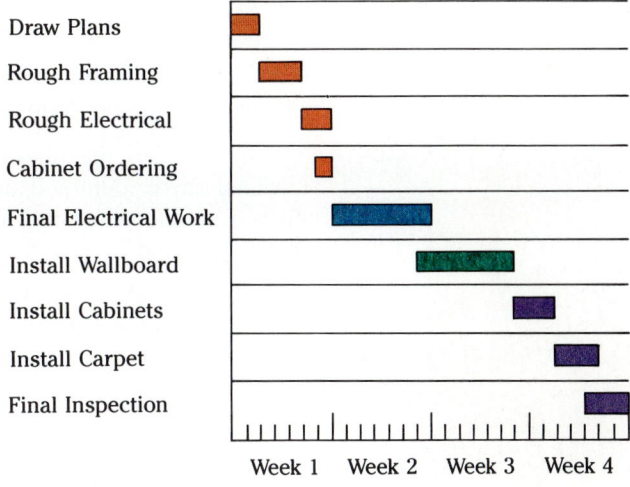

FIGURE 5.2   *Gantt Chart for Lil'America Builders*

Draw Plans
Rough Framing
Rough Electrical
Cabinet Ordering
Final Electrical Work
Install Wallboard
Install Cabinets
Install Carpet
Final Inspection

Week 1   Week 2   Week 3   Week 4

Source: Adapted from J. G. Monks (1982), *Operations management: Theory and problems*, New York: McGraw-Hill, 549.

concerned with the structure of an organization and with designing processes that would make its operations rational, ordered, predictable, efficient, and effective. Classical organization theorists viewed organizations as giant machines created to achieve goals, and they believed in a basic set of universal laws, or principles, that would design and run those "machines" effectively. Two primary contributors to classical organizational theory were Henri Fayol and Max Weber.

Henri Fayol   Henri Fayol (1841–1925) worked for fifty-eight years with Commentry-Fourchambault, a French coal and iron processing organization. His perspectives on management grew out of this experience and his formal training as a mining engineer. Fayol attributed his success as a manager to the methods he used rather than to personal talent. He felt that other managers could be as successful as he was if they had appropriate guidelines for managing complex organizations.

Fayol paid particular attention to managerial activities. Although he believed that all managers perform all five of the managerial functions he identified—planning, organizing, directing, coordinating, and controlling, he also recognized that the nature of managerial work differs from manager to manager according to such factors as the size of an organization and a manager's location in its hierarchy.

Fayol identified six major activities of organizations:

1. *Technical activities* involving primarily production and manufacturing
2. *Commercial activities*, such as buying, selling, and exchange, that require knowledge of the market and competitors
3. *Financial activities* used to search for and make optimum use of capital
4. *Security activities* to safeguard property and people against theft, fire, and flood and to prevent strikes, felonies, and other forms of social disturbance

5. *Accounting activities* that gather and provide clear, precise information about an organization's economic position
6. *Managerial activities* including planning, organizing, directing, coordinating, and controlling organizational activities

In addition to the attention he gave each of the six management activities, Fayol identified an underlying set of fourteen principles he believed should guide the management of organizations and which he himself followed:

1. *Division of labor*—improve levels of efficiency through specialization, resulting in reduced learning time, fewer activity changes, and increased skill development
2. *Authority*—the right to give orders should always carry responsibility fitting to its privilege
3. *Discipline*—relies on respect for the rules, policies, and agreements that govern an organization; should be achieved by the clear and fair presentation of all agreements between an organization and its employees
4. *Unity of command*—each employee reports to only one superior, thus avoiding confusion and conflict
5. *Unity of direction*—one manager for each organizational plan and a single plan for operations within the organization that deal with the same objective
6. *Subordination of individual interest to the common good*—the needs of individuals and groups within an organization should not take precedence over the needs of the organization as a whole
7. *Renumeration*—wages should be equitable and satisfactory to employees and superiors
8. *Centralization*—levels at which decisions are made should depend on the specific situation; no level of centralization or decentralization is ideal for all situations
9. *Scalar chain*—the relationship among all levels in the organizational hierarchy and exact lines of authority should be unmistakably clear and followed at all times
10. *Order*—there should be a place for everything (and everyone), and everything (and everyone) should be in its place
11. *Equity*—employees should be treated with kindness and justice
12. *Stability of tenure*—the employee population should be stable so that people can learn the nature of their jobs and the larger context within which their jobs are performed
13. *Initiative*—subordinates should be encouraged to conceive and carry out their ideas
14. *Esprit de corps*—teamwork, a sense of unity and togetherness, should be fostered and maintained

Fayol felt that the application of these principles should be flexible enough to match each specific organizational situation:

For preference I shall adopt the term principles whilst dissociating it from any suggestion of rigidity, for there is nothing rigid or absolute in

Max Weber saw the bureaucratic organization as that organizational form most capable of attaining the highest degree of efficiency and superior precision, stability, and reliability.

management affairs, it is all a question of proportion. Seldom do we have to apply the same principle twice in identical conditions; allowance must be made for different changing circumstances, . . . [6]

Despite Fayol's call for flexibility, many of the managers who adopted his fourteen principles applied them rigidly. It is the strict application of Fayol's principles that characterizes the classical approach to organizational management. As a result, the principles of esprit de corps and initiative failed to become an integral part of the classical approach to the practice of management. For Fayol, however, the flexible application of these fourteen principles helped him guide the nearly bankrupt Commentry-Fourchambault back to prosperity.

Max Weber   Max Weber (1864–1920), a German lawyer and sociologist, was convinced that there was an appropriate design for an efficient and effective organization and developed a model for this "rational organization" (see Figure 5.3).[7] In Weber's organization, labor should be divided according to specialization. Each employee's authority and responsibility should be clearly defined as the official duties of the position and not as the duties of the particular individual who holds that position. Weber also proposed that a well-defined hierarchy be set up to eliminate ambiguity and to specify the nature of relationships among jobs within an organization.

Weber's vision of an ideal organization included an elaborate set of rules specifying the rights and duties of employees and a second set of rules containing the procedures involved in each work situation. These

FIGURE 5.3   *The Anatomy of Weber's Bureaucracy*

Goals of a Bureaucratic Model

- Speed
- Precision
- Order
- Unambiguity
- Continuity
- Predictability

Structure of the Bureaucratic Model

- A division of labor is based on functional specialization.
- A well-defined hierarchy of authority exists.
- A system of rules specifies the rights and duties of employees.
- A system of rules and work procedures specifies the methods for dealing with work situations.
- An interpersonal network is characterized by the impersonality of interpersonal relations.
- Selection into the organization is based on technical competence and organizational need.
- Promotion inside the organization is based on technical competence and comprehensive knowledge of the organization, which comes through seniority.
- Employment is intended to reflect a lifetime commitment to a career.
- A clearly specified career path to the top of the organization is provided for those who qualify.
- Office management consists of the creation and maintenance of extensive written records of organizational transactions.

rules were to be applied uniformly throughout the organization. As a result, Weber's bureaucratic organization would be impersonal, and employees would be managed without personal affection or enthusiasm for individual or personal accomplishments. Managers were to conform to this atmosphere of impersonality and were to avoid giving special individual considerations.

According to Weber, the bureaucratic organization would provide a clear career path for competent individuals. Written rules would govern all major activities, and all management activities and decisions would be documented. A bureaucratic organization would be impersonal, rigid, and routine in meeting its goals of speed, precision, order, unambiguity, continuity, and predictability.

Contributions and Limitations

Although the classical school of management did not provide a totally unified approach to management, there were many similarities among the views expressed by Babbage, Taylor, the Gilbreths, Gantt, Fayol, and Weber. Classical management was, to a very large extent, prescriptive in nature: it described how people should manage organizations. Just as engineers specify the appropriate way to build bridges, managers were to follow a rational approach and a set of principles to build and operate organizations. Through their work to identify "one best way," systems were developed that led to greater organizational productivity. In some ways, these systems still characterize contemporary bureaucratic organizations.

Another contribution of these early management pioneers is that their efforts to create an ideal organization spurred additional scientific inquiry into management and organizational systems. Although the various contributors to the classical school of management agreed on many issues—such as the importance of a division of labor, order, the development of standard operating procedures, and centralization of authority, there were also a few areas of disagreement. For example, there were radical differences in thinking about supervision in the technical core. Fayol talked about "unity of command"; Taylor called for functional supervision. Fayol argued that each employee should report to and be directed by only one superior to avoid confusion and conflict; however, Taylor believed that employees should have multiple supervisors so that they could benefit from various types of specialized knowledge.

Another area of disagreement became evident when managers put the prescriptions from the classical contributors into practice. Fayol instructed managers to apply his fourteen principles flexibly, making adjustments to fit each situation. In practice, however, classical management tended to be closed and rigid. Similarly, Taylor called for friendly labor-management relations, but the typical classical approach was often cool, impersonal, and adversarial. Unfortunately, many contemporary organizations have become slaves to a set of inflexible bureaucratic principles and have grown large and sluggish as a result.

The classical school of management thought has a number of critics. Many argue that its description of organizational members as rational and economically motivated is incomplete. These critics claim that when managers ignore the social needs of workers, organizations do not provide adequate motivation and reinforcement programs. If managers think of organizations as machines rather than social systems, they treat employees as resources to be manipulated for organizational ends. The result has been confrontation between labor and management, as managers direct and control employees, work methods, and the pursuit of organizational goals.

A second area of criticism of the classicists revolves around their attempts to identify universal principles for efficient management. Although many of the classical principles of management may be appropriate for organizations operating in simple, nonturbulent environments, they are less well suited to conducting business in shifting and heterogeneous environments (see Chapter 2).

The Behavioral School

The classicists' preoccupation with the mechanics of organizations left a void. This space was filled by behavioral management theorists, who viewed organizations from social and psychological perspectives. The contributors to the **behavioral school** were concerned about the welfare of employees and wanted to treat them as much more than just cogs in the industrial wheel.

Early Contributors

Instead of viewing organizations as machines with perfectly designed mechanical systems, behavioral thinkers envisioned a social system. In this social system was a people-to-people and people-to-work network so smoothly linked and efficient that it would accomplish organizational goals. Effective management of this social system would require managers to understand the nature of individuals, groups, and their patterns of interaction.

Robert Owen was an early industrialist who saw the need for effective human resource management.

Robert Owen British industrialist Robert Owen (1771–1858) was one of the first managers to recognize the need for good overall management of an organization's human resources. Owen called for managers who treat workers with respect and dignity, better working conditions, reduced hours of work, meals for the workforce, and restrictions on the use of children as a source of labor.

Hugo Munsterberg, the "father of industrial psychology," taught managers to use psychological principles to enhance organizational effectiveness.

Hugo Munsterberg After establishing a psychological laboratory at Harvard in 1892, Hugo Munsterberg (1863–1916) concentrated on applying psychological concepts to organizational settings. Considered the father of industrial psychology, Munsterberg documented the psychological conditions associated with different levels of productivity. He taught managers to use empirical psychological findings to match workers with jobs and to motivate these workers after placing them in jobs.[8] In his ground-breaking book, *Psychology and Industrial Efficiency*, published in 1913, Munsterberg popularized the notion that managers can use psychology to enhance organizational effectiveness.

Walter Dill Scott suggested that employees are not only motivated by economic rewards, but also by a set of social needs.

Walter Dill Scott While on the faculty at Northwestern University, Walter Dill Scott (1869–1955) argued that managers were not effectively using the human factor in organizations. Although Scott agreed that employees are economically motivated, he emphasized that they are also social creatures with needs for recognition and membership in social groups. Scott argued that if managers did not consider employees' social needs, organizational effectiveness would be hindered. He believed that managers had placed a great emphasis on developing the technology for getting work done and not enough on developing good employee selection and supervision. Scott asserted that management should work at improving employee attitudes and motivation as a means to increase worker productivity.

Mary Parker Follett called on organization members to take orders from the situations they face.

Mary Parker Follett Management philosopher, consultant, and educator Mary Parker Follett (1868–1933) called mangement "the art of getting things done through others" and wrote about the issues of power, authority, leadership, and coordination.[9] She believed that a natural order between management and employees could be achieved through leadership. This leadership was not, however, to be accomplished through the traditional use of formal authority by superiors over subordinates. Rather, Follett asserted that a manager's influence and power should flow naturally from his or her knowledge and skill. She also encouraged managers to coordinate work activities through personal contact rather than through impersonal structured work systems or written rules, as advocated in Weber's bureaucratic model.

Chester Barnard One of Chester Barnard's (1886–1961) major contributions to management comes from his discussion of formal and informal organizations. A formal organization is an entity managers consciously create to achieve organizational goals. An informal organization arises spontaneously as employees interact and form bonds. Whereas classical management thinking asked managers to focus on the design and management of the formal organization, Barnard's work sensitized managers to the informal organization's ability to aid communication, provide leadership, maintain cohesiveness, and strengthen individual feelings of integrity and self-respect.[10]

A Transition: The Hawthorne Studies

Between 1924 and 1933, a series of worker productivity studies was conducted at the Hawthorne Plant of the Western Electric Company in Chicago. These studies, widely known as the Hawthorne studies, have strongly influenced the course of behavioral management theory (see "A Closer Look: The Hawthorne Studies").* Prior to the Hawthorne studies, managers had increased productivity primarily through developing better

Chester Barnard informed managers of the advantages of informal organizations.

*The Hawthorne studies have been much discussed and often misrepresented. The discussion here is consistent with the review of the Hawthorne studies published by the Academy of Management as part of their celebration of 100 years of modern management: R. G. Greenwood and C. D. Wrege (1986), The Hawthorne Studies, in D. A. Wren and J. A. Pearce II, eds., *Papers dedicated to the development of modern management*, Chicago: Academy of Management, 24–35.

A CLOSER LOOK

The Hawthorne Studies: Shedding Light on Worker Productivity

A series of studies conducted at the Hawthorne Works of the Western Electric Company near Chicago, usually referred to as the Hawthorne studies, has had a significant impact on the management of work.[1] A set of studies involving illumination levels was conducted at the Hawthorne plant between November 1924 and April 1927 by D. C. Jackson and G. A. Pennock. These studies were intended to identify lighting levels that would produce optimal productivity. In the first illumination experiment, however, productivity increased when illumination was increased and when it was decreased. Overall, productivity bounced up and down without an apparent direct relationship to illumination level.

A second illumination study had an experimental group which experienced illumination changes and a control group for which illumination was held constant. In this experiment, production increased in both groups to an almost equal extent. In yet a third illumination experiment, lighting levels were decreased over time. As a result, productivity levels increased for both experimental and control groups (at least until an extremely low level of illumination was reached).

The first major study of the Hawthorne studies themselves was conducted over a twenty-four-experimental session between April 25, 1927, and February 8, 1933. These relay assembly test room (''RATR'') experiments explored the degree to which variations in length of rest periods, of the working day, and of the working week influenced productivity. As was the case for the illumination study, productivity fluctuated during the various stages of the RATR experiments. Again, these variations in productivity could not be explained by the expected factors.

Many reports of the Hawthorne studies suggest that any change conducted during the studies increased productivity. This is not exactly true, and it is not the primary reason that these studies are so important. The importance of the RATR and Hawthorne experiments is a function of how researchers and scholars explained the unexpected findings. As early as September 1928, an extensive interviewing program elicited comments from workers that helped identify the causes of fluctuations in productivity. Conclusions as to why the Hawthorne effects occurred vary. According to Elton Mayo, for example,

What actually happened was that six individuals became a team and the team gave itself wholeheartedly and spontaneously to cooperation in the experiment. The consequence was that they felt themselves to be participating freely and without afterthought, and were happy in the knowledge that they were working without coercion from above or limitations from below.[2]

Mayo seemed to feel that the experiments satisfied workers' needs and shifted their attention from personal problems to productivity.

George Pennock, who conducted the RATR experiments, has stated that

Emotional status was reflected in performance; and the major component of this emotional condition was attitude toward supervisor. The inference from these studies was inescapable that the dominant factor in the performance of these employees was their mental attitude.[3]

Another perspective on the Hawthorne effects comes from the independent writings of Whitehead and Chase, who both suggested that a major reason the ''Hawthorne effect'' produced increases in productivity was that being a part of the experiments made the workers feel important.[4] Even members of control groups felt important; thus, their productivity was said to increase as a result.

1. R. G. Greenwood and C. D. Wrege (1986), The Hawthorne studies, in D. A. Wren and J. A. Pearce II, eds., *Papers dedicated to the development of modern management*, Chicago: Academy of Management, 24–35.

2. E. Mayo (1945), *The social problems of an industrial civilization*, Boston: Division of Research, Graduate School of Business Administration, Harvard University, 72–73.

3. G. A. Pennock (1930), Industrial research at Hawthorne: An experimental investigation of rest periods, working conditions and other influences, *Personnel Journal* 8: 297.

4. T. N. Whitehead (1938), *The industrial worker* (2 vols.), Cambridge: Harvard University Press; S. Chase (1941), What makes workers like to work? *Reader's Digest*, 15–20.

tools and improving machines and work methods. The Hawthorne studies focused on the relationship between worker productivity and such factors as the illumination of the work place, the length of coffee breaks, the length of the workday, and the nature of pay plans. The researchers expected that improvements in these work environment factors would yield improvements in productivity.

Surprisingly, the results of these studies were often inconsistent with expectations. In fact, at times, productivity actually increased when decreases were expected (such as when illumination levels were decreased). In an attempt to understand the confusing pattern of results, the Hawthorne researchers interviewed a large number of workers. The interviews suggested that a human/social element operated in the workplace and that productivity increases were as much an outgrowth of group dynamics as of managerial demands and physical factors. The importance of employees as social beings was firmly established.

Another result of the Hawthorne studies was the suggestion that social factors might be as powerful a determinant of worker productivity as were financial motives. Classical management theorists expected each employee in a group to maximize pay by producing as many units as possible. Instead, Harvard professor Elton Mayo observed that informal work groups emerged with their own leaders, influence systems, norms for appropriate behavior, and pressures for conformity to maximum and minimum acceptable levels of performance. Any individual who produced above the maximum level was considered a "rate-buster" and was pressured by co-workers to slow down. Anyone who produced under the minimum level was a "chiseler" and urged to speed up. The social pressures within the group powerfully affected workers' productivity.

The Hawthorne studies failed to uncover a simple relationship between improvements in physical working conditions and increases in worker productivity, but they emphasized the importance of human considerations for worker effectiveness and documented, for the first time, the tremendous power of an informal work group and the social environment on workers' attitudes and behaviors. The studies provided a transition between the classical and behavioral management schools of thought. The classicists were task oriented and thought managers should enhance productivity through technical systems. The emerging human relations (behavioral) approach to management focused on employees and directed managers to guide individual needs for recognition and peer interaction. A social model of employees was beginning to compete with the rational economic model of the classical management school.

The Human Relations Movement

Rising negative reactions to the impersonality of scientific management and bureaucratic theory, combined with evidence from the Hawthorne studies, helped ignite the **human relations movement.** Turning from task-oriented styles of management, advocates focused on employees in the belief that satisfied workers would be productive workers. A manager following the guidelines of the human relations movement would be supportive and paternalistic, creating and nurturing cohesive work groups

A manager following the guidelines of the human relations movement creates and nurtures cohesive work groups.

and a psychologically healthy environment for workers. This social model, thus, proposed that increased productivity depended on the degree to which an organization could meet workers' needs for recognition, acceptance, and group membership.

The Behavioral Science Movement

Two factors distinguish the **behavioral science movement** from the classicists and human relations advocates. First, behavioral scientists stressed the need to conduct systematic and controlled studies of workers and their attitudes and behaviors. Second, they emphasized that empirical observation of the human side of organizations should take place through research techniques, such as field and laboratory experiments. Behavioral scientists considered both the classicists' rational/economic model and the social model espoused by human relations advocates to be incomplete representations of workers; thus, they presented a model that suggested that employees have a strong need to grow, to develop, and to maintain a high level of self-regard.

Abraham Maslow   In 1943, psychologist Abraham Maslow (1908–70) advanced a theory of human motivation that was later adopted by many managers (see Chapter 14 on motivation).[11] Maslow identified five sets of human needs arranged in a hierarchy of their importance to individuals (see Figure 5.4). These needs range from physiological needs (such as the need for food and water) to self-actualization needs (the need to develop one's capabilities fully).

Maslow's need hierarchy theory had specific implications for managers. To motivate people, an organization must offer its members the opportunity to satisfy their active personal needs. Maslow helped manag-

FIGURE 5.4
Maslow's Hierarchy of Needs

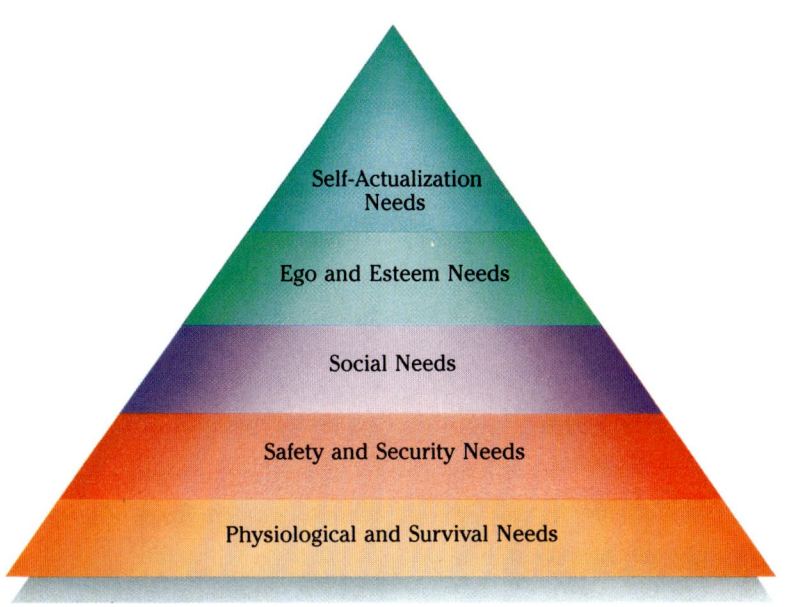

Abraham Maslow was the architect of the hierarchy of human needs.

ers identify the types of needs that employees have, the order in which employees are likely to satisfy these needs, and the specific actions that organizations can take to try to satisfy these needs. For example, organizations can help employees meet their physiological and security needs by providing a base salary with which they can buy food and shelter. Organizations can offer benefit programs, such as retirement plans, to help employees meet their safety and security needs. Maslow, thus, provided a rational model of human behavior based on workers' needs.

Maslow's work suggests that employees have some needs that can be satisfied by earned wages, but it also makes clear that employees are social beings with needs for acceptance, warmth, and caring that can come only from associating with others. Maslow's work places the needs for self-esteem and self-actualization as growth needs at the top of the hierarchy. These growth needs can be strong motivators of human behavior, particularly when physiological, security, and social needs are reasonably satisfied. Recognition of growth needs calls for a different style of management from that proposed by classical or human relations advocates.

Douglas McGregor   Douglas McGregor (1906–64) first presented his ideas on Theory X and Theory Y management in a classic article, "The Human Side of Enterprise."[12] McGregor called the traditional approach to management "Theory X." **Theory X** describes the worker as inherently disliking work, lacking ambition, resistant to change, gullible, dull, and indifferent to organizational needs. Theory X includes the following propositions:

1. Management is responsible for organizing the elements of productive enterprise—money, materials, equipment, people—in the interest of economic ends.
2. With respect to people, this is a process of directing their efforts, motivating them, controlling their actions, and modifying their behavior to fit the needs of an organization.
3. Without this active intervention by management, people would be passive—even resistant—to organizational needs. They must, therefore, be persuaded, rewarded, punished, and controlled—their activities must be directed.[13]

In contrast, the **Theory Y** view of management suggests that people like work, are motivated to achieve objectives to which they are committed, and are capable of self-direction and self-control. People are not considered passive or resistant to organizational needs by nature, although they may have become so as a result of their experiences in organizations. According to the Theory Y approach to management:

The essential task of management is to arrange organizational conditions and methods of operation so that people can achieve their own goals best by directing their own efforts toward organizational objectives.[14]

Raymond Miles, from the University of California at Berkeley, called for expanded employee involvement in organizational affairs.

Managers can do this by creating structures and processes that encourage employees to become actively involved in executing their organizational roles; thus, the Theory Y approach involves strategies that enable employees to exercise self-direction and self-control. The decentralization and delegation of authority, job enlargement, participative and consultative management, and the use of goal setting are some of the management practices a Theory Y manager can use to encourage and facilitate desirable subordinate behavior.

McGregor's Theory Y, like the work of Maslow, focuses managers' attention on an employee model that is more complex than either the rational/economic model of the classicists or the human relationists' social model. Theory Y depicts employees as having complex motivational patterns, with behavior strongly influenced by their need to exercise self-direction and self-control in pursuit of their full human potential.

Other Contributors to the Behavioral Science Movement Rensis Likert from the University of Michigan and Harvard's Chris Argyris concentrated on how organizational and management systems affect employees' attitudes and behaviors. Both advocated the development of open and flexible organizations. Argyris, for example, argued that classically designed organizations (bureaucracies) make demands on employees that are incompatible with the needs of growing, self-actualizing individuals.[15] Like Likert, he suggested that management should create organizational systems that permit a greater opportunity for employees to exercise self-direction and self-control.

During the early 1960s, Raymond Miles, from the University of California at Berkeley, called for expanded employee involvement in organizational affairs. Believing that the employee group is a major untapped resource in organizations, Miles suggested that managers involve workers in decision-making and departmental functions to increase organizational performance. According to Miles, when performance increases, employees derive satisfaction that heightens their willingness to become even more involved in organizational activities.[16]

Contributions and Limitations

Proponents of classical management theory envisioned increases in organizational control, efficiency, and effectiveness as stemming from developments in the technical and mechanical side of an organization, but the behavioral school introduced the importance of personal and social considerations to the management task. It stimulated managers' thinking about employees and the need to design organizations that were more open and flexible than Weber's bureaucratic model. Many of the concepts introduced by the behavioral school of thought are influential in contemporary organizations. American companies with a reputation for excellence treat human resources as central to their success and growth.[17] It has been claimed that the success of Japanese organizations lies in their integration of employees into the organizations' technical systems.[18]

Behavioral management thinking has several limitations, however. First, it lacks a good language for communicating the importance of its ideas to

Thomas A. Mahoney

Thomas A. Mahoney is the Frances Hampton Currey Professor of Organization Studies in the Owen Graduate School of Management at Vanderbilt University. His research, teaching, and consulting interests focus on the managing of human resources in work organizations, particularly in relation to organization design, planning, and the motivation and reward of behavior.

1. What are one or two of the most significant changes you have seen in the management literature over the last twenty to twenty-five years?

One significant change has been the specialization of subject matter. What used to be termed "management" is now examined as organization behavior/organization management, production/operations management, and strategic management. Each functional specialization within management has developed independently of the others. A second change has been the shift from descriptive reporting of managerial practice to theory testing. There is more of a focus on the empirical testing of theoretical propositions.

2. Who do you feel was (is) the management philosopher who has contributed most to our understanding of management? What was this person's greatest contribution?

Two who have jointly contributed to our knowledge of managing organizations are Chester Barnard and Herbert Simon. Their concepts of the employment contract with inducements and contributions and of satisficing behavior provide a framework for a richer understanding of the management of coalitions and organizational decisions.

3. In what areas have management scientists given us the greatest insights into management? In what areas is our understanding the least developed?

Management science has provided a sound framework for optimizing decisions in well-structured situations, by providing guides to optimizing decision making. Unfortunately, we know much less about managing unstructured situations and decisions. Much of managing is an art of coalition formation, the exercise of political influence, and guiding behavior in unstructured situations. Management science currently provides little guidance in these issues.

4. Identify one or two of the most significant contributions the study of management has made to management practitioners.

Most of the contributions to management practice have occurred within functional specialties, such as employee selection, performance appraisal, group decision making, and the like. Somewhat unfortunately, contributions to management decision making have been most notable in influencing well-structured, quantifiable, and short-term decisions. Attention is focused on the problems we best know how to address, rather than on less easily analyzable problems, which may actually be more critical.

managers. Behavioral scientists often use a jargon that is not easily understood, and many of their theories are highly abstract. Second, behavioral scientists have not done well at getting the attention and respect of key managers in top positions. As a consequence, many managers still see organizations as mechanical systems, or purely in terms of the financial bottom line. The third limitation is that, in many ways, behavioral management theorists still assume that there is "one best way" to manage, but some managerial situations may call for the classical perspective, whereas others require the behavioral perspective. This dilemma is addressed by contemporary management theorists.

Contemporary Management Thought

The past few decades have been marked by the refinement, extension, and synthesis of both classical and behavioral management thinking. **Sociotechnical systems theory,** for example, tries to counteract the one-sided approach taken by the classical and behavioral schools by balancing the technical and social-psychological sides of an organization.[19] The perspectives of both classical and behavioral management have been combined and incorporated in a number of new management models.

The Systems Perspective

One of the contemporary approaches to management perceives an organization as a complete system of related parts. A **system** can be defined as a set of interrelated elements that functions as a unit for a specific purpose. **Systems theory,** therefore, is presented in this discussion not as a separate theory of management but as a way of viewing organizations. Systems theorists see organizations as complex networks of interrelated parts that exist in an interdependent relationship with the external environment.[20]

This interrelationship affects all components of an organization's internal environment (see Chapter 3). Managers from different departments need to communicate with one another, and they need to understand the degree to which the activities of their own departments affect and are affected by the activities of other departments. When an automaker's accounting department reports increased revenues from the sale of luxury sedans, for example, its marketing department can be instructed to expand the advertising campaign for that model, and production departments can be told to increase the number of cars made during the next fiscal quarter. The boundaries between an organization's internal divisions must be open for such give-and-take of information.

The relationships among internal organizational systems also call for an open relationship between an organization and its external environment.[21] Managers are expected to be sensitive to the needs of the environment as they take resources from and interact with it while pursuing organizational goals (see Chapter 2). For example, logging companies reseed areas they deforest and restaurants heed customers' growing demands for nonsmoking areas.

Two of the three contemporary theories on organizational management—contingency perspectives and the McKinsey 7-S framework—were derived from a systems-theory perspective. The next section discusses these theories.

Contingency Perspectives

You will recall that both classical and behavioral management theorists searched for the "one best way" to manage. Contemporary theorists, however, see such an approach as too simplistic. They believe that, although a particular managerial strategy may succeed in some situations, it may fail in others; therefore, strict adherence to one approach can have disastrous results.

According to various **contingency perspectives,** the techniques appropriate for a manager to use depend (are *contingent*) on the situation. Although managers always need to plan, organize, direct, and control, they need to do so situation by situation. A contingency theory of decision making, for example, might suggest that the centralized authority and highly directive leadership style found in the classical approach is effective when a manager has a well-developed body of knowledge that defines the most effective way of proceeding. For example, if workers and managers have a body of knowledge that defines an effective way to convert iron ore into pig iron, there is very little need for them to collaborate in deciding which techniques should be used to perform this task.

When there is a high level of environmental uncertainty and little or no developed knowledge to guide work methods, however, a different decision-making strategy is needed. A manager who faces high levels of environment-based and task-based uncertainty needs to use more consultative and participative decision strategies. The *Miami Herald* editor's decision to publish personal information about Gary Hart during the 1988 presidential campaign, for example, could have required meetings between the newspaper's editor, reporters, campaign officials—even the newspaper's owner. The ability to diagnose a situation and to be flexible about adopting an approach is critical in a number of contingency models.

Contingency perspectives, thus, suggest that as situations vary, the consequences of a particular approach to planning, organizing, directing, and controlling events also vary. The resulting challenge facing management scientists is to identify, understand, and explain these critical contingencies. For managers, this challenge has three aspects (see Figure 5.5). First, managers must develop diagnostic skills that allow them to identify situational demands and characteristics. Second, they must

FIGURE 5.5
Demands on Effective Management:
Contingency Perspectives

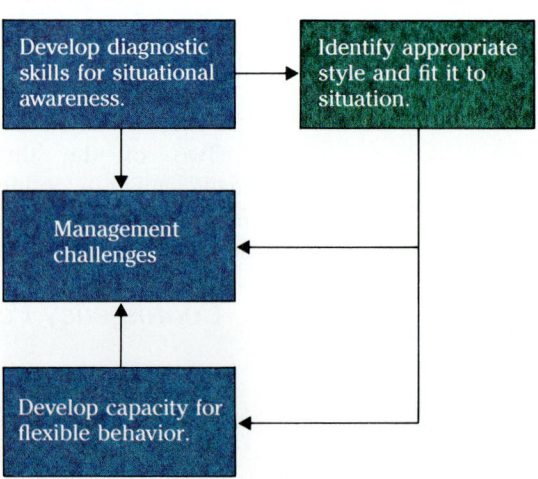

identify a management style appropriate for the demands of the situation. Finally, they must develop the flexibility to move from one managerial style to another as demands change.

Contingency theories identify some of the critical situational forces that call for particular approaches to management; thus, becoming familiar with various contingency models helps managers overcome the first challenge, diagnosing the situation. Contingency theories can also specify appropriate management styles for a given situation. For example, managers can learn that complex jobs are more appropriate for employees who are motivated by needs for achievement and autonomy than for those motivated by a need for security. Good managers, of course, must also be able to perform in the fashion indicated—even when it runs counter to their natural inclinations. This final step, tailoring behavior to match the demands of the situation, is crucial to good management (and quite difficult for most people).

Throughout the remainder of this book, contingency perspectives guide discussion of the management process, from planning through controlling. These perspectives show the usefulness, as well as the limitations, of the earlier classical and behavioral approaches. Given the complexity of modern organizations, effective managers must rely on contingency theories to go beyond the simplistic strategies of the past.

The McKinsey 7-S Framework

A second contemporary perspective on organizational management to come from a systems-theory perspective is the **McKinsey 7-S framework.** It is the product of an association between two sets of authors, Thomas Peters and Robert Waterman and Richard Pascale and Anthony Athos, who worked in conjunction with McKinsey and Company, a large management consulting organization.[22] Their research into America's effective organizations revealed that there are seven interdependent factors in organizations that must be managed harmoniously, because a change in one necessitates adjustments in the other six.

The critical components in the McKinsey 7-S framework—*S* factors—include the following:

1. *Strategy*—the plans or courses of action that allocate an organization's scarce resources and commit it to a specified action, over time, to reach identified goals—for example, Coca-Cola's decision to increase its control over its distribution system by purchasing JTL, the nation's largest Coca-Cola bottler

2. *Structure*—an organization's design, such as the number of its hierarchical levels, its divisions, and the location of authority within them

3. *Systems*—proceduralized reports and routinized processes, such as those governing the standard operating procedures for handling depreciation of an organization's assets and absenteeism.

4. *Staff*—important personnel groups within an organization, described demographically (for example, the ages of engineers, the functional background of M.B.A.'s)

FIGURE 5.6
The McKinsey 7-S Framework

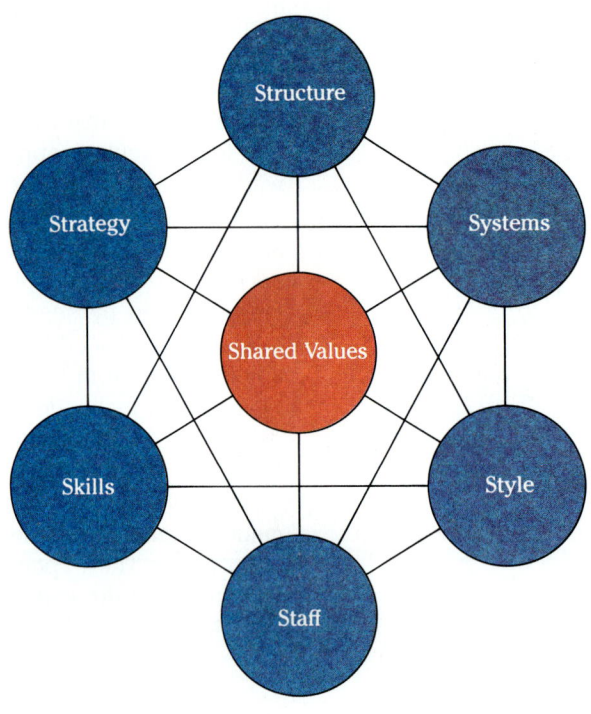

Source: T. L. Peters and R. H. Waterman, Jr. (1982), *In search of excellence: Lessons from America's best-run companies*, New York: Harper & Row, 10.

5. *Style*—the way key managers behave when pursuing an organization's goals; also refers to an organization's cultural style (for example, consultative or dictatorial)

6. *Skills*—the distinctive capabilities of an organization's key personnel

7. *Superordinate goals (shared values)*—the significant meanings or guiding concepts that an organization instills in its members, such as when organization members are encouraged to experiment with new methods even if they risk failure[23]

Because of their interdependent relationship, a change in one *S* factor alerts managers to the need for adjustment of the others. A change in an organization's strategy, for example, may call for a change in its structure. According to the McKinsey model, effective managers achieve a good fit among these seven variables (see Figure 5.6).

The Theory Z Perspective

During the 1970s and 1980s, American business organizations were seriously affected by Japanese competitors and by American productivity problems. Japanese organizations were generating products of higher quality at less cost and carving serious inroads into American markets. Often, Japanese managers appeared to be a step ahead of their American counterparts.

American scholars identified a number of management practices common to Japanese organizations that appeared to account for much of

It has been claimed that the success of Japanese organizations lies in their integration of employees into their technical systems.

their effectiveness. Whether these practices could be transplanted successfully to American organizations was an issue for debate. Some argued that unique cultural differences would prevent American organizations from adapting Japanese management practices. Others felt that the Japanese practices could be successful in American organizations, often noting that they were basically American in origin anyway.

In 1981, management professor William Ouchi offered **Theory Z** to integrate the merits of the Japanese (Theory J) and American (Theory A) management styles (see Figure 5.7).[24] Theory Z is less a major theory of management than it is a set of organizational and management style characteristics. As summarized in Figure 5.7, Theory Z emphasizes terms of employment, decision making, responsibility, evaluation and promotion, control, career paths, and concern for employees. Some successful American organizations that practice Theory Z management include Eastman Kodak, Hewlett-Packard, IBM, and Procter & Gamble. For example, until recently, IBM prided itself on finding ways to relocate, rather than laying off, its workforce in times of decline.

Theory Z is not a contingency theory of management. Ouchi seems to suggest that this style of management is universally better than the traditional American approach and prescribes Theory Z as appropriate for almost any management situation. In fact, in many ways, Theory Z reflects a return to the outdated "one best way" thinking of behavioral management theory. In the tradition of behavioral management, Theory Z

FIGURE 5.7 A Comparison of American, Japanese, and Theory Z Organizations

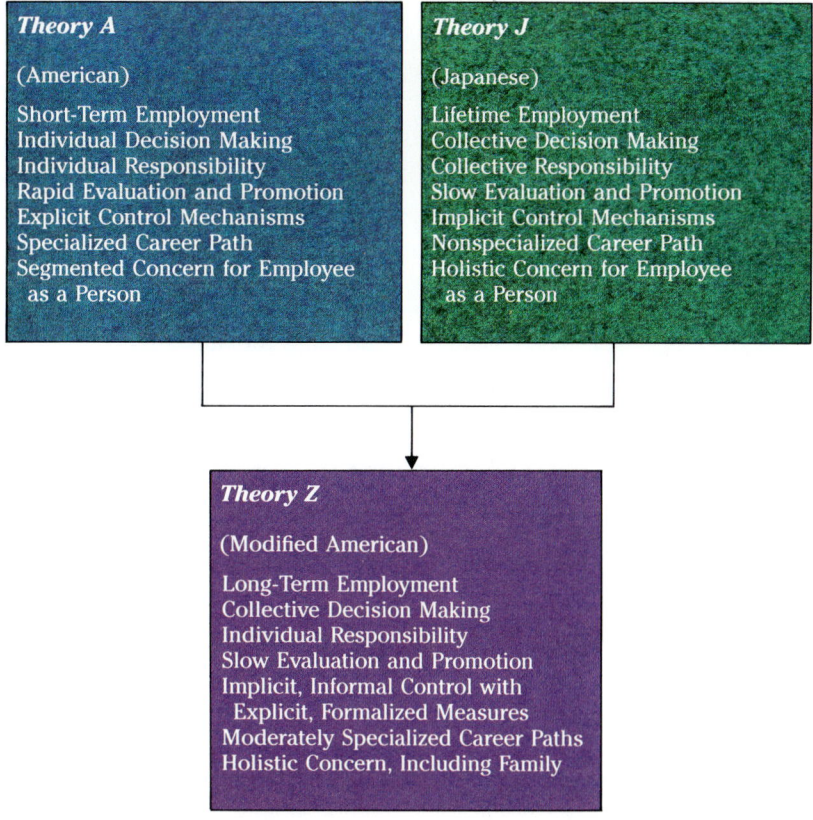

Source: Adapted from William Ouchi (1981), *Theory Z*, Reading, MA: Addison-Wesley, 58.

identifies employees as a key component of organizational productivity and effectiveness. It prescribes how employees "should be" managed so that organizational efficiency and effectiveness improve. Ouchi's universal management prescriptions call for long-term employment and a concern for employees' total life.

Theory Z is not a complete theory. It does not, for example, explain why certain management practices create an effective organization. Nonetheless, Ouchi's work has again heightened American industry's awareness of the variety of management techniques that may be effective under particular circumstances. (See "A Closer Look: Japanese Management Methods.")

Contributions and Limitations

Two major contributions have come from the contemporary schools of management thought. First, they have had a unifying effect, combining the technical side of organizations that the classicists examined and the social elements that were the focus of the behavioralists. This strong emphasis on multidimensionality has alerted managers to the interdependence of organizational subsystems and the importance of integrating them to achieve efficiency and effectiveness. Second, the contemporary era has sensitized managers to the fact that no one set of management principles is appropriate in all situations. Under some circumstances, the classical approach is effective. Under other circumstances, the behavioral model is effective. Under still others, managers should integrate and apply ideas from both the classical and behavioral models.

There are two primary limitations of contemporary management approaches. The first is that each perspective is more complex than either classical or behavioral theory. This complexity can make their use more difficult and their adoption less likely. The second limitation is that no contemporary management perspective has been thoroughly researched. It is, therefore, likely that, in their current state, these theories are incomplete. Despite these limitations, the contemporary perspectives appear superior to the behavioral and classical approaches because they build on the strengths but avoid many of the limitations of the older schools of thought.

Management: Art or Science?

The question of whether management is an art or a science has often been asked. The answers are diverse, and debate over the issue periodically surfaces in academic circles. In practice, a manager's job involves both science and art. A science is a body of knowledge that has evolved through controlled and systematic investigation. It provides descriptions, explanations, and predictions about the phenomena under investigation. There is a large body of scientific management literature based on such analyses. The art in management appears in the application of the knowledge derived by scientific investigation. Science discovers and documents; art creates.

A CLOSER LOOK

Japanese Management Methods: Arriving in Time to Develop Employee Loyalty

Most U.S. corporations have dealt with the demand for increased productivity, concerns over quality, and the need to enhance profitability by throwing millions of dollars at potential high-technology solutions. How have the Japanese dealt with the same problems? Although they have not been shy in applying new technology, the Japanese have emphasized the importance of management and the key role of employees in the successful development of business.

In 1982, for example, General Motors finally gave up and closed its plant in Fremont, California, because of apparently unresolvable problems with gross absenteeism, employee grievances, and wildcat strikes. The company eventually joined forces with Toyota Motor Corporation under a joint venture known as New United Motor Manufacturing Inc. (NUMMI), and Japanese managers reopened the Fremont plant. They introduced some new technology, but the primary changes involved management, delivery systems, assembly lines, and work teams run by the workers themselves—many of whom were former employees of the GM-operated plant.

How well have the new management approaches worked? The 2500 NUMMI employees are producing roughly the same number of cars that previously took twice as many GM employees to assemble, grievances have virtually disappeared, and absenteeism has dropped to around 2 percent. According to Joel D. Smith, a UAW representative at the NUMMI plant, "We have the same members, the same building, the same technology—just different management and a different production system."[1]

"Japanese philosophy is to make people . . . important."

The importance of strong employee loyalty appears to be paramount. To develop this loyalty, Japanese managers have created a situation of mutual trust by treating employees as equals. Gone are the executive parking lots, elite dining rooms, and fancy offices. Sometimes even the titles go, as at a U.S.-based Honda plant where employees are called associates rather than employees. Another important factor in the Japanese development of loyalty among American employees is minimizing layoffs. In fact, when business conditions were bad at a Japanese-managed tire plant in Danville, Kentucky, managers permitted a buildup of inventory, assigned some workers to house-cleaning tasks and actually shifted some of the production from one of their Japanese factories to the Danville plant to retain workers. According to D. William Childs, general manager of human resources at the NUMMI plant, "The Japanese philosophy is to make people an important item, as opposed to the typical U.S. philosophy that workers are just an extension of machines."[2]

Other modifications at the Fremont plant included a production change known as a "just-in-time" delivery system that typically keeps no more than a few hours of excess parts in inventory. Remaining supplies arrive just in time to be used. Job design changes are not only permitted but encouraged, as Japanese managers urge employees to find faster ways to perform their work with greater quality. Similar actions expand the nature of jobs for employees. Each employee does several jobs under the team system. They become more highly skilled. Work is spread out, making for a more flexible organization.

Will the success of these Japanese management techniques endure? Only time can tell, but many U.S. organizations evidently think so as more begin to experiment with just-in-time deliveries, team approaches, and so on. Some American managers have noted that many of the techniques described here actually originated in the United States in the 1930s and, therefore, are not Japanese but simply good management techniques. Regardless of their origin, most are clearly attributed to the Japanese today, and it is the Japanese who have stimulated their expanded use in the United States.

1. A. Bernstein, D. Cook, P. Engardio, and G. L. Miles (14 July 1986), The difference Japanese management makes, *Business Week,* 47.

2. A. Bernstein, et al., 49.

Just as artists need to master their crafts, business managers need to perfect their skills in dealing with people and in expressing themselves verbally; just as artists need visions and passion to realize them, managers need imagination and audacity to redesign their organizations; and just as great masters communicate their visions, great leaders inspire those who work for them.[25]

There is a body of management knowledge that has been developed through systematic and controlled inquiry, but managers who rely only on this knowledge deny the importance of feelings, hunches, intuition, and common sense. Effective managers expand knowledge and develop the personal skills and passion necessary to artfully apply that knowledge.

Schools of Management Thought in Review

Management theories should help managers understand and anticipate organizational events and, thus, allow them to manage more effectively and efficiently. There are several schools of management thought and, therefore, various approaches to the practice of management. Although no one grand theory has emerged from these schools to guide a manager's every step, each offers a distinctly useful perspective.

The classical school of management thought included the scientific-management movement and classical organization theory. It emphasized the economic rationality of decisions made by organizations and their members and the role of economic incentives as primary motivators. Classical management theorists, although occasionally paying lip service to the importance of a friendly labor-management climate, tended to focus on the mechanical side of an organization. Workers were treated as nonthinking, nonfeeling robots and were reduced to the role of cogs in the organizational wheel. The classicists felt that their prescriptions for designing and running the organizational machine defined the one best way to manage.

The Hawthorne studies provided a transition from classical to behavioral management theories, which emphasized the human side of organizations and the importance of personal and social factors as motivators. The human relations movement saw organizations as social systems and proposed that the way to increase productivity was to keep workers satisfied. The behavioral scientists saw employee involvement as the key to greater organizational efficiency and effectiveness. Like the classicists, behavioralists believed that their theories provided the one best way to manage organizations.

The contemporary school of management thought draws from the best of earlier theories. Although some contemporary theories, such as Theory Z, provide "new" management ideas, the most important recent advances develop contingency perspectives. Recognizing that organizations are not merely machines or social systems, contingency theories arising from this systems-theory perspective deal with both the technical and the human side of organizations. Managers must recognize the interdependence of these two systems when making decisions and performing other managerial duties.

Contemporary management theories propose that there is no one best way to practice management. Instead, managers must develop diagnostic skills to assess each situation, identify the appropriate managerial style for that situation, and be flexible enough to match their behavior to that demanded by the situation. The information they draw on to perform this balancing act is considered the fruits of the science of management. The manner with which they apply this knowledge can be considered an art.

Notes

1. G. D. Babcock (1927), *The Taylor system in Franklin management,* 2nd ed., New York: Engineering Magazine Company, 31.
2. C. Babbage (1832), *On the economy of machinery and manufactures,* London: Charles Knight, 132.
3. F. W. Taylor (1947), *Scientific management,* New York: Harper and Brothers.
4. F. W. Taylor (1912), *The art and science of shoveling,* testimony before a special committee of the U. S. House of Representatives.
5. Taylor, 1947.
6. H. Fayol (1949), *General and industrial management,* C. Storrs, trans., London: Sir Isaac Pitman and Sons, Ltd., 19.
7. M. Weber (1922), *The theory of social and economic organization,* A. M. Henderson and T. Parsons, ed. and trans., (1947), New York: Oxford University Press.
8. H. Munsterberg (1913), *Psychology and industrial efficiency,* New York: Arno Press.
9. M. P. Follett (1918), *The new state,* Gloucester, MA: Peter Smith.
10. C. I. Barnard (1938), *The functions of the executive,* Cambridge, MA: Harvard University Press.
11. A. H. Maslow (1957), *Motivation and personality,* New York: Harper & Row.
12. D. M. McGregor (November 1957), The human side of enterprise, *Management Review,* 22–28, 88–92; D. M. McGregor (1960), *The human side of enterprise,* New York: McGraw-Hill.
13. McGregor, 23.
14. D. M. McGregor (9 April 1957), The human side of enterprise, *Proceedings of the 5th Anniversary Convocation of the School of Industrial Management,* Cambridge, MA: Massachusetts Institute of Technology, 15.
15. C. Argyris (1957), *Personality and organization,* New York: Harper and Brothers.
16. R. Miles (1964), Conflicting elements in managerial ideologies, *Industrial Relations,* 4, 77–91; R. Miles (1975), *Theories of management: Implications for organizational behavior and development,* New York: McGraw-Hill, 42.
17. T. L. Peters and R. H. Waterman, Jr. (1982), *In search of excellence: Lessons from America's best-run companies,* New York: Harper & Row.

18. W. Ouchi (1981), *Theory Z: How American business can meet the Japanese challenge*, Reading, MA: Addison-Wesley.

19. E. L. Trist (1981), The sociotechnical perspective: The evolution of sociotechnical systems as a conceptual framework and as an action research program, in A. H. Van de Ven and W. F. Joyce, eds., *Perspectives on organization design and behavior*, New York: John Wiley & Sons, 19–75.

20. R. A. Johnson, F. E. Kast, and J. E. Rosenzweig (1963), *The theory and management of systems*, New York: McGraw-Hill.

21. *Ibid.*

22. R. T. Pascale and A. G. Athos (1981), *The art of Japanese management: Applications for American executives*, New York: Simon and Schuster; Peters & Waterman, 1982.

23. Pascale and Athos, 1981, 81.

24. Ouchi, 1981.

25. H. Boettinger (January-February 1975), Is management really an art? *Harvard Business Review*, 54.

Key Terms

classical school	sociotechnical systems theory
scientific management	system
behavioral school	systems theory
human relations movement	contingency perspectives
behavioral science movement	McKinsey 7-S framework
Theory X	Theory Z
Theory Y	

Issues for Review and Discussion

1. Who were the major contributors to the scientific management movement, and what were their respective contributions?

2. Name and discuss Taylor's six prescriptions for effective scientific management.

3. Explain the basic differences between the work of Taylor and his European counterparts, Henri Fayol and Max Weber.

4. What were the Hawthorne studies? What effect did they have on the practice of management?

5. Why do you think contingency theories of management emerged? How do these theories of management differ from the classical and behavioral schools of management thought?

6. Give an example of a situation involving a human resource and a marketing department that illustrates the importance of a systems-theory perspective.

7. Identify and discuss four attributes of Theory Z.

Suggested Readings

Bisesi, M. (1988). A review of *Theory Z: How American business can meet the Japanese challenge*. In Pierce, J. L. and Newstrom, J. W., eds. *The manager's bookshelf: A mosaic of contemporary views*. New York: Harper & Row, 263–67.

Dubin, R. (1981). Management: Meanings, methods, and moxie. *Academy of Management Review*, 7, 372–79.

Hunt, J. G. and Blair, J. D. (1987). Content, process, and the Matthew effect among management academies. *Journal of Management*, 13(2), 191–210.

Maidique, M. A. (1983). The new management thinkers. *California Management Review*, 26, 151–61.

Miles, R. E. (1975). Managers' theories of management. In Miles, R. E. *Theories of management: Implications for organizational behavior and development*. New York: McGraw-Hill, 31–50.

Robbins, S. P. (February 1977). Reconciling management theory with management practice. *Business Horizons*, 38–47.

Van Auken, P. M. and Ireland, R. D. (1979). An historical review of management philosophy. *Academy of Management Proceedings*, 39, 7–11.

CASE *A Job Interview with Sterling Manufacturing*

*By Phil Fisher of the University
of South Dakota*

Clayton Odland sat in disbelief as the personnel manager explained to him, "You see, our experience with young men such as yourself is that you will stay with us only long enough to gain some experience and then leave to go to work for a smaller company."

"How can he say that?" Clayton thought. "I want to work for Sterling. Where did I go wrong?" Shaken by the realization that he was not going to get a job offer, Clayton thought back over the events of the day to try to understand what he had said or done to make the personnel manager decide not to offer him a job.

Clayton's first interview with Sterling Manufacturing had been on the campus of State University, where Clayton was nearing the end of his senior year. Majoring in personnel management and scheduled to graduate with honors, Clayton had been sure that he would have many job opportunities, but the offer to visit a Sterling plant was especially exciting for him. Sterling was one of the largest manufacturers in the world, with plants located throughout the United States, Canada and Europe. Former Sterling executives served on the Cabinet of the President of the United States. A career with Sterling seemed to offer unlimited possibilities.

Despite Sterling's size and enormous prestige, at the on-campus interview Clayton had felt relaxed and confident. Donald Vodicka, the Sterling manager conducting the interview, was a State University graduate himself and had advanced to a position of considerable responsibility in the twelve years he had been with Sterling. An accounting graduate whose position was in the financial area at Sterling headquarters, he assured Clayton that he could arrange for him to visit one of Sterling's divisions to interview for a position in personnel management.

About two weeks after the interview, Clayton received a letter inviting him to visit a Sterling facility in Michigan. Now, as he sat in a red leather chair in the personnel manager's impressive paneled office, Clayton's mind raced back over the events of the day.

He had arrived at the Sterling building on schedule, traveling by cab from the hotel at which the company had made a reservation for him. The first person he met was Jim Pflanz, who was not much older than Clayton and had been working for Sterling for only a year. He talked about his work for Sterling, which mainly consisted of interviewing applicants for jobs and occasionally traveling to a college campus to interview seniors for management trainee positions. He also outlined Clayton's schedule for the day, which was to consist of a series of interviews with managers within the personnel department; lunch in the executive dining room; and a final interview with Mr. Merrigan, the head of the division's personnel department.

The second person Clayton saw that day was Luis Portillo. Mr. Portillo described the manner in which Sterling prepared its young management trainees for positions of responsibility. Clayton could expect to spend his first four to six years with Sterling in a series of appointments of six months' to two years' duration. He would probably spend some months interviewing job applicants, as had Jim Pflanz. He would probably have an assignment working in industrial relations as the first level of appeal in grievances filed by the union. He would no doubt spend some time learning the details of administering Sterling's pension and health benefits. The details of the company's training program varied somewhat for different people, but it was the company's policy to assure that its managers were well prepared through both experience and training before investing them with substantial authority.

Clayton asked Mr. Portillo about his responsibilities at Sterling. Mr. Portillo replied that he was responsible for reviewing the way departments were organized in the division. Clayton had enjoyed his college course in organization theory and asked about the possibility of a training assignment with Mr. Portillo. Mr. Portillo replied that he often did have a management trainee assigned to him, but as the work was rather complex and required some knowledge of the way in which the company worked, trainees were assigned there only after three or four years of experience.

At the close of Clayton's interview with Mr. Portillo, Jim Pflanz appeared and escorted Clayton to his next stop, which was with Stuart Davis. Mr. Davis worked in the industrial relations section, which was responsible for administering the labor contract that covered the employees of this division of Sterling. Mr. Davis described the functions of his department and the types of assignments typically filled by management trainees. Although apparently less intellectually challenging than the work of Mr. Portillo's department, the thought of having the opportunity to resolve real conflict gave the industrial relations department a lot of appeal to Clayton.

After Mr. Davis finished describing the industrial relations function, he asked Clayton if he had any questions. Clayton then asked what Sterling did to motivate its employees. At this, Mr. Davis seemed a little annoyed. As if he were explaining something to a child, he leaned forward and said, "Listen, it's very simple. Every job has a standard. If people meet that standard, we leave them alone. When they don't meet the standard, we take disciplinary action." This was not the approach favored by Clayton's professors at State University, but he did not comment.

At the close of their session, Mr. Davis escorted Clayton to the executive dining room, which was on the top floor of the building. He ushered Clayton into a richly appointed small restaurant, where they were joined by Mr. Portillo and three other men, including Richard Merrigan, the head of the personnel function for the division. Mr. Merrigan led the way to a table for six, where he took a seat at one end and invited Clayton to sit at his right hand. Clayton noted that Jim Pflanz had not joined them but supposed that he had other obligations.

The lunch was a heady experience for Clayton. The surroundings were sumptuous, befitting a corporation of Sterling's reputation, and the lunch was delicious. Two waiters hovered at their table, filling water glasses and coffee cups and attending to every word or gesture from Mr. Merrigan and the others. The conversation centered on labor problems in the division's plant in Great Britain and on Sterling's difficulty in dealing with British labor unions. The Sterling executives included Clayton in the discussion, explaining the differences in labor law between Great Britain and the United States. Clayton commented that it was too bad that relations between the company and its workers were so rigid.

At the close of the meal, Mr. Davis asked Clayton what he thought of the dining room. Clayton expressed his delight at so magnificent a place and Mr. Davis laughed. "Well, if you come to work here, it will be many years before you see the inside of it again." Clayton then understood why Jim Pflanz had not joined them.

After lunch, Clayton had one more interview before meeting with Mr. Merrigan. It was with one of the men who had joined them for lunch, and who, as it turned out, was responsible for administering the division's benefits. The work he described seemed terribly dull, more clerical than managerial, but Clayton could recognize the necessity to become familiar with it.

The final stop before checking out with Jim Pflanz was his interview with Mr. Merrigan. Despite the prospect of a long and probably often boring training period, Clayton was enthusiastic about the opportunity to someday be a member of the inner circle at this large, powerful company. He expressed that enthusiasm to Mr. Merrigan but immediately saw that the decision had already been made, and there would be no job at Sterling Manufacturing for Clayton Odland.

Questions

1. What school of management thought appears to underlie the management practices at Sterling Manufacturing?

2. How are these assumptions reflected in Sterling practices?

3. What school of management thought does Clayton Odland appear to ascribe to?

4. How did he express these assumptions?

5. What do you think would have happened if Clayton had gone to work for Sterling?

Lee Iacocca

Lee Iacocca has been fired as president of the Ford Motor Corporation, but he has also been credited with the turnaround of Chrysler. He has been called a skillful manager and mentioned as a possible presidential candidate. Others have characterized him as lucky and fortuitous. Iacocca has been described as "fast-talking," "straight-shooting," "blunt," "boastful," and "hard-hitting." Who is Lee Iacocca? What kind of manager is he?

Iacocca began working as a mechanical engineer at Ford. After entering sales, he quickly climbed the ladder to become general manager of a Ford division. As "Father of the Mustang," he was promoted to vice-president of the corporate car and truck group. Following accomplishments in the Lincoln-Mercury division and work with the Mark III, he was promoted to the presidency of Ford. Eight tumultuous years later, Iacocca was fired. Shortly thereafter he was brought into the battle-ridden, struggling Chrysler Corporation.

> *The starting point for good management is with the effective use of one's own time.*

Iacocca's management style and philosophy revolve around a number of concepts. The ability to identify, recruit, and surround himself with good people has been a key to Iacocca's success at Chrysler. According to Iacocca, a manager who surrounds him or herself with weak managers will not only have his or her own work to do, but will have to continually check up on the work of others. Hiring good people and delegating authority is critical to effective organizational management. Iacocca has also seen that teamwork is crucial. As a manager, he sees his role as one of developing teamwork through the use of his own interpersonal skills.

During his years as a serious student active in extracurricular pursuits at Lehigh and Princeton, Iacocca established the foundation of his management philosophy: effective use of time and communication. Iacocca's philosophy suggests that the starting point for good management is with the effective use of one's own time. Those who are good at managing their time effectively are self-motivated and, therefore, more productive. Through personal time management, people can be accountable to themselves. Self-motivation and personal accountability are important factors of success, especially for those in highly responsible and independent positions of management. Time management can facilitate a results orientation, promote a focus of the achievement of goals, and stimulate organized and creative thinking. Finally, managers serve as leaders and role models for those below them. A manager who uses self-direction and self-control effectively, through example, motivates others to do the same.

Managing others is not accomplished solely through delegation and role modeling. Iacocca is also a charismatic leader. He has brought a vision to Chrysler, and, through his interpersonal style, this vision has found its way to others. He has inspired people and built their confidence in themselves, in their organization, and in the product they produce. His strong sense of patriotism, in an industry embattled by foreign competition, has inspired others. He has been willing to take risks and make personal sacrifices at Chrysler, all in an effort to make the organization successful.

To manage time well, a manager must be disciplined enough to take time to organize. In Iacocca's life, this consists of taking time each week (Sunday evenings) to write out goals, priorities, and a timetable for the upcoming week. This weekly planning effort is always carried out with a vision toward long-range goals.

> *Iacocca is convinced that the ability to communicate is everything.*

Building on his strong beliefs in time management, goal setting, and evaluation of priorities, Iacocca has implemented a quarterly planning and review process. Each quarter, managers are asked to write down their goals and priorities and their plans for accomplishing them. These documents are shared with superiors to assure that their plans are realistic and consistent with the larger scheme of organizational activities. Iacocca believes that, through the interactive process between superior and subordinate, a team-oriented relationship will develop. Planning documents form the basis for quarterly reviews. According to Iacocca, the theory behind this procedure is that employees who set their own goals are more motivated and consequently more productive. The process makes the employee's activities more purposeful and organized.

Iacocca is convinced that the ability to communicate is everything. Obviously, this includes the ability to speak and to write precisely and clearly. In addition, managers must develop the ability to listen. Listening is especially important when attempting to solve problems. Good communication shows that management

cares and is open to the ideas of others. To a large extent, Iacocca sees communication as a tool through which managers motivate others to act, react, and work as a team pursuing the goals of the organization. Through open communication, people feel part of the team, which in turn prompts people to act more positively.

Iacocca's style includes elements of participative management. He believes in the use of a committee system. He wants every employee to know exactly where he or she fits into the organizational scheme of things. It is important, for example, that the production manager knows what the marketing manager is doing and vice versa. When Iacocca arrived at Chrysler, nobody understood the interaction and dependency among the different functions in the company. He suggested that the people in manufacturing, marketing, and engineering maintain constant communication

with one another. At Chrysler, they barely knew each other existed. Today the importance of dialogue permeates Iacocca's entire organizational system. Quality circles, for example, are used as a way of producing dialogue and involvement among production employees.

The ideal quality of a good manager, according to Iacocca, is decisiveness. A manager needs to gather information, set priorities and timetables, and act decisively. Participative systems help bring information, ideas, and people into the management process so they can act as managers and make effective organizational decisions.

Source: L. Iacocca with W. Novak (1984), *Iacocca: An autobiography*, Toronto: Bantam Books: R. E. Heller (1988), A review of *Iacocca: An autobiography*, in J. L. Pierce and J. W. Newstrom, eds., *The manager's bookshelf: A mosaic of contemporary views*, New York: Harper & Row, 145–49.

Planning

Student Learning Objectives

After reading this chapter, you should be able to:

1. Understand the four steps of planning and a manager's role as a planner.

2. Explain the concept of goals and understand how goals contribute to organizational efficiency and effectiveness.

3. Explain what is meant by multiple plans.

4. Explain a goal hierarchy.

5. Discuss MBO and associate it with one of the major schools of thought about management.

6. Distinguish among various types of plans.

7. Discuss the arguments for and against formal planning.

8. Understand why organization members often resist planning and discuss actions that can be taken to overcome this resistance.

9. Discuss the role of a planning specialist.

"*I*f you are good enough, it isn't really necessary to set aside time for formal planning. After all, 'planning time' takes away from 'doing time.'" Managers often make such statements to avoid developing a formal planning program; however, these are not valid claims. Consider the evidence from a relatively simple study conducted at General Electric.[1] This study provided hard evidence that the work units of managers who devote sufficient time to planning perform significantly better than the units of managers who do not.

Planning can influence the effectiveness of entire organizations, not just that of individual managers. Some years ago, the Calico Candy Company developed and produced a highly successful salt water taffy Santa Claus. Buoyed by this success, the company planned and manufactured a salt water taffy Easter Bunny and produced the Santa at Christmas again; however, this time Calico got stuck with its taffy as a result of a major planning error. Market research clearly showed that consumer preferences had shifted from taffy to chocolate. Rather than plan its product to meet this new preference, the company stayed with what had worked in the past. The result was a loss in excess of 200,000 dollars.[2] As this incident shows, planning is an important activity in managing organizations.

Introduction to Planning

This section will define planning and discuss why managers should plan. It will also explore how often managers actually do plan in a systematic manner.

Planning Defined

Planning is the process by which managers establish goals and define the methods by which these goals are to be attained. Plans have two basic components: goals and action statements. **Goals** represent an end state—the targets and outcomes—that managers hope to attain. **Action statements** reflect the means by which an organization moves forward to

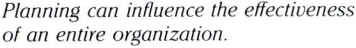

Planning can influence the effectiveness of an entire organization.

attain its goals. For example, during the summer of 1987, United Airlines set goals to make a market comeback and to deal with internal labor problems. As a part of its action statement, United considered putting pilots in its board room to increase their involvement in managing the company.[3]

Planning is an intellectual activity—a conscious act through which managers determine a course of action for pursuing a specific goal.[4] While planning, managers have to think about what has to be done, who is going to do it, and how and when they will do it. Planning also involves thinking about past events (retrospectively) and about future opportunities and impending threats (prospectively). It involves thinking about organizational strengths and weaknesses and involves decision making about desired states and ways to achieve them. Decision making and planning are not the same, however. Decisions can be made without planning, but planning cannot exist without decision making.[5]

Management's plans, whether highly developed or only the visions and intentions of managers, give meaning and direction to organizing, directing, and controlling. Planning is a fundamental activity that lays a foundation for the execution of other management functions.

Why Should Managers Plan?

> *The essence of planning is to see opportunities and threats in the future and, respectively, exploit or combat them as the case may be. . . . Planning is a philosophy, not so much in the literal sense of that word but as an attitude, a way of life.*[6]

Planning for organizational events, whether in the internal or external environment, should be an ongoing process—part of a manager's daily, weekly, and monthly duties. Managers should monitor their plans routinely. They should check to see if their plans need to be modified to accommodate changing conditions, new information, or new situations that will affect their organization's future. Managers need to administer their plans with flexibility. Clearly, the Calico Candy Company discussed earlier failed to monitor its plans in this way. By thinking of planning as a continuous activity, managers can formulate methods for handling future opportunities and threats. Managers engage in the planning process to give meaning and direction to organizational activity.

Managers have several reasons for formulating plans for themselves, their employees, and various organizational units: (1) to offset uncertainty and change; (2) to focus organizational activity on a set of consciously created objectives; (3) to provide a coordinated, systematic road map for future activities; (4) to increase economic efficiency via efficient operation and consistency; and (5) to facilitate control by establishing a standard for later activity.

Several forces contribute to the necessity for managerial planning. First, in the internal environment, as organizations become larger and more complex, the task of managing becomes increasing complex. Planning lets managers map out future activities in relation to other activities within their organization. Second, as an organization's external environment becomes increasingly complex and turbulent, the amount of uncertainty faced by a manager increases. Planning allows a manager to approach this environment systematically.

Do Managers Really Plan?

Managers should plan formally, but do they? Some observers contend that managers typically are too busy to engage in a regular form of systematic planning.

> When managers plan, they do so implicitly in the context of daily actions, not in some abstract process reserved for two weeks in the organization's mountain retreat. The plans of the chief executives I have studied seemed to exist only in their heads—as flexible, but often specific, intentions. . . . The job of managing does not breed reflective planners; the manager is a real-time responder to stimuli.[7]

Others disagree, however. After reviewing a number of studies focused on the degree to which planning and other managerial activities are inherent parts of managing, management professors Carroll and Gillen stated that "the classical management functions of Fayol, Urwick, and others are not 'folklore' as claimed by some contemporary management writers but represent valid abstractions of what managers actually do and what managers should do."[8]

Managers often are very busy people who act without having developed a systematic plan of action; however, many managers do plan systematically.[9] For example, many managers have developed systematic plans for how their organization will react to a crisis. United Airlines, for example, created a crisis planning group. The group developed United's crisis contingency plan book, which specifies what the airline's crisis management team should do in the event of a crisis. At the Los Angeles *Herald Examiner,* managers developed contingency plans that would allow the newspaper to go to press on time in the event of a power outage. In fact, when the power did go out at the *Herald,* the plan was set in motion, and the newspaper was printed at the facilities of the *Los Angeles Times.*[10]

Stages in the Planning Process

There are many models of the planning process. In all of them, an effective planning process appears future oriented, comprehensive, systematic, integrated, and negotiated.[11] In addition, an effective planning process involves organizational members in its evolution; it demonstrates an extensive search for alternatives and provides an analysis of relevant information; it follows a systematic and routinized procedure; and it is participative in nature.[12] This section will follow the stages in a model based on the framework provided by management scholars Harold Koontz and Cyril O'Donnell (see Figure 6.1).[13]

FIGURE 6.1   The Planning Process

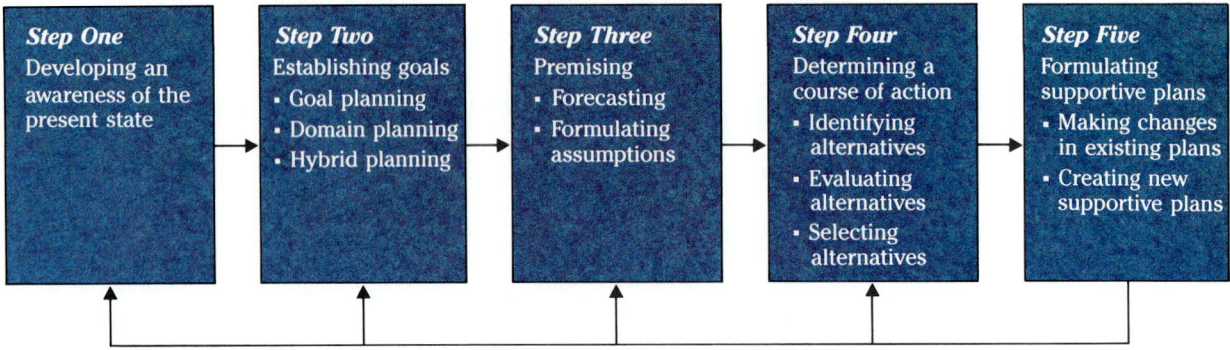

Source: Adapted from H. Koontz and C. O'Donnell (1972), *Principles of management: An analysis of managerial functions*, New York: McGraw-Hill, 113.

Step One: Developing an Awareness of the Present State

In the first step in the planning process, the awareness stage, managers create a foundation from which they will develop their plans for the next planning period. Some managers consider this awareness stage as a precursor to the actual planning process rather than as an actual part of the process.

This foundation is constructed by managers who take the time to define their organization's current location, pinpointing its commitments, recognizing its strengths and weaknesses, and setting forth a vision of expected gains. It is at this stage that an understanding of an organization and its history plays a critical role in that the past is instrumental in determining where an organization expects to go in the future. Henry Ford inscribed his view on the importance of history over the door to the Ford Museum: "The further you look back, the further you can see ahead."[14] The next step in the process, the setting of realistic goals, depends on the solidity of this foundation and on the accuracy of managers' perceptions.

In managing your education, you probably have already engaged in some planning. Before taking this management course, for example, first you had to create "a preplanning foundation" by finding out whether you had taken the necessary prerequisites and whether the course schedule fit your total academic program. You had to recognize the other demands on your time and other commitments you had made, and you had to take stock of your academic strengths and weaknesses. Such a review of past commitments and current strengths and weaknesses provides a planner with a foundation from which subsequent steps in the planning process can be taken.

Step Two: Establishing Goals

Specific goals are established during the second stage of planning. Your goal in this course might be to get a specific grade. An awareness of your strengths and limitations and the conditions under which you are operating helps you establish a reasonable goal (grade) and helps you create your action statement.

Managers set organizational goals at various levels. Many organizations, for example, consist of divisions, each of which is divided into departments, which, in turn, may contain additional subsystems, such as committees and work groups. For example, plans established by a university's Accounting Department's curriculum committee must fit within and support the plans of the department, which help contribute to the goals of the School of Business, whose plans in turn must support the goals of the university. Managers, therefore, have to develop an elaborate *network of organizational plans*, such as that shown in Figure 6.2, to achieve the overall goals of their organization. Effective total planning requires that managers in each subsystem of their organization engage in the planning process. As Figure 6.2 shows, these individual goals feed into and support the organization's central goals.

Not only do managers create plans at various levels within an organization, but they also create different kinds of plans. Not every organizational plan has a goal embedded within it. There is evidence of both goal and domain planning.

Goal vs. Domain Planning   In **goal planning,** people set specific goals and then create action statements.[15] For example, college freshman Barbara Burnett has decided that she wants a Bachelor of Science degree in biochemistry (the goal). She is constructing a four-year academic plan that will make this goal a reality. Barbara is engaging in goal planning. She

FIGURE 6.2
Network of Organizational Plans

When departmental goals in an organization's technical core are realized, they become the means by which the organization's divisions accomplish their goals. Accomplishing the divisions' goals, in turn, enables the organization to achieve its overall goals.

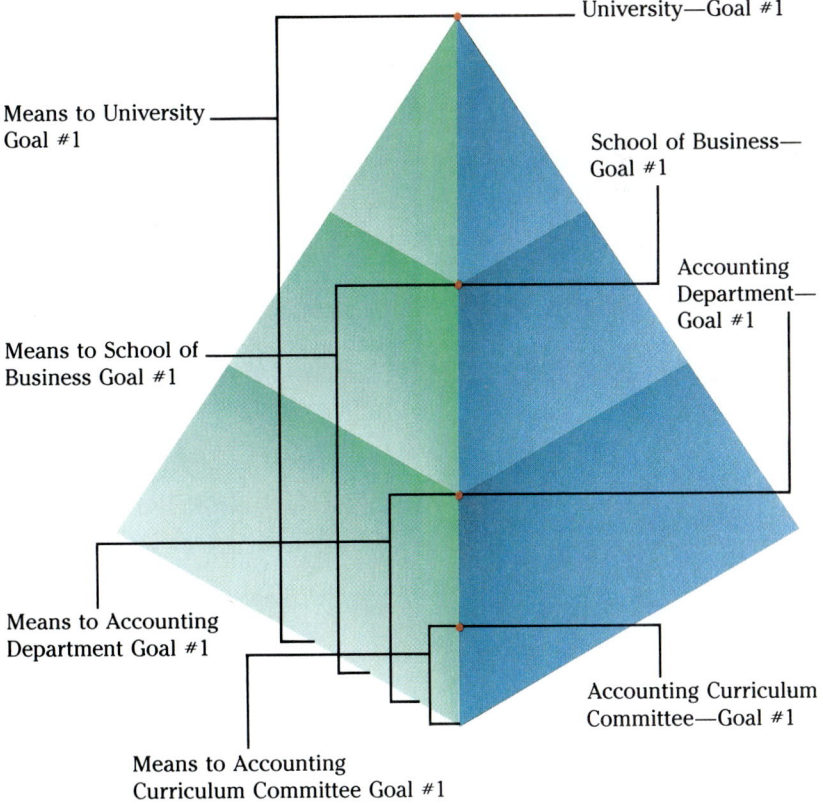

FIGURE 6.3
Goal and Domain Planning

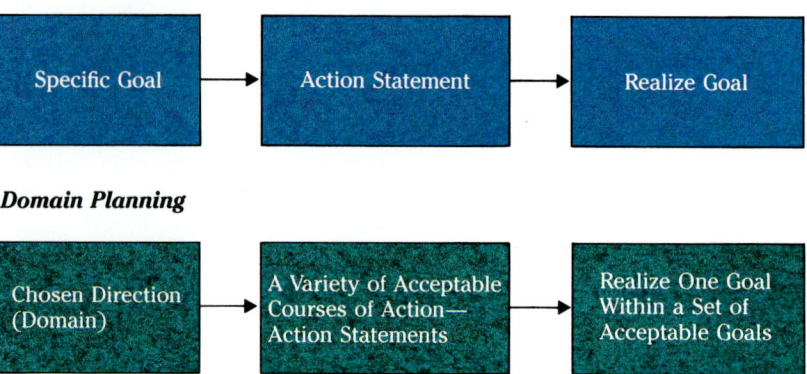

Goal Planning

| Specific Goal | → | Action Statement | → | Realize Goal |

Domain Planning

| Chosen Direction (Domain) | → | A Variety of Acceptable Courses of Action—Action Statements | → | Realize One Goal Within a Set of Acceptable Goals |

first identifies a goal and then develops a course of action to realize her goal.

Another approach to planning is domain, directional, planning.[16] **Domain/directional planning** is the development of a course of action that moves an organization toward one identified domain and, therefore, away from other domains. Within a chosen domain there may be a number of acceptable specific goals. For example, high school senior John Wade decides that he wants to major in a business-related discipline in college. During the next four years he selects a variety of courses from the School of Business curriculum but never specifies a particular major. After conveniently accumulating credits within this chosen domain, John accumulates enough credits to graduate with a major in marketing. John never engaged in goal planning, but in the end, he realized one of many acceptable goals within a particular domain. Unlike goal planning, which moves an organization toward a specific goal, domain planning simply moves an organization in a particular direction. This difference between goal and domain planning is illustrated in Figure 6.3.

It has been observed that, for many managers, some of the most important planning takes place in the absence of explicitly identified and specific goals;[17] thus, in the domain approach to planning, managers identify an acceptable general direction toward which their organization is to move. This approach is useful in those situations in which setting a specific goal would be difficult, impractical, or impossible. In many instances, the natural course of events leads to the realization of a particular goal within this chosen domain. To a large extent, the development of "Post-it" by the 3M Corporation reveals the domain planning model. In the laboratories at 3M, efforts were being made to develop new forms and strengths of cohesive substances. A weak cohesive material was developed with no known value. A 3M laboratory researcher, frustrated by page markers falling from his hymn book in church, discovered a weak cohesive material that would stick to paper for long periods of time but could still be removed without destroying the paper to which it was applied. Out of this came the now highly popular 3M product Scotch Post-it.

Domain planning provides a manager with more flexibility than does goal planning. If Barbara, the student who decided to pursue a major in biochemistry, wants to switch to chemical engineering in her junior year, the change would mean a considerable loss of credits in transferring to the new program; however, if Barbara had engaged in domain planning rather than goal planning, she might have pursued a Bachelor of Science degree in an unspecified major area related to chemistry. The courses required for the general chemistry domain are different from those needed for the specific goal of biochemistry. The domain planning model would have encouraged Barbara to choose courses during freshman and sophomore years that can cross over to satisfy some of the requirements for a number of different majors (including biochemistry and chemical engineering).

The presence of domain planning might support the contention that many managers are too busy to set specific goals or to plan systematically. Instead, managers engage in a variety of behaviors, moving their organization forward in a general direction expected to contribute to its well-being. Situations in which managers are likely to engage in domain planning include:

1. When there is a recognized need for flexibility (for example, when the payoff associated with a set of goals cannot yet be determined but managers must begin to act)
2. When people cannot agree on goals
3. When an organization's external environment is unstable and highly uncertain
4. When an organization is starting up or in a transitional period

Occasionally, coupling of domain and goal planning occurs, creating a third approach called **hybrid planning.** In this approach, planners move from domain planning to goal planning. They begin with the more general domain planning and establish their commitment to move in a particular direction. As time passes and their organization moves more closely toward its chosen domain, managers learn more about the strengths and weaknesses of their organization, about its environment, and about various payoffs associated with the possible outcomes. Managers can then identify increasingly specific targets within the selected domain and modify their action plans so as to move toward their chosen domain.

Figure 6.4 illustrates the dynamics of hybrid planning. In Stage I, planners pursue domain planning. Their movement from Stage I to Stage II represents an accumulation of knowledge, which narrows the domain. As they learn even more, the planners reduce the domain even further and enter Stage III. At this point, they can select a particular goal and create appropriate action plans; thus, John Wade, the university business student mentioned earlier, engaged in domain planning during his freshman and sophomore years, having chosen to graduate with a business-related major. During these first two years, John selected courses that provided the flexibility that allowed him to select any one of a number of business majors. During these two years, he collected additional information about each of the possible majors, about career opportunities, and so on; he began to narrow the domain. After taking a number of core business classes during his junior year, John's interest in marketing began to develop, and he entered Stage III, in which he constructed a goal-based plan that ultimately led to graduation with a major in marketing.

Some managers achieve success without moving from Stage I. In the mid-1980s, for example, a number of organizations succeeded by being in

FIGURE 6.4   The Dynamics of Hybrid Planning

As the stages progress, the number of goals within the chosen domain decreases. By Stage III, the planners have decided on a single goal and create an action statement that will move them toward that goal.

Stage I

Domain
Planning

Stage II

Domain
Narrowing

Stage III

●

Goal
Planning

In the mid-1980s, some organizations fell into success in the computer industry without developing specific goals.

the right place—the computer domain—at the right time, even though they never developed specific goals. Many of these lucky companies later failed, however, when their environments changed and they did not have specific goals and accompanying action plans to guide their reactions. For example, one of the "hottest" computers on the market for a short while was the Osborne. Osborne just happened to have the right computer at the right time; the Osborne computer fit the market demand. As the market changed, however, Osborne failed to plan and was not prepared to respond with a new generation of computers. Osborne found itself incapable of meeting market demands and eventually lost its market. Generally, success (organizational performance) is likely to be greater if a company reaches Stage III and establishes specific goals.

Consequences of Goal, Domain, and Hybrid Planning   Research evidence reveals that setting goals not only affects performance directly but also encourages people to plan more extensively. That is, once goals are set, people are likely to think more systematically about how they should proceed to realize these goals.[18] When people have vague goals, as in domain planning, they find it difficult to draw up detailed, systematic action plans, and, therefore, are likely to perform less effectively. Research evidence clearly suggests that performance is higher when goal planning has taken place.[19] (See "A Closer Look: Planning" for an example of successful goal planning.)

Although goal planning is generally preferable, many conditions seem to call for domain planning. Under such conditions, managers should combine goal planning with domain planning, which may take place as time passes and managers learn enough about the external environment to formulate meaningful, specific goals. This process may also take place at various hierarchical levels. For example, those at the institutional level might engage in domain planning, and those at lower levels might engage in goal planning (that is, formulating goals compatible with the chosen domain). Domain planning is likely to prevail at upper levels in an organization, where managers are responsible for dealing with the external environment and where task uncertainty is high. Goal planning is likely to prevail in the technical core, where there is less uncertainty.

A CLOSER LOOK

Planning: Rubbermaid Bounces Higher Every Year

If you had bought $1000 in Rubbermaid stock early in 1980, your investment would have been worth over $10,000 by 1987. During that seven-year period, you would have watched your company's sales double and its earnings triple, not bad for a company that makes boring rubber and plastic "stuff" for homes.

How has Rubbermaid achieved such strong performance, and why has it been recognized by *Fortune* as one of the country's most admired corporations year after year? Rubbermaid sets specific objectives, closely listens to consumers and retailers, and plans carefully.

The company has set and realized annual objectives of 15 percent growth in both sales and earnings per share; however, these objectives have not been realized without supporting planning. Rubbermaid expects new products (those less than five years old) to account for at least 30 percent of sales.

To support its expectations for new product sales, Rubbermaid develops and releases as many as 100 new products each year. Over 90 percent of these are successful. How is such a high hit rate obtained? According to *Fortune*, the company "maintains that enviable record by making a fetish of keeping in touch with customers. For instance, it tests color preferences year round through consumer focus groups in five cities, then confirms the results by quizzing people in shopping malls."[1]

Not all of Rubbermaid's market research is done by market researchers. Executives read letters sent by customers. Buyers visit the company's corporate offices, where they are wooed by these same executives. Executives willingly spend their time at these activities because customers and buyers generate product ideas and provide feedback about existing products, and these ideas are regularly converted into profit-making products, which are shared with executives in the form of bonuses.

Why aren't all companies as successful as Rubbermaid? Many give much of the credit to Stanley Gault, who took over as chairman and chief executive in 1980. Gault's formula for success is to watch the market and work at it twenty-four hours a day.

1. This quote is from page 77 of the article on which this "Closer Look" is based: A. Taylor (13 April 1987), Why the bounce at Rubbermaid? *Fortune*, 77–78.

Step Three: Premising

During the second step of the planning process, managers identify their organizational goals or domains. During the third step, they establish the premises, or assumptions, on which their action statements are built. The quality and success of any plan depends on the quality of the assumptions on which it is based. Even one outdated assumption can produce a poor or unrealistic decision. Throughout the planning process, assumptions must be brought to the surface, monitored, and updated.[20]

After managers derive information by scanning their organization's internal and external environments, they make assumptions about the likelihood of future events. They use these assumptions to develop action statements in the next phase of the planning process. For example, a manufacturing firm, planning to expand its scale of operations, might forecast changes in the prime lending rate. Basing its expansion plan on an assumption that the prime is going to rise in six weeks, the firm might borrow its needed capital within the next two weeks. While the company does not know for sure that the prime is going to rise, its forecast suggests an 80 percent chance of a rise. This assumption is built into the organization's expansion plans.

Through forecasting, organizations try to answer such questions as: "What will happen to the prime lending rate?" "What technological advances are on the horizon?" "How will consumers react to a proposed change in our product?" Forecasting may be based either on personal experience and expectation or on systematic, empirical research. In both cases, managers base their forecasts on assumptions. **Premising,** therefore, involves forecasting what is likely to happen inside and outside an organization. The forecasts go into the formulation of action statements to guide the organization in the future.

There are two types of forecasts. In one type, managers predict the consequences of a planned course of action. For example, managers in one organization might make a particular capital investment and ask what revenues are likely to be generated. This type of forecast helps managers define what an organization might expect to achieve as a result of a planned course of action. In the second type of forecast, managers make predictions about environmental events that might affect an organization's movement toward its goals. Managers use these forecasts to generate information for the development of their action statements. This second type of forecasting represents the premising activity, which is illustrated in Figure 6.5.

Organization members use either personal experience or empirical research to forecast events that will affect their organization's plans of action.

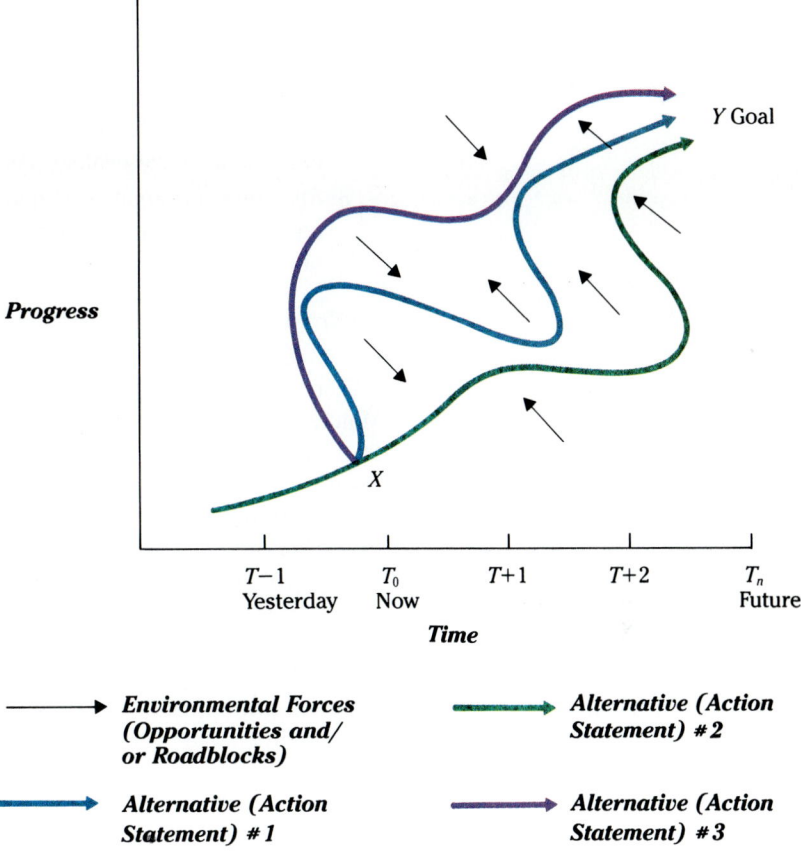

FIGURE 6.5   The Planning Diagram

The forecasting conducted at time zero (T_0) in the planning process identifies the internal and external environmental forces that are anticipated to operate on an organization as it travels from a starting point (point X) to the goal (point Y). Managers who recognize these forces can incorporate them into the assumptions that they make about the future and use them to determine alternative courses of action.

Progress

$T-1$	T_0	$T+1$	$T+2$	T_n
Yesterday	Now			Future

Time

→ **Environmental Forces (Opportunities and/ or Roadblocks)**

→ **Alternative (Action Statement) #1**

→ **Alternative (Action Statement) #2**

→ **Alternative (Action Statement) #3**

In sum, premising helps managers develop assumptions—premises—about future events. Managers use these premises to develop alternative courses of action.

Step Four: Determining a Course of Action

In the fourth stage of the planning process, managers decide how to move from their current position toward their goal (or into their identified domain). They develop an action statement that details what needs to be done, when, how, and by whom. The way in which an organization gets from its current position to its desired future position is determined by the course of action chosen by managers. There are three stages to the determination of a course of action:

1. *Determining alternatives.* Before a manager can select a course of action, he or she must know what the alternatives are. At this stage, a manager draws on research, experimentation, and experience to identify and develop a number of possible courses of action.

2. *Evaluating alternatives.* Once alternative courses of action have been identified, they must be evaluated in light of how well each

would help the organization reach its goals or approach its desired domain. Evaluating alternatives also includes determining the costs and expected efficiency of each. Evaluation can be difficult because of uncertainty about the future, various intangible factors, and inaccurate premises behind plans. Several techniques that managers can use to make evaluations will be discussed in Chapter 8.

3. *Selecting a course of action.* After identifying the alternatives and carefully considering the merits of each, managers must adopt a plan and select one course of action.

Step Five: Formulating Supportive Plans

The planning process seldom stops with the adoption of a general plan. Managers often still need to develop one or more supportive, or derivative, plans to bolster their basic plan and to explain the many details involved in reaching a broad, major plan. For example, suppose that an organization decides to switch from a five-day, forty-hour workweek to a four-day, forty-hour workweek in an attempt to reduce employee turnover. This major plan would require the creation of a number of supportive plans. Managers might find it necessary, for example, to develop a new plan for personnel policies dealing with the payment of daily overtime. New administrative plans would be needed for scheduling meetings, handling phone calls, and dealing with customers and suppliers. Even a new maintenance arrangement for cleaning the facilities would be required.

Typically, there are two kinds of supportive plans. The first involves changes in existing supportive plans. These are supportive plans that have been in use but need modification to support a new plan. Managers in the previous example may have to modify their definition of overtime to support a new four-day, forty-hour workweek. The second kind of subsidiary plan involves the creation of a new supportive plan. If, for example, an organization converted a plant from a traditional assembly line to one using a fully automated, computer-integrated manufacturing system, managers would need a new supportive plan for training employees to use the new equipment. They would need another new supportive plan for maintaining the new equipment.

Planning and Controlling

After managers have moved through each of the five steps of the planning process and have drawn up one or more specific plans, they must monitor and maintain these plans. In controlling, managers observe ongoing organizational activity, compare it to the goals formulated during the planning process, and take corrective action if they observe unexpected and unwanted deviations. Lake Superior Paper Industries has designed its management system around the sociotechnical systems (STS) theory. As their planned course of operation unfolds, they will monitor organizational activity by employing several STS sensing and auditing techniques. These monitoring systems will, for example, periodically monitor movement toward organizational goals. Cohesive work teams are important to the success of STS, and, therefore, work group cohesion will be continually monitored. Should problems begin to occur, participatively structured team meetings will be held to address ways of overcoming threats to group cohesiveness. The planning and controlling activities are closely interrelated. Planning feeds controlling by establishing the standards against which behavior will be compared during the controlling process. Behavior monitoring provides managers with input that can help them plan for upcoming planning periods. Managerial controlling will be discussed in more detail in Chapter 19.

Types of Plans

Managers create many different types of plans to guide operations and to monitor and control organizational activities. In this section, several commonly used plans are discussed: hierarchical, frequency-of-use (repetitiveness), time frame, organizational scope, and contingency plans.

Hierarchical Plans

There are three major hierarchical levels in an organization, you will recall: the institutional level, the managerial level, and the technical core. Plans drawn from hierarchical perspectives, therefore, are interdependent for each of these levels.

Strategic plans are generally associated with each institutional level of an organization. Strategic plans define the organization's long-term vision. They specify what business the organization is in and hopes to be in and how the organization intends to make its vision a reality. To a large extent, strategic plans define how an organization will integrate itself into its task environment. For example, following the Surgeon General's report on the health hazard of cigarette smoking in the 1960s, many firms in the tobacco industry adopted new organizational strategies. Managers at Philip Morris, R. J. Reynolds, American Brands, and Ligget and Meyers engaged in product diversification and acquired firms in the food, beverage, and petroleum industries as part of their strategy to maintain the survival of their organizations.

Managers use **administrative plans** to allocate organizational resources and to coordinate their organization's internal subdivisions. These plans, therefore, are associated with the organizational responsibility of middle management. For example, the plans made by the executive group at R. J. Reynolds to pioneer the development of smokeless cigarettes required the allocation of massive amounts of money over several years to sponsor the development and marketing of this product. Planning at this level—resource allocation, integrating the visions of the institutional level with the day-to-day activities of the technical core—reflects administrative planning.

Operating plans cover the day-to-day operations of an organization. As such, many operating plans are designed to govern the workings of the organization's technical core. For example, R. J. Reynolds will be required to revise its production plans for regular cigarettes in anticipation of a demand for their new smokeless cigarettes.

Middle managers use administrative plans to allocate organizational resources and coordinate internal subdivisions.

Frequency-of-Use Plans

Another category of plans is frequency-of-use, or repetitiveness, plans. Some plans are used repeatedly, and others are used for a single purpose.

Standing plans are designed to be used to cover issues that managers face repeatedly. For example, managers may be concerned about employees' tardiness, a problem that may occur often in the entire workforce. These managers, therefore, might decide to develop a standing policy to be implemented automatically each time an employee is late for work. The procedure invoked under such a standing plan is called **standard operating procedure (SOP).** Some of the most common standing plans are policies, rules, and procedures.

Policies   Most policies are standing plans. As broad-based statements of understanding or general statements of intent, **policies** provide limits within which decisions are to be made. Policies are types of plans that allow decision makers some discretion in carrying out a plan. For example, a policy statement pertaining to employees' acceptance of types of gifts and/or entertainment might be "No employee shall accept favors or entertainment from an outside organization which are substantial enough in value so as to cause undue influence over one's decisions on behalf of the organization." Such a statement provides employees the opportunity to decide what types of gifts and/or entertainment are acceptable.

Some policies originate from a conscious attempt to articulate a customary and general way of behaving. Some policies are put into place through verbal statements, and some are set forth in written organizational records. For example, managers might formulate this policy: "Except for token gifts of purely nominal or advertising value, no employee shall accept any gift from any supplier at any time." Such formal policies are likely to be written down and available to employees in company manuals and other customary printed guidelines.

In contrast, some policies are implied from the spoken statements or practices of managers. The top management group from the Radisson Corporation may make a practice of promoting from within merely for convenience, yet this practice may be interpreted as policy and rigorously followed by the managers of its various hotels. Because policies are general in nature and because they arise from formal statements and customary ways of behaving, it is important for managers to pay close attention to what they say, as well as to what they do. If, for example, it is common practice for managers to allow subordinates time off after they have completed a difficult assignment, employees will probably assume that this type of leave is company policy. If it is policy, employees will expect time off whenever they complete a difficult project. Managers, therefore, must exercise caution so that their spoken statements and customary practices are not interpreted as policy if they are not intended as such.

The fact that policies are usually general in nature is both an advantage and a disadvantage. Policies provide guidelines that clarify how employees are to do their jobs. Policies also provide employees with some flexibility in their approach to various organizational problems. This generality, however, tends to make policies rather vague. Control becomes difficult when people interpret policy meaning and purpose differently.

Rules **Rules,** like policies, are standing plans that guide actions. Rules specify what employees are supposed to do or not do. For example, many organizations have launched no-smoking campaigns and have developed organizational rules to support them. Unlike policies, rules do not permit organizational members to exercise individual discretion. Instead, rules specify what actions will be taken (or not taken) and what behavior is allowed or prohibited; whereas policies tell people how to think about decisions to be made regarding various actions, rules tell people the actions they are to take.

Procedures Like rules, **procedures** are standing plans that guide action rather than thinking. Procedures establish customary ways for handling certain activities: hiring an assistant, participating in a pension plan, ordering from a supplier, and the like. The major distinguishing feature of a procedure is that it represents a chronological sequencing of events. It specifies a series of steps that must be taken to accomplish a particular task. For example, Melissa Gulley, a student seeking admission into a specific degree program at the School of Business and Economics at the University of Minnesota-Duluth must follow this procedure: (1) she secures candidacy papers from the school's adviser for student affairs; (2) she obtains a current transcript from the registrar; (3) she completes the application-for-candidacy forms; (4) Melissa's adviser reviews the application form and indicates approval; (5) the application form is filed with and reviewed by the School's student affairs adviser; and (6) Melissa is informed of her acceptance.

Single-use plans are developed for unique situations or problems and are usually replaced after one use. Managers generally use three types of single-use plans: programs, projects, and budgets.

Programs **Programs** are single-use plans consisting of a complex set of policies, rules, procedures, and other elements necessary to carry out a course of action. With the rapid growth of computers, many organizations have implemented educational programs to familiarize employees with various computer systems.

Projects **Projects** have the same characteristics as programs but are generally narrower in scope and less complex. Projects are frequently created to support or complement a program. For example, Employers Insurance of Wausau provides traditional home, auto, and life insurance policies. Its managers have also developed nontraditional insurance coverage so they can consider insuring such activities as the construction of the San Francisco Bay Area Rapid Transit tunnel or the construction of a nuclear power plant on the San Andreas fault. Employers Insurance created a systems department to develop insurance packages for such nontraditional projects. Within the systems department, project teams develop insurance plans for each of these unusual proposals. At any time, the company is likely to insure several such unique projects within its overall program of insurance.

Budgets **Budgets** are single-use plans, expressed in numerical terms, that deal with the allocation and use of organizational activities for a specified accounting period. For example, the State of Maine's department of transportation's allocation of money to be spent for the purchase of office supplies and equipment during the 1989 fiscal year is a budget plan.

Sometimes called *numerized programs,* budgets are most commonly expressed in dollar terms. They also may be expressed as hours worked, as units sold, or in any other measurable unit.

Time-Frame Plans

Some activities that require planning are completed quickly. Other activites may not see completion for years. The classification of plans by time frame describes them as short-range, medium-range, or long-range.

Short-range plans cover activities that unfold relatively quickly. In most organizations, the short range is anything from the next several hours to the next several months. A newspaper may run a three-month campaign to boost circulation; a city government may plan street repairs over a two-week period; and a computer software company may run a crash, one-year program to develop a new database program. The two types of short-range plans are operating and reaction.

Johnson & Johnson quickly assembled an effective reaction plan when it was discovered that someone had tampered with Extra Strength Tylenol capsules.

As previously discussed, *operating plans* govern the day-to-day activities of an organization, but *reaction plans* are created to handle unforeseen circumstances. Johnson & Johnson put a reaction plan into effect after someone placed deadly cyanide in a few Johnson & Johnson Extra Strength Tylenol capsules. Because such tampering incidents previously were rare, Johnson & Johnson was caught off guard. Managers at Johnson & Johnson quickly assembled an effective reaction plan. It detailed how the organization was to react to the poisoning and any possible recurrences.[21] They realized, for example, that the use of certified mail would delay their communication with distributors to remove Tylenol from retailers' shelves, so their plan called for communication by electronic mail. The thoroughness of this plan showed the public and the business world how effectively Johnson & Johnson could plan, even under pressure. So thorough and responsible was the company's reaction that, many have argued, it has had long-term positive effects that have outweighed the negative effects of the original problem.

Medium-range, or intermediate, **plans** usually encompass a one-to-five-year period. **Long-range plans** generally encompass a period of more than five years. Figure 6.6 shows the responses obtained when organizations from various industries were asked to identify the time frame that they considered ''long-range.'' As you can see, the responses varied by industry. For example, organizations in the oil industry tend to develop more long-range plans for a decade or more into the future than do organizations in the machinery industry. The vast majority report

FIGURE 6.6   *How Long Is a Long-Range Plan?*

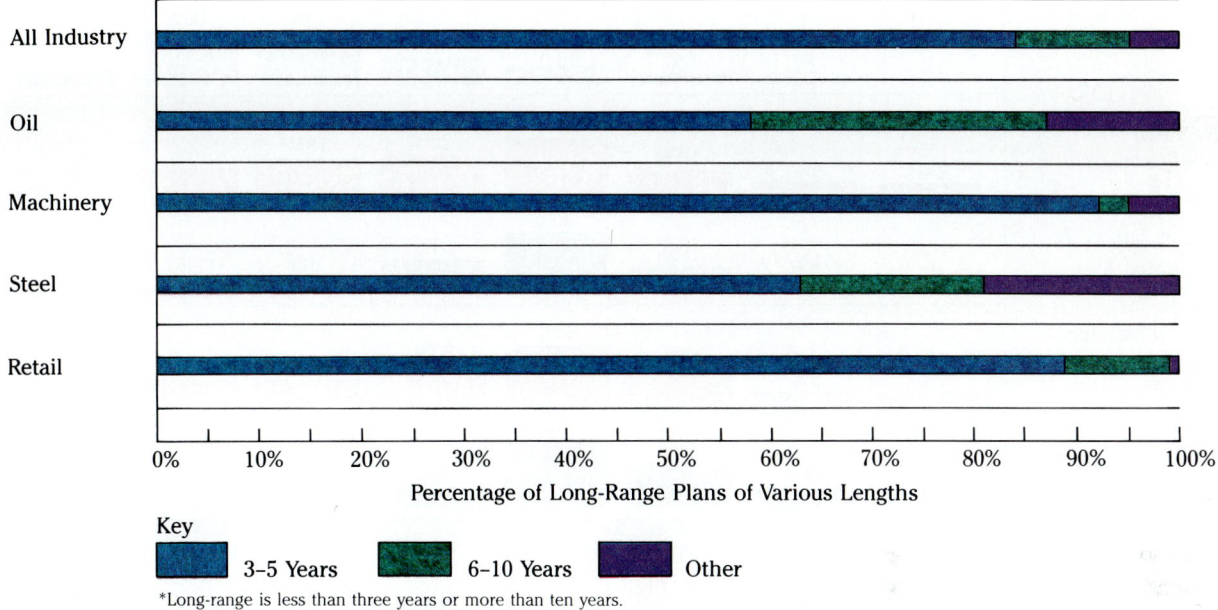

Key

■ 3–5 Years   ■ 6–10 Years   ■ Other

*Long-range is less than three years or more than ten years.
†Estimated

Source: L. W. Rue (December 1973), The how and who of long-range planning, *Business Horizons,* 29.

making plans classified as medium-range—three-to-five years in duration; thus, it appears that many organizations operate without formal plans for periods of time beyond five years.

Short-, medium-, and long-range plans differ in more ways than the amount of time they cover. Typically, the further a plan is projected into the future, the greater the uncertainty that planners encounter. As a consequence, long-range organizational plans are usually less specific than shorter-range plans. Also, long-range plans are usually less formal, less detailed, and more flexible than short-range plans in order to accommodate such uncertainty. Long-range plans also tend to be directional. For example, ten years ago a small manufacturer of tools developed a plan for the eventual use of robotics in manufacturing. Short-range plans, in contrast, tend to be goal plans. Two years ago, this same manufacturer developed a plan to implement a fully automated and computer-integrated system for manufacturing pliers.

The planning activity of managers at various hierarchical levels tends to vary along the time dimension. Managers at lower organizational levels spend much of their time in short-range planning. Managers at upper levels spend much of their time making long-range plans and thinking about the relationship between their organization and its external environment. Figure 6.7 depicts an ideal allocation of time for planning by people at various levels in a typical organization.

Neither the ideal condition nor the average organization actually exists. Managers' allocation of time to the planning process varies considerably across organizations of different sizes. Variations in organizational tech-

FIGURE 6.7   *"Ideal" Allocations of Time for Planning in a Typical Organization*

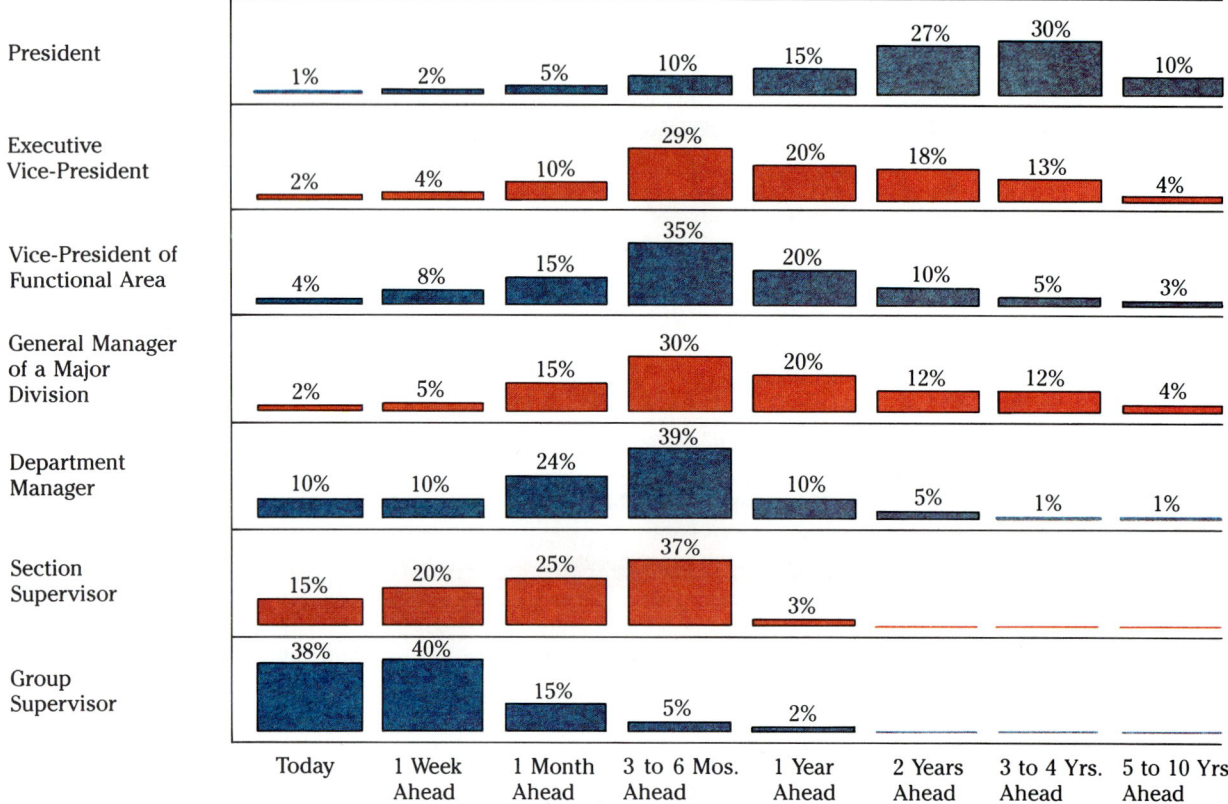

Source: G. A. Steiner (1969), *Top management planning*, London: Macmillan, 26.

nology and task environments also influence the degree to which managers engage in planning. For example, evidence suggests that as the level of environmental change increases, so, too, does the amount of uncertainty facing managers—with a consequent rise in the need for planning.

Organizational Scope Plans

Plans vary in scope. Some plans focus on an entire organization. For example, the president of the University of Minnesota advanced a plan to make the university one of the top five in the United States. The strategic plan for realizing this goal focuses on the entire institution (as opposed to a similar plan that might be focused on the health science unit).

Other plans are narrower in scope and concentrate on a subset of organizational activities. For organizations that operate multiple divisions or a number of different businesses, there are **business/divisional-level plans.** Divisional-level plans focus on the competitive position of a division in its market and on the ways in which the division can complement other divisions. During the late 1980s, Phillip Morris used revenues generated by 7Up to promote the growth of Miller High Life Beer.

INTERVIEW

Steven B. Fink

Steven B. Fink is one of the nation's leading authorities in the area of crisis management and is the author of *Crisis Management: Planning for the Inevitable.*

1. How does an organization plan for crises?

The best way for an organization to plan for a crisis is by practicing "worst-case scenarios." By identifying the worst things that can happen, managers of forward-thinking companies can advance to the next logical step and actually make contingency plans for dealing with particular crises. For example, if a worst-case scenario involves the inability of a company to transport goods to market, the contingency plan should involve alternative methods and costs of transportation and/or distribution.

2. Should crisis plans be part of the overall organization plan, or should a contingency plan replace the "standard plan" during a time of crisis?

Crisis-management planning should be part of the everyday management of a company; however, during times of crisis, the crisis-management plan should supercede other plans as common sense and other business plans dictate.

3. Do most organizations have complete business plans for both short-term and long-term purposes?

In a survey of Fortune 500 CEOs conducted for my book *Crisis Management: Planning for the Inevitable*, 89 percent agreed that a crisis in business is as inevitable as death and taxes, but fully 50 percent admitted that they or their companies did not have a written crisis-management plan in place.

"A crisis in business is as inevitable as death and taxes."

---

4. In developing organizational plans, how are goals chosen?

Goals should be chosen by priorities established by the company management.

5. What can go wrong when an organization does not have a well-developed set of plans?

In the same survey just cited, companies that experienced a crisis and had a plan in place at the time were able to recover and get back to routine business two-and-a-half times faster than companies that had no plan in place.

At a still narrower focus are **unit/functional-level plans.** Plans at this level are focused on the day-to-day operation of lower-level organizational units. For example, a marketing manager might create a plan for pricing decisions, and the Personnel Department might create a plan for handling the compensation of the organization's top performers.

Divisional-level and unit-level plans are also referred to as **tactical plans.** Tactical plans focus on subsets of an organization's overall programs, activities, and systems. They are designed to help an organization accomplish its strategic plans. For example, you may be familiar with tactical plans from a military point of view. Managers of a military maneuver standardize ways to handle recurring and predictable situations, such as feeding and moving the troops. These managers must also be able to cope with unique situations, such as a thunderstorm that prevents aircraft from completing a specific reconnaissance mission. Tactical plans developed to improve the functioning of organizations typically include policies, rules, procedures, programs, and budgets.

Contingency Plans

You will recall that the planning process is based on certain premises about what is likely to happen in an organization's environment. **Contingency plans** are created to deal with events that might come to pass if these assumptions turn out to be wrong. Contingency planning, thus, is the development of alternative courses of action to be implemented if events disrupt a planned course of action. A contingency plan allows management to act immediately if such unplanned occurrences as a strike, boycott, natural disaster, or major economic shift render existing plans inoperable or inappropriate.

During the early 1980s, the federal government deregulated the airline industry. Following this deregulation, competition for most favored routes intensified dramatically. As a consequence of this increased environmental turbulence and uncertainty, the importance of contingency planning for these firms increased. Even for those airlines that faced no immediate competition for a specific route, the development of a contingency plan that could be put into immediate operation if a competitor did emerge became a sound act of management. Two different contingency plans might have resulted, one to be implemented if a competitor came into the market with an airfare equal to that charged by the other airlines and a second plan to be implemented if a competitor came into the market with a lower fare and similar schedule. Airlines also develop contingency plans to deal with air tragedies. Although no airline plans to have terrorists attack one of its airplanes, contingency plans must be developed to guide action in case of terrorism. In reality, most contingency plans are never implemented, but when needed, they are of crucial importance. (See "A Closer Look: Contingency Planning.")

Goals

Goals are an inherent part of effective managerial planning. Although many studies have suggested that organizational performance improves as a result of formal planning, there are some inconsistencies in these observations.[22] Researchers have observed that setting specific and challenging goals contributes more to planning effectiveness and organizational performance than working under "no-goal" or "do-your-best-goal" conditions. They also have observed that comprehensive, communicated, negotiated planning contributes to optimal organizational performance, and vague goals and less effective planning significantly diminish performance.[23]

There are two types of organizational goals.[24] **Official goals** are an organization's general aims as expressed in public statements, in its annual report, and in its organizational charter. One official goal of a hospital, for example, might be to "heal the sick." Official goals are usually laudable statements created for the purpose of communicating in an abstract, ambiguous way to the external environment. They are oriented toward achieving acceptance by an organization's various constituent groups. **Operational goals** reflect managers' specific intentions.

A CLOSER LOOK

Contingency Planning: Oh, for a Better Plan

It sounded good. Boston legal firm McCabe/Gordon was new and bold. It chose a small number of legal areas in which to concentrate its work. It sought and obtained big, leading-edge cases. In 1986, the firm moved into new headquarters above Boston's harbor. "The offices were stunning, the lawyers among the brightest and best paid and the gleaming computer equipment seemed a beacon for the future."[1]

In May of 1987, McCabe/Gordon fell apart. Gone were the flashy offices. Gone were many leading attorneys who formed splinter groups and left the firm to practice on their own. The rising star had fallen.

What went wrong? The firm's failure cannot be tied to a lack of legal competence. These were good attorneys; rather, the business plan crafted for the firm appears at fault. "Their failing was not their specialties of bankruptcy and litigation or their marketing. It was most probably a combination of poor planning and bad luck."[2]

It seems McCabe/Gordon planned to concentrate on the cases of only one or two immense clients at a time. Most of these clients were located far from Boston. Rather than spend time developing a Boston-based group of regular clients, the firm went for flashier, highly publicized cases, wherever they might be found.

A problem with the McCabe/ Gordon plan was that the loss of even one of its large clients could deal a destructive blow. This is exactly what happened when the firm's extreme legal aggressiveness in a case for the billionaire Hunt brothers in Dallas was followed by their dismissal from the case. The firm was left with an insufficient caseload to support its large staff. Without a broad client base, another huge account was needed. Unfortunately for McCabe/Gordon, this time there weren't enough billionaires with legal problems to go around.

According to observers, the McCabe/Gordon plan was bold but too risky. They were done in by a lack of an adequate contingency plan should a client, such as the Hunts, be lost.

1. E. Bronner (12 May 1987), Boston's fallen legal star, *Boston Globe*, 45.
2. Bronner, 54.

These are the concrete goals that organization members are to pursue. Often they concern output or specific behavioral intentions.[25] For example, an operational goal for a hospital might be to increase the number of patients by 5 percent.

Functions and Dysfunctions

The importance of goals is apparent from the purposes they serve. Successful goals do the following:

1. Guide and direct the efforts of individuals and groups
2. Motivate individuals and groups, thereby affecting their efficiency and effectiveness
3. Influence the nature and content of the planning process
4. Provide a standard by which to judge and control organizational activity

TABLE 6.1 *Functions and Dysfunctions of Organizational Goals*

	For Organization	*For Individual*
Functions	Focus attention	Focus attention
	Rationale for organizing	Rationale for organizing
	Standard of assessment	Vehicle for personal goal attainment
	Source of legitimation	Personal security
	Recruitment through identification	Identification and status
Dysfunctions	Means to end can become real goals	Rewards may not be tied to goal attainment
	Measurement stresses quantitative goals at expense of qualitative ones	Difficulty in determining relevant performance evaluation criteria
	Goal specificity problem (ambiguous goals fail to provide direction; highly specific goals may constrain action and creativity)	Inability of individuals to identify with abstract, global goals
		Organizational goals may be incongruent with personal goals

Source: R. M. Steers (1977), *Organizational effectiveness: A behavioral view*, Santa Monica, CA: Goodyear, 21.

In short, goals help define organizational purpose, motivate accomplishment, and provide a yardstick against which progress can be measured.

A number of dysfunctional consequences are associated with goals:

1. The methods and means created to accomplish organizational goals may themselves become the goal (means-ends inversion).
2. The goals of an organization may be in conflict with the personal goals of employees or society.
3. Ambiguous goals may fail to provide adequate direction.
4. Goals that are too specific may inhibit creativity and innovation.
5. Goals and reward systems are often incompatible. Goals frequently lead people to do things for which rewards are unavailable, whereas rewards encourage people to do other things. For example, a university encourages faculty to be better teachers but rewards them primarily for good research.[26]

Table 6.1 summarizes the functional and dysfunctional aspects of organizational goals.

Multiple Goals and the Goal Hierarchy

Peter Drucker, management scholar, consultant, and writer, believes that to achieve organizational success, managers must try to achieve several goals and not be preoccupied with pursuing a single goal.[27] He has identified eight key areas in which corporate goals should be established: market standing, innovation, productivity, physical and financial resources, profitability, manager performance and development, worker performance and attitude, and public responsibility. Hewlett-Packard Corporation, for example, has established seven corporate goals, many of which overlap Drucker's areas of concern (see Table 6.2).

TABLE 6.2 *Hewlett-Packard's Corporate Goals*

Profit. To achieve sufficient profit to finance our company growth and to provide the resources we need to achieve our other corporate objectives.

Customers. To provide products and services of the greatest possible value to our customers, thereby gaining and holding their respect and loyalty.

Field of interest. To enter new fields only when the ideas we have, together with our technical, manufacturing and marketing skills, assure that we can make a needed and profitable contribution to the field.

Growth. To let our growth be limited only by our profits and our ability to develop and produce technical products that satisfy real customer needs.

People. To help our own people share in the company's success, which they make possible: to provide job security based on their performance, to recognize their individual achievements, and to help them gain a sense of satisfaction and accomplishment from their work.

Management. To foster initiative and creativity by allowing the individual great freedom of action in attaining well-defined objectives.

Citizenship. To honor our obligations to society by being an economic, intellectual and social asset to each nation and each community in which we operate.

From "New Look at Corporate Goals" by Y. K. Shetty, *California Management Review*, vol. 22, no. 2, 1979. Copyright © 1979 by the Regents of the University of California. Reprinted by permission of The Regents.

Organizations typically pursue many different goals at once. In large organizations, as you will see, various divisions and other internal units may pursue goals that actually conflict with the goals of other internal units. In most organizations, perhaps the most basic goal is to earn profits. The next most important goal is for an organization to grow. In a survey of corporate goals, managers also included capturing market share, meeting social responsibility, taking care of employees, and producing high-quality goals (see Figure 6.8).

In fact, most organizations have many different goals at the corporate level (see Table 6.3). Each internal subdivision is likely to have its own set of multiple goals focused on many of the same targets (for example, innovation and profitability). These goals are frequently in conflict, as might be the relationship between innovation and efficiency.[28] Managers must be able to integrate the network of goals and resolve internal conflicts.

All broad organizational goals—productivity, innovation, profitability, market share, and so forth—are likely to be broken down into subgoals at various levels within an organization. The complexities posed by many interrelated systems of goals and major plans can be illustrated by a **goal hierarchy** (see Figure 6.9).[29]

As Figure 6.9 shows, an organization sets corporate-level goals (A). Under this level are goal sets B and C for two organizational divisions B and C. Nested within the goals for divisions B and C are sets of goals (D through G and H through K) for departments. There is a further nesting of job-related goals (1 through 5 and 6 through 10) within each department. Managers must take care that lower-level goals combine to achieve higher-level goals; thus, innovation goals D through G combine to make goal B a reality, and goals B and C combine to make goal A a reality.

Each of the multiple goals identified by Drucker is likely to have its own hierarchy. These factors combine to define a complex network of

FIGURE 6.8 Stated Corporate Goals

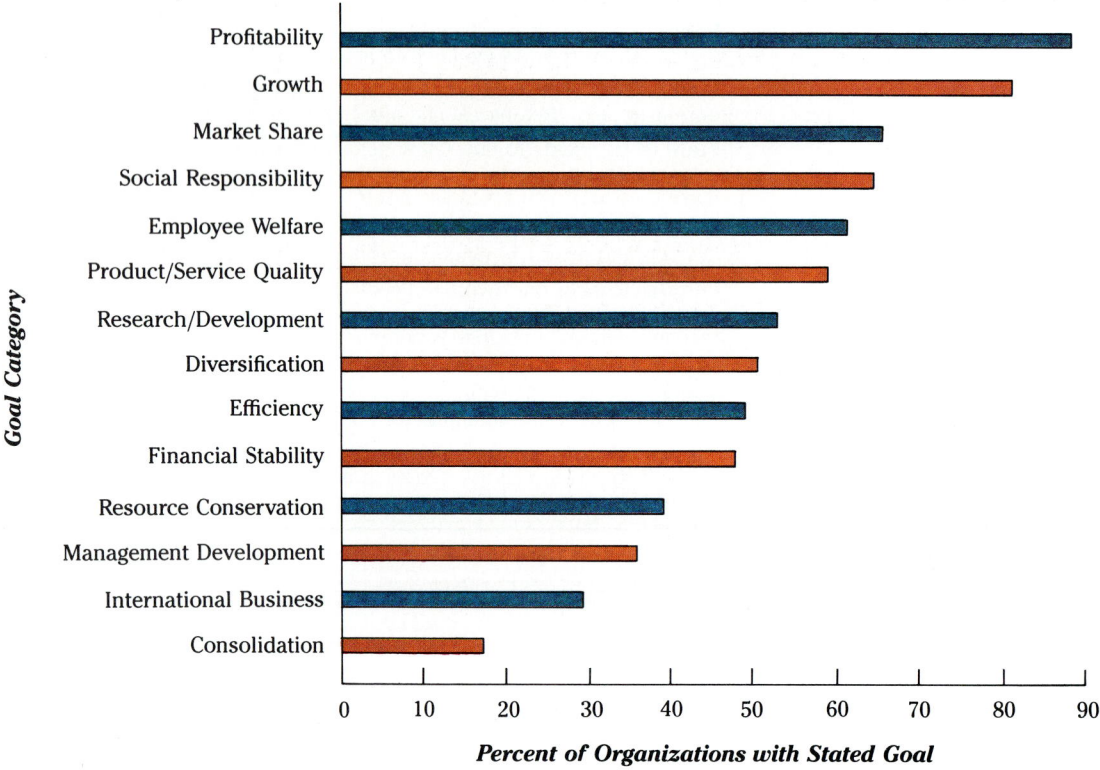

Source: Data from Y. K. Shetty (1979), New look at corporate goals, *California Management Review*, 22, 72.

organizational goals and a goal hierarchy. For a manager, as the goal hierarchy suggests, goal setting and planning can become very complex. For planning to be effective, there must be integration within and across the hierarchy.

Two models depict the process by which goals are formulated. According to one model, goals emerge from forces in an organization's external environment. According to the second model, goals emerge from forces in its internal environment.

The first model, presented by organizational sociologists James D. Thompson and William J. McEwen, takes a systems theory perspective and depicts an organization as functioning within and dependent on its external task environment.[30] As discussed in Chapter 2, an organization's task environment is made up of a wide range of individuals and groups, such as owners and investors, customers, suppliers, and regulatory agencies. All of these individuals and groups influence, are influenced by, or have a stake in an organization and its activities. This model suggests that managers pursuing their own instincts or general interests cannot set meaningful goals for organizational success. Instead, managers must understand the relationship between their organization and its task environment. Out of this delicate relationship between an organization and these groups, organizational goals emerge.

TABLE 6.3   Most Frequently Cited Goals of Corporations in Four Industrial Groups

Chemicals and Drugs		Paper and Containers		Electrical and Electronics		Food Processing	
Profitability	79%	Profitability	100%	Profitability	96%	Growth	91%
Social responsibility	74	Growth	94	Growth	88	Profitablity	86
Research and development	63	Social responsibility	59	Research and development	83	Market share	82
Growth	53	Efficiency	59	Product quality and service	75	Social responsibility	73
Product quality and service	47	Resource conservation	53	Social responsibility	67	Product quality and service	68

From "New Look at Corporate Goals" by Y. K. Shetty, *California Management Review,* vol. 22, no. 2, 1979. Copyright © 1979 by the Regents of the University of California. Reprinted by permission of The Regents.

The second model, presented by Richard M. Cyert and James G. March of Carnegie-Mellon University, concentrates on the internal dynamics of organizations.[31] This model depicts an organization as a set of coalitions, groups, and individuals with diverse interests, needs, investments in the organization, and goal orientations. These groups continually interact. They bargain, trade, and negotiate for favors and preferences. Through these political processes, organizational goals eventually emerge.

Clearly, both models explain part of how organizational goals are formed. Managers need to recognize the delicate and dependent relationship between an organization and its external environment. Goals must fit an organization into its external environment, while satisfying the needs of external constituent groups. In addition, goals must enable an organiza-

FIGURE 6.9   Goal Hierarchy

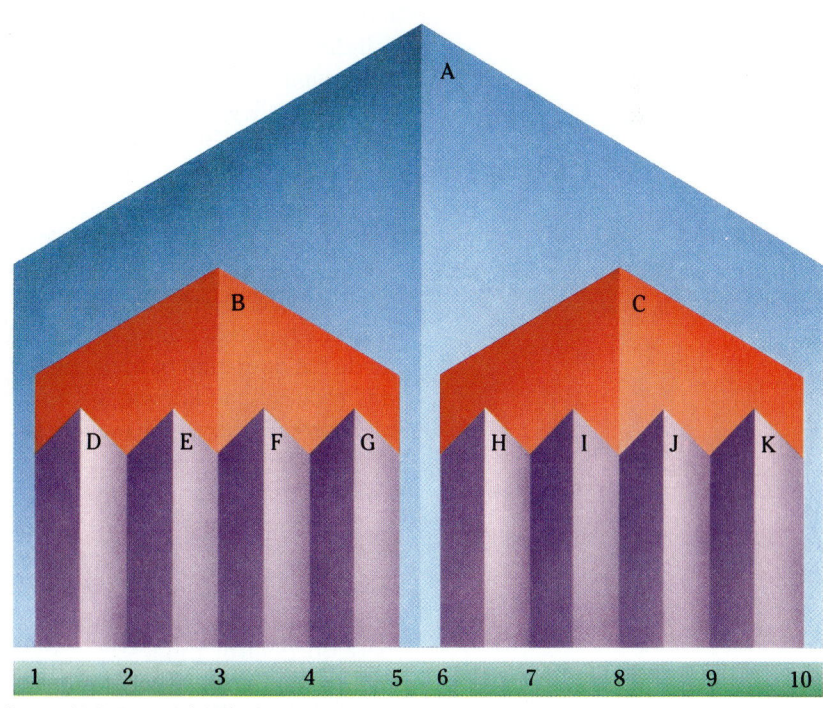

Source: M. D. Richard (1978), *Organizational goal structures,* St. Paul, MN: West, 27.

tion's internal components to work in harmony with one another. For example, the goals of its marketing department need to mesh with the goals of its production and finance departments. Finally, it is a manager's challenge to be able to balance these forces in order to preserve an organization.

What Makes Goals Work?

Much is known about the characteristics of effective individual goals (see Chapter 14). Although group and organizational goals have been studied less, it is probably safe to assume that most of what is known about individual goals also applies to group and organizational goals; therefore, effective organizational goals should:

1. Be difficult but reachable with effort
2. Be specific and clearly identify what is desired
3. Be accepted by and have the commitment of those who will help achieve the goals
4. Be developed by employees if this participation will improve the quality of goals and their acceptance
5. Be monitored for progress regularly

MBO: A Special Case

When people within an organization are personally committed to organizational plans, those plans are more likely to be accomplished. This truism is the philosophy underlying **Management by Objectives (MBO).**[32] MBO practitioners deal with employees from a human resource model and Theory Y perspective, assuming that employees are capable of self-direction and self-control. MBO is a management technique for increasing employee involvement in the planning and controlling activities. It is believed that, through involvement, employee commitment to a planned course of action will be enhanced, and performance will be more efficient.

Although there are many variations in the practice of MBO, it can be seen as a process through which an organization's goals, plans, and control systems are defined through collaboration between managers and their subordinates. Together they identify common goals, define the results expected from each individual, and use these measurements to guide the operation of their unit and to assess individual contributions.[33] In this process, the knowledge and skills of many organizational members are used. Rather than managers' telling subordinates "These are your goals"—the approach of classical management philosophy—managers ask subordinates to join them in deciding what their goals should be.

After an acceptable set of goals has been established for each employee through a give-and-take, collaborative process, the employee is asked to play a major role in developing an action plan for achieving these goals. In the final stage in the MBO process, employees are asked to develop control processes, to monitor their own performance, and to recommend corrections if unplanned deviations occur. At this stage, the entire process begins again. Figure 6.10 depicts the major stages of the MBO process.

FIGURE 6.10   The Management
by Objectives (MBO) Process

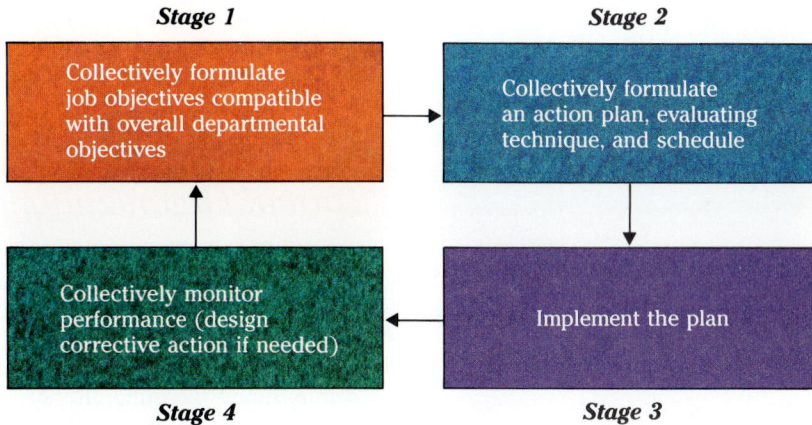

Stage 1

Collectively formulate
job objectives compatible
with overall departmental
objectives

Stage 2

Collectively formulate
an action plan, evaluating
technique, and schedule

Stage 4

Collectively monitor
performance (design
corrective action if needed)

Stage 3

Implement the plan

MBO has the potential to enhance organizational effectiveness. The following are four major components of the MBO process: 1) setting specific goals; 2) setting realistic and acceptable goals; 3) joint participation in goal setting, planning, and controlling; and (4) feedback. Research has shown that these components can play a meaningful role in achieving commitment to a course of action and organizational performance. In fact, research has clearly documented many instances in which MBO programs have increased organizational effectiveness, yet some managers have failed to adequately design or manage their MBO programs, and so, there have been failures. After reviewing 185 studies of MBO programs, one researcher concluded that they are effective under some circumstances, but not all.[34] For example, MBOs tend to be more effective in the short term (less than two years), in the private sector, and in organizations removed from direct contact with customers. For MBO programs to be effective, managers must be philosophically committed to the MBO concept, they must identify the conditions under which they propose to use such programs, and they must evaluate the likelihood of success. Among the factors that affect the success of an MBO program are the following:

- The intensity of upper-level managers' commitment to an MBO system: Half-hearted commitment is associated with a higher failure rate.
- The time element: Is there enough time for employees to learn how to participate in an MBO process—that is, to learn how to set meaningful goals, develop good action statements, and develop effective monitoring systems? Is there enough time for employees to learn how to assume responsibility in a new organizational context? Is there enough time for employees and managers to collaborate in a joint planning and controlling process?
- The legitimacy of the system: Is it integrated into an overall philosophy of management, or does it seem to be a gimmick to seduce employees into being more productive?
- The integration of employees' goals: Are goals for each employee integrated well enough into the goals of their larger organizational unit?

In light of the conditions that influence the effectiveness of an MBO program, management is challenged to provide an appropriate context for the design and maintenance of an effective MBO system.

Formal Organizational Planning in Practice

How many organizations actually engage in formal organizational planning? Studies indicate that in the 1950s, approximately 8.3 percent of all major American firms (one out of every twelve) employed a full-time long-range planner. By the late 1960s, 83 percent of major American firms used long-range planning. Today it is estimated that nearly all American corporations with sales over 100 million dollars prepare formal long-range plans.[35] Most have formal plans that extend five years into the future, and about 20 percent extend at least ten years.

Resistance to Planning

In spite of the advantages to be gained by planning, there is evidence that many managers do not plan or resist planning. Some of the common reasons for this problem include:

- Managers feel that there does not seem to be enough time to plan, that decisions need to be made at once.
- Because issues need immediate action, the movement from one crisis to the next results in continual postponement of planning.
- Managers feel that time that could be used for planning is so interrupted that attempts at planning are futile.
- Current reward and punishment systems within organizations do not encourage planning. These systems usually reward employees who solve current problems and punish those who ignore them. Managers are encouraged to attend only to immediate problems. Rewards and punishment for longer-range planning are less certain.
- Managers avoid planning because of the uncertainty associated with future events in rapidly changing, complex environments.

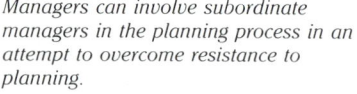

Managers can involve subordinate managers in the planning process in an attempt to overcome resistance to planning.

- Planning is difficult and complicated.
- Planning is costly and requires time, effort, and a variety of support systems.
- Some managers are reluctant to set goals for themselves and their organizational units for fear they may fail to reach those goals. They believe that this failure would be more obvious than if they had not set specific goals in the first place.
- Planning often involves change, and organization members may not want change.[36]

In spite of such resistance to planning, there appear to be several actions that can be taken to overcome this problem.

Overcoming Resistance to Planning

Some managers find planning so challenging that they simply choose not to attempt it at all. For example, approximately half of Britain's largest manufacturing firms have experienced difficulty getting their line managers to devote time to planning,[37] in spite of the many techniques that can lessen resistance, such as the following:

- Develop an organizational climate that encourages planning. Top managers should support lower-level managers' planning activities and serve as role models through their own planning activities.
- Train people in planning.
- Create a reward system that encourages and supports planning activity and carefully avoids punishment for failure to achieve newly set goals.
- Involve subordinate managers in the planning process and encourage them, in turn, to involve others, who will be affected, in their own planning.
- Open up information systems so that people have the information necessary to make plans.
- Provide the necessary support systems—such as personnel, computers, and money for the purchase of information—for planning.
- Use plans once they are created.

In order for managers to invest the time and energy needed to overcome resistance to planning, they must be convinced that planning does, in fact, pay off.

Does Planning Really Pay Off?

You may find planning difficult in your personal life. You plan to study this weekend for a test next week, but a friend from home comes into town. . . . Managers of organizations in complex and unstable environments may find it too difficult to develop meaningful plans, yet it is precisely conditions of environmental complexity and instability that produce the greatest need for a good set of organizational plans.

A logical question to ask is whether planning really pays off. A study of 199 corporations in 15 industries found that organizations facing complex

Many organizations have successfully involved employees in planning and controlling activities.

and unstable environments engaged in formal long-range planning. Several other studies have focused on the benefits of planning from a financial impact perspective. In general, they suggest that firms that engage in planning are more financially successful than those that do not.[38] For example, the median return on investment for a five-year period was 17.1 percent for organizations engaged in strategic planning, versus 5.9 percent for those that did not.[39] Similarly, of 70 large commercial banks, those that had strategic planning systems outperformed those that did not.[40]

Although planning clearly has observable benefits, it can be expensive. The financial commitment can be large for organizations with a formal planning staff. Even so, research evidence suggests that planning is warranted. It is imperative, therefore, that managers develop formal plans.

The Location of Planning Activity

Classical management thinking advocates a separation of "planning" and "doing." According to this school of thought, managers plan for technical core employees and formulate most of their organization's plans for the upper levels of the organization with little participation from lower-level managers and workers. In contrast, behavioral management theorists suggest involving organization members in drawing up plans that would affect them. Implementation of an MBO program is one means through which this participative planning can be realized. Researchers at the Tavistock Institute in England have promoted the idea of *"self-managed" work groups* as a means of expanding the level of employee involvement. According to this plan, work groups assume a major role in planning (as well as organizing, directing, and controlling) the work assigned to them. *Quality circles* generally consist of a group of workers (from the same and/or different departments) who meet regularly to work on production quality issues. The quality circle concept is a way of building an emphasis on quality at each stage of the manufacturing (service) process through the joint involvement of management and workers in planning and controlling activities. Many organizations—for example, Volvo and Motorola—have had successful experiences with employee involvement in the planning and controlling activities.

Planning Specialists

To keep pace with recent increases in organizational complexity, technological sophistication, and environmental uncertainty, many organizations now use **planning specialists.** Professional planners work singly or in groups to develop organizational plans and to help managers plan. Boeing, General Electric, Ford, and General Motors are among the many organizations with professional planning staffs. These specialists may serve as planning advisers to top management or may assist lower-level managers (for example, functional managers) with planning. Planning specialists helped develop United Airlines' crisis management plan. Some of the forces that have led organizations to create formal planning departments include:

- The recognition that planning takes time and that the presence of a planning staff can reduce a manager's workload.
- Highly competitive and rapidly changing environments frequently require an organization to make coordinated and systematic moves quickly. Professional planners develop contingency plans that can be implemented quickly to meet environmental changes.
- In highly centralized organizations, operating units are interdependent, and their planning must be integrated. A planning department can span organizations both horizontally and vertically to create highly integrated planning systems.
- Effective planning often requires more objectivity than employees with a vested interest in a particular set of activities can provide.
- Planning has become so sophisticated that specialists are needed.

There are two approaches to using a planning staff. According to one approach, a planning staff takes an advisory role as it assists line management in making plans. The planning staff is not asked to make plans for a company but to help line managers make plans.[41] The second approach calls for a planning staff to create a set of alternative plans in consultation with line managers. Line managers then make the final determination of which plans are to be implemented.

A planning staff's goals are varied.[42] Its primary responsibility is to assist line managers in developing strategies for achieving organizational objectives. It also should coordinate the complex array of plans created for the various levels within an organization. Finally, the planning staff should provide encouragement, support, and skill for developing formal organizational plans.

Planning in Review

Planning is the process through which managers establish goals and detail the methods by which these goals will be attained. There are five major stages in the planning process. First, an organization establishes its preplanning foundation, which describes the current situation. In the second step, the organization sets forth goals based on the preplanning foundation. In the third step, managers forecast what is likely to happen in the organization's internal and external environments in order to develop alternative courses of action. In the fourth step, managers identify possible courses of action for meeting their objectives, evaluate each alternative, and select a course of action. In the fifth step, planners develop the supportive plans necessary to accomplish the organization's major plan of action. Once implemented, that plan must be monitored and controlled so that it meets the goals established in the second step.

Goal development is an important part of the planning process. Goals developed for employees, for departments, and for an entire organization can greatly enhance the effectiveness of the organization. Evidence clearly reveals that performance is higher when organizations, as well as individuals, operate under difficult (but attainable) and specific goals.

Managers create many types of plans. These can be examined from the hierarchy, frequency-of-use, time frame, and organizational scope perspectives. Contingency plans to be used in case of unexpected events or wrong assumptions are critical in effective management in highly turbulent environments.

Plans reduce uncertainty and risk, focus attention on goals to be reached, and enhance understanding of the external environment. Although most major organizations now engage in formal organizational planning, many managers fail to plan appropriately. Fear of failure, lack of time, and uncertainty about the future are among the reasons given by managers for their failure to plan. A number of tactics have been developed to help managers overcome their resistance to planning, and formal planning staff positions have been developed. Although an organization's success is sometimes a question of being in the right place at the right time, sustained success requires careful, systematic planning.

Notes

1. S. J. Carroll and D. J. Gillen (1987), Are the classical managerial functions useful in describing managerial work? *Academy of Management Review,* 12, 38–51.

2. R. M. Fulmer and T. T. Herbert (1978), Decline and fall of Santa, in *Exploring the new management,* 2nd ed., New York: Macmillan, 65–66.

3. United once more (22 June 1987), *Time,* 46–47.

4. H. Koontz and C. O'Donnell (1972), *Principles of management: An analysis of managerial functions,* New York: McGraw-Hill, 113–14.

5. B. E. Goetz (1949), *Management planning and control,* New York: McGraw-Hill, 2.

6. G. A. Steiner (1969), *Top management planning,* London: MacMillan, 6, 7.

7. H. Mintzberg (July-August, 1975), The manager's job: Folklore and fact, *Harvard Business Review,* 51.

8. S. J. Carroll and D. J. Gillen (1984), The classical management functions: Are they really outdated? *Academy of Management Proceedings,* 44, 132–36.

9. T. A. Mahoney, T. H. Jerdee, and S. J. Carroll, Jr. (1963), *Development of managerial performance: A research approach,* Cincinnati: Southwestern; T. A. Mahoney, T. H. Jerdee, and S. J. Carroll, Jr. (1965), The jobs of management, *California Management Review,* 4, 97–110; J. A. Hass, A. M. Porat, and J. A. Vaughan (1969), Actual vs. ideal time allocations reported by managers: A study of managerial behavior, *Personnel Psychology,* 22, 61–75; R. V. Penfield (1975), Time allocation patterns and effectiveness of managers, *Personnel Psychology,* 27, 245–55.

10. S. Fink (1986), *Crisis management: Planning for the inevitable,* New York: AMACOM, 56, 64–65.

11. P. Lorange and R. V. Vancil (1977), *Strategic planning systems,* Englewood Cliffs, NJ: Prentice-Hall; Steiner, 1969.

12. K. G. Smith, E. A. Locke, and D. Barry (1986), *Goal setting, planning effectiveness and organizational performance: An experimental simulation,* unpublished manuscript, University of Maryland, College of Business and Management, College Park, Maryland.

13. Koontz and O'Donnell, 1972, 124-28.

14. J. K. Clemens and D. F. Mayer (1987), *The classic touch: Lessons in leadership from Homer to Hemingway,* Homewood, IL: Dow Jones-Irwin, 147.

15. Steiner, 1969, 7; M. B. McCaskey (1974), A contingency approach to planning: Planning with goals and planning without goals, *Academy of Management Journal,* 17, 281-91.

16. McCaskey, 1974.

17. McCaskey, 1974.

18. P. C. Earley, P. Wojnarocki, and W. Prest (1987), Task planning and energy expended: An exploration of how goals influence performance, *Journal of Applied Psychology,* 47, 107-14; P. C. Earley and B. Perry (in press), Work plan availability and performance: An assessment of prior training on subsequent task completion, *Organizational Behavior and Human Decision Processes.*

19. Smith, et al., 1986.

20. R. H. Kilman (1984), *Beyond the quick fix,* San Francisco: Jossey-Bass, 50-51.

21. Fink, 1986, 203-18.

22. J. S. Armstrong (1982), The value of formal planning for strategic decisions: Review of empirical research, *Strategic Management Journal,* 3, 197-212; J. S. Armstrong (1986), The value of formal planning for strategic decisions: Reply, *Strategic Management Journal,* 7, 183-85; W. F. Glueck and L. R. Jauch (1984), *Strategic management and business policy,* 2nd ed., New York: McGraw-Hill.

23. Smith, et al., 1986.

24. C. Perrow (1961), The analysis of goals in complex organizations, *American Sociological Review,* 26, 854.

25. P. E. Connor (1980), *Organizations: Theory and design,* Palo Alto, CA: Science Research Associates, 92-96.

26. R. M. Steers (1977), *Organizational effectiveness: A behavioral view,* Santa Monica, CA: Goodyear, 20-23.

27. P. F. Drucker (1954), *The practice of management,* New York: Harper and Brothers.

28. J. Hage (1965), An axiomatic theory of organizations, *Administrative Science Quarterly,* 10, 289-320.

29. M. R. Richards (1978), *Organizational goal structures,* St. Paul, MN: West, 27.

30. J. D. Thompson and W. J. McEwen (1958), Organizational goals and environment, *American Sociological Review,* 23, 23-30.

31. R. M. Cyert and J. G. March (1963), *A behavioral theory of the firm,* Englewood Cliffs, NJ: Prentice-Hall.

32. Drucker, 1954; A. P. Raia (1974), *Managing by objectives,* Glenview, IL: Scott, Foresman.

33. G. S. Odiorne (1979), *M.B.O. II,* Belmont, CA: Fearon.

34. J. N. Kondrasuk (1981), Studies in MBO effectiveness, *Academy of Management Review,* 6, 419-30.

35. J. J. Reitz and L. N. Jewell (1985), *Managing,* Glenview, IL: Scott, Foresman, 66.

36. Derived from L. V. Gerstner, Jr. (1980), Can strategic planning pay off? In R. A. Kerin and R. A. Peterson, eds., *Perspectives on strategic marketing management,* Boston: Allyn & Bacon.

37. J. Martin (1979), Business planning: The gap between theory and practice, *Long Range Planning*, 12, 2–10.

38. W. Lindsay and L. Rue (1980), Impact of the organization environment on the long-range planning process: A contingency view, *Academy of Management Journal*, 23, 385–404; D. Herold (1972), Long-range planning and organizational performance: A cross-valuation study, *Academy of Management Journal*, 15, 91–102; C. Saunders and F. D. Tuggle (1977), *Toward a contingency theory of planning*, presented at the 37th Annual Meeting of the Academy of Management, Orlando, Florida; S. S. Thune and R. House (1970), Where long-range planning pays off, *Business Horizons*, 13, 81–87.

39. E. H. Bowman (1976), Strategy and the weather, *Sloan Management Review*, 17, 53.

40. D. R. Wood and R. L. LaForge (1979), The impact of comprehensive planning on financial performance, *Academy of Management Journal*, 22, 516–26.

41. Steiner, 1969, 98.

42. Steiner, 1969, 117.

Key Terms

planning	programs
goals	projects
action statements	budgets
goal planning	short-range plans
domain/directional planning	medium-range plans
hybrid planning	long-range plans
premising	business/divisional-level plans
strategic plans	unit/functional-level plans
administrative plans	tactical plans
operating plans	contingency plans
standing plans	official goals
standard operating procedure (SOP)	operational goals
policies	goal hierarchy
rules	Management by Objectives (MBO)
procedures	planning specialists
single-use plans	

Issues for Review and Discussion

1. Define managerial planning.
2. What is the relationship between planning and decision making?
3. Identify and briefly describe each stage in the planning process.
4. Compare and contrast three different types of planning.
5. What is the difference between official and operating goals?
6. What are multiple goals. What is a goal hierarchy? How are these concepts related to one another?

7. Briefly describe the two different views of the goal formulation process and explain how they differ.
8. Describe the MBO process and the philosophy behind it.
9. What is the difference between a policy and a rule? Give an example of each.
10. Discuss whether planning really pays off.

Suggested Readings

Churchill, N. C. (July/August 1984). Budget choice: Planning vs. control. *Harvard Business Review*, 62, 150–164.

Drucker, P. F. (1959). Long-range planning: Challenge to management science. *Management Science*, 5, 238–49.

Fayol, H. (1949). *General and industrial management* (Chapter Four: Planning). London: Pitman.

Fink, S. (1986). *Crisis management: Planning for the inevitable*. New York: American Management Association. For a review, see Markham, S. (1988). A review of *Crisis management: Planning for the inevitable*. In Pierce, J. L. and Newstrom, J. W., eds. *The manager's bookshelf: A mosaic of contemporary views*. New York: Harper & Row, 285–90.

Hartman, S. J., White, M. C., and Crino, M. D. (1986). Environmental volatility, system adaptation, planning requirements, and information-processing strategies: An integrative model. *Decision Sciences*, 17, 454–74.

Odiorne, G. S. (October 1978). MBO: A backward glance. *Business Horizons*, 14–24.

Shetty, Y. K. (1979). New look at corporate goals. *California Management Review*, 22, 71–79.

CASE *Product Development Planning at Display Electronics*

By Phil Fisher of the University of South Dakota

The Display Electronics Corporation manufactures computer-driven electronic displays. These include such products as athletic scoreboards for college football stadiums; voting displays used by state legislatures; time-and-temperature signs used by banks; and larger displays sold as electronic billboards to coliseums, truck stops, and gambling casinos. In the early 1980s, opportunities for new products using this technology seemed endless.

Display Electronics grew as fast as company managers could develop marketing channels and raise funds to support the manufacture and sales of their new products. Despite this growth, company profits were irregular, and average return on sales was lower than company goals. Dr. Arthur Keene, the company president, became concerned that new product development was being driven more by technological than by economic considerations. Dr. Keene, who has a Ph.D. in electrical engineering, decided to put more emphasis on the profit potential of products at the earliest stage of development.

His first step was to create a marketing committee composed of himself, the vice-president for engineering, the vice-president for sales and two members of his staff, and a representative of the company's advertising agency. The function of this committee was to review all new product development projects twice a month. The project managers, usually electrical engineers, who actually managed the development of new products, met with the committee as their projects were being reviewed. The procedures to be followed by the committee and project managers were outlined in the memorandum by Dr. Keene titled *Product Design Procedure*.

Dr. Keene further outlined the information to be required by the marketing committee for evaluating new product proposals. He did this by setting the requirements for product development requests in the memorandum, titled *Product Development Request*, which became Display Electronics Form No. 44.

September 19, 1986

Product Design Procedure

1. All new product or product enhancement ideas are submitted to the marketing committee for consideration using Display Electronics Form No. 44.

2. Upon preliminary approval by the marketing committee, the idea is submitted to Engineering for design feasibility, estimated time and cost to complete the design, and estimated cost of the product. These data are presented to the marketing committee for final approval.

3. Upon final approval by the marketing committee, the development project is funded and scheduled for completion.

4. A project manager is assigned by the Engineering Vice-President to manage each design project. It is his or her responsibility to successfully complete the project on schedule and within budget.

September 19, 1986

Product Development Request

1. New Product _____   Product Enhancement _____
2. Purpose: (check all appropriate items)
   _____ Reduce manufacturing cost
   _____ Take advantage of new market
   _____ Another product in an existing product line
   _____ Uses existing parts and subassemblies
   _____ Uses existing distribution system
   _____ Improves product reliability
   _____ Other _____

3. Describe the new product idea. Carefully specify all key features.

4. Describe the market for the new product and the proposed method of distribution. Project total market size for the next five years.

5. Estimate the number of units that will be ordered and Display Electronics market share during the first year, the second year, and the third year. State product price at which these order quantities are feasible. State sensitivity of the market to product price. Carefully outline all assumptions made in arriving at your order projections.

6. List and describe all current and potential competitive products. Include company name, product description (brochures and manuals if available), market share, pricing, etc.

7. Describe the proposed marketing strategy for the new product (e.g. top of line, minimum first cost, complete system, etc.)

8. Describe the general manufacturing method and reference to currently used manufacturing methods.

9. Describe any unusual requirements and how these requirements are related to product success (e.g. critical product introduction date, special finish, size or weight, low power, etc.)

10. Additional comments as appropriate

Questions

1. What type of plans are being outlined in this case?
2. How does the planning process developed at the Display Electronics Corporation relate to the planning process stages outlined in this chapter?
3. Which organizational members are most likely to resist this process?
4. Do you see any other problems that might arise from the use of this planning process?

Decision Making

Student Learning Objectives

After reading this chapter, you should be able to:

1. Describe the nature of decision making.

2. Explain the various types of organizational decisions.

3. Differentiate among the many conditions under which decisions are made.

4. Distinguish among choice making, decision making, and problem solving.

5. Understand individual attributes, such as cognitive style, personality, and motivation, and how they affect decision making.

6. Compare and contrast the rational/economic (classical) and administrative (behavioral) models of decision making.

7. Describe the conditions under which managers should use groups for decision making.

8. Discuss the advantages and disadvantages of group decision making.

9. Identify and discuss the most common problems that managers face when making decisions.

10. Discuss the tactics that managers can use to make their decision making more effective.

*D*uring the late 1980s, the nation's air traffic controllers were on the verge of unionizing. One of their major grievances was that the powers within the Federal Aviation Administration (FAA) were making policy decisions about air safety without consulting those who were watching over the nation's airlines. Many claimed, for example, that the number of near collisions was rising dramatically and could be traced directly to these policy decisions.

In 1986, the spacecraft *Challenger* exploded, killing the seven people aboard and significantly setting back the United States space program. Those in control of the final decision to launch the *Challenger* claimed that they were not fully aware of lower-level engineers' long-expressed concerns over the booster's "O-rings" and concerns that the temperature on the morning of the launch was too low for safety.

What do these incidents have in common? Both characterize a closed system perspective of managerial decision making (closed and open systems were discussed in Chapter 2). In both incidents, the decision makers insulated themselves from critical information sources. These incidents highlight a significant challenge for management: developing effective organizational decision-making and problem-solving systems.

This chapter will introduce you to decision making. You will look at the decision-making process and learn that managers are more effective and less likely to make mistakes if they consciously choose to make decision making and problem solving targets of the act of managing. This chapter will discuss decision making by individuals and groups, identify problems that managers confront in making decisions, and provide suggestions for minimizing these problems.

The decision makers who launched the space shuttle Challenger *claimed they were unaware of information that might have prevented the explosion that killed seven crew members.*

The Nature of Decision Making

Decision making is the lifeblood of any organization and the very essence of management.[1] It is not unusual for a manager to face decisions about hiring and firing, product specifications, and return on investment all in the same business day. Some managers confront decisions rationally and coolly; others decide impulsively or with only part of the information that they should use. Some people avoid making decisions consciously; however, even such passive people actually have a definite philosophy about how to confront problems. These people probably are unaware that their philosophy of how to confront problems has a decision-making component: they have decided to run away from problems rather than to rationally select alternatives.

What Is Decision Making?

When faced with two or more feasible alternatives, a manager must decide which to select. **Decision making** is the process of identifying a set of feasible alternatives and, from these, choosing a course of action. **Decisions** are judgments which directly affect a course of action.[2] While still in high school, for example, Mary Pat Sitlington had to decide what to do after graduation—look for a job or seek further education. Deciding to

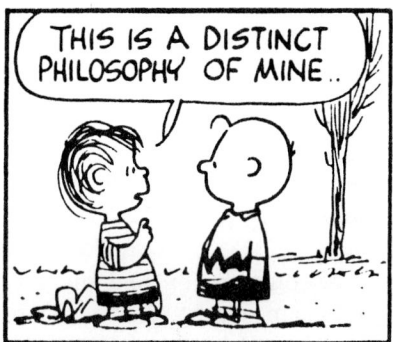

Reprinted by permission of UFS, Inc.

go to college, Mary Pat collected information about a number of schools, reviewed the material. narrowed the list to a number of alternatives, evaluated each alternative, applied to several schools, and then chose to attend St. Mary's College in Notre Dame, Indiana. In other words, Mary Pat did not merely "go to college." She made a decision to go to a particular institution.

Although many managers use the terms *choice making, decision making,* and *problem solving* interchangeably, these three activities are different.[3] **Choice making** refers to the narrow set of activities associated with choosing one option from a set of already identified alternatives. Choice making is involved when a manager selects one of five applicants to hire for a quality-control job opening. **Decision making** is an intermediate-sized set of activities. It begins with problem identification and ends with choice making. Decision making would be involved when a manager, faced with a large number of returned products due to defective manufacturing: 1) identifies three possible causes for the defective products, 2) concludes that the best way to deal with this problem is to have a quality-control inspector examine each product, and 3) selects an applicant to be hired for the new quality-control job. **Problem solving** refers to the broad set of activities that involves finding and implementing a course of action to correct an unsatisfactory situation. It includes not only decision making but also the implementation, monitoring, and maintenance of the decision. Problem solving would be involved if all of the choice-making and decision-making steps were followed, and if the manager implemented the chosen course of action and followed up to make certain that the addition of the quality-control person solved the problem of defective products being delivered to customers.

Many occasions give rise to the need for decisions.[4] First, a current state of affairs may fall short of a goal or an ideal.[5] A publisher, for example, may find that its book sales are not reaching target projections for the current fiscal year. Second, a problem or crisis may arise like that confronting managers of Procter & Gamble when their Rely tampon was accused of causing toxic shock syndrome among users. A third decision occasion may occur when managers want to take advantage of an opportunity. Du Pont, for example, is one of four companies pursuing the development of a sucrose polyester it hopes will become the food industry's next aspartame (NutraSweet). Accidentally discovered during research to help premature babies gain weight, this sucrose polyester is being substituted for fat in cooking. It can be used to create foods that retain their traditional taste—but not their calories, because the artificial substance cannot be digested by the human body. A fourth occasion for making decisions is, of course, to maintain the status quo—to preserve a high sales volume, to maintain suppliers' contentment, to keep a consultant, and so on. The fifth and final reason why managers make decisions is proactive in nature. Carrying out an entrepreneurial role, managers create new opportunities and ventures for their organizations. The decision by McGraw-Hill to purchase Data Resources was characterized by a search for new ventures that would contribute to McGraw-Hill's objective of serving the worldwide need for knowledge. Decision situations need not be limited to just one purpose. A hijacking, for example, can present a nation's government with a crisis but, simultaneously, offer the opportuni-

FIGURE 7.1 *Decision Making, Choice Making, and Problem Solving*

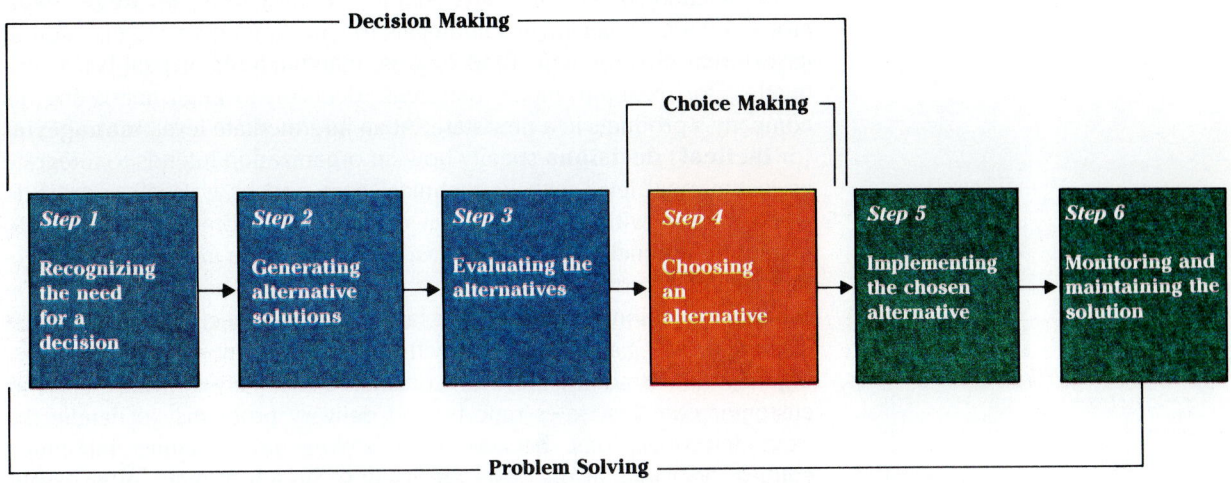

Source: Adapted from G. P. Huber (1980), *Managerial decision making*, Glenview, IL: Scott, Foresman, 8.

ty to forge a closer alliance with another government or to strengthen certain areas of its foreign policy. See Figure 7.1.

Many decision occasions force managers to make decisions quickly and under pressure. In all cases, decision making focuses on choosing an alternative that managers expect will lead their organization to a desired goal.

Types of Decisions

Every day managers must make many different types of decisions. When should an organization construct a new building? How should a company react to a competitor's price cut? Is it time to develop and market a new product? This section will discuss some of the many types of decisions that confront managers.

Means vs. Ends Decisions Decisions may be oriented toward means of achieving goals or toward the ends goals themselves. **Means decisions** concern procedures or actions undertaken to achieve particular goals—in other words, how a goal is to be reached. **Ends decisions** are oriented more specifically toward achieving a goal. For example, in the mid-1980s, IBM's goal (the result of an ends decision) was to reduce the size of its workforce. (It could be argued that the ends decision to reduce the workforce was itself actually a means decision directed toward the end of reducing costs and increasing flexibility.) To achieve this goal, the company decided to offer an early retirement program to encourage employees to leave the IBM workforce voluntarily. The means to reaching the ends goal of a reduced workforce was to encourage early retirement. In practice, means and ends decisions often are linked together. Ends decisions are more likely to be successful when they are combined with means decisions.

Decision Levels Managers make decisions that affect various levels of organizational responsibility. At the broadest level, **strategic decisions** reflect management's strategies for positioning an organization in its external environment. Brad Rogers, manufacturer of peat-based briquettes, for example, made a strategic decision to begin marketing his company's products in a new state. At an intermediate level, **managerial** (or **tactical**) **decisions** specify how an organization intends to integrate its institutional level with its technical core and how it will coordinate work systems within the technical core. Because Brad has decided to market the briquettes in other states, for example, he must make managerial decisions pertaining to resource allocations for the expanded organizational operations. At a narrower level, operating decisions, which were discussed in Chapter 6, deal with the day-to-day operations of an organization. Brad will have to coordinate the daily activities, such as customer contacts, sales reports, and delivery problems, to handle the expanded operations. Because organizations are dynamic, integrated entities, decisions at one level are likely to be felt at many other levels. Operating decisions ultimately affect strategic decisions, just as strategic decisions affect decisions made at lower levels.

Programmed vs. Nonprogrammed Decisions Some decisions cover routine circumstances and may turn into formal company policy. Other decisions cover special or novel circumstances. **Programmed decisions** are routines that deal with frequently occurring situations, such as requests for vacations by employees. In routine situations, it is usually much more efficient for managers to use a programmed decision than to make a new decision for each similar situation. In programmed decisions, managers make a real decision only once, when the program is created. Subsequently, the program itself specifies procedures to follow when similar circumstances arise. The creation of these routines results in the formulation of rules, procedures, and policies. Programmed decisions are not necessarily confined to simple issues, such as vacation policies or the appropriate dress for an organization's sales force; they also are used to deal with very complex issues, such as the types of tests that a doctor needs to conduct before performing major surgery on a patient with diabetes.

Nonprogrammed decisions generally are made in unique or novel situations. Nonprogrammed decisions are necessary when no prior routine or practice exists to guide the decision-making process. For example, when the first Sears employee with Acquired Immune Deficiency Syndrome (AIDS) was identified, a decision had to be made about whether the employee could continue to work as long as he was able. The decision required special consideration and could not have been made at that time simply by referring to a policy manual.

Conditions of Certainty, Risk, and Uncertainty Managerial decisions also can be characterized by the conditions of certainty and risk under which they are made (see Figure 7.2). Some decisions entail little uncertainty and little risk. Others entail great risk and very high levels of uncertainty.

FIGURE 7.2   Degree of Certainty and Decision Making

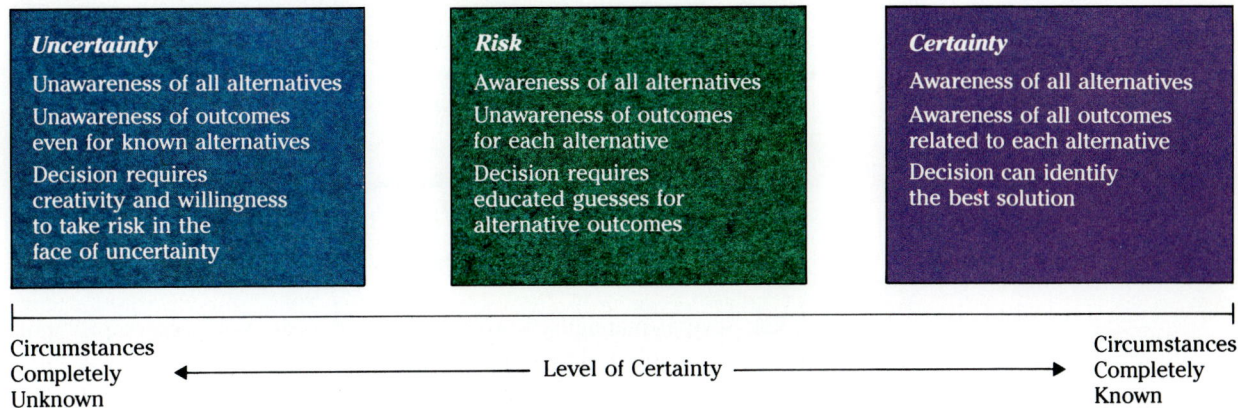

Uncertainty	**Risk**	**Certainty**
Unawareness of all alternatives	Awareness of all alternatives	Awareness of all alternatives
Unawareness of outcomes even for known alternatives	Unawareness of outcomes for each alternative	Awareness of all outcomes related to each alternative
Decision requires creativity and willingness to take risk in the face of uncertainty	Decision requires educated guesses for alternative outcomes	Decision can identify the best solution

Circumstances
Completely
Unknown   ◄——————— Level of Certainty ———————►   Circumstances
Completely
Known

When a decision maker is aware of all available alternatives and the factors (outcomes) associated with each, a state of **certainty** exists. Few organizational decisions are made under conditions of true certainty, but managers do face decisions that are relatively certain. Under these conditions, decision making requires the collection and use of accurate, measurable, and reliable information.

Managers who make decisions under conditions of **risk** also know all of the alternatives that are available. They do not know what will happen if they choose a particular alternative. They do, however, possess enough information to assign probabilities of occurrence subjectively to the various alternatives. When decisions are made under risk, managers must collect information that helps them estimate as accurately as possible the probable outcome of each alternative.

Under conditions of **uncertainty,** a decision maker is not aware of all possible courses of action, even though he or she may be aware of several. For those alternatives that can be identified, there is not enough information to permit the certain identification of probable outcomes. For example, when the British and French governments began developing the Concorde airplane, the newness of the venture meant that they had to make decisions under extremely high levels of uncertainty. Many aspects of the market's reaction and the plane's environmental impact did not surface during the planning stages.

Decisions made under high levels of uncertainty can be difficult, and they can make managers very uncomfortable, particularly those managers who have a low tolerance for ambiguity (see Chapter 13). On the positive side, however, decisions made under uncertainty can be very challenging, can provide opportunities for creativity, and can be especially rewarding when they lead to success.

Although many managers are perfectly comfortable making decisions under conditions of risk or uncertainty, they should always try to reduce the uncertainty surrounding their decisions. They can do so by conducting comprehensive and systematic research. The research can tell them more about their alternatives, give them a firmer basis for estimating possible outcomes, and help them look at best and worst alternatives. Imagine that manager Susie Carlisle is considering whether to finance a new building by taking a fixed interest rate loan of 10 percent or a variable rate loan that begins at 9 percent but could increase by 4 points. Susie might consider that, for the variable rate loan, the best case rate is 9 percent. The worse case rate is 13 percent. By taking this approach, she can at least reduce some uncertainty and get firmer support for her decision.

Decision Making: The Process and Managerial Practices

Ask several managers how they make decisions and solve problems and you probably will hear many say, "I don't know," "There are no rules; you just do it," and "I just do what feels right." In reality, good decision makers, acting either consciously or unconsciously, follow a fairly consistent pattern. Because this pattern can be identified, it can be applied to improve the quality of decisions. The following sections will identify a number of distinct stages in the decision-making process.

The Process

Earlier in this chapter, a distinction was made among decision making, choice making, and problem solving. This section will examine in greater detail the first four steps involved in the decision-making process (review Figure 7.1). These steps include: (1) recognizing the need for a decision (for example, problem awareness, definition, and understanding), (2) generating alternative solutions, (3) evaluating each alternative, and (4) choosing from among the alternative solutions (choice making). The remaining steps in Figure 7.1, implementing the chosen alternative and monitoring and maintaining the solution, are discussed at some length in Chapters 18, 19, and 20.

Step One: Recognizing the Need for a Decision   The first step in the decision-making process consists of recognizing that a decision is needed. (Much of the following discussion of the decision-making process will assume the existence of a problem. It is important, however, to remember that a number of occasions including opportunities as well as problems can give rise to the need for managerial decision making.) Problem recognition begins when a decision maker is alerted by a signal that a decision is needed. A tardy employee, slipping sales, an unusual hum in a computer console, or an angry supervisor may be signs that a problem exists. A manager may sense that something is wrong but cannot describe the problem yet. Sometimes people identify problems automatically. For example, suppose Tanya goes back to her dorm after a difficult examination to listen to music only to discover that her old stereo is not working. This sends her an obvious signal that she has a problem and that she needs to decide whether to have the old system fixed or to buy the new but expensive system that she wants.

One way to look at this first step of the decision-making process is in terms of the *detection of symptoms*. On the detection of a decision occasion, a decision maker needs to identify the problem exactly and

The first step in the decision-making process is to identify the problem and define the situation in detail.

define the situation in detail. He or she must come to understand why the situation is a problem, what are its causes, and what will be affected by it. In essence, the manager must develop an understanding of the anatomy of the situation.

To reach this detailed understanding, many decision makers find it useful to break a problem into a series of subproblems, analyze the subproblems, and then recombine them into an analyzed whole. Five guidelines aid the diagnostic process:

1. *Differentiate between events and the language used to describe them.* People's perceptions are often imprecise, and so is the language they use to describe their perceptions. Managers should make sure that they are looking at an event and not at how it might be interpreted— perhaps incorrectly—by others. For example, Eric Johns, a union leader, stated that "the labor-management conflict that has characterized this place for the past three years stems directly from management's continued exploitation of the workforce." This characterization of labor-management problems is not an objective analysis of the problems or their causes. It is more a description of the speaker's perception of events than of true causes and effects.

2. *Specify the degree of precision of available information.* Managers must identify whether the available information is fact or opinion, and they must evaluate the degree of certainty that surrounds the problem. For example, Sarah Morgan, a sales manager for Stringer Business Systems was overheard commenting to her boss, "Mark Johnson is lazy, and, as a result, he is by far our poorest salesperson." To diagnose the problem, the sales manager's boss must know whether he is dealing with the sales manager's opinion or with actual performance data.

3. *Determine underlying causes* rather than placing blame or giving credit. In other words, decision makers must try to understand rather than to judge, to investigate the dynamics of the situation, and to determine its cause. If Mark Johnson's performance is low, is it because he is lazy—or because he was assigned a difficult territory? In one organization, the marketing department blames the people in research and development (R&D) for failing to take into account customer preferences in their design of a new toothpaste that has not caught on. The R&D department blames marketing for not selling the product hard enough. Blaming, however, sheds little light on the real reasons the product has failed. Successful problem diagnosis entails looking for causes and not placing blame or giving credit.

4. *Look for several causes.* Problems and opportunities usually have several causes. When people identify only a single cause for a problem, they are probably overlooking information that might help them formulate a solution. A union leader who blames management for being exploitive, a sales manager who claims that a salesman's poor performance is due to his laziness, marketers who blame R&D for failing to consider consumer tastes, and R&D people who blame marketing for failing to sell a product are not only blaming, but they are stopping their analysis prematurely at a single cause of a problem.

5. *Be specific.* Managers should explicitly formulate their diagnosis of a problem and state it so that they and others can understand as clearly as possible what the problem is and why it has arisen. In the previous

example, it would have been helpful for Sarah Morgan to specify that Mark Johnson's poor sales performance is due to a lack of motivation, to the unattractiveness of the rewards that are associated with good sales performance, and to distractions caused by problems that he is having at home.[6]

Identifying and understanding a problem can be extremely difficult. Problems and crises frequently introduce uncertainty and discomfort. For these reasons, people sometimes avoid or take problem definition for granted. They tend to gloss over the first step in the decision-making process and rush to Step Two.

Step Two: Generating Alternative Solutions   After a problem has been identified, diagnosed, and understood, a manager is ready to move into the second stage of the decision-making process—the generation of a set of alternative solutions. (Chapter 8, "Tools for Planning and Decision Making," describes a number of useful techniques for identifying decision alternatives.) In developing these solutions, decision makers first must specify the goals that they hope to achieve through their decision. Are they trying to reduce costs? improve product quality? increase sales? Once they have determined their goals, they can search for alternative means of reaching them.

Alternative solutions generally fall into two categories: existing solutions and custom solutions. **Existing solutions** are alternatives that have been used (or at least considered) by other decision makers in similar situations. For example, many organizations purchase programs—compensation systems, for instance—that have worked well in other organizations. Existing solutions are frequently adapted, with or without modification, to new situations. Existing solutions sometimes prove an easy way out—even too easy a way out. Managers frequently rely more on existing solutions and their own previous experiences than on fresh information for making their decisions.[7] In failing to consider fresh information, managers might define problems poorly and identify solutions inadequately.

Custom solutions are developed specifically for a current situation. It is at this stage that creativity can be introduced into the decision-making

Reprinted with special permission of King Features Syndicate, Inc.

process, whether through a creative adaptation of existing alternatives, a combination of alternatives, or the development of new alternatives.

Step Three: Evaluating Alternatives Once managers have derived a list of alternative solutions, their task is to evaluate them. Research, experimentation, and drawing on experience are common tools for this stage of the decision process. To begin, they should estimate how well each alternative would meet the specified goals and objectives. For example, how well would each alternative be expected to reduce costs, improve quality, or increase sales? The goal is to evaluate how satisfactory each alternative is.

After evaluating how satisfactory the alternatives are, managers need to focus on their strengths and weaknesses, pros and cons, and latent and manifest consequences. In addition, it is important to evaluate the feasibility of each alternative. In doing so, managers should ask such questions as:

- How much would each alternative cost, both in money and in human resources?
- Would the alternative be acceptable to those who would have to make it work?
- What risks are associated with the alternative?
- Are there any legal, regulatory, social responsibility, or ethical barriers associated with the alternative?
- How would this alternative influence other aspects of the organization positively or negatively?

Step Three of the decision-making process usually eliminates many of the alternatives on the managers' list. Some are eliminated because they are not satisfactory. An alternative might be eliminated, for example, because evaluation suggests that it would increase rather than decrease costs. Other alternatives are eliminated because they offer too much risk or uncertainty. Increasing the size of the O-rings on the space shuttle's engine just before liftoff, for example, would be too risky an alternative if the effects of such a change have never been tested. Still other alternatives simply are not feasible. Evaluation might, for example, identify a law that prohibits an alternative or might suggest an adverse social consequence to a particular alternative.

Step Four: Choosing an Alternative If, after all of the possible solutions have been evaluated, managers have only one remaining viable alternative, their decision has essentially been made for them. Usually, however, several alternatives remain under consideration after the evaluation process; therefore, the final stage in the decision-making process involves making judgments and choices.

Some quantitative and qualitative tools to help managers select an alternative are presented in Chapter 8. The tools of the trade for decision makers can only help managers choose from among alternatives, however. Managers must ultimately decide what they want to accomplish in making a decision. There are three decision criteria: optimizing, maximizing, and satisficing. If managers hope to **optimize,** they want to find the

FIGURE 7.3   *Decision Strategies*

Outcome Preferences

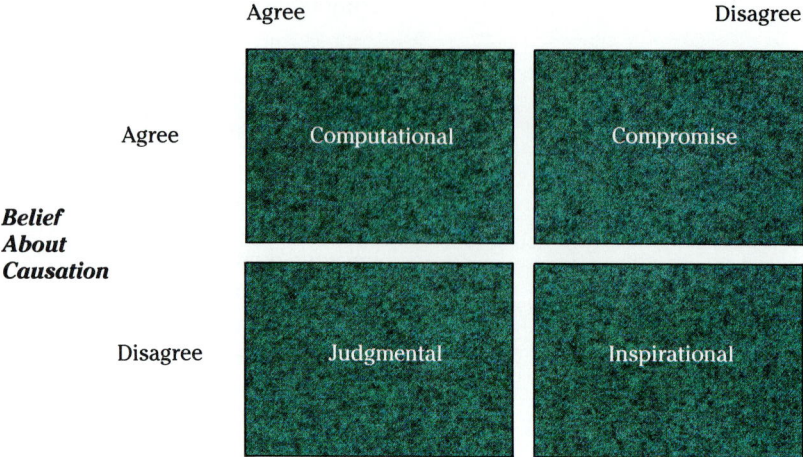

best possible decision. To **maximize,** managers must make a decision which meets the maximum number of criteria. To **satisfice,** managers try only to find the first satisfactory solution. As explained in later sections, different approaches to decision making promote the selection of one of these decision criteria. Each is unique, and the nature of the decision-making process can change substantially, depending on which approach a manager chooses. It usually takes more time, for example, to maximize than to satisfice—and still more time to optimize (if this is even possible).

A Contingency Approach: The Need for Flexibility   The variety of situations confronting managers calls for various approaches to decision making. As depicted in Figure 7.3, the appropriateness of a decision strategy is determined by two situational conditions: preferences about outcomes and belief about causation.[8]

The *computational* decision-making approach is a rational, mechanical process. Situations calling for the computational strategy include when there is agreement on the desired outcomes and the existence of a well-developed body of knowledge that instructs an organization on how to proceed. Under these conditions, relevant information, including facts regarding the problem and desired outcomes, is turned over to an expert, who may be a manager, staff manager, or subordinate. This expert interprets the existing body of knowledge, makes the decision, and directs others on how to respond. When Ford Motor Company detects a safety problem with one of its cars, managers do not solve the problem. Instead, engineers are instructed to apply the technology they control to develop an engineering solution to the problem.

The *judgmental* decision-making approach is used when managers agree on their goals but have no body of knowledge to guide them on how to achieve these goals. They, therefore, ask experts to share their knowledge, ideas, and opinions and to use their creativity to develop solutions in the face of uncertainty. The judgment resulting from that group's interaction is used to arrive at a decision. For example, when Chrysler's managers noted a drop in station wagon sales in the late 1970s, they sought a wide range of input and generated many alternative solutions. The judgmental solution they settled on from among the possibilities was to develop a minivan (possibly the best decision made by Chrysler in the last two decades).

In the *compromise* decision-making approach, individuals or groups who disagree about preferred outcomes bargain. This strategy calls for broad-based participation but a limit on the size of the actual negotiating group. In order to move forward effectively toward a resolution of their conflict over goals, each interest group selects a spokesperson to represent them in the group decision-making process. This strategy calls for participation through representation, with each coalition agreeing that its top priority must be resolution of conflict. In addition, it is important that each group have access to all relevant information and veto power over emerging decisions. The ultimate aim is to reach a compromise for which each group member feels ownership, such as when departments agree on a release date for a new product.

The *inspirational* decision-making approach is characterized by extremely high levels of uncertainty, because there is no agreement on either goals or methods. Such conditions frequently cause managers to procrastinate in the hope that the problem will go away. This type of decision situation calls for a commitment to finding a resolution to the impasse, for continued dialogue, and for the open and complete sharing of information. It also calls for creativity and intuition. Finding ways to reduce the national deficit, for example, calls for the inspirational approach. The structured techniques discussed in Chapter 8 can aid inspirational decision making.

The contingency decision model suggests that managers need to be flexible in their approaches to decision making. Under some conditions, they need to be able to make decisions and direct others. At other times, they need to allow other experts to make decisions and provide the needed directions. Still other conditions may call for any one of a number of group decision processes.

Research also suggests that there are several organizational factors that should be considered as managers decide on an appropriate decision-making strategy. Decision making is typically done on a hierarchical basis, with managers directing the activities of subordinates: when a decision is being made for a large department, when there is little task uncertainty, when there is an established set of procedures that defines how an activity should be performed, and when there is little interdependence among those who will be affected by the decision. Group forms of decision making are used effectively when there are high levels of interdependence among those who will be affected by the decision, when group size is small, and when task uncertainty is high. Finally, individual employees are likely to exercise high levels of discretion in the performance of their jobs under conditions of task uncertainty.[9]

Managerial Practices

Although the decision-making models described to this point show how decisions should be made, many managers do not actually follow these models. Many behaviors are not conscious in nature and are driven by habit. Many people have not learned when it pays to be systematic in decision making. A habitual or intuitive response is not necessarily bad; a

Intuition in Management: If It Feels Good, Do It

Decisions should be based on the best information available, coupled with a decision maker's best judgment and intuition. "What frightens me about business schools is that they train their students to sound wonderful. But it's necessary to find out if there's judgment behind their language."[1] This concern, expressed by Robert Bernstein, chairperson of Random House publishers, preceded his argument that the best managers must be more than "business-school-glib, number-crunching, fast-trackers."[2]

What is the all-too-often-missing element? *Intuition:* the ability to identify good decisions through gut feelings. Although there is no question that management is a science and that people can use sophisticated databases to provide the information they need to make decisions, these scientific techniques cannot replace a manager's intuition in making a final decision. Managers should take advantage of the scientific techniques available, but, as Roger Straus, president of Farrar, Straus & Giroux, says, it is a shame if the availability of scientific methods leads to "shunting intuition aside and going by the numbers."[3]

> *The best managers . . .*
> *are willing to use*
> *intuition as an important*
> *decision-making tool.*

So important is the role of intuition in management that Roy Rowan, writer and editor at *Fortune* magazine, has recently written a book entitled *The Intuitive Manager.*[4] In this book,

Rowan argues that, even though logic and analysis are important for effective management, "[T]he last step to success frequently requires a daring intuitive leap."[5] In today's business world, decisions rarely can be made with certainty. There is seldom one correct answer to a problem. The best managers recognize this and are willing to use intuition as an important decision-making tool. Eden Collinsworth, publisher of Arbor House enthusiastically agrees with Rowan that the most effective managers are not afraid to combine the intuitive art of management with science: "People may think of me as decisive and businesslike. I think of myself as artistic."[6]

1. R. Rowan (25 April 1986), The intuition factor, *Publishers Weekly*, 29.

2. *Ibid.*

3. Rowan, 30.

4. R. Rowan (1986), The intuitive manager, Boston: Little, Brown.

5. Rowen, The intuition factor, 30.

6. *Ibid.*

manager who has internalized the goals of an organization and has developed a good sense for the management process may be able to handle uncomplicated problems quite easily from instinct. In this approach lies part of the art of management. It is important for managers to be able to diagnose the situations that they face, to judge the importance of a decision, and to determine whether to decide systematically or instinctively. (See "A Closer Look: Intuition in Management.")

Not all decisions facing managers are of equal importance. A decision about a habitually tardy employee clearly differs from a decision about marketing a new product. Problems and opportunities may vary in terms of the size and length of a commitment stemming from a particular decision, the flexibility of the plans emerging from the decision, the amount of impact a particular decision carries, and who the decision affects. The need for a more systematic approach to decision making increases as the size and length of commitment expands, as the flexibility of plans diminishes, as uncertainty increases, and as the human impact of the decision rises.

Sometimes managers have to make decisions under extremely high levels of uncertainty. The problems, alternatives, solutions, and goals are ill defined. Cause-and-effect relationships are not clearly identified. The decision context is turbulent. The decision-making approach frequently used under these conditions has been called the "garbage can" model.[10]

Under such circumstances, problem identification and solution may not even be related to each other. Some problems are never solved, even when solutions are available. Solutions may be adopted independently of a recognized problem or in the absence of an agreed-on set of goals. Decisions are random rather than unfolding in a logical, organized, and systematic manner. The organization and its management process becomes like a garbage can into which problems, solutions, participants, and choices are haphazardly tossed. Occasionally, a problem, solution, participant, and choice happen to connect at one point; in that case, the problem may be solved.[11] Usually, though, the garbage can approach to decision making "stinks."

Despite the fact that a systematic approach to decision making has been proven effective, studies have shown that managers seldom progress smoothly through the stages of decision making.[12] The process is marked by frequent interruptions, delays, and periods of acceleration. Failures due to undesired results and poor planning frequently force a return to earlier stages of the process.

Individual Decision Making

Four general models of the individual as a decision maker have been identified (see Table 7.1).[13] The first of these, the *irrational person model*, suggests that many decisions stem from a variety of fears, anxieties, and drives.[14] The second model, the *creative/self-actualizing model*, assumes

TABLE 7.1   *Four Decision-Making Models*

The Irrational Person	The Creative/Self-Actualizing Person
Has a variety of fears, anxieties, and drives	Pursues total development of the inner self
Decisions are driven by the unconscious motives underlying these fears and anxieties	Decisions are driven by desire to develop the self even at the expense of external factors
The Rational/Economic Person	**The Administrative Person**
Is rational and deals with objective facts.	Is aware of only certain alternatives
Is economically motivated	Is limited by restricted cognitive capacity
Decisions are driven by objective rationality and a search for the best possible alternative	Decisions are driven by a desire to identify and select the first acceptable alternative.

that individuals pursue total development of their inner selves rather than look for an external goal, such as profit seeking.[15] Contemporary managers, however, deal mostly with the last two models: the *classical model* and the *behavioral model.*

A Classical (Rational/Economic) Decision-Making Model

Classical, or rational/economic, decision-making models were most popular during the early part of this century. They portray decision makers as rational in behavior, as dealing with objective and verifiable facts, and as economically motivated. They depict decision makers as completely informed; as infinitely sensitive; and, therefore, as making decisions under conditions of **objective rationality.** By knowing all possible alternatives and their probable consequences, decision makers rationally select the "one best" alternative. This classical decision-making model discounts as unnecessary the effects of the attitudes, emotions, or personal preferences of the decision maker.

A Behavioral (Administrative) Decision-Making Model

The ideal is different from the reality, however. Where the classical model argues that decision makers are aware of all possible alternatives, the behavioral, or administrative, decision-making theory proposes that this is seldom the case, and that it is unrealistic to think otherwise. According to this model, decision makers cannot possibly be aware of all consequences for each alternative, or their probabilities of occurring. Whereas classical theory argued that decision makers should make decisions that meet the greatest number of criteria, behavioral theory suggests that most decision makers actually choose the first satisfactory solution that they identify. That is, they satisfice.

According to Nobel-Prize winner Herbert Simon's administrative model of decision making, people operate in the realm of **bounded rationality.**[16] They try to behave rationally within the limits of their information-processing capabilities and within the context of their attitudes and emotions. They engage in restricted searches for information; have limited information-processing capabilities; rely on familiar sources of information; and, as a result, construct simplified models of reality out of which their decisions are made.

Individual Differences in Decision Making

People differ in their styles of making decisions. Some people make decisions quickly, others slowly. Some people consider a large amount of information before reaching a decision, others a small amount. Although it is not fully understood why people behave differently when making decisions, their cognitive and personality attributes appear to account for a number of these individual differences.

A person's decision-making style is affected by his or her personality and motivations. Some people make decisions quickly and confidently, while others are more cautious and careful to avoid risk.

Cognitive Attributes   An individual's cognitive attributes appear to affect the judgmental aspects of decision making. Relevant cognitive processes include intelligence, learning, remembering, and thinking. These cognitive attributes affect the ability to engage in inductive and deductive reasoning, to deal in the abstract, to handle information, and to generate ideas. They affect problem recognition, comprehension, and diagnosis; the storage, retrieval, and assimilation of information for the development of alternative solutions; and the capability of storing, retrieving, and processing information for the evaluation of alternatives. Differences in intelligence mean that people differ in their information-processing capacities. Some people can process only relatively small amounts of information before becoming overloaded, and they base their decisions on relatively small amounts of specific information. Decision makers with greater capacity tend to become more abstract decision makers.

Personality Attributes   Personality and motivational attributes tend to affect decision-making *style*. Style differences, for example, are reflected in the speed with which decisions are made, the level of risk taking, and the level of confidence attached to the decision once it has been made.

Several personality and motivational factors have been related to decision-making style. Those with a high propensity toward risk tend to make rapid decisions because they process less information and spend less time evaluating information before making a decision. People with dogmatic personalities possess fixed, narrow perspectives on life and, thus, often consider only the small set of alternatives that fits their existing view of the world. They make their decisions quickly and with great confidence, and they are highly resistant to change because they are convinced that they know how things are and should be. Individuals who are impatient and competitive tend to process information quickly and aggressively and, thereby, make decisions quickly. They are often better at making short-term decisions. People with calm, reflective personalities tend to be very good at long-term planning and decision making.

Decision makers also differ in their ability to accept uncertainty, a personality characteristic called *tolerance for ambiguity*. Not surprisingly, people with low tolerance for ambiguity are more likely to select alternatives with fairly certain consequences. They are not risk takers. In fact, people with very low tolerance for ambiguity tend to be *problem avoiders*. If something unexpected occurs, problem avoiders often ignore the first signs of a problem, causing them to function poorly at the symptom-detection stage of decision making; thus, they often progress far into a decision situation without being completely aware of the circumstances surrounding it.

At intermediate levels of tolerance for ambiguity are *problem solvers*. Rather than taking extensive steps to prevent problems, these individuals anticipate difficulties and deal with them as they arise. Such a person is usually one of the first to recognize the need for a decision and is likely to respond quickly. People who have a high tolerance for ambiguity tend to be *problem seekers*. Because problem seekers are so comfortable with novelty and uncertainty, they actually seek challenges of this type and derive great satisfaction from conquering uncertainty. Problem seekers often behave as entrepreneurs in an organization. They go out of their way to find potential opportunities and then attempt to develop decisions which capitalize on them.

Group Decision Making

Spotted on an old Volkswagen minibus in New Orleans was a bumper sticker that read: *GROUPS DO IT BETTER!!!* It is a common belief that groups make better decisions than do individuals. Many believe that two heads are better than one, that people involved in decision making feel a sense of ownership in the decision, and that group decision making is

TABLE 7.2   *Assets and Liabilities of Group Decision Making*

Assets	Liabilities
Greater knowledge and information	Negative social pressure
More perspectives on issues	Premature decisions
More alternatives identified	Individual domination
Great acceptance of decisions	Interference of personal goals
Better problem comprehension	

Assets or Liabilities
Disagreements can generate ideas or cause hard feelings.
Diverse interests can broaden perspectives or cause conflict.
Increased risk taking can be beneficial or costly.
Increased time spent can improve decisions or waste time.

Source: N. R. F. Maier (1970), Assets and liabilities in group problem solving: The need for an integrative function, in N. R. F. Maier, ed., *Problem solving and creativity: In individuals and groups*, Belmont, CA: Brooks/Cole, 431–44.

safer because everyone shares in the risk. For these and other reasons, group decision making abounds in organizations: committees are formed, task forces are constructed, and quality circles are installed. Groups often make excellent decisions, but they can make unwise and ill-fated decisions as well. Why the mixed results?

Group decision making has both assets and liabilities.[17] A thorough understanding of these assets and liabilities can help you, as a manager, determine when to encourage or discourage group decision making and how to improve the quality of group decisions (see Table 7.2). Perhaps that bumper sticker in New Orleans should have read: *GROUPS DO IT BETTER: SOMETIMES!*

Assets and Liabilities of Group Decision Making

What advantages do groups have over individuals in making decisions? Some assets of group decisions include:

- *A greater wealth of knowledge and information.* When many people are involved in decision making, they apply a greater accumulation of information and experience to the decision than that possessed by any one member alone.
- *More individual styles.* Most of us develop familiar patterns for decision making. If each individual possesses his or her unique way of searching for information, analyzing problems, and the like, group decision processes provide more angles of attack at each stage of the decision-making process.
- *A greater number of alternatives.* More people generate more potential solutions to a decision.
- *Increased acceptance of a decision.* Participative decision making breeds ego involvement. The more people who accept a decision and are committed to it, the more likely the decision is to be implemented.
- *A better comprehension of a problem and decision.* More people understand a decision when it is reached by a group. This factor is particularly important when group members are to be involved in executing the decision.

Group decisions also pose potential liabilities:

- *Social pressure* may encourage group members to support emerging ideas blindly or may discourage them from engaging in healthy disagreements. This desire to "not rock the boat" often causes groups to focus more on reaching agreement than on making a good decision.
- *Premature decisions* can result if groups tend to evaluate alternatives immediately. Groups often choose an apparently positive alternative as soon as it is identified and fail to consider other alternatives.
- *Individual domination* can occur within a group. If the ideas and opinions of one individual overwhelm other group members, the potential assets of group decision making are reduced. In addition, other group members can be resentful if they are prevented from participating fully.

- *Conflicting secondary goals* may get in the way of a group's primary goal. The primary goal of a group should be to make a quality decision. Frequently, however, individual members or one faction of the group wants its side to "win." When the desire to win conflicts with the group's primary goal, the quality of decisions suffers. Too much energy is devoted to winning and too little to finding a good decision.

Several group factors can serve either as assets or liabilities, depending on the specific situation:

- *Disagreement* between group members can provide the spark needed for the generation of new ideas, but it can also lead to hard feelings and threaten the existence of the group.
- *Diverse, conflicting interests* of group members can enhance the range of decision alternatives by providing a variety of perspectives on the situation under discussion. When deciding whether to manufacture and market a new product, for example, it can be useful to have a group with representatives from finance, marketing, production, and human resource departments. This diversity, however, can also produce conflict that threatens the group and, therefore, the quality of its decisions.
- *Risk taking.* Groups are prone to making decisions that are riskier than the decisions made by individuals. Although risky decisions are sometimes desirable (as in many entrepreneurial decisions), in other situations the costs associated with risk are too high.
- *Groups often require more time* than do individuals to come to a final decision. This tendency is a drawback because it uses more resources and slows the decision process. It can also be beneficial, however, if a group takes the time to understand the decision situation and to follow a good decision-making model thoroughly.

The arguments for and against group decision making suggest that choosing this approach requires careful thought. Managers must evaluate whether, for a particular situation, the assets outweigh the liabilities and whether they can simultaneously take advantage of the assets and control the liabilities.

Group Properties

Several characteristics of groups can influence the decision-making process. These characteristics include the size of the group, the physical arrangements used for group meetings, the degree of homogeneity within the group, and the level of cohesion within the group. For managers to use groups effectively as decision-making bodies requires that they manage each of these properties. They must consciously choose the size of the group, consciously construct a homogeneous or heterogeneous group, and decide whether working with a cohesive group is important to the process.

Group Size The size of a group can substantially influence group activity and effectiveness.[18] For example, a group of five to seven members is usually viewed as the optimal size. When a group is larger, group members' satisfaction declines, as does their ability to achieve a consensus and the participation level of individual members. Effective, efficient leadership emerges slowly and with difficulty. To capture the assets of group decision making in large groups, effective communication and coordination systems must be developed to link the members together.

Spatial Arrangements Researchers have repeatedly observed that where people are physically located when they interact strongly affects their behavior. For example, it affects the transfer of information, the conflict, and even the emergence of leaders.[19]

People sitting at a table tend to talk to those next to them and to those directly across the table, but people who sit at the opposite corners of long, narrow tables have difficulty speaking to one another. This restriction in the flow of information frequently splinters the group into cliques, and groups with cliques operate differently from those without them. Cliques may conflict with one another, with unpredictable results. Such a restriction might lead to creative decision making—but it can also induce guarded sharing of information. Cliques may become competitive rather than cooperative. They may be unable to achieve a consensus or to arrive at any decision.

Group Homogeneity/Heterogeneity Group members can be similar or different in such characteristics as education, work experience, aptitudes, and attitudes. Homogeneous groups and heterogeneous groups have both assets and liabilities.[20] For example, a homogeneous group encourages the building of good interpersonal relationships, and so, communication within the group tends to be better, group coordination is easier, and reaching consensus is more likely than in a heterogeneous group. Under most circumstances, homogeneous groups are also easier for managers to coordinate.

Heterogeneous groups have one major advantage, however, over homogeneous groups. Because the members of heterogeneous groups are different from one another, they bring to the group a greater variety of

Group size and spatial arrangements influence employee interaction and, subsequently, overall group effectiveness.

information and ideas. Research has frequently shown that decision quality increases as a result of such diversity.[21]

Group Cohesiveness   Group *cohesiveness* is the psychological glue that holds a group together (see Chapter 13). In a cohesive group, members are loyal to the group, tend to identify with each other, and want to work for group goals.[22] Effective and efficient decision making is usually more difficult to achieve in noncohesive groups than in cohesive groups. Noncohesive groups struggle more with communication, power relationships, and attempts to get to know and understand one another. The quality of decisions made in noncohesive groups may, however, benefit from the presence of conflict and the low levels of pressure toward conformity. Highly cohesive groups tend to make decisions that meet group needs, but unless these needs are consistent with those of the organization, a highly cohesive group may quickly and efficiently reach decisions that can damage the organization.

Group Phenomena

Managers should be aware of several interesting phenomena that affect group decision making.

Social Presence   You have probably noticed that you often feel and behave differently when there are other people around than when you are alone. This difference is due to the psychological and physical arousal caused by the presence of others. Have you ever been in a play or given a talk in front of a large group? Did your heart race? Did your palms sweat? Did you feel extremely alert? These are all reactions to the presence of others.

Under some conditions, decision making is enhanced (**social facilitation**) by the presence of others. Under other conditions, it is impaired (**social impairment**). The difference largely depends on the nature of the task, the level of arousal produced by the presence of others, and an individual's tolerance for high levels of arousal.

In general it has been observed that increases in arousal facilitate individual performance. For example, a person might be able to think of more solutions to a problem in the presence of others than when working alone. There is, however, a critical point at which additional arousal overwhelms the individual and performance suffers. This critical point differs from person to person and across tasks (as illustrated in Figure 7.4). For easy tasks, when people are dealing with familiar things, their performance improves, even with very high levels of arousal. For difficult or new tasks, however, performance begins to suffer at moderate or higher levels of arousal.

Managers should capitalize on this important psychological phenomenon in decision-making groups. If decision making involves simple, routine, or familiar situations, for example, managers should permit individuals to work in the presence of others—the resulting arousal will help increase their performance levels. If decision making deals with complex, difficult and unfamiliar situations, managers should urge the activity to be done privately, because the presence of others probably will

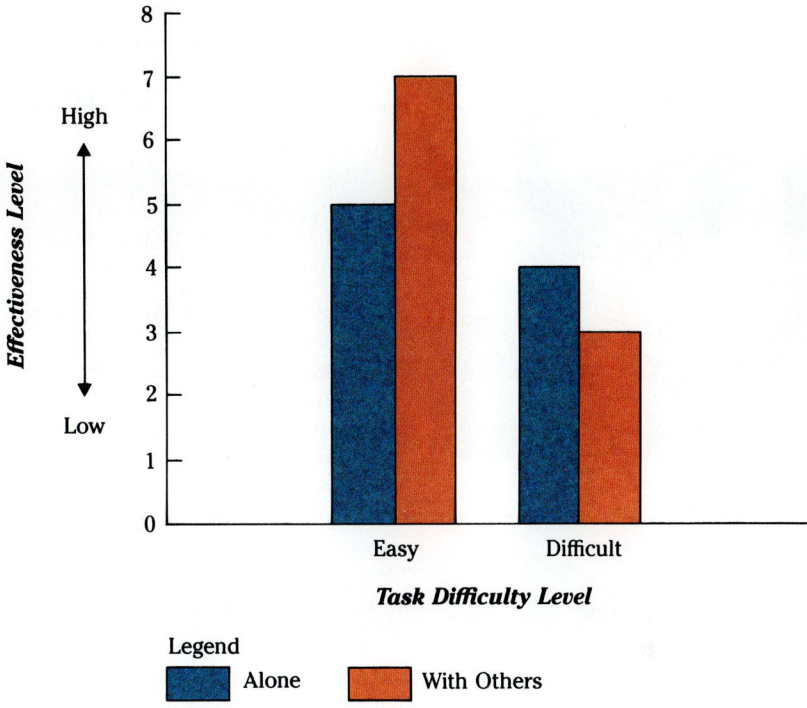

FIGURE 7.4 *The Effects of the Presence of Others on Task Performance*

Legend
Alone   With Others

impair effective decision making due to overarousal. It is important to recognize that overarousal in group settings may inhibit the ability of some individuals to perform to their capacity. Steps can be taken to reduce the likelihood of overarousal and to take advantage of the social facilitation process. For example, managers can direct individuals to write down their ideas in the presence of others rather than express them verbally.

Group Shift An interesting series of studies conducted by social psychologists has documented that group decisions often are riskier than those made by individual group members.[23] Although **cautious shifts** occur, it is far more common to find **risky shifts** in group decision making. Several factors explain why group shifts occur.

First, through group discussion and the sharing of ideas and information, *familiarization* with a decision situation increases for group members. As individual group members become more familiar with, and less uncertain about, decision goals and objectives and the probable outcomes of alternatives, they pursue alternatives that they previously considered too risky.

Second, *diffusion of responsibility* often occurs in groups. Because there are several people in a group, each individual tends to feel less personally responsible for the group's decisions. Because each believes that other group members are also responsible, each individual tends to accept decisions that are riskier than he or she would have made alone. Students in an investment class at the University of Wisconsin, for example, share the management of a portfolio worth over $200,000. As a group, the students tend to make investment decisions that are riskier than they would make individually. This shift seems to arise from a combination of the belief that "other group members will prevent a bad decision"

A CLOSER LOOK

Failure Through Isolation: The Challenger Disaster

Before January 28, 1986, twenty-four space shuttle flights had been successfully completed. There hadn't been as much as a single injury to any crew member. On that cold day at Cape Canaveral, final preparations were made for the twenty-fifth launching. On board were seven men and women who placed their lives in the hands of NASA decision makers. At 11:38 A.M. eastern standard time, the shuttle *Challenger* was launched into the bright Florida sky. Seventy-four seconds later, the shuttle exploded, and all seven aboard were killed.

What caused the fatal accident of the spaceship *Challenger?* Did the mechanical failure of an O-ring on one of the solid fuel booster rockets cost the lives of seven people? Yes and no. It is true that the explosion occurred when the O-ring failed, but most agree that the *reason* the accident occurred was because of a faulty

decision by NASA to launch under adverse conditions:

[I]t has become clear that the disaster represents a managerial failure. . . . [T]he tragically flawed decision to launch was no fluke. It was the almost predictable result of a pattern of mismanagement that has spread throughout the agency. . . . The people at the top ended up isolated, a grimly instructive example of a problem that can overtake any organization, governmental or corporate.[1]

Before the launch of *Challenger*, engineers at Morton Thiokol, the company that made the solid fuel booster, analyzed weather conditions and unanimously concluded that a launch would not be safe: the O-rings might fail. Repeatedly challenged by Lawrence Mulloy, chief of the solid rocket booster program at the Marshall Space Flight Center, Thiokol engineers repeated their concerns and stood their ground. Finally, Mulloy went over the heads of the engineers and convinced Joe Kilminster, Thiokol's vice-president for space booster programs to sign a launch go-ahead. The rest is history.

How could such a poor decision have been made? NASA was aware that failure of a primary O-ring probably would cause disaster. Engineers with presumably the greatest technical knowledge believed that the rings

might fail under the prevailing weather conditions. Apparently, Mulloy changed his decision strategy. He required "proof of probable failure" to abort a launch rather than "evidence of probable success" to initiate it. In addition, those top decision makers who made the ultimate decision to launch were isolated from the lower-level engineers and never informed about their concerns. The NASA decision makers had been lulled into complacency by their twenty-four successes.

Top decision makers were isolated from the lower-level engineers and never informed. . . .

The decision-making process was flawed: "This was an absolutely preventable thing. This accident never should have happened. Never."[2] "NASA's highest decision makers had either not heard about the contractors' fears or ignored them. So *Challenger* blasted into the Florida sky on its brief, one-way flight to oblivion."[3]

1. NASA's challenge: Ending isolation at the top (12 May 1986), *Fortune*, 26.
2. A serious deficiency (10 March 1986), *Time*, 38.
3. A serious deficiency, 42.

and the feeling that "if the decision does not work out well, the group will be blamed—not me personally."

Third, most groups have at least one member who is willing to make riskier decisions than are other group members. This can be any member of a group. These high risk takers also tend to be *risk persuaders*. They tend to dominate the group and effectively convince others to take greater risk; thus, the group decision tends to be almost as risky as that which would have been made by the greatest risk taker in the group. (See "A Closer Look: Failure Through Isolation.")

Finally, both risky and cautious shifts can be caused by *cultural values*. Many group members strive for approval and status in the eyes of other group members. To this end, they try to behave in a socially approved fashion. When the cultural values of a group (or organization) favor risk, individuals perceive this and take greater risks in the group than they would in making decisions alone. When group values favor caution, individuals take less risk in the group than they would alone. They hope to gain approval from the group by being on the leading edge of the group's values. Social psychologists refer to this as the *group polarization effect*.[24] Because each member of the group tends to be influenced in a similar fashion, the group decision is often either quite risky or quite cautious. Most people experience group polarization effects through social peer pressure, such as when they are influenced to drink more alcohol than they ordinarily would if alone and proceed to drive when they should not. The group known as SADD (Students Against Drunk Driving) is trying to capitalize on the same phenomenon in a cautious direction by presenting group values that discourage drinking and driving.

Groupthink **Groupthink** describes a phenomenon that can cause highly capable groups to make terrible decisions.[25] According to Irving Janis, groupthink (discussed more thoroughly in Chapter 13) is based on a group drive to obtain consensus at almost any cost. This desire for unanimity can be so strong that dissent is almost completely eliminated. Groups engaged in groupthink search incompletely for alternatives when they make decisions, and they only superficially evaluate the few alternatives that they do consider. They are unlikely to reexamine a decision in light of new information and seldom reconsider a rejected alternative. They rarely consult experts when making a decision. They ignore facts that do not support the group's position and overlook risks.

Groupthink was at work in the 1970s when U.S. President Richard Nixon and his advisers decided to launch a cover-up of the Watergate break-in. Despite clear evidence to the contrary, they refused to accept that the cover-up would fail. Group members rallied behind Nixon's claims that what they had done was for the good of the country, and they chose not to raise individual concerns in group meetings. When objections were raised, they were quickly quashed. As a result, Nixon's presidency faltered and failed.

In short, groupthink leads to bad—sometimes catastrophic—decisions. It is interesting to note that groupthink is more likely to occur in highly cohesive groups than in less cohesive groups. (Chapter 13 explores a variety of remedies for groupthink.)

When Should Groups Make Decisions?

Organizations are social systems; much of what goes on inside organizations takes place in groups. Because, as you have seen, group decision making has both strengths and weaknesses, managers must carefully consider whether to use individuals or groups in the decision-making process. Managers should consider the following guidelines:

1. If a problem is of moderate difficulty, groups have a clear advantage over an individual. When a problem is extremely easy, a single individual can probably solve it well. When a problem is extremely difficult, a group is likely to have trouble reaching a consensus—although it may ultimately produce a better solution.

2. Problems that can be divided lend themselves to group problem solving. Information about various facets of a problem can be collected by subgroups and later assembled during the final stages of the decision-making process.

3. Groups with five to seven members are the most desirable, and a range of four to ten members is acceptable. Groups that are too small cannot be highly productive. Groups that are too large tend to split into competing factions.

4. Groups made up of individuals who differ in experience, interest, and personal characteristics tend to be more productive than groups of similar individuals.

5. Partly structured interaction improves group functioning. Group leaders must encourage the free expression of ideas (from the majority as well as the minority) and prevent the premature evaluation of ideas.

6. Extreme status differences between group members—for example, president and secretary together—can inhibit group processes. Groups should be constructed without strong status differences, or various safeguards and inducements for low-status participants should be built into the process.

7. Groups that are too cohesive can bog down in groupthink and become overly concerned with presenting a united front to outsiders. Moderately cohesive groups with a good communication system and an appropriate set of norms can function effectively.[26]

The preceding guidelines should help managers obtain the best results from their groups; however, the creation of groups is no panacea for the problems of decision making, as they bring liabilities as well as assets into the process. The best managers recognize this and assign decision-making responsibilities to individuals or groups based on the characteristics of each situation.

Problems in the Decision-Making Process

Regardless of whether decisions are made individually or in groups, several problems confront managers in decision situations. Two of the most common are the tendency to misunderstand a situation and to rush the decision-making process.

Misunderstanding a Situation

To understand a decision situation, a manager must coordinate and organize a great deal of relevant information. If this information is incomplete or organized poorly, the manager may easily misconstrue the

Managers must coordinate and organize a great deal of information in order to understand a decision situation.

situation. Consider the case of Bill Bass, a manager inspecting information about a problematic product return level. If Bill sees information on returns organized by day of shipment and by quality-control inspector, he might conclude that the problem is linked to two particular quality-control inspectors who seem to have a heavy workload on Mondays. If the information is organized by customer, Bill will see that most of the returns are from one large customer whose regular standing order is always filled from the Monday morning production run.

Although it can be relatively straightforward to organize *concrete* information about costs, schedules, and units produced, the sheer quantity of such information can make it next to impossible to make sense out of it all. Giving meaning to *abstract* information is even more difficult. Because abstract information is more difficult to identify, it frequently goes unnoticed, and problems that appear through abstract signals—low job satisfaction, for example—often go unrecognized.

Perceptions which influence the understanding of decision situations vary from individual to individual. In addition, some individuals have limited information processing capabilities, which means they only partially understand situations. You often see what you are trained to see, or what you want or need to see. As a consequence, your perceptions of and reactions to situations aren't always accurate.

Managers may also misinterpret a decision situation if they mistake the symptoms of a problem for the problem itself. Diane Gray is a manager who has identified a problem of high absenteeism among her employees. High absenteeism may be only a symptom of an underlying problem. Perhaps employees are choosing not to come to work because they are highly dissatisfied. If so, any attempt by Diane to control absenteeism, such as docking her employees' wages for all unapproved absences, may force people to appear for work but does not address the underlying problem of job dissatisfaction. The problem, of course, remains and soon manifests in other guises, such as work slowdowns. To define this problem as high absenteeism is a mistake and hampers the decision-making process.

Rushing the Decision-Making Process

For many reasons, perhaps to save money or to avoid the uncertainty associated with problems, both individual and group decision makers often tend to rush the decision-making process. The results are inadequately defined problems, limited searches for and development of possible solutions, and inadequately evaluated courses of action.

For example, a company may rush to evaluate a situation before it has been fully defined. Perhaps the company has found that its sales were lower than desired. In a rush to attack the problem, the company defines the situation as a problem of too few sales representatives. Note that the problem has been defined in terms of its solution. Inadequate problem definition, in all likelihood, will adversely constrain subsequent stages in the decision-making process (for example, the development of alternative solutions). Is the problem too few sales representatives? The managers should cast the problem in the following manner: "Our sales volume is $500,000, but we targeted it at $750,000." With the problem defined as $250,000 of unmet targeted sales, the managers can generate more possible solutions. They might hire more sales representatives, advertise more or use different advertising strategies, or market the product in different outlets. With more possible solutions, the managers are closer to solving their real problem.

Because many decision makers dislike uncertainty, they tend to overlook unusual alternatives in favor of readily available and previously used alternatives. In their haste, decision makers often overgeneralize and assume that solutions from vaguely similar situations are appropriate for new situations. Decision makers also develop a similar familiarity with certain sources of information and alternatives. Although this approach is handy and fast, these comfortable alternatives limit the range of choices.

In their eagerness to make a final decision, many decision makers collapse the alternative generation and evaluation phases of the decision-making process into a single step. In the process, they inhibit idea "hitchhiking," wherein the first idea generated stimulates the development of a second idea, and so on. When ideas can surface completely, without being cut off by the evaluation process, they serve as catalysts for the development of other—perhaps better—ideas. The second problem associated with collapsing the generation and evaluation phases is that, often, people's first ideas and thoughts are only partly formed and fall short of their full potential. Early ideas should be permitted to surface and develop fully. When decision makers simultaneously generate and evaluate ideas, those ideas tend not to mature into fully formed possibilities for solutions.

Improving Decision Making

The decision-making process can be improved by changing the roles of the individuals involved. It can also be enhanced through organizational learning—capitalizing on developing and changing employees.

Charles Perrow

Charles Perrow is a professor of sociology at Yale University. Most of his work has been in organizational analysis, with some work on social movements. He is now concerned with long-range societal dynamics as the world increasingly develops a society of organizations.

1. In retrospect, what observations would you make about the decision-making process in complex organizations under conditions like the Three Mile Island nuclear incident, the ill-fated launch of the Challenger *space shuttle, or the Chernobyl nuclear accident?*

Contrary to the President's commission on the *Challenger* accident, I think the problem was with the goals of NASA rather than the process of decision making. NASA knew the risks it was taking but took them anyway, because NASA was increasingly changing from a scientific organization into one resembling the Defense Department and its contractors. No adequate decision-making process is possible in organizations with a high degree of interactive complexity, such as nuclear power plants. Even the best-run organizations are vulnerable to the incompatible demands of being both centralized and decentralized at the same time.

2. In general, what do you feel are the most common reasons for poor organizational decision making?

The major problem is the competing uses people in and outside of organizations want to make of those organizations. Poor decision making is quite secondary to this. Poor decision making is grounded in our limited rationality; in the incompatible goals or uses to which the organization is put; and, finally, in poorly designed structures, situations, or contexts that face the decision maker.

3. Are good organizational decisions usually due to one key individual or to a group of individuals?

Neither of the above. Good decisions are due to favorable environments and resources and to the well-designed contexts in which they occur. Individuals and groups respond in terms of the context they experience; the major task of top management is to shape that context so it will get the decisions it wants, even though an outside observer may feel these are bad decisions.

4. Can managers be taught to make decisions well? If so, how?

Certainly, to a limited extent. Teaching is valuable for almost anything, but I think this is the least difficult part of decision making. People with M.B.A.'s are productive because of the combination of their social background and the prestige of the institution they go to, which then puts them into contexts in which they can have more power. What they learn in school is relatively trivial.

Improving the Roles of Individuals

Managers can take a number of steps to improve the decision-making process. They can use heterogeneous groups, for example, to expand the information base and encourage the thorough definition of problems, searches for alternatives, and evaluations of alternatives. They can use a devil's advocate—that is, someone whose role is to look at alternatives and tentative decisions and challenge them. A devil's advocate helps a group focus on the possibly undesirable consequences of some alternatives or the possibly desirable consequences of others.

Most organizations, perhaps quite unintentionally, have reward and penalty systems that discourage employees from identifying occasions to make decisions. In most organizations, people are rewarded only for doing exactly what they are told to do—perform their jobs as they have been defined—and are discouraged from experimenting with new and different methods. As a consequence, many existing problems and opportunities go unnoticed. Some organizations do, however, encourage their employees to look for new opportunities and to explore potential decision opportunities. Almost any organization can develop an internal environment that makes it safe for members to pursue new ideas. Giving employees the freedom to try new things, plus the permission to fail or to be wrong occasionally, stimulates the search for solutions and for new ways of doing things. One organization that systematically encourages employees to search for new opportunities is 3M (Minnesota Mining and Manufacturing). 3M encourages many of its employees to devote a portion of their workday to searching for opportunities. One result of this policy was an employee's development of "Post-it" notes, a phenomenally successful product that met a previously unmet need.

Training organization members in systematic decision making, providing them with the tools for collecting the necessary information, and allowing adequate time for decision making can go a long way toward improving organizational decision making. Supporting these actions with reward systems that emphasize careful, effective decision making will reinforce their importance.

Organizational Learning

A fact of organizational life is that both internal and external environments are undergoing change. In addition, for most organizations, environments are becoming increasingly complex. In order for organizations to handle the challenges placed on their decision-making and problem-solving systems, they need to develop and maintain their capacity to learn.

Organizational learning consists of identifying and using ideas from other organizations, developing ideas within the organization, and regularly monitoring organizational events. The following actions can help an organization maintain or develop a healthy capacity to learn:

Organizational learning allows an organization to handle increasingly complex challenges to its decision-making and problem-solving systems.

- An explicit commitment to educational ideas
- The promotion of policies that emphasize curiosity, experimentation, and learning; permit failure; and reward discovery
- An allocation of organizational resources to support learning
- A system for collecting, storing, and processing information
- An opening of internal boundaries so that information can flow more freely, vertically, horizontally, and diagonally within the organization
- The creation of a participative philosophy and practices to support it so that organizational members become aware of what is learned and collaborate on decision making and problem solving[27]

IBM has done an excellent job of creating an environment that nurtures organizational learning. Corporate philosophy clearly states the importance of individual education as well as institutional learning. Managers create specific work assignments that encourage creativity in dealing with both new and existing problems and opportunities. The company devotes considerable time and money to the educational process. For example, IBM provides at least forty hours of management development training opportunities for all managers every year. The company has communication systems to share information learned by one division quickly and freely with other appropriate divisions. Employees have been encouraged to interact even more with the external environment in recent years. As a result, the company is learning from the activities of professional and other business organizations.

Organizations that can handle the vast number of decision-making and problem-solving occasions that confront them are strongly influenced by their ability to learn. When managers deliberately prepare their organizations to learn, they also prepare them to make decisions and solve problems effectively. For example, IBM's active support for the organizational learning process is one of the key reasons that the company has thrived, despite many changes in the business world.

Decision Making in Review

Decision making, the process through which a course of action is chosen, is distinguished from choice making, which is simply the stage of decision making when a choice is made from among previously defined alternatives. Decision making is also different from problem solving, which includes not only the entire decision-making process, but also the steps required to implement, monitor, and maintain the results of decision making.

In a four-step decision-making model, Step One involves recognizing that a decision is needed and defining the nature of the decision situation. Step Two involves generating a list of alternative solutions. Step Three consists of evaluating these alternatives. In Step Four, alternatives are chosen. Problem solving involves these steps, plus a fifth and a sixth step that implement the chosen decision and monitor and maintain its effectiveness.

Unfortunately, the systematic decision models often are not followed, for a variety of reasons. Furthermore, there are many differences from person to person in how decisions are made. Knowledge of these differences can help managers select decision makers wisely and improve their effectiveness.

There are both assets and liabilities to group decision making, as well as factors which can go either way. Awareness of these can lead to selection of an appropriate approach and improved effectiveness, regardless of which approach is taken.

Common decision-making problems include misunderstanding a situation and rushing decisions. Managers can counteract these problems by providing access to needed information, by training individuals and groups in systematic decision making, by providing adequate time for decision making, and by offering rewards that encourage effective decision making. In addition, the most effective organizations encourage and support organizational learning to improve the effectiveness of decision making over time.

Notes

1. B. M. Bass (1983), *Organizational decision making,* Homewood, IL: Irwin, 2; H. A. Simon (1960), *The new science of management decision,* Englewood Cliffs, NJ: Prentice-Hall.

2. Bass, 1983, 3.

3. G. Huber (1980), *Managerial decision making,* Glenview, IL: Scott, Foresman, 8–9.

4. Simon, 1960.

5. P. L. Koopman, J. W. Broekhuysen, and M. Meijn (1984), Complex decision making at the organizational level, in P. J. Drenth, H. Thierry, P. J. Wilems, and C. J. DeWolff, *Handbook of work and organizational psychology,* New York: John Wiley & Sons, 831–54.

6. A. Elbing (1978), *Behavioral decisions in organizations,* Glenview, IL. Scott, Foresman, 74–83.

7. D. Isenberg (1986), Thinking and managing: A verbal protocol analysis of managerial problem solving, *Academy of Management Journal,* 29, 775–88.

8. J. D. Thompson and A. Tudin (1959), Strategies, structures, and processes of organizational decisions, in J. D. Thompson, P. B. Hammond, R. W. Hawkes, B. H. Junker, and A. Tudin, eds., *Comparative studies in administration,* Pittsburgh, PA: University of Pittsburgh Press, 195–216.

9. A. H. Van de Ven (1977), A panel study on the effects of task uncertainty, interdependence, and size on unit decision making, *Organization and Administrative Sciences,* 8, 237–53.

10. M. D. Cohen, J. G. March, and J. P. Olsen (1972), A garbage can model of organizational choice, *Administrative Science Quarterly,* 17, 1–25.

11. R. L. Daft (1983), *Organization theory and design,* St. Paul, MN: West, 361.

12. H. Mintzberg, D. Raisinghani, and A. Theoret (1976), The structure of "unstructured" decision processes, *Administrative Science Quarterly,* 21, 246–75.

13. M. J. Driver (1979), Individual decision making and creativity, in S. Kerr, ed., *Organizational behavior,* Columbus, OH: Grid Publishing, 59–91.

14. S. Freud (1920), *A general introduction to psychoanalysis,* New York: Pocket Books.

15. C. Argyris (1957), *Personality and organization,* New York: Harper & Row; C. G. Jung (1957), *The undiscovered self,* Boston: Little, Brown; A. H. Maslow (1962), *Toward a psychology of being,* Princeton: Van Nostrand; D. McGregor (1960), *The human side of enterprise,* New York: McGraw-Hill.

16. H. A. Simon (1976), *Administrative behavior,* New York: Free Press.

17. N. R. F. Maier (1970), Assets and liabilities in group problem solving: The need for an integrative function, in Norman R. F. Maier, ed., *Problem solving and creativity: In individuals and groups,* Belmont, CA: Brooks/Cole, 431–44.

18. L. L. Cummings, G. P. Huber, and E. Arendt (1974), Effects of size and spatial arrangements on group decision making, *Academy of Management Journal,* 17, 460–75.

19. Cummings, et al., 1974, 463.

20. R. Hall (1975), Interpersonal compatibility and workgroup performance, *Journal of Applied Behavioral Science,* 2, 210–19; Huber, 1980; P. R. Laughlin and L. G. Branch, (1972), Individual vs. tetradic performance on

a complementary task as a function of initial ability level, *Organizational Behavior and Human Performance*, 8, 201–16.

21. J. P. Wanous and M. A. Youtz (1986), Solutions diversity and the quality of group decisions, *Academy of Management Journal*, 29, 149–59.

22. L. N. Jewell and H. J. Reitz (1981), *Group effectiveness in organizations*, Glenview, IL: Scott, Foresman, 5–6.

23. R. D. Clark III, W. H. Crockett, and R. L. Archer (1971), Risk-as-value hypothesis: The relationship between perception of self-others, and the risky shift, *Journal of Personality and Social Psychology*, 20, 425–29; J. H. Davis, P. R. Laughlin, and S. S. Komorita (1976), The social psychology of small groups: Cooperative and mixed-motive interaction, in M. R. Rosenzweig and L. W. Porter, eds., *Annual Review of Psychology*, 27, 501–41; L. B. Rosenfeld (1973), *Human interaction in the small group setting*, Columbus, OH: Charles E. Merrill.

24. E. Burnstein and A. Vinokur (1977), Persuasive argumentation and social comparison as determinants of attitude polarization, *Journal of Experimental Social Psychology*, 13, 315–32; J. M. Jellison and R. M. Arkin (1977), Social comparison of abilities: A self-presentational approach to decision making in groups, in J. M. Suls and R. L. Miller, eds., *Social comparison processes*, New York: Halsted Press, 235–57.

25. I. L. Janis (1971), Groupthink, *Psychology Today*, 5, 43ff; I. Janis (1982), *Groupthink: Psychological studies of policy decisions*, 2nd ed., Boston: Houghton Mifflin.

26. H. J. Reitz and Jewell L. N. (1985), *Managing*, Glenview, IL: Scott, Foresman.

27. J. W. Gardner (October 1965), How to prevent organizational dry rot, *Harper's Magazine*, 20–26.

Key Terms

decision making
decisions
choice making
problem solving
means decisions
ends decisions
strategic decisions
managerial (tactical) decisions
programmed decisions
nonprogrammed decisions
certainty
risk
uncertainty

existing solutions
custom solutions
optimize
maximize
satisfice
objective rationality
bounded rationality
social facilitation
social impairment
cautious shifts
risky shifts
group think

Issues for Review and Discussion

1. Briefly define decision making.
2. Identify and explain three types of decisions.
3. Identify and discuss the differences among the three types of conditions under which decision making takes place.

4. How are decision making and problem solving related?

5. Discuss the influence of personality and cognitive factors on individual decision making.

6. Identify the assets and liabilities associated with group decision making.

7. Identify three group properties that are known to influence decision making. Briefly discuss the role of each.

8. Define and explain groupthink.

9. Identify one major problem associated with managerial decision making. How can this problem be managed so that decision making is more effective?

Suggested Readings

Cotton, J. L., Vollrath, D. A., Froggatt, K. L., Lengnick-Hall, M. L., and Jennings, K. R. (1988). Employee participation: Diverse forms and different outcomes. *Academy of Management Review*, 13, 8–22.

Ford, C. H. (1977). The "elite" decision makers: What makes them tick. *Human Resource Management*, 16, 14–20.

Janis, I. L. (1983). Groupthink. In Blumberg, H. H., Hare, A. P., Kent, V., and Davies, M., eds. *Small groups and social interaction*, vol. 2. New York: John Wiley & Sons, 39–46.

Lindbolm, C. E. (1959). The science of muddling through. *Public Administration Review*, 19, 79–88.

Mintzberg, H., Raisinghani, D., and Theoret, A. (1976). The structure of "unstructured" decision processes. *Administrative Science Quarterly*, 21, 246–75.

Schweiger, D. M., Sandberg, W. R., and Ragan, J. W. (1986). Group approaches for improving strategic decision making: A comparative analysis of dialectical inquiry, devil's advocacy, and consensus. *Academy of Management Journal*, 29, 51–71.

Simon, H. (March 1965). Administrative decision making. *Public Administrative Review*, 31–37.

CASE *AgBanCorporation*

*By Lowell Bourne of Eastern
Illinois University*

Ken Ormiston, a successful business-man in Heartland, Iowa, had been a Director of AgBanCorporation since 1980. As he studied his briefing book for the directors' April 1986 meeting, he realized that the normally perfunc-tory vote to declare the 28-cents-per-share quarterly dividend would not be routine. In fact, Mr. Ormiston saw this as one of the most crucial votes he had cast during his tenure on the Board of Directors.

AgBanCorporation, headquartered in Heartland, Iowa, was a multibank holding company with twelve affiliate banks. Total consolidated assets amounted to just slightly more than $900 million. Ten of the affiliates with combined assets of $600 million were located in small farming communities along Iowa's southern border. The others were located in Heartland—a city of over 150,000 people with a diverse industrial base—and its sub-urbs.

Throughout the 1970s, AgBanCor-poration's earnings and assets grew at 12 percent per year. Although many observers considered AgBanCorpora-tion's management team to be one of the best in the Midwest, the firm's success during this period was largely due to the prosperity of its customers, especially farmers and those closely allied with agriculture. This period was characterized by strong grain prices, good growing conditions in AgBanCorporation's service area, and a general feeling of prosperity as agri-cultural land prices rose about 14 per-cent per year.

Unlike several agricultural lenders, AgBanCorporation maintained strin-gent lending standards during the 1970s and carefully secured its agri-cultural loans with ample collateral, usually land and/or major pieces of farm equipment. For example, a farm-er needing $50,000 to plant crops in the spring was required to provide collateral valued at $75,000 to secure the loan. Furthermore, the bank re-quired land buyers to have a 40 per-cent down payment.

Although these lending standards appeared tight at the time, they were insufficient to insulate the bank from the disaster which befell its borrowers during the early 1980s. The early 1980s were not good years for agri-culture in the United States. Other countries were becoming increasingly aggressive competitors, limiting the export opportunities available to U.S. farmers, and the strong dollar caused U.S. grain to be priced out of many foreign markets. Consequently, grain prices were low throughout the peri-od. Low grain prices coupled with ex-traordinarily high interest rates forced the price of agricultural land to re-verse its upward trend and to begin a seemingly endless downward slide.

The farmers in AgBanCorporation's service area would have had difficulty enough coping with these problems, but their situation was exacerbated by five consecutive years of well-below-average rainfall. Their crop production was far below normal in three of those years and almost nonexistent in two others. As a consequence, many of AgBanCorporation's loans to farm-ers, agricultural suppliers, and even area merchants became problems for both the borrower and the lender. Ag-BanCorporation's income statements, shown in Figure 7A, indicate the im-pact of these loans on the firm's prof-itability.

The first quarter of 1986 was a par-ticularly bad one from the standpoint of earnings. Many banks, including

FIGURE 7A   *AgBanCorporation Comparative Income Statements (in 000's)*

	1985	1984	1983	1982	1981
Interest Income	$93,899	$81,115	$72,372	$66,061	$52,929
Interest Expense	64,405	55,732	50,535	46,509	37,328
Net Interest Income	29,494	25,732	21,837	19,552	15,601
Provision for Loan Losses	7,391	4,910	2,168	2,116	1,242
Income After Provision for Losses	22,103	20,473	19,669	17,436	14,359
Other Income	8,174	5,947	4,045	3,629	2,931
Other Expense	27,033	23,845	17,954	15,859	11,839
Pretax Net Income	3,244	2,575	5,760	5,206	5,451
Tax Expense (Benefit)	(1,000)	(2,377)	48	20	1,028
After-tax Net Income	$4,244	$4,952	$5,712	$5,186	$4,423

AgBanCorporation, undertook reviews of their agricultural loan portfolios and concluded that many loans were uncollectible and several others were highly questionable. In most instances, the borrowers no longer had the capacity to repay their loans, and the value of the collateral had fallen to the point where it was insufficient to cover the loan. AgBanCorporation's review resulted in a 6.3-million-dollar provision for loan losses in the quarter to offset the large scale write-offs of agricultural loans and to strengthen the loan loss reserve. AgBanCorporation's first quarter 1986 financial statements were contained in Mr. Ormiston's briefing book and are shown in Exhibit 7B. After review by the Board of Directors, they were to be released to the public.

AgBanCorporation's Board of Directors meets quarterly. Standing items of business for each meeting are review of the financial statements for the quarter just concluded, review of the financial forecast for the next four quarters, dividend action, and approval of the press release containing the quarterly financial statements and the dividend action.

Two days prior to the meeting, each director receives a briefing book containing fairly detailed information concerning the meeting's agenda. In addition to including several routine items for the Board's consideration, the briefing book for the April meeting contained the material shown in Figures 7B through 7E concerning the standing agenda items.

FIGURE 7B   *AgBanCorporation Income Statement for the First Quarter, 1986 (in 000's)*

Interest Income	$22,365
Interest Expense	15,214
Net Interest Income	7,151
Provision for Loan Losses	6,318
Income After Provision for Losses	833
Other Income	5,046
Other Expense	7,641
Pretax Net Loss	(1,762)
Tax Expense	309
After-Tax Net Loss	$(2,071)

Questions

1. Since Chairman Mayvis has no reservations about declaring a dividend, why do you suppose Mr. Ormiston sees this as such a crucial vote?
2. Do you believe Mr. Ormiston should vote "For" or "Against" declaring the regular quarterly dividend? Explain your reasoning.
3. Why is it likely that some members of the board will vote for a different decision than they would choose if they were to make a decision alone?
4. What changes, if any, should be made in the press release prior to its being made public?

FIGURE 7C   *Memorandum for Your Eyes Only*

To: The Directors of AgBanCorporation
From: Bill Golladay, Controller
Subject: Earnings Forecast
Date: April 1986

My staff has prepared the following forecast of AgBanCorporation's after-tax net income during each of the next four quarters.

Period	Amount (in 000's)
2Q86	$100
3Q86	200
4Q86	200
1Q87	350

As usual, this forecast is the output of our own econometric model. Input data consists of national, regional, and local data as well as the firm's internal plans. We are 95 percent confident that 2Q86's actual net income will be within 7 percent of the forecast. The margin of error is 16 percent in the other forecasts.

After-tax net income will be depressed in each of these quarters due to anticipated loan losses of approximately $1 million per quarter. These write-offs will have a direct impact on earnings because of the desire to maintain the allowance for losses at its present level. We have very few unrealized gains in the securities portfolio, so earnings will not benefit to the previous extent from taking these gains.

To: The Directors of AgBanCorporation
From: Bob Mayvis, Chairman and CEO
Subject: Recommended Dividend Action
Date: April 1986

Despite the $2 million loss suffered by AgBanCorporation during the first quarter, I strongly recommend the declaration of a regular dividend in the amount of $.28 per share payable May 15, 1986, to common stockholders of record May 1, 1986. A dividend of $.28 per share has been declared and paid during each of the past sixteen quarters. A cash disbursement of $504,000 would result.

Maintenance of the dividend is important, in my opinion, for three reasons. First, the declaration of the regular dividend in the face of the loss is tangible evidence of your confidence in AgBanCorporation's financial health. Secondly, many of our stockholders count on our dividend for at least a portion of their living expenses. Inasmuch as many of these people have suffered a financial hardship from the area's agricultural problems, I see no reason to compound their plight by reducing or eliminating the dividend as long as the firm has the ability to declare it. Finally, maintenance of the dividend will provide some measure of protection against what I fear may be a precipitous drop in the price of our stock once the loss is announced. A substantial decline in the stock price would make it much less expensive for a "corporate raider" to acquire an influential position in our stock and, ultimately, rob us of our independence. Our stock is currently trading at $21 per share, or 69 percent of book value, whereas the stocks of our peers sell for slight premiums to book value. I fear this discrepancy may draw unwanted attention to us. We are somewhat vulnerable to a takeover because some of our stockholders, particularly those who joined us as a result of our merger with the suburban banks, feel uncomfortable with our exposure to the agricultural sector. They may be motivated sellers if the dividend is not maintained.

As you may remember, our 13 percent note held by the P————— Insurance Company contains a covenant prohibiting the declaration of dividends whenever our cumulative net income for the prior four quarters falls below $1 million. AgBanCorporation's net income for the four quarters ending with 1Q86 exceeds this amount; however, if the 2Q86 forecast by Bill's staff is anywhere near correct, and I fear it is, our net income for the four quarters then ending will not reach that minimum required by the covenant. I have no reason to believe that P————— will, even temporarily, waive the covenant.

FOR IMMEDIATE RELEASE

Heartland, IA—Today, AgBanCorporation reported a net loss of $2,071,000 for the first quarter of 1986. Chairman Bob Mayvis reported that the loss was caused by a substantial increase in the provision for loan losses resulting from an extensive review of the firm's ag-related loans. Net income is expected to be depressed until the agricultural sector improves. The Board of Directors declared a $.28 per share dividend payable May 15, 1986, to common stockholders of record May 1, 1986.

Tools for Planning and Decision Making

Student Learning Objectives

After reading this chapter, you should be able to:

1. Explain the difference between quantitative and qualitative planning and decision-making tools.

2. Understand why it is important for managers to balance the use of quantitative and qualitative tools.

3. Determine when to use each planning and decision-making tool.

4. Determine when planning and decision making should be carried out by one individual or by a group.

5. Recognize the benefits of qualitative tools over quantative tools.

6. Recognize the benefits of quantitative tools over qualitative tools.

7. Explain how a manager can master the use of both quantitative and qualitative tools but still be a poor planner and decision maker.

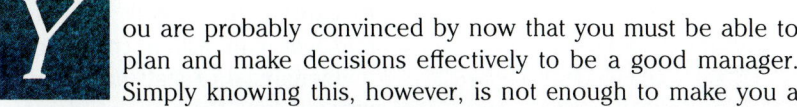

You are probably convinced by now that you must be able to plan and make decisions effectively to be a good manager. Simply knowing this, however, is not enough to make you a good manager any more than knowing that you must be able to work with wood and nails to be a good carpenter. You must have access to and know how to use a good set of tools to be a carpenter or a manager.

Consider this chapter your planning and decision-making "toolbox," in which you will find substantial help for planning and decision making. Some of these tools are **quantitative tools** that provide a way to examine, measure, and express information in numbers. The following are the quantitative tools discussed in this chapter:

- Inventory management
- Resource allocation (linear programming)
- Scheduling and sequencing
- Queuing theory
- Program evaluation and review technique (PERT) and Critical Path Method (CPM)
- Predicting/forecasting
- Break-even analysis
- Time series analysis
- Causal models

Typically, these quantitative tools rely on mathematical and statistical models, and many require sophisticated computer analyses. The computer programs used to solve many of the quantitative problems and examples contained in this chapter are provided on the easy-to-use software that accompanies the book *Microcomputer Software for Management Science and Operations Management* by Barry Render and Ralph Stair, Jr. (Boston: Allyn and Bacon, 1986).

Your toolbox also contains a number of **qualitative tools** designed for collecting and processing ideas, opinions, and judgments. Think of these as thought-processing procedures. They identify whether planning and decision making should be conducted by individuals or by groups and then offer structure to guide these activities. Both the quantitative and the qualitative techniques are effective.

Computer technology allows managers to quantify information in order to explore the effects of their decisions.

Quantitative Tools

As you saw in Chapter 1, effective management combines art and science. Quantitative decision-making tools are a significant aspect of the *science* of management. When high-speed computers made complex calculations feasible, a number of mathematical models were developed to help managers. These models typically use *objective measures* to quantify management information. They specify, in numeric terms, a picture of reality and treat information more objectively than intuition alone can do. Many of these procedures have been particularly useful to managers of production and operations (see Chapter 21).

One primary advantage of quantitative tools is that they allow managers to explore the effects of their decisions. By manipulating numbers, a manager can ask a sophisticated "what if" question and look at a mathematical or statistical model for the answer rather than putting the organization through an actual trial-and-error situation. A break-even model, for example, can demonstrate what would happen to an organization's profits if it closed one of its four plants, dropped one of its three product lines, and added a third shift of workers at the remaining plant to increase production of the two remaining product lines by 20 percent. The same model could then predict the effects on profits if production were to be increased by 15 percent or by 25 percent. By using these techniques, managers can anticipate the probable outcomes for various alternatives and plan accordingly.

It is important to note that quantitative models are no more effective than the quality of the assumptions on which they are built. In other words, if you build a poor mathematical model of reality, it will give very precise—but very inaccurate—estimates of the effects of management decisions. Although failing to use mathematical models handicaps a manager, relying too heavily on them ignores the *art* of managing. Managers have to capitalize on their intuition and personal skills, as well as on the precision of mathematical models.

Inventory Plans and Decisions

Cindy Mertes is the owner of Progressive Video Images (PVI). Her company offers consumers a number of services related to home video-tape systems. One such service is converting home movies into video-tapes. PVI also copies photographs and slides onto videotape and adds music and titles to produce a high-quality product.

Cindy Mertes has to decide how many blank VHS tapes to request in her next tape order. She expects to use a total of 10,000 VHS tapes during the next twelve months, and each tape costs her $4. Her standard weekly order is for slightly fewer than 200 tapes. Because she occasionally has a very busy week and runs short on tapes, Cindy has considered placing a larger order; however, to buy more tapes, she might have to borrow money, not only to pay for the tapes but also to insure the larger inventory against loss and to rent additional storage space.

With all of these considerations, Cindy is having a difficult time deciding how many tapes to order. To help her make the decision, she investigated the various costs associated with ordering and maintaining inventory. The following are some of the facts that she turned up:

1. PVI uses 10,000 VHS tapes per year.
2. Each tape costs $4 to purchase.
3. The administrative costs of placing and receiving an order (including payment for the merchandise and clerical, accounting, and stocking costs) average about $100 per order.
4. The cost of keeping tapes in inventory is about 12.5 percent of the value of the tape inventory per year, including the cost of insurance, rent, and interest on loans to purchase extra (stored) tapes.

Cindy was quite surprised to realize that it costs her $100 just to place and receive an order. Because she has been ordering tapes every week, PVI has been spending over $5000 a year for this expense alone. When she realized this, Cindy's first reaction was that she should borrow enough money to order a year's supply of tapes and to rent additional storage space; however, the 12.5 percent carrying costs associated with this plan caused her to reconsider. She wants to find the best number of tapes to order, a number that will balance all of these considerations.

Economic Order Quantity (EOQ) Cindy can answer her inventory problem by using a tool known as **economic order quantity (EOQ).** An **economic order quantity** is a mathematical model for identifying the amount of inventory to order when managers know their inventory use (*IU*), product cost (*PC*), cost of procuring inventory (*PI*), and annual inventory carrying costs (*CC*). The EOQ equation for determining the best inventory order is as follows:

$$EOQ = \sqrt{\frac{2 \times IU \times PI}{PC \times CC}}$$

To solve the equation and find the answer for PVI's current inventory dilemma, Cindy uses the information that she has uncovered:

Inventory annual use	$IU = 10{,}000$ units
Procuring inventory cost	$PI = \$100$
Product cost	$PC = \$4$
Carrying costs	$CC = 12.5$ percent

and plugs it into the EOQ formula:

$$EOQ = \sqrt{\frac{2 \times 10{,}000 \times \$100}{\$4.00 \times .125}} = 2000$$

As the equation shows, the best number of tapes for PVI to order is 2000. The EOQ is a simple model, and its advantages are obvious. Cindy should remember, however, not to become too dependent on the EOQ model (or any other model, for that matter). If reality differs from Cindy's assumptions, she may find herself with a bad solution. For example, Cindy could lose considerable money and competitiveness if the price of tapes drops right after she orders 2000 tapes. If the use of 8mm videotapes increases beyond her expectations, she could be stuck with thousands of VHS tapes and not enough money to buy 8mm tapes in volume. Because of such uncertainties, managers often solve the EOQ equation by using several sets of assumptions. In this way, they get an idea of how sensitive the solution is to variation in the assumptions.

Other Inventory Models Some inventory decision models are more intricate and sophisticated than the EOQ. They allow managers to manipulate more variables and, in turn, to control inventory and its attendant costs more carefully. The *production-run model*, for example, is useful for situations in which work is done in batches through production runs. The *planned shortage model* reduces inventory costs in situations in which periodic stock shortages are acceptable (although back ordering is sometimes necessary). The *quantity-discount model* is useful if suppliers offer discounts for purchases above a certain quantity. All of these models are used often by inventory managers.

Resource Allocation: Linear Programming

With **linear programming (LP),** another quantitative model, managers not only can control inventory but can also identify the appropriate quantity of product to manufacture. They can decide how many employees to hire, allocate advertising dollars, and plan any other task that involves minimizing an objective (for example, material waste or labor cost) or maximizing an objective (profit). LP helps managers calculate the best combination of resources and activities. The two requirements for using an LP model are that resources be limited (and known) and that two or more alternatives (products, advertising techniques, and so on) compete for these limited resources.

Encouraged by her successful use of one quantitative decision-making model to solve her inventory problem, Cindy Mertes, in the previous example, has decided to use the more sophisticated linear programming approach to solve a much greater problem. During the past six months, most of PVI's business has come from two of the company's services: converting movies to videotapes and custom editing customers' tapes. A problem has emerged, however: the employees who perform these two services are competing for equipment and other resources. Cindy hopes to solve this problem without having to acquire additional expensive equipment.

FIGURE 8.1   *Resource Usage at PVI*

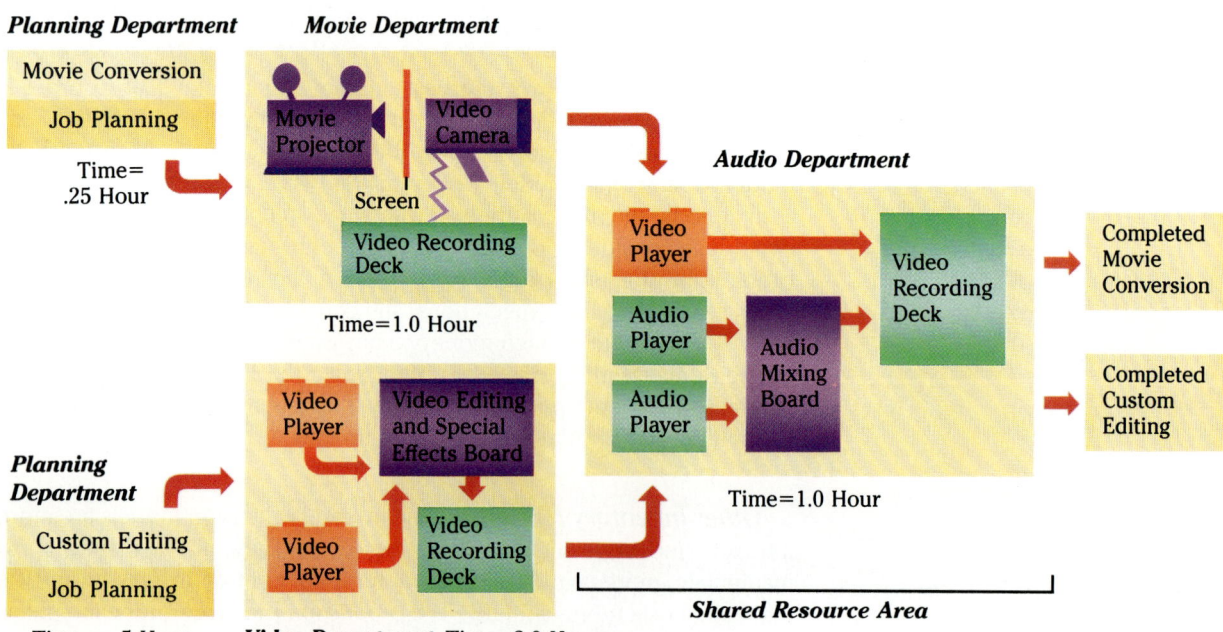

Note: All times shown are those required to prepare a one-hour-length completed product.

TABLE 8.1   *Production and Revenue Data for Conversions and Editing*

Department	Number of Hours Required per Hour of Completed Product		Capacity per Day (in Hours)*
	Movie Conversions (c)	*Custom Editing* (e)	
Planning (P)	.25	.50	16
Movie (M)	1.0	0.0	48
Video (V)	0.0	3.0	24
Audio (A)	1.0	1.0	48
Profit margin	$40	$150	

*Planning capacity based on hours worked by the two people who do planning. Video department capacity based on around-the-clock use of one available video room. Movie and audio department capacities based on around-the-clock use of two available rooms each.

A–V represent activities
1–18 represent beginning and ending points of activities

Figure 8.1 illustrates the processes involved in producing PVI's two competing services. As you can see, some equipment is used solely by employees converting movies to videotapes and some is used only by custom tape editors. The rest of the equipment, such as the audio mixing board, is used by both groups.

Table 8.1 lists some of the facts that Cindy identified by researching this problem. She has decided to use linear programming to identify the best combination of movie conversion and custom editing for using existing equipment and maximizing profits. Assuming that the resulting mix will be different from the current one, Cindy plans to reorganize the operation of PVI accordingly.

The movie department staff is currently producing forty-four hours of converted movies a day. In doing so, they are using the facilities of the movie department forty-four hours per day and need forty-four hours of audio department time. The video department staff is producing six hours of custom editing a day. To do so, they are using video department facilities eighteen hours a day and need six hours of audio department time. The present total demand for audio department facilities (44 + 6 × 50) has exceeded the total capacity of the audio department. This demand explains part of the conflict that has emerged between the movie and video groups. Competition for equipment has also led to some sloppy work, a number of missed deadlines, and the need to contract for audio work at another studio, which has proven very expensive ($150 an hour).

The following is a list of current daily profits and contracting costs for PVI:

1. Movie conversion profits   (44 units/day @ $40)   = $1760
2. Custom editing   (6 units/day @ $150)   =   900
3. Audio contracting costs   (2 hours/day @ −$150) = −300

    Total Current Daily Profits $2360

These look like pretty decent profits for one day of operations, but Cindy believes that profits could be increased and conflict reduced through a better business plan. Linear programming will help her determine if she can meet these goals, given the company's limited resources. The answer that she is looking for is the best combination of movie conversion and custom editing to maximize total profits. She insists that no equipment be scheduled for more time than is currently available. The equation that Cindy will solve by using LP is:

$$\text{PROFIT}_{\text{max}} = \$40X_c + \$150X_e$$

where

X_c = Units of movie conversions to be produced

X_e = Units of custom editing to be produced

Cindy is aware of several specific constraints as she tries to maximize profits. One of these is the capacity of her audio department. The planning department has two people, each working eight-hour days; thus, sixteen hours of planning time are available per day. The movie department has two staffs, each of which is available for twenty-four hours a day (three people, each working eight-hour days). The video department has one staff available for twenty-four hours a day. The audio department has two staffs, each of which is available for twenty-four hours a day. In LP, these constraints define "constraint equations" and are obtained using information from Figure 8.1:

$.25c + .5e$	16.0 (available planning department time)
$1.0c + 0.0e$	48.0 (available movie department time)
$0.0c + 3.0e$	24.0 (available video department time)
$1.0c + 1.0e$	48.0 (available audio department time)

By solving simultaneous linear equations with a computer program, Cindy determined that PVI should produce forty units a day of movie conversions and eight units a day of custom editing. (It is beyond the scope of this book to fully discuss simultaneous linear equations. In fact, computers can help you solve equations far more complex than those contained in this example.) This solution not only maximizes profits, it also eliminates the need for PVI to contract out audio work. Furthermore, it will significantly reduce the conflict between the video and movie staffs. When Cindy places these numbers into the first equation, she finds that her daily profits will be $2800:

$$\text{PROFIT}_{\text{max}} = (\$40 \times 40) + (\$150 \times 8) = \$2800/\text{day}$$

This figure represents an additional $440 a day of profits, a 19 percent increase that will amount to well over $100,000 a year more in profits.

Under this solution, both the video and audio departments will be operating at full capacity. The planning department will have two hours of excess capacity. Finally, the movie department will have a full eight hours a day of excess capacity. Cindy might wish to find alternative activities to take advantage of this excess capacity. She also might reduce work hours in those areas with unused capacity. She could even eliminate one eight-hour shift in the movie department.

The linear programming solution to Cindy's problem sounds almost too good to be true. Is it realistic? Many managers have a tendency to look at the precise mathematical results of these solutions and to assume that they provide a totally accurate reflection of reality. As you know, however, a mathematical solution is only as good as the assumptions on which it is based. If Cindy's estimates (shown in Table 8.1) are wrong, the solution will be wrong. She also has to make sure not to let a computer program inhibit her creativity. She needs to use the technique to find imaginative solutions. In fact, Cindy may run a whole series of linear programs, each based on different assumptions. She may ask, for example, what the best use of resources would be if she raised or lowered the price that PVI charges for either of the two services, what effect employee wage changes would have on the solution, and what would happen if she increased or decreased capacity in one or more of the four departments. Cindy can use LP to find the answers to all of these questions and then to select the solution that she thinks is best.

Scheduling and Sequencing

How many lines do you wait in during a typical week? Meg Malde-Arnosti of St. Paul, Minnesota, listed her waiting times during one week:

Line	Waiting Time (Minutes)
Parking lot checkout	7
Fast-food counter	4
Airport ticket counter	29
Taxi stand	12
Hotel check in	15
Gas station	6
Grocery store checkout	19
Football stadium entrance	14
Football stadium restroom	13
Physician's office	27

Time spent waiting in line can be extremely irritating. If this week is typical for Meg, she is spending over 130 hours a year waiting in line, the equivalent of over 16 workdays. At some point, she may give up on the gas station line and go to a less busy gas station. Perhaps next time she'll avoid the grocery store that kept her waiting 19 minutes for her to give *them* her money. Are the businesses involved so shortsighted that they can't staff adequately to reduce people's waiting times?

Queuing Models Most organizations would agree that, ideally, customers should not have to stand in long lines, but adding staff to avoid these lines costs money. **Queuing models**—a *queue* is a line—can help managers identify the best number of waiting lines. These models balance an organization's costs of having lines against what it costs to lose customers or their goodwill.

Greg's Wash and Buff is a car wash company that uses a state-of-the-art brushless car wash system. Greg's washes a large number of cars and usually has reasonable waiting times. Greg's also offers a hand-applied hard wax for $39.95. Although demand has been strong for the waxing service, most customers have been forced to wait in long lines for their wax jobs to be completed. This has generated a lot of negative talk about Greg's, and, recently, fewer customers have been asking for wax jobs. Greg's tried using an appointment-only system, but very few people made appointments. People seem to want their wax job "on demand." Right now, Greg's has only one person on staff who waxes cars. The managers have concluded that they must add a second person to the waxing staff or drop the service.

Donald Cole is a business student at the local college who works part time at Greg's. He has offered to conduct a computerized queuing analysis for both a one- and two-person waxing staff. He promises that each of these analyses will provide good estimates of the probability of idle worker time, the average number of cars in the system, the average time spent in the system, the average number of cars waiting in line to be waxed, and the average amount of time cars spend waiting in line. Donald has also promised to evaluate the financial advantage or disadvantage of adding a second person to the waxing staff.

Before he uses his microcomputer to conduct these analyses, Donald gets estimates of such factors as the amount of time it takes to wax a car, how often customers request wax jobs, and the cost of wages for waxers. He also gets an estimate that customer dissatisfaction, lost goodwill, and lost business amount to about $10 for each hour that a customer spends waiting in line for a wax job. By using these estimates and a computer queuing program, Donald finds that, even though a second waxer would spend a lot of time doing nothing and would have to be paid, a two-person waxing operation would substantially reduce waiting times for wax jobs and save Greg's $43 a day.

Sophisticated computer programs are available to handle considerably more complex queuing problems than that faced by Greg's. Usually, the more complex a problem, the more useful the model, because manual solutions are quite difficult to handle for complex problems.

PERT and CPM   While queuing models deal specifically with waiting time, *program evaluation and review technique* (PERT) and a closely related technique known as the *critical path method* (CPM) can be used to schedule and coordinate virtually any project that can be broken down into a series of interdependent tasks or activities. In fact, PERT was developed in the 1950s by the United States Navy to coordinate the efforts of over 3000 contractors involved in developing the *Polaris* nuclear submarine. The very similar CPM method was developed at Du Pont to control a number of its large and complex industrial projects.

PERT and CPM provide estimates of expected completion time for an entire project. They can also provide detailed information for each activity, including the earliest or latest start time and the earliest or latest finish time. PERT also identifies the amount of time that a specific activity can be delayed without the entire project being delayed. To conduct a PERT analysis, a manager must identify all of the tasks and activities required by the project and be able to specify which activities must be completed before others. Finally, for each activity, managers must estimate optimistic, pessimistic, and most likely completion times.

The primary difference between PERT and CPM is that CPM uses only one time estimate for each activity; thus, CPM can be used quite effectively for repetitive processes in which managers know the time of task completion with some certainty. PERT, in contrast, is better for nonroutine projects about which managers are fairly uncertain of the required completion time.

When managers use PERT or CPM, they construct a network to give them an overall picture of the flow of work that must be accomplished to complete the project. The network is made up of paths connecting the events and activities necessary to finish the project. All but one of the

When managers use PERT or CPM, they construct a network that shows the flow of work that must be accomplished to complete a project.

paths may have some slack time for completion before they jeopardize the overall completion of the project. The one path containing no slack time is called the *critical path* because it takes the greatest amount of time to complete; thus, completing the overall project takes the amount of time required to complete the critical path. Both PERT and CPM analyses identify the critical path through the network.

PERT can help identify critical stages of a project, activities that should receive attention early in the project, and potential bottlenecks. With this information, a manager can alter project plans—changing sequences of activities or modifying the way tasks are performed. If the publisher of this book, for example, conducted a PERT analysis and found that the preparation of artwork was expected to delay release of the book, additional artists could be assigned to the project.

Because PERT specifies when activities should be begun and completed, it can also be used as a control tool. By comparing actual progress to the PERT schedule, managers can spot performance problems before they seriously threaten a project. For example, the PERT model can easily identify how long an entire project will be delayed if a particular activity falls behind schedule by a certain amount of time.

An example of how PERT works is contained in "A Closer Look: PERT." There you will see how a contractor and his company used PERT to schedule the remodeling of the basement in a single-family dwelling. PERT makes it relatively easy for a manager to run several analyses by using different sets of assumptions. The contractor in this example could run an analysis to determine project completion time according to only his most optimistic or most pessimistic time estimates. He also could identify the time savings likely to result from designing a different work plan. What would happen to his project schedule, for example, if he subcontracted out some of the carpentry work? Usually, the more a manager uses PERT, the more accurate his or her time estimates become; it also becomes easier to identify current bottlenecks.

Predicting/Forecasting

Every day, managers must make decisions without knowing precisely what will happen in the future. PVI must buy tapes without knowing whether their price will drop, and a building contractor must schedule an electrical inspection in the hope that the electricians will have finished on time. Decision making requires making assumptions about the future, so managers must often rely on their subjective feelings and best guesses as they plan. The more accurate these feelings, the better prepared managers will be. Experience tends to improve managers' judgment and ability to forecast events. Several quantitative methods are available to help managers forecast events. The best managers combine intuition and the conscientious use of quantitative tools.

Break-Even Analysis **Break-even analysis** is the identification of the point at which sales *revenues* will equal the *total cost* of producing a product or service. Managers use break-even analyses primarily for financial planning. Sales that fall below the break-even point create financial losses; sales above the point produce profits.

A CLOSER LOOK

PERT: Scheduling for Lil'America Builders

Recently, Butch Ledworowski of Lil'merica Builders contracted to remodel the basement of a single-family home. So that he could identify a probable completion date and so that he could manage the project effectively, Butch conducted a PERT analysis. First he drew Figure 8A, called a PERT network, which showed the flow of work for the project. In this diagram, each arrow identifies a specific activity required by the project. The numbered circles indicate the beginning and end points of activities. Arrows indicate which activities must be completed before another activity begins.

For each activity, Butch provided optimistic, most probable, and pessimistic estimates of the time that would be required for completion.

Some of these estimates are shown in Table 8A.

Once Butch had a diagram of the work flow and estimates for each activity, he could use a PERT analysis to identify the following:

1. The critical path that would take the longest time to complete
2. The earliest possible starting and finishing day for an activity
3. The latest possible starting and finishing day for an activity without the project being delayed
4. The amount of slack time for each activity (that is, acceptable delay time that would not slow the entire project)

The results of a computerized PERT analysis for this project deter-

---

FIGURE 8A   PERT Network Used by Lil'America Builders

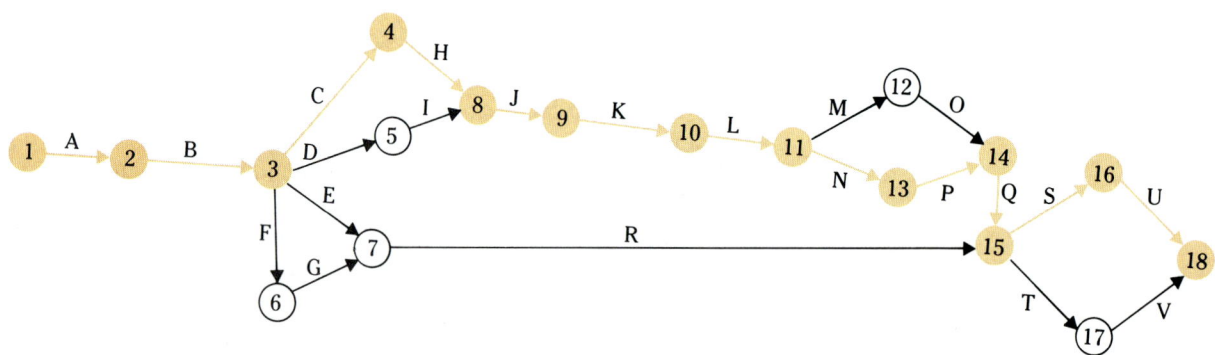

A–V represent activities
1–18 represent beginning and ending points of activities

mined that 22.4 working days could be expected for completing the critical path (and, thus, the entire project). Some of the estimates for individual activities appear in Table 8B below.

Butch used the results of the PERT analysis to tell the owners when they could expect their project to be completed, to schedule the various components of the job, and to monitor and control progress of the project.

TABLE 8A

			Time Estimates (Days)		
Activity	Description	Start, End Point	Optimistic	Probable	Pessimistic
A	Draw Plans	1,2	1.0	2.0	3.0
B	Rough Framing	2,3	2.0	3.0	4.0
C	Rough Electrical	3,4	1.0	2.0	3.0
G	Cabinet Ordering	6,7	0.2	0.5	1.0
H	Electrical Inspection	4,8	0.4	0.5	1.0
I	Heating Inspection	5,8	0.5	0.7	1.0
T	Install Cabinets	15,17	0.8	1.0	1.2
U	Install Carpet	16,18	0.8	1.0	1.5
V	Final Inspection	17,18	0.4	0.5	1.0

Table 8B

	Starting Day		Finishing Day		Slack
Activity	Earliest	Latest	Earliest	Latest	Time
A	0.0	2.0	0.0	2.0	0.0
B	2.0	2.0	5.0	5.0	0.0
C	5.0	5.0	7.0	7.0	0.0
G	6.0	9.7	6.5	10.2	3.7
H	7.0	7.0	7.6	7.6	0.0
I	6.0	6.9	6.7	7.6	0.9
T	20.3	20.8	21.3	21.8	0.5
U	21.3	21.3	22.4	22.4	0.0
V	21.3	21.8	21.9	22.4	0.5

To conduct a break-even analysis, managers must first estimate fixed costs, variable costs, and a sales price per unit. Fixed costs are costs incurred regardless of how many units of a product are produced. These usually include building costs, equipment and tool costs, insurance, and so on. Variable costs change, depending on how many units are produced, and include such factors as raw materials, labor, and supplies. Variable costs are usually expressed in terms of how much it costs to produce one additional unit of a product. Sales price per unit is simply the amount of revenue generated by each unit of sales. When these three pieces of information are known, the break-even point can be identified using either a graphical or an algebraic solution.

Recall that Cindy Mertes at Progressive Video Images used linear programming to identify the best allocation of company resources. The solution that she adopted left her with eight hours a day of excess capacity in the movie department. She has been looking for ways to use this excess capacity. Recently, a customer talked to Cindy about a special project that would involve the restoration of old movie films. Realizing that there might be a broad demand for this service, Cindy began investigating the market for movie restorations and the costs associated with doing them.

Cindy estimates the annual fixed costs of using the movie department for eight hours a day to be $40,000, including the cost of lighting, heating, cooling, and maintenance. She expects the variable costs for each movie restoration (including direct labor costs, supplies, and materials) to be $25. She feels that she can charge $75 for each restoration and that PVI has the time available to complete as many as 1600 restorations per year. What she wants to know is how many restorations PVI would have to do to break even and what the greatest potential profit would be for the operation.

Figure 8.2 plots the information that Cindy collected. The point at which the total costs (fixed plus variable) and total revenues lines cross is the break-even point. The break-even point is 800 restorations (units). In other words, annual sales below 800 units will generate losses, and sales of more than 800 will generate profits at the rate of $50 per unit (sale price of $75 less $25 variable cost). With a capacity for 1600 movie restorations a year, Cindy's potential profit for the operation is 800 × $50, or $40,000.

Although Cindy solved her break-even analysis on a graph, she could have used the following equation:

$$\text{Break-Even Point} = \frac{FC}{P - VC}$$

where

$$FC = \text{Fixed costs}$$
$$P = \text{Price per unit}$$
$$VC = \text{Variable cost per unit}$$

$$\text{PVI's Break-Even Point} = \frac{\$40,000}{\$75 - \$25} = 800 \text{ Units}$$

Notice how easy it would be for Cindy to repeat a variety of break-even analyses for different assumptions. She might ask what would happen to the break-even point if fixed costs were increased or decreased or what would happen if the market would bear only a charge of $60 per unit.

FIGURE 8.2 *Break-Even Analysis at PVI*

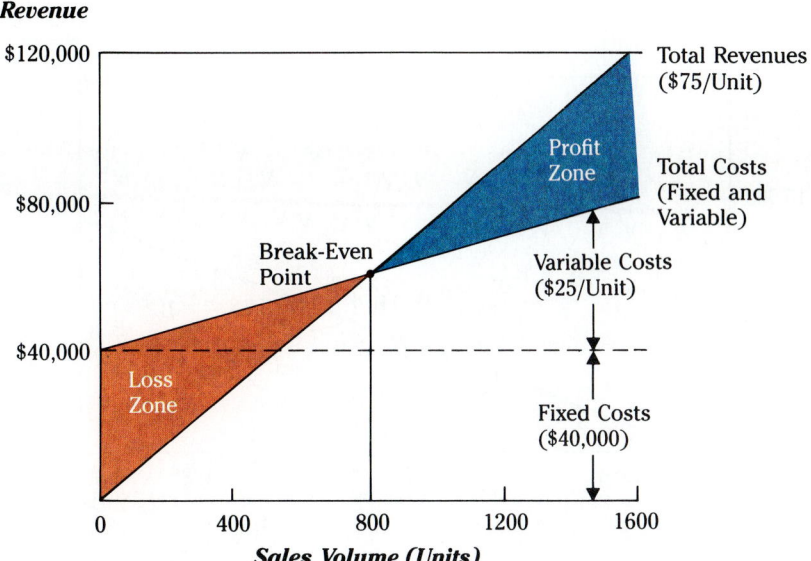

What if variable costs changed? What break-even analysis does not tell Cindy is whether this particular business venture would produce more profit than other possible ventures. It also does not tell her how much she loses in interest and lost opportunities before reaching the break-even point. She must make these judgments on her own, either subjectively or by using other quantitative tools available to managers.

Time Series Analysis Managers often must project future trends. **Time series analysis** examines past data for trends and forecasts what would happen in the future if the trend were to continue. This model must be used cautiously, however. Because it is based on the assumption that past trends will continue in the future, this model is most useful in stable environments.

PVI, which is considering opening a second facility, might use a time series analysis. Cindy thinks that opening a second facility makes sense because the home video market seems to be expanding rapidly and because her current facility is being used at nearly its full capacity. She is a bit concerned, however, about the future of the three most common home video formats (VHS, Beta, and 8mm). Because she must order equipment capable of handling the appropriate mix and volume of video formats, she would like to know how much the home video market is likely to expand and in which formats.

Time series analysis assumes that the past accurately projects future events. Cindy realizes the riskiness of this assumption in a market as volatile as that for home videos, but she needs the best estimates that she can get of future trends. Fortunately, very complete information is available for sales of each of the three video formats for each month of the last three years in Cindy's market area. She will use time series analysis to forecast for the next twenty-four months.

The particular type of time series analysis used in this example is a relatively simple and popular one known as *trend analysis*. Trend analysis develops a statistical equation from past performance and projects into

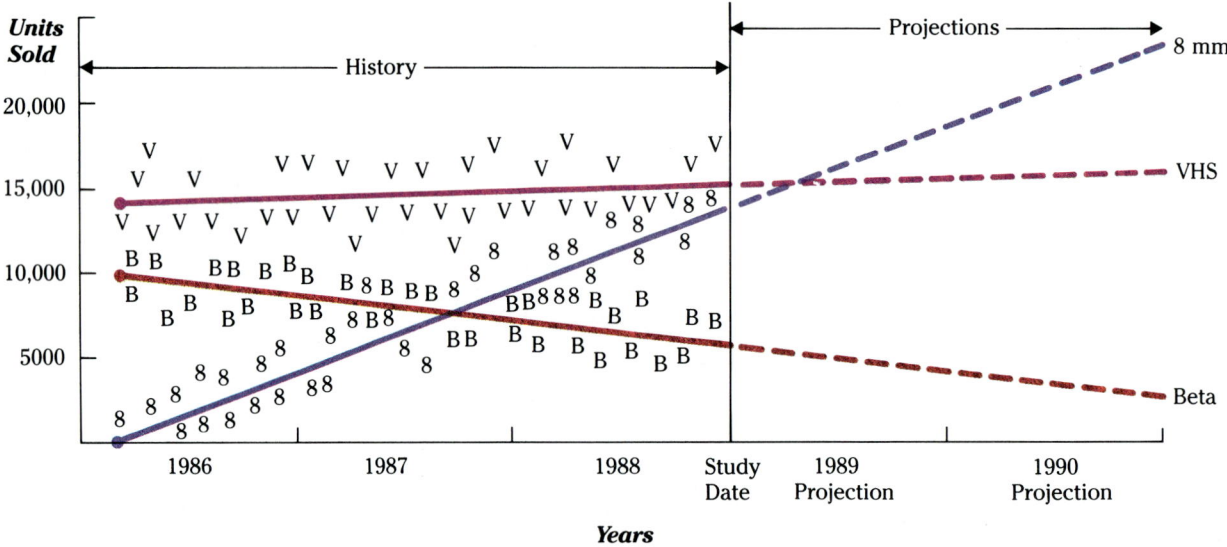

FIGURE 8.3   *Time Series Analysis Forecasts for Home Video Market*

the future. In Figure 8.3, the thirty-six-month history for PVI's market area is plotted for each of the three video formats. The solid line shown for each format represents the statistical solution that best describes its past trend. The dashed extension of each line shows the forecast for the next twenty-four months. These lines were generated by computer, but similar lines could have been drawn with a ruler through the center of the cluster for each product. The computer provides a more accurate solution of very complex trends.

These three forecasts suggest that the sale of Beta tapes declined steadily for the last three years and will continue to do so. VHS sales were and probably will continue to be high but relatively level, and 8mm sales were high and are projected to continue their rapid growth. The analysis also shows when—sometime during 1988—8mm sales are expected to exceed VHS sales. Figure 8.3 also suggests overall increases in the home video market. Because 8mm sales are increasing more rapidly than Beta sales are decreasing, Cindy can use this information in planning her second facility. Her first location has more than enough Beta capacity, so the second facility can ignore Beta and concentrate instead on the 8mm format to meet the expected demand. Cindy must be very careful, however. If 8mm prices drop substantially, 8mm sales might climb even more rapidly, and VHS sales might drop. It is also possible that the market could become saturated (how many video recorders will a family want in one home?). Because time series analysis assumes that past trends will continue, such effects cannot be forecast.

Many managers use more sophisticated time series analysis programs that can identify seasonal fluctuations (such as a holiday sales increase) and other nonlinear trends. These can often provide more precise forecasts than the simple linear projection shown in Figure 8.3.

Causal Modeling   Like time series analysis, **causal modeling** attempts to forecast future events in statistical terms. There is one very important difference between the two models, however. Time series analysis assumes that the past will predict the future without considering why past events occurred. Causal models document the causes of past events. These models use cause-and-effect relationships to predict and explain future events.

Suppose that the trends shown in Figure 8.3 were caused by a combination of the price of tapes in each format, the availability of prerecorded movies, and advertising. As long as none of these factors changes, future projections based on time series analyses should be reasonably accurate, but as soon as one or more of these factors change, time series projections become imprecise. Causal models take into account the probable effects of changes such as these.

The causal models used most often in business are based on a statistical procedure known as **regression analysis.** Regression analysis develops a mathematical model (equation) that describes the relationship of one or more causal variables to a variable that is dependent on the causal variables. A regression equation that explains the "causes" of student grades in college, for example, might look like the following:

$$Y = .001X_1 + .002X_2 + .3X_3 + .3$$

where

Y = College grade point average (GPA)

X_1 = SAT verbal score

X_2 = SAT quantitative score

X_3 = High school GPA

This equation was obtained by using regression analyses of the above information for a group of students who had already attended college. Once the equation is identified, it can be used to predict the probable college GPA for a student if his or her SAT and high school GPA scores are known. A college trying to decide whether to admit Randi or Bill could predict college GPAs for each and then select the candidate predicted to do better in college. Based on this prediction, Bill would be expected to earn a GPA average somewhat higher than Randi.

		Randi	Bill
X_1	SAT verbal	612	583
X_2	SAT quantitative	525	672
X_3	High school GPA	3.92	3.79

Randi: $Y = (.001)(612) + (.002)(525) + (.3)(3.92) + .3 = 3.138$

Bill: $\quad Y = (.001)(583) + (.002)(672) + (.3)(3.79) + .3 = 3.364$

Greg's Wash and Buff can provide an example of the use of regression analysis. Greg's wanted to predict how many wax jobs it would sell in a given month. The managers also wanted to determine the degree to which wax sales are determined by price, the time needed to get the job done, the advertising dollars spent promoting wax jobs, and the number of car washes sold per month. Greg's is a member of the Metropolitan Car Wash Association and has convinced thirty-nine other members to participate in the wax job study. Each car wash company will provide information about the number of wax jobs it sells and their wax price, time required to do wax jobs, advertising budget, and the number of washes sold per month. Regression analysis will then be used to solve the following equation (to identify the appropriate values for *A, B, C, D,* and *K*) and, thus, to find the importance of each factor in sales of wax jobs.

$$Y = AX_1 + BX_2 + CX_3 + DX_4 + K$$

where

Y = Number of wax jobs sold
X_1 = Price of wax job
X_2 = Average time in system
X_3 = Advertising budget
X_4 = Washes per month
K = A constant

When Greg's conducted the regression analysis on this information, the resulting equation captured the apparent cause-effect relationship among the four factors and actual wax job sales:

$$Y = (-4)X_1 + (-3)X_2 + (.1)X_3 + (.06)X_4 + 110$$

This equation represents the experience of the 40 car wash companies that participated in the study. Greg's managers tested the equation to see how well it applied to Greg's Wash and Buff. Greg's charges $39.95 per wash, has an average time in the system of 60 minutes, an advertising budget of $175, and does 10,500 washes per month. As shown, the equation predicted that Greg's should be selling 417.7 wax jobs per month.

$$Y = -4(39.95) + -3(60) + .1(175) + .06(10,500) + 110 = 417.7$$

Since Greg's actually sells about 450 wax jobs per month, the managers concluded that the prediction was quite good. How can Greg's Wash and Buff use this information? It obviously will help the managers understand why some car washes sell more wax jobs than others. More important, it will allow Greg's to identify what it can do to increase (or decrease) the number of wax jobs that it sells. Greg's can assume, for example, that it is likely to sell six additional car waxes for every 100 additional cars washed. It can also anticipate that reducing the price of a wax job by $10 would only increase demand by 40 wax jobs a month (-4×-10). Every $10 spent on advertising would probably lead to one additional wax job a month.

Perhaps most important, the equation suggests that reducing time in the system from 60 minutes to 22.5 minutes (as the earlier queuing example showed that adding a second waxer would do) would increase sales of wax jobs by 112.5 per month (-3×-37.5). The $4494.38 in additional revenue generated by these additional wax jobs ($39.95 $\times$ 112.5) would more than make up for the $1680 in wages paid each month to the second waxer ($56/day $\times$ 30 days).

By using information from the earlier queuing and regression analyses, Greg's developed a new business plan for its waxing operation. It hired a second waxer. It posted signs stating that the amount of time that customers would have to wait for their wax job to begin would average less than five minutes, and that a $5 discount would be given to anyone whose wax jobs was not completed within thirty minutes. Within three months, Greg's increased the sales of wax jobs from an average of 450 per month to over 600 per month.

The Pros and Cons of Quantitative Tools

The quantitative tools described in this chapter can help managers divide complex, difficult problems into smaller, more easily manageable parts. Managers can use these tools to learn things that they otherwise could learn only through risky trial-and-error experiments. These tools encourage managers to pay closer attention to the factors that influence the effectiveness of their business decisions. These tools identify the risks and potential payoffs of various decisions and promote a more systematic use of available information. They can save time and reduce the errors that often accompany purely subjective judgments. In short, quantitative tools can lead to better plans and better decisions.

The biggest problem with these tools happens when their use becomes detached from reality. Variables that are hard to measure are ignored. Projections are accepted despite indications from the environment that assumptions should be changed. A second problem is that even when they are accurate, quantitative tools can be expensive to use. Managers should use them only in situations in which their benefits are likely to outweigh their costs.

Many managers resist using quantitative tools because they personally resist change (as discussed in Chapter 20). Others go too far in the opposite direction and apply these tools too readily. A mathematical solution expressed to five decimal points can be totally worthless if the assumptions on which it is based are flawed.

The biggest challenge facing managers is to integrate these quantitative tools into the general management decision-making process. "No longer the exclusive toy of management scientists, decision analysis [the use of quantitative tools] is becoming an accepted managerial tool for solving everyday business problems."[1] Despite their increasingly widespread use, however, quantitative tools are seldom well integrated into the overall planning and decision-making process. What is needed now is broader recognition of the fact that the art of management improves when it is integrated with quantitative tools from the science of management.

Quantitative tools can save time and reduce errors that may occur as a result of purely subjective decisions; however, they must be used in accordance with the environmental reality of each situation in which a decision is made.

Qualitative Tools

Whereas quantitative tools generate mathematical or statistical solutions to managers' problems, qualitative tools help generate the information, ideas, and judgments that managers need for planning and decision making. Whereas quantitative (and some qualitative) techniques are focused on selecting the most desirable from among a set of options, qualitative tools focus most heavily on identifying options. The following is a list of some qualitative tools:

- Decision trees
- Brainstorming
- Synectics
- Delphi technique
- Nominal group technique

Decision Trees

The **decision tree** technique is special in that it is often used as both a leadership and a decision model. It is also special because its purpose is to help managers "decide how to decide." That is, a decision tree is a tool that helps a manager decide the extent to which subordinates should be involved in making decisions for particular situations.

Most managers have their own way of involving (or not involving) subordinates in planning and decision making. Some managers like to conduct these tasks in an autocratic and authoritarian manner. They develop plans and make decisions by themselves, without asking for information from subordinates. Other managers prefer to meet with subordinates as a group and to allow the group to have the final word. These two styles define the extremes on a continuum. In reality, neither of these two styles—nor any of the styles in between—is best for every planning and decision-making situation. Instead, managers should analyze each decision occasion and then select an approach that best fits it.

To help managers select the best planning and decision-making approach, Victor Vroom and Philip Yetton developed the "decision tree" model (see Figure 8.4). It helps managers select the appropriate amount of subordinate involvement. They described five approaches:

1. *Autocratic I (AI):* A manager makes plans and decisions alone, without any input from subordinates.

2. *Autocratic II (AII):* A manager asks for information from subordinates, who may or may not be informed as to why they are being asked. The manager then makes the plans and decisions alone.

3. *Consultative I (CI):* A manager shares the situation with subordinates and asks each individually for information and an evaluation of the problem. No group meetings are held. The manager makes the plans and decisions alone.

4. *Consultative II (CII):* A manager shares the situation with subordinates as a group and asks the group for information and evaluation of the problem. The manager makes the plans and decisions alone.

5. *Group (G):* A manager shares the situation with subordinates as a group and asks the group for information and evaluation of the problem. The manager accepts and implements the plan or decision agreed on by the group.

The best style in a particular situation becomes clear after a manager follows a "decision tree," such as that shown in Figure 8.4. To use the tree, begin on the left and answer question A. Depending on whether you answered yes or no to that question, follow the branch to the next question and repeat this process until you arrive at the right-hand end of a branch. Depending on your answers, you will have to answer between two and seven questions to arrive at the end of a branch. Next to the branch you will find a list of all of the appropriate strategies for your situation. If more than one alternative appears at the end of a branch, use either the one with the lowest costs or the one that you prefer if cost is not an issue. It is often possible to combine the characteristics of two or more acceptable strategies.

Preliminary evidence supporting the model, coupled with its favorable reception by many managers, warrants further examination.[2] Consider an

FIGURE 8.4 *Vroom-Yetton Decision Tree*

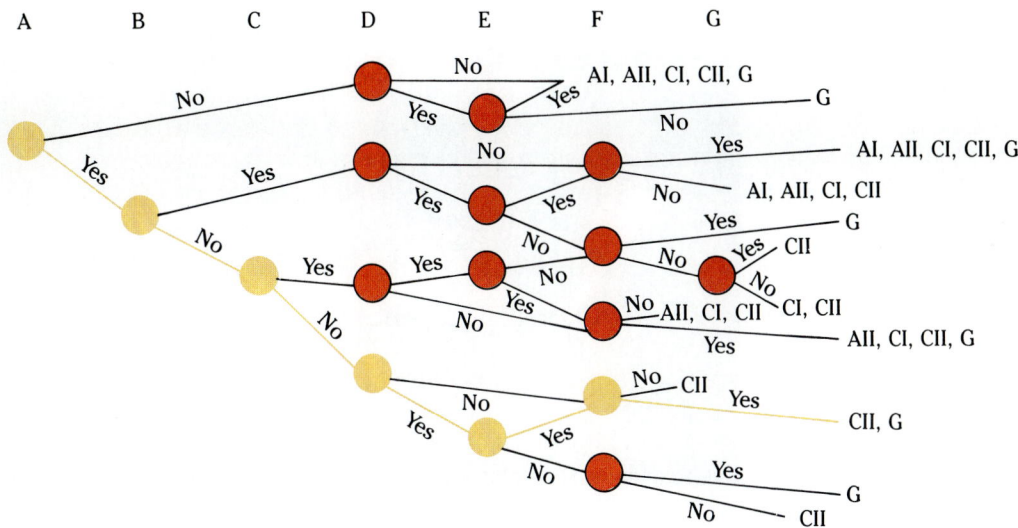

Questions
A. Is one solution better than another?
B. Is there sufficient information to make a high-quality decision without help from subordinates?
C. Is it clear exactly what problem needs to be solved?
D. Is acceptance by subordinates important for effective implementation?

E. If the decision is made independently of subordinates, will it be accepted by them?
F. Do subordinates share the organizational goals to be attained in solving this problem?
G. Is it likely that subordinates will disagree about the best solution?

Source: Adapted from V. H. Vroom and P. H. Yetton (1973), *Leadership and decision making,* Pittsburgh, PA: University of Pittsburgh Press.
Note: The highlighted path refers to the Wisconsin Tissue Mills example discussed in the text.

example of the model in actual use. Wisconsin Tissue Mills is a moderately large paper and paper products manufacturing company located in the Fox River Valley of Wisconsin. A few years ago, Vice-President of Manufacturing Bill New and other executives recognized that the company could make substantially more profits by improving quality and cutting costs at its plants. The question was not whether such steps should be taken but rather how they should be taken. Should Bill and his fellow executives identify the changes to be made, or should lower-level managers and professionals be involved in the planning process?

The approach used at Wisconsin Tissue Mills is consistent with the Vroom-Yetton decision tree. The highlighted path in Figure 8.4 identifies the branch of the decision tree that managers at that company followed for this situation.

- **A:** Is one solution better than another? **YES**
- **B:** Is there sufficient information to make a high-quality decision without help from subordinates? **NO**
- **C:** Is it clear exactly what problem needs to be solved? **NO**
- **D:** Is acceptance by subordinates important for effective implementation? **YES**
- **E:** If the decision is made independently of subordinates, will it be accepted by them? **YES**

In a brainstorming session, individuals describe any ideas they have for a potential solution to a problem. Others listen and react with more ideas. The object is to generate a wide range of potential creative solutions.

■ **F:** Do subordinates share the organizational goals to be attained in solving this problem? **YES**

Bill New and his executive colleagues identified two acceptable strategies that Vroom and Yetton would have called Consultative II (CII) and Group (G). The approach Wisconsin Tissue Mills finally selected resembles the CII approach, and it incorporates aspects of the Group approach. A number of quality groups were formed and given responsibility for identifying and evaluating possible actions for improving quality and reducing costs. The groups presented the executives with their plans, with estimates of the cost of their plans, and with projections of quality improvement and cost savings. The top executives then made a final decision on whether to implement each plan.

In such cases, the Vroom-Yetton model can prove very successful. At Wisconsin Tissue Mills, both management and employees were enthusiastic about the way the decision was handled, and the results were improved product quality, increased profits, and improved morale.

Brainstorming

Brainstorming is a technique designed to stimulate people to develop alternatives during the planning and decision-making process. Madison Avenue advertising executive Alex Osborn developed this technique in the 1950s after concluding that typical group decision-making processes inhibit rather than encourage creativity.[3] He observed that most groups discuss and evaluate an idea as soon as a group member generates it. Apparently, knowing that ideas will be evaluated immediately discourages people from developing and sharing ideas which are unusual and not yet well thought out. In short, it inhibits their creativity.

Brainstorming encourages the sharing of ideas in a setting free of the interruptions and risks of immediate evaluation and discussion. A set of basic ground rules governs a brainstorming session: no one may evaluate or criticize the ideas of others, and people are encouraged to be freewheeling in creating ideas. The more ideas produced, the better, and people are encouraged to "take off" on others' ideas ("hitchhiking").

To conduct a brainstorming session, the group is informed about the problem and asked to generate as many solutions as possible within a specified period of time. Participants are encouraged to suggest whatever comes to mind. It is emphasized that all ideas generated belong to the group, not to individuals. Criticism is forbidden.

All ideas from a brainstorming session are recorded for later evaluation either by the group or the manager (depending on which planning and decision-making strategy is being followed). Because the purpose of the technique is to generate many creative ideas, it is expected that many of the ideas eventually will prove to be of little use. The hope is that, among the many ideas offered, one or more will prove useful.

Some of the claimed advantages of the brainstorming technique include:

1. It reduces dependence on a single authority figure.
2. It encourages the open sharing of ideas.
3. It stimulates participation among group members.
4. It provides individual safety in a competitive group.
5. It maximizes output for a short period of time.
6. It ensures a nonevaluative climate.
7. It tends to be enjoyable and stimulating.[4]

How well does brainstorming work in practice? Compared to more traditional group processes, brainstorming works quite well.[5] The number and quality of ideas is better, and costs per idea generated tend to be more favorable. Through the brainstorming process, group members tend to focus on the task at hand, and, as a result, interpersonal conflict and pressures toward conformity decline. In addition, ideas generated by group members are likely to be accepted by the group.

Unfortunately, the aspects of brainstorming that help make it successful also create some problems. Because ideas are not evaluated, at the end of a brainstorming session the only product is a list of ideas. There is no plan, there is no solution, and the initial problem still exists. This lack of closure can create dissatisfaction among participants, especially when someone else (a manager or another group) evaluates the ideas that the brainstorming group has generated.

Many organizations use brainstorming because it appears to have many advantages in comparison to traditional group decision making and only a few drawbacks. There is some evidence, however, that individuals "brainstorming" alone would generate more and better-quality ideas than they would in a brainstorming group.[6] Even in a relaxed atmosphere, the presence of others may still inhibit the quantity and creativity of ideas generated by brainstorming group members.

Individual brainstorming is helpful in some situations, group brainstorming in others. A group session encourages each member to devote the necessary time to idea generation, and, because group sessions are often more enjoyable than solitary work, they can create an esprit de corps and satisfy people's social needs. Group sessions remind each member that others have many good ideas, and they can improve group commitment to ideas and increase communication within the group. When these factors are important, managers may use brainstorming groups rather than individual brainstorming.

Synectics

The Greek word *synectic* means "the joining together of different and apparently irrelevant elements."[7] The **synectic technique,** designed to develop creative ideas, attempts to integrate "diverse individuals into a problem-stating problem-solving group."[8] This technique gets people to focus on developing a single insightful solution and includes developing, evaluating, and critiquing ideas. Ideally, synectics produces a single, detailed potential solution to a problem. The strengths and weaknesses of the solution are identified during the process and attempts are made to resolve the weaknesses. As a result, a relatively complete plan often results from the use of the synectic process.

Synectics is based on the assumption that a person is divided into two parts. The first part is concerned about safety and is analytical, suspicous, logical, and cautious—and, thus, inhibits experimentation and creativity. The second part of a person, though, strives toward learning and is impulsive and sensation-seeking and likes to have fun. Because the self-censoring first part inhibits the creativity of the second part, the synectic approach is structured to encourage the impulsive, creative aspects of the individual to override his or her self-censoring tendencies. (See "A Closer Look: Synectics.")

The synectic technique includes the following steps:

1. *Problem statement and background information stage:* The group leader describes a general area of discussion but avoids identifying the specific problem. Creative thinking on the problem is encouraged. The leader presents background information on the problem and the goals associated with an ideal solution.

2. *Goal-wishing stage:* Group members are encouraged to wish for anything that comes to mind that could address the problem. As in brainstorming, in this "freewheeling stage," people are encouraged to generate wild ideas and to hitchhike. Exploring ideas and not evaluating them are of utmost importance at this stage.

3. *Excursion stage:* Participants are asked to forget about the specific problem. They are asked to generate ideas about a somewhat unrelated area that eventually might be related to the problem at hand.

4. *Forced-fit stage:* Participants take ideas from the excursion stage and force them to fit the initial problem. Although this often appears quite unusual and obtuse, it is intended to encourage creativity. In fact, evidence suggests that many great thinkers develop ideas from such experimental thinking.

5. *Itemized response stage:* The group picks one of the ideas generated during the forced-fit stage and pursues it further. The idea is dissected and only its positive aspects are identified. After all the positive aspects have been explored, the idea's limitations are addressed. This focus on the positive is intended to encourage productivity and creativity.

The outcome of the synectic process is a single unique plan or decision that has undergone considerable evaluation. The process tends to produce innovative ideas. The process also generates a list of the advantages

Synectics: A Phone That Can't Be Beaten (or Stolen)

Get several of your friends together and spend a half an hour brainstorming on the following issue: Identify ways to vandalize a pay telephone. Remember, feel free to come up with ideas that are as wild and unusual as possible. No matter how creative your solutions, they have probably all been used on phones owned by the New York Telephone Company. In fact, repairing and replacing damaged and stolen pay phones has become a major expense for the company during recent years.

New York Telephone decided to use the synectic approach to solve this vandalism problem. They enlisted the help of George Prince, developer of the synectic approach, and followed the five steps of the process.[1]

At the *problem statement stage*, the scope of the problem was described and it was agreed that an ideal solution to the problem would involve the total elimination of all pay phone vandalism and theft.

At the *goal-wishing stage*, a wide range of "wishes" was generated. One participant, for example, wished for an indestructible phone booth door that would open only after the insertion of money. Another participant wished that pay phones could be designed like punching bags, capable of withstanding repeated blows. An-

other wished the phones could be disguised as fire hydrants. This idea was hitchhiked on by someone who wished that the phone could be as indestructible as a fire hydrant. Continued discussion led to a wide range of creative ideas.

During the *excursion stage*, the leader suggested that the group follow up its ideas about indestructibility from the perspective of the Wild West. Discussion followed on the indestructibility of the bank safe, the indestructible relationship between a cowboy and his horse, and other equally "destruction-proof" ideas.

The *forced-fit stage* required participants to apply their Wild West ideas from the excursion stage to the problem of pay phone vandalism and theft in modern-day New York. When someone followed up on the idea of the impenetrable safe, for example, the suggestion was to build phones right into the walls of buildings. The

idea of the indestructible pillars of rock found in western canyons gave rise to a suggestion for designing phones with no external appendages.

At the *itemized response stage*, a single solution to the problem of vandalism and theft of pay phones was specified. The group documented its advantages, its possible drawbacks, and ways to reduce these limitations.

The solution was to design a pay phone that resembles a bank's automated teller and to build it into the wall of a building so that it fits flush with the wall. The phone should have no appendages, not even buttons. Instead of a handset, it would have a speakerphone. Instead of a dial or buttons, the wall would have touch-sensitive areas. If a caller wanted privacy, he or she could attach a Walkman-type headset.

1. G. Prince (1980), *Problem solving strategies: The synectic approach*, Del Mar, CA: CRM McGraw-Hill Films.

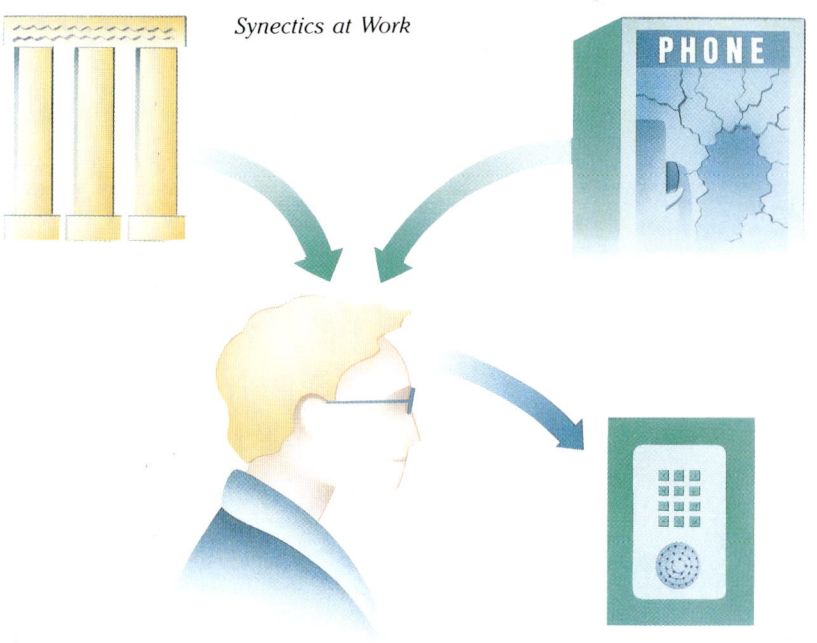

Synectics at Work

and disadvantages to the chosen plan or decision and suggestions for dealing with the disadvantages.

Although the synectic approach can be quite useful for creative planning and decision making, its cost is high. Furthermore, it produces only one potential solution to a problem. If that solution turns out to be unusable, the problem remains, and the process has failed.

The Delphi Technique

Solutions to problems that come from groups in which participants interact face to face often are of lower quality than solutions that come from individuals who work alone on the same problem. To address this problem, Norman C. Dalkey and his associates at the Rand Corporation developed the Delphi process.[9] The **Delphi technique** is a group process designed to bring information and the judgments of people together to facilitate planning and decision making. The Delphi process gathers information and opinions without physically assembling the contributors to the group effort, however. Instead, information is exchanged via mailed questionnaires. The Delphi technique is useful when a problem would benefit from group participation but it is not feasible to assemble individuals for a meeting because of time constraints, geographical dispersion, or desires to remain anonymous.

The Delphi technique, therefore, capitalizes on the combined creativity of a group of individuals but avoids the problems that often arise in face-to-face groups. The procedure allows for anonymity among participants and encourages feedback, even among geographically dispersed participants. A group coordinator orchestrates the process through a series of formal communications (usually by mail) to individual members (no two members communicate directly with one another). Although hundreds of individuals can participate in the Delphi technique, a maximum of thirty participants is usually desirable.[10]

Chemical Bank is a huge banking conglomerate with hundreds of individual banks under its umbrella. Suppose Chemical Bank were to encounter a significant decline in the amount of money being deposited at its banks. Suppose further that its executives concluded that the way to increase deposits would be through investment instruments beyond those traditionally offered, such as savings plans and certificates of deposit. What Chemical wants is not merely to copy the investment ideas of competitors but to create new investment instruments to bring in additional deposits. Top executives would like to hear ideas from some of Chemical's many banks throughout the country, but bringing them together to address this issue would be extremely difficult and expensive. The Delphi technique could help Chemical Bank identify and evaluate potential new investment instruments.

The Delphi technique generally consists of several stages:

1. *Development of the Delphi question and the first inquiry:* The coordinator prepares a written statement of the problem and sends it to each group member. With this statement, the coordinator sends a questionnaire requesting suggestions and potential solutions to the problem. At Chemical Bank, for instance, coordinator Matt Harr

selects twenty-five banks and appoints one banker from each to participate. Matt sends all twenty-five bankers a statement that reads, in part, "Chemical needs to identify potential new investment instruments to increase deposits at the banks." The questionnaire asks each banker in the Delphi group to present his or her ideas for potential new instruments and emphasizes that, at this stage, ideas need not be fully developed or completely evaluated.

2. *The first response:* Each participant, independently and anonymously, records his or her comments, suggestions, and potential solutions and returns these directly to the coordinator. At Chemical Bank, for example, the twenty-five participating bankers send their completed questionnaires directly to Matt.

3. *Analysis of the first response, feedback, and the second inquiry:* The coordinator prepares a written summary of all comments and sends this to each participant, along with another questionnaire. Depending on the nature of the first-round comments, this questionnaire might seek clarification of earlier comments, address apparent disagreements, or request more highly refined suggestions in particular areas. At Chemical, Matt reviews all twenty-five returned questionnaires and develops a single list that includes all suggestions from the Delphi members. He prepares and sends a second questionnaire to the participants that begins with the statement "Attached is a list showing all of the ideas the group has generated on potential investment instruments. Please review each of them, list suggestions on how you would refine each, and briefly evaluate the degree to which you believe the idea would be likely to generate increased deposits."

4. *The second response:* Each participant, again independently and anonymously, records his or her responses to the questionnaire and sends these directly to the coordinator. Each of the twenty-five participating bankers at Chemical completes the second questionnaire and returns it directly to Matt, who reviews this input, summarizes it, and makes yet another mailing.

5. *Continuation of the process:* The Delphi coordinator continues to follow this same procedure until a clear solution emerges, until a point of diminishing returns is reached, or until a vote is taken. Often, rather than take a formal vote, a statistical summary of the recommendations of group members is used. Research results suggest that stability of opinion is generally reached after four rounds.[11] When finished, Chemical Bank's Delphi group has produced a list of ideas for potential new instruments, refined descriptions of each, and an evaluation of each instrument's strengths and weaknesses. If desired, Matt could ask group participants to rate the promise of each idea so that he could include a statistical evaluation in his summary of the final results. (See Figure 8.5.)

Like the other qualitative decision tools, the Delphi technique has both strengths and limitations. As you have learned, the technique can involve large numbers of participants, even if they are physically separated from one another. The technique tends to produce a large amount of information and many high-quality ideas. Many of the dysfunctions of face-to-face

FIGURE 8.5   The Delphi Technique

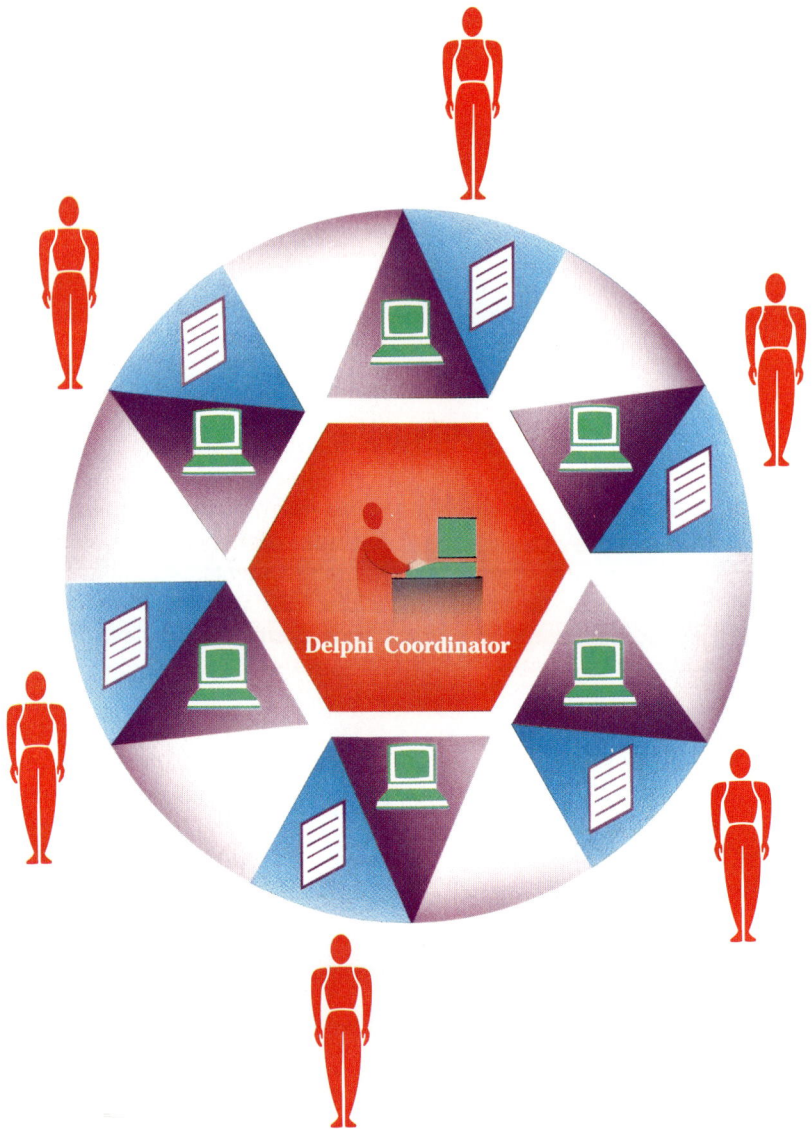

Delphi Coordinator

groups (such as pressure to conform and interpersonal conflict) can be greatly reduced; however, the technique is slow. In fact, it has been estimated that a minimum of forty-five days is required to complete a Delphi operation, although the use of computer networks and electronic mail systems can greatly reduce this problem.[12] The delays and the impersonality of the process do little to build group cohesiveness or commitment to the solution. In addition, group members need good written-communication skills to participate effectively in a Delphi exercise. Participants also have to be motivated to produce timely and constructive responses. Finally, the success of the technique requires a coordinator who is adept at interpreting, translating, and summarizing input from members at each stage of the process.

In a Nominal Group session, members attempt to identify solutions to an important problem. They do so by working alone to generate ideas, together to discuss the ideas, and then alone to vote on them. The result is a rank-ordered list of potential solutions.

Nominal Group Technique (NGT)

The **nominal group technique (NGT)** is a group decision-making process designed to generate a large number of creative potential solutions to a problem, to evaluate these solutions, and to rank them from best to worst. Since its introduction in 1971, the NGT has become extremely popular.[13] It has proved particularly useful when individual group members have some expert knowledge but none has the knowledge required to solve the problem completely. Improving the quality of paper products produced by Wisconsin Tissue Mills, for example, might require the expertise of engineers, production managers, purchasing agents, quality control analysts, and others. In fact, in response to the recommendations generated by the Vroom-Yetton decision tree, managers at Wisconsin Tissue Mills decided to form twelve NGT groups to develop ideas for product quality and profitability improvements.

The NGT is a highly structured, interactive process that was designed to capitalize on the strengths of group decision making and to control the inhibiting factors often associated with face-to-face groups. The NGT is a problem-solving and idea-generating approach designed for situations in which individual judgments must be identified and combined to reach a decision. It is not a technique for routine, noncomplex decision making.

The NGT process consists of at least four steps. It begins with a silent, individual generation of ideas. This is followed by a round-robin recording of these ideas. Next, ideas are discussed and evaluated sequentially by the group. Finally, there is a confidential vote on the relative importance of the ideas.

At the beginning of an NGT session, a "leader" presents a description of the problem to be addressed by the group. At Wisconsin Tissue Mills, the following statement was made:

Wisconsin Tissue recognizes the opportunity for employee groups to contribute further to cost reduction, production improvement, and

Andrew H. Van de Ven

as a standard operating group process for planning, problem solving, and decision making in contemporary organizations throughout the world.

"[NGT's] applications have gone far beyond our initial expectations."

Andrew H. Van de Ven is 3M Professor of Human Systems Management and director of the Minnesota Innovation Research Program. Professor Van de Ven's work is focused on the management of organization innovation, program planning, and group decision-making processes.

1. What impact has the Nominal Group Technique (NGT) had on management decision making?

Substantial. Andre Delbecq and I have found that the Nominal Group Technique has become incorporated

2. What have been the biggest disappointments and rewards in the use of the NGT?

The most significant benefit of the NGT is its reliability and robustness. Beyond our initial expectations, we have found that the technique consistently performs well, even when NGT leaders have had very little prior training. Its applications have gone beyond our initial expectations. My disappointment, if there is one, is that practitioners too often rely *only* on the NGT, to the exclusion of other group and organizational developmental processes, for addressing organizational change in their planning efforts. Andre Delbecq and I consider the NGT as but one step in a larger

process of program planning and organizational problem solving.

3. What impact has the Delphi Technique had on management decision making? How would you most like to change the Delphi?

The Delphi Technique is widely used and has had significant impact as a method for obtaining the opinions of individuals with respect to a wide variety of issues. The Delphi technique generates about the same number of ideas from group participants as the NGT, but it does not perform as well as the NGT in two important areas. Because people work face-to-face during an NGT session, the NGT generates both greater levels of satisfaction with the process and higher levels of motivation for involvement in subsequent steps of problem solving than does the Delphi Technique. To improve the Delphi technique, therefore, I would suggest using telecommunication conferencing methods to permit Delphi participants to interact and to discuss and evaluate the ideas they generated independently.

product quality. Specifically, what suggestions could your group make for actions or organizational changes at Wisconsin Tissue to
   facilitate cost reduction?
   improve production?
   enhance product quality?

Immediately, Step One—a silent generation of ideas—begins. Each group member works independently for five to ten minutes, generating and recording ideas. This phase of the process is identical to and has all the advantages of a short individual brainstorming session. This step provides time for people to search their memories and reflect on the problem. It avoids competition for the group's time and attention, it avoids pressures for conformity, it prevents the group from rushing toward a premature resolution, and it prevents the group from evaluating ideas as it generates them.

During Step Two, ideas are combined into a master list. First, the leader asks one member of the group to state an idea and records it on a list without discussing it. A second member of the group is then asked for one idea, and it is recorded. This process is continued round-robin, each member giving one idea at a time, until all ideas have been listed. No discussion is permitted yet, but hitchhiking is encouraged. The round-robin approach separates ideas from their creators and focuses attention on sharing rather than on evaluating ideas. Finally, this process prevents anyone from talking too much or becoming argumentative. Lists of ideas generated by employee groups at Wisconsin Tissue Mills typically contained more than thirty suggestions for quality and cost improvements.

In Step Three, the leader reads the first idea from the list and asks if any member would like to ask for or provide clarification of its meaning. Members then can briefly express their opinions about the strengths and weaknesses of the idea. Each item on the list is discussed sequentially in this way. The leader discourages attempts to select any idea as a solution, thus preventing the group from spending too much time on a single issue. This approach also prevents a single individual from dominating the group.

Step Four consists of a confidential vote on the merits of the various ideas. Each member of the group is asked to work alone and select a small number of ideas from the list (usually five to seven) that he or she feels are most important. Each member then rank-orders the ideas according to his or her personal evaluation and votes on them by assigning points based on his or her rank-ordering. Individual votes are recorded anonymously on index cards and submitted to the leader, who tallies them. After the voting, the ideas are rank-ordered. The aggregation of individual votes determines the relative importance of ideas. The voting assures that each group member has equal influence on the outcome of the session. At Wisconsin Tissue Mills, the voting process typically identified three or four ideas that were rated highly by most members of the group, another four or five ideas considered moderately promising, and about twenty ideas that group members agreed were less promising.

Some NGT groups go to a fifth step, another serial discussion of ideas. People share additional information and discuss the voting pattern. Sometimes this discussion is focused only on those ideas that were ranked relatively high by the voters. Finally, in a sixth step, the group conducts a final vote. Wisconsin Tissue Mills could have selected its top three or four ideas for further discussion and submitted these to a second vote.

The NGT can be an extremely effective tool. It generates a large number of ideas, many of which are of high quality. It also produces a lot of low-quality ideas, but these "wash out" based on the vote. People have strong feelings of accomplishment and commitment to the solutions arrived at by the group. Members also feel committed to their group, enjoy the process, and feel a strong sense of having done a satisfying job because they can clearly see the results of their work.

The NGT process also has costs, however. It takes a couple of hours to implement, and it requires advanced planning. The high level of structure reduces feelings of involvement for some members. This structure also reduces the direct interaction among participants and, therefore, does not work well when situations require negotiation between two or more parties. Furthermore, the process can succeed only if all members agree to abide by the rules. As noted by its creators, Andre L. Delbecq and Andrew H. Van de Ven, the technique is best suited for complex situations that require the judgment of a number of experts and for which no single person has the only "right" solution.

The Pros and Cons of Qualitative Tools

Qualitative tools can help managers perform a number of managerial tasks. The decision tree helps managers decide how to decide—whether to consult others or not. The decision tree presents managers with a systematic model for deciding how to make decisions about planning, organizing, directing, and controlling organizational resources. Brainstorming, synectics, Delphi, and the nominal group technique are structured, systematic processes for helping managers gather others' ideas and information. These processes facilitate creativity and probe the judgment of experts. Many of these techniques structure group interaction in ways that reduce the liabilities associated with group decision making, while simultaneously capitalizing on the assets that are associated with group processes (see Chapter 7).

Because each technique is designed for specific purposes, managers need to use them carefully in the appropriate settings. Used well, systematic approaches are helpful. Used badly, both qualitative and quantitative models may erode intuition, passion, and the art of management.

Tools for Planning and Decision Making in Review

Managers use a variety of tools as they plan and make decisions. Some of these tools are quantitative; they use mathematical and statistical models of planning and decision making. Others are qualitative; they concentrate on the generation and processing of ideas, opinions, and judgments. When used together, these tools can provide an effective combination of the science and art of management.

Some of the most popular quantitative tools available to managers include those intended for inventory management, resource allocation, scheduling and sequencing, and predicting or forecasting. Inventory models help managers balance inventory needs with the costs of procuring and maintaining supplies and products. Managers with resource-allocation problems can use linear programming to identify the best ways to use scarce resources. Managers with waiting-line problems can use queuing models to identify the best number of lines to maintain. Entire, complex projects can be organized, scheduled, and monitored using Program Evaluation and Review Techniques (PERT).

Other quantitative tools deal with predicting or forecasting events. Break-even analysis identifies the point at which revenues should equal the total cost of producing a product or service. Time series analysis projects past business trends into the future and assumes that past trends will continue. Causal models, such as regression analysis, identify the underlying reasons for past events and use these facts as the basis for predicting future events.

Useful qualitative tools include decision trees, brainstorming, synectics, the Delphi technique, and the nominal group technique. The decision tree helps managers determine the appropriate degree of worker participation in planning and decision making.

When the decision tree indicates that worker participation in planning or decision making is appropriate, managers can use one of the other qualitative tools to get workers' contributions. During brainstorming, a group of individuals generates as many innovative ideas as possible. During synectics, a group develops and evaluates a single, highly creative solution. The Delphi technique provides a way to capitalize on group processes without physically assembling the group members. Finally, the nominal group technique integrates aspects of all of these group approaches into an effective face-to-face approach for addressing single-issue problems.

Notes

1. J. W. Ulvila and R. V. Brown (September-October 1982), Decision analysis comes of age, *Harvard Business Review*, 140.

2. A. G. Jago (1982), Leadership: Perspectives in theory and research, *Management Science*, 28, 315–36; R. J. House and M. L. Baetz (1979), Leadership: Some empirical generalizations and new research directions, in B. M. Staw, ed., *Research in organizational behavior*, vol. 1, Greenwich, CT: JAI Press, 341–423.

3. A. F. Osborn (1957), *Applied imagination*, New York: Scribner's.

4. R. W. Napier and M. K. Gershenfeld (1985), *Groups: Theory and experience*, 3rd ed., Boston: Houghton Mifflin, 334.

5. D. W. Taylor, P. C. Berry, and C. H. Block (1958), Does group participation when using brainstorming techniques facilitate or inhibit creative thinking? *Administrative Science Quarterly*, 3, 23–47; J. K. Murnighan (1981), Group decision making: What strategies should you use? *Management Review*, 70, 55–62.

6. Taylor, et al., 1958.

7. W. J. Gordon (1961), *Synectics: The development of creative capacity*, New York: Harper & Row, 3.

8. *Ibid.*

9. N. C. Dalkey and O. Helmer (1963), An experimental application of the Delphi method to the use of experts, *Management Science*, 9, 458–67; A. L. Delbecq, A. H. Van de Ven, and D. H. Gustafson (1975), *Group techniques for program planning: A guide to nominal group and delphi processes*, Glenview, IL: Scott, Foresman; C. M. Moore (1987), *Group techniques for idea building*, Newbury Park, CA: Sage.

10. Delbecq, et al., 1975.
11. R. C. Erffmeyer, E. S. Erffmeyer, and I. M. Lane (1986), The Delphi technique: Empirical evaluation of the optimal number of rounds, *Group and Organizational Studies*, 11, 120–28.
12. Delbecq, et al., 1975.
13. A. L. Delbecq and A. H. Van de Ven (1971), A group process model for problem identification and program planning, *Journal of Applied Behavioral Science*, 7, 466–92; A. L. Delbecq and A. H. Van de Ven (1971), Nominal versus interactive group processes for committee decision-making effectiveness, *Academy of Management Journal*, 14, 203–11.

Key Terms

quantitative tools	causal modeling
qualitative tools	regression analysis
economic order quantity (EOQ)	decision tree
linear programming (LP)	brainstorming
queuing models	synectic technique
break-even analysis	Delphi technique
time series analysis	nominal group technique (NGT)

Issues for Review and Discussion

1. Describe the purpose of an inventory planning and decision model, such as EOQ (economic order quantity).
2. Discuss the information that a manager must have before using linear programming to solve a resource allocation problem.
3. Use PERT (Program Evaluation and Review Technique) to outline a plan for writing a term paper.
4. Select a technique that could be used by your college bookstore to project the demand for 5-1/4-inch floppy disks for the upcoming academic year, and explain your selection.
5. How could the student-body president at your college use the Vroom-Yetton model to determine the degree to which others should be involved in planning the annual budget? Explain your answer step by step.
6. Describe a situation in which brainstorming would be an appropriate qualitative tool for a manager to use.
7. Identify the two biggest potential drawbacks of the synectic approach to planning and decision making.
8. Under what conditions should a manager use the Delphi technique rather than the nominal group technique?
9. Discuss the pros and cons of quantitative planning and decision-making tools for managers.
10. Discuss the pros and cons of qualitative planning and decision-making tools for managers.

Suggested Readings

Anderson, J. C. and Hoffmann, T. R. (1978). A perspective on the implementation of management science. *Academy of Management Review*, 3, 563–71.

Boulanger, D. G. (1961). Program evaluation and review technique. *Advanced Management*, 26, 8–12.

Fox, W. M. (1987). *Effective group problem solving*. San Francisco: Jossey-Bass.

Levitt, T. (18 December 1978). A heretical view of management science. *Fortune*, 50–52.

Moore, C. M. (1987). *Group techniques for idea building*. Newbury Park, CA: Sage.

Murnighan, J. K. (1981). Group decision making: What strategies should you use? *Management Review*, 70, 55–62.

Napier, R. W. and Gershenfeld, M. K. (1985). *Groups: Theory and experience*, 3rd ed., Boston: Houghton Mifflin, 334–35.

Pender, B. and Stair, R. M., Jr. (1986). *Microcomputer software for management science and operations management*. Boston: Allyn and Bacon.

Vroom, V. H. (1972). A new look at managerial decision making. *Organizational Dynamics*, 1, 66–80.

CASE _Harvey Industries_

By Donald F. Condit of the Lawrence Institute of Technology

Harvey Industries, a Wisconsin Company, was incorporated in 1950 and specializes in the assembly of high-pressure washer systems and in the sale of repair parts for these systems. The products range from small, portable high-pressure washers to large, industrial installations for snow removal from vehicles stored outdoors during the winter months. Typical uses for high-pressure water cleaning occur for automobiles, airplanes, buildings, engines, ice cream plants, packing plants, swimming pools, and machinery. Harvey's industrial customers include General Motors, Ford, Chrysler, Delta Airlines, United Parcel Service, and the Shell Oil Company.

Although the industrial applications are a significant part of its sales, Harvey Industries is primarily an assembler of equipment for coin-operated self-service car wash systems. The typical car wash is of concrete block construction with an equipment room in the center flanked on either side by a number of bays. Cars are driven into the bays, where the driver can wash and wax the car, utilizing high-pressure hot water and liquid wax. A bill changer is available to provide change for the equipment and the purchase of various products from a coin-operated dispenser. These products include paper towels, a white-wall cleaner, and an upholstery cleaner. Harvey supplies its customers with all of the equipment, supplies, and products necessary for operation.

In recent years, Harvey Industries has been in financial difficulty, losing money in three of the previous four years. The most recent year's results are a loss of $17,174 on sales of $1,238,674.

The company employs twenty-three people with the management team consisting of the following key employees:

> President
>
> Sales manager
>
> Manufacturing manager
>
> Controller
>
> Purchasing manager

The abbreviated organization chart in Figure 8B reflects the reporting relationship of the key employees and the three individuals who report directly to the manufacturing manager.

The Current Inventory Control System

The current inventory control "system" consists of orders for stock replenishment being made by the stockroom foreperson, the purchasing manager, or the manufacturing manager when one of them notices that inventory is low. An order for replenishment of the inventory is also placed whenever someone (either a customer or an employee in the assembly area) wants an item that is out of stock.

Some inventory is needed for the assembly of the high-pressure equipment for the car wash and industrial applications. There are current and accurate lists of materials for these which are generally known well in advance of the scheduled time of production.

The majority of orders is for repair parts and supplies used by the car washes, such as paper towels, detergent, and wax concentrate. Because of the constant and rugged use of the car wash equipment, there is a steady demand for various repair parts.

The stockroom is well organized, with items stored in locations according to each vendor. The number of vendors is limited, and each vendor generally supplies many different stock items. For example, the repair parts from Allen Bradley, a manufacturer of electric motors, are stocked in one location. These parts are used to provide service for the many electrical motors used for car wash high-pressure pump and motor assemblies.

Because of the large number of repair parts, there are generally two employees working in the stockroom, the stockroom foreperson and an assistant, both of whom handle customer orders. Many customers come to Harvey's plant to get the parts or supplies they need. Other orders come by telephone and are shipped by United Parcel Service the same day.

Some inventory is stored on the shop assembly floor. This consists of low-value items, which are used every day, such as nuts, bolts, screws, and washers. These items do not amount to a large percentage of Harvey's purchases; unfortunately the assembly area is often out of one of these basic items, and this causes a significant amount of downtime for the assembly lines.

Paperwork is kept to a minimum. A sales slip listing the part numbers and quantities sold to a customer are generally filled out for each sale. If the assembly department needs items that

FIGURE 8B

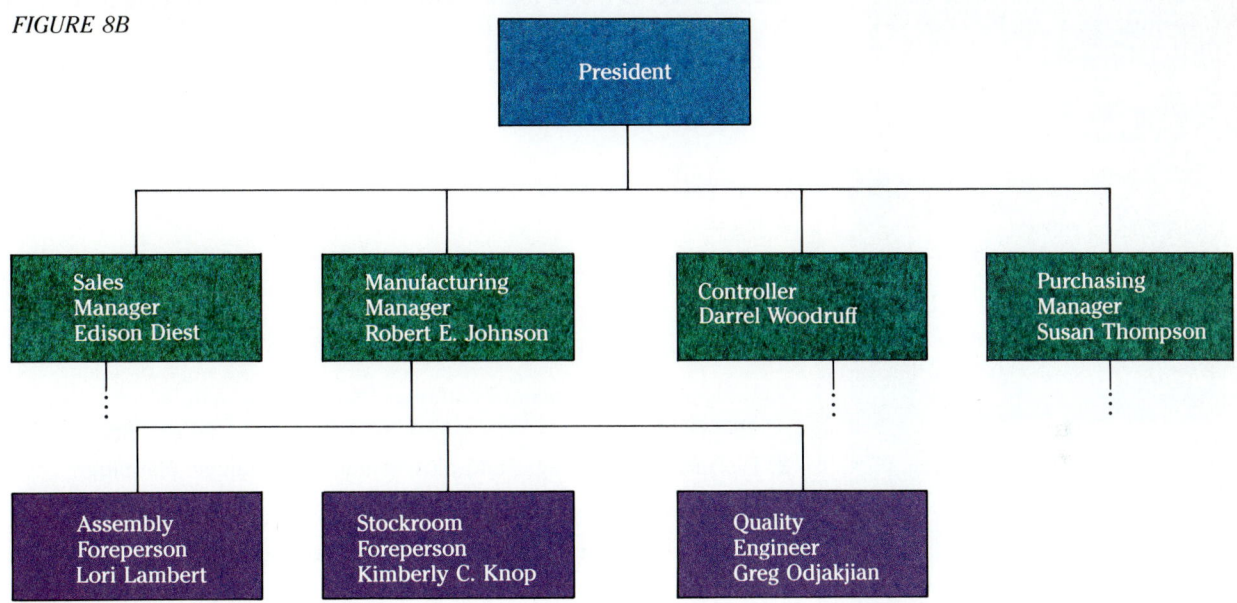

are not stocked on the assembly floor, someone from that department enters the stockroom and withdraws the necessary material. No paperwork is done for items removed for use on the assembly floor.

The company carries 973 different items in stock. Purchases amounted to $314,673 last year. Although the company does not use a computer, it does have accurate records on how much money was spent on each part last year. An analysis of that data showed that $220,684 was spent on just 179 of the parts.

Harvey Industries purchases items from both manufacturers and wholesalers. Fortunately these suppliers carry most of the items Harvey purchases in stock so that Harvey can usually replenish its inventory in two or three days after submitting an order.

Harvey Industries' recent losses have caused its auditing firm to become concerned about the company's ability to continue in business. Recently the company has been selling excess land adjoining its manufacturing facility to generate the cash to meet its financial obligations. Also of concern is the rising level of money tied up in inventory. At the last audit, inventory was valued at $124,324.

The New President

Because of the recent death of the owner, the trust department of a Milwaukee bank, as trustee for the estate, has taken over the company's affairs and appointed a new president, Cindy Herring. Cindy quickly identified many problem areas, among them inventory control. To solve the problem, she re-

tained a consultant to make specific recommendations concerning a revised inventory control system.

Questions

1. Pick a quantitative planning and decision-making tool you feel would be useful to Cindy. Briefly explain how and why this tool would be used.

2. Pick a qualitative planning and decision-making tool you feel would be useful to Cindy. Briefly explain how and why this tool would be useful.

3. What recommendations would you make to Harvey Industries' new president?

Strategic Management: Planning for Environmental Fit

Student Learning Objectives

After reading this chapter, you should be able to:

1. Understand the concept of strategic management and its importance.

2. Discuss the advantages and disadvantages of strategic planning.

3. Name and discuss the three levels of strategic planning.

4. Describe each of the nine steps involved in the strategic planning and implementation process.

5. Understand the three major problems addressed by a strategic plan.

6. Describe the various ways in which organizations can resolve strategic planning problems.

7. Explain the concept of strategic business units, the way in which they are classified according to market factors, and the appropriate strategies for use with each classification.

8. Describe the three generic approaches to organizational strategy.

9. Discuss the reasons for strategic planning in both small and not-for-profit organizations.

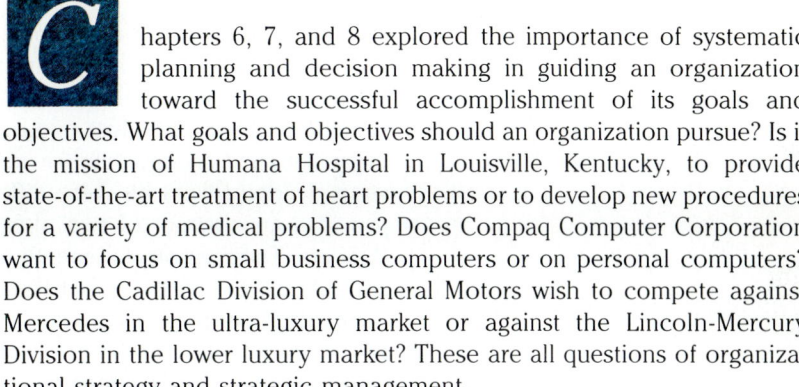

*C*hapters 6, 7, and 8 explored the importance of systematic planning and decision making in guiding an organization toward the successful accomplishment of its goals and objectives. What goals and objectives should an organization pursue? Is it the mission of Humana Hospital in Louisville, Kentucky, to provide state-of-the-art treatment of heart problems or to develop new procedures for a variety of medical problems? Does Compaq Computer Corporation want to focus on small business computers or on personal computers? Does the Cadillac Division of General Motors wish to compete against Mercedes in the ultra-luxury market or against the Lincoln-Mercury Division in the lower luxury market? These are all questions of organizational strategy and strategic management.

The Concept of Strategic Management

Strategic management is that part of the management process concerned with achieving an overall integration of an organization's internal divisions, while simultaneously integrating the organization with its external environment. Strategic management does this in two basic ways. First, it considers formulation—the planning that leads to the development of organizational goals and specific statements of action. Second, it involves implementation—the design and use of organizational subsystems and resources to operate strategic plans. Strategic management, then, formulates and implements tactics that try to match an organization as closely as possible to its task environment for the purpose of meeting its objectives.

Strategic Planning

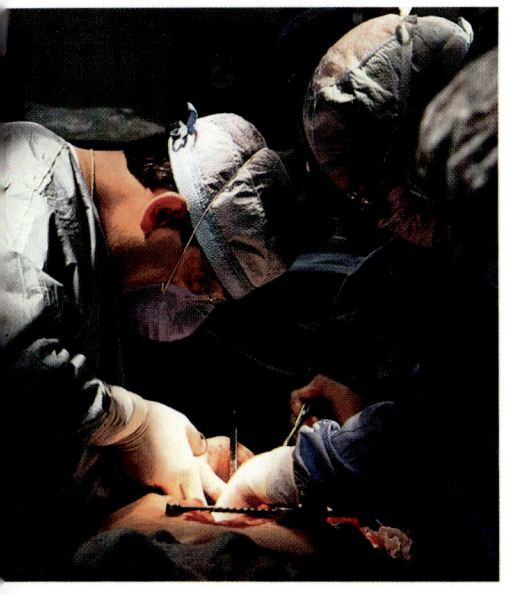

Is it the mission of Humana Hospital to provide state-of-the-art treatment of heart problems or to develop new procedures for a variety of medical problems?

Strategy is the art and science of combining the many resources available to achieve the best match between an organization and its environment. Top managers' active, conscious attempts to design a scheme to position an organization within its external environment are known as **strategic planning.** An organization's **strategic plan** outlines a long-term vision for the organization. It specifies the organization's reason for existing, its strategic objectives, and its operational strategies. An organization's strategic plan, thus, answers a set of fundamental questions: *What* business is it in or does it want to be in? *What* kind of organization is it or does it want to be? *How* is it going to operate to achieve this strategic position? A strategic plan, therefore, is a comprehensive framework that guides the decisions that determine the nature and direction of organizational activities.

An **organizational mission,** a statement that specifies an organization's reason for being, answers the question "What business(es) should be undertaken?" This mission is set forth in a **mission statement.** It encapsulates managers' vision for their organization based on its internal and external environments, its capabilities, and the nature of its customers or clients. The mission statement for Lil'America Builders, the small construction company mentioned in Chapter 8, simply states that the company is in and will remain in the business of home remodeling.

Note that a particular mission statement does not necessarily dictate specific strategic objectives or operational strategies. In fact, two different organizations can have almost identical mission statements (and even strategic objectives) but very different operational strategies. Table 9.1 provides an abstract of two alternative strategic plans for Lil'America Builders. The mission statement and strategic objectives in the two plans in Table 9.1 are identical, but the operational strategies are different.

Strategic objectives provide statements of definable and measurable accomplishments that, when realized, fulfill an organization's mission statement. Each of Lil'America's strategic plans, for example, shows six strategic objectives ranging from the amount of profit the company would like to earn per job to the percentage of business it wants to gain through the recommendations of satisfied customers (review Table 9.1). Finally, **operational strategies** specify the actions that are to be taken in order to accomplish these objectives. Lil'America has two different operational strategies, depending on which strategic plan it decides to use (review Table 9.1).

Characteristics of Strategic Plans Strategic plans have several characteristics:

1. They are *long-term* and position an organization within its external environment.
2. They are *pervasive* and cover many organizational activities.
3. They *integrate, guide, and control* organizational activities for the immediate and long-range future.
4. They establish *boundaries* for managerial decision making. Strategic plans are an organization's primary document and require that all managerial decisions be consistent with its goals.[1]

Thus, strategic plans set forth an organization's long-term goals; its intermediate objectives; and its purpose, or basic role, in society.

Strategy Components As managers construct a strategic plan, they must consider several important factors that relate to their organization:

- **Scope**—an organization's present and planned interactions with its environment. Scope also identifies the organization's domain, such as the markets in which it expects to compete, and the nature and character of these interactions, such as methods of competition. In constructing the strategic plan for Lil'America, for example, the owner had to consider: 1) whether he wanted to restrict the business solely to home remodeling (yes) and 2) how to obtain home remodeling customers (at least 50 percent through word-of-mouth) profitably (by controlling costs).

- **Resource deployment**—the internal distribution of an organization's resources, including how much money it will spend on research and development, for production, and so on in pursuit of its goals. At Lil'America, the owner decided to allot money for salaries high enough to retain skilled carpenters, purchase a microcomputer

TABLE 9.1   Strategic Plans for Lil'America Builders

Plan #1	Plan #2
A. Mission Statement	**A. Mission Statement**
We are in and will remain in the business of home remodeling	We are in and will remain in the business of home remodeling
B. Strategic Objectives	**B. Strategic Objectives**
1. For profits to constitute 15–20 percent of the charge to the homeowner for individual remodeling projects	1. For profits to constitute 15–20 percent of the charge to the homeowner for individual remodeling projects
2. To increase the dollar value of business conducted by 10–15 percent per year	2. To increase the dollar value of business conducted by 10–15 percent per year
3. To make project cost estimates accurate enough so that overruns average less than 3 percent of the project bid and underruns average less than 5 percent of the bid	3. To make project cost estimates accurate enough so that overruns average less than 3 percent of the project bid, and underruns average less than 5 percent of the bid
4. To make project completion time estimates accurate enough so that all projects are completed within five days of the initial scheduled completion date	4. To make project completion time estimates accurate enough so that all projects are completed within five days of the initial scheduled completion date
5. To be recognized as one of the top three remodeling contractors in the city based on the quality of work completed	5. To be recognized as one of the top three remodeling contractors in the city based on the quality of work completed
6. To obtain at least 50 percent of our business through word-of-mouth based on prior clients	6. To obtain at least 50 percent of our business through word-of-mouth based on prior clients
C. Operational Strategies	**C. Operational Strategies**
1. To hire highly skilled carpenters and pay them well enough to encourage long-term commitment to the company	1. To hire young, inexperienced carpenters, pay them moderately low wages, and teach them carpentry skills
2. To control costs by using subcontractors for all noncarpentry work (heating, electrical, wallboard, painting, carpeting)	2. To control costs by using subcontractors for heating and electrical work
3. To control quality by inspecting work quality and progress on all jobs at least once a day	3. To control quality by inspecting work on each job on completion of each major segment of the project
4. To schedule and control all jobs using PERT analyses*	4. To have the owner of the company schedule and control all jobs because of his experience in scheduling projects
5. To obtain a microcomputer to support the business and to use quantitative planning tools	5. To hire an accounting firm to meet financial responsibilities
6. To plan and monitor all project schedules according to a computerized PERT analysis	
7. To create and use a computer program to develop project bids based on input, such as number of square feet, type of existing construction, quality of materials, and so on	

Note: These plans have been simulated.
*PERT analysis is described in Chapter 8.

to run quantitative and planning analyses, and support development of a computer program to develop project bids.

- **Competitive advantages**—an organization's unique position, compared to other organizations in its task environment, such as exceptional skill in direct mail marketing or, as at Lil'America Builders, the owner's nearly fifteen years of fine workmanship in the community and many references from satisfied customers.

- **Synergy**—the positive results that will come from the combination of scope, resource deployment, and competitive advantages. (*Syner-*

FIGURE 9.1 *Strategy Components*

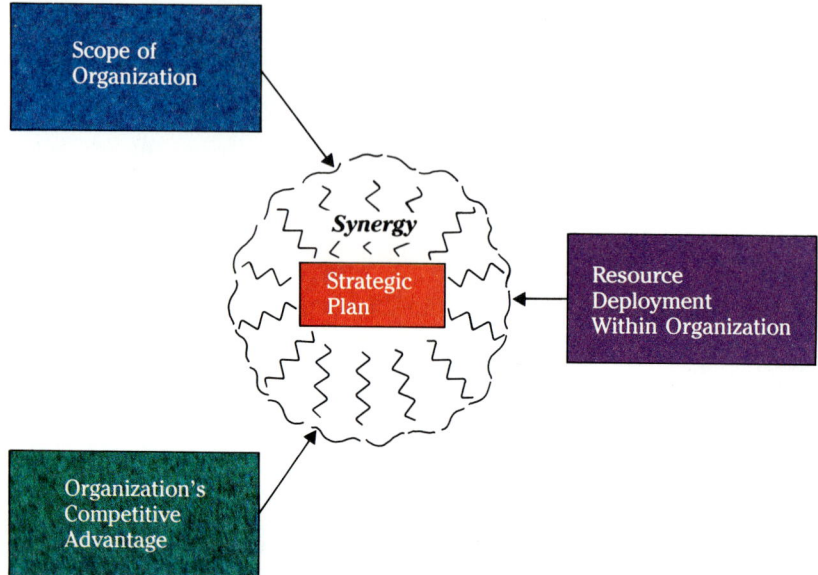

gy is a term taken from systems theory. It refers to the combined action of a number of different parts of a system such that their combined output is greater than that achieved from the sum of the parts alone.) Synergy can also stem from the integration of the internal components of an organization. The major business of Humana Hospital, for example, is routine hospital care, yet research activities conducted by Dr. William C. DeVries enabled Humana to perform its first artificial heart transplant in 1984. The strategic plan for the Humana chain of hospitals may be to count on the synergistic effects of this research with artificial hearts, to capitalize on media coverage of the transplant, and to expect the publicity to attract business and profitability for the corporation. (See Figure 9.1)

The Importance of Operational Strategies   While strategic objectives specify what an organization hopes to accomplish, operational strategies describe how this is to be done. For example, Lil'America's fifth strategic objective, shown in Table 9.1, is to be recognized as one of the top three remodeling contractors in the city based on the quality of work completed. Under Plan #1, the first and third operational strategies specify hiring and inspection policies designed to promote high-quality work by retaining skilled people and examining their accomplishments on a daily basis.

Operational strategies should be subordinate to strategic objectives and, therefore, should be specified only after strategic objectives have been chosen. Lil'America's third strategic objective regarding accurate cost estimates, for example, was established before the operational strategies for controlling costs—using subcontractors, microcomputers, and PERT analyses—were developed. Sometimes, though, managers must adjust operational strategies even if strategic objectives do not change, as would be the case if Lil'America's cost-control measures fail to enhance accurate cost estimates.

Many managers permit organizations to be driven by operational strategies rather than by the more important strategic objectives. By doing this, however, they undermine the sense of direction that people need to guide and coordinate organizational activities. They also make it more difficult to evaluate organizational effectiveness, because strategic objectives establish criteria of effective performance. Even when managers implement an operational strategy very well, its value to their organization is limited if it does not serve a higher strategic objective. An organization might do an excellent job of having the lowest prices in the marketplace for all of its products, but if the organization's objective is to lead the market in customer service, it has done the wrong thing well.

The Levels of Strategic Planning

In most organizations, strategic planning takes place at least three levels: corporate, business unit, and functional (see Figure 9.2).[3] At the corporate level, strategic planning establishes the organizational mission for an entire organization. At the business unit level, strategy defines how an organizational subunit, such as the Service Division at Sears, Roebuck and Company, interacts with its environment and performs in a particular business area. Finally, at the functional level, strategy determines how management intends to guide a particular functional area, such as marketing, finance, or production. Not only is it important that managers

FIGURE 9.2   Three Levels of Strategy

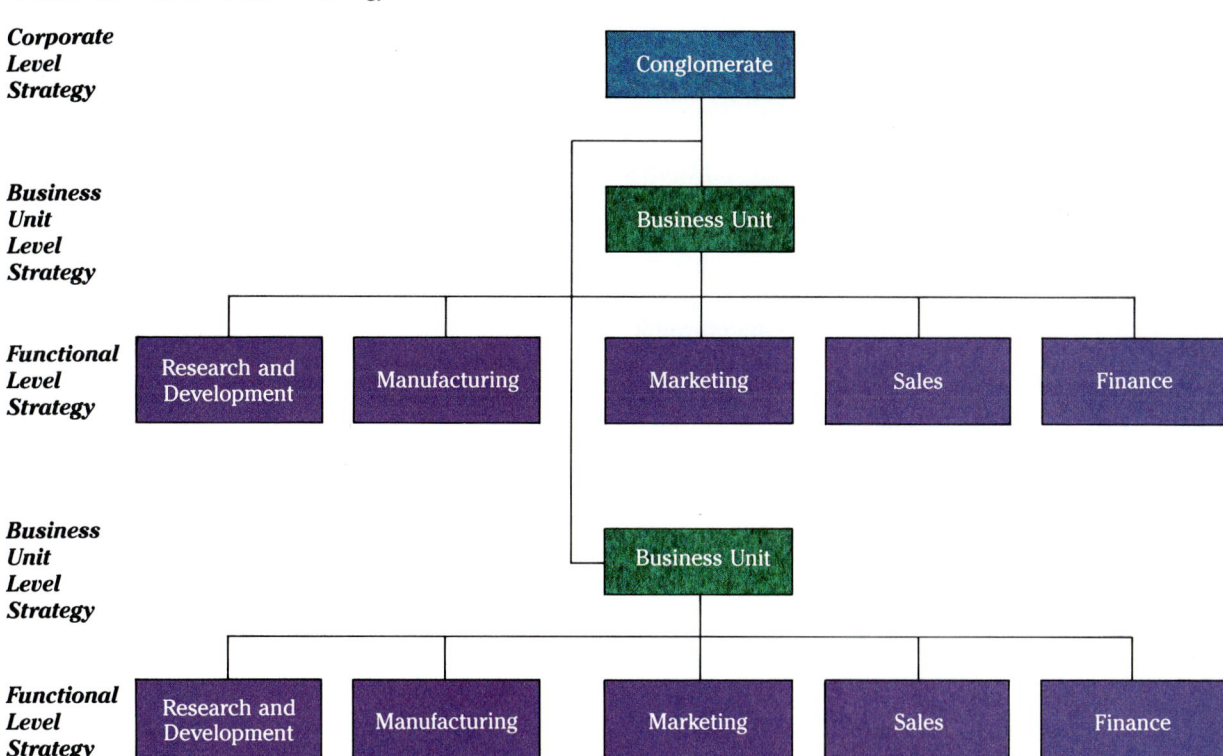

Source: Adapted from R. H. Hayes and S. C. Wheelwright (1984), *Restoring our competitive edge: Competing through manufacturing,* New York: Wiley & Sons, 28.

develop strategy at each of these three levels, but it is also critical that they integrate the levels to support and reinforce one another. It is important at Sears that the managers in the service division integrate their strategies with those developed by the major appliance sales division, which, in turn, complement strategies created by the advertising group, thereby contributing to the corporate-level strategy adopted for the entire national chain.

Corporate Strategy **Corporate strategy** addresses two major questions: "What businesses will the organization engage in?" and "How will resources be distributed among these businesses?" Usually plotted by top management, corporate-level strategy defines the domain of an organization and lets organization members know which priorities have been set. Corporate level strategy, for example, determined that Sears, Roebuck and Company would enter the real estate sales and home mortgage markets. The corporate level strategy also decided that Sears should distribute the DISCOVER consumer credit card. This level of strategic planning also determines how much of Sears' resources will be allocated to each of these ventures and how much to Sears' retail stores, catalog sales, and insurance businesses.

Business Unit Strategy A *business unit* (often referred to as a *strategic business unit*) is a segment of an organization with a distinct mission, external market, and strategy for dealing with that market. At Sears, for example, the service division can be considered a separate business unit. **Business unit strategy,** therefore, concerns the functioning of such an individual business within a corporation and specifies how the organization will interact with its task environment. At Sears, one business unit strategy specifies the plans for Sears' retail operations. Another business unit strategy defines the plans for its catalog sales business, and so on. These strategies define the relationship between the business unit and its task environment. Business-level strategy is primarily concerned with synergy and competitive advantage. Synergy at this level involves the means by which different business subdivisions can be integrated within the larger organization. Competitive advantage recognizes and takes advantage of the organization's unique position relative to its competitors.

Functional Strategy A **functional strategy** is a comprehensive plan for each major functional area (such as marketing, finance, and production) within a business unit. Functional strategy should support and conform to the strategy of the business unit. If, for example, the strategic plan for Sears' catalog business unit specifies that electronics should constitute 20 percent of catalog business, the catalog marketing department would identify potential customers for these products, while the buying department would obtain electronic products to be sold through the catalog. The integration of activities within the functional area (synergy) and competitive advantages are the key components of functional strategy.

The Allstate Insurance Group is a business unit within Sears, Roebuck and Co. Allstate's Direct Marketing Center provides direct mail and telemarketing services for the Sears family of companies as well as for other major corporations.

TABLE 9.2   Strategic Planning Styles

Style	Characterized By
Entrepreneurial	A strong leader, founder, or key organization member; an experience-, belief-, or intuition-based nature; bold initiatives and attempts to control the environment
Adaptive	The senior management group muddling through; a defensive nature; reacts to the environment
Planning	Managers and organizational planners; a systematic and rational nature; searches for environmental threats and opportunities and plans courses of action

Strategic Management Styles

The personalities and preferences of an organization's managers strongly influence the strategies that they develop. Managers have three distinct styles of strategic planning: entrepreneurial, adaptive, and planning.[4] Although there is no one best style in all cases, specific situations call for one of these three forms of strategic planning (see Table 9.2)

Entrepreneurial   In the *entrepreneurial style,* strategic planning is usually dictated by one individual in an organization. This person, typically the founder of the organization, develops a plan based on personal beliefs and experiences. These plans tend to be based on intuition and often involve substantial uncertainty and risk. The entrepreneurial approach is characterized by dramatic actions in the face of apparent uncertainty. With growth and the desire to win as driving forces, entrepreneurial strategists tend to view the environment as a malleable force to be confronted and controlled.

Sam Jacobson, founder of PDQ and Pick Kwik food stores, is an entrepreneur who helped pioneer the concept of drive-in convenience stores. Beginning with a single, small dairy store, Johnson based his retailing approach on the belief that customers would be willing to pay a higher price to obtain a needed product quickly and conveniently. The astounding success and spread of these convenience outlets across the nation are proof that he was right.

Adaptive   The *adaptive style* of planning has been called the "science of muddling through."[5] In contrast to the entrepreneurial style, which aggressively confronts the environment, the adaptive style reacts to changes in the environment. This strategy moves an organization forward timidly, defensively, and through a series of small (often disjointed) steps. The adaptive policymaker strongly believes in and accepts the status quo and seldom makes major changes in the organization's commitments or actions. Rather than trying to shape the environment, the adaptive manager monitors activities in the environment and reacts to them. SONY, for example, used an entrepreneurial style when it created the market for home videotape recorders with its Beta format. Subsequently, however,

Entrepreneurial strategists tend to view an uncertain environment as a malleable force to be confronted and controlled.

the company's style became more adaptive with the increasing popularity of the VHS format. Watching its Beta sales decline, SONY defensively issued a series of minor improvements and additional features to its machines before effectively abandoning the Beta format in 1988 and producing its own VHS product.

Planning   The *planning style* is characterized by the development of a comprehensive organizational plan. Managers who use this style assess the costs and benefits associated with various strategies and try to fit their organization into its external environment as rationally as possible. They analyze the environment, identify opportunities and threats, and formulate rational methods of coping with both according to the capabilities of the organization. The planning style provides a greater sense of direction than the other two approaches do. Sears' entry into the financial industry, for example, was a result of the comprehensive, systematic approach that characterizes the planning style of strategic management.

As you have learned, no one strategy works best for all organizations. In fact, approaches are likely to differ within an organization over time or across business units. The entrepreneurial approach may be appropriate for a small, new organization with a strong leader striving to find its niche in the marketplace. It might also work well for a distressed organization that needs a bold, new approach if it is to survive. The adaptive model may be the only choice available to an organization whose mission is specified and cannot be changed. Individual chapters of the Girl Scouts of America, for example, are largely bound by their national charter. Various government agencies are bound by congressional mandate, and many managers of various business units operate under strict control from their corporate offices. For most established organizations, the planning style serves well because it represents a conscious and systematic attempt to fit an organization into its task environment.

Some organizations use more than one style. The entrepreneurial style may work best in a research and development department where exploratory work is needed to identify new and unique products. An adaptive style may work best in a marketing department, because organizations often fit their marketing approach to the needs, values, and wants of their potential consumers. A planning style often works best for production departments, where an organization needs a systematic approach to product development. The rest of this chapter focuses primarily on the rational and systematic approach to strategic planning that is best characterized by the planning style.

The Advantages and Disadvantages of Strategic Planning

Strategic plans sometimes succeed—and sometimes create problems. They can offer organizations a number of advantages and disadvantages.

Advantages   There is growing evidence that strategic planning can make organizations perform more effectively. Studies have shown, for example, that organizations that engage in formal, long-term planning tend to outperform those that do not plan.[6] The mere act of planning, however, does not produce positive results. The effectiveness that has been associated with formal strategic planning arises instead from a number of planning attributes.[7] Successful formal strategic plans should be sophisticated, complete, integrated, specific, and appropriately structured and implemented.[8] In other words, they should meet the criteria described earlier: they should cover the long term, be pervasive, integrate and control activities within an organization for the immediate and long-term future, and establish boundaries for decision making.

The primary advantage of strategic planning is that it makes an organization more systematic. A systematic organization directs a greater percentage of its efforts toward specific objectives, which makes it more efficient than a less systematic organization. A strategic plan reduces guesswork on the part of managers because it tells managers specifically what the organization hopes to accomplish and how it plans to do so. A strategic plan also minimizes mistakes in individual decisions and plans by focusing on the overall strategy. Systematic strategic planning increases the chances of a good plan being identified because it develops a broad range of alternatives for an organization. Finally, managers tend to make better choices when they systematically compare the available alternatives.

Disadvantages   What are the disadvantages of such an effective tool as strategic planning? Probably the single biggest disadvantage—a major pitfall—is the potential misuse of the concept. Strategic planners can become so enthralled with their own importance that they fail to serve their organization. They can fall out of touch with the organization's realities and its environment and, subsequently, develop inappropriate plans.

Most observers have concluded that this is exactly what happened when R. J. Ferris, then CEO of United Airlines, developed a new strategy that would create Allegis, a "total travel partner" consisting of an airline (United), a car rental company (Hertz), and a hotel chain (Hilton). This strategy failed for a variety of reasons, among them the loss of United's identity as a premier airline. Under new leadership, United Airlines has tried to recover its prior identity but may succumb to a takeover attempt from its pilots—leaving Allegis without its prime holding. The parent company, currently shedding its Allegis identity, probably will sell both the car rental and hotel chains.

There are other potential problems associated with strategic planning that managers must work to prevent. One problem occurs when managers assume that a strategy is certain to succeed because it was so carefully developed. Managers then may be slow to react when the plan is failing. Sometimes plans stifle rather than facilitate the effects that were intended. Plans that have been carefully constructed and put into writing end up driving all future decisions, even though managers' instincts tell them that there is a need for an organizational change. Sometimes the desire to be systematic can stifle the instinct to change and inhibit the creativity that can flow from intuition. Charles Revson attributes to intuition his ability to pick product winners at Revlon. Paul Cook, while head of Raychem, claimed that "nearly all of his decisions were based on intuition," and the ones he regretted the most were the ones that were not.[9]

Former Allegis CEO Richard Ferris envisioned that passengers who traveled on United would also stay at a Westin or Hilton Hotel and rent a car from Hertz. This "fly-sleep-drive" strategy failed for a variety of reasons.

Lastly, even when effective, strategic plans cost both time and money and may not repay the investment for years. It takes considerable foresight to appreciate the value of a formal strategic planning program, particularly if an organization is already doing well.

The Strategic Planning and Implementation Process

By now you probably have a basic understanding of what strategic planning is. Does it work? It may not *always* work, but it *can* work. This is a process that covers several steps, from the initial examination of the current state of affairs, through the creation of a plan, to the final checks on how the plan is affecting daily performance (see Figure 9.3).[10]

Step One: Planning Awareness

The first step in developing a strategic plan is to take stock of the status quo: an organization's current mission; its goals, structure, strategy, and performance; the values and aspirations of the major stakeholders and power brokers of the organization; and the environment in which the organization is operating.

At this point, managers must review the *domain commitments* that they have made in previous plans. These commitments created groups with vested interests, allocated resources, and exerted other influences on decisions about the future. The organizational mission formed earlier has caused managers to establish commitments and groups that will exert

FIGURE 9.3 *The Strategic Planning Process*

The complete strategic planning process requires nine steps. As you can see, Steps Three and Four can be conducted concurrently. Note that Steps Three and Four must both be completed before Step Five can be completed.

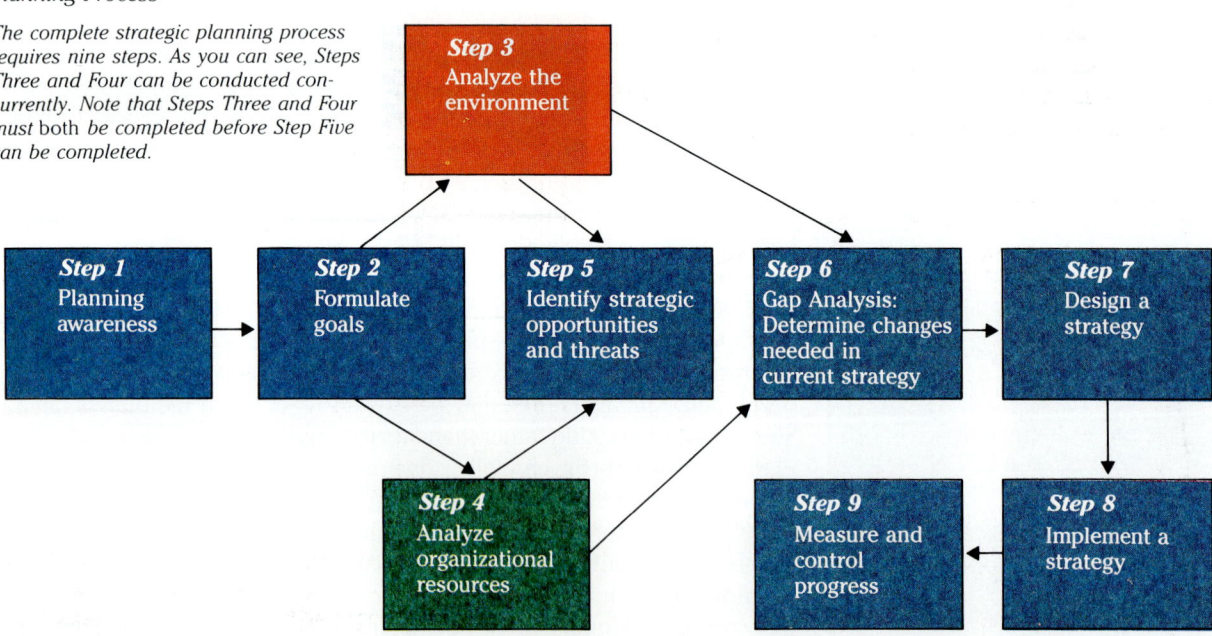

Source: C. W. Hofer (1986), *Strategy formulation: Issues and concepts*, 2nd ed., St. Paul, MN: West. While this particular model was developed primarily for the business unit level, it is useful for strategic planning at any of the three levels.

considerable influence on future decisions. Managers must also examine the goals, strategy, structure, and organizational performance accompanying the current mission. What the organization has set out to achieve, the methods used to reach these goals, and how well it has done so all have a major impact on the decisions that are about to be made in the next round of the strategic planning process. A final component to the planning awareness stage requires managers to understand the task environment in which the organization has been and will be operating.

When the owner of Lil'America initiated Step One of the strategic planning process, for example, he noted that: the organization was exclusively in the home remodeling business; it had been profitable for four years; the growth in profits had been slow but steady; employees were skillful and seemed committed to the organization; a strong base of satisfied customers existed but was not being fully utilized; and business was steady but jobs were seldom scheduled more than three months into the future, which left some questions about continuity. This type of assessment performed in Step One documents the point of departure for the future strategic plan.

Step Two: Formulating Goals

The second step in making a strategic plan is for managers to discuss and describe exactly what an organization wishes to accomplish in the future. Formulating goals requires managers to verify and affirm their organization's reasons for existence, define its mission, and establish strategic objectives. The beliefs, values, and aspirations of this dominant coalition will shape any new mission statement and accompanying goals and strategy.[11] Some managers, for example, are especially concerned about delivering new products and services and, thus, emphasize research and development goals. Managers who like to dominate a market might structure goals in terms of acquisitions and mergers. Socially responsible managers set goals expected to produce favorable social effects as well as profits. The Dayton-Hudson Corporation, for example, gives a fixed percent of its pretax profits to charity. Several firms, such as Calvert Social Investment Fund, now invest their clients' money solely in socially responsible companies with reputations for responsible environmental policies, nondiscriminatory hiring practices, and so on.

When formulating goals during Step Two of the strategic planning process, the owner of Lil'America concluded that he was basically happy with the nature of its business, the company's position in the home remodeling industry, and its degree of success. He felt, however, that the company's goals should be modified and specified. At this point, some of the goals he developed were to increase profits to a 15–20 percent margin per job, to increase the dollar volume of business by 10–15 percent per year, to gain wider recognition for the firm, and to capitalize more on word-of-mouth advertising.

Particularly for large organizations, the process by which goals are developed is complex. Individuals and groups, both internal and external to an organization, engage in a process of bargaining, and out of this exchange organizational goals emerge. The relative power of these various stakeholders in the organization determines the nature and character of the bargaining process and the goals that ultimately emerge.

Step Three: Analyzing the Environment

Once managers have formulated their organization's goals, they must look at the factors in the environment that might affect their ability to achieve them. What is out there that demands managerial attention? Answers to questions of this nature help managers develop their organization's strategy. An **informational (environmental) scan** is a process by which an organization collects information from the external environment about factors that have the ability to influence the organization. From the general environment, managers should gather international, political, cultural, technical, and economic information. Scanning the task envrionment provides information from suppliers, regulatory agencies, competitors, and customers. The main purpose of an environmental scan is to identify indicators of opportunities and threats to an organization so that managers can design a strategy to address them. This step may be conducted concurrently with Step Four (analyzing organizational resources). Both must be completed before Step Five can commence.

Managers get environmental information in several ways. The historical evaluation conducted in Step One often reveals important information. Sometimes the experiences of other organizations that have encountered similar situations provide valuable information. Managerial intuition can identify relevant factors, too. Unfortunately, it usually is easier for managers to look back and see that they should have investigated certain areas (but did not) than it is for them to anticipate which factors will turn out to be important. One problem facing managers is knowing what factors to focus on and how much forecasting will be necessary to develop an adequate amount of strategic planning information. When the external environment changes rapidly, these problems intensify.

For all of these reasons, scanning the environment can be a difficult and complicated process. Some information is available from government

TABLE 9.3   *The Focus of Environmental Scanning*

General Environment
1. *International information,* such as activities of foreign competition, resource availability, governments and interest groups, and international monetary events
2. *Political information* from local, regional, and national political developments
3. *Cultural information,* such as social movements and changes in values and societal needs
4. *Technical information,* such as technological innovations and licensing and patent information
5. *Economic information,* such as changes in rates of inflation, employment levels, and fluctuations in consumer prices

The Task Environment
1. *Supplier information,* such as resource availability and supplier behavior
2. *Regulatory agencies information,* such as current and pending regulatory activity
3. *Competitor information,* such as pricing strategies, advertising trends, and product/service characteristics
4. *Customers/market information,* such as distribution channels, market potential, pricing, and changes in customers' wants

and business publications. The value of the dollar relative to the Japanese yen, for example, is published daily in *The Wall Street Journal*. Other information is less concrete, however, and more difficult to assess, such as the policies and practices of OPEC and their influence on oil availability and pricing. Because of this complexity, many larger firms employ internal research units. Others rely heavily on consultants, whose job is to keep a close eye on specific industries.

Lil'America's scan of its environment revealed a number of pieces of information which subsequently influenced its strategic plan. Although undergoing a current spurt, the new housing market was expected to peak and level off soon due to an anticipated overbuilding of residential homes. Competition among builders for new residential housing was increasing, as commercial space was already overbuilt. The environmental scan also indicated that average income in the community had stabilized, but inflation was causing interest rates to rise. Current homeowners were unlikely to build a new home if they had trouble selling their old one due to oversupply and the prohibitive cost of borrowing money for a new one. All of these factors pointed to an increased market for home remodeling as homeowners chose remodeling over new construction. The environmental scan also indicated some potential problems, including an anticipated shortage of highly skilled labor.

It is particularly important that an informational scan detect trends and changes in the environment, especially as the rate of change in the external environment escalates. The informational scan provides managers with a set of assumptions on which to base a strategy. If, for example, forecasts predict a growth in the home remodeling market, subsequent strategic planning assumes that this will occur.

Step Four: Analyzing Organizational Resources

The promise of future possibilities is very exciting, but what is an organization capable of right now? That is the question that this fourth step of the strategic planning process must address. An organizational analysis, also referred to as an **organizational scan,** identifies an organization's present strengths and weaknesses by examining its internal resources. Whereas managers looked to the external environment during Step Three, they examine the internal environment in Step Four. This internal inspection typically focuses on such items as technological capabilities, human resource capacities, and an organization's culture and structure. The critical component of an organizational analysis is a description of what the organization does better or worse than its competitors. Managers, in other words, must answer, "For the goals we formulated in Step Two, what internal resources do we have that make us better able (or less able) to meet them than are our competitors?"

The assessment of current organizational resources at Lil'America indicated that the company possessed the technological capabilities, human resources, and financial strength not only to maintain the status quo but to move somewhat in the desired growth direction indicated in its new goals. It was clear, however, that the desired level of growth would require resources not currently in place, including advertising and other business acquisition methods, additional skilled human resources, and greater training. There was also an indication that if growth exceeded goals to any significant extent, additional management would be required to implement the strategy fully.

Step Five: Identifying Strategic Opportunities and Threats

Given the realities provided by the scan of the external environment in Step Three and the internal environment in Step Four, managers move to the fifth step. They identify their opportunities to meet their goals and the threats that could stymie them. Effective strategic planning must consider both elements.

In Chapter 8, for example, Cindy Mertes (owner of Progressive Video Images) seemed very systematic in her planning and decision making. Suppose that her scan of PVI's external environment reveals declining prices for raw materials, declining interest rates (the cost of borrowing money), low unemployment in the community, and increasing wages. In addition, a forecast based on information from the scan has projected a growth in market demand for video laser disks. Her analysis of organizational resources indicates that a full shift of highly skilled audio-video technicians is available. Cindy's scan also has detected dissatisfaction among her employees; they are arguing about who gets to use available equipment resources and are unhappy with Cindy's inability to resolve their conflicts.

Together, the environmental and organizational analyses help Cindy identify opportunities and threats to her business. She sees an opportunity in preparing prerecorded video laser disks as the market grows and as the costs of raw materials and borrowing money decline. Her employees have the skills and interests necessary to perform this work. She also sees some significant threats, however; one of which is a strong probability that her employees will unionize. Cindy expects unionization to increase labor costs and reduce her ability to manage her employees effectively.

In sum, managers involved in strategic planning should use the information that their scans provide to ascertain the opportunities and threats that might affect their organization in the future.

Step Six: Performing Gap Analysis

In this step of the strategic planning process, managers must find out how well their organization can meet the goals established in Step Two if they do *not* change their existing strategy. One way to determine if the current strategy is adequate is through gap analysis. **Gap analysis** identifies the expected gaps between where managers want the organization to go and where it will go if they maintain the current strategy. A performance gap is said to exist when managers must change goals and strategies to meet threats or to take advantage of opportunities. For example, Cindy Mertes' gap analysis revealed that her current strategy would almost certainly lead to the unionization of her workforce. This would run directly counter to her goal of maintaining a nonunion shop. This gap between her wishes and reality requires a change in strategy if she intends to meet her goal of maintaining a nonunion shop.

"I'd like to take this opportunity to analyze our conceptual arsenal, discuss our competitive strategies, and formulate a posture statement."

James Stevenson from the *Harvard Business Review*

Gap analysis points out areas in which an organization is likely to succeed, but its real value is in identifying the shortcomings in a present strategy and pointing to areas of necessary change. Gap analysis helps managers determine the cause of those gaps and, perhaps most importantly, makes managers sensitive to issues that must be addressed when designing a new strategy—the heart of Step Seven.

Step Seven: Designing Strategy

At the seventh step of the strategic planning process, managers answer whether a new strategy is needed, and if so, what it should be. If their gap analysis has identified no expected gaps, this step is simple. Managers reaffirm their existing strategic plan, congratulate themselves and others in the organization for a job well done, and continue with the existing plan. More often, though, gap analysis shows that at least some changes in strategy are needed; thus, managers usually have to identify new strategic alternatives, evaluate each of them, and select a new strategic plan.

The complexity of this process is influenced by the nature and the size of gaps. At times, managers need to make only minor modifications in existing goals and strategy. An image problem, for example, might be rectified by something as simple as a change in advertising or modernization of equipment to speed up product delivery. At other times, major changes in organizational strategy are required. An organization may have to enter a new market, redesign a product, or even merge with another organization to cope with changing competition.

It is at Step Seven that Cindy Mertes, having reviewed the results of the gap analysis from Step Six, questioned whether PVI would be able to succeed even if she were to make major changes. She therefore initiated a discussion with the owner of her leading competitor in the community. She shared her objectives, revealed her tentative strategic plan, and explained why she felt she had a good chance of executing that plan successfully. She gave reasons why she believed her success would threaten the competitor and how she felt the competitor was a threat to her. The competitor then explained the strategic plans for that organization, and the two of them discussed whether they could segment the market to avoid competing directly with each other. They also explored the possibility of merging to attack the overall market as a stronger force.

At Step Seven, managers must determine the specific actions necessary to accomplish their strategic objectives—not an easy task. The primary function of strategy, according to one professor of management, ". . . is to provide a consistent set of objectives and policies that restructures an ambiguous reality into a set of organizationally solvable subproblems."[12] Thus, if Cindy decides that PVI should prepare prerecorded video laser disks, the task at this step is to spell out exactly how to do that.

In identifying strategic options, managers typically take one of two approaches. Either they sit back, observe others, and then adopt a strategy used elsewhere, or they design a strategy that improves the fit between their organization and its task environment. After choosing a plan, one way that managers can evaluate it is to look for reasons why it might fail. There are four tests managers can use to judge whether their strategy is acceptable:

1. *The goal consistency test.* Does the proposed strategy have goals, objectives, and policies that are consistent with one another? Cindy's conclusion, for example, was that her goals, objectives, and policies were indeed consistent with one another and very much what she hoped to accomplish.

2. *The frame test.* Does the strategy focus managerial efforts and organizational resources on the issues or problems that have been identified as crucial? In Cindy's case, crucial issues were addressed well by organizational resources.

3. *The competence test.* Does the strategy solve problems using existing organizational resources and competencies? When Cindy measured her strategy with the competence test, results were mixed. Internal problems could certainly be solved using existing resources, both human and technical (equipment). The competencies of the employees were up to the task as well, but she was less certain that PVI would be able to compete effectively in the marketplace using only existing resources.

4. *The workability test.* Does the chosen strategy appear as though it will work? Are the resources available to enact the plan? Does what the managers know now suggest that these policies will achieve the desired objectives?[13] This test proved to be the biggest stumbling block for Cindy, because if her competitor decided to initiate a price war or other aggressive ploy, the plan might not work. Furthermore, she thought this was likely because following the new strategic plan would mean invading a market held by the competitor. These concerns drove Cindy to check into the possibility of merging PVI with its major competitor.

After evaluating the strategy options, management must "bite the bullet" and select one or more for implementation.

Step Eight: Implementing Strategy

How can the ideas from the strategic plan designed at Step Seven be put into action? That is the question that the eighth step addresses. No matter how good a strategic plan, it cannot fulfill its potential unless it is effectively implemented at each level of an organization. A corporate-level strategy must spawn compatible strategic plans for each business unit. Within each business unit, supportive functional strategies must be developed. As the overall strategy filters downward, managers at each level must follow the full strategic planning process to develop strategies for the major organizational subdivisions and each major functional area.

Consider, for example, what would happen if Sears decided to implement a strategic plan to combine its retail and catalog operations and allow customers to order and pay for purchases using their home computers and DISCOVER credit cards. The resulting new business would require a new business unit strategy. Within the business unit, the marketing department would need a functional strategy for promoting the idea. The computer department would need a functional strategy for developing hardware and software to support the system. Implementing the overall strategy would require the development of a number of compatible business unit and functional strategies.

Managers also must consider *who* in the organization must support the strategy for it to succeed. If people resist the new strategy, it is unlikely to operate efficiently. It is therefore important that management consider the attitudes, values, and goals of organization members when implementing a new strategy. Chapter 20 is devoted to the organizational development and change process required for Step Eight of the strategic planning process.

Step Nine: Measuring and Controlling Progress

How can managers tell if a strategy is being implemented as planned and if it is having the desired effect? At this final step of the strategic process, managers evaluate the effectiveness of the strategy in action. They check to see if it conforms to the strategy that they laid out in Step Seven and is accomplishing the goals that they set forth in Step Two. Managers also must control the progress of the implemented plan by making sure that appropriate work systems, such as those necessary for communication, are in place. Alfred A. Chandler, in his classic study of organizational strategy, notes that the effective execution of an organization's strategic plan hinges on an appropriate organizational design.[14] (See Chapters 10–12 for an exploration of organizational structure and design.)

The results of the evaluation and control measures conducted during this final step of the process tell managers if actions need to be taken to enforce a strategy that is not being followed or to modify a strategy that is not working. At this stage, managers can apply several criteria to gauge the success of a strategy (some of which are already familiar to you):

- *External consistency.* Is the strategy helping the organization respond to the demands of the external environment?
- *Internal consistency.* Is the strategy using organizational resources to achieve the goals set by management?
- *Competitive advantage.* Is the strategy enabling the organization to do things better than its rivals?
- *Degree of risk.* Is the risk inherent in the strategy consistent with the organization's preferences?
- *Contribution to society.* Is the strategy socially responsible?
- *Motivation.* Does the strategy contribute to the motivation, morale, and commitment of organization members?[15]

If managers discover during this final step of the strategic planning process that the plan being evaluated does meet these criteria, the chances are excellent that the strategy is working as intended.

This nine-step process seems long and complicated—it is. (Review Figure 9.3.) The strategic planning process is too important, however, to just "wing it." It is the primary tool that managers have for mapping the path their organization should take, for guiding it along that path, and for making sure that it arrives at the intended destination.

Perspectives on Strategic Management

Various scholars and managers have offered their perspectives on the process of strategic management. These perspectives are useful to planners who want to think through and develop a comprehensive, effective strategic plan.

Problems Faced: The Adaptation Approach

As you have seen, strategic plans must fashion a careful match between an organization and its environment. Professors Raymond E. Miles and Charles C. Snow discuss this match in their *adaptation* approach to strategic planning. They argue that the development of a match between an organization and its environment requires the solution of three basic kinds of problems: entrepreneurial, engineering, and administrative (see Figure 9.4).[16]

The *entrepreneurial problem* is to define an organization's mission. In new organizations, this problem is basically one of turning insight and vision into a product or service and delivering it effectively. This is what engineer Kenneth Harry Olsen did in the late 1950s when he decided that the world needed a small, rugged, inexpensive minicomputer to compete with the giant mainframes. In providing such a product through his Digital Equipment Corporation, Olsen laid the groundwork for the personal computer revolution.

In established organizations, the entrepreneurial problem is similar, but the new insight or vision must compete with established products or

FIGURE 9.4   The Adaptive Cycle

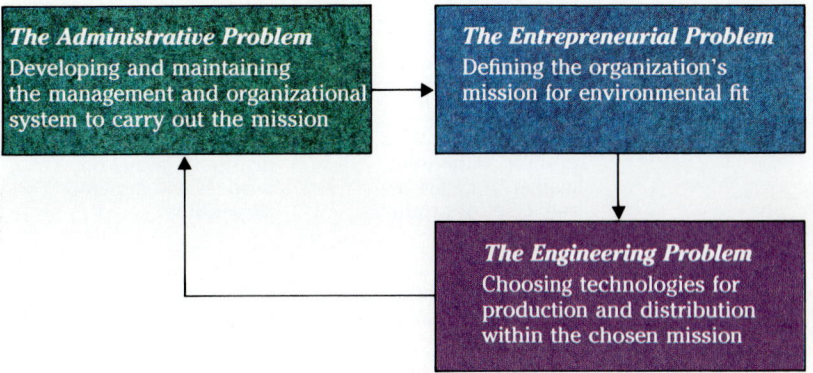

services and the organizational mechanisms that support them. For example, entrepreneur Ted Turner, owner of the Turner Broadcasting System, decided to purchase the MGM film studio for $1.6 billion in 1986. The idea of entering the film business was exciting, but the financial strain on his cable business proved substantial.

The *engineering problem* describes the creation of a way to implement the solution chosen at the entrepreneurial stage. Specifically, managers have to select technologies capable of producing and distributing their organization's products or services to the environment. In the hypothetical Sears example discussed earlier, the strategy was to combine retail and catalog sales and let consumers charge purchases to their DISCOVER credit card accounts using their home computers. An engineering solution to this entrepreneurial plan might require that all DISCOVER cardholders be given a phone number that their computers could dial to connect to the Sears system, a personal password to initiate the transaction, and software to help them order.

The *administrative problem* is one of developing, refining, and maintaining the management and organizational systems that let organization members carry out the strategic plan (see Chapters 10–12). In the Sears example, the administration solution could have managers (1) give the research and development department the task of creating the software that will enable the new system to work; (2) assign a subordinate to contact the telephone company, get the telephone number, and arrange the service that will allow DISCOVER cardholders' computers to dial Sears; (3) show clerical workers how to mail out postcards to DISCOVER cardholders, letting them know about the service; and (4) ask marketing personnel to fashion a campaign that tells the general public about this new advantage to owning a DISCOVER card.

Ways to Face the Problems: Strategic Approaches

Miles and Snow identified four distinct ways managers can approach the entrepreneurial, engineering, and administrative problems. Three of these—defender, prospector, and analyzer—are often associated with success (see Table 9.4). A fourth, the reactor approach, is usually considered a strategic failure, as you will see.

TABLE 9.4   *Strategic Approaches*

Type of Organizational Strategy	Problem		
	Entrepreneurial	*Engineering*	*Administrative*
Defender	How to "seal off" a portion of the total market to create a stable set of products and customers	How to produce and distribute goods or services as efficiently as possible	How to maintain strict control of the organization to ensure efficiency
Prospector	How to locate and exploit new product and market opportunities	How to avoid long-term commitments to a single technological process	How to facilitate and coordinate numerous and diverse operations
Analyzer	How to locate and exploit new product and market opportunities while simultaneously maintaining a firm base of traditional products and customers	How to be efficient in stable portions of the domain and flexible in changing portions	How to differentiate the organization's structure and processes to accommodate both stable and dynamic areas of operation

Source: Based on R. E. Miles and C. C. Snow (1978), *Organizational strategy, structure, and process,* New York: McGraw-Hill.

Defenders   Managers in **defender organizations** develop strategies that they hope will create and maintain a stable niche in the market for their organization's products or services. Perhaps the best known and most successful defender organization is McDonald's. The market chosen by McDonald's is narrow, confined to the fast-food consumer. (Although you may have seen children's McKid clothing, it is a Sears product line that uses the McDonald's name and logo by permission. McDonald's has not branched into the clothing business.) McDonald's is a model of efficiency in dealing with the engineering problem, and its strict control in dealing with the administrative problem is legendary.

A defender organization deals with its entrepreneurial problem by finding the right product or service, and it usually defines a narrow product or service line. Fiercely competitive, defenders attempt to seal off a portion of the total market and protect it from competitors. Engineering solutions tend to concentrate on the most efficient possible production and distribution of goods or services. Technological efficiency is central to a defender's success. Administratively, defender organizations tend to maintain strict internal controls to maintain their efficiency. To create a stable structure, their managers develop a bureaucratic organization with structured communications, top-down control, and an elaborate network of written standard operating procedures to regulate internal activities. Organizational resources are allocated to the product line to which the organization is committed and are not allocated to scanning the environment in search of new opportunities.

A defender strategy is best suited to organizations operating in relatively stable environments. If there is a major shift in its environment, a highly structured defender organization has difficulty being flexible enough to respond appropriately. Its tight structure and control also mean that new information is slow to reach managers. What is more, because of its narrow product or service line, the entrepreneurial problem is not considered a legitimate managerial challenge, and managers do little environmental scanning to seek new organizational opportunities.

Prospectors **Prospector organizations** are innovative. Unlike the managers of defender organizations, who seek to create market stability, managers of prospector organizations move rapidly from one domain to another in search of new opportunities. In addition, managers of prospector organizations attempt to create change within their own industry as a way of gaining an edge over the competition. Prospector organizations invest heavily in individuals and groups who scan the external environment in search of opportunities. They also are likely to invest heavily in research and development aimed at bringing about rapid changes in product or service characteristics. For example, the 3M (Minnesota, Mining and Manufacturing) Corporation invests heavily in individuals, groups, and research and development in an attempt to improve and develop new products that will keep the company on the leading edge of the industry.

In prospector organizations, managers devote substantial amounts of their attention to entrepreneurial activities. The engineering problem basically consists of avoiding long-term commitments to a single technology. In addition, prospector organizations do not allow their present technology to determine which products or services they will deliver in the future. They remain open to developing and adopting new technologies as they become available. The administrative problem centers around the methods used to facilitate rather than to control organizational operations. 3M, for example, encourages many of its people to use 15 percent of their time away from day-to-day operations for discovery. Organizational support for this type of strategy must be able to change quickly.

The biggest risk to prospector organizations is low profitability when resources are overextended. Rapid change may not allow time for management to develop internal economies of scale (that is, production in large enough quantities to bring down the costs of producing each unit). A prospector strategy clearly works best in an environment characterized by a high level of change.

McDonald's, a highly successful defender organization, has confined its market to fast-food consumers.

Analyzers **Analyzer organizations** are a true blend of both defender and prospector styles. They attempt to balance the risk and aggression of a prospector with the conservative, protective nature of a defender. In dealing with the entrepreneurial problem, an analyzer defensively maintains a solid base of existing products or services and customers. At the same time, however, it prospectively seeks new product or service opportunities and new market opportunities for its existing products or services.

One of the most successful analyzer organizations has been Procter & Gamble. Procter & Gamble operated as a defender organization for years, firmly establishing itself in the relatively narrow hand soap market. After decades of success with this approach, the organization began to incorporate prospector activities as it sought products to complement its soap business. Today, many of the products that it initially developed in its prospector mode, such as Crest toothpaste and Duncan Hines cake mixes, are now managed successfully with a defender approach. The company continues to use the prospector approach to identify and establish itself in new market areas, such as pharmaceuticals.

As a defender organization, Procter & Gamble operated for years within a narrow market for hand soap. Today the company uses the prospector approach to identify and establish itself in new market areas.

The engineering problem for an analyzer organization requires two separate solutions. For the stable portions of the business, it must emphasize the most efficient possible production and distribution of goods and services. For the dynamic aspects of the business, managers must be flexible and not commit themselves to a single technology. Because such different engineering approaches are necessary for the two aspects of their business, managers often divide the technical core of their organization into two parts. One part focuses on stable technologies to deliver well-established products or services in a standardized, mechanized, routine fashion. The other part tends to focus on development of new applications and often includes applications engineers, who rotate from one product design and development team to another.

The administrative problem for analyzer organizations also typically requires a dual solution. First, managers must design an organization that is flexible enough to accommodate the venture side of the organization. Second, they must design an organization that produces the administrative efficiencies associated with a bureaucratic (mechanistic) organization. The solution is for one administrative component to reflect the design of a defender organization and the second to reflect a prospector organization. This dual form of organization represents a blend of the mechanistic and organic organizations.

In many ways, an analyzer organization reduces risk—or "hedges its bets"—by conducting both stable and changeable businesses. It pays a price, however. Problems may crop up in at least one of the two areas at any given time. If problems arise in both areas at once, managers may become overwhelmed. A second price is the cost of running a dual technical core and management system. Finally, a third price comes in the fact that, whereas analyzer organizations are likely to show more growth than defender organizations, they also are less likely to realize the explosive growth sometimes obtained by prospector organizations.

Reactors **Reactor organizations** are so called because they tend to react to environmental events before they analyze the meaning and possible consequences of such events. Reactor organizations often fail because they develop strategy poorly, create an inadequate structure, and do not respond appropriately to changes in environmental conditions. In short, reactor organizations do not succeed because they do not systematically and effectively attack strategic planning and implementation. Their problems are aggravated because they often become even less aggressive after experiencing initial failure.

Reactor organizations do a poor job of both sealing off a stable market and identifying new opportunities. Their solutions to the engineering problem tend to be ineffective, in part because they have no strategy to guide them. After all, it is difficult to develop an engineering solution if managers do not know whether their organization's objective is efficiency or innovation. The administrative problem is handled equally poorly; often a reactor organization's design simply does not suit its needs. Although a reactor organization may limp along for a while, the only way it is likely to experience long-term success is by converting to one of the other three approaches and becoming a different kind of organization. This type of transformation usually occurs under the direction of a single strong individual who can guide the organization.

A CLOSER LOOK

Defender Organizations: Can MCI Analyze Its Way to Renewed Success?

A defender organization is one that creates a product or service in a fairly narrow area. By being fiercely competitive, a defender tries to seal off its portion of the total market and protect it from competitors, thus protecting a stable market niche. MCI is a good example of a company that has used the defender strategy to its advantage.

Almost twenty years ago, MCI selected a narrow service: cut-rate long-distance calls. At that time, American Telephone and Telegraph Company held a complete monopoly on long-distance telephone services in the United States. MCI brashly attacked, challenged the monopoly in court, won the legal battle, and established a 10 percent market share. By virtually all standards, MCI's selection of a defender stance succeeded immensely.

A defender organization generally does not fare well, however, if its external environment changes substantially—which is what has happened in the long-distance calling marketplace. In large part because of MCI's successful challenges, the Federal Communications Commission issued a series of rulings that decreased long-distance phone call rates by over 30 percent between 1984 and 1987. In 1986, MCI showed a $448 million loss. The question became: could MCI continue with a defender strategy and regain profitability? The answer was apparently not.

In its fight to recapture its previously successful position, MCI is trying an analyzer strategy, a combination of defender and prospector strategies. MCI, as a defender, is trying to retain its solid base of existing residential customers. As a prospector, MCI is pursuing new markets, among them corporate long-distance customers, toll-free users (with 800 numbers), and international calling. MCI is supporting its prospector side by using new technologies. The company has, for example, introduced computerized network phone services and added digital transmission lines that are ideal for computer communications.

Another aspect of the MCI analyzer strategy is to change its image. MCI has long prided itself on its image as a maverick, both in marketing and delivering services. Now it is shifting that image to a service-oriented company that customers feel they can influence, rather than the other way around. Recognizing that changes of this magnitude are difficult to accomplish alone, MCI struck an interesting deal that made IBM owner of 17 percent of MCI and gave IBM a position on the MCI board of directors. Among other advantages, this move let MCI capitalize on IBM's solid reputation as a service-oriented corporation.

A defender strategy served MCI well for almost two decades. It has served its purpose, and the organization has moved on. Overall, MCI's new analyzer strategy cut internal operating costs by $100 million in 1986 alone and, in 1987, reduced interest payments on loans by $15 million. Will the change from a defender organization to an analyzer organization achieve the desired results? Only time will tell, but observers seem to feel that this change gives MCI its best chance of success for the future.

This is what happened at Chrysler Corporation in the 1970s. The once-profitable organization had begun to flounder and to turn from a defender into a reactor. When Lee Iacocca took over Chrysler in 1978, he converted the corporation into an analyzer. In 1984, for example, Chrysler took prospective action in its risky introduction of minivans. By the late 1980s, Chrysler held most of the minivan market and was in the process of converting it into a defender operation. It was, at the same time, prospecting in joint ventures with Japanese organizations.

Ways to Configure an Organization: Business Portfolios

The nine-step strategic planning process does not automatically provide solutions to the strategic problem. Rather, it helps managers seek solutions systematically. Supplementing—not replacing—these nine steps is a technique that provides a framework for strategic solutions. When organizations that engage in many different businesses want a comprehensive approach to strategic planning, they sometimes adopt a *business portfolio* approach.[17] This technique was first developed by General Electric in 1971 in order to integrate its many businesses. Since then, the procedure has been refined by The Boston Consulting Group for use by other organizations.[18] The portfolio approach to strategic planning proceeds through three phases: (1) developing strategic business units, (2) classifying them using a portfolio matrix, and (3) selecting an approach to manage them.

Strategic Business Units In the first phase, an organization identifies its strategic business units. A **strategic business unit (SBU)** is a segment of an organization with a distinct mission, external market, and strategy (or potential strategy) for dealing with that market. In some organizations, SBUs are formally designated as divisions, departments, or subsidiaries. Regardless of its formal designation, an SBU is essentially a portion of an overall organization which could constitute a freestanding business. 3M, for example, is divided into a number of distinct divisions that operate as SBUs, such as Information Systems, Tape/Adhesives and Decorative Products, Chemicals, Film and Allied Products, and Electro-Telecommunications. In fact, 3M has SBUs within SBUs. 3M's Information Systems Division, for example, manufactures and markets a collection of office products. Within that division, several SBUs produce printers, deal with automated tellers, and so on.

The Portfolio Matrix In the second phase, the organization places each SBU into a portfolio matrix. A **portfolio matrix** categorizes an SBU according to its relative market growth and market share. The portfolio matrix is a classification scheme, developed by The Boston Consulting Group, that categorizes an organization's business units into one of four distinct categories (see Figure 9.5):

1. **Stars** are SBUs with a relatively large portion of a high-growth market. The compact disk SBU of SONY is a star, because it possesses the industry's largest share of the CD market, which is itself increasing at an extremely rapid rate.
2. **Cash cows** are SBUs with a large share of a low-growth market. The refrigerator SBU for General Electric is a cash cow because, although the overall market for refrigerators is not growing substantially, GE maintains a large share of that market.
3. **Question marks** (sometimes called *wildcats*) possess a relatively small share of a rapidly growing market. Western Union's computerized information service is a question mark for that corporation.

FIGURE 9.5   *The Business Portfolio Matrix*

Source: A. Gerald (June 1976), A note on The Boston Consulting Group concept of competitive analysis and corporate strategy, *Intercollegiate Case Clearing House,* ICCH 9-175-175.

There is no doubt that the market for on-line information services is growing rapidly, but Western Union presently possesses only a relatively small share of it.

4. **Dogs** are SBUs with a small portion of a low-growth market. Dogs are clearly not the glamorous part of a portfolio. In fact, they often cannot support themselves and drain cash from other parts of an organization. A recent study found that over 40 percent of SBUs can best be classified as dogs.[19]

Selecting a Business Approach   Once an SBU is identified and classified, the final phase of the portfolio approach involves selecting an approach to manage it. Managers often use one of four grand strategies to achieve long-term objectives: (1) growth, (2) stable growth or hold, (3) retrenchment or turnaround, and (4) divestiture.[20]

A **growth strategy** is required for stars and for question marks that an organization hopes to transform into stars. This strategy requires the organization to invest substantial amounts of capital in the SBU. Whether for advertising, product development, or expansion, money is used to increase the SBU's market share. Sometimes this approach even requires investments aimed at increasing the size and growth rate of the market itself. SONY's advertising for compact disks, for example, combines a pitch for CDs in general (to increase the market) and for SONY CDs (to increase market share).

A **stable growth,** or **hold, strategy** is appropriate for most cash cows and some dogs. Because substantial growth is unlikely for these SBUs, this strategy allocates only the resources necessary to maintain the status quo. Steps are taken to avoid loss of market share, whether the existing share is large (as for GE in the refrigerator market) or small, as it is for dogs.

Managers use a **retrenchment,** or **turnaround, strategy** to stimulate a market. When an SBU fails to perform as expected, as when a question mark fails to become a star, this strategy can be useful. It can also be useful when a valuable cash cow begins to lose ground or even when a dog has slipped, but the organization is not ready to abandon it. Managers can try to stimulate markets by finding new uses for existing products, by attempting to change the image of a product, or modifying a product in a search for a market niche. The drug Retin-A, for example, was sold for many years as an acne treatment. In the 1980s, research commissioned by its producer revealed the drug's potential for reducing wrinkles and reversing precancerous skin conditions, and sales of the drug soared.

In a **divestiture strategy,** managers get rid of an SBU that is financially unsuccessful and that is unlikely to respond to the retrenchment/turnaround strategy. It is also used when an organization cannot afford the investment required to produce a turnaround. An organization divests itself of an SBU either by selling it or by closing it. Divestiture is most common for dogs that no longer generate a profit and would be difficult to improve or when an organization believes its cash cow will stop producing soon, which is why General Electric divested its successful consumer electronics group as foreign competition increased.

Healthy SBUs also can be divested. A star SBU at the peak of its value, for example, can be sold to generate the large amount of cash needed to support other parts of the portfolio. Sometimes SBUs are divested to simplify managers' tasks, as when a defender organization finds itself with a star prospector SBU. To manage this SBU successfully, managers would have to adopt an analyzer approach and develop dual solutions to the entrepreneurial, engineering, and administrative problems. Faced with a problem of this complexity, many managers prefer to reap the profits from divesting the SBU.

Generic Strategies

A slightly different way of looking at strategies was developed by Michael Porter of the Harvard Business School.[21] Porter describes three generic strategies—cost leadership, differentiation, and focus—that are pursued by organizational managers. These three business-level strategies are known as **generic strategies** because they are applicable to a wide range of organizations. Porter argues that each of these strategies can produce above-average performance if they are used appropriately to establish a competitive niche in the market.

Cost Leadership Some organizations adopt a strategy of **cost leadership.** Managers find a market niche by selling their organization's products or services more cheaply than its competitor does. This strategy can work well if the product is much like the higher-priced competitor's. The Tandy Corporation, for example, introduced a line of IBM-compatible personal computers in the 1980s and marketed them primarily as cheaper versions of the IBM computer. By claiming that its computer was virtually identical to an IBM, Tandy conceded that its product was no better than IBM's. The strategy was to gain sales through price. Organizations can gain cost leadership by accepting reduced profits or by minimizing the cost (sometimes through high volume) of design, manufacturing, shipping, and sales.

Differentiation   The primary purpose of a **differentiation strategy** is to help an organization establish itself as different from the competition. Whether this differentiation is obtained in areas of quality, design, service, or another area is not important. What is important is that the strategy must clearly establish the difference, and the difference must be meaningful to consumers. Successful differentiation can both increase market share and the price that an organization can obtain for its products or services.

For example, although Tandy Corporation's Radio Shack computers competed with IBM through low cost, Compaq captured substantial portions of the personal computer market by offering a different computer. Theirs was the first mass-marketed personal computer to use the extremely fast 80386 chip. With earlier machines, Compaq differentiated itself from IBM by offering both graphics and text displays as standard equipment. Compaq's personal computer had built-in features, such as a battery-backed-up clock (an extra-cost option on the IBM). Thus, although Compaq's original strategy had been to compete in terms of price, it gradually shifted its strategy to one of differentiation.

Compaq captured a significant share of the personal computer market with video graphics and extremely fast 80386 microchip technology.

A CLOSER LOOK

A Turnaround Strategy: Disney Tires of Being Dopey; Results Not Just Mickey Mouse

The years between 1966 and 1984 were grim ones for the Disney corporation, despite the fact that its theme parks were still profitable. Its movie studios churned out mostly failures, and Disney images had pretty much disappeared from the TV screen. In 1984, Disney was considered ripe for a corporate takeover. "A revolution in the way Hollywood makes and sells movies had passed Disney by, leaving Mickey looking a bit moth-eaten and Sneezy a little shopworn."[1]

New owners . . . demanded a total management overhaul.

In 1984, things changed at Disney. New owners bought a 25 percent share of the corporation. In return, they demanded a total management overhaul and a new, aggressive strate-

gic plan. The results have been impressive. Michael D. Eisner, the new chairman and chief executive, and Frank G. Wells, the new president and chief operating officer, together with the rest of the Disney crew, began ". . . the formidable task of dragging Disney into the modern world of entertainment."[2] How have they done it? Through a two-part strategy designed to show growth and develop strength.

The first part of the turnaround strategy focuses on existing assets of the Disney corporation, including its theme parks, hotels, and cartoon characters. These have been marketed aggressively and have incorporated modern technologies, such as computer outlets for the Disney comics. The second part focuses on creating new properties. Disney has entered the modern world of movie entertainment with extremely profitable Touchstone Pictures, including *Outrageous Fortune, Who Framed Roger Rabbit?, Ruthless People, Tin Men,* and others. Disney's strategy also has been aimed at the small screen once again. The Disney Channel's subscriber base on cable TV has grown immensely in recent years, and Disney has had successes with network shows, such as *The Golden Girls.*

The new strategy is far from fully implemented. Recently, Disney divest-

ed itself of its real-estate unit for about $400 million, a $200 million profit in less than three years. To raise cash, Disney is trying to sell its Epcot Center property in Orlando, Florida, for over $1 billion. It plans to invest the money from these sales into what Eisner and Wells hope will be Disney's future star SBUs: new hotels, a $300 million combined movie studio and tour attraction, a new European Disneyland theme park, and other major entertainment investments. One likely acquisition for Disney would be a distribution channel for its movies—in other words, movie theaters.

The current strategic plan for Disney is quite different from its 1984 plan. After scanning Disney's external environment and internal capabilities, the managers who took control in 1984 targeted products and services that they believed would give Disney a solid base for its turnaround. They created a strategy, followed it, monitored its progress, and have revised it when necessary. Due to their sound strategy—if not to magic—the kingdom is healthy once again.

1. R. Grover, M. N. Vamos, and T. Mason (9 March 1987), Disney's magic, *Business Week*, 62.
2. *Ibid.*

Focus Some organizations adopt a **focus strategy,** in which they **focus** on a specific segment of a total market and concentrate their resources on competing within that segment. The segment might be a geographic location (American Family Insurance concentrates on the Midwest), a particular customer group (BMW concentrates on higher-income professionals), or any other identifiable segment of the market. This focus on only one part of the market is intended to lead to more efficient marketing of an organization's products or services.

Special Cases: Small and Not-for-Profit Organizations

You probably are convinced by now that strategic planning can benefit a large, profit-oriented organization; however, what about the tens of thousands of small and not-for-profit organizations throughout the country? Do they engage in strategic planning? Should they? If so, how can they? Research has shown that few of these organizations engage systematically in strategic planning, even though strategy is just as important to their success as it is to that of larger corporations. Many of the strategic planning techniques discussed in this chapter can be used by small and not-for-profit organizations. In addition, small organizations need to contemplate certain special considerations.

Small Organizations

To people in many small organizations, the strategic planning process appears complex, expensive, formal, and time consuming. For these reasons, managers of many small organizations avoid strategic planning; however, as Lil'America's experiences show, planning is valuable to organizations of all sizes.

The questions that managers of small organizations should consider are the same as those facing large organizations: *Where* are we? *How* efficient and effective have we been? *What* business are we in? *Where* do we want to go? *Can* we get there? *How* can we get there? *What* kind of competitive advantage do we have or can we create? *How* can we monitor our performance? The answers to these questions can be found by following the guidelines found in the strategic planning model presented in this chapter.

In some ways, strategic planning is easier in small organizations because they and their external task environments are generally less complex. In addition, because of the more manageable size of a small organization, strategic planning can often be conducted by one, or a few, managers. For these reasons, the strategic planning process can be considerably less formal, less complex, less costly, and less time consuming for a manager of a small and structurally simple organization than it is for a larger organization. On the other hand, because small organizations often struggle from day to day merely to survive, their managers find it difficult to take the time required to conduct strategic planning. As more and more managers of small organizations recognize that strategic planning saves time in the long run and enhances effectiveness, strategic planning will become more popular.

Not-for-Profit Organizations

Not-for-profit organizations, whether they are private or public, exist for many different reasons.[22] Some are large national organizations with far-reaching missions, such as the U.S. postal system. Others are concerns that affect only those people in the immediate community, such as a theater group dedicated to performing Shakespeare and other classical works. Most provide protection, social services, health care,

Strategic planning is as important in not-for-profit organizations as it is in for-profit businesses.

entertainment/recreation, and education. Although they may not operate for profits, these organizations still must be managed, and strategic management is an important part of this process.

Managers of not-for-profit organizations are less likely than their counterparts in for-profit organizations to engage in systematic strategic planning. Even when they do, their plans tend to be shorter term.[23] Lack of pressure from organizational stakeholders, near monopolistic conditions, and the absence of strong monetary pressures are among the reasons that many not-for-profit organizations have been able to ignore strategic management issues. Managers in many of these organizations infrequently reexamine their organization's mission, and because only a few individuals hold control, strategic planning is often ignored.

Some not-for-profit organizations, however, have recently begun to use strategic planning. One reason they are forced to do so is because they will fail if they don't, as was the case with American Players Theater in 1987. This small troupe performs Shakespeare and other classic plays in Spring Green, Wisconsin, during the summer months. Although it has gained national recognition for its productions and ticket sales have risen every summer, the organization could not pay its taxes and was threatened with foreclosure. Its founding director and primary actor left the company. In one last attempt to survive, the organization hired a business manager, who formulated a strategy that planned a systematic drive for corporate donations. The strategy also calculated how much money would be needed to make payments on outstanding and current taxes, what it would take to produce each play, and how much revenue could be anticipated in ticket sales. In 1988, American Players presented fewer plays because resources were too limited for a full season, but if the strategy works as anticipated, the troupe will be able to meet its financial obligations for 1988 and plan a 1989 season.

Economic factors can also encourage not-for-profit organizations to use strategic planning. During the energy crunch of the 1970s, for example, the federal government granted some communities money to support local bus service, which would reduce the number of individual drivers and, thus, conserve gasoline. In the 1980s, this federal funding diminished considerably, forcing communities to formulate plans to eliminate some routes, reduce service to others, and raise ridership rates. Likewise, as universities receive less money from state governments, administrators are forced to make plans that seek private donations to help meet organizational goals and to cut costs by curtailing certain programs.

Competition for services can also force even large not-for-profit organizations to use strategic plans. The U.S. postal service, for example, has operated at a loss for years—despite several rate increases—and has gained a reputation for slow service from uncaring employees. An increasing number of people choose to use competing services from such for-profit organizations as Federal Express and United Parcel Service because these companies promise a quality service at a good price. In response, postal administrators devised a strategy that extended branch hours past 5 P.M., established postal outlets in shopping malls during the busy Christmas season, and offered overnight mail service at competitive rates. It even considered eliminating Saturday delivery (among other options) to cut operating costs. Unfortunately, in recent moves that confounded many good strategic planners, the Post Office not only rolled back many of these service improvements but actually made service cuts, such as reduced lobby hours.

Although there are not yet any good strategic planning models specifically tailored to not-for-profit organizations, they can follow the guidelines presented in this chapter. Given their financial objectives, not-for-profit organizations should focus on efficiency rather than profitability. Managers of many not-for-profit organizations should attempt to generate income that exceeds organizational costs. This extra revenue can then be plowed back into the organizations, so that they can serve their customers better. In addition, measures of effectiveness are likely to concentrate on the degree to which an organization serves the external environment rather than on the degree to which the organization benefits from the environment.

Strategic Management in Review

Strategic management is systematic, long-term planning that positions an organization within its external environment. A strategic plan specifies the organization's mission (which businesses it will undertake), strategic objectives (the definable and measurable accomplishments associated with the mission), and operational strategies (the actions to be used to accomplish the objectives).

Strategic planning typically is performed on at least three levels. At the corporate level, plans are made for overall organizational activities. At the business unit level, planning focuses on the effective conduct of an individual business. Functional level planning specifies how individual functional areas (for example, marketing and finance) are to conduct their operations.

Phyllis A. Mason

Phyllis A. Mason of Baruch College teaches and conducts research in strategy, planning, and entrepreneurship. Formerly, she worked in the recording industry for thirteen years.

1. How common is it for organizations to assign a specific individual to the strategic planning function?

It's very common in large organizations. In small organizations, of course, it's less common because it's not considered cost effective. Most corporations have some sort of strategic planning department. Even medium-sized organizations frequently have strategic planning people.

2. Does systematic strategic planning really benefit an organization?

Yes and no. Strategic planning, like anything else, can be done well or done badly. Some research has shown strategic planning to be effective; some has shown it to be ineffective. I believe that, to a large extent, this reflects that organizations that plan well and organizations that plan poorly are mixed in the research samples. It has certainly been demonstrated that organizations that plan well have reaped benefits from that planning—such organizations as IBM, General Electric, GM, some of the major financial institutions, and financial service institutions. Organizations that are only interested in paying lip service to strategic planning probably get very little benefit from it.

3. If an organization were to develop a strategic planning unit, how would you recommend that it proceed?

The top managers of the organization must first give some good, hard thought to the objectives they expect their strategic planning unit to achieve and to the constraints they want to impose on that unit. The objectives have to be realistic. They have to be as broad as they need to be. For example, if the firm is really thinking about growing from a small regional company into a large national one, or is suddenly facing foreign competition for the first time in a big way, then dealing with that situation would be one of the objectives. The constraints should include, but not be limited to, the resources that will be allocated to the strategic planning unit and the size of the unit itself.

Once managers get the objectives and the constraints clear, they should hire someone who feels he or she can achieve those objectives within those constraints; let that person hire a staff and go to it. The crucial thing is that top management needs to communicate to the entire organization the objectives of the strategic planning unit, how the unit will work with the rest of the organization, the input that will be required from the rest of the organization, why the organization is doing strategic planning, how important it is to the organization's future, and so on. You have to get the whole organization plugged in to what's going on if the planning unit's output is to be effective and beneficial.

4. What conditions would indicate that a separate unit should be responsible for conducting strategic planning?

I think most businesses have found that strategic planning done by professional planners is far *less* effective than planning done by line managers. A few years ago, *Business Week* had a cover story called "The New Breed of Strategic Planner" that talked about how organizations that have turned over planning to professional planners have produced wonderful plans that do not get used.

There are two basic issues involved here. First of all is commitment. The line managers have to carry out the plans and should have their performance appraised based on their ability to plan and their ability to implement plans. If their input into the planning process is limited, whether voluntarily or involuntarily, they're not really going to understand what's going on. They are not going to be nearly as committed to implementing the plan as they are if they have input. The second thing is that line managers really have the best information. Professionals who have been trained in strategic planning in M.B.A. or Ph.D. programs know lots of techniques and produce marvelous planning documents, but line managers may not understand them.

It is essential that line managers do their own planning so they can put together plans they understand, plans that incorporate their best information, and plans they feel they will be able to implement. The role of the strategic planning unit, I believe, is, first of all, to provide a process, a system of planning. Second, it must provide basic information that the business units may need and not be able to provide for themselves, such as economic forecasts, other kinds of forecasts, and possibly some analysis.

The entrepreneurial style of strategic planning reflects bold initiatives. The adaptive style is defensive and allows the environment to shape an organization. The planning style reflects the systematic attempt to develop a comprehensive plan for positioning the organization within its task environment.

Implementing a strategic plan involves a nine-step process, which managers begin with a planning awareness stage. They proceed to formulate their organization's goals, analyze its external environment and internal resources, and identify existing and potential opportunities and threats facing the company. At this point, managers perform a gap analysis to see areas where the current strategy may fall short of meeting expectations, and they design a new strategy to address those shortcomings. After implementing the new strategy, managers must then measure and control its progress to see that it is being carried out as intended with the desired effects.

Strategic plans must address entrepreneurial, engineering, and administrative problems. These problems can be successfully tackled using approaches classified as prospector, defender, or analyzer. A fourth approach, reactor, usually leads to strategic failure.

In the business portfolio approach to strategic planning, strategic business units are classified by market share and market growth. Stars, cash cows, question marks, and dogs each have a potential role in the overall business portfolio. Recognition and appropriate management of these various types of business units are essential to the success of an organization.

Another way that managers can draw up strategic plans is according to a scheme of generic strategies. A cost leadership strategy stresses the low cost of products or services. A differentiation strategy concentrates on factors that distinguish a product or service from its competitors. A focus strategy is centered on a specific segment of the total market.

Although the managers of many small and not-for-profit organizations ignore strategic planning, they must fit these organizations into their environments. In doing so, they can benefit by following the models of strategic management presented in this chapter.

Notes

1. R. H. Hayes and S. C. Wheelright (1984), *Restoring our competitive edge: Competing through manufacturing*, New York: Wiley, 27–28.

2. D. E. Schendel and C. W. Hofer (1978), *Strategy formulation: Analytical concepts*, St. Paul, MN: West.

3. A. A. Thompson and A. J. Strickland III (1983), *Strategy formulation and implementation: Tasks of the general manager*, Plano, TX: Business Publications.

4. H. Mintzberg (Winter 1973), Strategy-making in three modes, *California Management Review*, 16, 44–53; H. Mintzberg (1973), *The nature of managerial work*, Englewood Cliffs, NJ: Prentice-Hall.

5. C. E. Lindblom (1958), The science of "muddling through," *Public Administration Review*, 19, 79–88.

6. D. M. Herold (1972), Long-range planning and organizational performance: A cross-validation study, *Academy of Management Journal*, 14, 91–102; D. W. Karger and Z. A. Malike (1975), Long range planning and organizational performance, *Long Range Planning*, 8, 6–64; S. S. Thune and R. J. House (1970), Where long-range planning pays off—findings of a survey of formal and informal planners, *Business Horizons*, 13, 81–87.

7. J. A. Pearce II, E. B. Freeman, and R. B. Robinson, Jr. (1987) The tenuous link between formal strategic planning and financial performance, *Academy of Management Review*, 12, 658–75.

8. J. S. Armstrong (1982), The value of formal planning for strategic decisions: Review of empirical research, *Strategic Management Journal*, 3, 197–211; Pearce, et al., 1987.

9. W. H. Agor (July/August 1984), Using intuition to manage organizations in the future, *Business Horizons*, 49; J. K. Clemens and D. F. Mayer (1987), *The classic touch: Lessons in leadership from Homer to Hemingway*, Homewood, IL: Dow Jones-Irwin, 116–22.

10. D. Schendel and C. W. Hofer (1979), Introduction to strategic management, in D. E. Schendel and C. W. Hofer, eds., *Strategic management: A new view of business policy and planning*, Boston: Little, Brown; A. D. Szilagyi, Jr. (1984), *Management and performance*, Glenview, IL: Scott, Foresman.

11. D. C. Hambrick and P. A. Mason (1984), Upper echelons: The organization as a reflection of its top managers, *Academy of Management Review*, 2, 193–206.

12. R. P. Rumelt (1979), Evaluation of strategy: Theory and models, in D. E. Schendel and C. W. Hofer, eds., *Strategic management: A new view of business policy and planning*, Boston: Little, Brown, 196–212.

13. Rumelt, 1979.

14. A. D. Chandler, Jr. (1962), *Strategy and structure: Chapters in the history of the American industrial enterprise*, Cambridge, MA: MIT Press.

15. These criteria are based on the ideas contained in A. D. Szilagyi, Jr. (1984), *Management and performance*, Glenview, IL: Scott, Foresman.

16. R. E. Miles and C. C. Snow (1978), *Organizational strategy, structure, and process*, New York: McGraw-Hill; R. E. Miles, C. C. Snow, A. Meyer, and H. Coleman (1978), Organizational strategy, structure, and process, *Academy of Management Review*, 3, 546–62.

17. B. Hedley (1977), Strategy and the business portfolio, *Long Range Planning*, 10, 9–15; Schendel and Hofer, 1978; I. C. Macmillan, D. C. Hambrick, and D. L. Day (1982), The product portfolio and profitability—a PIMS-based analysis of industrial product businesses, *Academy of Management Journal*, 25, 510–31.

18. A. Gerald (June 1976), A note on The Boston Consulting Group concept of competitive analysis and corporate strategy, *Intercollegiate Case Clearing House*, ICCH 9-175-175.

19. Hambrick, et al., 1982.

20. J. A. Pearce II (Spring 1982), Selecting among alternative grand strategies, *California Management Review*, 23–31.

21. M. E. Porter (1985), *Competitive advantage: Creating and sustaining superior performance*, New York: The Free Press.

22. R. Lachman (1985), Public and private sector differences: CEO's perceptions of their role environments, *Academy of Management Journal*, 28, 671–80; B. P. Keating and M. O. Keating (1980), *Not-for-profit*, Glen Ridge, NJ: Thomas Horton and Daughters.

23. M. S. Wortman, Jr. (1979), Strategic management: Not-for-profit organiza-tions, in D. E. Schendel and C. W. Hofer, eds., *Strategic management: A new view of business policy and planning*, Boston: Little, Brown, 353–81; Schendel and Hofer, 1979.

Key Terms

strategic management
strategy
strategic planning
strategic plan
organizational mission
mission statement
strategic objectives
operational strategies
scope
resource deployment
competitive advantages
synergy
corporate strategy
business unit strategy
functional strategy
informational (environmental) scan
organizational scan
gap analysis
defender organizations

prospector organizations
analyzer organizations
reactor organizations
strategic business unit (SBU)
portfolio matrix
stars
cash cows
question marks
dogs
growth strategy
stable growth, or hold, strategy
retrenchment, or turnaround, strategy
divestiture strategy
generic strategies
cost leadership
differentiation strategy
focus strategy

Issues for Review and Discussion

1. Describe the purposes of strategic planning and outline its advantages and disadvantages.
2. Identify the three levels of strategic planning and discuss why it is important to integrate planning across these three levels.
3. Discuss how analyses of the external environment and of organizational resources can identify strategic opportunities and threats.
4. What is gap analysis, and why is it a critical step in the strategic planning process?
5. Describe the relationship among the entrepreneurial, engineering, and administrative problems and how they are addressed by strategic planning.
6. Compare and contrast defender, prospector, and analyzer organizations. Explain why reactor organizations seldom succeed.
7. Why might an organization want to include stars, cows, *and* dogs in its business portfolio?
8. Discuss the special problems that face a manager of a small organization during strategic planning.
9. Suppose you are the director of United Way, a not-for-profit organization that receives public donations and distributes the money to other service organizations, such as the Boy Scouts of America. How would you incorporate what you know of strategic planning to fit the goals of your organization?

Suggested Readings

Agor, W. H. (1984). Using intuition to manage organizations in the future. *Business Horizons,* 27, 49–53.

Below, P. J., Morrisey, G. L., and Acomb, B. L. (1987). *The executive guide to strategic planning.* San Francisco: Jossey-Bass.

Buller, P. F. (Winter 1988). For successful strategic change: Blend OD practices with strategic management. *Organizational Dynamics,* 42–55.

Day, G. S. (1977). Diagnosing the product portfolio. *Journal of Marketing,* 41, 29–38.

Haspeslagh, P. (1982). Portfolio planning: Uses and limits. *Harvard Business Review,* 60, 58–74.

Huff, A. S. and Reger, R. K. (1987). A review of strategic process research. *Journal of Management,* 13, 211–36.

Kilman, R. H., Covin T. J., and Associates (1988). *Corporate transformation: Revitalizing organizations for a competitive world.* San Francisco: Jossey-Bass.

Knudsen, K. R. (1988). A review of *Coffin nails and corporate strategies.* In Pierce, J. L. and Newstrom, J. W., eds. *The manager's bookshelf: A mosaic of contemporary views.* New York: Harper & Row, 253–59.

Miles, R. E., Snow, C. C., Meyer, A. D., and Coleman, H. J., Jr. (1978). Organizational strategy, structure, and process. *Academy of Management Review,* 3, 546–62.

Miles, R. H. with Cameron, K. S. (1982). *Coffin nails and corporate strategies,* Englewood Cliffs, NJ: Prentice-Hall.

Mintzberg, H. (1987). Crafting strategy. *Harvard Business Review,* 65, 66–77.

CASE *Xexox Corporation*

By J. David Hunger, Thomas Conquest, and William Miller of Iowa State University

Xerox introduced the world's first convenient office copier in 1959, and its sales exploded, rising from $33 million a year to $3.6 billion by 1974. Its profits mushroomed from $2 million to $331 million, and the price of its stock soared from $2 a share to $172. The company grew to 100 times its former size. In that short period, photocopying machines dramatically transformed the nature of office work. Xerography made carbon paper and mimeograph machines obsolete and drastically reduced typing time. By the end of 1970, Xerox held the dominant position in the worldwide office copier market, with 95 percent of the market.

This monopolistic market share was seriously eroded in the 1970s, due to increased competition from many sources. Xerox had built its business by creating the plain paper copying market and then by protecting it with a solid wall of patents; however, in 1975, the company signed a consent decree with the Federal Trade Commission, in which Xerox agreed to license other companies wanting to use its process. Their seventeen-year patent protection was also expiring, and Xerox' technology could increasingly be used by anyone.

Recognizing that the copying industry was not going to continue to grow at its previous rate, Xerox positioned itself to become a major competitor in the "Office of the Future"

market by creating an office products division. In 1981, Xerox executives reported to their stockholders that the overriding corporate objective over the next decade was to be one of the leading companies in enhancing office productivity. "In order to accomplish this," the report said, "Xerox must maintain and strengthen its position of leadership in reprographics— as we refer to our total copying and duplicating business—*and* emerge from the 1980s as a leading systems company that is a major factor in automating the office."

Problems

By the autumn of 1982, the chief executive officer of the Xerox Corporation, David Kearns, was facing some difficult problems. His company had just suffered a 39 percent drop in third-quarter earnings. This was Xerox' fourth consecutive quarterly decline and the picture did not appear brighter for the current quarter. Much of the profit decline had been attributed to narrower profit margins brought on by steep price cutting on many copier models in response to increasing competition, especially from the Japanese. In addition, Xerox' profits had been reduced by severance costs of trimming its workforce; by the strength of the dollar, which eroded the values of its sales made abroad; and particularly by the sluggish U.S. economy. Xerox had reduced its workforce by 2174 employees in 1981, the first such reduction in the company's history. Further reductions occurred in 1982, with more predict-

ed for the coming year. Kearns had watched Xerox' share of the plain paper copier market slip from 95 percent to about 45 percent in 1982. In addition, Xerox stock had slipped to less than $40 in 1982.

Xerox' attempts to lessen its dependence on the competitive copier market by moving into the broader office automation area had been less than spectacular. The office products division had only one profitable quarter in its seven-year history and had losses of approximately $90 million in 1981. Kearns had admitted recently to market analysts that he did not expect the unit to be profitable until 1984. The division had recently been reorganized in an attempt to deal more effectively with some of the problems. Shortly after the reorganization, however, two of the key executives from the office products division resigned to form their own company.

The Office of the Future

The high cost of management, professional, and clerical workers in combination with the increasing capabilities of electronic office equipment established office automation as a major growth market for the 80s. White-collar salaries had become a huge and seemingly intractable cost of doing business. In 1980, 60 percent of the $1.3 trillion paid in wages, salaries, and benefits in the United States went to office workers. At the same time, the cost of electronic office equipment fell. Computer memory became cheaper at an annual rate of 42 percent over the five years prior to

1982 and the price of the logic chips that give computers their intelligence dropped about 28 percent a year.

Although office automation made sense in theory, the market did not develop as quickly as Xerox and others hoped. According to a competitor, Wang Laboratories, only 60 or so of the largest industrial corporations had acquired as many as 100 electronic office work stations; a much smaller number had linked them into networks.

Many reasons were given for the slow growth of this market. First of all, the recession caused many organizations to cut back on capital spending programs. Second, there was a lack of convincing studies on the savings associated with office automation. Third, in developing automation for managers and professionals, there was a problem in specifying exactly what steps or processes these individuals went through in doing their jobs. Fourth, top management did not feel comfortable with computer terminals on their desks. Fifth, there was uncertainty over the type of networking system that would prevail, and this made customers postpone purchasing networks. Finally, despite managers' universal desire to find better ways of doing work, office automation remained poorly understood.

Still, Dataquest, Inc., a California-based market research firm, estimated that U.S. shipments of equipment that could be linked to form electronic offices would grow 34 percent a year through 1986. Total revenues were predicted to grow between $12 and $15 billion.

This anticipation of a booming market for office automation brought dozens of companies into the competition. AT&T, IBM, and Xerox all declared the market to be a key to their future. In 1981, the top three minicomputer companies, Digital Equipment, Hewlett-Packard, and Data General, launched office automation systems within thirty days of one another. Analysts saw IBM, Wang, Digital Equipment, and Xerox as being in the best position to capture large pieces of this growing market, yet there appeared to be enough profitable niches to reward any company that could fill customers' needs.

Xerox Marketing

Xerox had traditionally been a single product line company, selling copiers to large businesses through its own sales and service force. This changed as it diversified its product line and redefined its customer base. The company revamped its copiers, offering a wider range of products to smaller businesses as well as larger companies. With their move into electronic office systems, a systems approach to marketing became necessary.

To meet the marketing problems associated with the company's new concepts, Xerox experimented with new distribution techniques. Independent distributors and dealers were contracted to sell products not only to end users, but also to original equipment manufacturers (OEMs), who resold the products as part of larger systems. These distribution systems reduced the company's expenses, thereby increasing margins while unburdening the company's own salesforce.

Xerox also planned to use retail chains, as well as its own retail stores, to reach small businesses. By 1982, it had already opened approximately thirty retail stores throughout the U.S. and had plans to open more. These outlets were named *The Xerox Store* and were designed to make small business operators comfortable in a store with a familiar name and reputation. In addition to selling Xerox' equipment, these outlets also carried brand-name equipment of other manufacturers, including competitors for home and office use. Most of this equipment complemented Xerox' own products and included Apple Computers, Hewlett-Packard calculators, Matsushita dictating machines, and a host of other products.

According to industry analysts, Xerox had three major marketing strengths. Its sales and service staff was the largest in the industry. The company had many financial resources to fund challenging, new product developments. Finally, the Xerox name was a household word, which gave customers a feeling of confidence about getting products serviced.

Analysts agreed that if the company had any weaknesses, it was a lack of expertise in marketing complex office products and systems. There were apparently great differences between marketing stand-alone copying machines and marketing more complex information-handling and processing systems. By 1981, Xerox had captured 13 percent of the word processor market but only about 1 percent of the small business office systems market.

September 1982

In September 1982, Xerox took the industry by surprise when it announced an agreement to acquire Crum & Forster, an insurance holding company, for about $1.65 billion in cash and securities. Crum & Forster was the nation's fifteenth largest property-casualty insurer, with $1.6 billion in premiums and $171 million in profits in 1981. The Xerox offer was twice the previous market price of the Crum & Forster stock.

Kearns gave several reasons for the acquisition: (1) Xerox believed that property-casualty insurance offered the best growth opportunities in the insurance industry. (2) the company perceived the acquisition as an expansion of Xerox' financial services, to complement the Xerox Credit Corporation. Formed in 1979 to help Xerox customers finance their purchases of Xerox equipment, this subsidiary had profits of about $35 million in 1981. (3) The acquisition would provide investment income, which Xerox needed to support its research in copiers, duplicators, and other office equipment.

Xerox watchers wondered whether the company had lost confidence in its office automation business. One analyst said, "My hunch is that office products may never be profitable for them. They've lost momentum." Kearns, however, disagreed, "This is a very aggressive strategy to grow this business with two market segments very different from each other. We concluded we could leverage the balance sheet at this time to branch out to other areas for a better return to our shareholders."

Questions

1. What are the major strategic planning issues that Xerox had dealt with in the late 1970s and early 1980s, following its consent decree with the Federal Trade Commission?

2. What evidence do you see here of corporate level strategic planning? Business unit level planning? Functional level planning?

3. What is your analysis of the Crum & Forster acquisition from a business portfolio standpoint?

4. From a strategy perspective, how would you have evaluated Xerox' quest in 1982 to be a dominant company in the "Office of the Future?"

5. Had Xerox CEO David Kearns asked you in 1982 to develop a strategic plan to take the company into the 1990s, what questions would you have asked him?

PART 3

Organizing

Sara Westendorf

From earning a B.A. in German and linguistics to receiving a B.S. in computer engineering, from having a career in social work to being a manager of design engineers, from Massachusetts to California—such has been the path of Sara Westendorf. Today while she heads a division at Hewlett-Packard, she is primarily concerned with doing things that are interesting and enjoyable, making sure that she is always in a position where she is learning something new. "My goal has always been to make the people and projects that I am responsible for successful. Doing a top-notch job will make the promotions come my way." In six years and after three promotions, thirty-five-year-old Westendorf is research and development manager for Advanced Manufacturing Systems (AMSO) at Hewlett-Packard.

Sex-role stereotyping (maybe), a caring for people (obviously), a drive to excel, perfectionism, and a problem-solving orientation have played major roles in Westendorf's career choices. Following graduation from high school in Amherst, Massachusetts, Westendorf worked as a nurses' aide in West Germany and then went on to earn a B.A. in German and linguistics from the University of Rochester. During this time, she did social work and eventually pursued an M.S.W. at Rutgers University. After two and one half years of developing caring relationships with the children and families who were a part of her case load, Westendorf began to experience frustration and, possibly, occupational burnout. She found herself dealing with problems for which her formal training had not equipped her, emotionally or technically.

She talks about working with a family with fifteen children aged fourteen and under. One of the babies belonged to the fourteen-year-old daughter, another to the twelve-year-old daughter. "Just as I was starting to feel good that the third grader with a truancy problem had achieved a perfect school attendance record for two weeks, two of the other children dropped out of school. Just as I was starting to feel good about the seventh grader staying away from liquor and dope for a week, the sixth grader overdosed on 'reds' and the mother spent the grocery money to get high herself." Experiences of this nature were taking their toll. As Westendorf tells it, "I would have done anything to help those kids, but frankly, the futility of my best efforts was so overwhelming that it seemed like the only way to preserve my sanity was to stop caring, in the same way many of the experienced social workers seemed to have done." Instead, Westendorf fantasized about becoming an engineer, and shortly thereafter she turned that dream into a reality.

> *She is always in a position where she is learning something new.*

At Princeton University and then at the University of Illinois, Westendorf turned her attention to designing functional computers. In 1976 she received a B.S. in computer engineering, and today she manages an engineering unit. Recognizing her need for formal training in business, economics, and management, she is planning on pursuing an M.B.A. degree.

Westendorf now manages R&D for Hewlett-Packard's Advanced Manufacturing Systems Operation. Formed in 1984, AMSO's mission is to apply HP's measurement and computation expertise in providing custom-integrated integrated testing systems that improve customers' product and process quality. AMSO produces integrated test systems with an aerospace/ military market focus and in-process/ service-bay vehicle analyses for the automotive industry.

AMSO is organized into four functional areas—manufacturing, marketing, finance, and research and development. The R&D unit is responsible for designing and implementing computer systems. Within the R&D unit, Westendorf's managerial responsibilities include providing the leadership the organization needs to meet its goals of profitability and customer satisfaction. She sees her success as largely dependent on the caliber and expertise of the people in her organization. As a consequence, she places a premium on human resource recruitment and development, and on providing an excellent working environment. She says, "If an engineering team has the right expertise for the job and the individuals are enthused about the project they're working on, then productivity, profitability, and customer satisfaction will follow." Westendorf sees her job as providing the right environment and developing a sense of enthusiasm and project commitment among her subordinates.

Westendorf's management style has significant roots in her educational experiences. Her social-work education and work experiences helped her develop several interpersonal skills that are necessary in the highly political and sensitive organizational environment. She also credits her experiences with giving her a sense of resourcefulness. "Working in agencies operating on shoestring budgets instilled the attitude of doing whatever it takes to get the job done." Finally, her frustration with social work left Westendorf with an appreciation for the importance of job satisfaction. "Enhancing your job satisfaction is important, because the more you enjoy your job, the better you'll do at it."

Westendorf's engineering education and work experiences provided her with another set of important ingredients of her management philosophy. Her technical background equipped her to understand the organization's product line. "No matter what business you're in, whether it's perfume or rifles, understanding your product line is essential to being successful in a management position." Understanding the customer is equally important. Westendorf feels that her engineering background helps her understand the product, and that this background provides her with the opportunity to better understand the customer and the needs the organization is attempting to fulfill.

"The more you enjoy your job, the better you'll do at it."

Several other factors—making it fun, making effective use of mentoring, keeping up a sense of humor, and managing by walking around—highlight Westendorf's management style and play an important role in her success:

Regarding fun—make sure you enjoy what you are doing. As a manager your enthusiasm about a project will inspire the workers and make them productive.

Regarding leadership—be willing to do whatever it takes. Leading through dedication and commitment to getting the job done will inspire others to do the same. Being boss does not mean you are any more important than everyone else; treating everyone equally is important in promoting a spirit of teamwork.

Regarding humor—especially in high-pressure situations, a sense of humor can do an amazing job of diffusing tension and promoting teamwork.

"Managing by Walking Around" (MBWA) is a management process that has become part of the Hewlett-Packard way. Westendorf notes that some decisions must be made in the privacy of one's own office, yet most decisions are best made with the involvement of employees. She says, "I find myself coming up to people and saying, 'I've been thinking about whether we ought to keep bidding minicomputer products into our system, or whether we ought to go to a lower-cost, PC-based controller, and I'd be interested in hearing your thoughts on the matter.'" This process accomplishes a number of things:

- You soon have a good feel for who knows what.
- Workers feel good that you cared enough to ask for their opinion.
- You will probably get some good information that will help you make the right decision.
- You will have more grassroots support for your decision from the people who felt involved in making the decision.
- If the decision is later questioned, you will know who to go to for back-up information.
- You will have effectively communicated to the trenches some of the issues you are wrestling with, and the "troops" seem to appreciate knowing these things.

Finally, Westendorf notes that MBWA is a good way to validate a decision once it has been made, or to see if there are any better ideas floating around before the decision is finalized.

What outstanding perspective makes Sara Westendorf a successful manager? According to her, it is "a results-oriented, can-do, get-the-job-done-no-matter-what-it-takes attitude."

Organizing and Coordinating Work

Student Learning Objectives

After reading this chapter, you should be able to:

1. Understand what managers do when they engage in the organizing activity.

2. Understand the difference between the formal and informal organization.

3. Distinguish among the classical, behavioral management, and work group approaches to the organizing of jobs.

4. Identify and differentiate the various approaches to departmentalizing jobs.

5. Discuss the interdependence of jobs and departments.

6. Identify the ways managers coordinate levels of an organization's hierarchy.

7. Identify the ways managers coordinate units at the same level in an organization's hierarchy.

8. Identify and discuss the problems managers face when integrating individuals, jobs, and organizational units.

*T*hink about all of the activities employees perform at your university: scheduling courses, cleaning windows, ordering supplies, maintaining student records, teaching classes, preparing food, photocopying, and so on. If you were to make a comprehensive list, you would probably identify several thousand different tasks. Without goals or a set of plans to provide direction, would the work get done? Would all necessary tasks be executed efficiently? Would you be willing to attend an unplanned, disorganized school and have to wait every day to see who showed up to teach you something, to clean the floor, to wash the blackboard, to serve you a meal, to check your blood pressure, or to mail student loan checks? With this approach, academic life would be chaotic for both students and employees. The managerial activity of organizing attempts to bring order and direction to the work of an organization. This chapter and the two that follow will discuss the ways that managers organize.

The Nature of Organizing

Organizations are systems created to achieve a set of goals through people-to-people and people-to-work relationships. Each system has its own external and internal environments that define the nature of those relationships according to its specific needs. A hospital, for example, has organizational needs that are different from those of a university, which are different from those of a museum or of the federal government. **Organizing** is what managers do when they design, structure, and arrange the components of an organization's internal environment to facilitate attainment of organizational goals. For example, to meet its goal of delivering high-quality health care, a hospital may organize both in- and out-patient facilities, locate its emergency room and trauma center on the first floor of the building to prevent delays in treating critical patients, prepare meal schedules, provide room cleaning services, and so forth.

Organizing creates the vehicle needed to reach a company's goals. When organizational goals are varied and complex, the organizing activity requires great sophistication. The housekeeping department within a hospital may set a goal to have all patient rooms cleaned by 3 P.M., which is different from the surgical department's goal of losing no more than 5 percent of its open-heart surgery patients. The people-to-people and people-to-work relationships created for housekeeping differ from those for the surgical unit. Each network in the system is organized as necessary to help the hospital achieve its overall goal of high-quality health service.

Managers organize by defining and coordinating work at a number of different levels: tasks are grouped to form jobs, jobs are combined into departments, and departments are organized into divisions (see Figure 10.1). For example, the tasks of answering phones and greeting visitors are part of the hospital's receptionist job. Secretaries open mail, type letters, and arrange meetings. Both the receptionist and secretary jobs are found in the hospital's clerical services department. Processing applications, interviewing and hiring job applicants, and conducting performance appraisals are tasks performed by job incumbents in the hospital's

Each organization has its own environments, which define its unique people-to-people and people-to-work relationships.

FIGURE 10.1   The Organizing Process

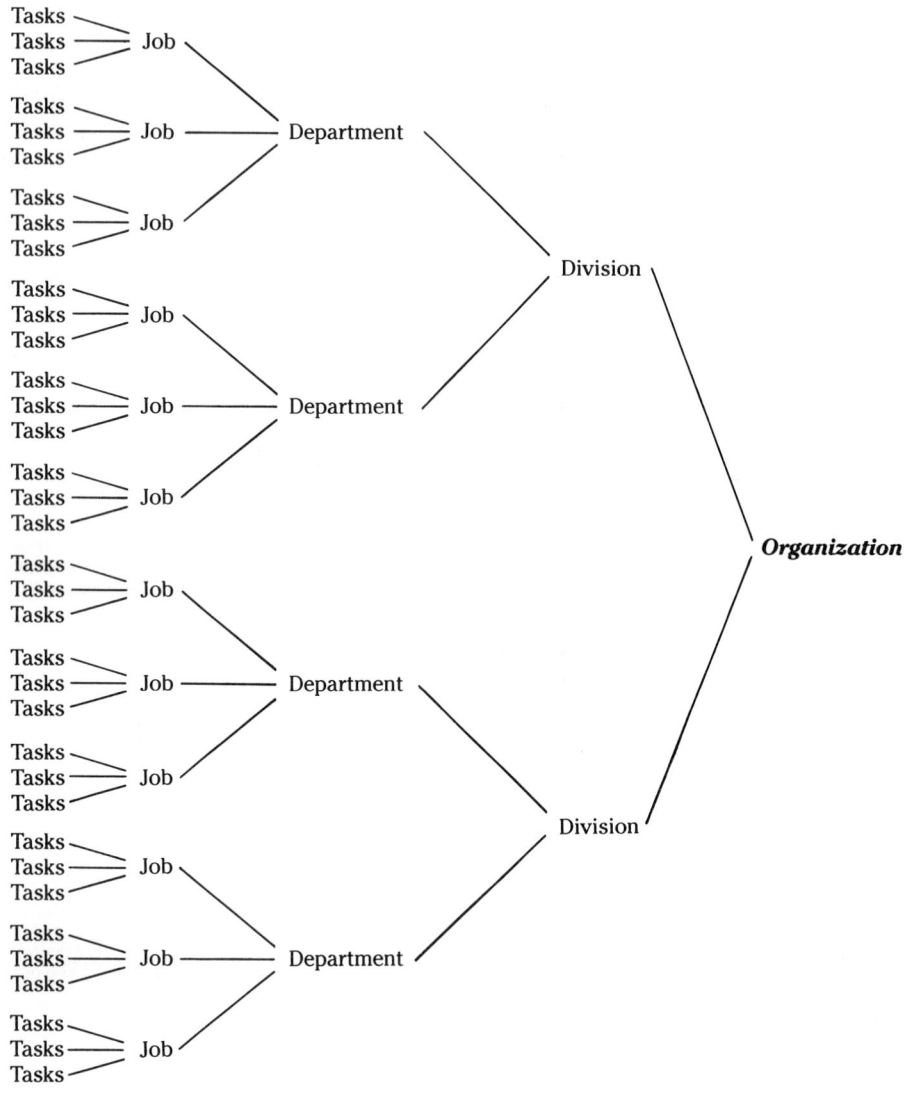

personnel department. Together, the clerical services and personnel departments form the hospital's administrative services division. The hospital's linen and housekeeping departments are part of its environmental services division.

Managers create a variety of systems to support the organization and coordination of tasks, jobs, departments, and divisions. Authority, communication, and coordination systems, for example, link and integrate an organization's jobs, departments, and so forth. The coordination system of a data processing subsidiary enables its representatives to present the following information at its parent company's annual meeting: the number of new customers who signed contracts for its services during the past year (provided by the marketing department), the amount of revenue these contracts generated (provided by the accounting department),

FIGURE 10.2   *Organizing Vertical and Horizontal Coordination Systems*

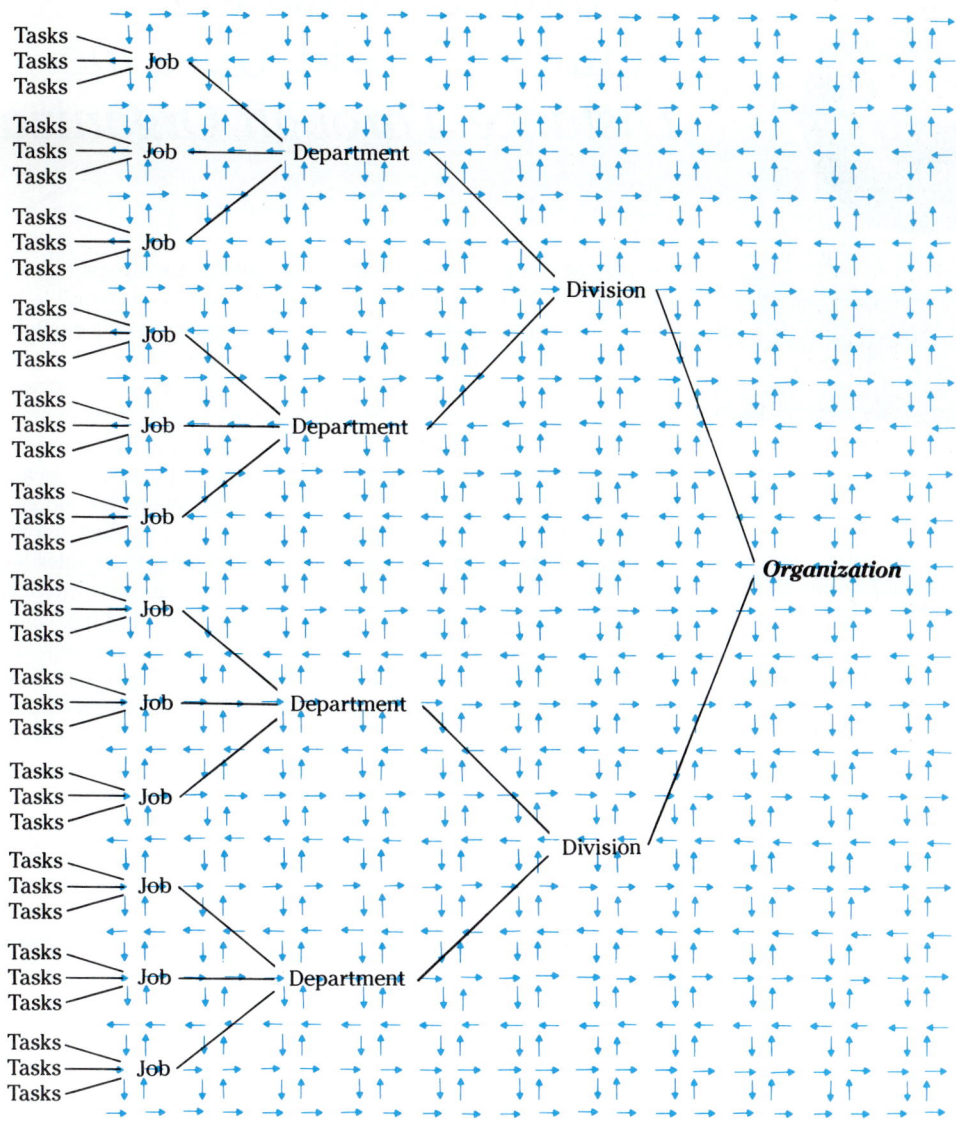

information on equipment downtime (from operations), and so forth. Managers must organize the systems needed to fulfill all of the organization's coordination needs (see Figure 10.2).

Within any organization, there are both formal and informal components. The **formal organization** exists as a result of the official structures and systems designed by managers through the organizing activity.[1] The formal organization usually contains a structured communication and command system that helps people pool their time, energy, and talents to reach common objectives. (See "A Closer Look: Formal Organization.")

The **informal organization,** in contrast, exists when two or more people interact for a purpose or in a manner beyond that specified by managers. Often, informal organizations evolve in a natural, unplanned manner, but they may also form intentionally, as when nurses in the

A CLOSER LOOK

Formal Organization: Runner's World *Goes the Distance Through Organization*

Runner's World magazine has a monthly circulation of well over a half a million copies and requires the services of over 100 full-time employees. To help these employees operate efficiently and effectively, *Runner's World* has a formal organization that specifies their responsibilities and clarifies the links among jobs and departments.

In 1966, *Runner's World* had no organization and no employees. In that year, seventeen-year-old Bob Anderson, tired of the lack of good information about running, produced a twenty-eight-page first issue of a magazine he called *Distance Running News*. Bob was writer, editor, publisher, and marketing manager—totally alone in the venture. He used $100 of savings to print and sell 1000 copies of his new magazine at $.75 per copy.

In 1967, Bob was still running the company alone; but he recognized

that one person alone could not guarantee the continued growth and success of the magazine. By 1970, he had moved the company from Kansas to California, changed the name of the magazine to *Runner's World*, developed an international network of part-time correspondents, and hired a full-time assistant.

Today, with over 100 full-time employees, Bob has created a formal organization designed to coordinate work in an efficient, effective manner. Bob still carries the titles of editor and publisher, but the organization now has an executive editor, a managing editor, a photo editor, a features editor, a columns editor, and a copyeditor. There are directors of production, creative arts, advertising, sales, circulation, and human resources. Each director has a staff.

> *Runner's World has a formal organization that . . . clarifies the links among jobs and departments.*

Job descriptions specify the responsibilities of each employee. People with similar jobs supporting a particular function (for example, advertising) are grouped into depart-

ments. Each department has a director, who is responsible for supervising the department's employees and managing its activities successfully. Directors report to executives, who coordinate related departments.

Bob and his managers created a variety of formal rules and regulations to encourage fair and consistent treatment of individual employees. At the same time, these rules and regulations set guidelines for the operation and coordination of jobs and departments. They specify who will make decisions and how they will be implemented.

Running requires one step at a time. Competitive running, however, requires coordination, stamina, and long-term planning. The same is true for the running of an organization. In 1966, Bob Anderson founded his magazine and developed it one step at a time. At its current world-class level, however, one step at a time is no longer enough. Today, Bob's main mission is to organize and coordinate the work of the organization and its individual members.

Source: S. P. Robbins (1983), *Organization theory: The structure and design of organizations*, Englewood Cliffs, NJ: Prentice-Hall, 3–5. Current facts were obtained from industry statistics and from *Runner's World*.

geriatric ward of a hospital meet to discuss problems they have with doctors and patients. As you will see in Chapter 13, each member of an informal organization has personal reasons for joining it. Because members of the informal organization exchange information, satisfy individual needs, and influence one another, the informal organization may have direct and significant implications for managers of the formal organization. Sometimes informal groups become formal groups, as would occur if the geriatric nurses just described organized a union.

In the formal organization, managers prescribe expected behaviors through job descriptions, rules, policies, and operating procedures. In contrast, informal behaviors arise from the needs, norms, values, and standards of organization members. The formal organization in a company that assembles bathroom exhaust fans, for example, might specify the time to show up for work, the type of clothing permissible, the method to be used to assemble bathroom exhaust fans, and the minimum number of fans that must be produced per hour. The informal organization, however, may define a social norm which states that employees should not produce more than a certain number of fans per hour.

Managers need to recognize that both formal and informal organizations exist and that both influence the overall efficiency and effectiveness of their organization. Rather than fight the informal organization, managers should try to benefit from it. Informal norms requiring ethical behavior, for example, can be useful, as can the informal communication "grapevine" that keeps people abreast of happenings at all levels of the formal organization.

Organizing Jobs

An organization achieves its goals through the work done by its members. To facilitate this, managers organize various tasks into jobs. Before the Industrial Revolution, the one dominant approach to job design was the craft approach. In the **craft approach,** a single skilled worker designed and built products one at a time from beginning to end. The craftsperson raised and sheared sheep, washed and carded the wool, dyed it with berries or blossoms that he or she had gathered, dried and spun it into yarn, and wove it into clothing.

Following the Industrial Revolution, however, the craft approach nearly disappeared. Wool clothing today is usually the result of the combined efforts of sheep ranchers, textile mills, weavers, and dyers—all of them separate enterprises, separate organizations, and separate workforces.

In the craft approach, a skilled potter designs and builds one product at a time from beginning to end. In contrast, clothing manufacturing is a collaborative process done by ranchers, textile mills, weavers, and dyers.

Although some potters, artists, weavers, and furniture makers still make individually crafted products, the craft approach has largely been replaced by four other approaches to job design: classical, behavioral, contingency, and work group. All four of these approaches are in use today.

The Classical Approach

In the **classical approach,** labor is divided into jobs made up of a small number of simple, repetitive, standardized tasks. Adam Smith first illuminated the economic advantages said to accompany the specialization, standardization, and simplification of work in his classic book *Wealth of Nations* (published in 1776).[2] In Smith's example of pin manufacturing, an inexperienced pin maker was expected to make no more than 20 pins per day using the craft approach. With division of labor, one worker drew the wire, a second cut it, a third straightened it, a fourth ground the point, and so on. With this approach and new equipment, a workforce of ten people could produce 48,000 pins a day.

Smith believed that labor should be highly divided so that each employee would perform only a limited number of activities that did not require elaborate skills. Smith gave five reasons for the effectiveness of designing jobs this way:

1. *Skill and dexterity development.* A worker who repeatedly performs the same activity improves over time.
2. *Time savings and production gains.* Workers are able to produce more if they do not lose time changing from one activity to another.
3. *Innovations.* People who specialize their efforts seem to find ways to do their job better, faster, and more cheaply.
4. *Specialized equipment.* Narrowly defined tasks can often be done by machines developed for that specific purpose.
5. *Training time and costs.* Employees can be productive almost immediately. It does not take long to train workers to perform a small number of simple tasks.

Succeeding generations of managers built on the idea of the division of labor. Charles Babbage, for example, saw that management could save money by paying for only those skills that it actually needed.[3] Instead of hiring one person to perform a job from beginning to end (the craft approach), organizations could divide the job into simple and complex tasks. Managers could hire people with a limited range of skills to perform simple tasks, and they could hire people with high levels of skill to perform the complex tasks, thus paying a high wage only where high skill levels were required. The work of such people as Smith and Babbage provided an economic rationale for ways to achieve high levels of productivity.

Today, managers routinely divide labor and design jobs along lines of work specialization, standardization, and simplification.[4] Frederick W. Taylor and other advocates of scientific management refined this approach and brought it to twentieth-century organizations.[5] As you saw in Chapter 5, Taylor believed that division of labor improved organizational effectiveness and efficiency. He advocated: (1) a division of labor that

FIGURE 10.3 *The Alleged Curse of the Classical Job Design Model*

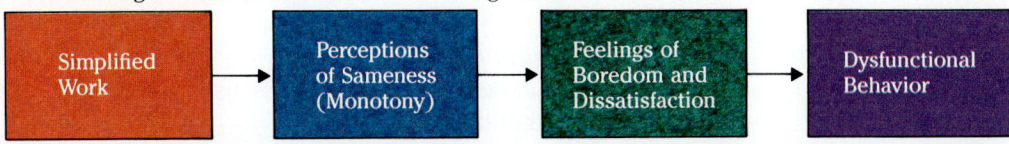

Simplified Work → Perceptions of Sameness (Monotony) → Feelings of Boredom and Dissatisfaction → Dysfunctional Behavior

separated management from the rank and file, (2) a division of labor within the ranks of management to achieve functional supervision, and (3) a division of labor among the rank and file. His work resulted in **vertical specialization,** which removes planning and controlling activities from production employees, and **horizontal specialization,** which creates many low-skill-level, repetitive jobs.

This classical approach to job design was seen as a way to greater productivity, efficiency, control, and standardization of work. For decades, its supporters touted that it increased labor effectiveness, lowered production costs, and made system performance more predictable. It is not clear how much these favorable results were a function of the division of labor or of the other changes that were ushered in by the classicists (such as wage incentive systems, the adoption of new technologies, and the increased ability of management to administer large complex production facilities).[6]

Critics have argued that jobs designed solely according to the classical approach may lead to problems for both organizations and their members. They have suggested that employees occupying simplified, low-skill-level, repetitive jobs eventually perceive them as monotonous and, thus, become bored and dissatisfied. Boredom and job dissatisfaction, they claim, eventually translate into absenteeism, turnover, and various other forms of output restriction (see Figure 10.3).[7]

Manufacturers of the Saab automobile have responded to these criticisms by eliminating the assembly line. Spokespeople for the company claim that, because its employees are no longer bored by the monotony of the assembly line, they care about the products that they make and will build a better-quality car.

The Behavioral Approach

The classical approach to job design tried to make organizations efficient and effective by making work simple, but in the late 1940s and early 1950s, behavioral management advocates suggested that perhaps the same objective could be attained by making work interesting. The **behavioral approach** rejects the idea of treating people as automated machines, continuously performing simple and repetitive activities. Behavioral theorists noted that, although machines have no emotions, people do. When people's feelings are negative, when their needs are not met and their motives frustrated, workers and their organizations suffer.

Adam Smith may have praised the advantages of pin straighteners and pinpoint grinders, but that approach places workers in an environment where they are continually asked not to think, to use only a few skills and abilities, and to do repetitive work. Under such conditions, employees eventually physically and psychologically resist this kind of world through escape mechanisms, such as the following:

- *Physical withdrawal.* Employees are late to work, absent from work, or quit.
- *Psychological withdrawal.* Employees care little about their work or the product, feel apathetic and dissatisfied, and are uncommitted to their job and the organization.
- *Physical resistance.* Employees may join a union, engage in work slowdowns and stoppages, or even commit sabotage.[8]

Job Enlargement and Job Enrichment   To interest and motivate workers, behavioral management advocates first introduced two alternative job design strategies.[9] **Job enlargement** adds breadth to a job by increasing the number and variety of activities performed by an employee. These efforts to reverse the effects of horizontal specialization are called *horizontal loading.* For example, an insurance clerk's job, which consists primarily of repeatedly completing one type of insurance application, can be horizontally enlarged by adding other forms to be typed, filing duties, and communication with clients and agents to maintain insurance histories. **Job enrichment** adds depth to a job by adding "managerial" activities (planning, organizing, directing, and controlling) to an employee's responsibilities. These efforts to reverse the effects of vertical specialization are called *vertical loading.* The insurance clerk's job could be enriched by allowing the worker to make decisions about accepting new policy applications, rejecting claims, and so on.

The Job Characteristics Model   An expansion on the ideas of job enlargement and job enrichment is found in J. Richard Hackman's and Greg Oldham's **Job Characteristics Model (JCM).** This model specifies the critical job components that lead to positive results for both an organization and its workers. According to the JCM, if a job has high levels of the five "core" components specified, a worker will perceive the job as meaningful, will develop a sense of responsibility for the outcome of the work, and will understand the results of his or her efforts. These three psychological states are expected to lead to job satisfaction; motivation; high-quality work performance; and a reduction in absenteeism, tardiness, and turnover behaviors. The following are the five core components plus two supplemental social-oriented components specified by the JCM:

1. *Skill variety*—the extent to which a job requires an employee to use a broad set of skills and abilities
2. *Autonomy*—the amount of independent thought, freedom, and discretion an employee is permitted to exercise in performing a job
3. *Task significance*—the degree to which a job affects the lives, well-being, and/or work of other people
4. *Task identity*—the extent to which a job produces a complete, identifiable piece of work (that is, the job is done from beginning to end and has a visible outcome)
5. *Job feedback*—the degree to which an employee receives information about the effectiveness of his or her task performance directly from the job as it is being performed

FIGURE 10.4   The Job Characteristics Model

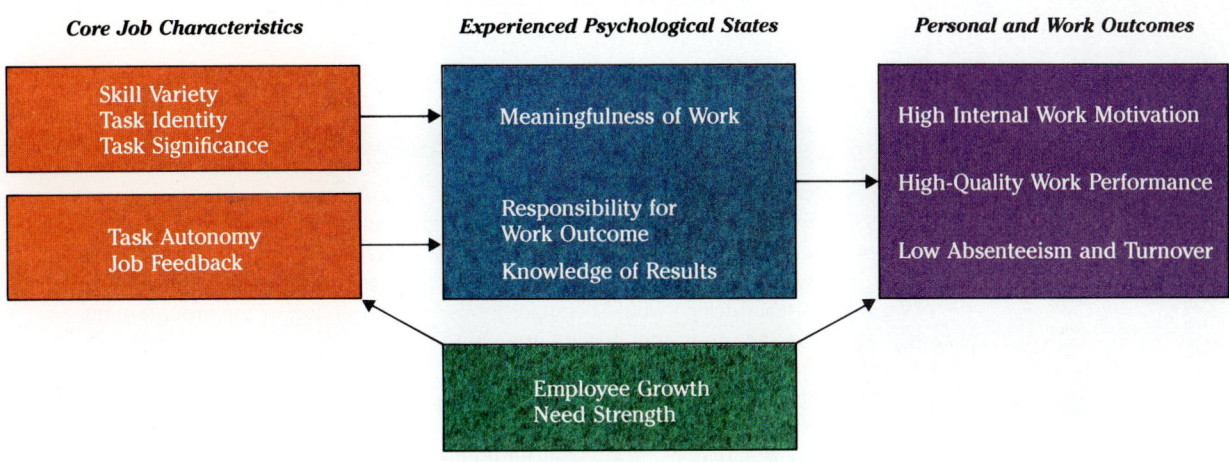

Source: J. R. Hackman and G. R. Oldham (1976), Motivation through the design of work: Test of a theory, *Organizational Behavior and Human Performance*, 16, 250–79.

6. *Agent feedback*—the degree to which a worker receives clear information about the effectiveness of his or her work from supervisors, co-workers, and/or clients

7. *Dealing with others*—the amount of human interaction an employee experiences while performing a job[10]

Hackman and Oldham encouraged managers to design jobs so they would contain high levels of each of these characteristics, particularly the first five, which they considered "core" (see Figure 10.4). Doing so, they argued, would avoid the problems inherent in the classical approach and, thus, would enhance organizational effectiveness. They also provided ideas that developed their model into a contingency approach.

The Contingency Approach

A number of management scholars have argued that neither the classical nor the behavioral approach to job design is universally most appropriate. According to the **contingency approach** to job design, managers should organize work and design jobs to fit the characteristics of the worker who will perform that job, the organization's technology, and other design characteristics of the organization.[11]

Initially, proponents of the contingency approach focused their attention on the fit between individual characteristics (such as an employee's work-ethic level) and job design characteristics. It was suggested that people have different needs and personality characteristics and, therefore, respond differently to job designs.[12] Some employees, for example, prefer routine jobs, while others respond more favorably to complex jobs. Accordingly, individuals with strong esteem, growth, and achievement needs (that is, higher-order needs) should be most compatible with complex jobs. People motivated primarily by lower-order needs, such as the need for security and social acceptance, are less likely to be excited

J. Richard Hackman

J. Richard Hackman is Cahners-Rabb Professor of Social and Organizational Psychology at Harvard University. He conducts research on a variety of topics in social psychology and organizational behavior, including the performance of work teams, social influences on individual behavior, and the design and leadership of self-managing units in organizations.

1. What should a manager pay more attention to—the design of individual jobs or the design of groups?

I don't think that's really the question. The real question is how to design motivating work that is consistent with organizational objectives. Sometimes that involves designing individual jobs; sometimes it involves designing autonomous work teams; and sometimes it involves designing an automated system for getting a piece of work done. The idea should be to design jobs that tap the resources of the people who are working in the organization, jobs that contribute to employee growth and development while also contributing to organizational objectives.

2. Are there conditions under which the design of individual jobs or the design of groups becomes particularly important?

In fact, sometimes there isn't any choice, or the choice is obvious. The only real error in such circumstances would be to go against the natural current. For example, for salespeople with a distinct geographical territory, a team design would be superfluous. On the other side, playing in a string quartet is a nice example of a team task; the interdependence at the core of the work can't be changed, so some situations clearly call for an individual design and others clearly call for a team design. It gets interesting in situations where you could go one way or the other. For example, in thinking about the work of an airplane cockpit crew, should you design a series of choreographed individual jobs or an intact team task? You see the kind of trade-offs that would have to be considered in making that decision. My advice is to actively think about that matter and not just "knee jerk" in one direction or the other.

Historically, there has been a "knee-jerk" reaction toward individual task design in traditional industrial practice, and in recent years there's been something of a "knee-jerk" reaction toward designing autonomous or self-managing work teams in new high-commitment-type organizations. I would encourage people on both sides of that fence to be a bit more thoughtful about the design choices they make because the choice will dictate, to a considerable extent, the organizational support structures and systems and the leadership style that will be needed. Also, the choice that's made will, over time, have an influence on the kind of organizational culture that emerges. Designers should be comfortable with the direction in which the design choices would move that culture—for example, toward a more individualistic or more collectivistic culture.

Finally, designers should keep in mind that a critical thing is to implement the choice well. In some organizations and with some technologies, it would be next to impossible to successfully implement either the individual option or the group option.

3. Your job characteristics theory has probably been generally more researched in the last ten years than any other theory. What's the good news or bad news about your research?

The good news is that I think we have pretty well tied down the fact that the characteristics of jobs really do make a difference—and it appears to be a very substantial difference—in the reactions people have to their work and to their behavior on the job. We've got that post in concrete, as it were, and can now move on from there to rather more interesting questions.

That leads me, of course, to the bad news, which is that we haven't moved on to more interesting questions nearly as vigorously as I would have hoped. We haven't, for example, really solved the individual differences question yet. It seems clear to observers of people at work that different people respond differently to motivating jobs, yet the growth-needs-strength measure Oldham and I developed doesn't seem to be quite right as the measure of whatever it is that accounts for those differences in responses. The dozen or so other measures that have been tried don't, in my view, quite capture it either, and so, we're still stuck with the question we were addressing a decade ago—namely, there are clearly individual differences in how people react to their work, but what are the key variables here, and how do they operate? We still don't know nearly as much as we ought to.

and motivated by the challenges of complex jobs. If Sandra Nossiter has a high need for achievement but is given a job filling ice cream cones at a snack shop, she is likely to become dissatisfied.

In addition to offering initial suggestions that managers consider the fit between individual differences and job design characteristics, many contingency approach proponents assert that structural characteristics of an organization should be considered as well. It has been argued that routine jobs are compatible with mechanistic (bureaucratic) organizations, while complex jobs have design characteristics that match the structure of organic organizations (see Chapter 2 for a discussion of mechanistic and organic characteristics). Researchers who study organizations have also noted that routine jobs are more likely to fit with routine technologies, while complex jobs fit nonroutine technologies and self-managing groups.[13] This means that a dynamic, organic organization using rapidly changing technologies is not likely to function well if jobs are overly specialized and routine. The incumbents of such jobs would be unlikely to keep up with the changing demands of such an environment. It also means that a mechanistic organization with simple, routine, unchanging technologies has little need for complex jobs. In other words, there is no need to buy a Lear jet to go to the neighborhood grocery store!

Because there is no one best way to design jobs, it appears that managers must use a contingency approach and consider the fit between job design, worker make-up, technology, and an organization's internal and external environments.

The Self-Managing Work Group Approach

So far this chapter has focused on the design of work for individuals. In the **self-managing work group approach,** groups of workers collaborate in performing and managing their work. As noted in the interview with J. Richard Hackman, some types of work are not well suited to group

A dynamic, organic organization using rapidly changing technologies is not likely to function well if jobs are overly specialized and routine.

performance. Other types of work are less well suited to being performed by a single individual. Still other tasks can be designed either for individuals or for groups. Automotive drive trains can be produced along an assembly line with individual job assignments or they can be assembled by teams of workers who produce the drive train at stationary work tables. Classes at your university can be taught by individual professors or they can be taught in teams.

In self-managing work groups, managers assign work to an entire group rather than to individual members of the group.[14] The group is given the authority to create the processes needed to accomplish their assigned work and to handle internal problems. For example, at Butler Manufacturing in Sioux City, Iowa, self-managing teams have replaced the traditional assembly line for the construction of grain driers.[15] Each construction team, operating autonomously, performs a wide variety of tasks. Team members change job assignments frequently so that eventually they learn the entire range of assembly activities. Quality inspection, employee training and development, work scheduling, assembly, and control activities are managed by the group through a combination of planned and spontaneous meetings. Team members handle many group personnel issues, such as hiring, performance appraisals, promotions, and treating behavior problems.

It has been argued that self-managing work groups provide all of the advantages of the behavioral approach and more. Work in a self-managing group is designed to offer variety, autonomy, significance, task identity, feedback, and opportunities for human interaction. Group members participate in their own management and, as a result, are more likely to accept, support, and actively pursue the procedures and goals set by the group. Participating in what traditionally have been management decisions tends to fulfill various growth needs and leads to satisfaction for many employees; however, this approach also moves organizational control from the hands of traditional managers to those of workers. Managers and workers must be able to accept this transformation, or the approach will fail. (See "A Closer Look: Work Teams.")

Departmentalization: Grouping Organizational Activities

Just as individual tasks need to be organized into jobs, jobs must be organized into larger units (such as work groups and departments) and work units into divisions. Otherwise, the control of jobs and the coordination and integration of work is extremely difficult. The process of grouping jobs into organizational units and those units into larger units is referred to as **departmentalization.**

Organizations use departmentalization to answer the question "What activities do we want to coordinate at one place in the organizational hierarchy?" For example, does Zimbrick, a large automobile dealer in the Midwest, want to locate (and therefore coordinate) all salespeople in one

Work Teams: Only People Can Give Wisdom to the Machines

The mechanization of muscle-power in the first Industrial Revolution led to simpler and simpler tasks that demanded little of workers except the use of their hands. Management neither expected nor wanted broader worker involvement. In the new Industrial Revolution now under way, capital consists of information technologies that require workers' mental commitment and responsibility for entire systems rather than for narrow tasks.[1]

Managers . . . loosen their control and encourage their workers to use their creativity.

Until recently, the majority of work performed in the United States was directed by the hands of people. Today, the bulk of work is guided by machines. When people were the instrument of production, managers were taught to control employees. Now that machines do the work, emphasis is shifting to teaching managers to loosen their control and encourage workers to use their creativity and initiative in controlling machines.

Modern plants in the United States rely heavily on robotics and other computer-driven systems for manufacturing. The Ex-Cell-O Corporation in Americus, Georgia, is typical. Ex-Cell-O manufactures a variety of plastic car parts, such as the shiny colored covers used for bumpers. In the past, each bumper cover was spray-painted by a worker. Now the job is done by robots—and quality and productivity are much higher. Employees at Ex-Cell-O's plant are responsible for operating and maintaining the robotics systems rather than for directly producing the goods.

The nature of work changes substantially when robotics take over production. Even though robotics and computerization have reduced the likelihood of a worker's making a simple production error, human errors in operating the technology can be magnified to dreadful levels: witness the nuclear accidents at Three Mile Island and Chernobyl. It is a fact of life in business today that "We're moving increasingly into dangerous, unforgiving technologies that can't be operated safely with uncommitted people."[2]

More and more organizations are turning to teamwork to nurture commitment to the organization and to manage the new technologies effectively. When Shenandoah Life Insurance Company placed employees into semiautonomous work teams of five to seven members, the time required to handle a policy conversion decreased from twenty-seven to two days. Overall, 50 percent more policies were handled with a smaller number of employees. Proctor & Gamble, a leader in the use of teams, claims that its team-based plants are 30 to 40 percent more productive than their traditional plants. Volvo's team-oriented plants in Sweden are reported to have production costs 25 percent lower than the company's conventional plants.

Procter & Gamble . . . claims that its team-based plants are 30 to 40 percent more productive.

Loosened controls, better use of employees' ideas, greater commitment, and stronger motivation go hand-in-hand in developing a more effective and more satisfied work force. Enlightened managers are discovering that one of the best decisions they can make is to allow workers to help make decisions. The solutions are not easy but the direction is clear: this is the decade of the worker!

1. J. Hoerr (20 April 1987), Getting man and machine to live happily ever after, *Business Week*, 61.
2. Lyman D. Ketchum in J. Hoerr, M. A. Pollock, and D. E. Whiteside (29 September 1986), Management discovers the human side of automation, *Business Week*, 71.

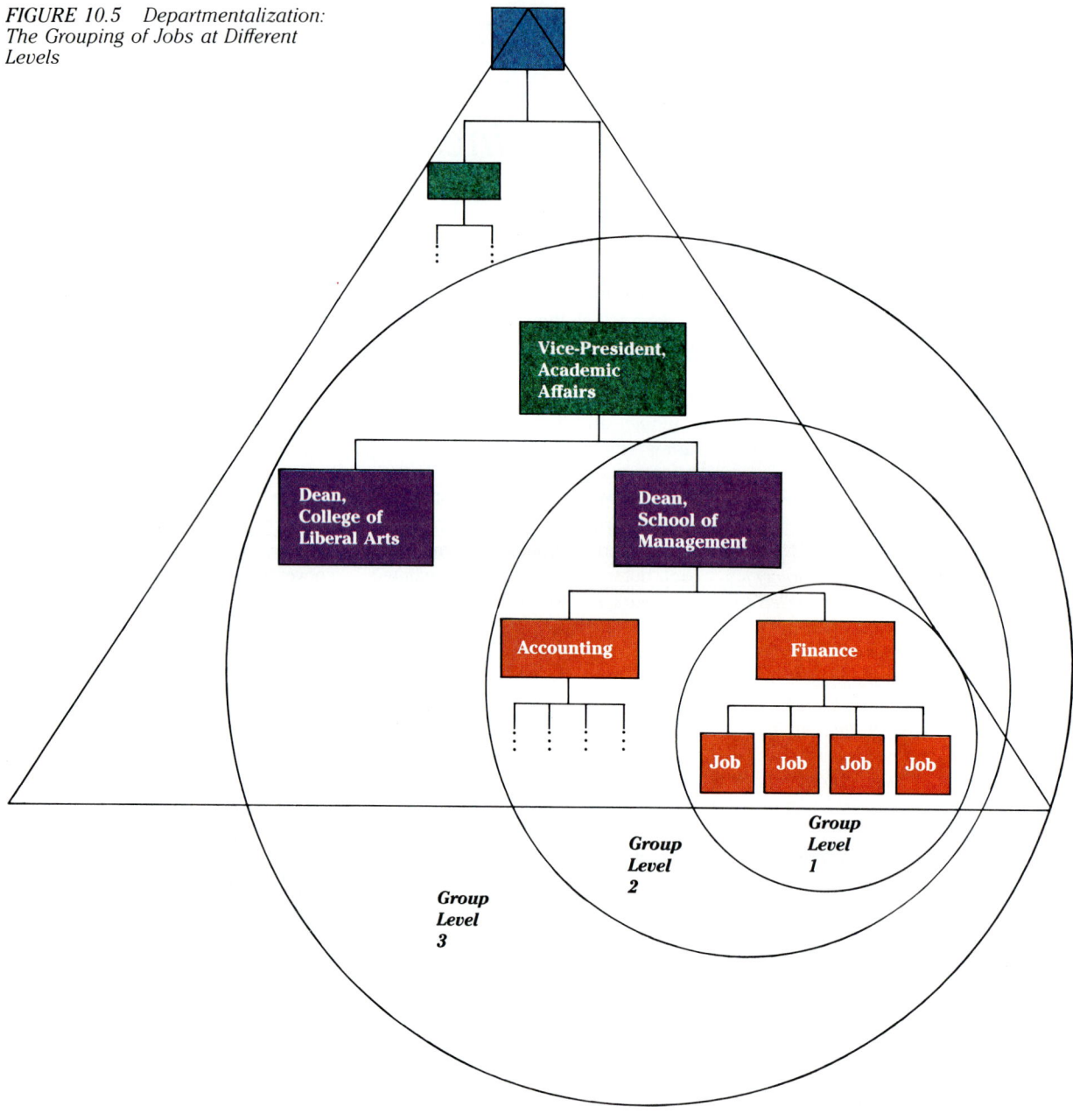

FIGURE 10.5 *Departmentalization: The Grouping of Jobs at Different Levels*

Vice-President, Academic Affairs

Dean, College of Liberal Arts

Dean, School of Management

Accounting

Finance

Job **Job** **Job** **Job**

Group Level 1

Group Level 2

Group Level 3

department, or does it want to coordinate new-car sales in one organizational unit and used-car sales in another? Should foreign and domestic car sales be combined? Should the purchasing department be coordinated with operations or with marketing? When a new job or group of jobs is created, where in the organizational hierarchy should these activities be managed? As shown in Figure 10.5, managers group activities at all levels of an organization. Chapter 12 deals with groupings at the very top of an organization. At that level, groupings refer not to department structure but to the superstructure of the entire organization. As you will see in that chapter, many of the strategies discussed here for developing structure are also used when developing superstructures.

Traditional Approaches

Through the years, managers have tried various ways to group (departmentalize) organizational activities. Two basic approaches to departmentalizing have dominated. The first approach groups activities that are within the same "family." That is, managers group activities by organization function, common products or services categories, geographical territories, customer or client groups, common processes or equipment used, or unique projects. These six family groupings represent the most traditional approaches to achieving departmentalization. The second approach to departmentalization groups activities based on the degree to which they are interdependent.

Departmentalization by Function Managers create **functional departments** by grouping activities according to the nature of the work performed. Activities that support an organization's operations system are placed in an operations department. Sales, marketing research, and advertising are grouped in a marketing department (see Figure 10.6). Although the names given to functional departments may vary from one organization to another, common terms in for-profit organizations are operations, marketing, finance, accounting, human resources, engineering, and research and development. Similar activities are coordinated from a common place in the organizational hierarchy. A marketing department, for example, controls only marketing activities. Each functional unit may be broken down further for coordination and control purposes.

FIGURE 10.6
Functional Departmentalization

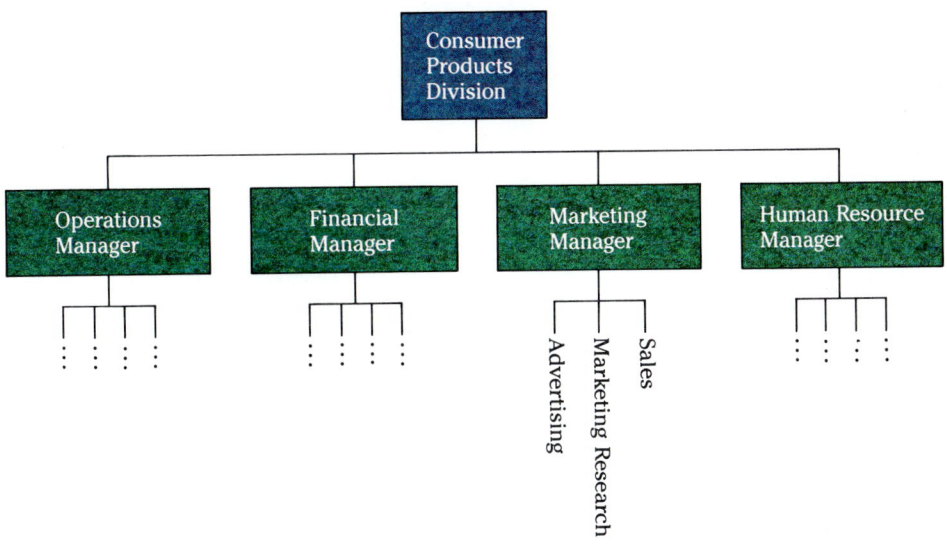

The functional approach to departmentalization is one of the most widely adopted approaches for grouping organizational activities because of its versatility. It can be used in both large and small organizations. It can be used at many different levels in the organizational hierarchy, from high levels (as was shown in Figure 10.6) or further down, such as the production and marketing departments that *The Wall Street Journal* has created within each of its major territorial offices.

Functional departments offer a number of other advantages. Because people who perform similar functions work together, they can specialize and benefit from one another's expertise. Decision making and coordination are easier, because managers need to be familiar with only a relatively narrow set of activities. Functional departments at high levels of the hierarchy use an organization's resources more efficiently because a department's activity does not have to be repeated across several organizational divisions. On the negative side, strong functional grouping may prevent people from seeing the totality of an organization. Communication and coordination across departments can be problematic, and, often, conflicts emerge as each functional department attempts to protect its own turf.

Departmentalization by Product/Service In **product/service departmentalization,** activities related to the development and delivery of a single product (or closely related group of products) are grouped together. Progressive Video Images, for example, has movie, audio, and video units (see Figure 10.7). When this system is combined with a territorial grouping, all activities for a product or service produced and delivered in one territory may be handled separately from the activities for the same product in a different territory. Progressive Video Images, thus, could have three movie departments: one in its northern territory, one in its southern territory, and one in its west European territory.

The product/service departmentalization approach can be logical and efficient. Procter & Gamble, for example, produces and markets both soap and food. Each of these product lines has unique technical and business properties and problems, so the company separates the activities that produce Ivory Soap from those that result in Crisco. Product/service departments also are useful when an organization wishes to treat product/service lines as independent business units. Managers can more readily assess the profitability of each product line; however, this approach has the potential disadvantage of creating destructive competition between

FIGURE 10.7   Product/Service Departmentalization at Progressive Video Images

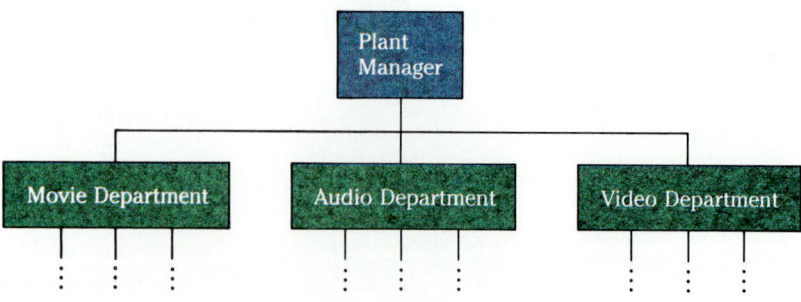

FIGURE 10.8
Territorial Departmentalization

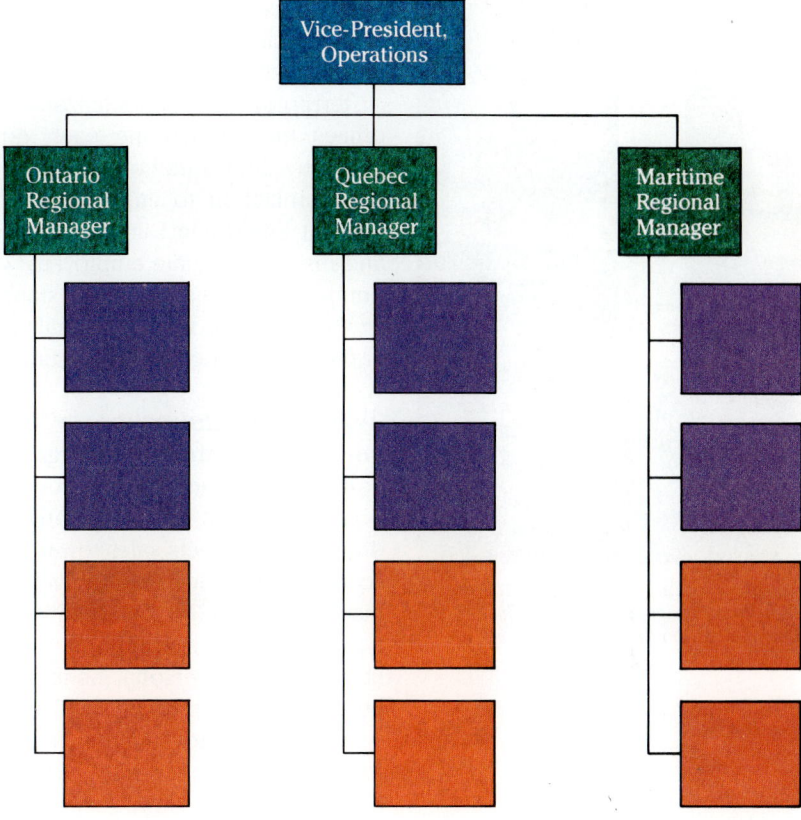

departments for organizational resources. People within product groups have a difficult time seeing the organization as a whole and, in fact, are encouraged to be responsible for *their* product line. Another potential disadvantage is that, if product/service departments are duplicated in each of an organization's territories, managers may not use standardized practices to run their departments. Although this may be necessary, it can create coordination problems among departments.

Departmentalization by Territory **Territorial (geographical) departmentalization** is often used when organizations have widely dispersed operations or offices. Retail outlets commonly have stores in communities throughout the nation (see Figure 10.8). Many American insurance companies also have regional offices throughout the United States. American Family Insurance, for example, has three separate territories, and the regional office in each handles the insurance issues that arise in its particular region.

The territorial approach has many logistical and practical advantages. It moves operations closer to raw materials, to distribution systems, and to customers. Sometimes geographic variations in laws, regulations, and customs change the nature of doing business enough so that territorial arrangements are necessary. For example, regulations on the sale and servicing of insurance differ from state to state, and each American Family Insurance Company regional office is responsible for complying with the

Banks typically organize their services into such customer groups as small business, commercial, and personal banking.

regulations within its own territory. Territorial departmentalization makes it easier for American Family to develop systems and train employees to cope with the requirements of the various states served by each region.

Territorial departmentalization has drawbacks, however. Territorial offices may undermine each other by competing for organizational resources, and sometimes geographical dispersion can make it difficult for an organization to enforce uniform standards. For example, the dress code at Electronic Data Systems headquarters in Texas prohibits beards and insists that male employees wear white shirts, but the company has not been able to enforce this standard in some of the organizations it has acquired outside of Texas. Finally, the physical separation of organizational divisions can create communication and coordination problems.

Departmentalization by Customer/Client Base **Customer/client departmentalization** organizes activities around the type of customer or customer needs served by an organization. The publishing house of Scott, Foresman and Company, for example, has a higher education division that directs sales toward professors and university bookstores. Its school division focuses on selling books to elementary and high school districts. Banks, too, generally organize their services around different types of customer groups (see Figure 10.9). It is common, for example, for banks to have personal banking, small business, and commercial (big business) departments.

The primary advantage to this approach is that it enables organizations to focus on and effectively serve the unique needs of identifiably different customer groups. Newsweek, Inc., for example, distributes the *Newsweek* magazine nationwide. It also prints *Newsweek Woman,* a version aimed at 700,000 female subscribers; *Newsweek Executive Plus,* a version aimed at 950,000 professional and managerial subscribers; and a number of international versions, such as *The Bulletin with Newsweek,* the best selling magazine in Australia. A drawback to departmentalization by customer is that sharing knowledge and resources among various departments can be difficult.

Departmentalization by Process/Equipment Somewhat related to functional departmentalization is **process/equipment departmentalization.** Consider an organization that manufactures a variety of paper products for home, office, and industrial use. One approach would be to form a department for each of these customer groups. Another approach would be to form departments by product types—cleaning, wrapping,

FIGURE 10.9
Customer/Client Departmentalization

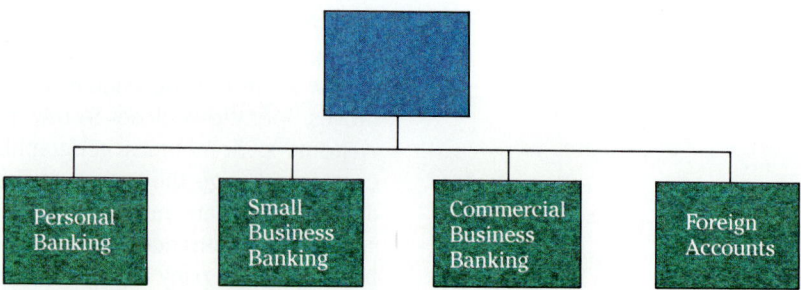

FIGURE 10.10
Departmentalization by Process/
Equipment at a Paper Company

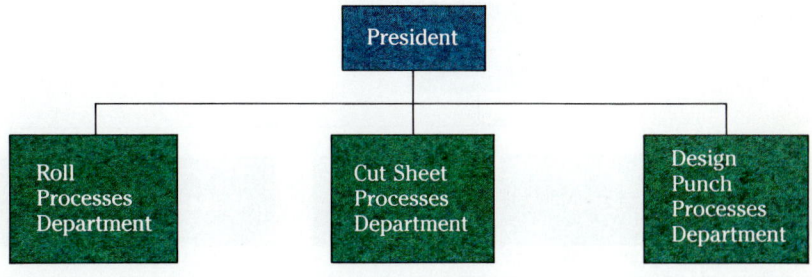

writing—but either of these strategies would lead to redundancy. Both the home and office departments, for example, would need the equipment used to manufacture rolled-paper products (paper towel rolls for home use and hand towel rolls for office dispensers). A process- or equipment-oriented department would run the equipment needed to make all rolled-paper products. Another department would run the equipment needed to make individual sheets of paper, and so forth (see Figure 10.10).

One of the advantages of process/equipment departmentalization is that it can reduce equipment costs. Paper-making equipment is extremely expensive. It would be wasteful to purchase two or three identical machines if one can do the job. It is not only the cost of acquiring equipment which is influenced, but the cost of staffing and maintaining it as well. Furthermore, when a given process is centralized in one department, an organization can usually be more responsive to technological changes. This approach is not without potential drawbacks, however. Having three product lines share one machine can create production scheduling problems. What happens, for example, if two product lines have rush orders at the same time? For these reasons, process/equipment-oriented departments often cause conflict among those who rely on them.

Departmentalization by Project **Project departments** are generally created to address specific, often unique organizational goals. They may, for example, have a design or developmental mission. A medical equipment manufacturer might form a project department to design an artificial heart. An engineering consulting firm might form a project department to report on the feasibility of constructing a rail system under the English Channel. In the aerospace industry, many organizations have created project departments to develop new technologies for the proposed Strategic Defense Initiative ("Star Wars") program.

People are brought into a project department because of their particular skills or unique expertise. They remain part of the project department until they have made their contribution; thus, people may join and leave the department at various times during its existence, so the membership at the end of the project may be different from what it was at the beginning. The project director is likely to be one of the few members who remains with the department until the project is finished. Once the project has been completed, the project department—having fulfilled its mission— ceases to exist.

Project departments typically have an organic management system. Not only are members of a project department likely to come and go as

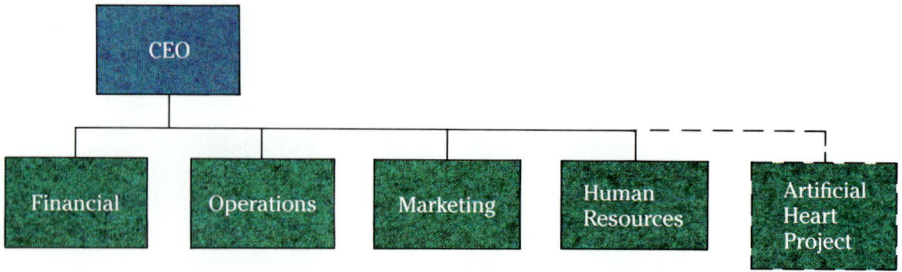

FIGURE 10.11A
New Department Approach
to Project Departmentalization

different stages of a project are worked on, but authority and positions of leadership shift as members bring their particular expertise to various phases of the project. In addition, the unit's communication, coordination, and control systems change frequently. The nature of the people-to-people and people-to-work relationships may change often to accommodate the uncertain nature of the project.

Managers can create a project department in a number of ways. One approach is to hire or transfer a group of employees to *form a new department* solely to work on the project at hand (see Figure 10.11A). In a second approach (illustrated in Figure 10.11B), organizations use members of a *standing project participant pool,* whose purpose is to work on an organization's special projects. Depending on their expertise and the time constraints involved, some pool members may be assigned to more than one project department at the same time. A third (albeit nontraditional) method managers use to create a project department involves the *matrix* approach. (The term *matrix* refers to an organizational arrangement in which two overlapping structures are used—see Chapter 12 for more details.) See Figure 10.11C. This type of project department is staffed with employees from various parts of the organization who may be released, either on a part-time or full-time basis, from their regular responsibilities. When they are required to perform their regular duties in addition to those of the project department, these individuals are account-

FIGURE 10.11B   Standing Project Department Approach to Project Departmentalization

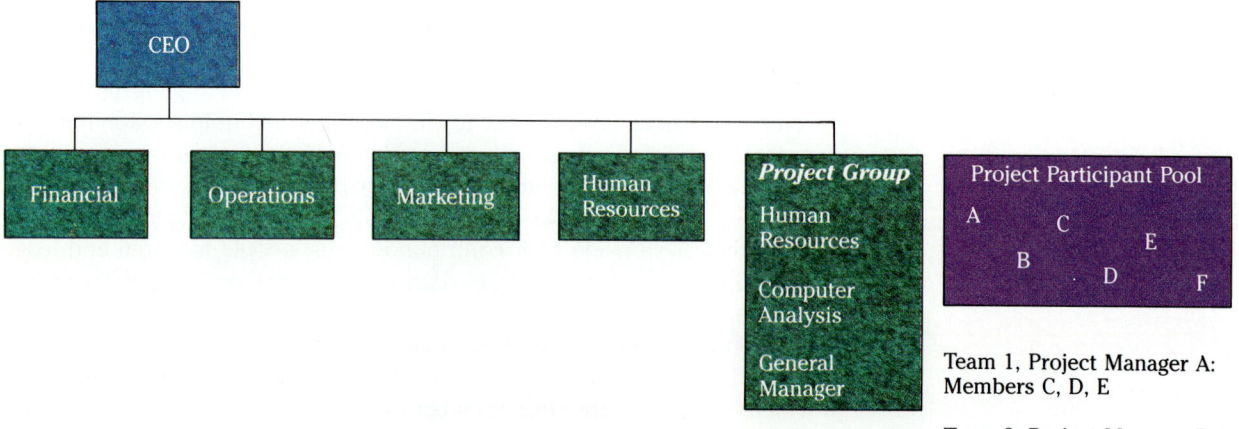

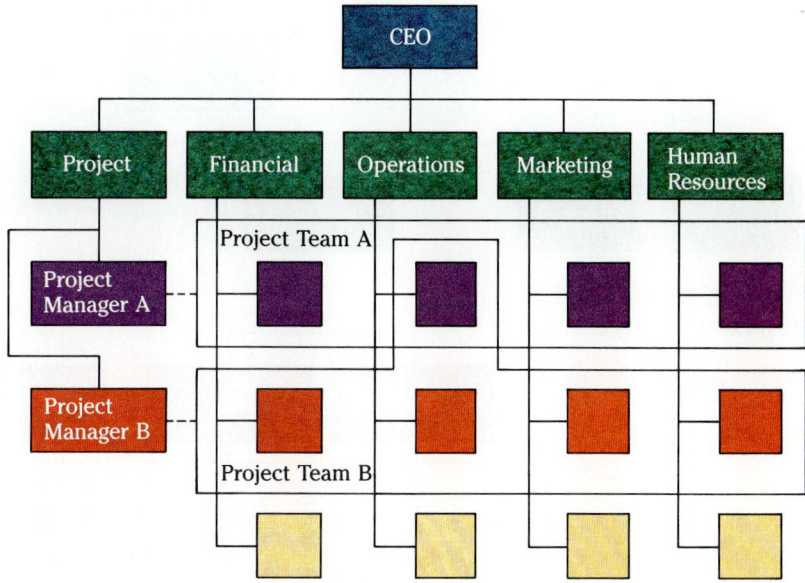

FIGURE 10.11C   Matrix Approach to Project Departmentalization

able to their home department as well as to the project department. The department developing an artificial heart, for example, may want the organization's marketing department to lend them Susan Hessney to conduct hospital surveys, operations employee Don Hull to conduct feasibility studies, and clerical employees Lucinda Thurley and Steve Sidwell from human resources for typing and filing tasks.

A primary advantage of creating a new department for a project is that it produces a group of people who are concentrating on a single organizational role and chosen for their ability to do so. The drawback is that, once the project is finished, they have no remaining organizational role to fulfill. A standing project department has the advantage of maintaining an inventory of qualified individuals ready for assignment, but this can be expensive when they are idle, and they tend to be out of touch with the regular operations of the organization. Finally, the matrix approach makes it easy to choose qualified members from almost anywhere in an organization who are familiar with a wide range of organizational issues, but this can be disruptive, because members must divide their time, attention, and energy between their regular and special assignments.

The Hybrid Approach to Departmentalization   Rather than limiting themselves to just one departmentalization strategy, managers in most organizations use a number of approaches. The **hybrid approach** calls for the simultaneous use of two or more departmentalization strategies. Figure 10.12 illustrates the hybrid approach to departmentalization that managers have taken at Comfort-Living Corporation, a home furnishings manufacturer and distributor. Bruce Nichols, owner of Comfort-Living, has organized top-level management according to organizational function and special projects. The operations department is subdivided by product

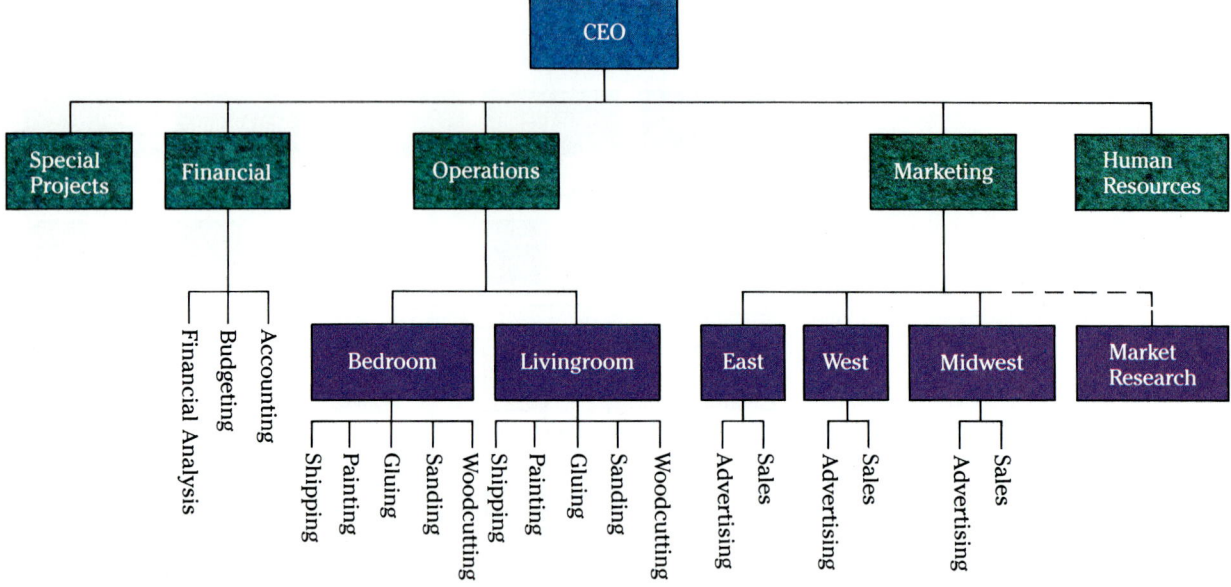

into bedroom and livingroom departments, which are further broken down by process/equipment departmentalization. Gloria Troy, supervising the marketing department's territories, also is currently heading up a special project department on market research.

To this point, this chapter has discussed creating departments that group families of activities or mix family groups. There is a second approach to organizing departments—the interdependence approach.

The Interdependence Approach

You will recall from Chapter 3 that the systems-theory perspective views each part of an organization as dependent on and interrelated with other organizational units. Operations managers, for example, need market information and financial resources from other departments to produce their organization's goods and services. As interdependence between jobs and organizational units increases, so do the costs and burdens of coordinating and controlling. Managers using an **interdependence approach** try to minimize these problems by grouping highly interdependent activities so that they are coordinated from a common point in the organizational hierarchy.[16]

There are four types of interdependence that can exist between employees and organizational units (see Figure 10.13).[17] The lowest form of interdependence is *pooled interdependence*, in which employees or departments basically act independently, each doing their own work within an organization and depending only minimally on others. A group of secretaries, for example, is likely to have pooled interdependence. Each does his or her own piece of work from beginning to end. They are interdependent, however, in that the contribution from each secretary is necessary to the effectiveness of the entire organization.

FIGURE 10.13 *Forms of Interdependence*

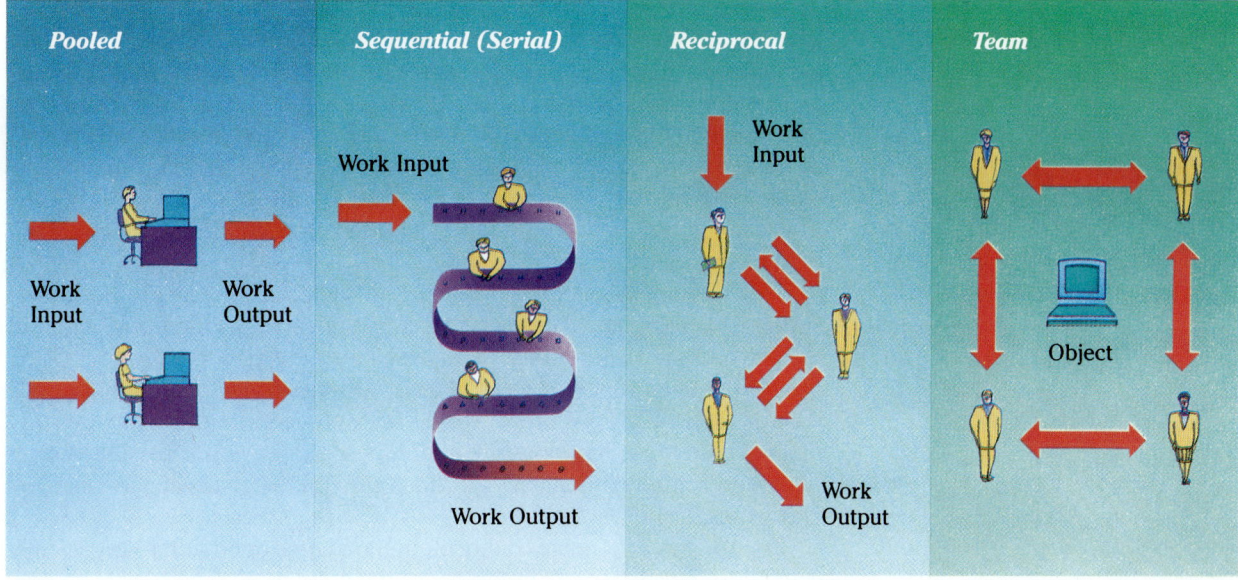

A second, and higher, form of interdependence represents a more complex relationship. Under *sequential,* or *serial, interdependence,* the object being worked on is passed from one worker or department to the next. The output of the first worker becomes the input for the second, whose output becomes the input for the third worker, and so on. This type of interdependence characterizes the assembly line.

A third form is *reciprocal interdependence,* in which the object being worked on is passed back and forth among workers before the process is completed. When seeing a dentist, for example, a patient usually checks in with a receptionist. The receptionist guides the patient to a dental hygienist, who cleans the teeth before the dentist checks them. The dentist often transfers the checked patient back to the hygienist, who takes X rays and sends the patient back to the dentist for repair work. Finally, the patient revisits the receptionist to pay the bill and, perhaps, to schedule a future appointment before leaving the office.

Team interdependence is formed when a group of workers interact simultaneously with one another and the object or person on which they are working. A hospital surgical team exemplifies team interdependence as the surgeons, surgical assistants, anesthesiologist, nurses, and other support personnel continuously interact to complete their complex task.

As the level of interdependence among organizational members becomes increasingly complex, the burdens associated with managing them also increase. A manager of reciprocally related activities, for example, must coordinate the flow of activities—the receipt of work to be done and the export of semifinished work—to and from several employees at the same time. A production delay by one employee affects the flow of work to and from others. This situation presents a manager with a much greater challenge than does planning the flow of work along an assembly line in which interdependence is sequential.

Managers attempting to use one of the interdependence approaches to departmentalization should start with jobs and organizational units that have the greatest and most complex forms of interdependence. Thus, a manager would first group all jobs with a team form of interdependence and then group jobs with reciprocally interdependent activities, followed by sequential interdependent jobs, and, last, pooled interdependent jobs. The same procedure should be followed in grouping organizational units within the hierarchy. Those with reciprocal interdependence should have, if possible, a common point of coordination in the hierarchy and organizational units.

The interdependence approach is, in fact, used by many hospitals. Groups requiring high levels of interdependence, such as the surgical team mentioned earlier, are organized into a surgical department composed of a wide range of types of jobs. A food service department might include dieticians, food preparation employees, and food delivery personnel, because these functions are interdependent; however, a maintenance department may consist only of those directly involved in the cleaning and repair of the physical facility.

The obvious advantage to the interdependence approach to organizing is that it removes barriers to the coordination of work. There must be one person in charge during surgery or the process would be drastically slowed. The primary problem with the interdependence approach is that it can be very difficult for one manager to direct such a wide range of individuals with diverse skills and needs. Often even the languages used by persons from different technical areas are unique.

Span of Control

How many individuals and activities can one manager coordinate? For example, how large a sales force can one sales manager supervise? How many managers of various personnel activities can a vice-president of human resources manage effectively? How many executive vice-presidents and their departments should report to the president of an organization?

Certainly there is a limit to the number of people and activities that any one manager can effectively manage, but what is that limit? **Span of control,** also referred to as *span of management* and *span of supervision*, refers to the number of subordinates and activities that a manager oversees. Span of control is an important consideration when departmentalizing. For example, a manager should not group all functionally similar or all reciprocally interdependent activities if it would create a span of control that was too large to handle.

During the classical management period, many people tried to determine an ideal span of control. Most argued in favor of greatly limiting a manager's span of control. Some proposed that limitations on a manager's attention, energy, and knowledge should restrict the span of control to five or six employees. Others argued that the nature of work and the limitations of the human brain should reduce the span of control as one moves up in an organization's hierarchy so that, at the top, a manager would be responsible for no more than six people but, at lower levels, a

There is a limit to the number of people and activities that one manager can handle.

wider span would be acceptable. A French management consultant demonstrated that an increase of one person in the span geometrically increased the number of possible relationships that a manager may be called on to handle. Thus, a manager with two subordinates may have to face six possible relationships, while a manager with four subordinates may face as many as forty-four possible relationships. When organizations grow rapidly, top-level managers might have to be limited to as few as three subordinates, but lower-level managers in static situations might be able to handle as many as thirty subordinates.[18]

In practice, managers have found a wide variety of ways to approach the span of control problem. Just as there is no one best way to design jobs, there is no universally ideal span of control. One health care provider might use managers in its occupational therapy department simply to assign patient case loads, leaving therapy strategies up to the therapist. In this case, one manager could supervise perhaps twenty or thirty occupational therapists, but if another health care provider had managers assign case loads, consult on therapy decisions, and provide training, they might need to limit the span of control to four or five people.

If a span is too limited, a manager's talents may be underutilized. Having an experienced, highly skilled manager supervise only a handful of employees performing routine work would not take advantage of the manager's capabilities. If the span is too large, a manager may have too much work to perform any of it effectively. Asking one manager to directly supervise the work of fifty staff accountants would be a mistake. It would be virtually impossible to effectively manage so many individuals and all of their projects at the same time.

From the perspective of subordinates, a span that is too large may prevent them from getting needed supervisory support. None of the fifty accountants mentioned earlier would be likely to get the training and support needed to perform effectively and to grow if one manager supervised them all. On the other hand, too small a span might result in too much supervision. In such cases, managers often baby-sit subordinates, not allowing them enough freedom to be effective.

FIGURE 10.14   *Span of Control and Shape of the Organizational Hierarchy*

A. Wide Span: Flat Organization

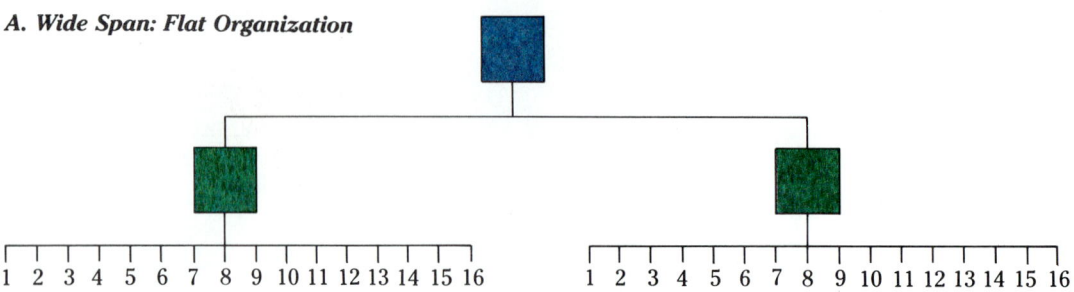

B. Narrow Span: Tall Organization

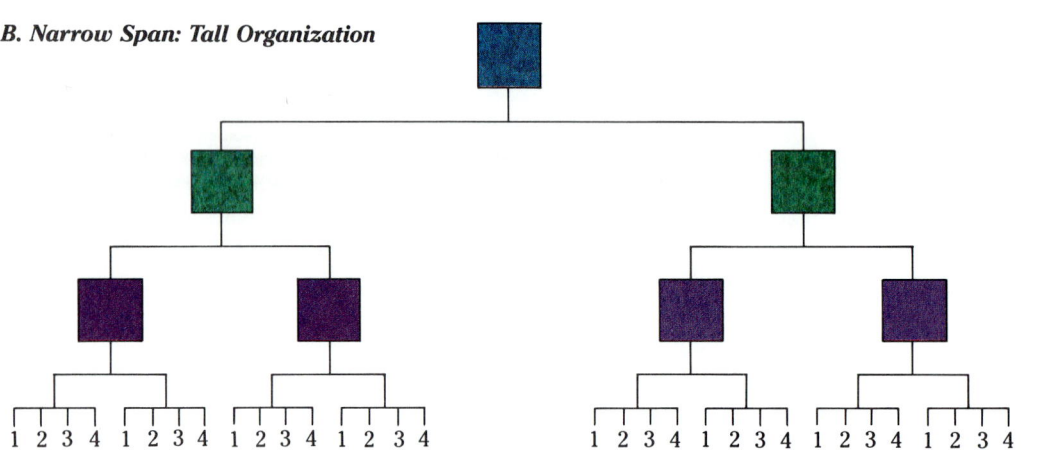

The size of a manager's span has other organizational implications as well. Figure 10.14A shows the structure for an organization with thirty-two production employees and a maximum span of control of sixteen. The shape of this organization is relatively flat, with only three managers and just two levels of management. Figure 10.14B shows what would happen if the maximum span of control were changed so that a manager handled only two groups of four employees. The result would be a taller organizational structure that contains one more level of management and four additional midlevel managers. The additional costs associated with this increase can be substantial. As this example suggests, decisions about the span of management are critical to an organization.

To avoid the costs associated with a large number of managers, an increasing number of organizations are using fewer levels of managers and a smaller top management group. This has resulted in broader spans of management, flatter organizational hierarchies, and wider organizational structures. For example, DANA Corporation, an auto parts manufacturer, changed its organizational structure by reducing the size of its management and administrative group from 475 to 84 people and by reducing the number of hierarchical levels from 15 to 5. Some organizations have adopted labor-management and self-managing work groups to help reduce the number of levels and positions in the hierarchy.

As you have seen, span of control influences an organization's size, shape, number of managers needed, and expenditures for running the structure. Because of the importance of span of control, managers should consider at least three factors when determining the span appropriate for their organization: the individual supervisor, the employee group, and the situation.[19]

The Individual Supervisor   Some managers believe that their subordinates are capable of self-direction and self-control; others do not. Those in the former group may be able to handle a broad span because their burden is lessened by allowing a degree of employee "self-management." Managers who believe in delegating authority and can do so effectively may be able to handle a larger span than managers who need to be intimately involved in each subordinate's work. For example, a consultant who has promised to conduct an organizational attitude survey will be free to take on additional consulting jobs if an assistant is able to prepare the survey for the consultant's approval.

In addition, a span decision must consider the experience level of an organization's managers. A person who has just become a manager, for example, may not be able to do more than merely keep up with the paperwork and a few subordinates. Managers who are seasoned veterans, on the other hand, may have time to prepare employees to work independently. Skills and training also influence span of control. For example, managers who have worked their way up the corporate ladder may be able to use their knowledge of the company to deal with a great number of people and situations.

The Employee Group   Employee competence is also a factor in the span of a manager's control. A highly professional group, a seasoned group, or a group of individuals with high levels of independence all permit managers a wider span of control than groups with less experience, competence, or independence. Thus, span of control for an accounting firm where all accountants are CPAs with at least five years of field experience can be much larger than that at a firm where most accountants are fresh out of college with no previous work experience. Generally speaking, span of control should be smaller when employees are relatively unskilled, poorly trained, or inexperienced.

The Situation   The nature of the situation also affects span of control. The more uncertain a task, for example, the smaller the span must be. The same holds true for highly interdependent tasks. In both cases, a narrow span of control provides managers and subordinates with the frequent and unrestricted communication they need to deal with coordination and control problems. Managers of research labs, for example, can supervise only a small number of assistants because of the daily need to evaluate and direct experiments. Contrast this with a regional sales supervisor whose primary contacts with twenty sales representatives are phone calls to check on weekly sales results and six "motivational" sales meetings a year.

FIGURE 10.15 *Indicators of Acceptable Span of Control*

The lower the score obtained when rating the nine statements, the lower the acceptable span of control. For example, if all nine statements are rated "strongly disagree," the span of control might be as low as three (or three subordinates for every manager).

	Strongly Disagree	Disagree	Neither	Agree	Strongly Agree
Managers					
1. Managers believe subordinates have the capacity to exercise self-direction and self-control.	1	2	3	4	5
2. Managers have highly developed managment skills, training, and experiences.	1	2	3	4	5
3. Managers accept an organizational philosophy/culture that encourages self-direction and control.	1	2	3	4	5
Employees					
4. Employees are, for the most part, professionals.	1	2	3	4	5
5. Employees have a strong need for independence.	1	2	3	4	5
6. Employees are experienced and have good skills and training.	1	2	3	4	5
Situations					
7. Worker's tasks are clearly defined and well understood.	1	2	3	4	5
8. There is little interdependence among tasks.	1	2	3	4	5
9. Information-processing needs are minimal.	1	2	3	4	5

Total Score =

Total Score/3 = _____ (Acceptable Span)

Information-processing needs also have a tremendous impact on span decisions. Can managers, for example, develop and communicate standardized operating procedures? If so, a wider span of control is possible. An area manager of a fast-food chain—Burger King, for example—may be able to oversee all of the outlets in a tri-state area because all stores follow the procedures set forth in the company's manual and require the same basic supervision. Contrast this with the desirable span of control for a manager in a company that owns food stores, clothing stores, and appliance stores. Clearly, the complexities inherent in such a wide range of businesses demand a smaller span of control. Figure 10.15 illustrates the kind of diagnostic tool managers can use to determine appropriate span of control.

Coordinating Organizational Activities and Units

When work is divided and various jobs and departments are created, someone must integrate and coordinate these organizational subsystems. Many management scholars consider the coordinating activity to be the essence of organizing. After all, the purpose of organizing is to achieve an integration among the diverse organizational parts and systems. **Coordinating** links two or more organizational units so that they work harmoniously together. Coordinating, for example, links the production of textbooks with the sale of textbooks; it connects the admission of students to a university with the supply of services needed to provide a high-quality education. Organizations have two basic coordination needs: vertical and horizontal.

Vertical Coordination

To meet organizational goals, managers must coordinate the institutional level with the technical core. **Vertical coordination** links organizational units that are separated by hierarchical level. For example, if Bruce Nichols, owner of the Comfort-Living Corporation, which was shown in Figure 10.13, decided to boost sales through increased advertising, he would tell Tom Bell, his marketing manager, to come up with a new ad campaign. Tom, in turn, would ask territorial managers to contribute ideas and provide Bruce with final recommendations. It would then be the marketing department's duty to launch the chosen campaign.

Managers can achieve vertical coordination in a number of ways. Some of the methods used include direct supervision, standardization, and goal statements.

Direct Supervision   In small, uncomplicated organizations or within individual organizational units, superiors and subordinates can meet face-to-face. This *direct supervision* enables people to communicate, offers them direction and assistance, and integrates activities across organizational levels. Thus, the president of a paper company might communicate directly with the vice-president of marketing who, in turn, talks to the director of sales.

Standardization   Another way managers coordinate work across levels in the hierarchy is by standardizing activities. Large spans of

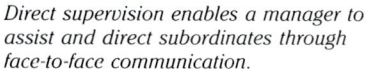

Direct supervision enables a manager to assist and direct subordinates through face-to-face communication.

control, high communication needs, desire for uniformity in operations, and physical dispersion all create pressure to standardize activities. Suppose, for example, that Julie Pearson is a manager at a collection agency whose span of control has gone from the supervision of five subordinates to twenty. This increase has made it increasingly difficult for her to deal face-to-face with each subordinate on all issues. If activities are standardized, Julie can handle this increase by developing *rules and procedures* to govern routine events. Subordinates could refer to these rules and procedures to find out what to do if someone claims they have already made the payment being requested (request a copy of a canceled check) or if a payment check is returned for insufficient funds (request a cashier's check to replace it). Of course, there will always be exceptions and unique events, for which rules and procedures have not been and, in fact, should not be created. At this point, the *exception principle* takes over, and managers should concentrate their efforts on matters that deviate from normal, such as a customer who threatens the physical safety of a collection agency employee.

Goal Statements   When the nature of work makes it difficult to designate the specific behaviors that are needed, managers can create a hierarchy of goals rather than specifying the behaviors that employees are to enact. A general manager of a publishing company, for example, might specify a goal of increasing sales by 15 percent in the next year. His or her vice-president of sales and marketing then assigns a sales goal to each of the division's regional managers. They, in turn, assign sales goals to their subordinates. This set of interrelated goals guides the actions of lower-level employees, and their accomplishments become the means through which the next higher level achieves its goals, and so on up to the top of the hierarchy.

Horizontal Coordination

Horizontal coordination occurs within a single hierarchical level. At most levels in the hierarchy, jobs and organizational units have varying degrees of dependency on one another and require coordination. Through horizontal coordination, for example, the efforts of manufacturing and sales departments are integrated, and shared resources are allocated. Horizontal coordination mechanisms, thus, make it possible for managers to coordinate organization members and units that do not have a hierarchical relationship with one another.

Manager and writer Henri Fayol talked about the need for creating horizontal coordination mechanisms. He noted that when conditions call for a frequent and rapid exchange of information, strict adherence to a chain of command can create bottlenecks in the hierarchy. For example, Meg Weant, a vice-president of marketing to whom five department directors report, may find that she does not have enough time to devote to each director. The span of control is simply too large, and the bottleneck slows down the communication process. To handle problems of this nature, Fayol devised his "gangplank principle" (see Figure 10.16).[20] Using the gangplank constructed by Fayol, a director of purchasing can ask the director of the finance department for permission to deviate from the allotted budget. This eliminates the need to work through higher-level managers for a budget change.

Horizontal coordination can be achieved in several ways.[21] In many instances, managers can use the same direct supervision, standardization, and goal statement techniques that bring about vertical coordination. Additional techniques include direct contact, liaisons, task forces/teams, integrators, managerial linking roles, and multiple command systems.

Direct Contact Perhaps the simplest way to achieve horizontal coordination is for two managers who have a common problem to communicate directly with one another. Direct contact is the simplest application of Fayol's gangplank principle. If Ann Stypuloski, a production manager, is having problems getting enough windshield glass to keep an automobile assembly line going, for example, she can call the purchasing manager directly to remedy the situation.

Liaison Roles When the volume of contact between two organizational units becomes extremely heavy, management may assign an employee to act as a *liaison* to facilitate communication between the units. An organization designing a new jet airplane, for example, might create a liaison to help integrate the efforts of those designing the jet's engine with the team that is responsible for designing the airframe.

Task Forces and Teams Direct contact and liaison roles work well in coordinating a limited number of organizational units, but when problems arise involving a number of organizational units, managers may have to form a *task force*. The task force is a temporary group that comes into existence to tackle a particular problem and dissolves when the problem is resolved. Its members are generally representatives from the several units experiencing the difficulty.

FIGURE 10.16
Fayol's Gangplank Principle

The gangplank represents the construction of bridges between horizontally separated units. These bridges enable managers at the same hierarchical level to work together to coordinate their units and, thereby, relieve the pressure on the managers above them.

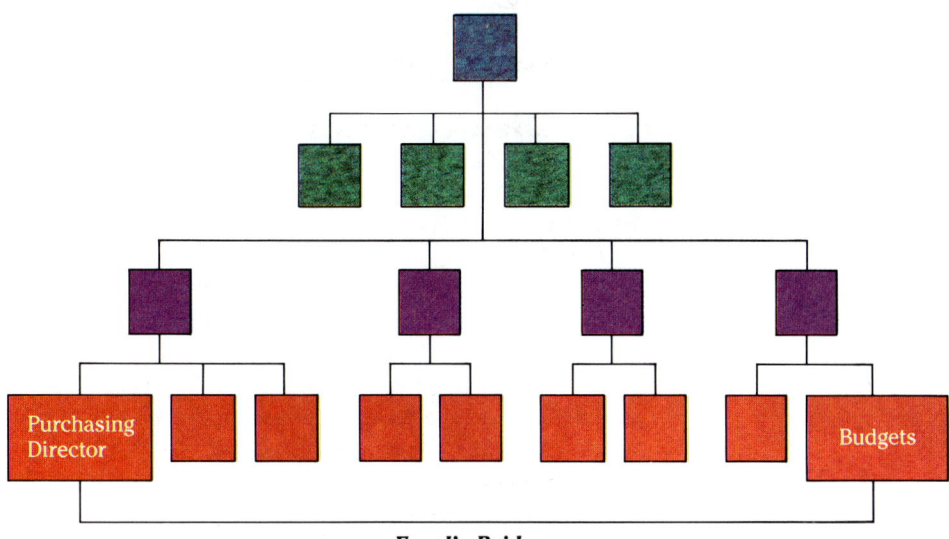

Fayol's Bridge

Suppose, for example, that a manufacturer of laser printers has a serious problem providing its customers with enough good-quality printers. The problem seems to lie in the design of the production process, the quality of raw materials, and unanticipated fluctuations in sales. Horizontal coordination is clearly needed. Management might create a task force dedicated to getting a sufficient number of good-quality printers to market. The task force might have members from the engineering, purchasing, operations (production), human resources, and sales departments. Using the decision-making tools discussed in Chapter 8 (perhaps the nominal group technique), the task force can identify the most significant factors contributing to the problem and specify a coordinated set of actions to deal with it. If the plan alleviates the problem, the task force, in all likelihood, would be dissolved.

Some problems need continual attention, not a one-time solution. A company that does customized production work, for example, has a continuing need for coordination between its sales department (which sells a customized product), the design department (which develops manufacturing plans), and its operations department (which actually produces the product). In this case, the task force does not disband but becomes permanent and is referred to as a *task team*.

Integrators   Under some conditions, managers acting as integrators must have enough leadership and power to influence the decisions made and actions taken by all of the interdependent units. People selected as integrators should have good political and conflict-resolution skills. They should thoroughly understand the units they are attempting to integrate, and much of their power base should come from their expertise. The role of an integrator is more complex than that of a liaison. Liaisons primarily encourage and facilitate an exchange of information so that coordination can be achieved between interdependent units. Integrators, on the other hand, are expected to provide leadership and directly influence the direction taken in the handling of mutual problems.

Managerial Linking Roles   When conditions are highly uncertain, an integrator alone may not be able to coordinate highly heterogeneous, interdependent organizational units. To deal with this type of situation, a linking manager must be given the formal authority to command action. Shifting from a reliance on the influence that stems from someone's expertise to actual, formal authority is a shift from an integrator to a managerial linking role. The integrator may say, "Here is a way to solve the problem, and this is why I think you should choose this solution." A linking manager, however, has the authority to say, "*Do* it this way."

Multiple Command Systems   Coordination is sometimes achieved when two or more independent units in an organization each have command authority over an activity. Creating two such command centers violates Fayol's principle of unity of command, yet there are times when it is necessary to adopt this strategy to bring about appropriate integration. Consider the case of Universe Products Limited, a manufacturer of electrical, chemical, mechanical, and aerospace products. Historically, the company coordinated all of its engineering and research activities out of its aerospace division; however, this functional grouping ultimately was unable to provide special engineering projects with adequate attention. To resolve this problem, management created a second command system for its space projects. Members of the engineering and research department are now accountable to both their functional (aerospace) boss and to a Venus, Mars, or Space-Lab project manager. (See Figure 10.17.)

Matching Coordination Techniques and Needs

Coordinating organizational units is seldom an easy task. As you have seen, high levels of interdependence between organizational units increase the difficulty of coordination. The degree of heterogeneity—the similarity or dissimilarity—of organizational units also may affect how easily they may be coordinated. The following four factors significantly affect management's ability to coordinate organizational units:

1. *Formality of structure.* The extent to which management systems are closed or open, mechanistic or organic, and flexible or rigid is an important factor in coordination efforts (see Chapter 3 on the internal environment for a discussion of these terms).

2. *Interpersonal orientation.* The style characterizing human interactions affects coordination attempts. Task-oriented departments tend to concentrate on task-based issues in their interactions with colleagues; relationship-oriented departments focus more on developing, maintaining, and engaging in social interaction. Some of these differences are a function of the nature of the work performed by a department. A production department that deals with the assembly of things, for example, may be more focused on task interactions than a marketing department, which deals with the persuasion of people.

3. *Time orientation.* The amount of time that elapses between the performance of a task and the time at which workers learn about the consequences of their actions influences coordination. Sales and

production departments, for example, generally deal with problems that provide rapid feedback, so employees' attention is usually focused on short-term matters. Research and development departments deal with longer-term concerns, and feedback about the results of their work may be delayed for many years.

4. *Goal orientation*. The extent to which the goals of each organizational unit are compatible has an impact on coordination efforts. Production departments, for example, face high inventory costs for excess production, but sales departments face losses if inventory is too low to fill orders. The sales department wants a large inventory; the production department wants a smaller one.[22]

If each organizational unit had the same internal environment and the same interpersonal, time, and goal orientations, coordinating would be a relatively straightforward task, but differences between organizational units in these factors can cause conflict and operating incompatibility. The challenge facing managers is to find ways of integrating highly diverse

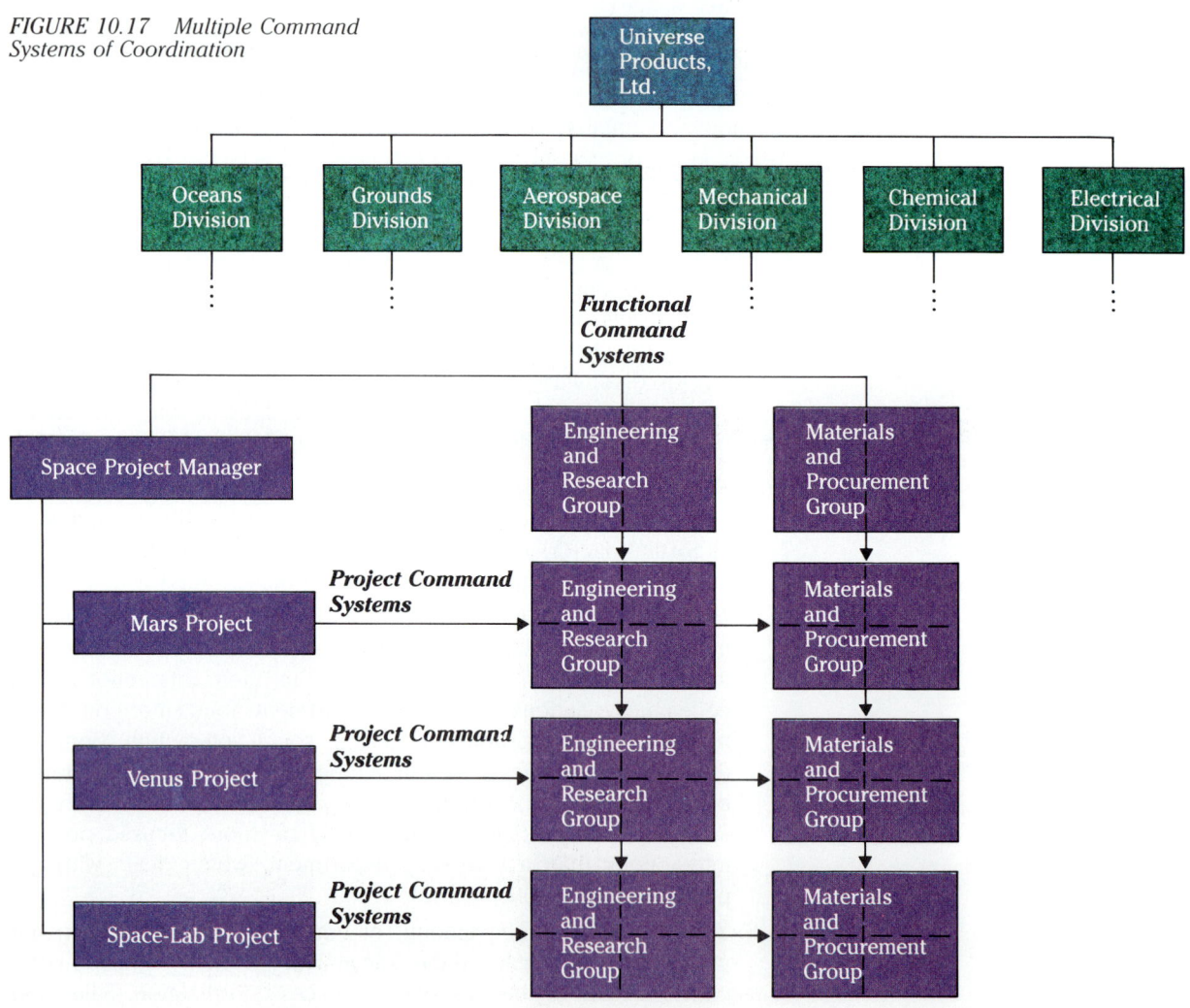

FIGURE 10.17   Multiple Command Systems of Coordination

TABLE 10.1 *Evaluation of Coordination Techniques*

Coordination Strategy	Coordination Needs							
	Size	Complexity	Span of Control	Inter-dependence	Uncertainty	Internal Differen-tiation	Communi-cation Needs	Horizontal Communica-tion Needs
Direct supervision	L*	L	L	L-M	L-M	L	L	L
Rules and procedures	M-H	L-M	H	L	L	L	H	L
Goal statements	?	M	?	L-M	H	?	L	?
Direct manager contacts	L-M	M	?	M	M	L-M	L-M	M
Liaison roles	L-M	M	?	M	M	L-M	L-M	M
Task force/team	M	M-H	?	M-H	M-H	H	M	M-H

*Amounts of Coordination: L = Low   M = Medium   H = High   ? = Uncertain

Note: This table indicates the conditions under which each coordination strategy is expected to work well. Direct supervision, for example, is expected to work well with low size, low complexity, and low span of control. Further information relating to these issues may be found in M. Tushman and D. Nadler (1978), Information processing as an integrating concept in organizational design, *Academy of Management Review*, 3, 613–24; J. G. March and H. A. Simon (1958), *Organizations*, New York: Wiley; A. H. Van de Ven, A. L. Delbecq, and R. Koenig, Jr. (1976), Determinants of coordination modes within organizations, *American Sociological Review*, 41, 322–38; and P. R. Lawrence and J. W. Lorsch (1967), *Organization and environment*, Homewood, IL: Irwin.

organizational units. Fortunately, there are techniques available to help managers coordinate organizational systems.

Selecting Coordination Techniques In selecting coordination techniques, managers first must assess the needs of the situation and then identify the technique (or combination of techniques) that can satisfy those needs. The better the match, the better the organizational effectiveness.[23] Table 10.1 illustrates many of the coordination needs faced by managers and the ability of each type of technique to meet those needs.

In addition to a technique's ability to meet an organization's coordination needs, its cost—both in time and money—should also be considered. The simpler approaches, such as rules and procedures and direct supervision, tend to be less expensive. When groups are involved, costs go up. When complex horizontal solutions are added to vertical solutions, costs rise still further. The more expensive techniques should be used only when less expensive alternatives will not suffice.

Organizing and Coordinating Work in Review

Organizing is the management function of designing an organization and its internal systems with people-to-people and people-to-work interaction patterns. This design must take into account the formal organization created by managers and the informal organization that arises spontaneously as organizational members interact. The primary purpose of organizing is to integrate various organizational units so that an entire system is efficient and effective.

The first step in organizing is to group tasks into jobs. Before the Industrial Revolution, one worker crafted an entire product from start to finish, but that craft approach has been replaced by four approaches in use today. The classical approach is based on a strict division of labor that tries to increase productivity by concentrating on work specialization, standardization, and simplification. The behavioral approach focuses on employees and tries to make jobs more interesting through job enlargement and enrichment. The contingency approach to job design tries to match a job to workers and the organization. The self-managing work group approach attempts to increase productivity by allowing workers to participate in the managerial processes that accompany production.

The next step in organizing is to group jobs into larger units and then place those units into larger organizational divisions. This is called departmentalization, and managers can choose one of two basic approaches to this activity. The first is to group jobs according to the activities performed. Managers taking this approach group according to organizational function, territory, product/service, customer/client group served, process or equipment used, and projects. In the second approach to departmentalization, managers group activities based on the nature of interdependence between jobs and organizational units. In practice, most organizations use a hybrid approach to combine methods of departmentalization.

A third part of the organizing process requires managers to decide how many people one manager can supervise effectively. This is known as a manager's span of control, and it affects the size of the various organizational units and the shape of the organization's overall hierarchy. There is no ideally sized span of control. The nature of the task, the managers involved, and the characteristics of subordinates combine to help determine the appropriate span for a given organizational situation. The degree of interdependence between jobs and organizational units also is likely to play a major role in determining where in the organizational hierarchy to place jobs and departments.

Coordinating is another, perhaps the most important, major organizing activity. There are two ways in which coordinating must be done in organizations. Vertical coordination links people and activities from different levels of the hierarchy. Horizontal coordination links people and activities from the same organizational levels. There are numerous techniques managers can use to achieve both vertical and horizontal coordination. Choosing a technique or combination of techniques depends on the specific coordination needs of an organization.

Notes

1. C. Barnard (1938), *The functions of the executive*, Cambridge, MA: Harvard University Press.
2. A. Smith (1776), *The wealth of nations*, New York: Modern Library, Inc.
3. C. Babbage (1832), *On the economy of machinery and manufacturers*, London: Charles Knight.

4. J. L. Pierce and R. B. Dunham (1976), Task design: A literature review, *Academy of Management Review*, 1, 83–97.

5. F. W. Taylor (1947), *Scientific management*, New York: Harper & Brothers; F. B. Gilbreth and L. M. Gilbreth (1910), *Applied motion study*, New York: Sturgis and Walton Co.; H. L. Gantt (1910), *Work wages and profits*, New York: The Engineering Magazine Co.

6. J. L. Pierce (1980), Job design in perspective, *The Personnel Administrator*, 25, 67–74.

7. M. R. Blood and C. L. Hulin (1967), Alienation, environmental characteristics and worker responses, *Journal of Applied Psychology*, 51, 284–90; J. L. Pierce, 1980.

8. C. Argyris (1957), *Integrating the individual and the organization*, New York: Wiley.

9. F. Herzberg, B. Mausner, and B. Snyderman (1959), *The motivation to work*, New York: Wiley; F. Herzberg (1968), One more time: How do you motivate employees? *Harvard Business Review*, 46, 54–62.

10. J. R. Hackman and G. R. Oldham (1975), Development of the job diagnostic survey, *Journal of Applied Psychology*, 60, 159–70; J. R. Hackman and G. R. Oldham (1976), Motivation through the design of work: Test of a theory, *Organizational Behavior and Human Performance*, 16, 250–79; J. R. Hackman and G. R. Oldham (1980), *Work-redesign*, Reading, MA: Addison-Wesley.

11. Hackman and Oldham, 1975; Pierce and Dunham, 1976; C. I. Hulin and M. R. Blood (1968), Job enlargement, individual differences and worker responses, *Psychological Bulletin*, 69, 41–55; Argyris, 1957; F. Herzberg (1966), *Work and the nature of man*, Cleveland: World.

12. R. W. Griffin (1982), *Task design: An integrative approach*, Glenview, IL: Scott, Foresman; Pierce and Dunham, 1976; Hulin and Blood, 1968.

13. L. W. Porter, E. E. Lawler III, and J. R. Hackman (1975), *Behavior in organizations*, New York: McGraw-Hill; J. L. Pierce, R. B. Dunham, and R. S. Blackburn (1977), Social systems structure, job design, and growth need strength: A test of a congruency model, *Academy of Management Journal*, 22, 223–40; J. L. Pierce (1984), Job design and technology: A sociotechnical systems perspective, *Journal of Occupational Behavior*, 5, 147–54; J. W. Slocum, Jr., and H. P. Sims, Jr. (1980), A typology for integrating technology, organizations, and job design, *Human Relations*, 33, 143–212.

14. M. Bucklow (1972), A new role for the work group, in L. E. Davis and J. C. Taylor, eds., *Design of jobs*, Middlesex, England: Penguin; Hackman and Oldham, 1980.

15. Hackman and Oldham, 1980, 165–68.

16. J. D. Thompson (1967), *Organizations in action*, New York: McGraw-Hill.

17. Thompson, 1967; A. H. Van de Ven, A. L. Delbecq, and R. Koenig, Jr. (1976), Determinants of coordination modes within organizations, *American Sociological Review*, 41, 322–38.

18. V. A. Graicunas (1933), Relationships in organizations, *Bulletin of the International Management Institute*, Geneva: International Labour Office, in L. Gulick and L. Urwick, eds., *Papers on the science of administration*, New York: Institute of Public Administration, 1937, 181–87; L. Urwick (October 1955), Axioms of organization, *Public Administration Magazine*, 348–49; R. C. Davis (1951), *Fundamentals of top management*, New York: Harper & Row.

19. J. C. Worthy (January 1950), Factors influencing employee morale, *Harvard Business Review*, 61–73; D. D. Van Fleet and A. G. Bedeian (1977), A history of the span of management, *Academy of Management Review*, 2, 356–72; J. G. Udell (1967), An empirical test of hypotheses relating to span of control, *Administrative Science Quarterly*, 12, 420–39.
20. H. Fayol (1916), *General and industrial management*, London: Pitman.
21. J. R. Galbraith (1974), Organization design: An information processing view, *Interfaces*, 4, 28–36.
22. P. R. Lawrence and J. W. Lorsch (1967), *Organization and environment*, Homewood, IL: Irwin.
23. Lawrence and Lorsch, 1967.

Key Terms

organizing
formal organization
informal organization
craft approach
classical approach
vertical specialization
horizontal specialization
behavioral approach
job enlargement
job enrichment
Job Characteristics Model (JCM)
contingency approach
self-managing work group approach
departmentalization

functional departments
product/service departmentalization
territorial (geographical) departmentalization
customer/client departmentalization
process/equipment departmentalization
project departments
hybrid approach
interdependence approach
span of control
coordinating
vertical coordination
horizontal coordination

Issues for Review and Discussion

1. Define organizing and discuss its purpose.
2. Specify the differences between formal and informal organizations.
3. Identify and differentiate among the four approaches managers use to design jobs.
4. Identify and briefly describe six different forms of departmentalization.
5. What is the hybrid approach to departmentalization?
6. What is task interdependence, and how does it influence the grouping of organizational activities?
7. Identify the two basic coordination needs that organizations have, and discuss the three different mechanisms that managers use to meet them.
8. Identify and discuss the four factors that affect the integration among organizational units.

Suggested Readings

Dow, G. K. (1988). Configurational and coactivational views of organizational structure. *Academy of Management Review,* 13, 53–64.

Griffin, R. W. (1982). *Task design: An integrative approach.* Glenview, IL: Scott, Foresman.

Hackman, J. R. (1977). Work design. In Hackman, J. R. and Suttle, J. L., eds. *Improving life at work.* Santa Monica, CA: Goodyear, 96–162.

Manz, C. C. and Sims, H. P., Jr. (1987). Leading workers to lead themselves. *Administrative Science Quarterly,* 32, 106–28.

Pierce, J. L. (1980). Job design in perspective. *The Personnel Administrator,* 25, 67–74.

Reynolds, E. V. and Johnson, J. D. (1982). Liaison emergence: Relating theoretical perspectives. *Academy of Management Review,* 4, 551–59.

Scott, W. G. (April 1961). Organization theory: An overview and an appraisal. *Academy of Management Journal,* 7–26.

Wall, T. D., Kemp, N. J., Jackson, P. R., and Clegg, C. W. (1986). Outcomes of autonomous work groups: A long-term field experiment. *Academy of Management Journal,* 29, 280–304.

By Toni Stenger of the University of Wisconsin-La Crosse

R. H. Merriam, Inc., was formed in 1920 by Russ Merriam. It was a residential construction plumbing company until the 1950s, when the company expanded into commercial and service plumbing. The company had thirty to forty employees at that time, but it lost money, and Russ Merriam was forced to cut the company down to a ten-person staff. It stayed at that size until Russ Merriam's death in 1975. His son, Dennis Merriam, then acquired a majority interest in the company. At that time, the company had $600,000 in sales and ten employees.

By mid-1987, annual sales had grown to $2.3 million, and the company employed a small office staff and eighteen to twenty members of Local No. 31 of the Plumbing and Pipe Fitters Union. These employees installed and maintained all conduits for fluid materials, including water systems, cooling systems, and heating systems. Plumbers worked with pipes that carried oil, gas, or water. Steam fitters specialized in steam pipes.

Dennis Merriam's company grew both because the community in which it was located grew (population 70,000) and because Merriam instituted several changes in operations. He saw a need for a plumbing contractor with enough resources to provide commercial construction projects, such as hospitals, motels, and schools with high quality and rapid installations. These projects tied up large amounts of capital, and the investors usually were interested in how quickly the construction could begin generating revenues. Because to the investors, quality and speed were the highest priorities, the lowest bid was not always the prime concern in choosing

a plumbing contractor. To keep his employees working and to keep his cash flow even, Marriam took about one third of his revenues from smaller installations, such as public swimming pools and retail stores. In this market, the company competed with smaller, nonunion contractors, and work usually was awarded to the lowest bidder. Merriam sometimes took these jobs on a break-even basis.

R. H. Merriam, Inc., became well known as a reliable provider of commercial plumbing and heating/cooling installations in the surrounding four states. The company did little or no advertising; most contracts were obtained through word-of-mouth recommendations from satisfied general contractors. (Most construction jobs are bid and supervised by general contractors, who then subcontract some of the specialized work, such as plumbing. Merriam itself sometimes subcontracted parts of its work.)

Merriam had very few competitors of its size and resources in the area. Of the thirty-seven plumbing contractors in its home community, only three others were of comparable size; therefore, larger commercial construction projects offered an opportunity with few competitors. Under a uniform labor agreement, Merriam and its competitors used union employees and paid the same hourly wages and benefits.

Managing the Workforce

All of Merriam's plumbers were members of the union, including all forepersons and the general foreperson, William Tobey. The company also employed three "helpers." Helpers usually were not allowed by the union contract, but Dennis Merriam had won this concession by presenting evidence that they were necessary for the company to stay

competitive with those contractors which did not employ union labor.

Most of Merriam's employees had been with the company for a long time and were, Merriam believed, of top quality. The contract did reserve to Merriam the right to discharge incompetent employees.

One of the strictest limits on Merriam's discretion was the contract requirement that seniority alone determine most staffing (except foreperson) and pay decisions. There was no formal performance-appraisal system. Furthermore, Merriam felt that most of his plumbers were too comfortable in their highly paid trade (wages and benefits totalled $20 an hour) to be financially motivated.

The union contract specified the tasks that helpers, journeymen plumbers, and forepersons could perform. The forepersons ran each job on its site and handled day-to-day operating problems. Usually they were responsible for converting the blueprints into the materials order for the job and for supervising the loading of materials into trailers that were hauled to job sites. They were not involved in bidding nor in financial control of projects.

William Tobey, the general foreperson, was responsible for estimating most new jobs, with Dennis Merriam's final approval. He also worked with each foreperson to make certain that each job was running smoothly. He was supposed to visit each site at least weekly. Often he had to run to supply houses to obtain parts unexpectedly needed by the various forepersons. He also occasionally served as foreperson for smaller local projects. Figure 10A illustrates the company's organizational structure.

The forepersons were supported by a small office staff. Betty Ellis, the receptionist, also handled all bookkeeping, such as billings, payroll, ac-

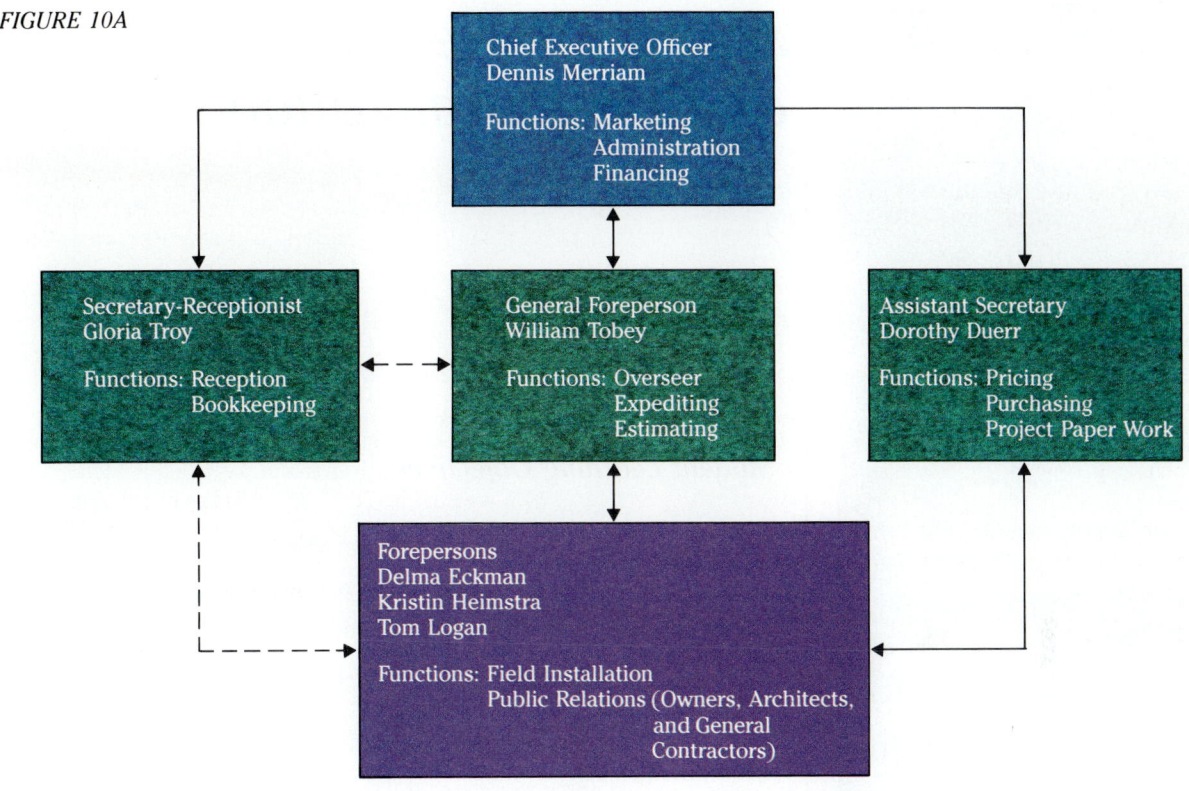

counts payable, and taxes. She also kept labor and other records. Dorothy Duerr, the purchasing agent, obtained prices for and purchased all materials for the jobs and controlled all paperwork in the ordering process. She also worked with the forepersons to coordinate procurement. Dennis Merriam, the chief executive officer, did everything else that needed doing. Merriam used no computer inventory-management or planning systems, but he was considering choosing a total computer system.

A Typical Day at R. H. Merriam

The state of operations at R. H. Merriam can be captured in a description of a few typical moments at the office.

Dennis frantically tells Dorothy to find a Fisher housing, (a special part) that can be delivered to the project

site of the steam pressure reducing station within two weeks. Dorothy, in self-defense, claims that Kristin Heimstra, the project's foreperson, should have stipulated that a Fisher part was required on the project and that the project was already on a tight deadline. "I was only trying to save the company money by substituting with the less costly Hoffman," she explains. "How was I to know the engineer would reject it and we'd have to order another part? This thing has an eight-to-ten-week delivery time."

The phone rings. It's Delma Eckman, another site foreperson, reporting that he can't find a part that was supposed to be in the trailer and that the three journeymen plumbers can do nothing more until that part arrives. Dennis yells over to William Tobey, "Get on the horn and find a half-inch coupling for Delma and get it out to the site quick. These guys are each costing us $20 an hour to sit and wait."

Gloria Troy pops in to say that Tom Logan, the Oslo Motel project foreperson, is on the phone and wants to know if Dennis will be at the final check-out for the project. "Yeah, I'll be there, but I'm not sure when. There just aren't enough hours in the day. I just wish I could get things under control around here and stop spending so much time doing crisis management."

Questions

1. What are some of the symptoms of lack of organization and control at R. H. Merriam, Inc.?

2. What kind of organizational structure would you recommend for the company?

3. What recommendations would you make so that Dennis Merriam could "get things under control around here"?

Authority, Delegation, and Decentralization

Student Learning Objectives

After reading this chapter, you should be able to:

1. Distinguish among influence, power, and authority.

2. Understand the major views on the meaning of authority.

3. Identify and understand the need for the various types of authority.

4. Understand the processes through which influence is exercised inside organizations.

5. Discuss how, when, and why organizations use delegation.

6. Distinguish between centralized and decentralized authority.

7. Identify conditions that determine whether an organization should have a centralized or decentralized authority system.

8. Determine when formalization of authority is necessary and how to develop it.

The last chapter began a discussion of the managerial activity of organizing. It examined the ways in which managers organize tasks into jobs and jobs into departments. You saw that a major part of the organizing process involves coordinating individuals, jobs, departments, and various hierarchical levels. This chapter continues the discussion of the organizing process with an examination of such questions as: Who is in charge? Who makes commitments on behalf of the organization? How? These are questions of influence, power, and authority. The answers depend, in part, on the type of authority system that management creates to distribute and use its power, influence, and authority.

Deciding what type of authority system to create is a major challenge facing managers. For example, two Midwestern utility companies can be compared. In one, the president of the organization accepts or rejects all appointments of new employees. In the second organization, the authority for making these decisions is given to employees in the human resources department, several levels below the president. This chapter will look at the nature of organizational power and authority, at several types of authority systems, and at the processes managers use to transfer authority from one organization member to another.

Managerial Influence: Power and Authority

Inexperienced managers often assume that their organization's work *will* be successfully accomplished because formally defined jobs and departments specify how the work *should* be done. Things work this way for some people, in some jobs, at some times, but usually they do not. In most situations, formal job definitions and coordinating strategies are not enough to get the work done. Organizations must somehow galvanize their workers into action, and, to do so, they must use influence. **Influence,** therefore, is a person's ability to produce results and to bring about a change in his or her environment. People derive influence from interpersonal power and authority.

People derive influence from interpersonal power and authority.

Interpersonal Power and Its Sources

The people inside organizations influence one another and shape organizational events. Managers, for example, can tell subordinates what to do and, in many cases, how to do it. Nonmanagers can share ideas for cost-cutting measures with supervisors or encourage co-workers to form a union. It is **interpersonal power** that enables individual organization members to exert influence over others and over their organization.[1] There are several types and sources of interpersonal power, and these are discussed in more detail in Chapter 15. Some of the more visible forms of power in the work environment include:

- *Reward power*—the power a person has because people believe that he or she can bestow rewards or outcomes, such as money or recognition, that others desire
- *Coercive power*—the power a person has because people believe that he or she can punish them by inflicting pain or by withholding or taking away something that they value
- *Referent power*—the power a person has because others want to associate with or be accepted by him or her
- *Expert power*—the power a person has because others believe that he or she has and is willing to share expert knowledge that they need
- *Resource power*—the power a person has because others believe that he or she has and is willing to share resources, such as information, time, or materials, that they need
- *Legitimate power*—the power a person has because others believe that he or she has a right to influence them and that they ought to obey.[2]

In practice, many organization members have—and need—more than one form of power. For example, when a manager makes a decision and directs others, employees usually follow this directive because of the legitimate power given to the manager by the organization; however, what if the new manager is Fred Kooperstein, the company president's son, and employees resent "this young hotshot who only got the job because of his dad"? What if the new manager is Patricia Quinlan, a newly graduated M.B.A. from Northwestern University, whose blue-collar subordinates do not think a "college kid" can possibly know how they should do their jobs?

In these and other cases, legitimate power alone might not be enough. In reality, workers seldom give automatic and unconditional compliance to any manager. (After all, did you always do exactly as your parents told you? Do you always do exactly what your professor asks?) If workers react to Patricia by slowing production, they are using coercive power to force higher-level management to replace her. The secretary who wanted to be promoted to Fred's position may use resource power to hamper his directives by delaying the typing of his reports.

To reinforce their legitimate power, then, managers also must use other forms of power. If workers think that Fred has the ability to fire them, their perceptions may give him coercive power. If Patricia tells her subordinates that she will pay a year-end bonus to any employee whose use of new tools leads to an increase in production output, she is using expert and reward power if the employees believe her and follow through. Many public and private organizations have formal reward-and-punishment programs that managers can use to enhance legitimate power. Merit raises are given to reward high levels of performance, for example, and workers can be suspended without pay if they fail to show up for work without first having notified their supervisor.

It has been argued that formal power insulates management from reality and prevents organizations from functioning effectively.[3] According to a **strategic-contingency model of power,** those people and organizational units most capable of coping with an organization's critical problems and uncertainties acquire power. For example, when an organization is embroiled in a number of lawsuits that threaten its existence, its legal department probably will gain considerable power and influence over decision making in the organization. As power flows to those who grapple with organizational problems and uncertainties, the organization adapts to these problems and uncertainties; thus, power may shift as the organization moves from one problem area or uncertainty to the next.

Authority

Many equate authority with legitimate power. Max Weber, the famed sociologist, saw **authority** as the legitimate right of a person to exercise influence.[4] According to Weber, this perception that someone has the legitimate right to exercise influence can stem from such sources as legal systems, situational demands, relationships between people, tradition, and charismatic personalities. In the United States Army, for example, anyone wearing a lieutenant's uniform possesses the right to command privates, and privates have the obligation to comply. Contrast this with a project department, where influence is based on the expertise that each participant brings to a task. The next sections will look at the various types of authority found in organizations and their sources.

Classical View of Authority   One view of authority arises from the classical approach to management. According to **classical authority theory,** authority is the *institutional right* of organizations to act, to decide, and to exercise influence. What this means for organizations in the United States is that the institutions of private property and private enterprise give the owners of organizations the right to run their organization as they see fit, so long as they do not violate the rights of others. In most large organizations, the owners transfer a significant portion of these ownership rights to the people who operate the organization on behalf of the owners. A group of stockholders, for example, transfers rights to a board of directors, which, in turn, transfers a large portion of its rights to a chief executive officer, who then transfers some rights to lower-level officers, and so on.

Eventually, all organization members in management positions possess some formal authority to act, to decide, and to exercise influence. People at the institutional level, by virtue of their organizational position, possess the right to exercise control over the organization. They retain the right to make strategic decisions and may pass along the right to make operational

FIGURE 11.1
Classical View of Authority

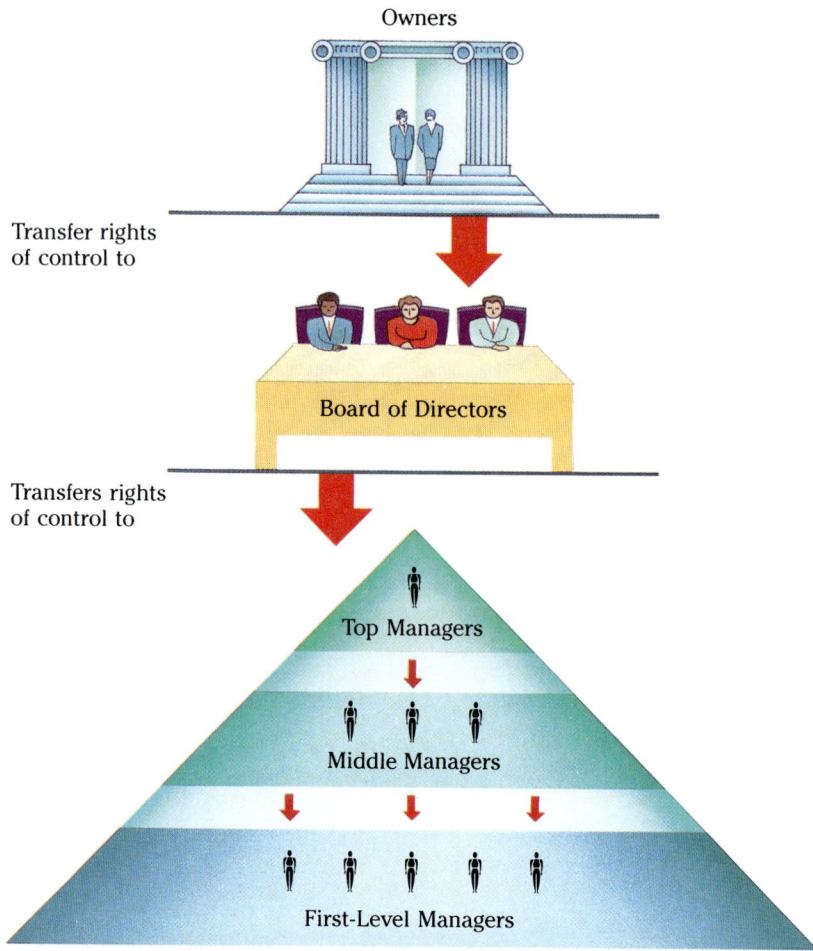

Owners

Transfer rights
of control to

Board of Directors

Transfers rights
of control to

Top Managers

Middle Managers

First-Level Managers

decisions to managers in the technical core; thus, from this classical perspective, authority flows from the top down (see Figure 11.1).

Review the example of the authority relationship between the lieutenant and the private, this time from the classical authority view. The lieutenant has the institutional right, vested by the army, to issue orders to the private. The classicists might also argue that, in a rationally designed authority system, one person at the top of the organization is and should be ultimately in charge of and responsible for all organizational affairs. As the sign on President Truman's desk said, "The buck stops here."

Acceptance View of Authority   There is a second perspective on authority that is oriented more toward people's relationships than is the classical view. In the **acceptance view of authority** proposed by Chester Barnard and other behavioral management advocates, authority flows upward from subordinates to superiors, based on the nature of the relationship between people and their perception of this relationship.[5] According to the acceptance view, the relationships between employees and their superiors become authoritative when the subordinates view those relationships as legitimate. Subordinates consider relationships legitimate and, therefore, authoritative and will comply with a superior's request when four conditions are met:

1. The subordinate understands the nature of the request.
2. The subordinate perceives that the request is consistent with the goals and values of the organization.
3. The request is compatible with the subordinate's personal interests.
4. The subordinate is mentally and physically capable of complying with the request.

In other words, if Don Reynolds, sales manager, asks the salespeople in his department to prepare a report outlining their sales prospects for the upcoming year, the salespeople will accept the request as legitimate, will consider Don's request for action authoritative, and will comply if: 1) they understand what information Don wants included in the report; 2) they know that the company needs the information included in their reports to facilitate its overall strategic plan; 3) they have personal reasons to want the company to succeed, perhaps so they will be able to earn larger commissions; and 4) they can retrieve the information they need to analyze past performance, assess market trends—and find the time to sit down, write the reports, and deliver them to Don's desk.

These four conditions define what is acceptable to an employee and, thus, identify an employee's *zone of acceptance*.[6] Managers must be sure that their requests fall within their subordinates' zone of acceptance. Otherwise, their requests are likely to be met with resistance or at least something less than full support.

Situational View of Authority A third perspective is the **situational view of authority** proposed by Mary Parker Follett. She argued that, rather than one person's giving orders to another; both should agree to take orders from the situation. Under these conditions, ultimate authority would reside in the will and consent of the people who perform a particular task. Like Barnard, Follett treated acceptance as the key to establishing authority relationships. Unlike Barnard, however, Follett strongly emphasized the importance of considering each situation according to its particular demands. It is the knowledge and skills of people in relation to the task being executed that determines who will exercise authority, not those people's positions in the organizational hierarchy. Authority in a project department, for example, may change hands more than once, depending on whether a project is in the development stage, the experimental phase, or in the process of generating a final report.

Exercising Authority

In all three views of authority, it is how subordinates perceive a manager's legitimacy that is important. When people perceive attempts at influence as legitimate—whether because of hierarchical right, the nature of the relationships between people, or the situation itself—they concede its authority and willingly comply. Although many managers treat authority as an institutional right that flows from the top downward, effective use of formal authority depends on whether subordinates will accept directives. It is, therefore, imperative that managers place their directives within subordinates' zone of acceptance so that they will try to achieve the organization's goals.

The acceptance view of authority is oriented toward people's views of their working relationships.

One of the simplest approaches a manager can take to find out what an employee considers acceptable is to ask. Some secretaries, for example, consider running personal errands or working late to be outside their zone of acceptance. Other secretaries find it acceptable to do both, as well as sharpen pencils and make coffee. Asking a job applicant during an interview whether he or she is willing to perform these tasks in addition to the specified clerical duties is a simple method managers can use to predict whether requests for these sorts of activities will be resisted or granted.

Another way to ascertain an employee's zone of acceptance is to observe his or her behavior. If an employee refuses to join the company's softball team, does not attend the company's annual picnic or end-of-the-year banquet, and never chips in to buy a retiring employee or hospital-ized co-worker a gift, it probably will be futile for the manager to ask the employee to attend a fund-raising benefit on noncompany-paid time. This employee is clearly demonstrating that only those duties specifically related to the job and performed for pay are within his or her zone of acceptance.

In organizational situations in which formal superior-subordinate rela-tionships exist, managers may often rely on the power of formal authority to encourage workers to comply, keeping in mind that directives must fall within the zone of acceptance. What about the many situations in which formal superior-subordinate relationships do not exist, however? For example, the interaction patterns of employees assigned to committees and task forces often are not prescribed in advance. Much influence, in fact, is informal. The people at the lower levels of organizations may not have an institutional right to exercise influence, but they often accumulate considerable power and, therefore, the ability to influence.[7] Consider, for example, the power exercised by the person who controls the appoint-ments of the President of the United States. This individual screens the information that the President gets before he or she makes a major decision and, thereby, substantially influences decisions. Many corporate secretaries wield great power by deciding how much and which pieces of mail the boss will see and by screening the boss' telephone calls.[8]

The sources of power in any organization, thus, are varied. Some are subtle, some obvious. Some are planned, formal parts of the organization-al structure. Some are spontaneous and informal outgrowths of particular personalities in particular situations. Managers should be aware of the complexities of power and cultivate a climate that will use it to further the goals of their organization. Specifically, managers should:

1. Determine where in the organizational hierarchy they want authority to lie. Specify exactly who is to be in charge of which subordinates and which tasks.
2. Take action to ensure that legitimate power is achieved. Communi-cate reasons for authority assignments and make sure authority relationships flow logically from tasks. Encourage and guide the spontaneous development and use of power that flows from new and unanticipated situations so that it reflects a concern for the welfare of people and the organization.

At Apple Computer, the management system encourages employees to challenge decisions made by others.

3. Supplement legitimate power (authority) by developing other sources of power, such as reward systems that allow people in positions of assigned authority to encourage and positively reinforce various forms of behavior.

Compliance

You have learned that organizational members comply with formal authority if they accept it as being legitimate and if it falls within their zone of acceptance. There is another consideration as well. To a large extent, they have *learned* to do so. Societal norms and values teach children how to react to authority, starting with their parents as authority figures and continuing with teachers and employers. In some societies, authority is expected to be accepted almost automatically. In others, it is the norm to question authority. Even within a single society, subcultures often have their own norms. In the military subculture of the United States, for example, authority is to be accepted without question. One of the themes of the activist college subculture during the 1960s and early 1970s, however, was "Question authority!"

Likewise, the ability to question authority differs from organization to organization. At PepsiCo, for example, decisions are made by top-level managers and are expected to be accepted by lower-level managers. Contrast this with Apple Computer, where the "buy-in management" system obliges people to challenge decisions, forcing the initiator(s) to prove that their ideas are sound.[9]

As organization members learn to comply with the requests of those in positions of authority, their learning is further shaped by the consequences of their compliance or lack of it. Those who have been rewarded for complying are more likely to comply in the future. Those who have been disappointed—punished or not rewarded—are less likely to comply in the future. In addition, as will be discussed in Chapter 13, some individuals are more likely to comply with authority as a result of personality factors. People who have strong authoritarian personalities, for example, tend to expect their subordinates to comply with their influence attempts, just as they submit to the influence of their superiors.

Of course, organization members do not always comply with authority. Many employees are fired, suspended, and demoted because of their disregard for authority. Even Lee Iacocca, the man credited with rejuvenating the nearly bankrupt Chrysler Corporation, was fired from the presidency of the Ford Motor Corporation after numerous clashes with the company's chairperson. Sociologist Amitai Etzioni has suggested that the type of authority managers use produces a predictable compliance response.[10] Managers who rely on *coercive* power, for example, ultimately alienate employees. The manager who resorts to such threats as "That report better be on my desk by Friday or you can forget about that promotion you've been wanting" is bound to alienate the subordinate. Managers who use *remunerative*, or reward, power get an instrumental or calculative response from employees. In other words, employees choose tasks that promise them a reward and ignore those that do not. For example, employees who will work overtime if their supervisor promises to pay them at twice their normal salary might refuse the extra work if they are asked to do it for regular or no pay.

Even though management theories differ somewhat in the details as they address the role of managerial influence, one important universal message comes through. The ability to influence organization members is an important resource that must be used if a manager is to succeed. Saying "I am the boss" may help but alone is seldom powerful enough to achieve adequate influence. Organizations must provide managers with the influence tools they need, and managers must use these tools effectively. (See "A Closer Look: The Redistribution of Authority.")

Authority Relationships

As part of the organizing activity, managers must design an organization's authority system. This design creates **authority relationships** between people and between people and their work. There are three different types of authority found in these relationships: line, staff, and functional authority.

Line Authority

Line authority is a *command* authority. Line authority gives a manager the organizational right to make decisions and to commit the organization to action. Line authority is represented by the chain of command: an individual positioned above another individual in the organizational hierarchy has the institutional right to make decisions, issue directives, and expect compliance from the lower-level employees in his or her span of control. Figure 11.2 traces the line authority for claims adjusting in an insurance company. In this figure, the regional operations director has direct responsibility for providing claims service to the insured. Authority for this service flows directly from this director to a regional claims manager, to branch managers, to claims managers, and then to claims representatives who provide the actual claims service.

Staff Authority

Staff authority is *advisory* authority.[11] It is the authority that comes in the form of counsel, advice, and recommendation. Unlike line managers with formal command authority, people with staff authority—for example, staff managers—derive their power primarily from their expert knowledge and from the legitimacy they can establish for themselves in their relationships with line managers. A hospital's lawyer, for example, cannot dictate a contract that is negotiated between the personnel department and its unionized employees. Instead, the lawyer, in a staff capacity, advises the hospital's contract negotiators about the advisability of the language contained in the contract. Similarly, the legal department at Employers Insurance of Wausau offers advice to the claims, underwriting, and human resources departments.

A CLOSER LOOK

The Redistribution of Authority: Can It Help Saturn Run Rings Around Toyota and Intel Chip Away at the Competition?

There is no question about who holds supreme authority in a traditional U.S. auto plant. A plant manager has virtually total authority, and he or she alone decides whether to share this authority with anyone else; however, if General Motors' plans for its new Saturn facility are fully executed, a new day will dawn in corporate America. With its new Saturn plant, GM intends to cut labor hours in half and bring the costs of its cars closer to those of its Japanese competitors. Although robotics are expected to increase effectiveness, GM also plans a radical redistribution of power through the widespread use of participative management. According to GM Chairperson Roger B. Smith, this project will be "the key to GM's long-term competitiveness."[1] According to Richard G. LeFauve, president of the Saturn subsidiary of GM, the success of this venture will depend heavily on such practices as the team approach to work.

Work groups at the new Saturn plant will consist of a handful of employees who will elect their own boss and will decide who does which jobs. Each work unit will use a personal computer to coordinate the maintenance of equipment, the ordering of supplies, and the administration of

work and vacation schedules. Workers will be paid a salary instead of an hourly wage and can earn substantial bonuses for good performance. If a work group needs another member, candidates will be interviewed by the work group members themselves.

In short, power at the Saturn plant will lie in the hands of the workers. If cutbacks are needed, employee committees will decide whether to issue layoffs or to curtail work hours. Such questions are unlikely to arise, however, because almost 5000 of Saturn's 6000 workers will be protected from layoffs unless a "catastrophic event" should occur. Why does GM expect this bold experiment to work? Because, along with authority and power, workers will be responsible for controlling costs, managing quality, and making the plant profitable. The company is convinced that employees have the capabilities to do so if given the opportunity and sufficient support.

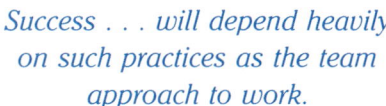

Success . . . will depend heavily on such practices as the team approach to work.

Although not at as daring a level as at the Saturn plant, semiconductor giant Intel is also redistributing power in hopes of enhancing organizational effectiveness. The company has simply "grown too big and its markets too turbulent for one manager to control it so closely,"[2] The once-profitable Intel, with its highly centralized structure, posted operating losses

of $255 million in 1985–86 alone. Intel's chief executive, Andy Grove, has stated publicly that corporate giants must become agile or die. Although Grove admits that it is hard to follow his own advice, he is decentralizing Intel along product lines and placing power in the hands of managers in each of the company's three major operating units. Grove's hopes? To restore confidence to the company, return it to money-making status, and position it to respond quickly to market opportunities. General Motors and Intel, previously profit-making leaders in the United States, have seen hard times in recent years. How do they "spell relief"? DECENTRALIZATION

1. W. J. Hampton (16 March 1987), Will Saturn ever leave the launchpad? *Business Week*, 107.
2. J. W. Wilson (16 March 1987), Can Andy Grove practice what he preaches? *Business Week*, 68.

FIGURE 11.2 Line Authority

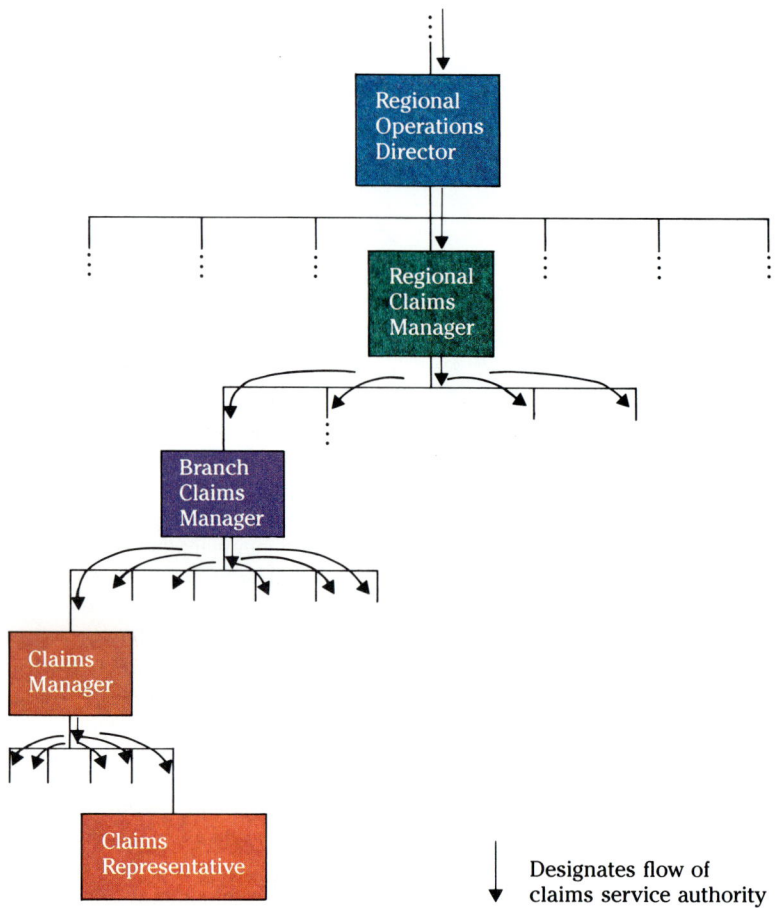

Designates flow of
claims service authority

Although people generally associate staff authority with staff personnel and departments, staff authority is not limited to this context. A line manager may be asked formally to serve as an organizational adviser to other line managers and, thereby, to exercise staff authority. In addition, staff managers may have line authority within their own staff department. A chain of command connects staff department members who are hierarchically separated. As noted, the legal department at Employers Insurance has staff authority in its relationship with a number of other departments in the organization, yet managers within the legal department also have line authority over nonmanagers in the legal department.

Organizations often have trouble getting their line managers to listen to and accept advice from staff personnel. Line managers often feel that staff people are isolated from the realities of their department and that, therefore, their advice is of limited value. In addition, because line managers are responsible for the action taken, many want to make their own decisions about what needs to be done, how, and why.

To solve this problem, many organizations have formally modified the role of staff personnel and the type of authority that they are permitted to exercise. These variations in staff authority include compulsory staff consultation, concurring authority, and functional authority for staff personnel. These tactics are intended to move staff personnel from a purely advisory role toward broader authority (see Figure 11.3).

Compulsory staff consultation forces line personnel and staff personnel to discuss issues before taking action. Under this system, for example, a purchasing agent would be required to contact the legal department before signing an agreement to buy raw materials. Through this arrangement, organizations hope to create better-informed line managers who take advantage of the resources of staff members.

Some organizations have tried a slightly different approach to make sure that their line managers listen to staff departments. They assign a staff member **concurring authority.** That is, a designated staff member can formally approve or disapprove an action that is to be taken. For example, if the quality inspection department has concurring authority, the production manager will have to obtain the approval of the quality inspection department before making changes in production methods. Concurring authority, in effect, gives staff the right to veto actions proposed by line managers.

Functional Authority

The third way of expanding staff authority is to vest staff members with functional authority, which also may be given to line managers. When this is done, a staff manager is able to utilize more powerful functional authority instead of relying solely on staff authority.

Functional authority is the right to direct or control specific activities that are under the span of control of other managers. Functional authority allows a manager (line or staff) to command specific processes, practices, and policies related to the activities undertaken by personnel in other departments. The human resources department, for example, may create policies guiding an organization's compliance with equal employment regulations. As managers in such departments as marketing and operations promote and hire employees, the human resources department makes all final decisions to assure compliance with the organization's

FIGURE 11.3
Variations in Staff Authority

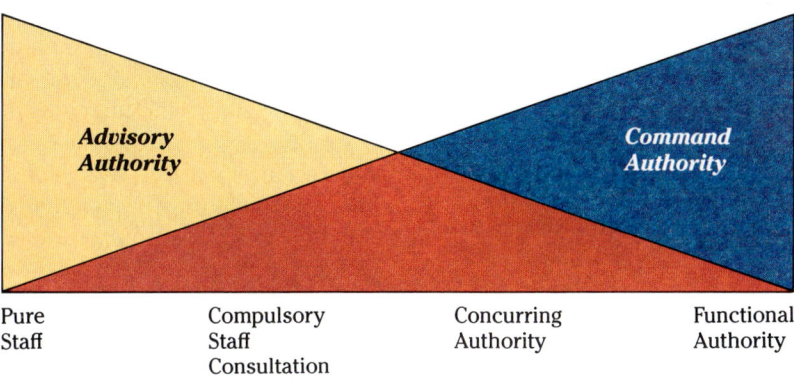

FIGURE 11.4   *Functional Authority*

(A)

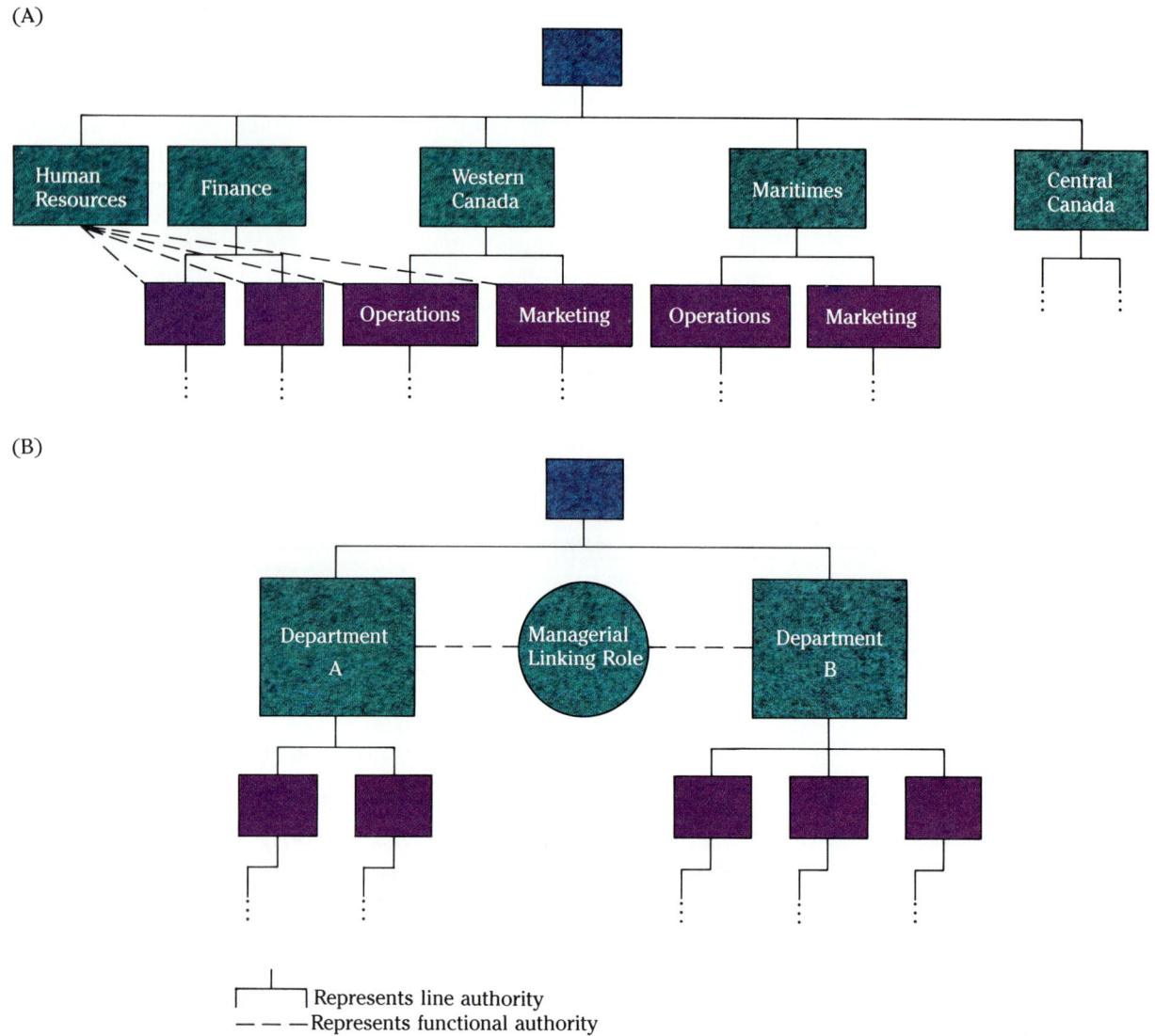

(B)

☐ Represents line authority

— — — Represents functional authority

equal employment opportunity policies (see Figure 11.4A). Whereas line authority runs vertically in a traditional organization, functional authority cuts across the vertical chain of command and flows horizontally and diagonally across the hierarchy.

In Chapter 10, you read about an example of functional authority in the discussion of managerial linking roles. Recall that organizations with two or more highly interdependent departments may assign someone to a special linking role to exercise authority over decisions on the points of interdependence between the departments. The department heads continue to exercise command authority over all other departmental matters. The managers who link the departments exercise their functional authority only over joint issues (see Figure 11.4B).

Delegating Authority

Managers may exercise line, staff, or functional authority; however, for any organization to function effectively, managers must transfer some of their formal authority to others. **Delegation** is the process managers use to transfer formal authority from one position to another within an organization and, thus, to put the authority system they have designed into place. Architects delegate authority to draftspeople, senior law partners delegate authority to junior lawyers, high-school principals delegate authority to vice-principals, and so on. Notice that delegating authority has not reduced the authority of the architects, senior partners, or principals. To delegate means to grant or to confer. To delegate does not mean to surrender authority. A manager who delegates authority in no way abdicates the institutional right to act on behalf of the organization.

From a subordinate's perspective, two things happen through the act of delegation. First, the subordinate *receives authority* from a superior, even though the superior retains all of his or her supervising authority. Second, the subordinate *becomes responsible* for carrying out the activities that have been transferred, even though the superior remains ultimately responsible for the performance of the task. For example, if Kelly Bell, purchasing manager for a national shoe distributor, authorizes Byron Hopkins, Midwest sales manager, to purchase a fleet of company cars: 1) Byron has the authority to make the purchase, even though Kelly retains the authority to execute the purchase and 2) Byron is responsible for performing the task and using the authority that has been delegated to him. Kelly remains ultimately accountable for the purchase, however, and for the way in which the organization's money is spent.

Delegation is not confined to a downward process in which authority is transferred from one level to those below it in the organizational hierarchy. Managers may delegate upward so that control can be exercised at a higher level. Kevin Carlson, for example, may have the authority to negotiate the sale of 10,000 tires to WalMart, but when WalMart asks for a guaranteed ten-day delivery schedule, Kevin may ask Elizabeth Hayes, his boss, to decide if the company should make such a commitment. Even though Kevin has the authority to make the decision, he delegates it upward to Elizabeth. Lateral delegation is also possible. If WalMart asks Kevin to sign a sales contract that guarantees his organization will not sell tires to any other company in the same city, Kevin can decide whether to sign, or he can delegate laterally by asking his organization's lawyer to decide if the contract would be legal. Authority delegation is lateral when line managers transfer authority to staff advisers or to people in other line departments.

Delegation generally is thought of as a transfer of authority from one person to another, but it also can operate to and from organizational units, such as departments, committees, and self-managing work groups. When authority is delegated to an organizational unit, a representative from that unit is usually called on to act on behalf of the unit, as when a committee chairperson accepts a charge from management to find a way to lower production costs. It is possible, however, for the group to accept a transfer of authority and its accompanying activities. For example, the self-managing work groups at Butler Manufacturing (discussed in Chapter 10) accepted the authority and responsibility for quality inspection, work scheduling, performance appraisals, and many other facets of the production process in addition to the actual assembly of the company's grain driers. These activities were delegated to the group and not to one specific individual.

A manager who delegates effectively retains authority but does not directly exercise it. A manager who chooses to delegate should step in only if the person delegated authority fails to act appropriately. Although Kelly Bell retains the authority to execute the shoe distributor's purchase of cars, she should allow Byron to make the purchase because she has delegated the authority and responsibility for the task to him. If Byron buys too many cars or cars that are too expensive, Kelly must exercise authority to block the purchase and must decide whether to give Byron a second chance to perform appropriately or to withdraw the authority she delegated to him.

How much authority can a manager delegate? Theoretically, managers can delegate the right to do anything that they have authority over, unless their source of authority prohibits doing so. For example, the president of a company may delegate authority over all hiring, firing, marketing, and production, but the president may retain the authority to make long-term strategic plans and to keep the company in compliance with the law. Realistically, to keep an organization functioning effectively, managers usually retain and manage critical tasks themselves and delegate as many others as possible.

There are a number of factors that influence managers' decisions to delegate authority.[12] These factors include:

- *Characteristics of the manager,* such as a need for dominance, need for control, and how much work the manager can handle

"All I need is a chair. I delegate everything."

- *Characteristics of subordinates*, such as their level of responsibility, trustworthiness, and capacity to work alone
- *Characteristics of the situation*, such as a project that becomes so complex or a company that grows so rapidly that the burdens of managing no longer can be borne by one person

Apple Computer, for example, started out as two young men tinkering in a garage. When their product became successful, their company grew beyond their own personal abilities to handle everything. They created jobs, hired people, and delegated authority.

In addition to delegating according to the characteristics of the manager, subordinates, and situation, many managers delegate authority because they consider developing employees to be one of their primary organizational responsibilities. These managers prepare employees for additional responsibilities and more challenging jobs by delegating increasingly important assignments. For example, when Donald Kendall was the chief executive at PepsiCo, he prepared John Sculley to assume the top position by first making him head of the company's international foods operation. Several other executives had previously failed to remedy the problems in this division, which included product difficulties, distribution problems, advertising weaknesses, and inefficient plants. Kendall's efforts to prepare Sculley for bigger and more complex challenges through the delegation process were successful; Sculley's actions wrought dramatic improvements in the division.[13]

Lastly, delegation is a tool that managers can use to become more effective by making their subordinates more effective. Many employees' skills are underutilized. If the managers give subordinates appropriate challenges and greater latitude within which to tackle them, it may result in increased employee motivation and effort.

The Delegation Process

There are four distinct stages in the delegation process, although it does not always unfold in an orderly fashion from one step to the next. Figure 11.5 depicts the stages in the delegation process. In the first stage, the delegator identifies a block of work to be transferred from one area in the organization to another and assigns this activity to an employee or group of employees. For example, Charlie Dawkins, founder of a medium-sized accounting firm on the East Coast, has been the coordinator of his community's annual holiday parade for eight years. He has elected to remove himself from direct involvement in this activity but wants his firm to continue to sponsor the event. Charlie decides to turn the activity over to the firm's vice-president, Laura Lance.

In the second stage of the delegation process, the delegator transfers authority—the organizational right to command—to the delegatee. Until this point, the delegator is the active participant, assigning activities and transferring authority. The subordinate is passive, listening to the delegator's requests and receiving authority. As often happens in organizations, Charlie combined the first and second stages by sending Laura a memo telling her of his decision and stating that, should she accept the assignment, she would have full authority to manage the parade.

FIGURE 11.5   *The Delegation Process*

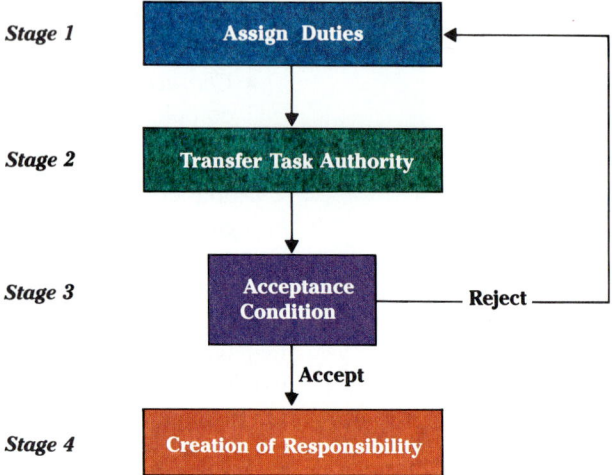

Charlie and Laura are now at the conditional third stage in the delegation process. At this stage, the delegatee either accepts or rejects the task assignment and the accompanying authority. If Laura refused the task, the delegation attempt would be blocked, and Charlie would have to start again by assigning the activity to someone else. If Laura does accept the assignment and authority, the delegation process continues.

The fourth, and final, stage in the process is the creation of an obligation on the part of the subordinate to perform the assigned tasks and to use the assigned authority properly. By accepting the assignment and its accompanying authority, the employee becomes accountable to the manager and is responsible for completing the assigned work. At this stage, both the delegator and the delegatee have authority to complete the task, and both are responsible for how the task is performed. Charlie shows Laura the procedures he has used over the past eight years to raise funds, drum up community support, solicit advertising, and coordinate other activities necessary to run the event. He then steps back to let Laura run the show. Laura probably will consult with Charlie from time to time about questions she may have, and Charlie may check occasionally on the project's status. Ultimately, however, Laura will produce the parade and will accept credit for a job well done. If things do not go well, however, she will have to answer to Charlie—who will have to respond to community criticism.

Barriers to Effective Delegation

In the best of all possible worlds, managers would delegate efficiently, and others would accept their new responsibilities with enthusiasm and carry them out to perfection. In the real world, however, the delegation process does not always go so smoothly. Some of the barriers to effective delegation reside in the abilities and beliefs of the delegator. Managers, for example, can be so poorly organized that they are incapable of planning the activities to be assigned. Even managers who are fully capable of delegating may not want to do so because they lack confidence in the abilities of others to do a job well, and they fear being held personally accountable for the work of others. Conversely, some managers may be afraid that others will do that delegated task so well that their success will be a personal threat. Some managers want so strongly to dominate and influence others that they resist delegating authority.

Another reason some managers do not delegate is that they fear losing control should conditions become turbulent. In fact, when an uncertain environment poses problems, threats, and crises that cry out for delegation and for opening up the system, many managers react in just the opposite fashion. They pull back the reins, reduce delegation of authority, rechannel information to themselves, and attempt to take personal charge. This phenomenon has been referred to as *threat rigidity*.[14]

Managers are not the only organization members who can have difficulty with the delegation process. Some of the barriers to effective delegation reside with those who would assume the new responsibilities. Some employees, for example, feel that they cannot handle additional responsibility. Others are reluctant to accept delegation because they fear that their managers will criticize them if they fail to execute the task well. Still others simply do not want any extra work. If workers perceive no benefit to themselves (whether from an organizational or personal reward system), managers may have difficulty inducing them to assume additional responsibility.

Overcoming Barriers to Delegation

No matter where they reside, the barriers to delegation are not easily overcome. Those at the top of an organization must create a climate in which delegation can be effective by encouraging managers to release some of their personal hold on authority and to inspire subordinates to pick it up. Managers must be persuaded to give others a chance to expand their organizational roles. In addition to providing the opportunity, delegators also must deliver the tools that delegates need to be successful. Managers must become resource providers, part of a support system, and trainers to prepare employees for expanded organizational roles. Equally important, managers must set aside the tendency to insist that delegated tasks be done their way. When assigning tasks and transferring authority, managers should grant permission for employees to experiment, to make mistakes, and to learn from those mistakes.

All of a manager's good intentions will come to naught, however, unless employees also want to expand their roles, to assume additional responsibilities, and to learn new skills. It is not enough for managers to give employees the opportunity to expand their horizons. Employees must give themselves permission to try new things, to make mistakes, and to seek the guidance and resources that they need to succeed in their new roles. For instance, when Charlie asked Laura to coordinate the holiday parade, she thought, "I've never done anything like this before. What if I fail? Wow, will I need help." When she decided to accept, she said to herself, "I'll give it a shot. I'll have to rely on Charlie a lot, but I'll try." Finally, employees may need to recognize that some organizations do not immediately reward workers who have taken on new responsibilities.

Delegating managers must act as resource providers, trainers, and members of a support system.

Jeffrey Pfeffer

Jeffrey Pfeffer, the Thomas D. Dee II Professor of Organizational Behavior at Stanford University, has also taught at the University of Illinois and the University of California, Berkeley, and has visited for a year at Harvard. He has written on power in organizations, organizational demography, organizations and environments, leadership, and wage structure and labor markets.

1. Historically, power in organizations seems to have shifted from production managers to marketing managers and appears to rest today with financial managers. Do you agree, and if so, why do you think this has happened?

Several studies have documented the shift you describe. The change has come about for several reasons. First, the distribution of organizations in the economy has changed, with a smaller manufacturing sector and a larger services—including financial services—sector. Second, because of changes in the financial markets and in share ownership, the crucial uncertainties faced by organizations have shifted. Third, business education itself, with its emphasis on financial analysis and quantitative methods, has contributed to this shift. Of course, it is important to recognize that this general trend masks a lot of variation across industries—engineers still dominate in many high-technology companies, and marketers still have control of many consumer-products firms.

2. Where do you expect dominant power to lie after the next shift?

There is evidence for the increasing importance of persons skilled in governmental and interorganizational relations. The proportion of lawyers in top management positions has increased rapidly, and many firms now routinely send high-level executives to serve in the Washington office for awhile to obtain valued experience in dealing with regulatory and political issues. Many firms now engage in joint ventures, including joint ventures with foreign partners, and the role of government and government policy in the economy remains quite significant.

3. What is the biggest problem encountered when managers delegate authority?

Frankly, the problem is most often delegating responsibility or accountability for some activities or results without delegating sufficient authority to accomplish the assignment. Managers are often unwilling to run the risk of things going wrong if others are given authority for decisions, and, moreover, share the natural inclination of all of us to think that we know best what should be done. The largest danger faced when real authority is delegated is that people at lower levels in the organization will not see the big picture—how their activities fit in with the overall objective; therefore, in trying to do well in their area of authority, they may engage in activities that, although excellent from a local perspective, lead to less-than-optimal performance from the perspective of the firm as a whole.

4. How can managers deal with this problem?

Information about the firm, its operations, its values, its performance, and particularly about the interrelationship among activities is invaluable in addressing this problem. Such information is shared through communication, which can occur informally through the use of task forces or teams, as well as through more formal written documents. The way to address this problem is to share information horizontally and to be sure that as many people as possible in the firm understand what it is trying to accomplish and as much as possible about how it works.

People in those organizations sometimes have to reward themselves by taking pride and pleasure in their own personal growth and development, at least for a while, but effective delegators should monitor their delegatees' actions and reward success. Otherwise, delegatees may conclude that their boss does not care whether they can do the job well or not.

Classical Principles for Effective Delegation

People's attitudes toward authority and responsibility have a long history of causing organizational problems. People like to accumulate and exercise influence over the individuals and events around them, but they often do not want the responsibility when things go wrong. Oliver North and John Poindexter, for example, accumulated and wielded a great deal of influence power during Ronald Reagan's presidency but tried mightily to avoid accountability for their actions during the hearings held after the surfacing of the Iran-Contra affair.[15] Such conflict between the desire to escape the consequences creates a delicate situation. Early writers on management tried to address this predicament by creating a set of principles that managers could use to guide the delegation process.

First, the principle of *parity of authority and responsibility* suggests that authority and responsibility should be equally balanced. That is, employees should not exercise more influence than they can be held accountable for, but they must have enough authority to do the work for which they are held accountable. Laura must not spend more money on the parade than the amount specified in her budget, but Charlie must give her the authority to spend the funds that the budget permits.

The second principle is that *responsibility is absolute*. It is a reminder that "to delegate" does not mean "to give away." Although people may want to relieve themselves of their responsibilities through the delegation process, the delegator retains ultimate responsibility for both the performance of the task and the way that the authority is used, even after work has been delegated. For example, it was discovered in 1987 that employees of Toshiba Machine, a Japanese high-technology firm, had sold equipment to the Soviet Union in 1984, which was expressly forbidden by agreement with the United States. The head of the Japanese company accepted full responsibility and resigned his position.

According to the *scalar principle*, lines of authority must be clear as they run from the very top of the organization to its lowest levels. Sometimes referred to as the "pecking order," these clear lines of authority show organization members the location and path of authority and responsibility in the organizational hierarchy. When H. Ross Perot owned Electronic Data Systems, he wanted every employee to be able to come to him if they had a problem they could not resolve at a lower level; however, they had to follow a pecking order, first trying to resolve their problem with their immediate supervisor, then their supervisor's boss, that boss' boss, and so on up the organizational hierarchy until they reached Perot. Otherwise, they were not allowed to speak to Perot.

The scalar principle can help management avoid **authority overlaps** that arise if two or more individuals or organizational units have the authority to perform the same activity. Consider the problems encountered by a large computer firm that did not have a clear scalar chain for hiring new employees. Each division manager had the authority to make job offers. Often, job candidates interviewed with two divisions of the company and received competing offers. This not only created a poor impression of the company but also increased hiring costs as candidates pitted one division against another. The scalar principle also helps management avoid **authority gaps** that can arise when authority has not been assigned for specific activities. Employees need to know, for example, to whom they should report a work-related injury or who is able to grant them permission to attend a seminar.

Finally, the principle of *unity of command* states that each subordinate should be accountable to only one superior.[16] The purpose of this principle is to concentrate authority over each employee so that workers do not face conflicting situations; thus, only one superior should assign activities, delegate authority, and hold a subordinate accountable for work accomplished.

Although these classical principles can serve as useful guides, they are not universally applicable to the delegating activity. They neglect an organization's occasional need to operate as a self-managing system. They tend to ignore the fact that people-to-people and people-to-work interactions must evolve out of the demands of the current situation.[17] They also ignore situations that require dual authority designs, such as a matrix structure; thus, there are cases in which management should violate these classical principles. (See "A Closer Look: Delegation.")

Decentralization of Authority

Some managers delegate authority extensively, others hardly at all. The extent to which formal authority is concentrated within the hierarchy of an organization determines its degree of **centralization.**[18] **Decentralization** exists when authority is diffused throughout an organization.[19] In the utility companies described earlier in this chapter, for example, hiring authority was centralized at the company in which the president approved the hiring of all new employees. In the second company, however, these decisions were made by members of the human resources department. The second company, thus, has a more decentralized structure. In practice, all organizations are somewhere between the two extremes of absolute centralization and absolute decentralization.

Decentralization: Its Nature and Importance

At the extreme, absolute centralization exists when authority is concentrated at a single, central point in the organization. A highly centralized organization is typically designed so that all important organizational decisions are made at a high level in the organization (see Figure 11.6A). Upper-level managers or advisers to the institutional level make the decisions considered important and provide directives for lower-level organization members to follow; thus a decision to adopt a merit pay system would be made at the top, with lower-level managers ordered to implement the plan.

With decentralization, authority is pushed down to the lowest possible hierarchical level (see Figure 11.6B). In a highly decentralized organization, authority is spread throughout the organization both horizontally and vertically. Very-low-level managers and nonmanagers are expected to

A CLOSER LOOK

Delegation: Dance to the Music or Pay the Piper

Delegating is one of the areas in which new managers are the weakest. It requires a clear understanding of the task at hand, the ability to communicate your expectations, and the skill to follow up on the task once it has been delegated.[1]

Busy managers must learn to delegate if they are to capitalize on the skills and knowledge of their subordinates, or else they will become immersed in details and unable to cope. According to Jack Smith, the director of support operations in the customer service division of Trans World Airline's information systems group, "People are motivated when they feel as if they are a part of the business and understand where they fit in. . . . We've found that sharing information and treating employees as business partners, not just workers, is highly motivating."[2]

In spite of its many advantages, though, many managers find it extremely difficult to delegate. One reason is that "a lot of people in . . . corporate life feel that delegating is an admission that there's something they can't do."[3] Delegation should be added to the list of important tasks that a manager does well. According

to Peter Drucker, "The greatest delegator was Franklin D. Roosevelt who, 'did' an absolute minimum."[4]

Delegation must be done well or the consequences can be devastating. Poor delegation can lead to legal, moral, political, and professional shambles, as people learned from the Iran-Contra affair, which derailed Ronald Reagan's presidency and the lives of many other people. Reagan conducted his administration according to his belief that "there's no limit to what you can do if you don't mind who gets the credit."[5] He recommended to managers: "Surround yourself with the best people you can find, delegate authority, and don't interfere as long as the policy you've decided upon is being carried out."[6] Even before the scandal emerged, however, *Fortune* noted, "Critics fault Reagan for not wading deeply into the substance of decision-making. . . . Management experts caution corporate leaders against disdaining detail to the extent Reagan does."[7]

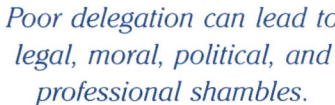

Poor delegation can lead to legal, moral, political, and professional shambles.

Things obviously went wrong for Reagan. According to Drucker, this outcome could have been anticipated because Reagan made "one of the most common but also most unforgiving management mistakes—[he] confused delegation of authority with abdication of responsibility."[8] For delegation to be effective, the delegatee must keep the delegator complete-

ly informed. One of the things that made Roosevelt such an effective delegator is that he required regular reports and upward responsibility. Reagan, however, allowed—and, in some cases, possibly required—his delegates to keep him in the dark. The results for Reagan, his administration, and the country were catastrophic.

1. D. C. Egelston (November 1986), How to manage a staff, *Business Week Careers*, 107.
2. *Ibid.*
3. John Sears, Ronald Reagan's former campaign manager, as quoted in A. R. Dowd (15 September 1986), What managers can learn from manager Reagan, *Fortune*, 35.
4. P. F. Drucker (24 March 1987), Management lessons of Irangate, *The Wall Street Journal*, 32.
5. Ronald Reagan as quoted in *Fortune* (15 September 1986), 36.
6. *Fortune*, 33.
7. *Fortune*, 35, 38.
8. Drucker, 32.

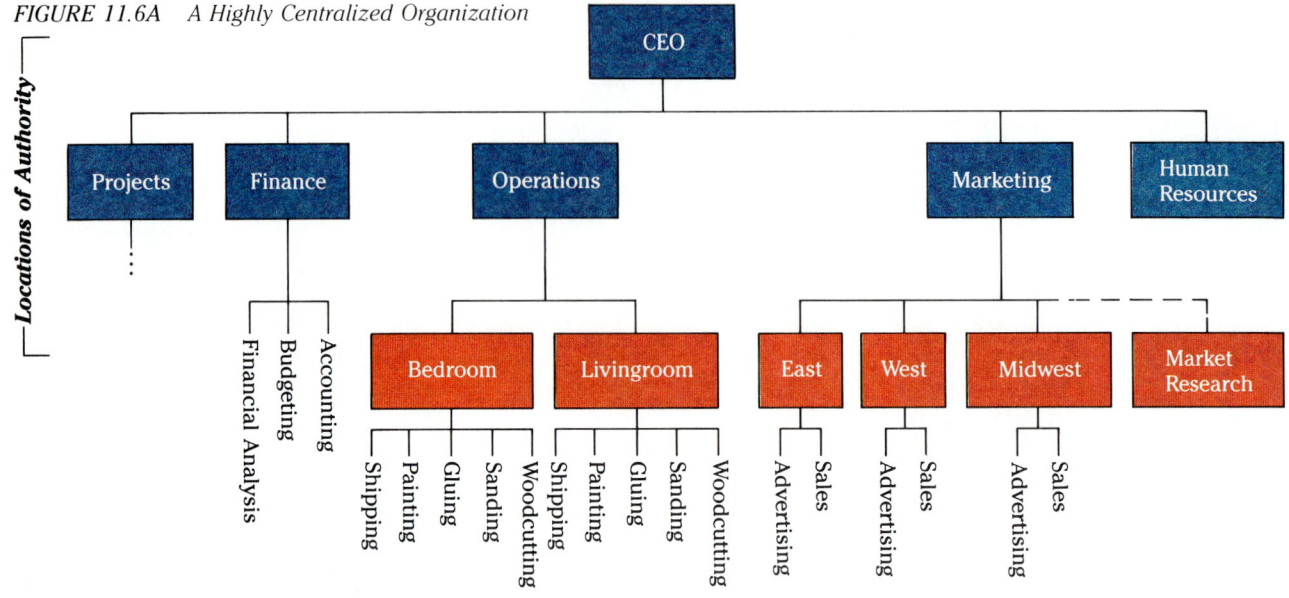

FIGURE 11.6A   *A Highly Centralized Organization*

make important decisions that pertain to their organizational units. In a decentralized organization, the decision to implement a merit pay system could be made within a single unit or department.

People often confuse decentralization of authority with delegation of authority or participation. *Decentralization* refers to the extent to which, by design, authority is spread throughout an organization and, thus, characterizes the organization's structure. *Delegation* is the process through which authority is transferred, thus enabling an organization to become increasingly decentralized. Like delegation, *participation* also involves a distribution of authority. In participation, though, superiors and subordinates make decisions together, whereas, in delegation, superiors transfer authority to subordinates so that they can make decisions independently.[20]

Organizations vary in the degree to which their work units, departments, and divisions are decentralized.[21] In fact, organizational units need varying degrees of centralization and decentralization to accommodate differences in the work they perform, the environments with which they have to deal, and so on. Reporting of on-the-job accident rates to the Occupational Safety and Health Administration (OSHA) usually needs to be centralized to facilitate effective, efficient reporting of inquiry statistics. Responsibility for the prevention of accidents, however, is often best decentralized to allow better control over hazardous situations. Before determining whether an organization or organizational unit should be made more decentralized, managers must first ascertain its current level of centralization. The questionnaire in Figure 11.7 shows some of the criteria for determining various degrees of centralization. The higher the score, the greater the centralization of authority.

Every organization needs an appropriate degree of decentralization to cope with the demands of its external environment, to coordinate activities within its formal structure, to do its particular kind of work, and

FIGURE 11.6B   *A Highly Decentralized Organization*

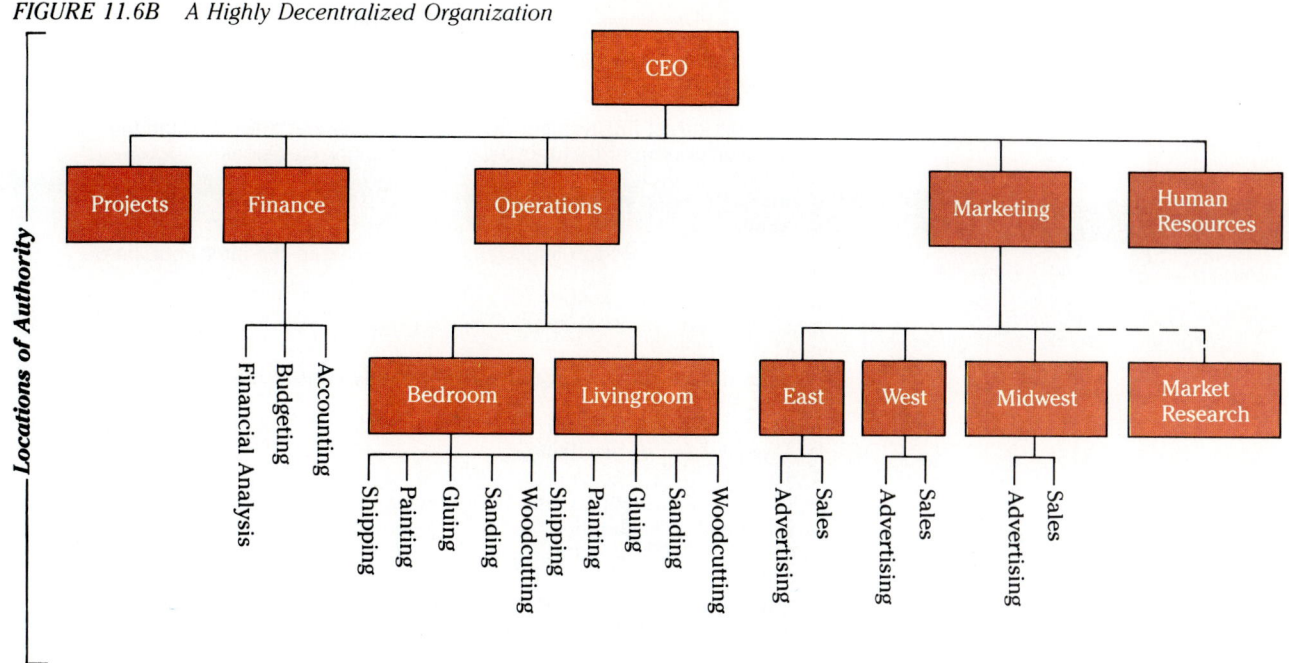

to manage the attitudes and capabilities of its members. The appropriate degree of decentralization enables an organization to:

- React in a timely fashion to changes in the external environment
- Deal with complex combinations of business activities
- Cope with organizational growth and change
- Place those most familiar with the work in positions to manage it
- Relieve managers of information and decision overload
- Motivate and improve the organization's human resources

Environmental uncertainty, turbulence, and organizational growth bring with them an increasing need for an organization to collect and process information. A decentralized structure allows a greater number of workers to monitor and react to these environmental conditions—more individuals have the authority to interpret and to make decisions on behalf of the organization. Decentralization is not a universally preferable way to design an organization's authority system, however. There are a great many reasons why centralization of authority may be a preferable arrangement in some cases. For example, under stable environmental conditions, centralization can let managers exercise needed control over organizational activities. The concentration of authority in the hands of a few organization members, as envisioned in Fayol's centralization, unity of command, and unity of direction principles, can help bring about consistency of operations, because only a limited number of people are providing direction to the organization. Military organizations operate this way out of necessity.

Managers must find the best match between the degree of decentralization and their organization's external and internal environments. The challenge facing managers is to balance the advantages of decentralization without losing the coordination, integration, and control advantages provided by centralization.

FIGURE 11.7   The Measurement of Centralization

Circle your response to each of the following items as they apply to the organization in question.

1. How much direct involvement does top management have in gathering the information input that they will use in making decisions?
   a. none   d. a great deal
   b. little   e. a very great deal
   c. some

2. To what degree does top management participate in the interpretation of the information input?
   a. 0–20%   d. 61–80%
   b. 21–40%   e. 81–100%
   c. 41–60%

3. To what degree does top management directly control the execution of the decision?
   a. 0–20%   d. 61–80%
   b. 21–40%   e. 81–100%
   c. 41–60%

For Questions 4 through 10, use the following responses:
   a. very great   d. little
   b. great   e. none
   c. some

4–10. How much discretion does the typical first-line supervisor have over
   4. establishing his or her unit's budget?
   5. determining how his or her unit's performance will be evaluated?
   6. hiring and firing personnel?
   7. personnel rewards (i.e., salary increases, promotions)?
   8. purchasing of equipment and supplies?
   9. establishing a new project or program?
   10. how work exceptions are to be handled?

Scoring: For all items, a = 1, b = 2, c = 3, d = 4, e = 5. Add up the score for all ten items. The sum of the item scores is the degree of centralization (out of a possible 50). Scores of 40 or above indicate high centralization; of 20 or below very low centralization (i.e., decentralization).

Source: S. P. Robbins (1983), *Organization theory: The structure and design of organizations,* Englewood Cliffs, NJ: Prentice-Hall, 88.

Determinants of Appropriate Decentralization

As you probably know by now, there is no one best way to accomplish a particular goal in management. There is no one best degree of decentralization for every organization, its units and various situations. There is no easy way to determine precisely the ideal level of decentralization for an organization. There are, however, several factors that managers should consider when designing their organization's authority system. Table 11.1 summarizes the conditions under which centralization and decentralization of authority are likely to be observed.

The External Environment   Decentralization is well suited to uncertain and rapidly changing external environments. The unpredictability of such environments demands that organizations acquire and process considerable amounts of information rapidly. Furthermore, they must respond quickly and appropriately to that information. Decentralization allows an organization to avoid the delays and information and decision overloads that would occur if all information had to be collected, analyzed, and responded to at a central source of authority. For example,

TABLE 11.1 *The Decentralization Decision*

Conditions	Appropriate Matches	
	Centralized	Decentralized
1. The External Environment		
Stability	Stable	Unstable
Uncertainty	Certain	Uncertain
2. The Organization		
Strategy	Narrow	Diverse
History/culture	Closed	Open
Growth rate	Slow	Rapid
Change rate	Slow	Rapid
Size	Small–med.	Large
Complexity	Simple	Complex
3. The Work		
Decision costs/risks	High	Low
Technology	Routine	Nonroutine
Task interdependence	Low	High
4. The People		
Upper managers—willing to "let go"	No	Yes
—confidence in lower managers	Low	High
Lower managers—managerial abilities	Low	High
—training needs	Low	High
—control desires	Low	High
—motivation needed	Low	High

authority must be decentralized in a fire brigade battling a blaze. Each group of firefighters working a particular part of a fire must be able to assess the needs of that location and have the authority to respond quickly. The fire chief would be overloaded if he or she retained all authority for all decisions, and the firefighters would be endangered if they could not react quickly when necessary.

The Organization Various features of an organization influence decisions about decentralization. The strategy pursued by an organization should influence the type of authority system that it creates. A strategy of product diversification, for example, dictates a need for decentralization, because the complexity of doing business in many markets would overwhelm a single manager. The history and culture of an organization tend to influence the level of decentralization as well. For example, organizations that grow from family ownership, such as the Ford Motor Company, are relatively centralized. So, too, are firms that have experienced slow growth under a strong leader. In contrast, organizations formed through acquisition and consolidations, as well as those that have grown rapidly, tend to be more decentralized.

Size and complexity also affect decentralization decisions. The larger an organization, the more it needs decentralization. Size eventually overwhelms an individual manager's span of control, and lower-level managers must take over some of the organizational decisions. Likewise, the more complex an organization, the more it needs decentralization. Regardless of its size, a complex organization needs decentralization to deal with its wide variety of organizational groups and types of decisions. Large and complex organizations, such as Procter & Gamble or IBM, need especially high levels of decentralization.

An organization's history and culture influence its level of decentralization. For example, Henry Ford's Motor Company is relatively centralized.

The Work The nature of the task is also relevant to decentralization. Some tasks are simply better performed under centralization, some under decentralization. Those that involve considerable interdependence, such as delivering a baby with a caesarean operation, are better suited to decentralization because it allows more careful monitoring of the work at a "local" level. The same is true for tasks that involve considerable uncertainty and nonroutine technologies and, thus, require frequent consultation, advice, or direction. For these reasons, research and development disciplines are usually quite decentralized. In contrast, routine and nonambiguous tasks, such as converting taconite pellets to ingots or rolled steel, are quite well suited to centralization, in which decision making is handled higher in the organization.

The People The right degree of decentralization for a particular organization is influenced as well by the characteristics of its managers. Upper-level managers are fully in charge under centralization; lower-level managers take over under decentralization. Decentralization is unlikely to occur, therefore, unless upper-level managers are willing to release some of their authority to and have confidence in the abilities of lower-level managers. Of course, decentralization is not appropriate if lower-level managers do not have the necessary abilities or motivation to make the required decisions. Through decentralization, however, lower-level managers can learn how to make these decisions. In fact, unless an organization is prepared to recruit externally for upper-level managers, at least some degree of decentralization is necessary if the organization is to develop a supply of highly skilled managers for the future.

The potential psychological effects of decentralization on lower-level managers should not be overlooked. To the extent that these managers like to exercise control over their work, they find decentralization satisfying. When employees' needs for control are met, they are likely to complete their work quickly and come to work regularly. There is also ample evidence that decentralization often improves the quality of the decisions that people make because it improves their motivation.

Decentralization can also pose disadvantages for lower-level managers. It places major responsibilities and the worries and burdens associated with this work directly on their shoulders. The result may be longer hours and more intense work, often increasing the amount of stress that workers experience.

Managers should take all of these considerations into account when making decentralization decisions. Often these factors point to the same conclusion, making the manager's task easier, but when signals are mixed, the decentralization issue becomes difficult. At that point, managers have to weigh the importance of each factor, as shown in Table 11.1, to arrive at a balanced decision.

Controls on Decentralization

As you have seen, the internal operations of many organizations are inefficient because managers are reluctant to delegate and decentralize. In addition, many managers centralized their authority system all the more tightly in reaction to those very conditions—uncertainty and turbulence—

that call for decentralization. To combat these problems, many organizations have found ways to decentralize and still maintain control over decision making through formalization and personal specialization.

Formalization   **Formalization** is the degree to which the norms of an organization are explicitly formulated.[22] Although the norms of an organization may be well developed and remain unwritten, most organization scholars agree that a higher degree of formalization is achieved when rules, procedures, instructions, and major organizational communications are contained in written documents, such as rule manuals and codes of conduct.[23] Many employees encounter this formalization when they receive their organization's handbook, which tries to control their behavior by defining members' rights and obligations.

In many organizations, decentralization of authority and formalization accompany one another. As managers delegate authority to people in lower organizational levels, they create a set of rules, policies, and procedures to guide the decisions made by lower-level employees; thus, decentralization gives a supervisor of reservation agents at Northwest Airlines considerable authority to make decisions about special customer requests. The supervisor must follow a set of formal, written guidelines when making these decisions, however. Formalization, thus, becomes a way of controlling the decision making of organization members.

Formalization also helps managers achieve consistency, coordination, economy, and standardization in their organization's operations. By prescribing expectations for employees, an organization can reduce variability and take steps to assure that decisions are being made within an acceptable range. For example, zone managers at Ford Motor Company must decide when to honor customer requests for car repair work beyond that normally covered by the car's warranty. Although zone managers are encouraged to use personal judgment in making their decisions, Ford provides guidelines so that decisions from zone to zone will not be dramatically different.

Specialists learn strong work skills and acceptable behavior in educational and apprenticeship programs.

Personal Specialization   **Personal specialization** (also referred to as *professionalization*) refers to the level of education, training, and experience of employees. Specialists are both willing and able to make decisions based on their professional training and expertise. A skilled teacher, a master carpenter, a physician, and a diemaker are all specialists with strong work skills and norms of acceptable behavior acquired through educational and apprenticeship programs. Organizations that rely on personal specialization to guide the decision processes need less formalization in order to achieve control.[24]

Many organizations rely on personal specialization to control delegated authority. For example, law firms rely on professional training to guide lawyers' job performance and their exercise of the authority given to them by the firm. Managers can trust that selected employees will use organizational authority appropriately and delegate it successfully if they are technically competent, guided by professional norms, and intellectually capable of diagnosing and solving task-related problems. Under such conditions, managers can create organizations that operate effectively and consistently, even with a decentralized authority system.

Authority, Delegation, and Decentralization in Review

Organization members are able to influence others in the organization to the extent that they have the power and authority to do so. Authority provides individuals (and groups) the right to influence others. Merely having the authority given to them by their organization may not be enough, however, for managers to influence subordinates. The ability to exert authority usually requires managers to develop an adequate interpersonal power base that adds to the legitimate power base derived from their position in the organization's hierarchy of authority. This is done by incorporating other sources of power, such as reward, coercion, and expertise.

Organization members continually try to influence one another as they pursue organizational goals. Organizations try to control these influence patterns by creating formal authority systems. There are three views of the types and sources of authority. The classical view holds that the people at the top of an organization's hierarchy have the right to influence members at lower levels, resulting in a downward flow of authority. The acceptance view maintains that authority flows upward, because employees must accept managerial influence as legitimate before they will comply. The situational view proposes that authority is neither up nor down. Instead, the question of who has authority depends on the characteristics of the specific situation. The one belief shared by all three views is that managers must see to it that employees perceive managerial directives to be legitimate. If they do, then workers tend to comply, in part because they have learned to do so. The type of compliance—or lack of it—that managers can expect to receive can be predicted according to the types of influence the managers used.

The authority system that managers design defines their organization's authority relationships. Line authority is a command authority that follows an organization's vertical chain of command. Organization members must comply with the people above them in the hierarchy who have the right to issue directives. Staff authority is an advisory authority that allows managers to influence through expert knowledge and experience. Functional authority is a command authority over a set of functionally related activities. Unlike the vertical flow of line authority, however, functional authority can also flow horizontally and diagonally within an organization.

Managers receive some of their line, staff, or functional authority because someone has transferred that authority to them through delegation. Although delegators may transfer authority and responsibility for certain tasks to others, the delegators remain ultimately responsible for the delegated activities. Delegating is a way to cope with large and complex workloads, but there are both managers and subordinates who resist delegation. Organizations must overcome this resistance by encouraging managers to develop, by training employees, and by providing the resources employees need to meet new challenges.

The amount of delegation that occurs in an organization determines its degree of decentralization. A highly decentralized authority system delegates authority to the points in an organization's hierarchy where decisions are implemented. Decentralization is appropriate for the high levels of environmental and task-induced uncertainty that accompany nonroutine technologies. An organization should determine the level of decentralization appropriate for its specific needs by examining the external environment; the history, size, and complexity of the organization; the work performed in the organization; and the people who do the work.

Essentially, authority, delegation, and decentralization are the means by which managers try to control the powerful effects of influence in organizations. Whether this influence is exercised in the direction intended depends, in part, on how well the authority system has been designed to match the characteristics of an organization.

Notes

1. The problems associated with defining power and the major approaches are discussed by: A. T. Cobb (1984), An episodic model of power: Toward an integration of theory and research, *Academy of Management Review*, 9, 482–93.

2. W. G. Astley and P. S. Sachdeva (1984), Structural sources of intraorganizational power: A theoretical synthesis, *Academy of Management Review*, 9, 104–13; J. R. P. French, Jr. and B. Raven (1959), The bases of social power, in D. Cartwright, ed., *Studies of social power*, Ann Arbor, MI: Institute for Social Research; D. J. Hickson, C. R. Hinings, C. A. Lee, R. E. Schneck, and J. M. Pennings (1971), A strategic contingencies' theory of intraorganizational power, *Administrative Science Quarterly*, 16, 216–29; G. R. Salancik and J. Pfeffer (1977), Who gets power—and how they hold on to it: A strategic-contingency model of power, *Organizational Dynamics*, 5, 3–21.

3. Hickson, et al., 1971; Salancik and Pfeffer, 1977.

4. M. Weber (1947), *The theory of social and economic organization*, Glencoe, IL: Free Press.

5. C. Barnard (1938), *The functions of the executive*, Cambridge, MA: Harvard University Press.

6. Barnard, 1938; H. A. Simon (1976), *Administrative behavior*, 3rd ed., New York: Macmillan.

7. D. Mechanic (1964), Sources of power of lower participants in complex organizations, in W. W. Cooper, H. J. Leavitt, and M. W. Shelly II, eds., *New perspectives in organization research*, New York: John Wiley and Sons, 136–49.

8. Executive secretary: A new rung on the corporate ladder (2 April 1986), *Business Week*, 74–75.

9. J. Sculley with J. A. Byrne (1987), *Odyssey: Pepsi to Apple*, New York: Harper & Row.

10. A. Etzioni (1965), Organizational control structure, in J. C. March, ed., *Handbook of organizations*, Chicago: Rand McNally, 650–77; A. Etzioni (1986), Leaders' control and members' compliance, in M. T. Matteson and J. M. Ivancevich, eds., *Management classics*, 3rd ed., Plano, TX: Business Publication, Inc., 227–33 (reprinted from *A comparative analysis of complex organizations*, 1961).

11. H. Stieglitz (1974), On concepts of corporate structure, *The Conference Board Record*, 11, 7–13.

12. C. R. Leana (1986), Predictors and consequences of delegation, *Academy of Management Journal*, 29, 754–74; F. A. Heller (1971), *Managerial decision making: A study of leadership styles and power sharing among senior managers*, London: Tavistock.

13. J. Sculley with J. A. Byrne, 1987.

14. B. M. Staw and J. Ross (1987), Behavior and escalation situations: Antecedents, prototypes and solutions, in L. L. Cummings and B. M. Staw, eds., *Research in organizational behavior*, vol. 9, Greenwich, CT: JAI Press 39–78; B. M. Staw, L. E. Sandelands, and J. E. Dutton (1981), Threat-rigidity effects in organizational behavior: A multilevel analysis, *Administrative Science Quarterly*, 26, 501–24.

15. W. Isaacson and M. Duffy (27 July 1987), Passing the buck: How the president's men attempted to evade accountability, *Time*, 8–9.

16. H. Fayol (1916), *General and industrial management*, London: Pitman. (The English translation came in 1949.)

17. M. P. Follett (1930), Some discrepancies in leadership theory and practice, in H. C. Metcalf, ed., *Business leadership*, London: Pitman; Salancik and Pfeffer, 1977.

18. R. H. Hall (1982), *Organizations*, Englewood Cliffs, NJ: Prentice-Hall; J. Hage and M. Aiken (1967), Program change and organizational properties: A comparative analysis, *American Journal of Sociology*, 72, 503–19.

19. C. R. Leana (1987), Power relinquishment versus power sharing: Theoretical clarification and empirical comparison of delegation and participation, *Journal of Applied Psychology*, 72, 228–33; D. M. Schweiger and C. R. Leana (1986), Participation in decision making, in E. Locke, ed., *Generalizing from laboratory to field settings: Research findings from industrial-organizational psychology, organization behavior, and human resource management*, Boston: D.C. Heath, 147–66; E. A. Locke and D. M. Schweiger (1979), Participation in decision-making: One more look, in B. M. Staw, ed., *Research in organizational behavior*, vol. 1, Greenwich, CT: JAI Press, 265–340.

20. Leana, 1987.

21. R. H. Hall (1962), Intraorganizational structural variation: Applications of the bureaucratic model, *Administrative Science Quarterly*, 7, 295–308; E. Litwak (1961), Models of organizations which permit conflict, *American Journal of Sociology*, 76, 177–84; P. R. Lawrence and J. W. Lorsch (1969), *Organization and environment*, Homewood, IL: Irwin.

22. Hall, 1982.

23. D. Pugh, D. J. Hickson, C. R. Hinings, and C. Turner (1968), Dimensions of organizational structure, *Administrative Science Quarterly*, 12, 65–105.

24. P. M. Blau (1970), Decentralization in bureaucracies, in M. N. Zald, ed., *Power in organizations*, Nashville, TN: Vanderbilt University Press; J. Hage and M. Aiken (1967), Relationship of centralization to other structural properties, *Administrative Science Quarterly*, 12, 72–91.

Key Terms

influence
interpersonal power
strategic-contingency model of
  power

authority
classical authority theory
acceptance view of authority
situational view of authority

authority relationships
line authority
staff authority
compulsory staff consultation
concurring authority
functional authority
delegation

authority overlaps
authority gaps
centralization
decentralization
formalization
personal specialization

Issues for Review and Discussion

1. Define influence, authority, and power and explain why organizations must manage each.
2. Compare and contrast the classical view of authority, the acceptance view, and the situational view.
3. Discuss the different means by which organization members gain the ability to influence organizational behavior.
4. Define delegation of authority and discuss the delegation process.
5. What issues should managers consider when deciding how to distribute authority through an organization's formal structure?
6. What forces do (and should) influence the degree of decentralization within an organization's authority system?
7. What role is played by formalization and personal specialization?

Suggested Readings

Barnard, C. I. (1986). The theory of authority. In Matteson, M. T. and Ivancevich, J. M., eds. *Management classics*, 3rd ed., Plano, TX: Business Publication, Inc., 211–19. (Reprinted from *The functions of the executive*, 1938.)

Etzioni, A. (1986). Leaders' control and members' compliance. In Matteson, M. T. and Ivancevich, I. M., eds. *Management classics*, 3rd ed., Plano, TX: Business Publication, Inc., 227–33. (Reprinted from *A comparative analysis of complex organizations*, 1961.)

Kanter, R. M. (1979). Power failure in management circuits. *Harvard Business Review*, 57, 65–75.

Kotter, J. P. (1985). *Power and influence*. New York: Free Press; McGee, G. (1988). A review of *Power and influence*. In Pierce, J. L. and Newstrom, J. W. eds. *The manager's bookshelf: A mosaic of contemporary views*. New York: Harper & Row, 158–67.

Nord, W. R. (1978). Dreams of humanization and the realities of power. *Academy of Management Review*, 3, 674–79.

Porter, L. W., Allen, R. W., and Angle, H. L. (1981). The politics of upward influence in organizations. In Cummings, L. L. and Staw, B. M., eds. *Research in organizational behavior*, vol. 3, Greenwich, CT: JAI Press, 109–50.

CASE *Leave of Absence*

By Joseph W. Leonard of Miami University and John Thanopoulos of the University of Akron

Custom Scales, Inc. (CSI) was formally established in St. Louis in 1964 as a manufacturer of industrial scales. During that year, Bill Ewing's small operation (Ewing's Scales) was taken over by a local group of bankers, who offered him 12.5 percent of the stock of CSI; the position of chief executive officer; and a sizeable salary in return for his business, which had been a family concern. He owned 100 percent of it, had no loans, and had a significant number of patented designs that were making unique inroads in the Benelux (Belgium, Netherlands, Luxembourg) markets. In fact, in 1963, his brother Steve, who was living in Brussels, sold the Ewing's Scales' entire production, almost $250,000 worth of industrial scales. At that point, Bill Ewing's operation employed a total of sixteen workers, plus his wife and sister-in-law, for general administration and accounting.

CSI proved to be an engineering and marketing success. Over the years, CSI increased sales by almost 20 percent annually and expanded both in the domestic and foreign markets, reaching sales of over $16 million in 1985; however, CSI never developed a management system necessary for a corporation of its size. Most practices and policies continued to be loosely administered, with most departments' growing independently and often instituting conflicting objectives. CSI's key personnel and their respective positions are presented in Figure 11A.

In January 1985, almost 60 percent of CSI's 424 employees were unionized by the International Brotherhood of Engineering workers (Local 76). The remainder was made up of salaried administrative and engineering employees, along with nonunion forepersons and technicians. Basically, all employees received the same fringe benefits package (insurance, vacation, sick leave, and so on), although the company had a less closely supervised atmosphere for the nonunion employees (coffee breaks, time off, no time clock punching, and so on).

The Situation

On August 9, 1981, Frank Capek (then age 28) was hired as an engineering technician at pay grade 4. Exactly two weeks later, Arnold Parker, 26, was hired also as a grade 4 engineering technician. Both men were employed in parallel positions within CSI's engineering department.

In January of 1983, Frank's wife and daughter were involved in a serious automobile accident. As a result of his family's mishap and in order to be of assistance during that period of suffering, Frank took all of his sick leave. Then, he exhausted his two-week vacation and, finally, he asked for a thirty-day leave of absence without pay. Under the circumstances, this leave of absence was granted, and Frank returned to his post in the first week of March after his wife and daughter had recovered.

In July 1983, Patrick Kelley was hired by CSI as engineering manager. During the following two years, Patrick had ample opportunities to evaluate Frank and Arnold and was convinced that both men were of equal talent and work ability. Furthermore, he was aware of the unfortunate accident that Frank's family had experienced, but he was not aware of the leave of absence that Frank had taken in February 1983.

Within the engineering department, two grade 5 positions were about to open. The first—on June 1, 1985 —was due to the resignation of Karen Bednarski, and the second—on September 1, 1985—was due to the retirement of Michael Anderson. Patrick concluded that Frank and Arnold were excellent choices for these positions. Since no promotion policies were established in CSI, the engineering department decided to use seniority as the only determining factor of promotion (grade 5 paid about 15 percent above grade 4).

Patrick Kelley decided to handle the promotion issue by himself. On June 9, 1985, he called the personnel department. Since William Young was extending his weekend by one day

FIGURE 11A   *Key Personnel*

Name	Position	Age	Years with CSI	Education
Bill Ewing	CEO	61	27	B.S.M.E.
Doug Gilbert	Production Manager	51	16	B.S.I.E.
Patrick Kelley	Engineering Manager	44	2	B.S.M.E.
Steve Ewing	Sales Manager	58	24	B.S.B.A.
Steve Spangler	Treasurer	36	3	M.B.A., CPA
William Young	Personnel Director	49	14	M.S.

(he often did this), Patrick asked James Marshall for some specific information. He wanted to know the exact dates and at which pay grades his nine technicians had joined the company.

Half an hour later, James called Patrick and gave him a complete list with names, ages, dates of entrance at CSI, and respective grades. The next morning the engineering manager, confident that he knew what he was doing, called both Frank and Arnold into his office and said, "As you can probably guess, I need a new grade 5 technician on July 1 to take Karen's place. She is leaving us at the end of this month. Since you have both been good employees of equal ability, I will follow strict seniority and promote you, Frank, on July 1 and you, Arnold, on September 1 to replace Michael Anderson, who is retiring." Neither Arnold nor Frank expressed any feelings about the promotions, and the discussion was quickly diverted to a drafting issue.

After discussing the matter that evening with his personal friend and lawyer, Jane Gunton, Arnold decided that he was (as Jane said) "getting the wrong end of the stick." The next morning, Arnold entered Patrick's office and adamantly complained that he had seniority. "I like Frank; he's a nice guy, but I have seniority over him; he took thirty days off when Sarah and his daughter nearly died when a drunk ran them off the road in a snowstorm." Before Arnold could explain his case in detail, Patrick interrupted him by saying, "Settle down, Arnold, I admit I didn't know about the thirty days. Let me check it out with William Young. I'll let you know by noon tomorrow at the latest." Seeing that it was not wise to prolong the conversation at that time,

Arnold left the engineering manager's office.

The engineering manager immediately went to William Young's office and closed the door behind him (so that James could not hear). Patrick explained the problem, and the two managers openly discussed the situation, quickly agreeing to the facts. William then replied, "Pat, it's your problem, not mine. You'll have to make the ultimate decision." Patrick countered, "I can't. This is a personnel matter. What do you think Custom Scales pays you for, playing golf two or three times a week on company time?" William snapped back, "I'm not going to sit here and listen to that line. Just leave my office and make this your decision. Leave me out of this. I'll support you either way." The engineering manager stormed out muttering to himself as he drew a peculiar stare from James.

Patrick immediately called Arnold into his office and told him that Frank and he were both being promoted to grade 5 on July 1. Arnold said, "Fine," and considered the matter as closed. The next morning the engineering manager issued a memo to both Frank and Arnold confirming the July 1 date and sent two copies to accounting and a copy to personnel.

About one week later, Steve Spangler, the treasurer, called Patrick, stating, "You can't promote both men in July. You'll be overexpended on your payroll; we can't tolerate that." Patrick replied, "I'm in charge of engineering. I have to run my department and have to get the most work out of my employees; I'm sure you can figure out a way to please those beancounters from Ross and Pickering (CSI's audit firm). Besides, that's your problem, not mine." Patrick hung up before Steve had time to reply.

Bill Ewing was out of the country on a personal vacation when all of this took place. As was customary, Doug Gilbert, production manager, was left in charge of CSI in his absence. Doug became aware of the situation through a conversation with Spangler over lunch the next day (Friday). The following Monday morning, he summoned Patrick, Steve, and William for a meeting. Patrick half-heartedly apologized to both Steve and William but insisted that there must be an easy way out of the situation and pleaded that July 1 stand as a promotion date for both technicians. All four men expressed a desire to keep the word of the incident from spreading and not to let Bill Ewing find out. They agreed to meet and work out a solution over drinks around 5:30 at the nearby "Aqua-Gate Lounge."

Questions

1. What was the origin of this problem? How could it have been avoided?

2. Explore the issue of Patrick's responsibility in making this decision. What responsibility did William have? Was Steve acting within his authority?

3. How has the history of this company contributed to the confusion surrounding this affair?

4. Are the four managers involved acting responsibly in not telling the CEO about the situation? What might be gained by bringing it to his attention?

Organizational Design

Student Learning Objectives

After reading this chapter, you should be able to:

1. Understand the importance of structural, process, and contextual dimensions to organizational design.

2. Describe the differences among functional, divisional, hybrid, and matrix forms of organizational design.

3. Identify the three key managerial roles found in a matrix organization and discuss their purpose.

4. Relate the importance of the classical (bureaucratic) model to organizational design.

5. Name and discuss two behavioral models of organizational design.

6. Identify the major features of organic organizations.

7. Describe the relationship between each of the major contextual features and organizational design.

*P*icture two houses. In the first, there are very few windows and doors, many corners, and small rooms; furniture is everywhere, and the hallways are crowded. The second house is open and spacious. The walls and furniture do not restrict movement. It has been said that organizations are like houses; just as an architect designs the features of a house, managers design the features of an organization. Architects create a house design to meet the needs of the family that will live in it. Managers create an organizational design to meet the needs of an organization and its members. This chapter will discuss **organizational design,** which is the creation of an organization's structure and the systems that help the organization operate. The chapter will also look at the reasons managers design organizations the way that they do.

Organizational Dimensions

Much like the design of a house and the anatomy of the human body, organizations are multidimensional systems. Some of these dimensions concern the structure of an organization, some define its processes, and still others concern its contextual features. Together, the structure and process features of an organization (or organizational unit) define its overall design. The contextual features are the primary determinants of that design. The development of an organization's design is a major purpose of the organizing function of management.

Structure

Just as an architect designs the features of a house, a manager designs the features of an organization.

Like the physical structure of a house, **organizational structure** identifies and distinguishes the individual parts of an organization and ties these pieces together to define an integrated whole.[1] Organizational structure differs from the physical structure of a house, however, in that it encompasses more than inanimate characteristics of walls, doors, and windows. Organizational structure includes the interaction patterns that link people to people and people to work, and, unlike a house, structural dimensions of organizations frequently change and evolve.

The most important components of an organization's structure include the following:

- *Decentralization of authority*—the degree to which decision-making authority is spread throughout the organization as opposed to being concentrated (centralized) at the top
- *Formalization*—the extent to which the norms of the organization are set forth in written records, documents, and procedure manuals
- *Standardization*—the extent to which work activities are described in detail and performed uniformly throughout the organization
- *Task specialization*—the degree to which organizational work is divided into narrow tasks, with extensive division of labor
- *Person specialization* (professionalism)—the level of formal education, training, and experience needed by the occupants of various organizational roles

- *Complexity*—the number of specialized job types or subsystems within the organization, the number of levels in the organizational hierarchy, and the number of geographical locations from which the organization operates
- *Stratification*—the degree of status differences among individuals and groups within the organization
- *Configuration*—the shape of the organization's structure, including the number of hierarchical levels; the spans of control; and the ratios of managers to technical employees, support to operating personnel, and the like

Consider the organizational structure of Progressive Video Images. Because Cindy Mertes makes most of the decisions from the top of the organization, the company has a centralized structure. There is a high degree of formalization attained through the organization's employee handbook, which outlines the company's policies on hiring, firing, paying, retiring, and the like. The tasks performed at the company are standardized in a manual that specifies the procedures that PVI's staff should follow when converting movies to videotapes and custom editing videotapes. Tasks in each of the movie, video, and audio departments are highly specialized, with each piece of film or videotape passing from person to person through a series of steps in which it is dubbed, spliced, and so forth. The people are somewhat less specialized. Some of Cindy's employees have had formal education in electronics or related fields, but most of them have gained their experience and expertise on the job. The organization is not very complex, as there are only three hierarchical levels and the number of specialized job types is small. PVI is still a small concern, with little stratification and a simple configuration. Cindy is the boss, and there are several other managers, but she and the supervisors of each department heed the recommendations of subordinates, who feel free to criticize and offer suggestions.

The structure of Progressive Video Images may differ dramatically from its competitors, from organizations in other industries, or from the original structure Cindy gave it when she founded the company. This is because managers have choices available to them when considering decentralization, formalization, standardization, and other structural component issues. Because there is no one best structure for all situations, a wide variety of structures exists. Managers choose and combine them as necessary when creating structures to serve organizational needs. Even units within the same organization often have different structures. For example, although the maintenance department at Upjohn Pharmaceutical is characterized by high levels of centralization, formalization, standardization, and task specialization, the company's research and development groups tend to be decentralized and informal, with relatively little standardization.

Process

Another dimension of an organization's design concerns the systems created to deal with organizational processes, such as decision making, coordinating, and communicating. Consider the decision-making process, for example. As part of management's planning function, decision making is done regardless of an organization's design; however, organizational design influences how this process is executed. For example, will the systems created enable employees to participate in the decision-making process, or will managers merely hand down edicts already "set in stone"? The coordinating process, as discussed in Chapter 10, is part of management's organizing function and is used to coordinate jobs, departments, divisions, and hierarchical levels within an organization. The systems designed to facilitate this can differ substantially, however. For example, a coordination system can be personal (based on direct contact between managers and subordinates, task forces, and so on) or impersonal (relying on written rules, policies, and standard operating procedures). The communication process is an important part of the directing function (see Chapter 15), and communication takes place regardless of the organizational design; however, the systems created affect the nature of the preparation and exchange of information. For example, will a particular organizational design allow a worker to speak directly with the president of the company or must that employee make all requests and suggestions through supervisors?

There is no one best way to design coordination, decision-making, communication, or other organizational processes to meet an organization's goals. Managers must examine the needs of their organization and design these processes so that they are consistent with and support the structure of the organization and the context in which it operates.

Context

When architect Cynthia Lockwood designs a house, she creates a structure and the systems that take into account the characteristics of the family that will live in the house. How many children are there, for example? Does anyone in the family use a wheelchair? She also considers the weather in that location. A house to be built in Marquette, Michigan needs a structure capable of supporting tons of standing snow on its roof and an excellent heating system. Contrast this with a house designed for southern Texas that needs only marginal snow protection and heating but absolutely must have air conditioning. Similarly, the structure and process dimensions that define an organization's design should be appropriate for the **organizational context,** or circumstances and conditions, within which it operates. Contextual design influences will be discussed in more detail later in this chapter. For now, you should note that some important contextual considerations include an organization's:

- *Goals*—its reasons for being and the missions that managers hope to realize
- *Size*—the magnitude of operations and the number of people employed
- *Technology*—the techniques used to transform raw materials (inputs) into products or services (outputs)
- *External environment*—suppliers, customers, regulatory agencies, competitors, and the like
- *People*—the beliefs, values, motives, and needs of its members, and the size, homogeneity, and cohesion of its groups

As managers make decisions about the types of structure and processes they will use, they must match these factors with the context of their organization. If they succeed, they will create an appropriate and effective design that can contribute to organizational success.

Organizational Superstructures

In Chapter 10, you learned the ways managers organize individual tasks into jobs, jobs into larger units (such as work groups and departments), and these units into divisions. If this perspective were applied to a house, an observer would start from the ground up, examining the way nails hold boards together, how the boards define the rooms, and the pattern of rooms that combine to create the house. From a design perspective, however, architects work in the opposite direction. Cynthia Lockwood begins by thinking about the overall design of the house—a one-story ranch? a two-story colonial? a split-level?—and then focuses on the pieces that combine to form rooms.

Managers are the architects of an organization's design. They, too, begin with the overall design and work downward to the level of jobs and tasks. An organization's **superstructure** defines the division of activities at the top of the organizational hierarchy and, thus, provides the primary structural form of the organization.[2] Since the superstructure is used at the institutional level, it is the dominant approach for the grouping of organizational activities. The superstructure reflects managers' attempts to balance the efficient, effective operation of its internal environment and its strategic response to the external environment. An organization's superstructure also specifies who has the power and legitimacy to guide its operations.

There are several superstructure designs available to managers. Consider first some traditional designs based on functional, divisional, and hybrid arrangements, and then the more complex approach known as the matrix superstructure.

Traditional Superstructures

The three most common traditional superstructures are the functional, divisional, and hybrid. Each is an appropriate design for particular combinations of goal, technological, and environmental conditions.

Functional Superstructures In a **functional superstructure,** upper-level managers are organized around the basic organizational functions similar to the departmentalization-by-function approach adopted at lower levels. One group is in charge of operations, one is in charge of marketing, one is in charge of finance, and so forth. In a functional superstructure, managers group functionally similar activities together and then connect them with other homogeneous groups through a hierarchical network. The organization shown in Figure 12.1, for example, uses a functional superstructure to group together all marketing activities, such as market research, advertising, and sales. The coordination of any of these activities with those of other functional areas must be done at a

Research personnel need to be creative, must focus on long-range time horizons, and require an open environment with no more than a moderate amount of tension.

FIGURE 12.1   A Functional Superstructure

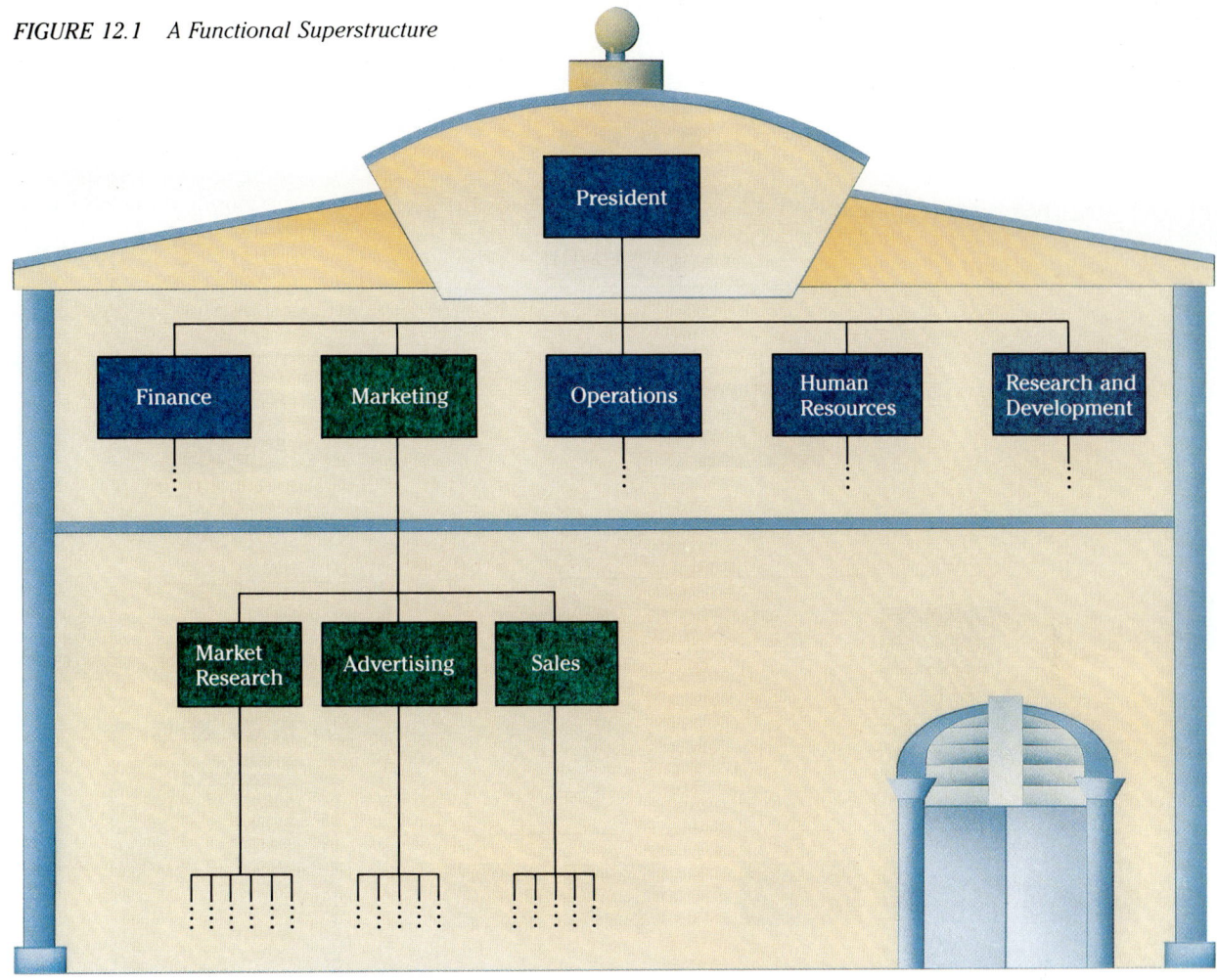

Note: The green portions identify the marketing functional group in the organizational superstructure.

higher level in the organization than if the functions were not separated by the structure.

The advantages noted in Chapter 10 for a functional approach to departmentalization also apply to a functional superstructure design. A functional arrangement is versatile; it is applicable regardless of size or position in the organizational hierarchy. Employees within a functional area are likely to have similar orientations to time, interpersonal relationships, values, and goals. This similarity promotes collaboration, specialization, economies of scale, efficiency, and quality *within* the functional area. When all of an organization's advertising experts are in the same group, for example, they can work together easily to generate creative ideas, negotiate better prices for advertising because of greater volume, and so on.

Likewise, the disadvantages of a functional superstructure are similar to those of functional departmentalization, most particularly in the tension it may create *between* units. An organization's research personnel, for example, need to be creative, must focus on long-range time horizons, and require an open environment with no more than a moderate amount of tension. Personnel in the organization's production department, on the

FIGURE 12.2 *A Territorial Divisional Superstructure*

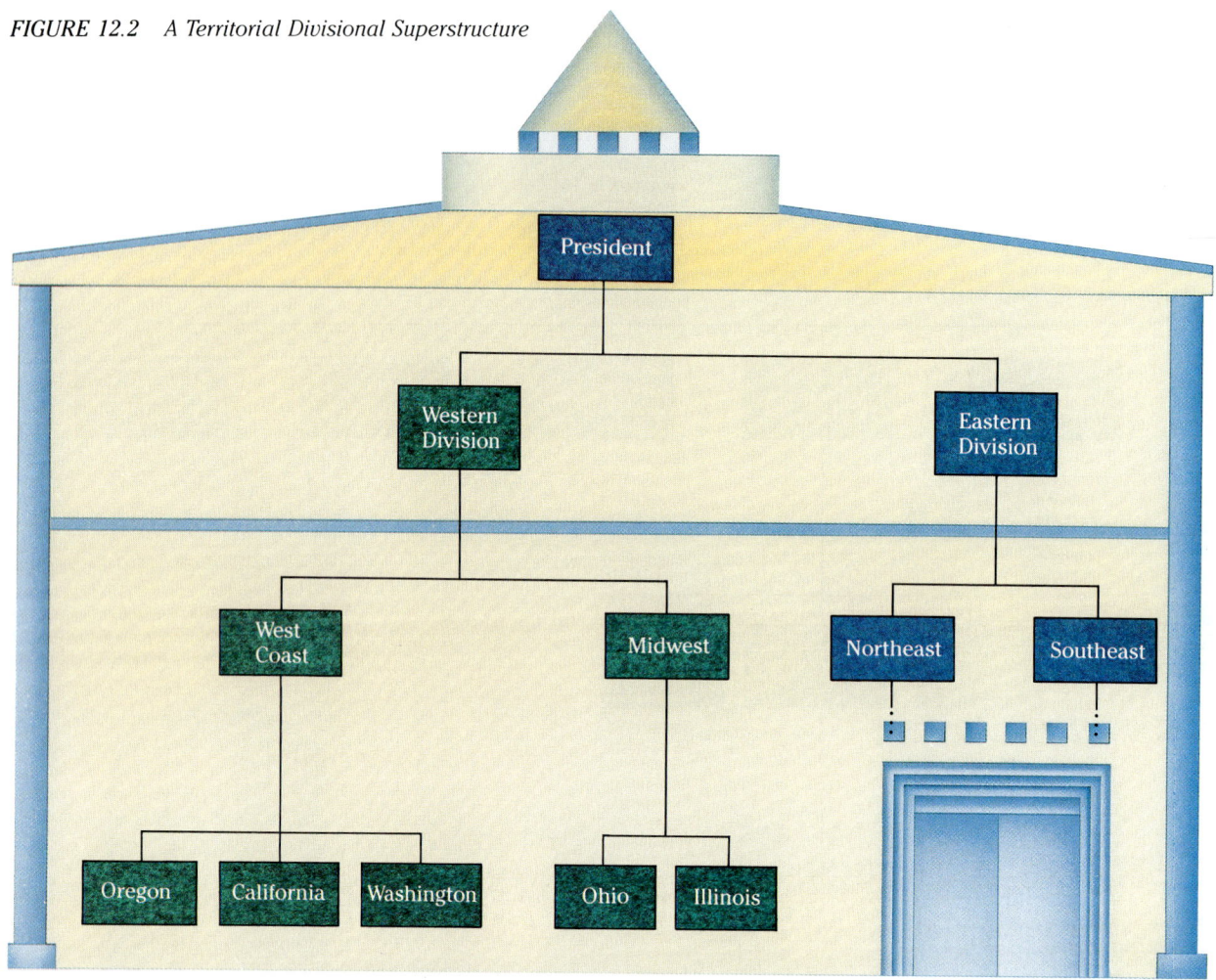

Note: The green portions identify the western division in the organizational superstructure.

other hand, have shorter time perspectives and goals centered on achieving immediately acceptable product quantity and quality. They thus may need a structure that emphasizes order, predictability, and control. Coordination of units in a functional superstructure can be complex, difficult, and complicated by the fact that members of various functional units often operate with different time, value, and goal orientations.

Divisional Superstructure When managers design an organization's superstructure according to *non*functional factors, such as territories, products, customer base, process, or projects, they create a **divisional superstructure.** Divisions most often created are product and territorial divisions, similar to the departmentalization approach for those groupings discussed in Chapter 10. Occasionally, divisional superstructures are also established on a customer/client basis. It is very rare, however, for a superstructure to be based solely on a process or project approach. These arrangements are usually reserved for use at lower levels of an organization. Figure 12.2 shows the superstructure of a retailing organization with operations in a number of different states. Figure 12.3 shows a product-based superstructure.

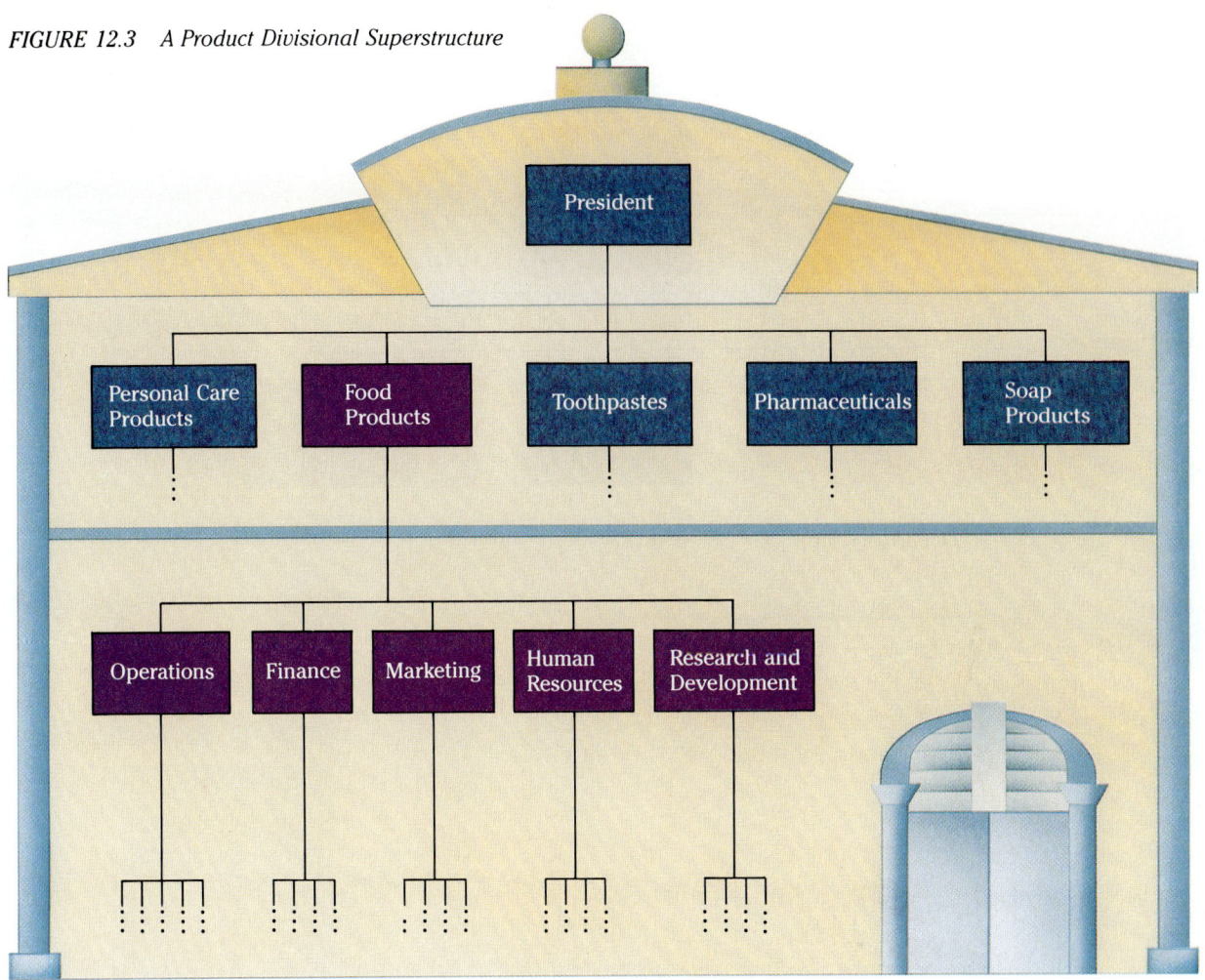

FIGURE 12.3   *A Product Divisional Superstructure*

President

Personal Care Products | Food Products | Toothpastes | Pharmaceuticals | Soap Products

Operations | Finance | Marketing | Human Resources | Research and Development

Note: The purple portions identify the food products division in the organizational superstructure.

One of the biggest advantages of a divisional superstructure design is that it can overcome both the inefficiencies caused by information overload and the bottlenecks that may affect upper-level managers in functional superstructures. For example, when chief executive officers are confronted with too much information to process, they tend to lose control over the internal operations of their organization and over some elements of strategic control. With a divisional superstructure, however, upper-level managers can divide the responsibility for internal and strategic control with divisional managers. For example, Michaelene Kelly, president of the bank shown in Figure 12.4, benefits from that firm's customer-based divisional superstructure. She uses input provided by the heads of the firm's personal, small business, and commercial divisions to focus on overall strategic issues. The three division heads take responsibility for strategic and operating issues within their own divisions; thus, internal control improves because day-to-day operating responsibilities are delegated to the divisions. The resulting reduction in demands placed on Michaelene allows her more time to manage strategic activities.[3]

A divisional superstructure lets managers exercise a high level of coordination within a division because those within a division usually

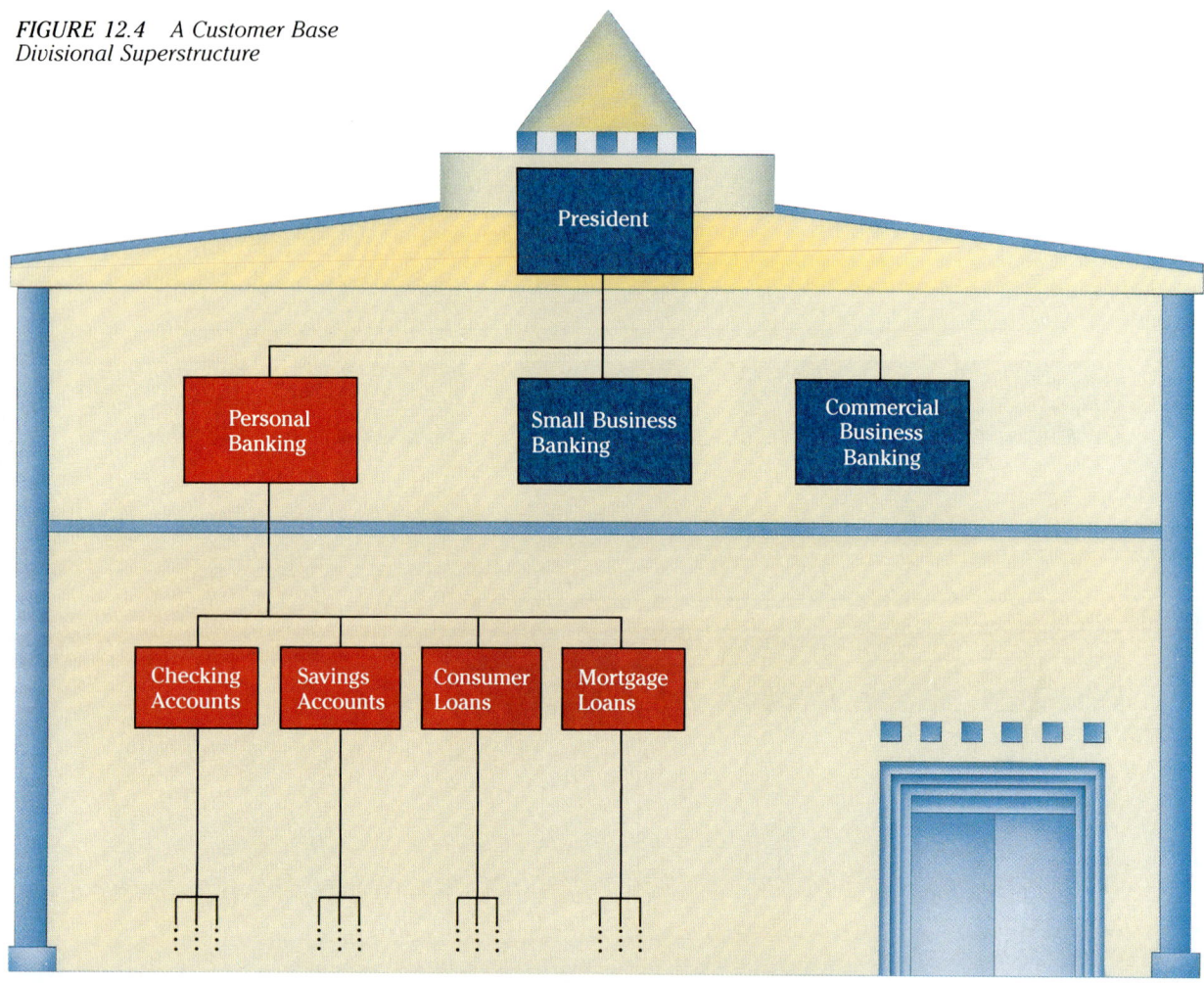

FIGURE 12.4 A Customer Base
Divisional Superstructure

Note: The red portions identify the personal banking division in the organizational superstructure.

share similar goals and areas of expertise. It also promotes opportunities for managers to exercise flexibility, adaptability, and specialization to meet the needs of each territory or product. The division that produces Procter & Gamble's paper towels, paper diapers, sanitary napkins, and other paper products has needs very different from those of its foods division, which develops no-cholesterol cooking oils and sugar substitutes. The type of flexibility required in such cases generally is missing from the functional superstructure that requires a high-level, powerful point of coordination in the organizational hierarchy.

Unfortunately, the divisional superstructure can lose the economies of scale associated with the functional grouping of activities. For example, instead of having one marketing program for the entire organization and all of its products, each division might have its own marketing unit. Sharing resources, such as equipment and personnel, among divisions is generally more difficult than under a functional arrangement. Reacting to this type of problem, General Motors recently reorganized its five divisions (Pontiac, Buick, Chevrolet, Cadillac, and Oldsmobile) into two groups. This reorganization was intended to lower the costs of maintaining five

FIGURE 12.5 A Hybrid Superstructure

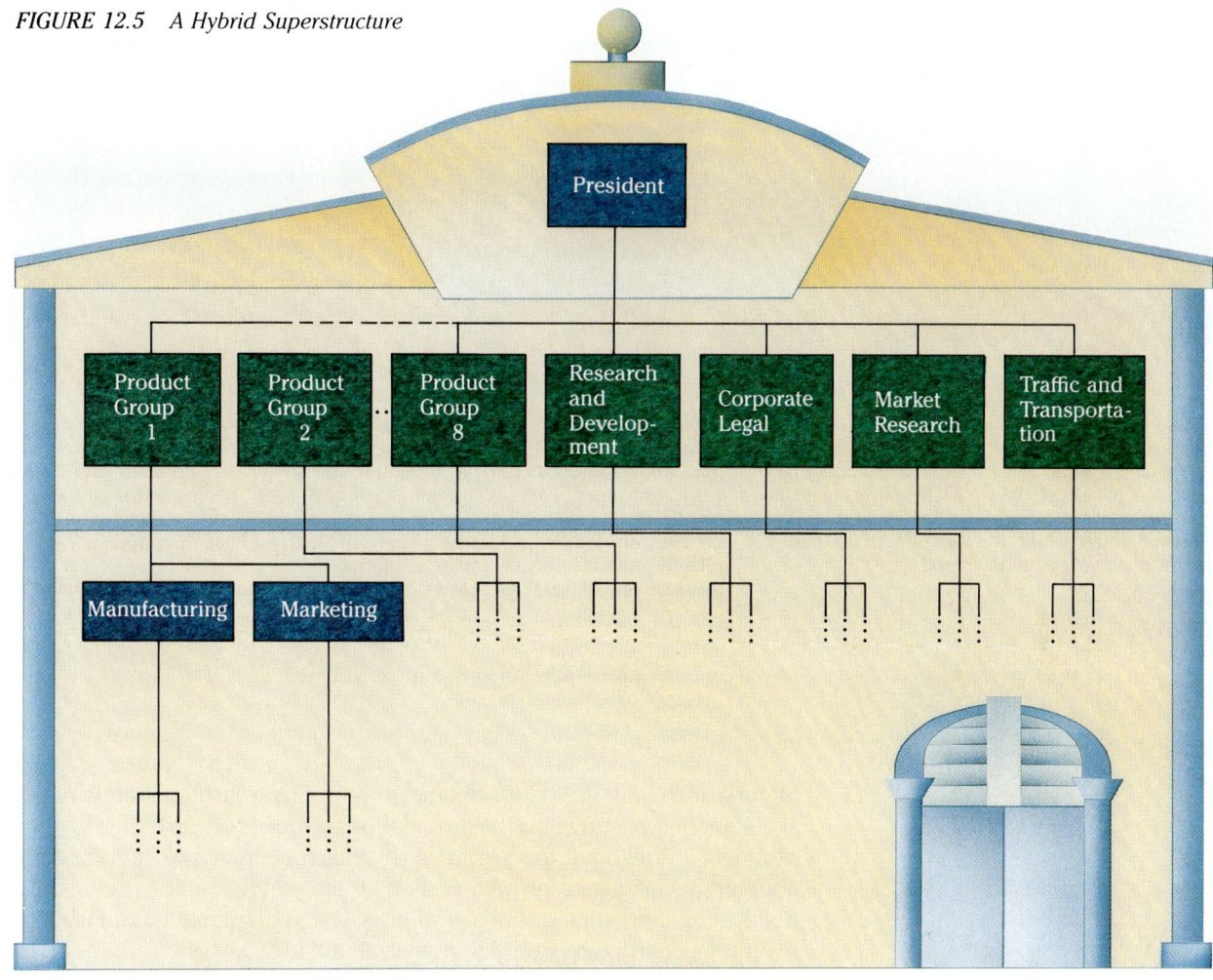

middle-management groups and to decrease the duplication of functional activities that existed in the five-division structure.[4]

Hybrid Superstructure Few managers adopt a pure functional superstructure or a divisional superstructure consisting of only one divisional basis (for example, product or territory). Instead, most combine the characteristics of two or more structural approaches to create a **hybrid superstructure.** The superstructure of Levi Strauss, for example, has such a hybrid form (see Figure 12.5). Near the top of this superstructure are eight product divisions (each containing its own marketing and manufacturing facilities) and four functional groups (consisting of research and development, corporate legal, market research, and traffic and transportation). The functional units serve each of the product divisions. For example, all research and development work for the eight divisions is done by the single R&D unit.

One of the advantages of a hybrid superstructure is that it lets managers of organizations that operate in uncertain environments innovate, as well as monitor and respond to environmental changes. Managers at Levi

FIGURE 12.6   *How the Corporation Has Evolved*

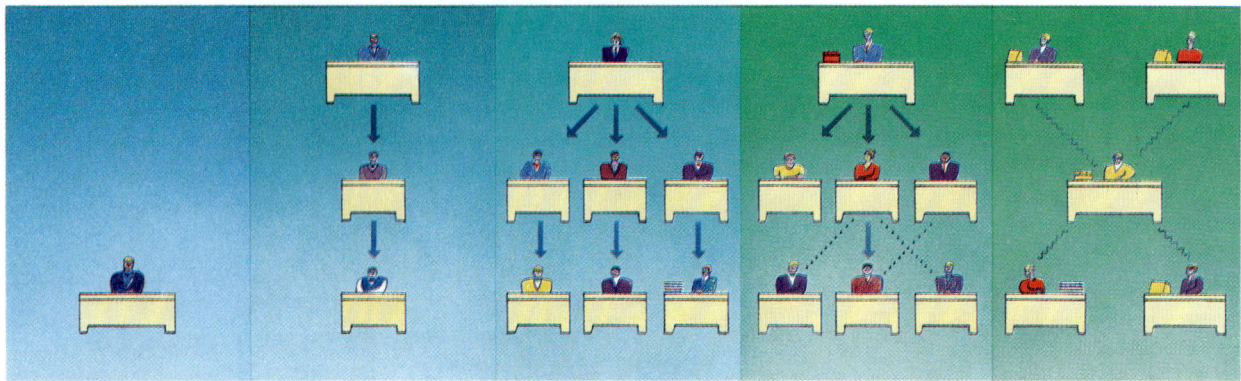

1800 Owner-managed —Small companies, generally making one product for a regional market, are controlled by one person who performs many administrative tasks.

1850 Vertical—Companies grow larger and hire more managers, each to oversee a stage of the chain from raw material to finished product.

1900 Divisional— Large companies organize around a series of vertical chains of command to manage each product, or group of related products, that the company makes.

1950 Matrix—Large companies with vertical structures add a second, informal reporting chain that links managers with allied responsibilities or managers working together on temporary projects.

2000 Network—Small central organizations rely on other companies and suppliers to perform manufacturing, distribution, marketing, or other crucial business functions on a contract basis.

Reprinted from March 3, 1986, issue of *Business Week* by special permission, copyright © 1986 by McGraw-Hill, Inc.

Strauss, for example, try to anticipate and shape fashion trends, while simultaneously struggling with the complexities of distributing their products throughout the world. A hybrid superstructure may also be adopted by managers of organizations that cannot support the costs of duplicating functional or other resources across divisional lines. Finally, a hybrid superstructure can give organizations high levels of efficiency by grouping particular units functionally and yet separating groups where necessary. It makes sense, for example, for Levi Strauss to be efficient by having just one legal group. It also makes sense to place manufacturing and marketing in each product division so that those functions can capitalize on the advantages of product divisions. Overall, a hybrid superstructure makes it easier for the Levi organization to manage its wide range of products and markets. (See Figure 12.6).

The Matrix Superstructure

Developed in the early 1960s to help solve the management problems emerging in the aerospace industry, a **matrix superstructure** uses two or more integrated, coexisting structures simultaneously. What distinguishes a matrix superstructure from a hybrid superstructure is its grid-like intersection of multiple lines of authority and responsibility. As is true at the departmental level, managers can create a matrix in many different ways. They can, for example, blend function with territory, territory with product, or function with territory with product. The company shown in Figure 12.7, for example, superimposes a product division over a function-

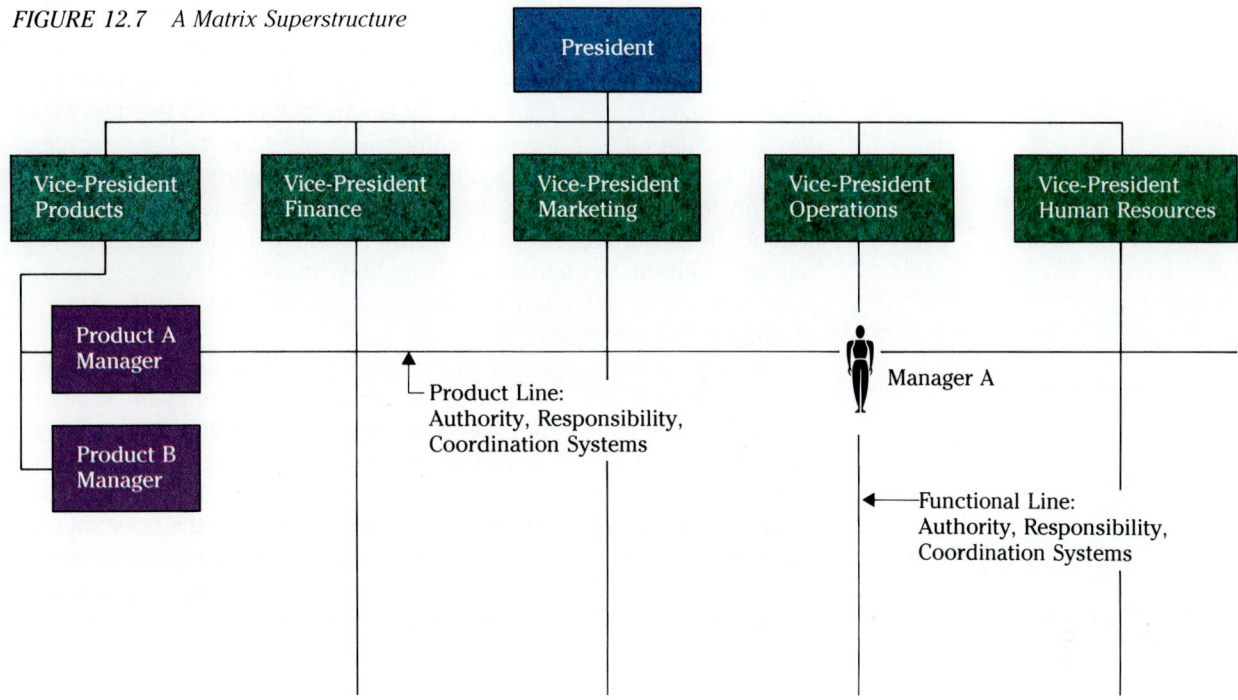

FIGURE 12.7   A Matrix Superstructure

al group to create its matrix superstructure. The functional finance, marketing, operations, and human resources units give the matrix a vertical structure, while the product division gives it a horizontal structure.

As shown in Figure 12.7, the matrix superstructure allows ready coordination and sharing of knowledge among those working with a particular product due to the horizontal product component of the structure. At the same time, the vertical structure provides similar benefits within each functional area. The major advantage, however, is that the intersection of the horizontal and vertical structures makes both product and functional expertise available to all parts of the organization, thus providing greater control over operations. The matrix approach differs from the hybrid approach used by Levi Strauss, in which *part* of its superstructure is product-based and part is function-based. At Levi Strauss, the two parts can interact through hierarchical levels when needed. In the matrix approach shown in Figure 12.7, however, *all* of the superstructure is *both* product- and function-based; thus, hierarchical connections are much less critical.

A major advantage to a matrix structure is its *dual authority system*, which allows all units to benefit from dual authorities and some employees (usually managers in the upper hierarchical levels) to be accountable to two bosses at the same time. In Figure 12.7, for example, Manager A is responsible to the vice-president of operations, as well as to the manager for Product A. Consider the potential advantages of this arrangement for a publisher of college textbooks. The project team formed to produce a book might include a project (book) director, an acquisition editor, a developmental editor, a production manager, and a marketing manager. The acquisition, developmental, production, and marketing team members report to the project director as well as to their respective functional bosses. The developmental editor, for example, reports to the director of developmental editing, the marketing manager reports to the director of marketing, and so on. Because the matrix superstructure gives equal authority to all important organizational groups, each member of the team benefits from the expertise of both the product (book) and functional managers. Product concerns, such as how the book looks, receive the same amount of attention as functional issues, such as the kind of advertising strategy to use.

The dual authority system also produces the major weakness of a matrix superstructure. For one thing, it violates the unity-of-command principle and creates the potential for role conflict and ambiguity, authority conflict, and responsibility gaps.[5] When the production manager reports that he or she needs more time to create a high-quality product and the marketing manager says that failure to produce the book on time will results in fewer sales, how does the project director reconcile this with the director of marketing? These problems and the structural complexity of the matrix have caused many managers to try and then abandon it; however, the matrix design remains popular among many of the giant firms, such as Honeywell, IBM, and General Electric.

Conditions Conducive to a Matrix Superstructure Although a matrix design can be beneficial under certain circumstances, it creates unnecessary complexity, confusion, and overhead if used inappropriately. Research and the experiences of organizations that have used this superstructure reveal that managers should only consider using a matrix design when their organization must respond to such conditions as:

- *Multiple external demands.* Many organizations operate in an external environment that pressures them simultaneously for, say, technical quality, new products, and new markets. Environmental pressure for technical quality can often be addressed through a functional structure. Demands for new products are often satisfied through a product division, and a call for new markets can be dealt with well through a territorial organization design, but what happens when two (or all three) of these demands are made simultaneously and are of essentially equal importance? The matrix design, with its use of simultaneous structures, is a natural way to address these complex demands.
- *Extensive information needs.* When an organization's external environment undergoes rapid, unpredictable change, its managers must perform timely, often complex environmental scans, quickly collect and process large amounts of information, and then prepare the organization so that it can respond effectively to these new environmental conditions. Sometimes the strong interdependence of several organizational units may cause the need for information processing and integration to rise. In these and other situations that call for upper-level managers to amass and analyze large amounts of infor-

INTERVIEW

Dave Gobeli and Erik Larson

Dave Gobeli and Erik Larson, both of Oregon State University, have written extensively on project management and innovation. They are currently involved in a worldwide study of project management practices.

1. What has encouraged so many organizations to adopt matrix structures?

Gobeli: There are two factors that have led to the matrix being the most popular form of organizational structure. First, a matrix structure naturally evolves in any organization as it grows and discovers the need for better coordination, especially within a traditional, functional structure. Second, matrix has been fashionable for many years, thanks to some academic and consulting organizations that may have been overzealous in its application.

2. Why have so many organizations abandoned the matrix?

Larson: First of all, our research indicates that reports on the demise of matrix structures are exaggerated. Matrix structures that grant the project manager considerable authority are still quite popular for product- or service-development efforts. Second, the principal reasons for abandoning matrix were breakdowns in coordination between functional and project managers and switches to speedier, ad hoc project teams, which are more easily managed.

3. Why does the bureaucratic approach have such a bad name? Is the reputation deserved?

Larson: Yes. The bureaucratic approach works best with routine, programmable activities. Developing a new product, such as a cardiac pacemaker, is not a routine activity. The bureaucratic method of delegating project segments according to functional expertise contributes to bottle-necks and poor integration, since there is no formal coordination mechanism and functional specialists tend to adopt a parochial view of the overall project.

4. What kind of organizational design would be most conducive to creativity and the design of new product/service ideas, and why?

Gobeli: A matrix design allowing a strong role for the project manager can be overlaid on a traditional organizational structure to increase the odds of success for product/service-development projects, and is probably the most effective structure for the majority of significant developmental projects; however, if the organizational resources are available and the organization simply *must* develop a truly creative new product/service for its survival, a project-team or "tiger-team" design is likely to be a better choice. This was how Apple developed the Macintosh computer and how IBM developed the PC. Both matrix and "tiger-team" structures require a strong, qualified project leader with experience and formal authority, since strong leadership is the key to all successful development projects.

mation, a matrix design allows more rapid information processing, because the points of intersection among the number of groups involved become natural points of coordination.

- *Shared resources requirements.* When several organizational units need the same resources, but they are too expensive or not available in sufficient numbers to be individually supplied for each department, a matrix superstructure can be extremely useful. If the project director of this book and the project director of a psychology book both need art developed for their texts, a superstructure can be created that has an art specialist at intersections in the matrix for all work units to share.[6]

FIGURE 12.8   *Key Matrix Superstructure Roles*

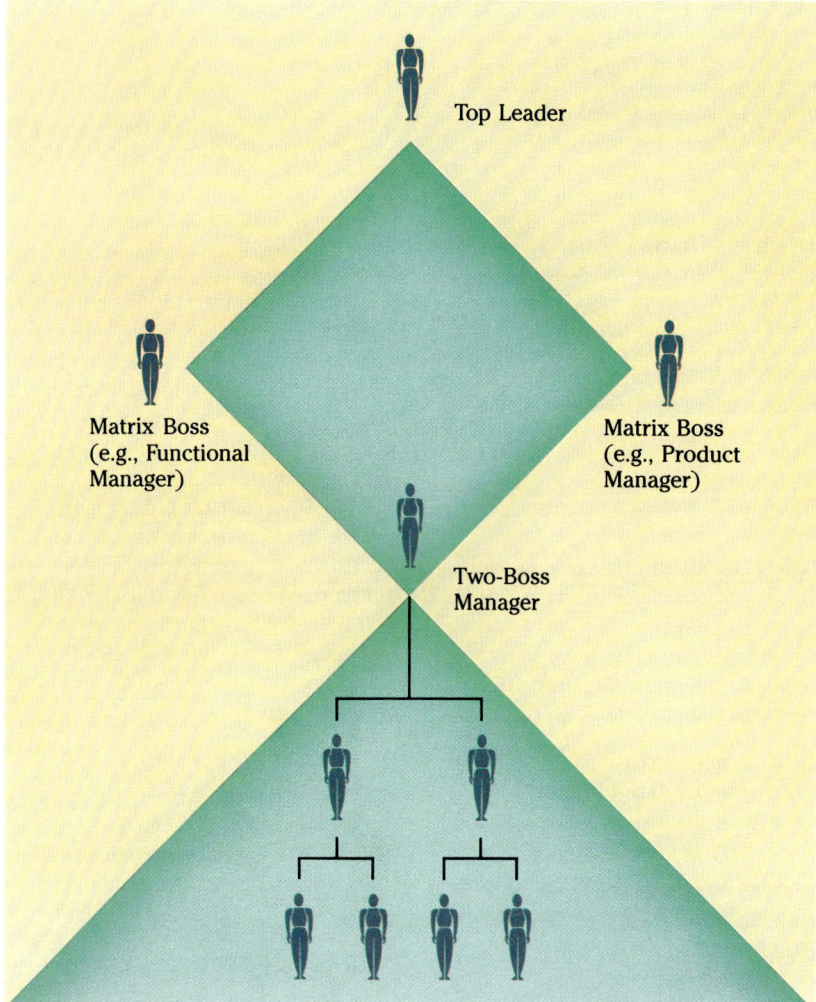

Source: Modified from S. M. Davis and P. R. Lawrence (1977), *Matrix*, Reading, MA: Addison-Wesley, 24, 27.

Key Management Roles in a Matrix Superstructure   A matrix superstructure, with its intersection of two authority systems, creates three key management roles.[7] These are referred to as top leader, matrix boss, and two-boss managers (see Figure 12.8).

- *Top leader.* A **top leader** heads the multiple command system of a matrix organization. It is his or her role to ensure a true balance of authority among the managers in the next layer—the matrix bosses. The top leader must delegate authority to matrix bosses and help them stay in direct contact with each other and with organization members so that they can resolve problems and benefit all components of the organization. The top leader is typically the president of the organization or the head of a major division.

- *Matrix boss*. A **matrix boss** manages one of the organization's overlapping systems. In the publisher example, one matrix boss is the project director and another is a functional manager, such as the director of marketing. Matrix bosses do not have complete control over their immediate subordinates (who are called two-boss managers) and the people they oversee. Because each shares control with at least one other matrix boss, these managers deal directly with one another to coordinate work and to solve problems. Matrix bosses work together on such matters as scheduling work, coordinating resources, and appraising employee performance.

- *Two-boss managers*. A **two-boss manager** is at the point of intersection of two or more of an organization's multiple structures and, therefore, is directly responsible to more than one matrix boss. In the publisher example, a marketing manager assigned to a book project is a two-boss manager, responsible to both the project (book) director and the director of marketing. To manager his or her own organizational unit successfully, the two-boss manager must be able to confront and influence senior managers when demands conflict, while remaining loyal to the matrix bosses. To reduce the anxiety, stress, and high levels of role conflict that this position may cause and, thus, increase the effectiveness of the matrix boss system, many organizations use liaisons to help the matrix bosses communicate with one another and to coordinate their expectations.

In sum, a matrix design is complex, may be difficult to manage, and can fill the lives of some of its managers with tension and role conflict. A dual-authority system requires matrix bosses and two-boss managers to form a consultative relationship, rather than the traditional superior and subordinate relationship. This relationship is a two-edged sword: it is beneficial, due to the professional atmosphere it can create, but problematic because of the absence of absolute authority. Although a matrix can produce a high level of conflict between two matrix bosses and a two-boss manager, the conflict, if effectively managed, can be worked to the organization's advantage by capitalizing on the varied skill and knowledge base of the managers. Even so, it is time consuming and often requires frequent meetings and conflict resolution sessions. These drawbacks are simply the price managers must pay if they are to benefit from the advantages of a matrix superstructure—a price well worth it for organizations requiring its special features but a waste of money for organizations that can use a simpler superstructure effectively.

Design Approaches

The functional, divisional, hybrid, and matrix superstructure designs all have their roots in three basic models. As you read about the classical, behavioral, and organic approaches to organizational design, remember that an organization is

Organizational Forms: The Coming of the Network Organizations

A new corporate look is emerging. Recently, a company called Ocean Pacific Sunwear generated $15 million in sales with only 67 employees; Electronic Arts, a software firm, $20 million in revenues with 75 employees; and Lewis Galoob Toys Inc., over $58 million in sales with just 115 employees. None of these organizations had even a single employee involved in the manufacturing of products. How could these companies perform that way? By using the newest corporate structure, the "network organization." A network organization maintains a very small central organizational structure. It then relies on other companies and suppliers to perform its manufacturing, marketing, distribution, or any other crucial business functions typically done in-house.

When Galoob selects a toy for its product line, it contracts with an outside firm—often in Hong Kong or China—to manufacture and package the product. The toys are then shipped to the United States, where they are distributed by commissioned manufacturers' representatives. Even accounts receivable are handled by an outside credit firm, so what do David Galoob, president of the com-

pany, and his brother Robert, executive vice-president, spend their time doing? Making critical decisions and coordinating the various organizations on which they depend. You might say that Galoob is an idea and coordination business. The Galoobs make their money by selling toys that never touch the hands of a Galoob employee.

Many network organizations in the United States arose out of their founders' desire to capitalize on lower labor costs found in other countries; however, many have extended this idea to capitalize on other potential advantages of the network structure. For example, network organizations need less capital and maintain lower overhead costs because they do not build their own facilities and they employ a minimum number of employees per dollar of sales. They can move more quickly on a product or service idea or can adapt other advanced technologies more easily than can their traditional counterparts. Network organizations also tend to support an entrepreneurial spirit. The focus is on creativity, and profitable ideas that might not emerge in a traditionally structured organization are encouraged.

Ocean Pacific Sunwear generated $15 million in sales with only 67 employees.

There are, however, some potential disadvantages to the network structure. Many firms, such as Tektronix,

which uses Seiko to manufacture its monitors, have discovered that their suppliers often compete in the same marketplace. A network organization usually has less control over production facilities than a traditional organization. If a supplier decides to sell its manufacturing capacity to a competitor, the network organization must look elsewhere. This decreased control can also affect a product's quality. If a supplier does not conform to the standards of the network organization, the network organization may not be able to remedy the situation quickly. Many people argue that networking causes a loss of the design and manufacturing expertise usually maintained by in-house production and that creativity and future product ideas are hampered.

Network organizations need less capital and maintain lower overhead costs.

No one knows for sure whether the network structure is here to stay. It is known, however, that

With less bureaucracy, they are well suited to an era in which managers and workers are demanding a bigger say in their jobs. . . . All in all, the network structure allows companies to zero in on what they do best and leave the rest to other experts."[1]

1. R. Brandt and O. Port (3 March 1986), And now, the post-industrial corporation, *Business Week*, 64, 66.

a formal collection of people that has been created for the purpose of accomplishing collective goals on a relatively continuous basis. The collection is characterized by a relatively identifiable boundary, norms of behavior, primary groups, channels of communication, task-related activities, [and] authority relationships . . . [8]

This means that managers must create a design for each formal organizational arrangement—work unit, department, and division—as well as for the total organization, keeping in mind the unit's or organization's purpose, technology, environment, and members.

Classical Design and the Bureaucratic Model

As you will recall from Chapter 5, classical management scholars, such as Henri Fayol, Frederick Taylor, and Max Weber, believed that a universal set of laws governed the efficient and effective functioning of organizations. The goals of their search were to identify these laws and to establish a set of principles to guide the organizing process. Although the members of the classical school did not agree on all issues, one major organizational design—the **bureaucratic model** most often associated with the work of Max Weber—emerged from the classical period.[9] Unfortunately, the term *bureaucracy* has become emotionally charged and synonymous with red tape and inefficiency.[10] This is too bad, because the bureaucratic model can create a high level of speed, order, predictability, and consistency of operations. Consider some of the characteristics that distinguish a bureaucratic design.

Characteristics of the Classical Bureaucratic Model
Few organizations have a purely bureaucratic design, but most possess at least some bureaucratic characteristics.[11] Chief among these is the emphasis on obeying one leader rather than many. This characteristic arises from Weber's well-defined hierarchy of authority, which specifies the lines of communication, command relationships, and the channels through which individual accountability should flow. A bureaucratic design, thus, centralizes its authority system and bases its legitimacy on inherent rationality. In a military setting, for example, it is rational for a field commander to possess the right to command troops into action. After all, there would hardly be time for a battalion to take a break during a firefight to see if members could agree on a course of action.

A second characteristic of an organization with a bureaucratic design is its reliance on a set of rules that specify employee rights and duties and on standard operating procedures to control work-related activities. This standardization and formalization delineates the relationship between the organization and individuals. It tries to ensure that each task is uniformly handled in accordance with Weber's belief that an organization should clearly define each member's role and should position him or her relative to other members. The U.S. Marine Corps, for example, clearly defines each of its ranks and the rights accompanying each. The corps also specifies in detail the procedures to be followed for work assignments, promotions, and so forth. In other words, the corps manages "by the book" to ensure efficiency and uniform (pardon the pun) procedures.

Other distinguishing features of the bureaucratic organization include:

- People selected to join the organization because of their technical competence: So that it can select employees on objective standards of competence, for example, the United States government bases selection decisions in part on the results of civil service exams.
- People advancing within the organization as a result of tenure and technical competence: For example, to avoid favoritism, the United States Post Office bases promotions on length of service and the development of job-related skills.
- Impersonal interpersonal relations: Application of organizational rules, standards, and procedures is uniform and administered without consideration of individual needs or personal preferences.
- Division of labor, individual specialization, and routine tasks: Each position is filled by an individual who will become an expert in the performance of a specific and limited number of activities.

As illustrated by the U.S. Marine Corps, when a bureaucracy runs well, it can be a model of order, stability, consistency, and predictability. Even when running well however, a bureaucratic design has drawbacks.

Problems with Bureaucracy   Although the rational approach espoused by the bureaucratic approach to design can work well for a mechanized organization in which people perform routine tasks under highly structured environmental conditions, it is less than ideal as environmental uncertainty increases and tasks become increasingly non-routine.[12] At Hewlett-Packard, for example, the development and design of information systems requires a much more open and flexible working environment than that which would be created by a highly programmed and controlled bureaucracy.

Another situation that does not lend itself to a bureaucratic design arises when the work in an organization is highly dependent on the creativity of people and their interdependencies.[13] For example, the collaborative creativity needed to identify and develop movie ideas at Disney's Touchstone Studios, for example, would be inhibited by the rigid structure of a bureaucracy. Some other problems frequently associated with the bureaucratic organization include:

- Human problems, such as alienation, frustration, low morale, and lack of motivation stem from a high level of division of labor and imposed control. Workers with strong affiliation needs, for example, feel that bureaucracies thwart, rather than satisfy, their need for socialization and group interaction.
- The social and psychological sides of the organization, such as the informal organization, tend to be ignored. For example, the informal organization and strong culture that contributes substantially to Hewlett-Packard's innovativeness and effectiveness would undoubtedly be stifled by the rigidity of a bureaucratic design.
- Rules and procedures frequently become ends in and of themselves, replacing original goals. Some claim that the Occupational Safety

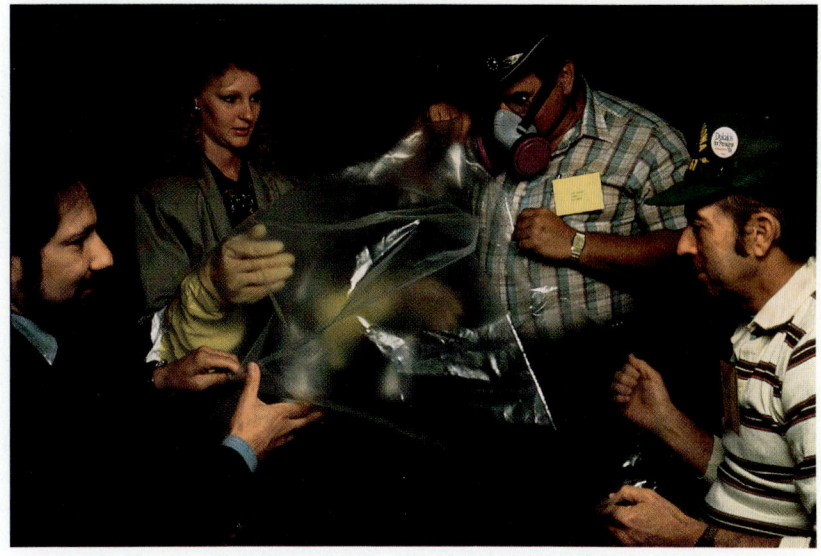

OSHA was created to identify and correct industrial safety risks. At an OSHA training conference, participants learn how to operate safety equipment, such as glove bags and respirators used in asbestos removal.

and Health Administration (OSHA) provides a good example of this. OSHA inspections were designed to identify and correct industrial safety risks, but the detailed schedules and rules specified by OSHA's bureaucracy have shifted the emphasis from a focus on safety to that of conducting the appropriate number of inspections.

- Communication inside the organization must follow the chain of command, frequently resulting in tedious and time-consuming delays for the flow of information. For example, Earl Karn is a distribution clerk who discovered a quality problem in the twenty-inch bicycles he was shipping at a large bicycle plant. As trained, he reported the problem to his supervisor, Karin Sandberg-Brennan. Following procedure, Karin reported the problem to the director of transportation, Melissa Graves Robin, who reported it to the director of quality control, Mindy Shumway. Mindy reported the problem to the manager of bicycle quality control, Philip Howrigan, who reported it to Mary Ellen Murnin, who supervises inspection of twenty-inch bikes. Mary confirmed the problem and informed the production team, who corrected the error. Had there not been such a bureaucratic chain of command, Earl could have gone directly to Mary, who could have remedied the problem quickly and efficiently. (If you think this example was painful to read, consider how frustrating it is to experience it in real life.)

- The organization becomes inflexible, incapable of responding quickly to environmental complexity and turbulence or to complex tasks and nonroutine technologies. For example, Du Pont responded to research that shows the ozone-depleting effects of chlorofluorocarbons (CBCs) by announcing that it will quit using them in its products. When asked *when* the phasing-out process would be completed, the company's spokesperson indicated a time frame somewhere near the year 2000.

Throughout the classical period, managers popularized the use of the bureaucratic organization. During the past few decades, however, managers have experienced increasing inefficiencies associated with this design. As a result, alternative designs have been adopted.

Behavioral Models

As you will recall from Chapter 5, such people as Hugo Munsterberg, Walter Dill Scott, Mary Parker Follett, and Chester Barnard argued that the classical approach to management fails to consider the human side of organizations. Their work led to the development of **behavioral models,** which focused less on the rational and mechanical aspects of organizational design and more on its social and psychological sides. Behavioral model designs and the contemporary models that followed did not reject all of the classicists' design ideas. Instead, they emphasized incorporating individuals and groups into the system as an integral part of managing. This section will examine two behavioral model design approaches referred to as sociotechnical systems theory and Rensis Likert's System 4 organization.

Sociotechnical Systems Theory Eric Trist and K. W. Bamforth's classic studies on alternative methods of coal mining suggested that managers should place substantial emphasis on the human side of their organization rather than focus strictly on its technical and mechanical side. Their research, and that of others conducted at England's Tavistock Institute, led to the development of the **sociotechnical systems theory,** a design perspective that proposes a more balanced approach to dealing with major organizational problems (see Figure 12.9).[14]

According to the sociotechnical model, managers should design organizations from two premises. First, they should recognize that two systems operate inside every organization: a technical system that focuses on the tasks that produce the organization's product or service and a social system that contains the people-to-people interactions that sustain both the formal and informal organization. The technical systems involved in the manufacture of paper, for example, include machines and such activities as debarking, grinding, washing, bleaching, and cooking the wood. The social system that runs the machines and performs these activities includes individuals and groups whose motivation, interest, ideas, insights, creativity, and needs also must be maintained. Unless managers pay attention to the social and psychological needs of this side of their organization, the technical side will not operate efficiently and effectively.

As you will recall from Chapter 2, every organization operates in an external environment. Because the survival and success of an organization depends on its environment, managers must design their organization to be open and responsive to that environment. The second premise of the sociotechnical systems model concerns the integration of an organization with its external environment.[15] In fact, it has been argued that the American automobile industry's lack of response to the external environment explains much of the success of the Japanese in the U.S. auto

FIGURE 12.9   *The Sociotechnical Systems Perspective*

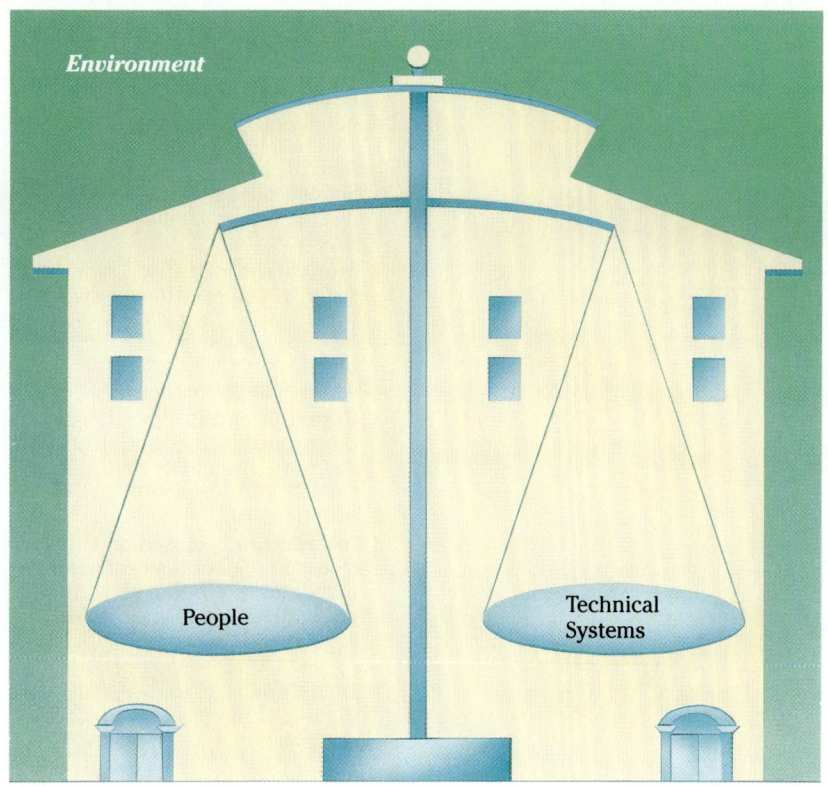

market. The socially sensitive Japanese auto manufacturers quickly recognized that American car buyers in the 1970s wanted fuel-efficient cars, and they responded with models to meet the demand. The technically oriented U.S. auto industry, however, focused too heavily on the machines and processes used inside the organization to fully notice this shift in consumer preferences. When they became aware of the new trend, their highly structured equipment orientation made it difficult to make the change quickly.

Likert's System 4 Organization   When he was a social scientist at the University of Michigan's Institute for Social Research, Rensis Likert found that there was a significant relationship between organizational design and effectiveness. Likert was most concerned with eight features of organizations: leadership, motivation, communication, interaction, decision making, goal setting, control, and performance goal setting. Through his research, Likert observed four design approaches that incorporate these features, which he referred to as Systems 1 through 4. Systems 2 and 3 have received little attention. The System 1 organization is similar to that of the classical organization's bureaucratic model. The most effective organization identified was classified as System 4.[16]

A **System 4 organization** emphasizes openness and has few boundary restrictions. People are not expected to adhere strictly to the chain of command in communicating information, coordinating work, or reporting accountability; thus, influence and information flow freely upward, down-

TABLE 12.1   System 1 and System 4 Organizations

System 1 Organization	System 2 Organization
1. **Leadership** shows little confidence or trust in subordinates, seldom soliciting their ideas and opinions. Subordinates are not free to discuss job problems with superiors.	1. **Leadership** shows confidence and trust in subordinates in most matters, soliciting their ideas and opinions. Subordinates are free to discuss job problems with superiors.
2. **Motivation** focuses on physical, security, and economic issues using fear and sanctions. Negative attitudes toward the organization are dominant among employees.	2. **Motivation** draws on a full range of motives through participatory methods. Positive attitudes toward the organization are dominant among employees.
3. **Communication** flows mostly downward. Information is often distorted, inaccurate, and viewed with suspicion by subordinates.	3. **Communication** flows throughout the organization in all directions. Information exchanged tends to be accurate and trusted by subordinates.
4. **Interaction** is closed and restricted. Subordinates have little influence on departmental goals, methods, and activities.	4. **Interaction** is open and extensive. All organizational members, managers and nonmanagers, can influence departmental goals, methods, and activities.
5. **Decisions** take place mostly at the top of the highly centralized organization.	5. **Decisions** take place at all levels of decentralized organization, often using group processes.
6. **Goal setting** is performed at the top of the organization. Group participation is discouraged.	6. **Goal setting** is based on group participation and emphasizes high but realistic goals.
7. **Control** is centralized and great importance is placed on apportioning blame for mistakes.	7. **Control** is decentralized and great importance is placed on self-control and problem solving.
8. **Performance goals** are usually low. Managers make little commitment to developing the human resources of the organization.	8. **Performance goals** are usually high. Managers are committed to developing the human resources of the organization through training.

Source: Adapted from R. Likert (1967), *The human organization,* New York: McGraw-Hill, 197–211.

ward, and laterally. Decentralization is the norm. There is an emphasis on participatory decision making, and employees are expected to engage in self and group control. Authority flows from the nature of people's relationships and is based on achieving acceptance, rather than stemming from hierarchical position. Table 12.1 summarizes the characteristics of a System 4 organization and contrasts them with a System 1 organization.

Structurally, a System 4 organization has a traditional hierarchy laced with a hierarchy of groups (see Figure 12.10). Each manager is a member of several groups. For example, Gina Saettone is the vice-president of the marketing division shown in Figure 12.10. Gina is a member of the firm's executive group, which is made up of the heads of the legal, operations, finance, and human resources departments. Gina also is a member of the

FIGURE 12.10 A Hierarchy of Groups

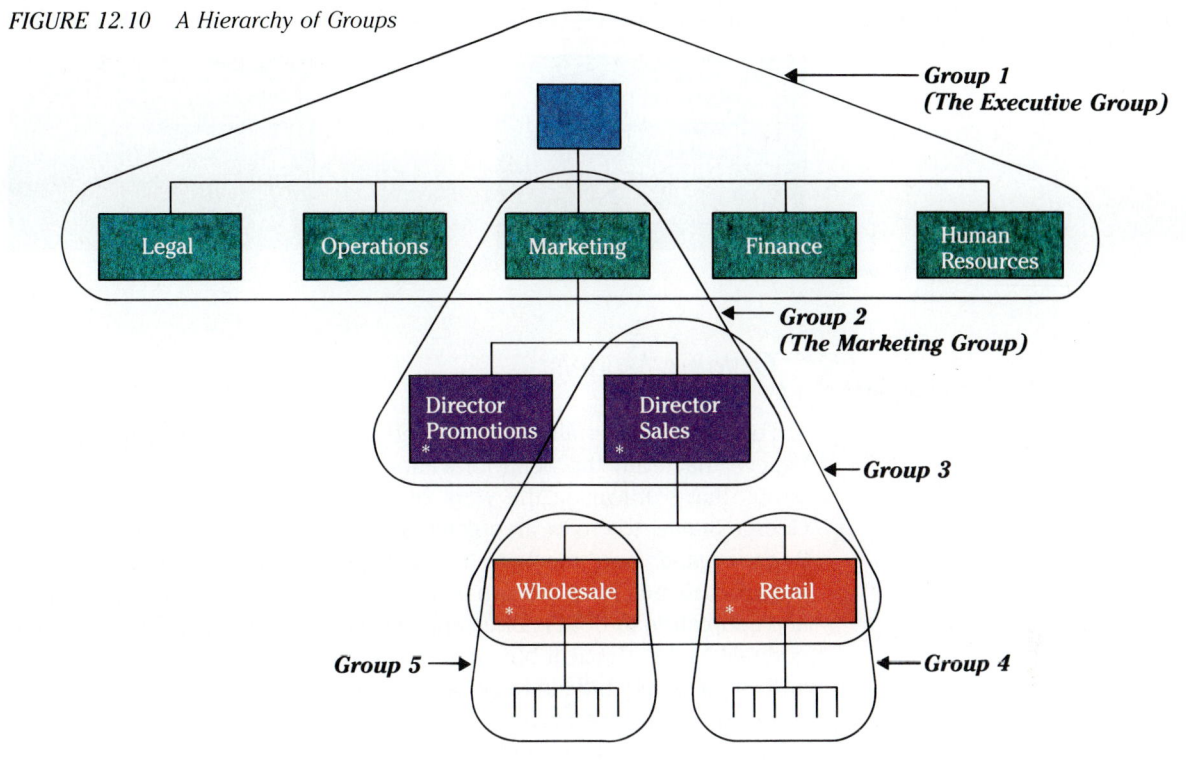

*Linking pin role

marketing group, which includes the directors of promotion and sales. She also belongs to a community relations group that has members both from other parts of the organization and from outside of the organization.

Their participation in and connecting function with so many groups imbues managers with **linking pin roles,** so that they become a major conduit through which information and influence flow. Gina represents the promotions and sales departments when decisions are made at the executive level. In addition, she can bring information about decisions made in operations or human resources back into the marketing group. As a linking pin, then, a manager connects the executive and marketing groups, which facilitates vertical, horizontal, and diagonal organizational relationships. This promotes problem-solving, planning, and controlling activities, because it brings together a wide range of people and knowledge when needed. It discourages one-on-one, superior-subordinate relationships because many individuals are included in critical activities. The design also encourages managers from various departments in the executive group to help each other with functional decisions.

In reality, Likert's System 4 organization is probably more a prescription for an ideal organization than a description of existing organizations. According to Likert, an organization's effectiveness should increase as it moves from a System 1 design toward System 4. The System 4 serves as a model toward which organizations may aspire.

FIGURE 12.11 *Structures of Organic and Mechanistic Organizations*

Organic ———————————————————— **Mechanistic**

High Complexity Low Centralization Low Formalization Low Standardization High Person Specialization High Task Specialization	Low Complexity High Centralization High Formalization High Standardization Low Person Specialization Low Task Specialization

Organic Models

For highly uncertain environments and technologies, some people believe that even the behavioral models are too rigid a design. These people have drawn on the work of British researchers Tom Burns and George Stalker to create an organic design (see the discussion in Chapter 2 on organic and mechanistic management systems).[17] An **organic organization** is fluid and dynamic and is capable of evolution, redesign, and adaptation to both internal and external environments. This is in stark contrast to the classical bureaucratic design, which is mechanistic, rigid, and changes very little in response to these pressures (see Figure 12.11).[18]

Consider the organization design of W. L. Gore and Associates, the company that produces and markets Goretex fabric. Each of the company's 28 plants employs no more than 200 people, all of whom are encouraged to work with every other employee in a kind of corporate free-for-all. There are few chains of command, few hierarchies, few titles, and few formalized rule and policy manuals. There is little fixed or assigned authority and responsibility. When people are hired, they are told to look around for something that they would like to do that will help the organization be successful. It sounds like anarchy, but Gore claims that its sales and earnings have been increasing at a 40 percent annual rate.[19]

Although W. L. Gore and Associates is an extreme example, an organic design does allow goals, rather than highly formalized rules or standard operating procedures, to direct employees. Authority is vested in individuals and groups as a function of the task that they are working on and the expertise that they bring to the task. The loosely coupled, decentralized hierarchical system changes as necessary to respond to environmental pressures, task needs, and participant expertise. Informal and spontaneous interactions facilitate the sharing of information and ideas. Participative decision making is common. Communication networks emerge and evolve to meet the needs of organization members and the changing nature of the tasks. Control systems are personal and rely heavily on feedback about process and outcomes.

Project teams and research labs often have organic designs. At the outset, the novelty of a project, such as developing a new laser-based communication system for General Dynamics, prevents managers from being able to create highly formal job descriptions, rigid hierarchical arrangements, or centralized authority and communication systems. In-

FIGURE 12.12   The Range
of Organizational Designs

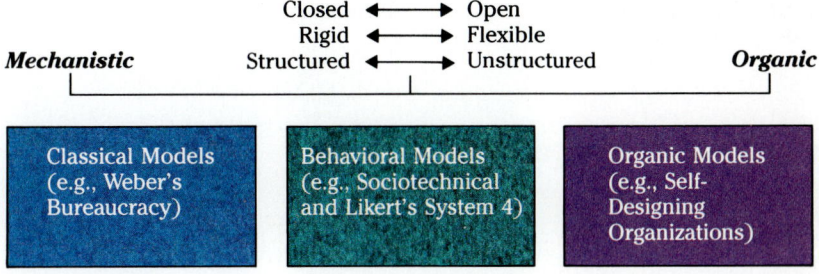

stead, team members have to experiment with various relationships as they go along and let the evolving situations dictate the most effective arrangements. Structural arrangements change as the team proceeds from one set of activities with one set of demands to another set with different demands.

One type of organic design that has received the attention of an increasing number of organization scholars in recent years has been the self-designing organization.[20] Described as a "tinkering organization," a **self-designing organization** continuously experiments and tries new ways to respond to environmental demands.[21] It continually appraises and revises itself in an effort to invent as well as to survive its future.[22]

Self-designing organizations are a breed apart. They value impermanence rather than permanence. They generate conflict, invent rather than borrow solutions to problems, pay little attention to tradition, and seek uncertainty. They permit work patterns to evolve to fit situations instead of designing patterns in anticipation of situational demands. Self-designing organizations are open, free, creative, alive (albeit often chaotic), and appeal to people who can thrive in that type of atmosphere. Others with a strong need for order, control, and predictability feel uncomfortable and frightened by the concept of self-design. It is too early to tell whether this organizational form will gain wide popularity in practice.[23]

The three basic approaches to the design of organizations and of their internal units can be placed along a continuum (see Figure 12.12). At one extreme are organizations with rigid hierarchies, centralized authority systems, formalized rules, and standard operating procedures. These bureaucracies are very mechanistic, with closed, rigid, and highly structured designs. At the other end of the continuum are organizations with very flexible hierarchies, decentralized authority systems, and loosely structured designs. These organic organizations, as seen in self-designing organizations, can evolve to meet increasing environmental uncertainty, such as that brought on by increased foreign competition and technological innovation. Between the two mechanistic and organic extremes are behavioral models, such as the sociotechnical system and System 4 organizations. System 4 organizations, for example, place a greater emphasis on open communication, lateral forms of influence and coordination, and participatory decision making than do mechanistic organizations, but they are not as open, fluid, and flexible as organic, self-designing organizations.

FIGURE 12.13
The Context-Structure Relationship

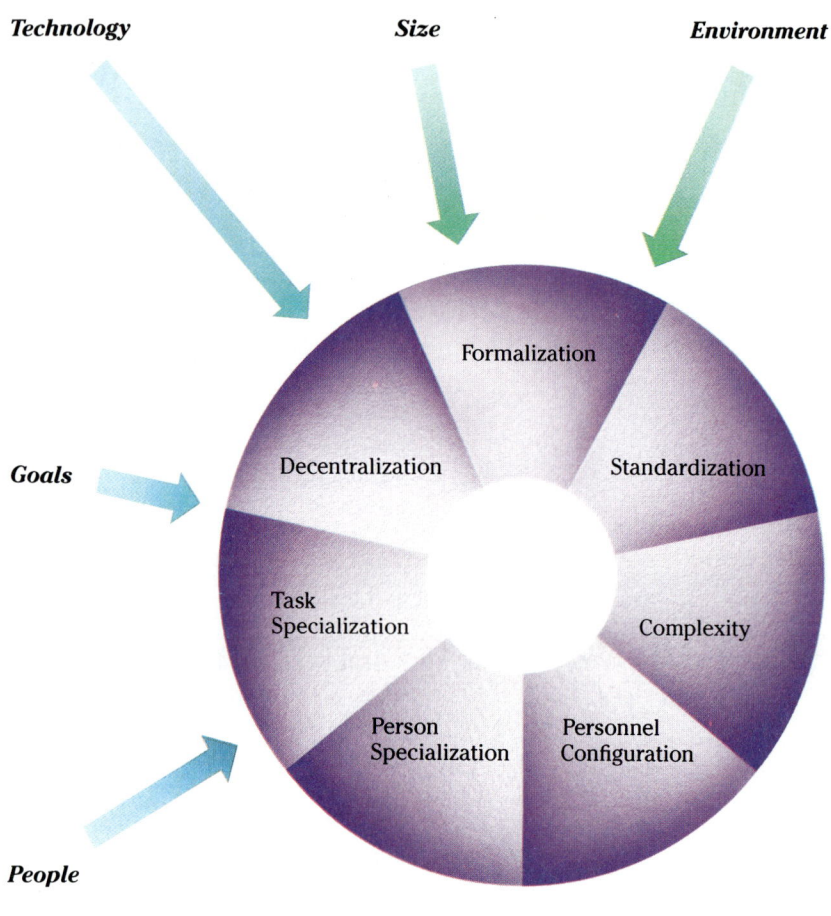

Design Influences

How do managers know whether to design an organization with high levels of centralization and formalization? Because no single design is universally effective, managers must examine the circumstances inside and outside of their organization to determine the most appropriate and effective design. In some cases, for example, highly mechanistic characteristics will be effective; in other cases, such a design could lead to the organization's demise. As noted early in this chapter, managers must consider several *contextual* factors, or contingencies, that influence design decisions: external environment, technology, goals, size, and characteristics of organization members (see Figure 12.13).

The External Environment

Particularly since the early 1960s, people who study organizations have stressed the importance of designing them so that they can respond to their external environments. For example, organizations operating in the fiercely competitive airline industry must contend with threats of organizational buyouts, price wars, changing schedules, and competition for lucrative routes. The uncertainty that accompanies such unstable and unpredictable environmental conditions requires a flexible organizational design, such as that found in the organic models. In stable environments, however, organizations have little need for flexibility. The continuity and lack of environmental change, thus, enable managers to use standard operating procedures, centralized authority systems, and other efficient characteristics of mechanistically designed organizations, such as are found in the bureaucratic model.

In addition to considering the design influence that the external environment exerts on an organization as a whole, managers must judge the effects of the individual external environments that surround each organizational unit.[24] As you will recall from Chapter 2, Paul Lawrence and Jay Lorsch observed that firms operating in stable environments had organizational units with similar structures and comparable time, goal, and interpersonal orientations, but firms operating in unstable environments often had highly differentiated structures, with varying time, interpersonal, and goal orientations. It is important that managers match the design of each unit to fit the conditions of its external environment. For example, Colgate-Palmolive's production department, operating under relatively stable environmental conditions, might do well with a mechanistic structure, while its marketing group, operating in a more turbulent environment, might need an organic structure. In fact, the greater the differentiation among units, the greater the need for the use of special integrators, task forces, permanent cross functional teams, and matrix superstructures.

In sum, "successful firms competing in complex and dynamic industries have been found to have organic structures, . . . whereas successful firms competing in simple and static environments are characterized by mechanistic structures. . . ."[25] Why? The organic approach gives managers the flexibility required to deal with environmental uncertainty and change; the bureaucratic model allows managers to streamline operations and compete in areas where efficiency, rather than innovation, determines success. These findings emphasize the need for managers to design an organizational structure in the context of external environmental influences.

Culture

The culture that permeates an organization and the attitudes toward authority within that culture often strongly influence organizational design. This effect is readily apparent in comparing organizations from around the world. For example, researchers have attributed many of the structural differences between British and American organizations to the fact that authority in British society often stems from tradition, whereas authority in the United States is based more on law and reason.[26] French organizational sociologist Michael Crozier attributes the strength of the bureaucracy in France to the value that society places on protecting individuals from those with power.[27] According to Crozier, the strong hierarchy, strict rules, and firmly established work procedures of the bureaucratic design keep authority figures from intruding into workers' daily lives. When compared to their German counterparts, American organizations emphasize individualism and the need for achievement, which is reflected in the design of many contemporary U.S. organizations.[28] Finally, Japanese organizations and their group management systems may reflect the dominant role of society over that of individuals in Japanese culture.[29]

Technology

People often define technology as the machinery that an organization uses, but, as you discovered in Chapter 3, an organization's technology includes any process or technique that converts inputs to outputs, whether it is turning high-school students into college graduates or transforming bolts of material into business suits.[30] Most organizations use one overall technology, but each unit within an organization also uses its own technology to accomplish its assigned task. For example, within a university, the routine technology used by the food service department to produce lunch in the cafeteria exists side by side with the nonroutine technology used in the biomedical research laboratory to pursue cancer research. The primary technology of the entire university is based on the development of new knowledge and its exchange through direct, interpersonal interaction; thus, this technology focuses on the creation, transformation, and exchange of ideas.

Pioneering work on the relationship between technology and organization design was done by British organization scholar Joan Woodward. In the early 1960s, she studied the relationship between technology and a number of organizational design features (span of control, hierarchical levels, decentralization of authority, and so on) in 100 British manufacturing firms.[31] Woodward classified firms according to three types of technology (depicted in Figure 12.14). In increasing order of technological complexity, they include:

FIGURE 12.14   *Woodward's Technology Classification Scheme*

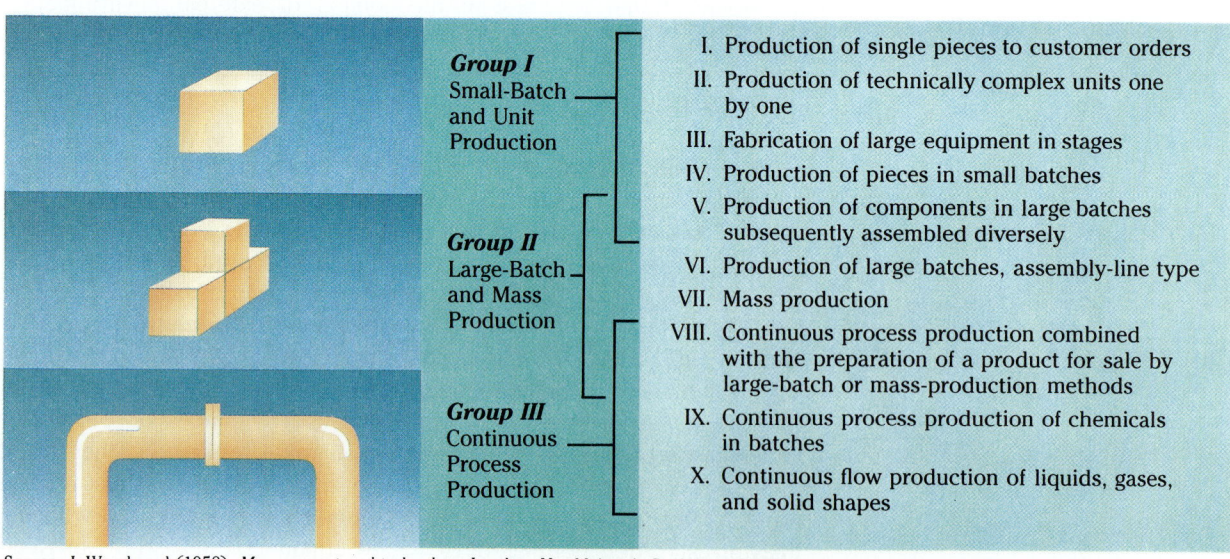

Group I Small-Batch and Unit Production	I. Production of single pieces to customer orders II. Production of technically complex units one by one III. Fabrication of large equipment in stages IV. Production of pieces in small batches
Group II Large-Batch and Mass Production	V. Production of components in large batches subsequently assembled diversely VI. Production of large batches, assembly-line type VII. Mass production
Group III Continuous Process Production	VIII. Continuous process production combined with the preparation of a product for sale by large-batch or mass-production methods IX. Continuous process production of chemicals in batches X. Continuous flow production of liquids, gases, and solid shapes

Source: J. Woodward (1958), *Management and technology*, London: Her Majesty's Stationery Office.

A petroleum refinery uses continuous process technology.

- *Unit or small-batch technology*—products are custom-made to a customer's specification and usually are produced in very small quantities; examples are tailor-made suits or custom-built vacation homes.
- *Large-batch and mass-production technology*—a large number of products are manufactured, assembly-line fashion, before production changeover to another type of product; examples are home appliances and automobiles
- *Continuous process technology*—products are generated in a continuous stream such that the beginning of the second product is not distinguishable from the end of the first; examples are the refining of petroleum and other chemicals

How does technology influence organizational design? Woodward noted that, as the technology became more complex, the number of hierarchical levels in an organization's structure increased. Span of control was also related to the type of technology. Top management's span increased as the technology became more complex. So did the size of the organization's staff. The span of control for lower-level supervisors was largest for organizations with large-batch or mass-production technologies. From these and other observations, Woodward noted that:

> *Successful firms inside the large-batch production range tended to have mechanistic management systems. On the other hand, successful firms outside the range tended to have organic systems.*[32]

In structuring organizations, managers must consider the technology that will be used. If it will be routine, a mechanistic (bureaucratic) design probably will be appropriate.[33] Organic designs, however, are better suited for organizations whose tasks and accompanying technology are nonroutine in nature.[34]

FIGURE 12.15 *The Strategy-Organization Design Relationship*

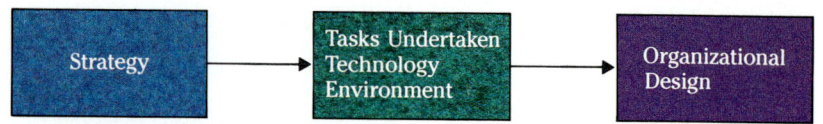

Goals

Alfred Chandler, while on the management faculty at the Massachusetts Institute of Technology, observed a close relationship between the types of goals pursued by an organization (its strategy) and its structure.[35] He analyzed the histories of such firms as General Motors, Standard Oil, Du Pont, and Sears and noted that each had used simple and centralized structures when dealing with limited product lines; however, as the firms took on more complex goals, adopted new products, entered new markets, and increased output, each decentralized their organizational structures.

Recent work shows that the strategies chosen by an organization's managers determine the tasks it undertakes, the technology it uses, and the environments in which it operates. Subsequently, these organizational attributes—tasks, technology, and environment—have a strong impact on the design adopted by the organization (see Figure 12.15).[36] The General Motors, Standard Oil, Du Pont, and Sears examples mentioned earlier all illustrate this finding.

The design that an organization adopts, in turn, places constraints on the goals managers are likely to adopt in the future. A mechanistic organization, for example, is likely to pursue goals that emphasize higher levels of productivity and operating efficiency. On the other hand, organizations that want to pursue innovation must be designed more openly and flexibly and must permit exchanges among individuals and groups that are highly heterogeneous in nature.[37]

Size

The size of an organization influences its design in many ways. As a department expands, a manager's span of control increases. As the span of control increases, coordination and control pressures mount. In response to these increased pressures, organizations frequently make structural changes. This reorganization often results in more organizational units, more hierarchical levels, and an even more complex organizational structure.

As organizations become larger, managers often increase the number of specialized departments (especially staff departments) and increase job specialization. Individuals often become responsible for the performance of a narrow range of activities. In the early days at Progressive Video Images, for example, employee Liz Phinney was involved in virtually all of the company's business activities. On a given day, she often would work on 35mm stills, 8mm movies, VHS videos, Beta videos, transfers from film to video, and so on. As the company grew, however, it developed specialized departments. Now Liz works exclusively at transferring 8mm movies to VHS videotape.

A CLOSER LOOK

Organizational Redesign: The Post Office Looks for New Zip, Kodak for More Snap

The Peter Principle holds that people rise to their personal level of incompetence. Robert J. Samuelson believes that "the same dynamic affects large companies; they tend to expand to their level of incompetence and inefficiency."[1] Many companies have been living proof of the organizational Peter Principle. They have diversified into areas where they are inept or, like Eastman Kodak Company, have focused too heavily on a small number of products, or, like the U.S. Postal Service, concentrated on operations at the expense of marketing.

For years, Kodak focused on what has now become a mature photo industry. After a ten-year low in profits and stiff competition from companies, such as Fuji Photo Film Company, Kodak has been trying to improve business by diversifying its narrow product line to include printers, optical memory systems, and new 35mm cameras. Perhaps more important, however, are changes in its corporate structure. According to Kodak's chairman, Colby H. Chandler, the company is being broken into a number of autonomous units that will market new products better and encourage additional new products to keep Kodak competitive.

Another familiar giant with problems is the U.S. Postal Service, which is finding that such organizations as United Parcel Service, Federal Express, and Purolator continue to grow at its expense. Postmaster General Preston Robert Tisch intended to turn the overgrown, 700,000-person bureaucracy into a more aggressive, businesslike provider of mail delivery services. According to Tisch, restructuring the organization was necessary to ". . . change it from an operating mentality to a marketing mentality."[2] Tisch initially agreed to local postmasters' suggestions for making Sunday deliveries in Manhattan's West Side to get rid of a backlog of mail, developed account teams to deal with major corporate customers, and took a more flexible approach to using automation. He seemed willing to admit error and bail out when mistakes were made, as the nine-digit zip code idea may prove to be. These and similar moves led *Business Week* to note that, "If Tisch leaves his mark on the Postal Service, it is most likely to be by making the organization more responsive to the public."[3]

Unfortunately, beginning early in 1988, Tisch was forced by Congress to take a number of steps that will make the Post Office less responsive. To save money, Sunday mail pick-up was terminated, lobby hours were shortened, and modernization was delayed. Congress won the short-term battle, Tisch resigned, and the new marketing orientation of the Post Office appears headed for an early demise.

The steps that both Kodak and the U.S. Postal Service (under Tisch's

guidance) took were designed to remedy their problems through restructuring. They were trying to capitalize on their organizational strengths and to eliminate their areas of organizational weakness. In effect, they were trying to become exceptions to the Peter Principle and rise to their true level of competence. Kodak may well succeed, but the meddling of Congress seems only to have shoved the Post Office further on the road to failure: calls for its privatization have begun.

1. R. J. Samuelson (8 September 1986), How companies grow stale, *Newsweek,* 45.
2. F. Seghers (24 November 1986), Bob Tisch is putting more zip in the Post Office, *Business Week,* 72.
3. *Ibid.*

Often accompanying increased specialization is greater standardization and formalization, more delegation of authority, and increased decentralization of structure. Employees at lower levels are permitted to make decisions to relieve upward pressure and bottlenecks in the hierarchy, but these decisions are guided by elaborate sets of policies, rules, and standard operating procedures. Upper-level management can then operate under the exception principle, handling only those issues that fall outside of the formal guidelines and delegating specific assignments to lower-level employees.

A final influence of size is its effect on coordination and control activities. Managers tend to rely increasingly on impersonal modes of coordination and control as organizational size increases. As a result, large organizations tend to be mechanistic in design.[38]

People

The attitudes, values, beliefs, commitments, and behaviors of organization members influence the design and, ultimately, the effectiveness of any organization. If employees are not good at self-direction and self-control, for example, the organization must rely on a mechanistic design.[39] If, on the other hand, an organization's employees are highly professional, organizationally committed, self-directed, and self-controlled, they work better with a less mechanistic design. Workers motivated by safety, security, and social needs tend to be comfortable in and work well with a bureaucratic organization design. Employees with strong growth needs, however, find more challenge and greater satisfaction in an organically designed organization.[40]

Several scholars who study organizations have argued that design is largely a function of the strategic preferences and choices of major organizational powerholders.[41] The values, beliefs, attitudes, and commitments of powerholders play a major role in shaping organizational design. Managers who subscribe to Theory X, for example, are likely to design tightly controlled, bureaucratic organizations to keep a watchful eye over the actions of workers they feel must be told exactly what to do and how to do it. Theory Y managers, on the other hand, believe in an individual's capacity to exercise self-direction and self-control and, thus, are more likely to adopt an organic design.

Personality factors also influence managers' design preferences. Such factors as authoritarianism (discussed in Chapter 13) can be particularly important. A manager with a highly authoritarian personality, for example, feels that power and status should be clearly defined and specified within organizations. This type of person, thus, is likely to create a centralized and formalized structure with a distinct hierarchy of authority.

Clearly, there is no one best organizational design. Good managers review an organization's internal and external environments, technology, goals, size, and other contextual factors when considering a structural design. They then should compare the compatibility of design alternatives with existing and anticipated conditions. Through this systematic approach, managers can select and implement an overall design with supporting superstructures and processes to meet the requirements of their specific organization.

Organizational Design in Review

As a part of the organizing process, managers must decide how to design the overall organization. Managers should consider structural, process, and contextual dimensions to arrive at an appropriate superstructure and accompanying systems. There are at least two types of traditional superstructures available to managers. A functional superstructure approach groups activities around the major types of tasks performed by an organization, such as operations, marketing, finance, and human resources. A divisional superstructure is based on arrangements similar to those used for departmentalization at lower levels: products, territories, customers, and so forth. A hybrid superstructure combines two or more of these approaches so that managers can benefit from the advantages of each.

Many managers of organizations that operate in complex, turbulent environments have come to rely on a newer design called a matrix superstructure. The matrix approach allows managers to overlap several organizational arrangements simultaneously. The intersections of authority in this complex arrangement requires three managerial roles: top leader, matrix boss, and two-boss managers. This structure has advantages, but it also creates many challenges for those who have to deal with its complexities.

The functional, divisional, hybrid, and matrix superstructure designs are based on essentially three models. The first perspective is the bureaucratic (mechanistic) structure approach advocated by classical management thinkers. It's design is relatively closed and rigid; it employs a high level of structured authority, communication, and coordination methods; and it uses many written standard operating procedures to control employee behavior.

To counter the classicists' concentration on the technical side of organizations, behavioral models emerged that stressed the human side of organizations. Sociotechnical systems theory advocates argued that organizations designed strictly from a mechanical perspective would be less effective than alternative designs. They called for the recognition of organizations as both technical and social systems that must be balanced. Similarly, Rensis Likert's System 4 design resulted in a network of interlocking groups, with managers' acting as linking pins to coordinate the flow of information and expertise. Both provide a structure that is more open and participatory than is the classical model.

The third model is based on organic design. Created to permit an organization's structure to evolve quickly in response to changes in the internal and external environments, the organic approach has resulted in self-designing organizations. These are extremely fluid, flexible organizations that "go with the flow." This arrangement has advantages for organizations that must cope with broad, changing foreign competition and technological innovation, but it may not be comfortable for workers who desire firm control and want procedures clearly outlined.

Managers contemplating various models and structures when designing organizations must take certain contextual factors into account. Environmental considerations, their organization's culture, the type and complexity of the technology to be used, their organization's goals, its size, and the attributes of organization members give rise to variations in organizational design. These contextual factors make certain approaches more suitable than others. To be most effective, a chosen design must be compatible with these factors.

Notes

1. R. H. Miles (1980), *Macro organizational behavior,* Santa Monica, CA: Goodyear 18; R. H. Hall (1987), *Organizations: structures, processes, and outcomes,* Englewood Cliffs, NJ: Prentice-Hall.

2. R. Robey (1982), *Designing organizations: A macro perspective,* Homewood, IL: Irwin.

3. R. E. Hoskisson (1987), Multidivisional structure and performance: The contingency of diversification strategy, *Academy of Management Journal,* 30, 625–44.

4. GM's shuffle: The calm before a slaughter (17 February 1986), *Business Week,* 35.

5. W. F. Joyce (1986), Matrix organization: A social experiment, *Academy of Management Journal,* 29, 536–61.

6. S. M. Davis and P. R. Lawrence (1977), *Matrix,* Reading, MA: Addison-Wesley, 11–24; R. B. Duncan (1979), What is the right organization structure? Decision tree analysis provides the answer, *Organizational Dynamics,* 7(3), 59–80.

7. Davis and Lawrence, 1977.

8. P. E. Connor (1980), *Organizations: Theory and design,* Chicago: SRA.

9. M. Weber (1922), *The theory of social and economic organization,* A. M. Henderson and T. Parsons, eds. and trans., (1947), New York: Oxford University Press.

10. P. M. Blau and M. W. Meyer (1987), *Bureaucracy in modern society,* New York: Random House.

11. E. Litwak (1961), Models of bureaucracy which permit conflict, *American Journal of Sociology,* 67, 177–84; R. H. Hall (1962), Intraorganizational structural variation: Application of the bureaucratic model, *Administrative Science Quarterly,* 7, 295–308.

12. Litwak, 1961; C. Perrow (1967), A framework for the comparative analysis of organizations, *American Sociological Review,* 32, 194–208; A. H. Van de Ven and A. L. Delbecq (1974), A task contingent model of work unit structure, *Administrative Science Quarterly,* 19, 183–97; W. A. Randolph and G. G. Dess (1984), The congruence perspective of organization design: A conceptual model and multivariate research approach, *Academy of Management Review,* 9, 114–27.

13. C. Argyris (1973), Personality and organization theory revisited, *Administrative Science Quarterly,* 18, 141–67; C. Argyris (1957), *Personality and organization,* New York: Harper & Row; W. Bennis (1965), Beyond bureaucracy, *Trans-action,* 2, 31–35; R. Blauner (1964), *Alienation and freedom,* Chicago: The University of Chicago Press.

14. E. Trist and K. W. Bamforth (1951), Some social and psychological consequences of the long-wall method of coal getting, *Human Relations*, 4, 3–38.

15. E. L. Trist (1981), The sociotechnical perspective: The evolution of sociotechnical systems as a conceptual framework and as an action research program, in A. H. Van de Ven and W. F. Joyce, eds., *Perspectives on organization design and behavior*, New York: John Wiley & Sons, 19–75.

16. R. Likert (1967), *The human organization*, New York: McGraw-Hill; R. Likert (1961), *New patterns in management*, New York: McGraw-Hill.

17. T. Burns and G. M. Stalker (1961), *The management of innovation*, London: Tavistock.

18. Litwak, 1961; Hall, 1962; G. Hage (1965), An axiomatic theory of organizations, *Administrative Science Quarterly*, 10, 289–320.

19. Classless capitalists (9 May 1983), *Forbes*, 122, 124.

20. B. L. T. Hedberg, P. C. Nystrom, and W. H. Starbuck (1976), Camping on seesaws: Prescriptions for a self-designing organization, *Administrative Science Quarterly*, 21, 46–65; B. L. T. Hedberg, P. C. Nystrom, and W. H. Starbuck (1977), Designing organizations to match tomorrow, *North-Holland/TIMS Studies in Management Sciences*, 5, 171–81; K. E. Weick (1977), Organization design: Organization as self-designing systems, *Organizational Dynamics*, 6(2), 30–46; A. Wildavsky (1972), The self-evaluating organization, *Public Administration Review*, 32(5), 509–20.

21. A. G. Bedeian (1984), *Organizations: Theory and analysis*, Chicago: Dryden Press, 499.

22. Hedberg, Nystrom, and Starbuck, 1977, 171.

23. Weick, 1977, 37.

24. P. R. Lawrence and J. W. Lorsch (1967), *Organization and environment*, Homewood, IL: Irwin.

25. Randolph and Dess, 1984, 121.

26. S. Richardson (1956), Organizational contrasts on British and American ships, *Administrative Science Quarterly*, 1, 189–207.

27. M. Crozier (1964), *The bureaucratic phenomenon*, Chicago: The University of Chicago Press.

28. A. Reudi and P. R. Lawrence (1970), Organizations in two cultures, in J. W. Lorsch and P. R. Lawrence, eds., *Studies in organization design*, Homewood, IL: Irwin.

29. W. G. Ouchi (1981), *Theory Z: How American business can meet the Japanese challenge*, Reading, MA: Addison-Wesley.

30. Randolph and Dess, 1984.

31. J. Woodward (1965), *Industrial organization: Theory and practice*, London: Oxford University Press.

32. Woodward, 1965, 71.

33. Perrow, 1967; Van de Ven and Delbecq, 1974.

34. J. W. Alexander and W. A. Randolph (1985), The fit between technology and structure as a predictor of performance in nursing subunits, *Academy of Management Journal*, 28, 840–59; J. V. Singh (1986), Technology, size, and organizational structure: A reexamination of the Okayama study data, *Academy of Management Journal*, 29, 800–812.

35. A. D. Chandler, Jr. (1962), *Strategy and structure: Chapters in the history of the American industrial enterprise*, Cambridge, MA: MIT Press.

36. H. Mintzberg (1979), *The structuring of organizations*, Englewood Cliffs, NJ: Prentice-Hall.

37. J. L. Pierce and A. L. Delbecq (1977), *Academy of Management Review*, 2, 27–37; M. Aiken and J. Hage (1971), The organic organization and innovation, *Sociology*, 5, 63–82; Burns and Stalker, 1961.

38. Singh, 1986.

39. D. McGregor (1960), *The human side of enterprise*, New York: McGraw-Hill.

40. L. W. Porter, E. E. Lawler III, and J. R. Hackman (1975), *Behavior in organizations*, New York: McGraw-Hill.

41. J. Child (1972), Organization structure, environment and performance: The role of strategic choice, *Sociology*, 6, 369–93; J. R. Montanari (August 1977), *Operationalizing strategic choice*, a paper presented at the 37th National Meeting of the Academy of Management, Orlando, FL; D. C. Hambrick and P. A. Mason (1984), Upper echelons: The organization as a reflection of its top managers, *Academy of Management Review*, 9, 193–206.

Key Terms

organizational design
organizational structure
organizational context
superstructure
functional superstructure
divisional superstructure
hybrid superstructure
matrix superstructure
top leader

matrix boss
two-boss manager
bureaucratic model
behavioral models
sociotechnical systems theory
System 4 organization
linking pin roles
organic organization
self-designing organization

Issues for Review and Discussion

1. Explain the roles of structure, process, and context in defining organizational design.

2. What are the differences between the functional and divisional forms of organizational superstructure?

3. What are some advantages of a hybrid superstructure? What are some disadvantages?

4. How is a matrix superstructure different from a hybrid superstructure? How are these differences intended to improve effectiveness?

5. Identify three major managerial roles that are found in a matrix organization and discuss each.

6. Compare and contrast the bureaucratic and System 4 approaches to organizational design.

7. Under what conditions is an organic design appropriate?

8. Explain how environmental conditions influence the design of an effective organization.

Suggested Readings

Hellriegel, D. and Slocum, J. W., Jr. (April 1973). Organizational design: A contingency approach. *Business Horizons*, 16(2), 59–68.

Joyce, W. F. (1986). Matrix organization: A social experiment. *Academy of Management Journal*, 29, 536–61.

Kets de Vries, F. R. and Miller, D. (1984). *The neurotic organization*. San Francisco, CA: Jossey-Bass.

Mintzberg, H. (January/February 1981). Organization design: Fashion or fit? *Harvard Business Review*, 59, 103–16.

Toffler, A. (1985). *The adaptive corporation*. Toronto: Bantam Books; Gribbins, R. E. (1988). A review of *The adaptive corporation*. In Pierce, J. L. and Newstrom, J. W., eds. *The manager's bookshelf: A mosaic of contemporary views*. New York: Harper & Row, 268–74.

Weber, M. (1947). The ideal bureaucracy. Parsons, T. and Henderson, A. M. trans., *The theory of social and economic organizations*. New York: Macmillan.

CASE *Arnco Products Company*

*By Kenneth L. Jensen
of Drury College*

The Arnco Products Company was founded in 1952 as a glass container supplier for the beer and soft drink segment of the beverage industry. Over the years, it branched into supplying other industries with glass containers. The first area was the dairy industry, which used returnable glass bottles for their delivery sales. Arnco then developed other forms of glass containers to allow it to expand into supplying food packers with jam and jelly glasses, which were reused by consumers. Eventually the company became known as a specialist supplier of reusable glass containers. In all of the industries to which it sold, Arnco maintained high quality levels and sold at prices higher than their competitors.

When Paul Greenstone became president of Arnco, he replaced his uncle, Ronald Joyce. Mr. Joyce was an engineer and designer who concentrated his efforts on operations, particularly quality control. It was his belief that high-quality products would sell themselves. Mr. Greenstone, on the other hand, had left a major manufacturer of consumer goods, where he had been the national sales manager. His strong suit was in the development of accounts and channels of distribution. He believed that sales representatives (reps) should cultivate major accounts by providing the types of services that such accounts demanded.

At the time Mr. Greenstone became the president of Arnco, company sales had been flat for several years. This came about because of the increased use of cans, plastic containers, and nonreturnable bottles in the beverage industry. The one favorable factor was the increased use of returnable glass bottles in states requiring deposits on all beverage containers for environmental reasons. Mr. Greenstone believed that there was a new opportunity for Arnco if the company could take advantage of it. He came to believe that the company should investigate the characteristics and requirements of its customers, as well as the ability of Arnco's sales organization to meet their needs. To do this, he asked his staff to do an analysis of Arnco's existing sales network and a study of customer buying patterns.

Arnco's Sales Organization

Arnco's sales force consisted of twenty sales reps organized on a geographical (territorial) basis. There were two regional managers supervising the sales reps. Each rep was expected to call on and service all accounts in his or her territory—an average of 100 accounts per rep. Two thirds of the accounts were in the beverage industry, with an increasing number of food packers and a decreasing number of dairy accounts.

Because of the broad diversity of customer requirements, Arnco's product line was quite extensive. Each rep sold all items in the line. This required a great deal of knowledge on the part of the sales force, for beer and soft drink customers had different product requirements than food packers. Beverage accounts were concerned more with the serviceability of the container. Food packers tended to be more concerned with print requirements for container labels.

Once an order was placed, Arnco shipped directly to customers from either of two warehouses. One was located at company headquarters in Lancaster, Pennsylvania. It served all accounts east of the Mississippi River. The other warehouse was in Denver, Colorado, and handled the remainder of the country. Orders were mailed in

FIGURE 12A *Arnco's Sales Organization*

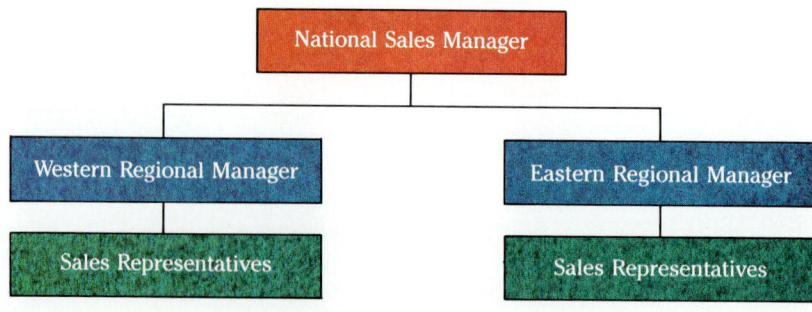

each day by the sales reps, processed at the warehouse, and then filled and shipped by truck to the customer. The order-processing time varied from one to four days, depending on the mail service and the volume of orders received on any one day. Truck delivery times varied from one to four days also; thus, total delivery time could vary from two to eight days once a customer placed an order.

Promotional efforts were totally concentrated in direct selling. No advertising had ever been used in the trade press, nor had direct mail ever been used. When calling on an account, Arnco's representatives tended to stress their product quality and the company's reputation to get the order.

Arnco's customers purchased glass containers either through negotiating the purchase or through letting the purchase out for bids. Customers who used the bidding process typically wanted products made to their specifications and required more time on the part of Arnco's sales representatives. Arnco's survey showed that nearly 25 percent of their accounts used the bidding process exclusively and that about three fourths used bids for 60 percent or more of their purchases. The survey also showed a strong relationship between the size of the customer and the use of competitive bidding, with the larger accounts using bidding more often than the smaller accounts.

The survey identified the importance of factors customers used to select their suppliers. The top five factors, in order of importance, were the following:

1. Quality
2. Speed of delivery
3. Service
4. Reputation
5. Price

The survey also showed that the larger customers who relied more on the bidding process placed more importance on speed of delivery than did smaller customers.

Another aspect of the survey examined competition from the customers themselves, who made some of their own containers. The survey showed that slightly fewer than 50 percent of their customers produced some of their own containers and that fewer than 10 percent made more than 40 percent of their required containers. None of their accounts produced more than 80 percent of their own containers.

After considering the results of the work done by his staff, Mr. Greenstone came to believe that the sales force would be more effective with a different organizational structure. He wondered what kind of structure was needed.

Questions

1. What do you think leads Mr. Greenstone to believe that the current structure needs improvement? What other changes might be made?

2. What are the most important aspects of the sales force's task environment?

3. What should be the basis for the sales force structure?

4. Prepare a new organizational chart for Arnco's sales force.

PART 4

Directing

Addison Barry Rand

After holding several sales jobs in suburban department stores, A. Barry Rand joined the Xerox Corporation as a sales trainee in 1968. After two years of hard work and self-denial, Rand's persuasive talents and passion for selling paid off. In 1970, Rand was recognized as the top salesperson in his district and ranked third among Xerox' national salesforce. Rand's twenty years with Xerox have been characterized by commitment, the setting of difficult goals, successful performance, and upward mobility. His performance record has positioned him as a possible candidate for the corporate presidency of Xerox.

Wanting to win—and winning—is a way of life for this manager.

After graduation from high school, Rand headed to Rutgers University to study medicine, yet his sights were really set on a career in sales. He transferred to American University and graduated in 1968 with a degree in marketing. After being recruited by IBM and EXXON, Rand chose to accept an offer as a trainee with Xerox. He saw Xerox as an organization that prompted individuality. It was an organization in which a young person who wants to win would have ample opportunity to do so. Wanting to win—and winning—is a way of life for this manager; as he says it, "I thought I was always supposed to win and that's the way life was supposed to be."[1]

Rand's strong sales performance helped put him in the spotlight at Xerox. Not only was he seen as a good salesperson, he understood marketing. Emerging opportunities gave him the chance to demonstrate managerial talents as well as a passion for excellence. These factors, and a little luck, enabled him to move rapidly through a number of marketing management positions. From 1980 to 1984, he was promoted from corporate director of major account marketing, into and out of vice-presidencies in account marketing and field operations, and into the vice-presidency of Xerox' Eastern operations. In January of 1986, Rand was named vice-president and general manager of Xerox' National Marketing Distribution Organization. He was elected a corporate officer in May 1986 and, in December of 1986 he was appointed to his present position of vice-president of Xerox Corporation and president of the company's U.S. marketing group. His corporate vice-presidency places him on a team of twenty top-level executives in the $13 billion multinational corporation.

As president of the U.S. marketing group, Rand is responsible for an operation that generates nearly $5 billion in sales and employs a salesforce of 33,000 people. For all practical purposes, his operation is responsible for the "bread and butter" of Xerox.[2] The division is responsible for marketing, direct sales and service of Xerox products, and services to major accounts and commercial customers throughout the United States. Rand is also playing a central role in Xerox' challenge to its Japanese competitors. In recent years, the Japanese have made major inroads into a market that once belonged to Xerox. Today, Xerox is positioning itself to take this market back, and Xerox chairman and CEO David T. Kearns has identified Rand as the man who will lead the "multinational giant's initiative against the Japanese."[3]

In response to this challenge, Rand has embarked on a major change in Xerox' strategy. This strategic change will necessitate a major change in the organization's internal culture. The essence of his strategy will be to place greater emphasis on customer satisfaction. Rand says, "We have got to develop an obsession with satisfying customers, . . . We've got to do everything we can to make sure that we get the affirmative vote of our customers."[4] According to Rand, Xerox historically has been an internally oriented organization. This internal orientation is reflected in the organization's drive for efficiency. The customer, says Rand, "doesn't necessarily care how lean we are. He cares about us meeting his needs."[5] Rand is steering Xerox toward building a customer-responsive product and a service-oriented organization. If he is successful, many speculate that he will become Xerox' next corporate president.

Being number one without giving the maximum is unacceptable.

Rand also finds himself responsible for meeting a number of the company's cost-cutting goals while increasing efficiency and productivity. Herein lies another part of his managerial philosophy. Instead of cutting costs by laying off a portion of the organization's workforce, Rand's approach is driven by the simultaneous achievement of cost cuts and the maintenance of employee morale and security.

Achieving excellence, driving for continual improvement, and exceeding expectations may be key forces behind Rand's motivation, hard work,

and successful track record. He credits his middle-class parents with instilling in him high expectations and the drives for achievement and continued self-betterment. In 1970, when he became Xerox' number-three national salesperson, his father might have asked why he was third and not second or first. When Rand looks at himself in the mirror, the face looking back says that if you gave your maximum effort, everything is okay, but being number one without giving the maximum is unacceptable.

Rand claims that his teamwork experiences with athletes of all ethnic backgrounds played a major role in preparing him for success in the corporate world. High expectations, ambition, preparation, and performance have enabled him to break into corporate management by the age of forty-three. These same factors are likely to carry him even higher and to more success in the decades to come.

At Xerox, Chairman and CEO Kearns sees Rand as a talented executive. "Barry has a tremendous amount of experience and he is an aggressive executive with a great background in marketing," says Kearns.[6] He believes Rand's drive, standards of excellence, aggressiveness, and experience with marketing will play a key role in Xerox' effort to combat the Japanese marketing challenge.

1. D. Narine (January 1988), Barry Rand—Xerox's $5 billion man, *Ebony*, 118.

2. J. P. Hicks (22 May 1987), A black's climb to executive suite, *Business Day: The New York Times*, D1, D4.

3. A. Edmond, Jr. (August 1987), Can this man keep team Xerox no. 1? *Black Enterprise*, 58.

4. Hicks, D1.

5. *Ibid.*

6. D. T. Kearns in Edmond, 60.

CHAPTER 13

The Nature of Organization Members: Individuals and Groups

Student Learning Objectives

After reading this chapter, you should be able to:

1. Understand the nature and purpose of the directing activity.

2. Understand the nature and organizational importance of individual needs.

3. Discuss the three approaches to ability management (selection, placement, and training).

4. Explain the importance to an organization of differences in personality.

5. Understand the nature of attitudes and how they can influence organizational effectiveness.

6. Discuss the four stages of the perceptual process and what is needed to effectively manage each stage.

7. Distinguish among types of groups and identify the factors that encourage group formation and cohesion.

8. Discuss the organizational impact of group cohesion, roles, and norms.

9. Understand the six major stages of group development.

*T*he third major management function, directing, is the process through which employees are led and motivated to make effective and efficient contributions to the realization of organizational goals. To execute the directing function successfully, managers must understand the nature of individuals *and* groups, much as they need to understand capital in order to execute financial activities. After all, an organization is a social system, and its work is accomplished through its individual members and through groups, such as work teams, project groups, committees, and quality circles. To direct people well, managers must understand their individual characteristics and learn how to guide the groups they form as they pursue organizational goals.

The Nature of Individuals

Susan Siegrist and Karlene McBride were classmates in high school and college. They both majored in business and graduated at the same time, but there the similarities between them end. Today, ten years after graduation, Susan Siegrist is performing well as the associate dean of a fine Midwestern university. She works closely with the treasurer and comptroller, oversees the preparation of the annual budget, and has close contact with the office of alumni. Karlene McBride, in contrast, has held over a dozen different jobs since graduating from college. She has never received a promotion at any of them. She is presently working as a publicist for the consumer product division of a large manufacturing firm. Her previous job was as assistant to the administrator of a small hospital. Before that, she worked in the real estate department of an insurance company. In each job, Karlene has felt increasingly less motivated and more dissatisfied with her responsibilities and her colleagues. Is the contrast between Susan and Karlene just a matter of fate? No; for the most part, each woman's motives, abilities, personality, and attitudes account

People enter an organization with a unique set of needs, abilities, attitudes, personality factors, and perceptual and learning styles.

for the differences between them. The psychological makeup of an individual has important implications for effectiveness on the job.

Susan Siegrist, Karlene McBride, and everyone else come into an organization with a variety of needs, abilities, attitudes, personality factors, and perceptual and learning styles. Together, these individual differences exert a tremendous influence over people's reactions to their work, over their ability to work effectively, and over the degree to which they serve the interests of their organization. People may be an organizational resource, but they are not standardized and automated machines. They are human and must be directed by managers who understand various human characteristics. The way in which managers work with (or against) employees' motivation, attitudes, skills, and abilities is crucial to an organization's success.

Motives

All individuals have needs, wants, desires, and expectations, or **motives,** which push them to perform various types of behavior. When people's motives are met, they feel happiness or satisfaction. When they are not, people feel unhappy or dissatisfied. Because of these consequences, individuals are continuously motivated to do things that satisfy their wants, needs, desires, and expectations and to avoid doing things that frustrate this satisfaction.

People often are not fully aware of the motives that shape their behavior. Susan Siegrist, for example, may not be aware that she is strongly motivated to work extra hours to become the best worker in her department because she needs to be recognized as an effective worker and thrives on promotions. Karlene McBride probably is not aware that she is strongly motivated to "slack off" at work so that her co-workers do not appear unproductive and accept her as one of the group.

Work-Related Motivation Motivation is an internal force that makes an organization member put forth a certain amount of effort to accomplish something. People are motivated, for example, to come to work, to remain on the job, to be good performers, to do things for the organization "above and beyond the call of duty"—or to skip work (and interview for another job or sleep late), to quit their job altogether, or to do as little for the organization as they can get away with.

Although motivation is not the only determinant of the way that employees behave, it certainly plays a central role. The level of employee performance appears to be determined largely by three factors: (1) accurate role perceptions (an employee knows what is to be done and how), (2) the skills and abilities to perform a task, and (3) the motivation to put forth the necessary effort to accomplish a task. Managers cannot elicit behavior from employees—selling products, serving customers, meeting budgets, and so on—unless they are motivated to engage in that behavior. In turn, employees' motivation is unlikely to be intense and appropriately channeled unless some of their needs, wants, desires, and expectations can be satisfied in the process. In short, organization members are motivated to meet their organizational responsibilities when they feel that doing so also meets their personal motives.

Employee performance appears to be determined by accurate role perceptions, the skills and abilities needed to perform a task, and the motivation to accomplish it.

As you undoubtedly know from personal experience, people have different motives, which change over time. Some things that are important to you today were not important to you five or ten years ago. Some things probably have been important to you for years and will continue to be important. You may have been motivated to become a manager for years because of a strong need to feel successful and effective, or because you have a flair for telling others how to get things done. In Chapter 14, you can read about several theories of motivation. In this chapter, you will learn a few theories of the needs underlying motivation.

Need Theories   Need theories focus on basic differences among people. Human needs are a central motivating force, which directs and governs the intensity of human behavior. People are motivated to satisfy their active needs. (See Chapter 14 for a thorough discussion of need theories.)

The work of Henry Murray and his associates at the Harvard Psychological Clinic during the 1930s led to the development of Murray's *manifest need theory*. According to this theory, people have many very specific needs.[1] They need, among other things, to succeed, to socialize, and to be loved. Unfortunately, the extreme specificity of Murray's theory made it unwieldy for use in organizations. His list of human needs was so long—consisting of hundreds of needs—that it included a separate need for almost every human behavior. Although of limited use to managers, Murray's work stimulated further research that has proven valuable.

One theory stemming from Murray's work has been particularly useful to organizations. Another group from Harvard University, David McClelland and his colleagues, has identified three central needs: the needs for achievement, for power, and for affiliation (belongingness).[2] People have needs to perform (at work, in school, in the family or community, and elsewhere), to control aspects of their environment and the people in it, and to belong to groups. Of these three needs, McClelland maintains, the need for power is the most important determinant of a manager's success. In addition, employees with a high need for achievement also tend to be strongly oriented toward personal success. Employees with a high need for affiliation often find it difficult to be assertive or to give others directions because they are afraid of offending people.

The understanding of human needs has been greatly enhanced by the work of such scholars as Abraham Maslow, Frederick Herzberg, and Clayton Alderfer. These people categorized needs into more workable groups and demonstrated the relative importance of needs. Perhaps most important, these scholars improved managers' ability to apply this knowledge in organizations.

Abilities

Performance, as you have seen, is a function of both a person's motivation and ability. Motivation accounts for the *desire* to perform; ability accounts for the *capability* to perform. Two people with identical levels of motivation perform at different levels if their levels of ability differ. For example, Sandra Rainer and Glen Wilson, two trainees in the accounting department of a textile mill, may both be highly motivated to achieve and succeed, but Sandra, who has a stronger mathematical ability, may work more effectively.

Of course, the performance of any job requires a combination of abilities. Sandra and Glen not only need mathematical ability but must be able to read and write, to follow directions, and to get along with others. Levels of various abilities differ substantially from person to person and can differ significantly across time for one individual. Sandra may have stronger mathematical skills than Glen, but Glen may have more persistence and a better ability to work with others. For large groups of people, statistics show what is called a *bell curve distribution* for almost any ability. The bell curve shows that, in the general population, the majority of people have average ability levels. Few people have abilities that approach very low levels and few have very high levels. This holds true for both physical abilities (strength, flexibility, and coordination) and intellectual abilities (thinking, memory, and reasoning). (See Figure 13.1.)

Different jobs, of course, require different types of abilities. Some jobs require conceptual abilities, some require interpersonal abilities, and some require technical abilities (see Chapter 1). Accounting trainees, for example, require a different mixture of these abilities than do investigative reporters or associate deans. The abilities that are relevant to the successful performance of a particular job depend on the nature of the job, on the design of the job, and on the types of technology available. The necessary mix varies not only from one job to another and across jobs at the same level in an organizational hierarchy, but from one level to another. It stands to reason that the higher up in the organizational hierarchy a manager rises, the stronger his or her conceptual and interpersonal abilities must be.

As a manager, you will need to exercise your ability to tell people what to do, how to do it, and when to have it done. You will have to motivate them to do as you ask and to meet the organization's goals. To do so, you must be capable of matching the demands of specific jobs to the abilities

FIGURE 13.1   *Ability Distributions*

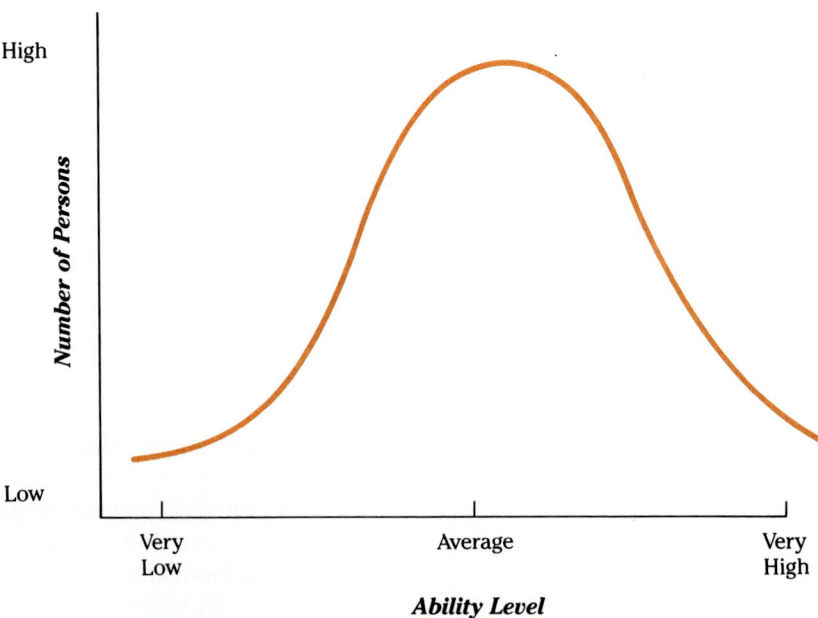

of your employees. If motivation is constant, one theory suggests that employee performance is primarily determined by the degree of correspondence between an individual's abilities and the ability demands of the job.[3] If the match between employee and job is not a good one, problems lie ahead.

Undermatching is what happens when an employee does not possess the abilities that his or her job demands. An accounting trainee with weak mathematical skills, a manager who shrinks from giving direction, and an investigative reporter whose interviewing techniques cause sources to withhold important information all are undermatched in their positions. In contrast, *overmatching* happens when an employee is overqualified for a job. A certified public accountant who accepts a job as an accounting trainee, an investigative reporter who is transferred to a proofreading job, and a vice-president of sales whose department is cut by two thirds all are overmatched in their positions. Employees who are undermatched cannot be high performers because they do not have the abilities to meet the demands of their job. Even extremely high levels of motivation cannot compensate for a lack of ability. Employees who are overmatched may lose motivation to perform, given the lack of challenge and opportunity on the job.

To avoid such problems, managers typically use three techniques referred to as selection, placement, and training to match the ability of employees with the demands of a job. *Selection* takes advantage of differences among individuals. Managers choose candidates with the necessary abilities for particular jobs by examining them. Whether through ability testing, job interviews, or other means, managers try to determine and select those who have the abilities needed to do a job. When Susan Siegrist interviewed for the job of associate dean, for example, she answered detailed questions about her experience in the area of financial management. *Placement* is the process of putting individuals into specific jobs within an organization; thus, an organization takes advantage of intraindividual (within person) differences by identifying a candidate's strong points and by placing that person in a job that will tap these abilities. Susan Siegrist was placed in—actually, promoted to—the associate deanship because she has strengths in dealing with finances as well as with her colleagues. *Training* deals with the potential differences within individuals by improving on employees' levels of ability. Susan is taking a course on institutional finance at the university's business school. This training not only strengthens her performance in her present job but makes her a stronger candidate for promotion.

Selection, placement, and training each contribute to the performance of organization members. Sometimes organizations perform these functions separately, but usually they make decisions about selection and placement at the same time. (Chapter 17 discusses these techniques further.)

Learning

Except on very simple tasks, a person's performance improves with time and training until he or she reaches a final level of competence. Like performance, the rate of learning (that is, the acquisition of skills) is influenced by a person's motivation and ability.

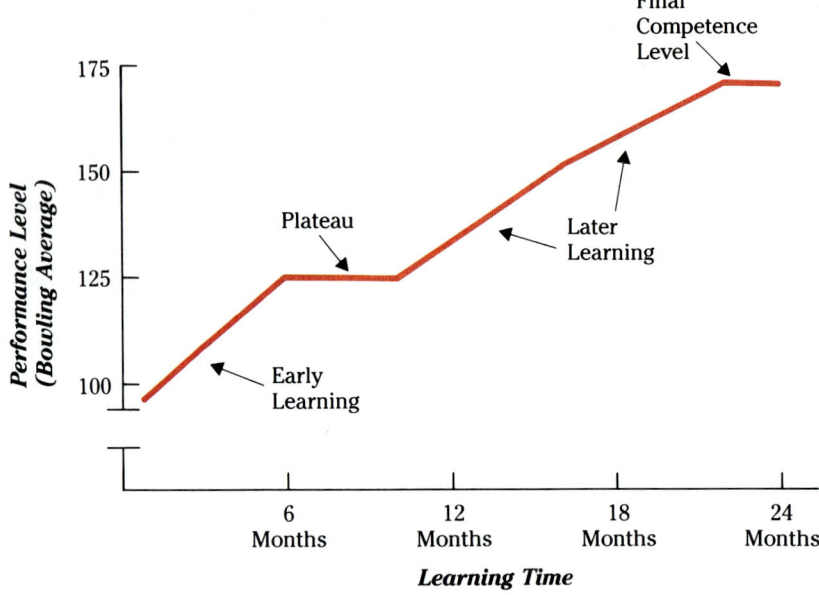

FIGURE 13.2 A Typical Learning
Curve for Bowling

It is interesting and important to note that learning seldom occurs at a steady rate. When you are learning a new task, for example, you have probably noticed that you seem to learn fairly quickly at the beginning, but then your speed tapers off. Sometimes, you reach a plateau at which, for some time, you seem to learn little, if anything. Then you break away from this plateau and learn fairly rapidly again until you reach your final level of mastery. Figure 13.2 illustrates such a learning curve for a person learning to bowl.

Managers must understand that, although plateaus are common, they are not a necessary part of the learning process. Plateaus usually follow a temporary lack of motivation, inefficient performance methods, or (often) poor training techniques. Although a plateau can provide brief respite from rapid learning, it clearly delays the point of reaching full proficiency. Appropriate training techniques and incentives can usually shorten or eliminate plateaus.

Figure 13.3 illustrates how ability and motivation can affect both the level and rate of learning for three people learning how to enter computer data. Donna has the lowest ability, the slowest rate of learning, and the lowest final proficiency level, and she takes the longest to reach that final proficiency level. Mark, who has higher ability than Donna, has a more rapid rate of learning and a higher final proficiency level, and he takes a shorter amount of time to reach that level. Randi's ability level is also high and about on par with Mark's, but she has received an incentive from the organization to learn data entry quickly. Her high ability level, coupled with her high motivation level (due to the incentive), have resulted in a rate and level of learning that are higher than those for Donna or Mark. The next chapter will explore the most effective ways for managers to enhance motivation.

The differences in people's skills and knowledge affect not only their speed and proficiency at performance skills, such as entering data or writing newspaper stories, but also their speed and proficiency with all kinds of skills and knowledge. People with strong abilities and motivation, for example, learn organizational policies, practices, norms, and cultures more rapidly than do those with lower abilities and motivation.

Personality

Although learning is determined by abilities and motivation, your general nature is determined in large part by your personality. **Personality** is a combination of the psychological characteristics and traits that make up each person's unique style of behavior. Psychologists think that personality characteristics tend to be quite stable over time and that significant changes, if any, usually occur only gradually. An employee who is impulsive and restless is not likely to become cautious and sedentary. An employee who is attuned to co-workers' feelings is not likely to become insensitive to them. An employee who is orderly and obedient is not likely to become disorderly and rebellious. Psychologists have identified many personality factors, some of which are of particular importance in an organizational context.

Locus of Control All people have experienced positive and negative consequences of their behavior. People receive praise, raises, and promotions. They also get criticism, demotions, and warnings. Although all people have experienced both success and failure, some people believe that their success and failure are determined by their own actions and abilities. They have what psychologists call an **internal locus of control.** Other people believe that other people, circumstances, or just plain luck account for their success and failure. They have an **external locus of control.**

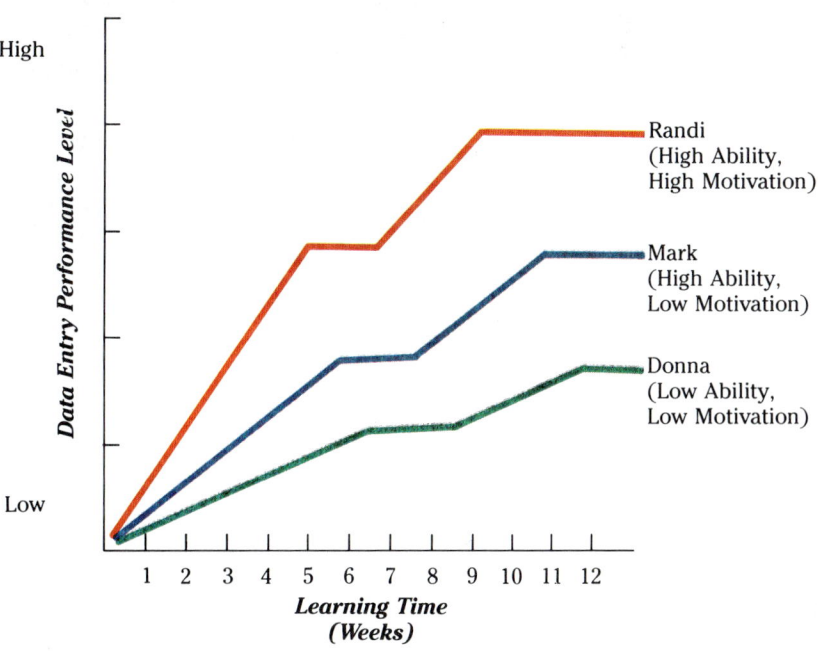

FIGURE 13.3   The Effects of Ability and Motivation on the Learning Curve

Individuals who have an internal locus of control believe that they determine their own fate. Because people with an internal locus of control believe that they have and will continue to have influence over their own effectiveness, they may be easier to motivate than people with an external locus of control. They are more likely to understand that success must be *obtained,* not just received. Employees with an internal locus of control are often effective because they actively seek success, seizing the initiative and expending personal effort to achieve it. Susan Siegrist believes, for example, that her hard work has paid off handsomely for her and will continue to do so as long as she puts in the time and effort that her position requires.

People with an external locus of control believe that factors beyond their motivation and abilities influence their destiny. Employees with an external locus of control can be tricky to motivate. Some believe that there is little point in working hard because they feel perpetually unlucky, think that "what will happen will happen," or believe that the cards were stacked against them from the beginning. People with an external locus of control, however, can be motivated to work effectively if given specific and appropriate direction. They also are not as likely to take failure personally, as are people with an internal locus of control.

Authoritarianism Another aspect of personality that affects job performance is a person's beliefs about authority. If your boss tells you to do something, will you do it without question? An **authoritarian** person believes that power and status should be clearly defined and that there should be an organizational hierarchy of authority. People with authoritarian personalities believe that organizations must concentrate authority in the hands of a small number of leaders and that this authority should be obeyed. They feel that orders and rules must be followed. Individuals with authoritarian personalities are generally willing to obey people of higher authority and to expect their subordinates to respond with similar deference.

Authoritarian leaders tend to be effective if they have authoritarian subordinates. Subordinates who are not authoritarian tend to examine the appropriateness of the orders that they receive, which frustrates an authoritarian leader. Authoritarian subordinates, in contrast, expect orders from the boss. They are likely to feel frustrated if they receive only suggestions or general instructions from an unauthoritarian leader. It is neither better nor worse for organization members to have authoritarian personalities. What is important is that an organization's leaders recognize the levels of authoritarianism that subordinates respond to best and manage them appropriately.

Dogmatism Another aspect of personality that influences how people do their work and relate to others is the level of dogmatism. A person high in **dogmatism** has a rigid belief system and sees the world from a narrow perspective. Some people are more open-minded than others. Some are comfortable considering lots of different perspectives and ideas. Highly dogmatic individuals are not. They feel uncomfortable when presented with ideas that are not consistent with their own views of the world. Within an organizational context, they like to know the rules and follow them closely. When faced with new ideas, they are likely to offer resistance. When faced with problems, they try to apply solutions that worked in a similar situation in their past experience. When they cannot call on experience as a guide for action, they may feel irritated and uncomfortable. Karlene McBride, who has gone unhappily from one job to another, has complained persistently that her bosses let people "get away with murder" and that the departments she worked in were "undisciplined" and "chaotic." It is likely that she is a fairly dogmatic person who needs to find work in a setting that is highly structured and rewards people for sticking to the rules.

Dogmatic personalities fit well in some positions and some organizations. They fit well into an organizational setting where there are few uncertainties and a fully specified course of action. They do poorly in settings involving uncertainty and a need for creativity. Dogmatic people can be very effective in routine tasks. They are unlikely to waste time, for example, thinking about alternative ways to view an already highly structured task. People low in dogmatism, in contrast, spend significant amounts of time and energy thinking about all sorts of alternatives. Unless creativity is needed on their jobs, much of their time and energy could be better directed toward the performance of already defined tasks.

Type A and Type B Personalities   One classification of personality types has important implications not only for how people work but also for their physical health and well-being. Some people, for example, are never late for an appointment. They are always rushed and very competitive. They walk fast, eat fast, and talk fast. They try to do several things at one time. They have what is referred to as a Type A personality. A **Type A personality** works intensely, impatiently, and under pressure. A **Type B personality,** in contrast, has a less-pressured style and tends to be more easy-going and relaxed. Lots of people in the corporate suite have Type A personalities. They got to where they are in the organizational hierarchy by dint of their driving ambition and competiveness, but they may be more likely than people with Type B personalities to suffer from certain physical and psychological problems. Some physicians, for example, believe that Type A people suffer more heart disease than do Type B people. In some

Although they seem to work well under pressure, Type A personalities may be likely to suffer from stress-related illnesses.

ways, Type A people resemble overworked machines: they break down and need frequent repair, but they do not want to take the time for it.

Type A people tend to work better under time pressure than do their Type B counterparts. Type A's do not always work well with others, however, because they tend to be impatient, aggressive, and highly competitive. A Type A person tends to focus on here-and-now issues but may fail to consider long-term concerns. Type B people, in contrast, are often better at long-term problem solving or planning. Type B's are more willing to take the time necessary to explore options; to evaluate alternatives carefully; and to develop well-thought-out, complete solutions. As is true for the other personality factors, what is most important to an organization about Type A and B personalities is that managers understand the relative strengths and weaknesses of each so that they can match individuals appropriately to organizational demands. (See "A Closer Look: Personality.")

Attitudes

In addition to differences in organization members' motives, abilities, and personalities, people also differ in their attitudes. Regardless of their source, employee attitudes can substantially influence motivation and various work behaviors.

What Is an Attitude? An **attitude** consists of the beliefs, feelings, and intentions about behavior that people have toward a person, event, task, or organization. The **cognitive component** of an attitude includes *what people think that they know* about a person, task, or the like and is generally descriptive. For example, John Miller is an investigative reporter who knows that his newspaper employs a number of editors, reporters, photographers, and fact checkers. The **affective component** of an attitude, is *how people feel* about a person, task, or the like and arises from their reactions to the cognitive component of the attitude. John is unhappy that his newspaper has too few photographers and too many editors. Finally, the **behavioral tendency component** of an attitude identifies *how people intend to behave* toward a person, task, or the like. John intends to quit unless the situation changes.

Because attitudes consist of all three components, and all three relate to one another, the attitudes that people hold are generally quite complex. For example, if a manager is concerned about a subordinate's attitude, that manager must first understand the attitude's various components. For example, a worker's cognitive component might include information about the size of the organization, the age of his or her manager, or the amount of money that the worker believes a co-worker earns. The affective component could include the worker's dislike of the organization's small size, concern that the manager is too young to exercise authority, and unhappiness that a co-worker is paid more. The behavioral tendency component could range from an intention to leave this small organization for a larger one, to ask for a reassignment to an older manager, or to request a raise. Because attitudes are related to a variety of motives and behaviors, in spite of the complexities involved, an effective manager must understand employees' attitudes and how and why they change.

How Are Attitudes Learned and Changed? Attitudes are acquired through learning. People are not born with them. They acquire attitudes gradually through personal experience; through learning based on information provided by others; and by associating one person, task, organization, or the like with another about which they already have formed an attitude.

Although firmly held attitudes are resistant to change, attitudes can and do change through the same processes by which they form in the first place. Managers who wish to understand and influence attitude change first need to recognize the relationship among the three attitude components and then decide how to change them. Managers, for example, can expose employees to new organizational experiences or give them information that will change their cognitions, feelings, or behavioral intentions.

Employee attitudes strongly influence behaviors within an organization. Some of the attitudes that researchers have found to be important to organizational functioning are job satisfaction, job involvement, and organizational commitment. These attitudes influence rates of employee turnover, absenteeism, tardiness, unionizing activity, and job performance. An attitude survey administered to Sears employees in Chicago, for example, showed that employee satisfaction with supervision, amount of work, kind of work, financial rewards, career future, and company identification was a powerful predictor of which employees came to work the day after a snowstorm paralyzed transportation systems.[4]

Many managers dismiss the importance of attitudes and conscious attempts to monitor, interpret, and manage them; however, they consider behaviors, such as job performance, absenteeism, tardiness, turnover, and various forms of union activity, quite important. It may seem easier to monitor and regulate poor job performance, high turnover, strikes, and absenteeism, but by taking this short-sighted, "bottom-line" orientation, many managers exert most of their effort on managing behaviors rather than attitudes. In failing to recognize the link between the two, managers are unable to take advantage of the fact that positive attitudes can create a basis for desirable behavior.

Job Satisfaction As you have seen, all attitudes have cognitive, affective, and behavioral tendency components. **Job satisfaction** is the affective component of people's attitudes toward their work. Job satisfaction has received tremendous attention in organizations; over 80 percent of organizations with 100 or more employees conduct satisfaction surveys. Job satisfaction can affect various behaviors (such as absenteeism and turnover), and it involves workers' personal feelings; thus, job satisfaction levels strongly influence an organization's effectiveness.

People's overall satisfaction with their jobs is composed of their feelings on many dimensions of the work and work environment. Eight dimensions that are important in almost any work setting are people's feelings about: the work itself, the amount of work, physical conditions, co-workers, supervision, compensation, promotions, and company policies and practices. Workers display all possible permutations of these components of overall job satisfaction. A worker may be highly satisfied with pay and promotional opportunities, for example, but dissatisfied with co-workers and supervisors.

Job satisfaction depends on a combination of factors, such as employees' feelings about their compensation, the work itself, and the company's policies and practices.

A CLOSER LOOK

Personality: Lots and Lots of Personality

Picture four adults sitting in a room answering over 100 questions on the order of "In a group, do you often introduce others or wait to be introduced?" and "Would you rather work under someone who is always kind or always fair?" The people then score the test, discover the label that corresponds to their personality type, and eagerly begin comparing notes. What is happening here? Is this the latest board game craze? The newest survey put out by *Good Housekeeping?* Possibly, but the chances are far greater that you are seeing employees take a personality test being administered by companies across the nation.

Known as the Myers-Briggs Type Indicator (MBTI), this increasingly popular personality test was completed by approximately 1.5 million people in 1986 alone, with nearly half of those at such companies as Apple, AT&T, Citicorp, Exxon, GE, Honeywell, 3M, and the U.S. armed forces. MBTI is based on a theory initially proposed by the Swiss psychologist Carl Jung in the 1920s and further developed by Katherine Briggs and her daughter, Isabel Briggs Myers. A person's answers to the test are divided and classified into sixteen different personality types (see Table 13A).

Why is this test so popular? Certainly one reason is that it is interesting to discover your personality classification and how it compares to that of others. Proponents of the MBTI argue that there is more to it than that, however. Knowledge of personality types can help managers understand why subordinates and co-workers behave the way they do and anticipate how they are likely to behave in certain circumstances. For

---

"Would you rather work under someone who is always kind or always fair?"

---

that reason, most businesses use the MBTI for developmental purposes, such as getting groups to work together more effectively. Understanding the personality types of group members helps managers assign roles best filled by particular personality

types. For example, the personality type often found in accountants and "numbers people" (ISTJ traditionalists) may be matched up with the "idea people" (ENTP conceptualizers) so that the plans developed during idea sessions can be translated into numbers and figures that might keep the company from making a disastrous move.

In some ways, the broad use of this test may be a fad, yet ". . . the theory may well be less significant than the communications it seems to foster. Talking about what type you are and what type I am and the differences between the two often proves to be an unthreatening way for people to raise and resolve problems."[1] Even if it does turn out to be a fad, the MBTI is at least based on a solid instrument, and it's fun, too.

1. Ideas and information for this "Closer Look" were obtained from T. Moore (30 March 1987), Personality tests are back, *Fortune,* 74–76, 80, 82.

TABLE 13A   The Sixteen Different Personality Types

	Sensing Types (S)		Intuitive Types (N)	
	Thinking (T)	Feeling (F)	Feeling (F)	Thinking (T)
Introverts (I) — Judging (J)	**ISTJ** Serious, quiet, earn success by concentration and thoroughness. Practical, orderly, matter-of-fact, logical, realistic, and dependable. Take responsibility.	**ISFJ** Quiet, friendly, responsible, and conscientious. Work devotedly to meet their obligations. Thorough, painstaking, accurate. Loyal, considerate.	**INFJ** Succeed by perseverance, originality, and desire to do whatever is needed or wanted. Quietly forceful, conscientious, concerned for others. Respected for their firm principles.	**INTJ** Usually have original minds and great drive for their own ideas and purposes. Skeptical, critical, independent, determined, often stubborn.
Introverts (I) — Perceiving (P)	**ISTP** Cool onlookers—quiet, reserved, and analytical. Usually interested in impersonal principles, how and why mechanical things work. Flashes of original humor.	**ISFP** Retiring, quietly friendly, sensitive, kind, modest about their abilities. Shun disagreements. Loyal followers. Often relaxed about getting things done.	**INFP** Care about learning, ideas, language, and independent projects of their own. Tend to undertake too much, then somehow get it done. Friendly, but often too absorbed.	**INTP** Quiet, reserved, impersonal. Enjoy theoretical or scientific subjects. Usually interested mainly in ideas, little liking for parties or small talk. Sharply defined interests.
Extroverts (E) — Perceiving (P)	**ESTP** Matter-of-fact, do not worry or hurry, enjoy whatever comes along. May be a bit blunt or insensitive. Best with real things that can be taken apart or put together.	**ESFP** Outgoing, easygoing, accepting, friendly, make things more fun for others by their enjoyment. Like sports and making things. Find remembering facts easier than mastering theories.	**ENFP** Warmly enthusiastic, high-spirited, ingenious, imaginative. Able to do almost anything that interests them. Quick with a solution and to help with a problem.	**ENTP** Quick, ingenious, good at many things. May argue either side of a question for fun. Resourceful in solving challenging problems, but may neglect routine assignments.
Extroverts (E) — Judging (J)	**ESTJ** Practical, realistic, matter-of-fact, with a natural head for business or mechanics. Not interested in subjects they see no use for. Like to organize and run activities.	**ESFJ** Warm-hearted, talkative, popular, conscientious, born cooperators. Need harmony. Work best with encouragement. Little interest in abstract thinking or technical subjects.	**ENFJ** Responsive and responsible. Generally feel real concern for what others think or want. Sociable, popular. Sensitive to praise and criticism.	**ENTJ** Hearty, frank, decisive, leaders. Usually good in anything that requires reasoning and intelligent talk. May sometimes be more positive than their experience in an area warrants.

TABLE 13.1   *Job Satisfaction Items from the Index of Organizational Reactions (IOR)*

The Index of Organizational Reactions

1. The people who supervise me have:
   a. Many more good traits than bad ones.
   b. More good traits than bad ones.
   c. About the same number of good traits as bad ones.
   d. More bad traits than good ones.
   e. Many more bad traits than good ones.

2. The supervision I receive is the kind that:
   a. Greatly discourages me from giving extra effort.
   b. Tends to discourage me from giving extra effort.
   c. Has little influence on me.
   d. Encourages me to give extra effort.
   e. Greatly encourages me to give extra effort.

3. How does the way you are treated by those who supervise you influence your *overall attitude* toward your job?
   a. It has a very unfavorable influence.
   b. It has a slightly unfavorable influence.
   c. It has no real effect.
   d. It has a favorable influence.
   e. It has a very favorable influence.

4. How much do the efforts of those who supervise you add to the success of your unit?
   a. A very great deal.
   b. Quite a bit.
   c. Only a little.
   d. Very little.
   e. Almost nothing.

Source: F. J. Smith, The index of organizational reactions, *JSAS Catalog of Selected Documents in Psychology*, 6, Ms. #1265.

A number of techniques allow the measurement of job satisfaction. The most popular of these are paper-and-pencil questionnaires. Examples of questions about people's satisfaction with supervision on the job appear in Table 13.1. Figure 13.4 illustrates the results that might be obtained in a job satisfaction survey of two departments. This type of survey can effectively identify those areas most in need of attention. It would appear from Figure 13.4, for example, that the company surveyed should examine why workers in the telemarketing division report relatively low levels of satisfaction with the work itself, with physical work conditions, and with compensation.

Job and Work Involvement   Attitudes of particular importance to organizations are their employees' involvement with work in general and with their own job in particular.[5] **Job involvement** concerns an employee's psychological involvement with a particular job. Employees who have a high level of job involvement are strongly psychologically attached to their jobs. John Miller, for example, often dogs a story for his newspaper for days on end, reluctantly taking breaks or diverting his attention. **Work involvement** refers to an employee's devotion to or alienation from work in general. John works harder at his reporting job than he has at almost anything in his life. His job involvement is actually stronger than his work involvement.

Both job and work involvement include three aspects. First, they include a person's conscious desire and choice to participate actively in

FIGURE 13.4   *Job Satisfaction Levels for Two Departments*

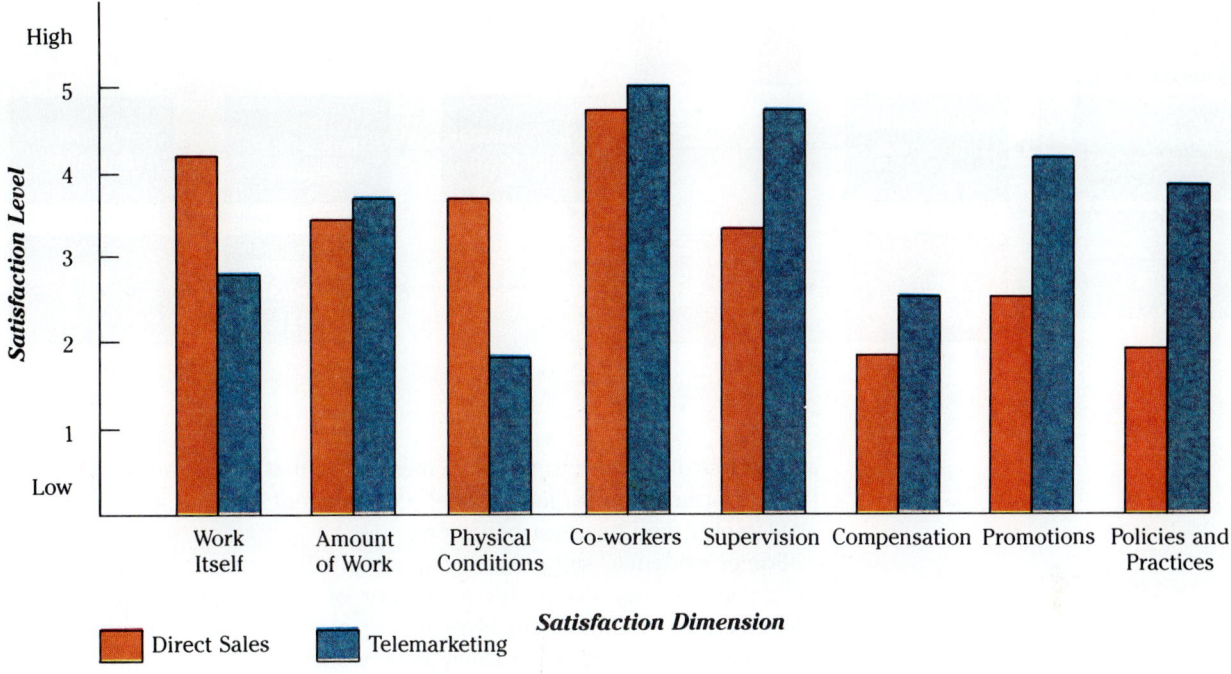

or to avoid a job or work in general. Second, they include the extent to which a person considers job and work central or marginal to his or her life. Third, they include how important the work or job are to a person's self-concept, because people evaluate who they are at least in part through reference to their work and job.

Job involvement is learned primarily from a person's experiences on a specific job. John has become deeply involved in investigative reporting while working for his present employer, a large city newspaper. Work involvement, in contrast, develops over a longer period of time and is based on a person's overall work experience. It develops out of people's experiences with work at school and in all of their jobs. Although job and work involvement are often similar—a person with strong involvement in one is likely to have strong involvement in the other—they can differ substantially. This happens when, for example, a person who has been highly involved in work over the years encounters a job for which he or she is overqualified. It also happens, as you have learned, when a person with relatively low work involvement, like John Miller, is sparked by a particular job and becomes highly involved in it.

Organizational Commitment   The organizational commitment attitude goes beyond that of job and work involvement. **Organizational commitment** is an active association between individuals and organizations such that committed employees are "willing to give something of themselves in order to contribute to the organization's well-being."[6] For example, John is moderately committed to his organization. Susan Siegrist is deeply committed to hers. A strong organizational commitment includes: 1) belief in and acceptance of an organization's values and goals, 2) willingness to put forth considerable effort on the organization's behalf,

FIGURE 13.5   *Organizational Commitment: Its Determinants and Consequences*

and 3) a strong desire to remain a member of that organization.[7] Much of the importance of organizational commitment lies in its effects on absenteeism and turnover behaviors.

Some evidence suggests that people who commit themselves to organizations may do so for a number of reasons. They may have a propensity to commit themselves to organizations, may possess certain personal characteristics, and may have worked in jobs that promoted a sense of responsibility.[8] By knowing about these factors, managers can choose employees who are likely to become committed. Managers can also use this knowledge to identify the types of work experiences that foster employee commitment. The potential importance of organizational commitment is illustrated in Figure 13.5, which specifies a number of the determinants and consequences of organizational commitment. This figure also makes clear that both the antecedents and consequences of organizational commitment involve a complex process.

Good managers understand a lot about the nature and psychological makeup of individuals. They use this knowledge to identify desired qualities in subordinates, to nurture their development, and to direct them to facilitate organizational effectiveness. The next section will explore the ways in which employees perceive their organizational experiences and the actions that managers can take to direct this perceptual process.

The Perceptual Process

A manager relies on subordinates to react to the policies, practices, and words of management. These reactions are guided by workers' motives, abilities, learning rates, personalities, and attitudes. Employees' reactions are also shaped by the way they perceive managers' actions and other events. **Perception** is the process by which a person gains information from the environment, organizes it, and derives its meaning. Managers, therefore, try to direct this perceptual process so that subordinates view managerial directives and other information as intended.

People react to their perceptions of an organization, whether or not they match objective reality. If subordinates perceive that their next sales

FIGURE 13.6   *The Perceptual Model*

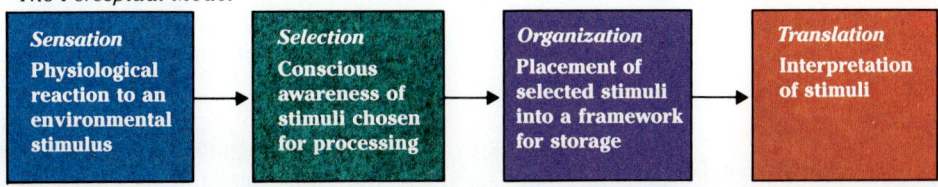

forecasts are due on your desk on Thursday, even though you, as a manager, may have told them Tuesday, then there has been a problem in perception. No matter how carefully a manager makes plans and guides subordinates, things are sure to go awry unless workers perceive these plans as the manager intends. For this reason, effective management involves the management of perceptions as well as the management of reality.

The perceptual process involves four distinct steps: sensation, selection, organization, and translation (see Figure 13.6). Before any environmental stimulus, such as a memo or a performance appraisal, is understood by an individual, it must pass through each of these four steps. At each step, perception of reality may either be distorted or processed as the message sender intended.

Sensation

Millions of environmental stimuli surround workers at any given moment. Some of these, such as a ringing telephone, have the characteristics and strength to produce a physiological reaction. The ringing telephone, for example, produces a sound in the appropriate frequency range and is of sufficient magnitude to stimulate the auditory nerve. *Sensation* is the physiological reaction of the body to an environmental stimulus. In effect, the sensation stage of perception is when the body acknowledges the presence of a stimulus. To avoid being overwhelmed by the magnitude of stimuli, people select only a small number of sensations to process further.

Selection

Because all stimuli that produce sensation are candidates for further perceptual processing, people use *selection* to reduce the number to a manageable subset. People weed out stimuli that are not relevant to their immediate motives and interests, stimuli with certain characteristics, and stimuli in certain contexts.

Characteristics of the Perceiver   Two people who sense a similar set of stimuli often select different subsets to process. Suppose that Vicki Barrett and Jane Kinney, co-workers at an insurance company, walk into the company cafeteria together. Vicki has an active need for food. She is very likely to pay attention to the food on display and probably does not even check to see whether there are any empty chairs available. Jane brought her lunch to work and has already eaten at her desk. She has come to the cafeteria to chat and unwind. Jane does not notice any of the appealing food but sees immediately that there are three or four chairs empty at tables where people from her department are sitting. In essence, people tend to select stimuli that are most relevant to their current motives and interests.

Characteristics of Stimuli   The nature of stimuli themselves can influence the selection decision substantially. *Intensity* is important because people are more likely to notice a loud voice or a bright light than a quiet sound or soft light. *Novelty* often makes people notice a stimulus that is different from the others with which they are familiar. *Repetition* influences selection because a stimulus that is encountered frequently is more likely to be selected than a stimulus encountered only once. *Changes in the stimulus* can increase the chance that it will be selected for further processing, which is why railroad crossings have flashing red warning lights instead of steadily glowing ones.

Characteristics of the Context   The *context* in which a stimulus is presented also plays an important part in the selection process. The number of stimuli present at one time affects selection: the more stimuli presented, the less likely a perceiver is to select a particular stimulus. A manager presenting a very important message to a subordinate, therefore, might deliver it in a face-to-face meeting rather than by sending it off in a memo that arrives with the rest of the employee's morning mail.

Contrast effects can also be quite powerful. A stimulus has a greater chance of being selected if it is distinctively different from those surrounding it, so a manager sending a memo to an employee might indent and italicize a paragraph containing the most critical message. There is nothing particularly novel about an indented paragraph or italics. They just contrast with the other stimuli present—that is, the margins and typeface in the rest of the memo.

Organization

Once a person has selected certain stimuli for further processing, he or she organizes and stores them until they can be translated. The process is somewhat like storing papers in a file cabinet until they are needed. The methods workers use to store information influence both how easily they can retrieve it later and the meaning that they ultimately derive from it. A secretary, for example, who takes the notes from every meeting and throws them in a random heap in a storage closet definitely influences his or her ability to prepare a quarterly report. Just as most secretaries select file folders, individual data files, or another organizational scheme for storing notes, *perceptual organization* places selected perceptual stimuli into a mental framework for storage and eventual use.

Managers can try to influence subordinates' organization of environmental stimuli in several ways. First, people are more likely to associate two stimuli if they are physically similar, so many offices use color-coded files and other materials. Second, because stimulus objects that are physically close to one another frequently are grouped together perceptually, it makes sense for managers to place related messages and materials physically together. (For example, put all of the accumulated information on Widget International, a story on the mayor's press conference, or profits since July in one file.) Third, managers can present related pieces of information at the same time so that workers associate the connected stimuli. Managers also can prevent dissimilar stimuli from being associated by letting some time elapse between the presentation of dissimilar stimuli. ("This is what I have for you on the Northwest sales territory. I'll get the material on the Midwest to you tomorrow.")

In short, a message that is effectively organized when it is sent is more likely to be effectively organized when it is received.

Translation

People use the translation stage of perception to give meaning to the various stimuli previously sensed, selected, and organized. The various factors that influence sensation, selection, and organization have already influenced to a great extent the meaning that a person derives from the resulting collection of information. In addition, a number of perceptual phenomena can distort the translation of stored stimuli. Most of us have had the disconcerting experience of our eyes "playing tricks" on us or of insisting, "But I was sure that you said Thursday, not Tuesday."

One distortion is called a *stereotype* effect. It occurs when a perceiver feels that a person, object, or event possesses the same properties as the group to which it belongs. Some managers, for example, like to hire workers from particular groups and avoid hiring others. Another distortion occurs when a specific stimulus influences a person's overall impression. It is called a *halo effect*. Because Susan Siegrist's financial computations are nearly always perfect, a halo effect might cause her boss to overestimate the quality of Susan's work in other areas. The halo effect can work in the opposite direction, too, causing managers to *under*estimate workers' contributions. Another perceptual phenomenon occurs when impressions are formed based on the order in which a perceiver obtains them. A *primacy effect* is created if a perceiver gives disproportionate weight to *first* pieces of information received about a person, event, or object; thus, the first few minutes of an interview with a job candidate may prove critical. If, however, a perceiver feels that it is the most recent information that counts, a *recency effect* may distort reality.

Another effect that may distort the translation of stored stimuli is perceptual readiness. *Perceptual readiness* occurs when a person experiences new events according to their anticipated, rather than actual, characteristics. If an employee expects management to be unfair and insensitive, for example, there is a strong likelihood that the worker will perceive these characteristics. Whereas someone without this perceptual readiness might interpret his or her boss' lateness to a conference as the result of, say, an unexpected phone call, a person who expects management to be insensitive interprets the boss' lateness as a snub. This phenomenon often leads to self-fulfilling prophecy (the process through which a person actually changes to match expected characteristics).[9]

Another factor that can distort the accuracy of perceptions is referred to as *projection,* in which someone "projects" his or her own characteristics onto another individual. Most frequently, projection occurs with negative traits, as is the case when an alienated employee sees other employees as alienated. Projection can also involve positive traits, however, which accounts for why employees who are committed to their organization often view co-workers as equally committed. Regardless of its nature, projection separates perceived reality from objective reality.

Perceptual defense is the tendency to defend existing perceptions against contradictory information. For example, if a subordinate believes that his or her boss is competent, fair, and highly ethical, the worker is likely to question claims from a co-worker to the contrary. Sometimes perceptual defenses cause people to deny or distort information that conflicts with their existing perceptions. At other times, a person may accept conflicting information but discount its importance or treat it as an exception to existing opinion.

By understanding that your own and other people's perceptions often are influenced by distortions, you actually improve your perceptual effectiveness. Although you are never likely to obtain completely accurate perceptions, understanding the source and the likelihood of perceptual errors can go a long way toward improving your perceptual capabilities.

Reducing Perceptual Errors

The previous section described a number of factors that influence the perceptual process. As a manager, how can you direct organizational events (such as rules, policies, and plans) so that employees perceive them as you or your superiors intended? To a certain extent, you can manage the perceptual process by following several steps:

1. Design stimuli so that they are likely to be sensed.
2. Assign attributes to stimuli that increase (or decrease) their chances of selection.
3. Encourage effective organization of stimuli by managing physical similarity and proximities in time and space, such as grouping only similar materials together or sending multiple messages only when they relate to the same topic.

There are also approaches you can take to enhance the accuracy of your own perceptions of organizational events.

1. Carefully and systematically select stimuli based on their content and the information you need. Try to discount superfluous, flashy, or catchy stimulus characteristics. ("Fresh from the ocean, snowy white, broiled to a sizzling turn, Atlantic halibut" is still fish. Order it only if you like fish as well as adjectives.)
2. Organize information according to similarity of content rather than solely according to physical similarity or nearness in time or space.
3. Try to focus on the facts and ignore irrelevant factors that might lead to distortion. (You may find orange ink jarring, but does the brochure in which it appears make the necessary points? Pay attention to those, not to the color of the ink.)

In short, managers can learn to influence the perceptual process systematically.

One last and important way to reduce perceptual errors is by *reality testing*. Compare your perceptions to reality, identify likely inaccuracies, and stay alert to the need to reconsider your perceptions. After formulating a perception about an employee, for example, a manager should compare his or her perception to another measure of the worker. Do other managers and co-workers agree with the perception? Is there a way to compare the perception to an objective measure, such as an actual count of the person's work output? Reality testing cannot prove whether perceptions are correct, because, for example, sources of comparison also could be flawed. Nevertheless, it and the other techniques described in this section can increase the accuracy of perception.

The Nature of Groups

Organizations are social systems. They cannot be treated as a mere collection of individuals acting independently of one another. Virtually all organizational goals are achieved by groups of individuals interacting. To be effective as a manager, therefore, you must understand the nature of groups.

Consider two situations faced by reporter John Miller, who has become involved with two groups during the course of his investigation of two major stories. Each story is being developed by a team of reporters, and each team has daily meetings to manage its investigation. John looks forward to the daily meeting of the first of these groups because the members respect and get along well with one another. Their meetings are efficient and effective. On the other hand, he dreads going to the second group's meeting because of its bickering, slow progress, and general ineffectiveness. Groups have their own personality: they can be more or less cohesive, more or less effective, and more or less successful in meeting organizational goals.

The Types of Groups

Formal groups are consciously created to serve an organizational objective.

A **group** is two or more people who interact, who perceive themselves to be a group, and who have a common purpose or work toward the accomplishment of a common goal. Groups differ according to how and why they were created. In organizations, **formal groups** are consciously-created to serve an organizational objective; departments and committees are formal groups. Typically, managers identify one or more objectives for a group and specify who will be members. John Miller, for example, is part of the metropolitan news department of his newspaper. Formal groups may also form, however, as the result of employee initiative in highly open and organic organizational settings.

Unlike formal groups, **informal groups** are not created by managers to serve an organizational objective. Informal groups arise spontaneously, such as when a few marketing managers regularly take their coffee breaks together, and group activity may or may not be helpful in reaching organizational objectives. Informal groups can evolve into formal groups, as would be the case if the group of marketing managers decided over coffee to design and submit a plan to take over a major competitor.

A **functional group,** either formal or informal, focuses on a general and continuing area of responsibility. Departments, such as personnel or accounting departments, are functional groups. A **project,** or **task, group** is created to accomplish a specific, defined task or collection of

A functional group, such as an organization's legal department, focuses on a general and continuing area of responsibility.

related tasks. Once the task or project is finished, the group disbands. A metropolitan school district, for example, may ask each of its elementary schools to form parent/teacher committees to study overcrowding and to devise plans to relieve the situation. Once those plans have been submitted to the school board, the committees disband. Similarly, when the two groups of investigative reporters with whom John Miller is working have finished their tasks, they will disband and be assigned to new investigations.

Groups, thus, serve various kinds of functions in organizations, and people tend to join and stay in groups for various reasons.

Group Formation and Cohesion

Several factors contribute to the formation, maintenance, and cohesiveness of a group. These factors make it attractive to be a member of a group and build the cohesive glue that holds the group together. This is particularly true when a person voluntarily joins a group, but these same factors are important for developing and enhancing cohesion even when participation in a group has been assigned by a manager.

People join some groups because they offer safety and security. Just as, thousands of years ago, membership in a cohesive group protected people from predators in the environment, membership in a cohesive group within an organization, such as a union, can protect members from harassment by those who oppose that group. People also join groups and become committed to them if they like the other members of the group. Nothing holds a group together so tightly as mutual affection and admiration. People also join and stay in groups whose activities interest them. Many groups can have high levels of cohesion even when members do not especially like each other if they enjoy the group's activities, and if belonging to the group is a requirement for participating in the activities.

People also join and stay with groups if belonging helps them achieve their goals. These goals can be personal, as when a worker joins the company's bowling team to learn how to bowl and to enhance his or her reputation as an involved employee. The goals can be social, as when a worker joins an organization to promote humanitarian treatment of political prisoners. Group membership can also provide participants with esteem and status. A new member can share in an established, respected group's esteem and status and build his or her own esteem in the eyes of group members. People take pride in serving on and being known to serve on prestigious committees and boards.

People also are attracted to groups because of the power they offer. A person may find opportunities in a group to influence other group members and, thus, acquire power. Neil Musgrave, for example, is an expert on microcomputer databases. His regional sales manager has just formed a task force to computerize the tracking of sales records. Neil quickly volunteered to join this group because he will have a chance to influence his boss with his expertise and his co-workers with his willingness to help. There is also power in numbers. A group of individuals is likely to exert more influence than is any one person working alone. A lone telephone operator's request that the company change to a flex-time schedule would probably not carry as much clout as would a petition from the company's entire workforce.

Groups are attractive to individuals and become cohesive when they satisfy needs that an individual would not be able to satisfy without belonging to those groups. For their part, managers must recognize that group cohesion often must be fostered, especially when they assign someone to participate in a group rather than asking for volunteers. Managers must identify members' needs and design groups that satisfy those needs. Otherwise, cohesion is unlikely to develop.

The Effects of Group Cohesion

Organizations often benefit when their members belong to highly cohesive groups. In some situations, however, cohesion can be dysfunctional. It is not enough for managers to foster cohesion. They must also direct the effects of that cohesion.

One effect of a high level of group cohesion is that members tend to be quite satisfied with their group experiences. After all, cohesion is, in large part, a function of the degree to which a group meets the needs of individual members. Group satisfaction is also related to the degree to which members of cohesive groups conform to group norms. Unfortunately, satisfaction does not cause performance. There are many happy but unproductive workers.

What about performance? Shouldn't cohesion enhance performance? In reality, cohesion may increase or decrease performance.[10] If the goals of a group match those of the organization in which it operates, organization members are likely to perform effectively. When, however, group goals are inconsistent with organizational goals, organizational goals will not be met, even if the group's goals are. The organization will not view the group as beneficial. You already know that highly cohesive groups are very effective at executing dysfunctional activities, such as work slowdowns or stoppages. You also know that highly cohesive groups can be quite effective at reaching high performance levels, should that be their goal. Managers need both to foster strong cohesion within a group and to direct it toward organizationally desirable goals.

Group Norms

In one of the two groups of reporters with whom John Miller works, daily meetings start promptly, members contribute relevant material, and joking and complaining take a back seat to finishing a story. In the other group, meetings usually start late, are often interrupted by irrelevant reports and complaints, and break down into bickering between members who want to investigate certain aspects of a story and those who think that the investigation should not "go looking for trouble." In each of these groups, different norms are operating.

Group norms stipulate the limits of expected and acceptable behavior for group members. They specify acceptable levels of performance, how members are to interact, what members must not do, and provide other guidelines for acceptable behavior. Sometimes norms are formalized into writing; more often they are passed from member to member verbally or through example. Different groups may have different norms, depending on the values of their members and the norms of their organization. For example, in some organizations it is acceptable for production workers to

Group norms guide employees' behavior, specifying how they should interact and perform their duties.

interact informally with executives. In others, it is not (in fact, some organizations separate these two groups to the extent of having "executive" and "nonexecutive" restrooms and cafeterias). Group norms, then, are the means by which groups guide and control the behavior of their members. As the Hawthorne studies revealed, group norms can influence work groups' effectiveness (see Chapter 5). Group members often pressure one another to work at a particular pace, for example. Members who work too hard are pressured, as are members who do not work hard enough.

Groups may have norms, but do group members honor them? Conformity to norms often varies substantially from person to person and from group to group. Conformity depends on many factors:

- *Personality factors*—an authoritarian personality, for example, encourages conformity.
- *Group size*—conformity tends to be greater in larger groups, particularly when the majority of group members have similar expectations for members.
- *Group unanimity*—greater agreement about norms leads to greater conformity.
- *Communication patterns*—decentralized patterns increase conformity.
- *Peer pressure*—direct pressure from other group members increases conformity.
- *Competence*—the more competent someone perceives group members to be, the more likely that person is to conform.
- *Past success*—groups with a history of success usually have greater conformity than those with a history of failure.
- *Cohesion*—more conformity occurs in highly cohesive groups.

Managers should be aware of the significance that group norms can have for an organization. They also should be aware of employees' conformity to these norms. Norms may signal sources of support or resistance to organizational activities. For example, when a group's norm is consistent with organizational goals, such as being courteous to customers, these norms can be a source of organizational strength. When "service with a smile" becomes a group norm and not just an organizational slogan, customers can expect to be greeted courteously. When John Miller's group aims to work as hard as possible to produce a thorough, balanced news story, the group's norms support the newspaper's goal of presenting thorough, balanced news to its readers. Managers can work to develop groups, to shape group norms, and to satisfy group needs that make these groups work as organizational allies. Groups whose norms are inconsistent with organizational goals can pose problems. A classic example of this is a group that sets an informal production ceiling below that desired by the organization.

Sometimes group norms become so powerful that they impair members' abilities to perceive information accurately. In such cases, groups begin to function in ways that can harm an organization.

Groupthink: A Special Problem

Irving Janis of Yale University has documented a special group phenomenon, **groupthink** (see "A Closer Look: Groupthink").[11] Groupthink happens when a group has illusions of invulnerability that lead it to accept excessive risks. Even when warned, members rationalize their way out of believing in impending problems. Group members also believe that the group's purpose is so righteous that they do not question the morality of its assumptions or tactics. They use negative stereotyping to degrade outsiders who question the group and put intense pressure on members to conform to group norms. If information from outside the group conflicts with the group's position, members protect it by developing what Janis has called "mind guards" to filter out the objectionable information. Groupthink produces such a strong desire for consensus and cohesiveness that it overwhelms a group's desire and ability to make realistic decisions.

Some of the potential consequences of groupthink include:

- Few alternatives are considered when solving problems.
- Reexamination of decisions is unlikely once they are made.
- Reexamination of a rejected alternative is unlikely.
- Outside experts are seldom used.
- Facts that do not support the group are ignored.
- Risks are ignored or glossed over.

Fortunately, managers can take steps to reduce the likelihood of groupthink. Most of these steps also can reduce the effects of groupthink once it occurs. Reducing groupthink, however, is much more difficult than preventing it in the first place, because groups engaging in groupthink seldom realize that they are doing so.

To prevent or reduce the effects of groupthink, managers can:

- Encourage each member of the group to evaluate ideas openly and critically.
- Ask influential members to adopt an initial neutral stance on solutions.
- Discuss plans with outsiders to obtain reactions.
- Use expert advisers to challenge group views.
- Assign a devil's advocate role to one or more group members to challenge ideas.
- Explore alternative scenarios for possible external reactions.
- Use subgroups to develop alternative solutions.
- Meet to reconsider decisions prior to implementation.

The Impact of Group Membership on Individuals

Group membership carries certain responsibilities. A member of any group or organization occupies one or more roles. Each **role** defines a set of expectations for a member's behavior. Once a role has been defined, its occupant is expected to fulfill these expectations.

Groupthink: Pearl Harbor—
Why the Fortress Slept

The early months of 1941: "MAGIC (the code name used for the intelligence branch which had cracked the Japanese secret codes) supplied plenty of warning signals showing that Japan was getting ready for massive military operations."[1]

March 1941: "A dawn patrol attack launched against Pearl Harbor from one or more Japanese aircraft carriers could achieve complete surprise."

November 27, 1941: "This dispatch is to be considered a war warning . . . an aggressive move by Japan is expected within the next few days. . . . Execute appropriate defensive deployment."

December 6, 1941: "I am certain the Japanese are going to attack Pearl Harbor."

In spite of these and other warnings, Admiral H. E. Kimmel, Commander-in-Chief of the Pacific Fleet, and his high-level group of naval commanders concluded that "there was no chance of a surprise air attack on Hawaii at that particular time." The result of their conclusions was felt at 8:00 A.M. (Hawaii Time):

Sunday, January 7, 1941: While most navy personnel were on weekend leave or just awakening in their bunks, the first wave of attack planes began to sweep over the island of Oahu. Bombs were dropped at will on the 96 unprepared American ships sitting at anchor in Pearl Harbor. Over 2000 men were killed. Thousands more were injured or missing. The U.S. Pacific fleet was devastated.

How could Kimmel and his group have ignored such clear warnings and left their fleet thus unprepared for attack? Because, according to Irving Janis, they allowed *groupthink* to convince them that Pearl Harbor was safe despite all evidence to the contrary.

> *"MAGIC supplied plenty of warning . . . that Japan was getting ready for massive military operations."*

This military group exhibited some of the classic symptoms of groupthink. Kimmel had surrounded himself with advisers who were extremely loyal to him. A highly cohesive group, these people interacted socially as well as for business purposes. Their feelings of personal security appeared to reinforce their perceptions of military security. The groundwork for illusions of vulnerability were firmly in place.

The group norm was "Pearl Harbor is safe." When warnings from outside the group suggested otherwise, group members focused on reasons to reject the warnings rather than reasons to accept and react to them. If

an individual member of the group expressed doubts (as Kimmel himself did on December 6, 1941), other members of the group quickly closed ranks to assure the doubter that all

> *"Over 2000 men were killed. . . . The U.S. Pacific fleet was devastated."*

was well. Their desire for uniformity and agreement with the group stance, combined with stereotypes they had formed of the enemy, allowed members to rationalize that all was well.

This naval group was not the only one so complacent. In fact, the views of Kimmel and his commanders were reinforced by apparently similar beliefs held by army commanders on Oahu and by President Roosevelt's War Council in Washington. Each group suffered from the groupthink phenomenon. In addition, the groups supported the development and maintenance of groupthink in each other by hesitating to share information that might upset the status quo of the other groups. Collective groupthink among the three main groups responsible for the defense of Pearl Harbor turned out to be a potent ally of the Japanese bombardiers.

1. Information for this "Closer Look" was obtained in an interview that the authors conducted with Irving L. Janis and from his book (1982) *Groupthink: Psychological studies of policy decisions and fiascoes,* 2nd ed., Boston: Houghton Mifflin, 72–96.

Each member of an organization occupies a role, a set of behavioral expectations defined by the organization.

People's perceptions strongly color the roles that they occupy in groups. First is the *expected role,* or the image of behavior that exists in the minds of others in the organization. A manager, for example, forms a mental picture of a subordinate's role. In the mind of a newspaper editor, an investigative reporter is expected to interview subjects and write stories. Expectations, however, may not match the *transmitted role.* This is the written or verbal description of the role given to the person expected to fill it. The editor may (or may not) describe the expected tasks to a reporter. The reporter, in turn, has a *perceived role,* that is, a definition of the role as he or she understands it. Finally, the *enacted role* is how the reporter (or other role occupant) actually fulfills it.

Ideally, there should be no significant contradictions among these four roles. In reality, there often are contradictions. It is the manager's job to see that the contradictions are kept to a minimum.

Role Ambiguity **Role ambiguity** is uncertainty about the requirements of a role. "Am I supposed to be a reporter or a writer?" John Miller may wonder. If employees are uncertain about their organizational roles, they are likely to feel stress, to be dissatisfied, and to perform poorly. Role ambiguity often creeps in because role specifications are deficient. Poor directions from a leader, an incomplete job description, or inadequate information from co-workers can all contribute to role ambiguity.

Individuals differ substantially in their *tolerance for ambiguity.* For some people, a moderate amount of ambiguity provides a challenge and is actually enjoyable. For others, even minor ambiguity can create major problems. Like other personality factors, tolerance for ambiguity can be formally measured via questionnaires, yet an astute manager often can discover subordinates' tolerance for ambiguity through informal observation. Some people, the manager may notice, "need everything spelled out for them" to perform well. Others thrive on the freedom to make some decisions on their own. It is important that managers clarify the roles of those employees with low tolerance for ambiguity so that they can meet the organization's expectations and do so comfortably.

Role Conflict **Role conflict** occurs when people occupy several roles whose expectations contradict one another or when the demands of the roles conflict with their personal preferences. Role conflict can cause even greater stress, satisfaction, and performance problems than role ambiguity.

There are three types of role conflict. *Interperson* role conflict occurs when role demands contradict personal values, beliefs, or preferences. If a marketing manager tells members of the sales force that their role includes providing kickbacks to customers, any salespeople who feel that this behavior is unethical will experience intraperson role conflict. *Intrarole* conflict occurs when role occupants receive mixed signals about their role. A subordinate who is told that quality is of the utmost importance to the organization receives mixed signals if he or she is then instructed to hurry and complete the work. *Interrole* conflict occurs when one person occupies different roles with conflicting expectations. A manager who is expected to be at an important company meeting, and to stay at home to care for a sick family member, and to fill out his or her income tax forms is experiencing interrole conflict.

Regardless of whether role conflict is present, sometimes there is simply too much to do, either because roles carry too many expectations or pose overwhelming demands. In these cases, people feel *role overload,* a particular form of role conflict. Regardless of its cause, role overload prevents people from meeting all of the expectations that their roles raise and can cause psychological and even physical discomfort as a result.

The job of managing role expectations falls jointly on the individual who holds the role(s) and the manager(s) who assign them. Managers should periodically evaluate and review role assignments, checking for evidence of role ambiguity, role conflict, or role overload. Employees should look for these same signs when accepting new roles and, occasionally, while executing old ones. If role problems are not corrected, stress, job dissatisfaction, and poor performance are the likely results.

Group Development and Facilitation

Like people, groups go through various stages as they mature, and their capacity for performance is not the same at each stage. Research in the area of group dynamics has identified six stages in group development (see Figure 13.7).[12] Perhaps more important for managers, there are steps that group leaders can take to facilitate the development of groups through these six stages.

FIGURE 13.7   *The Stages of Group Development*

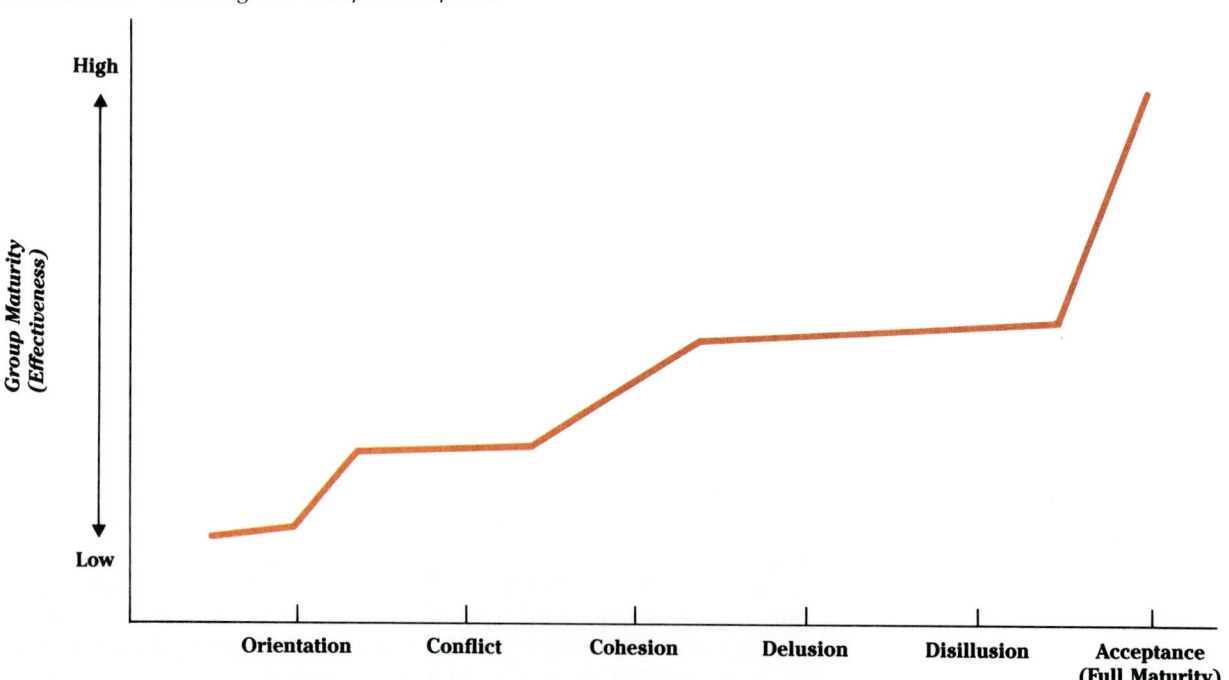

Source: Adapted from L. N. Jewell and H. J. Reitz (1981), *Group effectiveness in organizations*, Glenview, IL: Scott, Foresman, 20.

TABLE 13.2   Guidelines for the Orientation Stage

- Provide a strong leader who is willing and able to structure and guide the group.
- Offer group members the opportunity to share, discuss, and exchange ideas and information.
- Assign or have the group develop specific group goals.
- Assign or have the group define group roles for each member.
- Provide answers to members' questions about the group.

TABLE 13.3   Guidelines for the Conflict Stage

- Accept conflict as necessary for further group development.
- Allow conflict to emerge.
- Allow testing of group norms by members.
- Allow subgroups to form but maintain at least some total group interactions.

Orientation (Stage 1)

As a group first forms, members do not know each other within the group context (even if they know each other outside of the group). They are often uncertain about the group's purpose, individual personal agendas, rules, procedures, leadership, and their own roles as group members. During this first stage, members exchange information, ask questions about other group members, and attempt to define the nature of the group. A group leader or facilitator should try to complete this preliminary stage quickly and efficiently. Table 13.2 provides specific suggestions on how leaders can meet the needs of a newly formed group and turn it into a functioning body.

Conflict (Stage 2)

Following the orientation stage, a group enters a period of conflict as individual differences among group members surface. Often, group members compete for leadership and role assignments. They may disagree over procedures and over the merits of the group itself. Tension and hard feelings may arise. The group may divide into subgroups that set off in different directions. Because the conflict stage is unpleasant and often ineffective, many groups try to deny its onset or deal with its issues superficially; however, forcing a group to bypass the conflict stage greatly increases the chances of regression to this stage at a later date. It is far better to accept the stage as a necessary part of group development and to concentrate on effective ways to shorten its duration and minimize its impact (see Table 13.3).

Cohesion (Stage 3)

During the cohesion stage, group members work through personal differences, develop a set of norms, and agree on their roles. A group structure emerges, and operating procedures are established for guiding future activities. It is in this stage that a true sense of group identity emerges for the first time. Cooperation, low levels of emotionalism, and

Linda N. Jewell

Linda N. Jewell has been a manager, a management consultant, a management professor, and a facilitator for structured group experiences. She is the author or coauthor of a number of articles and books in management and psychology, including *Group Effectiveness in Organizations*.

1. You have described six stages of group development. Is it necessary for all groups to experience all six of these stages? If so, why?

The most effective and efficient groups have passed successfully through all of the developmental stages to reach maturity. Group development takes time, however, as well as considerable energy to work through the obstacles to maturity. There are many instances in which the time simply is not available or the improve-

ments in effectiveness and efficiency are not worth the time and energy. For example, short-term committees and groups, such as quality circles, that meet at intervals to solve a particular problem or brainstorm can be *sufficiently* effective and efficient even if they have not reached maturity.

2. You have pointed out that different types of leader behaviors are more effective for different stages of group development. Is it necessary to use different leaders, or can one leader effectively manage from orientation through maturity?

Not only is it possible for one leader to take a group successfully through the stages, it probably is necessary in most cases. Conflict over group leadership and member uncertainties about leader-member relationships are obstacles that must be overcome if a group is to reach maturity. Changing leadership at each stage of development would require the group to keep dealing with these same issues, making it difficult or impossible to move on to the later stages of group development.

3. If it is to attain maturity, a group apparently must move from a delusion to a disillusionment stage. What is your response to the manager who says, "Disillusionment is so unpleasant, I would rather leave my group at the delusion stage"?

It is not really possible to "leave" a group at the delusion stage of development. This stage is characterized by avoiding or glossing over interpersonal issues as members strive to maintain the group spirit they have achieved. All groups have problems, however, which are not solved by pretending they don't exist. If the group stays together, the delusion stage will become increasingly frustrating to some members, and group cohesiveness will begin to break down. At some point, the group will move into the disillusionment stage by itself.

4. What advice do you have for a nonleader member of a group who wishes to help the group reach maturity?

A few specific suggestions for an individual who wants to help his or her group achieve maturity include: (1) be fully active and participate in the group, so that other members know what you have to offer in the way of information, skills, and other resources; (2) encourage the active participation of other group members, especially any who appear to have opinions, information, and skills that are different from your own; (3) make an effort to interact with group members you do not know; and (4) avoid initiating or encouraging conflict over a personal agenda that is irrelevant to the group's purpose.

goal-directed activity are common characteristics of highly cohesive groups. Significant increases in group effectiveness are common during the cohesion stage (but remember that cohesive groups sometimes are dysfunctional). To harness the energy of a cohesive group, managers can follow several guidelines (see Table 13.4).

For many groups, the cohesion stage is so effective and gratifying that further development seems unnecessary. For groups that are to be relatively short-lived (such as a project group), this is not always a bad idea. Further significant improvement is likely only if a group manages to reach the full maturity stage of acceptance.

TABLE 13.4 *Guidelines for the Cohesion Stage*

- Provide a fair, nonpower-seeking leader who will work for the good of the group.
- Develop a system for addressing and resolving disagreements (conflict).
- Encourage a sense of group identity.
- Encourage written and/or public statements from the group as a whole.
- Develop and formalize a permanent operating structure to guide group actions.

TABLE 13.5 *Guidelines for the Delusion Stage*

- Accept delusion as a normal stage necessary for further group development.
- Avoid the onset of groupthink by watching for symptoms and taking corrective steps as needed.
- Avoid prolonged continuation of delusion by challenging the unrealistic bases of the delusion.

Delusion (Stage 4)

If a group develops beyond the cohesion stage, it is likely to evolve into a stage of delusion in which members believe that significant problems no longer exist. Group members delude themselves into believing that all is well and may become euphoric. After all, they have overcome the problems of conflict and gone on to achieve significant improvements in effectiveness during the cohesion stage. Sometimes the delusion stage is so enjoyable that it is difficult for a group to understand why it needs any further development. A group that stays at this stage, however, will not fulfill its potential, and there is a tendency for a group at the delusion stage to commit disastrous errors due to its false sense of perfection. It may even stumble into the groupthink phenomenon.

The onset of the delusion stage tends to be a natural consequence of the cohesion stage. After all, a group leader does not find it necessary to encourage delusion. The leader does have to control it, however. Table 13.5 presents ideas on how to manage this stage of development.

Disillusion (Stage 5)

For a group to advance to maturity, it must pass through the painful stage of disillusionment, in which the bubble of delusion bursts. Members are shocked into awareness of the problems that still confront the group. Significant improvements in group effectiveness are unlikely at this stage. Cohesiveness decreases, and members may be tempted to leave the group. Absenteeism and tardiness are common. Subgroups may emerge again, and interpersonal conflict is frequent. Members blame each other for allowing the group to be deceived by the delusion stage. Pessimism about the group's future grows.

The disillusion stage usually is quite unpleasant for group members. It seriously threatens the continued existence of the group. Should a group leader, then, try to avoid the disillusion stage if possible? No; this painful "group puberty" seems to be necessary if a group is to reach full maturity. If a group skips it, there is always pressure to return to this painful stage. It

TABLE 13.6 *Guidelines for the Disillusion Stage*

- Accept disillusionment as necessary for further development.
- Allow disillusionment to occur openly.
- Force development of disillusionment by identifying and presenting group problems.
- Allow subgroups to form but maintain at least some total group interactions.
- If the existing leader is unwilling or unable to manage conflicts, replace the existing leader with a directive leader who can do so.
- Emphasize how and why the group can mature effectively.

TABLE 13.7 *Guidelines for the Acceptance Stage*

- Provide a leader with good interpersonal skills who will work for the good of the group, either by replacing the existing leader or by changing the behavior of the leader.
- Encourage open, honest discussion of *issues*.
- Discourage differences that focus on personalities.
- Dissolve subgroups through rewards for commitment to the total group.
- Identify to the group the unique qualities and contributions of each group member.
- Develop communication channels to exchange information accurately and realistically.
- Use issue-oriented decision-making techniques.

is better to live through it and to manage its impact rather than trying to avoid it completely. Some strategies to help a leader direct a group through disillusion without becoming destroyed by it are shown in Table 13.6.

Acceptance (Stage 6)

With appropriate care and direction, a group moves out of the stage of disillusionment and into the acceptance stage, which takes the group into its full maturity. At the acceptance stage, members discuss their differences rather than fighting over them. They aggressively attack issues and deemphasize personal interests. Any divisive subgroups that may have formed tend to dissolve, and a stronger sense of group identity emerges. The distinctive qualities of each group member are recognized and appreciated. Communication flows freely. Time and resources are used effectively and efficiently. Group effectiveness increases more rapidly than ever before, as does members' satisfaction.

It is unfortunate that few groups ever reach the period of maturity realized during the acceptance stage. Some groups do not have the time. Others fail to nurture the development of this stage. Still others bog down in the problems of earlier stages of development (especially conflict and disillusionment). Shortcuts to group maturity seldom work.

The suggestions in Table 13.7 can help a group move into the acceptance stage. The successful path to maturity, however, begins when a group first comes together and requires careful management throughout its entire course of development.

Individuals and Groups in Review

Buildings are made of bricks and mortar, but organizations are made of people. Just as engineers must be familiar with the nature and characteristics of their building materials, managers must understand the nature of people. Likewise, they must know the effects of combining individuals into groups.

People react differently to the work experience, depending on the needs, abilities, personalities, and attitudes that they bring to and develop within an organization. They are motivated to satisfy their needs, but doing so changes the factors that motivate them. Abilities differ from person to person, as well as within each person. Managers must consider these differences when selecting, placing, and training employees. Because the very nature of individuals is formed by personality, understanding personality factors can help managers better utilize an organization's human resources. Finally, individual attitudes influence the way members approach their organizations. Are workers highly committed, for example, to the interests of the organization, or are they more highly motivated by personal concerns?

The reactions of people to their organizational environment is based on their perceptions of reality, whether or not this perception matches objective reality. The perceptual process has four steps: sensing environmental stimuli, selecting certain stimuli for further processing, organizing the selected stimuli, and translating the organized stimuli to derive meaning from them.

Groups can be formal or informal, functional or project oriented. They can bond firmly through cohesion or barely manage to stay intact. Many different factors attract individuals to groups and contribute to the development of cohesion. Cohesion can either benefit or injure an organization, depending, in part, on the nature of group norms and their level of consistency with the goals of the organization. Sometimes extremely high levels of cohesion can lead to groupthink, a phenomenon in which the members of a group act disastrously in the face of conflicting information.

Being part of a group has an impact on an individual. Group and organization members assume roles that carry particular expectations. Although roles are designed to clarify expectations, they often do just the opposite (thus creating ambiguity or conflict). Roles must be carefully defined and managed.

Groups differ dramatically in their nature and effectiveness. The most effective groups become competent only after passing through a number of stages of development. In the beginning (orientation stage), a group searches for its identity. Then the group usually encounters a conflict stage. Successful further development leads to cohesion and then to a period of delusion, when members falsely believe that all is well. When this bubble bursts, disillusionment sets in. Through careful management, however, the disillusionment stage can be turned into an acceptance stage. At this final point, full group maturity (and effectiveness) can be realized.

Managers cannot underestimate the importance of understanding individuals and groups of people. Trying to guide an organization without attention to its people would be similar to driving a car without caring for the engine and transmission. The difference, of course, is that the engine and transmission of organizations have psyches that require attention and care.

Notes

1. H. A. Murray (1938), *Explorations in personality*, New York: Oxford University Press.
2. D. C. McClelland (1961), *The achieving society*, Princeton, NJ: Van Nostrand; D. C. McClelland, J. W. Atkinson, R. A. Clark, and E. L. Lowell (1953), *The achievement motive*, New York: Appleton-Century-Crofts.
3. R. V. Dawis, G. W. England, and L. H. Lofquist (1967), *A theory of work adjustment: A revision*, Minnesota Studies in Vocational Rehabilitation, Bulletin 47, Minneapolis.
4. F. J. Smith (1977), Work attitudes as predictors of attendance on a specific day, *Journal of Applied Psychology*, 62, 16–19.
5. S. Rabinowitz (1981), Towards a developmental model of job involvement, *International Review of Applied Psychology*, 30, 31–50; S. D. Saleh and J. Hosek (1976), Job involvement: Concepts and measurements, *Academy of Management Journal*, 19, 213–24.
6. R. T. Mowday, L. W. Porter, and R. M. Steers (1982), *Employee organization linkages: The psychology of commitment, absenteeism, and turnover*, New York: Academic Press.
7. L. W. Porter, R. M. Steers, R. T. Mowday, and R. V. Boulain (1974), Organizational commitment, job satisfaction, and turnover among psychiatric technicians, *Journal of Applied Psychology*, 59, 603–9.
8. J. L. Pierce and R. B. Dunham (1987), Organizational commitment: Pre-employment propensity and initial work experiences, *Journal of Management*, 13, 163–78.
9. R. Rosenthal and L. Jacobsen (1968), *Pygmalion in the classroom*, New York: Hope, Rinehart & Winston; R. L. Dipboye (1982), Self-fulfilling prophecies in the selection-recruitment interview, *Academy of Management Review*, 7, 579–86.
10. R. M. Stogdill (1972), Group productivity, drive, and cohesiveness, *Organizational Behavior and Human Performance*, 8, 26–43.
11. I. L. Janis (1971), Groupthink, *Psychology Today*, 5, 43ff; I. L. Janis (1982), *Groupthink*, 2nd ed., Boston: Houghton Mifflin.
12. L. N. Jewell and H. J. Reitz (1981), *Group effectiveness in organizations*, Glenview, IL: Scott, Foresman.

Key Terms

motives	external locus of control
personality	authoritarian
internal locus of control	dogmatism

type A personality	group
type B personality	formal groups
attitude	informal groups
cognitive component	functional group
affective component	project (task) group
behavioral tendency component	group norms
job satisfaction	groupthink
job involvement	role
work involvement	role ambiguity
organizational commitment	role conflict
perception	

Issues for Review and Discussion

1. Why is it important for managers to understand the active needs of organization members?
2. Identify the major components of a basic ability-management program.
3. Discuss how differences in personality affect organization members' reactions to their experiences.
4. Why is it important for managers to care about the attitudes of organization members?
5. Identify and briefly describe each of the four major stages in the perception process.
6. Why should organizations be concerned about informal groups? How can such groups benefit an organization?
7. As the leader of a group, what steps could you take to develop cohesion within your group?.
8. As a group member, what can you do to reduce the likelihood that groupthink will develop?
9. How do group norms affect an organization?
10. Discuss the various sources of role conflict and suggest ways to reduce each type of conflict.
11. Briefly describe the actions you could take as the leader of a group to facilitate movement through each of the six stages of group development.

Suggested Readings

Janis, I. L. (1982). *Groupthink: Psychological studies of policy decisions and fiascoes,* 2nd ed., Boston: Houghton Mifflin.

Jewell, L. N. and Reitz, H. J. (1981). *Group effectiveness in organizations.* Glenview, IL: Scott, Foresman.

McCormack, M. H. (1984). *What they don't teach you at Harvard Business School.* New York: Bantam Books; Barber, A. E. (1988). A review of *What they don't teach you at Harvard Business School.* In Pierce, J. L. and Newstrom, J. W., eds. *The manager's bookshelf: A mosaic of contemporary views.* New York: Harper & Row, 89–96.

Mowday, R. T., Porter, L. W., and Steers, R. M. (1982). *Employee organization linkages: The psychology of commitment, absenteeism, and turnover.* New York: Academic Press.

CASE   *The Patterson Operation*

By James M. Todd and Thomas R. Miller of Memphis State University

Carrington, Inc., is an international company engaged in the production and distribution of pharmaceuticals, proprietary drugs, and cosmetics and toiletries. In its worldwide operations, Carrington employs over 15,000 people and has sales of over $500 million annually.

At the Mid-South plant of Carrington, Inc., management was faced with problems of low productivity, low employee morale, and high unit costs in the section responsible for the assembly of various kinds of packages containing assorted products made by the company. These "prepaks" or "deals," as they were referred to within the organization, were prepared to customer specifications. Each package might contain from 24 to 480 items, and the total number of packages for a customer ranged from 10 to 1500 units. Most of these packages were prepared so that the retailer could set them up as free-standing, point-of-sale promotional displays. Assembling the deals was essentially a job shop process, and prior to the events described here, the "assembly room," was located in a part of the main plant known as Section 10.

The employees in Carrington's manufacturing and assembly operations were unionized, and the firm used a Halsey 50-50 Incentive Plan, a time-saved bonus plan. Under the Halsey Plan, if a worker could produce the standard output in less than the standard time, that worker received a bonus of 50 percent of the hourly wage rate multiplied by the time saved. For example, an employee who completed ten standard hours of work in eight hours would be paid for eight hours plus one of the two hours saved; thus, if the hourly pay rate were $8, the worker would earn $72 for the day.

Problems with Section 10

The assembly of prepaks in Section 10 utilized roller type conveyor belts, which supplied each worker with the products to be included in a particular package. The working conditions were outstanding in that the work area was very clean, well-lighted, and air conditioned. An attractive cafeteria for employees was available in the same large building.

In spite of good working conditions and the chance to earn extra pay through the company's incentive system, the operation in Section 10 had encountered a marked trend of increases in unit costs and decreases in output per labor hour. In fact, over the most recent two-year period, cost figures revealed that the section was below the break-even point. Contributing to this deteriorating situation was low productivity and a failure of employees to meet the work standard. This latter problem was made particularly evident by the fact that no employees were able to earn a bonus under the incentive plan.

Discipline in Section 10 was poor, and supervisors constantly had problems. A number of grievances had been generated. Morale was not helped by the fact that employees quite often found themselves being moved from one assembly line to another. This tended to increase production costs because the employees had little chance of learning one operation before being moved to another. Workers in Section 10 lacked a spirit of mutual cooperation; an attitude of "that's not my job" was prevalent.

Working in Section 10 was unpopular. The manual labor there was perceived as harder than the automated work in other areas. Also, word had spread that no one could "make bonus" working there. Eventually, through the bidding system used by the organization, the workforce in Section 10 came to consist, in large part, of young, inexperienced employees; problem workers; and malcontents. As one manager described the situation, "Section 10 had the pits of the workforce."

A New Operation

Management at Carrington was also confronted with a severe space problem for its expanding operations. Several alternatives were considered, but none seemed to offer an economically feasible solution. In near desperation, a brainstorming session of managers led to a decision to move a large part of the assembly of the deals to a facility already leased by the company and presently used as a warehouse. This facility was located on Patterson Street, and for this reason the new deal room became known in the company as the "Patterson operation."

The new facility fell far short of providing work space and conditions comparable to those in Section 10. The building was located in an entirely separate area approximately three miles from the main plant in a neighborhood of run-down, low-income housing and other warehouse operations.

The building housing the Patterson operation had been thought to be acceptable only for warehouse use. It was an older brick structure with a number of large open bays for shipping and receiving. The building was dark, poorly ventilated, not air conditioned, and inadequately heated. It was poorly suited for use by workers involved in assembly operations. Temperatures averaged approximately 50 degrees during the winter months and well over 90 degrees in the summer. There was no cafeteria or food service, and employees either brought their own lunch or went to a small neighborhood grocery in the vicinity and bought food. Other worker facilities, such as rest rooms and break areas, were poor. In summary, conditions contrasted sharply with Section 10 and its clean, air-conditioned, well-heated facilities in a good neighborhood and with a first-class cafeteria available.

Despite these obstacles and seemingly against their best judgment, management, pressed for manufacturing space, decided on the move to the Patterson warehouse. Little money was spent on modifications.

Results of the Move

Moving to Patterson involved the transfer of approximately forty low-seniority employees from the main plant. All of these workers were managed by Fred Hammond, a new first-line supervisor.

As foreman, Hammond made some drastic changes in the assembly operation. He set up the assembly line so that individual workers could work on the same job until that particular order was completed. The situation was entirely different from Section 10, where an employee could work on as many as three different assemblies during the day. The repetition of working on the same line enabled workers to develop speed, which facilitated their earning bonuses.

The new foreman introduced some other innovations. He allowed employees the opportunity to influence decisions concerning their work hours and the times of their rest breaks. While at the main plant the playing of radios in a production area was not permitted, at Patterson it gradually became acceptable to have radios playing, usually at a high volume. Other "nonstandard" conditions existed at Patterson. Unlike Section 10, employ-

ees did not have to observe dress codes, wear bonnets, or refrain from wearing jewelry on the job. Because of the rather remote location of Patterson from the main plant, managers or supervisors visited the new facility rather infrequently. Where violations of company policies existed, management took a somewhat liberal attitude.

In order to have a place to eat or take a break, the employees got together and furnished a small room with enough tables and chairs to modestly equip a rather austere dining and rest break area. Eventually this room was air conditioned. The employees asked to get the company to furnish some paint so that they could repaint the room.

With these and other changes, a shift in worker attitudes began to evolve. Employees came to view Patterson as their own company. There was a willingness to assist others when possible. Productivity increased to such an extent that employees received bonuses. The jobs at Patterson became more popular, and the composition of the workforce changed from one of inexperienced workers to one in which older and more qualified people began to actively bid for the jobs. Over the first four years of operation, only one grievance was filed at the Patterson operation and, during the first year of operation, productivity was 32.8 percent higher than it had been in Section 10.

Fred Hammond was promoted and replaced by May Allison, who continued to run the operation in the same manner as Hammond. She continued to get the employees to participate in decision making. For example, the employees decided to change work hours at Patterson during the summer months. Work hours had been from 7:30 A.M. to 4:00 P.M.; the employees changed them to two hours earlier because of the nearly unbearable heat

of the late afternoon in the warehouse. This change in work schedule was not in accordance with company policy but was tolerated by management. The workers at Patterson really preferred an even earlier workday, but this was not feasible due to coordination problems in receiving goods from the main plant.

Another interesting development at Patterson was the formation of an employee softball team called the Patterson Warriors. Normally, the company fields a team composed of players from all units instead of from one particular section. Again, Patterson employees did this independently without reference to overall company policy.

Currently, work records at the Patterson operation concerning absenteeism, tardiness, and turnover are not better than in the main plant. In a few cases, they are slightly worse, although management does not consider this difference to be significant; however, the very low grievance rate, the high level of worker morale, and the better productivity are pleasant surprises to management.

The activities of the Patterson operation are fairly well known among the managers at the Mid-South plant of Carrington. Management reactions range from positive to negative, with other managers ambivalent about Patterson. All, however, seem to agree that it is, at least, interesting.

Questions

1. To what do you attribute the improvement in productivity at the Patterson operation as compared to Section 10?

2. What principles do you see at work here?

3. Why do you think that some managers at the main plant are negative or ambivalent about the Patterson operation?

Motivating Organization Members

Student Learning Objectives

After reading this chapter, you should be able to:

1. Identify and understand the four psychological foundations of motivation.

2. Name and describe the three traditional managerial approaches to motivation.

3. Discuss why, although each of the traditional approaches worked to some extent, none is adequate in today's organizations.

4. Explain why managers must know the needs of their employees in order to motivate them.

5. Describe ways to encourage desired behaviors and discourage undesired behaviors from a reinforcement theory perspective.

6. Understand how people evaluate the fairness of the outcomes they receive from organizations.

7. Identify the characteristics of goals that most effectively motivate performance.

8. Understand why people choose and actively pursue particular alternatives.

9. Name the steps an organization must take to help employees translate effort into performance.

*J*im Camp had just finished his first semester as a freshman at Hanover College. Last year, as a high-school senior, he scored in the 99th percentile when he took the Scholastic Aptitude Test (SAT). Despite this apparent high academic ability, he received a *C* in every college course during his first semester (except in calculus where he was not quite so fortunate). Jim's friend, Otis Taylor, received three *B*'s and an *A*, yet Otis' SAT scores were only in the 55th percentile.

Jim's SAT scores indicate that he had stronger academic abilities than did Otis. Despite this, Otis' academic performance was clearly superior to Jim's. How can you explain this discrepancy? The answer lies in differences in *motivation*. People's abilities and skills make performance possible, but motivation makes people choose to use those abilities and skills to accomplish things.

Recently, Blue Cross/Blue Shield of Illinois wanted to use selection tests to identify well-qualified applicants for its job openings. After investigating many abilities that were expected to be important determinants of performance, the organization identified several for each job group and tested for these when it selected employees. This strategy for hiring employees gave Blue Cross/Blue Shield a significantly improved workforce. Even after these steps were taken, however, management could still see major performance differences from person to person that could not be explained simply on the basis of differences in ability. When Blue Cross/Blue Shield investigated, it found that the major factor distinguishing the best of the employees from those performing at lower levels was motivation—the amount and direction of energy that employees exerted when performing their jobs.

The Nature of Motivation

As previously noted, ability provides a person with the capability to perform. Performance, however, is a function of both ability and motivation. Without adequate motivation, even the most capable person performs poorly. **Motivation** energizes, directs, and sustains human behavior. For Jim to get good grades, he must be motivated to do well in school.

Even the most capable employee must be motivated to perform well.

Although he probably would have failed his courses completely if he had lower abilities, he needs motivation to improve. Similarly, even the most capable employees must be adequately motivated to perform well. In fact, a survey of Fortune 500 chief executives identified employee motivation as one of the top three issues of concern to their organizations.[1]

Granted that motivation is important to performance, what determines a person's motivation level and direction? What can an organization or individual manager do to energize and direct—to motivate—an employee? This section examines the psychological foundations and traditional managerial approaches to motivation and explores several contemporary perspectives available to managers.

The Motivational Process and Its Psychological Foundations

Work motivation has been defined as the "set of energetic forces that originate both within as well as beyond an individual's being to initiate work-related behavior, and to determine its form, direction, intensity, and duration."[2] As you discovered in the section on motives in Chapter 13, people have basic needs, wants, expectations, and drives. These forces create a tension that propels people to pursue measures to relieve it. If their behavior is successful in reducing the tension, they feel rewarded—the energizing forces are satisfied (see Figure 14.1).

When managers attempt to motivate organization members, they rely quite heavily on several psychological theories. In fact, it is a series of psychological principles that underlie current management theories of motivation. The oldest of these principles is called *hedonism*. The principle of hedonism says that people are motivated to do things that are pleasurable and to avoid things that are unpleasant ("If it feels good, do it"). A manager who applies this principle should take steps to make experiences in the work environment—particularly effective performance—pleasurable. The greater the displeasure caused by working, the less motivating the experience will be; therefore, if your subordinates enjoy coming to work and performing well, they will be motivated to do so.

A second psychological perspective on motivation focuses on *instincts* (automatic predispositions to behave in a certain fashion). In the nineteenth century, Charles Darwin theorized that biological factors determine much human behavior.[3] Many scientists in his wake, including Sigmund Freud, based their theories of motivation in part on instincts. They argued that highly motivated individuals behave as they do because

FIGURE 14.1
The Motivational Process

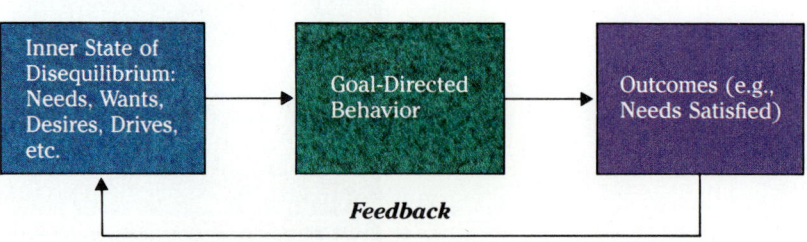

Reprinted with special permission of King Features Syndicate, Inc.

of natural or biologically acquired tendencies. According to this line of reasoning, some people find coming to work enjoyable because they were "born to work."

A third psychological perspective on motivation is known as *drive theory*. It states that people learn how to behave through personal experiences, and this learning drives their subsequent behavior. In organizations, people develop habits from actions that produced favorable results in the past, and they learn to avoid the experiences that have caused them problems. If, as a student, you have worked with a study group and consequently obtained good grades in a course, you will be driven to work with such a group again. If workers exert a lot of effort, perform at a high level, and are rewarded for doing so, it is likely they will be driven to repeat this behavior.

The final major psychological perspective used by current managers is one based on *cognition*. It says that people behave rationally based on what they think the future will bring. If they think a certain behavior at work will benefit them, they pursue it. If they think that it will not, they avoid it. From this perspective, a manager should try to create in the minds of workers the impression that behaving a certain way will benefit them. For example, even if Sarah has never been part of an autonomous work group, she will be motivated to participate in this new experience if her manager can convince her that it will provide something she desires (such as independence from hierarchical control or the opportunity to exercise peer and self control).

Traditional Managerial Approaches

Managers use several techniques as they attempt to motivate employees to perform well. Historically, three distinct approaches have been used. The first is based on economic factors, the second on social considerations, and the third on the nature of the work itself. Some managers use only one of these approaches. The best contemporary managers, however, incorporate aspects of all three.

Economic   The economic model assumes that people are rational in nature and that they are economically motivated. Unfortunately, it also assumes that work itself is distasteful to the majority of employees. This can and does result in many managers' taking the following approach:

My employees think their work stinks, and so do I. All work stinks. It may be necessary for most of us, but that doesn't make it pleasant. There's only one good way to get people to do something as unpleasant as work and that's to pay them. Since performing at a high level is even more unpleasant than performing at a low level, we have to pay more to motivate an employee to perform at a higher level than we would have to pay that same employee to perform at a lower level.

In keeping with the economic model of motivation, Frederick W. Taylor developed a financial incentive system, called the *differential wage rate system,* as a part of his approach to scientific management. If a worker produced nothing during the day, no wage would be earned; the more the worker produced, the more the worker would earn. In fact, money can motivate people to accept even unpleasant jobs, and it can motivate them to perform at a relatively high level.[4] Unfortunately, when managers rely too heavily on the power of the dollar, they fail to use other, possibly more effective, motivators.

Social   Whereas the economic model of motivation says, in effect, "Work stinks, so we'll pay you to make up for that," the social model says, "Let's make the work experience socially pleasant." If this can be done, proponents argue, workers will be both satisfied and motivated to perform their jobs effectively, because people are social and need acceptance and recognition. Managers who use this approach provide work opportunities that are socially rewarding: they offer opportunities for co-workers to interact, develop cohesive work groups, provide employees with recognition, and treat workers humanely. It is true that social factors can motivate and satisfy organization members, but just as the economic model overemphasizes money as a motivator, some managers overemphasize social factors and neglect other potential motivators.

The Nature of Work   Neither the economic model nor the social model of motivation addresses the nature of work itself. A more contemporary perspective on motivation deals specifically with the nature of work. A manager who uses this perspective believes that work can be interesting for organization members and that it is a manager's job to motivate employees by making the work interesting. In doing so, the manager focuses on employees' needs for esteem, growth, and personal development.

The nature-of-work model of motivation has been responsible for much of the job enlargement and job enrichment activity that has gone on during the past few decades (see Chapter 10). Again, it is unfortunate that many of the managers who have utilized the nature of work as an approach to employee motivation have done so at the exclusion of other motivating factors.

In sum, the economic, social, and nature-of-work models of employee motivation each focus on only a subset of an employee's total need structure. As a consequence, each has failed to achieve high and sustained levels of employee motivation. An effective motivational strategy should recognize that employees have a complex set of needs and that an effective long-term motivational strategy must address each set of needs or else it will have reduced effectiveness. The content theories, with their more complete treatment of a worker's complex need structure, provide a more comprehensive approach.

Content Theories

Content theories (also known as need theories) of motivation are based on the simple premise that all people have needs. Some needs are inborn, such as the need for food and water. These are called **innate needs.** Other needs, such as the need for self-esteem, are **acquired needs** learned through experience. Regardless of their source, if a person's needs are not met, he or she is dissatisfied. If these needs are met, people feel satisfied. Part of a manager's job is to determine which needs have not been met (and, thus, are active) among subordinates and to find ways for employees to meet these needs while simultaneously contributing to the achievement of the organization's goals.

Innate Needs

This section will examine some of the theories that are based on the concept of innate needs. The most useful and popular of these were set forth by Abraham Maslow and Clayton Alderfer.

Maslow's Need Hierarchy Theory   The most widely known theory of human needs was set forth by Abraham Maslow in his **need hierarchy theory.**[5] According to Maslow, people have a set of five innate needs (see Figure 14.2) that they try to satisfy in a particular order. The most basic

FIGURE 14.2
Maslow's Hierarchy of Needs

The lower-level needs are referred to as "deficiency" needs in Maslow's two-level version of the theory. He referred to the upper-level needs as "growth" needs.

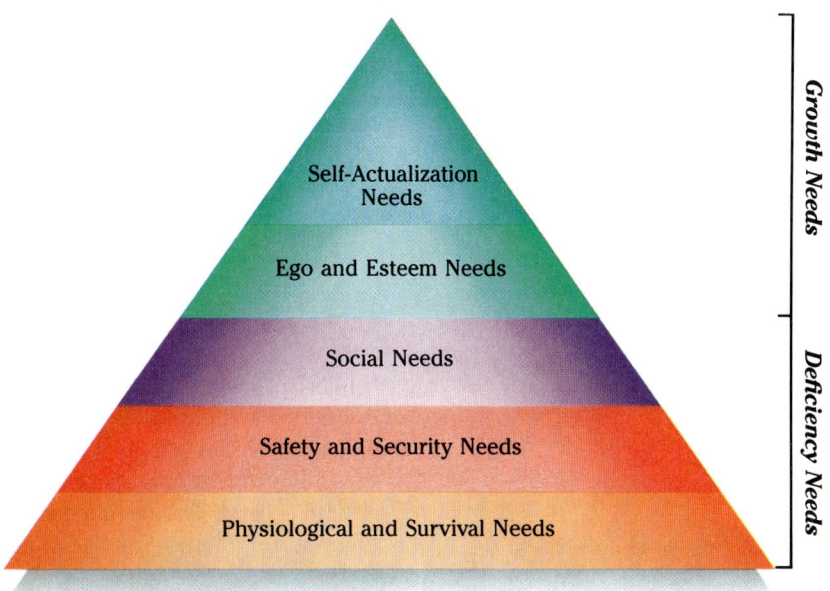

Self-Actualization Needs

Ego and Esteem Needs

Social Needs

Safety and Security Needs

Physiological and Survival Needs

Growth Needs

Deficiency Needs

Social needs include emotional needs for love, friendship, and affection.

human physiological needs have the greatest urgency and appear at the base of Maslow's hierarchy. As these needs are met, satisfaction results, permitting an individual to focus increasing amounts of attention on meeting higher-level needs. Most people move upward in the hierarchy as they attempt to satisfy unmet needs.

Physiological and survival needs include the most basic chemical needs for food, water, sex, sleep, and other physiological requirements. *Safety and security needs* involve the desire for protection from threats (including assault, robbery, disease, and extremes of temperature). *Social needs* include the need for affiliation and a sense of belonging, such as emotional needs for love, friendship, and affection. *Ego and esteem needs* involve the desire for self-respect, self-esteem, and the esteem of others. *Self-actualization,* the desire for self-fulfillment, involves the need "to become more and more what one is, to become everything that one is capable of becoming."[6] According to Maslow, most needs can be fully met, except for the need for self-actualization. No matter what you become or what you achieve, the self-actualizing need can always cause you to strive to become better and achieve even more.

Although Maslow initially proposed five levels to his hierarchy, he also discussed a two-level version. The lower of the two levels is shaded in Figure 14.2 and represents what Maslow referred to as *deficiency needs.* He called the higher-level needs *growth needs.* Motivationally, an individual tries to satisfy the deficiency needs before the growth needs. Many managers seem to believe that a person focuses on only one set of needs until it is completely satisfied and then moves on to the next level. Maslow, however, never proposed such a stringent perspective. Instead, he argued that the lowest, least-met need receives the majority of attention, while other needs receive less attention. In addition, Maslow noted that human behavior is influenced not only by an individual's need structure but also by other forces, such as society and the environment.

Alderfer's ERG Theory Maslow's ideas about the hierarchy of human needs are an important contribution to an understanding of how to motivate organization members effectively. More recently, Clayton Alderfer from Yale University refined the ideas of Maslow and others into a somewhat more useful perspective known as the **Existence, Relatedness, and Growth Theory (ERG).**[7] As Figure 14.3 shows, Alderfer presents a three-level hierarchy. It contains the same needs as those Maslow described, but Alderfer partitions them differently. His *existence needs* include the physiological and material safety needs identified by Maslow. *Relatedness needs* include all of Maslow's social needs, plus social safety and social esteem needs. *Growth needs* include self-esteem and self-actualization needs.

Four components—satisfaction progression, frustration, frustration regression, and aspiration—are the key to understanding Alderfer's ERG theory. The first of these, *satisfaction progression,* agrees with Maslow and refers to the process through which higher-level needs become increasingly important as lower-level needs are satisfied. The second component, *frustration,* occurs when a person attempts but fails to satisfy a particular need. The resulting frustration may make satisfying the unmet need even more important to the individual—unless he or she repeatedly fails to satisfy that need. In this case, Alderfer's third component,

FIGURE 14.3   *Alderfer's ERG Theory*

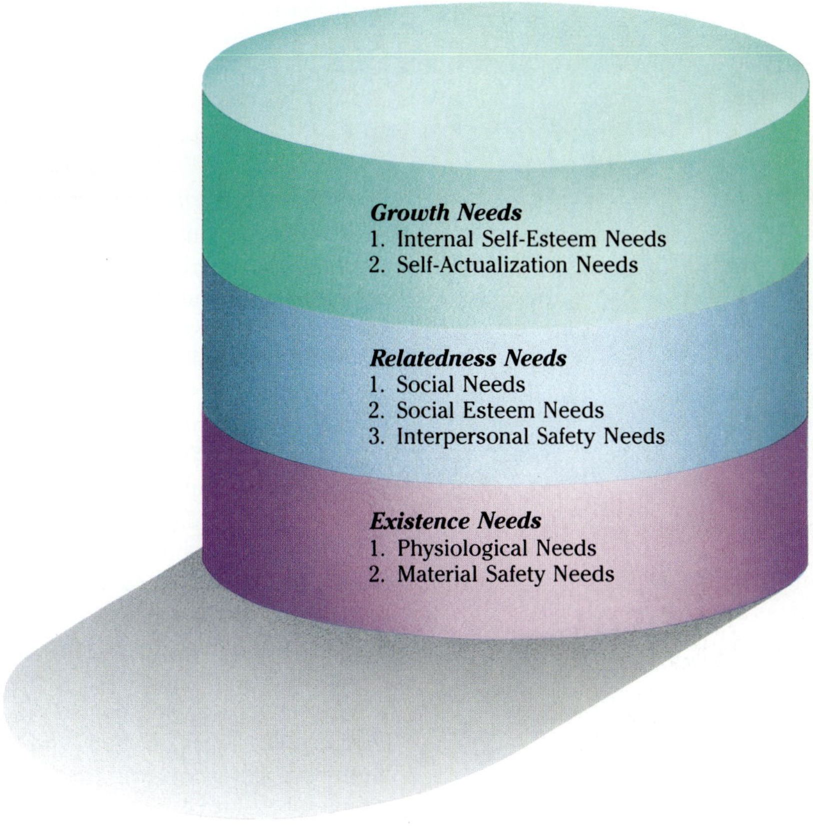

Growth Needs
1. Internal Self-Esteem Needs
2. Self-Actualization Needs

Relatedness Needs
1. Social Needs
2. Social Esteem Needs
3. Interpersonal Safety Needs

Existence Needs
1. Physiological Needs
2. Material Safety Needs

frustration regression, can cause a person who experiences repeated frustration to shift attention to a lower-level, more concrete and verifiable need. Lastly, the *aspiration* component of the ERG model notes that, by its very nature, growth is intrinsically satisfying. The more one grows, the more one wants to grow; therefore, the more a person satisfies the growth need, the more important it becomes, and the more strongly he or she is motivated to satisfy it.

Consider Tanya's experiences. After graduating from college, she took a job with a large retailing organization. Having no savings and shouldering thousands of dollars in college loans, she was initially motivated by her salary and benefits. As these satisfied Tanya's existence needs, she concentrated more on (and was motivated by) relatedness needs, especially the opportunities to develop friendships at work and to work effectively as a team player. After these needs were met to a reasonable degree, she shifted her attention to growth needs, focusing on the importance of significant job accomplishments. Repeatedly frustrated by a boss who denied her challenging assignments, Tanya ultimately stopped trying to meet her growth needs and concentrated once again on relatedness needs. The message to managers is that, if a worker fails repeatedly to meet the challenges of the job, he or she may become frustrated and regress to lower-level needs. Managers must understand that workers who are unable to satisfy a given level of needs are likely to redirect their attention elsewhere, perhaps to an area in which the results of their efforts are less valuable to the organization.

Of the two need theories, Maslow's is more widely known and more widely used in organizations. Alderfer's model, on the other hand, is potentially more useful because it provides a more contemporary perspective and incorporates much of the most recent knowledge about human needs and their role in organizations.

Innate Motivational Strategies   The innate need theories can be very useful to managers. To take advantage of them, managers first must assess those needs that are active in their workers and then provide opportunities to satisfy those needs. For employees who are strongly motivated by growth needs, for example, jobs might be redesigned and made more complex. Figure 14.4 identifies some of the rewards that have the potential to satisfy existence, relatedness, and growth needs. For example, employees with active growth needs can be motivated by managers who offer challenging jobs, creative opportunities, interesting work, and achievement opportunities. Employees with relatedness needs can be motivated by jobs that offer friendship opportunities, social recognition, a personal style of quality supervision, and the opportunity to work in teams. Employees with active existence needs can be motivated by job security, health insurance programs, and safe working conditions. These opportunities can motivate employees to join, to stay with, and to perform for an organization.

Most managers tend to use opportunities from only one of the three areas shown in Figure 14.4 when they try to motivate employees. ERG theory suggests, however, that good managers must be willing to meet a broad spectrum of needs and to use whatever tools are necessary to motivate employees.

FIGURE 14.4   ERG Needs and Organizational Opportunities

Growth Opportunities
- Challenging Job
- Creativity
- Organizational Advancement
- Responsibility
- Autonomy
- Interesting Work
- Achievement
- Participation

Relatedness Opportunities
- Friendship
- Interpersonal Security
- Athletic Teams
- Social Recognition
- Quality Supervision
- Work Teams
- Social Events
- Merit Pay

Existence Opportunities
- Heat
- Lighting
- Base Salary
- Insurance
- Retirement
- Air Conditioning
- Rest Rooms
- Cafeteria
- Job Security
- Health Programs
- Clean Air
- Drinking Water
- Safe Conditions
- No Layoffs
- Time Off

Acquired Needs

Not all human needs are present at birth. People also acquire needs through a learning process based on personal and organizational experiences. Because each person has different experiences, the type and strength of individual needs vary from person to person.

Henry Murray's work with the manifest need theory played a key role in focusing researchers' attention on the importance of acquired needs.[8] Building on Murray's work, researchers, such as David McClelland and John Atkinson, have strongly influenced the understanding of the important role of the needs for achievement, affiliation, and power within an organizational setting.[9] Each can be a powerful motivator of employee behavior. You might find it interesting to ascertain your own need for achievement, affiliation, and power by answering the nine questions in Table 14.1.

TABLE 14.1   *Measurement of Achievement, Affiliation, and Power Needs*

Directions: Read each of the following statements, which describe various things people do or try to do on their jobs. Then rate the statements in terms of how accurately each describes your own behavior when you are at work.

7 = Always   6 = Almost always   5 = Usually   4 = Sometimes
3 = Seldom   2 = Almost never   1 = Never

Need for achievement:

1. I do my best work when my job assignments are fairly difficult.	1	2	3	4	5	6	7
2. I take moderate risks and stick my neck out to get ahead at work.	1	2	3	4	5	6	7
3. I try very hard to improve on my past performance at work.	1	2	3	4	5	6	7

Need for affiliation:

4. When I have a choice, I try to work in a group instead of by myself.	1	2	3	4	5	6	7
5. I pay a good deal of attention to the feelings of others at work.	1	2	3	4	5	6	7
6. I find myself talking to those around me about nonbusiness-related matters.	1	2	3	4	5	6	7

Need for power:

7. I find myself organizing and directing the activities of others.	1	2	3	4	5	6	7
8. I strive to gain more control over the events around me at work.	1	2	3	4	5	6	7
9. I strive to be "in command" when I am working in a group.	1	2	3	4	5	6	7

RESULTS: To obtain your score on the need for achievement, add your answers to questions 1–3 and divide by three. To obtain your score on the need for affiliation, add your answers to questions 4–6 and divide by three. To obtain your score on the need for power, add your answers to questions 7–9 and divide by three. If your score on the need for achievement scale is between 18 and 21, you have a very high need for achievement. If your score on the need for affiliation or power is between 18 and 21, your needs in these areas also are quite strong.

Source: R. M. Steers and D. N. Braunstein (1976), A behaviorally-based measure of manifest needs in work settings, *Journal of Vocational Behavior*, 9, 251–66.

The need for achievement involves a desire to accomplish difficult and challenging objectives.

The Need for Achievement The **need for achievement,** which involves a desire to accomplish difficult and challenging objectives, is learned during childhood. High-need-for-achievement individuals find achievement satisfying whether or not anyone else even notices. They prefer relatively difficult challenges over simple ones but only if they perceive a reasonable likelihood of success. They value immediate feedback about goal progress and tend to become quite absorbed in a task until they succeed. For example, a basketball player with a strong need for achievement is likely to take shots with a 40–60 percent chance of success during practice. Similarly, a student choosing from among several job offers is likely to turn down those that are too easy or that have a limited chance of success in favor of an offer where success is possible but not assured.

Not surprisingly, people with a high need for achievement often perform better than those low in this need. High need for achievement, however, only contributes to performance under certain circumstances: the task at hand must be challenging (but achievable), feedback about performance must be provided, and the task must be at least somewhat interesting. When these conditions are not met, people with a low need for achievement may perform better because people with a high need for achievement are not interested in trying. Managers of high-achievement-motivation individuals must give them opportunities to succeed at challenging tasks and must provide feedback about progress toward success.

Managers can take systematic steps to capitalize on the need for achievement. A good place to start is in the employee selection process. If a job opening provides challenge, feedback, and opportunity for personal success, applicants high in the need for achievement are likely to perform better (because they need to achieve under challenging circumstances). A job that provides little challenge or, conversely, is virtually unachievable, is best filled by a person low in the need for achievement. Managers can make this information work for them by testing employees' need for achievement. Then they can transfer people to, or design jobs that will match the need-for-achievement levels of individual employees.

The Need for Affiliation The **need for affiliation** is the desire for warm and friendly relationships with others.[10] People with a strong affiliation need like to work and cooperate with others. They want to please people and to win their respect and affection. They seek approval and reassurance from others and are genuinely concerned about others' interests and feelings. Because of this, they are easily influenced by the norms and expectations of other individuals and of groups. Jeffrey Stephens is a supervisor at a meat processing plant. He goes out of his way to help his subordinates whenever he can. He does so because he genuinely wants to help and because he feels good when he does so. Jeffrey has a high need for affiliation.

People with a high need for affiliation are satisfied by organizational experiences that provide social opportunities; thus, they like to work closely with co-workers or customers. They are happy in groups. If forced to work alone, they become unhappy. A manager whose workers have strong affiliation needs must recognize that they will take steps to satisfy this need. If the manager does not offer opportunities for satisfaction in a way that benefits the organization, such as by placing these workers in work groups, they will try to satisfy their affiliation needs in another manner—perhaps by wasting time gossiping with co-workers.

When leaders and co-workers recognize, respect, and acknowledge high performance, workers with high affiliation needs are motivated to perform so that they can get this recognition and respect. When people's jobs give them lots of contact with others, people with a strong need for affiliation are motivated to get to work on time and regularly. If jobs offer little opportunity to interact with others, however, employees may miss work often because they look elsewhere for social opportunities. For example, Suzanne Sitlington, a sales representative at Scott, Foresman, has a very strong affiliation need. Her job puts her in contact with faculty members at colleges in the St. Louis area. This is highly motivating to her, in large part because it satisfies her affiliation need. If placed in a job in which she worked alone most of the time, Suzanne would probably spend a great deal of time seeking social interaction outside of the work environment.

In jobs in which group norms encourage low performance, people with strong needs for affiliation are likely to perform poorly. They are not likely to be "rate-busters" (people who perform above levels acceptable to the group). Performance can also be impaired when jobs provide opportunities for socializing that interfere with getting work done; thus, a job that allows plenty of socializing can be very satisfying to a person with a strong need for affiliation, but that person may spend considerable time socializing rather than working.

People with a strong need for affiliation like to work and cooperate with others.

What can managers do to deal with affiliation needs? First, they can assess the needs of both applicants and current employees. Then they can match the people with high affiliation needs to jobs that provide affiliation opportunities. High-affiliation-need individuals often make excellent salespeople, for example, and work well in teams. Low-affiliation-need people work best alone. Many systems analysts have low affiliation needs, as do many computer programmers and research specialists, who prefer to work alone. People with low affiliation needs should not be placed in jobs with distracting interpersonal activities, such as work teams.

The Need for Power   The **need for power** involves a desire to control others and to influence their behavior.[11] Depending on how it is used, this need can have a significant positive or negative effect on managerial success. There are two types of power, either of which (or a combination of which) can satisfy the need for power.

Personalized power seeking involves dominating others for the sake of domination. Often personalized power seekers overlook their organizational responsibilities in favor of personal concerns because they want power primarily to make themselves feel good about being powerful. A manager who tries to build an "empire" by developing a strong power base simply because he or she enjoys power is a personalized power seeker.

Socialized power seeking, on the other hand, involves acquiring power in order to benefit a group. Socialized power seekers use power to motivate and positively influence others and to help meet group goals. This is what office manager Mark Schmeling is doing when he uses his influence to convince the MIS manager to assign each of Mark's subordinates the microcomputers they need to manage their customer accounts effectively. Managers who deal with power needs through organizationally effective means, such as helping a work group succeed, are more likely to benefit an organization than are personalized power seekers.

Except under unusual circumstances, organizations should avoid hiring personalized power seekers. If managers discover people who act this way, they should place them in positions where they have very little contact with others. A person who behaves this way, for example, could be placed in a nonmanagerial job that is closely controlled and that offers little leeway for the use of power. In this way, they cannot manipulate people for the sake of manipulation. Socialized power seekers, however, should be sought for important leadership roles that will allow them to exercise power for the benefit of the organization.

Herzberg's Motivation/Hygiene Theory

Frederick Herzberg developed a unique perspective on employee needs.[12] He argued that different sets of needs play very different roles in the overall scheme of motivation and satisfaction in organizations. This perspective has strongly influenced motivational practices during the last three decades.

In the 1950s, Herzberg asked 200 accountants and engineers to think back over their work experiences and to identify those associated with: 1) extreme dissatisfaction and lack of motivation and 2) extreme satisfaction and motivation.[13] After analyzing these "critical incidents," Herzberg observed that certain issues were at the heart of dissatisfying experiences, and certain other issues were at the heart of satisfying experiences. He then concluded that people's needs could be grouped into two categories, which correspond to negative and positive experiences: hygiene and motivator needs.

Hygiene Needs **Hygiene needs** are not directly related to work itself. Instead they relate to the context of a job and consist of such factors as pay, working conditions, co-workers, supervision, and security (like the existence and relatedness needs included in Alderfer's ERG theory). Hygiene needs focus on the avoidance of pain and must be met to avoid dissatisfaction. Meeting these needs, however, does not necessarily provide satisfaction or motivation. Providing employees with clean working conditions, for example, will be satisfying initially. After a short while, though, the employees will take clean working conditions for granted, and they will no longer produce strong, long-term satisfaction or motivation. Dirty working conditions, on the other hand, will cause employees to be dissatisfied and eventually will reduce work motivation.

Herzberg often refers to hygiene needs as "dissatisfiers" because they are so often associated with dissatisfaction. In fact, Herzberg's research indicated that hygiene factors accounted for 69 percent of all reported dissatisfying experiences but only for 19 percent of the satisfying experiences (see Figure 14.5).

FIGURE 14.5   *Needs Associated with Satisfaction and Dissatisfaction*

Source: Data derived from F. Herzberg (1968), One more time, how do you motivate employees? *Harvard Business Review*, 46, 54–62.

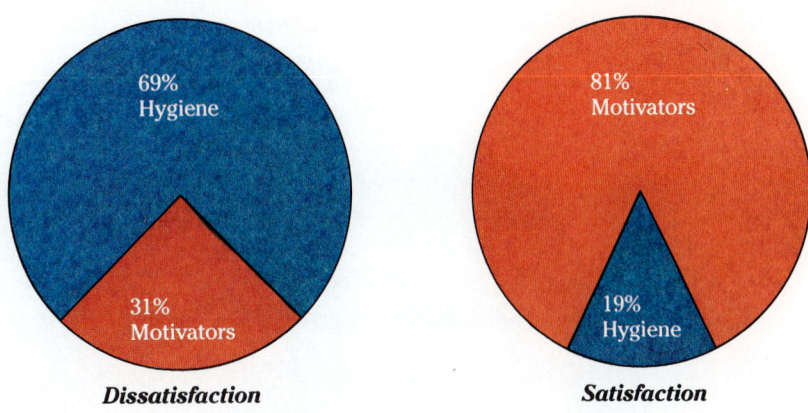

69%
Hygiene

31%
Motivators

Dissatisfaction

81%
Motivators

19%
Hygiene

Satisfaction

Motivator Needs   **Motivator needs,** such as achievement, recognition, responsibility, and advancement (like Alderfer's growth needs), center on a long-term need to pursue psychological growth. When motivators are present, employees are motivated to be high performers. For example, workers who achieve production goals, meet a sales target, or are assigned extra responsibility for a job well done are likely to have their motivator needs met.

Herzberg states that meeting motivator needs will produce satisfaction and, thus, he calls them "satisfiers." In fact, Figure 14.5 shows that motivator factors were involved in 81 percent of satisfying incidents but in only 31 percent of dissatisfying events. Probably Herzberg's biggest lasting contribution to management has been his creation of an awareness of the potential power of these needs for motivating and satisfying organization members.

Implications   Herzberg's work suggests a two-stage process for managing employee satisfaction and motivation (see Figure 14.6). First, managers should address hygiene factors so that relatively basic needs are met and employees are not dissatisfied. They must make sure that workers are adequately paid, that working conditions are safe and clean, that workers have opportunities for social interaction, and that treatment by supervisors is humane. When these conditions are met, employees should not be job dissatisfied and should not be motivated to avoid work or perform poorly. After these conditions are met, managers should proceed to the second stage and address the much more powerful motivator needs. They must make sure that workers experience recognition, responsibility, achievement, and growth. If motivator needs are ignored, neither long-term satisfaction nor high motivation is likely. When motivator needs are met, however, employees feel satisfied and are motivated to perform well.

Criticism   Although Herzberg's work contains important ideas for managers, his theory has been the subject of considerable controversy.[14] Critics claim that Herzberg's research results are open to alternative interpretations and that his subjects were not representative of the general workforce. Most importantly, it has been argued that, even if Herzberg is

FIGURE 14.6   *The Motivation/Hygiene Motivational Strategy*

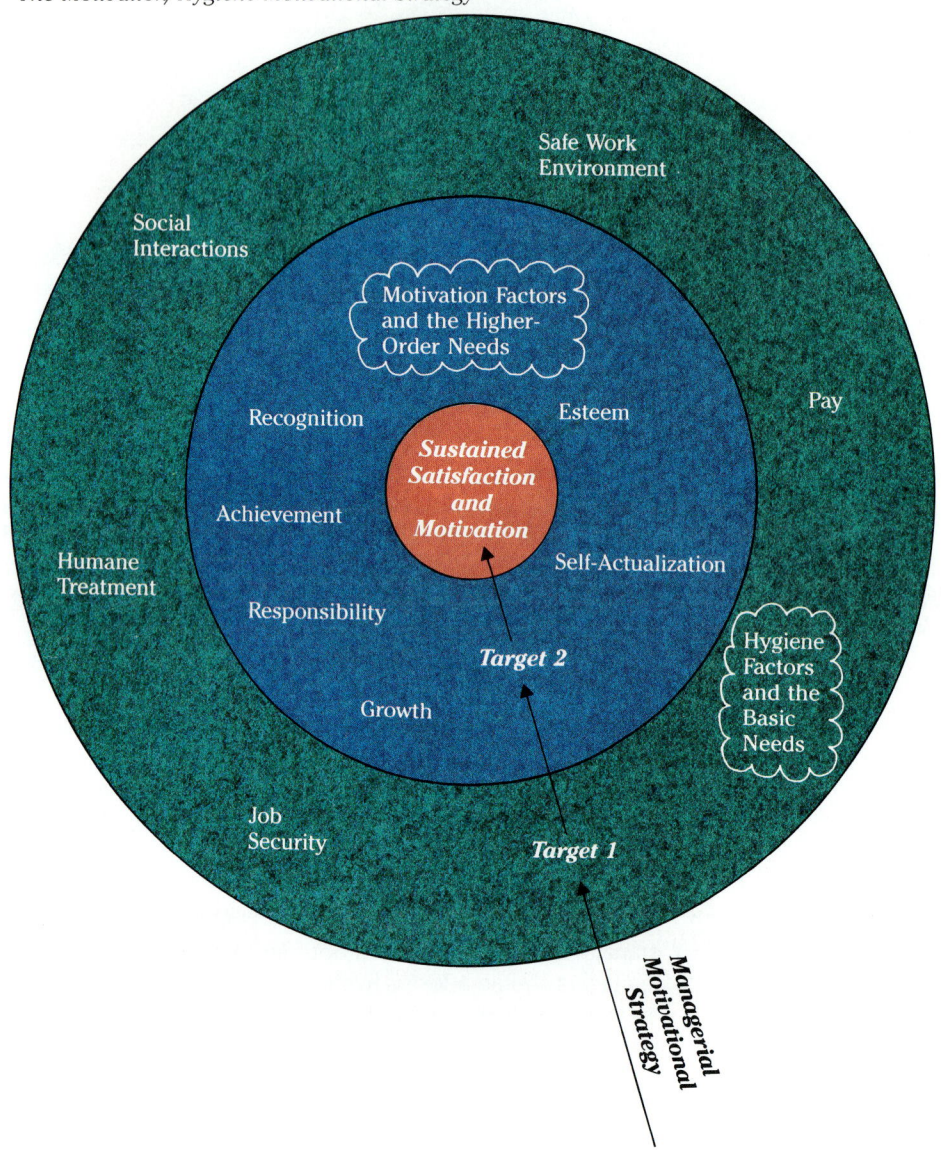

correct in noting that hygiene factors seldom produce satisfaction or motivation, this does not mean they *never* can do so.[15] Perhaps managers simply have failed to make hygiene factors work well as motivators. (Herzberg's research showed that hygiene factors were associated with satisfying experiences 19 percent of the time.) For example, appropriately administered monetary bonuses have been successful in motivating work attendance, performance, and satisfaction.[16]

Although it may be difficult for managers to use hygiene factors, such as pay, to motivate effective performance, they do have potential and should not be overlooked. "A Closer Look: Motivating Employees" examines how A&P grocery stores used a financial incentive system to improve employee productivity.

Content Theory Contributions

Although content theories differ somewhat in their details, they have more similarities than differences. Each deals with the importance of human needs and the dissatisfaction that occurs when they are unmet. Each shows that people are motivated to meet their needs, and, when they do so, they feel satisfied. The content theories, thus, explain why and how people are energized.

Content theories do not, however, provide enough guidance for a complete model of motivation. They do not specify exactly how managers can motivate workers, nor do they offer much guidance for understanding how people choose specific courses of action when faced with two or more alternatives, either of which could satisfy their needs. The reinforcement and process theories help complete this picture.

Reinforcement Theories

Managers often note that people repeat some behaviors more often than others. One employee, Diana Brown, for example, is frequently late for work, and another employee, Carol Pharo, is continually offering production improvement suggestions. What encourages people to behave in a particular way? According to **reinforcement theories,** a person repeats behaviors that result in desirable consequences and avoids behaviors that produce undesirable consequences. This idea reflects what is known as the *law of effect*.

If managers want to encourage people to repeat a particular behavior, reinforcement theorists say that they must provide a desirable consequence after the behavior is performed. A desirable consequence can be anything that satisfies an active need or that removes a barrier to need satisfaction. It can be as simple as providing a kind word or as major as offering a promotion. When it is necessary to discourage people from repeating a behavior, managers must provide an undesirable consequence, something which frustrates need satisfaction or removes a currently satisfying circumstance—such as a reduction in pay or a demotion.

Reinforcement theories build nicely on the knowledge provided by content theories. As a manager, you can use the content theories to help identify the outcomes your subordinates positively or negatively value. These factors are the energizers of human motivation. For example, if Suzanne Sitlington values relatedness opportunities, you can motivate her by offering social recognition for success. Reinforcement theories help you understand how to shape desired behavior by providing these positively or negatively valued outcomes—such as recognition and approval—to encourage or discourage particular behaviors.

A CLOSER LOOK

Motivating Employees: Workers Bag More Money, but A&P Reduces Labor Costs

In the late 1970s, rivals called Great Atlantic & Pacific Tea Co. the worst-run supermarket chain in the business. Shoppers were deserting A&P in droves. Managers doubled as baggers, and worker morale reached an all-time low. By 1982, after four straight years of losses, A&P had shrunk to 1,016 stores from 3,468 in 1974. But then A&P found an important resource: its employees.[1]

In a four-year period, A&P's operating profits increased 81 percent. The value of the stock doubled. Store sales jumped almost 25 percent. Employee satisfaction improved substantially. In fact, average overall earnings for employees also increased. What accounts for the turnaround at A&P? A large portion of this newfound success can be traced to a novel incentive plan which offers workers financial bonuses if they can help trim labor costs or increase sales volume.

In 1981, all eighty-one A&P stores in the Philadelphia area were closed for lack of profitability. A&P chairman, James Wood, believed that one of the reasons A&P had encountered such serious problems was the lack of ". . . motivation you find at a family business . . . . The idea of people get-ting a piece of what they are trying to achieve has always appealed to me enormously."[2] Accordingly, Wood worked with Thomas R. McNutt, president of the local United Food & Commercial Workers (UFCW) labor union, to develop the unique plan that they hope will be the salvation of A&P. Six of the stores were bought and reopened by employees, and another sixty stores were opened, at least in part, based on the viability of the new incentive plan.

How does this unique plan work? It starts with workers' accepting a 25 percent cut in pay in exchange for a store's promise of a bonus if labor costs can be cut to 11 percent of sales or less. In fact, if labor costs can be cut to as little as 9-1/2 percent of sales, the company presents workers with a bonus equal to 1-1/2 percent of all of the store's sales.

Profits increased 81 percent. . . . The value of the stock doubled. . . . Sales jumped almost 25 percent.

What do employees do to earn their bonus? They work harder, and they increase their productivity and efficiency. They also have twice weekly meetings with the store's manager, and they meet on a regional basis, during which time they make suggestions. Any suggestions that reduce labor costs directly or increase sales volume are welcome. Employees in Richmond, Virginia, for example, noticed that customers who came to the store during peak times and found checkout lines stretching into aisles would leave rather than deal with the congestion. The employees' suggestion: widen the aisles at the checkout counters. The results: more customers and greater sales. After heeding the suggestion of employees at a store in Philadelphia, managers noted sales soaring after ethnic foods were added to inventory.

The company has clearly benefited from the incentive plan, but so have employees. Thousands of employees who would otherwise have become unemployed through store closings have retained their jobs. Philadelphia workers now earn almost a dollar per hour more in base wages and bonuses than the average food store wage elsewhere in the city.

A&P's experience emphasizes that incentive plans can benefit both organizations and employees. To quote Thomas McNutt, "You'd be amazed at the willingness of people to participate when they can say anything without fear of reprisal."[3] A&P is now exploring the use of such incentive plans at more of its stores. They are now in place at almost 300 of the company's 850 U.S. stores. It is likely the plan will work elsewhere if employees accept it and believe that through their efforts they can benefit themselves as well as the organization.

1. C. S. Eklund (22 December 1986), How A&P fattens profits by sharing them, *Business Week*, 44.
2. *Ibid.*
3. *Ibid.*

FIGURE 14.7
The Basic Operant Learning Model

Stimulus → Response → Consequence

Operant Learning Theory

According to **operant learning theory,** people learn to behave in a particular fashion as a result of the consequences that followed their past behaviors.[17] The workers at A&P have learned to make suggestions at meetings because their managers follow up on these suggestions. When their suggestions work, the employees share in the increased profits that result. The learning process involves three distinct steps (see Figure 14.7). The first step involves the presentation of a *stimulus (S)*, which is any situation or event perceived by the individual that is followed by a response. For example, a work assignment is a stimulus. The second step involves a *response (R)*, which is any behavior that follows a stimulus. Working hard to meet a work assignment is a response. Finally, a *consequence (C)* is any event that follows a response and that makes the response more or less likely to occur in the future. If Colleen Sullivan receives praise from her superior for working hard, and if getting that praise is a pleasurable event, then it is likely that Colleen will work hard again in the future. If, on the other hand, the superior ignores or criticizes Colleen's response (working hard), this consequence is likely to make Colleen avoid working hard in the future. It is the experienced consequence (positive or negative) that influences whether a response will be repeated the next time the stimulus is presented.

When a consequence makes it *more likely* the response will be repeated in the future, **reinforcement** occurs. In the previous example, praise from Colleen's superior is a reinforcer. If a consequence makes the response *less likely,* **extinction** begins. Criticism from Colleen's supervisor could cause this. When this goes on long enough, the response eventually will disappear. At that point it is said to be extinct, which is what would happen if Colleen no longer worked hard at any assignment she were given.

As Table 14.2 shows, there are three ways to make a response more likely to recur: positive reinforcement, negative reinforcement, and avoidance learning. In addition, there are two ways to make the response less likely: nonreinforcement and punishment.

TABLE 14.2   *Ways to Change Behavior Using Operant Learning*

Ways to Encourage Behavior
1. Positive reinforcement
2. Negative reinforcement
3. Avoidance learning

Ways to Discourage Behavior
1. Nonreinforcement
2. Punishment

Making a Response More Likely Managers in any organization want to encourage desired behavior from employees, be it regular attendance, high productivity, or extra effort on special projects. One technique that managers can use to encourage desirable behavior is positive reinforcement. **Positive reinforcement** occurs whenever a positively valued consequence follows a response to a stimulus and makes future similar responses to the stimulus more likely. If a manager can provide subordinates with something of positive value after they respond in a desirable way to the managers' goals, they will be more likely to respond similarly in the future. For example, Eric, an employee of IBM, put in many extra hours on a project he knew was important to his manager. As a reward, he received a special recognition that IBM calls its "Dinner for Two" award. Eric could use this award to buy dinner for himself and a friend at any local restaurant. Impressed and delighted, Eric intends to work especially hard on future projects in hopes of receiving this or other rewards again. Positive reinforcement is encouraging him to repeat this desired behavior.

Another technique for making a desired response more likely is known as **negative reinforcement.** When a behavior causes something undesired to be taken away, the behavior is more likely to be repeated in the future. Elizabeth started her morning by slamming the "stop" button to silence her shrilly ringing alarm clock. She propped herself up on her pillows and began to read a magazine, which brought her mother running into the room with a lecture about Elizabeth's need to get ready for school. When Elizabeth put her magazine down and began to get dressed, her mother quit lecturing her and left the room. That evening Elizabeth went to her part-time job at the Embassy Suites hotel. Her duties were to clean the hotel's bathrooms, and Elizabeth found it very unpleasant work. That night, however, Elizabeth's boss informed her that, as a reward for being so reliable and efficient, she would be promoted to the bar area, where she would be responsible for preparing and serving hors d'oeuvres.

All three of Elizabeth's experiences involved negative reinforcement: pushing the button on the alarm clock made the obnoxious buzzer go away; getting dressed made her mother go away (no offense, Mom); and being an effective employee at the hotel made the undesirable work assignment go away. Managers can use negative reinforcement to encour-

Reprinted by special permission of NAS, Inc.

In using punishment as a technique for changing behavior, an airline might issue a one-day suspension for a mechanic who neglects to log a repair.

age subordinates to act in desirable ways by rewarding them with the removal of something unpleasant. The effect is much the same as the result achieved through positive reinforcement.

A third method of making a response more likely involves a process known as **avoidance learning.** Through avoidance learning, people learn to behave in a certain way to avoid encountering an undesired or unpleasant consequence. Many people learn to wake up a minute or so before their alarm clock rings so they can turn it off and avoid hearing the obnoxious sound of the buzzer. Some workers learn to get to work on time to avoid the harsh words or punitive actions of their supervisors. Many organizational discipline systems rely heavily on avoidance learning by using the threat of negative consequences to encourage desired behavior. When managers warn an employee not to be late again, when they threaten to fire a careless worker, or when they transfer someone to an undesirable position, they are relying on the power of avoidance learning.

Making a Response Less Likely   This section has talked about ways that a manager can encourage organization members to behave in a desired fashion. What techniques can managers use to discourage employees from repeating undesired behavior? Many managers feel that the best way to deal with an undesired behavior is to ignore it so that it will go away. This approach is what operant theorists call **nonreinforcement.** A subordinate is permitted to engage in an undesired behavior, but no consequence at all—positive or negative—follows that response. This lack of reward gives the person no reason to repeat the undesired behavior. This technique can take quite a while to discourage behavior, however, and sometimes does not succeed. For example, if a behavior is intrinsically satisfying, the nonreinforcement strategy is doomed to failure.

A much faster and less uncertain technique for changing behavior is the use of punishment. **Punishment** makes it less likely that a person will behave a certain way because the undesired behavior is followed by a distinctly undesirable consequence. A professor who wishes to discourage students from turning papers in late might lower the grades given late assignments by one letter for each day they are overdue. An airline might issue a one-day suspension without pay for a mechanic who completes required repairs on a plane but neglects to sign the maintenance logbook certifying that the repair had been made. Punishment provides a clear message: "Don't do this." For this reason, punishment usually causes behavior to change relatively quickly, particularly if the punishment is powerful.

Punishment clearly works more quickly than does nonreinforcement, but punishment has some potentially undesirable side effects. Although punishment effectively tells a person what *not* to do and stops the undesired behavior, it does not tell the person what he or she *should* do. In addition, even when punishment works as intended, the worker being punished often develops negative feelings toward the person who does the punishing. Although sometimes it is very difficult for managers to avoid using punishment, it works best when reinforcement is also used.

Schedules of Reinforcement and Punishment How often does a manager need to provide reinforcement or punishment? According to operant learning theorists, **continuous schedules of reinforcement**—reinforcing or punishing every time a behavior is shown—are the most effective for shaping behavior. People respond most powerfully when the consequence of their behavior follows quickly, reliably, and consistently. Employees who are rewarded for every production increase and students who are penalized for every late paper learn much more quickly than those whose feedback comes less consistently.

Of course, it is not realistic to expect that a manager, with many other responsibilities, can be available continuously for this purpose. Alternatives to continuous schedules, known as **intermittent schedules of reinforcement,** provide a consequence following some (but not all) responses. The most common intermittent schedules are known as fixed ratio, variable ratio, fixed interval, and variable interval. A *fixed ratio* reinforcement or punishment schedule reinforces or punishes *every* "nth" behavior, thus, a manager might give a subordinate a pat on the back every third time he or she executes a task appropriately. A company that rewards salespeople with a day off for every thousand units sold reinforces according to a fixed ratio. With a *variable ratio* reinforcement or punishment schedule, managers reinforce or punish *on average* one out of "nth" responses. A manager using this approach might sometimes provide that pat on the back twice in a row and at other times wait until four or five responses have been provided. A manager who sometimes gives a day off with pay to an employee who has worked weekends to complete a project but at other times offers only his or her thanks reinforces according to a variable ratio schedule.

Reinforcement can also be administered at time intervals. Managers who use interval schedules let a certain amount of time pass during which no reinforcement is offered, no matter how a subordinate behaves. After the interval ends, they offer reinforcement the next time the subordinate behaves in the desired manner. Managers who operate a *fixed interval* schedule maintain the same time period on a regular basis. Managers who operate a *variable interval* schedule reinforce or punish on an average of a particular time period. A supervisor who tours each work station every hour on the hour and makes favorable comments to employees who are working hard at that moment is using a fixed interval schedule. If the supervisor visits each work station on average once an hour—sometimes on the hour, sometimes at five minutes after the hour, sometimes at twenty minutes before the hour—and provides reinforcement at that time, he or she is using a variable interval schedule.

The various reinforcement schedules available to managers produce different effects. No one schedule is best in all circumstances. If, for example, the primary concern is to encourage a worker to learn something very quickly, a continuous reinforcement schedule works best, because the learner can see right away which behaviors will be reinforced. Ratio schedules are more efficient, however, and can be quite effective for maintaining behaviors once they have been learned (even though they are not as good at producing quick learning). Interval schedules of reinforcement, although seldom as effective as ratio schedules, may be useful when a manager cannot afford to spend the large amount of time and energy continuous or ratio reinforcement schedules require. With few exceptions, however, managers should choose a variable interval schedule over a fixed interval strategy because too many people learn to do what they are supposed to do only when the clock tells them their manager is about to appear.

Organizational Behavior Modification (OBM)

Individual managers can use the principles of operant theory to encourage or discourage certain behavior in their subordinates. The same principles can be used in a very systematic, organized way to produce broader changes in organizational behavior. The term **organizational behavior modification (OBM)** is used to describe the systematic application of operant learning principles to manage behavior within organizations. In addition to incorporating all of the principles of operant theory, OBM adds others to facilitate the management of behavior. For example, OBM makes it very clear to workers that they are choosing how to behave; thus, a manager using OBM can tell subordinates what he or she wants them to do and which consequences will follow if they do or do not choose to comply. OBM also takes advantage of *social learning*, in which people watch others and see which consequences follow their behavior. An employee who sees a co-worker rewarded for behaving in a certain way learns to behave similarly to try to be rewarded.

Managers who want to apply the principles of behavior modification can follow these steps:

1. Identify desired behaviors.
2. Identify potential reinforcers.
3. Choose appropriate learning techniques.
4. Choose appropriate reinforcement schedules.
5. Specify behavior → reinforcement links.
6. Measure behaviors accurately.
7. Follow planned behavior → reinforcement links.
8. Provide reinforcers soon after desired behavior occurs.

To begin the OBM process using the procedure just described, managers should identify the specific behaviors that they want from members in the program. For example, do they wish to motivate employees to generate money-saving ideas, reduce absenteeism, or increase their productivity? Management must specify exactly which behaviors are expected.

After identifying the desired behaviors, managers then should determine the reinforcers that employees will positively value. They must find out, through formal surveys or simple interaction, their subordinates' needs and interests and the value employees place on particular outcomes. Otherwise, something that they thought was a reward may backfire and punish behavior instead. Managers must consider two types of motivators when they try to determine outcomes: extrinsic and intrinsic.[18] **Extrinsic motivators** are based on rewards provided by someone other than the person being motivated. **Intrinsic motivators** arise from within the individual. If Joan Spaulding, data entry supervisor,

One way to begin the OBM process is to identify the specific behaviors that management expects from workers.

offers Floyd McCoy, key operator, a bonus in exchange for timely completion of a special project, she is using an extrinsic motivator to coax improved performance. If Floyd works hard to complete the project because he enjoys a difficult task or because it is a matter of pride, the motivation is intrinsic. This is also the point in the OBM process at which managers must decide whether the use of punishment is anticipated. If so, they must identify and prepare to use the consequences that are considered negative by employees.

Next, managers of the OBM process must choose appropriate learning techniques for their programs: positive reinforcement, negative reinforcement, punishment, or a combination of these. Once they have selected the learning devices, such as positive reinforcement, they must choose an appropriate reinforcement schedule—such as continuous reinforcement, ratio, or an interval schedule.

The next important step is to specify for employees exactly what behavior-reinforcement links have been chosen. Managers should tell workers, "If you behave this way, you will receive the following reinforcers" and "If you behave this other way, you will receive the following punishment." It is this stage that informs employees of the focus of the OBM program. It makes very clear what behavior is desired and what consequences the organization is prepared to provide for this behavior.

The last steps in an OBM program involve measuring how employees are actually behaving and providing the promised consequences in a timely fashion. If a person behaves as desired, reinforcement should follow quickly. If a worker behaves in an undesired manner so that punishment is necessary, it should be administered quickly. The effective use of OBM requires managers to behave systematically, following the many steps required in an orderly fashion. While OBM programs are never easy to design or administer, they can be strong motivators with excellent results.[19]

There is no question that OBM can shape the behavior of organization members, but is it ethical? After all, the steps in OBM lay out a systematic approach for controlling people so they will behave as an organization wants them to. Does this take away individuality and invade privacy? Is it humane? Does it open the door to wide-scale abuse of organization members?

The answer to all of the preceding questions is both yes and no. OBM can be used to manipulate people, but it can also be used for the good purpose of helping people behave the way that they want to. Many weight-reduction and quit-smoking programs apply OBM principles for the purpose of modifying personal behavior. Industrial safety programs use OBM to teach workers how to operate equipment safely. OBM programs teach salespeople effective techniques and provide rewards for successful sales.

Operant learning principles and OBM simply describe the processes through which people learn. The individuals who apply these processes can put them to ethical or unethical, harmful or beneficial, use. When used appropriately and explained fully to organization members, OBM can show employees that managers care. It lets workers know what is expected of them by their managers. It shows that managers are willing to help workers meet their organization's expectations and to reward desired

A CLOSER LOOK

OBM: Flying High at Scandinavian Airlines

Sales performance for reservations agents at Scandinavian Airlines was at an all-time low. A consultant hired to investigate and improve the situation found that agents were making firm booking offers during only 34 percent of potential sales opportunities. They were making round-trip bookings during only 17.5 percent of the opportunities. The only behavior that managers were measuring was the number of calls every agent took each day, and even this measurement was not being reinforced systematically.

An OBM program was designed to change the agents' behavior. The consultant helped the airline identify a desired response for agents: to provide specific booking offers to customers and to give customers supporting information to encourage them to book flights. The consultant developed a system that the airline could use to measure the frequency of each of these desired responses. Appropriate responses were reinforced through feedback, social recognition, awards, gifts, and special assignments. Inappropriate responses received nonreinforcement or mild punishment. Most reinforcement was provided using a combination of variable ratio and variable interval schedules.

The OBM program at Scandinavian Airlines seemed to be a tremendous success. Reservations agents offered customers specific bookings and gave

Appropriate responses were reinforced through feedback . . . and special assignments.

them the necessary supporting information 80 percent of the time. The number of successful round-trip bookings increased from 17.5 percent to over 30 percent. The financial impact for the airline was substantial, even considering the costs of the training required. OBM was working well at Scandinavian Airlines.[1]

1. For additional information, see E. J. Feeney, J. R. Staelin, R. M. O'Brien, and A. M. Dickinson (1982), Increasing sales performance among airline reservation personnel, in R. M. O'Brien, A. M. Dickinson, and M. P. Rosow, eds., *Industrial behavior modification: A management handbook,* Maxwell House, NY: Pergamon Press, 141–58.

behavior. In fact, it can be argued that managers behave unethically if they do *not* systematically use this knowledge: every time managers react or fail to react to the actions of subordinates, they influence workers' subsequent behavior. Unless managers use OBM, they may waste employees' time and energy and inadvertently encourage undesired behavior by failing to reward those who follow the rules and perform effectively.

Process Theories

Process theories go beyond content and reinforcement theories to provide a more complete understanding of human feelings, beliefs, and expectations. **Process theories** focus on the reasons people choose to behave in certain ways and the reasons they react as they do to organizational events.

Distributive Justice and Equity Theory

Lillie Chalmers has just been given a pay raise. It has increased her income from $30,000 a year to $31,800 and she is furious. Even though she normally likes her work, at the moment she is extremely dissatisfied. She is considering demanding a larger raise. She is half-inclined to quit her job. She is thinking that maybe it would be better to keep the job and the $31,800 but to quit working so hard. Why was Lillie happier yesterday earning $30,000 than she is today earning 6 percent more? When asked this question, she replied:

> My starting salary a year ago was $30,000, which I thought was reasonable pay for a new customer relations representative with a fresh MBA. During the last year, I have worked extremely hard and, if you ask me, have clearly shown that I am the most effective rep in the entire office. The value of what I give the company is much more than a lousy $30,000. I looked forward to today because I knew annual raises would be announced. I felt my effectiveness easily merited a 10 percent increase. When I found out I only got 6 percent, I checked with two of my friends who became reps about the same time I did. Keith Kastle, who isn't nearly as good as I am, also got a 6 percent raise. Mae Hedding, who is probably second best in the office, got a 9 percent raise and she doesn't even have an MBA. It just isn't fair!

Distributive Justice   One of the reasons Lillie reacted negatively to her pay raise involves what George Homans has called the principle of **distributive justice.**[20] Simply put, distributive justice is a question of fairness: does the person believe that a fair exchange has occurred between himself or herself and the organization? In Lillie's case, she clearly feels that she has given more to the organization than she has received. Because she feels that the organization is treating her unfairly, she is dissatisfied, and her future motivation is threatened.

Distributive justice can be written as a ratio:

$$\frac{\text{Outcomes (Self)}}{\text{Inputs (Self)}}$$

In weighing this ratio, a person making a fairness judgment about distributive justice includes any *outcomes* from the organization that he or she thinks are relevant: compensation, retirement benefits, enjoyment of the work, social interaction, prestige, and so on. *Inputs* include all the factors that the worker believes he or she provides to the exchange: level of effort, level of abilities, formal training, work effectiveness, and any other factors that the person chooses to include in this fairness judgment.

If this ratio equals 1, the exchange is considered fair. If it is below 1, it is considered unfair and causes dissatisfaction. When someone feels that the exchange has been unfair, he or she is motivated to obtain distributive justice, either by reducing inputs (as Lillie appears ready to do) or by increasing outcomes (as might happen if Lillie were able to negotiate a higher pay raise). If the ratio exceeds 1, it also should be considered unfair, although people generally do not get as upset as when the ratio falls below 1. Substantial overreward is usually required before people consider it upsetting and are motivated to bring about a change.

Distributive justice is a question of fairness between workers and their organization.

Equity Theory Lillie certainly was upset because of a lack of distributive justice, but she was also concerned about the unfairness she perceived when she compared her situation to that of her co-workers. **Equity theory,** as proposed by J. Stacy Adams, suggests that people compare their own distributive justice ratio to the ratio they perceive for other people (an individual, a group, one's self in another situation, or one's idealized self):[21]

$$\frac{\text{Outcomes (Self)}}{\text{Inputs (Self)}} \overset{?}{=} \frac{\text{Outcomes (Other Person)}}{\text{Inputs (Other Person)}}$$

The way in which people perceive this comparison influences their attitudes, motivation, and behavior.

When people perceive their ratio to be equal to the ratio of others, they see the situation as equitable (fair). When people feel that the situation is fair, they feel satisfied. When they feel satisfied, they are motivated to maintain the state of equity. To do so may require them to maintain high inputs, if that is what it has taken to obtain the state of equity.

People may perceive a situation to be inequitable (unfair) under two conditions. As previously noted, the first state, overreward, generally poses few problems. In this situation, people feel that their outcome-to-input ratio is greater than that of the people with whom they compare themselves. Whereas overreward does not usually cause a manager many difficulties (how likely is Mae to complain that her pay increase is too high?), *considerable* overreward can make people feel guilty. It also can motivate people to try to seek a state of equity, perhaps by increasing their inputs.

The second condition of inequity, underreward, does pose a problem for managers. In this situation, workers feel that those to whom they compare themselves are getting "a better deal," as illustrated in the following ratio:

$$\frac{\text{Outcomes (Self)}}{\text{Inputs (Self)}} < \frac{\text{Outcomes (Other Person)}}{\text{Inputs (Other Person)}}$$

When people perceive underreward, as Lillie did, they feel angry, tense, and dissatisfied and will be motivated to do something to reestablish a state of perceived equity.

In Lillie's case, she is considering reducing her inputs by lowering her performance to restore a state of perceived equity. Another solution would be to increase her outcomes, perhaps by demanding a raise. She also might try to change the situation of the people to whom she is comparing herself, by persuading Mae to work harder or by telling her boss about the times that Keith has cheated on his weekly status reports. Another alternative for Lillie in dealing with this perceived underreward is to change her perceptions and to decide that she is simply not as valuable to the organization as she had previously believed. She also might conclude that it is inappropriate to compare herself with Mae and Keith and identify another person with whom to compare herself. If all else fails, of course, Lillie can escape this unfair situation by leaving her job.

One of equity theory's shortcomings is that it does not fully specify which of these alternatives Lillie will choose to reduce her perceived inequity. Adams did, however, point out that most people have several preferences as they select an equity-reducing strategy. For example, people prefer to maximize their positive outcomes whenever possible. They prefer to avoid increasing their inputs when they can, and they usually keep as an action of last resort the alternative of quitting the job.

Together, the principles of distributive justice and equity theory can help managers recognize that organization members evaluate the outcomes they receive from the organization in a very personal manner. No matter how much workers value a pay raise or a promotion, for example, they may still react negatively if they think that the outcome was not fair relative to what they did to earn that outcome, or not fair when compared to the outcomes others in the organization have received for their efforts.

Motivating Through Goals

Goal theory specifies that particular kinds of goals motivate organization members most effectively. This theory applies many of the principles of the other theories in this chapter and is the simplest, most straightforward of all of the theories discussed here. In addition, although somewhat narrow in scope, it is also the most completely supported by research evidence.[22]

Important Goal Characteristics As Figure 14.8 shows, workers who have a goal, even if it is quite general, usually perform better than those who work without any goals at all. Furthermore, certain types of goals are more effective than others. The two primary goal characteristics which enhance the motivating power of goals are *goal difficulty* and *goal specificity.*[23]

People with difficult goals perform better than those with easy goals (note the third and fourth two bars in Figure 14.8), but goals that are perceived as impossible are not very effective.[24] Difficult goals must be considered reachable to be effective. A difficult goal also should be

FIGURE 14.8 The Effects of Goals on Performance

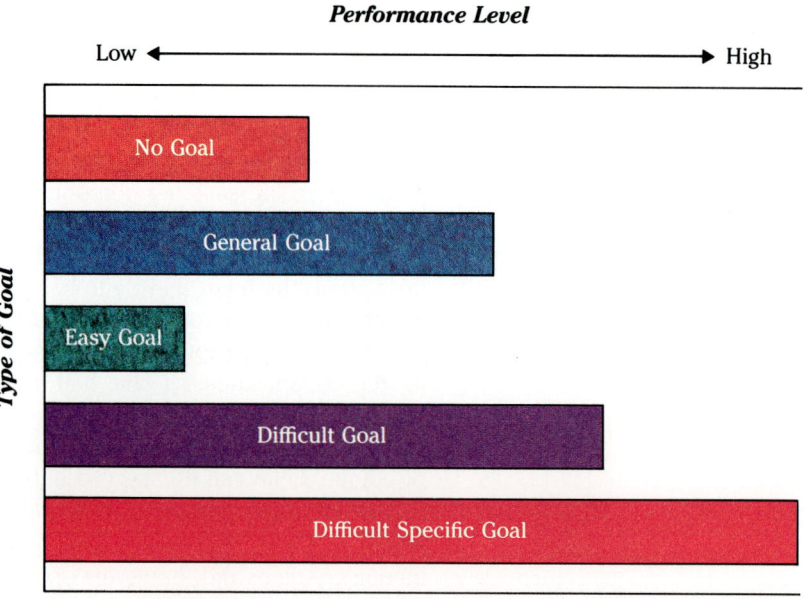

Barbara M. Karmel

Barbara M. Karmel, Ph.D., is president of the Reed Company, a management consulting firm she founded in 1982. The company provides specialized services to owner-managers of closely held businesses in many industry sectors and to partners of professional firms.

1. Which approaches to motivation do you see organizations using?

I see a stick-to-carrot ratio of 10:1. Managers often seem preoccupied with things that are too slow, inaccurate, or otherwise wrong rather than with looking for constructive, direct solutions to problems and for new windows of opportunity.

2. Which approaches do you see as most effective and why?

I suggest to managers of client companies that they consider the following menu of choices when they want to straighten out a wrong-headed employee. Let's call him Joe.

a. Peg the problem—what is really wrong? Does it really matter?
b. Help Joe figure out how to do it right. (If he had known how to do it right in the first place, he probably would have.)
c. Figure out what needs to be done by other employees or units to help Joe do it right and then motivate those people or units to help (with raw materials, supplies, updated information, moral support, and so on).
d. Watch intently for examples of what Joe does right and reward him for it by glance, bonus, smile, promotion, newsletter item, and so on.
e. Take care that a skill problem is not misdiagnosed as a motivational problem.
f. Replace managers who make repeated selection decisions that require remediation of their subordinates—after, of course, following steps (a) through (e) above for the manager.

3. What factors do you see interfering with a manager's ability to motivate employees?

A principle factor is that many managers have insufficient opportunity to observe a really good manager at work, managing—the learn-by-example component of management development; however, just observing good managers motivate others is not enough. Managers need assistance in order to interpret complex managerial behaviors, and in order to be able to identify specific behaviors that have motivational impact on an employee in a given setting and situation. Motivation is a touch game, not a power sport.

4. If there were one point you could convince all managers of, what would it be?

If your selection, retention, and placement (SRP) policies are effective, employee motivation and productivity will be generally tractable—that is, amenable to lasting improvement. Poor SRP practices, or poor documentation thereof, causes managers to spend most of their time curing "people problems" instead of managing output and developing opportunities.

specific to be maximally effective;[25] thus, the most commonly expressed goal, "I'm going to do my best," is not very effective because it is too general.

Even a goal that is both difficult and specific, however, is not very effective unless it is accepted by an individual who is committed to achieving it.[26] *Goal acceptance* is the degree to which you accept a goal as your own ("I agree that this report must be finished by 5 P.M."[27] *Goal commitment* is more inclusive, referring to one's level of attachment to or determination to reach a goal ("I *want* to get that report done on time").[28] Goals sometimes fail to motivate people when managers assign goals

FIGURE 14.9   A Model of Goal Setting

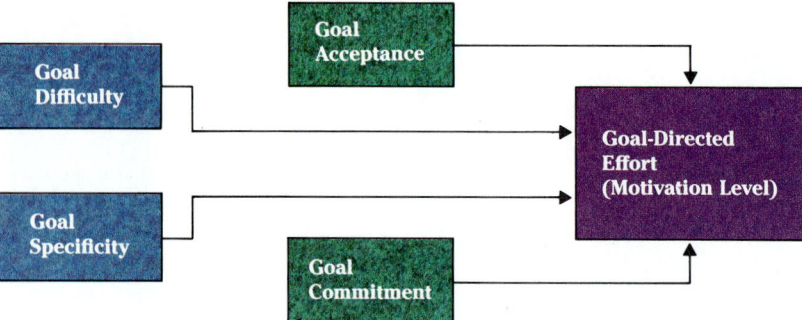

without making sure that subordinates have accepted or committed themselves to them. Figure 14.9 summarizes the conditions necessary to maximize goal-directed effort (motivation), a major contributor to subsequent performance.

A recent review of the goal-setting literature has identified three sets of factors that facilitate the development of goal commitment (see Figure 14.10).[29] These factors include:

1. External influences:
   - *authority*—being asked to do something by a person possessing legitimate authority increases goal commitment
   - *peer group influence*—group dynamics, such as peers acting as role models and group norms, can produce commitment to goals
   - *rewards and incentives*—commitment to goals is often the outgrowth of rewards and incentives that are associated with goal attainment

2. Interactive factor:
   - *participation*—participation can contribute to goal understanding and to a sense of goal ownership for those who want to be involved in the process[30]

3. Internal factors:
   - *expectancy of success*—perceptions of being able to achieve goals positively influences the commitment to those goals
   - *self-efficacy*—people who have a strong belief in their ability to accomplish goals are more likely to have strong commitment to these goals
   - *self-administered rewards*—self-generated feedback ("I did well") can lead to high goal commitment

A Manager's Role in Goal Setting   What can you do as a manager to encourage goal acceptance and commitment? Set difficult, specific, and reasonable goals and make certain that subordinates perceive them as reasonable. If necessary, provide employees with the training and support needed to make goals reachable. Offer feedback that lets people know when they are approaching the goal. Feedback reinforces employees for being on target or provides information that suggests a rechanneling of efforts. Avoid using threats. A positive, success-oriented approach is almost always more effective. Keep in mind that, whereas goal acceptance

FIGURE 14.10 *Determinants of Goal Commitment*

Source: Adapted from E. A. Locke, G. P. Latham, and M. Erez (1988), The determinants of goal commitment, *Academy of Management Review*, 13, 28.

occurs before people begin working on a task and can be encouraged through *promises* of reward, goal commitment can be nurtured throughout the performance period as workers *receive* rewards for progress.

Encourage the development of work group norms that contribute to goal commitment. Use legitimate authority to encourage the setting of specific and difficult goals. Stimulate workers to develop a sense of ownership in goals, thus producing goal acceptance and commitment.

Expectancy Theory

It is 8:30 on a Saturday morning. Kathleen Pratt is trying to decide how to spend her day. Her husband has asked her to go with him and another couple to a football game. Unfortunately, Kathleen has a final exam scheduled for Monday. Kathleen has until 9 A.M. to decide whether she will study until noon and then go to the game or skip the game and study all day. Which alternative will Kathleen choose, and how will she make this decision?

Expectancy theory states that Kathleen will make her decision by thinking through the implications of each alternative and choosing the one that is most attractive to her.[31] In fact, expectancy theory is a general model that can be useful in a wide variety of situations. Which job offer should you accept? Which classes should you sign up for? Should you go to work today or stay home?

In addition to stating that a person will select the most attractive alternative, expectancy theory specifies that the more attractive the selected alternative, the more highly motivated the individual will be to pursue it. If Kathleen concludes that staying home to study is only slightly more attractive than going to the football game, she will choose to stay home but will not be highly motivated to do so. In fact, it might be possible for her husband to change her mind without too much difficulty, but if staying home to study is much more attractive, Kathleen will choose to stay home and be highly motivated to do so. It will be very difficult for her husband or anyone else to convince her to go to the game.

Expectancy theory refers to the overall attractiveness of an alternative as the **Force** driving a person to choose that alternative. People consider three basic issues when they evaluate the attractiveness of alternatives:

FIGURE 14.11
Expectancy Perceptions

Alternative   **Expectancies**

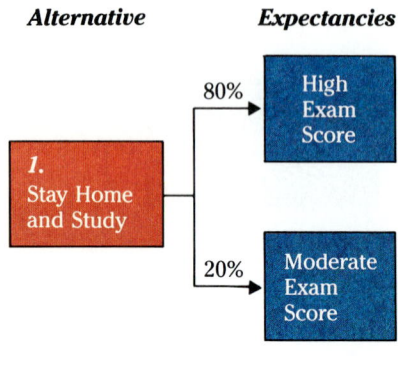

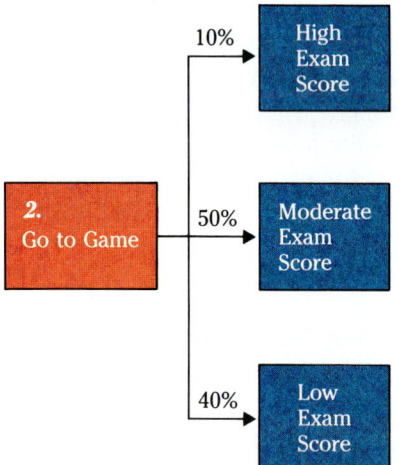

1. If I choose this alternative, what will my performance be? (expectancy perception)
2. If I perform at a given level, what outcomes will I receive? (instrumentality perception)
3. How much do I value each of these outcomes? (valence perception)

Expectancy Perceptions   For a given alternative, the **expectancy perception** is the perceived likelihood that the alternative will lead to a particular performance level. Consider Kathleen's expectancy perceptions as she evaluates the two alternatives:

1. If I study all day, I am reasonably certain that I will get a high score on the exam. Maybe there is a 20 percent chance that I will get only a moderately good score, but I see no chance of anything lower.
2. If I only study a few hours this morning and then go to the game, I see a very slim chance of getting a high exam score. I might have a 50-50 chance of getting a moderate score that way, but it is also quite possible that I could get a low exam score.

Figure 14.11 illustrates Kathleen's expectancy perceptions. Although these are important considerations, they are not enough to help Kathleen reach her decision. She needs to think through the consequences of the alternatives a bit further.

Instrumentality Perceptions   Kathleen has identified three possible performance levels: high, medium, and low exam scores. What outcomes might follow each of these performance levels? The **instrumentality perception** is the perceived likelihood that a given performance level will lead to one or more outcomes. Here are Kathleen's instrumentality perceptions:

1. If I get a high score on the exam, I am almost certain that I will be given an *A* for the course.
2. If I get a moderate exam score, I have equal chances of being given an *A* or *B* for the course.
3. A low exam score gives me no chance of an *A* for the course. In fact, a low exam score makes it pretty sure that I will get a *C* (although I suppose there is a chance that I could still get a *B*).

Kathleen is now close to making her decision. Only one final consideration remains: valence.

Valence Perceptions   **Valence** is the value attached to an outcome. How does Kathleen feel about her grades?

My current grade point average is 3.05. I know that I have to maintain at least a 3.00 to be admitted to the MBA program I just applied to. Although I value an A somewhat more than a B, I would be pleased with either an A or a B, since either helps me get into graduate school. A grade of C, however, would be a serious problem because it would drop my GPA below 3.0.

FIGURE 14.12 *Expectancy, Instrumentality, and Valence*

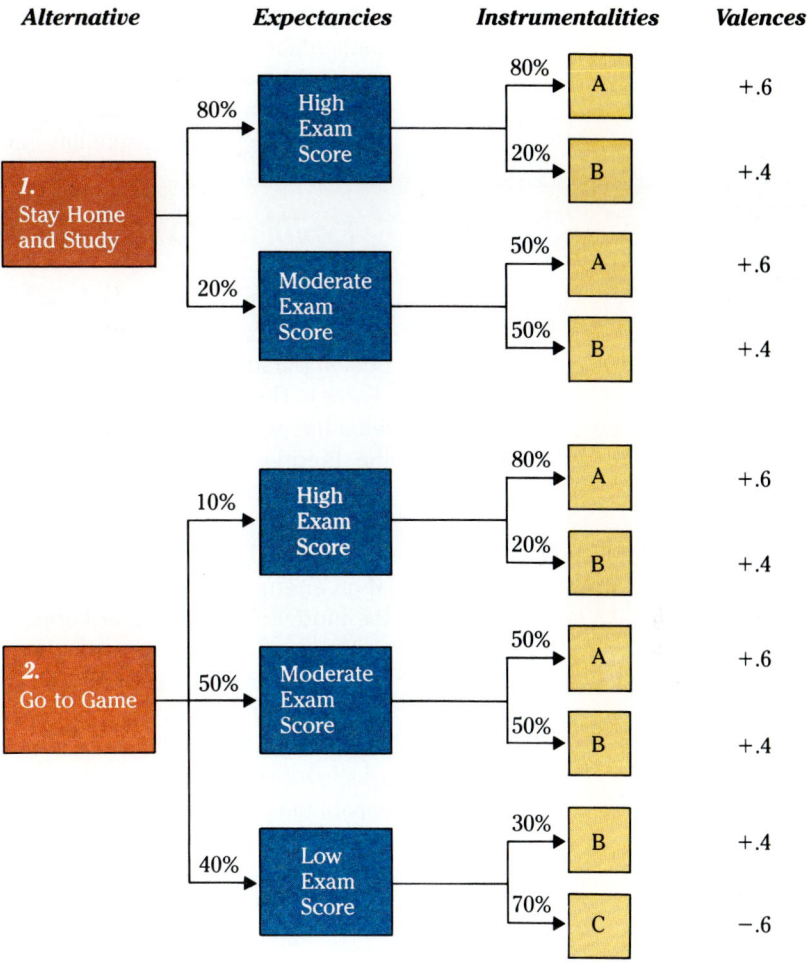

| Alternative | Expectancies | Instrumentalities | Valences |

Force Scores Figure 14.12 combines Kathleen's instrumentality and valence perceptions with the expectancy perceptions described earlier. Assuming that this figure includes all of the alternatives, performance levels, and outcomes considered by Kathleen in making this decision, it is now possible to identify quantitatively which alternative is more attractive and will be selected by Kathleen.

The following formula allows a quantitative evaluation of the two alternatives:

$$\text{Force} = \Sigma[(E \rightarrow P) \times \Sigma[(P \rightarrow O) \times (V)]]$$

where:

$E \rightarrow P$ are expectancy perceptions
$P \rightarrow O$ are instrumentality perceptions
V are valence perceptions

Using this equation, Kathleen's Force score for alternative #1 is +.548 and for alternative #2 is +.186. This means Kathleen considers alternative #1 to be almost three times as attractive as #2. She will choose #1.

It is unlikely that Kathleen sat down with paper and pencil and mathematically calculated a Force score. The theory states, rather, that the quantitative model captures the *character* of the decision-making process. As a person evaluates alternatives, he or she uses a combination of expectancy, instrumentality, and valence perceptions to arrive at a decision.

Expanded Expectancy Theory

Expectancy theory deals with the processes involved in choosing among alternatives. It also indicates that the enthusiasm with which a person pursues an alternative depends on how attractive the alternative is (Force). The expanded expectancy model shown in Figure 14.13 shows what happens after a choice is made by incorporating ideas from each of the theories discussed earlier in this chapter. This complete model, although somewhat complex, provides a realistic picture of how people react to their organizational experiences. (Notice that the three boxes on the model's left-hand side are the factors that determine the attractiveness of an alternative. Assuming that this is the chosen alternative, the rest of the model illustrates what happens next.)

The greater the Force score, the more highly motivated the person will be to expend energy pursuing that alternative. A high Force score, therefore, encourages strong commitment to a goal once it has been selected. A high Force score is also associated with a high level of effort, as shown in Figure 14.13. If an individual has the necessary personal capabilities, he or she can translate this effort into performance. Managers can use this to advantage if they provide employees with organizational support, such as materials and training to enhance their capabilities and, therefore, their likelihood of performing well.

The expanded expectancy model also demonstrates why performing at a high level is not sufficient to guarantee satisfaction. For workers to feel satisfied, all of the following conditions must be met:

FIGURE 14.13   *Expanded Expectancy Theory*

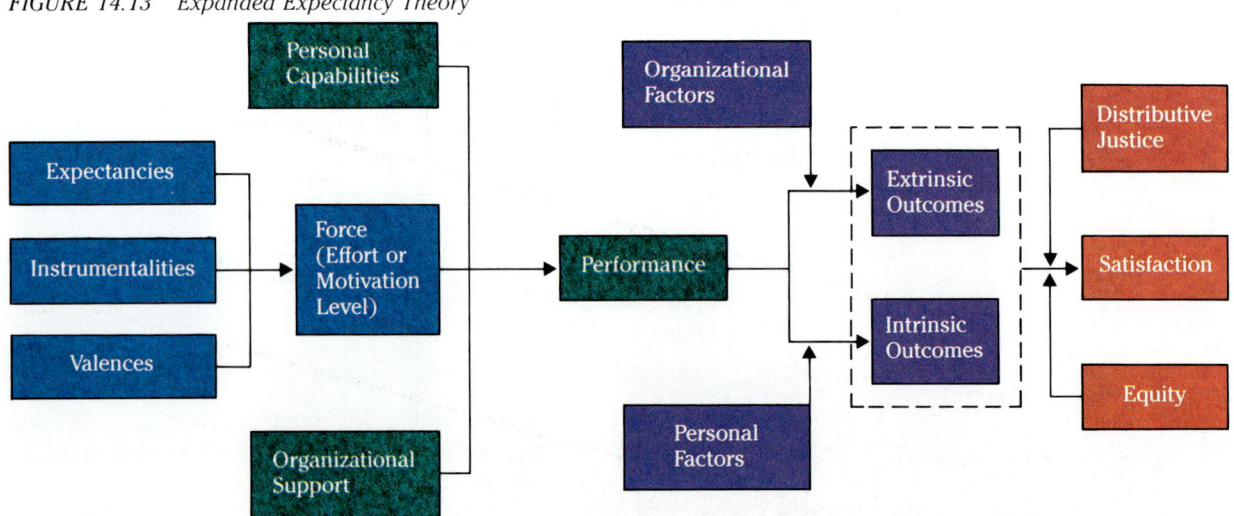

1. Valued outcomes, such as rewards, must be given to workers for successful performance.
2. Workers must value the experience of succeeding.
3. Workers must perceive that the value of the outcomes received in exchange for the effort expended is fair (the distributive justice evaluation).
4. Workers must perceive that their own situation compares favorably to that of others (equity comparisons).

If all of these conditions are met, workers will feel satisfied. Operant and other learning theories suggest that people repeat behaviors that in the past have led to satisfaction. Managers who want their employees to work hard must make certain that this effort translates into performance and eventually results in experienced satisfaction. If they do not, reasonable and rational employees will not choose to work hard in the future.

How Managers Can Use the Expanded Expectancy Model Most managers want their subordinates to choose to work hard. After persuading workers to choose that alternative, managers must follow through by seeing to it that the workers have the capabilities necessary to succeed and by providing the rewards promised. For example, Pamela Fullerton, a sales manager who has just convinced sales representative Mari Hall to choose a high sales goal and to devote considerable energy toward achieving that goal, cannot yet rest easy. The expanded expectancy model makes clear that Pamela must make sure that Mari has the capabilities needed to meet the goal. Does Mari, for example, have the interpersonal skills and the product knowledge required to make the sales? Is the organization's support—such as product samples, documentation of the products' merits, and appropriate supply and delivery mechanisms—adequate?

Pamela also must help sustain Mari's high effort and performance once they have been achieved. To do so, Pamela must identify outcomes—such as increased travel allotments, bonuses, and special recognition—that Mari values and must give them out in such in a way that Mari considers them a fair reward for her efforts. The rewards also must seem fair in comparison to those given to other salespeople.

If Pamela can meet all of these conditions, she is likely to have a highly effective, satisfied salesperson. If Pamela can convince Mari that hard work in the future—effort that translates into performance—will also lead to valued, fair, and satisfying outcomes, then Mari will again choose to work hard and, in all likelihood, will succeed again.

Motivation in Review

Almost any organization willing to spend enough money can staff its positions with individuals capable of performing its jobs effectively; however, being capable of doing something does not mean that workers will choose to do so and follow through to the point of effectiveness. It is motivation that energizes, directs, and sustains the human behavior necessary to turn a capable employee into an effective employee. Effective motivation of employees requires careful, systematic application of the principles derived from theories of motivation.

The psychological foundations of human motivation are based on four principles: hedonism, instincts, drive, and cognition. Traditional managerial approaches to motivation tried to capitalize on one or more of these psychological principles by satisfying various sets of human needs. The economic model of motivation dominant early in the century assumed that work is inherently unpleasant and that organizations should provide enough money to compensate employees for this unpleasantness. The social model of motivation assumed that the satisfaction of social needs would lead to effective performance. The nature-of-work approach argued that jobs that offer interesting, challenging work would motivate and satisfy workers.

Contemporary theoretical models offer more specific details. The content theories, such as Maslow's and Alderfer's need-hierarchy theories (and, to some extent, Herzberg's need theory), explain why individuals value outcomes as they do. The reinforcement theories show that providing or withholding valued outcomes following a behavior can encourage or discourage future repetition of that behavior. The process theories, such as distributive justice, equity theory, and goal theory, help managers understand some of the processes that organization members follow as they react to their work experiences.

Each of the theories presented in this chapter provides something useful for a manager who wants to motivate people. The expanded expectancy theory attempts to integrate the major points from each of the content, reinforcement, and process theories into a model that helps managers develop and maintain employee motivation, performance, and satisfaction.

Notes

1. M. McComas (28 April 1986), Atop the Fortune 500: A survey of the C.E.O.s, *Fortune*, 26–31.
2. C. C. Pinder (1984), *Work motivation: Theory, issues, and applications*, Glenview, IL: Scott, Foresman, 8.
3. C. Darwin (1964), *On the origin of species by means of natural selection, or the preservation of favoured races in the struggle*, Cambridge, MA: Harvard University Press (original papers presented 1859).
4. W. C. Hamner and E. P. Hamner (1976), Behavior modification on the bottom line, *Organizational Dynamics*, 4, 3–21.
5. A. H. Maslow (1943), A theory of human motivation, *Psychological Bulletin*, 50, 370–96.
6. Maslow, 1943, 382.
7. C. P. Alderfer (1972), *Existence, relatedness, and growth: Human needs and organizational settings*, New York: Free Press.
8. H. A. Murray (1938), *Exploration in personality*, New York: Oxford University Press.

9. J. W. Atkinson and D. C. McClelland (1948), The projective expression of needs, II. The effect of different intensities of the hunger drive on thematic apperception, *Journal of Experimental Psychology*, 38, 643–58; D. C. McClelland, J. W. Atkinson, R. A. Clark, and E. L. Lowell (1953), *The achievement motive*, New York: Appleton-Century-Crofts.

10. J. W. Atkinson and A. C. Raphelson (1956), Individual differences in motivation and behavior in particular situations, *Journal of Personality*, 24, 349–63; R. C. DeCharms (1957), Affiliation motivation and productivity in small groups, *Journal of Abnormal Psychology*, 55, 222–76; D. Birch and J. Veroff (1966), *Motivation: A study of action*, Monterey, CA: Brooks/Cole; R. M. Steers and D. N. Braunstein (1976), A behaviorally based measure of manifest needs in work settings, *Journal of Vocational Behavior*, 9, 251–66.

11. D. C. McClelland (1975), *Power: The inner experience*, New York: Irvington; D. C. McClelland, W. N. Davis, R. Kalin, and E. Wanner (1972), *The drinking man: Alcohol and human motivation*, New York: Free Press.

12. F. Herzberg, B. Mausner, and B. Snyderman (1959), *The motivation to work*, New York: Wiley; F. Herzberg (1968), One more time: How do you motivate employees? *Harvard Business Review*, 46, 54–62.

13. Herzberg, et al., 1959.

14. V. H. Vroom (1964), *Work and motivation*, New York: Wiley; R. J. House and L. A. Wigdor (1967), Herzberg's dual-factor theory of job satisfaction and motivation: A review of the evidence and a criticism, *Personnel Psychology*, 20, 369–89.

15. House and Wigdor, 1967.

16. R. J. Bullock and E. E. Lawler III (1984), Gainsharing: A few questions and fewer answers, *Human Resource Management*, 23 (1), 23–40; E. A. Locke, D. B. Feren, V. M. McCaleb, K. N. Shaw, and A. T. Denney (1980), The relative effectiveness of form methods of motivating employee performance, in K. D. Duncan, M. M. Gruneberg, and D. Wallis, eds., *Changes in working life*, New York: John Wiley & Sons, 363–88.

17. B. F. Skinner (1953), *Science and human behavior*, New York: Free Press; B. F. Skinner (1969), *Contingencies of reinforcement*, East Norwalk, CT: Appleton-Century-Crofts; B. F. Skinner (1971), *Beyond freedom and dignity*, New York: Bantam Books.

18. R. N. Kanungo (1987), An alternative to the intrinsic-extrinsic dichotomy of work rewards, *Journal of Management*, 13, 751–66; L. Dyer and D. F. Parker (1975), Classifying outcomes in work motivation research: An examination of the intrinsic-extrinsic dichotomy, *Journal of Applied Psychology*, 60, 455–58.

19. Hamner and Hamner, 1976.

20. G. C. Homans (1961), *Social behavior: Its elementary forms*, New York: Harcourt, Brace, and World.

21. J. S. Adams (1965), Inequity in social exchange, in L. Berkowitz, ed., *Advances in experimental social psychology*, vol. 2, New York: Academic Press; also see R. T. Mowday (1987), Equity theory predictions of behavior in organizations, in R. M. Steers and L. W. Porter, eds., *Motivation and work behavior*, New York: McGraw-Hill, 89–110.

22. E. A. Locke and G. P. Latham (1984), *Goal setting: A motivational technique that works!* Englewood Cliffs, NJ: Prentice-Hall.

23. E. A. Locke (1982), Relation of goal performance with a short work period and multiple goal levels, *Journal of Applied Psychology*, 67, 512–14; G. P. Latham and J. J. Baldes (1975), The practical significance of Locke's

theory of goal setting, *Journal of Applied Psychology,* 60, 187–91; G. P. Latham and E. A. Locke (1979), Goal setting—A motivational technique that works, *Organizational Dynamics,* 68–80, 77.

24. Locke, 1982.
25. E. A. Locke, K. N. Shaw, L. M. Saari, and G. P. Latham (1981), Goal setting and task performance: 1969–1980, *Psychological Bulletin,* 90, 125–52, 129.
26. Locke, 1982; H. Garland (1983), Influence of ability-assigned goals, and normative information of personal goals and performance: A challenge to the goal attainability assumption, *Journal of Applied Psychology,* 68, 20–30; J. R. Hollenbeck and H. J. Klein (1987), Goal commitment and the goal setting process: Problems, prospects, and proposals for future research, *Journal of Applied Psychology,* 72, 212–20.
27. Locke, Shaw, Saari, and Latham, 1981.
28. E. A. Locke, G. P. Latham, and M. Erez (1988), The determinants of goal commitment, *Academy of Management Review,* 13, 23–39.
29. Locke, et al., 1988.
30. M. Erez and P. C. Earley (in press), Comparative analysis of goal setting across cultures, *Journal of Applied Psychology.*
31. Our treatment of expectancy theory is based primarily on the work of Lyman Porter and Ed Lawler, although many others have contributed to various aspects of this theory, c.f., L. W. Porter and E. E. Lawler (1968), *Managerial attitudes and performance,* Homewood, IL: Irwin; V. H. Vroom (1960), *Some personality determinants of the effects of participation,* Englewood Cliffs, NJ: Prentice-Hall; Vroom, 1964; J. Galbraith and L. L. Cummings (1967), An empirical investigation of the motivational determinants of task performance: Interactive effects between instrumentality-valence and motivation-ability, *Organizational Behavior and Human Performance,* 2, 237–57.

Key Terms

motivation	nonreinforcement
content theories	punishment
innate needs	continuous schedules of reinforcement
acquired needs	intermittent schedules of reinforcement
Maslow's need hierarchy theory	
Existence, Relatedness, and Growth (ERG) theory	organizational behavior modification (OBM)
need for achievement	extrinsic motivators
need for affiliation	intrinsic motivators
need for power	process theories
hygiene needs	distributive justice
motivator needs	equity theory
reinforcement theories	goal theory
operant learning theory	expectancy theory
reinforcement	Force
extinction	expectancy perception
positive reinforcement	instrumentality perception
negative reinforcement	valence
avoidance learning	

Issues for Review and Discussion

1. Identify and describe each of the four psychological principles of motivation.
2. Describe the economic, social, and nature-of-work approaches to motivation.
3. Describe the type of worker who would *not* be motivated by the nature-of-work approach to motivation; by the social approach.
4. Discuss how an organization can identify outcomes that motivate members.
5. Outline an organizational behavior modification program to reduce absenteeism among workers at your favorite restaurant.
6. Use equity theory to describe a situation in which you might be unhappy even though you received an *A* in a course.
7. Explain why the goal "I'm going to do my best" is not effective for motivating high performance.
8. According to expectancy theory, how does a worker determine the attractiveness of an alternative?
9. From an expectancy theory perspective, identify five reasons that high effort can lead to low performance.

Suggested Readings

Herzberg, F. (1968). One more time: How do you motivate employees? *Harvard Business Review,* 46, 54–62.

Kerr, S. (1975). On the folly of rewarding A, while hoping for B. *Academy of Management Journal,* 18, 769–83.

LeBoeuf, M. (1987). *The greatest management principle in the world.* New York: Berkley Publishing.

Locke, E. A. and Latham, G. P. (1984). *Goal setting: A motivational technique that works!* Englewood Cliffs, NJ: Prentice-Hall.

McClelland, D. C. (November-December 1966). That urge to achieve. *THINK Magazine,* 19–23.

McGregor, D. M. (November 1957). The human side of enterprise. *Management Review,* 22–28, 88–92.

Martinko, J. J. and Moss, S. (1988). A review of *The greatest management principle in the world.* In Pierce, J. L. and Newstrom, J. W., eds. *The manager's bookshelf: A mosaic of contemporary views.* New York: Harper & Row, 109–16.

CASE *Jack Dobbins' Problem*

By David Kenerson of the
University of South Florida

Jack Dobbins left the vice-president's office feeling elated as well as concerned about the new responsibilities he was about to assume. Ralph Barnes, State College's vice-president and comptroller, had just told Jack of the Executive Committee's decision to appoint him superintendent of buildings. Jack was concerned because Mr. Barnes had gone into considerable detail about the many management and morale problems among the college's custodial workers and their supervisors.

The Situation

State College is located in a rural area just outside of St. Louis, Missouri. It is one of several universities run by the state and is less than ten years old. In this short time it has grown rapidly to 9500 students, the majority of which live off campus and commute to school each day.

The superintendent's major function is to plan, organize, direct, and control the activities of about eighty employees and supervisors involved in keeping all college buildings, except for the dormitories, in a clean and orderly condition. There are ten major buildings ranging in size from 24,000 square feet to 137,000 square feet. Total square footage under the jurisdiction of the superintendent amounts to 1,025,000. This space includes classrooms, faculty offices, administration and library buildings, student center, and the like.

Of the eighty employees in the department, sixteen are women, and sixty-four are men, including the four male supervisors who report to the superintendent. Starting wages are $11,000. Employees can only receive one raise per year, usually on July 1 at the beginning of the fiscal year. It is within the superintendent's authority to grant raises up to a maximum of 10 percent the first year, 7 percent the second year, and 5 percent the third and subsequent years. To qualify for the maximum, however, employees have to receive a performance rating of "outstanding". The work week is forty hours. Vacation leave of ten working days is allowed while sick leave is accrued at the rate of one day per month to a maximum of thirty days. Group life insurance and medical and hospitalization insurance are available through payroll deduction at employee expense. Employees participate in the state retirement system under which both the state and the employee contribute. The total budget for the department amounts to about $1,015,000, with $900,000 for wages and salaries and $115,000 for supplies and materials.

Turnover among employees is unusually high. In July and August of the previous year, turnover amounted to 15 percent and 20 percent respectively. Typically, in this type of work in universities, turnover averages 75 percent per year. Most of the employees at State College hold second jobs outside of the college.

Departmental Work Organization

There is no organization chart for the department, but it appears to Jack Dobbins that it would look pretty much like the chart shown in Figure 14A. Work is assigned on the basis of special tasks. Although supervisors are assigned responsibility for different buildings, night crews are specialized into floor-mopping crews, followed by waxing and buffing crews. Supervisors decide when particular floors are to be mopped, waxed, and buffed and coordinate and schedule the different crews in proper sequence. The day crews work largely on rest-room detail in all buildings, with special groups assigned for carpet cleaning, window washing, and straightening and cleaning up meeting rooms before and after meetings.

Jack Dobbins' Background

Jack Dobbins is a retired military officer with twenty years' service in various posts as a management analyst and operations and training officer. As a young man, he graduated from a Midwestern engineering school. On resigning from the military, he enrolled in an MBA program to earn a degree in management. Now at forty-five he is looking forward to a new career in a new environment in a field in which he feels his experience, knowledge, and training could be most effectively used.

During the last hour and a half in his talk with Mr. Barnes, he has learned much about the current problems of the department. Harry Kraft,

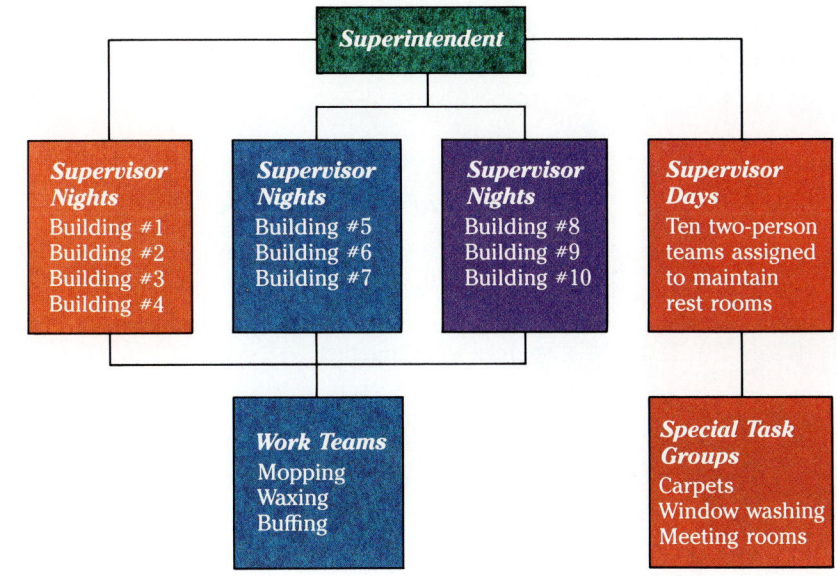

the superintendent he is replacing, had come to State College when the first students were admitted. He is fifty-five years old, of limited education, and with a varied background as a supervisor in construction firms. When the college was small with only a few buildings and few employees, he had been reasonably successful; however, four months ago, Harry fired one of the supervisors, with rather disastrous results. Rank-and-file employees were indignant and sent a petition all the way to the state capitol in an attempt to get Harry's decision reversed. Some were threatening not to come to work. Morale was low, turnover was high, and top officials of the college, as well as the department itself, were being deluged with complaints about the lack of good housekeeping in all buildings. Toilets were not adequately serviced, classrooms and offices frequently went untouched for a week at a time.

Although Jack is concerned, he is not dismayed because he feels strongly that his recent exposure to a wide variety of management courses will make it relatively easy to show substantial improvements in this department, despite the fact that no raises could be given to any employees before the next fiscal year eleven months away.

Questions

1. Analyze the custodial employees' situation using two different motivational theories.

2. Assuming Jack Dobbins has studied the same theories that you have, which, if any, are going to be of help to him?

3. What should Jack Dobbins do?

CHAPTER **15**

Interpersonal Factors in Organizations

Student Learning Objectives

After reading this chapter, you should be able to:

1. Explain the sources of interpersonal power and how these sources work together.

2. Describe how people use and abuse power.

3. Describe the major steps in the communication process.

4. Identify the common barriers to effective communication.

5. Enumerate ways to improve communication in organizations.

6. Identify conflict and explain why it occurs in organizations.

7. Discuss the various personal styles of conflict management and the situations in which each is appropriate or inappropriate.

8. Explain how organizational politics affect interpersonal behavior.

*B*ob Johnson and Elizabeth MacDonald both attended the University of Cincinnati, where each received an M.B.A. degree in accounting in 1979. Today, both Bob and Elizabeth are department managers at the Cincinnati Fan Company. Next week Elizabeth will become the company's new director of accounting. Missing out on this promotion has been the last in a long string of disappointments for Bob, who has considered his job an increasing struggle ever since he became a manager in 1984. He has concluded that management is not for him and has decided to accept a nonmanagement accounting job with Procter & Gamble.

When Elizabeth asks her subordinates to do something, they usually comply quickly. When Bob makes requests, he is never sure whether people will comply with them. Elizabeth's subordinates and co-workers always seem to understand her instructions, memos, and other communications. Bob's attempts at communication frequently elicit a puzzled "What do you mean?" Elizabeth and her workers function as a team; Bob struggles with almost constant conflict within his department. What has gone wrong for Bob?

Bob is failing as a manager because he cannot competently manage a variety of interpersonal factors. If an organization is to function effectively, its managers must direct subordinates' motivation and behavior toward meeting the organization's goals. Four interpersonal factors play a major role in this process: power, communication, conflict, and politics. This chapter discusses the role of these major interpersonal factors and the ways in which they can be managed effectively.

Just as there are many sources of electrical energy, there are many sources of interpersonal power.

Interpersonal Power

Electrical power lets people operate machines. **Interpersonal power** lets people influence other people. The greater your total supply of electricity, the greater your capacity to operate machines. The greater your total supply of interpersonal power, the greater your ability to influence others. Just as there are many different sources of electrical energy—water, coal, wind, and nuclear energy—interpersonal power has many sources. Just as it would be politically and ecologically undesirable for the United States to rely entirely on one source of electricity, it is not suitable for a manager to rely on just one source of interpersonal power. To build an interpersonal power base, managers must draw from all available sources.

In organizations, interpersonal power lets members maintain control over their own behavior and influence the behavior of others. Because everybody has some degree of power, your useful power is *relative* to the amount of power held by those whom you are trying to influence—or who are trying to influence you. Even individuals whose formal or informal power base is fairly small can influence others, as long as their power base is greater than that of the people whom they hope to influence. Power is important, but it is merely a *capability* until it is used. The amount of power that people have also changes over time. The next

TABLE 15.1   The Sources of Power

Type of Power	Description
Legitimate	Based on perceived authority: the *right* to influence
Reward	Based on perceived ability to provide/withhold rewards
Coercive	Based on perceived ability to provide/withhold punishment
Expert	Based on willingness to share/withhold desired expertise
Resource	Based on willingness to share/withhold desired information/resources
Referent	Based on charismatic attractiveness of power holder

section will take a look at the various sources of interpersonal power and explore their relative advantages and disadvantages.

Sources of Power

As you learned in Chapter 11, there are several major sources of social power (see Table 15.1).[1] A person's total power derives from a combination of these six sources, and a strength in one area can compensate for a weakness in another.

Legitimate Power **Legitimate power** exists when one person believes that another person has the right to influence him or her. Legitimate power is usually thought of as authority: the authority of a manager over a subordinate, of a board of directors over a manager, or of a teacher over a student. As you learned in Chapter 11, the hierarchy of an organization specifies that one person has the authority, or the organizational right, to tell another what to do. A manager's formal authority is typically limited to the right to influence only certain behavior, such as work-related activities, for a given group of organization members, usually subordinates. A machine foreperson can tell the machinists how many units to produce, for example, but he or she cannot tell the vice-president what to do. Legitimate power can also be derived informally. The leader of an informal work group or a social group may be recognized by other members of that group as having legitimate power over them: power to speak for them to their boss, to help them solve problems, and to suggest improvements.

A person holds legitimate power only when the individuals to be influenced accept his or her authority.

Like all other sources of power, legitimate power is in the eyes of the beholder. The fact that a manager is assigned a position of authority does not guarantee that others will respect his or her authority. For authority to translate into actual power, the individuals to be influenced must accept the manager's right to influence them. Until this happens, the manager has authority but no power.

Sometimes a formal leader cannot influence subordinates even with a reasonable amount of legitimate power. When this happens, the formal leader must develop additional sources of power. A good organization makes other forms of power available to the leader.

Reward Power   Managers have **reward power** if they can and will provide or withhold rewards from those whom they wish to influence. **Formal rewards,** such as increases in pay or receipt of a promotion, are stipulated by an organization to help its managers develop power. **Informal rewards** are provided from the leader's own resources. An elementary school teacher may use personal funds to purchase school supplies or treats to influence student behavior. A manager can provide an employee with special recognition, do an employee a favor, or send an employee to dinner at the manager's expense. Incorporating reward power, either formally or informally, is a common way to enhance a leader's legitimate power.

The way that managers use rewards influences the effectiveness of that source of power. Those to be influenced, for example, must be aware that the leader controls certain rewards and that the leader will use those rewards to influence behavior. A manager who gives all subordinates the same pay raise regardless of their behavior, for example, typically has much less reward power than a leader who gives raises on the basis of performance. As you learned in Chapter 14, giving across-the-board rather than performance-based raises is likely to lead to perceptions of inequity and reduced motivation to perform.

Coercive Power   Managers have **coercive power** if they can and will provide or withhold punishment from those whom they wish to influence. As with reward power, a manager holds coercive power over another person if that person believes that the manager has the *ability* to punish, can *control* the punishment, and is *willing* to provide or withhold that punishment. Managers who threaten punishment but never inflict it soon lose whatever coercive power they had.

Like legitimate and reward power, coercive power can be formal or informal. An organization can provide managers with the right to administer various forms of punishment, such as suspending or firing an employee or reducing an employee's pay. Other punishments can be administered by managers even if they have not been assigned the formal right to do so. A high-school drama instructor may publicly criticize a student actor. A manager can give a worker an undesirable work assignment.

Much of the coercive power found in organizations is based less on actual punishment than on the threat of punishment or on convincing bluffs. A manager, for example, may threaten to demote a subordinate unless his or her attendance record improves. If the subordinate believes the bluff, the manager establishes coercive power even if the manager does not have the authority to demote the employee or is unwilling to do so. As long as the subordinate does not call the bluff and discover the truth, the manager retains the coercive power.

Coercive power is like the punishment described in Chapter 14. That is, unpleasant consequences of behavior tend to reduce the recurrence of that behavior. Coercive power, like punishment, easily generates negative side effects, and managers who use this kind of power must use it carefully. Coercive power can create dissatisfaction and resentment. It can also lead to unexpected and undesirable results if employees fight back. It also can easily reduce the effectiveness of a manager's other power sources if employees resist the manager who inflicts punishment. (This effect is particularly true for referent power, which is based on the attractiveness of the power holder and is described later in this section.)

Expert Power Bill Huntsman, a chemistry instructor at the Madison Area Technical College, has used his knowledge of personal computers to generate record-keeping programs and to design computer demonstrations. His co-workers, seeing how fast Bill can complete his report cards at the end of the semester and how positively his students evaluate his classes, are eager to get copies of his programs. Further, by updating his knowledge with new computer languages and graphics programs, Bill is able to sustain his expert knowledge base and convince management to award him with requested assignments, such as curriculum development grants. Bill Huntsman has **expert power.**

For a manager to have expert power, the following conditions must exist: the employees to be influenced must believe that the manager possesses expert knowledge that they do not have; employees must want that expert knowledge; and employees must believe that the manager is willing to share (or withhold) the expert knowledge at his or her discretion. It is common for a person with little or no formal authority in an organization to become relatively powerful by acquiring skill in an area of great interest to others. Less-skilled members of the organization need the expert's help and, therefore, are willing to be influenced by this expert. By sharing such information when it is needed and by replacing this knowledge with new forms of expertise, an individual can develop and sustain power.

John F. Kennedy added substantially to his power base through great personal charisma.

Resource Power **Resource power** is the ability to influence others because they desire (nonexpert) resources that a manager controls. These resources could be information, time, materials, or anything else of value to the person who wants it. For a manager to have resource power, others must believe that she or he controls the resource and is willing to share it. Corporal Walter "Radar" O'Reilly in the movie and TV series "M*A*S*H," for example, possessed an incredible amount of resource power. Everyone—including his commanding officers—honestly believed that Radar could obtain virtually any resource if he chose to do so. For this reason, mild, unassuming Radar was capable of exerting tremendous influence over others in the M*A*S*H unit.

FIGURE 15.1   *Sample Power Profiles*

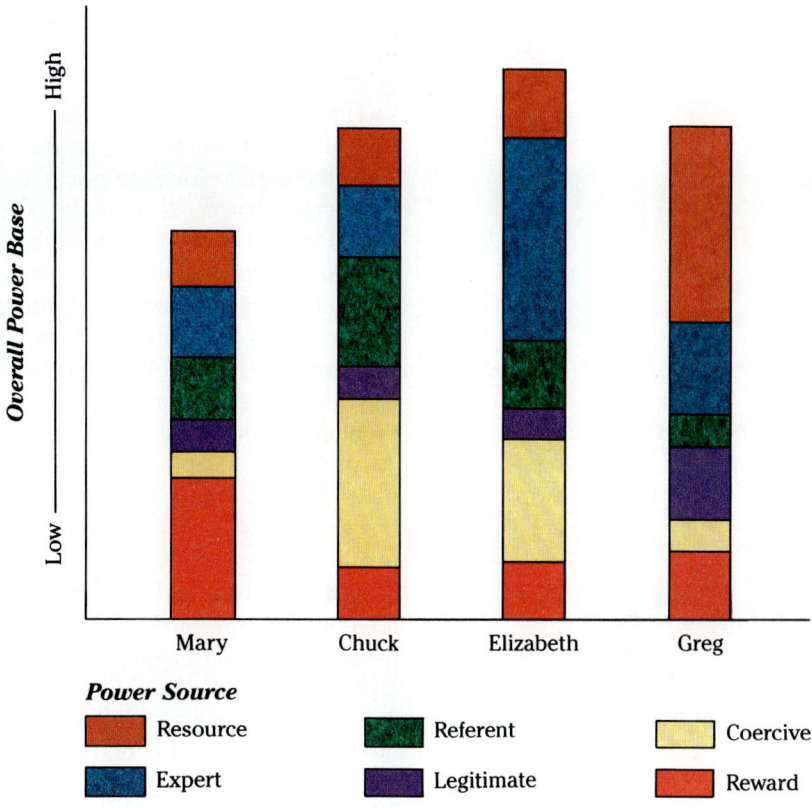

Power Source

■ Resource	■ Referent	■ Coercive
■ Expert	■ Legitimate	■ Reward

Referent Power   The final source of power commonly found in organizations is referent power. **Referent power** is the ability to influence another person because he or she wants to be associated or affiliated with the power holder. People are drawn to other people for a variety of reasons, including physical attractiveness, social attractiveness, fame, and prestige. Charisma often finds its base in referent power. Throughout the history of the United States, such politicians as John F. Kennedy have added substantially to their power bases through personal charisma. Like expert, informal reward, and coercive power, referent power is a potential source of power that almost anyone can use regardless of his or her legitimate power.

As you can see, an organization member may exercise power whether or not the organization has formally assigned him or her to a position of power. Although some individuals do have power by virtue of their formal position, many others possess power through acquisition.

The Coordination of Power Sources   As you have learned, managers develop a total power base by combining the various sources of power. An individual's overall power position is not, however, simply the sum of the power derived from each source. In reality, some combinations of power sources are synergistic: they are *greater* than the sum of their parts. Referent power, for example, tends to magnify the impact of other sources of power (particularly legitimate, resource, and expert power) because these are particularly valued when coming from a respected person.

Reward power frequently increases the impact of referent power because people tend to like those who reward them. In other words, certain power profiles may be more potent and effective than others.

The reverse can also be true. The power produced by some combinations of power sources can be *less* than the sum of the individual sources. As noted earlier, for example, high coercive power can dilute the impact of referent power. A manager who constantly threatens employees to obtain compliance usually becomes disliked and, therefore, has little referent power. At times, excessive use of legitimate power can also threaten referent power and other potential sources, such as expert, resource, and even reward power. This combination occurs when employees conclude that "being the boss"—having legitimate power—is not enough. A manager who repeatedly says, "Do it because I am the boss" eventually reduces his or her overall power base.

An individual's power profile, then, reflects his or her total amount of power and its various sources; thus, organization members have different power profiles. As Figure 15.1 showed, Elizabeth MacDonald has relatively little legitimate power, even though she has the highest overall power base. She is powerful because she is an expert at her job, because she has the power to give favorable job assignments to her department members, because she controls information that her department considers valuable, and because she recommends department members for seminars and conventions. She has relatively little formal authority in her department, however. Chuck and Greg have almost identical total power bases—but very different profiles. Chuck is long on threats (coercive power), whereas Greg is the one person in the department who always stays late to help others over the rough spots in their assignments (resource power). Mary probably cannot influence the other three very successfully in spite of her reward power—she officially recommends people for merit raises—because of her relatively low overall power base.

Uses and Abuses of Power

In January 1985, Tom Miller became the executive vice-president of a 500-employee service corporation. He developed a very strong overall power base out of a combination of legitimate, reward, and coercive power. Several ways in which Tom influenced other members of the organization include:

1. He asked his assistant to prepare a summary report of an impending business deal. The assistant worked until midnight to prepare the report on time.
2. He instructed the company's five division heads to develop and present him with a Management by Objectives program. They did so.
3. He asked his secretary to pick up his laundry on his way home. The secretary complied.
4. He asked a low-level staff accountant to spend a couple of hours tutoring his college-age son. The accountant obeyed.
5. He told the company's expense account manager to reimburse him for expenses for which he had no receipts (and which he had not actually incurred). The manager did so.

6. He asked all executives who earned frequent flyer awards from company travel to give them to his secretary "for company use." They did so, and Tom then used several of the awards on his family's vacation.

7. He invited an attractive woman from the human resources department to accompany him on an overnight business trip. She went. During the trip, Tom made repeated sexual overtures.

Tom soon found himself looking for a new job. He was fired by the president of the company, who used all but the first two items from this list as reasons for the termination. Tom Miller had power in the organization, which he abused.

Power can be used to encourage organization members to do things that they might not otherwise do. When that behavior has little, if any, relationship to legitimate organizational activities, the power is abused. Abuses of power raise ethical questions for which there are no easy answers. Although asking a subordinate to run a personal errand for a manager during the lunch hour is not an extreme case of abuse, it may not be an ethical use of the power that was developed to *serve the organization*.

It is not unethical for an organization to train its leaders to develop a power base. Power is needed to run an organization; however, each person who develops power is ethically bound to consider carefully the impact that this power will have on others. As you use power to influence the behavior of others, ask yourself: "Will this behavior hurt this person physically or psychologically?" "Am I exerting more influence than is necessary to fulfill the directing function?" "Am I using my power only for legitimate organizational purposes?" "Am I encouraging this person to do something he or she would prefer not to do?"

To close this discussion of interpersonal power, consider again the electrical power analogy. Many resources are required to generate both electrical and interpersonal power. Without the resources necessary to generate sufficient electricity, an electrical machine will not function effectively. Generating more electrical power than needed to run the machine, however, is a waste of resources. The same is true for interpersonal power. As a manager, you must determine how much interpersonal power is needed to direct the behavior of others effectively. The development of more than this amount of power is a waste of resources. Just as too much electrical power can damage an electrical motor, too much interpersonal power can damage working relationships. Egos and self-esteem are even more sensitive than are electrical motors.

Organizational Communication

Managers spend a great deal of time communicating with individuals and groups, both inside and outside of the organization. "Joe, here are the sales figures for your territory." "I'd like everyone in the group to take a look at this chart." "Well, group, our productivity is up." "Do you need more widgets?" Some managers communicate well; therefore, they become more effective. Others communicate poorly and become less effective. This section will focus on the role of communication in directing behavior in organizations.

The Communication Process

Communication is the process of transferring information from one person or group (the sender) to another (the receiver). *Effective* communication takes place when the information, or message, received matches the information the sender intended to transmit. Communication occurs, however, whenever a message is received—even if the received message is different from that which was intended; thus, two major communication-related problems are *communication failure* (no meaningful information changes hands) and *miscommunication* (the message received is different from the one intended). Signs of communication failure include such telltale remarks as "Oh, I guess I didn't hear you say that," "No, I never got that report," "He didn't have anything new to say," and "I have no idea of what she's talking about." Some signs of miscommunication include: A professor requests a ten-page paper and the student turns in a two-page paper. A manager says Wednesday, meaning the 15th of December, and the subordinate hears Wednesday, meaning the 22nd of December. A supervisor says, "Don't bother me with the small problems." A worker does not ask about a small planning detail and an entire project has to be started over from scratch.

Managers communicate—well or badly—for many different reasons. They often communicate to provide receivers with needed information. From a control perspective, communication clarifies duties, authority, and responsibilities for organization members. Managers also often communicate to motivate employees' commitment to organizational objectives. Communication allows them or their employees to express their feelings. In fact, most communication serves more than one of these functions. It transmits information and it motivates. It expresses feelings and it informs.

The complexity of the communication process increases as the number of purposes of communication increases. In turn, increased complexity makes distortion more likely. Despite the increased risk of distortion, however, complex communications are often necessary, and they can be quite effective. Bill Cornett, for example, is a manager concerned about his organization's ability to fill a major order. He decides to send a message to production workers that:

- Shows that there is a large upcoming order
- Relates that large orders have been poorly handled in the past
- Indicates who is responsible for filling the upcoming order
- Motivates by promising that success at filling this order will contribute to the company's success and, thus, the size of the profit-sharing pool for production workers
- Conveys the manager's feelings about the importance of the upcoming order

Bill's fairly complex communication serves several different purposes. It provides information, clarifies duties, motivates, and expresses feelings.

Components of Communication

The communication process has five components: ideation, message encoding, channels/networks, message decoding, and a received message (see Figure 15.2). Communication begins when a sender identifies the need to send a message, formulates the message, and places it in the channels needed to transmit it. Communication concludes when a receiver accepts the message and interprets its meaning.

Ideation, the first step of the communication process, involves a manager's decision to communicate and the development of the nature and content of the intended message based on the manager's reasons for communicating. "I'm worried about that order," Bill Cornett thinks. "I'd better let my people know."

Encoding is the second step: converting an intended message into a transmittable form, such as speech, a written message, computer code, or any other form that can be sent to a receiver. A manager must be careful during the encoding stage, or the message sent will be different from the one intended. "I'd better note exactly who is responsible for filling the new order, or we'll have the same problems as last time," Bill thinks as he makes notes for his message.

Once a manager has encoded a message, he or she must send it. Bill decides to send the message to the department secretary for typing and copying. When it is finished, Bill intends to distribute copies to each worker personally, to post a copy on the bulletin board, and to send a copy to his supervisor. Messages are sent through **communication channels.** Any medium capable of transmitting a message is a communication channel, including mail systems, phone lines, and computers. Networks tie channels together to facilitate the flow of information. It is imperative that a manager choose channels and networks appropriate for the nature of the message and of sufficient quality to preserve its integrity. Writing a letter but forgetting to mail it halts the communication process quickly.

Decoding, the fourth step, is the process by which a receiver interprets a message to derive meaning from it. As you read this book, you are decoding the messages that were encoded and transmitted to you in book format. As his subordinates read Bill's memo, they interpret his message. Managers must recognize that effective communication depends as much on the receiver as on the sender. Whether or not the meaning that a receiver derives from a message matches the intentions of a sender, once the message is decoded, the message has been received.

The decoding process is influenced heavily by the perceptual processes discussed in Chapter 13. For a message to be noticed by a receiver, for

FIGURE 15.2 *The Communication Process*

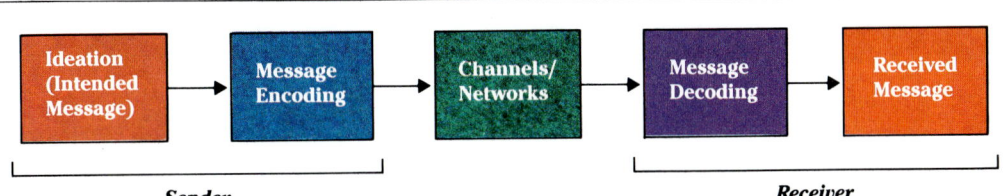

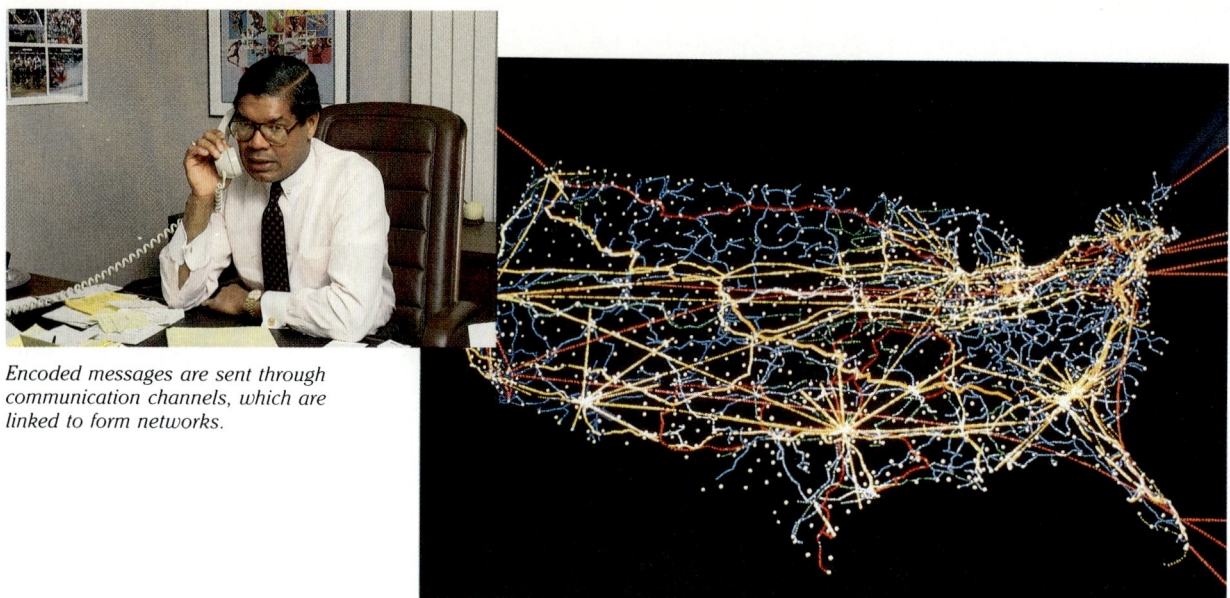

Encoded messages are sent through communication channels, which are linked to form networks.

example, it must be loud enough, bright enough, or different enough to get the receiver's attention. Once a message is noticed, it must be special enough for the intended receiver to decide to take the time to decode it. Most people in organizations are inundated with messages in the form of memos, phone calls, reports, and so on. Some of these are ignored; others are attended to. Many people, for example, throw away mail that is sent bulk rate without bothering to open it, but they read all of their express mail. As a manager, you must make certain that your important messages will be selected by receivers.

The decoding process is often distorted by receivers' perceptual characteristics. For example, if the messages that you receive from a particular subordinate usually contain good ideas, your first reaction to any message from this person is likely to be positive, even if a particular message contains bad ideas. Other receiver characteristics, such as stereotypes or perceptual readiness (discussed in detail in Chapter 13), can also influence the way a message is decoded.

Clearly, the communication process is in no way simple. Effective communication requires careful planning and considerable skill. As a manager, you must do more than plan what you want to say. You must also choose your words carefully and send them appropriately. Furthermore, you need to consider the receivers and design your message so that they will notice the message, choose it for decoding, and interpret it as you intended.

Communication Channels

Selecting a communication channel to transmit a timely, accurate, complete, and understandable message is very important. People are channels who use speech, sight, and body motions to communicate. Mechanical channels go beyond the capabilities of the human body and include newsletters, magazines, telephones, radio, television, and computers. At this moment, messages about the process of management are coming to you through a textbook—a mechanical channel that is more

A CLOSER LOOK

Creative Communication: The Annual Report

Every shareholder of every publicly held corporation in the United States receives a copy of the company's annual report. One section of the annual report contains financial figures that must conform to specific standards set by the Securities and Exchange Commission (SEC) and the Financial Accounting Standards Board. These figures also must be examined by auditors who certify they are factually accurate. As a result, this section usually provides a fairly forthright picture of the company's finances.

Virtually every annual report, however, also contains other information, often in the form of a message from the chairperson, that is not subject to audit. According to *Business Week*, this message "doesn't always give a brutally frank version of the year's events. . . . Part of the challenge is learning how to translate this verbiage."[1] To this end, *Business Week* offers some illustrated translations of common messages from the chair.

1. G. Weiss (23 March 1987), Reading between the lines of an annual report, *Business Week*, 164.

Illustrations reprinted from March 23, 1987 issue of *Business Week* by special permission, copyright ©1987 by McGraw-Hill, Inc.

WHEN THEY SAY THIS:
The uncertain regulatory climate poses challenges for our business.
THEY MAY MEAN THIS:
The SEC has subpoenaed our records and our lawyers are scared to death.

We can prosper only by being better managed than our competitors.
If we can sell below cost long enough, we'll have the field to ourselves.

Your company is now posed for earnings growth.
We lost so much money earnings can't get worse.

We're seizing the growing opportunities for global out-sourcing.
We're moving production to the Far East, where wages are dirt-cheap.

We are vigorously seeking creative techniques to bring our costs in line.
We are going to slash salaries by 20% and cash in our pension plan.

Last year we substantially strengthened the ranks of our senior management.
After the latest series of indictments, heads rolled.

efficient than your instructor's sitting down with you and your classmates individually and imparting such information. Audio or video recording is also an alternative. In fact, for students with visual or learning disabilities, this book will be translated by Recording for the Blind (Recording for the Blind, Inc., 20 Rozel Road, Princeton, NJ 08540).

Most managers have personal preferences among the various communication channels available. Some believe that face-to-face communication is best whenever possible. Others rely almost entirely on memos. More and more managers use computer channels as a first choice. In reality, there is no single best communication channel. Because of their differences in capacity, modifiability, duplication, speed, feedback, and appropriateness, some channels convey particular messages better than others.

Channel Capacity Channel capacity is the amount of information that a channel can transmit without significant distortion. A duplicating machine has greater capacity than a scribe, and a television broadcast has greater channel capacity than a memo. Capacity is particularly important when time is limited.

Channel Modifiability Modifiability is the degree to which the transmission can be changed while in progress. Changes might involve content or speed, for example. A number of universities are now presenting lectures on television for many of their lower-level classes. Although this is a very efficient channel for this purpose, its modifiability is much lower than it is for a live lecture from a professor because students cannot stop a TV show to ask questions. A TV lecture presented using a video recorder can greatly increase modifiability if students can replay a passage or freeze an important frame on the screen.

Channel Duplication Duplication involves the use of subchannels to repeat or elaborate on a message. A speaker making a presentation to a group of business associates may use a projector to place key terms on a screen at the front of the room while discussing the terms in more detail. Television and other audiovisual channels provide great opportunity for duplication because they can provide written, pictorial, and audio messages all at the same time. The greater the complexity and importance of a message, the greater the need for duplication.

Channel Speed The speed at which a message can be sent is often important. If it is 2 A.M. and you notice that the house across the street is on fire, you probably will not send a letter to inform the owner of this observation, but if you want to send birthday greetings to your neighbor, you probably will not rush over in the middle of the night and yell "happy birthday!" through the bedroom window. In organizations, communication channels for safety devices at work must have great speed, as must any message for which significant delay could be costly.

Channel Feedback Some channels allow for feedback and, thus, bilateral (two-way) communication. A telephone, for example, allows information to flow in both directions. Feedback is usually not necessary if a message involves only a simple piece of information. The time and temperature announcement provided by your local phone company is a channel designed to allow only one-way communication, because people don't need to talk to the speaker, but police emergency lines cannot be answered by "Leave a message. We'll get back to you when we return." For managers, feedback can be very important. It allows a sender to determine if the intended message was received, lost, or distorted during the communication process. It also allows a sender to function as a receiver and vice versa. Managers can choose their words much more carefully and effectively when they can see and hear the reactions of receivers as they listen.

Channel Appropriateness   Although most managers pay attention to such factors as channel capacity, modifiability, and duplication, many often overlook channel appropriateness. If a female student wants to tell her male instructor that she thinks he is an excellent teacher, should she send a note on flowery, perfumed stationery? Could this choice of a communication channel influence the way the message is decoded? If a manager wants to persuade a job candidate to accept a job offer, should the manager's secretary call the candidate with the job offer, or would a personal call from the manager be more effective? In addition to evaluating the more objective characteristics of a channel, a manager should think about whether the channel(s) under consideration are appropriate to the message.

Communication Networks

Each communication between two people or groups is called a *linkage*. A **communication network** is a series of interconnected linkages. Together, these linkages connect individuals or groups for communication purposes. The number of linkages in a network is important because each linkage tends to introduce some distortion. In a hierarchical organization, if the president wants to send a message to a first-level supervisor, he or she might give the message to a vice-president, who gives it to a division head, who passes it down the chain of command until it reaches the first-level supervisor. Direct communication from the president to the first-level supervisor would probably have been more accurate and more efficient, because it would eliminate the opportunity for the message to be lost or distorted as it passed through each linkage.

Formal Communication Networks   Because there is no single best network for all communication needs, most organizations use a variety of networks. Communication networks can send vertical (supervisor to subordinate), horizontal (supervisor to supervisor), and diagonal flows of information (see Figure 15.3).

Vertical communication can flow downward, upward, or in both directions. It cuts across organizational levels and may allow feedback, as shown in Figure 15.3. Vertical communication represents the transfer of information between individuals in superior-subordinate positions. When an employee reports on sales calls to the district manager, and when the manager tells the employee which calls to make in the next sales period,

FIGURE 15.3   Vertical, Horizontal, and Diagonal Communication Channels

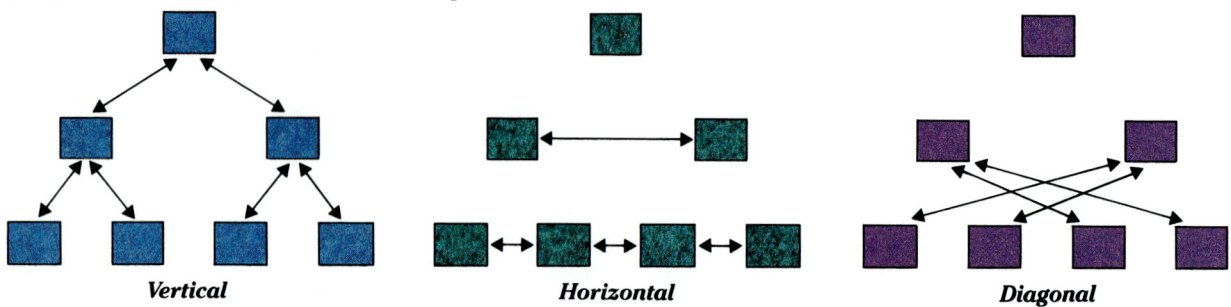

Vertical   **Horizontal**   **Diagonal**

they are engaging in vertical communication. Similarly, a professor who tells a student to bring a case analysis to class, and a student who says that the case analysis is all but complete are communicating vertically.

Horizontal communication represents the flow of information between individuals or groups who occupy positions at the same hierarchical level. When the head of the radiology department consults with the head of the oncology department at a hospital regarding the purchase of new equipment, a horizontal communication has transpired. When a vice-president of marketing shows other vice-presidents the story boards for a new advertising campaign, the communication is horizontal.

Diagonal communication is a third form of communication in organizations as information flows across *both* vertical and horizontal components. Diagonal communication occurs when a salesperson receives information from the vice-president of human resources or when the head of research and development solicits information from one of the organization's purchasing agents.

Managers can choose from among many types of networks when creating a communication system within their organization. If they adhere to classical management theory, for example, they may design very rigid communication networks in which employees are discouraged from talking with anyone except their immediate supervisors. Such a system enables supervisors to maintain control over subordinates and to remain highly informed about various activities in their departments. Managers in more open systems, such as those found in organically designed organizations, are likely to design very open and flexible communication systems. Individuals are therefore encouraged to seek and transmit information as dictated by the nature of the task on which they are working.

Different networks have different characteristics.[2] In some, information flows quickly. In some, information flow is channeled to the right place at the right time. In other networks, the accuracy of the information is distorted in transmission. Figure 15.4 illustrates five of the most common networks.

The *chain* is the simplest of networks. Although it can be used for a horizontal communication network—for example, interdepartmental communication—it is more often used vertically. In the vertical configuration, the person with the greatest power is usually located at the top of the chain. Although the chain allows the possibility of feedback, many linkages can exist between a sender and receiver, which makes distortion likely. Even when they are accurate, chain networks tend to be slow and subject to information overload. Such a network usually produces relative-

FIGURE 15.4   Communication Networks

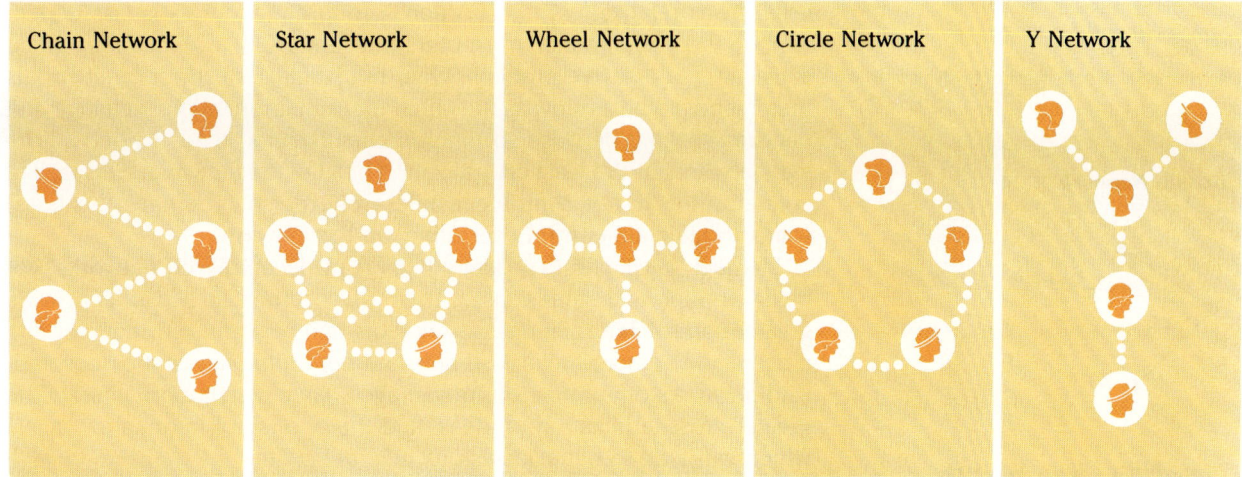

Chain Network	Star Network	Wheel Network	Circle Network	Y Network
Person can communicate directly only with persons one step higher or lower in chain.	Any person can communicate directly with any other person.	All communication must flow through person at hub of wheel.	Person can communicate only with persons adjacent in the circle.	Person can communicate only with persons one step higher or lower in chain; most communication flows through key person.

Source: Based on B. L. Hawkins and P. Preston (1981), *Managerial communication*, Glenview, IL: Scott, Foresman.

ly slow decisions, and the quality of those decisions depends highly on the leader of the network.

The *Y* network is a modification of the chain. Two equal-status members are positioned either at the top (as in Figure 15.4) or at the bottom (in an inverted *Y*). Like the chain, the Y network allows feedback in a relatively inefficient manner. The Y is not quite so slow as the chain and is not subject to as much distortion, because fewer linkages are required, but the improvement is not great. Decision quality is still heavily dependent on the leader. The Y introduces a measure of centralization, one member's having direct access to three other members, but this results in considerable information overload for the person in the center.

The *circle* network allows each member to communicate directly with two other members. This improves decision quality and speed somewhat over the chain and Y networks because of greater information exchange, but feedback is still difficult and distortion tends to be undesirably high. There tends to be some problems of information overload for all members.

The *wheel* network has the greatest amount of centralization of all the networks considered here. The person in the center of the wheel can communicate directly with all other network members; he or she is their only direct communication contact. This centralization speeds communication, especially decision making. Information overload can be substantial for the person in the center of the wheel, although it is usually not a problem for other members. Dependence on the leader for decision quality is high.

The *star* communication network, which allows any member to communicate directly with any other member, is among the best in some

FIGURE 15.5   *Grapevine Networks*

Single-Strand Network

Gossip Network

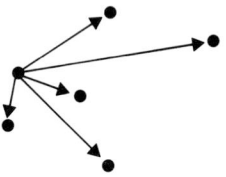

Probability Chain Network

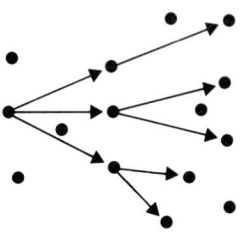

Cluster Network

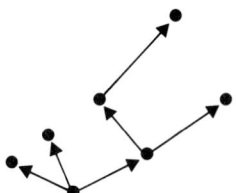

ways. It tends to produce the highest-quality decisions, for example, and usually has relatively little distortion. Group effectiveness is less dependent on the leader than in most other networks, and information overload is usually not a severe problem. One disadvantage of the star network is that it tends to be as slow as the chain for both information exchange and decision making because so much communication tends to occur. The star network has the least centralization of all of the networks. This lack of centralization is not a problem unless one person (perhaps the boss) wants to maintain control over others in the network.

Member satisfaction is usually highest in decentralized networks. For highly routine and simple tasks, the more centralized networks provide greater control, information coordination, and performance accuracy and efficiency. For more highly complex and nonroutine tasks, the decentralized networks offer numerous advantages. They permit more interaction, greater cross-fertilization of ideas, and the pooling of information, all of which can lead to better decisions.

Informal Communication Networks   Although the communication networks discussed so far are formal and created by organizations, informal networks also exist. Informal networks are created by employees and are often referred to as "the grapevine." They emerge through natural and spontaneous human interaction—they "flow around water coolers, down hallways, through lunch rooms, and wherever people get together in groups."[3] They do not necessarily follow the same pattern as formal channels do, nor do they necessarily carry information that management wants transmitted. They are not easy to control, they transmit information rapidly, and they often carry rumors.

Although an informal network could use the structure of any of the formal networks, grapevines usually conform to one of the four communication patterns shown in Figure 15.5.[4] The *single-strand* pattern is the same as a chain and is the least complex and least accurate at passing on information. In this network, Person A passes along a message to Person B, who, in turn, passes along the message to Person C, and so on until someone terminates the chain. The *gossip* network is often used when one person believes that he or she has some "very interesting" information to pass on. This individual seeks out a number of individuals and proceeds to pass on the information to each.

The *probability chain* network represents an almost random transfer of information. Person A is basically indifferent in selecting people to receive information and communicates to whomever happens to be handy. In turn, the people with whom A has communicated tell others at random what they have heard. The *cluster* network, in contrast, represents a careful and systematic selection of individuals to whom the information will be transferred. The cluster network is the dominant grapevine system in organizations.

Managing Communication Effectively

Unfortunately, there is no one best approach to communication. An approach that works well in one situation may be atrocious under other circumstances and, as you have seen, there are many opportunities for

INTERVIEW

Michael J. Marx

Michael J. Marx is president of the consulting firm Selection Sciences, Inc., in San Francisco. He is an expert in organizational communications and organization and management assessment.

1. How widespread are communication problems in organizations?

If we define communication as the process of transmitting information from at least one person to another in a way that results in understanding, I think communication problems are quite widespread. Organizations typically need communications to be accurate, complete, and timely. Although they often meet these standards, too often in the most sensitive situations they do not.

2. What are some of the most serious communication problems usually experienced?

At a macro level, the most serious communication problems involve the exchange of information between senior management and the rest of the organization. Particularly in economically difficult times, management often fails to communicate what it sees as the problem, how it plans to deal with the problem, and the role employees play in the process. The resulting uncertainty felt by employees can have devastating effects on day-to-day and future operations of the organization. At a micro level, the most serious communication problem involves managers' and supervisors' failing to clearly define and communicate performance expectations, performance standards, feedback, and reinforcement.

3. To what extent are communication problems due to individuals? To groups?

The majority of communication problems are due to individuals, not groups. In fact, groups often act to ensure that individual communications are more accurate, complete, and timely. When individuals communicate with each other, their different backgrounds, specialties, values, and personalities color their messages and interpretations of others' messages. In groups, the need to get consensus often requires members to have mutual understanding of what is being said.

4. Realistically, what can an individual manager do to improve communication in his or her organization?

Realistically, the individual manager can be more precise when communicating the overall unit goals, individuals' roles, and standards of performance expected. This provides a clear set of expectations against which performance can be measured. When conflict, misunderstanding, or poor performance occur, they can be judged and resolved by referring to the objectives which have been defined.

5. In what aspects of communication do managers tend to be most effective?

Managers often excel in their ability to build relations with other managers in interdependent departments. They are often good in presentation-, negotiation-, and relation-building skills, which require an ability to communicate effectively. In short, they are best when communicating laterally, weakest when communicating upward or downward.

things to go wrong. A message may be poorly formulated, such as when a manager is not sure what to say, or encoded poorly, as when a manager chooses the wrong words. Often, two or more sources of distortion have compounding effects; thus, a poorly encoded message sent over inadequate channels through an inappropriate network can produce disastrous results. Making the correct choices can be very difficult for a manager. Table 15.2 contains suggestions to guide managers along each step of the communication process so that they can avoid the barriers to effective communication.

TABLE 15.2   A Guide for Systematic Communication

1. Establish the intended message and communication objective(s).
2. Establish the communication needs of the message.
3. Appraise the characteristics of the receiver(s).
4. Identify the available communication channels and networks.
5. Identify noise in the environment likely to interfere.
6. Evaluate the adequacy of each channel for the communication needs.
7. Evaluate the adequacy of each network for the communication needs.
8. Select channel(s) and network(s) for use.
9. Reduce noise in the environment if necessary/possible.
10. Encode the message to match the channels, networks, and receivers.
11. Carefully send the message.
12. Obtain feedback (was the message received as intended?).
13. Follow up if necessary with additional communication.
14. Learn from your communication experiences.

Note that a final step in effective communication takes place after the message has been received. The final step is *learning*. Every communication experience can teach you something. You may learn about new channels or networks. You may discover additional strengths and weaknesses of channels and networks. You might learn more about your ability to encode messages or about the characteristics of your receivers. Take advantage of every opportunity for enhancing your communication effectiveness.

Interpersonal Conflict

Karin Matthiesen is angry, frustrated, and determined to get back at Craig Gagstetter. Karin and Craig are sales representatives for the Lepley Calculator Company. For years, there has been an informal agreement that Karin would have sole rights to sell the company's products at grocery stores, and Craig would have the rights to sell to discount retail stores. In the past year, three grocery "megamarkets" have opened in the area. Each time, Craig has made the first contact with the megamarket and obtained large, profitable sales. Karin told Craig to stay away because she "owned" the grocery stores. Craig responded by arguing that the megamarkets are not grocery stores because they sell not only groceries but also a wide range of discount retail products for cars, homes, and recreation. Karin retaliated by invading the Kmart stores that Craig had been selling to because they sell a few food products. Things have gotten so bad that the two sales representatives are spending almost as much time fighting as they are selling calculators.

What has happened in the relationship between Karin and Craig? Their conflict hurts both them and their company. Could this conflict have been prevented? What should their manager do now that the conflict has escalated to such a damaging level? This section will explore the reasons that conflict occurs and will identify methods that managers can use to keep conflict from becoming destructive. Conflict is and will continue to be a part of organizational life whenever people work together. It is not possible to *avoid* conflict, but it is possible to *manage* it.

The Nature and Causes of Conflict

Conflict exists when two or more people have incompatible goals, and one or both believe that the behavior of the other will prevent his or her own goal attainment. The presence of incompatible goals alone is not sufficient to produce conflict. Conflict does not occur until the behavior of one of the parties interferes with the efforts of the other. Good managers possess the skills to minimize conflict and to emphasize the benefits of the conflict that does emerge.

Clearly, conflict often produces negative effects, such as decreased performance, lowered satisfaction, aggression, and anxiety. It wastes time, uses energy, and limits effectiveness. In some situations, however, conflict can be beneficial. As noted in Chapter 13, conflict within a group can help members resolve underlying problems so the group can move on to a more effective stage of development. Conflict between groups can increase within-group cohesion and can instigate needed organizational change. Not all conflict needs to be avoided, but all conflict needs to be managed.

In organizations, incompatible goals may come about for a variety of reasons. The needs and values or personalities of workers might clash, for example. If one member of a work team is intense, aggressive, and highly energetic, while another member is slower, less aggressive, and less intense, they may clash. Incompatible goals are often created through job assignments or the structure of an organization. It is common, for example, to find incompatible goals between a quality control department and a production department in a manufacturing organization. The production department often concentrates on quantity, while the quality control department focuses on quality.

Other factors, such as limited resources, job design, and organization structure, can also create an atmosphere that increases the probability of conflict. Organizations with limited resources are more likely to experience conflict as their members and departments fight to obtain a share of the limited resources. A job design or organizational structure that makes individuals or departments interdependent also increases the likelihood of conflict. Under these circumstances, by definition, the goals of one person or group cannot be reached without the cooperation of the other. Neither Karin nor Craig can sell calculators unless the company's shipping department consistently delivers products on time. The shipping department, in turn, can do little unless the production department provides the goods.

The Conflict Process

Conflict does not suddenly appear in full bloom; it evolves from a series of occurrences. It begins when a person experiences frustration—and it may never end. Even when a conflict is resolved, a conflict aftermath remains (see Figure 15.6).[5]

FIGURE 15.6   *The Conflict Process*

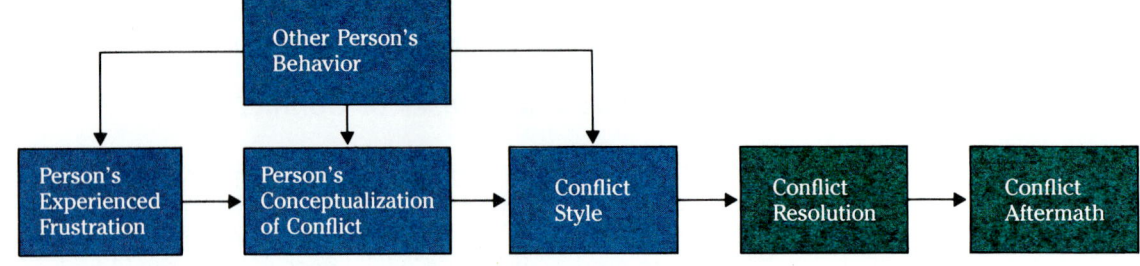

Experienced Frustration People first may become aware of the evolution of conflict when they experience frustration. This frustration can concern anything of importance: not receiving a promotion, receiving only a small pay raise, or having difficulty accomplishing a work objective. In fact, when people are prevented from or have difficulty accomplishing anything of value, they are likely to experience frustration. Karin was frustrated because Craig's invasion of her territory prevented her from reaching her sales goals and earning bonuses. Frustration, regardless of the cause, commonly leads to dissatisfaction, anxiety, anger, depression, and aggression.

The magnitude of conflict is usually in proportion to the magnitude of the frustration experienced. As conflict escalates, so does the amount of frustration. As conflict is reduced, frustration also decreases. Similarly, if a conflict is not fully resolved, some level of frustration remains. People who feel residual frustration retain much of the anxiety, anger, dissatisfaction, depression, and aggression created by the conflict. In fact, accumulated residual frustration often contributes to the development of future conflict, particularly with those who have been involved in conflict before.

Conceptualization of Conflict After experiencing frustration and other negative effects of conflict, people can try to figure out why the conflict is occurring and what it means. To do this, they might ask themselves such questions as:

1. Why do I feel this frustration?
2. What is the underlying cause of this conflict?
3. What has the other party done to contribute to my frustration?
4. What have I done to contribute to the other party's frustration?
5. What would I like to obtain that I am currently being prevented from obtaining?
6. What do I think the other party would like to obtain that he or she is currently being prevented from obtaining?
7. How do I expect the other party to behave during the remainder of this conflict?
8. How do I plan to behave during the remainder of this conflict?

Answers to these questions help people conceptualize the nature and meaning of the conflict. In reality, not everyone considers this many questions about the nature of a conflict. In fact, some ask only one question: "Why is he or she doing this to me?" The more systematic and analytical managers are, however, the more questions they will ask about the nature of a conflict. Managers' perceptions about these issues influence their subsequent behavior. As you know from Chapter 13, as well as from your personal experiences, perceptions are not always accurate. They get distorted for many reasons. Karin may perceive that Craig has invaded her territory because she has refused to see him socially. In fact, he may have done so out of desperation as the sales of calculators have shifted from discount retail stores to the check-out counters of supermarkets.

Conflict Styles   After people have conceptualized a conflict, they can take action to deal with it. The actions they engage in, of course, influence the reactions and behavior of the others involved in the conflict. Conflict behavior can take many forms, depending on the levels of cooperation and assertiveness of those involved. As shown in Figure 15.7, various combinations of cooperativeness and assertiveness create five distinct styles of conflict behavior: competing, collaborating, compromising, avoiding, and accommodating.

The *competing* conflict style is marked by high levels of assertiveness but little cooperation. It is an aggressive strategy, often combative in nature, and makes use of a person's power base to try and overcome the interests of the other party. Competitors pursue their own goals intensely without concern for the other person's interests. They often make the first move in a conflict to try and gain control of the situation and thus increase their chances of winning. If Karin were to adopt a competing style, she would take whatever steps were necessary to meet her own goals while she tried to prevent Craig from reaching his.

The *collaborating* conflict style involves attempts by the participants to satisfy both (or all of) their interests. They may try to solve the problems at the source of the conflict, to identify why the conflict exists, and to learn what can be done to deal with this cause. Collaborators usually

FIGURE 15.7   *Conflict Behavior Styles*

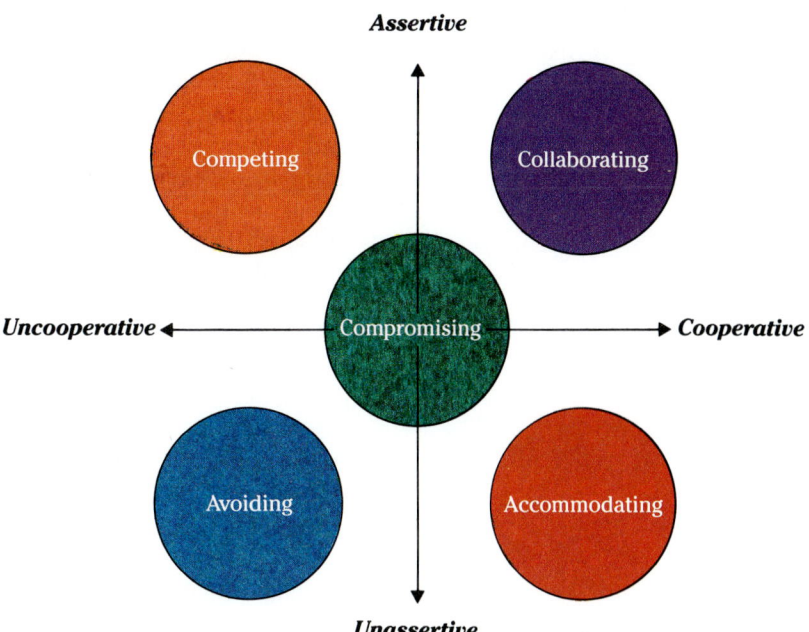

make it clear to the other person that they want a conflict resolution that satisfies everyone's interests; thus, collaborating strategies can produce what University of Wisconsin management professor Alan Filley has referred to as "win-win" solutions, because both parties get most of what they want.[6] Karin and Craig could collaborate if they agreed to figure out why problems arose and to develop a mutually acceptable and beneficial solution.

Despite the common belief that a compromising approach to conflict resolution is desirable, it often is a poor choice. The *compromising* style produces a mutually acceptable but less than optimal solution for both parties. Each makes concessions, and disagreements are often resolved through sacrifice by one or both parties. This typically leads to "lose-lose" solutions, because both parties have to give up something valuable to them. In fact, often the biggest loser is the party most willing to compromise. A compromiser interacting with a competitor often fares poorly in conflict resolutions. If Karin agreed to give Craig one megamarket in exchange for two Kmarts, both would lose something in the compromise.

A person who chooses to be both uncooperative and unassertive in conflict situations uses an *avoiding* style. This person attempts to withdraw from conflict rather than resolve it. Avoiders often ignore their own personal interests as well as those of the other party. The seriousness of the problem is discounted, and the person denies concern over the conflict. Often the avoider feels there is no point in even trying to resolve the conflict, believing that resolution is unlikely.

A person with an *accommodating* conflict style tries to satisfy the interests of the other party at his or her own expense. This is a passive, even somewhat submissive, approach to conflict management. The accommodating individual tries to discover what the other party wants and then tries to meet those needs. Rather than fight for his or her own interests, the accommodator surrenders. This tends to produce a "win-lose" solution, because the other party is given what he or she wants by the accommodator, who gets nothing in return but resolution of the conflict. Although this resolution may remove some of the existing frustration from the conflict, it often creates new frustration as the person admits his or her impotence.

Although most people have a dominant conflict style, in reality, few people use only one of these styles. Usually people choose a dominant style but incorporate aspects of the other styles as well. From one conflict to another, their dominant style may differ, depending on how they conceptualize the situation.

The Other Person's Behavior   It is Craig's behavior that first caused Karin to sense frustration. Karin's behavior and reactions affected Craig, who reacted to these. Clearly, there would be no conflict without the presence and behavior of another person. Your perceptions of another person's style substantially influence your own choice of conflict style. You are likely to behave differently, for example, if you perceive the other person to be accommodating than you probably would behave if you perceived him or her to be competing. In conflict situations, it is important to remember that you and the other person simultaneously perceive and react to each other's behavior. It is unlikely that anything you do in a conflict situation will go unnoticed by the other person.

Conflict Aftermath   Think back to the last big conflict that you were involved in. The fact that you can remember this conflict is proof that things are not the way they were before the conflict. The conflict process leaves an aftermath that costs both the competing parties and their organization. During the aftermath of a conflict, people may change, depending on how fully each party attained his or her goals and how much each was frustrated. Their feelings of satisfaction, motivation, trust, and cohesiveness, for example, are likely to be affected. If Karin wins the conflict with Craig, and he is prohibited from selling to any of the megamarkets, what will this victory for Karin do to the future of their working relationship and to the effectiveness of the company? Regardless of the outcome of the conflict, its presence costs the organization time, energy, and money. Clearly, the conflict consumed Karin and Craig's time. It cost their company money due to sales lost while Karin and Craig fought. The company also lost some of the effectiveness and productivity of Karin and Craig's manager, Dorian Ring, as he spent time trying to referee the dispute.

The aftermath of conflict can also be positive. Conflict resolution often leads to needed organizational change, stronger feelings of cohesion, and greater individual or group maturity. Dorian suggested that Karin and Craig find a collaborative way to settle their dispute. Eventually they arrived at a solution in which Karin created and then became the manager of a new mail-order division. Craig then acquired Karin's grocery stores. Karin finds her new job much more rewarding than her previous job, and Craig is pleased to have the expanded market. By working out the solution together, each gained respect and admiration for the other.

Managing Conflict Effectively

Managers must select an approach for handling every conflict situation. Sometimes they make this selection carefully and systematically. At other times, they do so haphazardly. Fortunately, it is possible to understand many of the factors that influence how people actually choose a strategy for managing conflict. More important, it is possible to identify *effective* strategies for managing specific conflict situations.

Factors That Typically Influence Strategy Choice   The way that managers decide to handle a conflict depends in part on the kind of person that they are and in part on their perceptions of the situation and the behavior of the conflicting parties. Together, these factors operate as shown in Figure 15.8.[7]

Most people favor one of the five conflict styles discussed in this chapter because it matches their personality, or because it has worked well in the past. All else being equal, people are more likely to choose that style than any other. Because a natural style of conflict management is not necessarily the best, people involved in conflict often need to modify their style to deal more effectively with specific conflict situations and the behavior of the other person. Managers embroiled in conflicts between

FIGURE 15.8   *Conflict Strategy Choice*

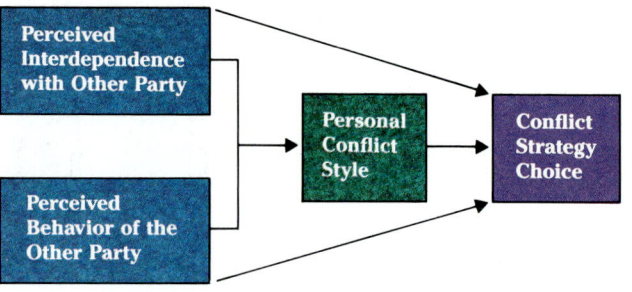

subordinates must encourage them to make such changes. Karin and Craig can thank Dorian for intervening in their conflict and for suggesting that they make the shift to the collaborative style that led to their "win-win" solution.

When an employee is dependent on another, he or she is likely to become cooperative during a conflict; however, if an employee believes that another person is dependent on him or her, the employee is likely to become more assertive. A person's choice of strategy, therefore, may change according to the degree of interdependence in the conflict situation. The behavior of the opposing party also influences a person's conflict strategy. Someone is less likely to be collaborative, for example, if the other party is using a competitive style. Managers must be aware of the styles used by conflicting subordinates to anticipate and manage conflict effectively in their organizations. It was by listening to and talking with Karin and Craig that Dorian was able to recognize the need for the switch to a collaborative style. Their acceptance of his suggestion made a good resolution possible.

Choosing Appropriate Strategies   People's typical choices in conflict situations are not necessarily good ones. For this reason and because there is no one best conflict strategy, the best conflict manager is aware of all of the various strategies and the factors that make them more or less effective. Effective conflict management, then, is a matter of carefully conceptualizing the conflict situation and reacting appropriately. A competing style might be quite appropriate, for example, when quick, decisive action is vital and the other person in the conflict has a history of attacking noncompetitive opponents. An accommodating style might be more fitting when people discover that they were wrong, when they know that they will lose no matter what, or when future relations with the other person are more important than the outcome of the conflict at hand. Table 15.3 provides further suggestions for situations in which each of the five conflict styles might be appropriate.

Politics

Webster's dictionary defines **politics** as "the art or science concerned with guiding or influencing . . . policy . . . with winning and holding control . . . [and] competition between competing interest groups or individuals for power and leadership."[8] Politics is active in every organiza-

TABLE 15.3 *Appropriate Situations for Conflict Management Styles*

Conflict-Handling Styles	Appropriate Situations
Competing	1. When quick, decisive action is vital—e.g., emergencies 2. On important issues where unpopular actions need implementing—e.g., cost cutting, enforcing unpopular rules, discipline 3. On issues vital to company welfare when you know you are right 4. Against people who take advantage of noncompetitive behavior
Collaborating	1. To find an integrative solution when both sets of concerns are too important to be compromised 2. When your objective is to learn 3. To merge insights from people with different perspectives 4. To gain commitment by incorporating concerns into a consensus 5. To work through feelings which have interfered with a relationship
Compromising	1. When goals are important but not worth the effort or potential disruption of more assertive modes 2. When opponents with equal power are committed to mutually exclusive goals 3. To achieve temporary settlements to complex issues 4. To arrive at expedient solutions under time pressure 5. As a backup when collaboration or competition is unsuccessful
Avoiding	1. When an issue is trivial or more important issues are pressing 2. When you perceive no chance of satisfying your concerns 3. When potential disruption outweighs the benefits of resolution 4. To let people cool down and regain perspective 5. When gathering information supersedes immediate decision 6. When others can resolve the conflict more effectively 7. When issues seem tangential or symptomatic of other issues
Accommodating	1. When you find you are wrong—to allow a better position to be heard, to learn, and to show your reasonableness 2. When issues are more important to others than to you—to satisfy others and maintain cooperation 3. To build social credits for later issues 4. To minimize loss when you are outmatched and losing 5. When harmony and stability are especially important 6. To allow subordinates to develop by learning from mistakes

Source: Based on Table 1 of K. W. Thomas (1977), Toward multidimensional values in teaching: The example of conflict behaviors, *Academy of Management Review*, 2, 487.

tion as individuals and groups promote their own best interests. Organizational politics has been defined as "the management of influence to obtain ends not sanctioned by the organization or to obtain sanctioned ends through non-sanctioned influence means."[9] Coalitions form, labor and management bargain, and payments are made "on the side." In fact, it has been suggested by a noted organization scholar that organizations are political coalitions in which decisions are made and goals are formed through the bargaining processes that unfold between individuals and groups.[10] Good managers must recognize the importance of organizational politics and either act to reduce their importance or skillfully play the political game themselves.

Politics and Interpersonal Behavior

In theory, people's behavior in organizations is guided by rational, logical reasoning for the purpose of furthering *organizational* interests. In practice, however, much behavior is motivated and guided by organiza-

A CLOSER LOOK

Conflict Management: Disagree with Your Boss? Let Your Peers Settle It

"I don't agree with you, but you're the boss." These words have been spoken millions of times to thousands of bosses. In recent years, however, a number of progressive companies have decided that simply being higher in the organizational hierarchy does not necessarily make a boss right. These companies have created a variety of "speak up" and "open door" policies. Typically, these policies allow a worker to skip over his or her boss and go directly to a higher-level manager to appeal an action that the employee considers unfair or unwise.

For many organizations, such as IBM, speak up and open door programs have worked well. For many others, however, employees have viewed these grievance systems as a waste of time. Convinced that managers would almost always support lower-level management decisions, employees have not felt it worthwhile to complain.

Some progressive organizations, such as Federal Express, Digital Equipment, General Electric, and Borg-Warner have therefore created peer review panels to resolve employee grievances. According to *The Wall Street Journal,* most peer review panels contain peers of both the aggrieved employee and his or her manager.[1] On a typical panel, however, peers outnumber managers three to two. How do the panels work? A couple of examples follow.

An employee at Control Data Corporation was fired. According to his boss, the employee refused to cooperate in a performance improvement program. According to the employee, however, the "boss's idea of feedback consisted of verbal abuse and threats."[2] The employee appealed to a peer review panel. After taking statements from both parties, the boss was overruled, and the employee was reinstated with back pay.

Simply being higher in an organization does not make a boss right.

Consider a case at Deseret Generation & Transmission Cooperative of Salt Lake City. When Leesa Story was passed over for a job in a power plant control room, she claimed that she was treated unfairly when a man with less experience was given the job instead of her. She complained to her boss and then to her boss' boss. They refused to budge. She appealed to the peer board. The board reversed the decision of management and awarded the promotion to Ms. Story.

Peer appeal boards are clearly risky business. They threaten to undermine the authority of management, but they also promise to open communication, to create a trusting atmosphere, and to keep managers on their toes. Such boards may also "help deter union organizing, and perhaps most importantly, stem the rising number of costly lawsuits claiming wrongful discharge and discrimination."[3] Is there a risk that peer boards will give away too much to complaining employees? So far, it does not appear likely. Often peers are tougher on complainants than even a boss would be. In fact, in the majority of cases to date, peer boards have sided with management.

1. L. Reibstein (3 December 1986), More firms use peer review panel to resolve employees' grievances, *The Wall Street Journal,* 25.
2. *Ibid.*
3. *Ibid.*

tional politics as individuals and groups strive to have their own way for the purpose of furthering their own interests.

In early 1988, the Lepley Calculator Company merged with The Electronic Abacus. Both companies manufactured and marketed electronic calculators and had often competed head to head in the same marketplace prior to the merger. After the merger, the companies formed a new management team with members from both of the previous companies and created a management council to make significant decisions for the new company.

On February 15, 1988, the first meeting of the council took place. During that meeting, the primary focus was on how best to serve the needs of the new organization. It was very difficult, however, for the members of the committee to forget that they had once been a Lepley or Abacus employee. Coalitions clearly existed and vested interests endured. Former members of each company seemed intent on demonstrating that their company had been the better of the two and, thus, should play the dominant role in the new organization. Such political issues could not be ignored, and they could not be allowed to supersede the interests of the new organization. Sandy Manly, president of the new company, deemed effective management of the political issues within the council to be essential or the company would suffer significantly.

Although politics can benefit an organization, organizational politicians (just like government politicians) can become so enamored of winning that they slight the purpose of their primary role. The acquisition of individual or group power is of utmost importance to such people. Organizational politicians obtain gratification by showing others in the organization just how powerful they are. Kent Merrill, former general manager of The Electronic Abacus, had a political decision to make as he sat on the management council. He could serve as a rallying person for the council members from his former company and attempt to imbue that group with the strongest power base. On the other hand, he could side with Grand Odokara, former president of Lepley, and attempt to acquire political power by siding with the new regime. His decision was based as much on personal interests as on consideration of what would be best for the company.

It is widely believed that organizational decisions, such as whom to promote, where to locate a new facility, and how to administer pay, are influenced by political issues.[11] It is also commonly believed that such political considerations damage an organization and its members. Even so, most managers believe that they must be politically effective to succeed.

Living in the Political Environment

What can you do about organizational politics? First, you cannot ignore them. Recognize that individuals and groups are interested in the acquisition of power and probably will use this power to serve their own interests. Be aware of the fact that decision making is often based not only on the merits of an issue, but also on the political consequences. Does the accounting department, for example, want to hire additional workers to help the organization function effectively or to build power for the accounting department? Be sensitive to the political concerns and interests of various individuals and groups as you evaluate the probable effects of alternative decisions. In short, learn about the political realities of your organization and anticipate their effects.

A second tactic used by some is to take advantage of organizational politics. Supporting a politically powerful member of an organization can yield payoffs. If pay raises and promotions are influenced by people's political stance, learning the "party line" and behaving accordingly probably will increase wages and enhance employees' positions. Combining forces with other individuals or groups to build a political power base that dominates less powerful interests can also be effective.

Third, if you decide to play the political game, be aware of the possible ramifications. You cannot gain political advantage without expending energy that could be used for other purposes, such as increased performance. Furthermore, reliance on political support can be costly if the political view that you espouse falls from power. If your favored status in an organization is heavily influenced by affiliation with a strong political leader, for example, what happens to you when that leader is replaced by a political opponent? You undoubtedly will lose whatever political benefits you were enjoying. When you must stand on your capabilities rather than on your politics, you may also find that the energy you devoted to the political cause may have prevented you from being an effective, competitive organization member.

Rather than play the political game, you might wish to reduce the role of politics in your own life. Avoid using power solely as a show of force. Use power for organizational purposes when you need to, but do not flaunt it. Unfortunately, others may feel your behavior is politically motivated even if it is not. Take care to explain the reasons for your actions and be sensitive to the political concerns and awareness of others. Encourage open decision making and problem solving, because decisions made behind closed doors are often politically suspect.

A fourth alternative is to try to reduce the role of politics in an organization as a whole and to diffuse responsibility throughout the organization rather than center it in the hands of a favored few. This atmosphere makes the development of strong political coalitions less likely. Where political power does exist, try to channel that power toward the accomplishment of organizational rather than special-interest objectives.

As a member of an organization, you must decide whether to use or diffuse political power. You should realize, however, that failure to recognize and deal with the political realities of organizational life will decrease your effectiveness, be it as employee or manager.

Interpersonal Factors in Review

Interpersonal factors affect a manager's ability to direct the behavior of organization members. These factors include interpersonal power, communication, interpersonal conflict, and politics.

Every member of an organization can accumulate legitimate, reward, coercive, expert, and referent power. Some of these sources can be fed by formal organizational policies and practices, but others must be nurtured by individuals. Regardless of its source, power is "in the eyes of the beholder." You will not have reward power, for example, unless the person you wish to influence perceives that you have the ability to provide rewards and that you are willing to provide or withhold them. Development of an appropriate power base requires careful coordination of the various sources of power. Some combinations of sources can produce very strong power, such as fusing referent power with reward power. Other combinations are self-defeating, as when a manager combines referent and coercive power.

Communication is an intricate but critical organizational process. The communication process includes the formulation of an intended message, the encoding of that message, the transmission of the message through channels and networks, and the decoding of the message by receivers. Distortion can occur at each step of the process. Managers must be very careful to match their communication choices to each situation for their message to be received and interpreted as intended.

Conflict is a situation in which two or more people have incompatible goals, and one or both believe the other will prevent his or her own goal attainment. A person going through the conflict process first experiences frustration, then tries to conceptualize or understand what is happening, reacts to his or her perceptions, and lives with the aftermath.

In reacting to conflict, people choose one or a combination of styles: competing (trying to win at all costs), collaborating (trying to see that both parties win), compromising (finding a solution in which both parties renounce something), and avoiding (withdrawing from the conflict altogether). Most people have a dominant conflict management style that they typically rely on. This style can and usually should be altered according to the opponent's behavior and the degree of interdependence between the opponents. The most effective managers are aware of the conflict styles available to them, and they select those styles that are appropriate for a given conflict situation.

Finally, much behavior in organizations is influenced by political considerations, so an awareness of these issues is essential. Each person must decide how to respond to political pressures in organizations. Some available choices include learning to play the political game, avoiding politics as much as possible, and trying to diffuse the importance of politics in a specific organization.

Notes

1. J. R. P. French, Jr. and B. H. Raven (1959), The bases of social power, in D. Cartwright, ed., *Studies in social power*, Ann Arbor, MI: University of Michigan Press; D. Mechanic (1964), Sources of power of lower participants in complex organizations, in W. W. Cooper, H. J. Leavitt, and M. W. Shelly II, eds., *New perspectives in organizational research*, New York: John Wiley, 136–47; G. R. Salancik and J. Pfeffer (1983), Who gets power—and how they hold onto it: A strategic-contingency model of power, in R. W. Allen and L. W. Porter, eds., *Organizational influence processes*, Glenview, IL: Scott, Foresman, 52–71.

2. A. Bavelas (1950), Communication patterns in task-oriented groups, *Journal of the Acoustical Society of America*, 22, 725–30.

3. K. Davis (1969), Grapevine communication among lower and middle managers, *Personnel Journal*, 48, 269–72.

4. K. Davis (September-October 1953), Management communication and the grapevine, *Harvard Business Review,* 43–49.

5. K. W. Thomas (1976), Conflict and management, in M. D. Dunnette, ed., *The handbook of industrial and organizational psychology,* Chicago: Rand-McNally.

6. A. C. Filley (1975), *Interpersonal conflict resolution,* Glenview, IL: Scott, Foresman.

7. This model was discussed in C. J. Riggs (1983), Dimensions of organizational conflict: A functional analysis of communication tactics, in R. N. Bostrom, ed., *Communication yearbook 7,* Beverly Hills, CA: Sage.

8. *Webster's ninth new collegiate dictionary* (1985), Springfield, MA: Merriam-Webster, 911.

9. B. T. Mayes and R. W. Allen (1977), Toward a definition of organizational politics, *Academy of Management Review,* 2, 672–78.

10. J. G. March (1962), The business firm as a political coalition, *Journal of Politics,* 24, 662–78.

11. J. Gandz and V. Murray (1980), The experience of workplace politics, *Academy of Management Journal,* 23, 237–51.

Key Terms

interpersonal power
legitimate power
reward power
formal rewards
informal rewards
coercive power
expert power
resource power
referent power

communication
communication channels
communication network
vertical communication
horizontal communication
diagonal communication
conflict
politics

Issues for Review and Discussion

1. Identify the major sources of organizational power.
2. Discuss how the various sources of power can work with or against one another.
3. Describe the major steps of the communication process.
4. What are the most common barriers to effective communication in organizations?
5. Why does conflict occur in organizations?
6. Describe the stages in the evolution of conflict.
7. Identify the five major styles of conflict management.
8. Why does politics emerge as an issue in organizations?
9. How can you capitalize on politics in organizations?
10. How can you reduce the impact of organizational politics?

Suggested Readings

Blanchard, K. and Johnson, S. (1981). *The one minute manager*. LaJolla, CA: Blanchard-Johnson; Manz, C. C. (1988). A review of *The one minute manager*. In Pierce, J. L. and Newstrom, J. W., eds. *The manager's bookshelf: A mosaic of contemporary views*. New York: Harper & Row, 104–9.

Cavanagh, G. F., Moberg, D. J., and Velasquez (1981). The ethics of organizational politics. *Academy of Management Review*, 6, 363–74.

Davis, K. (1969). Grapevine communications among lower and middle managers. *Personnel Journal*, 48, 269–72.

Filley, A. C. (1975). *Interpersonal conflict resolution*. Glenview, IL: Scott, Foresman.

French, J. R. P., Jr. and Raven, B. H. (1959). The bases of social power. In Cartwright, D., ed. *Studies in social power*. Ann Arbor, MI: University of Michigan Press.

Gandz, J. and Murray, V. (1980). The experience of workplace politics. *Academy of Management Journal*, 23, 237–51.

Murray, V. and Gandz, J. (December 1980). Politics at work. *Business Horizons*, 11–23.

CASE   *The Open Door*

*By Mabry Miller and Thomas
Pursel of Drake University*

The U.S. Navy has an airborne weapons evaluation facility located on an Air Force base in New Mexico. The primary mission of the command is to test weapons used with various types of aircraft deployed throughout the fleet. As a secondary mission, it provides personnel administration services for Naval personnel assigned to inter-service commands in the vicinity and to many retired naval personnel located in central New Mexico. At the time of the incidents related here, the organizational structure for the facility was as shown in Figure 15A.

Background

The technical requirements of the primary mission were accomplished in the nuclear engineering, special applications, and surface applications departments. The other departments fulfilled a supporting role. The secondary missions were coordinated by the administrative support department (ASD). For example, the command might be called on to provide color guards, escorts, and pallbearers for military funerals or to provide units to participate in civic events, such as parades. The military personnel who actually took part in these events were, of necessity, provided by the aircraft maintenance department. These events tended to occur on weekends, holidays, and other times that would normally be off-duty hours.

All departments formally reported through the executive officer. Navy regulations also provided that department heads had direct access to the commanding officer for matters related to the mission of their departments. In reality, however, the nuclear engineering, special applications, and surface applications department heads dealt almost exclusively with the technical director, who had complete—or nearly complete—autonomy, depending on the incumbent commanding officer's management style. The technical director and the three technical department heads were all senior civilian employees, as were most of their assigned engineers and analysts. All were long term-employees with an average of fifteen years' service at the facility. In contrast, military personnel were usually assigned for only two-year tours of duty.

As indicated in the organizational chart, the personnel mixture of the facility was approximately 50 percent military and 50 percent civilian. Most of the military personnel were assigned to the ASD and aircraft maintenance. With the exception of pilots, who were assigned to management positions, all of the personnel in the ASD held nonaviation ratings. In contrast, all personnel in the aircraft maintenance department were in positions which required aviation ratings.

The facility occupied space in two widely separated locations. The commanding officer, executive officer, technical director, and three departments—flight operations, finance/logistics, and aircraft maintenance—were located in the main hangar. All other departments were located in an area requiring a lower security clearance. The nuclear engineering, special applications, and surface applications departments needed to be accessible to visitors. The ASD also needed to be accessible because it was responsible for servicing the needs of Navy personnel assigned to other commands in the area and the needs of retired naval personnel living in the area.

This separation prevented the incidental interactions normally associated with cohesive military or civilian units. A particular source of resentment was the assignment of personnel from the aircraft maintenance department to funerals, parades, and other ceremonial functions by the ASD. These personnel blamed the ASD for ruining their weekends and holidays.

Captain Rahl

Captain Rahl had been recently assigned as the new commanding officer. Having previously served a two-year tour at the base as a department head, he was aware of the latitude normally granted to both civilian and military department heads by previous commanding officers. Captain Rahl, however, insisted that he should be involved in every detail. In addition, he wanted to be thought of as being completely accessible to every member of the facility on any matter. To accomplish this, he instituted an "open door" policy, whereby he was accessible to anyone on the same day they requested to speak to him.

Shortly after Captain Rahl established his open door policy, Petty Officer Jones of the aircraft maintenance department asked to speak to the captain. Captain Rahl then advised Commander Smith, who was head of Jones' department, that Jones had scheduled an interview; however, he did not invite Smith to be present, nor did he discuss the interview with Smith afterwards. After this, Jones often spoke privately with Captain Rahl without Smith being advised either by Jones or Rahl that the conversations were taking place.

When it was seen that Captain Rahl really honored his open door policy, the members of other departments, from the lowest-ranking sailor to the most senior petty officer and civilian

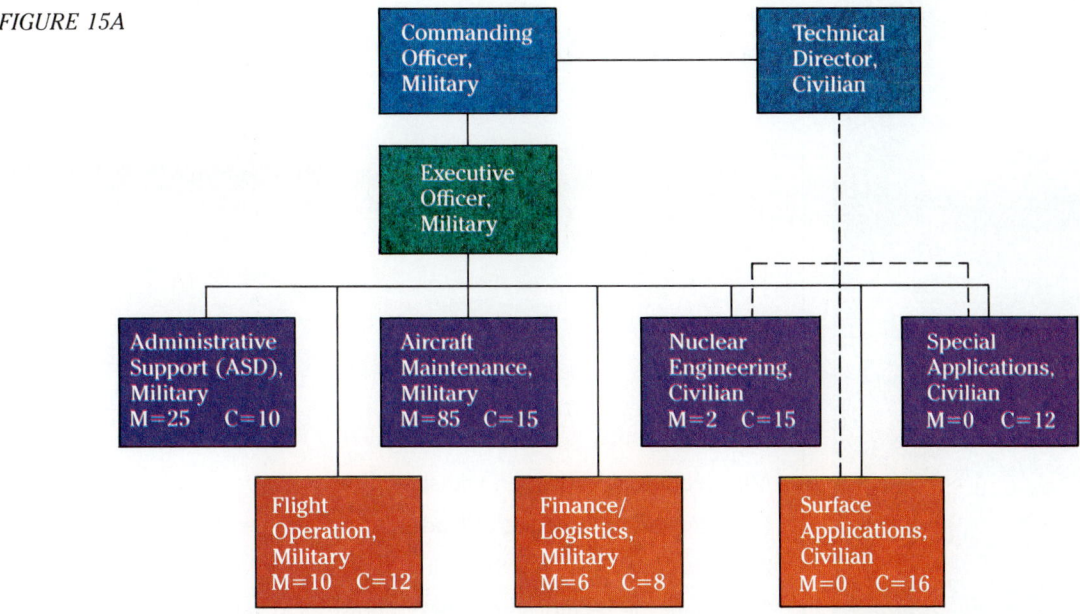

Note: The term *Military* or *Civilian* within each block denotes the status of the department head. *M* indicates the number of military personnel assigned to the department and *C* indicates the number of civilian personnel.

employees, took advantage of the opportunity for personal discussions with the commanding officer.

Not long after his conversations with Petty Officer Jones, Captain Rahl called Commander Smith into his office and said, "I understand that favoritism is being shown in the assignment of personnel for special functions on weekends and holidays. Morale in your department is not what it should be because some of your people are being treated unfairly. Straighten this out or I'll have to make note of it on your fitness report [performance evaluation]." Smith sought in vain to learn the source of the Captain's information, to obtain specific details, and to refute the accusation. He was simply advised to "Shape up your ship."

As the Captain's open door policy gained momentum, no department head, civilian or military, was immune from "Rahl's Rockets." Even though formal grievance procedures were readily accessible, the Captain's open door became the accepted channel for the resolution of perceived problems within the command.

This had a dramatic effect on the department heads. Commander Green of the ASD, who felt her department had been particularly victimized, made this private assessment:

It would be bad enough if problems that I can easily handle were taken to the commanding officer merely to speed up routine actions, but it appears that some people are trying to earn credit with the 'old man' or to embarrass someone who is totally unaware that a problem exists. The results are devastating. Personnel in the departments affected have withdrawn from all but the most essential contacts with the rest of the facility. Inaction is deemed to be safer than an unpopular action which is essential, or an action which can be misinterpreted. As a consequence, productivity and morale are both suffering. Requests for early reassignment have been received from practically all military personnel in the ASD and not a single person has reenlisted upon completion of obligated service. This includes many who have many years of service.

The same results occurred with civilian personnel in the ASD and in the nuclear engineering, special applications, and surface applications departments. Many sought new positions in other activities or simply resigned. The technical director and two of the three technical department heads resigned during Captain Rahl's tour of duty.

Questions

1. What barriers to effective communication are present in the situation described in this case?
2. Discuss the motives which led Captain Rahl to establish his open door policy.
3. Has the open door policy helped or hindered the flow of effective communication in this organization? Why?
4. What alternative to the open door policy could Captain Rahl have used to get good information about department performance?
5. What would you recommend to Captain Rahl?

Leadership

Student Learning Objectives

After reading this chapter, you should be able to:

1. Understand the nature of leadership and the leadership process.

2. Explain and describe the trait perspective on leadership.

3. Explain the relationship between power and various forms of leadership.

4. Distinguish between Theory X and Theory Y leader attitudes.

5. Understand the behavioral perspective on leadership.

6. Discuss how situational theories of leadership can help managers.

7. Discuss the concept of substitutes for leadership.

8. Describe what is meant by charismatic leadership.

9. Summarize the ideas for effective leadership from trait, behavioral, and situational theories of leadership.

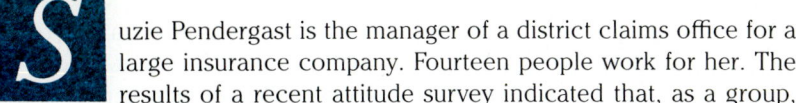

Suzie Pendergast is the manager of a district claims office for a large insurance company. Fourteen people work for her. The results of a recent attitude survey indicated that, as a group, these fourteen people have extremely high job satisfaction and motivation. Conflict is rare in Suzie's office. Furthermore, productivity ratings indicate that her group of employees is among the most productive of all claims groups in the entire company. After reviewing these facts, the company's vice-president of human resources visited the claims office in an attempt to discover the secret to her success as a manager. Suzie Pendergast's peers, superiors, and subordinates all gave the same answer: she is an outstanding leader of people. She gets the most possible from her workers and does so in such a way that they enjoy working for her.

There is no magic formula for becoming a good leader. As this chapter will show, however, there are many reasons that some people are better leaders than others.

The Nature of Leadership

There are many definitions of leadership. Most people agree that **leadership** is an interpersonal process involving the exercise of influence within a social system, such as a group, family, community, or work organization. In work organizations, effective leadership influences individuals and/or groups to achieve organizational goals.

The Leadership Process

The leadership process is a complex and dynamic exchange consisting of four components: leaders, followers, the context within which the process takes place, and resulting by-products. A leader, as defined by Webster's, is a person who takes charge of or guides a performance or

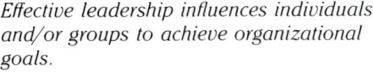

Effective leadership influences individuals and/or groups to achieve organizational goals.

activity. A follower is a person who performs under the guidance and instructions of a leader. The context is the situation—formal, informal, social, military, emergency, routine, and so on—surrounding a leader-follower relationship. The nature of the leadership process varies substantially with the context in which it occurs. For example, the context is very different for the leader of a recreational softball team than it is for a military commander on a battlefield, and leadership tactics that work in the first context might fail miserably in the latter. The by-products of leadership can include animosity produced by a punitive leader's actions and respect for an able leader's decisions.

As shown in Figure 16.1, the leadership process is interactive. Leaders influence followers, followers influence leaders, and all are influenced by the context in which the exchange takes place. The by-products of any leader-follower exchange can influence future interactions.

In some cases, leadership exchanges produce positive by-products. **Transactional leadership** describes the interactions between a leader and follower in which both give and receive something that is valued.[1] These reciprocal exchanges take place within the context of a mutually interdependent relationship between the leader and the follower, resulting in an interpersonal bonding between them.[2] Consider the case of Margie Van Handel, who manages a small company that specializes in designing computer systems for small business. Cheryl Gillespie, who works for Margie, is extremely knowledgeable and keeps up-to-date on all of the latest microcomputer software developments. Cheryl's technical expertise and long hours of dedicated work have contributed substantially to Margie's success. Cheryl has likewise benefited, receiving excellent career development advice, moral support, and interesting work assignments from Margie.

FIGURE 16.1   The Leadership Process

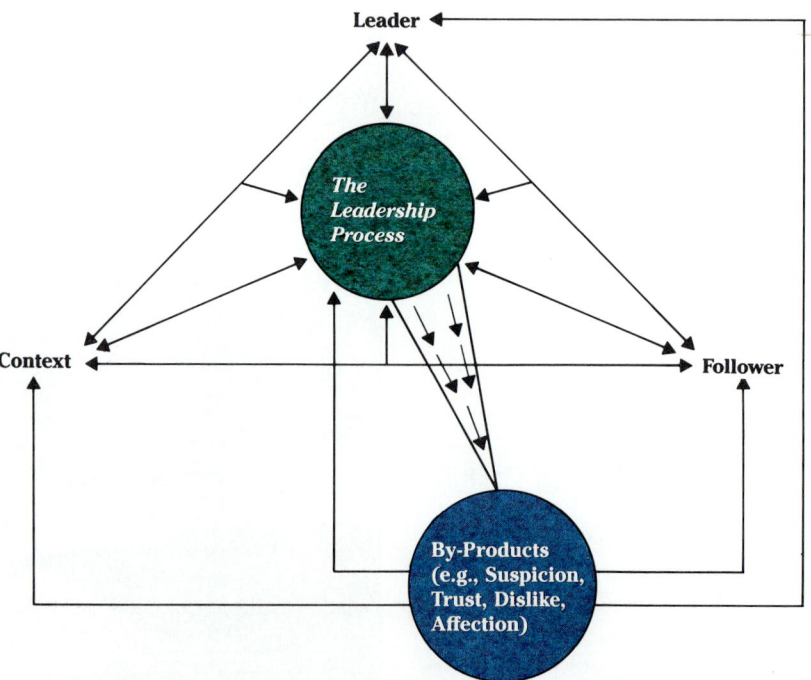

Leaders

Leaders provide direction, as does Leonard Bernstein in his unique role as symphony director.

Leaders hold a unique position in their groups, exercising influence and providing direction. As a symphony director, for example, Leonard Bernstein is a part of the symphony. His role, however, is distinctly different from that of other symphony members. He is responsible for coordinating the sounds and the tempo for the group of musicians. In this capacity, his identity within the group is unique.

Two kinds of leaders can usually be identified in organizations: formal and informal. A **formal,** or **designated, leader** is an individual appointed *by the organization* to serve in a formal capacity as an agent of the organization. Suzie Pendergast is the formal leader of the claims office, and Leonard Bernstein is the formal leader of the symphony. As you learned in Chapter 1, practically every manager is called on to act as a formal leader as part of his or her interpersonal role assigned by the formal organization.

An **informal leader,** in contrast, becomes a leader because *group members* choose him or her as their natural leader. Athletic teams often have informal leaders, who exert considerable influence on team members, even though they hold no official (formal) leadership positions. In fact, most organizational work groups contain at least one informal leader. Informal leaders can benefit or harm an organization, depending on whether their influence encourages group members to behave consistently with organizational goals.

The terms *leader* and *manager* are, therefore, not synonymous. Informal leaders, for example, often have considerable leverage over their colleagues but are not designated as managers by the organization. An informal leader's role does not include the total set of management responsibilities because an informal leader does not exercise all of the functions of planning, organizing, directing, and controlling. Leaders who are also managers find that leadership falls under the directing function.

Power and Leadership Styles

Because leadership includes influencing others, power is an essential ingredient for effective leadership. So important is power to the exercise of effective leadership that many leaders (and writers about management) treat leadership as little more than the development and application of interpersonal power. As you learned in Chapter 15, power is not always based entirely on the authority derived from a formal position within an organization's hierarchy. As you will remember, there are at least five sources of power aside from legitimate power: reward, referent, coercive, expert, and resource. Good leaders, whether formal or informal, develop many sources of power. Relying on legitimate power (authority) alone is seldom sufficient. Consider the ways in which the use of power is reflected in leadership styles.

The Tannenbaum and Schmidt Continuum   In the late 1950s, Robert Tannenbaum and Warren Schmidt developed a continuum depicting different degrees of power and influence exercised by a manager in a leadership position (see Figure 16.2).[3] As leadership style slides from left

FIGURE 16.2   Tannenbaum and Schmidt's Leadership Continuum

Boss-Centered Leadership   **Subordinate-Centered Leadership**

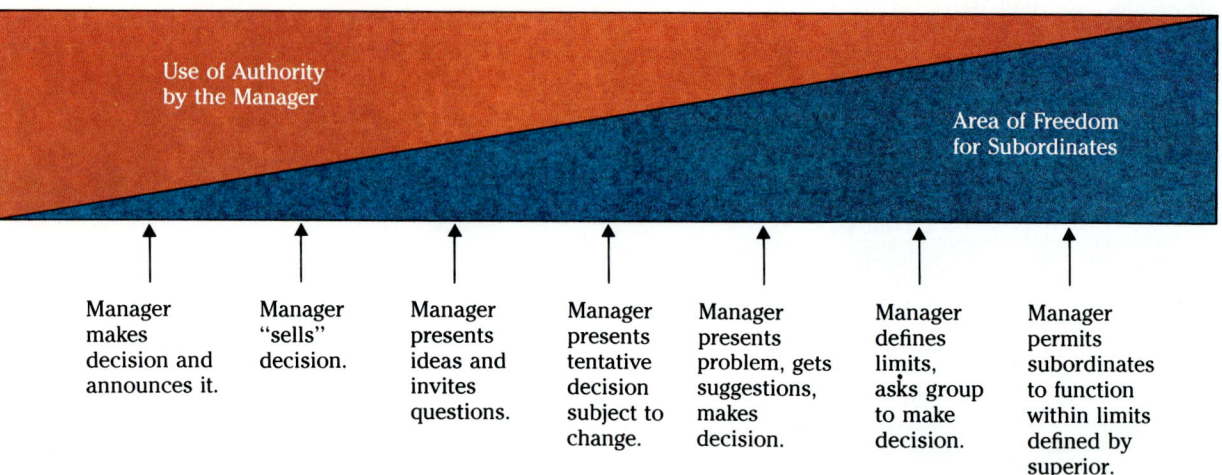

Use of Authority
by the Manager

Area of Freedom
for Subordinates

| Manager makes decision and announces it. | Manager "sells" decision. | Manager presents ideas and invites questions. | Manager presents tentative decision subject to change. | Manager presents problem, gets suggestions, makes decision. | Manager defines limits, asks group to make decision. | Manager permits subordinates to function within limits defined by superior. |

Source: Modified from R. Tannenbaum and W. H. Schmidt (May-June 1973), How to choose a leadership pattern, *Harvard Business Review*, 167.

to right, the authoritarian (boss-centered) role of the manager declines, and the amount of power and influence exercised by employees in the decision-making process increases. At the extreme left side of this continuum, for example, is a leader who operates out of a highly authoritarian position, makes decisions alone, and announces these decisions to subordinates. At the extreme right side of the continuum is a leader who engages in participative leadership, with the leader and group acting as a single social unit. At the center of the continuum is a leader whose consultative decision-making style encourages both the leader and subordinates to play active roles in making decisions and assuming joint responsibility for those decisions.

By the early 1970s, Tannenbaum and Schmidt had expanded their model to suggest that leaders should use their power in a manner consistent with: (1) the personality of subordinates, (2) subordinates' expectations about the behavior of the leader, (3) the ability of the work group to solve problems, and (4) the willingness of subordinates to accept responsibility.[4] In other words, they said, there is no one best way to be an effective leader. Leaders must use power appropriate to the circumstances.

Management professors Keith Davis from Arizona State University and John W. Newstrom from the University of Minnesota-Duluth further expanded Tannenbaum and Schmidt's power continuum to include an additional power position (see Figure 16.3). A *free-rein leader*, also referred to as a *laissez-faire leader*, avoids power and responsibility.[5] A free-rein leader exists primarily as a contact person or consultant to a group and provides members with information and other resources they may need to accomplish their tasks. Free-rein leaders tend to give assignments to work groups and offer support as needed but otherwise leave the group alone. Under this "hands-off" form of leadership, subordinates assume operating authority, define their own work goals and procedures, and resolve performance-related problems as they occur.

FIGURE 16.3 *Leader Style and the Distribution of Power*

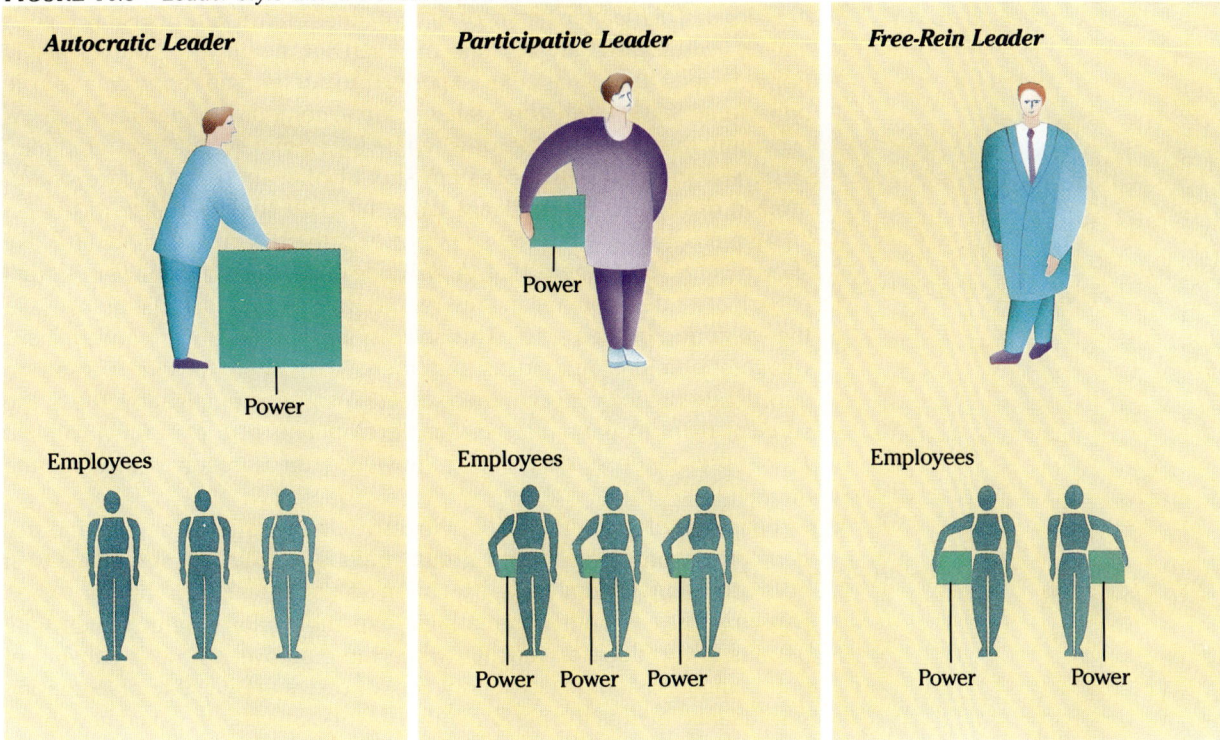

Autocratic Leader

Power

Employees

Participative Leader

Power

Employees

Power Power Power

Free-Rein Leader

Employees

Power Power

Directive/Permissive Leadership Styles Jan P. Muczyk and Bernard C. Reimann of Cleveland State University recently suggested that a contemporary approach to leadership and power should distinguish between making decisions and executing them.[6] They note that *directive* leader behavior refers to the degree to which a leader lets employees execute decisions once they have been made. At one extreme, for example, are permissive leaders who let subordinates carry out role assignments as they see fit. At the other extreme, directive leaders specify how activities are to be executed. *Participative* behavior refers to the degree to which a leader lets employees become involved in the decision-making process. Autocratic leaders use position power and make decisions; democratic (participative) leaders endorse employee involvement at each step of the decision-making process. Combinations of the directive and participative leadership styles result in four types of leadership and uses of power (see Figure 16.4).

The first cell in Figure 16.4 shows the directive autocratic leadership style. A *directive autocrat* retains power, making unilateral decisions and directing the activities of subordinates with close supervision. This style of leadership is seen as appropriate when circumstances require quick decisions and subordinates are new, inexperienced, or underqualified. A doctor in charge of a hastily constructed shelter for victims of a tornado may use this style to command nonmedical volunteers.

Cell 2 in Figure 16.4 shows a permissive autocratic style. A *permissive autocrat* mixes his or her use of power, retaining decision-making power but permitting subordinates to exercise discretion in the execution of decisions. This leader behavior is recommended when decision time is limited; when tasks are routine; or when the employee group is highly trained and, thus, has the expertise to determine appropriate role behaviors. Steve Orth, the manager of a computer software house, is executing this type of behavior when he tells a highly skilled programmer, "I have decided that this program should offer the option of keyboard, mouse, or joystick input. Please write the code to accomplish this."

Also employing a mixed use of power is the directive democratic style shown in Cell 3 of Figure 16.4. A *directive democrat* shares power through participative decision making but retains the power to direct employees in the execution of their roles. This style is appropriate when followers have valuable opinions and ideas but there is a need for one person to coordinate the execution of these ideas. A surgeon might allow the entire surgical team to participate in the development of a plan for a surgical procedure. Once surgery begins, however, the surgeon is in complete charge.

Finally, Cell 4 identifies the permissive democratic style. A *permissive democrat* shares power with group members, soliciting involvement in both decision making and execution. This style is appropriate when participation has both informational and motivational value, when time permits group decision making, when the employee group is capable of improving decision quality, and when followers are capable of exercising self-management in the performance of work. Steve Orth would have been acting as a permissive democrat if he had asked his programmers to help choose the input devices to be supported by the computer program and then allowed them to write the code executing the decision.

FIGURE 16.4   *Leader Behavior and Uses of Power*

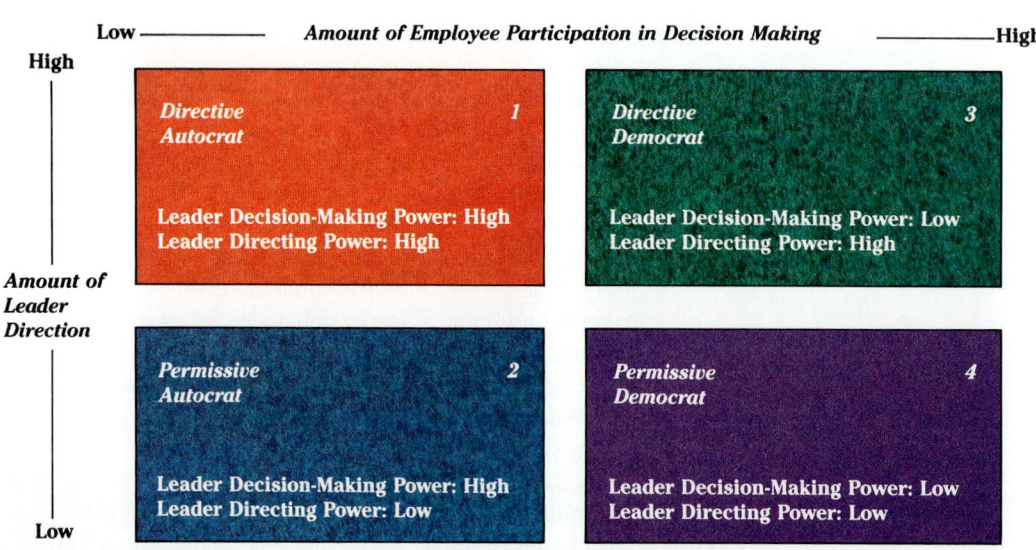

Source: Modified from J. P. Muczyk and B. C. Reimann (1987), The case for directive leadership, *The Academy of Management Executive*, 1, 304.

Trait Approaches to Leadership

One of the oldest approaches to the study of leadership is known as the **trait approach.** Those who follow a trait approach attempt to identify physiological, psychological, attitudinal, and ability traits associated with effective leaders. Proponents of this approach believe that certain people are "born leaders," and organizations should, therefore, select leaders who possess the appropriate physical and intellectual characteristics.

Leader Trait Research

The great person approach states that some people, such as Napoleon Bonaparte, are born with the attributes of great leaders.

In the late nineteenth century, researchers began a serious search for the specific traits that characterized "the great person." The **great person approach** to leadership states that some people are born with the necessary attributes to be great leaders. Alexander the Great, Julius Caesar, Joan of Arc, Napoleon, Mahatma Gandhi, and Mao Zedong are cited as naturally great leaders, supposedly born with a set of personal qualities which enabled them to become effective leaders.

Three questions guided the research efforts of the trait theorists during the 1930s and 1940s. First, they asked whether specific traits of great leaders could be identified. Second, they asked whether it was possible to select people for leadership positions by identifying those who possess the appropriate traits. Finally, they asked whether someone could learn the traits that characterize an effective leader. It was assumed that a finite set of individual traits—age, height, social status, fluency of speech, self-confidence, need for achievement, interpersonal skills, attractiveness, and so on—distinguished leaders from nonleaders and successful leaders from unsuccessful leaders.

Ralph Stogdill was a pioneer of the modern study of leadership.[7] He studied physical characteristics (such as appearance, height, and weight), demographic characteristics (such as age, education, and socioeconomic background), personality characteristics (such as dominance, self-confidence, and aggressiveness), intellective factors (such as intelligence, decisiveness, judgment, and knowledge), task-related characteristics (such as achievement drive, initiative, and persistence), and social characteristics (such as sociability and cooperativeness). Stogdill observed that:

> The average person who occupies a position of leadership exceeds the average member of his group in . . . (1) intelligence, (2) scholarship, (3) dependability in exercising responsibilities, (4) activity and social participation, and (5) socio-economic status.[8]

Later, after reviewing several hundred studies of leader traits, Stogdill described the successful leader this way:

> The [successful] leader is characterized by a strong drive for responsibility and task completion, vigor and persistence in pursuit of goals, venturesomeness and originality in problem solving, drive to exercise initiative in social situations, self-confidence and sense of personal

TABLE 16.1 *Traits Expected to Characterize Good Leaders*

Pleasant appearance	Intelligence
Good grooming	Self-confidence
Moderate weight	Interpersonal sensitivity
Adaptability	Tactfulness
Alertness	Persuasiveness
Assertiveness	Fluency
Cooperativeness	Creativity
Ambition	Dependability
Aggressiveness	Judgment
Enthusiasm	Achievement orientation
Persistence	Extraversion
Stress tolerance	Integrity
Responsibility	Persistence

Source: Derived from lists provided by G. A. Yukl (1981), *Leadership in organizations*, Englewood Cliffs, NJ: Prentice-Hall; A. G. Jago (1982), Leadership perspectives in theory and research, *Management Science*, 28, 317.

identity, willingness to accept consequences of decision and action, readiness to absorb interpersonal stress, willingness to tolerate frustration and delay, ability to influence other persons' behavior, and capacity to structure social interaction systems to the purpose at hand.[9]

Table 16.1 identifies some of the traits found to differentiate leaders from nonleaders. At the time, these findings were used to guide managers in the selection of leaders. More recently, however, it has been recognized that, although statistically significant, many of the effects which were attributed to certain leader traits were quite small and of limited practical value. It has also been noted that, even though certain traits increase the likelihood that a leader will be effective, they do not guarantee effectiveness. In fact, the demands of the situation in large part determine the qualities, characteristics, and skills most important for a leader to be effective. For these reasons, the notion that leaders are born, not made, has been put to rest.

Theory X and Theory Y

During the 1950s, Douglas McGregor presented a unique view on leadership that quickly became very popular among managers.[10] McGregor's work resembled that of earlier trait theorists in that he argued that effective leaders had certain identifiable characteristics. Unlike the earlier trait theorists, however, McGregor focused on the attitude and belief structures of leaders. He felt that most leaders adopted one of two basic attitude and belief structures about employees, which, in turn, influenced how they fulfilled their leadership role (see Table 16.2).

As you learned in Chapter 5, a leader who subscribes to Theory X assumes that the average individual dislikes work and is incapable of exercising adequate self-direction and self-control; thus, a Theory X leader is likely to engage in a highly controlling leadership style, treating each employee like a cog in the machinery of the organization. Theory X-oriented managers frequently create simple jobs, use routine technologies, and design organizational structures characterized by low levels of participation, high levels of authority centralization, and formalized operating procedures. Such managers concentrate on the ability of people to *do* and deemphasize the need for them to *think*. Theory Y leaders, in contrast, believe that people have a creative capacity and both the ability and desire to exercise self-direction and self-control. They typically allow employees to exercise significant amounts of discretion in their jobs and to participate in departmental and organizational decision making. Suzie Pendergast, the district claims manager, is a Theory Y leader. She permits her employees to accept or reject claims, schedule work and vacation time, and handle departmental grievances. Suzie's philosophy is that her employees are creative, resourceful, and responsible, and she, therefore, does not have to make these intradepartmental decisions on their behalf.

Researchers from the University of California at Berkeley examined Theory X and Theory Y beliefs among 3600 managers from 14 countries.[11] They found that most of the managers held assumptions about human nature that could best be classified as Theory X. Even though managers tended publicly to endorse the merits of participatory management, most of them doubted their subordinates' capacities to exercise self-direction and self-control and to contribute creatively.[12] Theory X and Theory Y attitudes may explain why some leaders behave considerately toward employees (Theory Y), whereas others concentrate on task-oriented behavior (Theory X). As McGregor has pointed out, however, a Theory Y perspective is often more effective in motivating workers to meet an organization's goals.

TABLE 16.2   *Theory X and Theory Y Assumptions*

Theory X
1. The average human being has an inherent dislike of work and will avoid it if possible.
2. Because of their dislike of work, most people must be coerced, controlled, directed, or threatened with punishment to get them to put forth adequate effort toward the achievement of organizational objectives.
3. The average human being prefers to be directed, wishes to avoid responsibility, has relatively little ambition, and wants security above all.

Theory Y
1. The expenditure of physical and mental effort in work is as natural as play or rest.
2. External control and the threat of punishment are not the only means for bringing about effort toward organizational objectives. Workers will exercise self-direction and self-control in the service of objectives to which they are committed.
3. Commitment to objectives is a function of the rewards associated with their achievement.
4. The average human being learns under proper conditions, not only to accept but to seek responsibility.
5. The capacity to exercise a relatively high degree of imagination, ingenuity, and creativity in the solution of organizational problems is widely, not narrowly, distributed in the population.
6. Under the conditions of modern industrial life, the intellectual potentialities of the average human being are only partially utilized.

Source: D. McGregor (1960), *The human side of enterprise*, New York: McGraw-Hill, 33–34, 47–48.

A CLOSER LOOK

Leadership: The Leader of Tomorrow—What Is She Like?

If you look at research on leadership from the first third of this century, you will find a profile of the person thought most likely to be an effective leader. The leader should stand six feet tall, weigh around 175 pounds, have well-conditioned (but not bulky) muscles, be "ruggedly handsome," and well groomed. The research did not usually say so outright—it was simply *assumed*—that the ideal leader was a man.

Even today, many people assume that men can lead and women cannot. "Mention women in management and the instant association in the minds of many men (and women) is: Women have babies . . . women can't be counted on to make a full-time, open-ended commitment to their careers."[1] Such beliefs are strongly rooted in age-old stereotypes, which resist change even in the face of contradictory evidence: the thousands of women who manage effectively every day.

Felice N. Schwartz is the president of Catalyst, an organization that helps organizations further the careers of women. As she says, "A significant number of working women are determined to reach the top of their field. Many of the most gifted and able leaders of the future will be women to

whom career is primary, women who are ready to make the same trade-offs that male leaders traditionally have made. Companies that do not spot and groom these women are short-sighted."[2]

Employers who are smart enough to identify and develop women as managers will soon benefit.

Ms. Schwartz notes that there has always been a shortage of individuals with the capabilities to become effective leaders. She predicts that this shortage will worsen as the United States economy shifts further into service industries where leadership is critical and as many of the young people entering the workforce increase their interests in nonwork activities. "Within a few years, as the effects of an aging baby boom are felt, the [leadership] talent of women will become indispensable. Companies that start now to develop the leadership potential of women will have a competitive edge."[3]

The task of identifying and developing effective leaders is not an easy one, and finding female leaders is particularly challenging for the traditional male CEO. "The very qualities that bespeak motivation—determination, drive, aggressiveness, single-mindedness—still tend to provoke discomfort and uncertainty . . ."[4] Employers who are smart enough to identify and develop women as managers will soon benefit by obtaining ". . . the difference between getting employees who simply put in their hours and those who perform with enthusiasm and effectiveness."[5] They will capture the best people available for leadership positions, generate important female role models for the next generation of female leaders, provide motivating evidence that anyone can advance in the organization, and create a healthier, more socially responsible environment.

1. F. N. Schwartz (8 June 1987), Don't write women off as leaders, *Fortune*, 185.
2. *Ibid.*
3. *Ibid.*
4. *Ibid.*
5. Schwartz, 188.

Ralph Stogdill helped identify leader behaviors associated with effective group performance.

Behavioral Approaches to Leadership

As interest began to wane in identifying critical leader traits, researchers turned their attention to studying *observable* leader behavior. Rather than arguing that effective leadership was a function of who a leader was or with which traits a leader had been endowed, researchers suggested that effective leadership was a function of a leader's *behavior*. During the late 1940s, major leader behavior research programs were launched at Ohio State University and at the University of Michigan. These programs focused on activity patterns, managerial roles, and a range of leaders' behaviors that could be directly observed and, perhaps, changed.

The Ohio State University Studies

During the late 1940s, a group of Ohio State University researchers, under the direction of Ralph Stogdill, began an extensive and systematic set of studies that attempted to identify leader behaviors associated with effective group performance. Data were collected from a large number of civilian and military employees describing the behavior of their supervisors. These data led to the identification of two major sets of leader behaviors: consideration and initiating structure.

Consideration is the "relationship-oriented" behavior of a leader. It is instrumental in creating and maintaining good relationships with subordinates. Consideration behaviors include being supportive and friendly, representing subordinates' interests, communicating openly with subordinates, recognizing subordinates, respecting their ideas, and sharing concern for their feelings.

Suzie Pendergast, for example, often behaves considerately toward the members of her department. When the corporate office told her that three new counties were to be added to her geographic region and two new claims personnel were to be assigned to her office, she realized this would almost certainly require at least some reassignment for everyone in her district. As soon as Suzie heard the news, she called a meeting of everyone in her office. She explained what was going to happen, acknowledged that the transition would be rough, and encouraged people to come and discuss their concerns.

Initiating structure involves "task-oriented" leader behaviors. It is instrumental in the efficient use of resources to attain organizational goals. Initiating structure behaviors include scheduling work, deciding what is to be done (and how and when to do it), providing direction to subordinates, planning, coordinating, problem solving, maintaining standards of performance, and encouraging the use of uniform procedures. When a new computer system was installed, Suzie Pendergast provided initiating structure for members of her department:

As you all know, I have been trained by our corporate management information systems department on the new computer system. I would like to take this opportunity to explain the new system. On April 21, a computer terminal will be installed on each of your desks. You will use the system to record the information that you would normally enter by hand on the old form 23A. To sign on to the computer, simply press the key labeled "alert" and then enter your employee ID when asked to do so by the computer. You are to use the computer for all noninjury settlements. Continue to use the old method for injury settlements. . . .

After the importance of consideration and initiating structure behaviors were first identified, many leaders believed that they had to behave one way or the other. If they initiated structure, they could not be considerate, and vice versa. It did not take long, however, to recognize that any combination of these two behaviors was possible. As shown in Figure 16.5, a leader's behavior can include any combination of consideration and initiating structure.

The Ohio State studies were important because they identified two critical categories of behavior that distinguish one leader from another. Both consideration and initiating structure behavior can have a significant impact on employee work attitudes and behaviors. Unfortunately, the effects of consideration and initiating structure are not consistent from situation to situation.[13] In some of the organizations studied, for example, high levels of initiating structure increased performance. In other organizations, the amount of initiating structure seemed to make little difference. Although most subordinates reported greater satisfaction when leaders acted considerately, consideration behavior appeared to increase performance in some studies but had no clear effect in others.

Initially, these mixed findings were disappointing to researchers and managers alike. It had been hoped that a profile of the most effective leader behaviors could be identified so that leaders could be trained how

FIGURE 16.5   A Contemporary View of Initiating Structure and Consideration

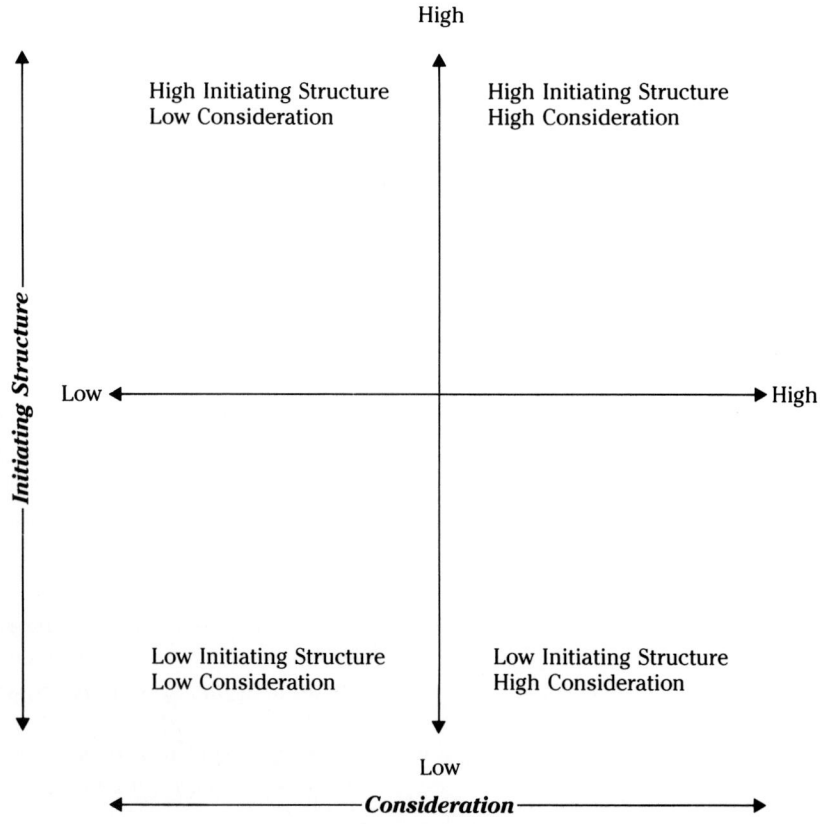

to behave. Research made clear, however, that there was no one best style of leader behavior for all situations.

The University of Michigan Studies

At about the same time that the Ohio State studies were under way, researchers at the University of Michigan also began to investigate leader behaviors. As at Ohio State, the Michigan researchers attempted to identify behavioral elements that differentiated effective from ineffective leaders.[14]

The two types of leader behavior that stood out in these studies were job-centered and employee-centered. **Job-centered behaviors** were devoted to supervisory functions, such as planning, scheduling, coordinating work activities, and providing the resources needed for task performance. **Employee-centered behaviors** included consideration and support for subordinates. These dimensions of behavior, of course, correspond closely to the dimensions of initiating structure and consideration identified at Ohio State. The similarity of the findings from two independent groups of researchers added to their credibility. As the Ohio State researchers had done, the Michigan researchers at first proposed that job-centered and employee-centered leader behaviors were mutually exclusive, at opposite ends of a continuum. They also found later that any combination of the two was possible.

Subsequent research at Michigan identified two additional behaviors associated with effective leadership. First, effective leaders were found to adopt an active leadership role by setting goals and basic guidelines for subordinates while still allowing subordinates to decide how their job was to be done and how to pace themselves. For example, as you saw, Suzie Pendergast provided her employees with company guidelines on processing claims and let them handle all aspects of the process, as long as they met departmental goals and followed organizational guidelines. Second, effective leaders were found to exert influence upward to obtain resources and the support needed for their subordinates. As it turns out, this was something Suzie Pendergast also did quite well. When she discovered, for example, that her employees were uncomfortable about using a new computer system, she convinced her boss to allow each member of her department to spend a day at corporate headquarters learning how to use the new system.

The studies at Michigan were important because they reinforced the importance of leaders' behaviors. They provided the basis for later theories that identified specific, effective matches of work situations and leader behaviors.

System 4 Leadership

Influenced heavily by the work of his University of Michigan colleagues, Rensis Likert identified the *System 4* approach to organization design (see Chapter 12).[15] According to Likert, a System 4 leader should provide:

- *Supportive behavior.* This includes understanding, supporting, dealing with subordinates' problems, providing recognition, keeping subordinates informed, and showing appreciation (similar to the

Job-centered behaviors are devoted to planning, scheduling, and coordinating work activities.

considerate behavior identified in the Ohio State University leadership studies). A supervisor should deal with each subordinate in such a way that the subordinate "will view the experience as supportive and one which builds and maintains his or her sense of personal worth and importance."[16] Suzie Pendergast, for example, was behaving in a supportive fashion when she took the time to give her followers advance notice of the impending changes and when she offered her assistance to help them cope with the new arrangements.

- *Group methods of supervision.* Supervision is exercised through group meetings instead of one-on-one relationships. Likert suggested that effective leadership is group rather than individual oriented. Managers should guide group discussions along paths that are supportive, constructive, and problem oriented. When Suzie met to inform subordinates of the new territorial and staff assignments, she was capitalizing on the effectiveness of the group method.

- *High performance goals.* For effective group performance, a leader should guide the group toward setting high (although realistic) and specific performance goals. Suzie's long-standing practice of meeting with each of her followers to set specific, difficult, but reachable goals shows her familiarity with this third System 4 behavior.

- *Linking-pin functions.* As discussed in Chapter 12, managers in their role as formal leaders become central points for collecting, dispensing, and coordinating information and influence among organizational units. Through this system, communication, influence, interest representation, cohesiveness, and organizational decision making are enhanced. Suzie fills this role in part by attending a weekly meeting of all managers at her district claims office. At these meetings, Suzie shares information on the claims department with managers of other departments and negotiates the resources needed by her department.

- *Technical expertise functions.* The leader serves as a source of expert knowledge for subordinates, thereby making their work more effective. Whenever claims technicians encounter a difficult claim, they come to Suzie for advice. Her followers know that she is an avid reader of the trade journals and attends monthly update sessions on company claims practices.

Likert reasoned that the leadership behaviors associated with System 4 would produce favorable attitudes toward leadership, open channels of communication, create group cohesiveness and cooperation, motivate employees, and ensure a high level of reciprocal influence between leaders and subordinates. As you can see in Figure 16.6, this interactive process should enhance organizational and group effectiveness (high productivity, both in quantity and quality and low rates of absenteeism, turnover, and grievance).

The Managerial Grid(R)

Much of the credit for spreading knowledge about important leader behaviors to managers must go to Robert R. Blake and Jane S. Mouton, who developed a method of classifying styles of leadership compatible with many of the ideas from the Ohio State and Michigan studies.[17] In their

FIGURE 16.6
Likert's Leadership Process Model

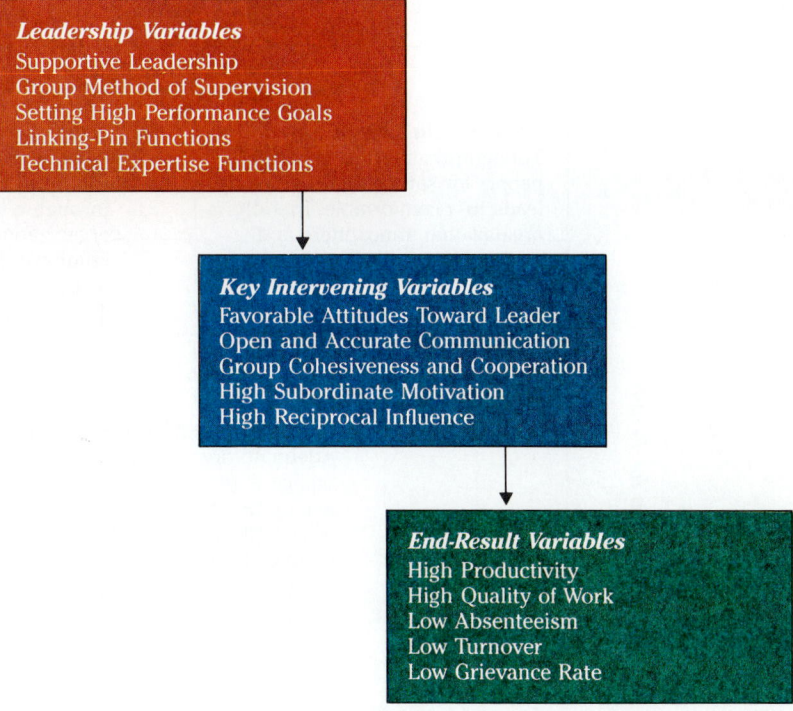

Leadership Variables
Supportive Leadership
Group Method of Supervision
Setting High Performance Goals
Linking-Pin Functions
Technical Expertise Functions

Key Intervening Variables
Favorable Attitudes Toward Leader
Open and Accurate Communication
Group Cohesiveness and Cooperation
High Subordinate Motivation
High Reciprocal Influence

End-Result Variables
High Productivity
High Quality of Work
Low Absenteeism
Low Turnover
Low Grievance Rate

From *Leadership in Organizations* by Garl A. Yukl, p. 117. Copyright © 1981 by Prentice-Hall, Inc. Reprinted by permission of Prentice-Hall, Inc., Englewood Cliffs, New Jersey.

classification scheme, *concern for production* involves an emphasis on output, cost effectiveness, and (in for-profit organizations) a concern for profits. *Concern for people* involves promoting friendships, helping subordinates with work, and paying attention to issues of importance to employees. As their Managerial Grid(R) shows, any combination of these two leader behaviors is possible (see Figure 16.7). The combinations produce five distinct styles of leadership:

- *Country club* (1,9). A country club leader emphasizes concern for people but devotes little time and energy to production.
- *Impoverished* (1,1). An impoverished leader shows a low level of concern for both people and production.
- *Organization person management* (5,5). This leader demonstrates a moderate concern for both people and production.
- *Authority-obedience* (9,1). An authority-obedience leader shows a low concern for people but has a strong production orientation.
- *Team* (9,9). A team leader, also commonly referred to as a 9,9 leader, simultaneously shows a strong regard for employees and a strong production orientation.

Blake and Mouton contend that the team leader (9,9) style is universally the most effective. Furthermore, they claim that experienced managers prefer the team style of leadership in many types of situations.[18] The fact that the 9,9 style may be preferred, however, does not mean that it necessarily is effective. Unfortunately, although the Managerial Grid(R) is appealing and well-structured, research evidence suggests that there is no universally effective style of leadership (9,9 or otherwise).[19]

FIGURE 16.7 *Blake and Mouton's Managerial Grid(R)*

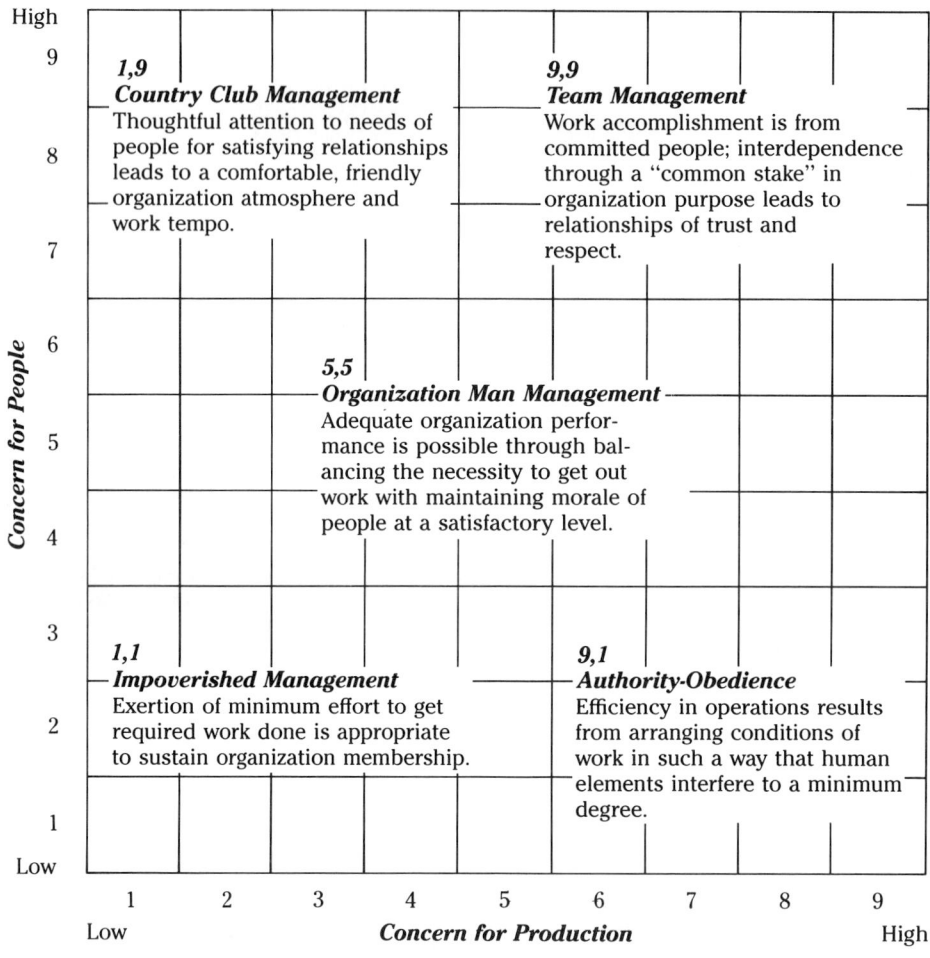

Source: R. R. Blake and J. S. Mouton (1985), *The managerial grid III*, Houston, TX: Gulf, 11.

Situational Approaches to Leadership

Geoff Priest was a drill instructor (DI) for the United States Marine Corps. Tough and extremely task-oriented, he became one of the most effective DIs in the corps. Geoff's leadership style was tough and straightforward. He wasted little time talking with recruits; he talked *at* them. Rather than discuss recruits' problems, he told them to keep their problems to themselves. He carefully and completely explained what was expected of his subordinates and then demanded compliance.

At age forty-five, Geoff Priest retired from the Marine Corps with a full pension. Anxious to continue working and to supplement his pension, he accepted a job as a supervisor in a small manufacturing plant. Convinced that he knew the most effective way to lead subordinates, Geoff treated his subordinates, who belonged to a union, in the same way that he had treated Marine recruits. The results were disastrous. Satisfaction among workers plummeted, absenteeism increased, productivity dropped, and many grievances were filed against Geoff by his subordinates. How could Geoff have been such an effective leader in the Marine Corps but so unsuccessful in his new leadership role?

As you have seen in this chapter, many people have assumed—erroneously—that there is one most effective leadership style regardless of the situation; however, different situations demand different leadership qualities or behaviors. As early as 1948, Ralph Stogdill stated that "the qualities, characteristics, and skills required in a leader are determined to a large extent by the demands of the situation in which he is to function as a leader."[20] Geoff Priest learned this lesson the hard way.

Because the characteristics of a situation are so important, it is necessary to identify them and then specify the appropriate match of leader traits or behaviors. One such situation-contingent behavioral approach, the Vroom and Yetton normative theory of leadership, was discussed in Chapter 8 on decision-making tools because it focuses primarily on the conditions under which leaders should select particular types of decision-making strategies. Two other well-known situational approaches to leadership are Fiedler's contingency model and House's path-goal theory.

Fiedler's Contingency Model

One of the earliest and best-known situation-contingent leadership theories was set forth by Fred E. Fiedler from the University of Washington.[21] This theory is known as the **contingency theory of leadership.** Fiedler classified leaders according to an underlying trait, described situations that leaders face, and identified optimal matches between leaders and situations. According to Fiedler, organizations must do the same thing: assess the leader, assess the situation, and construct proper matches between the two.

Fred E. Fiedler developed a popular contingency theory of leadership. His work helped show the importance of good leader-situation matches.

The Leader Trait   Fiedler measured traits by asking leaders about their **least preferred co-worker (LPC).** Leaders described the person with whom they *least* wanted to work along a number of dimensions, such as pleasant/unpleasant, friendly/unfriendly, cold/warm, open/closed, untrustworthy/trustworthy, kind/unkind, and sincere/insincere. These descriptions are presented in Figure 16.8. The most recent interpretation of the LPC score is that it reflects a leader's underlying disposition toward others.

Fiedler states that leaders with high LPC scores are *relationship oriented*. They tend to evaluate their least-preferred co-workers in fairly favorable terms. These individuals, it is argued, need to develop and maintain close interpersonal relationships. Task accomplishment is a secondary need to this type of leader and becomes important only after the need for relationships is reasonably well satisfied. In contrast, leaders with low LPC scores tend to evaluate the individuals with whom they would least like to work fairly negatively. They are *task oriented* rather than relationship oriented. Only when tasks are accomplished in an effective and efficient manner are low LPC leaders likely to work on establishing good social and interpersonal relations.

The Situational Factor Some situations favor leaders more than others do. To Fiedler, situational favorableness is the degree to which a leader has control and influence and, therefore, feels that he or she can determine the outcomes of a group interaction.[22] Three factors work together to determine how favorable a situation is to a leader:

- *Leader-member relations*. The quality of the relationship between a leader and followers is the strongest determinant of situation favorability. This relationship reflects the leader's degree of acceptance by the group and the members' level of loyalty to the leader. Group

FIGURE 16.8   Fiedler's LPC Scale

Think of the person with whom you can work least well. This may be someone you work with now or someone you knew in the past. It does not have to be the person you like least well but should be the person with whom you had the most difficulty in getting a job done. Describe this person as he or she appears to you.

	8	7	6	5	4	3	2	1	
Pleasant	8	7	6	5	4	3	2	1	Unpleasant
Friendly	8	7	6	5	4	3	2	1	Unfriendly
Rejecting	1	2	3	4	5	6	7	8	Accepting
Helpful	8	7	6	5	4	3	2	1	Frustrating
Unenthusiastic	1	2	3	4	5	6	7	8	Enthusiastic
Tense	1	2	3	4	5	6	7	8	Relaxed
Distant	1	2	3	4	5	6	7	8	Close
Cold	1	2	3	4	5	6	7	8	Warm
Cooperative	8	7	6	5	4	3	2	1	Uncooperative
Supportive	8	7	6	5	4	3	2	1	Hostile
Boring	1	2	3	4	5	6	7	8	Interesting
Quarrelsome	1	2	3	4	5	6	7	8	Harmonious
Self-Assured	8	7	6	5	4	3	2	1	Hesitant
Efficient	8	7	6	5	4	3	2	1	Inefficient
Gloomy	1	2	3	4	5	6	7	8	Cheerful
Open	8	7	6	5	4	3	2	1	Guarded

Note: LPC score is the sum of the answers to these sixteen questions. High scores indicate a relationship orientation; low scores, a task orientation.

Source: F. E. Fiedler and M. M. Chemers (1974), Leadership and effective management, Glenview, IL: Scott, Foresman.

A CLOSER LOOK

Failed Leadership: The Bottom Line Is Not Enough

In 1982, 1983, and 1984, Dravo Corporation, an international engineering and construction firm, lost money. In an attempt to turn the company around, Dravo named Thomas F. Faught, Jr., president and chief executive officer. He cut costs. He reduced employment by almost 50 percent. In both 1985 and 1986, Dravo made money. The value of the company's stock increased over 50 percent. Faught clearly had started the company on a fiscal turnaround. These and other actions led business analysts to conclude that the company had been put back on a successful path.

In January 1987, however, Faught was fired by the Dravo board of directors. Why in the world would the company rid itself of the person who had engineered its comeback? Simply put, there is more to management than making money. Mr. Faught was fired, in large part, because he was not a good enough *leader*.

Apparently, Mr. Faught remained distant from all but a few top managers. In his interactions he was often erratic, alienating and eventually driving away a number of key members of the organization. "Mr. Faught's lieutenants complained that he gave contradictory orders and ruled by fear."[1] He gave himself a raise while freezing or even cutting the salaries of subordinates. "One month he would be demanding from a subordinate completion of existing orders and the next fuming that the subordinate wasn't finding new business. . . ."[2]

The effects were more problematic. For instance, James P. Kelly, senior vice-president to Mr. Faught, was considered one of the company's most talented managers. He tried to reason with Faught but finally left Dravo and soon lured away a number of other key Dravo employees. Kelly found that he "was able to pick up the best Dravo people because they were so disenchanted."[3] Dravo may have been doing well financially for the first time in years, but managers were so unhappy with the company's leadership that they chose to leave.

Leadership is part of only one of the four major functions of management—directing—but without effective leadership, managers will find it difficult to exercise their other functions. As Dravo's experiences showed, performance is not just a matter of profit.

1. S. H. Lubove (24 February 1987), Dravo seeks leadership to pursue turnaround strategy: Chief's downfall shows how performance isn't judged only by profit, *The Wall Street Journal*, 6.
2. *Ibid.*
3. *Ibid.*

member support, an ability to work well together, loyalty, and dependability are some of the attributes that enhance situational favorableness for a leader.

- *Task structure.* The second most important determinant of situation favorability is the degree of structure of the task to be performed. A highly structured task provides a detailed, unambiguous goal, and this structure clarifies how to achieve this goal. Situational favorableness rises as the amount of task structure increases.

- *Position power.* Fiedler uses the term *position power* to refer to a leader's direct ability to influence subordinates. Position power may include legitimate, reward, coercive, expert, resource, and referent power (the sources of power discussed in Chapter 15). The presence of position power enhances situational favorableness.

FIGURE 16.9   *Fiedler's Contingency Model Leader-Situation Matches*

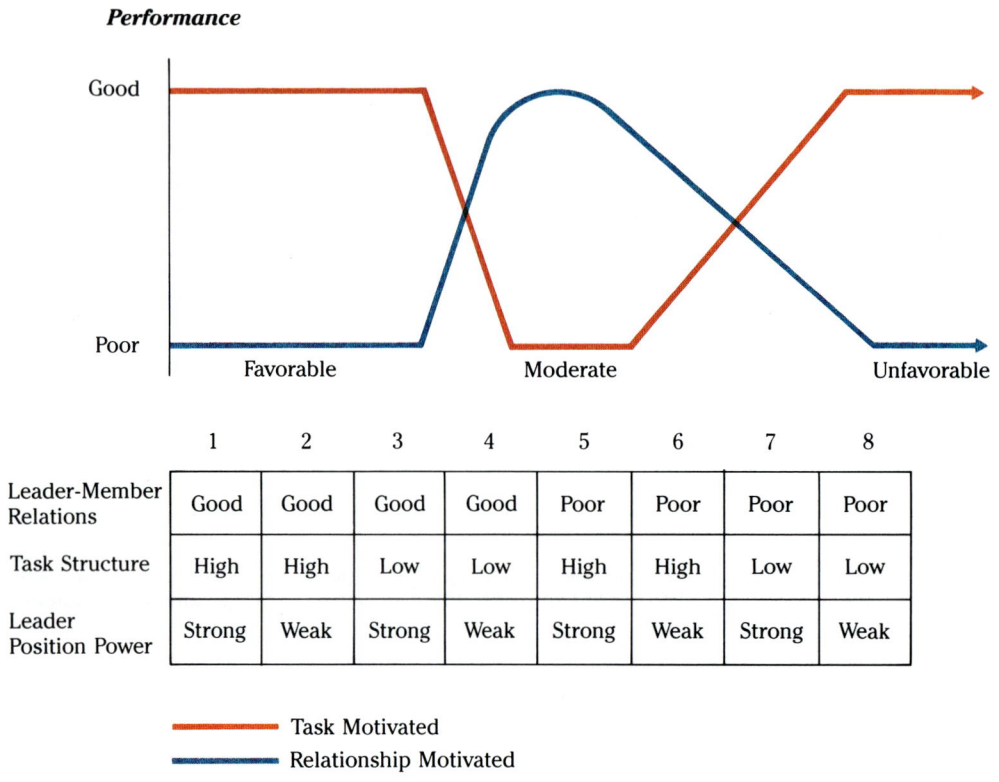

Performance

	1	2	3	4	5	6	7	8
Leader-Member Relations	Good	Good	Good	Good	Poor	Poor	Poor	Poor
Task Structure	High	High	Low	Low	High	High	Low	Low
Leader Position Power	Strong	Weak	Strong	Weak	Strong	Weak	Strong	Weak

———— Task Motivated
━━━━ Relationship Motivated

Source: F. E. Fiedler and M. M. Chemers (1974), *Leadership and effective management*, Glenview, IL: Scott, Foresman.

The situation is most favorable for a leader when the relationship between the leader and group members is good, when the task is highly structured, and the leader's position power is strong (Cell 1 in Figure 16.9). The least favorable situation for a leader exists when the relationship between the leader and group members is poor, the task is unstructured, and the leader's position power is weak (Cell 8) in Figure 16.9). The types of leader behavior needed to achieve high levels of group performance under favorable conditions are not the same as the types of behavior needed to achieve group performance under unfavorable conditions. Fiedler argues that appropriate leader behavior can be obtained by choosing a leader with the LPC score that matches the situation.

Leader-Situation Matches   Some combinations of leaders and situations work well and others do not. In search of the best combinations, Fiedler examined a large number of leadership situations, ranging from those on high-school basketball teams to those among boards of directors. He studied ROTC cadet officers, supervisors in a steel plant, bomber crews, and many others. Results of this research indicate that relationship-oriented (high LPC) leaders are quite effective under conditions of intermediate favorability, such as those shown in Cells 3 through 6 in Figure 16.9, but ineffective in highly favorable (Cells 1 and 2) or highly unfavorable (Cells 7 and 8) situations. Fiedler attributes the success of relationship-oriented leaders in situations with intermediate favorableness to the leader's nondirective, permissive attitude in a situation where a more directive attitude could lead to anxiety in followers, conflict in the group, and a lack of cooperation.

For highly favorable and unfavorable situations, task-oriented leaders (those with a low LPC) are very effective. Under highly favorable conditions, the leader-member relationship is good, task structure is high, and leader position power is strong. As tasks are accomplished, a task-oriented leader is likely to allow the group to perform its highly structured tasks without the imposition of more task-directed behavior from the leader. The job gets done without the need for the leader's direction. Under unfavorable conditions, task-oriented behaviors, such as setting goals, detailing work methods, and guiding and controlling work behaviors, move the group toward task accomplishment.

What about a leader with a mid-range LPC score? This type of leader can be quite effective under many different circumstances, sometimes more effective than either high or low LPC leaders.[23] Middle LPC leaders, it appears, are neither preoccupied with task accomplishment (as low LPC leaders might be) nor preoccupied with establishing relationships (as high LPC leaders might be). Consequently, they may find it easier to deal with the task of being a leader and adjust leadership style as the nature of the situation changes. Under conditions of low favorability, for example, a middle LPC leader can be task-oriented to achieve performance but show consideration for and allow employees to proceed on their own under conditions of high situational favorability.

Fiedler argued that most leaders have a relatively unchangeable, dominant leadership style, be it task or relationship oriented. Because he feels it is difficult to change a person's leadership style, Fiedler argues that job situations should be designed to fit the leader rather than the other way around.[24] Managers must place leaders into leadership situations carefully or modify the work situation if they want a favorable match between a leader and a situation.

Controversy Over the Theory   Fiedler's theory of leadership has generated controversy among those who study leadership in organizations. As some see it, Fiedler's theory characterizes leaders through reference to attitudes or personality traits (LPC) but explains the effectiveness of leaders through reference to their behaviors. Fiedler assumes that leaders with a certain trait (high or low LPC) will behave in a particular fashion.

Most research on Fiedler's theory has been conducted by Fiedler and his colleagues, many of whom are Fiedler's students or former students. Unfortunately, little of this research has provided complete tests of the model. Those tests which have been conducted have often produced mixed or contradictory findings.[25] Perhaps of most concern has been a lack of clarity about the true meaning of the LPC measure. Look at Figure 16.8 one more time and ask yourself what those items really measure.

The fact is, Fiedler's theory can often identify appropriate leader-situation matches, and this is very useful, but it is not clear why the theory works. Fiedler's theory is, therefore, considered by many to be a "black

According to the path-goal theory, leader behavior should match the work environment.

box'' theory of leadership. It describes the elements that enter a ''box'' (attitudes toward others) and shows the product that leaves the box (leader effectiveness). Hidden from the viewer, however, is the process inside the box which transformed the original components into the final product. In the case of Fiedler's theory, missing is the explanation of how attitudes determine effectiveness through behavior.

The Path-Goal Theory

Robert J. House and Martin Evans, from the University of Toronto, have developed a useful leadership theory that strongly agrees with one of the principles underlying Fiedler's theory of leadership—but forcefully disagrees with another. House and Evans accept the notion that the type of leadership needed to enhance organizational effectiveness is contingent on the situation in which a leader is placed. A leader may, therefore, be effective in one situation but quite ineffective in another. Whereas Fiedler argues that a leader's trait (LPC) determines whether leader and situation produce a healthy match, House and Evans focus on the observable behavior of the leader. Also, whereas Fiedler feels that the situation must fit the leader, House and Evans believe that healthy leader-situation matches can be obtained either by matching the situation to the leader or by modifying the behavior of the leader to fit the situation.

The model of leadership advanced by House and Evans has been called the **path-goal theory of leadership** because it suggests that an effective leader provides subordinates with a *path* to a valued *goal*. According to House:

> *The motivational function of the leader consists of increasing personal payoffs to subordinates for work-goal attainment, and making the path to these payoffs easier to travel by clarifying it, reducing road blocks and pitfalls, and increasing the opportunities for personal satisfaction enroute.*[26]

Effective leaders, therefore, provide rewards that are valued by employees. These rewards may be pay, recognition, promotions, or any other reward that gives employees an incentive to work hard to achieve performance goals. Effective leaders also give clear instructions so that ambiguities about work are reduced and employees understand how to do their jobs effectively. They provide coaching, guidance, and training so that employees can perform the task expected of them. They also remove barriers to task accomplishment, correcting shortages of materials, inoperative machinery, or interfering policies.

According to path-goal theory, different kinds of leadership are appropriate for different kinds of situations. First, leader behavior must match the work environment, which can differ, for example, in the extent to which jobs are structured. If a leader is supervising experienced employees who work on a highly structured assembly line, the leader does not need to spend much time telling the workers how to do their jobs—they already know how. The leader of a group of laborers excavating an archeological site, however, will need to spend a great deal of time telling the workers how to excavate and care for the relics they uncover. Second, leader behavior must match the characteristics of those being led. The leadership style that motivates employees with strong

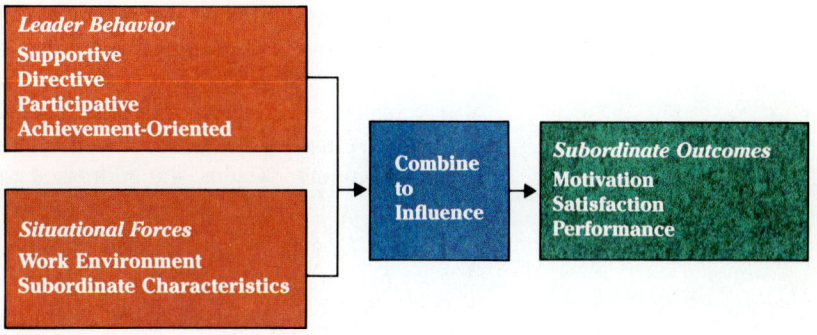

FIGURE 16.10 The Path-Goal Leadership Model

needs for autonomy, for example, is different from the style necessary to motivate and satisfy employees with weaker needs for autonomy. For example, a group vice-president who leads executives with strong needs for autonomy must use a different style of motivating and directing from a drill sergeant who teaches enlistees to clean their weapons.

The challenge facing leaders is basically two-fold. First, they must analyze situations and identify the most appropriate leadership style. Second, they must develop the capacity to be flexible enough to use different leadership styles as appropriate. The degree to which leadership behavior matches situational factors will determine the level of subordinate motivation, satisfaction, and performance (see Figure 16.10).

According to path-goal theory, there are four important dimensions of leader behavior, each of which is suited to a particular set of situational demands.[27] Examples of good matches between leader behaviors and situational demands are depicted in Table 16.3.

Supportive Leadership Effective leaders demonstrate concern for the well-being and personal needs of subordinates. Supportive leaders are friendly, approachable, and considerate to individuals in the workplace. (Note the similarity to what the Ohio State studies called "consideration" and the Michigan studies called "employee-centeredness.") Supportive leadership is especially effective when a subordinate is performing a boring, stressful, frustrating, tedious, or unpleasant task. Leaders who are understanding, considerate, and supportive say, in effect, "I care about you as a person" and can help relieve subordinates of some of the

TABLE 16.3 Leader Behaviors to Match Situational Needs

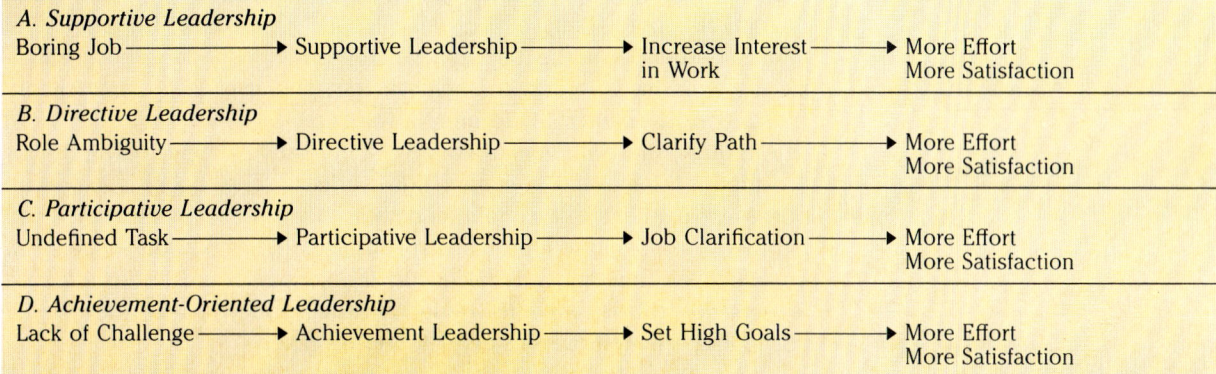

A. Supportive Leadership
Boring Job ⟶ Supportive Leadership ⟶ Increase Interest in Work ⟶ More Effort / More Satisfaction

B. Directive Leadership
Role Ambiguity ⟶ Directive Leadership ⟶ Clarify Path ⟶ More Effort / More Satisfaction

C. Participative Leadership
Undefined Task ⟶ Participative Leadership ⟶ Job Clarification ⟶ More Effort / More Satisfaction

D. Achievement-Oriented Leadership
Lack of Challenge ⟶ Achievement Leadership ⟶ Set High Goals ⟶ More Effort / More Satisfaction

unpleasantness of the experience. If a task is difficult and a subordinate has low self-esteem, supportive leadership can reduce some of the subordinate's anxiety, increase his or her confidence, and increase satisfaction and determination as well. For example, when Suzie Pendergast noticed that her employees were worried about learning a new computer system, she addressed these concerns.

Directive Leadership Effective leaders set goals and performance expectations, let subordinates know what is expected, provide guidance, establish rules and procedures to guide work, and schedule and coordinate the activities of employees. (Note the similarity to what the Ohio State studies called "initiating structure" and the Michigan studies called "job-centeredness.") Directive leadership is called for when there are high levels of role ambiguity, such as when the ultimate goal and/or the means to achieve that goal are unclear. A directive leader says, in effect, "Here is the way to do your job well." This can increase employees' effort, job satisfaction, and job performance by removing uncertainty and providing needed guidance. Steve Orth effectively uses a directing leadership style with a new group of programmers hired to develop a computer program. He tells them what language and program structure to use, specifies the characteristics of the new product, makes work assignments, and provides a schedule for the project's completion.

Participative Leadership Effective leaders consult with subordinates about job-related activities and consider their opinions and suggestions when making decisions. Participative leadership is effective when tasks are unstructured. By saying, "Let's work together to identify the best way to do this job," a participative leader helps subordinates learn more about the task and increase their confidence. This increased confidence, improved performance, and participation itself increase satisfaction. Participative leadership is used to great effect when leaders need help in identifying work procedures and where followers have the expertise to provide this help.

Achievement-Oriented Leadership Effective leaders set challenging goals, seek improvement in performance, emphasize excellence, and demonstrate confidence in subordinates' ability to attain high standards. If a task lacks inherent challenge, a leader who sets challenging goals for the employee and says, "This is what I would like you to do. I know it will be difficult, but I believe you can succeed" increases the amount of interest and effort on the job. Achievement-oriented leaders, thus, capitalize on employees' needs for achievement and use goal-setting theory (described in Chapter 14) to great advantage.

Although the path-goal theory is still relatively new, research has provided a fair amount of support for its ideas.[28] The theory is important because it explains why certain leaders do better in some situations than in others, and because it provides specific guidelines on *how* leaders can be effective. The theory is based on the simple premise that effective leaders control the rewards valued by their subordinates, they clarify goals, and they remove obstacles to performance.

Substitutes for and Neutralizers of Leadership

Relatively recently, several factors have been discovered that can substitute for or neutralize the effects of leader behavior (see Table 16.4).[29] Sometimes it is an employee's characteristics that make leadership less necessary, as when a master craftsperson or highly skilled worker performs up to his or her own high standards without needing outside prompting. Sometimes it is a task's characteristics that take over, as when the work itself—solving an interesting problem or working on a familiar job—is intrinsically satisfying. Sometimes the characteristics of an organization make leadership less necessary, as when work rules are so clear and specific that workers know exactly what they must do without help from the leader.

Substitutes for leadership behavior can clarify role expectations, motivate employees, or satisfy employees (making it unnecessary for the leader to attempt to do so). In some cases, these substitutes supplement the behavior of a leader. The presence of a highly professional workforce is a good example of this. Standardized accounting practices, for example, are established by the accounting profession. A good accountant knows and follows these standards and does not need a leader to develop or administer the guidelines. In other words, some substitutes act as substitutes when they are necessary but do not interfere when not

TABLE 16.4   *Substitutes and Neutralizers of Leader Behavior*

Substitute or Neutralizer	Leader Behavior Influenced	
	Supportive Leadership	Instrumental Leadership
A. Subordinate Characteristics:		
1. Experience, ability, training		Substitute
2. "Professional" orientation	Substitute	Substitute
3. Indifference toward rewards offered by organization	Neutralizer	Neutralizer
B. Task Characteristics:		
1. Structured, routine, unambiguous task		Substitute
2. Feedback provided by task		Substitute
3. Intrinsically satisfying task	Substitute	
C. Organization Characteristics:		
1. Cohesive work group	Substitute	Substitute
2. Low position power (leader lacks control over organizational rewards)	Neutralizer	Neutralizer
3. Formalization (explicit plans, goals, areas of responsibility)		Substitute
4. Inflexibility (rigid, unyielding rules and procedures)		Neutralizer
5. Leader located apart from subordinates with only limited communication possible	Neutralizer	Neutralizer

Source: Based on G. A. Yukl (1981), *Leadership in organizations*, Englewood Cliffs, NJ: Prentice-Hall, 163.

Standardized accounting practices can be used as a substitute for leadership.

needed. Effective leaders can use them to good advantage. When an accounting manager need only say, "Follow standard procedures" to provide much of the structure needed by the organization's accountants, for example, it allows the manager to spend more time on other leader behavior.

Neutralizers of leadership are not always so helpful; they prevent leaders from acting as they wish. A computer-paced assembly line, for example, prevents a leader from using initiating structure behavior to pace the line. A union contract that specifies that workers be paid according to seniority prevents a leader from dispensing merit-based pay. Sometimes, of course, neutralizers can be beneficial. Union contracts, for example, clarify disciplinary proceedings and identify the responsibilities of both management and labor. Leaders must be aware of the presence of neutralizers and their effects so that they can work at either eliminating troublesome neutralizers or take advantage of any benefits that accompany them (such as the clarity of responsibilities provided by a union contract). If a leader's effectiveness is being neutralized by a poor communication system, for example, the leader might try to remove the neutralizer by developing (or convincing the organization to develop) a more effective system.

Charismatic Leadership: A Trait Reborn

Ronald Reagan, Jesse Jackson, and Evita Peron have something in common with Martin Luther King, Jr., Corazon Aquino, and Winston Churchill. The effectiveness of each of these leaders is (was) due in part to **charisma,** a special personal magnetic charm or appeal that arouses loyalty and enthusiasm. Each exerted considerable personal influence to bring about major events.

Sociologist Max Weber showed an interest in charismatic leadership during the early 1920s, calling charismatic leaders people who possess legitimate power that arises from "exceptional sanctity, heroism, or exemplary character."[30] Today, there is renewed interest in people who can "single-handedly" effect changes in even very large organizations.

The charismatic leadership phenomenon involves a unique interplay between the attributes of the leader and followers' needs, values, beliefs, and perceptions.[31] At the extreme, leader-follower relationships are characterized by followers': unquestioning acceptance, trust in the leader's beliefs, affection, willing obedience, emulation of and identification with the leader, emotional involvement with his or her mission, and feelings of self-efficacy directed toward the leader's mission.[32] What are the characteristics of these people who can exert such a strong influence over their followers? Characteristics of a charismatic leader include a strong need for power and the tendency to rely heavily on referent power as the primary power base.[33] Charismatic leaders also are strongly self-confident and convinced of the rightness of their own beliefs and ideals. This self-confidence and strength of conviction tend to make other people trust a charismatic leader's judgment, unconditionally following

Steven Kerr

Steven Kerr is Dean of Faculty at the University of Southern California's Business School and is president-elect of the Academy of Management.

1. Many who have read your comments on substitutes for and neutralizers of leadership conclude that these create problems for leaders. Is it possible for leaders to use substitutes or neutralizers to their advantage?

Neutralizers are unlikely to be viewed positively by a leader and, to the extent they are consciously constructed, will probably be by someone who desires to limit a leader's power and influence over subordinates—a leader's leader, for example, or the subordinates themselves. Substitutes for leadership, on the other hand, are often employed by an effective leader to his or her own advantage. One example might be for a leader to make use of subordinates' formal training and expertise as substitutes for guidance the leader is for some reason unable to provide personally. As another example, a leader may elect to use a formula-based reward system as a substitute for personal salary judgments that would inevitably appear to subordinates as arbitrary.

2. There has been discussion in the business press recently of the resurgence of the charismatic leader. Should organizations seek charismatic leaders and, if so, why?

While most effective leaders are able to clarify goals and paths to goals, charismatic leaders are uniquely able to *create* goals and articulate them in a way that galvanizes subordinates and those who are not subordinates—indeed, those who may not even be members of the organization. Charismatic leaders, therefore, can have an extraordinary impact on even the most bureaucratic enterprise. Because a charismatic leader's power base is inherently personal, that is, vested in the leader's personality rather than in the office per se, the death or retirement of a charismatic leader is usually followed by a dramatic drop-off in the organization's energy level and sense of purpose. This circumstance, coupled with the fact that charismatic leaders typically spend little time grooming their successors, means that replacement of a charismatic leader is one of the most difficult tasks confronting any organization.

3. How important is leader behavior as a determinant of organizational effectiveness?

The impetus to study substitutes and neutralizers began as a reaction against the relatively weak results typically obtained by our theories and models of leadership. These weak results do not mean that leader behavior is never an important determinant of effectiveness; rather, they remind us that substitutes and neutralizers in many organizations negate the potential power of hierarchical leadership. As I have mentioned before, our field would greatly benefit from the development of a different kind of situational theory of leadership, which would explicitly restrict its predictions to those situations in which formal leadership really should make a difference.

the leader's mission and directives for action.[34] The result is a strong bond between leader and followers, a bond built primarily around these attributes of the leader's personality. Charismatic leaders also are likely to:

- Manage their followers' perceptions of the leader's competence. This appears, for example, to be at least one objective of the frequent meetings conducted by Lotus Development's CEO Jim Manzi and chairman Mitchell Kapor with all Lotus employees during the late 1980s.
- Articulate ideological goals for followers that anchor the group's goals and mission in deeply rooted values, beliefs, and aspirations, as Corazon Aquino did in requesting support by reminding Filipinos that "the support is not for me, but for your country, for yourselves, and your prosperity. . . ."[35]
- Paint exciting visions of the future to make current work more exciting, inspirational, and meaningful. Consider Ronald Reagan's "lift up America" theme repeated throughout his two presidential campaigns in the 1980s.
- Encourage followers to rely on and have hope for the future. Recall Martin Luther King, Jr.'s, ". . . dream that one day this nation will rise up and live out the true meaning of its creeds . . . we will be free one day."[36]
- Set high goals and expectations for followers, while expressing confidence in their ability to achieve these ideals. Oral Roberts apparently convinced followers that he was willing to stake his life on the conviction that they would generate over $8 million.
- Instill a strong belief in group members that they possess the ability to meet the leader's high expectations. In his first inaugural address, for example, Franklin Delano Roosevelt inspired Americans to recognize ". . . that we cannot merely take, but we must give as well; that if we are to go forward we must move as a trained and loyal army willing to sacrifice for the good of a common discipline. . . . We are,

TABLE 16.5 *Behavioral Characteristics of Charismatic and Noncharismatic Leaders*

	Noncharismatic Leader	Charismatic Leader
Relation to Status quo	Essentially agrees with status quo and strives to maintain it	Essentially opposed to status quo and strives to change it
Future Goal	Goal not too discrepant from status quo	Idealized vision which is highly discrepant from status quo
Likableness	Shared perspective makes him or her likable	Shared perspective and idealized vision makes him or her a likable and honorable hero worthy of identification and imitation
Trustworthiness	Disinterested advocacy in persuasion attempts	Disinterested advocacy by incurring great personal risk and cost
Expertise	Expert in using available means to achieve goals within the framework of the existing order	Expert in using unconventional means to transcend the existing order
Behavior	Conventional, conforming to existing norms	Unconventional or counternormative
Environmental Sensitivity	Low need for environmental sensitivity to maintain status quo	High need for environmental sensitivity for changing the status quo
Articulation	Weak articulation of goals and motivation to lead	Strong articulation of future vision and motivation to lead
Power Base	Position power and personal power (based on reward, expertise, and liking for a friend who is a similar other)	Personal power (based on expertise, respect, and admiration for a unique hero)
Leader-Follower Relationship	Egalitarian, consensus seeking, or directive	Elitist, entrepreneur, and exemplary
	Nudges or orders people to share his or her views	Transforms people to share the radical changes advocated

Source: Modifed from J. A. Conger and R. N. Kanungo (1987), Toward a behavioral theory of charismatic leadership in organizational settings, *Academy of Management Review*, 12, 641.

I know, ready and willing to submit our lives and property to such discipline because it makes possible a leadership which aims at a larger good.''[37]

Table 16.5 summarizes a number of the behavioral characteristics of charismatic and noncharismatic leaders.

Today there is renewed interest in people who can bring about major organizational transformations, such as Lee Iacocca did when he saved Chrysler Corporation from bankruptcy.[38] **Transformational leadership,** so-called because the leader inspires enough strategic change in an organization actually to transform its identity, relies on leaders' charisma and ''deeply held personal value systems that include such values as

Reprinted with special permission of King Features Syndicate, Inc.

justice and integrity."[39] John Welch of General Electric, for example, has been the transformational leader guiding the metamorphosis of GE during the late 1980s. Welch divested the company of many historically key product lines that had lost their previous value and began the construction of a new corporate identity. Of at least equal importance were the changes in the GE culture nurtured by Welch.

Although there has been little empirical research on charismatic and transformational leadership, many people believe that major organizational events can be influenced by the leadership efforts of people with such magnetic personalities. Most attention until now has been focused on charismatic leadership at the top of organizations. It will be interesting to learn whether charismatic leadership is a significant factor at other levels in the organizational hierarchy.

Leadership in Review

Leadership is a primary vehicle for fulfilling the directing function of management. Because of its importance, theorists, researchers, and practitioners have devoted a tremendous amount of attention and energy to unlocking the secrets of effective leadership. They have kept at this search for perhaps a greater period of time than for any other single issue related to management.

Organizations typically have both formal and informal leaders. Their leadership is effective for virtually identical reasons. Leadership and management are not the same. Although effective leadership is a necessary part of effective management, the overall management role is much larger than leadership alone. Managers plan, organize, direct, and control. As leaders, they are engaged primarily in the directing function.

There are many diverse perspectives on leadership. Some managers treat leadership primarily as an exercise of power. Others believe that a particular belief and attitude structure makes for effective leaders. Still others believe it is possible to identify a collection of leader traits that produces a leader who should be universally effective in any leadership situation. Even today, many believe that a profile of behaviors can universally guarantee successful leadership. Unfortunately, such simple solutions fall short.

It is now clear that there is no one best way to be an effective leader in all circumstances. Rather, the nature of the situation dictates the type of leadership most likely to work well. Fiedler focuses on leader traits and argues that the favorableness of the leadership situation dictates the type of leadership approach needed. He recommends selecting leaders to match the situation or changing the situation to match the leader. Path-goal theory focuses on leader behavior that can be adapted to the demands of a particular work environment and subordinate characteristics. Path-goal theorists believe that leaders can be matched with the situation as well as the situation changed to match leaders. Together, these theories make clear that leadership is effective when the characteristics and behavior of the leader match the demands of the situation.

Aspects of subordinates, tasks, and organizations can substitute for or neutralize many leader behaviors. Leaders must remain aware of these factors, no matter which perspective on leadership they adopt. Such awareness allows managers to use substitutes for and neutralizers of leadership to their benefit rather than be stymied by their presence.

Finally, in recent years, there has been a renewed interest in charismatic leadership and its transformational effects on organizations.

Although a great deal is currently known about the determinants of effective leadership, there is still much to be learned. Each of the theories presented in this chapter is put into practice by managers every day. None provides the complete answer to what makes leaders effective, but each has something important to offer.

Notes

1. G. A. Yukl (1981), *Leadership in organizations*, Englewood Cliffs, NJ: Prentice-Hall.
2. B. Kellerman (1984), *Leadership: Multidisciplinary perspectives*, Englewood Cliffs, NJ: Prentice-Hall; F. L. Landy (1985), *Psychology of work behavior*, Homewood, IL: Dorsey Press.
3. R. Tannenbaum and W. H. Schmidt (March-April 1958), How to choose a leadership pattern, *Harvard Business Review*, 95–101.

4. R. Tannenbaum and W. H. Schmidt (May-June 1973), How to choose a leadership pattern, *Harvard Business Review*, 162–75.

5. N. R. F. Maier (1965), *Psychology in industry*, Boston: Houghton Mifflin 157; K. Davis and J. W. Newstrom (1985), *Human behavior at work: Organization behavior*, New York: McGraw-Hill.

6. J. P. Muczyk and B. C. Reimann (1987), The case for directive leadership, *The Academy of Management Executive*, 1, 301–11.

7. R. M. Stogdill (1948), Personal factors associated with leadership: A survey of the literature, *Journal of Applied Psychology*, 25, 35–71; R. M. Stogdill (1974), *Handbook of leadership: A survey of theory and research*, New York: Free Press.

8. Stogdill, 1948, 63.

9. Stogdill, 1974, 81.

10. D. McGregor (1957), The human side of enterprise, *Management Review*, 46, 22–28, 88–92; D. McGregor (1960), *The human side of enterprise*, New York: McGraw-Hill.

11. M. Haire, E. E. Ghiselli, and L. W. Porter (1966), *Managerial thinking: An international study*, New York: Wiley.

12. R. E. Miles (1975), *Theories of management: Implications for organizational behavior and development*, New York: McGraw-Hill.

13. E. A. Fleishman (1953), The description of supervisory behavior, *Personnel Psychology*, 37, 1–6; E. A. Fleishman and E. F. Harris (1962), Patterns of leadership behavior related to employee grievances and turnover, *Personnel Psychology*, 15, 43–56; A. W. Halpin and B. J. Winer (1957), A factorial study of the leader behavior descriptions, in R. M. Stogdill and A. C. Coons, eds., *Leader behavior: Its description and measurement*, Columbus: Bureau of Business Research, Ohio State University; J. K. Hemphill and A. E. Coons (1975), Development of the leader behavior description questionnaire, in R. M. Stogdill and A. E. Coons, eds., *Leader behavior;* S. Kerr and C. Schriesheim (1974), Consideration, initiating structure, and organizational criteria—an update of Korman's 1966 review, *Personnel Psychology*, 27, 555–68.

14. D. Katz and R. L. Kahn (1952), Some recent findings in human relations research, in E. Swanson, T. Newcomb, and E. Hartley, eds., *Readings in social psychology*, New York: Holt, Rinehart, and Winston; D. Katz, N. Macoby, and N. Morse (1950), *Productivity, supervision, and morale in an office situation*, Ann Arbor, MI: Institute for Social Research; F. C. Mann and J. Dent (1954), The supervisor: Member of two organizational families, *Harvard Business Review*, 32, 103–12.

15. Yukl, 1981, 114–18; R. Likert (1961), *New patterns of management*, New York: McGraw-Hill.

16. Likert, 1961, 103.

17. R. R. Blake and J. S. Mouton (1964), *The managerial grid*, Houston: Gulf; R. R. Blake and J. S. Mouton (1981), *The versatile manager: A grid profile*, Homewood, IL: Dow Jones-Irwin; R. R. Blake and J. S. Mouton (1984), *The new Managerial Grid III*, Houston: Gulf.

18. R. R. Blake and J. S. Mouton (1981), Management by Grid(R) principles or situationalism: Which? *Group and Organization Studies*, 6, 439–55.

19. L. L. Larson, J. G. Hunt, and R. N. Osborn (1976), The great hi-hi leader behavior myth: A lesson from Occam's razor, *Academy of Management Journal*, 19, 628–41.

20. Stogdill, 1948, 63.

21. F. E. Fiedler and M. M. Chemers (1974), *Leadership and effective management*, Glenview, IL: Scott, Foresman.

22. F. E. Fiedler (1976), The leadership game: Matching the men to the situation, *Organizational Dynamics*, 4, 9.

23. R. B. Dunham (1984), [Interview with Fred E. Fiedler], *Organizational behavior: People and processes in management*, Homewood, IL: Irwin, 368; J. L. Kennedy, Jr. (1982), Middle LPC leaders and the contingency model of leadership effectiveness, *Organizational Behavior and Human Performance*, 30, 1–14.

24. F. E. Fiedler (September-October 1965), Engineering the job to fit the manager, *Harvard Business Review*, 115–22.

25. See, for example, the supporting results of M. M. Chemers and G. J. Skrzypek (1972), Experimental test of the contingency model of leadership effectiveness, *Journal of Personality and Social Psychology*, 24, 172–77, and the contradictory results of R. P. Vecchio (1977), An empirical examination of the validity of Fiedler's model of leadership effectiveness, *Organizational Behavior and Human Performance*, 19, 180–206.

26. R. J. House (1971), A path goal theory of leader effectiveness, *Administrative Science Quarterly*, 16, 324.

27. R. J. House and T. R. Mitchell (Autumn 1974), Path-goal theory of leadership, *Journal of Contemporary Business*, 86; R. J. House and G. Dessler (1974), The path-goal theory of leadership: Some post hoc and a priori tests, in J. Hunt and L. Larson, eds., *Contingency approaches to leadership*, Carbondale, IL: Southern Illinois University Press.

28. J. B. Miner (1980), *Theories of organizational behavior*, Hinsdale, IL: Dryden Press, 350.

29. S. Kerr (1977), Substitutes for leadership: Some implications for organizational design, *Organization and Administrative Sciences*, 8, 135–46; S. Kerr and J. M. Jermier (1978), Substitutes for leadership: Their meaning and measurement, *Organizational Behavior and Human Performance*, 22, 375–403; J. P. Howell and P. W. Dorfman (1981), Substitutes for leadership: Test of a construct, *Academy of Management Journal*, 24, 714–28.

30. S. N. Eisenstadt (1968), *Max Weber: On charisma and institution building*, Chicago: University of Chicago Press, 46.

31. J. A. Conger and R. N. Kanungo (1987), Toward a behavioral theory of charismatic leadership in organizational settings, *Academy of Management Review*, 12, 637–47.

32. House and Baetz, 1979; Conger and Kanungo, 1987.

33. R. J. House (1977), A 1976 theory of charismatic leadership, in J. G. Hunt and L. L. Larson, eds., *Leadership: The cutting edge*, Carbondale, IL: Southern Illinois University Press.

34. A. R. Willner (1984), *The spellbinders: Charismatic political leadership*, New Haven, CT: Yale University Press.

35. A. F. Pater and J. R. Pater, eds., (1987), *What they said in 1986. The world book of public opinion*, Beverly Hills, CA: Monitor Book Company, 277.

36. H. Peterson (1965), *A treasury of the world's greatest speeches*, New York: Simon & Schuster, 839.

37. Peterson, 1965, 749.

38. B. M. Bass (1985), Leadership: Good, better, best, *Organizational Dynamics*, 13, 26–40; N. M. Tichy and D. O. Ulrich (Fall 1984), The leadership

challenge—a call for the transformational leader, *Sloan Management Review*, 26, 59–68.

39. K. W. Kuhnert and P. Lewis (1987), Transactional and transformational leadership: A constructive/developmental analysis, *Academy of Management Review*, 12, 650.

Key Terms

leadership
transactional leadership
formal, or designated, leader
informal leader
trait approach
great person approach
consideration
initiating structure

job-centered behaviors
employee-centered behaviors
contingency theory of leadership
least preferred co-worker (LPC)
path-goal theory of leadership
charisma
transformational leadership

Issues for Review and Discussion

1. Define leadership and distinguish between leadership and management.
2. Discuss the relationship between power and variations in types of leadership.
3. What has been learned from the universal leader trait perspective?
4. Both the Ohio State University and University of Michigan leadership studies identified central leader behaviors. What are these behaviors and how are they different from one another?
5. Blake and Mouton's work with the Managerial Grid(R) identified several leadership types. What are they and how does this leadership model look from the perspective of situation theories of leadership?
6. Identify and describe the three situational variables presented in Fiedler's contingency theory of leadership.
7. What are the four leadership behaviors in the path-goal theory of leadership?
8. What are substitutes for leadership? What are neutralizers? Give an example of each.
9. What are the distinguishing features of charismatic leadership?

Suggested Readings

Bennis, W., and Nanus, A. (1985). *Leaders: The strategies for taking charge*. New York: Harper & Row.

House, R. J. (1977). A 1976 theory of charismatic leadership. In Hunt, J. G. and Larson, L. L., eds. *Leadership: The cutting edge*. Carbondale: Southern Illinois University Press.

Loden, M. (1985). *Feminine leadership: Or how to succeed in business without being one of the boys*. New York: Time Books.

Manz, C. C. and Sims, H. P., Jr. (1988). *Superleadership: Leading others to lead themselves to excellence.* Englewood Cliffs, NJ: Prentice-Hall.

Manz, C. C. and Sims, H. P., Jr. (1988). A review of *Superleadership: Leading others to lead themselves to excellence.* In Pierce, J. L. and Newstrom, J. W., eds. *The manager's bookshelf: A mosaic of contemporary views.* New York: Harper & Row, 327–35.

Rubenfeld, S. (1988). A review of *Feminine leadership: Or how to succeed in business without being one of the boys.* In Pierce, J. L. and Newstrom, J. W., eds. *The manager's bookshelf: A mosaic of contemporary views.* New York: Harper & Row, 97–103.

Schriesheim, C. A. and Von Glinow, M. A. (1977). The path-goal theory of leadership: A theoretical and empirical analysis. *Academy of Management Journal,* 20, 398–405.

Yukl, G. A. (1981). *Leadership in organizations.* Englewood Cliffs, NJ: Prentice-Hall.

CASE *Which Style Is Best?*

By W. D. Heier of Arizona State University

The ABC Company is a medium-sized corporation which manufactures automotive parts. Recently, the company president attended a leadership seminar and came away deeply impressed with the effect various leadership styles could have on the output and morale of the organization.

In mulling over how he might proceed, the president decided to use the services of Paul Patterson, a management consultant, who was currently reviewing the goals and objectives of the company. The president told Paul about the leadership seminar and how impressed he had been and that a leadership survey of the company was desired.

They determined that the division headed by Donald Drake should be the test case and that Paul would report to the president on completion of that survey. Some of the notes made by Paul in his interviews with the key managers in Drake's division follow.

Amy Allen

Amy is very proud of her section's output. She has always stressed the necessity for good control procedures and efficiency. She is very insistent that her subordinates fully understand project instructions and that follow-up communications be rapid, complete, and accurate. Amy serves as the clearinghouse for all incoming and outgoing work. She gives small problems to one individual to complete, but, if problems are large, she calls in several key people. Usually, her employees are briefed on what the policy is to be, what part of the report each subordinate is to complete, and the completion date. Amy considers this as the only way to get full coordination without lost motion or an overlap of work.

Amy considers it best for a boss to remain aloof from her subordinates and believes that being "buddy-buddy" tends to hamper discipline. She does her "chewing out" and praising in private. She believes that people in her section know where they stand.

According to Amy, the biggest problem in business today is that subordinates do not accept responsibility. She states that her people have lots of opportunities to show what they can do but not many try very hard.

Amy commented that she does not understand how her subordinates got along with the previous section head, who ran a very "loose ship." Amy stated that her boss is quite happy with the way things go in her section.

Bob Black

Bob believes that every employee has a right to be treated as an individual and espouses the theory that it is a boss' responsibility and duty to cater to employees' needs. He noted that he is constantly doing little things for his subordinates and gave, as an example, his presentation of two tickets to an art show to be held at the City Gallery next month. He stated that the tickets cost $5 each but that it will be both educational and enjoyable for the employee and his wife. This was done to express his appreciation for a good job the man had done a few months back.

Bob says he always makes a point of walking through his section at least once each day, stopping to speak to at least 25 percent of the employees on each trip.

Bob does not like to "knock" anyone, but he noted that Amy Allen ran one of those "taut ships." He stated that Amy's employees are probably not too happy, but there is not much they can do but wait for her to move.

Bob said he had noticed a little bit of bypassing going on in the company but that most of it is due to the press of business. His idea is to run a friendly, low-key operation with a happy group of subordinates. Although he confesses that his section might not be as efficient in terms of speedy outputs as other units, he considers he has far greater subordinate loyalty and higher morale, and his subordinates work well as an expression of their appreciation of his (Bob's) enlightened leadership.

Charlie Carr

Charlie says his principal problem is the shifting of responsibilities between his section and others in the division. He considers his section the "fire drill" area that gets all of the rush, hot items, whether or not they belong in his section. He seems to think this is caused by his immediate superior's not being sure who should handle which jobs in the division.

Charlie admits he has not tried to stop this practice. He stated that it makes the other section heads jealous, but they are afraid to complain. They seem to think Charlie is a personal friend of the division manager, but Charlie says this is not true.

Charlie said he used to be embarrassed in meetings when it was obvious he was doing jobs out of his area but he has gotten used to it by now, and apparently the other section heads have also.

Charlie's approach to discipline is to keep everyone busy and "you won't have those kinds of problems." He stated that a good boss does not have time to hold anybody's hand, like Bob Black does, and tell them what a great job they are doing. Charlie believes that if you promise people you will keep an eye on their work for raises and promotion purposes, most of the problems will take care of themselves.

Charlie stated that he believes in giving a subordinate a job and then letting him or her do it without too much checking on the work. He believes most of his subordinates do their jobs reasonably well.

If Charlie has a problem, it is probably that the role and scope of his section has become a little blurred by current practices. Charlie stated that he thinks he should resist a recent tendency for "company people above my division manager's level" to call him up to their offices to hear his ideas on certain programs; however, Charlie is not sure that this can be stopped without creating a ruckus. He says he is studying the problem.

Don Drake

As division manager, Don thinks things are going pretty well, since he has not had any real complaints from his superiors in the company, beyond the "small problem" type of thing. He thinks his division is at about the same level of efficiency as the other divisions in the organization.

His management philosophy is to let the section managers find their own level, organizational niche, and form of operation and then check to see if the total output of the division is satisfactory. He stated that he has done this with his present section heads. This was the policy being used when Don was a section head, and it has worked fine for him.

Don considers his function to be that of a clearinghouse for division inputs and outputs. He sees his job basically as a coordinating one, coupled with the requirement for him to "front" for the division. He believes that subordinates should be allowed to expand their job activities as much as they are able to do so. Don noted that Charlie Carr had expanded greatly as a manager since Don had arrived. Don frequently takes Charlie with him to high-level meetings in the company, since Charlie knows more about the division's operations than anyone else.

Don noted that both Amy and Bob seem to do a credible job in their sections. He has very little contact with Amy's employees but occasionally has to see one of Bob Black's workers about something the employee has fouled up. This results from the fact that Bob considers such a face-to-face confrontation between a division manager and lower-level section employees a good lesson to impress on subordinates that they have let down their boss. Don Drake said he is not too keen on this procedure but that Bob considers it a most valuable training device to teach employees to do a good job every time, so Don goes along with it.

Questions

1. How would you characterize the leadership styles of each of the managers described in this case?
2. Where would you place each on the Managerial Grid?
3. Which of the four would you prefer to have as a boss?
4. Which of the four appears to be the most effective? least effective?

Human Resource Management

Student Learning Objectives

After reading this chapter, you should be able to:

1. Understand how the human resource function supports the overall strategy of an organization.

2. Explain how economic, labor market, legal, and labor union factors influence the nature and effectiveness of the human resource function.

3. Understand how strategic planning applies to human resource planning.

4. Explain why job analysis is required for the successful design and execution of most human resource activities.

5. Describe the process for obtaining and keeping staff members.

6. Explain why training and development programs are needed even when an excellent staffing program exists.

7. Understand the purposes, techniques, and problems associated with assessing performance.

8. Discuss the forms of cash and noncash compensation and the ways in which they are used to motivate and reward employees.

9. Explain why unions exist and how they interact with the management of organizations.

*O*rganizations are systems of people who interact. To realize their goals, organizations must depend on those people. Organizational success and survival, therefore, largely depend on how well the people in the organization perform, that is, on how well human resources are managed. How does an organization identify the types of people it needs and then convince them to join it? What does it take to train them, to evaluate their performance, and to encourage them to stay with the organization and contribute to its mission? All of these tasks fall within the realm of **human resource management.**

In most organizations, the management of human resources is a joint venture. It involves all of the managers in an organization, plus a human resource department (often called a personnel or industrial relations department). In most cases, individual managers do the everyday hiring, training, evaluating, and promoting. The human resource department usually identifies standards and provides resources to managers, including performance appraisal forms, training, information about how to select employees, and so on.

For many years, some managers considered personnel departments to be an organization's weak link. They felt that such departments had little to offer and created more problems than they solved. Part of the reason for this reputation was the fact that few personnel managers were professionally trained in the personnel function. Over the last couple of decades, however, human resource departments have earned a much better image. Managers now recognize the importance of the function and demand high-quality human resource employees and programs. Organizations are beginning to measure and document the economic impact of human resource activities.[1] Increasingly effective professional organizations, such as the American Society for Personnel Administration, the American Society of Training and Development, and the Industrial/ Organizational Division of the American Psychological Association, keep human resource managers well informed on developments in their field. The available tools and techniques have been improved, and, although

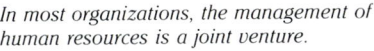

In most organizations, the management of human resources is a joint venture.

they are still far from perfect, there are now serviceable models for all human resource activities. Today it is the rule, rather than the exception, for the human resource function to be accepted and respected by managers.

The Role of the External Environment

The external environment affects every level of an organization, and it affects human resource management with strength and directness. Human resource managers must cope with at least four important components of the external environment economic forces, labor markets, laws and regulations, and labor unions. The top part of Figure 17.1 identifies these four major external influences. (This figure and much of the general approach to human resource management presented in this book are based on H. G. Heneman III, D. P. Schwab, J. A. Fossum, and L. D. Dyer (1986), *Personnel/human resource management*, 3rd ed., Homewood, IL: Irwin.) The bottom left side of the figure shows two kinds of activities that human resource managers engage in: support and functional. Support activities include analyzing individuals and jobs, assessing outcomes (such as performance), and planning human resource activities. Functional activities include staffing and overseeing compensation plans, labor relations, and aspects of the working environment. The middle panel of the bottom portion of the figure shows the need for these activities to match workers' abilities to job requirements and to enhance motivation through rewards. If these are matched appropriately, workers achieve the objectives shown on the bottom right side of the figure.

Economic Factors

Business organizations operate in a marketplace. They must respond sensitively to economic changes. The level and health of economic activity in the external environment, for example, strongly influence the volume of business that an organization does. This volume, in turn, affects the types and numbers of employees that the organization requires. If new car sales slump, for example, steel orders decline and the need for employees at steel mills drops substantially. At the same time, auto repair shops may hire extra staff members to keep older cars running.

Another structural factor in the economy that affects organizations concerns geographical differences in business conditions. Labor is cheaper, for example, in certain Southern states than on the Eastern seaboard. When considering new plant sites in the United States, organizations take these human resource costs into consideration. Similarly, increasing labor costs have contributed to the development of robotics to reduce the number of employees needed to staff an assembly line.

Economic factors also influence the demands that the overall organization places on a human resource department. In response to tight financial conditions during the 1980s, human resource departments have been called on to identify and implement work design, training, and motivational programs to enhance productivity and increase the value of

FIGURE 17.1   *The Human Resource Management Model*

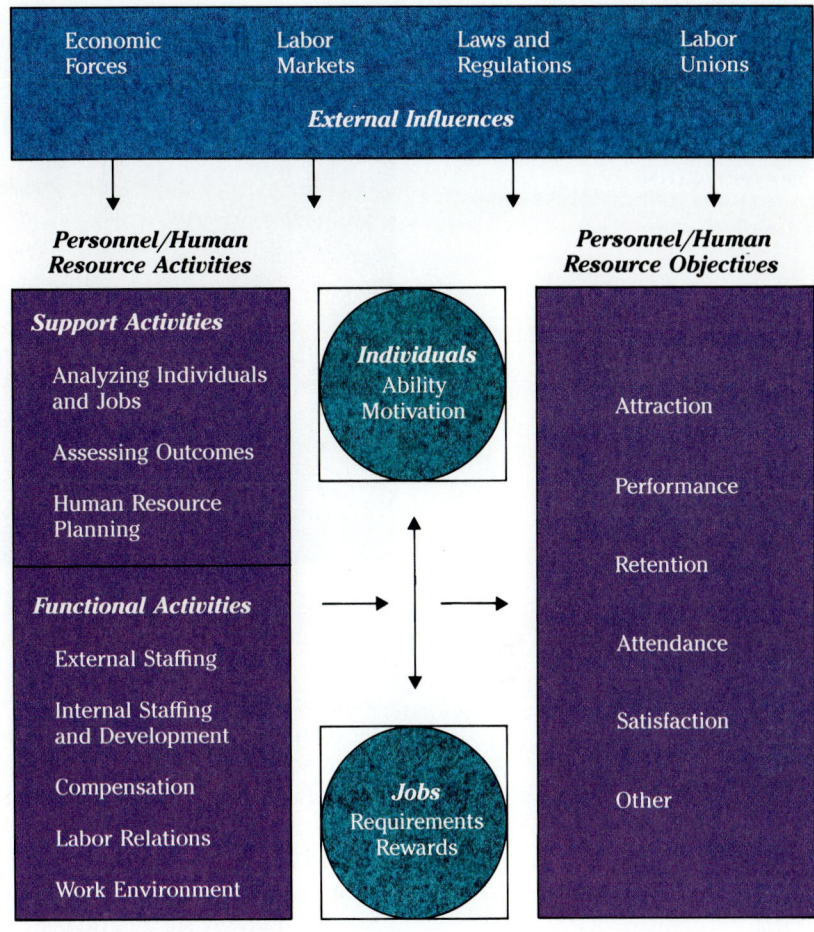

Source: Based on H. G. Heneman III, D. P. Schwab, J. A. Fossum, and L. D. Dyer (1986), *Personnel/human resource management*, 3rd ed., Homewood, IL: Irwin, 8.

work output per employee. Human resource departments also have dealt with difficult financial conditions by designing and implementing early retirement programs to help reduce payroll costs.

Labor and Legal Factors

Economic factors, of course, influence the number and types of workers whom organizations hire, keep, or let go. Economic factors, therefore, are critically important influences in the nation's labor market.

Labor Markets   The **labor market** defines the numbers and types of people present in the workforce. The labor market typically is described in terms of the number of employed and unemployed individuals in various labor groups, such as skilled, unskilled, professional, and technical. It is also typically described in terms of the characteristics of the people in these groups, such as their age, gender, and level of education.

The labor market influences virtually every aspect of human resource management. Jobs, recruiting programs, training programs, and even

Young job applicants often find it difficult to break into the workforce because they lack experience and skills. In El Paso, however, students at the Job Corps Center are trained to be mechanics, cooks, and nurse's aides. Of those who have graduated from the program, 96 percent have been placed in jobs.

work schedules must draw on the talent available and address the personal needs and work interests of those people. In some cases, for example, companies must offer alternative work schedules, such as job sharing or flextime, or design jobs in particular ways to attract and retain certain segments of the labor market.

The Bureau of Labor Statistics (BLS) in the U.S. Department of Labor collects and publishes labor market information, as do various state and local agencies.[2] BLS Area Wage Surveys provide labor supply information and wages by geographic area. The Bureau of the Census publishes the results of monthly surveys on unemployment rates. These sources categorize labor market information for human resource managers. They also reflect changes in the workforce; thus, human resource managers have seen the trend for women to remain in the labor force during their childbearing years. They have seen that older workers are becoming more willing to retire early, birth rates are dropping, and the overall workforce is getting older. To manage human resources effectively for an organization, human resource managers must not only recognize these changes in the labor market but anticipate them as well. The design of jobs, the nature of compensation, training programs, and retirement programs all depend on the profile of workers brought to the organization.

Legal Factors Human resource managers must juggle a number of legal considerations. As illustrated in "A Closer Look: Separations," which discusses lawsuits brought by former employees against employers, managers do not have complete discretion in hiring, managing, and letting workers go. They must conform to certain legal requirements:

- *Hours/wages.* Laws govern the number of hours that some employees can be asked to work and specify the minimum wages they must be paid. Laws also decree that time-and-a-half pay must be given to employees who work more than a certain number of hours (usually forty) per week. The U.S. Fair Labor Standards Act enforces such

A CLOSER LOOK

Separations: The High Cost of Terminating Employees

What does singer Diana Ross have in common with insurance broker Larry W. Buck? Both have been embroiled in an increasingly common type of lawsuit brought by people involving terminated employment. Larry Buck felt that he was fired from his job without warning. When he found it difficult to get another job in the insurance industry, he decided to hire an investigator to find out why. Posing as a manager who was considering hiring Buck for a responsible position, the investigator taped interviews with Buck's former employer, in which Buck was said to be

. . . ruthless, disliked by his co-workers, and a failure as a business man. . . . [a] classical sociopath, a zero, a Jekyll-and-Hyde person who was lacking in . . . scruples."[1]

Buck sued, the case went all the way to the U.S. Supreme Court, and his former employers were forced to pay him $605,000 in lost wages and other damages, plus a $1.3 million penalty.

Although the amount awarded Buck may be an exception, the fact that he won is not. Of employees filing such suits in California during a seven-year period, 72 percent won. When the suits went all the way to a

jury decision, former employers ended up paying an average of $582,000 per award—not counting the tens of thousands of dollars that the companies spent to defend themselves.

Singer Diana Ross was on the losing end of a lawsuit filed by a former employee. Ross had circulated a letter that read, "If I let [employees] go, it's because either their work or their personal habits are not acceptable to me. I do not recommend these people. . . . "[2] She then named seven former employees. One of them sued for libel, arguing that she had left employment voluntarily and on good terms, and that the letter implied otherwise. The employee won, and Ross settled out of court.

Former employees ended up paying an average of $582,000 per award.

What can a manager do to protect an organization against such lawsuits? The first thought might be to just refuse to say anything about the circumstances surrounding an employee's termination; however, silence is not golden in this case. In several recent cases in which companies have refused to release information about why an employee was terminated, employees have sued—and often have won. Why? The courts found that former employees were, in essence, forced to tell potential new employers the reasons they had been terminated. When former employers could not prove the facts underlying this "com-

pelled self-publication," the employees won.

Singer Diana Ross was on the losing end of a lawsuit filed by a former employee.

Is the answer never to terminate an employee, no matter what? Of course not, but managers must make good decisions about letting people go. They should not act in haste. They should keep good records that document systematic performance appraisals and exit interviews. When hiring, they should tell employees whether they can be fired without cause and tell them the organization's policy on providing recommendations. In short, they should stick to the facts and make sure that they can support them in writing.

1. G. Stricharchuk (2 October 1986), Fired employees turn the reason for dismissal into a legal weapon, *The Wall Street Journal*, 31. For more information on this topic, see: J. Hoerr (28 March 1988), It's getting harder to pass out pink slips, *Business Week*, 68; I. M. Shepard and R. L. Duston (1987), *Workplace privacy: Employee testing, surveillance, wrongful discharge, and other areas of vulnerability*, Washington: BNA.

2. J. B. Copeland, B. Turque, L. Wright, and D. Shapiro (16 February 1987), The revenge of the fired, *Newsweek*, 46.

standards for most private employers who do interstate business. Other legislation, such as The Walsh-Healy Act and the Davis-Bacon Act, apply to organizations with federal contracts. Most other employees are covered by the laws of the state in which they do business.

■ *Worker safety.* Of the laws that apply to worker safety, the most notable is the Occupational Safety and Health Act (OSHA) and the Federal Mine Safety Act. These laws dictate that employers have a duty to provide workers with safe working conditions and have succeeded in greatly increasing worker safety in the workplace. Unfortunately, part of the cost of safety in the workplace is a massive amount of paperwork. In fact, OSHA regulations often are the bane of a human resource manager's existence. Many managers feel that OSHA's basic requirements are consistent with their organization's objectives but that the administrative procedures demanded are unreasonable. Although most organizations agree with the spirit of these laws, many disagree significantly with specific safety requirements.

Most workers are covered by the Social Security Act, which provides health- and retirement-related financial assistance.

■ *Financial protection.* There are also laws designed to protect employees financially in case of disability, retirement, and other conditions. The Federal Unemployment Tax Act requires that financial benefits be paid to most workers who lose their jobs through no fault of their own. State workers' compensation laws require that financial benefits be paid to employees who become temporarily or permanently disabled while at work. The federal Employee Retirement Income Security Act (ERISA), although it does not require pension plans for all workers, rigidly regulates the administration of such plans when they are offered. Except for federal and railroad employees, most workers are also covered by the Social Security Act, which provides retirement benefits, benefits for the totally disabled and their children, health insurance (Medicare), and certain other health- and retirement-related financial assistance.

■ *Discrimination.* A host of federal and state laws, regulations, and executive orders protect certain subgroups in the labor force. In a nation dedicated to principles of equal opportunity and nondiscrimination, human resource managers must become familiar with the laws and regulations that enact these principles. The Civil Rights Act of 1964, Title VII and its subsequent amendments, provide the broadest coverage by prohibiting employment discrimination on the basis of race, gender, religion, color, or national origin. The Age Discrimination in Employment legislation and its amendments protect most workers between the ages of forty and seventy from being treated differently from younger workers. The Equal Pay Act of 1963 requires that men and women be paid equally for jobs that require equal skill, effort, responsibility, and working conditions.

Many other laws and regulations place additional constraints on employment practices, and human resource practices must conform to them all. Human resource managers must be fully conversant with many labor-law issues.

Labor Unions   Labor unions have a substantial influence on human resource management. Labor laws in the United States guarantee most employees the right to form and join unions. These laws also specify the types of activities permitted by the unions, the rights of union members, and enforcement procedures. The collective bargaining agreement between an organization and its unionized members is called a *union contract*. This agreement specifies the conditions of employment and work requirements agreed to by both the organization and the union, and neither side can alter any of the terms specified in a signed contract unless the other party agrees. Although the interests of unions and management may often be consistent, many issues negotiated between the two seem to result in a "win-lose" situation. When the union "wins" a demand for higher wages or shorter work weeks, for example, management loses money or productive work time. Later sections of this chapter will deal more extensively with labor-management relations and the laws that regulate them.

Basic Activities

It probably seems that coping with external factors would keep any human resource manager busy. The primary work for a human resource manager, however, is within an organization, with the workers. It is analyzing jobs, finding the appropriate staff to hold those jobs, training and developing the people hired, and appraising their performance. Each of these tasks is an essential component of a human resource manager's role.

Job Analysis

Newspaper publisher, reporter, photographer, typesetter, delivery truck driver, real-estate broker, office manager, title searcher, lawyer, tax collector, salesperson, assembly line worker, and shop supervisor—all of these are jobs. A **job** is a collection of tasks that can be performed by one person. **Job analysis** is the process of identifying and defining those tasks and their associated responsibilities and requirements. In turn, the information gathered in a job analysis lets human resource managers develop job descriptions. At a minimum, a **job description** should list the duties and responsibilities that managers expect the holder of that job to accomplish, the procedures that the job holder should follow in carrying them out, and the qualifications—education, skills, and experience—that a person needs to accomplish these duties and responsibilities.

Job description is something that interests Kathy Holt, director of administrative services at a 750-bed hospital in Georgia. The hospital has a human resource department, but Kathy sometimes performs human resource activities. In fact, she and the human resource department often work together on these tasks.

Kathy's department includes the legal services group for the hospital. One of her legal clerks, Sandra Lynn, is planning to retire. Kathy asked the

FIGURE 17.2   Sample Job Description: Legal Clerk

4/15/88

Title: Legal Clerk III   Grade: C
                                           Hours: 7:30 A.M.–4:00 P.M. (Some Flexibility)
Minimum: $12,580/year   Division: Legal

The Duties of This Position Involve the Following:

1. Answer telephone, screen calls as required, take messages or refer for proper handling.
2. Make photocopies and overhead transparencies as requested.
3. Utilize typewriter, work processor and personal computer for typing needs of the Legal Division staff (reports, letters, memos, charts, etc.).
4. File and maintain records as assigned, including maintenance of sublicense agreements file and list.
5. Assist in preparation of materials for printing, production, and mailing.
6. Distribute completed work, photocopies, and research files as needed.
7. Maintain inventory of office supplies and replenish as needed.
8. Provide assistance and support to Legal Division secretaries.
9. Other duties as assigned.

Qualifications:

High-school diploma plus one year office experience. Two-year secretarial certificate may be considered in lieu of experience. Sixty wpm typing speed, excellent oral and written communication skills, excellent organization skills, proofing/editing efficiency, and ability to work under pressure required. Word processing, personal computer, telephone and dictaphone experience required. Additional relevant experience may be considered in lieu of educational requirements as stated.

human resources department to prepare a job description for the job of legal clerk so that she can hire someone to replace Sandra. Figure 17.2 shows the one-page job description that Kathy was given.

The Importance of Job Analysis   Kathy now knows that she needs a legal department clerk. She first checks the job description before making recruiting plans. Is the best plan to hire from outside the company or to promote someone with strong skills? Should the clerk earn more or less than secretaries in the department? To answer these and other questions, Kathy and the human resource manager will depend on job analysis. Virtually every human resource activity is influenced by the results of job analysis. For this reason, job analysis is considered to be the *core* of human resource operations. Managers depend on job analysis to identify the qualifications that job applicants should have. If job analysis indicates, for example, that a particular job requires formal training in chemistry, recruiting efforts would concentrate on chemists. When trying to choose one of many candidates, managers are guided by job analysis information that specifies the abilities required for the particular job. For the chemist's position, job analysis might suggest selecting applicants primarily on the basis of their analytical, long-term planning and supervisory skills because those were identified as most critical to successful job performance.

The results of job analyses also help human resource managers identify natural "ladders" of progression through an organization. The managers can track the development of skills necessary for workers to advance from one job to another. Managers also need this kind of information for training and development programs. By comparing the skill requirements of a job to the skills of the people already doing the job (the job incumbents), human resource managers can find the people and areas of skill that could benefit most from training. Furthermore, job analysis helps managers *focus* training on those factors most important to successful performance. For the chemist's job, for example, training would concentrate on chemical analysis, long-term planning, and supervision.

Managers also use job analyses to identify which aspects of people's work to monitor in conducting performance appraisals. How well people are meeting the responsibilities of their jobs influences individualized training and counseling, as well as the distribution of rewards. Furthermore, virtually all cash compensation in the United States is based on either a formal or informal **job evaluation** (the process of determining the relative value of jobs). Job evaluation, in turn, is based on the work requirements identified in a job analysis. Without job analysis, it would be extremely difficult to evaluate jobs accurately.

Job Analysis Techniques There are thousands of job analysis techniques in use today. They differ substantially in their methods of collecting job information, their focus of analysis, and their expression of results. The range of jobs covered by job analysis techniques also varies. Some techniques are designed for small subsets of jobs. Others are intended for very broad use. Unfortunately, job analysis techniques also vary substantially in quality. Without high-quality job analysis information, a human resource program cannot meet the organizations' needs. Some good techniques that human resource managers use for conducting job analyses include the following practices.[3]

- **Direct observation**—watching workers during a continuous observation period to identify every relevant activity. Direct observation of an assembly line job, for example, might reveal that a worker picks a bolt from a bin, uses a power driver to insert the bolt into a frame carried by the assembly line, and then attaches a gasket to the frame using a screwdriver. Direct observation can be a very good way of examining jobs that require little abstract thinking, planning, or decision making and is often used with jobs in which the same set of activities is repeated frequently. (It only takes 20 seconds, for example, for a worker to assemble a bathroom fan, resulting in over 1400 repetitions per 8-hour shift.)

- **Work sampling**—a variation of the direct observation approach, in which a human resource manager periodically samples workers' behavior on jobs that have relatively long cycles, that have irregular patterns of activity, or that require many different tasks. For the job of tax accountant, for example, a human resource manager could examine the job behavior of twenty or thirty tax accountants on a given day or pick twenty or thirty days of the year at random and observe the job behaviors of one or two tax accountants during those days. (Few organizations want to wait very long for the results of a job analysis, however, so this latter approach is seldom used.)

- **Critical incidents**—another variation of the direct observation method that examines only those job behaviors leading to successful or unsuccessful performance. Incidental activities are given little emphasis. This technique can be conducted by an outside observer, a supervisor, or a job incumbent. Using employees to identify actions that they feel have led to effective or ineffective job performance can be more efficient and cost-effective than paying an observer for the extensive time often required to conduct a critical incident analysis. This approach is somewhat more practical than other direct observation approaches, particularly when a long period of time may pass before activities are repeated.

- **Interviewing**—discussions between a job incumbent or supervisor and a human resource manager to identify important aspects of a job that are not obvious through direct observation. Direct observation of a research chemist, for example, would reveal only that the chemist picks up and moves beakers, applies heat, takes measurements, and makes notes in a lab book. This method fails to identify the more important aspects of this job, such as analytical thinking and problem solving. Through an interview, however, the chemist or a supervisor could describe the important requirements of the job.

- **Structured questionnaires**—standardized forms that elicit answers about a job, the activities it involves, and other relevant data. Questionnaires can generate broad data relatively inexpensively and allow the direct comparison of job requirements across a large number of jobs. Many standardized questionnaires are scored by computers that also can be programmed to analyze the ability requirements for jobs and evaluate jobs, as well as describe job activities. Some questionnaires, such as the Comprehensive Occupational Data Analysis Program (CODAP) developed by the U.S. Air Force, elicit information about hundreds of tasks (see Figure 17.3).[4]

  The Position Analysis Questionnaire (PAQ) is probably the best-known structured job analysis questionnaire. Developed at Purdue University, the PAQ assesses a variety of job behaviors found in a wide range of jobs.[5] The PAQ is not appropriate, however, for middle- or upper-level managerial or professional jobs because it does not adequately address such factors as long-term planning. Other instruments, such as the Management Position Description Questionnaire (MPDQ) and the Professional and Managerial Position Questionnaire (PMPQ), have been developed to deal with these types of jobs.[6] Figure 17.4 illustrates the results of a PMPQ analysis that the human resource department at Kathy Holt's hospital prepared for the job of chief legal counsel in her department. It identifies the areas of responsibility most important for this job and shows how these requirements compare to those for a national sample (expressed as percentiles on each dimension).

Staffing

Job analysis tells what *a* person must be able to do to carry out a job, but **staffing** is the process of finding *the* person to do it well. Human resource managers look within and outside of their organization to find people who meet the specified requirements, narrow the field to candi-

FIGURE 17.3 CODAP: A Checklist Approach to Job Analysis

Duty A. Arranging for Appointments, Meetings, or Events

Scale for Time Spent

1 = Very much *below* average
2 = *Below* average
3 = Slightly *below* average
4 = Average
5 = Slightly *above* average
6 = *Above* average
7 = Very much *above* average

	Time Spent	√ If Performed
A1. Coordinate *or** prepare agenda items (prior to typing) for meetings and conferences.		
A2. Distribute agenda *or* minutes of meetings.		
A3. Maintain either personal diary *or* appointment schedule for others.		
A4. Make physical arrangements for meetings after being given time and place (such as scheduling rooms, reserving public address equipment and other equipment).		
A5. Make travel arrangements (such as transportation and hotel arrangements).		
A6. Notify participants of time and place of meetings as directed.		
A7. Remind meeting *or* conference participants of required action.		
A8. Schedule appointments for either supervisors *or* others in your office.		
A9. Schedule events such as court hearing dates *or* surgery.		

*The word *or* is used to mean *either* coordinate or prepare. If you do either of these two things, you √ the task as performed. This same meaning is used throughout the task inventory. If you do any part of a task with *or* in it, √ the task as performed.

Source: A. J. Gandy and W. Maier (1979), *Utah clerical linkup study: Comparison of federal and state jobs*, Washington, DC: Office of Personnel Management.

dates who appear to have those abilities, and try to develop them into effective organization members. Staffing also describes the processes that human resource managers go through to separate members from organizations through layoffs, firings, and retirement.

External Recruiting When searching for viable job candidates, managers can look either outside or inside their organization. Human resource managers perform **external recruiting** when they find a qualified pool of candidates from outside their organization. External recruiting consists of five steps:

FIGURE 17.4   PMPQ Job Analysis

Job: Chief Legal Counsel

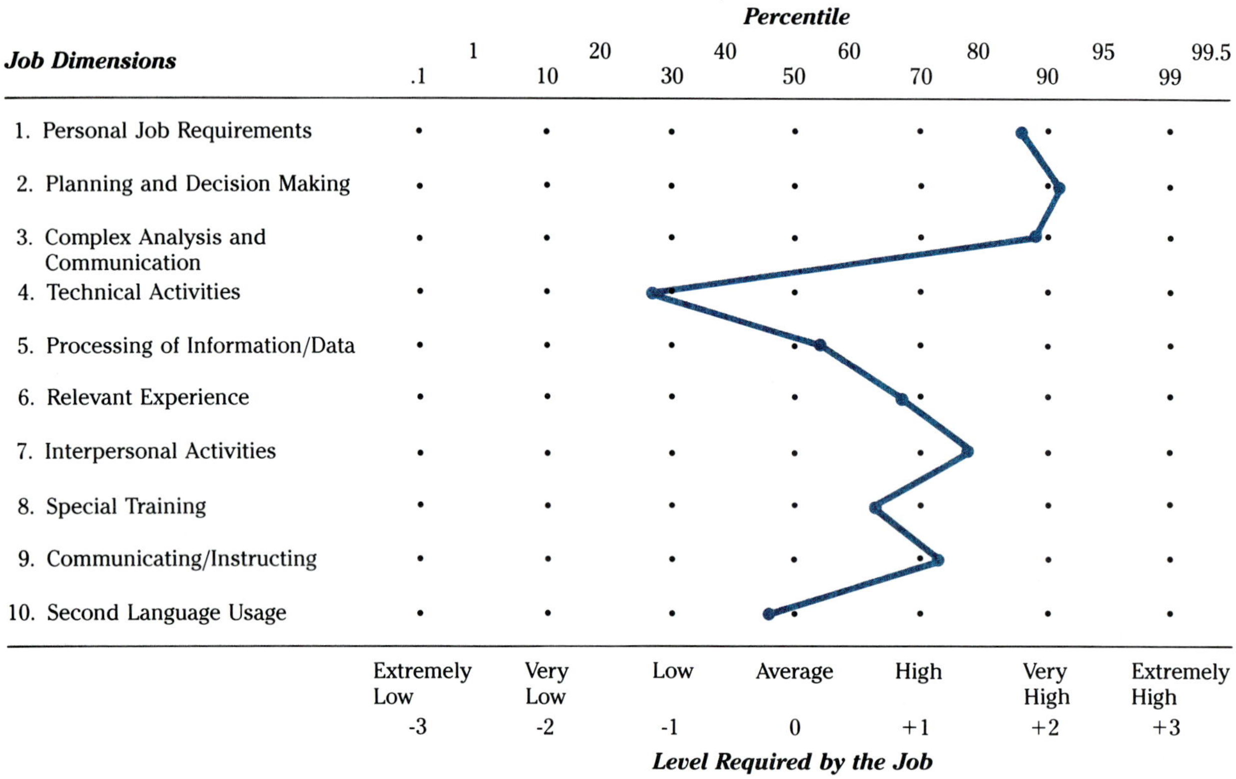

Percentile

Job Dimensions								
	1	20	40	60	80	95	99.5	
	.1	10	30	50	70	90	99	

1. Personal Job Requirements
2. Planning and Decision Making
3. Complex Analysis and Communication
4. Technical Activities
5. Processing of Information/Data
6. Relevant Experience
7. Interpersonal Activities
8. Special Training
9. Communicating/Instructing
10. Second Language Usage

Extremely Low	Very Low	Low	Average	High	Very High	Extremely High
-3	-2	-1	0	+1	+2	+3

Level Required by the Job

1. *Planning.* How many people does the organization need? How many people are likely to meet the requirements? How many of those are likely to take a job if it is offered? Human resource managers use this first step to see how many and what kind of people the organization is going to need by examining current and expected job vacancies. Some organizations have developed **yield ratios** to estimate how many applicants are likely to qualify for the job opening and accept the job if it is offered.[7] Yield ratios often run as high as 100:1, which means that managers would have to evaluate 100 applicants for only 1 job opening.

2. *Strategy development.* Once managers know the types and numbers of candidates to contact, they must develop a strategy to tell them where, how, and when to look. *Where* to look for candidates depends on the nature of the job in question. A potential legal clerk can probably be found within a local community, for example, but the search for a new chief legal counsel may extend to the entire state. *How* to look for candidates also depends on the type of job. Executive search firms, for example, can be used to find professional and managerial employees. Advertising and direct applications can be used to find blue-collar workers (see Table 17.1). *When* to look for candidates depends on how long it will take to complete the search. The search can include advertising, checking résumés,

TABLE 17.1   *How to Find Job Candidates*

Type of Job	*How to Look*
Blue-collar	Direct applications, advertising
Clerical	Advertising, direct applications, employee referrals
Sales	Advertising, private employment agencies, employee referrals
Professional/technical	Advertising, private employment agencies, educational institutions
Managerial	Advertising, private employment agencies, executive search firms

Source: *Recruiting policies and practices* (1979), Washington, DC: Bureau of National Affairs.

issuing invitations for and conducting interviews, screening candidates, and so forth. Managers can use the PERT technique discussed in Chapter 8 to estimate the total time that a search will require by identifying the expected length of each of the recruiting activities, their interdependencies, and the steps most critical to the overall timing.

3. *Searching.* Once they have planned the strategy, human resource managers begin the search process. They seek and get applications; they exchange information with job applicants. Part of the information that they give out is about the job and the organization itself. How realistically human resource managers portray the job and the organization is important in the search. They must be made to sound attractive enough to lure candidates, but overstatements can lead to disappointment and poor performance if the candidates who are hired later discover that the reality of the job differs significantly from the promise. There is growing evidence that realistic information about the strengths and weaknesses of the job can lead to higher satisfaction and lower turnover rates in the long run.[8] Further, honesty at this step may protect an organization if an ex-employee later files a lawsuit (review "A Closer Look: Separations").

4. *Screening.* After applications are received, human resource managers screen them to identify those candidates who meet the basic qualifications for the job. The legal clerk, for example, must have personal computer and word processing experience, so the candidate with a B.A. who has worked as a receptionist in a law office but cannot type is screened out. By comparing applicants' qualifications to the needs identified through job analysis, human resource managers reject applicants who have little chance of performing the job successfully. As they concentrate on finding people with the knowledge, skills, abilities, and interests required to perform the job, managers must avoid discriminating on the basis of gender, race, or religion. After the screening process has reduced the pool of applicants to only qualified candidates, a selection process (described later in this section) is used to choose the one person to hire for the job.

5. *Program evaluation.* Like any other strategic plan, the recruiting program must be monitored, evaluated, and controlled. Human

resource managers must determine whether recruiting activities have occurred as planned and assess the results. How many candidates were contacted and at what cost? How effective was the search from equal employment and affirmative action perspectives? These types of evaluations let managers identify the strengths and weaknesses of their organization's external recruiting program and allow them to make changes for the future.

Internal Recruiting   External recruiting means looking outside an organization for potential employees. **Internal recruiting** means trying to find employees already inside the organization who are qualified for new job openings. Internal recruiting involves the same five steps used for external recruiting: planning, strategy development, searching, screening, and program evaluation. In fact, most organizations integrate internal and external recruiting, at least to a degree, as when a company places a classified ad in a local newspaper and posts the job opening on an employee bulletin board. An organization's hiring policies, often specified in an employee handbook and union contracts, usually dictate the degree to which current employees will be given priority over candidates from outside the organization for new openings.

Human resource managers can use one of two systems for internal recruiting. **Closed recruiting systems** let managers select the types of people (and, sometimes, even the specific individuals) who will be considered for a vacancy. A closed recruiting system gives managers a tremendous amount of reward power and can greatly enhance their influence on the behavior of organization members. **Open recruiting systems** publicize job openings so that any employee who meets specified minimum requirements can apply. Although somewhat slower and more costly than closed recruiting, the open approach reduces the power held by individual managers. More important, open systems can improve employee motivation and morale if employees believe that they will at least be considered for relevant job openings.

Selection   The purpose of external and internal recruiting is to identify a pool of qualified candidates for a job opening. Managers use a **selection** process to evaluate each of these candidates, to make predictions of the probable levels of job performance by each, and to choose a candidate for the job. Any technique or procedure for choosing from among candidates is referred to as a **selection device.** A wide range of selection devices are available to give human resource managers information on which to base their decisions. These selection devices include:

- *Application blanks*—forms that ask for personal information as well as information about previous training and work experiences. Figure 17.5 shows the application form used by Kathy Holt's hospital. Many states have laws that limit the types of questions which can be asked on the application to avoid possible discrimination on the basis of age, race, religion, marital status, and so forth.[9] (For this reason, many organizations no longer ask date of birth and gender questions).

FIGURE 17.5   *Application Blank*

Application for Employment

We are an Equal Opportunity Employer. Our personnel policy is intended to ensure equal treatment to all individuals with regard to rate of pay and all other conditions of employment regardless of race, religion, color, national origin, sex, physical or mental handicaps and age.

PLEASE PRINT OR TYPE, ANSWER ALL QUESTIONS. If information is not applicable write "NA", if answer is "none" write "none"

PERSONAL DATA

Name (as it appears on Social Security card) Last	First	Middle	Today's date

Present mailing address Street or RR City State Zip	Area code and phone no.

Permanent address through which you can always be contacted	Area code and phone no.

Social Security Number	Date of birth (1)	Sex: (2) ☐ Male ☐ Female	U.S. citizen ☐ Yes ☐ No	If not U.S. citizen, check Immigrant ☐ Non-Immigrant ☐ Visa Classification _____

MILITARY

This company adheres to Section 38 USC 2012 of the Vietnam Era Veterans' Readjustment Assistance Act, and has an Affirmative Action Plan to employ and advance in employment qualified veterans. If you qualify under the Act and would like to be considered under Affirmative Action, please tell us.

Date entered service	Date separated	Branch of service	RESERVE STATUS Active: Inactive:

Occupation in the service

PHYSICAL CONDITION

This Company adheres to Section 503 of the Rehabilitation Act of 1973 and has an Affirmative Action Plan to employ and advance in employment qualified handicapped individuals. If you have such a handicap and would like to be considered under Affirmative Action, please tell us. Besides identifying your handicap, also include: (1) any special methods, skills and procedures which might qualify you for positions that you might not otherwise be able to do because of your handicap, and (2) accommodations which would enable you to perform the job properly and safely.

Please identify handicap: _____

List special methods or accommodations needed due to handicap: _____

Information obtained shall be kept confidential and is voluntarily submitted. Refusal to provide it will not subject you to discharge or disciplinary treatment.

EDUCATION

	Name and location of school	Major subject	Hours in class	Hours credit	Grad-uate?	Degree	Date of Graduation
High School							
College							
College							
Graduate School							
Other: Business, Service, Trade, Correspondence, etc.							

High School average	Approximate college grade point average for each separate year 1st Yr. 2nd Yr. 3rd Yr. 4th Yr. 5th Yr.	Cumulative grade point average ——out of possible——	Approx. standing in class:	Out of total class of:

What year in school are you? (Freshman, sophomore, etc.)

WORKING EXPERIENCE

Give details of work experience, including apprenticeships, summer work, and misc. jobs. LIST MOST **RECENT** WORK EXPERIENCE **FIRST.**

Name of employer, address and nature of business	From (Mo.) (Yr.)	To (Mo.) (Yr.)	Wages or salary	Your position and nature of duties	Reason for leaving
	May we contact for reference? ☐ Yes ☐ No				
	May we contact for reference? ☐ Yes ☐ No				

WORK REFERENCES

Check Appropriate square
☐ Full-Time Employment
☐ Summer Employment
☐ Part-Time Employment

From the job assignments listed below, please check your first job preference (Check only one box). Your application will be considered for all openings within the job group you have selected. Your application will be further considered in other areas based upon the Company's need and your experience and training.

Date available for employment

Salary Required $

Geographic Preference

Are you willing to travel on a regular basis?

☐ Management
☐ Management Staff
☐ Professional Staff
☐ Sales/Marketing

☐ Systems
☐ Clerical

Specific position applied for:
_____

Data Processing & Clerical Applicants Only	List machines you have operated and extent of ability to operate.
	Steno, Clerical, Data Processing Skills. Typing speed Shorthand speed Keypunch speed

(1) The AGE DISCRIMINATION IN EMPLOYMENT ACT of 1967 prohibits discrimination on the basis of age with respect to individuals who are at least 40 but less than 70 years of age. Our personnel practices will conform with applicable state age discrimination laws.

(2) Executive Order 11375 prohibits discrimination with respect to sex. Our Company personnel practices conform to this Order and only request that this information be provided for record keeping purposes.

- *References and recommendations*—information sought from some-one other than the candidate about his or her past performance record. Kathy contacted the current employer of each of the three leading candidates for the legal clerk job. Two were rated as "perfectly acceptable employees." The third was rated "almost irreplaceable." Sometimes references and recommendations are honest, helpful, and reliable. They genuinely help managers identify good potential employees and screen out others. References and recommendations can be unreliable and lack validity, though, if the source allows personal opinions and feelings—positive or negative—to override objective evaluation of the candidate. They can also be costly to the source if, for example, the information prevents the candidate from receiving a job (review "A Closer Look: Separations").

- *Interviews*—question-and-answer sessions held between candidate and prospective employer. Kathy Holt personally interviewed each of the three leading candidates for the legal clerk job. Although probably the most commonly used selection device, interviews often fail to identify the most qualified candidate because of time constraints and managers' personal biases and poor interviewing techniques. For an interview to produce valid information, interviewers must be properly trained to use a structured approach that asks the same relevant, job-related questions of each candidate, questions that are written out in advance and scored on a standardized rating scale. Under these conditions, an interview can produce valid information.

- *Tests*—a wide range of instruments used to examine candidates' abilities, skills, behaviors, and attitudes. The best tests assess those factors that the job analysis identifies as necessary for the candidate to perform well on the job and to do so in a standardized manner. The three top candidates for the legal clerk job were each given a typing test and a dictaphone test.

- *Assessment centers*—environments in which managers conduct a simulation of the job in question over a two- or three-day period. Typically, a panel of observers independently rates each candidate on a standardized scale on a number of dimensions identified by job analysis as important parts of the job. A typical simulation tool used in assessment centers is the "in-basket" exercise. Kathy Holt's three top legal clerk candidates, for example, were given in-baskets containing identical samples of mail, phone messages, and reports and given an hour to respond to its contents. Observers rated how effectively each candidate handled the material. Other assessment center exercises often involve role playing and participation in group exercises.

Career Development   Up to this point, this discussion has centered on matching one person to one job at one specific time. Organizations and job candidates are increasingly looking beyond the immediate job in question, however. Job candidates want to know what their promotion possibilities are if their performance is satisfactory. Organizations want to know who will be available to fill job openings all along their career paths. By considering the jobs that probably will open up in the future as they evaluate candidates, human resource managers can develop career plans that benefit the overall and long-term staffing strategy of the organization. When employees know that their organization has a systematic career development plan, it helps them evaluate opportunities realistically within the organization. It can also improve morale. Career development plans usually identify probable career paths, from entry-level jobs to considerably higher levels (see Figure 17.6).

The most effective career development plans identify career paths, along with estimates of how likely it is that an employee will advance to higher-level jobs. They should also depict estimates of the amount of time it typically takes employees to reach each step along the path. By meeting with supervisors or career counselors, employees can see how they fit into a generic path, such as that shown in Figure 17.6.

Separation Issues   Sometimes human resource managers must ask employees to leave an organization. They have to ask employees to leave when the organization needs fewer or different types of employees or when employees are not meeting the requirements of their job. Asking employees to leave an organization is (perhaps euphemistically) called *separating* them. Methods include:

- *Layoffs*—stopping someone's employment temporarily or permanently through no fault of the employee. When orders fall at a car manufacturing plant, workers are laid off. When city budgets are tight, police are laid off.
- *Dismissals*—ending someone's employment "for cause." Usual causes include habitual tardiness; poor performance; and undesirable behavior at work, such as sleeping on the job, fighting, or using drugs.
- *Retirement*—allowing (usually) older employees to leave an organization in good standing. Although retirement can be required at certain ages in some states, most retirements occur voluntarily. Federal law prohibits mandatory retirement before age seventy, except for some executives and policymakers and for certain types of jobs, such as airline pilot. It is because of Sandra Lynn's retirement that Kathy Holt is seeking a legal clerk.

Training and Development

Organizations identify and hire people who match their requirements as closely as possible, but the match is seldom perfect. Usually, employees hired through even the best staffing programs need to be taught how to apply their abilities and skills to the requirements of the specific job. This instruction, which prepares an employee for a job, is known as **training.** In contrast, **development** usually refers to preparation that extends beyond the present job, such as the instruction the employee will need if the design of the current job changes or if the employee changes jobs through transfer or promotion.

FIGURE 17.6   Career Paths in an Insurance Company

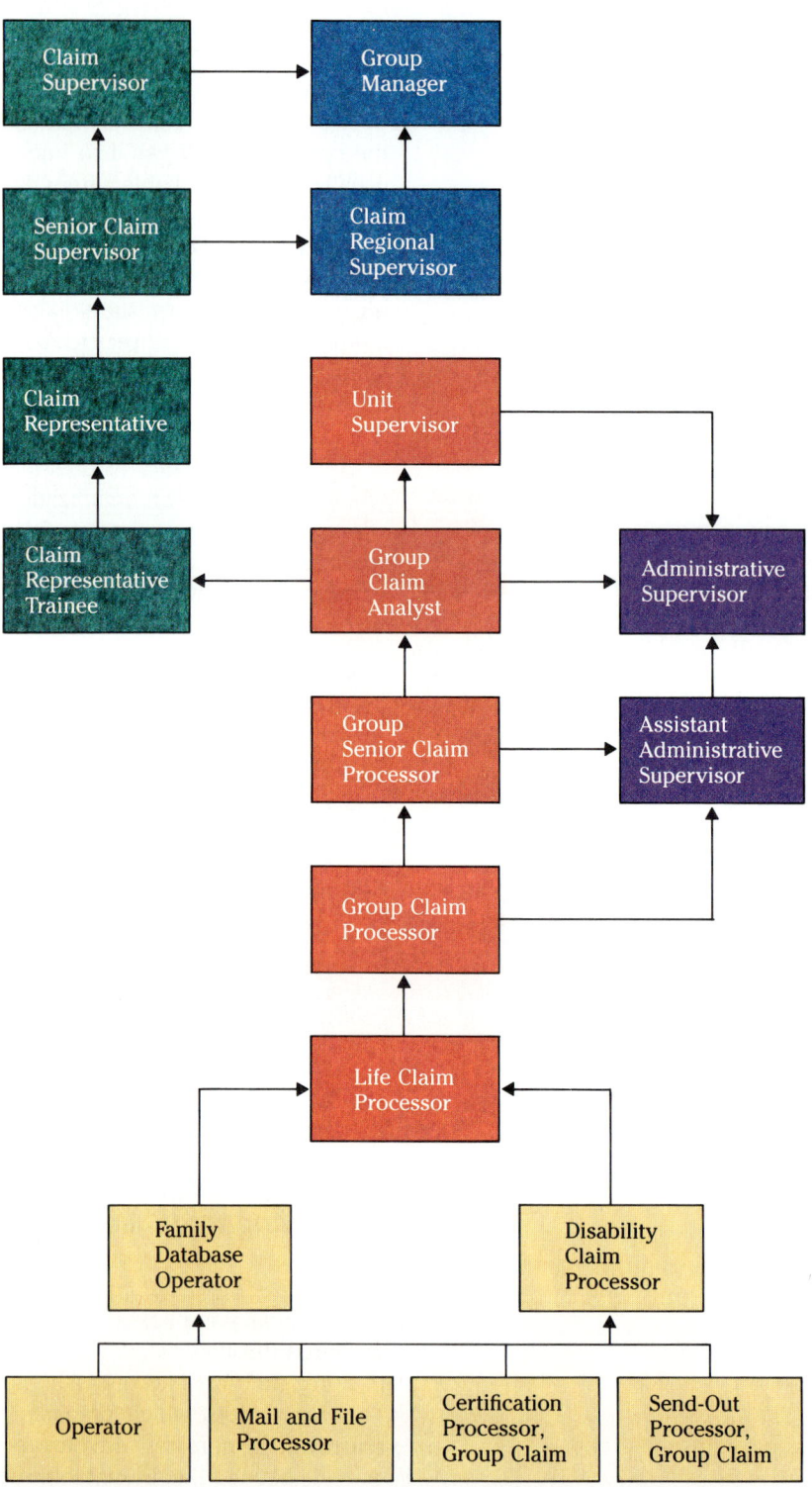

Source: M. London and S. A. Stumpf (1982), *Managing careers*, Reading, MA: Addison-Wesley, 140.

Employees hired through even the best staffing programs need training and development.

Determining Training and Development Needs As you will see in the next section of this chapter, managers planning a human resource strategy follow the same nine-step process that is used to create any strategic plan (described in detail in Chapter 9). The results of their analyses of organizational resources, analyses of strategic opportunities and threats, and gap analysis reveal most of an organization's training and development needs. In addition, managers also need to conduct two other reviews to define an organization's training and development needs.

First, managers must identify particular *areas* that have or may develop performance problems. If there are extreme quality control problems on a particular assembly line, the organization may have to train workers in that area. If the organization can expect to be short of qualified first-level managers, the human resource manager should begin to prepare some nonmanagerial employees to make the transition into management. Good human resource plans, in other words, anticipate needs rather than react to problems once they take hold. Aware of the pharmacy department's plans to automate prescription records, for example, the director of human resources at Kathy Holt's hospital ordered computer training for pharmacy employees six months before the new system was installed.

After learning where problems are likely to occur, human resource managers focus on the specific *types* of training needed. Here, too, job analyses often are useful. Managers can compare job requirements to the abilities of employees and, thus, pinpoint the types of training required. A manager analyzing a robotic technician's job, for example, might determine that the ability to work a computer keyboard is essential. If the employees who are or who will become robotics technicians do not know how to use a keyboard, they should receive training *before* they are placed in the new job.

In planning employee development, human resource managers also can create formal career paths that draw on a progression of closely related skills for each succeeding job. The presence of career paths helps managers plan how to use each employee over a series of years. It also helps employees aspire to appropriate future jobs and prepare for them. The legal clerk that Kathy Holt hires, for example, can take advantage of the hospital's continuing education policy to gain paralegal training if he or she would like to progress along a nonmanagerial path. The clerk also could take managerial courses to prepare to manage the legal division's clerical staff.

Training and Development Methods   Managers conduct training and development in several ways (see Table 17.2), usually while employees are on the job. Much of this on-the-job training and development is informal, but there is a growing tendency toward formal and standardized procedures.

On-the-job training consists mostly of coaching, special assignments, and job rotation. *Coaching* occurs as a supervisor guides a subordinate through the day-to-day activities of a job. The supervisor observes the subordinate at work and provides suggestions for maintaining or improving performance. For example, a unit supervisor in an insurance company would coach a claims analyst; a head bank teller would coach a trainee. Employees sometimes get *special assignments*, such as membership in a task force or responsibility for a particular project, so that they can learn or refine skills for their current job or for a future job. For example, a teacher who wants to be promoted to an administrative position takes an assignment in a task force to devise a community outreach program. *Job rotation* systematically moves a subordinate through a series of relatively brief job assignments. These changes are not promotions but an opportunity for an employee to broaden his or her abilities, skills, and knowledge about the organization. A person hired as a group claim analyst in an insurance company might spend some time processing group life claims, then disability claims, then health claims, so that he or she will better understand the workings of the organization.

Organizations are increasingly turning to *off-the-job training*, including information presentation, information processing, and simulation.[10] With *information presentation*, employees are given information via written material, films, videotapes, lectures, or computer. For example, the computerized instruction modules developed to accompany this text use this method, which has proved to be both popular and effective for job training.[11]

TABLE 17.2   *Examples of Training and Development Methods*

On-the-Job	Off-the-Job
Coaching • Tutoring • Role modeling	Information Presentation • Written/visual materials • Lectures
Special Assignments • Projects • Task forces	Information Processing • Conference groups • Discussion groups
Job Rotation • Departmental transfers • Functional transfers	Simulations • Role playing • Vestibule training

To manipulate information—to generate ideas and discussions, for example—rather than merely to learn facts is the goal of *information processing techniques*. In discussion groups, employees meet with management development trainers, who are likely to supplement the information presented in training manuals and lectures by guiding trainees in experiential exercises; discussing case studies; and helping them complete questionnaires to learn more about themselves, such as what kind of leaders they are. Information-processing techniques are useful for presenting complex material, and they often increase trainees' motivation.

Simulation techniques give trainees a chance to encounter important aspects of a job in a safe environment, where they are free to perform inexpertly or to make mistakes. Airline pilots, for example, can practice landing planes under various weather conditions without risk to life or limb. Physicians can practice on computer-simulated patients—diagnosing their symptoms, prescribing treatment, and noting reactions—without placing real patients at risk. Although simulation techniques usually are the most expensive training and development techniques, they tend to be the most effective. Learners can solve real cases, play roles to be faced on the job, and practice coping with business scenarios that depict real issues. Some simulations construct a work experience identical to the real job but call for no actual output. Known as **vestibule training,** this method is used by American Family Insurance to teach employees how to use the company's computers for processing insurance applications. Computer terminals are set up in a training workroom, and trainees follow the same procedures as they will use on the job. The only difference is that the applications processed by trainees are simulated.

Performance Appraisal

How well are subordinates doing? What exactly are they doing well? What needs improvement? Does anyone need to be promoted, warned, or trained? Answering these questions is one of the most important—and most difficult—tasks that managers face. **Performance appraisal** is the process of evaluating how effectively employees are fulfilling their job responsibilities and contributing to the accomplishment of organizational goals. It is not surprising that performance appraisal is so difficult. To appraise performance effectively, a manager must be aware of the specific expectations for a job, monitor employees' behavior and results, compare the observed behavior and results to expectations, and measure the match between them. In most cases, a manager must also provide feedback to employees, a process that can raise strong feelings.

Although they may be difficult to conduct, performance appraisals are extremely important to an organization. They tell organizations whether their selection devices are effective. They show where training, development, and motivational programs are needed and later gauge whether these have been effective. In fact, many organizational policies and practices are evaluated, in large part, through their impact on performance. Performance appraisals, after all, are the basis on which managers make decisions about compensation, promotion, and dismissal. They also use feedback about people's performance to recognize them for a job well done and to motivate them. In short, without good measures of employees' performance, managers find it very difficult to identify and encourage organizational effectiveness. Because formal performance appraisals are so important, the vast majority of organizations conduct them.[12]

Appraisal Techniques Job analysis is the foundation on which performance appraisal rests. It is a job analysis that identifies the standards and expectations against which employees' performance is measured. Effective appraisals require managers to be astute observers, keen analysts, and sensitive communicators of feedback.

Managers have two ways of comparing actual to anticipated performance. They can try to assess an employee's output through *objective methods* based on verifiable physical objects or events. One objective measure of performance used by the Producers Color lab in Detroit, for example, is the amount of film scrap produced while processing a movie. Sales performance can be measured by how much of a product or service is sold, either in units or in dollars. Objective methods can be quite useful because numbers are readily understandable and easy to explain.

For most jobs, though, objective measures are neither possible nor adequate. For instance, in some jobs, performance—and measurable output—is the combined effort of many workers. How, for example, is a manager to determine who made the steel at a steel mill? In other cases, an objective count says nothing about quality of performance. An artist's performance is not judged on the number of paintings completed in a year. Even when the results of a job are an observable and quantifiable product, such as the number of widgets produced, such factors as quality must be taken into account. Does it matter if a worker turned out more widgets than anyone else on an assembly line if 25 percent of the widgets are defective?

For these reasons, managers often use *subjective methods* to judge performance instead of or in addition to objective measures. In one subjective approach, the *comparative method,* supervisors compare the perceived performance of each employee to the perceived performance of co-workers. The results let the supervisors rank the employees' performance levels in one of two ways. Supervisors can use *straight ranking* and simply list the employees from best to worst, or supervisors can use *forced distribution* by creating categories (such as average, above average, and superior) and place a certain number of employees into each category.

Both types of rankings can identify the "best" and the "worst" workers, but it is important for managers to remember that they compare only relative performance. Even the highest performer could be falling short of organizational expectations. Conversely, it is possible that the lowest-ranked employee is meeting organizational goals quite well (if not as well as the "stars" above him or her). Another limitation of comparative methods is that they may identify overall performance levels but fail to identify the specific strengths and weaknesses of individual employees. Sandra Lynn, the retiring legal clerk, was ranked somewhat lower than other clerks in the legal division because she did not always complete assignments on time. This did not reflect the fact that the other clerks only typed what was given to them, leaving proofreading and revising to the

For some jobs, objective measures say nothing about quality of performance.

FIGURE 17.7 Traditional Rating Scale

Behavior	Unsatisfactory	Questionable	Satisfactory	Outstanding
A. Quantity of Work	1	2	3	(4)
B. Quality of Work	1	2	(3)	4
C. Work Initiative	1	(2)	3	4
D. Efficiency	1	2	(3)	4
E. Overall	1	2	(3)	4

Employee Rated: Jean Smith
Rater: Susanne Rowe

attorneys, whereas Sandra took the time to proofread her work and draft memos suggesting possible changes and corrections.

The *absolute standards approach* is another subjective method, but in this approach, managers compare the performance of each employee to a certain standard instead of to the performance of other employees; thus, they rate the degree to which performance meets the standard. There is a variety of absolute standards or rating approaches to performance appraisal. In the *traditional approach,* managers use job analysis to identify important performance dimensions. They then develop a rating scale with several grades of performance and use the scale to compare a worker's performance to the standard. Figure 17.7 shows the traditional rating scale used by Kathy Holt and other managers at her hospital.

Behaviorally anchored rating scales (BARS) have been developed to improve the accuracy and usefulness of absolute standards rating scales.[13] The BARS approach also uses a scale for each relevant dimension of performance, but this scale has anchors at various points along it. For each performance dimension that is to be evaluated, specific and observable behaviors that reflect varying degrees of performance effectiveness are described. A rater chooses the description of behavior most characteristic of an employee's actual performance (see Figure 17.8). Although the BARS approach is an improvement in the quality of performance ratings, it has not eliminated many of the problems with appraisals described in the following section.

Identifying and Dealing with Appraisal Problems
Because most performance appraisals rely in large part on subjective methods, they are influenced by the perceptions of raters. Because they are subjective, many of the perceptual problems discussed in Chapter 13 can emerge in the appraisal process. For example, some supervisors base their ratings entirely on first impressions of an employee's performance, and others base them on only very recent job performance. Halo effects disturb ratings when a single positive or negative characteristic of an employee's performance is allowed to influence the ratings. Some supervisors distort performance ratings because of prejudices or stereotypes against people of certain race, gender, religion, age, or other characteristics.

Performance ratings also pose other problems. One of the most severe is their unreliability. If two or more raters are doing an appraisal, or if

FIGURE 17.8 *Behaviorally Anchored Rating Scale*

Supervising Sales Personnel

Gives sales personnel a clear idea of their job duties and responsibilities, exercises tact and consideration in working with subordinates, handles work scheduling efficiently and equitably, supplements formal training with his or her own "coaching," keeps informed of what the salespeople are doing on the job, and follows company policy in agreements with subordinates.

Effective	9	Could be expected to conduct full day's sales clinic with two new salespeople and thereby develop them into top salespeople in the department.
	8	Could be expected to gve his or her sales personnel confidence and strong sense of responsibility by delegating many important jobs to them.
	7	Could be expected *never* to fail to conduct training meetings with his or her people weekly at a scheduled hour and to convey to them exactly what is expected.
	6	Could be expected to exhibit courtesy and respect toward his or her sales personnel.
	5	Could be expected to remind sales personnel to wait on customers instead of conversing with each other.
	4	Could be expected to be rather critical of store standards in front of his or her own people, thereby risking their developing poor attitudes.
	3	Could be expected to tell an individual to come in anyway even though he or she called in to say he or she was ill.
	2	Could be expected to go back on a promise to an individual whom he or she had told could transfer back into previous department if he or she did not like the new one.
Ineffective	1	Could be expected to make promises to an individual about his or her salary being based on department sales even when he or she knew such a practice was against company policy.

Source: Adapted from J. P. Campbell, M. D. Dunnette, R. D. Arvey, and L. V. Hellervik (1973), The development and evaluation of behaviorally based rating scales, *Journal of Applied Psychology*, 57, 15–22.

raters use two or more different techniques, the results may disagree. Some raters are more lenient than others. Some raters do not like to differentiate among employees and, therefore, tend to rate all employees quite similarly.

How can managers do a better job of appraising performance? Improvements require an integrated set of actions. First, raters should be taught to recognize and avoid the pitfalls just discussed. Rating instruments also must be improved and raters trained in how to use them properly. Then, dimensions of performance and the scales for rating them must be described unambiguously so that the raters understand what they mean. The rating process should involve standardized procedures, and the raters must be motivated to follow them. Finally, top-level managers must recognize that rating performance is an important part of every manager's job, and they must assess managers in part on how effectively they rate subordinates. Pay and promotions for managers also should be based, in part, on the effectiveness of their performance appraisals.

Compensation and Benefits

Money can motivate workers to meet goals. Although people join organizations for a variety of reasons, including their desire for interesting challenges, enjoyable interactions with other people, and simply a need to get away from home, being paid for their efforts is certainly a major attraction. Organizations pay their members in two ways, through cash compensation and benefits.

Cash Compensation

Organizations compensate people in cash to attract them in the first place, to keep them, to motivate and reward their performance, and to give them feelings of satisfaction. To accomplish these objectives, managers use pay levels, pay structure, and individual pay.

Pay Level **Pay level** is the relationship between an organization's rate of cash compensation and the general level for comparable jobs in the labor market. Pay level varies with many different factors, such as the supply and demand for workers and the financial health of an organization. "Wage leaders" are organizations that generally pay employees more than other organizations pay for similar jobs in the same labor market. "Wage trailers" pay less than average for the market; thus, a wage leader pays computer analysts 15 percent more an hour than a neighboring wage trailer. The wage leader, therefore, is likely to attract more applicants for computer analyst positions and to keep those it already has, although the wage trailer may attract workers with other enticements, such as better working conditions and more interesting projects.

Because decisions about pay levels have major implications for organizations as a whole, managers should include them when designing a human resource strategy. For example, they may have to offer high pay levels to recruit employees in a tight labor market. When labor is plentiful, unemployment is high, and jobs are highly structured and controlled, organizations may be able to offer lower pay levels. Managers must keep abreast of prevailing pay rates. Much of the information necessary for determining these comes from **wage surveys** that contain summarized information on prevailing pay practices collected from organizations within a given labor market.

Pay levels vary by region and by the size of the employing organization. Figure 17.9 shows the survey information for the chief pharmacist job at hospitals with over 500 beds in the Southeastern part of the United States. The median figure indicates that 50 percent of the organizations surveyed paid more than $35,500 for chief pharmacists and 50 percent paid less than $35,500. The column labeled "first quartile" indicates a pay level higher than in 25 percent of hospitals; the "third quartile" figure indicates a figure higher than in 75 percent of the hospitals surveyed. Because of its need for a stable workforce and its ability to pay, Kathy Holt's hospital has chosen to pay 5 percent more than prevailing practice in the labor market; thus, at the time of the survey shown in Figure 17.9, it set the middle of its pay range for the chief pharmacist job at 105 percent of $35,500 ($37,275).

FIGURE 17.9   *Sample Pay Survey Results*

Chief Pharamacist

Directs, coordinates, and supervises all activities in the hospital pharmacy in the purchase, receiving, storing, compounding, and the dispensing of pharmaceuticals. As necessary, assists in the dispensing of medication and maintenance of inventory, records, files, and references, and consults with and advises medical staff regarding drugs and pharmaceuticals.

Region	Bed Size	Average Salaries			Weighted Average Salary	Average Salary Range	
		First Quartile	Median	Third Quartile		Minimum	Maximum
United	0-100	$27,500	$31,700	$35,400	$32,900	$25,600	$36,300
States	100-300	31,700	34,600	38,700	35,600	27,900	39,700
	300-500	36,000	38,500	41,800	38,700	30,100	43,400
	500 and Over	37,000	42,600	45,300	38,100	31,000	45,700
Northeast	0-100	27,700	30,800	32,000	33,900	24,300	35,100
	100-300	29,900	32,000	36,000	32,800	25,600	36,600
	300-500	33,800	37,200	41,900	37,700	29,700	43,400
	500 and Over	35,100	40,000	43,500	40,300	30,800	45,200
Southeast	0-100	27,000	32,800	38,500	32,500	27,100	37,200
	100-300	31,500	34,300	39,300	35,000	28,500	40,500
	300-500	35,300	38,800	40,100	37,500	29,100	42,200
	500 and Over	31,900	35,500	49,200	33,900	28,600	42,900
North	0-100	26,000	30,800	33,300	30,200	24,100	34,500
Central	100-300	33,600	34,600	37,400	36,100	27,700	39,800
	300-500	35,500	37,000	39,500	37,700	29,100	42,400
	500 and Over	38,100	43,000	45,100	38,800	31,500	46,300
South	0-100	28,400	33,000	35,400	32,000	25,500	36,500
Central	100-300	29,500	35,200	38,200	33,600	26,700	39,200
	300-500	36,900	40,000	42,400	39,600	30,500	43,300
	500 and Over	39,900	42,000	45,900	42,900	31,600	47,500
West	0-100		41,000		36,800	28,600	39,800
Coast	100-300	35,700	39,000	42,200	38,600	31,200	42,600
	300-500	42,100	45,900	53,800	47,000	37,500	51,100
	500 and Over		45,500		46,600	35,600	48,600

Source: *Hospital and health care report* (1984/85), 9th ed., Fort Lee, NJ: Executive Compensation Service, Inc., a subsidiary of the Wyatt Company, 104.

Human resource managers can get information about pay levels from many different sources, such as the U.S. Bureau of Labor Statistics, the American Compensation Association, and the American Management Association. In addition, many industry groups collect data relevant to their own industries, as do some organizations. The National Association of Independent Insurers, for example, surveys pay levels for a wide range of insurance industry jobs. Many professional associations also conduct surveys focused on specific occupational areas. For example, the American Society for Personnel Administration surveys pay levels in human resource jobs.

Pay Structure   Whereas pay level involves the comparison of the amount of cash compensation offered by one organization to that of another, **pay structure** describes the relative values and pay ranges for each job in the same organization. Pay structures specify the minimum, midpoint, and maximum pay levels for each organizational job or groups of jobs (also called *pay grades*). Table 17.3 contains part of the pay structure from the legal department at Kathy Holt's hospital (the legal clerk III job is a C pay grade).

Pay structures are developed and priced by combining the results of wage surveys and an organization's human resource goals with the

TABLE 17.3   Sample Pay Structure

Pay Grade	Annual Pay Range		
	Minimum	Midpoint	Maximum
A	10,200	12,000	13,800
B	11,220	13,200	15,180
C	12,580	14,800	17,020
D	14,280	16,800	19,320
E	16,065	18,900	21,735
.			
.			
.			

information provided by job evaluation. Job evaluation, as you saw earlier, is the process of determining the overall value of a specific job relative to the value of other jobs in the pay structure. For example, human resource managers at Kathy Holt's hospital used job evaluations to compare the relative value of the jobs legal clerk I, II, and III; secretary I and II; legal aides I and II; and so on. Generally, job evaluation is based on the results of job analysis and resulting job descriptions. The content of jobs is compared to standards (sometimes called *compensable factors*) that indicate the value of jobs based on their importance to the organization.

Of all the procedures used to conduct job evaluations, the point method is the one most widely used today. The **point method** identifies a group of compensable factors, which typically parallel factors in job analyses, and assigns points to each job according to the level of responsibility for each factor. A rater then adds the points and arrives at a total for each job. For most of the structured job analysis approaches described earlier, there are computerized methods of converting job analyses into points. Table 17.4 provides an example of the point method of job evaluation. Note how each job is rated in each of four areas to arrive at an overall point value for each job. The total number of points indicates the relative overall value (responsibility level) of the evaluated job.

Once jobs have been given points, jobs with approximately the same numbers of points are usually grouped into grades. The legal clerk III job, for example, was grouped with jobs—such as secretary II—and placed in job grade C. Human resource managers then check the pay surveys for each grade and set midpoints for pay ranges for each job grade based on the organization's decision to lead, trail, or match market pay levels. Finally, they assign minimum and maximum levels of pay within each

TABLE 17.4   The Point Method of Job Evaluation

Job	Compensable Factor				Total Points
	Skill	Effort	Responsibility	Job Conditions	
File clerk	50	45	60	50	205
Receptionist	70	60	70	45	245
Medical secretary	85	75	85	60	305
Lab technician	100	80	95	55	330

range. It was through this process that a pay range of $12,580 to $17,020 was determined for the legal clerk III job shown in Figure 17.2. Usually they adjust pay structures annually to take into account changes in market compensation and in job design.

Individual Pay   Once pay ranges are established for jobs, how does a manager determine what to pay an individual? Decisions about **individual pay** usually are based on a combination of factors. Workers usually are paid according to *qualification level*, that is, their prior work experience, if any, and their level of skills. For example, a legal clerk with five years of experience is likely to earn more than a novice. Workers also are paid based on *seniority*, that is, the length of time that they have worked for an organization or in their current job. The legal clerk III hired to replace Sandra Lynn will probably earn less than Sandra or her co-worker, a legal clerk III who has worked at the hospital for three years. Finally, workers are paid for their actual performance on the job—their *merit*. As you learned in Chapter 14 and other chapters in this book, pay based on performance can motivate workers to perform effectively.

For jobs in which it is possible to measure performance objectively, **incentive** systems are sometimes used. With a piece rate plan, for example, employees are paid a certain amount for each unit of work produced. Some organizations have production bonuses that pay "extra" when a worker produces more than a standard amount in a given time period. Commission plans for salespeople provide compensation based on the amount of product or service sold. In situations in which individual output is difficult to assess, group plans sometimes are appropriate. The supervisor of a team assembling the bathroom exhaust fans mentioned earlier, for example, could be paid a low hourly wage but receive a production bonus based on the output of the team working on his or her assembly line.

Some organizations use bonus systems not only to pay individuals for high productivity but also to reward them for offering cost-saving suggestions and other unique contributions. Profit-sharing systems pay each employee a bonus based on the profits that an organization earns. When the plans are designed properly and the bonuses are significant, most bonus plans increase workers' general satisfaction with their organization and encourage them to stay. Profit-sharing plans seldom motivate workers to improve their performance significantly, however, because few employees honestly believe that they can significantly influence their organization's profits.

Benefits

Many employees get benefits (noncash compensation) as well as cash compensation from their organizations. Benefits can include almost anything from medical insurance to retirement plans and vacations to college tuition for workers' children. The U.S. Chamber of Commerce Research Association develops annual estimates of the cost of benefits for American organizations. Twenty years ago, organizations spent an amount equal to about 30 percent of cash compensation on benefits for employees. Today, the figure is closer to 40 percent.

Day-care benefits are becoming increasingly popular.

What do organizations hope to receive in exchange for the millions of dollars that they spend on benefits? Some organizations have a simple paternalistic motivation: they want to protect and provide for their employees. For example, they offer health care and life insurance policies. Most organizations, however, view benefit costs as a business investment. They expect benefits to help them attract qualified job candidates and persuade them to accept positions. They hope that benefits will encourage employees to keep their jobs, to retire contentedly, and to feel satisfied with their work.

Types of Benefits   Organizations offer an extremely wide range of benefits. Some benefits that many employees have come to think of as standard include:

- *Time not worked*—pay for "time off," such as coffee breaks, holidays, and vacations
- *Insurance*—primarily coverage for disability, medical care, and death
- *Retirement*—private plans, such as savings, thrift, and stock options, offered in addition to the 7.51 percent of cash compensation that most organizations must contribute to Social Security
- *Income maintenance*—insurance and other policies that continue an employee's income in case of unemployment or disability

Other forms of benefits are not yet so firmly established as to be considered standard in most cases. Fitness and wellness programs, such as memberships in health clubs or on-site exercise facilities, have become extremely popular. Some employees want day-care benefits for their children. Increasing numbers of organizations are setting up "employee assistance programs" to provide counseling and treatment, such as self-improvement seminars, stress-management programs, and financial and tax planning.

Flexible Benefits   Usually, benefits are offered to all full-time employees in an organization regardless of whether they are likely to use or even want them. In the last ten years, however, more and more organizations have begun to offer benefit plans that allow employees the flexibility of choosing plans that meet their own personal needs. These plans are often called **cafeteria plans,** because employees choose benefits much as they would choose a meal in a cafeteria line. Every benefit is priced, and employees are told how much money their organization will give them to spend. Employees can spend their money however they please, choosing day care over dental coverage, life insurance protection for dependents over increased health policies, and so on.

In some cafeteria plans, organizations specify a set of benefits that everyone must receive, and employees spend their money to add on to these "core" benefits. Sometimes organizations do this to avoid imbalances, as would occur if, for example, only older employees chose retirement coverage. Sometimes organizations specify core benefits because managers have strong beliefs about certain issues, such as the feeling that employees should take at least one week's vacation each year.

Flexible benefit plans can work, but they must be developed, introduced, and administered carefully. If employees are properly educated and the extra administrative burdens that the plans impose are handled appropriately, flexible plans can deliver more benefit value to employees than standard, fixed plans that allow little choice.

Designing and Evaluating Benefit Systems It is beyond the scope of this chapter to describe fully how to design and evaluate benefit systems. The process is intricate and important, and it should be conducted systematically if an organization is to receive the best return on this type of investment.[14] Generally, human resource managers must design and evaluate benefit systems by examining alternative benefits and their value to employees. They must check the costs and benefits of any potential plan. A benefit plan contributes to an organization's objectives primarily to the extent that employees perceive that it is better than the plans available elsewhere.

Labor-Management Relations

Labor unions developed to protect employees from undesirable management practices. Unions concentrated on improving health and safety conditions at work, controlling the hours employees could be asked to work, protecting job security, and, of course, improving pay.

Union Formation

Research indicates that employees vote to join a union when they are dissatisfied with their ability to meet their economic and noneconomic goals at work.[15] They may feel that their working conditions are unsafe or that their pay levels are exploitative. The National Labor Relations Board (NLRB) has established specific rules that union organizers must follow when trying to start a union for a group of employees. Organizers begin by encouraging employees to sign *authorization cards* stating that they wish to be represented by a union. When a sufficient number of cards has been signed (usually 30 percent of the employee group), the NLRB identifies a *bargaining unit* (the employees to be covered if the union prevails) and conducts a *representation election*. If a majority of employees votes to establish the union, the NLRB certifies it to act as the employees' representative. If not, at least one year must pass before another representation election can be held.

Collective Bargaining

Winning a representation election gives a union the right to require an organization to negotiate agreements that cover wages, working hours, and the terms and conditions of work. Table 17.5 contains a wide range of items in these categories. It shows the broad impact that a union can have on the human resource function.

Before an existing labor contract expires, the union and employer must notify each other and the Federal Mediation and Conciliation Service if they plan to negotiate changes in the bargaining agreement. They then meet and try to reach a new agreement. The union identifies and bargains on items that represent the concerns of its membership. The employer tries to negotiate terms favorable to the organization. If the two parties agree on terms, a renegotiated contract is presented to union members for their approval, known as a **ratification vote.** If union employees vote to

TABLE 17.5   Items Mandatory for Bargaining

Wages	Stock-purchase plan	Partial plant closing
Hours	Workloads	Hunting on employer forest reserve
Discharge	Change of employee status to	where previously granted
Arbitration	independent contractors	Plant closedown and relocation
Holidays—paid	Motor carrier—union agreement	Change in operations resulting in
Vacations—paid	providing that carriers use own	reclassifying workers from
Duration of agreement	equipment before leasing	incentive to straight time, or cut
Grievance procedure	outside equipment	workforce, or installation of
Layoff plan	Overtime pay	cost-saving machine
Reinstatement of economic strikers	Agency shop	Plant closing
Change of payment from hourly	Sick leave	Job-posting procedures
base to salary base	Employers insistence on clause	Plant reopening
Union security and checkoff	giving arbitrator right to enforce	Employee physical examination
Work rules	award	Union security
Merit-wage increase	Management-rights clause	Bargaining over "bar list"
Work schedule	Cancellation of seniority on	Truck rentals—minimum rental to
Lunch periods	relocation of plant	be paid by carriers to
Rest periods	Discounts on company products	employee-owned vehicles
Pension plan	Shift differentials	Musician price lists
Retirement age	Contract clause providing for	Arrangement for negotiation
Bonus payments	supervisors' keeping seniority in	Change in insurance carrier and
Price of meals provided by	unit	benefits
company	Procedures for income tax	Profit-sharing plan
Group insurance—health,	withholding	Company houses
accident, life	Severance pay	Subcontracting
Promotions	Nondiscriminatory hiring hall	Discriminatory racial policies
Seniority	Plant rules	Production ceiling imposed by
Layoffs	Safety	union
Transfers	Prohibition against supervisor	Most-favored-nation clause
Work assignments and transers	doing unit work	Vended food products
No-strike clause	Superseniority for union stewards	
Piece rates	Checkoff	

Source: R. Richardson (1979), Positive collective bargaining, in *ASPA handbook of personnel and industrial relations*, D. Yoder and H. G. Heneman, Jr., eds., Washington, DC: Bureau of National Affairs, 7-120–7-121.

A union's primary tool is a strike.

accept the agreement, it goes into effect. If they reject the agreement, the union must either hold a second vote or go back to the bargaining table for another round of negotiations with management.

Bargaining Impasses

If the two sides fail to sign a contract, an *impasse* is said to exist. If requested, the Federal Mediation and Conciliation Service will provide an impartial third party, known as a **mediator,** to work with the bargainers to identify a mutually acceptable agreement. The mediator does not have the power to force an agreement, only to help the sides reach one. If the parties do not request a mediator, or if the mediator cannot get them to agree, one or both parties may take more forceful actions to encourage the other side to agree to their terms.

The primary tool of the union is a **strike.** Not all strikes are alike. If a contract has expired, employees can legally refuse to return to work until an agreement is reached, an arrangement known as an *economic strike.* In the late 1980s, the contract between the nurses' union and Kathy Holt's hospital expired. The union demanded a clause in the new contract that would reduce the patient-to-nurse ratio at the hospital. When the hospital refused to agree, the union called a strike, and the nurses refused to work. After the local media presented editorial comments favoring the nurses, hospital management agreed to the desired clause. The nurses returned to work. Sometimes a union calls an *unfair labor practice strike* to try to force an employer to conform to agreed-upon terms. Such a strike was threatened by the nurses' union a year later after the hospital had not fully kept its promise to lower the ratios. A *wildcat strike,* although unauthorized and illegal, is sometimes conducted by union members in violation of an existing contract.

Organizations have their own tools. Under certain circumstances, they can conduct a **lockout** by closing down operations and refusing to offer work to union members until an agreement is reached. Sometimes an organization hires nonunion members, called **scabs,** to work in place of striking union members. These actions, although legal, usually generate bitter reactions by union members.

Grievance Activities

A union contract specifies agreed-upon conditions of employment. If a union member feels that part of a contract has been violated, he or she may file a **grievance** that describes the alleged violation. An employee designated to represent the union members, known as a **steward,** attempts to resolve the grievance by meeting with the complaining employee's supervisor. If this does not lead to satisfaction, higher-level representatives of the union and the organization typically meet to develop a solution. Finally, if the employee does not feel that the issue has been resolved, the grievance can be submitted to an outside third party, called an **arbitrator.** This step, called **binding arbitration,** is the last available remedy. Both parties are obligated to conform to the findings of the arbitrator.

Public-Sector Considerations

The kinds of labor-management relations just discussed are those characteristic of private-sector organizations. In the public sector, things are somewhat different. In most states, for example, it is illegal for public employees to strike, a fact that clearly can limit union power substantially. Instead of allowing strikes, many states require binding arbitration, fact finding, or voluntary arbitration. One disadvantage to these methods is that they are slow. Employees sometimes must work for long periods of time without a contract, and mountains of paperwork build when the delayed contract is finally signed. Sometimes arbitrators must work according to guidelines that some people feel are detrimental. For example, guidelines for teachers' contracts in Wisconsin say that arbitrators must choose the proposal of either the school board or the teachers' union but not a compromise solution. The obvious advantage of and prevailing rationale for these methods is that agreements can be reached without work stoppages, and, as the argument goes, public-sector employees—such as police, firefighters, and teachers—are so important to the social welfare that they must not strike.

Human Resource Strategic Planning

Human resource managers must try to match organization members to particular jobs so that these people's individual needs are met and so that the match benefits the organization. To achieve this match, human resource managers follow a systematic approach—strategic planning. In Chapter 9, you saw that strategic planning is needed at three levels of an organization: corporate, business unit, and functional. Human resource planning is an example of strategy at the functional level, designed to support an organization's overall strategic plan by managing the people who perform the daily activities it requires. Chapter 9 discussed a nine-step strategic planning process that could guide strategic planning at any of the three levels (see Figure 17.10). Consider some of the issues that a human resource manager considers at each of the nine steps.

Step One: Planning Awareness

At this first step of the planning process, human resource managers get a sense of past activities. What goals were spelled out? How were people to reach them? Did they? How well? Human resource managers examine previous methods of job analysis, staffing, training, appraising performance, and so forth. At this step, human resource managers also review the number of employees, their mix and nature, the degree to which unions have been involved, and their treatment of and by the organization. They identify any formal organizational policies concerning human resource management and any practices, even informal ones, that define the current practice of human resource management in an organization.

FIGURE 17.10   *The Strategic Planning Process*

Source: Based on C. W. Hofer (1986), *Strategy formulation: Issues and concepts,* 2nd ed., St. Paul, MN: West.

Step Two: Formulating Goals

Because a functional strategy should support and conform to the strategy of the business unit and corporation, many human resource goals are formulated at the corporate or business unit level of strategic planning. Recall from Chapter 4 IBM's socially responsible, corporate-level decisions when it converted its typewriter plant in Kentucky from a traditional labor-intensive assembly plant to one that uses robotics. This decision clearly meant that the size and nature of the labor force at the plant would change. Corporate strategy also dictated that all displaced employees be offered other jobs within IBM. Human resource managers had to formulate goals to support the higher-level strategy by, for example, creating training programs to give employees the skills needed for their new jobs.

Step Three: Analyzing the Environment

In the third step, human resource managers check conditions in the external environment that have a bearing on the strategy they are to pursue. This scan is comprehensive: it covers economic factors and trends, such as regional labor costs; supply and demand of needed employees; and new laws and regulations, such as those covering equal pay for *comparable* (not just equal) work. This environmental scan may also evaluate union negotiations at other organizations and the success or failure of unions in bargaining on important issues.

William J. Colucci

William J. Colucci has held various staff and executive personnel positions since joining IBM in 1968. These have included both domestic and international assignments in manufacturing, development, field sales, and marketing organizations. In his current position, which he assumed in January 1988, Mr. Colucci is responsible for all personnel activities within IBM United States.

"The human resource function must anticipate . . . and adapt. . . ."

1. What do you consider the most significant personnel/human resource advances made by IBM?

As business conditions have changed in IBM, we have been able to avoid layoffs through workload rebalancing, employee retraining, and the use of hiring alternatives. The voluntary nature of these efforts and the flexibility of our employees have enabled us to meet our changing resource needs.

Our human resource policies and the benefits we provide our employees have been responsive to the changing demographics and expectations of our workforce. For example, our child and elder care referral programs, extended leaves for personal and family care, and individualized work schedules help our employees balance work and home life challenges.

At IBM, we are willing to change everything but our basic beliefs, the most important of which is "respect for the individual." All of our personnel policies and practices are built on this principle. Through management training, and a broad range of employee communication vehicles, IBM continues to maintain a positive employee relations environment.

2. What is today's biggest challenge to effective human resource management?

We face three major challenges: first, anticipating and adapting our policies and practices to the changing business and legislative environment; second, developing affordable personnel strategies that are responsive to our employees and to our company; and third, continually looking for ways to educate and motivate our employees in order to maintain quality, productivity, and customer service.

3. How do you expect personnel/ human resource management to change during the 1990s?

American businesses will be challenged to become more productive with fewer resources as we face increased foreign competition. Our role will be to find ways to meet these new requirements without causing undue disruption and hardship to the workforce.

As new legislative initiatives are introduced which affect the workforce, the human resource function must anticipate, influence, and adapt to these changes.

Significant changes in the demographics of the workforce have occurred in the last twenty years, and more will occur at a faster pace. Our challenge is to modify our policies and practices in order to meet societal expectations, while at the same time providing cost-effective support of the business process.

The key is to constantly maintain an open and positive relationship with employees so, when change occurs, there is understanding and receptivity.

Step Four: Analyzing Organizational Resources

At this step, human resource managers assess their organization's existing human resources. How many employees are currently working at the organization? What kinds of abilities, work experiences, and motivation do they possess? Human resource managers check performance levels, turnover rates, attendance levels, job satisfaction, and so on. At this step, managers project changes in human resources, such as whether a large number of employees is likely to retire soon or be needed in new middle-management positions.

Step Five: Identifying Strategic Opportunities and Threats

Top-level managers use the results of their environmental and organizational analyses to draw conclusions about opportunities for and threats to their organization. Human resource managers also need to answer the question "Given what the organization hopes to accomplish, how can its existing human resources and policies help or hinder it?" For example, expected labor shortages in a particular location can threaten an organization's goal of opening branch offices in that area. If part of the organization's strategy depends on retaining skilled employees to avoid the costs of hiring and training new workers, employee dissatisfaction with its compensation and benefit plans could cause many of them to leave. Human resource managers might pinpoint a benefit that could attract employees, or they might identify a particularly bright and highly motivated group of employees for a special work assignment. At this stage, too, an organization that anticipates significant growth might identify its employees with managerial potential.

Step Six: Performing Gap Analysis

At this step, human resource managers examine the gaps between where the organization *wants* to go and where it *will* go if its human resource strategy is not changed. Gap analysis might reveal, for example, that the organization will fail to recruit the number of qualified engineers that it needs given current pay practices or that performance problems will arise if training programs are not changed. Table 17.6, for example, shows the results of a gap analysis that compares the supply of and demand for four important categories of workers in a company that plans to add robotics to its assembly lines. This analysis reveals that, even though an

TABLE 17.6   *Gap Analysis: Labor Supply and Demand*

Job Category	Labor Demand	Labor Supply	Gap
Unskilled material handlers	75	145	70 (Surplus)
Skilled assembly workers	150	130	−20 (Shortage)
Robotics tehcnicians	40	12	−28 (Shortage)
Repair technicians	15	8	− 7 (Shortage)
Totals	280	295	+15 (Surplus)

overall surplus of fifteen employees is expected, shortages are anticipated for three of the four job categories. This information is important at the next step of the planning process, when human resource managers must design strategies to cope with the disparities that their gap analysis reveals.

Step Seven: Designing Strategy

At this step, managers specify actual policies and practices. For each of the major activities, such as staffing and training, managers detail actual methods and expected results. If gap analysis forecasts a shortage of skilled robotics technicians, for example, the human resource strategy might specify recruiting skilled technicians, modifying compensation practices to keep current technicians, and training existing unskilled employees to become skilled technicians. Human resource strategic plans typically outline both specific objectives ("reduce benefit costs by 5 percent") and actions to accomplish the objectives ("adopt a benefit plan that requires employee contributions to major benefits, such as health insurance").

Step Eight: Implementing Strategy

This stage in the human resource planning model calls for putting the strategy into effect (see Chapter 20). Because human resource strategies usually affect every member of an organization, implementation effectiveness is critical—but seldom easy. One reason is that people frequently resist change in general. Another reason is that employees often view the ideas that come from human resource departments as attempts to do something *to* rather than *for* them. Most people simply do not like to be controlled, and they may perceive the plans of human resource managers as intrusively controlling.

Step Nine: Measuring and Controlling Progress

At this step, human resource managers must engage in two types of activities. First, they must measure how well the plan has been implemented. Are managers using the new system, for example? Are they providing the necessary feedback to employees? Are they following the rules for rating employees? Did turnover really drop after an on-site day-care center was built? Did performance actually increase after a bonus pay plan was introduced? In short, did the strategy work? Second, if managers conclude that the plan is not being followed, they must act to enforce it. They may need to reassess the plan to determine why it is not working and, perhaps, revise their goals or operational strategy. (See "A Closer Look: Human Resources and Computers.")

The Reality

The strategic planning process described in this section portrays an ideal way to manage human resources for mature, progressive organizations. In reality, very few organizations manage human resources this systematically or in such a sophisticated fashion. How thoroughly manag-

A CLOSER LOOK

Human Resources and Computers: Should HR Managers Chip Away at HR Information?

All organizations must manage the human resource function. Most organizations, even small ones, are using computers to find new and creative ways to facilitate organizational effectiveness. It seems natural that these two realities should blend and produce computer programs that help manage the human resource function. In fact, organizations routinely use computers to keep track of payroll rosters, compensation, and distributions of the workforce. Seldom, however, do HR managers systematically use computers to conduct and track job evaluations or performance reviews, nor is the computer used much to track health and safety records or career path and profile information.

> *All organizations must manage the human resource function.*

HR managers commonly use computers to monitor payroll, compensation, employment history, and other recordkeeping information. Managers who use computers as a human resource tool state that they do so to save time and increase management

efficiency, objectives that can be accomplished by computerized recordkeeping. Very few HR managers profess to use computers to enhance decision making or to improve human resource effectiveness. This restricted view of the computer's capability may be why computers are least used in such areas as career development, job evaluation, and performance review. It is these areas in which the human resources function can contribute to employee development and enhance organizational effectiveness.

> *What is needed is for managers to expand their domain of expectations.*

Although the majority of managers in human resource departments agree that computerized human resource systems are very useful for an organization, only about one fifth of the top managers who manage nonhuman resource functions feel this way. Worse, less than one seventh of the managers of departments unrelated to human resources think that computers can save their organization money or augment decision making. These and other findings from a survey of 325 organizations using computerized HR systems seem to indicate that

the status of human resources information systems will not have changed substantially in the future unless top management sees more advantages in

computerized human resources information systems. If the present climate does not change, practice will continue to lag behind what is technically possible.[1]

What does the future hold? Technically, the hardware and software is there to support expanded human resource uses of the computer. The Bureau of National Affairs, for example, offers a 1988 computer program that allows managers to determine easily what their organization's minority hiring record has been, plant by plant, or the overall effect on payroll if all manufacturing employees were to receive a 6 percent raise, among many other features.[2] There is nothing to prevent the development of programs that would enable an employee to sit at a computer and explore the experiences, abilities, and skills required to pursue various career options in his or her organization. In sum, it is not the lack of capability that stymies expanded use of computers in the human resource area. What is needed is for managers to expand their domain of expectations. The potential is there. It awaits only the interest.

1. L. L. Moore and C. J. Clavadetscher (August 1985), Computerized HRIS: Still simmering on the back burner, *Personnel,* 11.
2. HR Pro, a BNA software product.

ers are able to plan and execute human resource activities depends in large part on their organization's stage of development. Just as groups begin with an orientation phase and go through several stages on their way to group maturity (recall the discussion of group development in Chapter 13), organizations also pass through levels of development.

Table 17.7 shows five stages of human resource management typically found in organizations. The strategic planning model discussed in this

TABLE 17.7   The Human Resource Strategic Matrix

Components	Stage I Initiation	Stage II Functional Growth	Stage III Controlled Growth	Stage IV Functional Integration	Stage V Strategic Integration
Manager awareness	Aware of function's administrative role	Aware of function's broad role but not committed	Aware; often frustrated at fragmentation	Cooperative and involved	Integrated
Management of the personnel function	Loose, informal; often none	Personnel manager; program orientation; manage, conflicts among subfunctions	Personnel executive; business orientation; control, measurements, goals	Function orientation; department goals; planning, long-range direction, line/staff relations; collaborative	Company orientation; consistent and integrated with business strategic direction
Portfolio of programs	Basic salary and benefits administration; basic recordkeeping; nonexempt hiring	Many new programs added responding to business needs in comp. benefits, training, etc.; revisiting basic programs	Management control programs; budgets, ROI; portfolio reevaluated in measurable and analytical terms; advanced compensation	Interdisciplinary programs; focus on department goals and direction; productivity; change management; succession planning	Cultural and environmental scanning; long-range planning; emphasis on effectiveness and efficiency in direct response to business needs
Information technology	Manual employee profile; recordkeeping	Automated salary and basic profile; advance recordkeeping	Automate personnel work; mainly profiles, EEO, tracking; basic metrics	Utilize computer for projection; planning, analysis, and evaluation	Planning tools, research, and analysis; long-range issues and "what-if" questions linked to the personnel and the organizational database
Personnel skills	Administrative routine and housekeeping	Functional specialists	Increased professionalism in function and managerial skills	Integrating activities; skills in systems, planning, and analysis	High-level involvement in organization; skills dealing with macro issues
Awareness of internal and external environment	Not aware	Aware of environment and corporate culture but do not incorporate them into function's activities	Aware of risks and opportunities in environment; address some in programs	Aware of; react and incorporate into planning process; environmental changes identified	Systematically search for impact the environment has on organization; take an active role in making and shaping decisions

Source: L. Baird and I. Meshoulam (1988), Managing two fits of strategic human resource management, *Academy of Management Review*, 13, 124.

section is most consistent with the strategic integration stage (Stage V) shown in the table. Other less advanced, but perhaps more common, approaches are found in the descriptions of Stages I through IV. Stage I, for example, is appropriate for new organizations in which line managers and their administrative staff members handle most human resource management activities, concentrating primarily on basic recruiting and compensation programs.[16] As organizations expand, line managers become too busy to recruit and train people, and they lack the specialized knowledge and contacts they need to do so. For an organization at this phase in its development, Stage II is an appropriate level of human resource activities. Stages III and IV address organizational situations when rapid expansion slows, competition for resources intensifies, and diversification points to the need for decentralization of authority.

In other words, although managing human resources should be approached as systematically as possible,

> *no one best way exists. The practice of human resource management should fit the firm's business needs. Managers should be cautious about adopting what they perceive as state-of-the-art programs and approaches simply because these work well in other organizations. How well these programs will work is determined by how well they fit the organization's needs.*[17]

Human Resource Management in Review

The purpose of the human resource function is to match the abilities and motivation of individuals with the requirements and rewards associated with jobs. If done well, the human resource objectives of attraction, performance, retention, attendance, and satisfaction will be met. To meet these objectives, human resource managers must, among other things, pay attention to all of the economic, labor market, legal, and union factors in the external environment that can influence the process.

The task at the core of human resource management activities is job analysis, which uses direct observation and structured questionnaires to gather information and to document the responsibilities and associated requirements of jobs within organizations. All other human resource activities—staffing, training and development, performance appraisal, motivation and reward programs, and labor management relations—are built on the foundation that job analysis provides.

Staffing is the human resource activity that locates, selects, and prepares career paths for organization members (including separating them from the organization when necessary). Human resource managers are also responsible for training and developing those people hired and then appraising their performance on the job, usually through a combination of objective and subjective methods. Of course, organization members expect to receive something for their efforts, and it is part of the human resource function to determine what that compensation ought to be. Usually it takes the form of cash and benefits, with human resource managers' determining the specific pay levels for employees.

If workers belong to a union, managers do not have total discretion over the working conditions and amount of pay that they can offer. Bargaining agreements, called contracts, specify these and other terms of employment that the workers and the organization have endorsed. If the two sides cannot agree on a contract, an outside party may be brought in to help them reach agreement. In extreme cases of disagreement, union members who work for private organizations may stop working and go on strike. The organization may retaliate by hiring nonunion workers or strike the first blow by locking employees out of the workplace. In the public sector, laws usually govern the settlement of management-labor disputes and prevent strikes by public employees.

Organizations cannot be managed effectively unless the human resource function is also managed effectively. Planning is essential, and the model for strategic planning used in Chapter 9 can be adapted to human resource management. Following this nine-step approach helps managers plan a functional human resource strategy that supports the overall strategy of the organization.

Notes

1. B. D. Steffy and S. D. Maurer (1988), Conceptualizing and measuring the economic effectiveness of human research activities, *Academy of Management Review,* 13, 271–86.

2. This information is described in the U.S. Department of Labor, Bureau of Labor Statistics (1976), *BLS handbook of methods,* Bulletin 1910, Washington, DC: U.S. Government Printing Office.

3. Information on job analysis techniques can be found in the following sources: U.S. Department of Labor, Manpower Administration (1972), *Handbook for analyzing jobs,* Washington, DC: U.S. Government Printing Office; S. E. Bemis, A. H. Belenky, and D. A. Soder (1983), *Job analysis,* Washington, DC: Bureau of National Affairs; E. L. Levine (1983), *Everything you always wanted to know about job analysis,* Tampa, FL: Mariner.

4. R. E. Christal and J. J. Weissmuller (1977), New comprehensive data analysis programs (CODAP) for analyzing task factor information, *JSAS Catalog of Selected Documents in Psychology,* 7, ms. no. 1444, 24–25.

5. E. J. McCormick, P. R. Jeanneret, and R. C. Mecham (1972), A study of job characteristics and job dimensions as based on the position analysis questionnaire (PAQ), *Journal of Applied Psychology,* 56, 347–68.

6. W. W. Tornow and P. R. Pinto (1976), The development of a managerial job taxonomy: A system for describing, classifying, and evaluating executive positions, *Journal of Applied Psychology,* 61, 410–18; J. L. Mitchell and E. J. McCormick (1979), *Development of the PMPQ: A structured job analysis questionnaire for the study of professional and managerial positions,* West Lafayette, IN: Department of Psychological Sciences, Purdue University.

7. R. H. Hawk (1967), *The recruitment function,* New York: American Management Association.

8. J. A. Breaugh (1983), Realistic job previews: A critical appraisal and future research directions, *Academy of Management Review*, 8, 612–19.

9. C. M. Koen, Jr. (1984), Applications forms: Keep them easy and legal, *Personnel Journal*, 63(5), 26–29.

10. H. G. Heneman III, D. P. Schwab, J. A. Fossum, and L. D. Dyer (1986), *Personnel/human resource management*, 3rd ed., Homewood, IL: Irwin, 398–403.

11. K. W. Wexley (1984), Personnel training, *Annual Review of Psychology*, 35, 519–51.

12. Bureau of National Affairs (1983), Performance appraisal programs, *Personnel Policies Forum*, 135.

13. P. C. Smith and L. M. Kendall (1963), Retranslation of expectations: An approach to the construction of unambiguous anchors for rating scales, *Journal of Applied Psychology*, 47, 249–55; J. P. Campbell, M. D. Dunnette, R. D. Arvey, and L. V. Hellervik (1973), The development and evaluation of behaviorally based rating scales, *Journal of Applied Psychology*, 57, 15–22.

14. For a description of one such approach, see: R. B. Dunham and R. A. Formisano (April 1982), Designing and evaluating employee benefit systems, *Personnel Administrator*, 29–35.

15. W. C. Hamner and F. J. Smith (1978), Work attitudes as predictors of unionization activity, *Journal of Applied Psychology*, 63, 415–21; J. M. Brett (1980), Why workers want unions, *Organizational Dynamics*, 8(4), 47–59.

16. L. Baird and I. Meshoulam (1988), Managing two fits of strategic human resource management, *Academy of Management Review*, 13, 118.

17. Baird and Meshoulam, 1988, 125.

Key Terms

human resource management	development
labor market	vestibule training
job	performance appraisal
job analysis	pay level
job description	wage surveys
job evaluation	pay structure
direct observation	point method
work sampling	individual pay
critical incidents	incentive
interviewing	cafeteria plans
structured questionnaires	ratification vote
staffing	mediator
external recruiting	strike
yield ratios	lockout
internal recruiting	scabs
closed recruiting systems	grievance
open recruiting systems	steward
selection	arbitrator
selection device	binding arbitration
training	

Issues for Review and Discussion

1. What are the major goals of the human resource function?
2. Identify major factors of the external environment and explain how they influence the effectiveness of the human resource function.
3. Describe the steps in developing a human resource plan.
4. What are the primary reasons for conducting job analyses?
5. Describe the most important goals and functions of the following activities: external recruiting, internal recruiting, selection, career development, separation.
6. How can an organization identify its training and development needs?
7. Discuss why the performance appraisal and feedback process is troublesome to so many managers.
8. Explain why cash compensation is usually a more effective performance motivator than is noncash compensation.
9. Briefly describe how the presence of a labor union changes the nature of the human resource function.

Suggested Readings

Breaugh, J. A. (1983). Realistic job previews: A critical appraisal and future research directions. *Academy of Management Review*, 8, 612–19.

Brett, J. M. (1980). Why workers want unions. *Organizational Dynamics*, 8(4), 47–59.

Cascio, W. F. (1987). *Costing human resources: The financial impact of behavior in organizations*. Boston: PWS-Kent.

Kravetz, D. J. (1988). *The human resources revolution: Implementing progressive management practices for bottom-line success*. San Francisco: Jossey-Bass.

Latham, G. P. (1988). Human resource training and development. *Annual Review of Psychology*, 39, 545–82.

Levine, E. L. (1983). *Everything you always wanted to know about job analysis*. Tampa, FL: Mariner.

Shepard, I. M. and Duston, R. L. (1987). *Workplace privacy: Employee testing, surveillance, wrongful discharge, and other areas of vulnerability*. Washington: BNA.

Zimmerman, J. H. (April 1986). Human resource management at MCI. *Management Review*, 49–51.

The River City Library

By William Ross of the University of Wisconsin at La Crosse

John Switzer, the head of the River City Citizens' Library Board (CLB), had a problem. His board was charged with evaluating the performance of the library director, who was responsible for the daily affairs of the library. The board had just finished the director's performance evaluation for the previous year, and the entire process left John dissatisfied, although he could not put his finger on the problem.

John called the River City personnel office to see if they would develop a new performance evaluation form for the position of library director. The personnel director explained that her employees were unable to accept new projects at that time and recommended that he hire a consultant. After several phone calls, John obtained the necessary authorization from the proper city officials and arranged a meeting with Fred Sawyer, a private consultant.

Meeting with the Consultant

At the meeting, John explained that the CLB was supposed to supervise the library director, and that he had misgivings about using the existing performance appraisal system.

Fred: So, you'd like my firm to design a new performance appraisal system the board can use to evaluate the library director?

John: Right. I called you because nobody on the board knows how to tackle this situation, and the people at the city personnel office have their hands full with other things.

Fred: How often do you get a chance to observe the library director at work?

John: That's the problem. No one on the board has any formal education in library matters; we all have other jobs. What we know about the library, we've learned from serving on the board. Unless we're also on special committees, we only see the library director at monthly meetings, so we really don't see him at work. He just reports to us.

Fred: Do you have a copy of a job description that I could have?

John: Yes, a job analysis was conducted about a year ago by the city personnel department. Here's the job description they created. [See Figure 17A.]

Fred: What type of performance appraisal have you been using?

John: It's one we borrowed from another library. [See Figure 17B.] We set up a three-member CLB personnel committee. Each member did ratings individually and then discussed them jointly. Then, they made a final rating based on the average of the three.

Fred: What happened to the average ratings made last year?

John: We sent one copy to the library director. A second copy went into his personnel file at city hall. The third copy went to me. I could go before the city and use the ratings to argue for a raise or bonus for the library director if the ratings were high or no raise at all if he received low ratings. Let me emphasize that, while there are problems with the library, we feel that the director is doing an effective job, so there is no hidden agenda. This is not an attempt to replace the library director by changing the rules. We just aren't sure that the present system is adequate. If it is, that's fine. If you know of something better, then we'd like to hear about it.

Fred: OK, I'll see what I can do. I'll need to talk to the other board members and to the library director. I may also ask you for other information later. Otherwise, I'll get back to you in about three weeks.

Organizational Problems

Fred reviewed the job description John gave him and interviewed several city officials, including the library director. Fred discovered a growing list of organizational problems. The relationship between the library and other city agencies was deteriorating. Library staff members refused to cooperate with other departments' requests, and sometimes even disregarded their own director's orders. Complaints were mounting and there was talk of the library employees' unionizing. One person who worked in another city agency even said that "things at the library are out of control."

The library had recently undergone a number of changes. Chief among these was that the library had been a private, nonprofit organization until the city assumed responsibility for it two years before. New facilities were built, the collection was enlarged, and a museum was added. More staff members were hired, doubling the number of library employees in a short time. An extremely well-liked head librarian retired after many years of service, and the city then established higher qualifications for a more professional library director. For the first time, the library was required to use citywide personnel procedures and to follow city personnel rules.

The mayor appointed local residents to a nine-member CLB to set policy, to approve major projects, and to provide general supervision to the library director. John met with the mayor every six months to brief him on library projects and to explain anticipated future library needs. The CLB also supplied the mayor's office with an annual report, which included the library director's performance appraisal. While the library director reported to the CLB, the position was made equal in status with other city department heads (for example, the police chief and the director of public works) and the director represented the library at bi-weekly executive council meetings called by the mayor.

The city provided about 80 percent of the library's annual operating budget of $1.2 million. A private trust fund had been established for capital improvements. Under the terms of the trust, the trustees, who were separate from the library board, were required to spend all of the interest from the trust, about $300,000 annually, but were prohibited from spending any of

the principal. Among city officials, only the library director had any regular contact with these trustees.

Recent Developments

River City CLB members were not experts in organizational change. Most were owners of small businesses, a few were attorneys, two were homemakers, and one was an elementary-school principal. They assumed that after an initial period of transition after the changes, relations with the library staff would improve; however, the situation continued to deteriorate. One female employee filed a complaint with the state Equal Employment Opportunity Commission, charging the library with sex discrimination by hiring a male library director rather than promoting the female head librarian. The library director reported increased bickering between the new staff members and older library employees, and, on a recent visit to the library, Fred overheard one staff member refer to the director as "the city's man."

The relationship between the library and other city agencies also worsened. For example, one agency head argued that the library budget should be cut because it received funding from the private trust. Fred reviewed the facts that he had uncovered during his inquiry. He realized that the problems facing the CLB went far beyond an inadequate performance appraisal system. He wondered whether he should try to address these other problems, and if so, how he should begin.

Questions

1. Is the job description for the library director's position adequate? Explain.
2. Are the performance appraisal form and procedures adequate? Why or why not?
3. The consultant believed that a poor relationship existed between the library staff and the city. What caused this? What can be done?
4. If you were the consultant, what recommendations would you make to the Citizens' Library Board?

FIGURE 17A   Job Description: Library Director

A. RESPONSIBILITIES:

Listed below is a brief description of the library director's duties for each of several dimensions. In each instance it is suggestive, not inclusive, of the director's duties in that area.

Dimension I. Managing the Library Staff

1. Develops and implements equitable personnel policies
2. Motivates the staff to achieve high goals and evaluates their performance as appropriate
3. Contributes to employee job satisfaction, low absenteeism, and a low grievance rate and handles grievances that do occur in a proper and timely fashion
4. Contributes to staff selection, training, and development
5. Sees that staff organization and use are efficient
6. Ensures that physical facilities are maintained by proper personnel

Dimension II. Planning, Implementing, and Maintaining Projects

1. Establishes priorities
2. Works with the Library Board to establish long- and short-range plans
3. Presents well-developed ideas clearly and concisely to the Board
4. Provides the Board with sufficient information for planning and monitoring projects
5. Is willing to make the difficult decisions that are necessary to fully implement Library Board policies
6. Establishes guidelines and actively sees that projects stay within those guidelines

Dimension III. Coordinating Work with Other Agencies

1. Sees that library policies and procedures are consistent with those of the city
2. Coordinates plans with appropriate city agencies
3. Gives presentations to and/or attends relevant governmental committee meetings
4. Coordinates City Library work with that of the county and of the regional library system as necessary
5. Actively works to maintain harmony between the library and other city agencies
6. Sees that physical facilities are maintained and repaired by the appropriate city agencies

Dimension IV. Budgeting

1. Adequately researches budget proposals
2. Sees that budget proposals are explained clearly to the Library Board
3. Sees that budget covers necessary expenses
4. Ensures that adequate funds are requested for unanticipated contingencies
5. Proposes budget to the city in a clear, concise, and effective manner
6. Maintains the library's share of the overall city budget
7. Effectively communicates special library needs before the Washington Board (the private fund trustees)

Dimension V. Professional Activities

1. Actively participates in state library system activities
2. Is active in the regional library system
3. Is involved in professional organizations
4. Does not allow professional activities to unduly interfere with the administration of the library
5. Keeps abreast of current laws and procedures affecting library administration
6. Maintains high ethical standards

Dimension VI. Customer Service

1. Communicates services to the public
2. Solicits public input to better identify and meet customer needs in developing the library collection
3. Is visible to the community
4. Seeks to increase circulation rate in all areas of library service
5. Promotes the Friends of the Library Organization

B. QUALIFICATIONS:

Essential Knowledge and Abilities

1. Advanced administrative ability
2. Knowledge of local, state, and library law
3. Ability to communicate effectively with people from diverse backgrounds
4. Ability to speak effectively in public
5. Extensive knowledge of modern library organization, procedures, policy, aims, and service
6. Considerable knowledge of current and world literature and a diverse liberal arts background
7. Ability to plan, motivate, direct, and coordinate the work of others

Training and Experience

1. Masters of Library Science from an accredited library school
2. Five years' progressively responsible public library experience
3. Eligibility for Grade I state library certificate
4. Administrative or supervisory experiences

FIGURE 17B   *Library Director Evaluation*

Library Directory _____   Date _____

Board President _____

Directions: Circle the response that *best* reflects the consensus of
the Board with regard to each of the following items:

	Always true	True most of the time	True about half of the time	Seldom true	Never true	Not enough information to rate	Board Comments (Required for a rating of 1 or 2)
Library Director	5	4	3	2	1	0	
1. Presents proposals to the Board in a clear and concise manner	5	4	3	2	1	0	
2. Provides Board with sufficient information that members can make intelligent decisions	5	4	3	2	1	0	
3. Effectively plans projects	5	4	3	2	1	0	
4. Anticipates crises and takes appropriate preventive action	5	4	3	2	1	0	
5. Delegates work to subordinates	5	4	3	2	1	0	
6. Meets deadlines	5	4	3	2	1	0	
7. Effectively identifies budgetary needs and keeps expenses within the budget	5	4	3	2	1	0	
8. Maintains harmonious working relationships with other government agencies	5	4	3	2	1	0	
9. Effectively manages library staff	5	4	3	2	1	0	
10. Performs all duties conscientiously	5	4	3	2	1	0	

Overall Performance Rating   (Outstanding) 5   4   3   2   1   0 (Unsatisfactory)

Acknowledgment of Receipt and Discussion   _____

                                                                   Library Director

PART **5**

Controlling

John Sculley

After receiving an M.B.A. from the Wharton School at the University of Pennsylvania, John Sculley went to work for PepsiCo. Sculley arrived at about the time Pepsi developed the goal of taking on Coke in a marketing battle, with the objective of surpassing its archrival in market share. Sculley was placed on the fast track, and, with his marketing skills, he responded successfully to each of the challenges presented to him. After a series of rapid promotions, he was moved to the presidency of PepsiCo's international foods operation. This promotion was a major challenge for him, since this division, with all of its problems and complexities, had been the dead end for many executives before him. Donald Kendall, then the CEO of PepsiCo, was grooming Sculley as his eventual replacement.

Innovation must be carefully managed.

The international foods operation was characterized by inefficient plants, unsanitary conditions, terrible products, poor distribution, and nonexistent advertising. Sculley successfully tackled the operation, and three and one half years later he was promoted to the presidency of PepsiCo, Frito-Lay, and the food group.

John Sculley claims that the more difficult and challenging the task, the greater the satisfaction he derives from task accomplishment. Sculley appears to be driven by intrinsic rewards—feelings of accomplishment and success he gives to himself while responding to challenging tasks. Like most individuals with a strong need for achievement, Sculley possesses a need to feel in control of things. At PepsiCo, Sculley became bogged down in numerous contractual squab-

bles, began to feel a lack of challenge, failed to find intrinsic rewards in the myriad tasks he was working on, and experienced a growing sense of helplessness. He eventually left PepsiCo and journeyed to Apple Computer, fascinated with the computer whiz-kid entrepreneur, Steven Jobs. Sculley saw Apple as an organization in which he could make a difference. The team of Sculley and Jobs would be one in which Sculley would teach Jobs management and marketing skills, and Jobs would teach Sculley about his vision for a world wrapped up in the information age—a new social, cultural, economic, and technological revolution.

The early months at Apple were exhilarating. Creativity was emphasized by everyone; they were working on the cutting edge, learning about the ways that people process information; everyone was involved in the decision-making process; and there was an intense sense of commitment and direction that seemed to bind the organization together. A highly intrinsically motivated individual himself, Sculley was fascinated by the intrinsic motivation of the Apple employees who surrounded him. The commitment level was high, people were energized, and excitement filled the organization.

After one and one half years of Apple prosperity, major problems began to emerge. As he worked on these issues to no avail, Sculley began to doubt himself, and once again that feeling of helplessness began to set in. People around him began to criticize him for allowing Steven Jobs to become more and more involved in day-to-day decision making, the very job, they claimed, for which Sculley had been hired.

Sculley thought about leaving Apple, but then threw aside his feelings of helplessness and took a number of major steps in order to regain control. He replaced Apple's product structure with a functional structure. He removed Steven Jobs from his position as general manager of Macintosh and eventually fired him—the man who had brought him to Apple. He repositioned the Macintosh computer line for businesspeople, and he instituted massive layoffs. Running the risk of stifling creativity, he became directive and reduced the level and form of participation that had characterized Apple during its early stages of existence.

Sculley strongly believes that it is important for a manager to have a clear vision for the organization and views on how to position it within its external environment. It is also critically important that the manager communicate that vision to his or her subordinates. A key to effective leadership is that the manager must clearly understand his or her strengths and weaknesses and attack problems with these strengths.

Sculley suggests that an innovative organization does not manage itself. If an organization is going to grow and continue to be innovative, the process of innovation must be carefully managed. Management has the responsibility to be proactive. According to Sculley, there are six general principles that can be used to manage creativity.[1]

First, *the safer you can make a situation, the higher you can raise the challenge.* An environment that is risk free, coupled with easy goals, breed arrogance and complacency; therefore, management needs to create an environment in which people are not afraid of making mistakes and must simultaneously make the task confronting them extremely difficult.

Second, *do not give people goals; tell them which way to go.* In order to get people to have creative ideas,

management needs to avoid specifying where it wants to be tomorrow based on extrapolations from where it was yesterday. Instead, people need to envision what tomorrow will be like and then come back to today and design ways to get there.

Third, *encourage contrarian thinking.* There is a need for low levels of dissent within an organization; there should be a modest amount of tension between discipline and anarchy. Instilling a measured amount of anarchy into an organization encourages people to express varying opinions without worrying about the implications. Tension properly placed between points of view brings out the best in people. Dissention stimulates discussion and influences decision making for the better.

Fourth, *build a work environment to extend not just people's aspirations but also their sensibilities.* There are tools that foster creativity, and the major tool is an environment that is conducive to fun and to thinking in nonstandard ways. The work environment should be egalitarian, informal, relaxed, devoid of symbols of management, and open, while possessing a culture (norms, values, symbols) that reflects creativity. It is the relaxation at the level of consciousness that is the seed for creativity at the level of the subconscious mind.

Fifth, *build emotion into the system.* "Defensiveness is the bane of all passion-filled creative work."[2] Problems need to be thought about in positive instead of negative terms. Large and public reward systems that provide immediate reinforcement of major breakthroughs can contribute to the creation of emotion within the system. For example, reward problem finding as well as problem solving.

Sixth, *encourage accountability over responsibility.* Creative people need to feel free to let their creative

instincts work. As a result, organizational responsibility should be attached to the desired outcome, namely the production of creative ideas. Accountability should be attached to the results of the work assigned to people.

According to Sculley, "while management demands consensus, control, certainty, and the status quo, creativity thrives on the opposite—instinct, uncertainty, freedom, and iconoclasm."[3] If Sculley's early successes in managing creativity at Apple continue, it would seem that he has developed an effective means to mesh the demands of management and the needs of innovative organization members.

1. Sculley's lessons from inside Apple (14 September 1987), *Fortune*, 108–19.
2. *Fortune*, 119.
3. *Fortune*, 118.

Source: J. Sculley with J. A. Byrne (1987), *Odyssey: From Pepsi to Apple*, New York: Harper & Row; D. A. Greenberger (1988), A review of Odyssey: From Pepsi to Apple, in J. L. Pierce and J. W. Newstrom, eds., *The manager's bookshelf: A mosaic of contemporary views*, New York: Harper & Row; Sculley's lessons from inside Apple (14 September 1987), *Fortune*, 108–19.

Organizational Effectiveness

Student Learning Objectives

After reading this chapter, you should be able to:

1. Understand why there is disagreement about the meaning of organizational effectiveness.

2. Identify various criteria that can be used to measure organizational effectiveness.

3. Discuss four major systematic approaches to assessing effectiveness and identify the major differences among these perspectives.

4. Describe important limitations presented by each of the four major approaches to assessing effectiveness.

5. Understand the competing values perspective on organizational effectiveness and the way in which it incorporates the merits of each of the four major approaches.

6. Describe each of the four models of effectiveness included in the competing values perspective.

7. Consider how organizational life cycles can help managers decide which of the four competing values models is most appropriate for their organization.

*T*his book has identified management techniques that should contribute to the effectiveness of organizations. Most people would agree that the development and maintenance of an effective organization requires careful and systematic planning, organizing, directing, and controlling. Beyond this general agreement, however, the waters get murky. When comparing two organizations, for example, how does a person know which is more effective? In 1987, General Motors had $101.8 billion in sales compared to Ford Motor Company's $71.6 billion. Does this make GM more effective than Ford? In 1987, Ford had a $4.6 billion profit compared to GM's $3.5 billion profit. Does this make Ford more effective? In 1987, Ford's profits equaled 6.5 percent of sales compared to GM's 3.5 percent. A "little" shop named Weingarten Realty had only $60 million in sales, but almost 30 percent of this was profit. Does that make Weingarten Realty a more effective organization than either GM or Ford?

The Nature and Importance of Organizational Effectiveness

Previous chapters in this book have addressed the planning, organizing, and directing functions of management. This part of the book examines the fourth function: controlling. As you learned in Chapter 1, the controlling function involves monitoring both the behavior of organization members and the effectiveness of the organization itself, determining whether plans are achieving organizational goals, and taking corrective actions as needed. To execute the controlling function, managers must understand the nature of organizational effectiveness, because organizational effectiveness is largely what they must control. This section on the controlling function, thus, begins with an examination of organizational effectiveness. Chapters 19 and 20 follow up by exploring methods for controlling organizational behavior and effectiveness.

To execute the controlling function, managers must understand the nature of organizational effectiveness.

Webster's defines *effectiveness* as the production of or the power to produce a desired result. Management scholars and managers have a much harder time agreeing on a definition of *organizational effectiveness*. Many managers in the private sector, for example, consider organizational effectiveness to be reflected by the bottom line (profits). Defining organizational effectiveness strictly in terms of dollars and cents, however, fails to capture the complexity of organizational operations and the full meaning of effectiveness. After all, managers in the public sector sometimes overspend their current year's budget to justify a larger budget request for the next year. This chapter explores a wide range of definitions of organizational effectiveness and offers an integrated model that permits organizations to define effectiveness in ways that are relevant to them. As you will see, these definitions focus on the degree to which organizational goals are met.

Assessing Effectiveness

Managers have used a wide range of specific criteria to assess organizational effectiveness. They have also used four systematic approaches in defining organizational effectiveness. This section explores these traditional criteria and approaches. The next section presents an integrating perspective that can guide managers in selecting effectiveness criteria that are appropriate to their particular organizational situations.

Potential Criteria

Just as it is difficult to agree on the definition of organizational effectiveness, selecting criteria to use in assessing organizational effectiveness is not an easy task. There is a tendency to use a single criterion or a limited number of effectiveness criteria, and many managers select a criterion because it "looks right." Many managers, for example, concentrate on profit because it seems to be an intuitively appropriate measure of organizational effectiveness. As you will see, however, excellent arguments can also be made for using such effectiveness criteria as employee job satisfaction and flexibility in adapting to changing environments. Table 18.1 presents thirty of the many criteria managers have used to assess organizational effectiveness.

Few organizations will find all of these criteria to be appropriate indicators of effectiveness. Most organizations, however, should be evaluated along many of these dimensions. Despite this, many managers take a rifle approach to assessing effectiveness, often aiming at only one of these criteria (see Figure 18.1). The problem with this approach is that a manager who uses a single indicator might miss information that has an important bearing on organizational effectiveness. Focusing only on sales volume, for example, could permit a manager to classify an organization as effective even if it is losing money or experiencing other major problems.

One reason for the use of such a narrow approach is that managers frequently adopt criteria largely according to their personal interests and values. Compounding this is the fact that managers tend to choose criteria

TABLE 18.1 *Criteria and Measures of Organizational Effectiveness*

1. *Overall effectiveness.* The general evaluation that takes into account as many criteria facets as possible. It is measured usually by combining archival performance records or by obtaining overall ratings or judgments from persons thought to be knowledgeable about the organization.

2. *Productivity.* Usually defined as the quantity or volume of the major product or service that the organization provides. It can be measured at three levels: individual, group, and total organization via archival records or ratings or both.

3. *Efficiency.* A ratio that reflects a comparison of some aspect of unit performance to the costs incurred for that performance.

4. *Profit.* The amount of revenue from sales left after all costs and obligations are met. Percentage return on investment or percentage return on total sales are sometimes used as alternative definitions.

5. *Quality.* The quality of the primary service or product provided by the organization that may take many operational forms, which are determined largely by the kind of product or service provided by the organization.

6. *Accidents.* The frequency of on-the-job accidents resulting in lost time.

7. *Growth.* Represented by an increase in such variables as total work force, plant capacity, assets, sales, profits, market share, and number of innovations. It implies a comparison of an organization's present state with its own past state.

8. *Absenteeism.* The usual definition stipulates unexcused absences, but even within this constraint there are a number of alternative definitions.

9. *Turnover.* Some measure of the relative number of voluntary terminations, which is almost always assessed via archival records.

10. *Job satisfaction.* Has been conceptualized in many ways but the modal view might define it as the individual's satisfaction with the amount of various job outcomes that he or she is receiving.

11. *Motivation.* In general, the strength of the predisposition of an individual to engage in goal-directed action or activity on the job. It is not a feeling of relative satisfaction with various job outcomes but is more akin to a readiness or willingness to work at accomplishing the job's goals. As an organizational index, it must be summed across people.

12. *Morale.* The model definition seems to view morale as a group phenomenon involving extra effort, goal communality, commitment, and feelings of belonging. Groups have some degree of morale, whereas individuals have some motivation (and satisfaction).

13. *Control.* The degree, and distribution, of management control that exists within an organization for influencing and directing the behavior of organization members.

14. *Conflict/cohesion.* Defined at the cohesion end by an organization in which the members like one another, work well together, communicate fully and openly, and coordinate work efforts. At the other end lies the organization with verbal and physical clashes, poor coordination, and ineffective communication.

15. *Flexibility/adaptation.* Refers to the ability of an organization to change its standard operating procedures in response to environmental changes.

16. *Planning and goal setting.* The degree to which an organization systematically plans its future steps and engages in explicit goal-setting behavior.

17. *Goal consensus.* Distinct from commitment to the organization's goals, consensus refers to the degree to which all individuals perceive the same goals.

18. *Internalization of organizational goals.* The acceptance of the organization's goals. The belief that the organization's goals are right and proper.

19. *Roal and norm congruence.* The degree to which organization members agree on such things as desirable supervisory attitudes, performance expectations, morale, and role requirements.

20. *Managerial interpersonal skills.* The level of skill with which managers deal with supervisors, subordinates, and peers in terms of giving support, facilitating constructive interaction, and generating enthusiasm for meeting goals and achieving excellent performance.

21. *Managerial task skills.* The overall level of skills with which managers, commanding officers, or group leaders perform work-centered tasks and tasks centered on work to be done—not the skills used when interacting with other organization members.

22. *Information management and communication.* Completeness, efficiency, and accuracy in analysis and distribution of information critical to effectiveness.

23. *Readiness.* An overall judgment concerning the probability that the organization could successfully perform some specified task if asked to do so.

24. *Utilization of environment.* The extent to which the organization interacts successfully with its environment and acquires scarce and valued resources necessary to its effective operation.

25. *Evaluations by external entities.* Evaluations of the organization, or unit, by the individuals and organizations in its environment with which it interacts. Loyalty to, confidence in, and support given the organization by such groups as suppliers, customers, stockholders, enforcement agencies, and the general public would fall under this label.

26. *Stability.* The maintenance of structure, function, and resources through time and, more particularly, through periods of stress.

27. *Value of human resources.* A composite criterion that refers to the total value or total worth of the individual members, in an accounting or balance sheet sense, to the organization.

28. *Participation and shared influence.* The degree to which individuals in the organization participate in making the decisions that affect them directly.

29. *Training and development emphasis.* The amount of effort that the organization devotes to developing its human resources.

30. *Achievement emphasis.* An analog to the individual need for achievement referring to the degree to which the organization appears to place a high value on achieving major new goals.

Source: Adapted from S. P. Robbins (1983), *Organization theory: The structure and design of organizations,* Englewood Cliffs, NJ: Prentice-Hall, 22–23.

FIGURE 18.1   *The Rifle Approach to Assessing Organizational Effectiveness*

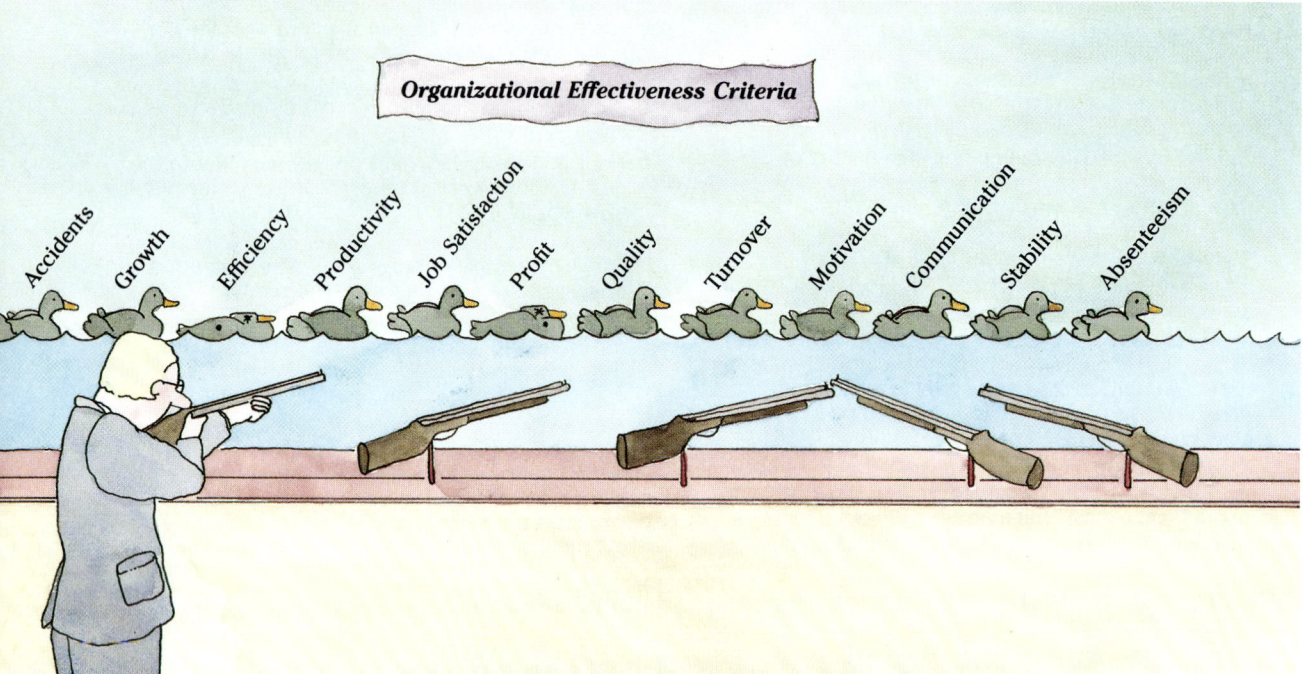

Organizational Effectiveness Criteria

Accidents   Growth   Efficiency   Productivity   Job Satisfaction   Profit   Quality   Turnover   Motivation   Communication   Stability   Absenteeism

that make them look good; thus, economically oriented managers of organizations that are generating high sales might choose a criterion such as profit to gauge organizational effectiveness, whereas human relations-oriented managers in organizations with low turnover levels might focus on such criteria as job satisfaction, motivation, or cohesion.

Although an overly narrow approach to measuring effectiveness is ill-advised, so is the opposite approach. Some managers overreact by using a shotgun approach that aims at every criterion in sight (see Figure 18.2 on page 650). Managers who adopt too many criteria may lose sight of important individual criteria. If, for example, morale is just one of thirty effectiveness criteria being used, it is easy to overlook its importance. As you will see later in this chapter, some criteria are significantly more important than others under certain circumstances.

One of the first challenges facing managers is to identify and use the proper mix of criteria to assess organizational effectiveness. Managers should take a focused approach that does not rely on too few or too many criteria, selecting only those that are relevant to their particular organization, based on its current stage of activity and development. The integrated perspective discussed later in this chapter is designed to help managers do exactly this.

This discussion will begin by considering the four major systematic approaches that managers have used to assess organizational effectiveness: goal attainment, systems, internal processes, and strategic constituencies. As you read about these four approaches, remember that they describe how managers have assessed organizational effectiveness in the past, not necessarily how they *should* do so.

A Goal Attainment Approach

The most widely used method of assessing organizational effectiveness is a **goal attainment approach.** The goals referred to are considered **ends goals:** what is an organization trying to accomplish? Managers using a goal attainment approach, thus, evaluate organizational effectiveness by assessing the degree to which one or more specified goals are met. Consider, for example, a company that sets a goal of clearing $5 million in profits in 1990. If it has accomplished this goal by the end of the year, the company will have been effective from a goal attainment perspective—even if that $5 million was accumulated through a combination of aggressive marketing, deceptive pricing techniques, and extensive employee layoffs.

Under what conditions has a goal attainment approach worked reasonably well? Managers often use a goal attainment approach when:

- An organization has specific outcome-oriented goals (this holds true for any organization, whether it is a football team trying to win the Super Bowl or a branch of the military attempting to recruit enlistees).
- Specific goals are stated, defined, and understood by management.
- Management agrees that the stated goals are appropriate indicators of effectiveness.
- It is possible to measure the degree to which goals are being met.
- The number of goals is small enough to be manageable.

Advantages Because a goal attainment approach uses observable, measurable statements and outcomes, managers can use this approach relatively easily. In addition, although reaching agreement on organizational goals can be difficult, it nevertheless may be easier to agree about *which* goals to aim for than to concur about *how* to reach them. Managers may also like a goal attainment approach because it allows them to obtain regular feedback about progress toward goals. Managers can regularly see, for example, how close they are to reaching targeted sales quotas or profit margins. In addition, as you learned in Chapter 14, appropriate goals can be quite motivating. Consider, for example, the goal attainment approach NASA has used to generate many important consumer goods.

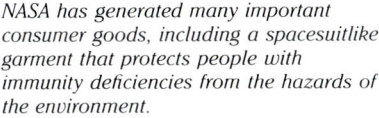

NASA has generated many important consumer goods, including a spacesuitlike garment that protects people with immunity deficiencies from the hazards of the environment.

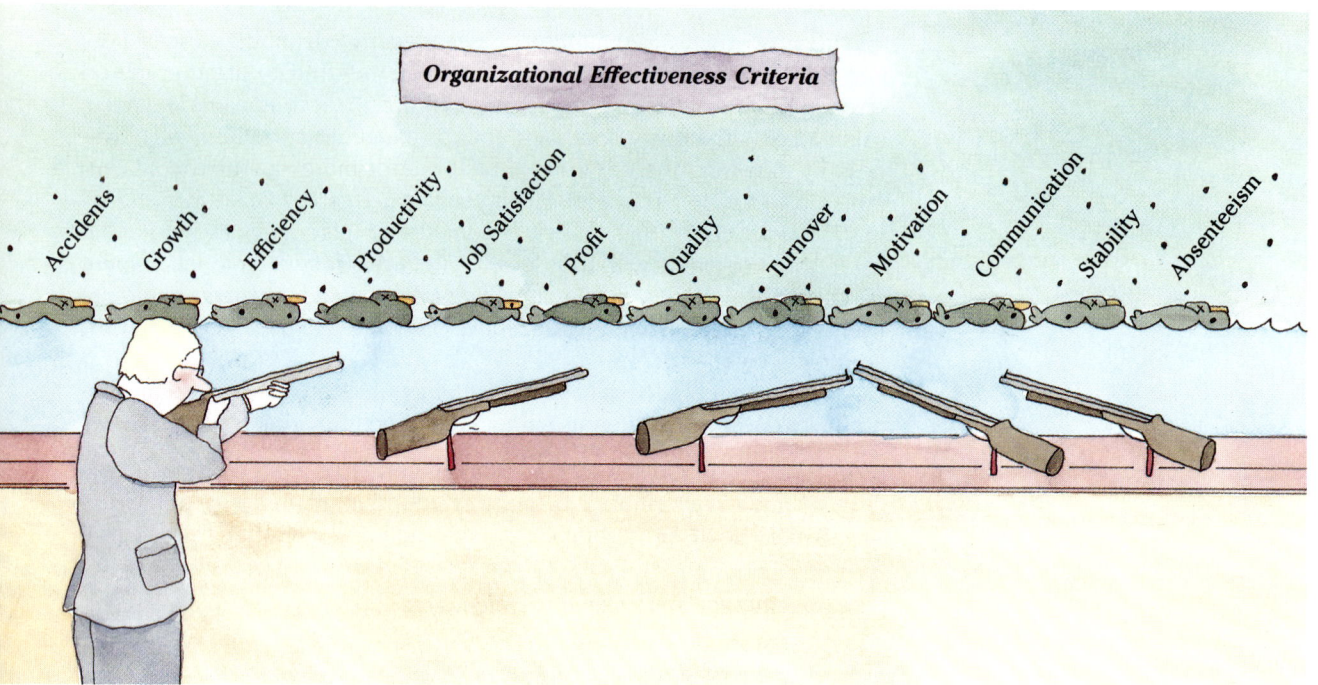

The legislation that created NASA in 1958 specifically directed the agency to find a way to disseminate to the general public the technology developed under its programs. With that goal in mind, NASA was very effective, as indicated by its introduction of such innovations as lightweight insulating materials used in sportswear, blankets, and sleeping bags; hang gliders; quartz crystal clocks and watches; fogless ski goggles, diving masks, and vehicle windows; studless winter tires; and compressed freeze-dried foods.

Limitations   When managers use a goal attainment approach as the sole indicator of assessing effectiveness, they may condone or mask a variety of inappropriate, abusive, and even unethical behaviors. Consider one instance in which goal attainment blinded managers to some of the serious repercussions of inappropriate organizational behavior. For twelve consecutive years, the Boise Cascade Company met or exceeded its major ends goal of a 20-percent growth in earnings per share per year. To meet this goal, however, the company repeatedly took on risky projects and ignored the warnings and protests of various environmental groups. These actions and other factors eventually led to bankruptcy and a forced reorganization of the company.

Complicating the use of the goal attainment approach is the fact that it is sometimes difficult to reach agreement on the goals to be pursued. For example, whose goals should be considered most relevant—the board of directors'? the officers' of the organization? all high-level managers'? the goals of a subcoalition of this top executive group? When an organization has multiple goals, as is usually the case (see the discussion of goal hierarchy in Chapter 6), who assigns their relative importance? Who resolves conflicts between goals, as might occur when short-term and long-term goals are at odds with one another? Problems of this nature, along with the fact that ends goals seldom address the means to the ends, limit the usefulness of the goal attainment approach to assessing organizational effectiveness.

If managers can deal with the limitations presented by a goal attainment approach, this perspective can provide a reasonable assessment of major aspects of organizational effectiveness. Using this approach well, however, requires at least the following from organizations:

1. Ensuring that management receives input from all individuals who have a major influence on formulating official goals, even if they are not part of senior management
2. Including recognition of all goals attained (by observing the behavior of organization members) whether or not they were included in the official goals set forth by management
3. Recognizing the necessity of both short- and long-term goals
4. Insisting on tangible, verifiable, and measurable goals rather than relying on vague statements that merely mirror general expectations
5. Viewing goals as dynamic entities that change over time, rather than as rigid or fixed statements of purpose[1]

A Systems Approach

In contrast to managers who use a goal attainment approach and focus on *what* is accomplished, managers who use a **systems approach** to assess organizational effectiveness care mostly about *how* things are accomplished. This approach is also goal oriented, but the goals referred to are **means goals:** how should an organization and its members behave? Managers using a systems approach, thus, evaluate organizational effectiveness by assessing the degree to which their organization acquires resources, processes these resources, and distributes the resulting goods or services in order to maintain environmental stability and balance.[2] Consider, for example, an organization that sets means goals that define a particular mix of products and the use of an aggressive marketing strategy. If the organization met these goals, it would be considered effective according to the systems approach, even if its profits were low.

Perhaps a personal analogy will help differentiate the goal attainment and systems approaches. Suppose you were planning to drive your car from Chicago to Denver. The goal attainment approach for measuring effectiveness might focus on such ends goals as reaching Denver by noon on Thursday and keeping trip expenses under $150. The systems approach, on the other hand, might focus on such means goals as not exceeding the speed limit and driving between 350 and 400 miles each day. If you reach Denver Thursday night and spend over $150 to do so, your trip has been ineffective according to a goal attainment approach. If, on the other hand, you get to Denver by noon Thursday, having spent no more than $150, but had to drive for 24 hours at 75 miles per hour to make it because you were snowbound in Nebraska for a day, your trip has been ineffective from a systems approach.

Why do some people favor a systems approach over a goal attainment approach? According to some advocates, a systems approach is appropriate because:

- Goals are attained only when an organizational system operates effectively; therefore, managers should concentrate on assessing system effectiveness rather than on determining whether a profit was made or a particular sales goal was reached. Had NASA operated according to a systems approach, for example, the agency would have been concerned with gathering people, material, and technology and transforming them into astronauts, spacecrafts, and flying missions. The fact that those people, machines, and activities generated information that could be spun off into consumer products would have been of little interest.

- An organization is a collection of interdependent segments, all of which must perform well or the overall organization will suffer. Just as your car's ignition, cooling, power train, and other systems must work well to make it to Denver on time, an organization's communication, decision-making, and other systems must work well for it to be effective (see the discussion of systems theory in Chapter 5).

- Organizational success requires awareness of and appropriate interaction with the external environment, including financiers, suppliers, customers, regulatory bodies, and labor unions (see Chapter 2).

- A systems approach is based on the belief that an organization's survival and effectiveness depend on its ability to replenish the resources it consumes. Raw materials must be replenished, exiting employees must be replaced, and outdated information (on customer needs, technological processes, and regulatory requirements) must be refreshed. From a systems approach, for example, the Weyerhaeuser Company would be classified as having a high level of organizational effectiveness in conducting its forest products business. Managers at Weyerhaeuser stay informed of current and developing environmental regulations, make sure that trees are planted to replace those harvested, research market trends, and regularly evaluate and update as necessary the technologies used by the company to conduct business.

Advantages   A systems approach can be beneficial to organizations in a number of ways. Whereas ends goals may be preferable for *evaluating* effectiveness, means goals are preferable for *controlling* effectiveness. They specify what must be done in order to increase an organization's chances of reaching its ends goals. When only ends goals are used as effectiveness criteria, managers cannot assess performance until their organization successfully reaches or clearly fails to reach its goals. With a means goals approach, however, performance assessment can be ongoing. A sales manager using a systems approach can determine, for example, that sales staff in the eastern division are not pursuing initial contacts with the prescribed follow-up phone calls. It is clearly desirable to correct this situation before receiving a poor quarterly sales report from the eastern division.

Another advantage to a systems approach is that it reminds managers that the long-term health and success of their organization requires ongoing attention to more than short-term goals. You will recall that managers using a goal attainment approach could consider an organization effective because it meets its $5 million profit goal, even if the goal is achieved through distasteful and unethical means. Managers using a systems approach would argue that this type of behavior damages an organization's long-term effectiveness by threatening the stability of its customer base and human resource supply and motivation. In other words, although the company meets one ends goal, its customers may lose interest in making future purchases from an organization they find disreputable. The company may also have difficulty recruiting new employees, while experiencing seriously strained relations with current employees because of irresponsible layoffs.

Another way in which the systems approach can benefit an organization is by raising managers' appreciation of the interdependency of various organizational activities and segments. It is clear from a systems approach, for example, that a poorly trained secretarial staff damages the performance of executives, just as the late arrival of raw materials restricts a production department's ability to construct a product. A final advantage of a systems approach is found in situations in which specific ends goals are difficult to define or cannot be measured. What, for example, are the specific, measurable ends goals for the U.S. Senate? for a student counseling center? for a police department? Although ends goals could be set for each of these organizations, a systems approach can provide a more useful perspective on effectiveness. The effectiveness of a city's police department, for example, should be assessed by how it interacts with the public, as well as in terms of its success at writing a specified number of parking tickets or at reducing the crime rate.

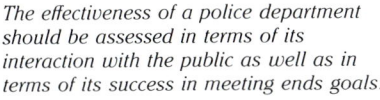

The effectiveness of a police department should be assessed in terms of its interaction with the public as well as in terms of its success in meeting ends goals.

Limitations   The advantages just discussed would seem to indicate that a systems approach can significantly benefit organizations; however, its deemphasis of ends results can be problematic. There is a danger, for instance, that managers might forget that the reason the systems approach is so useful is because it provides the means to a desired end. If the means become the sole indicators of effectiveness, problems can arise. A restaurant, for example, can have adequate supplies of fresh food, employ competent cooks, and offer courteous service—in short, maintain its systems effectively—but if customers do not come in, it will go out of business.

As noted in the discussion of goal attainment, it is usually more difficult to define and agree on the means than on the ends. Most football coaches would agree that winning is an important end, for example, but relatively few would be able to agree on the appropriate means to accomplishing that end. Similar problems confront managers who use a systems approach to assess organizational effectiveness. Even if turning a profit is an agreed-on ends goal, obtaining agreement on the means to reaching this end can be quite an arduous undertaking. How, for example, would an organization resolve the differences between a manager who seeks profit through specialization and a manager who believes diversification is the route to success?

Finally, one of the overriding concerns many managers have with a systems approach is that organizations can sometimes meet ends goals without meeting means goals. Of even greater concern is the fact that means goals can be met without achieving ends goals. Promoters of a systems approach respond to these arguments by saying that, in the first case, achievement is likely to be maintained only in the short run, with a long-term price to pay (as would be the case if an organization meeting its $5-million profit goal were to lose its customers and dissatisfied employees). In the second case, they would characterize the failure to meet ends goals as emerging from poor planning that results in a selection of inappropriate ends goals. For example, a sales organization that follows means goals and canvasses each territory appropriately, pursues initial contacts with follow-up phone calls, and arranges the correct number of demonstrations should be able to sell the number of products specified by the ends goals unless the ends goals themselves are unreasonable.

An Internal Processes Approach

An **internal processes approach** defines effectiveness as the degree to which organization members are integrated with organizational production and management systems to function smoothly with a minimum of internal strain. According to this approach, in an effective organization communication flows freely, members trust management, and the organization is benevolent toward members.[3] An effective organization identifies and satisfies employee needs, nurtures cohesion, reduces dysfunctional interpersonal conflict, and treats the integrity of internal systems (such as communication, work coordination, group functioning, and safety systems) as its most important concern. Managers can gauge effectiveness with the internal processes approach by assessing the degree to which these systems are working appropriately for organization members. A communication system, for example, can be evaluated by the timeliness and accuracy of its information exchanges. An examination of accident records and inspection results can reveal safety system results. A survey program—such as the one used by Sears to assess employees' attitudes toward such factors as leadership, work design, physical working conditions, and communication—can reveal the extent to which employees are satisfied.

An internal processes approach and a systems approach are similar in that both look at an organization's systems. An internal processes approach, however, has a much narrower scope that focuses on an organization's *members;* thus, managers using an internal processes approach must satisfy the needs of organization members, both as the *means* to accomplishing goals and as an *end* in itself.

Advantages   According to psychologist Bernard Bass, organizational effectiveness evaluations should include an assessment of the degree to which the organization is of value to its members and the degree to which the organization and its members are of value to society. PVI, for example, is one of only three companies in its geographical area that specializes in small, custom video services. The organization's employees appreciate the chance to work for Cindy Mertes, owner of the company, given how well she treats them and the stiff competition for jobs. Members of the community, who have steadily increased their usage of camcorders, value the speedy service and reasonable prices PVI charges to convert home movies into videotapes and to custom-edit the tapes. Although relatively few organizations include such factors in their explicit definitions of organizational effectiveness—perhaps because they fail to see their relevance to other effectiveness criteria—some organizations devote considerable resources to achieving these forms of effectiveness. PVI, for example, pays the tuition and related expenses of employees who wish to further their education. Formalizing an internal processes approach as a measure of organizational effectiveness often leads to more humane treatment of organization members and greater social responsibility.

The widely popular quality of work life (QWL) movement is an affirmation of the importance of the internal processes approach to organizational effectiveness.[4] Organizations institute QWL programs to make the work environment more compatible with their employees' physical, social, and psychological needs. Typical QWL programs focus on maintaining safe and healthy environments, developing human capacities, improving employees' self-esteem, and balancing personal-life demands with work-life demands.[5]

Another potential advantage of an internal processes approach is that it can facilitate organization members' development of ideas for change within their organization.[6] Some changes are thrust on an organization; others are generated by an active search for improvement. The ability of an organization and its members to adapt to change may, thus, be indicative of organizational effectiveness. An internal processes approach that integrates organization members and organizational systems can result in an environment conducive to change. Organizations that demonstrate respect for individuals, support freedom of opinion, and nurture trust foster workers who are willing to invoke and respond well to change (see the discussion of change in Chapter 20).

Limitations Critics of the internal processes approach argue that the integration of members and systems does not always lead to the achievement of ends goals. In fact, apparent internal health (such as extremely high cohesion levels in an organization) can sometimes help *create* problems. The damaging phenomenon of groupthink (discussed in Chapters 7 and 13), for example, emerges under seemingly healthy conditions of group unanimity and support.

Although not as serious a concern as when healthy internal processes fail to achieve ends goals, another potential limitation of this approach is that the reverse can also happen. That is, organizations with unhealthy internal processes (such as high levels of conflict) sometimes succeed in meeting ends goals. A classic example of this was the New York Yankees, whose organization during the 1977 and 1978 seasons was characterized by "lack of team discipline, fights among players and between players and coaches, threatened firings, turnover in key personnel, and lack of cohesion. . . ."[7] Despite this, however, the Yankees won the World Series both years. Clearly, the 1977 and 1978 Yankee organization would be rated as ineffective with regard to its internal processes but as very effective with regard to its ends goals.

These observations only reinforce a conclusion that this approach to defining effectiveness is too narrow. Healthy internal processes should be treated as only one aspect of effectiveness. The relationship between the health of internal processes and attainment of ends goals is symbiotic in nature. Managers should not treat either factor as an end in itself but should allow the two factors to complement and nurture one another. If either dies, eventually so will the other.

A Strategic Constituencies Approach

The newest of the four approaches, a **strategic constituencies approach,** assesses effectiveness by evaluating the degree to which the needs of an organization's constituents have been satisfied.[8] An organization's constituents are its stakeholders—that is, suppliers, customers, unions, regulatory bodies, and any other group whose cooperation is required for the organization to survive. According to this approach, achieving effectiveness involves three steps:

1. Identifying critical constituents
2. Identifying the important demands of each of these critical constituents
3. Satisfying these demands

At PVI, Cindy's strategic constituencies include the bank that loaned her the capital to purchase supplies, the wholesale outlets that sell her tapes at reasonable prices, employees who transform customers' tapes into the desired products, and—of course—customers who want to use PVI for movie conversion and custom editing. PVI can be considered effective from a strategic constituencies approach if it can meet the needs of each of these groups.

A strategic constituencies approach overlaps somewhat with the other three approaches to organizational effectiveness. Managers trying to satisfy critical constituents may, for example, need to develop and pursue

Organizations may be unable to identify constituents who pose a possible threat until the threat has emerged.

specific goals related to constituent satisfaction. In most cases, satisfying constituents also requires managers to focus on internal processes and on integrating organization members with organizational systems. What distinguishes a strategic constituencies approach from the other approaches is its concentration on one primary ends goal (to satisfy constituent needs) rather than on other goals or on the means by which this ends goal is achieved.

Advantages   The primary advantage of a strategic constituencies approach is that it focuses an organization's attention and planning efforts on the groups in its environment without which it cannot succeed. Furthermore, this approach provides a systematic method for identifying these groups and their needs. Investors will not fund an organization unless it helps meet their needs, suppliers will not furnish resources if the organization fails to satisfy their needs, employees will not come to work unless the organization offers need satisfaction, and customers will not purchase products and services unless their consumer needs are met.

Limitations   The most obvious drawback to a strategic constituencies approach is that identifying critical constituents can be extremely difficult. In many cases, organizations may be unable to identify constituents who pose a potential threat until after the threat has emerged, as when a previously minor stockholder makes an unanticipated takeover bid. Furthermore, the importance of a particular constituent can change in rapidly shifting environments. Prior to the Arab oil embargo of 1973, for example, suppliers of domestic oil were only moderately important constituents of oil-using firms in the United States. They became much more critical constituents during the embargo, however, when many foreign supplies were cut off.

A strategic constituencies approach poses other difficulties as well. Managers must perform a delicate balancing act to satisfy the needs of strategic constituencies that have conflicting demands. For instance, suppliers may demand a higher price for raw materials at a time when consumers demand a lower price for the finished product. Sometimes a constituent may not disclose its needs, making it difficult for an organization to assess how well it has met those needs. Organization members may disagree about who the organization's critical constituents are. A marketing department, for example, might consider its clients to be the organization's most important constituent group—to the consternation of the human resource department, which views organization members as the dominant strategic constituency. If agreement cannot be reached on who is important, it is unlikely that the needs of many constituents will be well met.

In conclusion, the strategic constituency approach adds a valuable dimension to the definition of organizational effectiveness by focusing attention on the importance of groups that must be satisfied if the organization is to succeed. The approach must, however, be used in combination with other approaches to assessing effectiveness. Table 18.2 summarizes the main emphasis of each of the four systematic approaches presented in this section and gives examples of effectiveness statements for each.

TABLE 18.2 *Four Systematic Approaches to Assessing Organizational Effectiveness*

Approach	Characterized By	Sample Effectiveness Statement
Goal attainment	Focus on the degree to which ends goals are met	"The company was effective, having met its profit goal of $5 million."
Systems	Focus on how systems acquire, process, and export processed resources (i.e., means goals)	"The company was effective, having obtained necessary resources, produced a supply of products, successfully marketed these products, etc."
Internal processes	Focus on the integration of members with systems producing a smoothly functioning organization	"The company was effective, having good communication systems, satisfied employees, cohesive employee groups, and little internal conflict."
Strategic constituencies	Focus on the degree to which the needs of the organization's constituents have been met	"The company was effective, having identified and met the needs of critical constituents, including suppliers, employee unions, customers, and regulatory bodies."

An Integrated Approach to Controlling and Managing Organizational Effectiveness

The four approaches just presented are the most common approaches used by U.S. organizations in recent years to define, measure, and control effectiveness. Although each approach addresses critical effectiveness issues, each also has significant limitations. What is worse, the approaches are often used in inappropriate situations. An organization that is just getting started, for example, sometimes uses a goal attainment approach to specify what it expects its first-year results to be. Any of the other three approaches would be a better choice at a time when the organization should be concentrating on the future. The **competing values perspective** on organizational effectiveness attempts to address these problems by integrating ideas from the four systematic approaches.[9]

Development of the Competing Values Perspective

The competing values approach takes its name from the belief that what a person values or considers effective depends on who that person is and what he or she represents. If an organization has yearly sales of $1 million, its sales managers may consider it to be effective. The human resource director at the same company, on the other hand, may consider it ineffective if its unethical sales practices caused three top salespeople to

Kim S. Cameron

Kim S. Cameron is Associate Professor of Organizational Behavior and Industrial Relations in the Graduate School of Business Administration and Associate Professor of Higher Education in the School of Education at the University of Michigan. He is the author or coauthor of numerous publications on organizational effectiveness, organizational life cycles, managing decline, and management skills.

1. Do organizations formally adopt definitions of organizational effectiveness?

Yes, they do, but these definitions are seldom important in guiding managerial or organizational action. For one thing, official company definitions of effectiveness are almost always so general as to be meaningless. Mission statements or credos that define effectiveness as service to customers, contribution to society, highest-quality products, and so on are largely constructed for public-image purposes or to meet legal requirements. A second problem is getting constituencies to agree about which criteria are most important. For example, a company's stockholders may define effectiveness as return on assets or earnings per share, whereas its managers may define it as product quality or meeting production schedules.

2. Do organizations really monitor effectiveness?

I don't think I have ever seen an organization that didn't monitor its effectiveness in some way. Some organizations rationally and systematically gather data to evaluate effectiveness. Others rely more on informal or impressionistic information. The trouble is, the indicators of effectiveness being monitored are almost always those that justify current organizational behavior. In a recent study of automobile manufacturing plants, for example, I was amazed by the variety I found in the indicators of effectiveness being monitored. In almost every case, the plant picked criteria on which it was doing well to justify its effectiveness. In areas where plant performance wasn't so high, effectiveness criteria were often ignored. Colleges and universities also differ widely in what they monitor. Some use prestige rankings, some use starting salaries of graduates, some use service to the community, and some even use football records. It is well known that a winning football season dramatically increases alumni donations. A common rule of thumb seems to be: If it makes you look good, measure it and make it official.

3. What effect do managers have on an organization's effectiveness?

Through my investigations of decline in manufacturing firms, institutions of higher education, and the financial services industry, I have become absolutely convinced that management makes a difference. Despite economic or demographic trends, and despite the turbulence of the external environment, good managers can improve organizational effectiveness. Bad managers, on the other hand, can lead their organizations into decline. Failing to provide a clear vision or future direction for the organization; not giving employees opportunities for growth and initiative, being insensitive to organizational culture; demonstrating personal insecurity, jealousy, and self-aggrandizement; and being unable to manage interpersonal and intergroup conflict are the most common characteristics exhibited by bad managers.

> *"A common rule . . . seems to be: If it makes you look good, measure it and make it official."*

4. Which important criteria of effectiveness do organizations most often neglect?

Those not championed by some constituency. Because different constituencies value different criteria of effectiveness, organizations constantly must respond to multiple demands for performance. It is difficult for any organization to be all things to all people, so they tend to ignore effectiveness criteria unless one or more constituencies demand it. Until foreign products of significantly higher quality became available to American consumers, for example, not many U.S. manufacturers monitored quality as a criterion of effectiveness. Now, because of the insistence of vocal constituencies, most organizations place a high priority on quality.

FIGURE 18.3
Organizational Life Cycles

**Stages of Development
(Life Cycles)**

resign in disgust. Competing values create different and potentially conflicting goals among organization members and constituents. According to this perspective, there is no single goal against which effectiveness should be measured, and a consensus on the importance of goals is unlikely to be reached. The competing values perspective acknowledges a number of important effectiveness measures and specifies a viable way to deal with this fact consistent with an organization's stage of development and the values held by its key members.

The Importance of Organizational Life Cycles In choosing a model of organizational effectiveness, managers must take an organization's **life cycle** stage into account. The competing values perspective considers four stages, or cycles, to be important (see Figure 18.3):

1. *Entrepreneurial* ("birth") stage—the focus is on collecting from the external environment resources needed for an organization's survival and the support of future activities

2. *Collectivity*—the concentration is on activities revolving around informal communication, informal structure, the development of cooperation among members, and building members' commitment to the organization

3. *Formalization*—the emphasis is on stability, efficiency of operations, and rules and procedures to guide operations

4. *Elaboration of structure*—the attention is refocused on the external environment and opportunities for additional growth

As you will discover in the next section, the competing values perspective offers four models of effectiveness. None of them is best for all organizations at all times, but each is well suited to particular stages of the organizational life cycle. Later in this chapter, you will see how managers can determine which model(s) to emphasize based in part on their organization's stage of development.

Critical Values and Effectiveness Criteria The developers of the competing values perspective examined the many criteria used by others to define effectiveness. They identified three sets of competing values that appeared to influence which criteria managers choose to use in assessing effectiveness:

1. *Flexibility vs. control*—the degree to which an organization values flexibility over control. If innovation, adaptability, and change are important to an organization, flexibility is emphasized. If, on the other hand, order, consistency, and maintenance of the status quo are more important, the organization will accentuate control.

2. *People vs. organization*—the degree to which the organization values the well-being of organization members vis-à-vis the development and promotion of the organization. The competing values approach does not assert that these two must conflict with one another, merely that an organization should determine which it wishes to emphasize as it assesses effectiveness. When managers believe that the feelings and needs of organization members are of utmost importance, they express a value similar to that promoted by the internal processes approach to organizational effectiveness.

3. *Means vs. ends*—the relative importance of each type of goal to the organization. If ends are valued more highly, a perspective similar to that found in the goal attainment approach is favored. If means are preferred, managers maintain a perspective such as that presented in the systems approach.

As shown in Figure 18.4, the three sets of critical values can be placed into eight possible combinations. Each combination of values is associated with a particular type of effectiveness criterion. An organization that values *O*rganization over people, *E*nds over means, and *C*ontrol over flexibility, for example, would probably want to include criterion set 1 (OEC) in its assessment of effectiveness, because its emphasis on productivity and efficiency is consistent with that particular combination of values. As shown in the figure, a manager might measure this effectiveness criterion by assessing the amount of output generated by the organization or by looking at the ratio of output to input.

Because the developers of the competing values perspective believed that no one effectiveness criterion is adequate, they grouped the eight effectiveness criteria shown in Figure 18.4 into compatible combinations. This results in four models that managers can use to assess effectiveness in organizations (see Figure 18.5). Recall that the four systematic ap-

FIGURE 18.4
A Three-Dimensional
Model of Organizational
Effectiveness

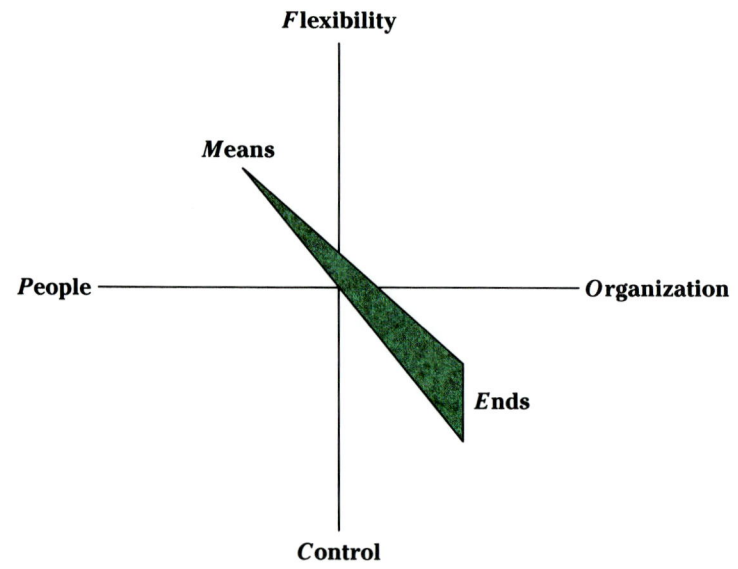

The Eight Cells	The Eight Criteria
OEC	1. *Productivity/efficiency*—volume of output, the ratio of output over input
OCM	2. *Planning and goal setting*—the amount of emphasis on the planning, objective setting, and evaluation process
OFE	3. *Resource acquisition*—the capacity to capture assets and develop external support
OFM	4. *Flexibility-readiness*—the ability to adapt to shifts in external conditions and demands
PCE	5. *Stability-control*—Smoothness of internal conditions, continuity, equilibrium.
PCM	6. *Information management-communication*—sufficiency of information flows, adequacy of internal orchestration
PFE	7. *Value of human resources training*—the enhancement and maintenance of overall staff capacity
PFM	8. *Cohesion-morale*—the level of communality and commitment among the staff members

Source: Based on R. E. Quinn and K. Cameron (1979), *Organizational life cycles and the criteria of effectiveness*, working paper: SUNY-Albany. The three-dimensional model shows the three value sets. The eight cells represent the ways the value sets can be combined. The criterion to the right of each cell is often used to measure effectiveness for that particular combination of values.

proaches discussed earlier were *descriptions* of how some organizations have assessed effectiveness. The four models proposed by the competing values perspective are *prescriptions* of what organizations should do to evaluate effectiveness. Unfortunately, relatively few organizations have followed these prescriptions thoroughly.

FIGURE 18.5
Four Models of Effectiveness

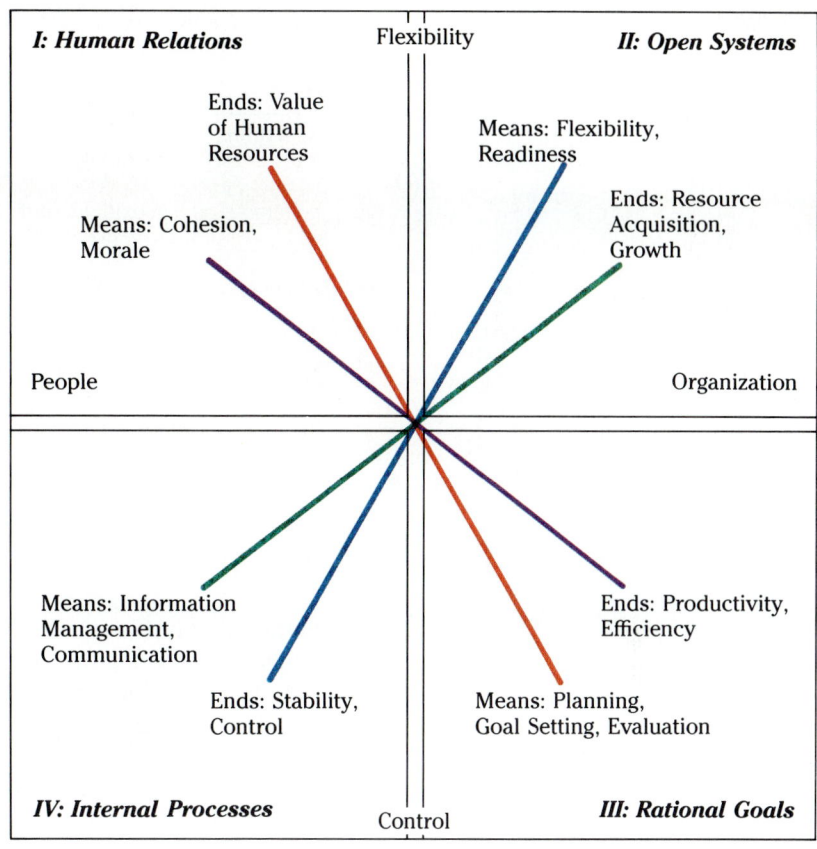

I: Human Relations   Flexibility   II: Open Systems

Ends: Value of Human Resources

Means: Flexibility, Readiness

Ends: Resource Acquisition, Growth

Means: Cohesion, Morale

People   Organization

Means: Information Management, Communication

Ends: Productivity, Efficiency

Ends: Stability, Control

Means: Planning, Goal Setting, Evaluation

IV: Internal Processes   Control   III: Rational Goals

Source: Based on R. E. Quinn and K. Cameron (1979), *Organizational life cycles and the criteria of effectiveness*, working paper: SUNY-Albany.

Four Models of Effectiveness

This section describes the four models of effectiveness proposed by the competing values perspective and shows how managers can assess effectiveness using each. Table 18.3 lists the four models of effectiveness proposed by the competing values perspective, as well as the value set from which each is derived and the means and ends effectiveness criteria appropriate for each. As you read, you will notice that some of these models have names similar to the four systematic approaches discussed earlier in the chapter. Do not let these (or other) similarities between the four *models* and the four *approaches* confuse you. The four models are more complete and potentially more useful than their predecessors.

The Human Relations Model   The **human relations model** characterizes an organization that values the well-being of its members over the development and promotion of the organization itself. This model is further characterized by the beliefs that flexibility is necessary for innovation, adaptation, and change and that the need for flexibility is more important than the need for control and maintenance of the status quo.

TABLE 18.3   *Models, Values, and Effectiveness Criteria*

Model	Values	Effectiveness Criteria	
		Means	*Ends*
Human relations	People and flexibility	Maintaining cohension and morale	Value and development of human resources
Open systems	Flexibility and organization	Maintaining flexibility and readiness	Growth, resource acquisition, and external support
Rational goals	Organization and control	Planning, objective setting, and evaluation	Productivity and efficiency
Internal processes	Control and people	Information management and coordination	Stability and equilibrium

Source: Modified from S. P. Robbins (1983), *Organization theory: The structure and design of organizations*, Englewood Cliffs, NJ: Prentice-Hall, 39.

Given this orientation, managers should assess the effectiveness of means goals by measuring the degree to which cohesion and morale are developed and maintained among organization members. Cohesion can be measured by evaluating the degree to which organization members like each other, work well together, communicate fully and effectively, and successfully coordinate work with each other. Morale can be measured by evaluating the degree to which members feel they are important to the organization; share goals; are committed to the organization and its interests; and, as a group, desire to contribute to the organization.

Managers adopting a human relations model assess the effectiveness of ends goals by measuring the value and development of an organization's human resources. They can, for example, assess the economic worth of the organization's workforce. In this assessment, managers would value trained, experienced, skilled workers capable of producing at high levels more highly than they would less-skilled, less-experienced, less-accomplished members who probably could not produce as much. (If you are wondering why any organization might prefer a workforce with lesser value, consider that a more valuable workforce tends to cost more. An organization must believe that a greater investment in human resources will yield a greater premium, or it will not pay more for its workforce.)

Just as investors judge the worth of their stocks by whether they increase in value, another indication of the economic worth of an organization's workforce is whether it improves over time. An organization that is unable to retain valued employees and replaces them with less-skilled, less-experienced, or less-accomplished employees would see a decline in the worth of its workforce and be considered ineffective under a human relations model. On the other hand, an organization that recruits, retains, and improves its members increases the worth of its human resources and, thus, its effectiveness. The human relations model, by its nature, considers the worth of a workforce as indicative of an organization's chances of functioning effectively.

Managers adopting a human relations approach value trained, experienced, skilled workers capable of producing at high levels, even though such a workforce tends to be more expensive for an organization.

The Open-Systems Model An open system of management, as described in Chapter 2, characterizes an organization that is sensitive and responsive, capable both of receiving information from and projecting information to the external environment. Managers of an **open-systems model** organization, thus, value the need for flexibility over the need for control, as do managers using the human relations model. The open-systems model, however, emphasizes organizational development and promotion over the well-being of organization members.

Given this orientation, managers should assess the effectiveness of means goals by measuring the degree to which their organization maintains flexibility and readiness for change. Flexibility can be measured by determining how easily the organization can alter its policies and practices in response to changes in its environment. Managers can make changes in standard operating procedures relatively quickly in a flexible organization. Managers in a less-flexible organization must "move heaven and earth" to change the way work is performed. Readiness for change can be assessed by determining how easily the organization can perform alternative tasks if called on to do so and by measuring the degree to which workers are receptive to change (see Chapter 20).

Ends goals in an open-systems model focus on organizational growth, the acquisition of needed resources, and the procurement of external support for the organization. Managers, thus, can measure the production capacity of the workforce, assets, sales levels, market share, and (in for-profit organizations) profits. Managers can assess resource acquisition by, for example, evaluating the degree to which sufficient raw materials, inventories, and employees are obtained from the environment and by evaluating the cost of doing so. External support can be measured by the degree to which critical external constituents—suppliers, customers, regulatory agencies, and so on—are loyal to the organization, have confidence in it, and provide support when needed.

A CLOSER LOOK

Organizational Effectiveness: Who's on First?

The competing values perspective stresses that there is no universal goal against which organizational effectiveness can be measured. The criteria appropriate for judging one organization's effectiveness should differ from those used to judge another, depending on each organization's values, life-cycle stage, and so on. Sometimes, however, people want to compare the effectiveness of one organization to that of another. Is a "blue chip" company still considered strong, for example? Which companies are poised for rapid growth and which are ripe for a takeover bid? *Business Week*, *Fortune*, and other publications generate lists each year to satisfy readers' demands to know what the "top" companies are.

> *The criteria appropriate for judging one organization's effectiveness should differ from those used to judge another. . . .*

To compile these and other comparison lists, standard criteria of effectiveness must be adopted. Five standard criteria will be used here to examine the effectiveness of three well-known companies: Du Pont, Merck, and Amoco. In 1987, these companies were similar in market value, ranging from $19.5 billion to $21.2 billion. Their CEOs received similar compensation: $1.4 million, $1.4 million, and $1.0 million, respectively. Deciding which company is most effective is not an easy task. Which company comes out on top depends on the effectiveness criterion that is used. As you examine the five accompanying charts, look at how the lead changes according to whether the criterion is sales revenues, profits (income after expenses), margin (profit as a percent of sales), sales growth (the increase in sales over those from the previous year), or profit growth (the increase in profit over that from the previous year). Note, for example, that Du Pont comes out on top on the basis of both sales and profits. Merck, however, excels on the basis of sales growth and margin, while Amoco appears best in terms of profit growth. This illustrates the importance of using more than one effectiveness criterion to understand an organization's overall effectiveness.

As you examine the charts, you will note that they (and many of the "top" lists published) are based mostly on ends criteria. Understanding how ends effectiveness is obtained, however, would require examination of means criteria. Although it is more difficult to compare means criteria than ends criteria across organizations, some means measures can be compared. In fact, when *Fortune* publishes the results of its annual survey of America's most admired corporations every January, many of the criteria examined are means criteria. It is very likely that Merck's success on ends criteria is largely attributable to its strong means performance. Of the 300 companies included in *Fortune's* survey, Merck ranked first overall; first in the ability to attract, develop, and keep talented people; second in quality of products and services; second in community and environmental responsibility; and, no lower than fifth on any criterion.[1]

1. E. C. Baig (19 January 1987), America's most admired corporations, *Fortune*, 18–31.

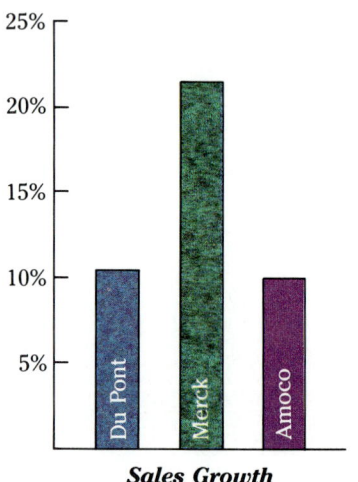

Sales Growth

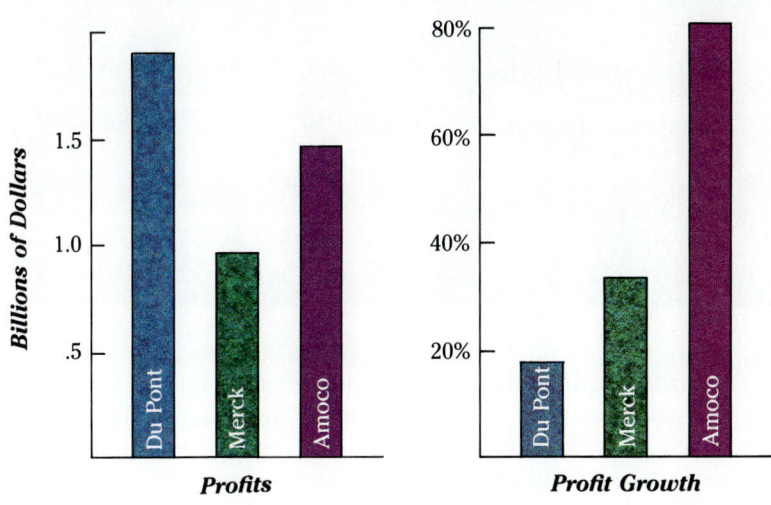

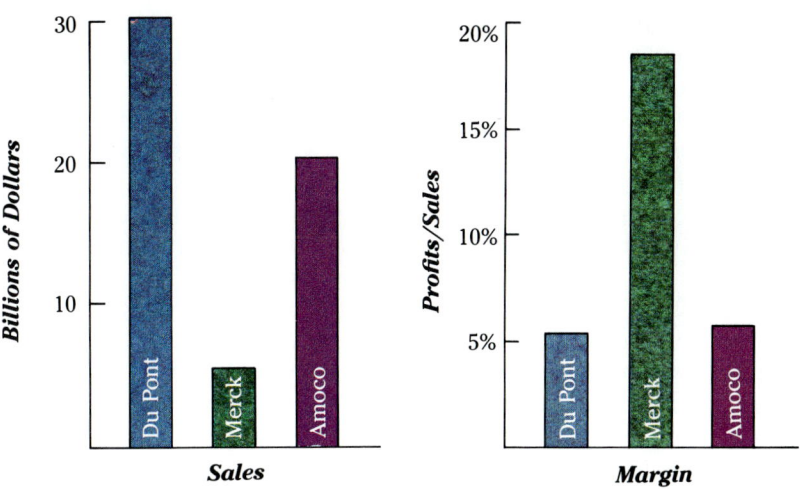

Managers can measure efficiency by comparing productivity to production costs. The greater the productivity per dollar of cost, the greater the organization's efficiency.

The Rational Goals Model   When management values an organization over its members and control over flexibility, its focus is considered to be on rational goals. Like the open-systems model, the **rational goals model** is concerned with organizational development and promotion. Unlike the open-systems model, however, the rational goals model values control, consistency, and maintenance of the status quo more than it values flexibility.

This combination of values results in means goals that focus on organizational planning and the setting of objectives—in short, a focus on setting and reaching rational goals. Managers assessing the effectiveness of an organization's planning techniques can measure the degree to which the organization follows the planning procedures suggested in Chapters 6 and 9 as they plot its course for the future. For example, does the organization establish objectives, premise (forecast and formulate assumptions), determine a course of action, and then formulate supporting plans for the plotted course of action? Managers also can evaluate these goals to determine the degree to which they are properly formulated, specific, difficult, and reachable.

The important ends goals in the rational goals model usually involve productivity and the efficiency of operations. Generally, managers measure productivity by assessing the amount of goods or services generated in a specific amount of time. This assessment of productivity can be conducted for individual members of the organization, for specified groups, and for the overall organization. Managers can measure efficiency by comparing productivity to the costs of producing products and services. The greater the productivity per dollar of cost, the greater the organization's efficiency.

The Internal Processes Model   Like the traditional internal processes approach, and similar to the human relations model, the **internal processes model** of organizational effectiveness values the well-being of organization members. Unlike either of them, however, the internal processes model described here shares the rational goals model's emphasis on the value of control, consistency, and the status quo over flexibility.

One set of means goals important in an internal processes model involves information management. Managers can assess the effectiveness of their information-collection and distribution processes by measuring the completeness and accuracy of information received from and delivered to their external and internal environments. Managers can also take into account the efficiency with which the information is collected. The effectiveness of other information-management means goals should include assessment of the adequacy of the organization's analysis and interpretation, as well as the adequacy of its communication of information, evaluations, and directives.

Another important set of means goals for this type of model involves coordination processes. Managers should determine how well the activities of individuals and groups within their organization are coordinated. How aware, for example, are organization members of their individual and group responsibilities? Do they understand how to interact with other individuals and groups to serve the organization?

Ends goals in the internal processes model relate to an organization's stability and equilibrium. Managers can assess stability and equilibrium by measuring the degree to which their organization maintains its structure, distribution of functions, and allocation and utilization of resources over time. Particularly important is the degree to which these factors remain unchanged in the face of stress or external threats.

Guidelines for Managers

As you can see, each of the four models advocated by developers of the competing values perspective provides a way for managers to assess organizational effectiveness. Confounding the situation, however, is that characteristics of all four effectiveness models can be found, to a degree, in almost any organization. Furthermore, as you have learned, not all key members champion the same model, because they hold different values. The obvious question for managers is "Which model of effectiveness should I favor?" The answer, in part, is based on an organization's level of maturity.

An organization in the *entrepreneurial stage*, for example, often is best served by the open-systems model of effectiveness. After all, the organization's chances of survival depend on how flexible it is (a means goal in the open-systems model) and whether the organization exists for reasons beyond the personal interests of a few individuals. The ends goals of growth, resource acquisition, and external support that characterize the open-systems model are also appropriate for this stage in an organization's life cycle. In its entrepreneurial stage, for example, Apple Computer should have gauged effectiveness by measuring how well it maintained flexibility and readiness for change and by measuring its growth rate, the adequacy of the resources it obtained, and the level of support it received from those outside the organization. Not only were these appropriate measures of effectiveness for Apple in its early years, but they were based on goals that had to be accomplished in order for the company to advance to the next stage in its life cycle.

The *collectivity stage* of an organizational life cycle is consistent with the characteristics of the human relations model of effectiveness. At this point in an organization's life cycle, that model's means goals of maintaining cohesion and morale match the organization's emphasis on informal communication and structure and the development of cooperation and commitment among organization members. The human relations ends goals relating to the value and development of human resources also fit well, because the organization is trying to build a strong "family" of members during this stage. The onset of this life cycle stage was particularly noticeable at Apple in the early 1980s, given the company's rapid growth and the high visibility of its revolutionary product line. During the collectivity stage, Apple was proud of its human relations orientation and devoted tremendous amounts of resources to developing employee morale and cohesion. Even its advertising revealed the company's emphasis on its members.

For organizations in the *formalization stage,* the combined use of the internal processes and rational goals models could be appropriate. An organization at this point in its life cycle usually becomes somewhat conservative relative to its earlier stages, and the combined use of these models offers the control the organization seeks as it concentrates on efficiency and stability. As Apple entered this life cycle stage during the mid-1980s, managers were faced with the company's first quarterly loss and employee layoffs. Particularly between 1985 and 1987, after John Sculley took control of the company, Apple shifted its means criteria to systematic and rational planning, formal objectives, careful information management, and comprehensive internal coordination. Ends effectiveness criteria became measures of productivity, efficiency, and stability. For most of this period, the combination of means and ends goals enabled the company to become profitable again.

As an organization matures further, it may find that it has become too stable, too conservative. When it reaches the *elaboration of structure stage*, it must again become flexible and open to change in its search for new growth opportunities, additional resources, and new and continuing sources of external support. This point in the life cycle encourages a return to the open-systems model of effectiveness so that the organization can take advantage of any opportunities it finds. In practice, however, organizations at full maturity are unlikely to adopt the open-systems model as a sole perspective on organizational effectiveness, even if they did so during their entrepreneurial stages. Instead, they may adopt an open-systems model and—perhaps to a lesser extent—both the internal processes and rational goals models. As a result, the process of definition and measurement of organizational effectiveness can become quite complex.

Apple has not abandoned the rational goals and internal processes models that served it so well during the mid- to late 1980s, but John Sculley appears ready to incorporate some open-systems characteristics in his plans for the company's future.[10] Developing new products, capitalizing on rising interest in such issues as desktop publishing, and

TABLE 18.4   *Life Cycle Stages and Matching Effectiveness Models*

	Entrepreneurial Stage	Collectivity Stage	Formalization Stage	Elaboration of Structure Stage
Characterized By	Emphasis on collection of resources needed for survival and future activities	Emphasis on informal communication and informal structure	Emphasis on stability and efficiency	Emphasis on monitoring the external environment
	Use of resources to find creative, innovative business methods and/or products/services	Development of cooperation among members and the building of commitment of members to the organization	Development of rules and procedures to guide operations; use of a conservative approach	Searches for opportunities for renewal and further growth; attempts to become less conservative
Appropriate Effectiveness Model	Open-systems model	Human relations model	Internal processes model combined with rational goals model	Open-systems model and, to a lesser extent, internal processes model and rational goals model

spending over $150 million a year on research are some indications that Apple is taking the open-systems effectiveness criteria seriously.

Another possible avenue for mature organizations is to create a unit or division targeted for growth and development and to use an open-systems model of effectiveness for that unit but to continue to emphasize internal processes and/or rational goals models for the remainder of the organization. This, in effect, is what IBM did when it created an independent business unit to develop the IBM PC. In fact, IBM's success in this venture contributed heavily to Apple's problems in the early 1980s and is a testimony to this model's potential usefulness.

As you can see, an organization's stage of development significantly influences the models of organizational effectiveness managers adopt, or, rather, it should. Managers too often allow themselves to choose a model based strictly on personal values, sometimes selecting inappropriate models as a result. Steven Jobs, one of the founders of Apple, successfully used the human relations model at the company for years. When his preference for this model matched the company's needs, Apple was successful. As the company matured beyond the collectivity stage, however, Job's insistence on this model and the company's conservative behavior contributed to its profitability problems.

In sum, managers should assess the dominant life cycle stage of their organization and choose effectiveness criteria from a model compatible with that stage. This only means that one (or perhaps two) models should be emphasized during certain life stages, not that all other effectiveness criteria are irrelevant. In fact, many internal problems encountered at Apple during its formalization stage were due largely to the company's failure to attend to the effectiveness criteria used during the two earlier life cycle stages. To quote former employees, "It's just another big, boring company." "Why bother? You're a cog in a wheel."[11] Table 18.4 summarizes the characteristics of each of the four stages of development and

A CLOSER LOOK

Managers and Effectiveness: Do Managers Matter?

In 1988, Maria Castañeda of Texas A&M University and Nancy Johnson, vice-president of corporate research for American Family Insurance, conducted a study to find out whether the performance of individual managers influences the effectiveness of their work units. Approximately seventy-five American Family district claims managers (DCMs), who oversee the investigation and settlement of claims filed by or against the company's policy holders, participated in the investigation.

Performance was defined as the degree to which a manager fulfilled each of ten major managerial responsibilities identified through job analysis (see Chapter 17), three of which

were planning, directing, and controlling. (The terminology in this "Closer Look" is consistent with that used elsewhere in this book, even though different terms were sometimes used in the study at American Family.) How well each DCM performed each of ten managerial behaviors was rated by his or her boss. Seven measures of effectiveness involved various business outcomes of the manager's unit, three of which were productivity, employee satisfaction, and financial effectiveness. Productivity was assessed by the number of claims handled by the technicians working for the DCM. Employee satisfaction was measured by surveying the technicians. Financial effectiveness was assessed by measuring annual loss payments and expenses.

The results of the study showed little relationship between the managers' performance and four effectiveness criteria of customer retention, customer satisfaction, customer attraction, and timeliness of claims service. All of the management behaviors examined, however, were related to at least one of the three effectiveness criteria of productivity, employee satisfaction, and financial effective-

ness. Perhaps most importantly, managers who were better at planning, directing, and controlling had more effective work units. The better managers planned, the more satisfied were their employees. Managers who directed better than their peers also had employees who were more satisfied and more productive and who contributed more to the company's financial effectiveness. Lastly, the better managers executed the controlling function, the more satisfied and more productive were their employees (who contributed more to financial effectiveness).

> *The better managers planned, the more satisfied were their employees.*

It would appear from this study that managers *do* matter. Better managers have more effective work units. These findings are helping American Family Insurance improve managerial selection and training programs to obtain a result desired by every organization: improved organizational effectiveness.

indicates which model (or combination of models) of effectiveness is appropriate for that point in an organization's life cycle.

Different models of effectiveness might be appropriate for different parts of an organization. The criteria for assessing the effectiveness of a research and development department, for example, nearly always favor the values expressed by the open-systems and/or human relations models of effectiveness, regardless of the life cycle of the overall organization. An audit or quality assurance department, on the other hand, usually needs a rational goals model. An appropriate match is the key to success.

Organizational Effectiveness in Review

There is no universally accepted definition of organizational effectiveness. This is unfortunate, because managers need to know what organizational effectiveness is in order to control it. This ambiguity is evident in the haphazard way managers often try to assess organizational effectiveness— by taking aim at one (or perhaps only two or three) criteria, such as improved morale or increased profits. This approach, however, ignores a large number of other potential criteria. Some managers go the other way, evaluating many criteria but paying sufficient attention to none.

In recent years, managers have used four major systematic approaches to assessing organizational effectiveness. Each is driven by a particular vision or definition of organizational effectiveness. The diversity of these approaches reveals the need for managers to consider both where their company is going (ends goals) and how it intends to get there (means goals).

A goal attainment approach, which evaluates effectiveness by assessing whether specified ends goals are met, has been the most widely used approach. The systems approach concentrates on the means goals organizations use to achieve ends goals and, thus, examines the degree to which organizations successfully acquire and transform important resources. A less-common approach, the internal processes approach, assesses effectiveness by measuring whether organization members are well integrated and the organization is functioning smoothly. Finally, the strategic constituencies approach concentrates on the degree to which the needs of critical organizational constituents, such as suppliers and customers, are satisfied.

Because each of the four approaches has merit, they are integrated by the competing values perspective on effectiveness. This perspective observes that organizations define effectiveness differently depending on the values held by key organization members. This difference in values led to the development of four models from which managers should choose to assess an organization's effectiveness: human relations, open-systems, rational goals, and internal processes. Each model can be used individually or in combination with others.

Organizations usually select an effectiveness approach or model based on their managers' values, but total reliance on personal values can lead to poor choices. The competing values perspective states that managers should evaluate the life cycle of their organization to identify the model of effectiveness most appropriate for its stage of development: entrepreneurial (creation), collectivity, formalization, and elaboration of structure. Appropriate measures of effectiveness are different for organizations in different stages of the cycle.

Managers should examine the models to identify and define the most appropriate effectiveness criteria for their organization. Unless they do so systematically, they are likely to join the many others who have fallen into the trap of using convenient or readily available effectiveness criteria that they personally value, rather than using the most appropriate criteria.

Notes

1. S. P. Robbins (1983), *Organization theory: The structure and design of organizations,* Englewood Cliffs, NJ: Prentice-Hall, 27.

2. E. Yuchtman and S. E. Seashore (1967), A systems resource approach to organizational effectiveness, *American Sociological Review,* 32, 891–903; E. Yuchtman and S. E. Seashore (1967), Factorial analysis of organizational performance, *Administrative Science Quarterly,* 12, 377–95.

3. B. Bass (1952), Ultimate criteria of organizational worth, *Personnel Psychology,* 5, 157–73; B. S. Georgopoules and A. A. Tannenbaum (1957), The study of organizational effectiveness, *American Sociological Review,* 22, 534–40; W. Bennis (1966), *Changing organizations,* New York: McGraw-Hill.

4. G. Dessler (1986), *Organization theory: Integrating structure and behavior,* 2nd ed., Englewood Cliffs, NJ: Prentice-Hall.

5. R. E. Walton (1973), Quality of work life: What is it? *Sloan Management Review,* 15, 11–21.

6. Bennis, 1966.

7. R. E. Quinn and K. Cameron (1983), Organizational life cycles and shifting criteria of effectiveness: Some preliminary evidence, *Management Science,* 29(1), 33–51.

8. J. Pfeffer and G. Salancik (1978), *The external control of organizations,* New York: Harper & Row.

9. J. Rohrbaugh, G. McClelland, and R. Quinn (1980), Measuring the relative importance of utilitarian and egalitarian values: A study of individual differences about fair distribution, *Journal of Applied Psychology,* 65, 34–49; K. S. Cameron and D. A. Whetten (1981), Perceptions of organizational effectiveness over organizational life cycles, *Administrative Science Quarterly,* 26, 525–44; Robbins, 1983.

10. K. M. Hafner with G. Lewis (19 January 1987), Apple's comeback, *Business Week,* 86.

11. K. M. Hafner (19 January 1987), Apple is getting a few gray hairs, *Business Week,* 88.

Key Terms

goal attainment approach	competing values perspective
ends goals	life cycle
systems approach	human relations model
means goals	open-systems model
internal processes approach	rational goals model
strategic constituencies approach	internal processes model

Issues for Review and Discussion

1. Discuss the rifle approach to organizational effectiveness and explain how it differs from the shotgun approach.
2. Identify the primary drawback of the rifle approach and the primary drawback of the shotgun approach.

3. Present an example of a goal attainment approach to organizational effectiveness for an organization at which you have worked.

4. Describe how a systems approach to effectiveness would differ from an internal processes approach for an organization such as McDonald's.

5. Describe a strategic constituencies approach to effectiveness for a college fraternity or sorority and identify at least two important factors that would be overlooked in using such an approach.

6. Develop a brief argument that could be presented to the Board of Directors of Ford Motor Company, making clear how a competing values perspective could benefit that organization.

7. List the main similarities and differences among the four models in the competing values perspective.

8. Briefly explain why a large, complex organization must often use different criteria of effectiveness for different parts of the organization.

9. The competing values perspective argues that an organization's life-cycle stage should dictate the model of effectiveness it uses. Construct an argument against this.

Suggested Readings

Goodman, P. S., Pennings, J. M. and Associates, eds. (1977). *New perspectives in organizational effectiveness*. San Francisco: Jossey-Bass.

O'Toole, J. (1987). *Vanguard management*. New York: Berkley Publishing.

Peters, T. J. and Waterman, R. H., Jr. (1982). *In search of excellence*. New York: Harper & Row.

Peters, R. (1987). *Thriving on chaos*. New York: Alfred A. Knopf; Noe, A. W. (1988). A review of *Thriving on chaos*. In Pierce, J. L. and Newstrom, J. W., eds. *The manager's bookshelf: A mosaic of contemporary views*. New York: Harper & Row, 320–26.

Quinn, R. E. and Cameron, K. (1983). Organizational life cycles and shifting criteria of effectiveness: Some preliminary evidence. *Management Science*, 29(1), 33–51.

CASE   *The Night Shift*

By Cyril Ling of the University of Wisconsin-Whitewater

Jean McDuff, the night nursing director of St. Amos Hospital, was disturbed by a memo from the hospital administrator, Paul Seay. Reports from the controller's office indicated that linen replacement costs, particularly for bed sheets, had doubled within the past three months due to shortages. A check by the day staff of laundry room procedures and nursing floor supplies had not accounted for the continued shortages. Paul's memo concluded, "In view of rising operating costs, I suggest that you institute immediate close checks on all your personnel."

The hospital had two main sections of eight floors each, including fifteen nursing units and an operating room, and one small wing consisting of three nursing units. Soiled linen was collected from two main laundry chutes in the basement of the main sections and from linen hamper trucks in the adjoining wing. The hospital laundry operated at peak capacity for eight hours, six days a week, starting at 9 A.M. Daily supply orders were filled and checked by the laundry manager before the laundry closed at 5 P.M. The night shift ran from 11 P.M. to 7 A.M. At 11 P.M., the night orderlies began distributing loaded hampers to each of the nursing units and the operating room. Floor personnel stored the linen in closets during the night as time permitted. The empty hampers were returned to the basement chutes by orderlies before they checked out at 6:30 A.M.

The night shift was a close-knit group, and its employment turnover was the lowest in the nursing department. Since the hospital was located in the far southwest corner of the city, many of the night employees, including several members of the professional nursing staff, carpooled from downtown areas. Many of the night-shift nurses' aides and orderlies were long-time employees; some were related to other employees or were second-generation St. Ames employees.

Jean MacDuff, being of ample proportions, was affectionately referred to as "Miz Mac" directly and "Big Mac" indirectly. With her approval, the night shift's 2:30 A.M. break had become a respected ritual; employee birthdays, anniversaries, and pay raises were always celebrated with food and fellowship between the units. Henry Sharon, the head orderly, often wrote a poem in honor of special occasions. Of undetermined age and handicapped with an artificial leg, Henry was the most agile and light-hearted worker on the night-time staff. He proudly carried his keys dangling from his belt, which indicated that he was in charge of laundry cart deliveries. He had been at the hospital for more than twenty years, and he tutored new orderlies with skill and understanding. Many student nurses also learned much from Henry in handling difficult patients and deaths.

Because of the size of the hospital and her many administrative duties, Jean considered Paul's directive to be an impossibility. On rounds that evening, she simply read the memo to each of the nursing unit supervisors and asked them to observe the handling of linen closely, to report any irregularities, and to make suggestions for changes. That night during the break, Jean asked Henry if he had noticed any outsiders hanging around while the linen hampers were being moved from the laundry. Henry reminded her that there were six exits in the hospital, which fire regulations stated must be kept open at all times, and that only one night watchman was on duty, usually at the emergency entrance. No suggestions or ideas were reported to Jean by any of the night personnel. Since there was no apparent shortage of clean linen during the 11-to-7 shift that evening, Jean and the night shift did nothing further about the linen problem.

Two weeks later, a second memo from Paul advised, "Due to continued shortages in linen sheets, effective immediately, all linen closets on nursing units will be kept tightly locked. Sheets will be dispensed only upon request by the nursing unit supervisors, and delivery and storage of the next day's linen must be personally supervised by the supervisor in each unit."

This regulation was met with much opposition and resentment from night staff, because it would require so much time and personnel. Orderlies unloading floor linen hampers were often called from the floor, and patient calls could not be handled promptly as a result of the regulation. With the extra work, the 2:30 A.M. break was frequently delayed until 3 or 4 A.M., and on some floors was omitted entirely. On two occasions, Paul was observed counting hampers and checking the basement laundry room at 6 A.M. Empty hampers often filled the service elevators when the day shift reported for duty; Henry

Sharon explained to Jean that his orderlies no longer had time to get the empty hampers back to the basement, because the floors were too slow in unloading them. Nurses' aides reported frequent backaches from so much heavy unloading and complained that they could not guide the hampers, even when they were empty and blocking the hallways.

Absenteeism, which had never been a problem on the 11-to-7 shift, became more frequent, and several aides asked for transfers to the day shift. Jean questioned one very capable aide who resigned from the hospital. She said, "It's just no fun working here like it used to be. Everybody's got to be so careful and looking at each other. What do they think we would do with those missing sheets anyway, Miz Mac? We're all double-bed sleepers! You can ask anybody!"

The following month, the hospital began using linens with its name printed in large blue letters in the middle. In spite of the addition of two new guards at employee exits and the checking of all personal parcels, linen losses continued, although at a reduced rate.

About three weeks later, Jean resigned as night nursing director, complaining that she simply "couldn't take all this bickering and suspicion anymore."

Six months later, Paul still had not found a qualified replacement for Jean. Nursing care during night hours had been reduced sharply, and many staff doctors admitted acutely ill patients to the hospital only if private-duty night nurses were available.

Questions

1. Which of the four approaches to assessing organizational effectiveness was Paul using?
2. How might other approaches have helped him devise a better solution to the problem of the missing linen?
3. How would you have handled this problem?
4. Describe how you would go about identifying an appropriate organizational effectiveness model for use in the hospital.

CHAPTER 19

Control Methods and Their Effects

Student Learning Objectives

After reading this chapter, you should be able to:

1. Define the managerial function of controlling and discuss the levels at which controlling activities take place.

2. Identify the targets of the control activity.

3. Distinguish among the four steps of the integrated control process and understand why an effective control system must include all four steps.

4. Explain why it is important to integrate strategic planning and controlling.

5. Understand the advantages and limitations of cybernetic and noncybernetic control systems.

6. Discuss the various time perspectives that may be found in a control system.

7. Recognize the specific characteristics of good control systems and explain how each can improve the effectiveness of the control system.

8. Identify some of the most important positive and negative effects of control systems on organization members, and explain the importance of this knowledge for managers.

Marianne Rowe is an assistant manager at Burger Barn #382 in Greensboro, North Carolina, one of 750 virtually identical fast-food restaurants in the Burger Barn chain. The parent organization has established a collection of very detailed ends and means goals for each restaurant in its chain, including the amounts of sales and profits each restaurant must generate per square foot, exactly how much each hamburger patty should weigh, and the word-for-word greetings employees should give customers. Robert Frank, the company's national franchise director, sends a report to each franchise at the beginning of every quarter that recaps the previous quarter's activity for that store and specifies corrective actions for the next quarter.

Yesterday Marianne received the report for store #382. It noted that her franchise met its sales goals for the preceding quarter, did not achieve its profits goals, treated customers according to procedure, and exceeded its food wastage allowance. As always, the report detailed the actions Marianne and her manager should take to improve performance. When Marianne met her friend Lois at a restaurant after work that night, she told her about the report. Lois asked Marianne how she felt about working for a company with so many rules and procedures to follow, and Marianne replied:

> *Actually, most of the time I like having the rules to depend on. They tell the people working for me how to do their jobs, and I can almost always anticipate what the other assistant managers will or won't do. Sometimes the rules do get on my nerves, though, especially if I feel the company uses them to treat me like a machine instead of a person. When I really get mad (and my boss isn't around), I get even by putting extra meat in the hamburgers and giving the staff complimentary meals.*

Robert Frank's quarterly reports are part of the control process used by the Burger Barn chain. When Marianne feels overly controlled by the process, she vents her dissatisfaction and hurts the company's profitability by putting too much meat in the hamburgers and by giving free meals to employees. Maintaining an organization's control systems while taking into account the reactions of members to the control process are an integral part of a manager's job.

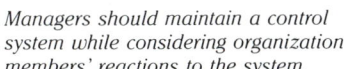

Managers should maintain a control system while considering organization members' reactions to the system.

The Control Process

In Chapter 18, you learned that the primary reason managers exercise control is to make their organization as effective as possible; therefore, **controlling** is defined as the process of monitoring and evaluating organizational effectiveness and initiating the actions needed to maintain or improve effectiveness. The control system in the Burger Barn chain, for example, collects information about the franchises through a variety of monitoring systems, including company observers who pose as customers. It then sends this information to Robert Frank for evaluation, who provides feedback and instructions for improvements to the stores' managers in his quarterly reports.

The Need for Control

Like the managerial functions of planning, organizing, and directing, controlling is a complex activity that managers must perform at many organizational levels. Upper-level managers, for example, must monitor their organization's overall strategic plans, which can only be implemented if middle-level managers control the organization's divisional and departmental plans, which, in turn, rely on lower-level managers' control of groups and individual employees (see the discussion of goal hierarchy in Chapter 6). While Robert Frank is controlling franchise effectiveness in the Burger Barn organization, Marianne's boss is controlling the effectiveness of Barn #382, and Marianne is controlling the effectiveness of her shift.

Although there is a continual and universal need for control in organizations, the importance, amount, and type of control vary across organizational situations. Probably the most important influence on the nature of an organization's control systems is the amount of environmental change and complexity.

Organizations that operate with relatively stable external environments usually need to change very little, so managers eventually are able to control such organizations using a set of routine procedures. Routines are not necessarily simple, however. In fact, the rigid control systems usually incorporated into the bureaucratic model often can be put in place and used for a long time. Consider, for example, the controls used to regulate the means goals of a large bank and its branch offices. There are rules and procedures governing loan-making decisions, cash handling, dress codes, treatment of customers, and so forth.

With greater levels of environmental change, however, controlling requires more continual attention from managers. Traditional routines and rigid control systems are simply not adequate for such conditions, as U.S. investment firms discovered on October 19, 1987, when their computerized trading programs were unable to cope with dramatic and unanticipated changes in the stock market. From the crash's aftermath arose stronger, more flexible control systems that rely on human intervention, as well as computer programs, to deal with the volatile environmental conditions of the U.S. economy.

The amount of environmental complexity also affects the nature of control systems. Simple environments contain a limited number of highly similar components that are relatively easy to control through common sets of rules and procedures that address similar goals. Here, too, rigid bureaucratic systems provide adequate control. The same control system, for example, can be used at almost every branch office of a large bank.

Control systems become increasingly important as complexity increases. When organizations grow larger, diversify product lines, or encounter a more heterogeneous task environment, for example, managers' needs for up-to-date information and coordination among organizational activities intensify. The complexity that calls for increased control, however, also requires open, organic systems that can respond quickly and effectively to complex environments. In such complicated situations, organizations often specify the use of flexible systems as a means goal: "To allow us to manage the complexities of our organization, we must

FIGURE 19.1   Need for Control

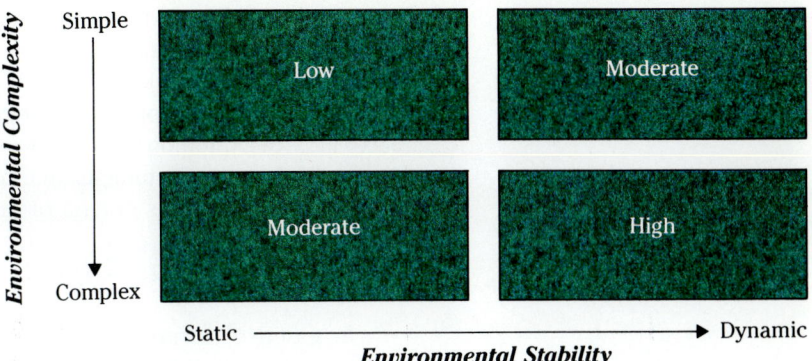

remain flexible and open." Other control activities shift to ends goals, such as, "We want to increase market share 10 percent in each of our divisions." Flexibility allows substantial choice as to how ends goals will be met: "Each division may decide how to achieve its 10-percent increase in market share." Figure 19.1 shows the level of control needed by organizations under different environmental conditions.

A Traditional Control Model

Traditional control models suggest that control is a process consisting of four steps (see Figure 19.2). The first step in the control process consists of *establishing standards*. Standards are the ends and means goals against which organizational activities are compared and are established during the planning process; thus, planning provides the basis for the control process by providing standards of performance.

The second step in the control process consists of *monitoring* actual organizational behavior and results by measuring what has actually taken place. Questions to be answered at this step include determination of *what* should be measured, *who* should do the measuring, *when*, and *how*.

The third step in the controlling process consists of *comparing actual behavior and results against standards*. Similar to the gap analysis performed during the strategic planning process (see Chapter 9), this third step in the control process provides managers with the input (information) needed for the fourth and final step.

The final step consists of *evaluation and action*. Initially, this step of the control process is judgmental in nature as managers interpret the meaning of the comparative information provided by the third step. Based

FIGURE 19.2   *The Traditional Control Model*

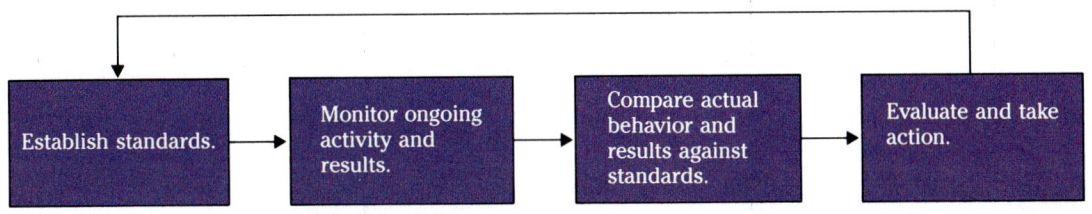

on their conclusions about the relationships between expectations and reality, managers make decisions. They might, for example, decide to maintain the status quo, change the standard, or take corrective action.

Later in this chapter, an integrated control model is presented. It expands the traditional model to deal with the complexities of today's organizational environments and the needs of managers to monitor better both ends and means criteria of organizational effectiveness.

Organizational Targets

In essence, control affects every part of an organization—the resources it receives, the output it generates, its environmental relationships, and all managerial activities (see Figure 19.3). As you learned in Chapter 3, some of these managerial activities—operations, marketing, financial, and human resources—are conducted in all organizations. Consider the targets of control in each of these essential functional areas.

Operations Control   Managers in charge of an organization's operations function control the activities necessary to transform resources into goods and services. Two common targets of operations control are productivity and quality. To control productivity and quality, managers have devised a number of operations control systems, such as design controls, product controls, service and use controls, materials controls,

FIGURE 19.3
Targets of the Control Function

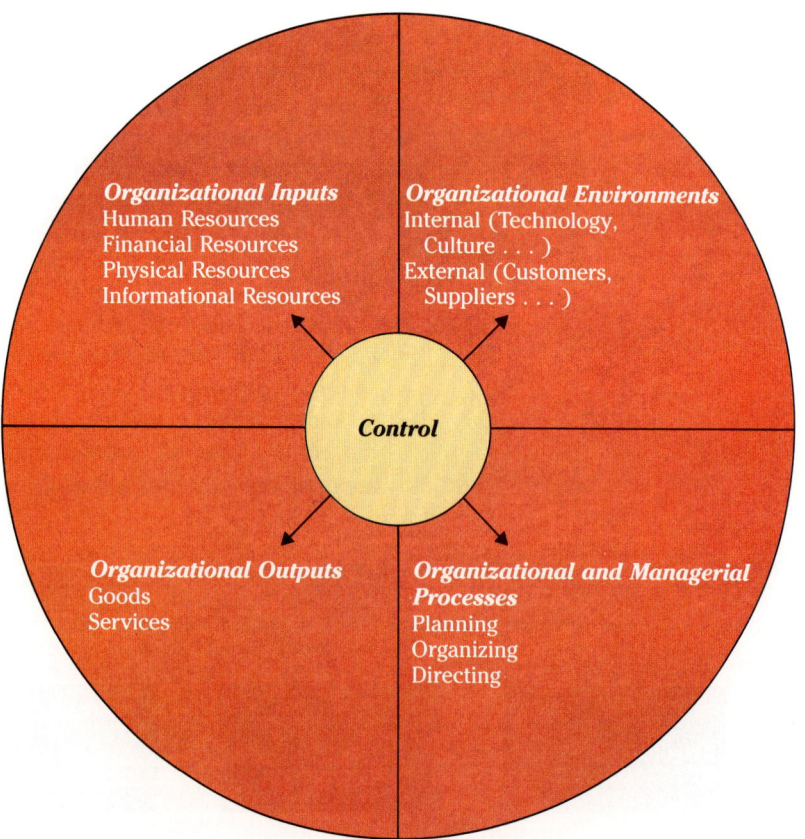

Organizational Inputs
Human Resources
Financial Resources
Physical Resources
Informational Resources

Organizational Environments
Internal (Technology, Culture . . .)
External (Customers, Suppliers . . .)

Control

Organizational Outputs
Goods
Services

Organizational and Managerial Processes
Planning
Organizing
Directing

Product control is one system managers have devised to control productivity and quality.

inventory controls, production controls, and employee behavioral controls.[1] Operations specialists for the Burger Barn chain, for example, designed food preparation systems that are quick, efficient, and sanitary while producing tasty food. They also created control systems to monitor whether Burger Barn employees follow the procedures to be used with these systems.

Marketing Control   Managers in charge of an organization's marketing function control activities that place its goods and services into the market. Marketing control systems often focus on regulating sales, prices, costs, and market share.[2] Quantitatively based quotas, for example, are commonly used to define sought-after market share, sales volume, and units to be sold by the marketing department. It was the Burger Barn marketing department that identified the prices each Barn would charge for food items and the dollars in sales expected per square foot of restaurant space. Marketing managers also use advertising to try to control consumers' opinions about an organization's goods or services.

Financial and Budgetary Control   Managers who oversee financial, operating, and nonmonetary budgets control activities at a number of different levels within an organization. At an individual level, for example, Robert Frank is given a travel budget that regulates how much he can spend on hotel rooms and meals when traveling to the franchises. The department he manages operates under an annual budget that governs how much money it can use to recruit and hire employees. The chain has an annual operating budget that specifies how much each Barn can spend for hamburger meat, condiments, paper supplies, labor, maintenance, and so forth, as well as a nonmonetary budget that defines the number of hours each company manager will donate to charity.

Managers create budgets with a number of characteristics to facilitate control. Usually, for example, budgets are created by upper-level managers, who distribute them to managers at the appropriate operating levels. This top-down approach is one means by which upper-level managers control the activities of subordinates and lower-level organizational units. A more participatory alternative is the "bottom-up" approach, in which unit managers prepare budget requests and submit them to department heads. The department heads integrate unit requests into a departmental budget request, which they submit to division heads, and so on up the organizational hierarchy until the requests reach upper-level managers for action.

In some organizations, zero-base budgeting has been integrated into the budget preparation and control process. Under the **zero-based budgeting** system, the fact that an item was approved in a prior budget does not guarantee that it will be included in a new budget. Unit managers are required to justify each element of their budget every time one is prepared, and their review and defense provides the basis for the control activity. For example, when Sue Talarczyk, human resource manager for the Burger Barn chain, prepares her budget for next year, she must justify her request for employee training funds, even though she received money for that purpose in this year's budget. Her explanation must show why training will be needed, what it will cost to provide, and why it will cost that much.

Human Resource Control Managers who oversee the human side of organizations control activities involving individuals, groups, and the nature of people-to-people and people-to-work interactions. Two common targets of human resource control are the regulation of managerial and nonmanagerial activities carried out on behalf of an organization and the improvement of its human resources so that its people can respond to and initiate new organizational ventures.[3] Sue Talarczyk, for example, has implemented control systems that specify, monitor, and control employee selection procedures, training and development programs, performance appraisals, compensation methods, and so on.

Controlling Ends and Means Goals

Whether the need for control is high or low, whether the target is marketing or operations, the essential purpose of the controlling function is to monitor and enhance organizational effectiveness. As you learned in Chapter 18, both ends goals (*what* an organization is trying to accomplish) and means goals (*how* an organization and its members behave) contribute to the overall effectiveness of organizations. Good control systems allow managers to evaluate effectiveness based on the degree to which both ends goals and means goals are met. Robert Frank, for example, wants to know whether Burger Barn #382 achieves its sales and profit (ends) goals each quarter and whether it accomplishes this by greeting customers with the specified speech, by serving hamburgers that weigh between 4.0 and 4.1 ounces, by wasting no more than .8 percent of its food, and by following other rules and procedures (means goals). Specific ends and means goals differ, depending on the effectiveness model chosen by an organization, but all of the integrated models discussed in Chapter 18 (human relations, open-systems, rational goals, and internal processes) take both ends and means goals into account.

Managers who monitor and evaluate the effectiveness of an organization by assessing the degree to which it is meeting ends and means goals must arrive at one of four conclusions based on the use of their control systems. Figure 19.4 shows the four possible conclusions and the ways in which managers should respond to their findings.

Both Ends and Means Goals Are Met In this situation, the control system has shown managers that their organization is getting where it wants to go (achieving ends goals) by following the planned policies and procedures for doing so (meeting means goals). This is a confirmation that the organization's strategic and operational plans are appropriate, and no corrective action is needed. Managers might, however, want to take steps to ensure that organization members continue to follow policies and practices. (Although it is possible that the strategic planning process might identify the need to change future ends or means goals in response to changes in the organization's environments, this is part of the planning function, not the controlling function.)

Neither Ends nor Means Goals Are Met This conclusion indicates that an organization is not getting where it wants to go and that it is not following the policies and procedures specified by its strategic and operational plans. Clearly, correction is needed. From a control perspec-

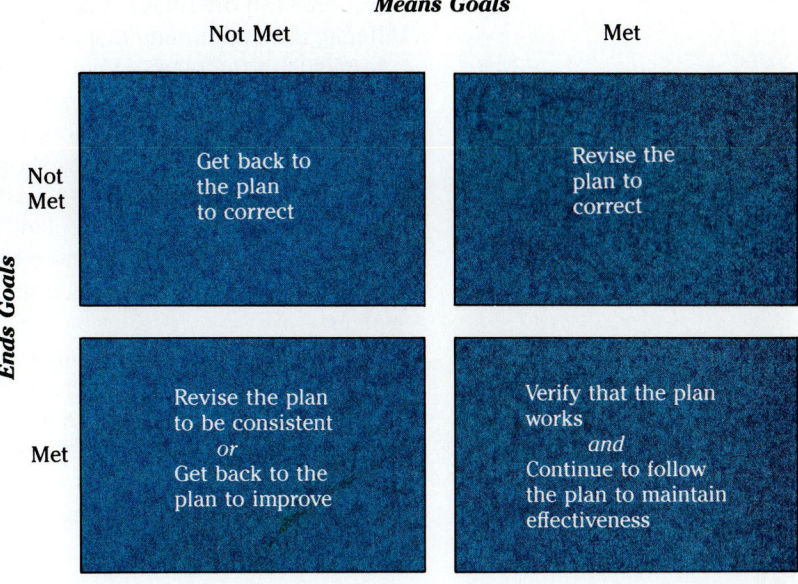

tive, the appropriate response is for managers to get the organization back on track. If means goals are appropriate, and managers can compel organization members to pursue them as specified, ends goals should be met. From a planning perspective, managers who receive a report that neither ends nor means goals have been met should also reassess their goals to verify that they are appropriate.

Means Goals Are Met but Ends Goals Are Not In this situation, the control system has revealed that the organization is following its operational plans, but ends goals are not being met. This would be the case, for example, if Marianne and her manager were to abide by all of the policies and practices but nevertheless fail to meet profit goals. From a control perspective, the appropriate response to this conclusion is primarily to provide feedback to planners that operational plans are not working and may have been inappropriate or incomplete. From a planning perspective, managers must determine why their successfully followed plans have failed to produce the desired ends.

Ends Goals Are Met but Means Goals Are Not In this situation, ends goals are being met, but the policies and practices specified by means goals are not being followed. Sometimes this is referred to as "succeeding in spite of yourself," because an organization achieves its ends goals even though it "does everything wrong." If Marianne's franchise met sales and profits goals despite serving five-ounce hamburgers and wasting 1 percent of the food, other stores in the chain might consider this to be the case. Sometimes, however, this situation indicates that organization members believe the operational plans are bad and choose not to follow them. In other words, they do what they feel they *ought* to do rather than what they are *told* to do.

In this situation, the control system is again very important in providing feedback to planners. From a planning perspective, there are two possible responses to the finding that ends goals are met but means goals are not. If managers determine that members' actual behavior has achieved better results than the planned behavior would have, the formal plans were not appropriate. In this case, strategic and operational planners should modify their plans to incorporate actions that have proved to be successful. Perhaps the Burger Barns should start serving larger hamburgers, for example, or change the food wastage allowance. If, however, managers determine that their original plans were appropriate and that ends criteria would have been met even more had the plans been followed, the control system should be used to get organization members to follow the original plans.

As you can see, the control function operates in tandem with the planning function. Managers use strategic and operational planning systems to define the ends and means goals to be monitored. They use control systems to monitor and enforce these plans, as well as to provide feedback that lets planners know whether the plans have achieved the desired results or if a change is needed.

An Integrated Control Model

As you now know, managers should evaluate effectiveness based on the degree to which both ends and means goals are met. Figure 19.5 contains a comprehensive four-step model of the control process. In this model, managers assess the degree to which their organization has met

FIGURE 19.5   An Integrated Organizational Control Model

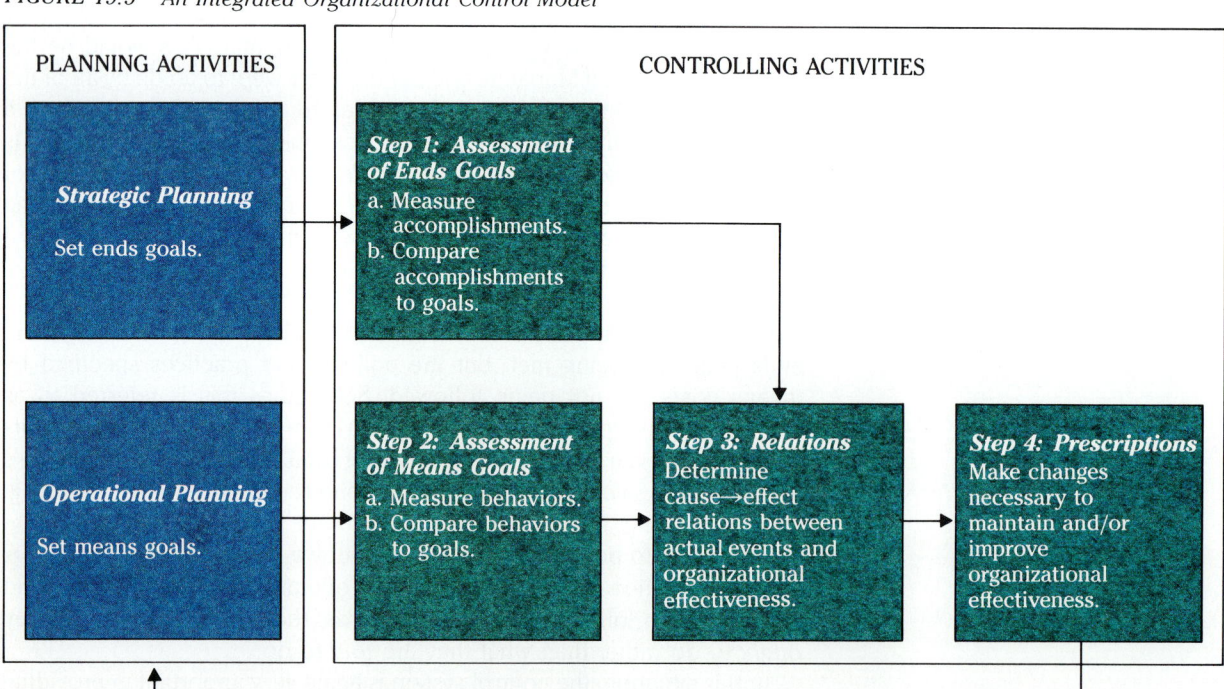

both ends and means goals established during the planning process. They examine the relationship between means behavior and ends results and develop prescriptions for maintaining strengths and correcting weaknesses. Consider these steps through the eyes of Butch Ledworowski, owner of Lil'America Builders.

Step One: Assessment of Ends Goals

At Step One, managers measure actual organizational accomplishments and compare them to planned ends goals. Because Lil'America is an organization in the collectivity stage of its life cycle, Butch has chosen to emphasize a human relations model of effectiveness (see the discussion of life cycle characteristics in Chapter 18). Ends criteria, thus, are focused on the value and development of human resources. In addition, Butch developed a number of specific ends effectiveness criteria, including a profit goal of 15-to-20 percent on each construction project and a completion goal for each project within five days of the scheduled deadline. To assess Lil'America's effectiveness, Butch measured each ends effectiveness criterion and arrived at the results shown below in Table 19.1.

Butch was generally pleased with the degree to which ends goals were met. Human resources showed a high value, half of his employees showed growth, and profits averaged within the 15-to-20 percent range. Butch noted substantial room for improvement, however. Only half of his employees improved their competence and productivity, and 10 percent actually declined in value. Some projects had a profit margin as low as 4 percent, and most projects were not completed within the five-day tolerance.

The purpose of Step One of the control process is to identify what happened, not why it happened or what to do next. This is one of the reasons managers should not gauge organizational effectiveness solely by assessing the degree to which ends goals are met. If an organization is concerned only with ends goals, as would be the case with the goal attainment approach (see Chapter 18), this step would constitute the complete assessment of organizational effectiveness. If Butch stopped at this point, he would never know why many of Lil'America's projects fail to be completed on time or how to improve the situation.

TABLE 19.1 Assessment of Ends Goals at Lil'America Builders

Effectiveness Criteria	Assessment Results*
Value of human resources	70 percent highly valued (strength); 30 percent about average
Development of human resources	50 percent growth (strength); 40 percent stable; 10 percent decline (weakness)
15–20 percent profit	Average of 17 percent (strength)—projects ranged from 4 percent to 23 percent
Completion within five days of schedules	Average of eleven days late (weakness)—ranging from three days early to twenty-three days late

*Simulated

TABLE 19.2 *Assessment of Means Goals at Lil'America Builders*

Effectiveness Criteria	Assessment Results*
Employee morale	Consistently high (strength), except for apprentice carpenters (weakness)
Employee cohesion	Consistently extremely high (strength)
Hire and retain highly skilled carpenters	New hires all highly skilled; no losses of highly skilled employees (strengths)
Assign work to most highly qualified employees	Consistently yes (strength)
Use subcontractors for noncarpentry work	Subcontractors used for 70 percent (strength); 30 percent done by employees (weakness)
Inspect work quality in progress on all jobs at least once a day	Average inspection 1.7 days (weakness)
Schedule all jobs using PERT analysis	Yes for all projects over $7500 (strength)
Monitor all project schedules using PERT analysis	No (weakness)
Create and use a computer program to develop project bids	No (weakness)

*Simulated

Step Two: Assessment of Means Goals

At Step Two, managers measure actual behaviors and compare them to planned means goals. Given the human relations model of effectiveness used by Lil'America, means goals value employee morale and cohesion and specify these as necessary to the achievement of the company's specific ends goals. Table 19.2 shows the means goals established by Butch and the results obtained from his measurements of effectiveness.

Once again, Butch has reason to be pleased. Employee morale and cohesion were high, highly skilled carpenters joined and stayed with the company, subcontractors did most of the noncarpentry work, quality inspections were performed close to target, and PERT analysis (described in Chapter 8) was used to schedule projects with budgets over $7500. Again, however, Butch noted some less effective areas. The company failed to use PERT to monitor project progress, and the computer program for constructing project bids was not developed as planned.

As for Step One, the purpose of Step Two of the control process is to identify what happened. By itself, it does not permit Butch or any other manager to conclude whether adherence to the plan accounted for the successes detailed in Step One, or whether deviations from the plan caused the weaknesses identified. If an organization is concerned only with means goals, as would be the case with the systems approach (see Chapter 18), this step would constitute the complete assessment of organizational effectiveness. If Butch stopped at this point, he would never know if meeting means goals contributed to meeting ends goals.

Step Three: Examination of Ends and Means Goals Relationships

Step Three of the control process explores probable relationships between behaviors (the degree to which means goals are met) and results (the degree to which ends goals are met). At this stage of the control process, managers try to answer the question "What effect did behaviors aimed at means goals have on the attainment of ends goals?" Although it is possible for some organizations (particularly large ones) to examine the relationships between means and ends goals statistically, most such examinations are performed subjectively by one or more key analysts. For Lil'America and other small organizations, the analyst is likely to be the owner. For larger organizations, the analyst might be a CEO or a group of key executives. Sometimes analysts are members of a strategic planning staff. Another popular alternative is to ask someone from outside the company, usually a consultant, to conduct this analysis.

Butch has examined the ends and means goals relationships for the strengths shown in Tables 19.1 and 19.2. He attributes the high morale and cohesion levels among the company's employees to Lil'America's policy of hiring, developing, and retaining highly skilled people. He also credits part of this success to the practice of using subcontractors for much of the work that Lil'America's highly skilled carpenters would find undesirable. Finally, he believes that these strengths arise in part from the informal leadership style within the organization and the respect that he and other managers show for employees' capability and judgment.

In analyzing the relationship between means goals and the weaknesses revealed in Table 19.1, Butch believes that the 30 percent of employees best described as "average," the 40 percent whose skills remained stable during the year, and the 10 percent whose skills actually declined can be explained by the practice of assigning challenging work activities to the best-qualified employees. Although this policy is satisfying to the highly qualified employees, it reduces the opportunity for skill development

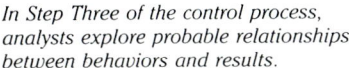

In Step Three of the control process, analysts explore probable relationships between behaviors and results.

among the less highly skilled employees. It also poses a risk should the company continue to grow and need a larger number of highly skilled employees or should some of the most highly skilled employees be lost.

In analyzing the remaining weaknesses, Butch has concluded that failure to achieve some of his means goals did, in fact, contribute to the company's lack of success in meeting some ends goals. For projects in which profitability sank below target, Butch faults the original cost estimates. He further believes that their accuracy would have been better had the company developed and used the computer program to construct bids as planned. The project completion overrun is blamed both on the company's failure to monitor progress using the PERT charts as initially planned, and on the lack of daily quality inspections. Too often employees spent time correcting errors that would have been detected earlier if the inspections had been conducted as often as planned.

In short, Step Three of the control process can yield a great deal of useful information. It provides answers to questions relevant to any organization, namely: "Why have we been successful? What lies behind our failures?"

Step Four: Prescriptions

In Step Four, managers use the cause-and-effect conclusions reached in Step Three to determine what actions their organization can take to maintain effectiveness already achieved and improve effectiveness where needed. Often, these actions can be categorized into three main groups:

1. If means criteria were planned, followed, and helped achieve ends goals, they should be retained to maintain organizational effectiveness.

2. If means criteria were planned but not consistently followed, they should be retained and followed more consistently to improve organizational effectiveness.

3. Some means criteria should be added or changed. Sometimes the determination of cause-and-effect relationships shows that a means activity helped achieve an ends goal even when the activity was not specifically intended to do so. In that case, this new means criteria should be added to the organization's plan. At other times, the relationship analysis shows that planned means criteria failed to produce ends results. In such cases, the criteria should either be changed or eliminated.

The prescriptions Butch created for Lil'America are shown in Table 19.3. The two means goals that were followed consistently and helped achieve ends goals were hiring and retaining highly skilled carpenters and using PERT for project scheduling. These should be continued. Other means goals, such as hiring subcontractors for noncarpentry work, conducting quality inspections, and using a computer program to construct project bids, were followed inconsistently or not at all. Because greater ends effectiveness would result if these goals were more strictly heeded, Butch should encourage greater adherence to them. Butch made two changes to the means criteria. First, less-qualified employees should

TABLE 19.3 *Prescriptions for Effectiveness at Lil'America Builders*

Means Criteria Followed and to Be Continued
- Hire and retain highly skilled carpenters
- Use PERT for project scheduling

Means Criteria Not Consistently Followed That Should Be
- Subcontract all noncarpentry work
- Develop and use computer programs for project bids
- Conduct daily quality inspections on each project
- Use PERT for monitoring project progress

Means Criteria to Be Added or Changed
- Continue using informal leadership style showing respect for employee capability and judgment
- Periodically assign advanced work to less-qualified employees for training purposes

be assigned advanced work periodically so that they can develop and improve their skills. Second, Butch's leadership style is formally specified and included among the planned means criteria.

Variations in Control Systems

Whereas all good control systems should follow an integrated control model such as that just described, not all control systems are identical. Control systems differ in terms of the degree to which they are self-managing (cybernetic) as opposed to externally managed (noncybernetic). They also can be distinguished by the point in the process at which control is exercised: prior to beginning work, during the work process, or after work is completed. This section will examine these variations, as well as the appropriateness of their use in different situations.

Cybernetic and Noncybernetic Systems

Control systems differ in the amount of outside attention required for them to operate effectively (see Figure 19.6). Systems using **cybernetic control** are based on self-regulating procedures that automatically detect and correct deviations from planned activities and effectiveness levels. Control systems that are operated completely independently from the work system itself involve **noncybernetic control.** They rely on external

FIGURE 19.6 *The Cybernetic Continuum*

| Maid Services | Football Refereeing Without Instant Replays | Football Refereeing with Instant Replays | Computerized Tax Preparation System | Generating Station Coal-Flow Control System |

Totally Noncybernetic ← → *Totally Cybernetic*

A CLOSER LOOK

Controlling Employee Behavior: Here's Looking at You, Kid

In the United States, when over 1.5 million employees talk, more than 14,000 employers listen—at the keyhole, that is.[1] The amount of eavesdropping on employees' phone calls is exceeded only by the amount of surreptitious monitoring of employees' computer workstations. It has been estimated that more than one third of the 15 million Americans using workstations are being monitored by the computer itself.[2] At Pacific Southwest Airlines (PSA) and other airlines, for example, computer monitoring programs tell managers how much time each reservation agent spends with a caller, the intervals between calls, and how long the agents are away from the phones for bathroom breaks and the like. The same optical scanners that tell cash registers in grocery stores how much items cost are used to control clerks and inventories by checking how many items are handled per minute. Computers at *The New York Times* keep track of clerks who accept advertising over the phone. In addition to electronic surveillance, there is the traditional company spy, like the ordinary passenger who really is an airline employee on board to observe flight-crew behavior.[3]

These examples are just a few of the ways in which managers are trying to control workers' behavior. Allan Clyde, president of Clyde Digital Systems, brags that his company's software monitoring program "permits total surveillance of all users, all of the time."[4] Some computerized control programs deliver (sometimes subliminal) messages to boost productivity, such as, "You're not working as fast as the person next to you."[5] The companies that use these programs, as well as the firms that develop them, claim that they greatly facilitate the effectiveness of organizational control. R. Douglas MacIntyre, senior vice-president of Management Science America, says that his company's programs ". . . are letting management make better, quicker decisions based on facts, not emotions."[6] Some employees like programs that reward them financially for typing the most keystrokes, booking the most reservations, and so forth. Many employees feel the monitoring helps identify and eliminate poor co-workers. One flight attendant, for example, is not bothered by reports that her behavior is monitored by spies, "because I know I do my job. . . . Maybe if they checked a little more they'd spot the ones who don't."[7]

When over 1.5 million employees talk, more than 14,000 employers listen— at the keyhole.

Other workers and their representatives are less pleased. One national worker advocacy group, 9 to 5, believes that surveillance systems invade workers' privacy, cause stress, and show a lack of trust and concern for employees. Employees complain that the feeling of being watched makes them "a nervous wreck. . . . The stress is incredible. . . . It's a very oppressive way to work."[8] Because it appears these systems are here to stay, however, perhaps the best approach is to come to an agreement on their use. Managers who want both to use monitoring devices and to maintain good working relations with subordinates should consider following these guidelines:

1. Tell employees when their work will be monitored and why
2. Create reasonable work standards that account for different types of tasks and for short-term variations in employee performance
3. Monitor and measure employees' performance only as often as is necessary to make effective calculations
4. Allow employees to have complete access to their own records[9]

1. I. M. Shepard and R. L. Duston (1987), *Workplace privacy*, Washington, DC: Bureau of National Affairs, 59.
2. S. Koepp (28 July 1986), The boss that never blinks, *Time*, 46.
3. A. S. Blask (April 1988), Ghost riders in the sky, *Frequent Flyer*, 80f.
4. Koepp, 47.
5. *Ibid.*
6. Koepp, 46.
7. Blask, 86.
8. Koepp, 47.
9. Shepard and Duston, 66.

monitoring systems, in much the same way that a manufacturing company might use a separate quality control department to monitor and enforce quality standards rather than allowing production crews to perform this activity.

Cybernetic Control Everyone is quite familiar with—and, in fact, personally operates—a number of highly sophisticated cybernetic control systems. One of these determines the body's need for oxygen, assesses whether the supply is adequate, and causes action (breathing) to maintain an adequate supply. Few organizational control systems are totally cybernetic, but some come close. The control system for a coal-fired electrical generating station at Detroit Edison, for example, uses computers to monitor the flow of pulverized coal into the burning chamber. The computers speed up or reduce the flow as necessary to maintain adequate feeding speeds.

Although totally cybernetic systems are difficult to design for many organizational activities, they have a number of distinct advantages. The cybernetic portions of the control system at the generating station are able to identify and document deviations much more rapidly than any human worker could. Furthermore, unlike people, cybernetic systems can provide this analysis consistently and for long periods of time without getting tired and subsequently losing effectiveness. Finally, cybernetic control systems are often much more cost effective. Only a few employees are required to operate the entire electrical generating station, primarily because significant portions of the control process are conducted by computerized cybernetic control systems.

The mere automation or computerization of a *work* system does not necessarily mean that the *control* system is cybernetic. The drone submarine sent to explore and photograph the sunken Titanic was fully automated, but humans on the surface monitored the effectiveness of the sub's operations and its adherence to the planned mission. To be

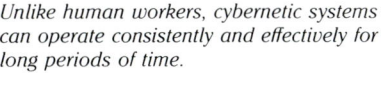
Unlike human workers, cybernetic systems can operate consistently and effectively for long periods of time.

classified as a cybernetic system, a work system must have built-in automatic control capabilities, although the built-in control need not be machine-based. A group of workers who control their own activities without assistance from people outside the group would constitute a cybernetic system.

Noncybernetic Control With so many advantages inherent in cybernetic control systems, why would an organization want to use noncybernetic controls? Sometimes it is not possible to develop a completely cybernetic system. Universities, for example, have not yet developed cybernetic systems for monitoring and correcting teaching effectiveness. Even the cybernetic control system at the Detroit Edison generating plant relies on noncybernetic controls in nonroutine situations. When an alarm alerts the staff at the plant that something has gone wrong, a human worker must find the cause (perhaps by inspecting the coal conveyors, pulverizers, or feeders) and solve the problem. Using human capabilities and intelligence to pinpoint the cause of and solve an automatically detected problem represents the use of noncybernetic control systems.

Sometimes it is possible, but not economically or socially feasible, to use a cybernetic system. Technology currently exists, for example, to enable Burger Barns to use a completely cybernetic system to control food preparation, delivery, and payment. Customers could go up to the counter, gaze at the menu, and press the buttons next to their menu choices. Automated systems could prepare the food, signal the customer to pick it up at a designated delivery station, and require the customer to insert payment into a receptacle before releasing the meal. The cybernetic system could automatically monitor and control the adequacy of the supply of these products and conduct appropriate financial audits of payments received. Possible? Yes. Economically feasible? No. Socially acceptable? Probably not yet. The cost of products would probably have to rise dramatically to support the expense of such a system.

Resistance One of the most common reasons cybernetic systems are not used more today is simply one of personal preference. Managers, for example, want to exercise personal control over their organization rather than delegate this control to self-managing systems. Employees and labor unions often believe that cybernetic approaches reduce both the quantity and quality of jobs available to workers. Sometimes there is simply a reluctance to use a machine for tasks that people associate with human performance. For example, the automated teller machines now commonly used to dispense money were initially greeted by severe customer resistance.

Many enlightened managers are discovering that, if used properly, cybernetic systems in appropriate areas can free them for noncybernetic control in more appropriate areas. A computer system that monitors operator input and detects and "announces" errors can relieve managers from monitoring much of the input process. Managers who spend less time on monitoring activities have more time to concentrate on training and motivating subordinates.

Time Perspectives

Organizations can introduce the control activity at three stages in the work process: prior to, during, or after performance of a work activity.[4] Inasmuch as some work systems are better suited to a particular approach, managers should examine the advantages and disadvantages of each before implementing a control design.

Precontrols Control activities that occur before input enters the system or prior to the beginning of an activity are usually referred to as **precontrols** (or preaction controls). These control systems consist of taking steps before the transformation stage of organizational activity is reached.[5] In other words, precontrols are designed to prevent deviation from a desired plan of action before work actually begins. For example, Phoenix Steel, a manufacturer of iron beams for the construction industry, ensures the quality of its finished product by making certain that only acceptable grades of iron enter the fabrication process. Grade point averages and other screening mechanisms control the types of students who enter the Harvard Graduate School of Business. Cindy Yates, a china buyer for a large department store in San Francisco, experiences precontrol before each purchasing trip. The company allots her a fixed budget that provides the resources she needs to buy Mikasa, Noritake, and other patterns but prevents overexpenditures by placing a ceiling on the amount of money Cindy can spend.

Concurrent Control Managers use **concurrent control** to be certain that deviation from the planned course of action does not occur while work is in progress. Two common forms of concurrent control are steering controls and screening controls. *Steering controls* occur after work has begun but before it is completed. They are intended to keep the work operation on track and to make adjustments if deviation occurs. Managers at Detroit Edison, for example, use a thermostat to monitor the burning chamber and to adjust the heat as necessary to keep temperatures within acceptable limits. At Lil'America, Butch visits each construction site and watches his carpenters, offering advice and instruction as they work.

The primary advantage of steering controls is that they help managers discover deviations quickly and reduce the impact of mistakes. The primary drawback is that steering controls require substantial resources. Clearly, it takes greater resources to have a supervisor monitor the entire work process than it does to have that supervisor work on other tasks and merely confirm that the work was done correctly. Another limitation is that steering controls are reactive rather than preventive in nature. For example, Butch cannot correct his carpenters until he sees them make a mistake. Because a reactive system often cannot make changes quickly, preventive precontrols may sometimes be more effective. When Butch tells carpenters in advance how to do a job, he is using a preventive precontrol system.

Because it is difficult and costly to monitor every organizational activity, managers often try to identify critical "go, no-go" stages of organizational activity and to subject them to *screening controls*. Each

Steering controls are intended to keep work operations on track and to make adjustments if deviations occur.

stage represents a juncture at which the recovery cost for undetected errors is critical. As each of these identifiable steps is completed, managers use screening controls (also referred to as yes/no controls) to assess work performed to that point and to judge whether progress is adequate. If it is, a "go" or "yes" decision is made to proceed to the next stage. At Lil'America, for example, Butch always inspects carpentry work after walls have been framed. Unless he approves the work, electricians cannot begin wiring the structure.

Screening controls are often used to follow up on the use of steering controls. Butch uses steering controls when he watches carpenters do framing work, but he always follows up with screening controls. Screening controls are attractive because they usually require relatively few resources. They also prevent errors from damaging subsequent steps of the work process or becoming very difficult to correct. It takes little of Butch's time, for example, to examine a framed wall; this prevents expensive rewiring and reframing, which would be necessary if mistakes are found later on.

Postaction **Postaction controls** are exercised after the entire set of work activities has been completed to produce a product or service. Managers use postaction controls to examine the output and answer such questions as "Does the engine perform as planned?" "Was the strategic plan followed?" and "Was the desired level of effectiveness achieved?" At the Burger Barn, for example, postaction controls assess the volume of sales per square foot of restaurant space. Although postaction controls play an important role in future planning, their primary function is to provide feedback by describing the degree to which previous activities have succeeded. Butch Ledworowski, for example, uses postcontrols to assess how closely to schedule a project is completed and the percent of profit realized from the project.

A Hybrid Control System Although precontrol, concurrent, and postaction control systems are important, in practice most managers use multiple control systems to govern work activities at many different points in time. At Burger Barn #382, for example, Marianne must be sure that the raw meat, hamburger buns, milkshake mix, and other foods arrive on time and in good condition. Once the food has arrived, her crew has to prepare it properly and serve it promptly. The facility must be cleaned, and customer supplies of napkins, straws, and so forth must be restocked several times each day. Money has to be collected and dispersed and employees and creditors paid. Obviously, a precontrol system alone cannot monitor and control each point, nor can a concurrent control system handle the entire job. Marianne and her manager use multiple control systems to address the interconnected components of the work process at their franchise.

A *hybrid control system* is used by most managers to integrate precontrol, concurrent, and postaction control systems. Precontrols help an organization prepare for tasks that have not yet begun. Concurrent controls provide guidance while work is underway. Postaction controls assess the effectiveness of the entire process, thus preventing flawed work from leaving the organization and/or reducing the likelihood of similar errors being repeated in the future. Some of these controls may be cybernetic. Hybrid systems sound good because they are. There are only two potential drawbacks: they are costly due to their complexity, and they may create dysfunctional reactions if workers feel they are being overly controlled (as when Marianne put too much meat in the hamburgers and gave the staff free meals).

Characteristics of Effective Control Systems

As you have learned, good control systems should monitor organizational effectiveness by assessing the degree to which an organization has met both ends and means goals. Successful control systems have certain common characteristics. First, a good control system systematically incorporates each of the four steps of the control process described in this chapter (review Figure 19.5) and adequately addresses each of the organizational targets discussed earlier (review Figure 19.3). Next, to the extent possible, an effective control system takes a hybrid approach so that precontrol, concurrent, and postaction control systems can be used to monitor and correct activities at all points in an organization's operations. Consider some of the other characteristics of a good control system.[6]

Information Characteristics

Without good information, managers cannot assess whether ends and means goals are met. They cannot determine the relationship between them or provide feedback to strategic planners. The control process itself—and certainly all effective control systems—are thus based on timely, accurate, objective information that can be sent to the appropriate organization members.

Accuracy If the information provided by a control system is not accurate, all subsequent control actions are at risk. Inaccuracies can occur due to imprecise or inappropriate information collection techniques (for example, asking Marianne to estimate food wastage once a week), carelessness in handling information (such as trying to remember food wastage percentages instead of writing them down at the end of each day), intentional distortion (such as lying about the amount of wastage), unintentional distortion (because of personality factors and perceptual biases), or a variety of other factors. Inaccurate information can have disastrous results if it is used as the basis for evaluation and planning. A good control system, thus, must provide information that is both appropriate and grounded in reality.

Objectivity Whenever possible, control systems should use objective information. Whenever subjective information is used, the possibility of distortion is increased. Furthermore, managers are more likely to accept and respond positively to feedback based on objective information than to subjective feedback. At the Burger Barn, for example, Marianne would much rather hear, "The $4500 per day that Barn #382 sells ranks twelfth among all franchises" than "Your store is doing fairly well compared to the rest of the chain." The preference for objective information does not mean, however, that managers should disregard abstract signals. A normally open, loyal employee who suddenly becomes very closed and uninvolved is showing signs of a potential problem that must be recognized and addressed, even though the signs are not highly concrete or quantifiable.

Timeliness   No matter how accurate or objective a manager's information is, it is not very useful unless it can be obtained and used on a timely basis. After all, an announcement that all franchises in the Burger Barn chain should switch soft drink distributors as of May 1 is not very effective if Marianne does not receive her copy until May 7. Advertisements for express shipping and fax machines to the contrary, timeliness does not necessarily mean that *all* information has to be obtained quickly. It does mean, however, that information must be obtained prior to the time it will be needed for evaluation and action.

Distribution   Accurate, objective, and timely information is of little use unless it arrives at its destination. Job assignments, delegation of authority, and the nature of individual and group responsibilities clarify that there are certain individuals who have a "need to know." Upper-level managers must receive actual and projected sales information to devise and modify strategic plans. Human resource directors must have access to current labor market information and government regulation updates. Supervisors responsible for screening control activities need information concerning the quality level reached at each stage of the production process to make go, no-go decisions. Many otherwise good control systems fail simply because they do not put information in the hands of those who need it.

Appropriateness of Focus

Many managers seem to become almost obsessed with the need for control systems: they develop control procedures for virtually all work activities and outcomes. Such an approach is dysfunctional for two reasons. First, it wastes resources. An organization that tries to control every behavior of every employee, for example, might require one supervisor to watch over every nonmanagerial organization member. Would this be economical? Second, as will be discussed later in this chapter, a control system that is too "nitpicky" often creates negative feelings and reactions among employees (see "A Closer Look: Evading Control").

When evaluating whether a control system is right for a particular organization, managers should ask the following questions:

1. "Does the control system deal with important issues?" A good control system focuses on significant ends and means goals and disregards minor issues. Is it really necessary, for example, for all of Lil'America's carpenters to use the same brand of hammers or all Burger Barn employees to wear the same make of shoes?

A CLOSER LOOK

Evading Control: Games People Play

Carlton Arthur works for the bridge inspection office in a Western state. His boss, Peter Johnson, decided last year that all bridges in the state should be inspected at least every other year, and he assigned each inspector a monthly quota of bridges to inspect. To make sure all bridges were inspected as required by the quota, Peter required the inspectors to paint a control number on the side of each bridge after each inspection, log the entry in a control book, and turn in their control books for review at the end of each month.

Carleton and his co-workers soon found that they could not possibly complete the number of assigned inspections in a month. Initially, they simply turned in their logs showing that they were failing to meet their quotas while they continued to make comprehensive bridge inspections. When Peter started to place inspectors on probation for substandard performance, however, some of the inspectors began to "pad" their logs by listing inspections that they had not actually conducted. As part of his control system, though, Peter examined some of the bridges at random. Discovering that the painted control numbers were missing on some bridges that had been logged as inspected,

he terminated an inspector for falsifying records. Now inspectors inspect every other bridge, but they paint the inspection number on every bridge and log each entry.

Carleton and his co-workers are players in the "let's see who can beat the system" game. They and other employees who systematically try to circumvent control systems are sometimes able to fulfill the letter of the law but clearly not its spirit. The increased use of computerized monitoring systems may have eliminated some such players but has promoted increased creativity from others. Some computers have been fooled when people have left machines running while the workers are away from their desks. Students who are required to complete computerized exercises as a course requirement have evaded control by using a word processor to type a facsimile of the verification printout. Typists whose performance is monitored by the number of keystrokes entered on computers have placed staplers on the keyboard to produce keystrokes (and deleted the nonsensical characters afterwards).

Sometimes, employees try to "pull a fast one" because they are lazy.

Usually, however, workers try to circumvent control systems they consider unfair, unreasonable, or offensive. Bypassing the rules without getting caught is one way to strike back at a dehumanizing control system. Unfortunately, many organizations respond to these types of actions by further tightening controls, making them even more offensive and oppressive. The dehumanizing factor aside, it often would make good economic sense for organizations to look at the cause underlying the behavior they are trying to control. At one of the Burger Barns, for example, a manager reprimanded for exceeding the food wastage allowance instructed employees to allow unsold food to remain on the shelf for ten minutes rather than the specified eight minutes before throwing it out. Who knows how many customers never returned because they were unhappy with their cold hamburger but did not want to complain?

In short, managers should consider whether a stringent control system will be accepted by workers. So-called foolproof systems may end up being foolhardy if they fail to acknowledge that the object of control is a thinking individual with feelings.

2. "Is the control system placed at critical junctures in the work process?" For example, do Butch's go/no-go decisions focus on issues that are critical to the overall success of the organization?
3. "Can managers do anything about these issues to improve their organization?" An effective control system focuses on areas where corrective action is within management's control. A disciplinary system, for example, should recognize the difference between voluntary absenteeism (a behavior that managers may be able to change) and absences caused by accidents and illness (events over which managers have little control).

Practicality

In designing a control system, managers must keep a firm grip on reality. Something may have worked well for another organization or look wonderful in print, but unless it is applicable to the organization in question, it will not work well there. Some practical characteristics to look for in a control system include feasibility, flexibility, the likelihood of acceptance by organization members, and the ease with which the system can be integrated with planning activities.

Feasibility   No matter how well designed, control systems must be feasible. Ends and means goals must be reachable and perceived to be realistic by the people responsible for achieving them. The control system must also be economically viable. An elaborate computerized tracking network for the Burger Barn chain may have the potential to accomplish the company's goals precisely, but if its costs outweigh its benefits, what good is it? In practice, most managers design control systems that are less effective than they could be if money were no object, because the managers must make the system cost-effective.

Flexibility   As you have learned, some organizations can get by with a rigid control system because they change relatively little over time. A control system designed for a company such as Minnesota Power usually remains appropriate for quite a while, because the company continues to buy the same supplies (coal) from the same supplier (Peabody Coal Company) to generate the same product (electricity) to sell to the same customers (users throughout northern Minnesota). Most organizations and their environments, however, change substantially and, thus, need flexible control systems that can adapt to additional product lines, modified production procedures, updated sales methods, and altered management techniques. In 1987, for example, Oscar Mayer acquired Kemp Foods. The flexible systems used to regulate the company's hot-dog and lunch-meat product lines were easily adapted to controlling Kemp's imitation seafood products.

Acceptance   As you will discover in the next section, control systems do not work well unless they are accepted by organization members. Managers must agree that the ends and means goals focused on by the control system are appropriate, that the information collected and used by the control system is fitting and proper, and that the specific

TABLE 19.4 *Checklist for Evaluating Control System Characteristics*

	Inadequate	Unknown	Adequate
Follows Stage 1 of control process	————	————	————
Follows Stage 2 of control process	————	————	————
Follows Stage 3 of control process	————	————	————
Follows Stage 4 of control process	————	————	————
Incorporates precontrols	————	————	————
Incorporates steering controls	————	————	————
Incorporates screening controls	————	————	————
Incorporates postcontrols	————	————	————
Information accuracy	————	————	————
Timeliness of information	————	————	————
Objectivity of information	————	————	————
Appropriate distribution of control information	————	————	————
Appropriate focus	————	————	————
Feasibility (economically and organizationally)	————	————	————
Flexibility	————	————	————
Acceptance	————	————	————
Is well integrated with planning	————	————	————

techniques used to exercise control are suitable. Nonmanagers must believe that the control system is functional, desirable, and fair. As described in "Closer Look: Evading Control," without acceptance from its members, an organization runs the risk of having managers and nonmanagers who appear to comply with the rules but actually invent creative ways to circumvent the system whenever possible.

Integration with Planning A good control system facilitates the link between planning and controlling activities. The planning function establishes the ends and means goals that are enforced by the control system. The control system generates the feedback that planners need when they create and revise strategy. Feedback from the control system used at the Burger Barns, for example, revealed that stores that put more meat in hamburgers sold significantly more burgers. In addition, stores that spent more money on landscape design and upkeep had greater drive-through sales. Based on this information, new plans called for larger burgers and better landscaping at all Burger Barns.

Table 19.4 lists many of the characteristics discussed in this section. Managers can use such checklists when they evaluate current or planned control systems.

The Impact of Control on Organization Members

This chapter has stressed the importance of the controlling function to an organization. Control systems enforce an organization's strategic plan, monitor effectiveness, identify the need for change, and guide the planning and implementation of such change. What does the controlling function do for or to the organization's members, however? If designed well, control systems can have many positive effects both for organizations and for the people who work in them.[7] Unfortunately, sometimes a number of dysfunctional effects are also achieved (see Table 19.5).

Positive Effects

In the directing section of this book (Chapters 13–17), you learned about a wide range of factors that influences the motivation and performance of organization members, as well as their satisfaction and such behaviors as absenteeism and turnover. Many of the techniques discussed in those chapters can be enhanced by control systems that provide adequate structure, appropriate feedback, and effective goal-setting programs.

Structure   Both precontrols and concurrent controls provide employees with information that describes what is expected of them by their organization. As you learned in Chapter 16, when workers want clarification of what they are expected to do, a leader can improve both their performance and satisfaction by providing initiating structure. The guidance provided by a structured control system can likewise be received favorably. In her conversation with her friend Lois for example, Marianne remarked that one thing she liked about the rules was how they enabled her to predict the behavior of the other assistant managers at the Burger Barn.

TABLE 19.5   *The Impact of Control on Organization Members*

Potential Positive Effects of Control
- Clarifies expectations
- Reduces ambiguity
- Provides feedback
- Facilitates goal setting
- Enhances satisfaction
- Enhances performance

Potential Dysfunctional Effects of Control
- Consumes resources
- Creates feelings of frustration and helplessness
- Creates "red tape"
- Creates inappropriate goals
- Fosters inappropriate behavior
- Decreases satisfaction
- Increases absenteeism
- Increases turnover
- Creates stress

Feedback provides the guidance employees need to correct ineffective behavior.

Another potential and related benefit employees can receive from the structure of a good control system is that it tends to reduce the uncertainty of a work situation. For many people, excessive ambiguity is both dissatisfying and stressful.[8] For these people, knowing what is expected of them only partially fulfills their needs. They also want to know how to perform what is expected of them, and a control system's structure can provide this information. If reduced ambiguity lessens their stress, workers are likely to be more satisfied with their work experience. As you will recall, Marianne also liked the fact that her subordinates could depend on the rules to tell them how to do their jobs.

Feedback   It has long been known that most employees react quite favorably to the timely provision of accurate feedback about their effectiveness.[9] Feedback provides the guidance employees need to correct ineffective behaviors. Perhaps more importantly, feedback can be very rewarding. People who have a need to succeed are gratified when feedback tells them that they are, in fact, succeeding. Feedback can improve job performance if workers use it to adjust their goals appropriately. Both concurrent and postaction controls provide employees with feedback about the appropriateness of their behavior and the degree to which their work is producing successful results. When Butch watches a carpenter at work and comments on how well he or she is doing or suggests a change, he is providing feedback that can be both satisfying and helpful.

Goal Setting   You have already seen that goal setting can be an important contributor to effective management. A good control system is very useful for identifying appropriate goals. Consider the control system used by the sales company at which Nancy Flannery works. It specifies an expected sales volume (ends goal) that helps her work toward a specific, difficult sales goal (means goal). Precontrols help her understand how to achieve the desired sales level by providing such means goals as specific sales calls to make and promotional specials to offer. Concurrent controls and postcontrols provide feedback that helps Nancy monitor her progress. The combined effects of goal setting and feedback about goal progress are particularly powerful.

Dysfunctional Effects

Unfortunately, control systems can also produce dysfunctional side effects. Excessive controls are quite simply a waste of money and energy. Peter Johnson, for example, needs a larger travel budget because he must personally inspect bridges under a new control system (review "A Closer Look: Evading Control,"). His inspectors spend the time they could have used to inspect bridges in logging entries, painting numbers, and griping about the unfairness of the situation. Not only do excessive controls waste money because they fail to enhance effectiveness, but they can also create additional problems. For example, Carleton and his co-workers have changed from good corporate citizens who kept accurate records and conducted comprehensive inspections into harried workers who falsify log entries. Worse, unsuspecting motorists travel over what might be unsafe bridges.

The vast amount of paperwork and documentation called for by an excessive control system usually also causes the dysfunctional effects of frustration and helplessness. The "red tape" created by many universities' control systems, for example, wastes students' time. Standing in lines for hours—sometimes in different buildings—they wait to pay dorm fees, purchase meal tickets, rent parking spaces, pay tuition, and register for classes. Their frustration and dissatisfaction is mirrored by many organization members who question the competence, the reasonableness, and perhaps even the intelligence of supervisors who insist on maintaining excessive control.

Another dysfunctional result of poor control systems can be seen in their effect on goal-setting programs. Whereas a good control system can help design and monitor valuable goal-setting programs, a poor control system can accomplish quite the opposite. A control system focused on ends and means goals can motivate workers to establish inappropriate individual goals. For example, the ends goal Peter Johnson established of having all bridges inspected within two years was unreachable, and his monthly inspection quotas (means goals) were unobtainable. Peter's insistence on maintaining these inappropriate goals was evident in his reactions when the inspectors failed to meet them. Consequently, Carleton and his co-workers focused on preserving their jobs as a primary goal, rather than on conducting quality inspections.

In addition to encouraging the formation of inappropriate goals, organizational control systems often emphasize and reward behaviors that, although not necessarily inappropriate, may hinder more productive behavior. Managers who concentrate on workers' attendance, for example, may not promote desirable behaviors, such as creativity, cooperation, and team building.[10] Although there is nothing wrong with encouraging attendance, a control system that fosters attendance (by punishing tardiness), because it is easier to measure than creativity, tends to encourage rigid, uncreative behavior (on the part of employees who are almost always at work). An advertising agency that controls attendance but not creativity would soon be in serious trouble.

Even when control systems help identify appropriate goals and encourage appropriate behavior, rigid adherence to narrow goals can also create problems. Large numbers of specific concrete goals, for example, tend to inhibit creativity. The vast amount of time organization members must spend tending to concrete goals leaves them little time or energy to create. According to Apple CEO John Sculley, managing creativity is best done in an open, relaxed, and informal atmosphere.[11] It is particularly important, thus, for organizations that depend on creativity to avoid excessive controls. It is not only creativity that suffers, however. Every minute used taking attendance in a classroom is one less minute available for teaching. Every hour a police officer spends completing paperwork is one less hour available for public service. Use only the goals you need, no more.

The Need for Personal Control

Organizations clearly have a need to control their members and operations, but individuals also have a need for personal control, a need to believe that they have the "ability to effect a change, in a desired direction, on the environment."[12] Sometimes organizations make people feel they have too little control. Colleges and universities, for example, tell students which classes they are allowed to take and when, what grades they have to maintain, how to behave outside the classroom, and so on. Work organizations tell members when to come to work, how many hours to work, what to wear, how to behave, when to take breaks, when to eat lunch, how to perform their jobs, how to improve performance, and many other things. The challenge facing managers is to strike a balance between the amount of control the organization needs to assert and the amount of personal control needed by its members.

Finding the optimum balance between organizational and personal control is not an easy task, however, because most employees desire more

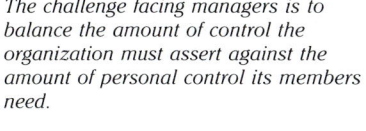

The challenge facing managers is to balance the amount of control the organization must assert against the amount of personal control its members need.

INTERVIEW

David B. Greenberger

David B. Greenberger is on the management and organization faculty at The Ohio State University. Much of Professor Greenberger's research has been focused on the topic of personal control in organizations.

1. What evidence is there to suggest that organization members want to control their work experiences?

Before answering this question, it is important to understand what I mean by *control.* This type of control, personal control, refers to the degree to which members see a link between their actions and outcomes; therefore, control is a perception, and the degree to which they see themselves as having control may or may not be based in reality.

In psychology there is much evidence that people want control. In fact, a number of researchers have suggested that control is a fundamental, intrinsic component of motivation. Just as important, evidence suggests that people suffer a variety of negative consequences when they don't possess control. These consequences include higher levels of stress, depression, lower productivity, and lower levels of job satisfaction.

2. How do organization members react when they feel they are controlled by their organization more than they would prefer?

Since it is clear that most people want control at work, this poses an interesting problem for organizations. If employees do not believe that they are capable of obtaining all the control they desire, they may still try to obtain it. If their organization gives them the opportunity to obtain control in ways consistent with organizational goals, then this desire for control can benefit the organization. If it does not provide employees with opportunities to increase control — or makes them feel as if they have lost control — then the organization may find that employees perform less effectively, take more

days off, and may even engage in industrial sabotage.

3. How can managers balance an organization's need to control members with members' need to control themselves?

This common approach suggests that control is a zero sum phenomenon, but the issue of control is probably much larger than most managers envision. Management can and probably should keep control over its members, but management must also allow them to feel a sense of accomplishment and success at work. This can be achieved by allowing members to participate in decision making, but it also can be achieved by removing obstacles to successful task completion.

4. What are the implications of control for the day-to-day running of organizations?

Management must be less concerned with losing control than with providing opportunities for individuals to derive their own control. A good example may lie with increasing opportunities for creativity and intrapreneurship. More organizations are starting to recognize the advantages of these kinds of programs.

personal control than their organization allows them. People will strive to gain greater control "in spite of (and frequently because of) the barriers and constraints the organization places on the attainment of personal control."[13] This is an important point for managers to consider, because such attempts can result in either functional or dysfunctional reactions. Positive effects include those discussed earlier, such as the more effective use of goal setting and feedback. Dysfunctional reactions can include decreases in satisfaction, increases in absenteeism and turnover, increases in stress, and possibly even sabotage.

Repeated failures to gain personal control do not necessarily discourage workers from continuing to want it. They may, however, develop what has been called *learned helplessness*.[14] People who learn that they are helpless to influence their work environment are likely to be the source of low productivity, low quality, high absenteeism, dissatisfaction, and possibly turnover. They tend to react with depression, anxiety, stress, frustration, hostility, anger, and alienation. Furthermore, once helplessness has been learned, people often continue to behave helplessly, even if the environment changes to permit them greater control; thus, managers must prevent subordinates from developing learned helplessness because it will be very difficult to reverse. They should do so by allowing workers to control the aspects of their work lives that they can adequately control and by using only the amount of organizational control actually needed. Butch instructs his highly skilled carpenters to frame a wall, for example, but he does not attempt to control how this is done (his best carpenters know how to do it).

In Search of Balance

It might seem that managers should just accede to workers' persistent demands for greater personal control. After all, possession of personal control can be intrinsically motivating, encouraging people to work hard because they enjoy exercising their control as they work. It has been noted, however, that intrinsic motivation is most likely to be high for people whose exercise of personal control actually translates into high performance.[15] Research has shown that indiscriminantly providing employees with large amounts of personal control increases performance only to a certain point. When the control possessed exceeds an individual's capacity to use it, performance can actually suffer.[16] In other words, if Marianne Rowe's boss gives her a lot of control and she exercises it but still fails, Marianne probably will not be highly motivated because use of her control leads to failure, not to success.

If an organizational control system that is too excessive does not work, and if giving workers all of the personal control they desire is not effective, what should managers do to achieve the proper balance? First, because people need to possess personal control, managers should give them an appropriate amount. Next, managers should take steps to make certain that workers given control believe they can use it effectively. Managers should also help them translate their effort into successful performance. (The techniques and managerial skills discussed in the directing section of this book—Chapter 13–17—can help managers in these endeavors.) Last, managers must recognize that organizational control systems influence the personal control perceptions of organization members. These, in turn, change workers' behavior and attitudes.

By interviewing and/or surveying employees, managers can learn more about organization members' needs for control. Through organizational scans (see Chapter 9), managers can determine the amount and location of control already existing within the organization, as well as areas needing control. The objective then becomes one of achieving the best possible match between organization members and their work environment.

Control Methods and Their Effects in Review

The primary purposes of the controlling function are to monitor the extent to which an organization's plans are being followed and their effectiveness, as well as to identify when and where it is necessary to take corrective action. These are ambitious tasks. To accomplish them, organizations construct control systems that touch nearly every aspect of an organization's functional areas, its relationships with the external and internal environments, and its relationships across different hierarchical levels.

The control process consists of four steps. In Steps One and Two, managers determine the extent to which ends and means goals have been met. In Step Three, managers examine the relationships between means and ends. Step Four of the control process is where managers develop prescriptions based on the relationships unveiled in Step Three. These prescriptions are designed to correct problems, to maintain strengths, and to provide feedback to an organization's planners as they plot the strategic changes necessary to maintain or improve organizational effectiveness.

Whereas all control systems have the same general purposes, they differ in other ways. Some control systems, known as cybernetic systems, are self-managing. Noncybernetic systems require regular external supervision to be effective. Other variations in control systems include the point at which control activities are applied. Precontrols occur before work has begun and are designed to prevent deviations from the strategic plan. Steering controls occur while work is in progress and are designed to help provide direction for those doing the work. Screening controls, which also occur while work is in progress, guarantee that each step in the process is successfully completed before the next step is begun. Postaction controls occur after work is completed and provide feedback about how well the work was or was not accomplished, thus identifying changes to be considered should similar work be necessary in the future. A hybrid control system engages a variety of control activities at many points in time.

Although there are variations in control systems, all good systems have characteristics that enable them to work well in a given organization. Managers evaluating the adequacy of a control system, thus, might wish to gauge its adequacy in providing accurate, timely, objective information to appropriate people in the organization. They also should examine whether the system focuses on the most critical aspects of their organization's condition in a feasible, flexible manner that will be accepted by organization members. Because of the importance of the information it provides, a good control system should also be integrated with planning activities.

Any control system can produce both positive and dysfunctional effects on organization members. If it is well designed, a control system helps provide needed structure and feedback and can facilitate the development and execution of effective goal-setting programs. The result of this can be a satisfied, motivated, productive workforce. Inappropriate control systems, however, can produce dysfunctional effects, including frustration, dissatisfaction, and poor performance. Being aware of a control system's potential effects on organization members can help managers capitalize on its positive aspects, reduce the impact of dysfunctional effects, and promote workers' acceptance of the system.

Notes

1. D. H. Holt (1987), *Management: Principles and practices*, Englewood Cliffs, NJ: Prentice-Hall, 546–81.

2. W. H. Cunningham, I. C. M. Cunningham, and C. M. Swift (1987), *Marketing: A managerial approach*, Cincinnati, OH: South-Western, 785–89.

3. H. C. Carlson (1979), Personnel control systems, in D. Yoder and H. G. Heneman, Jr., eds., *ASPA handbook of personnel and industrial relations*, Washington, DC: The Bureau of National Affairs, Inc., 31–56.

4. W. H. Newman (1975), *Constructive control*, Englewood Cliffs, NJ: Prentice-Hall, 6.

5. H. Koontz and R. W. Bradspies (June 1972), Managing through feedforward control, *Business Horizons*, 25–36.

6. Newman, 1975; W. H. Newman (1984), Managerial control, in J. E. Rosenzweig and F. E. Kast, eds., *Modules in management series*, Chicago: Science Research Associates, 1–42; W. H. Newman, J. R. Logan, and W. H. Hegarty (1985), *Strategy, policy, and central management*, 9th ed., Cincinnati, OH: South-Western; W. H. Sihler (1971), Toward better management control systems, *California Management Review*, 14, 33–39; E. P. Strong and R. D. Smith (1968), *Management control models*, New York: Holt, Rinehart.

7. M. S. Taylor, C. D. Fisher, and D. R. Ilgen (1984), Individuals' reactions to performance feedback in organizations: A control theory perspective, in K. M. Rowland and G. R. Ferris, eds., *Research in personnel and human resources management*, Greenwich, CT: JAI Press, 81–124.

8. R. L. Kahn, D. M. Wolfe, R. R. Quinn, J. D. Snoek, and R. A. Rosenthal (1964), *Organizational stress: Studies in role conflict and ambiguity*, New York: Wiley.

9. E. A. Locke and G. P. Latham (1984), *Goal setting: A motivational technique that works*, Englewood Cliffs, NJ: Prentice-Hall.

10. Interview with Steven Kerr appearing in R. B. Dunham (1984), *Organizational behavior: People and processes in management*, Homewood, IL: Irwin, 147; S. Kerr (1975), On the following of rewarding A, while hoping for B, *Academy of Management Journal*, 18, 769–83.

11. J. Sculley with J. A. Byrne (1987), *Odyssey: Pepsi to Apple*, New York: Harper & Row.

12. D. B. Greenberger and S. Strasser (1986), Development and application of a model of personal control in organizations, *Academy of Management Review*, 11, 164.

13. Greenberger and Strasser, 1986, 174.

14. J. B. Overmier and M. E. P. Seligman (1967), Effects of inescapable shock upon subsequent escape and avoidance learning, *Journal of Comparative and Physiological Psychology*, 63, 28–33; M. J. Martinko and W. L.

Gardner (1982), Learned helplessness: An alternate explanation for performance deficits, *Academy of Management Journal,* 7, 195–204.

15. C. D. Fischer (1978), The effects of personal control, competence, and extrinsic reward systems on intrinsic motivation, *Organizational Behavior & Human Performance,* 21, 273–88.

16. M. H. Bazerman (1982), Impact of personal control on performance: Is added control always beneficial? *Journal of Applied Psychology,* 67, 472–79.

Key Terms

controlling
assessment of ends goals
assessment of means goals
examining ends and means goals
  relationships
control prescriptions

zero-base budgeting
cybernetic control
noncybernetic control
precontrols
concurrent control
postaction controls

Suggested Readings

Bazerman, M. H. (1982). Impact of personal control on performance: Is added control always beneficial? *Journal of Applied Psychology,* 67, 472–79.

Greenberger, D. B. and Strasser, S. (1986). Development and application of a model of personal control in organizations. *Academy of Management Review,* 11, 164.

Greenberger, D. B., Strasser, S., and Dunham, R. B. (in press). Personal control, performance, and job satisfaction. *Organizational Behavior and Human Decision Processes.*

Martinko, M. J. and Gardner, W. L. (1982). Learned helplessness: An alternate explanation for performance deficits. *Academy of Management Journal,* 7, 195–204.

Merchant, K. A. (1982). The control function of management. *Sloan Management Review,* 23(4), 43–55.

Newman, W. H. (1984). Managerial control. In Rosenzweig, J. E. and Kast, F. E., eds. Modules in management series. Chicago: Science Research Associates, 1–42.

Taylor, M. S., Fisher, C. D., and Ilgen, D. R. (1984). Individuals' reactions to performance feedback in organizations: A control theory perspective. In Rowland, K. M. and Ferris, G. R., eds. *Research in personnel and human resources management.* Greenwich, CT: JAI Press, 81–124.

Issues for Review and Discussion

1. Define *controlling* and explain the relationship between it and each of the managerial functions of planning, organizing, and directing.
2. Identify the different levels and targets of the control activity.

3. Identify and discuss each step of the control process.
4. Distinguish between cybernetic and noncybernetic control systems and list the advantages and drawbacks of each.
5. Identify, compare, and contrast the different time perspectives found in control systems.
6. Name the common characteristics of all effective control systems.
7. Identify and discuss three positive and three dysfunctional effects often associated with control systems.
8. How does the desire for personal control affect managers, and how can they balance it with organizational control systems?

CASE *The Two Edges of Control*

Adapted from R. S. Schuler and
D. R. Dalton (1985), Case prob-
lems in management, *3rd ed., St.
Paul, MN: West, 184–86.*

"Tom, do you have a minute?" asked David Morrison.

"Sure, come in," responded Tom Davidson, plant manager of Mayberry Manufacturing. "What do you have on your mind?"

"I'll tell you, Tom. At times it is just frustrating as can be around here. Sometimes you can't get a straight answer from anyone. There are times when absolutely no one can seem to help you," answered David with some irritation.

"What specifically is bothering you, Dave?"

One Story

"It's just one thing after another. For instance, two days ago one of my employees asked me for a six-week leave of absence for surgery and a recuperation period. Frankly, I was not familiar with the leave policy around here. I must have asked a half a dozen people, including the shift supervisors, what the policy is. They told me there is no specific policy and that I will have to use my best judgment on the matter. I am to examine the circumstances of the request and decide accordingly. I thought I had better check with you before I acted in one way or another on the request for the six-week leave," explained David.

"Ordinarily, I wouldn't bother you with something like this. I just can't seem to find a policy anywhere."

"Well, I appreciate the fact that you checked with me. The advice you've received, however, is essentially correct. We don't have a specific policy for leaves of absence. In the past, they have been handled on a case-to-case basis. I will say this, though. I don't think that this request has come at a very opportune time. As you know, we have a large order due for delivery and we'll need every employee we can get. In fact, I'll be very surprised if we get through this without paying a lot of overtime. Obviously, I hate to see us give any employees that much time off when we'll have to replace them with employees on overtime at time-and-a-half pay," said Tom.

"You haven't heard the half of it," continued David. "Yesterday, another employee requested a six-week leave of absence as well. It seems that this employee's daughter works for a major airline and can get tickets to Europe for very reasonable rates. I don't know exactly what is happening there, but apparently the airline is in the middle of some kind of promotion for their overseas flights and employees are entitled to an extraordinary discount. To hear my employee tell it, this is the dream of a lifetime—the opportunity to visit Europe for very little money. There's no telling when, if ever, the employee will have this opportunity again."

"Given our circumstances," said Tom, "I can hardly see how that leave of absence could be justified."

"Well, I really have a problem," replied David. "Both of these are excellent employees. At first, I thought that I could justify the leave of absence on medical grounds for the surgery but would have trouble with the vacation; however, I looked into the matter more carefully and it turns out that the surgery is elective—this is not a life-threatening situation. The surgery could be put off for a time. Interestingly, the vacation really can't be put off. Well, of course, it *can* be put off, but only at great expense. We can be sure of one thing. The vacation is at least as important to the one employee as the surgery is to the other. I really wish we had a policy on this. It would make things a lot easier for me." David finished with some irritation.

"I see your point, Dave, but let me share a problem I recently had that involves policy."

Another Story

"We were talking about overtime a few minutes ago. Our corporate headquarters recently sent a memorandum to all department heads concerning the use of overtime. The memo essentially stated that, in the future, no overtime could be authorized without the personal permission of the plant manager. In this case, of course, such permission would have to come from me. Let me remind you that I did not send the memo to the department managers. That memo was sent by corporate headquarters. I was, as you would expect, notified of the memo," Tom explained.

He continued, "Now, in the past, any department manager could authorize overtime for his or her department if the need should arise. Evidently the corporate offices are concerned about the amount of overtime that has been authorized and are seeking to control it by having all overtime okayed by me before its use. The company is trying to reduce costs, and the reduction of overtime is a high-priority item.

"This worked fairly well for awhile. Of course, the department heads did not especially like the new policy. The policy did, however, reduce overtime somewhat. The department heads were a little more careful. For the most part, I approved any overtime that was requested. I think that the department heads just thought it over a bit more carefully before they called me.

"This all came to an unfortunate conclusion last Friday. As it happened, I was out of town that day. At the same time, two unforeseen circumstances caused a problem in the shipping department. First, there was an unusually high incidence of employee absenteeism, so shipping was very shorthanded. Second, there was a delay in sending the finished goods from production to the shipping department. In other words, they were short of people, and the goods they were to send out were coming in late. It became absolutely obvious to Ms. Bates, head of the shipping department, that there was no way that all

of the orders were going to be dispatched by Friday's deadline. The following Monday was a holiday. So, if these orders didn't go out on Friday, they would not be processed until Tuesday. The sum of this is that the orders would go out four days late."

"What happened?" asked David.

"Nothing, and that's the problem," replied Tom with some exasperation. "Ms. Bates tried to reach me, but I was, of course, out of town. She knew that in the past, orders that were not processed by the deadline have been returned by customers and subsequent orders canceled. The memo clearly stated that my personal permission was required to authorize overtime. She badly needed that overtime so the orders could be processed Friday and not wait until Tuesday. If she had authorized the overtime, she would have exceeded her authority. If she didn't, we ran the risk of product returns and cancellation of future orders."

"What did she do?" asked David.

"Oh, she took the safe course. She did not use the overtime," answered the plant manager disgustedly. "It would seem, Dave, based on your recent experiences and mine, that policy is a two-edged sword."

Questions

1. What type of control is exemplified by the corporate policy on approval of overtime? Is this the kind of control being sought by David Morrison?

2. Since a policy on granting leaves of absence would restrict David's freedom to act, why does he seek such a policy?

3. Why does Tom Davidson refer to policy as a "two-edged sword?"

4. What should David do about the leave requests? What should he do to prevent a reccurrence of the overtime authorization problem? to prevent reoccurrence of the problem with leave requests?

Organizational Change and Development

Student Learning Objectives

After reading this chapter, you should be able to:

1. Identify the five primary reasons change does and should occur in organizations.

2. Understand the difference between proactive and reactive change.

3. Describe the major types of change that occur in organizations.

4. Describe the range of reactions people have to organizational change and the reasons underlying their reactions.

5. Identify and describe the relative strengths and weaknesses of the seven major techniques for developing support for organizational change.

6. Understand the special role of organizational development (OD) and how it can enhance organizational effectiveness and benefit organization members.

7. Describe the major stages of a systematic approach for planning and managing organizational change.

It is not enough for a manager to have a good idea. He or she must also possess the skills to make that idea work well.

This book has offered techniques that help managers effectively execute organizational planning, organizing, directing, and controlling. When creating a new organization, managers can choose from these techniques to develop an appropriate model for managing the organization. Few of you, however, will have the opportunity to create a new organization from scratch. Instead, most of you will use the knowledge you have obtained during this course to change an existing organization from what it is to what you want it to be.

Organizational change can occur for several reasons. Sometimes a manager decides a change would be advantageous, as when installing a new machine promises greater efficiency. Under other circumstances, managers are forced to make a change, as when a legal entity issues new regulations governing the way an organization does business. Regardless of the cause, there are complex issues common to all change. As a manager, you will discover that it is not enough to have a good idea—you must have the skills to make that idea work well. This chapter is designed to give you those skills by exploring some of the causes of organizational change, the types of changes managers are likely to face, and the potential reactions of organization members to change. This chapter will also explore the ways managers can develop support for organizational change; some organizational development techniques for developing structured, systematic changes; and a step-by-step model for planning and managing the change process. As you will see, managing change is not easy, but it is necessary if an organization is to succeed.

This chapter on change and organizational development is included in the section on controlling because change is generally the final step of the controlling process. In the earlier steps, managers observe actual organizational behavior (ends and/or means) and compare observed behavior with expectations (standards). Through this comparison process, managers can determine how effective their organization has been and whether change is needed to maintain or enhance effectiveness.

Why Change Occurs: Forces to Change

Organizational change does not occur spontaneously. It takes place when the forces encouraging change become more powerful than those resisting change. Most organizations face an incredible number of factors that "invite" them to change. These *forces to change* can be either **internal forces** (emanating from within an organization) or **external forces** (coming from outside an organization). A new strategic plan specifying product diversification, for example, can be a potent internal force driving change. So, too, can a decision to implement quality circles to improve organizational effectiveness. A new technological development from outside an organization can provide a powerful external force to change, such as the way in which the creation of compact audio disks (CDs) revolutionized the recorded music industry. The emergence of the Occupational Safety and Health Administration in response to public pressure was a potent external social force that changed the safety practices of thousands of U.S. organizations.

FIGURE 20.1 *Major Forces to Change*

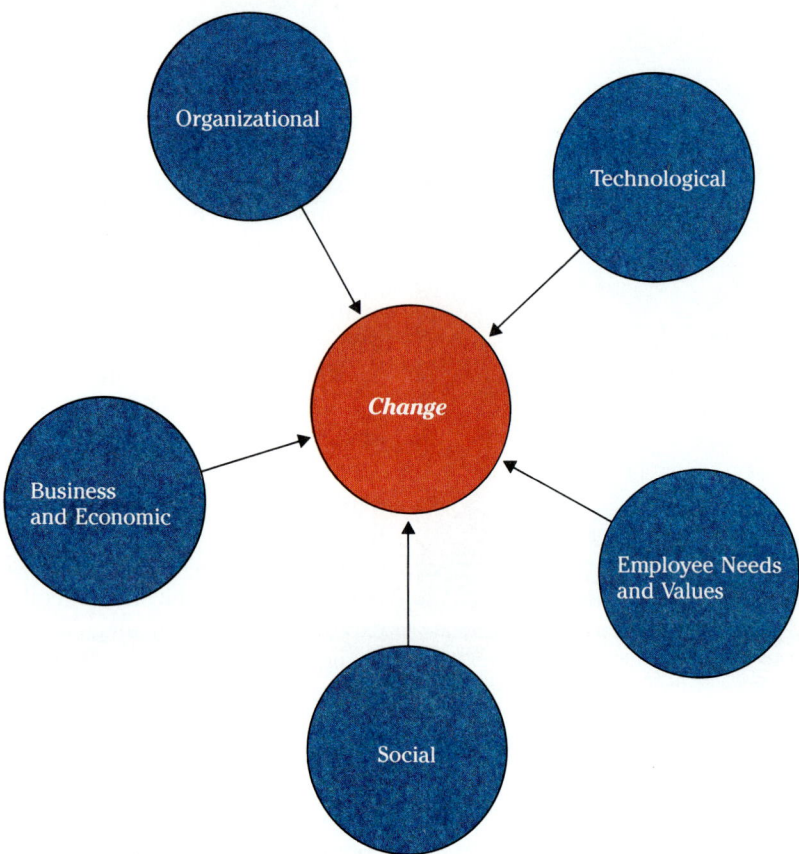

It is often more useful to categorize forces to change based on their nature (see Figure 20.1). Consider some of the most common forces to change.

Technological Forces

All organizations use a variety of technologies to produce their goods and services. Most of these technologies are subject to modification. Significant alterations and advancements in existing technologies may compel organizations to change. The development of "metal" tape to improve the sound quality of cassettes, for example, was a technological change that required the recording industry to retrain employees so that the accuracy of recordings would rise to the level permitted by metal tapes. Technological change can arise from both internal sources (as when organizations develop their own new technologies) and external sources (as when organizations acquire technologies from sources outside the organization).

Employee Needs and Values

An effective organization cannot exist without considering the needs and values of its members. Organizations attract members by offering them things they value, including pay, benefits, and interesting work. Organizations retain these workers and motivate them to perform effectively by promising and providing additional valued outcomes. Indeed, this is the thrust of the directing section of this book (Chapters 13–17). What happens, though, if organization members change their minds about what is of value to them?

Many organizations have discovered in recent years that workers are leaning less toward traditional financial rewards and more toward quality-of-life alternatives. It is not uncommon, for example, for organization members to desire greater flexibility in scheduling their work and to want such benefits as onsite child-care facilities. Changes in employees' needs and values can be an extremely strong force driving organizational change.

Social Forces

It is not only people inside an organization who exert pressure to change. The general public also can bring about change, sometimes simply by altering customer interest for products. Society's increased appreciation of health and physical fitness, for example, has caused many food companies to market products containing less salt, fewer calories, and lower cholesterol. At other times, social pressures go beyond indicating what is merely desirable and define what is acceptable. Society, for example, demands that American businesses stop discrimination against employees on the basis of gender, age, race, and sexual preference. Societal pressures are increasingly causing organizations to provide meaningful work experiences and to allow worker participation in management decision making.

Business and Economic Forces

On a regular basis, business and economic factors, such as inflation rates, gross national product, money supplies, interest rates, and industry competition, exert a tremendous pressure for organizational change. Extremely high interest rates plagued the United States in the early 1980s, for example, causing organizations to restrict expansion, reduce borrowing to finance new ventures, and minimize unsold inventories. This, along with the accompanying recession, led to reduced workforces; increased ratios of number of employees per manager; and, in many cases, the removal of complete levels of management in organizations. Demands for productivity and quality also increased. Indeed, many American methods of doing business changed substantially during this period. American car makers launched joint ventures with Japanese auto manufacturers, for example. Mergers and acquisitions flourished, producing larger corporations.

The entire economy does not have to shift, however, for business and economic factors to drive change in an organization. The year 1987 was a tough one for *The Wall Street Journal* and the Dow Jones business publications group, of which it is a member. Ad linage was down for the entire year—in some months it was as much as 15 percent lower than for the year before—necessitating some important changes in the organization. After Dow Jones conducted a major budget review, eight top editors were given new responsibilities in 1988, and other measures were taken to save money and improve the effectiveness of the newspaper.

Society demands that American businesses stop discrimination against employees on the basis of such factors as gender and age.

Organizational Forces

Often the organization itself is the primary force behind a change. During the planning process, for example, key decision makers may decide to branch into new product areas, implement a Management-by-Objectives program, or install a new communications system. Sometimes these changes are prompted by an organization's belief that there may be a more appropriate or effective way to accomplish its objectives. Sometimes an organization's control system reveals that strategic plans are not being followed and that changes must take place to correct the situation. Some of the unique characteristics of organizationally driven change are discussed in the organization-development section later in this chapter.

Review

The five forces just described seldom operate individually. Instead, the total force driving change is typically a combination of two or more of these individual forces. For example, have organizations introduced robotics solely because technological advances have made it possible to do so? Not likely. Rather, economic constraints, employees' desire for more challenging work, and the demands of society for better-quality products have combined with the availability of new technologies to encourage the development and implementation of robotics.

Types of Change

Regardless of their content, all changes occur either in reaction to a driving force(s) or on a proactive, planned basis initiated by an organization. Either type of change can involve technological, structural/procedural (administrative), and human components.[1] Changes can also be distinguished based on the degree to which they are innovative or simply different from what was previously done in the organization. This section will take a brief look at the various types of change organizations often encounter.

Reactive vs. Proactive Change

Reactive change occurs when the forces driving change provide so much pressure that an organization *must* change. The failure of existing equipment or systems, for example, is a powerful impetus for change. Consider two issues that faced United Airlines in 1986. One was increased competition from Continental Airlines. Probably a more influential issue was the discovery that much of the equipment acquired from Pan Am to start up United's Trans-Pacific service was unreliable. Flights were frequently canceled, and customers were angry. The result was a reported $13.1 million loss for the airline in the fourth quarter of 1986.[2] United took a reactive stance, spending an unplanned $70 million on repairs, new interiors, and new engines. Some workers suffered pay freezes; others were laid off. Expenditures were slashed almost across the board. Even when it eventually leads to favorable results—as United Airlines obviously hoped it would—unplanned, reactive change is seldom welcomed by organizations because it usually results in poorly coordinated, inefficient management that plays havoc with virtually any strategic plan.

Proactive change occurs when an organization's managers conclude that a change would be desirable (as opposed to necessary). Generally, proactive change is more orderly and more efficient because it is planned (although, as noted in previous chapters, not all planning is done well). The section on organizational development later in this chapter deals primarily with proactive, planned change.

Change and Innovation

"All innovation is change, but not all change is innovation."[3] Despite the fact that the majority of writers about change and innovation tend to equate these two concepts, it is important to differentiate them. Change involves any modification of an organization's established ways of operating. An organization that replaces its word processors and laser printers with manual typewriters is initiating a change, but hardly an innovative one. **Innovation** occurs when an organization is the first or an early user of an idea among its set of similar organizations.[4] The first airline to provide scheduled service in orbital altitudes will be innovative; the first hospital to use the newly discovered treatment for AIDS will be innovative; and the first organization to use a "heads-up" system (one that projects operational and control system display information so workers can keep their heads up while working) to operate an assembly line will be innovative.

Because innovation provides more excitement, more challenge, and more uncertainty than most change, managing innovation requires special care. The importance of nurturing support for innovative change and managing the change process systematically is heightened when change involves not only the introduction of something different into the organization but also something new.

Technological Changes

Some of the most visible and dramatic changes made in organizations during the last decade introduced new technologies. Organizations increasingly use robotics in manufacturing processes. Computers are leading to paperless offices. Even the nature of teaching is changing through technological advances. The days in which students could be confident of arriving in the classroom to see and hear their professor speak to them "live" may be numbered. Some universities now present lectures to students in a videotaped format, giving students a choice of whether to watch it in the classroom or at home on cable television.

For better or for worse, technological change is occurring today at an unprecedented rate (see Figure 20.2). The most common technological changes involve new equipment, new work procedures, new methods of processing information, and other automation.

A CLOSER LOOK

Technological Change: Kellogg's Profits Snap, Crackle, and Pop

Tony the Tiger may not strike you as the high-tech type, but innovation got Tony where he is today. Frosted Flakes' developer, the Kellogg Company, was founded on an experimental idea, and Americans have been chomping on the results for almost 100 years.

In the 1890s, W. T. Kellogg was the manager of a sanitarium in Battle Creek, Michigan. Kellogg, a vegetarian, was committed to providing healthy diets for his patients and eventually came up with a hardy but unpalatable whole-wheat meal. Although able to convince many members of his captive audience to eat the unappetizing concoction, there was little danger of taking the world by storm. Kellogg, therefore, set out to find a way to retain the nutritional value of the meal but make it more appealing. It turned out that using a set of rollers to flatten day-old wheat dough produced dry, attractive little flakes as opposed to the original mushy concoction.

The result has shaped the cereal market for nearly a century, but Kellogg has not kept ruling the breakfast table by sticking to one tried-and-true product. Continued development of new methods for manufacturing and handling no-sugar, no-preservative cereals made it possible to market

"health foods" to the masses. The Nutri-Grain line of whole-grain cereals, for example, created a new market niche. Super-secret, advanced techniques resulted in Crispix, a product that competitors spent years trying to duplicate. With it, Kellogg introduced the first cereal product in history that combines two separate grains. Similar technological breakthroughs produced Raisin Squares—a crispy cereal with a chewy fruit center—another good seller with only very recent competitive look-alikes.

Kellogg is not afraid to change its production methods for existing product lines. It was among the first to use statistical sampling to check the quality of products. It involves production workers in the generation of ideas for improving quality and decreasing costs. It has been willing to introduce new equipment, but only after its effectiveness has been carefully evaluated. So committed is Kellogg to this idea, in fact, that it has a plant in Canada that tests experimental equipment and production methods before replacing existing equipment.

The results seem well worth the planning and execution complexities that accompany change. In 1987, Kellogg rated second in market value among the 31 food processing companies ranked by *Business Week* and 62nd among all U.S. companies.[1] Sales increased 14 percent over the previous year, and profits soared 24 percent. Margin (profits as a percent of sales) were 10.4 percent compared to the top-1000-company composite of 4.9 percent. Return on invested capital was 28.7 percent compared to the 1000-company composite of 12 percent. Tony the Tiger is not the type to let success go to his head, though. According to Kellogg Chairman William E. LaMothe, " . . . [W]e look at

ourselves as a small company dealing with giants. . . . We spend a lot of time talking about small things that top management in more diversified companies probably don't get involved with."[2]

To avoid missing an opportunity, the company reevaluates its strategic plan every year, even when it appears to be succeeding. New products and innovative manufacturing and marketing methods just keep coming. About the only thing that has not changed at Kellogg is Tony's famous slogan, and it could just as easily be applied to the company's operations as to the taste of its cereals: They're G-R-R-REAT!

1. The Business Week top 1000 (15 April 1988), *Business Week*, 171ff.
2. R. Mitchell (30 March 1987), The health craze has Kellogg feeling G-R-R-REAT, *Business Week*, 53.

FIGURE 20.2 *Rate of Technological Change*

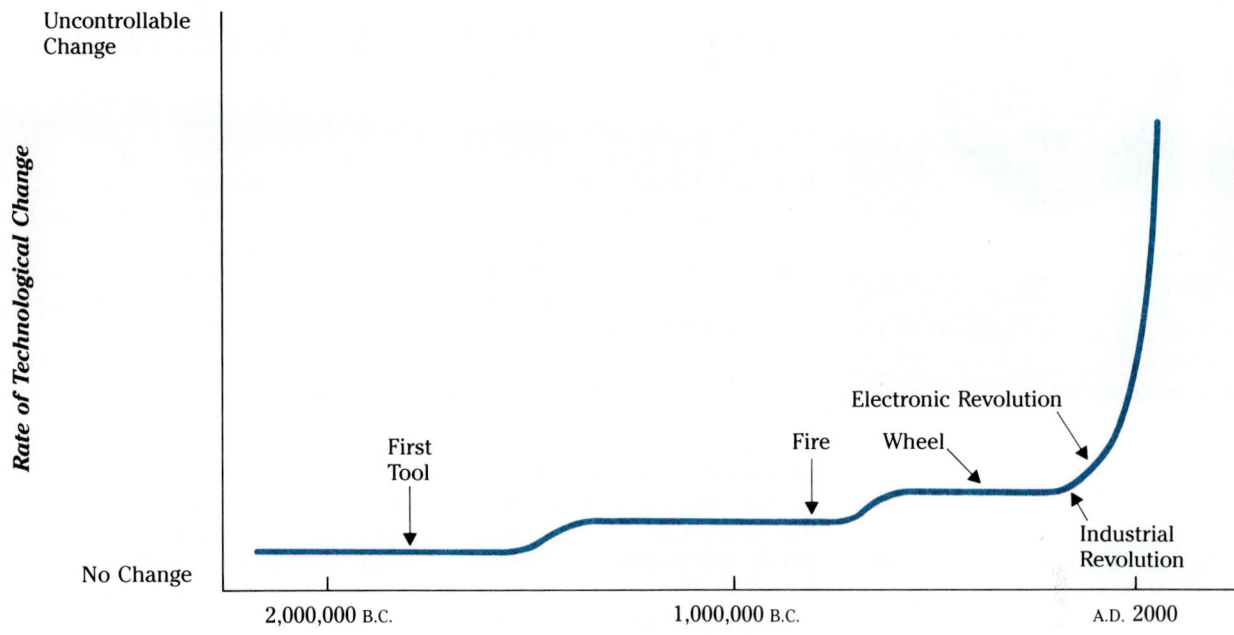

Source: R. B. Dunham (1984), *Organizational behavior*, Homewood, IL: Irwin, 465.

Structural/Procedural Changes

While changes in technology focus on the tools used to accomplish work objectives, structural changes concentrate on an organization and the methods it uses to coordinate work (as described in Chapter 12). For example, movement from a functional form of organization (such as one based on finance, operations, marketing, and so forth) to a divisional form (such as one centered on product lines, customer groups, or territories) is a structural change. Less far-reaching structural changes include situations in which an organization increases or decreases the degree to which authority is delegated or the span of control of its managers. Structural organizational changes have been very popular in recent years as organizations struggle to find effective coordinating work designs (see "A Closer Look: Restructuring").

People-Oriented Changes

Technological changes attempt to improve organizational effectiveness by using better tools. Structural changes try to improve effectiveness by using the tools better. Tools, however, are used by people. No matter how marvelous the technology or how well suited the structure, success cannot be achieved without the appropriate contributions of individual organization members. For this reason, many organizational changes concentrate on people-oriented changes, such as improving the skills, attitudes, motivation, and behaviors of organization members (see the discussions of people-oriented issues in Chapters 13–17). These factors are so important that they constitute a major part of the work conducted by organizational development specialists.

A CLOSER LOOK

Restructuring: Changes Contribute to Eczel Excellence

"Bust-ups? Oh, no! The whole company gets blown to smithereens, as if by dynamite. What crazy, wasteful destruction!"[1] Although a common attitude, bust-ups (separating a corporation into its component parts, often selling off the pieces) and the restructuring that usually follows do not have to portend doom and gloom. Many bust-ups benefit more than hurt the economy and the individual business involved.

Eczel is a fast-growing organization that distributes office supplies to a variety of large corporations. Until 1985, Eczel was a subsidiary of Crown Zellerbach Corporation, then a huge forest products company. In 1985, however, Sir James Goldsmith gained control of Crown Zellerbach and got rid of everything but Eczel, which he felt had great potential. Goldsmith installed Al Dunlap as the new opera-

ting head of Eczel, and Dunlap initiated major structural changes almost immediately. He reduced Eczel's twenty-two distribution centers, each with its own vice-president, to four centers and four VPs. He also created a highly centralized buying center to replace Eczel's inefficient, decentralized buying operation. These and other structural changes, accompanied by a new "this company is important" approach to management, have turned Eczel's deep losses into profits. Why couldn't giant Crown Zellerbach do the same? Because, according to Dunlap, "We operate it like it's the only company in the world."[2]

New bosses attribute . . . success to " . . . being liberated from the three layers of bureaucracy between them and a decision."

Eczel's success following restructuring is not an isolated case. Goldsmith also took over and broke apart Diamond International, whose egg-carton manufacturing business has flourished as an independent entity. Its new bosses attribute much of their success to ". . . being liberated from the three layers of bureaucracy between them and a decision. . . .

[T]hey can make instant product improvements instead of waiting months for the go-ahead."[3] Consider a former TRW subsidiary that, as part of the TRW conglomerate, scrapped 24 percent of the aircraft turbine parts it manufactured because they failed to meet specifications. After the business was sold to Precision Castparts and given a new boss, the scrap rate was cut in half, orders skyrocketed, and the company became profitable. Why? The business was managed systematically, focusing on quality and providing a new structure to support this focus.

Bust-ups and restructurings offer opportunities for organizations to make changes that can yield improvements. They do not, however, guarantee improved effectiveness. It is up to managers to provide the systematic strategic planning and implementation of change that produces the results. Given this fact, it is not surprising that today's most popular topics in executive education programs focus on strategic planning and the management of organizational change.

1. M. Magnet (2 March 1987),
Restructuring really works, *Fortune*, 41.
Other facts for this "Closer Look" were
also derived from pages 38ff of this article.
2. Magnet, 43.
3. Magnet, 42.

One of the most noticeable changes of this type involves replacing organization members, which is sometimes done if existing employees are unable to function effectively with new technologies or in a new environment. At other times, organizations will replace members in an attempt to bring in "fresh blood" and new ideas. Replacing employees can also send a message to the external environment, as is often the case when a CEO is replaced. Some observers, for example, feel that the replacement of R. J. Ferris as the CEO of Allegis was intended to say "We are a new corporation that wants to work with—not against—you" to United Airlines employees and "Now we can serve you better" to its customers.

Much people-oriented change in organizations involves training and development activities to improve the value of existing organization members. Some of the most powerful people-oriented changes focus on motivation in hopes of energizing employees and directing these energies appropriately. Behavior modification and goal setting are examples of motivational approaches. The people-oriented approach to organizational change can be said to "value human fulfillment highly and expect improved organizational performance to follow on improved human functioning and processes."[5]

Technostructural and Sociotechnical Changes

It is often fairly easy to distinguish between technological, structural, and people-oriented changes in theory. In reality, however, organizational change is rarely so neatly categorized, representing instead a combination of these approaches. Accordingly, hybrid approaches that "affect the work content and method and . . . the sets of relationships among workers" have been developed to reflect certain combinations of the three specific types of change.[6] **Technostructural changes,** thus, involve concurrent changes in organizational technology and structure. **Sociotechnical changes** involve changes in people and technology.

As you may have guessed, even these distinctions are seldom made so clearly in practice. In fact, most changes using either of these hybrid titles involve changes in all technological, structural/procedural, and people-oriented change areas. Rather than fighting over the appropriate label to assign a given change, it is more important to use all three areas of potential change effectively.[7]

Reactions to Change

Organization members notice and react to changes of any type. Their reactions can range from quite positive and supportive to quite negative and very resistant. In fact,

> . . . [P]eople experience change in all manner of ways. For some, a particular change will bring satisfaction, joy, advantage, a sense of job well done; for others, that same change may bring disadvantage, pain, sadness, even humiliation. Still others may barely perceive the change at all, experiencing it indifferently at most.[8]

The Range of Reactions

Because not even good change ideas work well unless they receive favorable reactions from organization members, managers must understand the types of reactions that might result from a planned change (see Figure 20.3). Consider each possible reaction and its importance to managers.

FIGURE 20.3   *Continuum of Change Reactions*

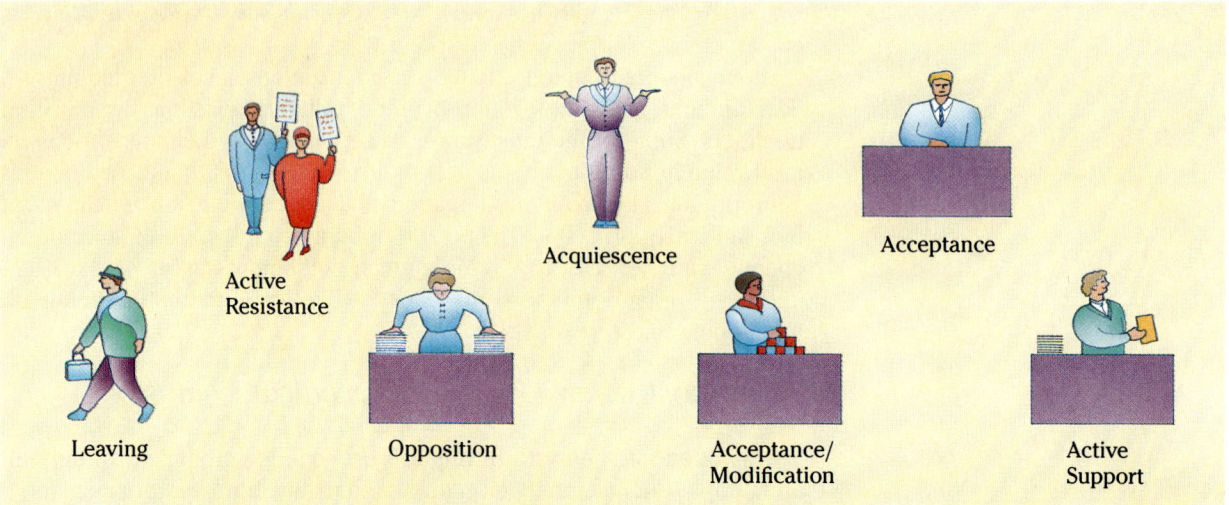

Leaving the Organization   Usually, the most extreme reaction an organization member shows to a change is to leave the organization. For example, following the introduction of a major organizational change, such as a merger or transfer in job assignment, many workers go because they believe the change is so obnoxious that staying would be intolerable. Sometimes organization members depart even if the change is a good one because they find it personally difficult to cope with the change. Many of the employees who left Apple Computer after John Sculley took over in 1985 appear to have done so because they had learned to love the open, informal Apple of old and could not tolerate the expected constraints of the new Apple.

It should be noted that, although leaving an organization may be the most extreme reaction to change, it is not necessarily the most damaging one to the organization. Indeed, things probably proceed more smoothly if the most adamant opponents of a change leave rather than stay to fight it.

Active Resistance   Workers who actively resist a change may try either to prevent it from occurring or to modify its nature. At its extreme, active resistance sends the message "No, I will not do this." Active resistance often goes beyond personal defiance and includes attempts to encourage others to resist the change. Many organizational changes have been scuttled by active employee resistance. A strike by a trade union is a good example of group-oriented active resistance.

Opposition   Somewhat less extreme than active resistance is behavior that can be labeled "opposition."[9] Usually somewhat passive in nature, opposition behavior might result in no more than simple "foot dragging" to delay implementation or to bring about a scaled-down version of a proposed change. Opposition is a tactic commonly used by those who control resources that are necessary for the change to be made. By withholding essential resources, people can slow or modify a change quietly without having to actively or aggressively make their dislike for the change known. For example, an air traffic controller who informs the Congressional Oversight Committee through an anonymous tip of a planned change in control procedures that he or she feels may reduce safety margins falls into the opposition category. (A public whistleblowing, as described in Chapter 4, would be considered more of an active resistance maneuver.)

Acquiescence Opposition reactions tend to occur when those affected dislike a change and engage in passive resistance to delay or modify it. Sometimes, however, those opposed to a change feel powerless to prevent or alter it and, thus, allow the change to occur without interference. This acquiescence to an unwanted change may arise from an impending sense of its inevitability—like death or taxes, about which human beings supposedly can do little or nothing. People put up with the inevitable as best they can, shrugging their shoulders, gritting their teeth, and steeling themselves to face a "tragic" event.[10]

Acceptance/Modification Still farther to the right on the continuum shown in Figure 20.3 is the first of the reactions that are positive instead of negative. Organization members who demonstrate an acceptance/ modification response accept a change to a certain extent but have some reservations about it. For example, suppose manager Marie Archer has been told that her employer intends to move the company's headquarters out of state. Marie supports the idea of moving operations because local taxes and other restrictive ordinances are hurting the company's ability to compete in the marketplace. On the other hand, she is worried that the change may alienate many of its major customers and adversely affect its supply and delivery systems. At a personal level, she would rather not move her family too far from friends and relatives. One option available to Marie is to accept the need for a relocation but to try to persuade her employer that there are sound reasons for finding a different site in the same state. Acceptance/modification responses to change usually can be characterized as "bargaining over details (albeit, perhaps, important ones), rather than over principles."[11]

The acceptance of a change is characterized by passive support. Employees who accept, for example, new technology in their work environment are likely to participate in the change but not likely to actively promote it.

Acceptance Even farther to the right on the continuum is a more clear-cut acceptance of change. This type of reaction is likely when people are either indifferent toward the change (that is, they do not *dislike* it), or they agree with it. Acceptance reactions to change are characterized by passive support. If asked whether they like the change, for example, workers might agree that they do—but they are unlikely to volunteer such information. If asked to participate in the change, they will cooperate—but they probably will not initiate participation.

Active Support Why would people only passively support a change they might like? They may have no reason to be actively supportive. The final point on the continuum defines an active support of change. In this situation, organization members choose to engage actively in behaviors that increase the change's chances for success. Active supporters often initiate conversations explaining why they support the change and think it is a good idea. These conversations may even be aimed at encouraging others to support the change. For example, when American Family Insurance decided to implement work teams for services employees at its office in Eden Prairie, Minnesota, a group of workers promoted the idea with banners and a party celebrating the change. Active support also includes "pitching in" and making the change work.

It is important to emphasize that the reactions shown in Figure 20.3 lie along a continuum. Consider the label *acceptance*, for example. Clearly, a workforce that approves of a change is more likely to support it actively than a workforce that merely does not dislike it. Both situations, however, can produce primarily passive acceptance behaviors in individuals. There is also a big difference between active supporters who make favorable comments about a change and those who work overtime to make the change succeed. In reality, an individual's reaction to change can fall along any point on the continuum.

The Underlying Causes

Why is there such a wide range of reactions to organizational change? Why do some people react to a given change with active support while others simply passively accept the change, and still others actively resist it? The answers to all of these questions are not known, but many major determinants have been uncovered (see Figure 20.4). People's support of or resistance to change depends heavily on how they answer the following questions:

1. Will this change cause me to gain or lose something of value?
2. Do I understand the nature of this change?
3. Do I trust the initiators of this change?
4. Do I agree with the advisability of this change?
5. Given my personality, personal values, and attitudes, how do I feel about this change?[12]

In other words, although some people occasionally resist change just to be difficult, most people usually react to change based on rational, logical considerations. In fact, it can be argued that the majority of resistance to change occurs because people have lived through changes that caused them problems or prevented them from satisfying important needs.[13] Knowing this should help managers anticipate when support or resistance is likely and encourage them to manage actively the development of support for change.

Gain or Loss of Value People who review a proposed change and conclude that its introduction will cause them to lose something of value have a vested interest in resisting the change. Workers, therefore, resist changes that cause them to lose status, restrict their promotional opportunities, reduce their control over their work, produce an undesired change in the nature of their work, reduce enjoyable interactions with co-workers, or threaten anything else that they value. The greater the expected loss, the more likely they are to resist. Their resistance will be most active if they feel they can influence the change.

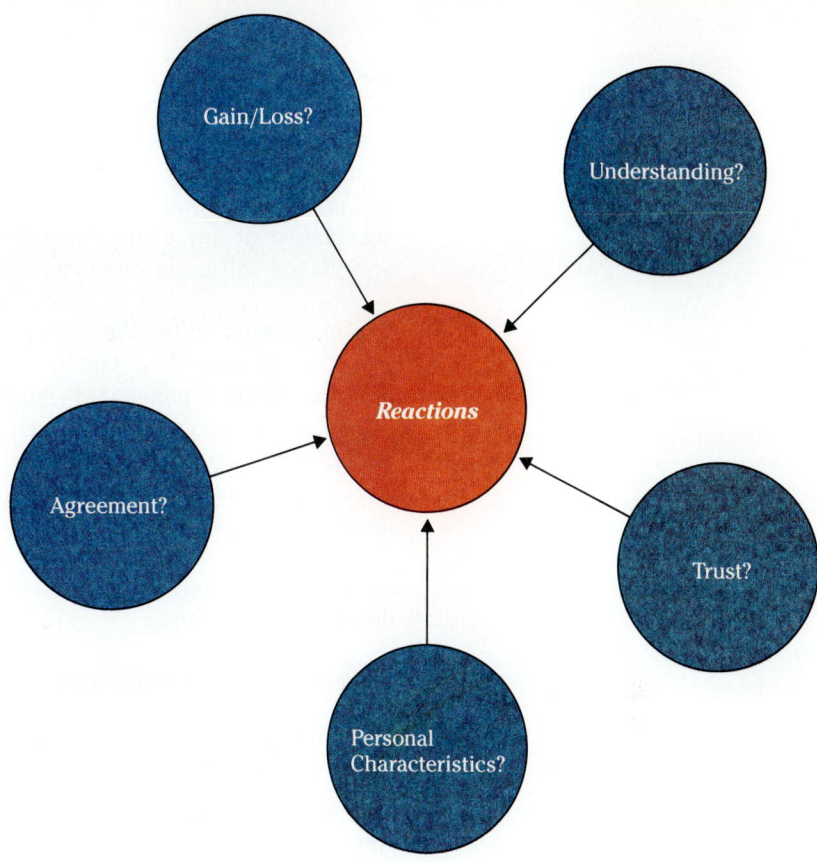

FIGURE 20.4 *The Causes of Reactions to Change*

Many times a proposed change wins the support of those affected by offering something of value, such as a job redesign effort that makes jobs more interesting or leads to greater pay and recognition. The more people expect to gain from a change, the more they will support it.

Understanding of the Change Because most people have some fear of the unknown, they are less likely to support a change if they do not understand it. If organization members are confused about the implications of a particular change, they are likely to assume the worst and react accordingly. For example, workers who are told only that a flextime work schedule will be introduced may not understand that they will be able to select their work hours. If they assume incorrectly that supervisors will assign arbitrary (perhaps undesirable) hours, the employees may fight the introduction of the new schedule.

It is important to note that merely understanding a change does not guarantee support for it. In fact, sometimes the more completely people understand an idea, the more reasons they discover to dislike it. If you assume a change would be well received if it were understood, however, you can usually make workers' support of it more likely by increasing their understanding.

Trust in the Initiators of Change Organizations vary substantially in the degree to which members trust management. If a change is proposed when trust is low, a natural first reaction is to ask, "What is really going to happen and how is this change going to harm me?" When the initiators of change are not trusted, virtually any change tends to be received negatively. When trust is high, employees are more likely to support a proposed change. It is interesting to note that, under conditions of distrust, organization members often resist changes, even when they are understood and promise something of value. Members fear that acceptance of any change could set a dangerous precedent or that its acceptance will make members feel indebted to the initiators.

Agreement with the Change It is amazing that organizations planning change often fail to assess who is likely to agree with the introduction of a change and who is apt to disagree. It is clearly logical to expect that those who think the change is a good idea will be more likely to support it than those who feel the change is a bad idea.

Disagreement with a proposed change can be of two types. The first possibility is that those who disagree about the merits of a change are examining the same information but simply reaching different conclusions. The second alternative is that the two parties are considering different information.

Personal Characteristics A number of personal characteristics affect support for or resistance to a change. People who lack confidence in the skills they will need following the change may be resistant. Instructors, for example, might resist teaching a televised class because they are afraid that their appearance or ability to hold viewers' attention will not be good enough. A confident person, however, may see the same change as a new opportunity for success. Introduction of a computerized inventory control system may be well received by a manager who feels the new system can help improve his or her sales performance. Sometimes a change is resisted to "save face," particularly if the resister had been a supporter of the "old way."

A number of personality characteristics can cause people to support or resist a change. Because change is usually believed to introduce additional uncertainty into the work environment, their tolerance for ambiguity can influence their reactions. Workers who have a low tolerance for ambiguity and believe that a change would push uncertainty beyond their personal comfort level may resist a change as a defensive reaction. On the other hand, organization members who have a high tolerance for ambiguity may welcome the uncertainty associated with change as something that will make their lives more interesting.

Highly dogmatic (closed-minded) individuals are likely to support a change actively if it is consistent with their view of "how things should be." On the other hand, when presented with changes that challenge their personal points of view, resistance is often swift and strong. Less dogmatic, more open-minded individuals are usually receptive to a wider range of potential changes without prejudice but may spend a great deal of time exploring alternatives and carefully evaluating their many merits and weaknesses. Although this is often a healthy response, it can be time consuming and costly.

The degree to which people have authoritarian personalities can also influence whether they support or resist a change. An individual with a strong authoritarian personality tends to be supportive of organizational change when its initiator is considered to be in a position of authority to order the change. If the initiator is not considered to have legitimate authority, however, resistance is very likely. Managers trying to gain the support of workers with highly authoritarian personalities, therefore, should have "the boss" initiate the change, even if it was designed by someone else. Organization members low in authoritarianism, on the other hand, probably do not care who initiates the change but have a tendency to evaluate its merits before making a decision to support or resist the change.

In addition to the influence of these and other personality attributes, workers' attitudes toward change itself can also play an important role in shaping their reactions to the change process. Although still somewhat exploratory, the eighteen items listed in Figure 20.5 are believed to assess the cognitive, affective, and behavioral tendency components of a person's attitude toward change and, thus, help managers anticipate workers' probable reactions to changes in general. Cognitive items concentrate on whether a person believes change tends to produce positive or negative effects. Affective items measure the degree to which a person enjoys change. Behavioral intent questions deal with the degree to which a person tends to support or resist change.

Review Although the five categories of underlying causes just discussed seem to operate independently, this is usually not the case. Particular combinations of these factors can be especially powerful. What kind of reaction, for example, would emanate from a highly dogmatic person who does not trust management, expects personal loss, and disagrees with a change? The person will probably actively resist the

FIGURE 20.5   *Measuring Attitudes Toward Change*

Cognitive Items	Strongly Disagree	Disagree	Neither Agree nor Disagree	Agree	Strongly Agree
1. Changes usually benefit the organization.	1	2	3	4	5
2. Most of my co-workers benefit from change.	1	2	3	4	5
3. Change often helps me perform better.	1	2	3	4	5
4. Other people think that I support change.	1	2	3	4	5
5. Change usually helps improve unsatisfactory situations at work.	1	2	3	4	5
6. I usually benefit from change.	1	2	3	4	5
Affect Items					
7. I look forward to changes at work.	1	2	3	4	5
8. I don't like change.	5	4	3	2	1
9. Change frustrates me.	5	4	3	2	1
10. Change tends to stimulate me.	1	2	3	4	5
11. Most changes are irritating.	5	4	3	2	1
12. I find most changes to be pleasing.	1	2	3	4	5
Behavioral Intent Items					
13. I usually resist new ideas.	5	4	3	2	1
14. I am inclined to try new ideas.	1	2	3	4	5
15. I usually support new ideas.	1	2	3	4	5
16. I often suggest new approaches to things.	1	2	3	4	5
17. I intend to do whatever possible to support change.	1	2	3	4	5
18. I usually hesitate to try new ideas.	5	4	3	2	1

change or leave the organization. How about a highly dogmatic and authoritarian person who agrees with the change proposed by a trusted boss and believes that the change will benefit him or her personally?

Developing Support for Change

The preceding section dealt with the types of reactions that might accompany change and explored some of the reasons for these reactions to help you anticipate the types of reactions you are likely to encounter as a manager. This section explores ways to develop support for an impending change—ways to avoid resistance or reduce it when possible through such methods as education and communication, participation and involvement, facilitative support, emotional support, incentives, manipulation and co-optation, and coercion.

Education and Communication

Simple education and communication about an impending change can often contribute significantly to the development of support and the avoidance or reduction of resistance. The purpose of this technique is to provide information: *what* the change is, *when* it is to be introduced, *how* it will be introduced, and *why* it is considered necessary. Education and communication can also reveal the logic behind the change, as well as the objectives it is intended to accomplish. The informational methods of education and communication appear to be the most commonly used by managers to overcome change and are based on the assumption that people ". . . will act rationally in the face of factual information; moreover, given adequate information they will recognize the problem and develop a mutually agreeable solution because the facts are so compelling."[14]

How do education and communication address the underlying causes of resistance to a change? First, they can reduce misunderstanding about the change and the worst-case assumptions often made in the presence of misunderstanding. Education and communication can also clarify the ways in which the change can benefit organization members. Because

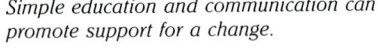
Simple education and communication can promote support for a change.

effective communication can improve understanding and clarify the potential advantages of a change, it can also increase agreement with the advisability of the change (although communication about bad ideas will reveal that the ideas are bad). Finally, education and communication can increase employees' trust of management. This occurs when the education/communication is viewed as an honest, straightforward attempt to describe the impending change.

Although this technique can be very powerful, it does have some potential drawbacks. Education and communication typically require a significant investment of time, effort, and money. In addition, at least a reasonable level of existing trust is needed, or the method may appear to be an attempt at manipulation.

Participation and Involvement

Education and communication *give* information to organization members about an impending change. Participation and involvement, on the other hand, *ask* members for information. There are two primary reasons for using participation and involvement. The first of these is to elicit information from members that might help improve the quality or effectiveness of a change. The second reason is to increase the likelihood that employees will accept the change and become committed to its success. Employees can be involved in the change process either at the stage of designing the change or during the planning and implementation phase; thus, under appropriate circumstances, participation and involvement can improve the change, promote its acceptance, and enhance its support.

Participation and involvement influence the same causes of change reactions as education and communication, but usually in a more powerful way. Active participation substantially increases understanding of a change. Personal concerns about potential losses can be dealt with during the design stage, and because members help design the change, they are more likely to agree about its advisability. Trust can also be substantially enhanced, since management is saying, "We trust you and value you enough to ask you to help us with this important task."

Given the potential power of participation and involvement, what are their possible drawbacks? Almost without exception, participation/ involvement is one of the most expensive and time-consuming techniques available to managers. This simply represents a cost, however, not a risk. A manager of change must simply do a cost/benefit analysis and decide whether this cost is justified, given the potential benefits of the participation and involvement process.

One of the biggest risks of this technique is that organization members may make suggestions that managers choose not to pursue, thereby alienating rather than gaining their cooperation. What does a manager do if workers design a bad change? Implementing the change could intentionally introduce poor quality; rejecting it risks creating resentment.

This approach to developing support is most appropriate under conditions in which change initiators do not possess all of the information needed to design or implement a change. It is also quite useful if managers expect significant resistance from the organization members who will be affected by the change but need their acceptance and

Facilitative support consists of the assistance an organization provides its members to help make a change effective.

commitment to make the change work. Participation and involvement work best when those involved in the change are willing and able to participate and if they ". . . have some sense of what they want to do but do not have all the means to do it."[15]

Facilitative Support

Organizational change does not occur in a vacuum. In fact, most change efforts fail unless they are adequately supported. Facilitative support consists of the assistance an organization provides its members to help make a change effective. This support can be provided to individuals or to groups. An individual who lacks some of the skills required to operate a new computer system, for example, might be offered a training program. Other types of facilitative support include tools, materials, and advice. Mechanics required to conduct car tune-ups reasonably expect to be provided with an appropriate set of automotive tools, diagnostic equipment, and technical manuals. If an organization intends to introduce new technology to conduct tune-ups of electronic ignition or fuel injection systems, initiators of the change should plan to identify the tools and equipment that will be needed to implement the change and provide them to the mechanics.

Sometimes the facilitative support needed is somewhat less tangible. There may be, for example, organizational barriers that interfere with the effective implementation of a change. Consider a change that involves the introduction of autonomous work teams. Existing policies might discourage employees from leaving their desks to talk with other employees. An existing computer system might be set up so that only one member of the department is authorized to use it. The autonomous work team approach, however, requires employees to initiate interaction with other team members and necessitates computer access by all members. When the organization removes existing barriers to these behaviors, it is providing facilitative support for the change.

The provision of appropriate facilitative support can make the difference between moderate and major success for a change program. It not only directly facilitates effectiveness, it does so indirectly by reducing employee fears about facing new techniques and procedures. It also shows that the organization is competent enough to plan ahead and caring enough about employees to provide the support needed in the face of change.

Emotional Support

When faced with major changes, most employees require support that goes well beyond the technical aspects of facilitative support. In many cases, emotional support can be at least as important as facilitative support. As noted earlier, it is natural for employees to be concerned about potential personal losses and to fear that they may be unable to work effectively with a change. Emotional support addresses these personal concerns. Often a formal program of emotional support is best. This might take the form of an employee assistance program that provides individuals with the opportunity to discuss their fears and concerns with a counselor. Sometimes emotional support is provided through group meetings that encourage the open expression of concerns and fears and provide a straightforward treatment of them. In the majority of cases, however, emotional support comes primarily from a member's immediate supervisor and co-workers. Oftentimes alerting these people to the need for such support is all the person initiating the change has to do.

Emotional support can be thought of as a method of removing potential stumbling blocks to change and of increasing support. It does so by honestly addressing concerns resulting from a change and by once again saying, "This organization cares about its members."

Incentives

A major reason people choose to support or resist a change involves their judgment of whether they will personally gain or lose because of the change.[16] Management can emphasize the potential for personal gain by providing incentives when the change is implemented. People are more likely to support a change that benefits them personally and are more likely to resist a change that costs them something.

Management can provide incentives in two ways. First, the person initiating change can identify people who are likely to lose something of value when a change is implemented and give them compensation for their loss. For example, a person who suffers because of a change may be provided an additional pay increment, some time off, an extra vacation day, or a particularly desirable work assignment. When an organization provides compensatory incentives, it is saying, "I know this change will hurt you, and I want to do something to make up for it."

Although the compensatory approach can be helpful and can demonstrate that an organization cares about employees, it comes with some very substantial risks. If managers provide incentives to workers because they expect the workers to resist, how does this differ from blackmail? Furthermore, it does not take long for people to figure out that the way to obtain special rewards is to show signs of potential resistance. If it becomes known that "the squeaky wheel gets the grease," organizations suddenly discover a large number of squeaky wheels.

A second way to provide incentives is to design a change in such a way that the change itself benefits organization members. The introduction of a performance appraisal and merit pay system, for example, allows good employees to gain larger pay raises. The redesign of jobs can provide a substantial incentive for employees who value more interesting, challenging work. Whenever possible, such "built-in" incentives should be used over compensatory incentives. Although there may be times when the compensatory approach cannot be avoided, incentives inherent in a change tend to be more powerful and benefit the organization for longer than one-time compensatory changes.

Manipulation and Co-optation

Manipulation involves the systematic control or distortion of information provided to organization members about a change. Information (accurate or inaccurate) is provided that makes a change appear to be one that members should like and support. Information that might discourage support is withheld or distorted. Some managers of change believe that it is perfectly acceptable to provide only part of the information related to a change as long as the change information selectively provided is accurate. In fact, such an approach is probably just as common in the management of change as it is in political campaigns. It can be argued that knowingly presenting information that will produce a distorted picture of a change is just as unethical as lying about individual facts.

Ethical judgments are personal concerns. Someday you may encounter a situation in which it is important that a change be accepted, and manipulation is your only alternative. You should know, however, that this approach is risky. There is no easier way to damage trust and assure resistance—for both the immediate change and for future changes—than to have employees discover that they have been intentionally deceived.

Co-optation is a special type of manipulation, which, on the surface, appears very similar to participation and involvement. With the participation and involvement approach, the initiators of change want to nurture employee support for change. They benefit from employee input. In other words, they care about employees' ideas and support. In co-optation, a change initiator wants to nurture support but is not interested in genuine employee input. Employees, thus, might be asked to participate, or even lead others in adapting to change, creating the impression of participation and involvement. In fact, however, their ideas are neither wanted nor given serious consideration.

This is not always done deceitfully. Indeed, many people are happy to accept a figurehead role during the design or implementation of a change because it makes them look good. They accept such a position because it benefits them personally with full knowledge that the change agent does not really care about the ideas rising out of such participation. The biggest risk faced in using co-optation is that the people deceived will discover the truth. Reactions to such discoveries can be quick, strong, and actively resistant. The damage can last for a significant amount of time. Another risk in creating a figurehead is that others in the organization may believe the role and allow themselves to be influenced by the figurehead—hardly what the initiator of the change had in mind.

Coercion

Often the most forceful, powerful, and quickest technique for developing support (at least on a short-term basis) is coercion. The principle underlying the use of coercion is very simple: "Do this or else." For coercion to work, organization members must believe that resistance to a change would result in punishment, either through the loss of something of value or at a significant cost to them. Recall the discussion of avoidance learning in Chapter 14. Avoidance learning encourages people to behave (or not to behave) in a certain way in order to avoid a negative consequence that would otherwise result.

Coercion can be either implicit or explicit. Implicit threats occur when organization members are led and/or allowed to *believe* that adverse consequences are likely if they resist a change. Explicit coercion occurs when members are told specifically that a negative consequence *will* occur if they resist or fail to support a change. Coercion can involve

TABLE 20.1   *Advantages and Drawbacks of Change Techniques*

Technique	Advantages	Potential Drawbacks
Education and communication	After being convinced, members often assist with implementation.	It costs time and money.
Participation and involvement	Participants' input can be useful, and they are likely to be supportive.	It has heavy time costs; it can lead to poor change suggestions and disillusionment if ideas are not followed.
Facilitative support	It enhances the successful implementation of change.	It costs time and money for support materials and training programs.
Emotional support	It is relatively inexpensive; it is a good way to help with personal adjustment problems.	It is often done nonsystematically, resulting in time and cash outlays that may not remedy the problem.
Incentives	It can "head off" major resistance before it arises.	It can be expensive and can encourage resistance in hopes of gaining "compensation."
Manipulation and co-optation	It works fairly rapidly without substantial cost.	It is unethical and can destroy trust if workers find out they have been intentionally misled.
Coercion	It is usually the fastest method; it suppresses resistance regardless of cause.	It decreases satisfaction, increases resentment, and makes other techniques less effective.

threats of the loss of jobs, promotion, pay, recognition, or anything else that organization members value.

Coercion can be quite effective, and managers sometimes use it when support is needed because a change must be implemented quickly to avoid great loss. There are some problems, however. First, people who are coerced to behave in a particular way often seek alternative ways to regain control; thus, workers who are forced to support a change they dislike may react by increasing absenteeism, lowering performance, or possibly even engaging in organizational sabotage (see Chapter 19). Coercion usually results in reduced satisfaction and increased resentment. An organization's ability to use many of the other techniques for managing change is reduced, as most employees lose respect for a coercive change manager.

Many of the techniques for developing support discussed in this section are used extensively during the organizational development efforts discussed in the next section. Indeed, their use should be considered when implementing any organizational change. Table 20.1 summarizes these approaches and emphasizes that each has advantages and potential drawbacks. In most situations, managers will want to choose an appropriate combination of techniques to most effectively manage change. Table 20.2 provides examples of situations in which each technique may be appropriate.[17]

TABLE 20.2 *Techniques for Developing Support/Reducing Resistance and Examples of Appropriate Uses*

Technique	Common Uses
Education and communication	When knowledge would help alleviate fears due to inaccurate or sketchy information
Participation and involvement	When change initiators need information from others to design change and when the probability of resistance is high
Facilitative support	When people lack the necessary skills or tools to be effective following change
Emotional support	When people have personal concerns and anxiety about a change that supportive reassurance could help alleviate
Incentives	When key people will resist the change unless they benefit from it
Manipulation and co-optation	When change is absolutely necessary and all other techniques would be ineffective or too costly
Coercion	When change must occur quickly and the initiators have significantly more power than the resistors

The Special Role of Organizational Development

This chapter has dealt with a wide range of issues relating to the effective management of change in organizations. This information can be useful whether the change you deal with is reactive or proactive, mandated or voluntary, or involving the introduction of a minor piece of new technology or a complete reorganization. These techniques for managing change discussed in this chapter have been developed and refined to a large extent by a group of individuals referred to as *organizational development (OD) specialists*. OD specialists tend to apply these techniques in a particular manner and for a particular purpose. In general, they attack substantial, often organization-wide, issues for the purpose of achieving a planned, systematic improvement of organizations.

What Is OD?

Michael Beer, a well-known OD specialist from Harvard University, defines organizational development as "a process for diagnosing organizational problems by looking for incongruencies between environment, structures, processes, and people."[18] Although this may sound like a very broad or loose description of what has developed into a distinct discipline over the last thirty years or so, it can be argued that the openness of OD provides the breadth and flexibility necessary for the effective enhancement of organizations.

Organizational development specialists apply a variety of theories from psychology and organizational behavior. The OD process consists of a series of planned actions designed to improve the effectiveness of an organization and/or the well-being of its members. OD practitioners refer to these actions as *interventions*. An OD specialist conducts an analysis of an organization's problems and needs and then plans an intervention. Specific interventions could involve anything from individual or group counseling sessions to organization-wide structural changes. It is unfortunate that the openness that has given OD its strength almost doomed it in the eyes of managers. In the 1960s and 1970s, the use of sensitivity training (T-groups) designed to encourage the open expression of feelings through words and actions and other explorative methods led to stereotypes of OD as "group grope, flakey, and soft."[19] More recent trends in OD that have helped counteract this stereotype include: 1) a more systematic integration of the OD process and the enhancement of organizational effectiveness; 2) a focus on the importance and development of organizational culture as a means of enhancing organizational effectiveness; 3) concentration on the management of interpersonal, intergroup, and interorganizational conflict; 4) better research on the principles driving OD and on the effectiveness of OD interventions; and 5) the development of better guiding theories.[20]

This section will explore some of the specific techniques OD practitioners use. For now, it may be useful for you to think of such people as organizational doctors. What does a medical doctor do when a patient comes in for a general checkup or with a specific concern? A good physician talks to the patient to identify apparent health weaknesses and strengths. He or she then conducts a more formal assessment using the tools of the medical trade to assess the condition of each major component of the patient's body. If problems are found, more extensive diagnostic techniques are used in an attempt to find the source(s) of the apparent problems. Based on this information, a diagnosis is made and alternative treatment plans are identified. These alternatives are discussed with the patient and, based on the patient's preferences and the physician's expert opinions, a course of treatment is undertaken. If treatment goes beyond the expertise of the examining physician, he or she seeks assistance from other experts. The patient's progress is assessed periodically and treatment is adjusted if necessary; if all goes as planned, the patient improves.

An organizational development specialist ("Dr. O") follows a virtually identical procedure. When an organization asks an OD specialist for an assessment of overall organizational health or for help with a particular problem, Dr. O talks to critical representatives of the organization to

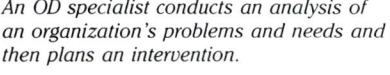
An OD specialist conducts an analysis of an organization's problems and needs and then plans an intervention.

obtain more details about apparent organizational weaknesses and strengths. He or she then conducts a more formal assessment, using such tools as surveys and interviews, to identify the affected components of the organization. In the problem areas, Dr. O extends the depth of the diagnosis to determine the source of the organizational problem (for example, is it based on technology or structural or people problems?). Based on this information, Dr. O identifies potential interventions that might remedy the problem(s) and discusses them with key organization members. Based on the organization's preferences and Dr. O's opinions, appropriate interventions are undertaken. When necessary, the OD specialist might ask for help from engineers, accountants, psychologists, or others who possess the knowledge and expertise needed to effectively design and implement the necessary organizational changes. Throughout the intervention period, Dr. O assesses the organization's progress, fine-tunes the interventions as necessary, and guides the improvement of organizational effectiveness. As is the case with medical doctors, Dr. O sometimes succeeds and sometimes fails, but the treatment of every organization, whether it leads to success or failure, enhances the doctor's ability to treat future patients.

Who Practices OD?

Traditionally organizational development was practiced primarily by consultants who were typically referred to as *change agents*. These consultants tended to be trained in a behavioral science, such as psychology or sociology, although similar training is now being offered by many management programs in business schools. More often than not, they were academics. Only a relatively small number of organizations had in-house OD specialists. Although OD specialists still conduct the majority of organizational development work, beginning in the 1980s the biggest growth in the OD area has occurred among managers. It is only just recently that OD concepts, values, and methods have been found to a substantial degree in the general practitioner-oriented management literature. Now it is relatively common to see reports of managers driving OD activities that have led to innovative plant designs, participative management, collaborative union-management activities, and the use of employee task forces.[21]

Common OD Activities

This section has mentioned some of the tools and techniques often used during OD activities. Because OD involves such a flexible, adaptive process, it is very difficult to create a list of tools that are always used. Your medical doctor does not use every available tool each time you visit his or her office. The same is true for Dr. O. The next section of this chapter provides an overview of the process often followed by OD practitioners working with organizations. Before you read that section, however, you should become aware of some of the specific techniques OD practitioners often use as they follow the change-management process (see Table 20.3). These common activities reflect some of the most basic values and assumptions inherent in the OD process.[22] These values and assumptions include, for example, the belief that people in

TABLE 20.3   *Frequently Used OD Techniques*

Technique	Examples
Organizational diagnoses	Interviews, surveys, group meetings
Team building	Improvement of existing groups; creation of teams for problem solving
Survey feedback	Provision of survey results to members; interpretation of results by members
Education	Classroom training for "sensitivity" skills and interpersonal skills
Intergroup activities	Communication development; conflict reduction
Third-party peace making	Negotiation, mediation by "outsider" for interperson and intergroup conflict
Technostructural/sociotechnical activities	Joint examination of technology, structure, and people systems
Process consultation	Observation of groups in action with immediate feedback on processes observed
Life/career planning	Future oriented—development of personal goals and acquisition of skills to help individuals fit into the organization and the organization match individual needs
Coaching	Nonevaluative feedback to individuals describing how others see them
Planning and goal setting	Training of individuals to improve personal-planning and goal-setting effectiveness; emphasis on individual's place in the overall organization

organizations seek satisfaction of high-level needs, personal development, and growth. It is also believed that people wish to contribute to organizational effectiveness and are capable of doing so. OD values tend to stress that group relationships have the major impact on the satisfaction and productivity of individual members and that groups are the key to organizational success. Finally, OD specialists tend to assume that the design, structure, policies, and practices of organizations influence the attitudes and behaviors of their members and that management must recognize this and be prepared to change these factors to benefit both the organization and its members.

How Effective Is OD?

How well does organizational development actually work? It is hard to say. Most OD activities need to remain open to change while underway in order to adapt to organizational and individual complexities. The problem is that such flexibility can make it very difficult to judge the success of an intervention. Many OD practitioners choose not to collect evidence that could be used to assess their effectiveness. Perhaps they are too busy with the intervention itself to conduct an independent "research" study at the same time, or perhaps they are so convinced they will be successful that they do not see the need for doing so. The literature contains many case studies reporting apparently successful OD interventions.[23] Reports of success, however, tend to be based on subjective rather than objective evaluation. Although there is certainly nothing wrong with subjective evaluation of OD interventions, the use of such reports to guide future OD work is limited by the lack of substantiating evidence.

There have been several attempts in recent years to assess the effectiveness of typical OD interventions.[24] John Nicholas, after reviewing sixty-seven OD studies and their impact on "hard criteria," such as costs, productivity, quality, and absenteeism, and after noting some potential confounding effects, concluded that some interventions succeeded while others did not and that "the single most apparent finding of this research is that no one change technique or class of techniques works well in all situations."[25] Barry Macy and his colleagues conducted an excellent overview of fifty-six OD intervention studies. Overall they identified positive effects on productivity. Unfortunately, they also found that OD interventions sometimes produced (at least in the short term) negative effects on such factors as work involvement and job satisfaction.

Many OD interventions have been conducted well and have produced moderate to substantial positive effects. Others have been conducted less well and have often done damage to an organization and its members. Some OD practitioners expect too much from their interventions and to promise too much. They should have a more realistic set of expectations; less puffery in the promotion of OD activities; and improved, more systematic documentation of the effects of their interventions. Finally, the OD interventions that prove most effective tend to follow a systematic approach, such as that presented in the next section, and are begun without prejudice about the nature of needed organizational change. The best OD practitioners appear to be those who practice the trade systematically and follow the principles that give OD so much promise.

The Future of OD

It appears likely that OD techniques will become even more popular and more widespread as organizations face greater uncertainty and greater demands for effectiveness. There is a trend toward the use of more systematic approaches and more precise tools. More managers are "buying in" to the OD concept, which will lead to more widespread use of the techniques and more manager-oriented OD work. Academic institutions are now teaching general managers that managing change is and will continue to be an important part of their management duties. Michael Beer and Anna Elise Walton suggest that OD should move away from structured, preprogrammed, consultant-centered interventions toward the "general manager . . . [as] the central character in the drama of organization development."[26] They also argue that OD consultants must become more expert on business issues in addition to honing their OD skills. It has even been argued that OD practices should be integrated with the strategic planning process to ". . . enhance both the quality of strategic decision making and the implementation of strategic decisions."[27] Beer and Walton further suggest that the values and approaches of OD may help alleviate the belief that a choice must be made between concern for organizational effectiveness and concern for the well-being of employees.

INTERVIEW

Chris Argyris and Donald L. Hawk

Chris Argyris is the James Bryant Conant Professor of Education and Organizational Behavior at Harvard University. Over the past thirty years he has written extensively on organizational learning, change, and development. Donald L. Hawk is executive vice-president and manager of the administration department for Texas Commerce Bancshares, a seventy-bank holding company headquartered in Houston, Texas.

1. Why do some organizations succeed while others fail?

Hawk: Long ago, Peter Drucker said, "The purpose of an organization lies outside itself." Organizations that do not adapt to changing environments wither and die. The more congruent an organization is with its environment, the greater its potential success.

2. What is a learning organization?

Argyris: Learning is the ability to detect and correct error. It is important to recognize that organizations can learn and, therefore, be able to make changes. A learning organization is capable of creating matches between the design and implementation of its actions and the actualization of its intended behaviors; thus, a learning or-

ganization is one that is capable of creating matches between intentions and actuality.

3. What is it like managing change in the banking industry today?

Hawk: The banking industry is changing rapidly. Deregulation has increased the quantity and quality of competition and product alternatives. In such a situation, change is almost thrust on industry participants. The critical issue becomes one of determining priorities—which among the many things that *could* be changed *should* be changed first?

With an industry in such flux, conscious decisions must be made about the kinds of change to be accomplished. While the goal is always to make organizational changes that are congruent with the external environment, just keeping up can be a real challenge during a period of rapid change. A thoughtfully planned change implemented too late has no value. Consequently, every attempt must be made to institutionalize a change as quickly as possible. This can best be done by creating organizational systems that stimulate or reinforce behavior. Careful attention must be paid to compensation systems in particular, to make sure they reinforce the change sought to the extent practical.

4. Should organizational change focus on making changes in people or changes in organizational systems?

Argyris: Both. People changes and system changes appear to be suited to differing circumstances. When the problem you are dealing with is routine, when the people have the skills that are required to solve the problem

at hand, and when the correction that is needed is do-able, then I believe system change is more effective. Under these conditions you can then create a system—a policy and a set of behavior requirements that you know people can achieve. Efforts to bring about change by making alterations in the system are difficult to achieve, however, when you are dealing with old but wrong ways of doing things that have been accepted (legitimized), or when you are dealing with organizational defense routines, skilled unawareness, and skilled incompetence. Under these types of conditions, organizational change is more likely to be effective when efforts are made to change the people. It is under these conditions that old, inappropriate routines need to be changed, defense mechanisms need to be broken down, awareness needs to be created, and competencies need to be developed. System changes would bring about bewilderment, ambiguity, and a perpetuation of defensiveness.

Planning and Managing the Change Process

To this point, the chapter has discussed the reasons for organizational change, the most common types of change, and the types of and reasons for the reactions to change. The chapter has also explored some techniques for reducing resistance to change and developing support. It is now time for an overview of a systematic procedure for the planning and management of the change process, using the four-stage procedure shown in Figure 20.6.

The change process begins with the identification of the nature of a change. This is followed by planning for implementation of the change. Next, the change is implemented. After implementation, people begin to assess the success of the change process and identify needed alterations. The key to effective management of change is the use of a *systematic* and orderly change process.

Change Identification

The first stage of the change process involves the recognition of a need for change and the identification of the nature of the needed change(s). Normally the need for change is indicated by the forces to change discussed at the beginning of this chapter. This need may be manifested in a variety of ways. Employee complaints might identify the need for change, or a regularly scheduled attitude survey might provide an early warning that a change is needed. Similarly, drops in performance or productivity or increases in absenteeism or turnover may indicate the need for change. Many other factors, including sales problems, labor-management difficulties, or external criticism can signal a need for organizational change.

Once a need for change has been identified, the nature of the necessary change(s) should be clarified. Sometimes the signals that indicated the need for change suggest the general nature of the change, while at other times they also reveal the specific types of change needed. An increase in turnover in one office, for example, might indicate that a turnover-management change is needed. On the other hand, exit-interview complaints of poor supervision may more precisely identify the nature of the needed change. Sometimes a needed change is identified quite specifically, as might be the case when a machine breaks down and cannot be repaired.

During Stage One (change identification), it is important to specify—at least in a general sense—the objectives of a proposed change and the criteria that will be used to determine whether these objectives will be met. At times the change can be very specifically and completely identified at Stage One. At other times, however, the final planning of the change will carry over to Stage Two (implementation planning). This might be the case, for example, when significant employee input is needed to design the change.

FIGURE 20.6
The Systematic Management of Change

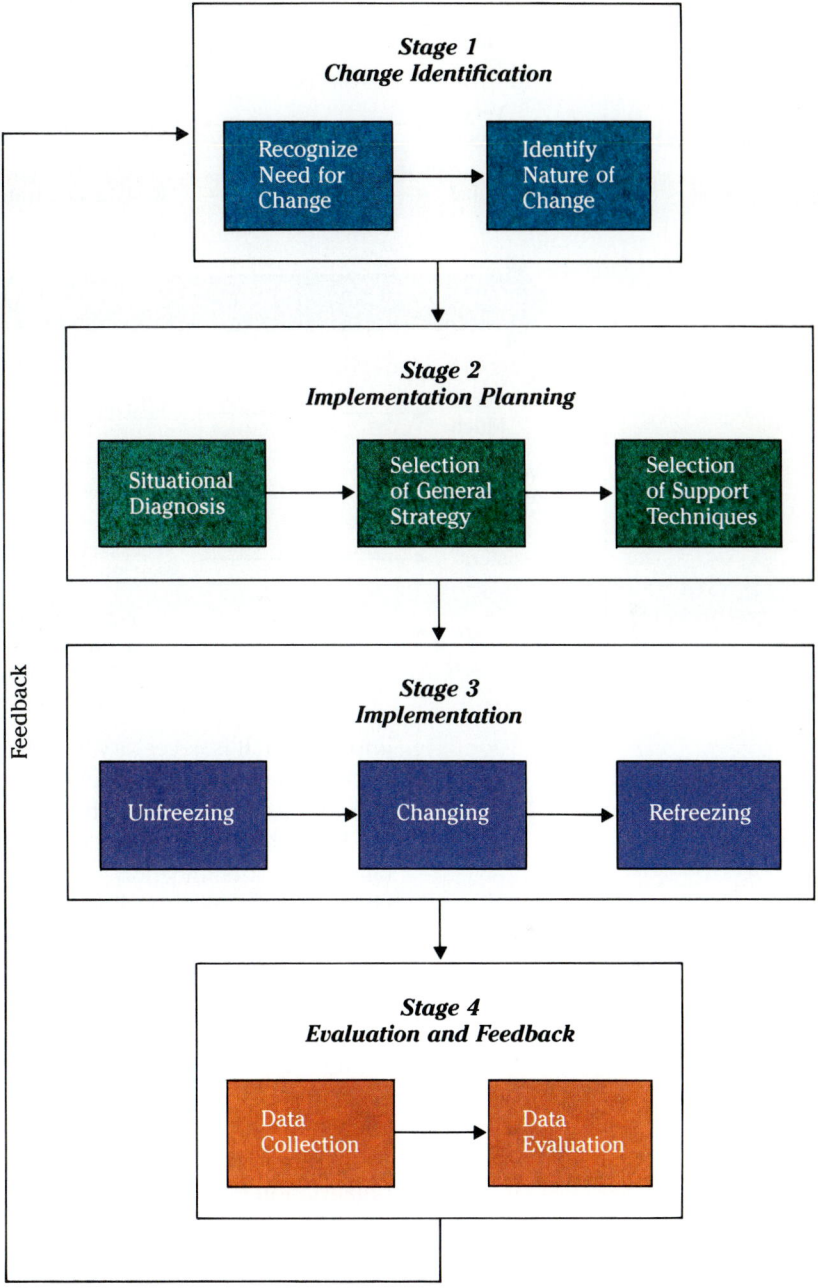

Implementation Planning

The second stage of the change process includes a diagnosis of the situation in which the change is likely to occur, the selection of a general strategy for managing the change, and the choice of specific techniques to be used to develop support for and reduce resistance to the change. The situational diagnosis involves the collection of a broad range of

FIGURE 20.7   *General Change Strategies*

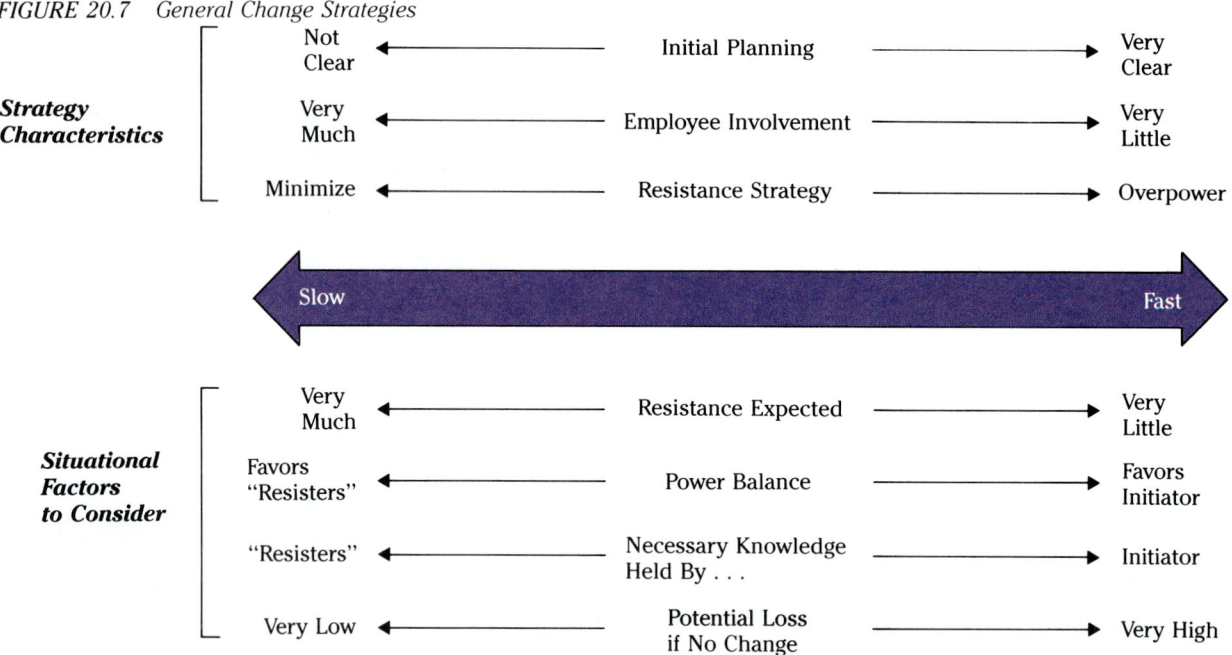

information. It is necessary, for example, to identify where the change will be implemented and which organization members will potentially be influenced by the change. It is also appropriate to identify who possesses the information needed to effectively design the change. Equally important is the identification of the key individuals who must support the change for it to work well and the identification of those who are likely to support or resist the change. It is critical not only to identify *who* is likely to support or resist the change, but to learn *why* they are expected to do so. Finally, further assessment should be made of the expected risk(s) and benefit(s) of making the change.

Next, a general change strategy should be selected (as shown in Figure 20.7). Decisions must be made, for example, concerning how quickly the change must be implemented. Furthermore, a decision must be made about how completely the plan should be designed before it is revealed to organization members. Also at this stage, initial decisions should be made about the desired level of participation and involvement of organization members. Finally, a decision should be made about whether resources will be expended to minimize resistance and develop support or used instead to overcome resistance should it emerge.

The final step of implementation planning involves the selection of techniques for developing support and reducing resistance. The information obtained from the situational diagnosis, along with the choice of a general change strategy, should aid in the selection of these techniques. In choosing from the available alternatives, care should be taken to construct what is most likely to become an effective package of techniques. An organization might, for example, choose to combine participation and involvement with the provision of facilitative support to encourage general support for an impending change that might be worrisome to employees.

Implementation

Once a change has been identified and implementation planning completed, it is time to finally implement the change. Psychologist Kurt Lewin has specified a widely accepted and very useful model for the implementation of change.[28] Lewin specifies three necessary steps for effective change implementation: unfreezing, changing, and refreezing.

The *unfreezing* component of change implementation involves the systematic upsetting of equilibrium between the forces driving change and those discouraging change. It is argued that the greater the dissatisfaction with the current state of affairs, the greater the motivation to change and the lower the resistance to change. When necessary, steps should be taken to *create* a need for change if it does not currently exist. One way to accomplish this is to provide members with information that will help them understand the need for change.[29] This information might consist of descriptions of the forces driving change, of the indicators that change is needed, and/or of the proposed change's potential for improvement over the status quo.

The second step identified by Lewin is referred to as *changing*. At this step, the change is introduced. If the change involves a new machine, it is put in place. If the change involves new work procedures, they are adopted. It is important that the changes be implemented only after unfreezing has occurred, or the organization and its members will not be ready for the change and will be more likely to resist it.

The final step identified by Lewin is known as *refreezing*. This involves taking action to restabilize the situation and encourage the long-term acceptance and success of the change. It is at this step that people involved in the change must become aware of and experience the positive consequences associated with the change.

Evaluation and Feedback

The final stage of the systematic management of change is extremely important for the long-term success of the organization. Unfortunately, it is the stage that is often overlooked by managers. In the first step of this stage, data should be collected to assess the degree to which the intended change was effectively implemented and to measure whether the specified objectives for the change were achieved.

The second and final step of Stage Four involves evaluation of the data collected. Here, managers should compare what was accomplished by the change to what was desired. When discrepancies exist, plans should be made for potential alterations of the change or processes by which the results of the change are managed. Based on this evaluation, feedback should be provided and, if necessary, the change process should begin again from Stage One.

Careful adherence to a systematic approach to the management of change (such as that presented here) can greatly increase your chances of being an effective change manager. Change must occur for organizations to succeed. Today, more than ever, a key factor that distinguishes effective managers from less effective managers is an ability to manage change well.

Organizational Change and Development in Review

This chapter observed that organizational change is occurring, will continue to occur, and must occur to maintain organizational effectiveness. A large amount of change occurs because of pressure from technological forces, employee needs and values, social forces, business and economic forces, and organizational forces.

It was noted that change can be reactive when the forces driving it are so strong that it becomes *necessary* to change. Change can be proactive when an organization assesses its status and concludes that change would be *desirable*. Innovation is a special type of change that occurs when an organization is the first or an early user of an idea.

A wide range of organizational change is possible. Some changes involve the introduction of new technologies; others focus primarily on organizational structure and procedures. Still other changes are people oriented. Many of the most effective changes—often referred to as technostructural or sociotechnical—involve combinations of these three types of change.

Many reactions to change are possible. A change might be actively resisted, actively supported, or anything in between. The reason for this is that people faced with a change react based on whether they expect to personally gain or lose something of value because of the change. Their reactions are also influenced by how well they understand the change, whether they trust the initiators of the change, and whether they agree to the advisability of the change. Finally, reactions to change are influenced by the personal characteristics of members.

The chapter discussed the importance of developing support for a change and reducing resistance and offered a number of suggestions for doing so. These suggestions included education and communication, participation and involvement, facilitative support, emotional support, incentives, manipulation and co-optation, and coercion. The strengths and potential drawbacks of each tactic were discussed, along with appropriate situations for their use.

The chapter briefly discussed the special role of organizational development. OD is "a process for diagnosing organizational problems by looking for incongruencies between environment, structures, processes, and people." OD systematically applies knowledge about change management to facilitate and enhance organizational effectiveness and the quality of the work experience for organization members. OD is still an evolving area that shows much promise for the future. Much of this promise will be realized only if individual managers embrace the concepts of OD.

Finally, the chapter presented a systematic procedure for planning and managing the change process. Four stages are included in this process, beginning with the identification of the nature of a change. Stage Two involves planning for implementation of the change. Stage Three comprises the actual implementation of the change. Stage Four involves the evaluation of the results of the change process and the identification of necessary fine-tuning for change.

In many ways, this chapter is the most important one in this text. If you have any ideas that are worth implementing, you must implement these ideas well or they will fail to realize their potential. It is clear that good ideas only work well when they are managed effectively. Regardless of your ultimate field of interest, you should recognize that one of the major factors that distinguishes excellent managers from adequate ones is the degree to which they are able to design and effectively manage organizational change.

Notes

1. H. J. Leavitt (1964), Applied organization change in industry: Structural, technical, and human approaches, in W. W. Cooper, H. J. Leavitt, and M. W. Shelly II, eds., *New perspectives in organization research,* New York: John Wiley & Sons, 55–71.
2. Will customers pledge Allegis? (May 1987), *OAG Frequent Flyer,* 30ff.
3. Based on a similar quote by J. L. Price (1972), *Handbook of organizational measurement,* Lexington, MA: D.C. Heath, 118.
4. This definition is consistent with that provided by S. W. Becker and T. L. Whisler (1967), The innovative organization: A selective view of current theory and research, *Journal of Business,* 40, 462–69.
5. F. Friedlander and L. D. Brown (1974), Organization development, *Annual Review of Psychology,* 25, 325.
6. Friedlander and Brown, 1974, 320.
7. Leavitt, 1964.
8. C. A. Carnall (1986), Toward a theory for the evaluation of organizational change, *Human Relations,* 39, 745–66.
9. Carnall, 1986.
10. B. Moore (1978), *Injustice: The social bases of obedience and revolt,* New York: MacMillan, 490.
11. Carnall, 1986, 756.
12. Many of the issues covered in this section are based on those discussed by J. P. Kotter and L. A. Schlesinger of Harvard University in (March/April 1979), Choosing strategies for change, *Harvard Business Review,* 106–13 and in J. P. Kotter, L. A. Schlesinger, and V. Sathe (1979), *Organization: Text, cases, and readings on the management of organizational design and change,* Homewood, IL: Irwin. In addition, both Kotter and Schlesinger graciously submitted to interviews with one of the authors of this text to discuss some of their ideas. It should be noted that these authors organized these issues somewhat differently and focused primarily on reasons for resistance. Treatment of these issues in this textbook has been expanded to include reasons for support as well as for resistance.
13. L. W. Mealiea (1978), Learned behavior: The key to understanding and preventing employee resistance to change, *Group & Organization Studies,* 3, 211–23.
14. P. E. Connor (1988), Strategies for managing technological change, *Harvard International Review,* 10(2), 11.

15. Connor, 1988, 10.

16. Mealiea, 1978.

17. Some of these are based on Kotter and Schlesinger, Choosing strategies for change, 11.

18. M. Beer (1980), *Organization change and development: A systems view,* Santa Monica, CA: Goodyear, 7; M. Beer and A. E. Walton (1987), Organization change and development, *Annual Review of Psychology,* 38, 339–40.

19. M. Sashkin and W. W. Burke (1987), Organization development in the 1980's, *Journal of Management,* 13, 410.

20. Sashkin and Burke, 1987, 393–417.

21. M. Beer and B. Spector (1985), Corporate-wide transformations, in R. Walton and P. Lawrence, eds., *HRM trends and challenges,* Boston: Harvard Business School Press.

22. W. L. French and C. H. Bell, Jr. (1978), *Organizational development: Behavioral science interventions for organization improvement,* 2nd ed., Englewood Cliffs, NJ: Prentice-Hall.

23. Z. E. Barnes (February 1987), Visions, values, and strategies: Changing attitudes and culture, *The Academy of Management Executive,* 33–42; R. N. Beck (February 1987), The theory practice gap: Myth or reality? *The Academy of Management Executive,* 31–32; J. J. Renier (February 1987), Turnaround of information systems at Honeywell, *The Academy of Management Executive,* 47–50.

24. B. A. Macy, C. C. M. Hurts, H. Izumi, L. W. Norton, and R. R. Smith, (1986), *An assessment of U.S. work improvement and productivity efforts: 1970–1985,* 46th Annual Academy of Management Convention, Chicago, IL; J. Nicholas (1982), The comparative impact of organization development interventions on hard criteria measures, *Academy of Management Review,* 9, 531–43; W. M. Vicars and D. D. Hartke (1984), Evaluating OD evaluations: A status report, *Group Organizational Studies,* 9, 177–88.

25. Nicholas, 1982, 540.

26. Beer and Walton, 1987, 362.

27. P. Buller (Winter 1988), For successful strategic change: Blend OD practices with strategic management, *Organizational Dynamics,* 43.

28. K. Lewin (1947), Frontiers in group dynamics, *Human Relations,* 1, 5–41; K. Lewin (1951), *Field theory in social science,* New York: Harper & Row.

29. W. G. Bennis, D. E. Berlew, E. H. Schein, and F. I. Steele (1973), *Interpersonal dynamics: Essays and readings on human interaction,* Homewood, IL: Dorsey Press; D. A. Nadler (1981), Managing organizational change: An integrative perspective, *The Journal of Applied Behavioral Science,* 17, 191–211.

Key Terms

internal forces	innovation
external forces	technostructural changes
reactive change	sociotechnical changes
proactive change	

Issues for Review and Discussion

1. Describe how the five forces to change combine to create the need for organizational change.

2. Why is it important to differentiate planned (proactive) change from reactive change?

3. If your college proposed a major change in the grading system so that all courses would be graded pass/fail only, do you think all students would react to this proposed change in an identical fashion? Consider the various underlying causes for reactions to change discussed in this chapter, and explain why you would expect a variety of reactions.

4. Briefly describe which of the techniques for developing support for change discussed in this chapter might be useful for an organization planning to change from traditional assembly-line production to a heavily automated operation.

5. Prepare a brief presentation explaining why Organizational Development should be required training for all managers.

6. Prepare a brief presentation explaining why Organizational Development *should not* be required training for all managers.

7. In your own words, summarize the systematic procedure, presented in this chapter, for the planning and managing of organizational change. Briefly note why each stage and each step is necessary.

Suggested Readings

Beer, M. and Walton, A. E. (1987). Organization change and development. *Annual Review of Psychology,* 38, 339–40.

Buller, P. (Winter 1988). For successful strategic change: Blend OD practices with strategic management. *Organizational Dynamics,* 42–55.

Connor, P. E. (1988). Strategies for managing technological change. *Harvard International Review,* 10(2), 10–13, 42.

Connor, P. E. and Lake, L. K. (1988). *Managing organizational change.* New York: Praeger.

Kanter, R. M. (1985). *The change masters.* New York: Touchstone.

Kilmann, R. H., Covin, T. J., and Associates (1988). *Corporate transformation.* San Francisco: Jossey-Bass.

Naisbitt, J. and Aburdene, R. (1985). *Re-inventing the corporation.* New York: Warner; Boal, K. (1988). A review of *Re-Inventing the corporation.* In Pierce, J. L. and Newstrom, J. W., eds. *The manager's bookshelf: A mosaic of contemporary views.* New York: Harper & Row, 275–81.

Sashkin, M. and Burke, W. W. (1987). Organization development in the 1980s. *Journal of Management,* 13, 393–417.

CASE *Guarantee Corporation of America*

*By Randall B. Dunham of the
University of Wisconsin*

The Guarantee Corporation of America (GCA) was founded in Denver, Colorado, in 1958. The company developed, marketed, and supported a single product: mortgage insurance. This product protected the lender should a borrower default on a mortgage loan. The willingness of lenders to make loans with as little as a 5-percent downpayment greatly increased the number of mortgages being issued, and the desire of lenders to reduce their risk on such loans made mortgage insurance attractive. Soon, most lenders required mortgage insurance when downpayments were less than 20 percent of the purchase price of a home. What was the catch for borrowers? They had to pay the cost of the mortgage insurance, a condition most first-time home buyers considered fair and one that lenders and GCA found great. GCA did quite well, competing effectively in the booming market created by the expanding population and the growing desire of baby boomers to buy homes as soon as they could possibly afford to do so. In fact, GCA did so well that a large financial corporation bought the company in 1975 and continued to operate it as GCA, a wholly owned subsidiary.

GCA maintained its home offices in Denver, but about half of its 250 employees were spread across the country where they could better sell and service policies. All administrative (filing, reporting, clerical, and secretarial) services were performed by a centralized office administration department in Denver. The manager of this department, Mary-Jo Kovach, joined GCA in 1982 as an accountant and was promoted to management in 1985.

When the company conducted an employee attitude survey in June 1986, the survey of the twenty members of the office administration department, as a group, had the following results: satisfaction with physical work conditions, pay, promotional opportunities, and the work itself was a little above company averages; satisfaction with co-workers and supervision was far above company averages; and satisfaction with amount of work and company policies and practices was noticeably below company averages. Group cohesion was the highest of any department in the company.

Mary-Jo was proud of her department and her work. She felt her group was performing well, especially in light of the fact that conditions were considerably less than ideal. By January 1987, her comments to a friend showed her rising concern over the situation:

When I accepted this promotion, I didn't realize what I was getting myself into. My department is understaffed and constantly subjected to conflicting demands from the marketing and policy services departments. My boss tells me to give equal treatment to both departments, but each acts as though the other doesn't exist. Worse, both act as if we do nothing but wait for them to drop work into our laps. Expectations for turnaround time on correspondence, major reports, and other information processing are totally unrealistic. I do everything I can to protect the members of my department from unreasonable demands, even though this sometimes makes us appear unresponsive to the needs of the people we are here to serve. Some days the stress gets to me so much that my stomach is just tied up in knots. Given the circumstances, we are doing an exemplary job, but nobody appreciates this.

When Carolyn Larson became executive vice-president of GCA in April 1987, she held a series of group meetings with members of each department to seek information on the "state of the company." She heard many favorable comments about the quality of the GCA product, the superb sales force, and the appropriateness of GCA's strategic and operational plans. She also heard the following from Bob Ley, Vice-President of Marketing:

Our office administration department is a joke. I can't tell you how many potential sales we have lost because they failed to get our proposals out on time. Every time I send work over, I tell them it is a top priority but they seem to treat every piece of work as though it's just another meaningless task. What really irritates me is when they do the unimportant work and leave the important stuff undone. I don't get it—what's wrong with them?

Dave Womble, vice president of policy services, added his comments:

I hate to be blunt but Mary-Jo has got to go. Her department doesn't have to sell policies, and they don't have to service them. All they have to do is keep track of them, and they can't even do that. What's needed for that department is a manager who is not afraid to manage employees. Mary-Jo spends too much time protecting her underlings and not enough time demanding work out of them.

When Carolyn followed up with Mary-Jo to get her response to the comments from Bob and Dave, Mary-Jo said:

I can understand how Bob and Dave would feel that way. To tell you the truth, I don't think we are meeting their needs well, but they do little to help. Telling me everything is a top priority doesn't help me plan. We are understaffed, underrespected, and I must admit, poorly organized. I would like to turn the department around, and I think I could if I could get some help and support to do so.

Based on this and other input, Carolyn decided to give Mary-Jo a chance to turn her department around. She told Mary-Jo that if she would make a wholehearted effort to succeed, she would have Carolyn's full support. Specifically, Mary-Jo would have to produce within two months:

1. A rank-ordered list of the primary problems her department encountered in trying to meet the needs of the company

2. A rank-ordered list of the primary internal problems within her department

3. A list of criteria against which the effectiveness of the department should be evaluated

4. A strategic plan for developing the department into an effective group

5. A plan for implementing the strategic plan

6. A strategy for assessing the degree to which the plan worked

The next morning, when Carolyn arrived at work, she found Mary-Jo's office empty of all personal effects and the following note:

Dear Ms. Larson:

I wish you the best of luck in managing the operations of GCA. I have been managing the office administration department as effectively as was humanly possible, given the unreasonable demands placed on the department and the lack of adequate top managerial support. What you have asked me to do in two months in addition to my current overwhelming responsibilities is exactly what you should have done to help my department succeed. Asking me to do your work for you is of little help. It is with deepest regret that I resign my position with GCA, effective immediately.

Sincerely,

Mary-Jo Kovach

Mary-Jo Kovach

Questions

1. What would you have done if you were Mary-Jo?

2. Did Carolyn do the right thing? What would you have advised her to do?

3. Using the model for planning and managing change presented in this chapter and any other resources you feel necessary, describe how the six items presented to Mary-Jo by Carolyn could be addressed.

4. Who from GCA should be involved in addressing the six items?

PART 6

Special Topics

MANAGER PROFILE

Mary Kay Ash

Her organization is characterized by a humanistic management philosophy. A free and entrepreneurial spirit is encouraged and rewarded, and emphasis is placed on self-esteem, self-confidence, and an endless stream of self-competition. She motivates her employees with public praise and an elaborate reward system. Rewards of increasing value are given for increasing performance, and as employees climb upward, pins, diamonds, fur coats, and pink cadillacs await them. If a person slips downward while trying to achieve, the rewards slide down as well. The system is designed so that people can compete with themselves, not with others or with a bureaucratically defined performance standard. People set goals, compete with themselves, and are rewarded for their effort and performance.

> *She motivates her employees with public praise and an elaborate reward system.*

The founder and chairperson of this organization is its corporate symbol, its heroine. The company is Mary Kay Cosmetics, and the woman at the helm is Mary Kay Ash. A woman with an entrepreneurial spirit—a sense of drive, the need to succeed, and a strong sense of self-confidence—born out of a need to overcome myriad obstacles confronted during childhood, Ash developed a "you can do it" conviction. This conviction is the cornerstone of her cosmetics empire.

As a young child, Ash nursed her tubercular father, cleaned house, cooked, and attended school while her mother worked long days managing a restaurant. "When I was growing up, we had very little and I had to work hard. That experience made me want to excel and to work hard. We had plenty of love and my mother always encouraged me by saying, 'You can do it, Mary Kay! . . . You can do it.'" Sacrifice and hardship carried her past high-school graduation, when a lack of money prompted her to go to work instead of to college. Starting out as a salesperson with Stanley Home Products, it was not long before she was recognized as one of Stanley's top performers.

While achieving forms of personal success at work, Ash continued to face a series of hardships. Divorce, rheumatoid arthritis, an emotional breakdown, and facial paralysis scarred her life and yet made her strong in a unique way. She has woven this strength of character into her management style and organizational culture. Ash developed a strong sense of competitiveness and a desire for recognition. In 1963 she founded Mary Kay Cosmetics, Inc. Today as founder and chairperson, she heads an organization with over $300 million in revenue, selling a facial care system to over 180,000 beauty consultants.

Self-competition, rewards for achievement (once a year at the annual Mary Kay seminar, diamonds, mink coats, and "Mary Kay Pink" cadillacs are presented), and peer recognition are an integral part of her management system. Her objective is to create a work environment that encourages and brings out the best in people. She awards people with the diamond bumblebee, which symbolizes the personal ability to overcome great odds—aerodynamically the bumblebee cannot fly, yet it does. Ash attempts to bring out this spirit in the people with whom she works. Her management style emphasizes the creation of a humanistic work environment in which self-strength is a core component.

William MacPhee writes that entrepreneurs are characterized by vision, resourcefulness, and self-confidence. They are risk takers—managers of odds, constraints, and obstacles. They are the types of people who make things happen. As a manager, Ash values goal setting and self- and time management. She manages her own day with a set of goals and an agenda that tackles the most challenging task first. Her problem-solving style consists of breaking problems down into manageable pieces, so that they can be dealt with one issue (piece) at a time until the entire problem has been resolved.

Entrepreneurial spirit is valued in the Mary Kay organization. People are encouraged to establish their own goals and try to exceed them. Achievement is nurtured, while control that stems from the bureaucracy is minimized. Ash's operating philosophy encourages striking a balance between the need to nurture the entrepreneurial spirit and certain elements of managerial necessity.

"By eliminating stress . . . you can . . . inspire productivity."

It has been said that Ash's management style is built around seven basic principles, the Mary Kay "Golden Rules of Management":

1. *Recognize the value of people:* "People are your company's number one asset. When you treat them as you would like to be treated yourself, everyone benefits."

2. *Praise your people to success:* "Recognition is the most powerful of all motivators. Even criticism can build confidence when it's 'sandwiched' between layers of praise."

3. *Tear down the ivory tower:* "Keep all doors open. Be accessible to everyone. Remember that every good manager is a good listener."

4. *Be a risk taker:* "Don't be afraid. Encourage your people to take risks, too, and allow room for error."

5. *Create a stress-free workplace:* "By eliminating stress factors, fear of the boss, [and] unreasonable deadlines, [etc.] . . . you can increase and inspire productivity."

6. *Develop and promote people from within:* "Upward mobility for employees in your company builds loyalty. People give you their best when they know they'll be rewarded."

7. *Keep business in the proper place:* "At Mary Kay Cosmetics, the order of priorities is faith, family and career. The real key to success is creating an environment where people are encouraged to balance the many aspects of their life."

MacPhee concludes his look at Ash and her company by noting that "Mary Kay Cosmetics has a people philosophy." The organizational culture is one that "encourages self-esteem and self-confidence" through its slogan, "You can do it." Management encourages "free spirited [and] visionary thinking."

Source: W. MacPhee (1987), *Rare breed: The entrepreneurs, an American culture,* Chapter 2, Chicago, IL: Probus, 21–36.

Management Information Systems (MIS)

Student Learning Objectives

After reading this chapter, you should be able to:

1. Understand what a management information system is.

2. Understand the components of a system.

3. Explain the purpose of an MIS.

4. Understand the relationship between an MIS and various stages in the decision-making process.

5. Explain how an MIS can serve as a support system.

6. Understand the relationship between an MIS and routine and nonroutine decisions.

7. Understand artificial intelligence and expert systems.

By Thomas Duff of the University of Minnesota at Duluth

*I*t has become clear that a third certainty can be added to the two that Benjamin Franklin identified over 200 years ago, near the end of the eighteenth century. At that time, Franklin said that the only two certainties in life are "death and taxes." Today almost all Americans would add "change" to Franklin's list.

In the preface to his book *The Future of American Business*, the futurist, Marvin Cetron, said that "countries, companies, and individuals will endure wrenching transitions as the twentieth century gives way to the twenty-first." He also stated his belief that the rate of technological change will not slow down but will, in fact, increase so that "the tempo of change will be absolutely blistering." The certainty and rapidity of change will probably have a greater impact on managers and management practices than on society in general. According to Cetron:

> *This will put a premium on management's ability to make speedy decisions. At the same time, the stakes riding on those decisions will climb because more activities will become increasingly capital-intensive. Running tomorrow's companies won't be a task for the timid.*[1]

Ironically, one of the factors perpetrating the rapidity of change in general—technology—will be the tool that contributes most to managers' ability to make speedy decisions based on timely and accurate information.

It is becoming increasingly difficult to find an organization that does not have one or more computers at its location or access to one at another location. The decreasing cost and overall improvements in computer and communications technologies have made them a part of most organizations. Where computers are present, most of the information about an organization's activities is increasingly being provided by computer-based information systems. For example, most of the crucial information about a retail grocery store's operation is computer based today. Information about inventory levels, stock ordering, advertising expenses and results, unit and dollar sales volume, employee work schedules, payroll, and other planning and control functions are all computer based. As computers have become more intricately involved in the processing, storing, and distributing of information, more attention has been paid to developing formal systems of organizing and managing organizational information. As managers become more actively involved in using the formal systems, the systems started to be called *management information systems*.

The decreasing cost and overall improvements in computer technology have made it a part of most organizations.

What Is a Management Information System?

There may be as many different definitions or descriptions of an MIS as there are textbooks written on the topic. Some people prefer to use a very short, simple definition; others insist on a longer definition laced with technological jargon. Stated most simply, a **management information system** is a system that provides managers with information that enables them to make better decisions and to improve their job performance.

An MIS provides managers with information that enables them to make better decisions and to improve their job performance.

The idea of an organization having an MIS has been around for a long time. Managers have always sought as much information as possible to make decisions while carrying out their planning, organizing, directing, and controlling activities at various levels in an organization. A variety of manual tools and methods were used to create and distribute information before the advent of office machines, such as typewriters, electronic calculators, and copiers. The increasing use of machines changed the type of information provided to managers and the way it was provided. As noted, the pervasiveness of the computer and telecommunications technologies in today's organizations has changed information systems even more dramatically. You will read more about why computer hardware and software are important parts of the MIS in contemporary organizations later in this chapter. For now, you might think about why the word *computer* does not appear in the definition of MIS used here.

Since the words *managers*, *information*, and *systems* are used in the definition of an MIS, it would seem that they must be an integral part of the concept. The next sections define and discuss how *information* and *system* are usually defined by those who develop and maintain an MIS.

Information

You have probably heard or read about things like the information explosion or information society. While you may have a general idea of what those things mean, how would you define *information?*

As it will be used in this chapter, **information** consists of meaningful data. Data are basic facts or figures. More accurately, some people feel, **data** are representations of facts pertaining to people, things, ideas, and events. The facts are represented by symbols, such as numerals or letters of the alphabet. Data can be groups of symbols combined in a particular way. The words you are reading now consist of data—alphabetic symbols combined to represent facts.

In order to get information from data, they must be processed and presented in a way that a user finds meaningful. The foundation of any information system is data processing. It is hoped, for example, that the combinations of data you are reading have been processed and are being presented in a way that makes them meaningful to you. As you read the words, you are taking in data, processing them, and trying to derive meaning from them. The mental data-processing techniques you use are much more complicated than even those used by the most sophisticated computers available today. The goal of your processing activities and that of a computer are the same, however; both are trying to make data meaningful or to create new information from them.

Like alphabetic characters, numerals are data until they are processed or combined so they become meaningful. When a person buys something with a charge card at a department store, several data items represented by numerals are collected. The credit card or account number, an identification number for the purchased article, the article's price, the amount of tax, and the total amount of the charge are recorded. Each of these is a meaningless data item individually. When they are combined in a particular manner and recorded together, they become information about a business transaction.[2]

Even small organizations collect and process large amounts of data as they complete their production and marketing activities, keep track of customer and employee activities, make and receive payments, and carry out other activities. To be useful, all of these data must be accurately recorded after they are collected and must be organized and stored so that they can be easily processed and become meaningful data— information. All data related to a certain transaction or individual are combined to create a record; closely related records are combined to form a file. The data in all the records and files are considered to be the base of an organization's data, sometimes called its *database*.

Organizations collect and process large amounts of data as they make and receive payments.

Almost all routine business data-processing activities are done by computers today because machines can do them much faster and with greater accuracy than humans can. One of the most important contributions computer technology and software have made to the area of information systems is the development of the database concept. As used in computer jargon, a **database** is an organization's computer data files that are structured and stored so they can be easily processed and used by those who need information about the organization. The power and processing speed of computers have been primarily responsible for the increasing amount of information available to managers in organizations and to society in general. As the amount of information has increased, organizations have found it necessary and beneficial to study different ways of systematically organizing and distributing it. This has resulted in an increased interest in the terminology and development of systems within organizations.

Systems

In simple terms, a **system** is a set of related parts that work together in an organized way to achieve a stated purpose or purposes. The parts are often called *components*, and their relationship is described as being interdependent or dynamically linked. Each one affects and is affected by the other components.

You live and work in a variety of systems. For example, there are legal, economic, and political systems. Business firms and other organizations have systems that are more familiar to those who work in them. Accounting, inventory, and payroll systems are smaller, less complex systems than an economic system, for example and people deal with them more directly. General systems theory, first formulated by von Bertalanffy in the 1930s, identifies and describes principles that are applicable to systems in general. He felt that there were models, principles, and laws that apply to systems or to their components no matter what the particular discipline (physical, biological, or social), the nature of the components, or their interrelationships.[3]

The eight basic characteristics of a system are shown in Figure 21.1. An organizational system has a long-term purpose (or purposes) and short-term goals or objectives. The goals or objectives are developed to achieve an organization's purpose. The purpose and goals or objectives provide a basis for determining how well the system is functioning. There is input to the system—people, machines, material, energy, capital, and the like. The system's components perform the processing (transforming) of input into outputs. The basic components of a system are people, machines, buildings, and so on. There are, of course, interactions and interrelation-

FIGURE 21.1
The Characteristics of a System

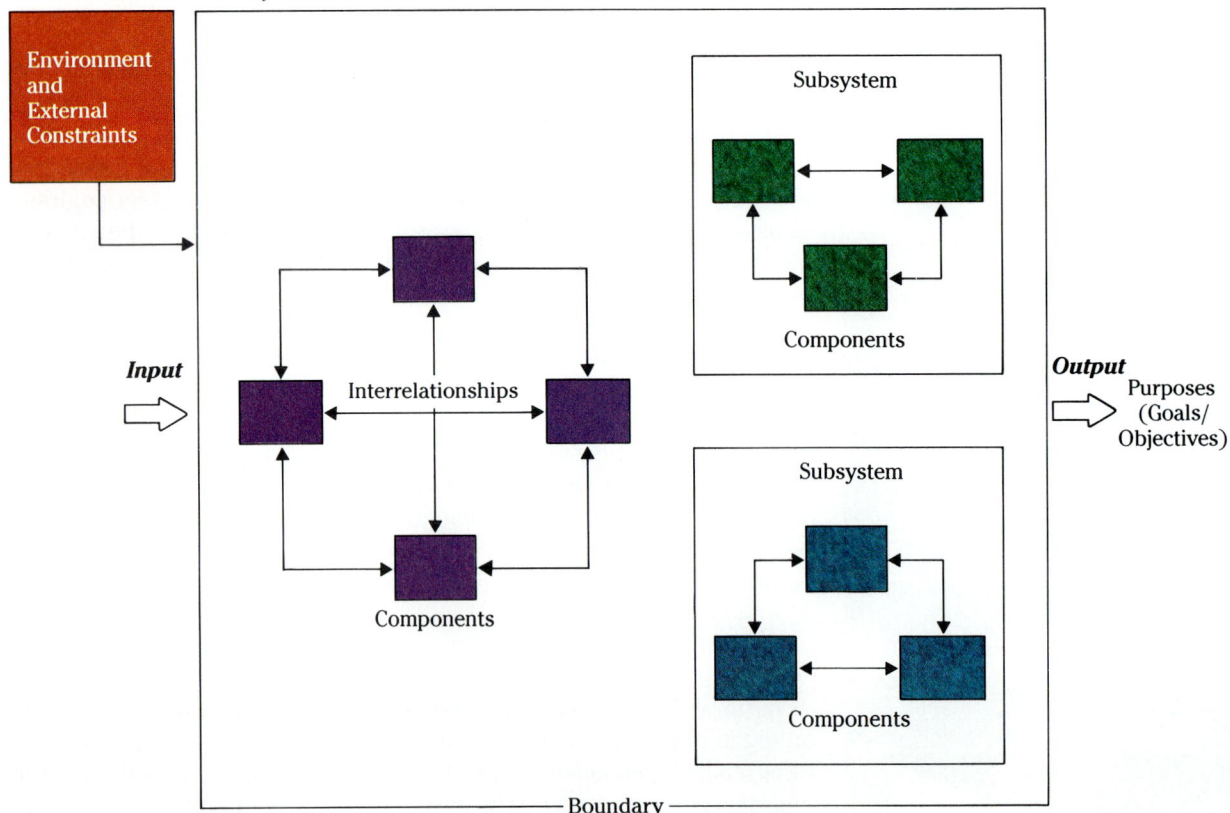

Source: Adapted from M. Ahituv and S. Neumann (1986), *Information systems for management*, 2nd ed., Dubuque, IA: Wm. C. Brown, 83.

ships among these components. The boundaries of a system define its limits. The system is inside, and the environment in which the system exists is outside the boundaries. Determining the boundaries is sometimes difficult. Each system is affected by external constraints imposed by its environment. For example, businesses must cope with rules and regulations established by federal and state agencies for hiring, safety, and a variety of other activities. Finally, note that there are usually several subsystems within a system. The process of systems analysis consists of breaking down systems into their subsystems and studying their components and the nature of their interrelationships until the smallest subsystems needed are identified.

The college or university where you are completing this class is an example of a system. One of its major purposes is to improve society in general. It has probably set some research and service goals or objectives that will benefit the local community, the state, and perhaps the nation or the world, depending on its size and overall mission. The school's goal or objective with which you are most familiar and that most directly affects you is the one related to educating people. For this particular goal or objective, the process is called *education*. Students like you are the input; professors, support staff, classrooms, computers, and printed material are the components; and people with baccalaureate or graduate degrees are the outputs. There is a variety of interrelationships among the system components, of course, and there are physical boundaries as well as boundaries for the system's activities. Colleges and universities function in specific geographical, political, and educational environments that impose constraints on the system in general. Government rules and regulations related to student financial aid, admission standards, and affirmative action are examples. For public institutions, an annual operating budget allocation from the state legislature is a significant constraint. Finally, the system of one campus may be operating as a subsystem of a larger overall system, and there are subsystems functioning on each campus.

There are probably separate subsystems for the academic, student-life, business, and plant-services activities on most campuses, and each of these subsystems can be broken down into smaller, more specific subsystems. For example, the academic subsystem on a campus usually functions under a unit called Academic Affairs, or something similar, that consists of the various collegiate units. These units carry such titles as Business, Liberal Arts, Science and Engineering, Education, and so on. Each of these collegiate units or subsystems is made up of departments or programs. Accounting, Economics, Finance, Management, and Marketing are common names for departments in a School or College of Business. Art, Chemistry, English, Mathematics, Music, Physical Education, and other such departments are subsystems in other collegiate units.

From your point of view, it may be most important that data representing the fact that you completed this course be recorded on your transcript. For the system as a whole, it is very important that enrollment data for you and others in this course be accurately reported by department, collegiate unit, and campus. This and other types of data are processed to provide information used by the system's managers as they plan, organize, direct, and control the resources and activities in the academic subsystem and the subsystems within this unit.

The amount and type of computer hardware and software can provide clues to the quality of an MIS.

The Purpose of an MIS

The ultimate purpose of an MIS is to improve job performance and decision making in an organization. An MIS is developed and operated to improve the performance of managers and by providing them with the information they need to make decisions. An MIS should provide the type of information top management needs to develop long-range plans and objectives for an organization. It should also provide information that will help managers organize, direct, and control their organization's resources so they are used most efficiently and effectively to achieve those objectives.

The amount and type of computer hardware and software and the speed with which a system can process data may provide some clues to the quality of an MIS; however, the most important criterion for judging the success of an MIS is its ability to support the improved performance of the people in the organization in which it is operating.[4] It is generally agreed that one of the keys to improving the performance of managers in today's organizations is to "get the right information to the right person at the right time." One might sum up the purpose of an MIS in precisely that way.

Providing Appropriate Information to Managers

Managers at all levels are involved to varying degrees in planning, organizing, directing, and controlling activities in an organization. Since the ultimate goal of an MIS is to help managers improve their performance, it should provide them with the information they need to carry out their managerial activities. That is easier said than done, however. Managers in each of the functional areas and at each of the hierarchical levels in an organization may require some special information to aid them in making decisions unique to their particular position.

Except in very small organizations, there are at least several different managers. Each may be responsible for making decisions related to specific functional areas and at different hierarchical levels in the organization. A production manager and a marketing manager in the same firm may use some of the same information, for example; however, they will also want some very different information, or at least will want it presented in a different way, as they plan, organize, direct, and control the resources and activities unique to their respective functional areas. A first-line supervisor at a furniture company needs detailed information, such as raw materials requirements, personnel availability, and shipping dates to direct and control the production of sofas. The president of the company, on the other hand, may be interested in furniture sales trends in general, the availability and price of timber, and the predictions for general economic activity in the nation in making long-range plans for the organization.

Even at the same hierarchical level in the same unit, there may be different amounts of time devoted to planning, organizing, directing, and controlling activities by different managers. Also, as you are aware, one of the key distinctions between managers at different levels is the amount of time they spend at each of the different managerial activities. An information system, therefore, must be designed to serve many different managerial needs for information.

What factors determine the kind of information managers need to make decisions and how can an MIS be used to provide the appropriate information? The next sections attempt to answer that question by discussing how the MIS concept relates to the decision-making process identified by Herbert Simon and the various types of managerial activity identified by Robert Anthony.

The Decision-Making Process

Research has shown that a stimulus makes a person aware that a decision must be made. Three general types of situations trigger the decision-making process: the belief that a problem exists, the emergence of a crisis, or the availability of an opportunity. It is in these contexts that managers, like others, seek information. They need information to help them make decisions about how to solve problems, resolve crises, or take advantage of opportunities.

Once a stimulus signals the need to make a decision, the process continues through three stages, according to Herbert Simon—the intelligence, design, and choice stages. An organization's MIS should collect and process data to provide information that will help managers during all three stages.

Intelligence   During the intelligence stage, a decision maker collects, classifies, processes, and arranges information so that it is available for use during the next two stages of the process. In Simon's description, the term *intelligence* is used as it is in the military. The basic purpose of this stage is to gather information to determine as accurately as possible what is going on internally (within the system or subsystem) and in the general external environment of the sociocultural, economic, technological, legal/political, or international domains. It may gather such information itself, obtain it from government agencies, or purchase it from one of the many private firms that collect and sell such information as a service to others.

Managers receive periodic reports that are routinely produced and distributed by their organization's data-processing, or information-services, unit. These reports provide periodic information about such things as quantities or dollar value of goods or services produced and sold and the cost of raw materials, human resources, and other things used to produce and sell them. The content of the reports, as well as the number and frequency of them, should be based on an analysis of the needs of the managers in the organization. These reports provide much of the information managers seek during the intelligence stage.

Periodic reports are usually designed to meet the perceived needs of several managers in an organization. To best serve the perceived intelligence needs of each manager, however, an MIS should also provide an opportunity for the manager to collect additional information. An MIS should allow each manager to easily access, combine, and manipulate as much information as he or she feels is needed to provide the most accurate picture of a problem or opportunity and the internal and external environment in which an upcoming decision will be made.

In today's organizations, most of the information managers seek during the intelligence stage is gathered and presented by a computer-based system. Managers who are not able to use terminals or microcomputer technology to access the computer-based system directly are dependent on others to get the information they desire. Managers who are familiar with and able to use the technology of the computer-based system can search through the available information in whatever way they feel will generate the most meaningful results. This provides them with an advantage in securing the type of information they feel will best help describe the conditions under which they must make planning, organizing, directing, and controlling decisions.

Design During the design stage, the decision maker and others outline alternative sets of action that can be taken to address the problem or opportunity, given the conditions identified during the intelligence stage. Each of the possible alternatives is assessed to determine the pros and cons on the basis of established criteria. The data and information collected during the first stage—about the organization's activities and the environment in which it is functioning—are now used in various ways to try to forecast the outcomes of the alternatives.

To assist managers at this stage, an MIS should provide planning and forecasting models that are easy to use and understand. Management-science and information-system professionals have developed programmed models and analytic tools to forecast, predict, and assess outcomes. In order to use these successfully, managers must know enough about the models and tools to be able to select the appropriate one for each situation, and they must have accurate data and information for the variables involved. They may be directly involved in entering the data and running the models, or they may simply be provided with the results.

In addition to allowing them to search, combine, and manipulate data to meet their unique needs, current database systems allow managers to develop their own models. Models are built in the computer by writing program commands using English words and syntax, which are more familiar than those required in a procedural programming language, such

LOTUS is a popular and powerful design-stage tool. It can be used on microcomputers and is relatively easy to learn and to use.

as COBOL. A manager develops a model using commands from a "Fourth-Generation Language" (4GL), such as IFPS (Interactive Financial Planning System) or Focus. These systems and their 4GLs enable users to develop a model for a situation based on their understanding of current and future conditions. LOTUS and other electronic spreadsheets are also popular design-stage tools because they are powerful planning devices, they can be used on microcomputers, and they are relatively easy to learn and to use. An MIS assists managers in the design stage by providing them with information and tools or the ability to gather information and develop tools that can be used to identify, explore, and assess the possible outcomes of as many alternative actions as the managers wish.

If more information about the problem, opportunity, or internal or external conditions is needed at this stage, the manager can return to the intelligence stage. Herbert Simon views the decision-making process as a series of loops through the intelligence and design stages rather than a sequential process. In other words, managers can return to the intelligence stage and gather additional information from the database if they feel it is necessary to do so to satisfy their needs at the design stage.

Finally, it is important to note that the models and analytic tools an MIS provides for use during the design stage do not replace human decisions makers; they aid or support managers at this stage. It is appropriately descriptive that the term *decision support system* (DSS) is frequently used to describe these and other tools used in the design and choice stages.[5]

Choice   Choosing a set of actions to take is the final stage in Herbert Simon's model. No matter how much quantitative and statistical analysis can be done in a situation, decisions often come down to qualitative judgments by those who must make a final choice. This occurs for many reasons. First, the trade-offs among alternatives are not always easy to measure in monetary terms. Second, because decisions in the areas of planning and organizing are usually based on the future, uncertain outcomes are involved, and the probabilities of their occurring are often assigned subjectively. In addition, there are usually conflicting interests among those who have helped move the process through the intelligence and design stages. The more people involved in making recommendations on a final choice, the more the probability of disagreement increases because there are more interests represented and more subjective judgments involved.

Given this situation, it is difficult to say how an MIS can provide support at this stage; however, there are some simulation tools and other software packages that can help by providing answers to "what-if" questions. For example, a model might be built with IFPS and used to project what would happen to total revenue, costs, and profits in an organization if there was an increase or decrease in the rate of inflation or federal income taxes. Depending on the product or service involved, it might be based on the number of cars sold, the birth rate in a region or state, or the number of new homes built during a certain period of time.

Because the role of an MIS is one of support at this stage, the tools used are considered to be part of the decision support system also. There is a considerable amount of research and development activity among MIS and computer professionals related to providing support tools to aid managers in the choice stage. They have been trying to develop tools that mimic how humans make the final choice in the decision-making stage. Artificial intelligence and expert systems, which will be discussed later in this chapter, are two areas in which research and development have been involved. Again, it is important to note that final choices are made by humans; machines and software packages only provide support for human decision makers.

Routine and Nonroutine Decisions

Herbert Simon and others who investigated the decision-making process made another important contribution to MIS development by identifying the differences between routine (programmed) and non-routine (nonprogrammed) decisions. According to Simon:

> *Decisions are programmed to the extent that they are repetitive and routine, to the extent that a definite procedure has been worked out for handling them so that they don't have to be treated* de novo *each time they occur . . . Decisions are nonprogrammed to the extent that they are novel, unstructured, and consequential. There is no cut-and-dried method of handling the problem because it hasn't arisen before or because its precise nature and structure are elusive or complex, or because it is so important that it deserves a custom-tailored treatment.*[6]

The terms *structured* and *nonstructured* are also commonly used to describe the two general categories of decisions identified by Simon. As you would expect, decisions do not usually fall clearly into a category. Instead, decisions can be placed somewhere on a continuum running from routine to nonroutine, and the role of an MIS changes as the nature of each decision shifts.

Routine Decisions   Routine decisions are usually quantitative in nature; the factors involved and the outcomes can be clearly defined, and the timelines involved are usually short. Such decisions are based on clear logic, are repetitive, and are made at low levels in an organization. In essence, the conditions under which they are made are very structured. Examples of routine decisions include when to send an overdue notice to a customer, when to reorder an inventory item, what premium to charge an insured party, and when to buy or sell a stock. As Herbert Simon's terminology implies, routine decisions are those for which a rather definite procedure has been developed to choose an appropriate alterna-tive given certain information about conditions or variables involved.

Once there is agreement about the alternative to choose under certain conditions, a computer can be programmed to make routine decisions. That is, instructions for making such decisions can be written into a computer system, and the computer can compare the conditions for each subsequent case and make the decision. For example, a computer can be programmed to compare the amount of cash requested from an account through an automatic teller machine and the amount of funds available in the account. After making the comparison, the computer can decide whether to provide the amount of cash requested. In this and other cases, a computer program substitutes for a human decision maker; however,

A computer can be programmed to make routine decisions.

keep in mind that a human being must originally set up the procedure for making the decision and put the instructions into the computer system.

In its early years and through the 1970s, the focus of much MIS activity was directed toward programming computers to make routine decisions. Managers working with MIS professionals identified procedures to be used for making routine decisions, and the guidelines for making the decisions were converted to computer programs. The majority of the activity was focused on relieving managers of the responsibility for making routine decisions because there was greater benefit to be gained, more quickly at less cost, in this area. Currently, the focus of activity has switched to providing support for managers as they make nonroutine decisions.

Nonroutine Decisions   While they can provide some help, computers and software are not widely used by managers as they make nonroutine decisions. These decisions usually involve the use of intuition, common sense, and trial-and-error. They are also made over longer periods of time and affect longer periods of time than routine decisions do. The important factors about the conditions and outcomes related to the problem or opportunity involved are vague and usually more qualitative than quantitative. The conditions under which nonroutine decisions are made may only be present once or, at best, are encountered infrequently. Since the specific procedure used to make such decisions may have limited, if any, future application, developing a procedure that can be formalized and computerized usually will not meet the cost-benefit test applied by most organizations.

Some of the computer-based models and simulations described earlier can be used to help managers who are involved in nonroutine decisions, but most of these are management-science and operations-research models that are appropriate for routine, but not nonroutine, situations.

Although there are more sophisticated definitions, **artificial intelligence (AI)** can be defined as the ability to program computers so they can be used for tasks requiring the human characteristics of intelligence, imaginations, and intuition. Computers are programmed in this way to make them more human than machine in nature. AI systems have a knowledge base similar to that of a human being and are able to communicate in a natural human language rather than in a machine language. Some of the "natural language" products being used in AI today allow a user to ask questions of a system in the same English syntax he or she would use with another human being. The system then does its best to understand the question and present a response. If the system becomes confused, it asks for more information from the user to clarify the question. Such products as INTELLECT, CLOUT, and GURU certainly do not enable a computer to substitute for a human being; however, many MIS professionals believe they are the forerunners of natural languages and artificial intelligence that will continue to become more human in nature. If they are correct, future managers may be able to communicate with a computer using everyday English, much as communication is carried on with other human beings.

Knowledge, or **expert, systems** may be thought of as computer programs that store representations of human knowledge about a specific subject and process it in various ways to draw conclusions. Of all the research and development efforts in the AI area, the work on these systems has produced the greatest return. Such systems currently exist for specific areas of medicine, geology, chemistry, computer configuration, and diesel engine repair. An expert system that helps airlines decide what price to charge for each seat on each flight in order to maximize revenues is also being heavily used. The system weighs such factors as date and time of departure, prices charged by competing airlines for service on the same route, number of passengers using the flight in the past, and so on. It then suggests how many seats should be offered in each price range in order to maximize the revenues. Such a system helps managers bring more structure to nonroutine situations and suggests an appropriate decision in such cases.

While the work done to develop AI and expert systems to their present state is admirable, the systems are not being widely used for a number of reasons. Many managers feel that these systems can be applied to a very limited class of decisions, that they are time consuming and expensive to develop and maintain, and that they simply are not well suited to managerial decision making. Even the harshest critics of AI and expert systems, however, point out that research in these areas is useful because of the help it may give managers in the future.

Managers who are higher up in an organization's hierarchy are generally involved in making more nonroutine or unstructured decisions than those in the lower levels. Usually the more unstructured the decision, the less relevant or directly related information there is available from an MIS to support the decision maker. Periodic reports and other routine information generated by the data-processing system provide only a small portion of the information managers need to make nonroutine decisions.

Decisions at Different Levels

As you know, research and investigation have indicated that there is a difference in the types of decisions made by managers at different levels in an organization. Robert Anthony's work in the area is representative. He classifies managerial activity and decision making into three categories—strategic planning, management control, and operational control—each directly related to a hierarchical level in an organization. In addition, he believes the decisions made by those at various levels are sufficiently different to require different types of information.[7]

Senior Managers (Strategic Planning) Anthony refers to the activity and decisions at the senior-manager level, the top of the organizational hierarchy, as *strategic planning*. The strategic planning process usually involves a small number of people in the highest levels of an organization. The complexity of the situations with which these managers deal and the nonroutine, creative way in which they handle them make it difficult to know what type of information they need.

Because strategic planning deals with broad policies and goals, senior managers have a crucial need for information that addresses the relationship of their organization to its environment. Strategic planners usually need summarized, aggregated information, much of it obtained from external sources. The scope and variety of the information are large, but the requirements for accuracy are not particularly stringent. The decisions made at this level are nonroutine and nonrepetitive, which means that the demand for the information occurs only once or infrequently.[8]

In order to meet the needs of senior managers, an MIS must gather, process, and provide information about conditions outside an organization. Further, the MIS must be structured so that senior managers are comfortable using the system to obtain data or information to meet their unique needs while making nonroutine decisions. Because senior managers are relatively highly paid and make decisions that have a major impact on an organization, MIS professionals must work with them to ensure that they are using the system efficiently and effectively.

Middle Managers (Management Control) Robert Anthony refers to the second category of managerial activity as *management control*. He defines it as "the process by which managers assure that resources are obtained and used effectively and efficiently in the accomplishment of the organization's objectives."[9] This type of activity is performed by middle managers.

Decision makers in this category generally require summarized information that compares present and past performance. Although the need is mostly for internal information, there is also some need for external information. The decisions made here are somewhere between routine and nonroutine; they are often referred to as being *semistructured*. Part of the decision-making process is structured, while part is not. It is important to note that much of the information needed at this level is obtained through interpersonal interaction.[10]

To serve the needs of middle managers, an MIS should provide several types of periodic internal reports, exception reports, and perhaps some forecast and historical information. In addition, it should be structured so middle managers, like senior managers, can easily use the system to obtain information they might need for their unique organizing, directing, and controlling activities. For example, middle managers may need information to help them develop personnel policies, build and monitor budgets, and determine an appropriate marketing mix.

Operating managers can use an MIS to plan and implement production or to exercise inventory control.

Operating Managers (Operational Control) Anthony refers to the managerial activity of lower-level or operating managers as *operational control*. He defines this as "the process of assuring that specific tasks are carried out effectively and efficiently."[11] Operational control is primarily concerned with tasks rather than with people and deals with very short-term activities.

In this area, there is a need for well-defined, detailed, and accurate information that is usually narrow in scope. The information is used frequently, so it is often available and reported routinely through the data-processing system. Many of the decisions at this level are routine and lend themselves to structured approaches.[12]

To meet the needs of operating managers, an MIS provides a variety of information designed to help them direct and control the resources and activities for which they are responsible. Almost all of the information needed at this level is provided through regular internal reports, detailed transaction reports, procedures manuals, and the like. Operational managers need this type of information to plan and implement production, to exercise inventory control, and to manage credit and other types of activities at the lower levels of an organization.

Figure 21.2 shows the information needs of managers by management level and general type of decision. It summarizes the major points made in this section related to getting the right information to the right person.

The Types of Organizational Information Systems

As an MIS has been described in this chapter, it is the broadest, most comprehensive information system in an organization. This type of MIS includes both computer-based information and information collected or provided to managers in another way. The emphasis in this chapter and in most of the information-system discussions today is on how managers get and use computer-based information. In fact, when hearing or reading about an organization's MIS, it is almost certain that the discussion is related only to the formal, structured MIS. Even though this is true, remember that managers receive information from both the formal MIS and from informal networks within and outside of the organization. Managers use both informal and computer-based information while making decisions.

Informal Information

Decision makers at all levels are influenced by the informal information they pick up consciously or accidentally. This is information communicated through informal, oral, and subjective conversations. It is difficult to pin down how big a factor such information plays in managerial decision making. It has little, if any, influence on the routine decisions made at the operational level; however, it may be given some consideration in various management control situations and has its greatest influence in nonroutine decisions made at the strategic-planning level.

FIGURE 21.2
The Information Needs of Managers

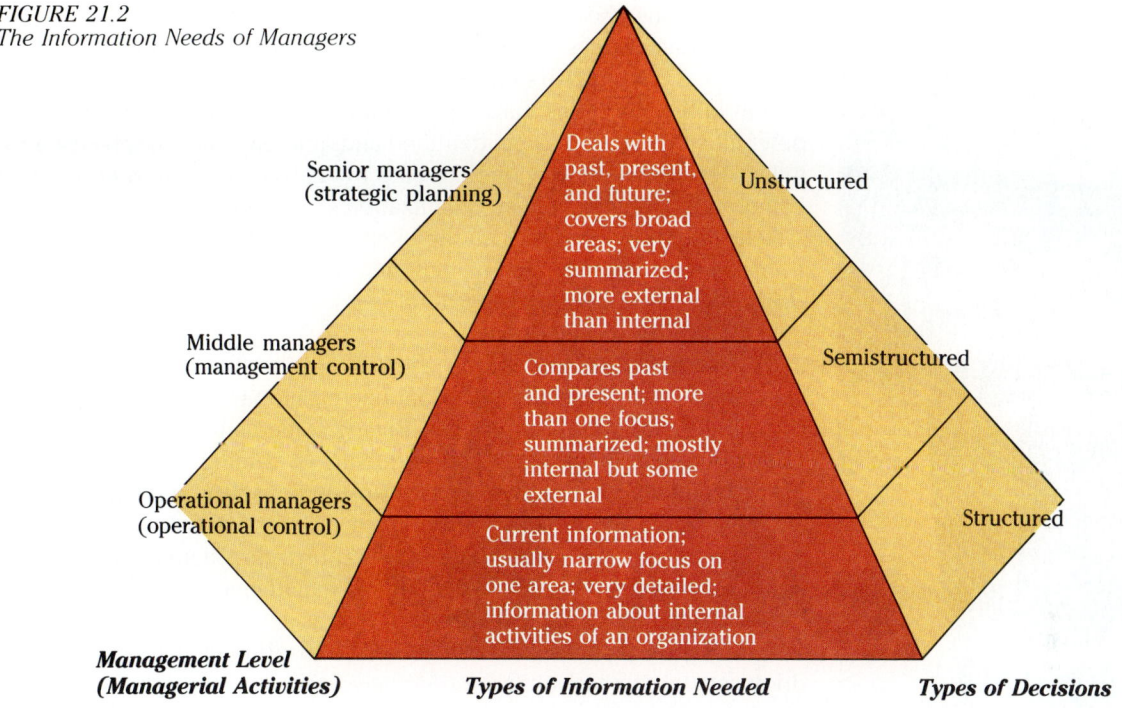

Senior managers (strategic planning)

Middle managers (management control)

Operational managers (operational control)

Deals with past, present, and future; covers broad areas; very summarized; more external than internal

Unstructured

Compares past and present; more than one focus; summarized; mostly internal but some external

Semistructured

Current information; usually narrow focus on one area; very detailed; information about internal activities of an organization

Structured

Management Level (Managerial Activities)   **Types of Information Needed**   **Types of Decisions**

Some believe informal information is the most important factor in decision making. Henry Mintzberg, one of the supporters of this belief, has studied the content of managers' information and what they do with it. He says:

> The evidence here is that a great deal of the manager's inputs are soft and speculative—impressions and feelings about other people, hearsay, gossip, and so on. Furthermore, the very analytical inputs—reports, documents, and hard data in general—seem to be of relatively little importance to many managers.[13]

J. F. Rockart agrees that a great deal of information must be dynamically gathered as new situations arise for top executives, and that much of it is not computer-based but is communicated informally. Based on his MIT team's study of critical success factors among chief executives, however, he points out that there are also data that should be supplied regularly to chief executives through a computer-based information system.[14]

Computer-Based Information

In almost all of today's organizations, quantitative data related to the production and sale of goods or services is recorded, processed, stored, and distributed by a computer. Large mainframe and supercomputers process data and create information for large organizations, such as the Department of Defense, the Social Security Administration, General Motors, and Exxon. Similarly, microcomputers are now being used to do the same thing—but on a much smaller scale—for farmers, bakeries, churches, and PTAs. Computers provide a fast, accurate way of handling

Large mainframe and supercomputers, such as the CRAY-2, process data and create information for large organizations

and processing the data in organizations. The information that is the output of data-processing activities is part of an organization's MIS.

Just as a computer-based information system is one subsystem of an overall MIS, subsystems make up a computer-based system. A number of different subsystems may be identified and different terms may be used for them, depending on how one chooses to analyze an organization. Three common subsystems of an organization's computer-based information system will be described in the next sections and referred to as a *transaction-processing system*, an *information-reporting system*, and a *decision-support system*.

A Transaction-Processing System In business and accounting vocabulary, a transaction is an economic event that affects the resources or financial position of a business. Buying something, paying an invoice, selling a good or service, and reducing or adding to inventory are examples of transactions. A **transaction-processing system (TPS)** in an organization records, processes, and manages data related to these everyday business activities. Data files that provide a detailed description of an organization's activities are built and maintained in a TPS. This set of files and the data it contains are referred to as an organization's database.

A TPS provides information to be used for printing standard business documents, such as purchase orders, invoices, and employee paychecks. Management information that is produced by a TPS usually takes the form of a listing of transactions or business events that have occurred recently or are scheduled to occur. As you might expect, the information output by a TPS is most frequently used by managers for making structured decisions at the operating level. Since it is usually very detailed, current information focusing on one area of internal activities of an organization, it best meets the needs of managers at this level. In addition to providing the information needed for operational control decisions, a TPS is important because the database it contains is the basis for the information provided in the other two computer-based subsystems.[15]

An Information-Reporting System Since the usual output of a TPS is related to the daily activities at the lower levels of an organization, it does not provide much decision-making support for middle and senior managers. These managers need more general types of information. An **information-reporting system** in an organization meets these needs; it retrieves, sorts, pools, and manipulates transaction data in other ways to produce summary or management reports. The information is summarized, aggregated, and otherwise transformed in such a way that it is quite different from the original transaction data. In fact, additional data or information may be added to the transaction data in order to create meaningful reports. One of the major advantages of a computer-based information system is that, once it is programmed to prepare an organization's most frequently used reports, it can prepare them repeatedly without additional work. The system is programmed and designed to start the preparation of these reports in various ways and to prepare them very efficiently.

The reports produced are of most value to middle managers in an organization. *Periodic reports* about various activities are prepared and distributed after a specified period of time has elapsed—perhaps daily, weekly, monthly, quarterly, or annually. *Exception reports* are distributed when an "exception" occurs. For example, a manager may be reminded that sales in a region are more than 15 percent below a goal or that labor costs are more than 20 percent above a budgeted amount for a project. *Demand reports* are distributed to managers who ask for specific information because they wish to analyze a particular issue in more depth. These and other prespecified reports compare summarized information related to past and present activities within an organization. The information they provide is used mostly by middle managers in their management-control roles as they monitor business activities, spot problems and opportunities, and analyze specific issues. Some of these reports, or specific information from several of them, may be combined to create even more summarized reports. The summarized reports are then used by senior managers as part of a decision-support system.[16]

A Decision-Support System A **decision-support system (DSS)** in an organization consists of the data, information, and reports of the TPS and information-reporting system. In addition, it includes a variety of computer software that enables managers to access and use information in the other two systems to produce desired output that is not routinely available. The software usually includes programs designed to do standard data processing and analysis, modeling, and forecasting and to apply statistical techniques. There is little structure to a DSS because it is intended to be used by individual managers in whatever way they feel is most helpful in a given situation. They may use it to obtain information for decisions that arise only occasionally or have never arisen previously, or they may use it to analyze the available alternatives in a particular situation. Managers may add information or alter some presented from the TPS and information-reporting system. They may do this on the basis of information collected from informal networks or external sources so that the variables and a model or simulation more accurately reflect current conditions. Perhaps each of the alternatives requires that different data be retrieved, that a variety of models or statistical techniques be used, or that different output be produced.

As is evident, a DSS is probably of most value to senior managers who make many nonroutine, one-time-only decisions in their role as strategic planners for organizations; however, a DSS could be helpful to middle and operational managers in certain situations. A DSS should support a variety of decision-making processes, since managers often use various techniques for different situations. All parts of the DSS must be designed and developed so managers can learn about and use them easily. Otherwise, the DSS will not be used to support decision making in an organization. In his article proposing a framework for the development of DSS, R. H. Sprague, Jr., puts it this way:

> *Finally, a DSS should be easy to use. A variety of terms have been used to describe this characteristic including* flexibility, user-friendly, *and* nonthreatening. *The importance of this characteristic is underscored by the discretionary latitude of a DSS's clientele . . . The user of a DSS has much more latitude to ignore or circumvent the system than the user of*

a more traditional transaction system or required reporting system. Therefore, the DSS must "earn" its users' allegiance by being valuable and convenient.[17]

What Do Managers Need to Know to Use an MIS Effectively?

Now that you have a better idea of what an MIS is and what it can do, you must think about what you need to know as a manager to use an MIS effectively in an organization. As you know, the tasks performed by managers involve varying amounts of planning, organizing, directing, and controlling. The conventional targets of information-system applications have been an organization's planning and controlling activities. (These are the activities Anthony has identified as strategic planning, management control, and operational control.) While it is generally agreed that an MIS can also be helpful to managers in their organizing and directing activities, relatively little formal work has been done to develop standard applications and tools for using information from a computer-based system in these areas.

An MIS should be user friendly; however, people developing the computer-based parts of such systems have complained that the system must be "user seductive" to get some managers involved. As is true for most management- and decision-support resources in an organization, an MIS is an essential tool for managers to use in order to improve their performance. To use an MIS effectively, managers must be familiar with the process of management and the roles that managers play. They must also be able to understand and apply some of the traditional principles of management, and they must possess some basic technical and decision-making skills.

Technical Skills and Knowledge

Until recently, most managers knew very little about computers and other information-system technology. There are no generally established criteria for what a manager needs to know about computer-based systems to use them effectively. Knowing about bits and bytes, storage size and processing speed, computer architecture and compatibility, and other technical aspects of the system may be helpful; however, there is no empirical evidence to indicate that possessing technical knowledge makes managers more effective users of computer-based information systems. It is still advantageous for a manager to be proficient at a keyboard; however, the advent of systems that allow one to touch the screen or to use voice actuation for input may soon change that. A manager also needs to know enough about using a system to be able to easily access data, programs, and communication devices. These are really the only technical skills needed. They are not difficult to master for anyone who is willing to invest time to learn them. A relatively small investment of time in learning the necessary skills will pay large dividends in time saved in the long run.

Computer Fluency

Managers and others concerned with organizational behavior believe that technical people need to build a better understanding of organizations. Managers must take a more sophisticated approach to assessing the potential organizational consequences and opportunities that technology produces. In a 1985 publication of the American Management Association, P. G. W. Keen pointed out: "*Sophisticated* is not the same as *detailed*. The real issue is how little, not how much, managers must understand about IT."[18] Keen suggested that managers need "computer fluency" not "computer literacy." Literacy suggests little more than confidence building through a crash course on personal computers. This narrows the issues to the visible aspects of technology—hardware, software, and perhaps individual uses. Fluency, on the other hand, relates to understanding choices and consequences.[19]

Managers need a vocabulary for reviewing choices related to the use of information technology in organizations. As long as managers are not fluent in this area, technical factors will drive decision making, and technical people will control the debate related to the choices involved. Technical people tend to understate the importance of nontechnical dimensions, because their role is to direct the use of technology. They are not prone to worry about what they consider to be highly ambiguous and contentious business and organizational problems. It is the responsibility of managers to ensure that nontechnical issues are factored into decisions in this area.[20]

Managers have tended to consider computers as strange and magical. They have been largely uninformed and lack confidence in making decisions related to the development of computer-based information systems; therefore, delegating such decisions to technical people has been rational. Even today, managers can evade involvement, but they must not be allowed to do so. Keen and others believe that managers at all levels must become actively involved in the choices being made related to informational technology (IT) and computer-based information systems.

Managers who invest just a small amount of time in learning to operate a computer-based information system reap the reward of time saved in the long run.

Management Information Systems in Review

Information systems, their roles in organizations, and the development and use of a management information system have been described in this chapter. Appropriate information must be provided to managers in the context of the decision-making process in general, as well as in relation to routine or nonroutine decisions. An MIS also serves different functions based on the varying types of decisions made by managers at different hierarchical levels in organizations. Organization members must consider the components of a decision-support system, their place in the overall organizational information system, and their use by managers.

Transaction-processing systems, information-reporting systems, and decision-support systems are important subsystems of an overall organizational information system. Each of these computer-based subsystems supports managerial decision making in a specific way. The chapter closes with a brief discussion of the type of computer fluency—technical skills and knowledge—managers need in order to be able to use organizational information systems effectively. The ultimate goals of an organizational information system and the managers who use it are congruent. The system and the managers are both concerned with getting the right information to the right decision makers so that the best possible decisions are made.

Notes

1. M. Cetron (1985), *The future of American business*, New York: McGraw-Hill, xiv–xv.
2. D. R. Adams, G. E. Wagner, and T. J. Boyer (1983), *Computer information systems: An introduction*, Cincinnati, OH: Southwestern, 48–50.
3. N. Ahituv and S. Neumann (1986), *Principles of information systems for management*, 2nd ed., Dubuque, IA: Wm. C. Brown, 74–76.
4. R. H. Sprague, Jr. (December 1960), A framework for the development of decision support systems, *MIS Quarterly*, 4:4.
5. Adams, et al., 1983, 36–42.
6. H. A. Simon (1960), *The new science of management decision*, New York: Harper & Row, 5–6.
7. R. N. Anthony (1965), *Planning and control systems: A framework for analysis*, Boston, MA: Harvard University Graduate School of Business Administration.
8. A. G. Gorry and S. Morton (Fall 1971), A framework for management information systems, *Sloan Management Review*.
9. Anthony, 1965, 69.
10. Gorry and Morton, 1987, 70.
11. Anthony, 1965, 69.
12. Anthony, 1965, 70–71.
13. H. Mintzberg (July-August 1976), Planning on the left side and managing on the right, *Harvard Business Review*, 54.
14. J. F. Rockart (March-April 1979), Chief executives define their own data needs, *Harvard Business Review*.
15. T. H. Athey and R. W. Zmud (1986), *Introduction to computers and information systems*, Glenview, IL: Scott, Foresman, 265–67.
16. Athey and Zmud, 1986, 267–68.
17. Sprague, 1960, 141.
18. P. G. W. Keen (1985), Computers and managerial choice, *Organizational Dynamics*.
19. *Ibid.*
20. Keen, 1985, 463, 478.

Key Terms

management information system

information

data

database

system

artificial intelligence (AI)

knowledge, or expert, systems

transaction-processing system (TPS)

information-reporting system

decision-support system (DSS)

Issues for Review and Discussion

1. Explain what a management information system is and discuss the purpose served by an MIS.
2. What role can an MIS play in each stage of the decision-making process?
3. Comment on the observation: "MIS should not be a decision-making system, but rather a decision-support system."
4. What is the relationship between an MIS and hierarchically based managerial decisions?
5. Identify three organizational information subsystems. What role does each play?
6. Compare and contrast artificial intelligence and expert systems.

Suggested Readings

Keen, P. (January 1985). A walk through decision support. *Computerworld.*

Magee, J. F. (Winter 1985). What information technology has in store for managers. *Sloan Management Review.*

McGarrah, R. E. (September-October 1984). Ironies of our computer age. *Business Horizons.*

Millar, V. E. (January 1984). Decision-oriented information. *Datamation.*

Porter, M. E. and Millar, V. E. (July-August 1985). How information gives you competitive advantage. *Harvard Business Review.*

Power, D. J. (September 1983). Impact of information management on the organization. *MIS Quarterly.*

Shoor, R. (June 1986). The new breed of executive information user. *Infosystems.*

Wrapp, H. E. (July-August 1984). Good managers don't make policy decisions. *Harvard Business Review.*

Operations Management

Student Learning Objectives

After reading this chapter, you should be able to:

1. Identify the types of operation processes and describe how the management tasks are different for each.

2. Show how the design and use of the operating function are central to the attainment of an organization's goals and objectives.

3. Understand important concepts (such as just-in-time) that are shaping current operating decisions.

4. Distinguish between the different types of production processes.

5. Discuss the concept of world-class operations.

6. Define the interrelationships among operations and other functions in an organization, such as marketing, finance, human resource management, and research and development.

7. Define the competitive operations objectives and explain how they can be used for competitive advantage.

8. Describe the decisions involved in designing and using an operating system.

By Peter Billington of Northeastern University

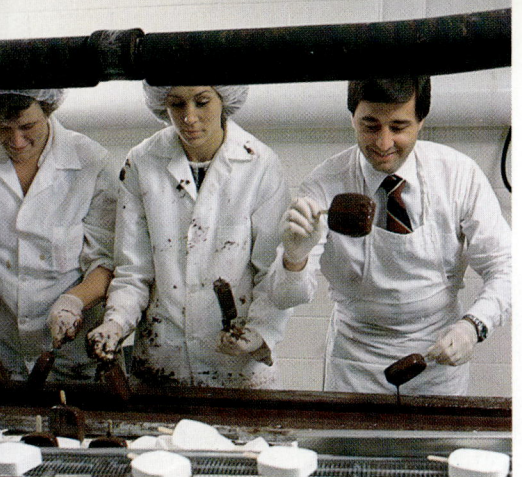

Every organization has an operating function that produces a product or delivers a service that is useful to customers.

very organization, whether manufacturing or service, for-profit or not-for-profit, has an operating function that produces a product or delivers a service. Operations management is the process of designing, planning, organizing, directing, and controlling this operating function.

The central task of an operating manager is to transform resources into products or services that are useful to customers. The design and use of an operating system must complement the overall objectives of an organization. The operating function should be designed and used in a way that gives an organization a competitive advantage, whether this means faster delivery, higher quality, or another attribute of its product or service.

Operating managers have recently seen significant changes in operations management philosophy due to the success of foreign competitors in the domestic market. Managers are now applying important concepts used by foreign competitors, such as just-in-time and total quality control, to domestic operations.

The Transformation Process

An operating function, shown in Figure 22.1, consists of resources, a transformation process that converts the resources into products or services, and a feedback loop. "Random" events are external and internal environmental events that occur but may be out of the control of management. Resources consist of labor, material, technology, information, and management. The *transformation process* changes these resources into products and services for customers. Examples of transformation processes include assembly lines, information gathering and transmitting, college lectures and assignments, hamburgers being made at a fast-food restaurant, and patient care and diagnosis at a hospital.

A *feedback loop* is needed to monitor output, which is measured and compared to a standard. If a product or service does not meet the standard, the loop is completed to make resource adjustments. Quality control is an example of this. At the end of a production line, the product is measured to ensure that it meets quality-control specifications. If it does not, then a change must be made. Possible changes include getting better

FIGURE 22.1 Schematic Diagram of an Operating System

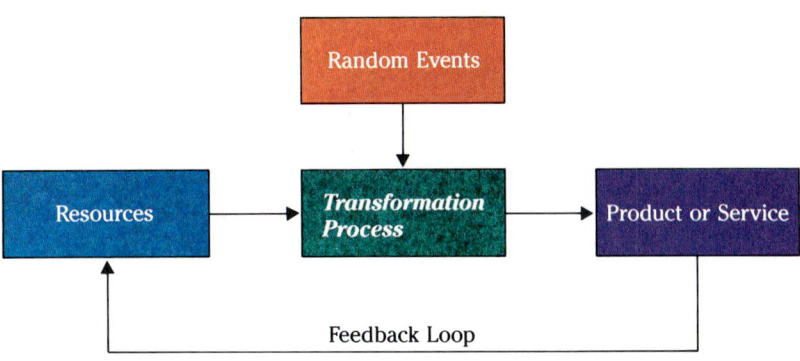

TABLE 22.1   Component Elements of the Operations Function in Several Organizations

| Organization | Inputs | Transformation Processes | Outputs | | Feedback Loops |
			Products	Services	
Fast-food restaurant	Food Labor Grill Building	Cooking Mixing Assembling	Burgers Fries Drinks	Seating areas Drive-up window Speed of delivery	Customer returns Inspections
Hospital	Medicines Physicians/nurses Diagnostic equipment	Surgery Therapy Treatment	Bandages Pacemakers Prostheses	Patient wellness	Customer surveys Patient returns
Automobile manufacturer	Steel Rubber Glass Labor Machines/tools Conveyors	Metal stamping Welding Molding Assembling Painting	Automobiles Service parts Service manuals	Service training Warranty Financing	Warranty charges Inventory levels Quality-control inspections Customer surveys

University	Textbooks
	Faculty
	Students
	Classrooms
	Computers
		Lectures
		Exams
		Assignments
		Writing
			Diplomas
			Books
			Research papers
				Educating
				  students
					Alumni donations
					Job offers to students
					Teacher/course
					  evaluations

raw materials, increasing inspection of the raw materials, purchasing new machinery, and training workers.

Table 22.1 provides examples of operating system components for a variety of organizations. Organizations that are typically considered to be service providers produce many products; similarly, many operations that are typically considered to be manufacturers provide many services. For example, a typical automobile manufacturer produces cars, trucks, and spare parts. It is easy to overlook the fact that successful competition in the automobile business also requires a significant output of services. General Motors, for instance, has a division that provides financing of purchased cars. More importantly, every auto manufacturer must provide extensive service training and a large amount of information through service manuals, availability updates, and price lists of parts. If an auto company did not provide this service component, very few consumers would want to purchase its cars.

Management Decisions

Management of the transformation process entails a wide range of decisions. Management must make decisions about product design, the type of production process, the type of equipment to use, workers' skill and pay levels, the location of the operation, the operation's capacity (or size), and the layout inside the facility. After design decisions have been made, the system must be used. Utilization decisions fall into three types: planning, managing (organizing and directing), and controlling. Managers must plan how the system will be used, organize and direct its use to produce goods and services, and then control the system using feedback loops.

All of these decisions must be coordinated through an organizational structure that allows an operating system to produce products or services in a way that meets organizational goals. It is important for managers to ensure that all of these activities are coordinated. As an example of what could happen if this were not done, consider the role of a purchasing agent in an auto company. If the paint buyer does not coordinate the purchase of blue paint with the production schedule for blue cars, one of several things could happen: production might come to a halt when the blue paint runs out; fewer blue cars might be produced than needed; or more blue paint might be produced in a hurry, often for higher cost.

Operating Function Objectives

An organization can produce a product or deliver a service that has a combination of features—whether low prices, fast delivery, or something else—that sets it apart from its competitors. These features can be translated into the objectives of the operating function in four dimensions: (1) the *cost* per unit to produce a product or service (low vs. high), (2) the ability to produce a product or service with a certain *quality* or features (high customization vs. a commodity product), (3) the *flexibility* to change the product design and volume (quickly vs. slowly), and (4) the *dependability* to deliver a large volume of the same product (high reliability vs. low).

It is generally considered impossible to succeed in all four of these dimensions at the same time. Most operating systems can succeed in two of these dimensions, which define the systems' distinctive competence. For example, consider the difference between a producer of four-door sedans and a producer of custom-made race cars. The operating system that delivers the sedans can do so at a relatively low cost and with high dependability. The cars are affordable to a large segment of the population and are readily available. The cost of the custom-made race cars is very high, but the manufacturer can produce cars that meet drivers' high-quality specifications and that can be redesigned and rebuilt almost on a whim. Table 22.2 compares the production process dimensions for these different automotive products.

As Table 22.2 shows, the processes needed to produce these two types of cars are very different. Sedans are produced on a high-volume assembly line with many automated processes. Many of the jobs on an assembly line are for low- to medium-skilled workers. The assembly line

TABLE 22.2   *Product/Process Objectives*

Objectives of the Production Process	Sedan	Race Car
Cost	Low	High
Quality/features	Standard	Customized
Flexibility	Slow (model changes once a year)	Fast (can be redesigned and rebuilt quickly)
Dependability	High volume of same product, fast delivery from dealer's lot	Low volume, every car different, longer lead time to custom build

process results in low cost and high dependability in delivery. On the other hand, the product features are not minutely customized as they are for race cars. An auto assembly plant is rarely slowed down for a prolonged amount of time, since the cost per car would go up dramatically.

Race cars are produced in a small shop that can create parts to specifications. The labor must be highly skilled to run the equipment to produce parts to exacting detail. Such a shop also has high flexibility to change the race cars' design; it can produce different types of race cars, since it has skilled labor and the equipment to make virtually any type of car. On the other hand, the cost is very high and the yearly volume of cars produced is small.

An assembly line is not a proper process for producing customized race cars, and a small shop is not a proper place to produce a high volume of low-priced cars. It is important to recognize that each product is being produced by the process that is appropriate for the type of car and the customer. Neither of these production processes is capable of meeting more than two operating objectives. It is impossible, for example, for a small race-car shop to have high quality, high flexibility, and low cost or volume dependability. It can excel at two operating objectives, which set this operation apart from other car producers.

Operations for Strategic Advantage

Organizations try to gain competitive advantage over their competition. A **competitive (strategic) advantage** is a quality of a product or service that will induce customers to choose it over the competition. Advantages are not just marketing gimmicks, but are tangible benefits for customers. For example, a fast-food restaurant's advantage is its convenience, both in its location and in its ability to deliver a low-cost meal quickly.

An operating function must be designed and used to provide competitive advantage. If the kitchen and serving facilities of a fast-food restaurant were not designed around the concept of quick delivery of low-cost food, the restaurant would have no competitive advantage; thus, the design and use of the operating function is central to an organization's strategic and competitive advantage.

An overall organizational strategy must be linked to operations to ensure that the organization's operation system can produce products or services that allow the organization to attain its goals. If an organization has a top-down view of operations, managers can use a series of steps to link strategy with operations:

1. Analyze the external environment to determine the competitor's strengths and weaknesses.
2. Assess the organization's internal environment—its strengths and resources. This will highlight, among other things, what the operating system is best at doing. For example, what type of materials can it work with (metal, plastic, and so forth), how flexible is the equipment, and can it produce custom products or only standard designs?

Fast-food restaurants attempt to gain competitive advantage by offering customers convenient locations and quick, low-cost meals.

3. Formulate an overall organizational strategy considering the external environment (competition) and the internal environment.

4. Set an operating strategy in light of the overall organizational strategy; the overall strategy sets a foundation for the operating strategy. For example, if customer service is important, will there be a need for many small facilities near customers, or can fast delivery from a central location be effective?

5. Design an operating system to meet the organization's objectives. Specific decisions regarding location, process design, and inventory procedures must be made.

6. Plan to use the operating system to meet the objectives by making decisions about where to locate inventory and how to schedule production to meet customer delivery requirements.

7. Manage the operation to ensure that it produces products or services according to plans and the overall strategy.

The design utilization of the operating function is important to an organization's overall competitive ability. Managers must analyze the abilities of their organization's existing operating system to see if it can carry out the organization's strategy.

Contemporary Strategy Factors

In today's global marketplace, it is important for organizations to be able to compete with foreign firms in domestic markets and in other countries. Rapid transfers of information and products among countries break down advantages that may have been inherent in domestically based companies. For example, foreign banks now compete in the U.S. market with U.S.-based banks, and many large U.S.-based banks have branches in other parts of the world.

Due to the globalization of competition, a new set of factors shapes the operating environment. Capacity, location, and other factors were previously considered key to successful competition. Although still important, those factors are now not as important as:

- Shorter new product lead time
- Faster inventory turnover (less inventory)
- Shorter delivery lead time
- Higher quality
- More flexibility
- Better customer service
- Less waste
- Higher return on assets

Companies that are successful in meeting all or some of these objectives are at a competitive advantage. Note that these factors are all operationally based. It is no longer adequate to have only the best advertising campaign or the lowest cost to compete successfully. Consumers are now demanding higher quality, better service, and faster delivery.

It is apparent that managers must pursue a course of continuous improvement in the operating process. It is no longer enough to meet the competitor's position, since the competition may be improving the product or process. This also suggests that the management tasks required to be successful with this new form of competition will be different from former operating functions in which managers were able to focus exclusively on the operating function. The new factors require that managers concentrate more on activities outside of the operating function. For example, operating managers should have more contact with marketing managers, first to understand what marketing advantages would be useful and then to translate those advantages into improved operating systems. Would shorter delivery times be a competitive advantage and a good marketing tool? If so, how can the operating system be designed and used to accomplish faster delivery?

Operating managers must be prepared to make changes continuously, since product innovations and technological innovations in operating processes are occurring rapidly. It is no longer important to be a good "housekeeper" of a production system, as that process may be likely to change. Competition is forcing managers to reduce inventory, increase quality, and speed up delivery lead times.

Service Industries and Manufacturing

Historically operations management has focused on the manufacturing part of business. Most concepts and techniques in operations management were first developed for manufacturing. This was a natural extension of the fact that at one time the manufacturing sector was the largest part of the U.S. economy. Now the service sector of the economy is larger than the manufacturing sector. Not only do banks and insurance companies provide services as their primary products, but many manufacturing companies provide a large amount of service that is necessary to sell their products.

Service companies have "production" departments that have delivery objectives similar to manufacturers. A fast-food restaurant must deliver a

Service organizations have "production" departments with delivery objectives similar to those of manufacturers. A restaurant, for example, must deliver meals to customers within a certain amount of time.

hamburger in a certain amount of time. A hospital has a limited number of patient beds and certain objectives regarding the average length of stay.

Service providers must have operations systems and must make the same types of decisions regarding product design, capacity, location, and so forth that manufacturers make. There has been a lag in the implementation of many operations-management concepts among service industries. Hospitals have been slow to implement inventory control procedures, for example. Since a hospital does not want to run out of medical supplies, managers are motivated to retain large inventories. On the other hand, a large stock of inventory is very costly to maintain, and, in the era of cost containment in the medical industry, it is no longer acceptable. Inventory-control procedures are being applied to the medical industry, with the dual objectives of reducing costs and maintaining high availability of inventory.

In the 1970s, many jobs in manufacturing industries were lost to foreign competition. The causes of this phenomenon are complex and varied; the simple view is that the quality of foreign-made products improved while the quality of U.S.-made products did not. Now U.S.-based manufacturers are improving the design and reliability of their products to remain competitive. Service industries have had a significant historical advantage over manufacturing. At this stage in the history of the service economy, many sectors do not have a significant foreign threat. Service industries should learn from manufacturing industries, however, that foreign competition will probably arise, and it may represent lower costs and higher quality. The service industries must learn how to design and produce their services for continuing improvement. The study and application of sound operations management in the service industries will ensure their continuing ability to compete effectively with foreign-based companies.

Interaction of Operations with Other Functions

The operations function must interact effectively with all other functions in an organization. The competitive advantage an organization wants to achieve is best found through the coordinated efforts of all functional areas. In the marketing area, for example, the ability to deliver a product or service more quickly than the competition can provide a tremendous marketing advantage. Marketing managers must, therefore, ask operating managers about operational improvements that could be fruitful. In the other direction, if marketing plans to promote a product to increase sales, operating managers must be told so that the proper level of production can be set and the proper amount of inventory can be determined. Failure to do this could result in customers' looking for a product that is not available.

Marketing managers must also interact with operating managers in such areas as new product design, product redesign, sales forecasting, and delivery lead time. As an example of product design, the Chrysler Corporation was a leader in the mid-1980s with the introduction of minivans designed to meet the needs of families who need seating and extra cargo space in a car, while at the same time providing a vehicle that drives more like a car than a truck. This new product design required a joint effort of product designers, marketing, and manufacturing to ensure

Marketing managers interact with operating managers to create strategies to gain competitive advantage through such activities as product delivery, design, and redesign.

that the minivans could be produced in sufficient volume at reasonable cost. In contrast, General Motors did not introduce a minivan (other than a redesigned full-size van) until several years after the Chrysler product came out, partly due to the lack of manufacturing facilities to produce that type of product.

Research and development functions are active in new product design, product redesign, and the design of substitutions for raw materials and parts. The redesign of a product may have a direct impact on the production process: different types of material require different types of equipment. New products must be considered in light of the particular strengths and capabilities of the existing production process.

The financial function also interacts significantly with the operations function. In manufacturing organizations, the major assets are usually inventory, plant, and equipment. The finance managers in most firms must know the planned levels of inventory in order to determine inventory financing. Finance managers can assist operating managers in determining the expected benefits of new equipment and the location of new facilities.

The accounting department is responsible for operating a system of collecting and analyzing the cost of producing products or services. Operating managers need accurate information about the cost of production so they can make the proper decisions regarding new product cost estimation, equipment purchasing, and scheduling for improved productivity.

Types of Processes

This chapter has discussed two types of cars, sedans made on an assembly line and race cars made in a small shop. These two production processes have very different functions, produce very different products, and result in very different sets of management activities. Figure 22.2 shows how different products relate to various process structures. Generally, a facility falls on the diagonal from the upper left to the lower right. This ensures a good match of product and process: the process produces the desired product with high efficiency. It is not unusual to find an organization that is not on the diagonal; this is not necessarily an

FIGURE 22.2   *The Product/Process Matrix*

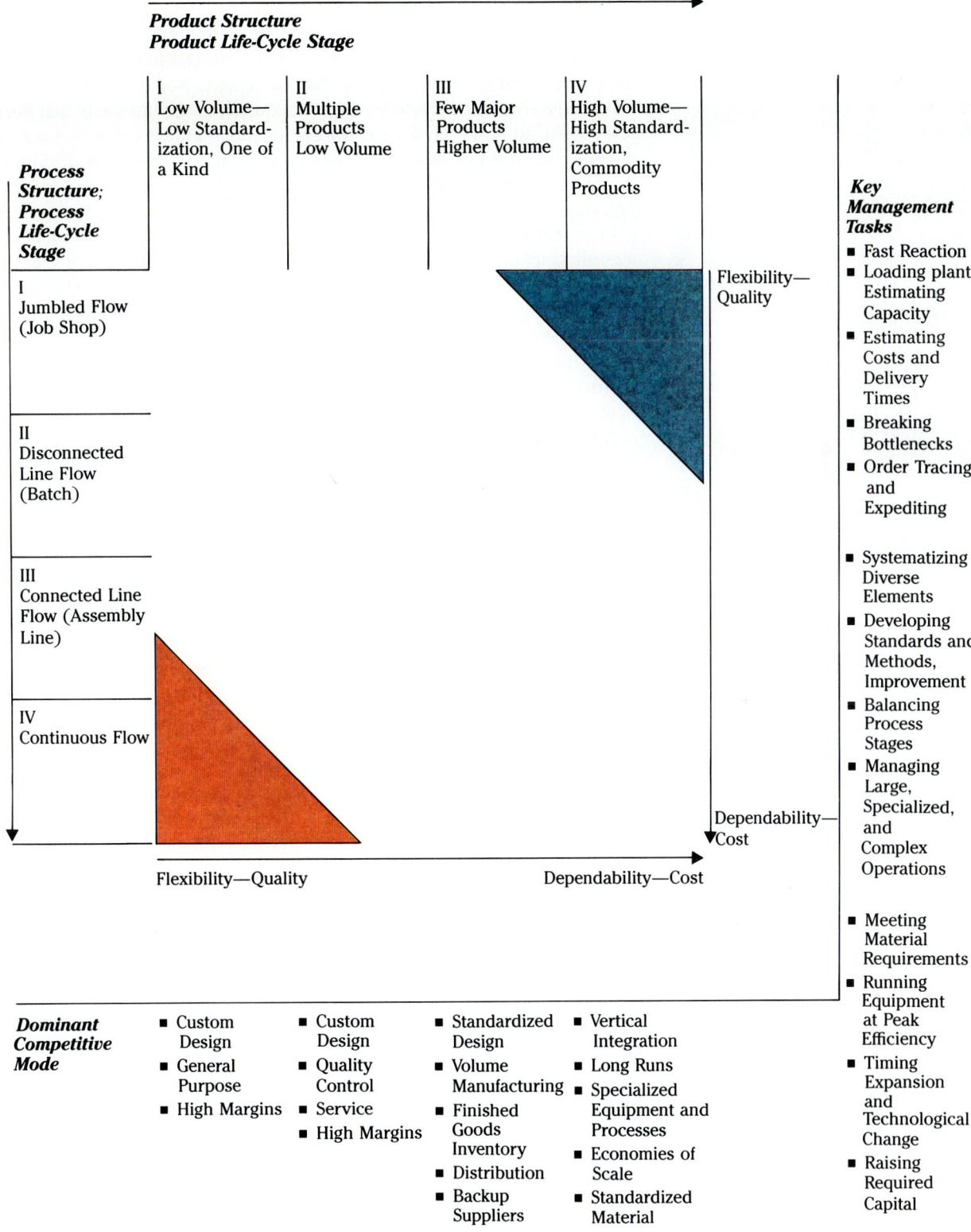

Product Structure
Product Life-Cycle Stage

	I Low Volume— Low Standard- ization, One of a Kind	II Multiple Products Low Volume	III Few Major Products Higher Volume	IV High Volume— High Standard- ization, Commodity Products

Process Structure; Process Life-Cycle Stage

I
Jumbled Flow
(Job Shop)

II
Disconnected
Line Flow
(Batch)

III
Connected Line
Flow (Assembly
Line)

IV
Continuous Flow

Flexibility—Quality

Dependability—Cost

Flexibility—
Quality

Dependability—
Cost

Key Management Tasks

- Fast Reaction
- Loading plant, Estimating Capacity
- Estimating Costs and Delivery Times
- Breaking Bottlenecks
- Order Tracing and Expediting

- Systematizing Diverse Elements
- Developing Standards and Methods, Improvement
- Balancing Process Stages
- Managing Large, Specialized, and Complex Operations

- Meeting Material Requirements
- Running Equipment at Peak Efficiency
- Timing Expansion and Technological Change
- Raising Required Capital

Dominant Competitive Mode	■ Custom Design ■ General Purpose ■ High Margins	■ Custom Design ■ Quality Control ■ Service ■ High Margins	■ Standardized Design ■ Volume Manufacturing ■ Finished Goods Inventory ■ Distribution ■ Backup Suppliers	■ Vertical Integration ■ Long Runs ■ Specialized Equipment and Processes ■ Economies of Scale ■ Standardized Material

Source: W. Hayes and S. Wheelwright (January-February 1979), Link manufacturing process and product life cycles, *Harvard Business Review*, 137.

incorrect position, as long as the organization can exploit its product/process combination to competitive advantage.

In a **job shop,** work centers are arranged around particular types of equipment or functions. Examples of job shops include photocopy centers, universities, and hospitals. Each job, or customer, flows through the process from function to function according to requirements that may be different for each customer. An engineering student takes one set of courses, a business student another; both may share some similar functions, such as taking English and math courses. A job shop allows a high degree of customization and is very flexible.

In a **repetitive process,** functions are arranged in a sequence according to product specifications. An auto assembly line is a classic example. Each car made on the line is assembled in exactly the same sequence and with the same components. The tools and equipment are arranged in a line according to where they are needed to produce the cars. This process results in a high volume of products that are all approximately alike and in relatively low costs due to the specialized equipment that is placed where it is needed.

A **batch** (or **disconnected-line) process** falls midway between a job shop and a repetitive line. Products or services can be produced in a line manner but are usually processed in large batches because of a particular feature of the product or process. For example, soup is made in large batches since it must cook for a certain amount of time. After a certain soup is prepared in a large kettle, it then flows out to the canning operation. The next batch, possibly of a different soup, can then be made in the same kettle (after cleaning, of course). This operation shares some of the characteristics of a job shop in that there is some flexibility in the types of products. The operation also has some characteristics of an assembly line in that all types of soup must go through the same process (mix, cook, can).

A **continuous process** operating system is a higher-flow version of a repetitive line. It is called *continuous* because the product flows continuously through the process. Examples are sugar refining and oil refining. This results in very high volume with very little variability in the final product: a sugar refinery makes sugar (with perhaps white and brown

A continuous-process operating system creates very high volume with very little variability in final product.

variations) in high volume in a plant that can do nothing else. The result is low cost and high dependability of volume output.

Generally an operation does not rely strictly on one type of process. A fast-food restaurant, for example, may have a batch process (the grill on which hamburgers are cooked), a repetitive process (the assembling of the burgers), and then a job shop (counter workers who custom-assemble the final product).

Key Management Tasks

Job shop, repetitive, batch, and continuous processes require different management tasks, some of which were shown in Figure 22.2. A job shop, since it may involve many different jobs moving in many different routes, requires managerial skills in scheduling production, tracing orders, estimating capacity, and determining costs and delivery times. For instance, the manager of a hospital emergency room is concerned with the scheduling of patients, doctors, and nurses. Since each patient has a different illness or injury with varying degrees of severity and patients arrive randomly, the emergency room must have a scheduling system that moves the most critically ill or injured patients through the facility most efficiently and effectively.

A repetitive operation (such as an assembly line), due to its high volume of standard product, requires management skills in determining the timing of expansion and technological change; in managing large, specialized, and complex organizations; in running equipment at peak efficiency; and in raising the capital to pay for expensive equipment and facilities. For example, since an auto assembly plant is usually dedicated to one or two basic models, managers spend little time making decisions about which models to produce in any one day or week. On the other hand, managers must deal with the complex task of ensuring that the thousands of parts necessary for each car are available at the right time. Changes in the process, such as the addition of a new painting facility, involve major decisions that may take years to move from planning to implementation. Changes in technology are major ones that must be made at the appropriate time, or competitors may gain an advantage.

Competitive Differences

Each of the four operating processes has different competitive abilities. A job shop can produce custom products and services with a large amount of flexibility, while a continuous process is capable of delivering large volume at low cost. Generally an organization that produces custom products should use a job shop. An organization that provides a high volume of standardized products should use an assembly line. Note how the four operating function objectives described earlier in this chapter are positioned on the product/process matrix in Figure 22.2. On one extreme, a job shop is capable of quality (customized) products, with the ability to be flexible in the amount of production and the variety of products. A photocopy center is a classic job shop. Each customer has a slightly different product, whether in quantity of copies required or in the configuration of the processing (four copies of one page or one copy of four pages, stapled, and so on). A copy center is very flexible in quantity and product variety, while able to produce a custom (high-quality) product. On the other extreme, an order to copy 10,000 posters could not be handled efficiently at a standard copy center. That type of job is better done by a commercial printer with high-speed presses. The result would be lower cost and high dependability in delivering a large quantity of identical copies.

Designing and Using the Operations Function

Operating managers must first design an operating system, then use it to produce products and services. Design and use decisions must be made within the framework of an organization's strategy to gain a competitive advantage. These decisions also should be made to ensure that the operating functions are fully integrated with other organizational functions, such as human resource and financial management.

Integrated Operations

A typical product or service goes through the following sequence of activities:

1. Product and process design
2. Planning and control system design
3. Production or delivery
4. Distribution
5. After-sales service and support

All parts of an operating system should be designed and used in harmony with each other. If a purchasing agent buys low-quality parts, there may be a negative impact on the reliability of the product after it is produced and sold. If the purchasing agent, design engineers, and warranty department had discussed the product or service before the purchase, there would be a clear understanding and coordination of efforts between these functions to ensure a reliable product.

It is necessary to integrate these five activities in dealing with vendors and customers. For example, when product designers are working on a design, they must approach materials vendors to find out the types of available products. Automobile designers approach radio vendors to identify the latest radio technology so that the proper wiring can be designed into the cars.

Design Decisions

Design decisions are long-term and usually made by upper or upper-middle managers. Decisions about the location and size of a facility are not easily changed once it is built.

Product and service design, although not usually carried out within the operations function, has a major impact on how a product will be produced or a service delivered. For example, air conditioning is standard on luxury cars and is factory installed. In less expensive cars, it may be an option that can be either factory or dealer installed. An inexpensive car must be made with the proper placement of holes and supports so that an air conditioning unit can be easily installed by the dealer. A luxury car will not need this, since all air-conditioning units are factory installed.

Process design involving the type of process and types of equipment must be coordinated with product design. For example, in the fast-food industry, there have been different approaches to marketing and producing hamburgers. One large chain produces a standardized product, while another at one time advertised that customers could have a burger "their way." The design of a product (standardized vs. customized) results in different production processes. The "have-it-your-way" hamburger chain has a process that allows customization without excessive costs, while the other chain has a process that produces exactly the same product every time.

Capacity is the maximum amount of product or service that can be delivered in a stated time frame—for example, 400 cars per shift on an auto assembly line and 100 customers per hour at a restaurant. An operation's capacity must be matched to the expected or anticipated demand. For large operations, such as auto assembly, this is a difficult decision: extra assembly plants waste money if they are not used, yet insufficient capacity when demand is high results in lost sales. The capacity decision is often combined with the location decision, since it is possible to balance production between one large, central plant and many small, scattered plants.

Organizations can locate near customers, near sources of raw material, or near sources of labor. The **location decision** is a function of the nature of the product or service, the type of inputs, and other factors. A supermarket must be located near its customers; a furniture manufacturer may be located near sources of lumber and labor; some colleges are located near customers, while other colleges are located where the founders started them.

The **layout** of a facility is a function either of the product or process used in production. A product layout arranges the processing equipment or functions in sequence as they are needed in production. An assembly line is an example: a car is assembled in a certain sequence, which is a function of its design, and the processing equipment must be arranged in that order.

Process layout groups equipment according to the functions it serves. A college typically locates administration in one building, the college of arts and sciences in another, the college of business in another, and the gymnasium in another. This is done because each customer (or student) travels a different path through the college each day, and it would be impossible to arrange the buildings or classrooms in a sequence for more than a few students.

Finally, jobs must be designed around the type of processing equipment being used, and the wage scale must be tailored to the skill level required to accomplish the jobs. For example, you would not want to hire a high-cost gourmet chef to cook hamburgers at a fast-food restaurant. Conversely, you would not hire a fast-food cook for a gourmet restaurant. The skill levels, pay scales, and final products are different.

Utilization Decisions

Utilization decisions are short term; they may be constrained by the design of a system and fall into planning, managing, and controlling activities. Before the plan for each product, department, and machine is determined, the plan for the entire operating system, known as an **aggregate plan,** is created. It is easier to forecast the demand for an "aggregate" measure each month, such as the total student semester hours for an entire college, than to forecast activity in individual departments and programs. An aggregate plan is used to plan for the utilization of the operating system at this aggregate level for each month during the coming year.

Based on the forecast for total cars, General Motors can plan the total car production for each of its assembly plants for each month for the next year, balancing the cost of inventory, back orders, and changing production rates. This allows the corporation to plan the number of workers it needs each month, raw material and parts purchases, and inventory levels.

The determination of which employees will work when and at which machines or departments and the determination of the work that will flow through the operating system is known as **scheduling.** Decisions must be made on a day-to-day, sometimes hour-to-hour, basis on which products or jobs to produce, which jobs should be expedited, which patients should be examined first, and so forth.

Inventory is a measure of physical goods that are produced and not yet sold. Inventories can include raw materials and purchased parts, work-in-process (WIP), and finished goods. Since inventory can be very costly to store, many decisions must be made regarding the scheduling of production to increase or decrease inventory. For example, inventory could be kept in raw-material form and finished products made only when customers demand them; at the other extreme, products could be produced and kept in finished-good form for rapid delivery. This is not an easy decision, since it is possible that a finished product may become obsolete or damaged if it is not sold, yet inadequate inventories could lead to lost sales for customers in a hurry to obtain the product. For example, auto dealers maintain a large inventory of cars on their lots for fast delivery, but at the end of each model year, they usually have some leftover cars that have not sold due to unpopular color, lack of key features, or low demand. On the other hand, a car can be ordered and produced to customer specification, but that takes several weeks.

Quality assurance and control relates to the fact that it is important to produce a product or service that meets customer expectations. Inspection of the service or product during its production can ensure that it will meet specifications. Proper design assures that the product or services will serve the desired needs.

More emphasis is now being placed on the role of **purchasing** in determining the quality of products or services. Purchasing agents at one time were merely required to find the lowest-cost suppliers of raw materials, parts, and services. Now managers recognize that using the lowest-cost supplier may not result in the lowest cost if many defective supplies must be discarded or returned or if low quality causes customer

Inventory is a measure of physical goods that are not yet sold. Since storage costs can be high, many decisions must be made about the scheduling of production to regulate inventory.

dissatisfaction in the final product. The role of purchasing is to work with vendors to supply the best product at the lowest cost.

Finally, **distribution systems** include warehouses and delivery systems, such as truck and rail operations. Decisions must be made regarding the location of warehouses and inventory and the best way to transport that inventory to customers.

World-Class Operations

Due to the competitive disadvantage of many U.S.-based companies, a significant revolution in the way operating systems are managed has been occurring since 1980. Through the 1970s and 1980s, Japanese manufacturers produced higher-quality products at lower prices and took over significant market shares in many industries. The response to this has been a study of several Japanese methods that have contributed to their superior market position. Contrary to popular opinion, the Japanese advantage was not gained solely through cheap labor rates and government subsidies. It was usually gained through superior production systems that resulted in high quality at low cost.

The ability to produce a product or service that can compete successfully anywhere in the world is known as **world-class operations.** Since the usual application of this principle has been in the manufacturing sector, it has been called *world-class manufacturing (WCM)* in the popular press. It is apparent that the concepts used in WCM are applicable to service industries, so the term *WCM* is not entirely accurate; world-class operations would be more appropriate.

This significant change in operations entails very different approaches to how operating managers manage. World-class operations focus on three key areas: inventory planning and scheduling, quality, and automation and process technology. These areas are addressed through just-in-time management, total quality control, and computer-integrated operations.

Just-in-Time (JIT)

The concept of **just-in-time (JIT)** applies to the way in which inventory is managed and production is scheduled and involves a particular philosophy of managing. In the "requirements era" in the United States, from the 1970s to the present, computerized systems have been used to determine the best schedule of production and location of inventory. During that time, Japanese managers were developing the key JIT philosophy: inventory is a fundamental liability that must be reduced. Inventory hides problems and costs that are not readily noticed.

This view of inventory forces managers to think of ways to reduce inventory problems rather than determining the best place to store inventory. For example, suppose that a hamburger restaurant chef decided to produce 100 cheeseburgers to place in inventory at the front counter to meet lunchtime demand. After the inventory of 100 burgers was delivered to the front, the first customer noticed that there was no cheese on the cheeseburger. On inspection it was discovered that there was no cheese on any of the burgers; the chef made an error. Unfortunately, most of the 100 burgers had to be discarded, since there was small demand for hamburgers.

Now consider what would have happened if the chef had made a smaller batch of 10 rather than 100 and had made 10 small batches to meet the demand as it occurred during lunch. Obviously, the inventory level would be much smaller. Although the first defective cheeseburger would have been discovered at about the same time as before, only 10 hamburgers would have to be discarded. When the chef received feedback that cheese had been omitted, he or she could have made an immediate correction, added cheese to the next batch of 10, and made no more cheeseless cheeseburgers.

Notice that this inventory reduction through smaller batch size also results in improved quality, a reduction in waste (and consequently cost), and a reduction in space requirements for holding the inventory. Also consider that the chef would have been more productive, since the 100 cheeseburgers would not have had to be made again. The inventory of 100 cheeseless cheeseburgers might also have inconvenienced customers, a cost (perhaps of future lost sales) that is hidden and very difficult to detect.

JIT is difficult to implement, however, because managers have historically used inventory to compensate for uncertainties in demand. In addition, inventory hides problems, and few managers want problems to arise, since they are spending too much time already handling problems. If the system can be designed to deliver a product or service quickly, however, there is little need for inventory.

A manager can begin to move toward JIT with a deliberate reduction of inventory. A reduced inventory eventually causes problems to surface. JIT managers actually welcome these problems, since they indicate the reasons for having excessive inventory. Solving the problems allows even further reductions of inventory.

The overall effect of JIT is to improve the total operating process, not just to reduce inventory. Quality improvement and scrap reduction are typical in a JIT environment, with resulting productivity improvement. It is very difficult to argue against the success of this technique when you consider the success of the Japanese-dominated industries that produce automobiles, cameras, and electronic home consumer products, all characterized by high quality and lower price.

Total Quality Control (TQC)

For a JIT system to work well, the quality of incoming parts and supplies must be high. Since production occurs in small batches with little inventory to cover any variation in production rate, there can be no defective parts, or the production process will not meet demands. In a JIT system, if defective parts come into the process, they are discovered quickly.

The basic premise of **total quality control (TQC)** is that quality is everyone's responsibility, not just the responsibility of a quality control department. That is, everyone must work together to determine how

The premise behind total quality control is that quality is everyone's responsibility.

quality can be improved. The quality of a final product or service has a direct bearing on how customers perceive the product.

Like JIT, TQC requires a philosophy of continual improvement through the discovery of problems, which are then corrected, with a resulting increase in quality. This is counter to the conventional quality wisdom that has endured for many years in this country: quality can be "inspected in." That is, if you inspect the product or service at many points in the process, you can remove products or services that do not meet standards. This attitude ignores the time wasted in producing defective products, with resulting productivity decreases and larger amounts of scrap. The TQC approach is different: find the problems and fix the process so that only defect-free products are produced. This results in reduced scrap and higher productivity.

In conjunction with JIT, TQC can help reduce costs (scrap, warranty costs, and so on) while improving quality. This also is a concept that runs counter to conventional wisdom: higher quality is believed to mean higher cost. This wisdom does hold regarding the features of a product, say a Cadillac vs. a Chevy; higher quality (more features) does mean a higher price (from higher cost). Lower costs, however, result if a car is produced that meets specifications, whether it is a Cadillac or a Chevy.

Computer-Integrated Operations

Recent advances in electronic technology have resulted in a significant improvement in the ability to control manufacturing and service processes by computer. For example, an automated bank teller can accept deposits, dispense cash, and show account balances. This process links account balances and can be used to show the bank's immediate cash positions to its financial controllers. Various functions within the bank are integrated by computer.

In manufacturing, product design can be assisted by engineering design software, which can provide machines with procedures for producing parts. Computer-controlled equipment that is scheduled with computer-driven systems can then produce products with little human intervention. This technology allows a new degree of flexibility—in both volume and product variety—in the production of high-quality parts and products. With computer-integrated operations, there is no need for inventory, since units can be produced on demand.

An earlier section of this chapter discussed the four objectives of an operating system in relation to a key result: it may not be possible to achieve more than two of the objectives at a time—for example, both low cost and high flexibility in design and volume. This old approach, which was shown in Figure 22.2, indicates that low cost is usually combined with large volume (in a repetitive process) and that high flexibility is not possible with either. Computer-integrated technology combines high flexibility, high customization, and low cost.

Why haven't computer-integrated operations taken the world by storm? Progress has been slow due to cost and complexity of the equipment and software needed to accomplish integration and due to uncertainties about this type of generally unproven technology. This is an area, however, that is advancing very rapidly and deserves the attention of operating managers who must observe competitors' use of the technology.

The three areas of world-class operations—just-in-time, total quality control, and computer-integrated operations—are linked, although the third concept does not need to be implemented to gain the advantages of the first two. Significant implementation of the first two has begun in the United States, while the implementation of computer-integrated operations is still in its infancy, due to the new technology. These three topics are revolutionizing the management of manufacturing and can also be applied to service functions.

Today's operations managers are concerned with systems that must not only be operated on a day-to-day basis but also encompass increasing complexity and change. Product and process innovation is changing, and managers must be capable of changing along with it.

Operations Management in Review

Operations management is concerned with the production of goods and the delivery of services. Inputs of material, information, labor, and capital are used in the transformation process to produce useful goods and services. Many decisions must be made in designing a production system, in planning and managing its use, and in controlling it.

The design and use of a production system are crucial to successful competition in a rapidly changing global economy. Continual improvement is required to maintain a competitive edge. Both service and manufacturing operations can benefit from using the latest concepts of operations management.

An operating system must be integrated with other important functions, such as marketing, finance, accounting, and human resource development. The management of the process is highly dependent on the type of product or service and the type of delivery system used. There are different types of production systems; each type competes differently, and different management skills are required for each.

Global competition has forced organizations to determine how to compete with world-class operations. The best Japanese techniques of just-in-time and total quality control are now being applied in U.S. companies with excellent results. Computer integration requires new management tasks and results in more competitive advantages for organizations that can produce products and deliver services more quickly, at higher quality, with more customization, and at lower prices. These new concepts are changing the way managers must think about and manage operating systems.

Key Terms

competitive (strategic) advantage
job shop
repetitive process
batch (disconnected-line) process

continuous process
capacity
location decision
layout

aggregate plan
scheduling
inventory
quality assurance and control
purchasing

distribution systems
world-class operations
just-in-time (JIT)
total quality control (TQC)
computer-integrated operations

Issues for Review and Discussion

1. In your own words, define operations management.
2. What is the role of operations in an organization?
3. Watch a television commercial and list the attributes that are presented to induce you to buy the product or service. Which of those attributes are a direct result of the design and utilization of the operating function?
4. Think of the different types of restaurants in which you have eaten. Which ones could be considered job shops? batch processes? assembly lines? Do the objectives of those restaurants match the process objectives? Place the restaurants on the product/process matrix in Figure 22.2.
5. Many people who cook at home shop for food about once a week, buying enough for a week's worth of consumption. Other people eat in a cafeteria, thus avoiding the purchase of food ahead of time. Discuss these two different approaches in terms of JIT, TQC, and inventory management.
6. Discuss the operating objectives of the college in which you are enrolled in relation to a competing college. Use the operations objectives of cost, quality, flexibility, and dependability. Which of these does your college use as a competitive advantage? What form of production process does your college use? Does this fit its objectives?
7. How can computer-integrated operations increase a company's ability to compete?

Suggested Readings

Chase, R. B. and Aquilano, N. J. (1985). *Production and operations management: A life cycle approach*, 4th ed., Homewood, IL: Irwin.

Ferdows, K. and Skinner, W. (Fall 1987). The sweeping revolution in manufacturing. *Journal of Business Strategy*, 64–69.

Gunn, T. S. (1987). *Manufacturing for competitive advantage.* Cambridge, MA: Ballinger.

Hayes, W. and Wheelwright, S. (January-February 1979). Link manufacturing process and product life cycles. *Harvard Business Review*, 133–40.

Hayes, W. and Wheelwright, S. (March-April 1979). The dynamics of process-product life cycles. *Harvard Business Review.*

Schonberger, R. J. (1982). *Japanese manufacturing techniques—nine hidden lessons in simplicity.* New York: The Free Press.

Stevenson, W. J. (1986). *Production/operations management*, 2nd ed., Homewood, IL: Irwin.

Vonderembse, M. A. and White, G. P. (1988). *Operations management, concepts, methods, and strategies.* St. Paul, MN: West.

International Management

Student Learning Objectives

After reading this chapter, you should be able to:

1. Describe the roles of an international manager.

2. Explain why companies go abroad.

3. Discuss importing and exporting.

4. List the major factors that must be considered when managing in an international environment.

5. Understand the managerial problems and opportunities of joint ventures.

6. Describe how and why wholly owned subsidiaries need highly trained international managers.

7. Identify the basic tasks of an international human resource manager.

8. Describe the basic tasks of an international marketing manager.

9. Understand why the tasks of an international finance manager are so complex.

By Heidi Vernon-Wortzel of Northeastern University

*B*ritish businessman and business raider Jimmy Goldsmith, owner of France's second largest publishing company, sent Goodyear Tire & Rubber Company executives and Wall Street scrambling with his $5 billion bid to take over Goodyear.[1] What do Bertelsmann and British Petroleum have in common? Both are foreign-owned corporations that have recently acquired American-based firms, Doubleday Publishing and Purina Mills respectively.[2] GE and Toshiba have formed a consortium for the conduct of joint research and development. France recently let Sweden's L. M. Ericsson purchase Compagnie Generale Construction Telephoniques—and 16 percent of the French telecommunications market—while Britain's electronic group GEP PLC merged with Dutch electronics giant Philips.[3]

Between 1975 and 1979, world trade increased by approximately 32 percent. By 1980 the volume of world trade exceeded one trillion U.S. dollars; compare this to $800 billion in 1975.[4] Foreign investments by U.S. firms grew from approximately $12 billion in 1950 to approximately $280 billion in 1985.[5]

Such events and information clearly suggest that international trade can be a major factor in organizational management. This chapter defines international management and discusses various ways of "going international." You will consider a number of differences between the practice of management in domestic and international settings. As you look at the different arrangements companies make when they go abroad and the tasks that are involved, you'll see that executives need to develop special managerial skills to cope effectively in the international business environment.

No country in the world can be economically self-sufficient, and no company, however small, can ignore foreign competition. Fifty years ago, few managers predicted today's high degree of interrelationship among

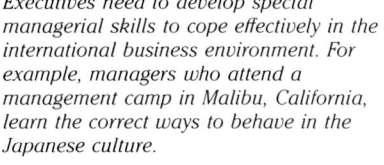

Executives need to develop special managerial skills to cope effectively in the international business environment. For example, managers who attend a management camp in Malibu, California, learn the correct ways to behave in the Japanese culture.

trading countries. Few would have foreseen the rise of the small Asian countries to their powerful position in world business, or the concomitant decline of U.S. power.

International management is the process of carrying out the managerial functions of planning, organizing, directing, and controlling in a business that operates in more than one country. An international manager's task is far more complex than that of a manager who operates in a single country. This book has suggested throughout that management consists of planning, organizing, directing, and controlling organizational resources in the pursuit of organizational goals. Managers engage in interpersonal, informational, and decisional activities. You have learned that management unfolds within two different contexts—the internal and external environments.

In considering international management, the definition of management will not change. International management and operations simply change due to new elements in an organization's general and task environments. "Going international" means that both the internal and external organizational environments are more complicated, given the presence of a greater variety of sociocultural, political, legal, economic, and technological factors. An organization's task environment also becomes larger and more complex as a result of an increase in the number and variety of customers, suppliers, competitors, regulatory agencies, and allies.

The International Environment

Sociocultural, legal/political, economic, and technological systems represent four major factors that exert a force on an organization's international operations (see Figure 23.1). International managers are challenged in their attempts to deal with these forces as they manage both the internal and external organizational environments.

Sociocultural Factors

The manager of an international operation may carry out his or her tasks in a domestic headquarters or in a foreign subsidiary. Regardless of where this manager actually works, he or she will have to be sensitive to the cultural differences among subsidiary locations. Doing business in New York is not like doing business in Saudi Arabia. Doing business in the United States is quite different from carrying out the functional-area tasks in England or even Canada. An international manager must consider the social and cultural elements of his or her home country as well as those of a host environment. Rules of behavior and differences among institutions can vary substantially from one country to another. Most people take their own culture for granted and rarely think about why they behave in a particular way. It is only when they leave their culture and deal with the different expectations abroad that they think about what culture is and what changes they have to make in the way they manage and conduct business.

FIGURE 23.1
The International Environment

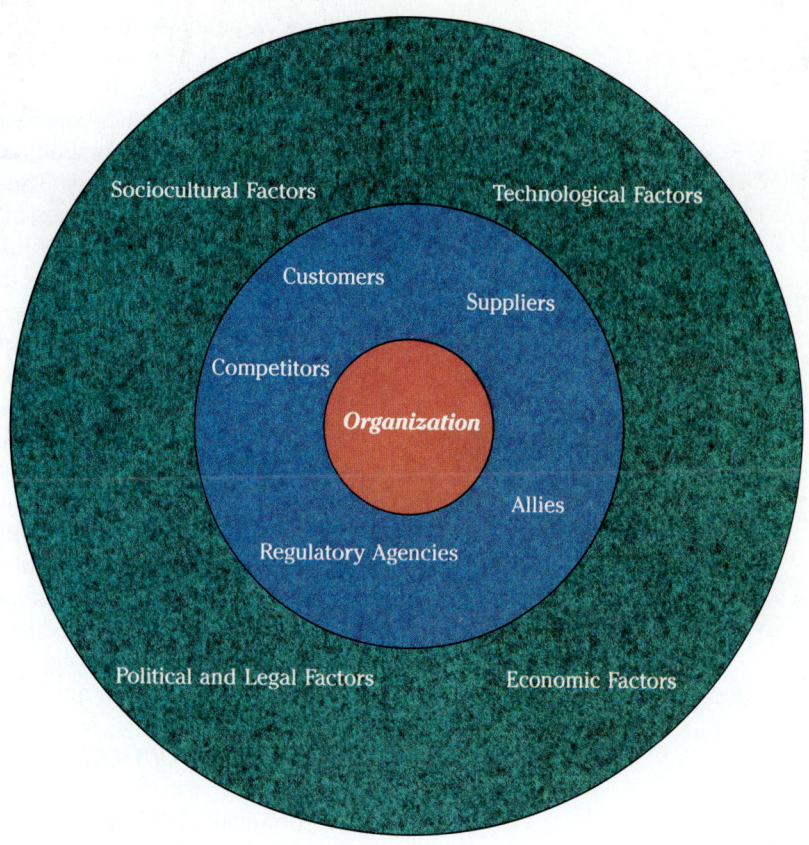

Culture can be defined as a complex whole that includes knowledge, belief, art, morals, law, customs, and any other capabilities and habits acquired by people as members of society.[6] Geert Hofstede calls culture a "collective programming of the mind."[7] People within a particular culture think, feel, and react in unconsciously patterned ways that give them a collective personality. A culture is made up of such components as language, religion, attitudes, education, norms, social organization, property, government, law, and community organization.

Rules of behavior are passed from generation to generation through the *enculturation process*. Language and the many forms of nonverbal communication transmit elements of culture so subtly that individuals are not usually aware that they act in response to the norms of their own culture.

Business culture in the United States can be quite different from that in other nations. Consider a few differences between the introduction protocol of Japanese and American managers. The use of business cards is common to both Japanese and Americans, although American managers rely on it far less than do the Japanese. A Japanese business meeting begins with a card-exchange ceremony, in which people exchange cards that include their name and rank within their companies. This exchange occurs even if the businesspeople do not expect to meet again. Japanese businesspeople bow to one another in a ritual called *ojigi*.[8] The depth of each bow depends on the prestige of each of the individuals engaged in the ceremony. If a person is greeting his superior, he bows lower than does the superior.

The lesson for an American businessperson in Japan is always to carry a card with his or her name, company, and position in English on one side and in Japanese on the other. The American should not bow. Americans are rarely aware of the nuances of rank in Japan. Furthermore, Japanese businesspeople understand the use of the handshake and will feel far more comfortable shaking hands than trying to engage in an exercise that requires intimate knowledge of the Japanese culture. The first few minutes of the simple act of meeting a foreign counterpart are so different from culture to culture that it is easy to understand that there are many potential cultural pitfalls for an international manager.

Other cultural elements relevant to organizational transactions include the amount of space people from different cultures like to maintain around them, what constitutes being "on time," and what subjects can be covered in "small talk." Knowing what is appropriate can make the difference between a successful transaction and a failure. The basic cultural differences among organization members from different countries can be learned. It is not necessary, or even possible, for a manager to learn every element of a foreign culture, but it is critical to learn enough about a host country's culture to avoid major gaffes.

Legal and Political Factors

The political and legal systems of a country are dimensions of the general environment that influence international management. Firms simultaneously operating in several countries have to deal with a variety of legal/political systems.

The legal/political systems of the world can be positioned along a continuum ranging from democratic systems to totalitarian systems. Democratic systems rely on a representative form of government. People and organizations operating in such systems play active roles through the electoral process, influencing national priorities, policies, and laws and electing individuals and groups to serve as their representatives. Under totalitarian systems, countries are frequently governed through dictatorships and/or single-party rule. Organizations are permitted to play a minimal role in governmental policy and regulation.

Organizations operating in a country are obligated to abide by its legal/political system and not strictly by the legal/political system of the home country. A number of legal/political factors can have a major impact on an organization's international operations. Some of the issues to be considered include governmental stability, terrorism, and laws and regulations governing foreign investment and international trade.

Economic Factors

World economies fall somewhere along a continuum between free-market economies and centralized-planned economies. Free-market economies basically operate under the laws of the marketplace and the dynamics of supply and demand. The economic systems of the United States and Canada are free-market economies.

A sufficient, accessible knowledge base within a host country enables an organization to deliver its products efficiently and effectively.

Organizations operating in a centralized-planned economy will find that the central government makes basic economic decisions for the entire nation. Resource allocation, pricing and distribution, wages, and production quotas are defined in accordance with a master societal economic plan.

The challenges and responsibilities associated with carrying out the task of management are quite different under these two economic systems. In order to be successful, international companies must adapt their management practices to accommodate the realities of this external environment.

There are other economic factors that influence the nature of operations across various countries. Management should consider a country's infrastructure, with a focus on such factors as its education, communication, and transportation systems; the country's level of economic development; exchange rates and the government's trade, monetary, and fiscal policies; and the country's resource and product markets.

Technological Factors

Another component of an organization's foreign and general environment that significantly influences the organization's operations are technological in nature. Technological dimensions consist of the availability of equipment, machinery, and components that will be used in the transformation of the firm's inputs into outputs. Is there a sufficient, accessible knowledge base within the host country that will enable the organization to deliver its product efficiently and effectively?

It should be apparent that the external environment within which an organization operates is complex. This complexity increases dramatically as the organization enters foreign markets because of the complex interaction among many sociocultural, legal/political, technological, and economic systems.

International Management Functions

As you have seen, "going international" makes both an organization's general and task environments more complex; thus, the management process is also more complex. Environmental scans needed to aid in the decision-making and planning process are more complicated; new kinds of organizational structures are needed; directing strategies have to cope with a variety of cultural differences; and organizational control systems need to be larger, more elaborate, and capable of integrating a greater variety of information.

Planning and Controlling

International planning and controlling require setting objectives and designing strategies and policies for a company that may face constraints unique to its host country or countries. Foreign laws and regulations may subject the company to forces beyond its control. An international manager, therefore, approaches the planning function knowing that he or she will have to provide a framework to help the firm reach its objectives in many different environments. An international manager may be able to state objectives in broad terms without much more difficulty than his or her domestic counterpart, but when specific objectives require directions and guidelines for employee action, the manager will have to consider the constraints and opportunities in each country in which the company is located.

The international planning and controlling functions take place in a context characterized by multiple and varied languages, political systems, currencies, governmental regulations, business climates, cultural value sets, and diverse and distant sources of information.[9] In this context, it is easy to see that successful planning efforts will be highly dependent on "good information." Given the increased environmental segmentation that accompanies international activities, it is incumbent on managers to make a major investment in a good information-retrieval system that is sensitive to environmental issues.

International managers must make international strategic planning an integral part of their overall long-range strategic planning. Without intense planning and detailed observation of operations, an international firm is subject to great risk. The international controlling function is influenced by many of the same opportunities and constraints as the planning function. Multiple environmental factors dictate the types of control systems that are effective in different locations and cultures.

Organizing

The organizing function is approached from the same perspective in the international context as in the domestic context. For example, characteristics of the environment, technology, people, and size of the system serve to influence organizing decisions. It is as important for there to be an environment-structure match for a firm operating only in Washington, DC, as it is for a firm with international operations.

For small firms or organizations that are just beginning to enter the international arena through importing or exporting, structural arrangements are likely to be very simple. As the scale of international operations increases and becomes more complex, specialized departments may have to be created. Further growth in international operations may lead to the creation of an international division within the organization. Finally, an organization can develop a truly multinational organizational structure. The evolution of international organizational structures is illustrated in Figure 23.2.

Multinational organizations generally have one of four basic structural arrangements. These four structures are illustrated in Figures 23.3A–23.3D on pages 806–9.[10] You may wish to refer to Chapters 10 and 12 as you study the structures.

1. The *multinational geographic structure* involves a territorial form of departmentalization. A world headquarters coordinates international operations and assumes major responsibility for strategic operations, but day-to-day operations are managed by territorial divisions.

FIGURE 23.2   *The Evolution of an International Organization Structure*

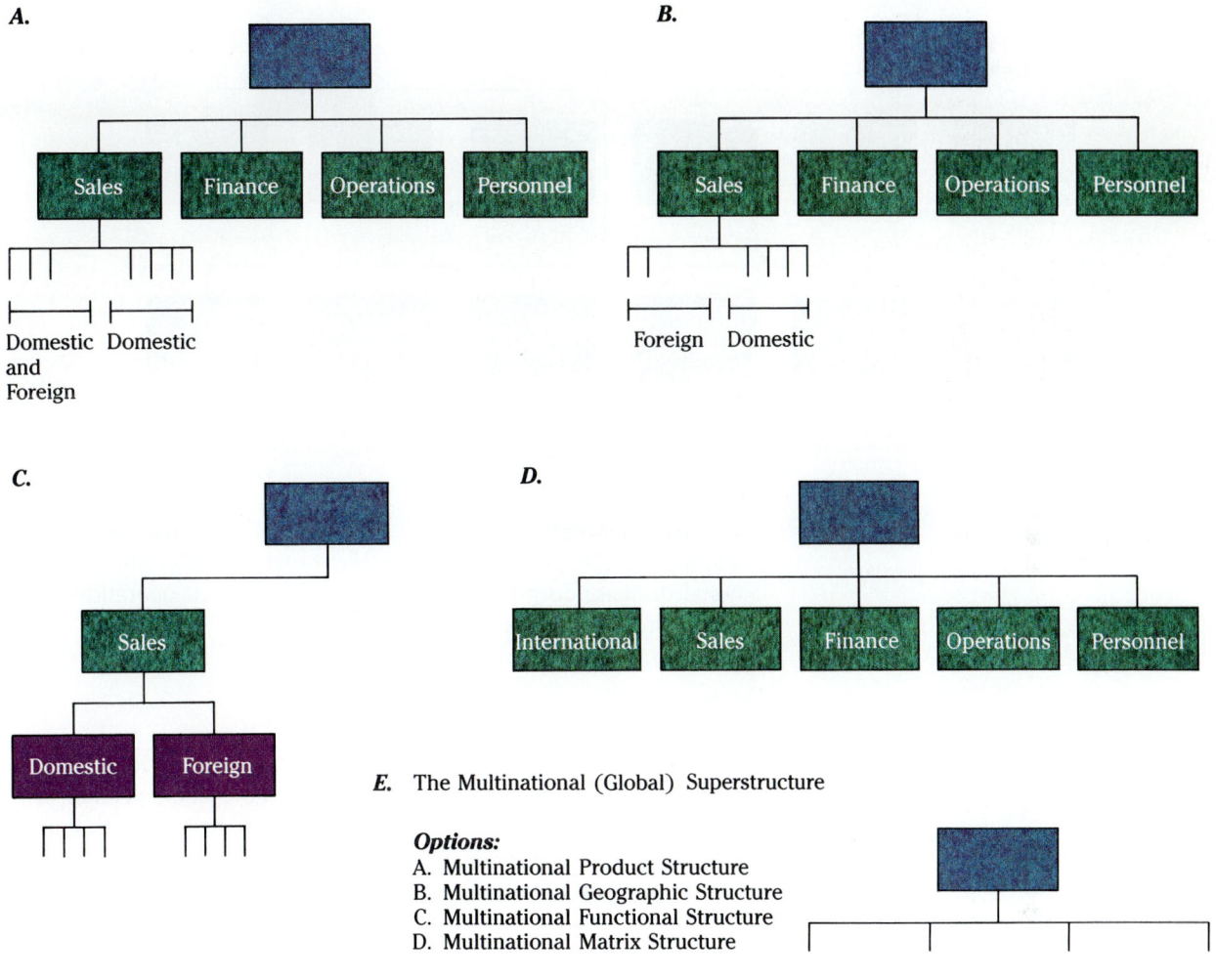

A.

Sales | Finance | Operations | Personnel

Domestic and Foreign   Domestic

B.

Sales | Finance | Operations | Personnel

Foreign   Domestic

C.

Sales

Domestic   Foreign

D.

International | Sales | Finance | Operations | Personnel

E.   The Multinational (Global) Superstructure

Options:
A. Multinational Product Structure
B. Multinational Geographic Structure
C. Multinational Functional Structure
D. Multinational Matrix Structure

Each of these divisions is organized to take advantage of environmental resources in its foreign location.

2. The *multinational product structure* also involves a large world headquarters that functions much like the headquarters in a multinational geographic structure; however, the international operations are organized around a firm's major product lines. It would not be unusual for the product divisions to use geographic departmentalizations to handle the diversity in product demands that may stem from different cultures.

3. The *multinational functional structure* is patterned after the functional form of departmentalization. Each manager is in charge of one of the organization's major functional areas, such as finance, and controls worldwide operations in that area.

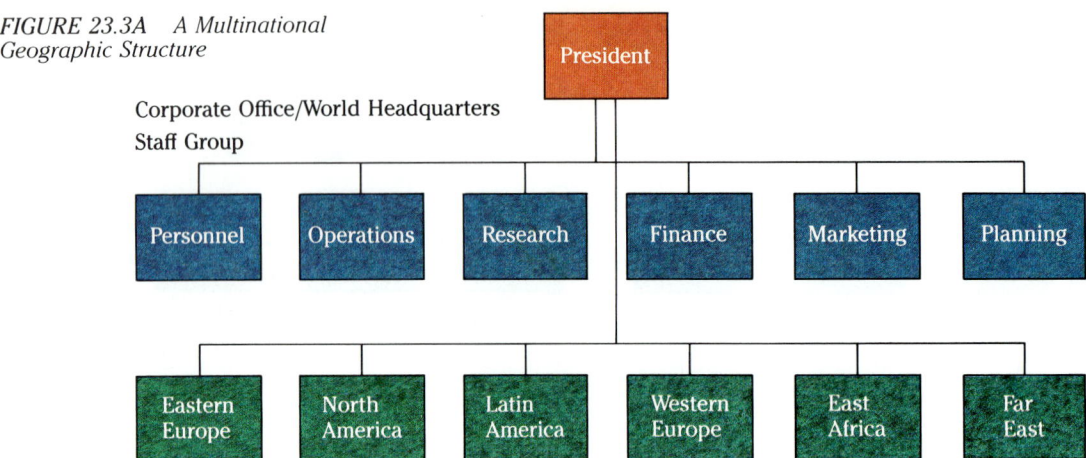

FIGURE 23.3A   *A Multinational Geographic Structure*

Corporate Office/World Headquarters
Staff Group

| President |

| Personnel | Operations | Research | Finance | Marketing | Planning |

| Eastern Europe | North America | Latin America | Western Europe | East Africa | Far East |

4. The *multinational matrix structure* simultaneously uses a product and a geographic structure. Across the organization's entire international domain, coordination is achieved among all operations and within product lines and geographical locations.

Directing

Once a company has been designed and the plans developed, the plans must be carried out. In order to guide and move employees to help the organization meet its objectives, a manager must provide leadership to people from other countries and must communicate with them and motivate them in ways that may be very different from the methods used in the home country. An international manager must know what incentives are appropriate, what constitutes supportive behavior, and how to give feedback in such a way that foreign managers are encouraged to meet the organization's goals. Imagine how an American manager might motivate an employee in a culture in which monetary rewards are not considered important. An international manager must understand what foreign employees value.

It cannot be assumed that U.S. models of motivation, leadership, political and communication processes, and group management are equally effective across cultural boundaries. International managers, therefore, must carefully develop directing strategies that are anchored in the specific culture in which their organization is operating.

Why Do Companies Go International?

Managers thinking about investing abroad, purchasing from foreign manufacturers, or simply exporting goods to another country find themselves in a situation fraught with uncertainties and risks. Why, then, contemplate entering international business? Why not be content to

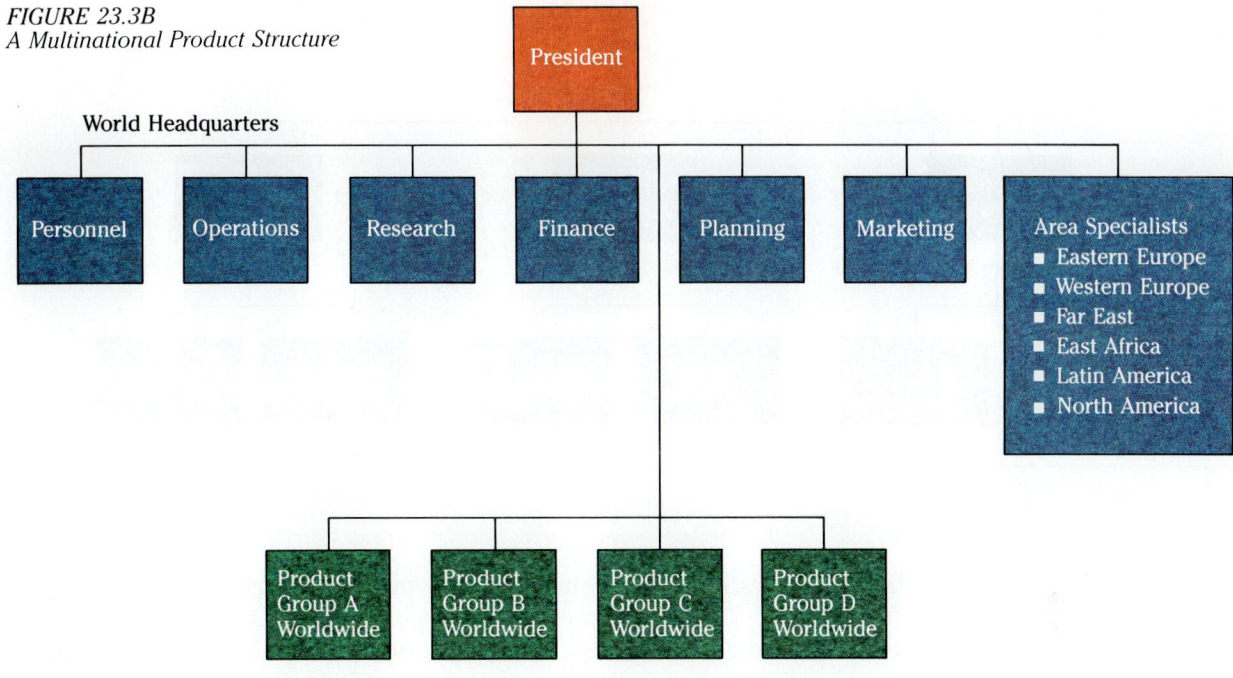

FIGURE 23.3B
A Multinational Product Structure

World Headquarters

President

Personnel | Operations | Research | Finance | Planning | Marketing

Area Specialists
- Eastern Europe
- Western Europe
- Far East
- East Africa
- Latin America
- North America

Product Group A Worldwide | Product Group B Worldwide | Product Group C Worldwide | Product Group D Worldwide

---

operate in an environment that is familiar, comfortable, and at least reasonably predictable? The answer is that in the United States or in any other country there is no domestic environment that has not felt the impact of foreign competition, and there is no organization so small that there are not opportunities to be found abroad.

Some of those opportunities can be exploited even by very small firms. If you are a manager contemplating expansion to other countries, you might look at the example of Otto Clark whose little company, Clark Copy International Corporation, was able to win a contract with the Chinese despite fierce competition with American, German, and Japanese conglomerates. In 1981, Clark won a twenty-year $5.5 million contract to deliver desktop copiers and parts to China because he was able to win the trust of the Chinese and respond quickly to their needs.[11]

There are opportunities for very large, diversified firms as well. Walking through the Guangzhou (Canton, China) Foreign Trade Center you might see the Jolly Green Giant staring at you from a huge poster and suggesting, in Chinese characters, that you buy niblet corn and tiny green peas. Western expatriates working in China are making the bulk of the purchases, but surely some Chinese with foreign currency are developing a taste for Western food. A tiny market for Western foods today can be a huge market tomorrow.

Foreign Companies in the United States

Increasingly, foreign companies are snatching U.S. domestic markets. The Bertelsmann Group of Germany now owns Doubleday Publishers; Nissan Foods makes the dry ingredients for oceans of noodle soup in a factory a few miles up the road from Campbell; and Benetton of Italy

FIGURE 23.3C
A Multinational Functional Structure

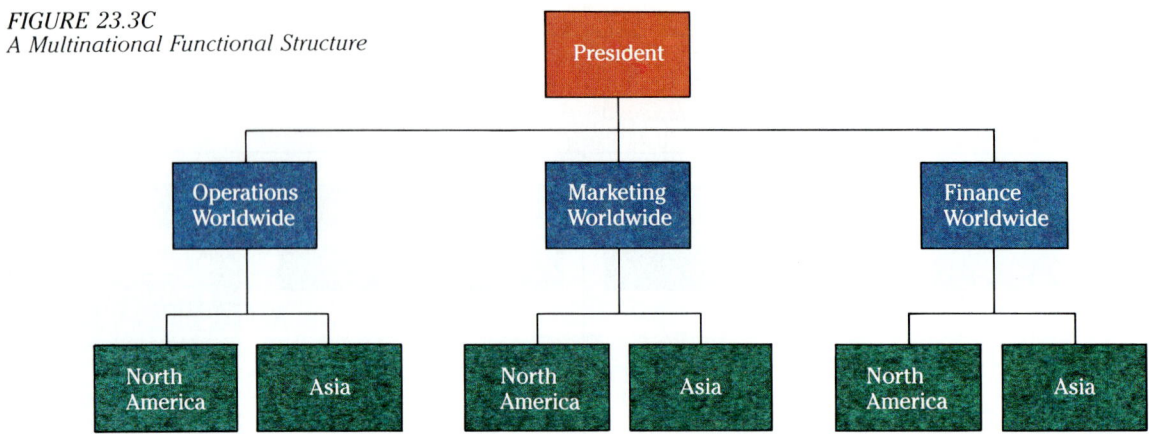

dresses American teenagers, their younger siblings, and even their parents.[12] The British have become major investors and competitors in the United States. In 1986, British companies spent $14 billion gobbling up U.S. firms and, in the first nine months of 1987, spent $24 billion.[13] British Petroleum now has the controlling interest in America's largest oil field in Alaska. Hanson Trust PLC has acquired Kidde, Inc., which is best known for Jacuzzi whirlpool baths and Farberware cookware.[14]

Managers in every type of business are well aware of Japanese investment in the United States. This investment ranges from Nissan automobile factories to YKK zippers to commercial real estate. Although the Japanese are still behind the British and Dutch in terms of total investment in the United States—and in 1987 only accounted for about 11 percent of foreign investment—they are investing in industries that can make in the United States what they now export from Japan.[15] Japanese motorcycles, automobiles, televisions, and photocopiers are all being made in the United States and are not subject to import barriers, such as tariffs or quotas. Increasing numbers of U.S. managers and workers are now working for Japanese bosses in Japanese-owned buildings.

There are obvious reasons that foreign investment from Britain, Japan, or elsewhere is important to an American manager. Home-turf competition increasingly comes from foreign-owned companies that are often better organized, better financed, and "hungrier." As foreign investment grows, American managers can find themselves on the defense unless they, too, develop a global perspective.

U.S. Firms Competing Abroad

One of the most common reasons for firms' deciding to go international is for *market* reasons. Saturated domestic markets and perceptions of opportunities to expand sales by entering foreign markets prompt many organizations to become involved in international activity. Some organizations go international in order to acquire *resources* that are needed for the

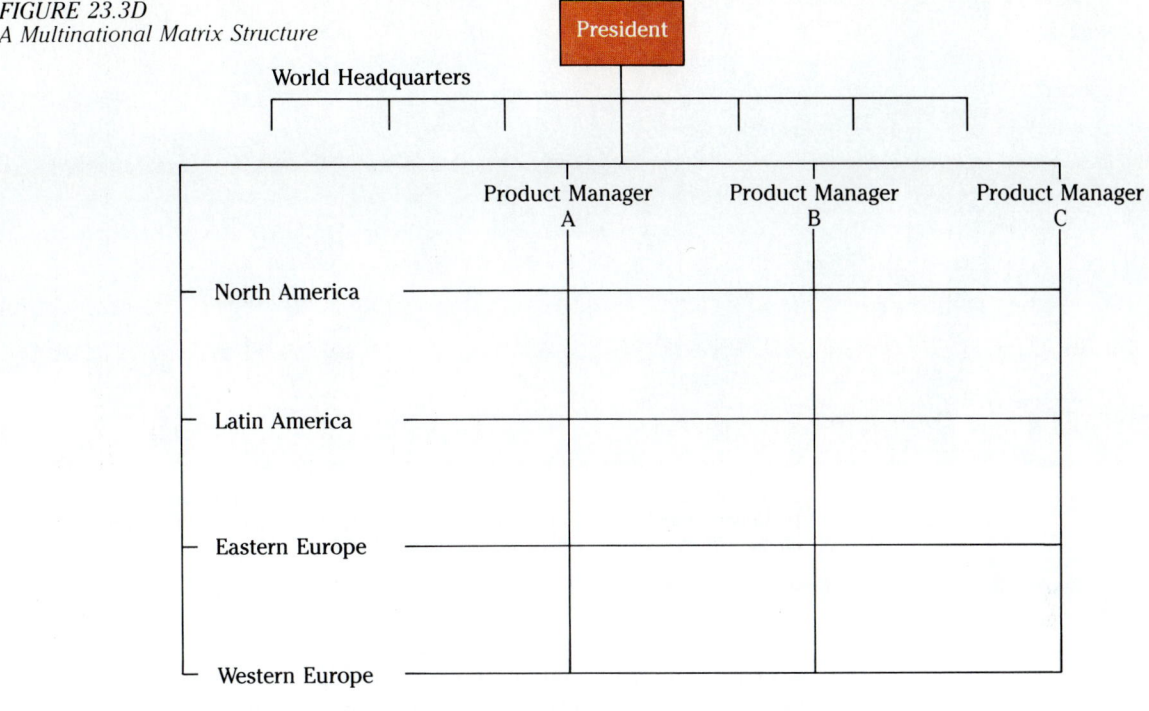

FIGURE 23.3D
A Multinational Matrix Structure

World Headquarters

President

Product Manager A

Product Manager B

Product Manager C

North America

Latin America

Eastern Europe

Western Europe

production of goods or for access to products to sell that are not available domestically. Many firms have gone international for *production* factors. In many instances lower labor costs in other countries can lower a firm's production costs. Finally, in many instances, firms enter the international arena simply because their major *competitors* have decided to expand into foreign operations. Fear that the competition might enjoy lower costs and/or higher sales gains may prompt a firm to follow its competition to these new and foreign markets.

International business is certainly not new to American firms. American entrepreneur Isaac Singer manufactured his sewing machine in Scotland only twenty years after he invented it in Boston. In the late nineteenth and early twentieth centuries, many other American firms began to move abroad with their operations and grew rapidly in size and strength. Even so, just twenty-five years ago, about one quarter of the companies on *Fortune*'s 500 list had no overseas manufacturing subsidiaries.[16] Today, virtually all *Fortune* 500 firms have a substantial overseas presence. Many American managers and entrepreneurs of firms much smaller than the *Fortune* 500 have realized the opportunities offered by foreign investment and have taken advantage of them.

Consider, for example, Scott Karppinen of Hibbing, Minnesota. At peak production, his company makes 1.6 billion chopsticks a year, or 7 million pairs a day. The entire output of the factory is exported to the Far East. Other American companies have had long traditions of overseas business, not just in marketing but in manufacturing as well. General Motors has had

Some organizations enter foreign markets to seize new sales opportunities. For instance, the Japan Branch of the American Family Corporation surveys untapped Japanese markets in an effort to expand its insurance sales.

a major manufacturing presence in Europe since the 1920s, when it bought Opel. In 1987, GM management embarked on a turnaround strategy to streamline European operations and coordinate activities by imposing a new corporate structure on all European operations. GM's major competition in Europe comes not just from European car companies but, importantly, from Ford.

While there are endless examples of companies that have seized opportunities abroad, there are still many more like General Electric and Maytag that have decided to not enter the fray in certain product categories. The big appliance market is an example. GE and Maytag decided not to compete for worldwide market share in washing machines and other "white goods"; however, Sweden's Electrolux aggressively pursued in the same markets and made $5.1 billion in 1987. Electrolux (no relative of the American firm by the same name) also snatched White Consolidated in the United States and used its brand names of Frigidaire, Tappan, and White-Westinghouse to compete with GE and Whirlpool in U.S. markets.[17]

In sum, a growing number of American firms are heeding the advice of the Business Roundtable that exhorts American companies to get involved abroad. In the report of its Policy Committee, the Roundtable urged U.S. managers to remember that: "The major responsibility falls on each company to stress the development of strategies and methods in a framework of global and long-term performance. . . . The major responsibility falls on each company to foster effective and timely development of competitive products."[18]

There is one irrefutable fact with which U.S. firms must deal. Like foreign companies, they no longer have the luxury of dependence of domestic markets. They *must* go abroad. The questions are through what mechanism and how effectively will they carry out their management tasks?

Linkages Abroad

There are many arrangements that firms can make as they go abroad. At one end of the spectrum, a manager can simply choose to pack up a product and ship it to an importer in another country, where that importer will take all of the responsibility for marketing, thereby relieving the company of many marketing decisions. On the other hand, the manager can decide to manufacture abroad and use the company's resources to market the firm's products. International managers may enter into licensing agreements with foreign counterparts or become involved in complex product trades with a foreign government. In the largest corporations, an international manager may be involved with a complex web of international arrangements. To a major extent, the kind of arrangements into which a manager enters is determined by his or her company's product lines and by the size of its overseas operations.

Exporting and Importing

Organizations can enter international business by exporting or importing goods and/or services. International trade through **exporting** (selling goods to buyers in another country) or **importing** (buying goods from sellers in another country) is perhaps the simplest level of international operation. Few changes need to be made in an organization's organizing and directing functions. Planning is, of course, influenced by the importing/exporting strategy, and some control systems may have to be adjusted to accommodate such operations.

Most firms begin international business simply through **direct exporting,** or selling their goods overseas. Apple Computer started selling personal computers in Japan almost as soon as it sold them in the United States. Alcoa exported 25 million pounds of beverage-can sheeting to Japan in 1988.[19] Direct exporting does not necessarily require a great commitment of financial or human resources by a firm, nor does it require extensive international management expertise. Often a company will appoint a sales manager to handle the export business; this manager may work alone when the volume is small and create a new department as the export component of the business grows. This individual or department deals with the tasks of billing and shipping, but these activities are carried out in a familiar domestic environment. If the volume of exports warrants, a direct exporter may even set up its own sales company in the major markets to which it exports. The sales company uses the name of the parent company and bills customers in local currency.[20]

Indirect exporting involves making goods within one's own country but using an intermediary to sell them abroad. Such intermediaries are located in the country to which the goods are being sold, and they typically do all of the work associated with the sales. They may sell for a manufacturer, buy for a customer, or work for their own accounts. They have no say in the management of the exporting firm or in the customer's firm and are generally paid a commission for their services. A variation on indirect exporting is the export management company (EMC). EMCs typically operate on a buy-and-sell basis and handle their own financing.

Organizations can enter international business by exporting goods to buyers in other countries or by importing goods from sellers in other countries.

EMCs may obtain financing for a manufacturer, select markets for the goods, handle documentation relating to the transactions, and even consolidate shipments of various goods from a single supplier or of goods going to a single buyer from various sellers. The exporting company is thus relieved of having to develop its own in-house international management skills.

Some firms import goods and services from another country for domestic distribution. For example, Haskels Winery purchases a wide assortment of wines from around the world for resale in the Minneapolis/ St. Paul metropolitan area. Importing simply involves buying products or materials from another country for use or sale in the company's home country. Management skills must be developed to the extent that international purchasing arrangements must be effectively chosen and executed; in other aspects, buying from foreign sources is quite similar to buying from domestic sources, except that appropriate duties and tariffs must be considered in financial planning.

Joint Ventures

A **joint venture** is a company formed by two or more parent firms, which may be located in the country of one of the parents or anywhere else. There are many reasons for companies to form joint ventures. In some cases, they want access to a market and are forced, by a host government, to take on a local partner. In China, for example, there are very few freestanding foreign companies. The Chinese government, in an attempt to gain access to foreign technology and to enjoy income from foreign sales by exporting the joint venture output, insists that investors team up with local partners. Early in 1986, Orlando Helicopter Airway Company of Florida and Guangdong No. 3 Machine Tools Factory formed a joint venture to make Guangdong Province's first helicopters.[21] Northwest Engineering Company of Wisconsin announced that its Scottish subsidiary, Terex Equipment, Ltd., signed a twenty-year joint-venture agreement with the Inner Mongolia Second Machinery Company to manufacture trucks for use in road building and mining.[22]

In other cases, the joint venture gives one partner access to technology in return for a monetary compensation. In Korea, Daewoo automobile division is in a joint venture with General Motors (U.S.), Opel (West Germany), Isuzu (Japan), and Nissan (Japan) to make cars to export to the United States. Daewoo gets sales and technical cooperation from GM and technical cooperation from the German and Japanese partners.[23]

Honeywell Bull is a company that was formed in 1987, when Minneapolis-based Honeywell spun off its information systems division to a newly formed joint venture owned by Bull (French), NEC (Japan), and Honeywell. Honeywell Bull plans to be a world player in the computer business and will not limit its activities to any of the parent countries. The reasons for the joint venture in this case were complex. In part, the joint venture was designed to meet aggressive challenges from IBM and Digital Equipment in the computer field. Bull, an acknowledged leader in marketing open systems, networking, and turnkey solutions, had marketing expertise that Honeywell lacked. Honeywell knew technology, while

Bull was strong in serving the government and the banking and insurance industries. NEC's expertise was in research and development of top-of-the-line mainframe computers.[24] Managerial tasks, in this case, are shared by the partners and each tries to work the joint venture into its own organizational objectives.

There are many reasons that an international manager should consider a joint venture arrangement. Gains from technological cooperation and the achievement of scale economies are well known. Telecommunications is one industry in which there are examples of joint ventures that give the partners scale economies and a way of handling high entry costs. Steel is an industry in which joint ventures for technology transfer are taking place. In 1986, U.S. Steel and Pohang Iron and Steel Company of South Korea announced a joint venture. California Steel Industries is a joint venture of Japanese and Brazilian interests located in Southern California.[25] In these cases, the Korean and Brazilian partners got access to technology they would not have had otherwise.

Another benefit of a joint venture is the possibility of avoiding nontariff barriers. For example, the Chinese Jiangsu Provincial International Economic and Technical Cooperation Corporation is in a joint venture with Kingsboro Holding Company in Barbados.[26] Since the United States has a Caribbean Basin Initiative that offers Caribbean countries preferential access to U.S. markets, textile goods coming from Barbados are not subject to the same quotas that goods coming from China would encounter.

Still a third benefit is to gain access to an internal market that would not otherwise be available and to thus gain the economic and political advantages that partnership can bring. Investment risks can even be eliminated through the use of a partner's existing infrastructure of local marketing and distribution resources. China's state planning system has traditionally handled all of the marketing and distribution of joint-venture output. The foreign partners contribute technology, foreign currency, and training.

Joint ventures can also present many problems for managers. Many joint ventures fail or are terminated when one partner's contribution of technology does not prove to be as good as expected, or when partners cannot get along. Problems also arise when partners fail to deliver on their part of the agreement, or when owners who have promised to contribute resources or information cannot get their own personnel to deliver what has been promised.[27] Many of these problems can be avoided or solved when firms plan ahead and are firmly committed to making the venture work. Joint ventures are complex organisms that require trust on the part of all participants, careful selection of managers, and nurturing by parent firms.

Licensing Agreements

In a **licensing agreement,** a licensor gives a licensee the right to use a patent, trademark, copyright, technology, or other asset in return for a royalty or fee. A licensing agreement usually lasts for five to ten years, after which time the technology belongs to the licensee. There are both benefits and risks for the licensor in such agreements. The benefits of a licensing agreement is that it circumvents import barriers that may limit the quantity or add excessively to the price of the product. Licensing carries little or no political risk for the licensor. The worst that can happen is that the royalties will be lost. Small manufacturers, particularly, find it advantageous not to have to commit precious resources to building a plant overseas.[28] When a license is granted to a firm in a developing country, however, the risks involved in licensing agreements may be unacceptable, as was discovered by U.S. pharmaceutical manufacturers. The United States has consistently pressured the South Korean government to reform its patent law. When U.S. companies have licensed their patents to Korean pharmaceutical companies, they have encountered local Korean laws that grant process patents covering the techniques of production but which do not grant patents for the product or substance. When a popular U.S. product is licensed to a Korean firm, it is usually imitated within two to four years, because a competitor can legally produce the same products with a slightly different process. The licensor has little legal recourse.[29]

Licensors, in some cases have found that the royalties over the five-to-ten-year period of the license do not compensate for the fact that they have created strong competitors in world markets by entering the licensing agreement. Intangible assets licensed to a foreign firm are not protected automatically if that foreign firm wants to sell the product elsewhere. The licensor must protect the product by registering it in every foreign country in which it is sold. Even then, it may not be protected. Many of the risks and problems encountered in a licensing agreement can be overcome by drawing up a careful contract. It is highly desirable for a licensor to cover all of these issues prior to granting the license, since it is extremely difficult, if not impossible, to win a case in host-country courts.

Franchising is a relatively new form of international management. A franchisor licenses an entire business system to an independent franchisee in another country.

Franchises

Franchising is a form of investment that is relatively new in international business. It is actually a variation on a licensing agreement. A franchisor licenses an entire business system, as well as industrial property, to an independent person (a franchisee).[30] In **franchise** arrangements, the franchisor retains the right to inspect the franchisee's operations and to prohibit activities that may harm the product or service. For instance, McDonald's keeps a close eye on its overseas operations. When customers in Thailand stores wanted Filet-O-Fish sandwiches, the president of international operations tasted cod substitutes until he found one that was satisfactory. Franchisees sometimes come up with some new menu ideas, such as the Egg McMuffin. This combination of tight control over operating systems and encouragement of new ideas has resulted in 2300 international outlets.[31] Some of the other more readily identifiable American franchises outside the United States are Holiday Inn, Avis, Dunkin Donuts, and Kentucky Fried Chicken. Such products as Coca-Cola and Pepsi-Cola have always established franchised bottling operations when they have gone outside the United States.

Wholly Owned Subsidiaries

A **subsidiary** is an entity that is legally separate from the parent company and is organized under the laws of the country in which it is located. In a **wholly owned subsidiary,** the parent company owns 100 percent of the voting stock but its liability is generally limited to the assets of that subsidiary. Many companies, both U.S. and foreign owned, prefer to have total control over subsidiaries so that foreign governments do not have access to their technology or control over strategy.

Companies that have a variety of overseas linkages, of which a significant number are wholly owned subsidiaries, are often referred to as **multinational corporations (MNCs)** or multinational enterprises (MNEs). MNCs are large and have a substantial proportion of the workforce outside the home country. There is no magic number of linkages to define an MNC, but it is generally agreed that if a company has more than six foreign operations, it can be considered a multinational. MNCs hire local personnel to be managers, to work in factories, and to run operations. Although many strategic decisions for the firm are made in the home country, the sheer number of host-country personnel is substantial.

Some MNCs can be characterized as "multidomestic" companies. These companies are really a collection of individual domestic companies, where competition in one country is essentially unrelated to competition in another. An example of a "multidomestic" MNC is the Fuller Company. H. B. Fuller, a Minneapolis-based maker of paints, adhesives, and coatings, has 43 plants in 27 countries. Fuller's 1986 earnings were $18.9 million, and more than half of its operating profits were from foreign business accounts. This company customizes its products in foreign plants run by local people. It is a successful and thriving company that fosters close connections to customers and quick delivery of goods on a country-by-country basis.[32]

In the last decade, the pattern of international competition has changed somewhat. In some key industries, the environment now is dominated by a small number of worldwide competitors. Multinational corporations that respond to world markets through a unified strategy are referred to as **global enterprises.** Michael Porter defines a global industry as one in which "a firm's competitive position in one country is significantly influenced by its position in other countries."[33] Some of the manufacturing industries in which the global pattern is exhibited include television, copiers, semiconductors, automobiles, and pharmaceuticals. These global enterprises have two main characteristics: common strategy and common resources.

Global enterprises have a common strategy for all operations, both domestic and international. For example, the IBM headquarters sets policy for all its subsidiaries around the world. The management reorganization IBM announced in January, 1988, will have an impact on every part of the company, wherever it is located. Strategic moves into software and services will be part of the managerial plan worldwide.[34]

Global enterprises also have common resources. Technology, financing, managerial expertise, copyrights, and patents are used by the company in any or all subsidiaries. IBM's move into building voice and data networks will be felt worldwide, and the technology that goes into building the capability will be available to all of the subsidiaries taking part in the effort.[35] Digital Equipment Corporation (DEC) operates nearly twenty separate businesses selling the same products and services in Europe. In each subsidiary, there is a chief executive who is responsible for his or her own plans, yet headquarters determines the strategy, overall organization, and allocation of technology. Caterpillar Inc. headquarters transferred resources by shifting some of its U.S. forklift production to a subsidiary in Leicester, England, in 1985 (in order to reduce costs). Del Monte plans to be processing fresh fruit in its subsidiary in Cameroon by 1989 in an effort to develop new markets. All of these subsidiaries have headquarters in the United States, where the allocation of resources is made for the firm worldwide.

Wholly owned subsidiaries, whether of a multidomestic or global firm, have to conform to labor laws, wage laws, and hiring practices of their host countries. They also have to pay taxes and, in general, act very much like local firms. These firms also have the most involved and difficult management tasks and, to succeed, must develop the specific abilities that international management entails.

Countertrade

Countertrade is playing an increasingly important role in global trade. Managers find themselves having to consider arrangements that include the exchange of goods for goods. **Countertrade** involves simultaneous importing and exporting. It might occur when one country does not have easy access to foreign currency yet needs to engage in international trade. In 1986, an economist at the U.S. Department of Commerce estimated that by the year 2000 countertrade would account for one third of all world trade. Other estimates reach as high as one half.[36]

Barter, the exchange of goods for goods, is the simplest form of what has turned into an elaborate and complex set of linkages. Developing countries that face foreign exchange difficulties when they try to sell their goods in developed-country markets, or find that developed-country markets are protected, are turning increasingly to countertrade. These arrangements can be extremely complex and very often include investment, technology transfer, and compensation trade. Briefly, countertrades can include situations in which foreign suppliers are required to market developing-country goods abroad (counterpurchase) or are required to take goods as payment (buy-back). For example, early in 1987, two French companies, Dumez and Fougerolle, helped construct a steelworks in Nigeria in return for oil. In another arrangement, Caterpillar Inc. took iron ore from a Central American country in return for machinery.[37]

Managers are not unanimous in their attitudes toward the opportunities in countertrade. Some firms absolutely refuse to get involved with it. Other companies enter countertrade deals when there seems to be a good opportunity to make a deal. Still others aggressively seek countertrade agreements as part of a global strategy. To a significant degree, a company considering countertrade can enhance the likelihood of a favorable deal through careful planning and organizing. If countertrade adds significantly to a firm's overall profitability, the firm might consider organizing an internal countertrade unit. This unit identifies products that are suitable for countertrade, undertakes the negotiations, and contracts for the purchase and delivery of countertrade products. A critical part of the countertrade unit's job is to plan, organize, direct, and control the procurement and disposal of the goods.[38]

International Human Resource, Marketing, and Financial Management

You have seen that international operations can take place on large and small scales and that international managers are faced with numerous factors that vary from host country to host country. This section will take a detailed look at three organizational functions that are strongly influenced when they are undertaken in international firms. While you should not lose sight of the fact that all international managers must consider a wide range of forces in carrying out organizational functions, you will see that sociocultural forces have a major impact on human resource management and marketing management. Legal and economic factors, likewise, play major roles in international financial management. By considering these three functions, you can begin to examine some of the specific decisions international managers must make.

International Human Resource Management

Of all the functional areas of management, the management of human resources is most affected by the cultures of the host countries in which the firm has operations. This section will look specifically at international staffing as a part of the human resource management function. Issues of staffing, compensation, benefits, labor relations, and management technique will be very different, depending on the firm's strategy in managing subsidiaries and the national cultures in which the subsidiaries operate.

One of the most fundamental decisions that headquarters has to make is whether the subsidiary will be staffed primarily with managers from the home country, the host country, or both. When the staffing of subsidiaries is based on putting home-country personnel in place, it is called an **ethnocentric staffing** policy. Companies usually choose this policy because they want tight control by headquarters. Home-country managers, they insist, are more likely to communicate with headquarters and more likely to understand the overall goals of the firm. U.S. firms that insist on using home-country managers abroad usually focus on placing them in the finance area because they want their entire firm to adhere to the same financial standards.

Japanese firms are well known for using Japanese managers wherever subsidiaries are located. Their rationale is that Japanese is a very difficult language that few outsiders speak, and communication with headquarters would be impeded by having a local manager at the top of the subsidiary. Another reason for ethnocentric staffing in Japanese subsidiaries is that the managers need to have overseas experience for upward career moves. Very recently, Japanese organizations have been increasing their use of highly enculturated local managers, but only because of host-country insistence.

U.S. managers who are sent abroad by their companies often find that their careers back at headquarters are sidetracked and that the adaptation that was necessary to function abroad has little relevance at home. It has been estimated that it takes home-country managers about six months before they are functioning well in a foreign environment, and a significant number never adjust to the change. Failure of U.S. executives to stay for the term of their assignment is calculated at between 5 and 14 percent. The overwhelming reason for an early return is the inability of executives' families to adjust to their new environment.[39] The failure rate among Japanese executives is almost nonexistent, since loyalty to the company is the primary concern of Japanese managers, and their families are often left at home.

Host-country staffing, or **geocentric staffing,** is increasingly common. Host countries, particularly developing countries, insist that managers be locals, and there are compelling reasons for corporations to adopt this policy. Host-country managers are not as expensive to maintain as home-country executives; there is no long-term training and there are no extra payments for housing, schooling, and moving. Salaries for local managers are based on host-country scales, which are often considerably lower than in the home country. Local managers experience no language barriers and are more aware of the political and economic situations in their own country.

On the other hand, it can be argued that host-country managers may not be able to communicate easily with headquarters and may not understand the overall goals of their firm. Their local educational system may not have prepared them as well as their home organization would like. This situation is of particular concern when it comes to the finance and accounting functions, which usually have to be in accord with the parent company. Poor technological preparation is another negative attribute of some host-country managers. A graphic example of a managerial breakdown because of poor technological preparation occurred in Bhopal, India. The Indian government insisted on maintaining a policy of staffing local managers who simply disregarded the gauges that told them poisonous gas was escaping at a Union Carbide plant in 1984, with disastrous results.

Host-country nationals who head subsidiaries may perceive that they are superior to others in their organization and may be reluctant to "get their hands dirty." They may have built-in cultural biases about hiring minority groups, different ethnic or religious groups, or women. Finally, host-country managers may be stuck at the top of the subsidiary. It is unlikely that they will be brought to headquarters and integrated into the overall structure of a multinational. A French person would not have any difficulty in moving to headquarters in another European country, but it is probable that an Indonesian would encounter institutional barriers in moving to headquarters in Holland.

Polycentric staffing is staffing with executives from any country if they are the best people available. The concept makes very good sense; a global organization should pursue a global human resource management policy. If a Japanese manager of a U.S. subsidiary in Japan has the finance skills that are needed in Taiwan, it should make sense to send him or her there. If the skills of an Italian marketing manager of a French firm are needed in Hong Kong, why not buy him or her an airplane ticket? The possession of excellent functional skills does not necessarily ensure that an effective manager has been selected, however. A firm that wants to build an international management force must embark on a broad (and expensive) training program. Salaries have to be adjusted for living conditions, taxation, and currency fluctuations. There has to be a firmwide commitment to upward mobility of these managers in the corporation as a whole, so that regular transfers are rewarded. Finally, host-country governments have to be persuaded to accept the fact that the company does not hire host-country personnel unless they fit the needs of the company as a whole.

Combination staffing policies are a combination of ethnocentric, polycentric, and geocentric patterns. A major staffing consideration is a firm's product mix. In consumer products, it is advantageous to use local managers who understand local tastes and culture. For industrial products, it is less important that the manager be a local. It may be preferable to have a home-country manager in place who can quickly process information about the technology. Banks and other service industries tend to have a large number of home-country nationals in foreign subsidiaries so that local information is incorporated more quickly.

International human resource management is composed of much more than just staffing. All of the issues concerning compensation, benefits, and labor relations fall under this functional area. In many ways, the success of a company rests on how effectively it selects and manages its personnel.

International Marketing Management

An international marketing manager carries out activities that may be as basic as exporting to one customer abroad, or may encompass selling a number of products in many countries. He or she makes decisions about the "4 P's": product, promotion, price, and placement (or physical distribution). The marketing mix has international dimensions and may have to be tailored to the needs of foreign customers.

Market research helps a firm decide what is possible in terms of marketing abroad. Some of the elements that should be explored before entering a foreign market are competition, economic environment, consumption patterns, social customs, religious influences, transportation, legal systems, and political climates.[40] Data should be collected systematically, recorded carefully, and analyzed expertly. Market research can be done by personnel from headquarters who are sent abroad, or by managers already in overseas subsidiaries. Other alternatives are to hire a foreign research firm or a multinational research firm to assess potential markets. Finding the right group to do the job is essential to the success of the marketing effort.

Marketing managers must analyze research data to assess the suitability of a product in a foreign market. Even when a product is standardized and does not change when introduced abroad, foreign consumers may have certain expectations that will affect sales.

Product Every marketing manager knows it is dangerous to assume that just because a product sells well in the home-country it will sell well abroad. A marketing manager must use data collected by researchers to assess the suitability of the product in the chosen market. There are certain products that are considered to be standardized and, therefore, acceptable across cultures. For example, baby powder in New York should be the same as baby powder in Tokyo, and a bottle of Coke in Denver is basically the same as a bottle of Coke in Beijing. There are three fundamental questions an international marketing manager should ask about a product before it is introduced abroad:

1. Should the company sell the same product abroad that it sells in the home market?
2. Should the company change or adapt the product it sells at home to the specific needs of people in different cultures?
3. Should the company develop a completely new product?

Even when a product is standardized and does not change when it is introduced abroad, users may have different expectations that will affect sales. For example, the Japanese found the idea of talcum powder quite acceptable when it was introduced, but Johnson & Johnson could not sell it in the shaker can so familiar to Americans. It took the company a while before it discovered that Japanese mothers liked the powder but not the container. Since Japanese homes are typically very small, they were afraid the powder might get into food or onto furniture. When the powder was packaged in a cardboard box with a puff, Japanese mothers bought it. Even Coke ran into problems when it tried to find an advertising slogan in China in the 1920s. The company tried to find the Chinese characters that would correspond with the English pronunciation of Coca-Cola. The characters that eventually went on the bottle were translated to mean "bite the wax tadpole."[41]

Marketers know that, in general, cultural differences are more likely to affect tastes in consumer products than in industrial goods. Alternatives for changing consumer products to meet local needs include altering the physical characteristics of the product to meet local environmental needs. For example, American refrigerator manufacturers had a very difficult time selling their product in Japan until they discovered that their refrigerators' compressor was much louder than in Japanese refrigerators. They were able to muffle the sound and sell the product. Another strategy is to alter both the physical features of the product and the promotional message to sell it. Many messages on greeting cards are culture bound. An easy way to change the product is to take the message off of the card altogether and let consumers write their own.

Usually, marketing managers in multinational corporations adapt products when they go abroad. Sometimes they find that they can make simple changes, such as putting less salt in a canned soup or rewiring an electric appliance. Other times, no matter what they do, their products do not sell in a foreign environment. American consumers may be quite comfortable cooking an entire dinner in a microwave oven. Microwave-adapted products will not find a ready market, however, in cultures in which economics do not support widespread purchases of microwave ovens, where food is prepared by stirring over high heat (as in the Orient), or in cultures that value cooking "from scratch." Market research, done effectively, helps uncover adaptation needs and product requirements.

Promotion Promotion is the second part of the marketing mix. The fundamentals of developing an international promotional strategy include: "(1) determining the promotional mix (the blend of advertising, personal selling, and sales promotion) in national markets; (2) determining the extent of worldwide standardization; (3) developing the most effective message(s); (4) selecting effective media; and (5) establishing the necessary controls to assist in achieving worldwide marketing objectives."[42]

The stories of promotional efforts gone awry are legion. David A. Ricks has written books that chronicle many of the marketing blunders companies can make. As he points out, cultural norms in presenting products vary widely. General Motors, in marketing a car in Belgium, intended to promote the car as having a "Body by Fisher." Instead, the Flemish translation was "Corpse by Fisher."[43] Braun developed its promotional strategy for an electric razor carefully. A Norwegian magazine advertisement showed the sleek, high-tech razor lying against a formal shirt and black tie. The translation of the text was "To indulge in a little bit of luxury is not the same as wasting money." In the United States, the copy would have stressed performance and styling—not thrift.

French advertisements for body cream and beauty products often show a nude woman in what, by American standards, is considered a sexually provocative pose. When the same companies advertise in the United States, they conform to U.S. norms and clothe the models. In the United States, advertisements for female sanitary products are now quite candid and acceptable in the print media and on television. These same ads would be both insulting and illegal in the Middle East.

It is important to remember that media vary widely across cultures. While most people in developing countries listen to radios, they may not be able to read. Even if they can read, they may not have access to magazines or newspapers. In West Africa, for instance, buses are traveling billboards and are a very effective means of getting messages to the public, a fact that is not likely to be obvious to a foreign firm.

Pricing Of the 4 Ps, pricing is most likely to baffle an international marketing manager, yet pricing policy is a critical part of a manager's job. Managers must consider the prices permitted by the market, by competition, and by government regulation. They must deal with different tariffs from country to country that change the price of their product. For example, a $15,000 car made in the United States and exported to South Korea will, with Korean-imposed duties, taxes, and fees, cost over $40,000.

Sometimes a manager has control over the price of a good in a foreign market, and at other times that price is largely dictated by host governments. Some governments refuse to allow companies to discount or to raise prices. Until 1987, the Japanese government presented American cigarette companies with a frustrating dilemma. The Japanese tobacco monopoly added charges to American cigarettes to make them prohibitively expensive to all but the most determined consumers. Although the Japanese agreed to pricing changes, they used a multilevel intermediary structure to ensure that the distribution of American cigarettes would continue to be slow and inefficient.

Pricing decisions must take the costs of intermediaries into account. In Japan, there are often several levels of intermediaries, all of whom take a markup on a product. In the United Kingdom, Campbell Soup's distribution costs were 30 percent higher than in the United States. The reason was that English grocers purchased in such small quantities that an extra level of wholesalers was paid to facilitate handling small lots.[44]

An international marketer who makes pricing decisions deals with an extremely complex combination of factors. There are multiple competitors, multiple costs, and widely varying government regulations. A manager must take all of these factors into account when determining policy, yet remain flexible enough to allow for price movements.

Physical Distribution Every product, regardless of where it is marketed, must go through a physical distribution system. This system includes the physical handling of goods; the passage of ownership; and the buying and selling negotiations among producers, intermediaries, and consumers. An international manager must understand the channels available in each market. The key elements include: "(1) the availability of middlemen, (2) the ability and effectiveness of the alternatives in performing the functions, (3) the cost of their services, and (4) the extent of control that the company can exert over the middlemen's activities."[45]

Some American companies have had frustrating experiences with the complex Japanese system, but others have managed to forge arrangements that are quite satisfactory. Levi Strauss has set up its own independent system. Goods that the company imports into Japan are sent to its own distribution center; salespeople contact retailers directly and arrange for products to be delivered by trucks. Department stores in

Every product, regardless of where it is marketed, must go through a physical distribution system.

Japan, unlike their U.S. and European counterparts, often carry designer items in an exclusive relationship. If a designer makes an arrangement with one store, none of the others will carry the same line.[46]

International Financial Management

There are major issues that make the tasks of an international financial manager different from those of a financial manager who works solely in a domestic environment. An international financial manager works in an environment in which there are political and sociological differences. He or she deals with foreign exchange rates in foreign markets. There is substantial risk to a company when foreign exchange rates change. Also, an international financial manager has access to funds outside the home country.

Foreign Exchange Consider what happens when companies are involved in the exchange of foreign currencies. When goods are exported from the home country, they are priced in home currency. For example, a tractor made by John Deere is priced in dollars. If the tractor is sold in France, its price is converted to francs. There must be a standard method of converting dollars to francs. You can find the exchange rate on any given day by looking in *The Wall Street Journal* or on the financial pages in any other large newspaper.

Say that a John Deere tractor costs $50,000 when priced in the United States. In 1982, 1 U.S. dollar could be exchanged for about 10 francs, so the tractor would cost a French road builder 500,000 francs. In 1989, the exchange rate of 6 francs to a dollar means that the road builder only has to pay 300,000 francs for the same tractor. Obviously, this illustration is very simplistic. It does not take into account any shipping, marketing, or other costs that are normally added to the price of items; however, it

When currency values fluctuate, companies' competitive positions change at home and abroad. A finance manager's task is to reduce or eliminate foreign exchange risk.

illustrates why American goods imported to France were much cheaper to the French in 1988 than they were 6 years earlier.

The case of Goodmark Foods, Inc. of Raleigh, North Carolina, offers another example. The company sells Slim Jim beef sticks to an importer in Japan. With the dollar at 134 yen instead of 150 yen, each beef stick is cheaper for the Japanese consumer and, therefore, more attractive to the Japanese importer, who stands to make a greater profit.[47]

When companies deal in multiple currencies, they must convert their accounting statements from one currency to another. Subsidiaries normally keep their records in the monetary units of the country in which they are located. For instance, Mitsubishi International, a New York-based subsidiary of a large Japanese trading company, keeps its books in U.S. dollars. When the headquarters of Mitsubishi in Tokyo wants to determine the corporation's overall profits, the books of Mitsubishi International, like the books of all of the foreign subsidiaries, must be consolidated into a statement for the entire firm. In order to do that, all of the books must be converted from the currencies of the host countries into yen.

Foreign Exchange Risk Management For international finance managers, anticipating and responding to changes in exchange rates is the most exciting and challenging part of their job. When currency values fluctuate, as they have done dramatically since the early 1980s, companies find that their competitive positions change both at home and abroad. The task of a finance manager is to use techniques that reduce or eliminate foreign exchange risk. The measure of the foreign exchange risk is called *exposure*. There are three major kinds of exposure: transaction exposure, economic exposure, and translation exposure.

Every company has obligations that must be settled in the near future. These obligations include the purchase and sale of goods and services or the borrowing and lending of funds in foreign currencies. The exchange rates may change between the time an obligation is incurred and the time it is to be settled. **Transaction exposure** is the potential gain or loss on the future settlement of that obligation and refers to immediate or very-near-term effects on cash flows.

Financial managers have to look out for the long-term financial health of their company. To some extent, that health depends on how the firm's earning power will be affected in the future by unexpected changes in the exchange rate. **Economic exposure** refers to long-term effects on cash flows. Economic exposure cannot easily be measured or predicted and is potentially devastating to a company that does not plan effectively. If you were the financial manager of a U.S. subsidiary in Mexico in 1982, you would have been involved in a situation of economic exposure. In that year, President Lopez Portillo devalued the peso, nationalized commercial banks, and froze the dollar assets of U.S. corporations. Companies, such as Ford, were forced to shut down Mexican operations because of a Mexican rule that the value of a company's imported raw materials and parts (in U.S. dollars) could not exceed the value of its exported products (also in dollars). The shutdown resulted in an 8-percent decline in Ford's vehicle output in Mexico. Other companies could not get parts from the United States because they could not use their dollar assets in Mexican banks. All foreign companies in Mexico suffered economic exposure.

Most companies manage economic exposure by diversifying operations into different countries and by financing internationally. It makes sense, therefore, for a firm to be prepared to shift sources of production or financing into countries where currency is undervalued. In 1989, with the low dollar, firms doing business abroad might reasonably be expected to consider shifting some of their production to the United States (if other variables, such as cost and prices, warrant this). Discussions have been held by Airbus Industry, Netherlands' Fokker, and the Lockheed Corporation about making commercial aircraft in the United States to cut the high costs of manufacturing in Europe. West Germany's Siemens has already shifted production and exported $430 million in U.S.-made goods in 1987.[48]

As mentioned earlier, the financial statements of subsidiaries must be prepared in home currency before the individual components can be added to the account balances of the parent firm. When the exchange rate changes, so does the amount earned by the subsidiary in home-currency terms. That "translation" of currencies results either in a gain or a loss relative to the translation the last time the calculation was made. The accounting rules in the parent country determines whether the amount is added or subtracted from net income in the income statement. **Translation exposure** reflects changes in the accounting or balance sheet of the firm.[49]

Import and Export Financing   Exporters and importers have a wide range of financial services available to them, and it is important for an international financial manager to understand what they are and how they work. Commercial banks with international facilities handle the collection for the payment of goods. When a transaction is completed, the seller will be paid for the goods through the bank.

Except in those rare instances in which a buyer pays for goods before they are delivered, the terms of an export transaction are negotiated between the buyer and seller. The instrument that is used between a buyer and seller is called a **letter of credit (LC).** Say that a U.S. buyer agrees to buy goods from a Taiwanese shirt manufacturer. Under the terms of their sales contract, the shirt manufacturer is to be paid through a letter of credit. The American buyer arranges with her own bank to open a letter of credit that is usually, but not always, irrevocable if the terms of the letter of credit are met. The LC establishes an account in favor of the seller. For example, if the American buyer agrees in the sales contract the Taiwanese shirtmaker will be paid $4000 for the shirts, she sets up an LC for that amount by having her bank fill out a standard letter-of-credit form that guarantees payment for the goods. The buyer's bank sends this letter to the manufacturer's bank, where it is held until the terms of the contract are met. It is possible for the manufacturer to borrow against the LC to finance the purchase of materials and the payment of workers. In essence, the LC becomes the collateral against which a loan is made by the manufacturer's bank to the manufacturer. The buyer usually will not be required to pay for the goods until she has received the shipping documents from the Taiwanese manufacturer. The manufacturer, on the other hand, will have to prepare shipment of the goods within the delivery date stipulated. Once shipment is completed, the manufacturer will

Many managers are realizing that there are major opportunities in foreign markets. Whether they are located in a domestic or in a foreign environment, international managers must deal with the sociocultural, legal/political, economic, and technological forces that influence business operations.

present all of the documentation to his bank for payment under the terms of the letter of credit. In due course, the manufacturer's bank will send the documentation to the American buyer's bank, where the money has been deposited, and the bill will be settled. The buyer will use the shipping documents to take possession of the shipment in the United States.

It is critically important that buyer and seller documentation be drawn up with the greatest care. In addition to an LC, other necessary documentation includes commercial invoices, bills of lading, and insurance certificates. The commercial invoices must be signed by the exporter and must describe the goods exactly as they are described in the LC. A bill of lading serves as a document of title to the goods at the destination, and it shows that shipment has taken place as stipulated in the LC. An insurance certificate, which is usually called for in an LC, must be issued by an insurance company or its agents, and the sum for which the cargo is insured must be the same as in the LC.[50]

The tasks involved in international financial management are concerned with making the maximum profit for the firm, just as they are for a purely domestic firm. International operations complicate the task and add such tasks as developing an adequate financial information system and juggling multiple currencies. Perhaps the most important task for the international financial manager is to reduce the risks of exposure.

International Management in Review

In the international arena, managers must effectively carry out the planning, organizing, directing, and controlling functions in one or more foreign countries. Whether an international manager is located in a domestic or foreign environment, he or she must deal with various forces that influence business operations in foreign countries. These forces are created by sociocultural factors, legal and political factors, economic factors, and technological factors. In international business, planning and controlling demand high-quality information gathering and processing. A business may be organized along geographic, functional, or product lines, or it may involve a matrix organization that coordinates functions and products in various geographic areas. Directing strategies must be based on factors present in the country in which the business operates.

No U.S. company can completely ignore the opportunities and risks involved in international business. Managers are increasingly aware of the impact of foreign competition at home; many American companies are now partially owned by foreign investors. In addition, many American managers are realizing that there are major opportunities in foreign markets and that it may be more cost effective to use foreign human and production resources than to maintain strictly domestic operations.

Companies can enter international trade simply through exporting or importing goods and services. Managers can also form joint ventures with foreign companies, in which they trade technological and marketing expertise. They may also participate in licensing agreements, in which they give a foreign operations rights to use a process or product for a limited period of time—usually five to ten years. Several well-known American companies, such as McDonald's, Kentucky Fried Chicken, and Avis, have established numerous franchise arrangements. A foreign franchisee operates a business that is directed and controlled by the parent franchisor.

Large companies frequently have foreign subsidiaries, many of which are wholly owned. A wholly owned subsidiary may be completely staffed and operated under host-country policies, but 100 percent of its stock is owned by its domestic parent company. Multinational companies and global enterprises encompass many wholly owned subsidiaries.

Both small and large companies may participate in international countertrade. Countertrade involves importing and exporting goods in exchange for one another; it can involve pure barter or complex systems of product and monetary exchange. For example, a U.S. company may send machinery to Brazil in exchange for iron ore, which it may, in turn, send to France in exchange for plastic products.

Three areas that have special complexities for international managers are the organizational functions of human resource, marketing, and financial management. International staffing can be conducted by placing home-country managers in foreign locations (ethnocentric staffing), by using host-country managers in host-country operations (geocentric staffing), by placing managers from various countries in operations where their functional expertise is deemed most useful (polycentric staffing), or by using a combination of these approaches. International marketing management involves making decisions concerning products, pricing, promotion, and physical distribution based on forces operating in foreign environments. International financial management is heavily influenced by fluctuating currencies and monetary conversions.

Notes

1. The two worlds of Jimmy Goldsmith (1 December 1986), *Business Week*, 42.
2. Europe goes on a shopping spree in the States (27 October 1986), *Business Week*, 54.
3. Hands across Europe: Deals that could redraw the map (18 May 1987), *Business Week*, 64–65.
4. N. J. Adler (1986), *International dimensions of organizational behavior*, Boston: Kent; International Monetary Fund and ACLI International, Inc., *Wall Street Journal* (28 May 1981), 50.
5. *Survey of Current Business* (February 1981), 50–51, and (August 1981), 22.
6. Adapted from E. B. Tylor (1978), Primitive culture, in V. Terpstra, ed., *The cultural environment of international business*, Cincinnati, OH: South-western.
7. G. Hofstede (1980), *Culture's consequences*, Beverly Hills, CA: Sage.
8. M. Otsubo (Spring 1986), A guide to Japanese business practices, *California Management Review*, 28 (3), 28.
9. G. Hofstede (Summer 1980), Motivation, leadership, and organization: Do American theories apply abroad? *Organizational Dynamics*, 9, 46–49.
10. G. H. Clee and W. M. Sachtjen (November-December 1964), Organizing a worldwide business, *Harvard Business Review*, 42, 102–7.
11. J. Curley (26 April 1982), Small firm outmaneuvers big-time rivals in winning copier sales from the Chinese, *The Wall Street Journal*.
12. The Buying of America (June 1987), *World Press Review*, 16–18.
13. British firms big spenders in U.S. (11 October 1987), *Boston Globe*, A9.

14. *Ibid.*

15. L. Uchitelle (7 April 1987), Japanese funds still pour in, *The New York Times,* D1, 5.

16. R. Vernon (1971), *Sovereignty at bay,* New York: Basic Books, 11.

17. On the verge of a world war in white goods (2 November 1987), *Business Week,* 91, 94.

18. *American excellence in a world economy: A summary of the report* (15 June 1987), Washington, DC: The Business Roundtable, 7.

19. Foiling Japan in the aluminum market (30 November 1987), *Business Week,* 108B.

20. D. A. Ball and W. H. McCulloch, Jr. (1985), *International business,* Plano, TX: Business Publications, 985.

21. N. Fletcher (10 December 1988), U.S., China form joint venture to manufacture helicopters, *Journal of Commerce,* 58.

22. N. Fletcher (24 November 1987), Joint ventures held key to succeeding in China, *Journal of Commerce,* 5A.

23. South Korea's carmakers count their blessings (3 January 1987), *The Economist,* 45.

24. S. Greenhouse (19 May 1987), Challenge for Honeywell Bull, *The New York Times,* D1, D6.

25. B. Mongelluzzo (1 May 1987), West Coast steel users in a bind, *Journal of Commerce.*

26. Orienting the Latin connection (February 1988), *South,* 21.

27. K. R. Harrigan (July 1987), Why joint ventures fail, *Euro-Asia Business Review,* 6 (3), 20–26.

28. F. R. Root (1982), *Foreign markets entry strategies,* New York: AMACOM, 97–100.

29. Patents battle (February 1986), *South,* 48.

30. Root, 1982, 122–23.

31. R. Johnson (18 December 1987), McDonald's combines a dead man's advice with lively strategy, *The Wall Street Journal,* 1.

32. M. J. Pitzer (16 November 1987), Fuller's worldwide strategy: Think local, *Business Week,* 169.

33. M. E. Porter (Winter 1986), Changing patterns of international competition, *California Management Review,* 28 (2), 11.

34. Big changes at Big Blue (15 February 1988), *Business Week,* 92–98.

35. *Ibid.*

36. C. Bates (Summer 1986), Are companies ready for countertrade? *International Marketing Review,* 28.

37. J. R. Wills and A. P. Palia (October 1987), Managing countertrade, *Euro-Asia Business Review,* 6 (4), 45.

38. Wills and Palia, 44–48.

39. A. M. Gilmore (1986), Are U.S. expatriate managers prone to failure? *Business Intelligence Program,* Menlo Park, CA: SRI International, 8.

40. D. A. Ricks (1983), *Big business blunders,* Homewood, IL: Dow Jones-Irwin, 140.

41. Ricks, 1983, 38.

42. P. R. Caetora and J. M. Hess (1979), *International marketing,* 4th ed., Homewood, IL: Irwin, 417.

43. Ricks, 1983, 82.

44. Caetora and Hess, 1979, 477–78.

45. S. H. Robock and K. Simmonds (1983), *International business and multinational enterprises*, 3rd ed., Homewood, IL: Irwin, 450.

46. Keys to success in the Japanese market (1980), *JETRO*, 9–10.

47. R. W. Stevenson (18 November 1987), Dollar helps U.S. compete, *The New York Times*, D1.

48. U.S. exporters that aren't American (29 February 1988), *Business Week*, 7.

49. Robock and Simmonds, 1983, 536–44; A. I. Stonehill and D. K. Eitman (1987), *Finance: An international perspective*, Homewood, IL: Irwin, 33–45.

50. G. Tianwah (1984), *Guide to letters of credit*, Singapore: Rank Books, 10–69.

Key Terms

international management	multinational corporations (MNCs)
culture	global enterprises
exporting	countertrade
importing	ethnocentric staffing
direct exporting	geocentric staffing
indirect exporting	polycentric staffing
joint venture	transaction exposure
licensing agreement	economic exposure
franchise	translation exposure
subsidiary	letter of credit (LC)
wholly owned subsidiary	

Issues for Review and Discussion

1. Compare the tasks of a domestic manager with those of an international manager.
2. Why would a manager consider involvement in international business?
3. Explain the differences between direct and indirect exporting. Why would a manager choose one form over the other?
4. How could an organization use a joint venture for its foreign linkage? What are some of the benefits and drawbacks?
5. What is a licensing agreement? What use does it make of managerial expertise?
6. Explain the differences between global enterprises and multidomestic multinationals.
7. What is countertrade? Why do organizations use it?
8. Explain why the issue of culture is important to an international manager.
9. List three major staffing policies available to an international human resource manager.
10. How do the basic functions of an international marketing manager differ from those of a domestic manager?
11. Describe the basic function of an international financial manager.

Suggested Readings

Cole, R. E. (1980). Learning from the Japanese: Prospects and pitfalls. *Management Review*, 69, 9, 22–28.

Hayashi, K. (1978). Corporate planning, practice in Japanese multinationals. *Academy of Management Journal*, 21, 221–26.

Marsland, S. and Beer, H. (Winter 1980). The evolution of Japanese management: Lessons for U.S. managers. *Organizational Dynamics*, 49–67.

Schein, E. H. (Fall 1981). SMR Forum: Does Japanese management style have a message for American managers? *Sloan Management Review*, 55–68.

Schonberger, R. J. (1982). The transfer of Japanese manufacturing management approaches to U.S. industry. *Academy of Management Review*, 7, 479–87.

Wheelwright, S. C. (July/August 1981). Japan—Where operations really are strategic. *Harvard Business Review*, 67–74.

Zussman, Y. M. (Winter 1983). Learning from the Japanese: Management in a resource-scarce world. *Organizational Dynamics*, 68–80.

CHAPTER 24

Entrepreneurship and Intrapreneurship

Student Learning Objectives

After reading this chapter, you should be able to:

1. Define and discuss entrepreneurship and intrapreneurship.

2. Describe typical personal characteristics and experiences of entrepreneurs and intrapreneurs.

3. Describe the types of behaviors common among entrepreneurs and intrapreneurs.

4. Describe the key phases of the intrapreneurial process.

5. Discuss methods for facilitating and supporting intrapreneurship.

6. Describe and discuss the three major strategies available to entrepreneurs and intrapreneurs.

In the 1960s, Barbara Walden landed a minor role as an actress in the Paul Newman movie *What a Way to Go*. Anxious to see herself on the big screen, Barbara rushed to a movie theater when the film was released. What she saw was an attractive black woman who looked purple on screen because the makeup she used was formulated to compliment the appearance of white women. When her search for cosmetics better suited to black women failed to identify existing products, she decided to create her own. Beginning with a hair-styling lotion and expanding to a full line of personal care products, Barbara Walden Cosmetics now captures over $5 million in annual sales through national department store chains.[1]

Chuck House, an engineer at corporate giant Hewlett-Packard, worked on a project intended to develop a new cathode ray display for use by air traffic controllers. When the display failed to meet specifications, Hewlett-Packard management wanted to cut their losses and drop the project altogether. Chuck persevered, however, arguing that the display held promise for other markets. Working mostly on his own, Chuck identified potential market applications and customers. The result was success in three separate markets. Chuck had turned one failure into three successes.[2]

Both Barbara Walden and Chuck House are innovators. Each identified a need, developed products to satisfy the need, and made their products succeed in the marketplace through personal effort and perseverance. Barbara, who accomplished this on her own, is known as an *entrepreneur*. Chuck, who innovated within an existing organization, is known as an *intrapreneur*. This chapter explores the nature and importance of entrepreneurial and intrapreneurial activities and examines factors that contribute to their success.

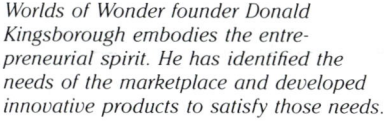

Worlds of Wonder founder Donald Kingsborough embodies the entrepreneurial spirit. He has identified the needs of the marketplace and developed innovative products to satisfy those needs.

Entrepreneurship

Entrepreneurship involves the development of a product or service idea and the creation of an organization to further its growth.[3] One word often used when discussing entrepreneurship is *innovative*. In fact, Peter Drucker, who wrote the stimulating book *Innovation and Entrepreneurship*, argues that the creation of an organization should not be considered entrepreneurial unless the new organization is also innovative.[4] Others, such as William Gartner of Georgetown University, acknowledge the fact that many of the most interesting entrepreneurial ventures are indeed innovative but do not believe that innovation is a requirement for entrepreneurship to take place. What entrepreneurship does require, of course, is a person whose ideas and energy make it happen. The first part of this chapter looks at what entrepreneurs are like and what they do.*

The Entrepreneurial "Type"

Jeff Lemieux was only fourteen years old when he received a $30 box of baseball cards that he built into a $10,000 collection and thriving business one year later. Orville Redenbacher was sixty-four when he first marketed his gourmet popcorn. Barbara Walden is a black woman. Dr. An Wang, founder of Wang Laboratories, is an oriental man. Obviously, there is no easy way to spot an entrepreneur at first glance. Nonetheless, many successful entrepreneurs share somewhat similar characteristics. Although it is sometimes difficult to separate factors, such as personality, from the behaviors that result, the next two sections briefly explore some of these factors.[5]

Personal Characteristics   One way to describe entrepreneurs is on the basis of their personal characteristics (see Table 24.1). Entrepreneurs, for example, tend to have a high need for achievement (review the need theories in Chapter 14) and perhaps gravitate toward entrepreneurial situations because they offer the person *a chance to compete against a standard of excellence*. Success (and, therefore, satisfaction of the need) depends on the effectiveness of the individual entrepreneur. A strong need for achievement may, thus, encourage certain individuals to select entrepreneurial situations they perceive as offering greater opportunity for personal achievement than would most opportunities with someone else's organization. Once in the situation, the challenge to succeed becomes a powerful motivator.

A high need for achievement is particularly powerful when coupled with a low fear of failure. Put quite simply, many entrepreneurs love to achieve but are not afraid to fail. They recognize that success requires some risks and are not devastated by periodic failures. Some people, in fact, make their initial forays into entrepreneurship only after a failure. Consider, for example, Louis Centofanti, former Carter Administration official, who developed a revolutionary way to clean up PCBs after being

---

*More research has been conducted on the characteristics of entrepreneurs than on those of intrapreneurs. It appears, however, that the vast majority of characteristics of entrepreneurs also apply to intrapreneurs. Indeed, many of the examples in this section are of intrapreneurs.

TABLE 24.1   *Personal Characteristics of Successful Entrepreneurs*

High need for achievement	High self-confidence
Low fear of failure	Optimism
Low need for power	Determination
Strong internal locus of control	High energy level
High tolerance for ambiguity	Strong individualism

fired by the Reagan administration in 1981.[6] By the late 1980s, Centofanti had turned his invention into USPCI, the fifth-largest hazardous waste company in the United States.

Many nonentrepreneurs assume that the search for power is important to entrepreneurs. Often, however, the most successful entrepreneurs actually have a low need for personal power. It appears that power is important only to the extent that it facilitates successful goal attainment rather than as an end in itself. Bill Gates, cofounder of Microsoft, for example, hired professional managers to help run the growing computer software company (sales for 1987 were $349.9 million), because he "learned at a young age that you've got to give up power to get power."[7]

Successful entrepreneurs also tend to have a strong internal locus of control (review Chapter 13). In other words, they believe that their accomplishments are due primarily to their own capabilities and efforts. Failures are attributed to a lack of capability and/or adequate effort. Particularly when combined with a high need for achievement, an internal locus of control can produce powerful effects. People possessing this combination of characteristics value achievement but believe it cannot be obtained without personal effort. One example can be found in Kenneth Olsen, founder of Digital Equipment Corporation. After more than thirty years at the helm of the giant company, Olsen still

> *draws strength from nuts and bolts. He can spend hours sweating the homely, low-tech details of DEC's computers—making sure, for example, that the plugs and connectors on the backs of DEC machines are neatly laid out.[8]*

Tolerance for ambiguity is another quality characterizing many successful entrepreneurs. They are able to cope with the tremendous amount of uncertainty typically present in entrepreneurial situations. In fact, although those with low tolerance for ambiguity might be threatened and frustrated by this amount of uncertainty, many entrepreneurs actually find it stimulating and challenging. Scott McNealy, the thirty-three-year-old cofounder of Sun Microsystems, for example, relishes situations that depend on courage and intuition. McNealy attributes one of Sun's most recent successes—a new microprocessor licensed to AT&T, Xerox, and Unisys—to an abrupt strategy change based on "90% assumption and 10% fact."[9]

Other characteristics sometimes mentioned when discussing entrepreneurs include self-confidence, optimism, determination, high energy levels, and a strong sense of individualism. Consider the comments of entrepreneur Mortimer Levitt, who founded the Custom Shop Shirtmakers chain in New York:

> *What I'm getting at is that here I'm it. I'm responsible only to Uncle Sam and our two unions. Other than that I am in complete authority. This*

Scott McNealy, cofounder of Sun Microsystems, relishes situations that call for courage and intuition. Hardworking McNealy has led his company through the troubled computer market at a quarterly growth rate of 30 percent.

really hit home recently when I examined an offer from some venture capitalists. Usually I don't even listen to buyout offers because I have no interest in selling. But a close friend was involved this time, so as a courtesy I gave it a good listen. But the more I listened, the less I heard. We never got down to discussing a selling price, but even if they paid me $200 million, I'd lose my identity. And that's what it boils down to, I suppose: Here I know who I am. . . .[10]

Personal Experiences The characteristics just discussed help identify people most likely to succeed as entrepreneurs. There is a second set of factors that facilitates these individuals' success, and these revolve around their personal experiences. Although less is known about these factors and their importance than about the personal characteristics of entrepreneurs, it appears that certain experiences are common among entrepreneurs prior to becoming entrepreneurs (see Table 24.2). It has been argued that these life experiences may contribute to the development of interest in entrepreneuring and to the nurturing of the capabilities to do so effectively.[11]

One of the first common early experiences is that they encounter difficulty working for someone else. It is not always possible to determine whether the entrepreneur-to-be caused this difficulty or the experience encouraged the person to set out on his or her own. It makes sense, however, that people with the personality profiles just discussed would want to avoid situations in which someone else controlled their ability to succeed and/or treated failure as something from which to refrain at all costs. Scott McNealy, for example, quit his job at a large corporation after ten months because management put him on a strategy team when what he really wanted to do was "make something." McNealy started up Sun Microsystems with a business school buddy and "built the first 25 Suns by hand . . . [with] the skinned knuckles to show for it."[12]

Many entrepreneurs mention challenging educational experiences as instrumental in their road toward entrepreneurship (even though some insist that their real education did not begin until after graduation). To an extent, these educational experiences simply provide students with early opportunities to be an entrepreneur by allowing them to solve a difficult or challenging class problem. In 1947, for example, MIT student Ken Olsen worked with other students as part of the research team that developed the Institute's first computer. In addition, educational experiences may help entrepreneurs-to-be develop some of the personal characteristics (such as need for achievement) that later become important.

Running an organization early in life is an experience in the background of many entrepreneurs. For some, this takes the form of leading a special project group for a student organization. In eighth grade, for example, Bill Gates headed up a programming group that developed a

TABLE 24.2 *Personal Experiences Before Becoming Entrepreneurs*

Difficulty working for someone else
Challenging educational experiences
An early experience running an organization

computerized payroll system for the school. Planning and coordinating a club fundraising event is the first entrepreneurial experience for many. Others create a business either while still in school or shortly after graduation. Jeff Lemieux now rents store space for his Jeff's Sports Cards enterprise. Most entrepreneurs, in fact, begin their first organization before turning thirty.

A number of other life experiences have also turned up as entrepreneurial antecedents. Being first-born in a family, for example, appears to increase the probability of becoming an entrepreneur. So does having a supportive spouse. Together, these have been cited as factors that provide the opportunity and support needed to experience and succeed at such activities.

Entrepreneurial Behaviors

It appears that entrepreneurs not only have different personal characteristics and experiences but they also engage in different behaviors than do those less likely to become entrepreneurs. Some of these characteristic behaviors are shown in Table 24.3.

Many of the behaviors shown in Table 24.3 might be expected, given the characteristics of entrepreneurs discussed earlier. It is not surprising, for example, that entrepreneurs set specific goals for themselves and their organizations, become committed to these goals, and persevere until succeeding or recognizing that success cannot be obtained. If failure does result, the entrepreneur is typically willing to accept responsibility for the failure. For example, cofounder of Liz Claiborne Inc. Jerry Chazen blames himself for failure of the company's high-hemlined dresses, saying, "I should have known better. . . . It was the biggest boo-boo that I know of in my 35 years in the business."[13] This pattern of behaviors is quite consistent with a high need for achievement and strong internal locus of control. So, too, is the choice of goals that provide moderate, but not extreme, risks.

Entrepreneurs spend much of their time engaged in problem-solving behaviors. This is consistent with a high self-confidence that lies in the belief that solutions can be found if sought hard enough. Maybe it is the entrepreneur's high tolerance for ambiguity that makes it tolerable to wallow in uncertainty in search of solutions. Solutions that emerge are often innovative due, perhaps, to the entrepreneur's willingness to try new ideas in the face of failure coupled with the desire to demonstrate a sense of strong individualism.

The behaviors just presented are descriptions of how entrepreneurs actually tend to behave. As you will see later in this chapter, these behaviors often (but not always) match prescriptions for how entrepreneurs *should* behave to be effective.

TABLE 24.3   *Typical Entrepreneurial Behaviors*

Goal-oriented behavior	Moderate risk taking
Commitment to goals	Acceptance of responsibility
Perseverance	Innovative behavior
Problem-solving behavior	

In the solo phase, an intrapreneur typically works alone to determine if an idea will clearly benefit customers and if it is compatible with the organization's resources and overall strategy.

Intrapreneurship

As you will recall from the example of Hewlett-Packard engineer Chuck House, not every person who identifies a need, develops products to satisfy the need, and makes the products succeed in the marketplace through personal effort and perseverance is an entrepreneur. **Intrapreneurship** takes place when individuals who identify the need for (often innovative) change in an organization create the environment in which the change can succeed and champion the implementation of the change.[14] Rather than creating a new organization in which to develop an idea, as entrepreneurs do, intrapreneurs create a new climate within their existing organization to further the idea's growth. In practice, this often means stimulating a willingness for risk taking and change in the organization.

The Intrapreneurial Process

The intrapreneurial process involves both creative and analytical activities. Together, these create the new ideas and develop what has been called the "intraprise" necessary for their successful implementation. Table 24.4 presents the four phases of intrapreneuring. Managers should encourage workers through all four phases for maximum facilitation of the emergence and success of intrapreneurial activity.

Phase 1: The Solo Phase   In this stage of the process, intrapreneurs typically work alone. First, they must identify the intrapreneurial idea. Next, they begin to develop the idea and submit it to three feasibility tests:

1. Will the idea provide a clearly identifiable benefit for customers or clients?
2. Is the idea compatible with the organization's resources and overall strategy?
3. Is the idea and its potential implementation compatible with the intrapreneur's personal character and skills?

If the idea passes these tests, the next phase begins.

Phase 2: The Network Phase   In this stage of the process, intrapreneurs share the idea with other members of the organization. Seeking feedback on the idea's merits, intrapreneurs ask for suggestions on how to capitalize on existing strengths and identify the idea's potential weaknesses.

TABLE 24.4   *Intrapreneurial Phases*

Phase 1:	The Solo Phase
Phase 2:	The Network Phase
Phase 3:	The Bootlegging Phase
Phase 4:	The Formal Team Phase

Phase 3: The Bootlegging Phase In this stage of the process, intrapreneurs start to build an informal team that will pursue the idea. Typically, this group maintains independence by remaining informal and, often, by operating outside of the (physical and psychological) walls of the organization. The purpose of this phase is to refine the idea before its formal presentation to the rest of the organization.

Phase 4: The Formal Team Phase At this phase, the intraprise becomes a visible organizational entity, usually subjected to the organization's "normal" policies and practices for the first time. Prior to this phase, the idea was primarily a concept. It now begins to harden into reality.

Why People Become Intrapreneurs

Given that intrapreneurs typically have almost all of the characteristics and behaviors of entrepreneurs, why would a person choose to develop his or her ideas within someone else's organization rather than starting a new one? According to Gifford Pinchot, it may be very difficult under certain circumstances

> to develop the new business independently of the corporation. This is true whenever the new venture (or intraprise) requires access to proprietary technology, the firm's marketing system (e.g., company name, distribution channels), production facilities, financial resources, or managerial capabilities.[15]

Given the entre- or intrapreneur-to-be's strong need for achievement, it makes sense that the person might choose to become an intrapreneur rather than start from scratch if the organization can help improve the chances of success.

The potential advantages of intrapreneuring may be outweighed, however, by the restrictions of freedom typically imposed in larger organizations. Intrapreneurs-to-be may also be frustrated by existing organizational structures that are designed for stability rather than for change. These two restricting factors can be compounded further by the relatively limited potential for monetary rewards relative to those possible with a major entrepreneurial success. Organizations looking to capitalize on the potential benefits of intrapreneurial activity, then, should seek ways to overcome these barriers.

Developing a Supportive Environment

It has often been argued that large organizations in the United States must take a lesson from small business entrepreneurs if they are to continue to succeed, yet much of the impetus driving entrepreneurs seems to be tied to avoidance of working for someone else. How, then, can larger organizations enjoy the benefits of entrepreneurship? In part, by shifting the focus of workers' behaviors and, in part, by encouraging, supporting, and rewarding intrapreneurial behavior systematically. In other words, managers must find ways to convince workers to become intrapreneurs rather than entrepreneurs.

Formal sponsors ensure that intrapreneurs are provided with needed funds, that their work is accepted politically, and that they are free to think and create.

Pinchot identifies a number of steps that managers should take to create an environment that supports intrapreneurial activity. These include:

1. *Sponsorship.* Formal sponsors can be anyone, from an intrapreneur's immediate supervisor to the president of the company, identified and empowered by an organization. Formal sponsors, although not always directly involved in the intrapreneurial activity, make such activity possible. They do so by ensuring that needed funds are provided, that political acceptance of the work occurs, and that the intrapreneur is free to think and create. In short, the sponsor frees the intrapreneur from the hassles of the organization.

2. *Self-selection.* Managers should recognize that it is virtually impossible to command someone to become an intrapreneur. They should, therefore, focus on identifying likely candidates for intrapreneurship (that is, those who might choose to be and succeed at being intrapreneurs) and allow it to occur.

3. *No hand-offs.* Managers should allow intrapreneurs and their teams to stay with projects as long as possible. When managers say, "Thank you for the idea. Now we will hand it off to someone else to develop," organization members probably will feel inhibited and less likely to generate future ideas. Moreover, hand-offs tend to reduce commitment to and effective development of ideas that are generated.

4. *The doer decides.* Managers should allow intrapreneurs and their groups to make as many decisions as possible rather than concentrating decision making at higher levels. The purpose of this is to facilitate rapid development of ideas as well as commitment to them.

5. *Corporate slack.* Managers should allow individuals the time and freedom to explore new ideas. Tight controls inhibit creativity by removing the opportunity for it to occur.

6. *Ending the home-run philosophy.* Home-run hitters are nice, but a collection of base hits is usually more desirable in the long run. Put in other terms, big ideas should not be discouraged, but an organization that only supports big ideas is unlikely to get many small ideas. Small ideas are the ones that sustain an organization.

7. *Tolerance of risk, failure, and mistakes.* The kinds of people who make good intrapreneurs are people who like to take risks, who can live with failures, and who accept mistakes as learning opportunities. Managers who permit this facilitate intrapreneurship.

8. *Patient money.* Managers must recognize that ideas take time to mature. Withdrawing financial support too quickly when results do not appear is shortsighted. Doing so prevents potential successes from developing and discourages others from attempting innovation.

9. *Freedom from "turfiness."* Intrapreneurs are known for stepping on toes. When developing ideas, they frequently cross organizational boundaries. Managers must take care to see that the organization's culture discourages workers from digging in and protecting their own turf, because this erects barriers to innovation.

10. *Cross-functional teams.* Intrapreneurs should be encouraged to develop self-contained teams whose members possess all of the functional expertise needed by the venture. Managers should support these teams to reduce the need for hand-offs and to facilitate the development of ideas.

11. *Multiple options.* Intrapreneurs must be given flexibility in developing, producing, and marketing their products and services. If an organization's traditional methods match the needs of the new idea, fine. If not, other options should be permissible.

12. *An effective reward system.* Unfortunately, most organizational pay and career systems discourage and sometimes even punish intrapreneurial behavior. They must not be allowed to do so. Furthermore, rewards should be provided that can interest intrapreneurs without becoming dysfunctional for the organization. Promoting an effective intrapreneur to a managerial position, for example, is usually a mistake, because it significantly reduces the future intrapreneurial output from that person. It would often be better to provide direct financial rewards instead and/or to reward the intrapreneur by supporting his or her future endeavors. Managers should design systems that encourage, recognize, and reward intrapreneurial behavior.

13. *Use an intracapital system.* Intracapital is money that intrapreneurs may spend on a discretionary basis. In this way, intrapreneurs will have the financial support they need to develop ideas without encountering bureaucratic barriers to spending decisions. Pinchot recommends that a portion of funds generated by an intrapreneurial idea be funnelled back into the intracapital account of the intrapreneur for further discretionary intrapreneurial spending. This will reward the successful intrapreneur by providing support needed to pursue his or her valued ideas.[16]

The ideas just presented are not designed to guarantee intrapreneurial success. Their purpose is to offer opportunities for such success by providing a barrier-free, supportive environment. Unless managers follow these systematic steps, the probability that successful intrapreneurial activity will take place within an organization is greatly reduced.

Entrepreneurial and Intrapreneurial Strategies

Emphasizing that stereotypes of successful entrepreneurial efforts are too narrow, Peter Drucker described several alternative strategies that people can follow to identify and develop entrepreneurial or intrapreneurial ideas (see Table 24.5).[17] Each of these strategies has been used both by entrepreneurs and by intrapreneurs. To simplify the discussion of the strategies presented in the following sections, the term *entrepreneurship* will be used exclusively, although the strategies also apply to intrapreneurship.

Leadership in a New Market or Industry

Leadership in a new market or industry involves creating and then dominating a new product or service area. It is the approach most people associate with the idea of entrepreneurship and is referred to by Drucker as the "Fustest with the Mostest" (using the terminology of the Confederate Cavalry general who attributed his winning record to being first on the scene and with the most resources).

The approach also has been very successful. The entire plastics industry, for example, was created using this entrepreneurial approach.[18] In the 1920s, Du Pont (then a leading producer of explosives) hired chemist Wallace H. Carothers to develop synthetic fibers using polymer chemistry. At that point, no one had ever succeeded at doing so, and Du Pont funded Carothers for over ten years without success. Despite the years of failure, both Du Pont and Carothers kept searching for the big breakthrough. Finally, the first truly synthetic fiber was created and given the name *nylon*. The rest is history, thanks to Du Pont's massive manufacturing and marketing efforts. The "Fustest with the Mostest" strategy paid off.

The leadership in a new market or industry strategy has been successful in areas other than big business. Consider the case of the two surgeons

TABLE 24.5 *Entrepreneurial and Intrapreneurial Strategies*

Leadership in a new market or industry
Creative imitation
Entrepreneurial judo

In 1937, entrepreneur Wallace Carothers obtained a patent for the first synthetic fiber—nylon—which he developed at Du Pont's "pure" science laboratory in Delaware.

who, early in the twentieth century, decided to establish a medical center in the remote Minnesota town of Rochester.[19] Their goals were to create a center based on the then-unheard-of practice of staffing medical teams with outstanding specialists: to dominate the field in the treatment of complex medical problems, to attract the best physicians from throughout the country, and to attract patients who would pay extremely high fees for such superior medical care. They were the first to pioneer this approach to medical treatment and they did so in a big way. The two entrepreneurial physicians were named Mayo, and the clinic they founded is the renowned Mayo Clinic.

The aim of the Du Ponts and of the Mayos was the same: to create a new industry and to dominate it. They succeeded. So, too, did Hofmann-LaRoche, the pharmaceutical company that pioneered and dominated the vitamin market. So did Dr. An Wang who created, and for many years dominated, the word processing industry. So did the founders of Apple Computer. So have many others who have followed this strategy. The key to success with this strategy, Drucker says, is to aim high; set one goal and focus all effort on it. Succeed, and like Mayo and Du Pont, you've made history. Miss your target by even a little bit, though, and you are in big trouble. This is also a strategy that requires considerable attention even after the first success. When Apple, for example, failed to follow up appropriately after initially creating and capturing the personal computer market, such competitors as IBM, Compaq, and Radio Shack snatched large chunks of the personal computer market away.

Leadership in a new market or industry is risky, and most entrepreneurs prefer moderate risks. For these reasons, this may be the flashiest of approaches but it is not the most popular. The potential payoff must be quite large because the approach requires a large investment and sustained effort, but it promises only a small chance of payoff (albeit a potentially large one).

Creative Imitation

Drucker identified two strategies that he called "Hit Them Where They Ain't." The first of these is **creative imitation,** a strategy based on improving someone else's innovation. Although somewhat a contradiction in terms, this approach is used by entrepreneurs who understand the meaning and uses of an innovation better than its creator does.

According to Drucker, this is a market-driven, rather than product-driven, strategy, appropriate for a rapidly growing market in which a creative imitator can satisfy existing market demand better than a pioneer. Successful creative imitators capitalize on pioneers' success by perfecting and positioning a product or service more appropriately. This approach does not even require entrepreneurs to take customers away from the pioneers; instead, they can simply focus on customers new to the market. This approach has been particularly successful in high-tech areas where, according to Drucker, innovators "are least likely to be market-focused, and most likely to be technology- and product-focused. The innovators therefore tend to misunderstand their own success and to fail to exploit and supply the demand they have created."[20]

Creative imitation requires alertness, flexibility, an ability to read the market, and plenty of hard work. It, too, has been a successful entrepreneurial approach. Consider, for example, the over-the-counter painkiller market.[21] For years, aspirin dominated this market in spite of such side effects as nausea and bleeding. An alternative to aspirin, acetaminophen, was available, but only by prescription. When acetaminophen was approved for over-the-counter sales, it was quickly promoted as "the painkiller of choice for those with reactions to aspirin." The marketer of the drug quickly captured that relatively small market. Johnson & Johnson creatively imitated by positioning the drug as a safe, universal painkiller. In less than two years, Johnson & Johnson dominated the market with their version of the drug, which they named *Tylenol*. So successful was this effort, Tylenol even survived the Tylenol poisonings of recent years.

Another creative imitation success involves the now common digital watch. The Swiss watch industry was the first to develop and market a digital quartz watch when the availability of miniature semiconductors made such timepieces feasible. In fact, the Swiss succeeded in marketing digital watches as very expensive luxury items. The Hattori Company in Japan saw the opportunity for creative imitation. Recognizing a huge potential market for digital watches, they repositioned the product as a standard affordable watch. The result was dominance of the market by Hattori with its Seiko watches.

Other examples of creative imitation include IBM's success with personal computers following Apple's innovations. Indeed, IBM has used this strategy in other areas as well, including the photocopying market. Another example of a repeatedly good creative imitator in market after market of home products is Procter & Gamble. Although it has much less inherent risk than does the leadership strategy, creative imitators have to take care not to be too creative. This approach succeeds by filling an existing need in an existing market better than existing products and services, so entrepreneurs must keep their focus on the market rather than on a product or service.

Entrepreneurial Judo

Entrepreneurial judo is a strategy that capitalizes on the weaknesses of an organization that holds a leadership position. As with judo, the martial art,

> entrepreneurial judo first aims at securing a beachhead, one which the established leaders either do not defend at all or defend only half-heartedly. . . . Once that beachhead has been secured, that is, once the newcomers have an adequate market and adequate revenue, they then move in on the rest of the territory. In each case, they repeat the strategy. They design a product or a service which is specific to a given market segment and optimal for it.[22]

As does the martial artist, the person practicing entrepreneurial judo looks for weak points to attack. According to Drucker, organizational weaknesses are the result of five bad habits (see Table 24.6). The next sections examine these bad habits and the opportunities they present to entrepreneurs following this strategy.

TABLE 24.6   *Five Bad Habits to Attack with Entrepreneurial Judo*

The "not invented here" syndrome
Creaming the market
The misunderstanding of quality
The use of premium pricing
Maximization attempts

Five Bad Habits   When organizations fall into one or more of the bad habits shown in Table 24.6, they exhibit a weakness that facilitates an attack of an entrepreneurial judo artist. Furthermore, organizations with these habits tend to repeat them, making future use of judo even easier for ambitious entrepreneurs.

- *Bad habit #1: The "not invented here" syndrome.* This bad habit occurs when managers reject a new idea simply because it was invented by someone else. In 1947, for example, U.S.-based Bell Laboratories invented the transistor. Leading American manufacturers of radios and televisions delayed using the new technology, however, partially because it was invented by Bell and not by them. Conversion to transistors was planned for a couple of decades later. Akio Morita, president of Sony, read about the transistor and had no such qualms. Paying a paltry $25,000, Morita obtained a license to use the transistor in consumer electronics products. Through the quick and effective use of entrepreneurial judo, Morita captured the portable radio market for years to come.

- *Bad habit #2: Creaming the market.* Managers who fall prey to this bad habit attempt to skim the high-profit portion of the market, as Xerox did by concentrating on its customers who purchased the greatest number of the most expensive copy machines. Small users received relatively little attention, which left many feeling dissatisfied. Identifying this weakness as an opportunity, other American manufacturers and a number of Japanese competitors stepped in, courted, and won the small-user market. Exploration of this weakness was the stepping stone to bigger markets, and Xerox paid the price for its bad habit as it began losing some of its valued larger customers to increasingly successful competitors.

- *Bad habit #3: Misunderstanding quality.* Drucker argues that many organizations create a weakness by misunderstanding the meaning of quality. "Quality" in a product or service is not what the supplier puts in. It is what the customer gets out and is willing to pay for. Contrary to what most manufacturers believe, a product is not "quality" because it is hard to make and costs a lot of money. That is incompetence. Customers pay only for what is of use to them and gives them value. Nothing else is "quality."[23] The manufacturers of vacuum tube radios happily advertised the "quality" of their radios in the 1950s, citing the expertise, time, and materials required to build them. To consumers, however, the quality of a lightweight, reliable, inexpensive transistor radio assembled of relatively few parts by unskilled labor presented far greater quality. The message here is that strength is in the eye of the consumer and weakness in the methods of the producer.

When Xerox creamed the high-volume copier market, the competition stepped in and won over small users.

In a world of office copiers, are you suffering from tunnel vision?

RICOH

- *Bad habit #4: Premium pricing.* Premium pricing involves the use of the highest prices the market will accept. This may seem like a wonderful practice to an organization that has no competitors, but an excessive price makes an attractive target to an entrepreneur looking for a weak point to attack. When IBM priced its first personal computers relatively high, potential clone makers saw the opportunity to enter the market by providing low prices even if they could not compete with IBM on other bases. If clone makers believe they can produce a computer for $650 that is comparable to a machine IBM is selling for $3200, there is considerable room for attack. If, on the other hand, the IBM machine is selling for only $1200, the target looks much less attractive. The market leader who uses premium pricing may do quite well on a short-term basis but is vulnerable in the long term.

- *Bad habit #5: Maximization attempts.* The fifth of the common bad habits Drucker identifies involves attempts by an organization to maximize its product or service by making it "all things to all people." He again cites Xerox as an organization that allowed itself this weakness in the copier market. Concentrating on developing copy machines that could do almost anything, the company created machines that simply could not be used by many customers. When the competition offered small, simple, but functional machines for users with small, simple copying needs, they again hit Xerox where it hurt. Maximizing what a product can do may lead to a product that satisfies no one. A competitor who focuses on specific needs creates opportunities.

Three Opportunities for Entrepreneurial Judo   The five bad habits just described combine to create three principal opportunities for entrepreneurial judo. Challengers who wish to use entrepreneurial judo to attack established leaders' weak points can:

1. *Beat them to the punch.* Look for unexpected success or failure to which leaders are not reacting properly and deliver a new product or service before the leaders have a chance to do so.
2. *Undercut price.* Look for a rapidly growing market in which leaders try to cream the market and/or use premium pricing. Target the part of the market being slighted by the leaders and price your product lower.
3. *Seize the moment.* Look for a volatile market where the nature of products or services is changing quickly. Identify an area where leaders have not kept up with new demands and satisfy these demands before the leaders react.

The entrepreneurial judo strategy may not be as flashy as the leadership in a new market or industry approach, or as creative as the creative imitation approach, but it can be an effective, reliable (less risky) strategy. It seldom produces the same magnitude of results as the other approaches, but it has a much higher success rate and generally requires fewer resources to pursue.

Entrepreneurship and Intrapreneurship in Review

Entrepreneurship involves the development of a product or service idea and the creation of an organization to further its growth. Intrapreneurship involves identifying the need for change in an organization, creating the environment in which the change can succeed, and championing the implementation of the change.

Many entrepreneurs and intrapreneurs are characterized by particular personal or life experience factors. Many, for example, have a high need for achievement coupled with a low fear of failure and a strong internal locus of control. Often they have difficulty working for someone else, report encountering challenging educational experiences, and have early experiences running an organization. They engage in considerable goal-oriented behavior and possess high commitment to goals.

The intrapreneuring process is somewhat unique because its creative and analytical activities occur within an ongoing organization. It is a process that is becoming more and more critical to organizations, yet one that is often discouraged by organizational policies and practices. Thirteen steps were discussed which can create an environment conducive to intrapreneuring.

Three entrepreneurial and intrapreneurial strategies were presented and discussed. The first, leadership in a new market or industry, focuses on creating and then dominating a new product or service area. The second, creative imitation, concentrates on the creative improvement of someone else's innovation to serve a market better. The final strategy, entrepreneurial judo, capitalizes on the weaknesses of an organization to obtain a small entry point from which further inroads are attempted.

Notes

1. Based on information contained in L. Therrien, T. Carson, J. Hamilton, and J. Hurlock (22 December 1986), What do women want? A company they can call their own, *Business Week,* 60–62.

2. Based on information from G. Pinchot III (1985), *Intrapreneuring,* New York: Harper & Row.

3. Similar definitions are contained in W. B. Gartner (1985), A conceptual framework for describing the phenomenon of new venture creation, *Academy of Management Review,* 10, 696–706; K. H. Vesper (1980), *New venture strategies,* Englewood Cliffs, NJ: Prentice-Hall.

4. P. F. Drucker (1985), *Innovation and entrepreneurship,* New York: Harper & Row.

5. This section is based on ideas and findings from J. A. Timmons (1985), *New venture creation,* Homewood, IL: Irwin; G. Pinchot III (1985), *Intrapreneuring,* New York: Harper & Row; C. A. Kent, D. L. Sexton, and K. H. Vesper, eds. (1982), *Encyclopedia of entrepreneurship,* Englewood

Cliffs, NJ: Prentice-Hall; M. J. C. Martin (1984), *Managing technological innovation & entrepreneurship*, Reston, VA: Reston Publishing.

6. L. F. Centofanti (October 1986), So I said to myself, why not? *Venture*, 128.

7. R. Brandt (13 April 1987), The billion-dollar whiz kid, *Business Week*, 69.

8. America's most successful entrepreneur (27 October 1986), *Fortune*, 26.

9. S. Gannes (23 May 1988), America's fastest-growing companies, *Fortune*, 32.

10. Cited in J. G. Longenecker, J. A. McKinney, and C. W. Moore (Winter 1988), Egoism and independence: Entrepreneurial ethics, *Organizational Dynamics*, 64.

11. J. R. Mancusco (October 1974), What it takes to be an entrepreneur, *Journal of Small Business Management*, 16–22; J. A. Welsh and J. F. White (Summer 1978), Recognizing and dealing with the entrepreneur, *S.A.M. Advanced Management Journal*, 22–24.

12. Gannes, 1988, 33.

13. Gannes, 1988, 36.

14. Gifford Pinchot III has written a fascinating book on this subject appropriately entitled *Intrapreneuring*. Much of this chapter is based on an excellent review of that work prepared by Filip Caeldries and Arnold C. Cooper contained in J. L. Pierce and J. W. Newstrom, eds., *The manager's bookshelf: A mosaic of contemporary views*, 135–41. The concept is also discussed at length by Peter Drucker (although he uses somewhat different terminology).

15. Caeldries and Cooper, 137.

16. Caeldries and Cooper, 138–41.

17. Also see P. F. Drucker (1985), Entrepreneurial strategies, *California Management Review*, 27(2), 9–25.

18. Drucker, 1985.

19. Drucker, 1985.

20. Drucker, 1985, 18–19.

21. Drucker, 1985.

22. Drucker, 1985, 23.

23. Drucker, 1985, 21.

Key Terms

entrepreneurship	creative imitation
intrapreneurship	entrepreneurial judo
leadership in a new market or industry	

Issues for Review and Discussion

1. Discuss why you feel entrepreneurs and intrapreneurs are or are not the key to the future of American organizations.

2. Discuss steps that a college could take to encourage the development of entrepreneurs and intrapreneurs.

3. Describe the systematic steps that a large corporation, such as General Motors, could take to encourage intrapreneurial behavior. Would you recommend that GM do this?
4. If you were an entrepreneur looking for opportunities, which of the strategies described in this chapter would be most attractive to you? Explain why.
5. Discuss how a market leader could defend itself against entrepreneurs attempting to challenge it using the creative imitation strategy.
6. Discuss how a market leader could defend itself against entrepreneurs attempting to challenge it using the entrepreneurial judo strategy.

Suggested Readings

Drucker, P. F. (1985). *Innovation and entrepreneurship*. New York: Harper & Row.

Drucker, P. F. (Winter 1985). Entrepreneurial strategies. *California Management Review*, 27(2), 9–25.

Kent, C. A., Sexton, D. L., and Vesper, K. H., eds. (1982). *Encyclopedia of entrepreneurship*. Englewood Cliffs, NJ: Prentice-Hall.

Low, M. B. and MacMillan, I. C. (1988). Entrepreneurship: Past research and future challenges. *Journal of Management*, 14, 139–61.

Mancusco, J. R. (October 1974). What it takes to be an entrepreneur. *Journal of Small Business Management*, 16–22.

Pinchot, G. III (1985). *Intrapreneuring*. New York: Harper & Row.

Careers

Student Learning Objectives

After reading this chapter, you should be able to:

1. Define *career*.

2. Discuss life-span models, individual differences models, and organizationally based models of careers.

3. Identify the specific stages of Miller and Form's and Super's life-span models, and apply these to people in organizations.

4. Identify four common career patterns.

5. Explain the five career anchors identified by Schein.

6. Discuss Dalton and Thompson's career stages model.

7. Describe mentoring and networking in regard to career progression.

8. Apply the different career models to your own career development.

9. Discuss methods of increasing organizational effectiveness through the application of career theory.

By Ann Cope, in consultation with Gene Dalton, both of Brigham Young University

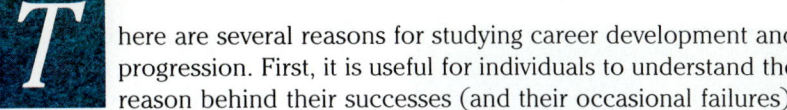

There are several reasons for studying career development and progression. First, it is useful for individuals to understand the reason behind their successes (and their occasional failures). It is not always clear why people in organizations are valued or promoted; this chapter clarifies many of the bases for such organizational decisions. Second, people in organizations need to understand ways in which they can assist and counsel other individuals toward successful and satisfying careers. There is always a need for better understanding and teamwork in merging individual goals with organizational needs. Third, a solid comprehension of career dynamics contributes to overall organizational effectiveness. As organizational needs are met in concert with individual career needs, organizations are better able to function.

Similarly, it is critical that people in management positions see the value of fostering the development of organization members. In this way, individual career needs can be met as people are given opportunities to grow, advance, and develop. Organizational needs are met as people's talents are best utilized, as planning for the future is carried out, and as managers anticipate organizational needs for new generations of leaders and managers.

Careers are very important for individuals, because, as Douglas Hall suggests, a career may represent a person's entire life in the work setting. He writes that for most, careers are a primary factor in determining the overall quality of life. The feelings of a seventy-year-old man illustrates this concept:

> *I enjoy working. I like to be around people. I coulda quit work five years ago. It's not that I don't like home, but it's monotonous to sit around. With your Social Security and what taxes I pay, I'm just as well off if I don't work. But I like to come down. I'm not saying I love people, but you miss 'em. . . . I think I've succeeded, if they didn't want me anymore, retirement wouldn't bother me. I'd go to the ball game, I'd go to the track, I'd do a little fishing.*[1]

It is critical that people in management positions see the value of fostering the development of organization members.

Definitions of Career

Once the importance of learning about and studying career development is realized, a question remains to be answered: what is a career? One definition could be that a career is a series of movements in an organization or a certain line of work or profession, such as a career as an accountant. Douglas Hall provides a more formal definition of **career**:

> *The career is the individually perceived sequence of attitudes and behaviors associated with work-related experiences and activities over the span of the person's life.*[2]

Inherent in this definition is the notion that careers are lifelong processes, but restricted to work-related activities. This definition requires further clarification. Specifically, Hall describes the phrase "attitudes and behaviors" as referring to: (1) a subjective career—changes in values, attitudes,

According to Douglas Hall, a career is an individually perceived sequence of attitudes and behaviors associated with work-related experiences and activities over the span of a person's life.

and motivation that occur as a person grows older—and (2) an objective career—the observable choices one makes and the activities one engages in, such as accepting or rejecting a particular job offer. Finally, Hall assumes that *career* does not imply success, failure, or rate of advancement.

A different explanation of careers is provided by Edgar Schein.[3] He suggests that a career can be thought of as a set of stages or a path through time that reflects: (1) an individual's needs, motives, and aspirations in relation to work and (2) society's expectations of what kinds of activities will result in monetary and status rewards. From Schein's definition is derived a career anchors model, which will be discussed later in this chapter.

Finally, Gene Dalton and Paul F. Thompson's definition of careers as sets of stages takes into account the role organizations play in an individual's career.[4] As individuals perform needed functions in organizations, they are valued and rewarded; however, if people fail to understand that career progression is to some degree dependent on organizational needs, they will often fail to advance or to feel rewarded and satisfied. Again, Dalton and Thompson's career stages model will be discussed later.

Each of these definitions of careers contributes a new dimension of understanding. In considering these different definitions, several frameworks have been devised to explain the ways in which individual careers progress and develop. Numerous theories take into account individual differences and properties of organizations. These theories can be categorized into life-span models, individual differences models, and organizationally based models of career development.

Life-Span Models

Life-span models of careers were constructed at a time when employees, mostly men, entered the workforce early in their lives and stayed in the workforce until retirement. Even so, the models are often applicable to modern employees, both men and women.

Because they are built around the biological life cycle, various life-span models exhibit a great deal of similarity. Life-span models provide such a broad framework that they accommodate a great diversity of empirical findings and points of view. In fact, other models can be enhanced when examined in terms of life-span models. The following quote from a fifty-five-year-old exemplifies the differences felt between workers at different points in their lives:

> *Some of the younger help, they seems to have the attitude, "I won't be here long." They say, "How long you worked here?" I say, "Oh, somewhat longer than you all." They says, "I don't want nobody's job that long." They don't feel like coming to work, they take the day off. Saturday, Sunday, Monday, it don't make no difference. . . . Wherein it was a rare thing for me to lose a day, years back. I don't lose any time now. I still think it's a wonderful thing to be employed.[5]*

This category of career models also makes clear that work-related organizations allow an individual to find a role or establish an identity as a competent, productive member of society. This is apparent in this society when people meet strangers; they often introduce themselves by stating what they do for a living or by naming the organization with which they are associated. These models also accommodate the fact that some individuals are unable to fit this role or to establish an identity as productive members of society.

These models also point out the efforts to hang on to a viable place in an organization among those past the midpoint in their careers. Finally, such models describe the period leading to and including retirement.[6]

Miller and Form's Life Stages Model

Delbert Miller and William Form were among the first to formulate a developmental model for careers.[7] They viewed a career as a series of social adjustments imposed on workers by a culture. Depending on the culture in which one lives, certain standard activities and vocations are desirable and acceptable; to function in the culture, an individual must adjust to these standards. These social adjustments fall into a pattern of five periods:

1. The **preparatory work period** characterized by socialization of a child at home and at school into the work patterns of society
2. The **initial work period** when the young worker is initiated into the work world through part-time employment
3. The **trial work period** beginning with the first full-time job and continuing to a more or less permanent work position
4. The **stable work period,** the period of job permanence
5. The **retirement period**

In the initial work period, a young worker is initiated into the labor force through part-time employment.

Miller and Form make it clear that not everyone goes through these stages successfully and achieves stability and security. Those who do might follow what they term a **stable career pattern,** in which they move from an initial job to a trial job and from there to stable employment. Some individuals develop an **unstable career pattern,** however, and never become established in one area, moving from trial jobs to stable situations but then back to trial jobs. Other individuals follow a **multiple trial pattern,** never staying in one field long enough to achieve stability, moving from one trial job to another.

In their explanation of what happens within and between these periods, Miller and Form emphasize the importance of social class in predicting and determining the occupational level attained. They cite research evidence that demonstrates a relationship between occupational level attained and the following five factors:

1. Parent's occupation
2. Worker's intelligence
3. Father's income and education
4. Accessible financial aid and influential contacts
5. Social and economic conditions in the general society

Because four of these five factors demonstrate a relationship between an individual's environment and occupational level, the accident of birth into a certain social class may be more of a determinant of an individual's attainments than anything the individual does (see Figure 25.1). With this view, a person's developmental pattern is determined largely before it even begins. Although this may be seen as a rather fatalistic approach, its implications for career counseling are enormous. The Miller and Form model should be used informationally to create a context in which to discuss career development in a number of possible directions.

Super's Model

Donald Super, an authority in vocational counseling, uses self-concepts to examine career development. He sees a career as a synthesis of a person's self-concept and the external realities of the work environment.[8] The synthesis develops as a person becomes aware of his or her self-concept, faces opportunities and requirements in particular occupa-

FIGURE 25.1   The Factors Involved in Determining Occupational Choice

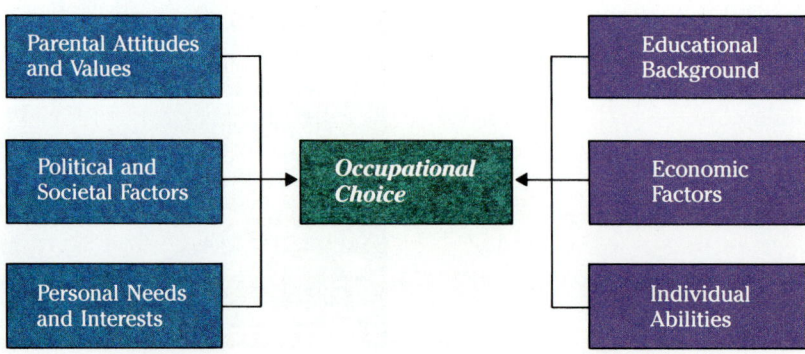

Source: D. C. Feldman (1988), *Managing careers in organizations,* Glenview, IL: Scott, Foresman, 29.

During the growth stage of Super's model, young people identify with key figures in the family and at school.

tions, and has experiences in implementing his or her self-concept by working. Career development, for Super, involves implementing a self-concept and testing it against reality. Not surprisingly, Super uses a life-span model fairly similar to Miller and Form's. He pictures career development as proceeding through five life stages, taken from a work by Charlotte Buehler.[9]

The first is the **growth stage,** extending from conception to approximately age fourteen, during which one's self-concept begins to form through identification with key figures in the family and at school. In this process, interests and capacities become more important with increasing social participation; adolescence is a time of developing a self-concept.

Second is the **exploratory stage,** ordinarily including the period from ages fifteen to twenty-five, during which self-concept is emerging and being tested against reality. In this stage, an individual retains aspects of the self-concept that bring satisfaction and rejects those that do not. This stage often includes the transition from school to working.

The third stage is the **establishment stage,** spanning the years from twenty-five to about forty-five, during which an appropriate field is found and effort is put forth to make a permanent place in it. During this stage, the tested self-concept is modified and implemented. There may be some trial or floundering early in this period, resulting in one or two changes before the life work is found or before it becomes clear that the life work will be a succession of unrelated jobs.

Fourth is the **maintenance stage,** stretching from forty-five to retirement. The main concern for an individual during this stage is to hold on to a place already made in the world of work. Usually there is little new ground broken; rather, there is a continuation along existing lines. In addition, an individual either preserves or feels nagged by his or her previously established self-concept.

Finally, there is a **decline stage.** In this stage, an individual moves out of an organization, concluding his or her work life. Consequently, there is an adjustment to a new self-concept.

Like Miller and Form, Super also postulates that environmental influences, such as family, disabilities, and economic factors, have a part in occupational choice. This is apparent if people follow in their parents' footsteps, if not by entering the same occupation, at least by choosing a similar work environment and socioeconomic level.

Individual Differences Model— Career Anchors

Through extensive research, Edgar Schein has formulated a model that describes the different needs, or "anchors," that individuals meet through their careers.[10] Schein's career anchors model was developed from a ten-to-twelve-year longitudinal study of forty-four male M.B.A. graduates from the Sloan School of Management at MIT. Part of the study included interviews focusing on detailed job histories of each person and the reasons for the choices each made. The forty-four interviews revealed a number of common ideas about what people are fundamentally looking for in their careers. These common themes can be defined as the underlying **career anchors** that pull people back if they stray too far from what they really want.

Schein's model of career anchors is based on the notion that "certain motivational, attitudinal, and value syndromes formed early in lives of individuals apparently function to guide and constrain their entire careers."[11] These basic combinations of needs and drives not only influence career choices, but also affect decisions to move from one company to another, shape what the individuals are looking for in life, and color their views of the future and their general assessments of related goals and objectives. These anchors are technical/functional competence, managerial competence, security and stability, creativity/entrepreneurship, and autonomy and independence (see Table 25.1).

This model holds some interesting implications for organizations. For instance, if career anchors do indeed function as stable syndromes in someone's personality, it is important for employing organizations to identify these syndromes early in an employee's career. The organization stands to gain by creating career opportunities that are congruent with the basic anchor needs of its human talent. For example, if an engineer works best with a large amount of autonomy and independence, an organization would benefit by providing an autonomous, independent atmosphere for that employee.

Anchor 1: Technical/Functional Competence

People with a **technical/functional competence anchor** are described as being motivated by the challenge of the technical work they do—financial analysis, engineering, marketing, strategic planning, or another area that can be related to technology or business. Their anchor is the technical field or functional area, not the managerial process itself. The following comment typifies the feelings of a person with this anchor:

TABLE 25.1 *Schein's Career Anchors Model*

Career Anchor	Characteristics	Typical Career Paths
1. Technical/functional competence	1. Excited by work itself 2. Willing to forgo promotions 3. Dislikes general management and corporate politics	1. Research-oriented positions 2. Functional department management jobs 3. Specialized consulting and project management
2. Managerial competence	1. Likes to analyze and solve knotty business problems 2. Likes to influence and harness people to work together 3. Enjoys the exercise of power	1. Vice-presidencies 2. Plant management and sales management 3. Large, prestigious firms
3. Security and stability	1. Motivated by job security and long-term careers with one firm 2. Dislikes travel and relocation 3. Tends to be conformist and compliant to the organization	1. Government jobs 2. Small, family-owned businesses 3. Large government-regulated industries
4. Creativity/ entrepreneurship	1. Enjoys launching own business 2. Restless; moves from project to project 3. Prefers small, up-and-coming firms to well-established ones	1. Entrepreneurial ventures 2. Stock options, arbitrage, mergers, and acquisitions 3. General management consulting
5. Autonomy and independence	1. Desires freedom from organizational constraints 2. Wants to be on own and set own pace 3. Avoids large businesses and governmental agencies	1. Academia 2. Writing and publishing 3. Small business proprietorships

Source: Adapted from E. A. Schein (1978), *Career Dynamics*, Reading, MA: Addison-Wesley, 124–60.

Briefly, what I need in a job is a specific goal, e.g., a computer system or program to solve some problem or a production schedule to be met which involves producing a concrete product. . . . In any case, I am convinced that I would never enjoy a position in sales—regardless of product or level in the organization. I much prefer to do the job—design the system, produce the car, etc.—than to sell it.[12]

These people's roots are in the analytical or technical work with which they are involved; promotion beyond such work is not important to people with this anchor. In fact, people with this set of needs would often rather leave a company than be promoted out of their technical/functional area. In terms of organizational titles, Schein writes that such people are often functional managers, technical managers, senior staff, junior staff, and external consultants.

Anchor 2: Managerial Competence

The people classified in this category clearly have as their fundamental motivation the need to be competent in the complex set of activities that make up the concept of "management." Schein identifies the most important components of the **managerial competence anchor** as:

1. Interpersonal competence—the ability to influence, supervise, lead, manipulate, and control people toward the more effective achievement of organizational goals

2. Analytical competence—the identification and solution of conceptual problems under conditions of uncertainty and incomplete information

3. Emotional stability—the capacity to be stimulated by emotional and interpersonal crises rather than exhausted or debilitated by them; the capacity to exercise authority without fear or guilt

The people with a managerial competence anchor usually fill a line or general manager's role, depending on their rank.

Anchor 3: Security

Individuals with a **security anchor** will probably remain with a certain company or in a particular geographic area for the greater part of their careers. Schein infers that their underlying need is for security and that they seek to stabilize their careers by linking them to given organizations or locations.

The implications are that individuals in this category accept organizational definitions of their careers to a greater degree than people with other anchors. These individuals must rely increasingly on organizations to recognize their needs and competencies; they trust organizations to do the best possible for them. This hope, however, is not always fulfilled. Often organizations can ask these people to do more while paying them less because of their need for stability. Some degree of personal freedom is lost, Schein writes, among those who are unwilling to leave a given organization. Such people are often quite willing to sacrifice some autonomy in their careers in order to stabilize their total life situation.

In interviews conducted for the research that yielded these career anchors of security and stability, the subjects spoke of their work, their families, their overall satisfaction with the geographical area where they have settled, and their sense of having achieved enough to satisfy themselves. They were not concerned with achieving brilliant success but rather with maintaining a degree of comfort.

Anchor 4: Creativity/Entrepreneurship

Some respondents expressed a strong need to create something independently of established organizations. Schein identifies this as the fundamental need operating in an entrepreneur, resulting in a desire to create a new product, develop a new service, or in some way invent something that can be clearly identified with the individual. It is interesting that people with the **creativity/entrepreneurship anchor** also exhibit a need for autonomy and independence, but there are important differences. All of the entrepreneurs identified by Schein strongly expressed the desire to be on their own, free of organizational restraints, but they did not leave the world of business to achieve their autonomy and creative goals.

Anchor 5: Autonomy and Independence

In Schein's research, these people had found organizational life to be restrictive, irrational, and/or intrusive into their private lives. Of the individuals who were viewed as having the **autonomy and independence anchor,** some left the world of business altogether, seeking

People with the creativity/entrepreneurship anchor desire to develop a new service or create a new product with which they are identified.

careers that provided more autonomy. Others remained with the business world by becoming consultants and operating on their own.

Superficially, those with the autonomy and independence anchor resemble those with different anchors. They seem similar to those with the creativity anchor, but they do not have the desire to create something that does not already exist. This group also resembles the technical/functional competence group in some respects; the difference between these two groups lies in the fact that no functional managers or staff roles are represented by those with the autonomy anchor. This anchor group is also distinguished from other groups by the fact that its members display little disappointment about missed opportunities. They are comfortable and happy in their work; they do not aspire for higher positions, and they greatly enjoy their freedom.

Implications of the Career Anchors Model

Not surprisingly, Schein found that the most successful in pure income terms was the managerial competence group. This is because climbing the managerial ladder is congruent with society's definition of success—organization executives are well paid and generally well respected. The creativity anchor group had the greatest net worth. Schein postulates that it perhaps is more important for those with a creativity anchor, often entrepreneurs, to build total assets than to consume what they have amassed. At the lowest end of the income scale was the autonomy-oriented group who had left large organizations. These included a freelance writer, a professor, and other people in vocations that allowed them plenty of freedom from institutions.

As Miller and Form theorize, Schein also uncovered some evidence in this study that family background, socioeconomic status, and other variables influenced the subjects' careers. Schein's population was a relatively highly educated group with a number of available options and, thus, the individuals studied were able to develop careers consistent with their needs and values. More highly educated people have more career alternatives. Some found opportunities to grow, to sharpen their skills, and to increase their abilities in organizations. Others were willing to trade time and/or loyalty to an organization for other things they wanted. Still others created organizations to achieve the goals central to their development.

This concept of career anchors is very useful in explaining the choices people make regarding their careers. There are several implications inherent in the model. First, organizations need to help employees recognize and work with their anchors toward more effective careers. Along with this, organizations would do well to create multiple paths and reward systems to permit effective use of employees' managerial, technical, and other professional talents. Business organizations can learn to identify individual career anchor orientations and subsequently steer individuals in the directions that will allow for the greatest amounts of satisfaction and productivity. In turn, these organizations will benefit from the fit between employees and positions, as employees are able to contribute more as their needs are filled.

An Organizationally Based Model— Career Stages

From years of study about professional employees, Gene Dalton and Paul F. Thompson developed a model of career stages.[13] Their model applies best to people they call "knowledge workers," or people in such professions as engineering, accounting, business management, and science. The principles also apply to other employees, however; those who work their way up in organizations by engaging in more highly valued activities typically move through the stages as well.

Traditional organizational models did not explain what Dalton and Thompson found in studying the careers of college graduates. For example, the pyramid model typified by most organizational charts suggests that authority, status, and pay increases come as a person moves higher up the chart. The implication is that a person should try to move up as quickly as possible. Also the pyramid model was often taken to imply that willingness to perform is the sole criterion for advancement, recognition, and reward.

Another model that has been used frequently to think about careers is the obsolescence model. This view holds that rapidly changing technology results in a rapid outdating of the skills of older professionals. New college graduates are hired to replace obsolete workers.

The obsolescence model implies that high performance can only be achieved by professionals who are constantly updated and reeducated through continuing education programs. Dalton and Thompson found in their studies, however, that high performers were no more likely to have taken continuing education courses than were low performers. The obsolescence model could not explain why some older professionals were classified as high performers and rewarded as such, while others were seen as having outdated skills.

In their study of 550 professionally trained employees, Dalton and Thompson found that high performance ratings were associated with taking on different activities and different relationships over time (see Figure 25.2). The key was not necessarily that professionals were continually moving up the pyramid; neither were they competing directly with new college graduates. Rather, the professionals who were rated as high performers throughout their careers played successively different roles in their organizations. They engaged in new activities and developed new skills. These new roles were valued by their organizations, and from this came high performance ratings.

In this extensive study, Dalton and Thompson found four distinct career stages, each different in the tasks people were expected to perform, the types of relationships, and the psychological adjustments. Stage I is identified as the apprentice stage, which is typified by people entering organizations and learning their duties. Stage II, called the independent contributor stage, is filled by people who are experts in certain areas and are no longer closely supervised. Stage III, the mentoring stage, is described as being a time to help other people in organizations develop and learn. Finally, in Stage IV—the sponsor stage—people determine policy and direction for organizations. Each of these stages is discussed further in Tables 25.2 and 25.3.

Stage I

Dalton and Thompson found that people in Stage I, the **apprentice stage,** typically lack experience and credibility and are under close supervision. They will perform routine duties and detailed tasks; however, to be successful, they must also exhibit initiative and innovation. The dichotomy between these two approaches can be difficult. There is a need to be reliable with detail work and at the same time to take initiative and be innovative. It is difficult, of course, to achieve a balance between a willing acceptance of routine assignments and an aggressive seeking out of new, more challenging tasks. A manager in a large national bank noted that:

FIGURE 25.2   Age and Performance: Managers' Evaluation of Engineers

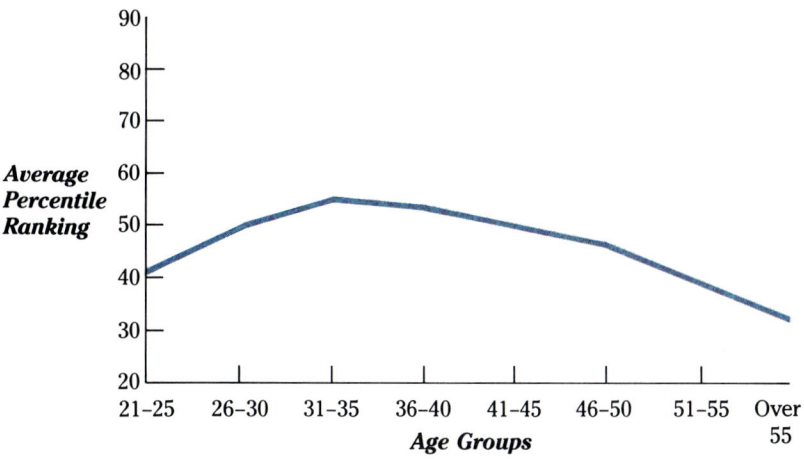

Source: G. Dalton and P. Thompson (1986), *Novations: Strategies for career management*, Glenview, IL: Scott, Foresman, 4.

TABLE 25.2 *Central Activities, Relationships, and Psychological Issues in Four Career Stages*

	Stage I	Stage II	Stage III	Stage IV
Central Activity	Helping, learning, following directions	Independent contributor	Training, interfacing	Shaping the direction of the organization
Primary Relationship	Apprentice	Colleagues	Mentor	Sponsor
Major Psychological Issues	Dependence	Independence	Assuming responsibility for others	Exercising power

Source: G. W. Dalton, P. H. Thompson, and R. L. Price (Summer 1977), The four stages of professional careers—a new look at performance by professionals, *Organizational Dynamics*, 23.

When a person leaves college or graduate school, he is automatically demoted from the senior level to freshman again. He's been the experienced student who's mastered the system, then all of a sudden he's forced back to the bottom of the heap. Many of our new MBAs have a rough time swallowing it. As students, they analyzed and discussed cases from the point of view of the president. Now they see themselves as the peons, doing all the detail work. Those that resist making this shift get off to a very poor start.[14]

Activities This stage involves three types of learning. First, a person in Stage I must learn to perform at least some of the organization's tasks competently. This can involve learning to run a computer, draw up an account, or perform another necessary task. Second, the person must learn which elements of the work are critical and which require the greatest attention. The person can focus attention on these activities, concentrating on learning the intricacies involved in the tasks.

Finally, people in Stage I must learn how to get things done using both formal and informal channels of communication. Successful Stage I people do all this while they are being closely observed for indications of competence and future potential. It is critical that they perform their duties thoroughly and well, even if the tasks appear small and menial, for two reasons: in order to learn the skills involved and because they are being closely watched.

Apprentices generally work on assignments that are part of a larger project or activity directed by a senior manager.

People in the apprentice stage generally work on assignments that are part of a larger project or activity directed by a senior manager or professional. It can be a frustrating experience, yet there is a need to learn from others' experiences. On the other hand, if an apprentice is impatient and attempts to undertake work he or she is not prepared to do, he or she earns a reputation for mediocre performance, which is hard to overcome.

Relationships The primary relationship an employee experiences in Stage I is that of subordinate. Stage I employees are typically low on the totem pole and must take direction and instruction from their superiors. Ideally, this person will work with a mentor, learning from observation

TABLE 25.3 *Characteristics of Career Stages*

Stage I	Stage II
Works under the supervision and direction of a more senior professional in the field	Goes into depth in one problem or technical area
Work is never entirely his or her own but assignments are given that are a portion of a larger project or activity being overseen by a senior professional	Assumes responsibility for a definable portion of the project, process, or clients
	Works independently and produces significant results
Lacks experience and status in organization	Develops credibility and a reputation
Expected to willingly accept supervision and direction	Relies less on supervisor or mentor for answers: develops more of his or her own resources to solve problems
Expected to do most of the detailed and routine work on a project	Increases in confidence and ability
Expected to exercise "directed" creativity and initiative	
Learns to perform well under pressure and accomplish a task within the time budgeted	

Stage III	Stage IV
Involved enough in his or her own work to make significant technical contributions but begins working in more than one area	Provides direction for the organization by: a. "Mapping" the organization's environment to highlight opportunities and dangers b. Focusing activities in areas of "distinctive competence" c. Managing the process by which decisions are made
Greater breadth of technical skills and application of those skills	
Stimulates others through ideas and information	Exercises formal and informal power to: a. Initiate action and influence decisions b. Obtain resources and approvals
Involved in developing people in one or more of the following ways: a. Acts as an idea leader for a small group b. Serves as a mentor to younger professionals c. Assumes a formal supervisory position	Represents the organization: a. To individuals and groups at different levels inside the organization b. To individuals and institutions outside the organization
Deals with the outside to benefit others in organizations—i.e., working out relationships with client organizations, developing new business	Sponsors promising individuals to test and prepare them for key roles in the organization

Source: G. W. Dalton and P. Thompson (1986), *Novations: Strategies for career management*, Glenview, IL: Scott, Foresman, 8,9.

and from trial-and-error the approaches, organizational savvy, and judgment that cannot be learned from textbooks. An apprentice performs detailed and often boring work in exchange for things that he or she can only learn from a mentor.

A mentor supports an apprentice and provides learning experiences. As an apprentice learns, he or she is given more responsibilities—but if the apprentice fails, he or she remains longer under supervision. A good mentor is often a model whom a Stage I employee can follow whenever he or she is unsure of how to solve a problem. In summary, this mentor instructs, provides opportunities for an apprentice to try his or her hand at new tasks, and makes sure the apprentice does not make important errors. A more in-depth discussion of mentors appears later in this chapter.

Psychological Issues   As mentioned previously, a person in Stage I must learn to be a subordinate and accept the dependence that comes with this role. An apprentice is "expected to willingly accept supervision and direction" and to "exercise directed creativity and initiative."[15] This can be difficult for new employees in organizations who have anticipated finishing their education so they could be free of the demands of professors and find some independence. Instead of freedom, new employees are confronted with high degrees of supervision, direction, and, of course, routine work. Consider the following experiences of two people in Stage I:

> *One 32-year-old lawyer reports that working on a famous and controversial securities default case means plowing through "hundreds of thousands of documents" to piece together events "in a given department in a given period of time. It's monotonous."*
>
> *A 27-year-old was proud to be helping manage a $7 billion money market fund. But after awhile, he tired of checking rates, making phone calls, and reinvesting maturing securities. "Whether it was $1 million or $100 million, the procedure was still the same." He quit when he decided that "except for the tension, a baboon could do what I was doing."[16]*

If apprentices learn to perform and stick with the seemingly endless routine work, they will be valued and rewarded by their organization. On the other hand, if they lose interest or do sloppy work, they may earn a poor reputation and have difficulty in subsequent career stages.

Stage II

Independence is the theme in the **independent contributor stage.** An individual makes the transition from Stage I by developing a reputation as a technically competent professional who can work independently to produce significant results. There is little if any supervision in Stage II, and people work with others only in coordinating projects.

Activities   Independent contributors have their own projects or areas of responsibility. This does not mean, however, that such people can work completely on their own individual projects, because projects often must be coordinated with other activities. In any case, Stage II employees are

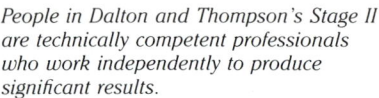

People in Dalton and Thompson's Stage II are technically competent professionals who work independently to produce significant results.

no longer closely supervised in regard to specified methods of getting work done. Instead, they are given general instructions and are left to complete work in whatever way is best. One young physicist's experience is insightful:

> *Since my early days at the laboratory, I'd always worked with Chuck Robinson on research projects. It took three years before I had confidence to submit a proposal on my own. But even with my own project, I never made a decision or wrote a final draft without consulting Robinson. When he took a six-month assignment in Kwajalein, I was paralyzed. I couldn't think for four months. Eventually, I figured out that I could get opinions from other people in the department and make a decision using their input. It was a major discovery for me to realize that I didn't need a boss to approve my decisions.*[17]

Independent contributors have developed a high level of professional skills and an area of specialization; they are very good in a certain area. The dilemma for those in Stage II is how much to specialize. A generalist is useful, but in order to be valued by an organization, a person needs to develop and demonstrate solid competence in a critical task area. If this does not happen, it becomes a major block to a person's career—in essence, the person remains in Stage I or is let go.

The best thing is to become a specialist, at least temporarily, in order to gain a reputation for expertise within a specialty, and to build a sense of competence and self-esteem, and to enhance visibility. Although some professionals are able to advance with technical inadequacies, workers unable to overcome this handicap are unlikely to do well in Stage II. An example of a professional who failed to develop an area of expertise follows:

> *Ted Barker was 27 years old when he was hired with an MBA from a prestigious business school. He moved very fast through his early career and within three years was promoted to vice president of consumer banking in Brazil. Two years later he was fired. He'd moved so fast that he knew almost nothing about the technical work of the bank. Senior management found serious problems with the mutual fund and the credit card systems. Barker didn't just not know what was going on, he didn't even know what questions to ask.*[18]

There are two approaches to selecting an area of specialization. The first is to focus on content, as does a CPA who concentrates on tax problems for banks, a scientist who focuses on testing, and a banker who concentrates on loans to utilities. The second approach is to focus on a set of specialized skills that can be applied in solving a variety of problems. These skills might be, for example, applying computer technology or dealing with clients. There is often a risk of becoming pigeon-holed in a phased-out specialty, but a good specialty is usually a solid base for a career.

Relationships   The main relationships in this stage are with peers. A professional can receive a great deal of support and information from his or her colleagues. Networking may become important for a Stage II employee, as mentor relationships may begin to fade. Independent contributors rely less and less on supervisors and mentors for direction;

often this attitude change is difficult to make both for the subordinate and the supervisor. The subordinate loses the direction and dependency that comes with a Stage I relationship, while the supervisor must learn to let go of a student and a helper.

Psychological Issues A person entering Stage II must make the transition from dependence to independence. He or she learns to develop personal ideas about what is required and about personal standards of performance. Help and guidance are less available from superiors but more available from peers and professional standards than during Stage I. Still, Stage II employees must learn to find a sense of confidence in their own judgment.

It is important that employees spend a period of time in this stage; problems arise when a person moves out of Stage II too quickly into a management position. Before moving into management, individuals need time to understand the technical aspects of the work they would be supervising. Otherwise, they risk undermining others' confidence.

It is interesting that Dalton and Thompson found that many professional workers stay in Stage II throughout their careers. In this stage, they are able to make substantial contributions and experience a high degree of personal satisfaction through the technical work they perform; however, high ratings tend to diminish with time for those in Stage II. As they get older, they are expected to begin filling new roles in their organization.

Stage III

Dalton and Thompson refer to Stage III as the **mentoring stage.** In this stage, a person begins to influence, direct, and develop other people. Additionally, those in the mentor stage develop broadened interests and capabilities; they are a natural source of ideas for people in Stages I and II.

Activities A mentor performs three roles, which are not mutually exclusive. The first is that of an informal mentor. People who might be mentors will be asked to do more work because of their demonstrated competency (which was most probably developed in Stage II). To accomplish this load, they need help, and apprentices in Stage II provide that help. For example, one technical mentor described his role in these words:

> *Right now I find the sponsors for our work. I do the conceptual thinking, develop the project, and then get someone to support it. After I get the job, then I must supervise and collaborate with others who do most of the actual work.*[19]

People in Stage II remain the driving force behind projects, and they work closely with those who do the detail work.

The second role enacted in Stage III is that of an "idea person." Stage III people may act as consultants for small groups, and others come to them for suggestions. From their past experience, they can pull information that will be helpful for others.

The third role is that of manager. Dalton and Thompson found this to be the most common role for someone in Stage III, as well as the most easily understood. Usually a Stage II manager will be no more than one or

two levels away from the work itself. A Stage III manager is more distant from the work and, thus, manages at a more abstract level. He or she deals more with concepts and less with technical activities. Nonetheless, he or she assumes responsibility for the technical work done by others.

Relationships   In Stage III, people learn to take care of others by mentoring and to assume responsibility for the work of subordinates. It is important that Stage III people work with the employees lower in the organization in order to tap their additional skills. In return for this help and loyalty, mentors need to learn to give independence. Aside from the mentoring relationship specifically, a person who has advanced to Stage III needs to demonstrate interpersonal skills in setting objectives, delegating, supervising, and coordinating. This person must satisfy many people, as he or she has responsibilities upward as well as downward. Always looking upward means losing loyalty from below. On the other hand, a Stage III individual needs to have influence with superiors to be able to obtain resources and provide ways for subordinates to perform their duties.

Psychological Issues   Psychologically, the Stage III person needs to develop a sense of confidence in his or her own ability to produce results and to help others do the same. Along these same lines, he or she needs to be able to build confidence in subordinates. If he or she feels threatened by the success of apprentices, he or she will not provide them with the guidelines and freedom needed for their progression. Somehow a balance must be found between directing them and providing them with freedom.

Furthermore, as mentioned earlier, a mentor needs to be willing and able to take responsibility for someone else's output. As a mentor, an individual assumes an obligation both to apprentices and to customers. Occasionally, a person begins to fill Stage III roles but then feels frustrated and unhappy. At times, the supervisory responsibility seems confining; in this case, a role may be found that allows for broad influence without supervising. On the other hand, a person who feels restricted by this role can move back into Stage II. In some organizations, this move is acceptable, while in others it is viewed as a demotion and a lowering of status.

One question that remains is how far a mentor can or should move from his or her technical expertise. One scientist describes his experience:

> *I assumed when I came here that being a good scientist was all that was necessary. Later, I found that science was more than just research. You have to conceive, sell, and direct a program. I began to do all those things and found myself in management mainly because I didn't want to work for the other guys they were considering. I want to stay close to technical work and maybe move back into it. Because I know it is difficult to move out of management into technical work, I have stayed close to my field, written papers, and still consider myself to be a scientist.[20]*

Since mentors rarely perform the tasks involved in a project, they must learn to derive satisfaction out of seeing apprentices moving away, becoming independent, or taking on new mentors. This may be a potential source of conflict or disappointment, especially for people in Stage III without a formal supervisory position that carries with it certain psychological supports and role clarity. As newer people in the organization begin to move through the stages, however, they no longer have strong needs for mentoring.

Dalton and Thompson discovered that to achieve a sense of long-term satisfaction, mentors meet challenges by broadening their thinking, by increasing knowledge by moving into new areas, and by applying present skills to new problems. They also derive satisfaction from social involvement and recognition from peers and by helping junior professionals further their careers. Organizational rewards, such as money and status, are at a fairly satisfactory level, given the positions Stage III people hold in organizations.

Stage III can be the climax of a career; some find Stage III viable and satisfying until retirement. The psychological and physical rewards may be substantial, and professionals enjoy a fairly high degree of status within organizations. Others may feel stagnated and hard-pressed to keep up with younger competitors. Some move on to Stage IV, where their roles again shift to meet another set of organizational needs.

Stage IV

People in the **sponsor stage** have an influence in defining the direction of an organization or a major portion of it. Some Stage IV professionals are in line management and others are not—all have a part in shaping the future of their organization. This influence is exercised in several ways—through negotiating and interfacing with key parts of the environment; through developing new ideas, products, markets, or services that lead the organization into new areas of activity; or through directing organizational resources toward specific goals.

Because these functions are so critical to the growth and survival of an organization, those who perform them are highly valued, and only those whose skill and judgment have been proven in the past are trusted to play Stage IV roles. Credibility is typically gained from reading the environ-

People in the sponsor stage influence the direction of an organization or a major portion of it.

ment and acting on that information. For example, top executive officers of business organizations are often paid many times the salaries of professionals subordinate to them.

Activities In Stage IV, a person performs at least one of three roles. The first of these, as in Stage III, is the role of manager. It is important, however, to remember that not all Stage IV professionals are managers. Managers in Stage IV are not as close to work processes as Stage III employees are. Upper-level managers are usually in Stage IV of their careers, while some middle managers are making the transition to this stage. They are usually not involved in guiding apprentices in Stage I, or even in supervising Stage II workers. They are not close enough to the details of daily work to perform these roles. Instead, they formulate policy and initiate and approve broad programs.

The second of the roles identified by Dalton and Thompson as being performed by those in Stage IV is that of intrapreneur. These are people with new ideas and a strong sense of direction for the future of their organization. Often because of their official positions, Stage IV people can bring resources—money and people—together to further their ideas. They may be considered mavericks in organizations, but as long as they are successful in their ideas and directions, they are valued.

The third role of people in Stage IV is described as "idea innovator." The biggest opportunities and the most significant breakthroughs most often originate with these people. An idea innovator may puzzle for years over a problem or idea before a solution finally presents itself. He or she may work quite closely with a manager or someone else to sell his or her ideas. Often Stage IV people have established a reputation outside their organization through professional achievements and/or publications. This outside reputation enhances their credibility within the organization and may allow Stage IV people to play key roles in recruiting and business development. In a world-famous research organization, Dalton and Thompson were told:

> *In my view, the senior project guys are clearly in Stage IV. Their projects are usually high visibility, high cost, high risk, or technically very difficult. When they screw up, the whole organization suffers. There is national interest, either positive or negative, in their projects. These people have a very strong influence on the internal and external system of this place. You might not think they have a lot to do with developing people, but they do. They find and develop people to work with them, and a successful and unsuccessful stint with one of them can make or break someone's career around here.[21]*

Relationships The first major relationship has to do with the selection and development of key people; this is one of the Stage IV person's basic ways of influencing the organization. He or she is not concerned specifically with getting new people started but does select and groom those from Stage II or III who show promise of performing Stage IV activities in the future. A Stage IV person's focus is on opening up opportunities, assessing work, and providing feedback for subordinates rather than on such mentoring activities as giving instruction. This person watches potential organization leaders, looking for strengths and weaknesses; he or she counsels them and guides them to areas where they can be most effective. Both managers and nonmanagers perform this Stage IV role. In fact, Dalton and Thompson found that most nonmanagers in Stage IV play a major role in developing many able managers.

The second primary relationship is directed to the outside of an organization. This relationship is critical because it brings current information about events and trends into an organization. Such a relationship can be seen in professional associations and legal and banking communities. In addition, a person's writing focused on major areas of concern to the organization can give further visibility.

Psychological Issues   A Stage IV person is invariably pulled away from organizational operations, although most managerial Stage IV people often stay close to at least some aspects. Because of this distancing, they must learn not to second guess subordinates on operating decisions. Instead, they must learn to influence those under them through ideas, personnel selection, reviews, resource allocation, changes in organizational design, and so on. It may be difficult to allow the distancing from day-to-day activities to take place, but it is necessary if people in each of the other stages are to function effectively.

People in Stage IV have broadening perspectives and lengthening time horizons. They have learned to think about their organization as a whole and to act in that framework, rather than to show concern for individual departments or divisions. It is important that they think of the needs of the organization beyond the time frame in which they are personally affected — their role is to plan for the next five to ten years and beyond.

Finally, Stage IV people must become accustomed to using power; they will be forced to exercise the power that comes with their position because so many others depend on them to fight for their programs. In addition, these people will need to form alliances and take strong positions without feeling permanent enmity toward those who differ. People in Stage IV can also use their power to direct their organization strategically in the proper direction. A vice-president and director of development stated:

> *I had never thought much about power or aspired to it. But when I got this job, I quickly found out that there were so many people depending on me to fight for their programs that I had to learn to line up support, build alliances, and take strong positions without feeling enmity with those with whom I differed.*[22]

Implications of the Stages Model

People in all four stages make an important contribution to their organization. Obviously, a number of people in each stage are necessary for organizational effectiveness, but as they grow older, they will be less valued if they do not move beyond the early stages. To maintain a high performance rating throughout a career, one should seek to move at least to Stage III. Depending on an organization's climate, people may move back and forth between stages, although for many this implies demotion.

Dalton and Thompson's model makes an important contribution in that Stages III and IV are not limited to formal management positions in most organizations—this is the distinction between the stages model and the pyramid or hierarchy model. This means that engineers and accountants, for example, can continue to work in their chosen fields without forgoing the organizational rewards that typically come with advancement into management.

Mentoring

From its origin in Greek mythology (Mentor was Odysseus' loyal friend and wise advisor), the word *mentor* has come to mean "wise and trusted counselor." In the corporate world, however, a **mentor** is a transitional figure who gives an apprentice a one-on-one education in subjects not learned in school. Mentors teach about the ins and outs of specific companies, help with real application of raw skills, work to protect apprentices, and help apprentices gain recognition when it is merited.

Mentoring can be very rewarding or very devastating to a career. No two mentoring relationships are alike. The following examples illustrate this idea:

Bob was an assistant branch manager in a bank. John Gilbert hired Bob and immediately took a liking to him. Before long, they were lunching together several times a week. Bob was given good assignments and eventually was asked to manage a department in the bank. Five years into Bob's career, John Gilbert was implicated in a major scandal. Even though Bob was never involved in any wrongdoing, he reported, "It was like having the plague. Nobody wanted to touch me, nobody wanted me near. Gilbert was fired, and since I was known as one of Gilbert's boys, suddenly management couldn't find a place for me. I had to leave the bank. In fact, I left banking. It was six months before I found a job as an accountant in a defense-related industry."

A mentor often becomes a role model for a protégé. Such identification tends to intensify the relationship and can make it more productive.

Jill Tanner was forty-five years old and the top-rated manager in a large manufacturing plant. She had been with the company for twenty-three years, having started as a secretary. When asked to attribute what impact her mentor had on her career, she replied, "Without Fred, I would be a career secretary. After I worked for Fred for six months, he told me that I deserved more. It took him three years to find a place where I could go that was not office work. He helped me get into accounting, and even though I didn't work for him anymore, he saw that I did well. Whenever there was an opening in a department, Fred would call me before it was announced and tell me to go after it. I know that he would work behind the scenes helping get the jobs. Today Fred and I are the best of friends. My husband and I vacation with Fred and his wife. I tell him about my work problems and he tells me about his. I haven't worked under his supervision for many years, but I still look at him as the boss."[23]

There are several characteristics of a mentor-protégé relationship. The first is common interests. People seem to find it easier to give feedback and suggestions to those with whom they can relate on another level.

Often people in these relationships spend time together outside of working hours.

Hand-in-hand with common interests is the idea of an emotional bond. Many people describing their mentors make such statements as, "He was almost like a father," or "He was more like an older brother."[24] For many, an apprentice-mentor relationship is more like a family tie than a formal work relationship. The negative aspect of such a bond occurs when a strong emotional relationship outgrows its usefulness on a business level and needs to be severed or changed.

A third characteristic is mutual identification. Apprentices often identify with their mentors as people they could look up to and use as role models. The identification tends to intensify the relationship, and in some cases, makes it more productive. The fact that successful mentoring relationships are formed through voluntary selection underscores the idea of mutual identification.

In light of these three characteristics, it is not surprising to learn that mentors and apprentices are not assigned. Many times it is natural for a boss to turn into a mentor, but this type of relationship develops over time and does not happen automatically. Dalton and Thompson write:

> In one of the companies we studied, 65% of those interviewed indicated that they had had a mentor at some point in their career; other studies have reported similar percentages. The voluntary aspect of the selection process suggests that the formal assignment of mentor is not likely to be very successful.[25]

Furthermore, mentors and apprentices both contribute to the relationship; there is a high degree of reciprocity. Both parties need to receive substantial benefits from the relationship if it is to endure. The mentor provides resources and information on current happenings and future opportunities and shows interest in the development of the apprentice. Additionally, the mentor acts as a role model—by teaching, influencing, and managing in large part by example. The apprentice learns much through observation.

A mentor provides a great deal of coaching—teaching another party how to work effectively in the organization. This includes sharing information not only about the work, but about the organization and how to get things done through the system. Mentors tend to protect their protégés; they must be willing to take public accountability for errors. Explicitly or tacitly, they have been a part of most of the decisions an apprentice makes.

Despite all of the advantages that can come from a successful mentor-protégé relationship, difficulties may arise. Specifically, in terms of female-male mentor relationships, K. Kram identifies several problem areas.[26] (Currently, most cross-gender mentor relationships have a male in the mentor role.) The problems Kram writes about include:

1. Collusion in stereotypical roles—men and women tend to assume traditional roles that may constrain behavior and reduce individual competence and effectiveness. Kram writes that "the challenge is to figure out how men and women can be freer to behave in a variety of ways that are most appropriate for a given work context."[27]

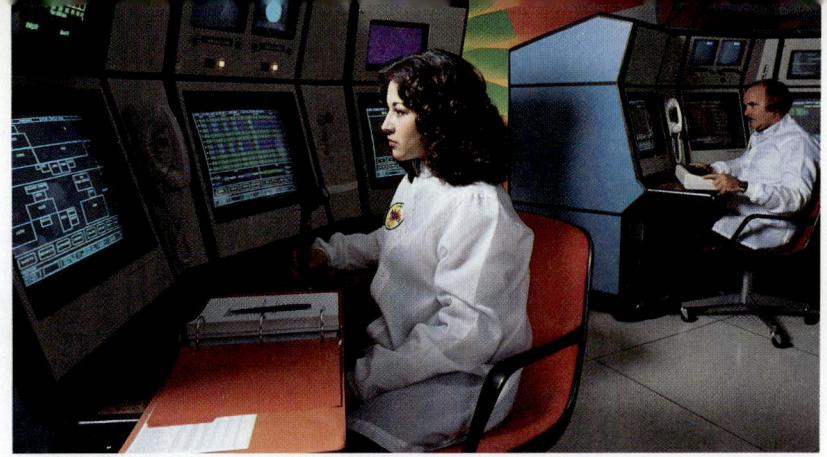

Women face dilemmas unique to being female in male-dominated organizations. For example, a male mentor may find it difficult to empathize and identify with a protégée.

2. Limitations of role modeling—women face dilemmas unique to being female in male-dominated organizations. Certain gender differences make it difficult for male mentors to empathize, to provide role modeling, and to identify with female protégées.

3. Intimacy and sexuality concerns; Kram notes that the mutual liking and admiration characteristic of all significant work relationships may lead to increasing intimacy and sexual tensions. The manner of dealing with them determines whether the relationship is strengthened or weakened by this complexity.

4. Public scrutiny and peer resentment—others notice the relationship and are interested in, if not suspicious of, motives. If rumors develop it can be destructive to one or more careers. Also, the possibility of favoritism can cause peers to resent the position of the new female protégée.

Networking

Networking is a process by which individuals gain social support from many directions. It can be seen as a supplement or even as an alternative to mentoring. A benefit of solid peer contacts is the network of associates that they provide. Peer support is important for any person in an organization; although most professionals enter the working world with certain standard skills, their respective strengths and weaknesses vary widely. Collectively, they form a broad pool of resources.

R. Keele observes that not every new member of an organization has a strong-tie relationship with a mentor.[28] Given this reality, people need to find other ways to gain stability and power in organizations. Forming networks with people in and out of an organization can provide the kinds of support needed.[29]

Such networks can be very effective in helping people tap resources in order to be successful in their careers. One implication is that organizations need to provide opportunities for employees from different areas to meet each other. That can be done at many levels—interdepartmental task forces, social events, transfers among departments, and so on. With this approach, individuals should have more successful careers that contribute greatly to organizational success.

Careers in Review

There are several reasons for studying career development and progression. First, it is useful for individuals to understanding the reasons behind their successes and failures. Second, people in organizations need to understand ways in which they can assist and counsel other individuals toward successful and satisfying careers. Third, a solid comprehension of career dynamics contributes to overall organizational effectiveness. Career development also contributes to the process of anticipating organizational needs for new generations of leaders and managers.

One definition of *career* is a series of movements in a company; *career* can also mean a certain line of work or profession, such as a career as an accountant. A more formal definition of *career* is given by Hall: a career is an individually perceived sequence of attitudes and behaviors associated with work-related experiences and activities over the span of a person's life. Schein contributes that a career can be thought of as a set of stages or a path through time that reflects (1) an individual's needs, motives, and aspirations in relation to work and (2) society's expectations of what kinds of activities will result in monetary and status rewards. Dalton and Thompson's definition of careers as sets of stages takes into account the role organizations play in individuals' careers.

Because they are built around the biological life cycle, life-span career models exhibit a great deal of similarity. This similarity exists whether the focus is on the society's forcing individuals to adapt to its needs or on individuals' forming an identity based on the choices and responses received from the environment.

Miller and Form were among the first to formulate a developmental model for careers. They viewed careers as a series of social adjustments that culture imposes on workers. This series of adjustments includes: (1) a preparatory work period, (2) an initial period, (3) a trial period, (4) a stable work period, and (5) a retirement period. In their explanation of what happens within and between these periods, Miller and Form emphasize the importance of social class in predicting and determining the occupational level a person attains.

Super, an authority in vocational counseling, uses self-concept to examine career development. He sees a career as a synthesis of a person's self-concept and the external realities of the work environment. The self-concept is synthesized through five stages: (1) the growth stage, (2) the exploratory stage, (3) an establishment stage, (4) the maintenance stage, and (5) the decline stage.

Schein formulated a model that describes the different needs individuals fill through their careers. These needs, called anchors, are managerial competence, technical/functional competence, security, creativity, and autonomy and independence. In satisfying the managerial competence need, the fundamental motivation is a need to be competent in the complex set of activities that makes up the idea of "management." In satisfying the technical/functional competence need, motivation comes from the challenge of the work that is done. The security need relates to remaining with a certain company or in a particular geographic area. Some people have a strong need to create something independently of established organizations. Schein identifies this as the fundamental need operating in an entrepreneur. Finally, those with autonomy and independence needs find organizational life to be restrictive, irrational, and/or intrusive into their private lives.

There are several implications inherent in Schein's career anchor model. First of all, organizations need to help employees recognize their anchors and work with them toward more effective careers. Along with this, organizations would do well to create multiple paths and reward systems to permit effective utilization of employees' managerial, technical, and other professional talents.

From years of study about professional employees, Dalton and Thompson developed a model of career stages. High performance ratings were associated with taking on different activities and relationships over time; high performers early in their careers were performing different functions from those in midcareer, and both sets of functions were different from those performed in late career. Dalton and Thompson found four distinct career stages, each different in the tasks people were expected to perform, the types of relationships they developed, and their psychological adjustments. Stage I is the apprentice stage, which is typified by people entering organizations and learning their duties. Stage II, called the independent contributor stage, is filled by people who are experts in a certain area and who are no longer closely supervised. Stage III, or the mentoring stage, is described as a time of helping people lower in organizations develop and learn. Finally, in Stage IV—the sponsor stage—people determine policy and direction for organizations.

In the corporate world, a mentor is a transitional figure who teaches an apprentice about the ins and outs of the company, helps with the application of raw skills, works to protect the apprentice, and helps him or her gain recognition when merited. Networking is a viable alternative or supplement to a mentor relationship. Networks can provide informational, appraisal, emotional, and instrumental social support.

Notes

1. S. Terkel (1974), *Working,* New York: Pantheon, 315–16.
2. D. T. Hall (1976), *Careers in organizations,* Pacific Palisades, CA: Goodyear, 4.
3. E. H. Schein (May-June 1975), How career anchors hold executives to their career paths, *Personnel.*
4. G. Dalton, P. Thompson, and R. Price (Summer 1977), The four stages of professional careers, *Organizational Dynamics.*
5. Terkel, 1974, 112.
6. Erik Erikson was one of the first to examine the way individuals grow in their capacity to deal with the world and with the crises they encounter as they live. According to Erikson, during adulthood each person faces the issue of "generativity versus stagnation." This is the time in life when a person either begins guiding the next generation or indulging themselves "as if they were their one and only child." Aside from this issue, Erikson's stages deal with trust, autonomy, initiative, identity, and intimacy. E. H. Erikson (1959), *Identity and the life cycle,* New York: International Universities Press, 97.

7. D. C. Miller and W. H. Form (1951), *Industrial sociology*, New York: Harper.

8. D. E. Super (1957), *The psychology of careers*, New York: Harper & Row.

9. C. Buehler (1933), *Der menschliche lebenshauf als psychologisches problem*, Leipzig: Hirzel.

10. Schein, 11–24.

11. Schein, 12.

12. E. H. Schein (1978), *Career dynamics: Matching individual and organizational needs*, Reading, MA: Addison-Wesley, 133.

13. G. Dalton and P. Thompson (1986), *Novations*, Glenview, IL: Scott, Foresman.

14. Dalton and Thompson, 1986, 22.

15. P. Thompson and G. Dalton (November-December, 1976), Are R&D organizations obsolete?, *Harvard Business Review*, 108.

16. *The Wall Street Journal* (18 December 1985), 31.

17. Dalton, Thompson, and Price, 28.

18. Dalton and Thompson, 1986, 51.

19. Dalton, Thompson, and Price, 30.

20. Dalton, Thompson, and Price, 31.

21. Dalton and Thompson, 1986, 128.

22. Dalton and Thompson, 1986, 161.

23. S. Hammond (1987), *A view of careers*, Brigham Young University working paper, 17–18.

24. Dalton and Thompson, 1986, 94.

25. Dalton and Thompson, 1986, 95.

26. K. Kram (1985), *Mentoring at work: Developmental relationships in organization life*, Glenview, IL: Scott, Foresman, 105–32.

27. Kram, 1985, 107.

28. R. Keele (1986), Mentoring or networking? Strong and weak ties in career development, in *Not as far as you think: The realities of working women*, L. L. Moore, ed., Lexington, MA: Lexington Books, 53–68.

29. J. S. House (1981), in *Work stress and social support*, Menlo Park, CA: Addison-Wesley, names four types of necessary social support that may be provided through strong mentoring ties and/or weak networking ties. These are emotional, appraisal, informational, and instrumental.

Key Terms

career
life-span models
preparatory work period
initial work period
trial work period
stable work period
retirement period
stable career pattern
unstable career pattern
multiple trial pattern

growth stage
exploratory stage
establishment stage
maintenance stage
decline stage
career anchors
technical/functional competence
  anchor
managerial competence anchor
security anchor

creativity/entrepreneurship anchor
autonomy and independence
  anchor
apprentice stage
independent contributor stage

mentoring stage
sponsor stage
mentor
networking

Issues for Review and Discussion

1. Define *career*.
2. What are some of the implications of measuring career success from an individual's perspective rather than from an organization's perspective?
3. What is career effectiveness? How may this be related to organization effectiveness?
4. Define *career stage*.
5. What are the periods identified in the life-span models of careers? How do these compare with Dalton and Thompson's career stages?
6. What are the pyramid and obsolescence models of organizations? How are they deficient in explaining careers of professionals?
7. How are career anchors useful in describing career development?
8. Based on your reading of Dalton and Thompson's career stages model, what organizational programs or policies might improve the career development of individuals at various stages in their careers?
9. How can bosses aid subordinates' career development?
10. What are the pros and cons of downward transfer?
11. How much control can an individual have over his or her own career?
12. Describe a mentor-protégé relationship. What does each participant contribute and receive?
13. How can networking be used to further careers? What kinds of support can networks provide?

Suggested Readings

Dalton, G. and Thompson, P. (1986). *Novations: Strategies for career management*. Glenview, IL: Scott, Foresman.

Derr, C. B. (1986). *Managing the new careerists*. San Francisco: Jossey Bass.

Hall, D. T. (1976). *Careers in organizations*. Pacific Palisades, CA: Goodyear.

Kanter, R. M. (1977). *Men and women of the corporation*. New York: Basic Books.

Kram, K. (1985). *Mentoring at work: Developmental relationships in organization life*. Glenview, IL: Scott, Foresman.

Levinson, D. (1978). *The seasons of a man's life*. New York: Alfred A. Knopf.

Miller, D. C. and Form, W. H. (1951). *Industrial sociology*. New York: Harper.

Schein, E. H. (1978). *Career dynamics: Matching individual and organization needs*. Reading, MA: Addison-Wesley.

Super, D. E. (1957). *The psychology of careers*. New York: Harper & Row.

Glossary

Absolute standards approach Subjective appraisal method by which managers compare the performance of each employee to a certain standard instead of to the performance of other employees. (Ch. 17)

Acceptance (Stage 6) Sixth stage of group development wherein members discuss their differences rather than fight over them. They aggressively attack issues and deemphasize personal interests. (Ch. 13)

Acceptance view of authority View in which authority flows upward from subordinates to superiors based on the nature of the relationship between people and their perception of this relationship. (Ch. 11)

Accommodating conflict style Conflict style in which a person tries to satisfy the interests of another party at his or her own expense. (Ch. 15)

Accommodation philosophies Philosophies in which social issues are addressed because they exist, even if demands to do so are not likely. (Ch. 4)

Accounting management System of management that plans, organizes, directs, and controls the successful execution of financial transactions between an organization and other parties. (Ch. 3)

Achievement-oriented leadership Effective leaders set challenging goals, seek improvement in performance, emphasize excellence, and demonstrate confidence in subordinates' ability to attain high standards. (Ch. 16)

Acquired needs Needs learned through experience. (Ch. 14)

Action statements Statements that reflect the means by which an organization moves forward to attain its goals. (Ch. 6)

Administrative plans Managers use administrative plans to allocate organizational resources and to coordinate their organization's internal subdivisions. These plans are associated with the organizational responsibility of middle management. (Ch. 6)

Administrative problem Problem of developing, refining, and maintaining the management and organizational systems that let organization members carry out a strategic plan. (Ch. 9)

Affective component Part of an attitude, which includes how people feel about a person, task, or the like and which aris-

es from their reactions to the cognitive component of the attitude. (Ch. 13)

Aggregate planning Planning for entire operating system done before the actual plan for each product, department, and machine is determined. (Ch. 21)

Allies Individuals and organizations with which an organization develops interdependent relationships and shares things important to all parties. (Ch. 2)

Analyzer organization True blend of the defender and prospector styles; attempts to balance the risk and aggression of a prospector with the conservative, protective nature of a defender. (Ch. 9)

Apprentice stage Stage in Dalton and Thompson's career model in which individuals enter organizations and perform detailed and routine tasks under close supervision. (Ch. 25)

Arbitrator Third party outside of an organization to whom a grievance can be submitted if an employee does not feel an issue has been resolved. (Ch. 17)

Artificial intelligence Computers' tasks requiring the human characteristics of intelligence, imagination, and intuition. (Ch. 21)

Assessment of ends goals Review of actual outcomes related to planned outcomes. (Ch. 19)

Assessment of means goals Review of actual processes and procedures used toward planned outcomes. (Ch. 19)

Attention directing Information reporting and interpretation in such a way that managers are shown where to concentrate on operating problems, imperfections, inefficiencies, and opportunities. (Ch. 3)

Attitude Beliefs, feelings, and intentions about behavior that people have toward a person, event, task, or organization. (Ch. 13)

Authoritarian person Person who feels that power and status should be clearly defined and that there should be an organizational hierarchy of authority. (Ch. 13)

Authority Legitimate right of a person to exercise influence. (Ch. 11)

Authority gaps Gaps that arise when authority has not been assigned for specific activities. (Ch. 11)

Authority overlaps Situations that arise if two or more individuals or organizational units have the authority to perform the same activity. (Ch. 11)

Authority relationships Relationships between people and between people and their work: line, staff, and functional authority. (Ch. 11)

Automation of equipment Extent to which the transformation process is performed by machines instead of by human beings. (Ch. 3)

Autonomy and independence anchor Need to be able to work without direction or restraints, often manifested in a departure from traditional jobs. (Ch. 25)

Avoidance learning Method of making response more likely. Through avoidance learning, people learn to behave in a certain way to avoid encountering an undesired or unpleasant consequence. (Ch. 14)

Avoiding conflict style Conflict style in which a person chooses to be both uncooperative and unassertive in conflict situations. (Ch. 15)

Batch (or disconnected-line) process Operating process that falls midway between a job shop and a repetitive line. Products or services can be produced in a line manner but are usually processed in large batches because of a particular feature of the product or process. (Ch. 21)

Behavioral approach Job design approach that rejects the idea of treating people as automated machines that continuously perform simple and repetitive activities. (Ch. 10)

Behavioral model Organizational design model that focuses less on the rational and mechanical aspects of organizational design and more on the social and psychological sides of an organization. (Ch. 12)

Behavioral school Behavioral management theorists viewed organizations from social and psychological perspectives. (Ch. 5)

Behavioral science movement Movement that stressed the need to conduct systematic and controlled studies of workers and their attitudes and behaviors. (Ch. 5)

Behavioral tendency component The part of an attitude that identifies how people intend to behave toward a person, task, or the like. (Ch. 13)

Bell curve distribution Statistic that shows that, in the general population, the majority of people have average levels of both physical abilities (strength, flexibility, and coordination) and intellectual abilities (thinking, memory, and reasoning). (Ch. 13)

Binding arbitration Process in which both parties are obligated to conform to the findings of an arbitrator. (Ch. 17)

Boundary roles Positions that link an organization to its external environment. (Ch. 2)

Boundary spanners Individuals who fill boundary roles. (Ch. 2)

Boundary-spanning process One means through which organizations conduct transactions with their external environment. (Ch. 2)

Bounded rationality Situation wherein managers try to behave rationally within the limits of their information-processing capabilities and within the context of their attitudes and emotions. (Ch. 7)

Brainstorming A qualitative tool; a technique designed to stimulate people to develop alternatives during the planning and decision-making process. Brainstorming encourages the sharing of ideas in a setting free of the interruptions and risks of immediate evaluation and discussion. (Ch. 8)

Break-even analysis Identification of the point at which sales revenues equal the total cost of producing a product or service. (Ch. 8)

Budgets Single-use plans, expressed in numerical terms, sometimes called *numerized programs*, that deal with the allocation and use of organizational activities for a specified accounting period. (Ch. 6)

Buffering Using techniques that enable an organization to maintain operations when there are shortages of raw resources and when there are peaks and valleys in demand for the organization's products. (Ch. 2)

Bureaucratic model Organizational design that bases its legitimacy on inherent rationality and relies on a set of rules that specifies employee rights and duties and on standard operating procedures to control work-related activities. (Ch. 12)

Business portfolio approach Approach to strategic planning that occurs when organizations that engage in many different businesses want a comprehensive approach to strategic planning. (Ch. 9)

Business unit Segment of an organization with a distinct mission, external market, and strategy for dealing with that market. (Ch. 9)

Business unit strategy Functioning of an individual business within a corporation; specifies how an organization will interact with its task environment. (Ch. 9)

Cafeteria plans Benefit plans that allow individual employees the flexibility of picking and choosing plans that meet their personal needs. Employees choose benefits much as they would choose a meal in a cafeteria line. (Ch. 17)

Capacity Maximum amount of product or service that can be delivered in a stated time frame. (Ch. 21)

Career Individually perceived sequence of attitudes and behaviors associated with work-related experiences and activities over the span of a person's life (Hall). (Ch. 25)

Career anchor Schein's description of the needs that individuals fill through their careers. (Ch. 25)

Cash cows SBUs within a portfolio matrix with a large share of a low-growth market. (Ch. 9)

Causal modeling Quantitative model that attempts to forecast future events in statistical terms. Causal models document the causes of past events. (Ch. 8)

Cautious shifts Tendency of groups to make decisions that are more cautious than an average individual's decision. (Ch. 7)

Centralization Extent to which formal authority is concentrated within the hierarchy of an organization determines its degree of centralization. (Ch. 11)

Certainty Situation wherein a decision maker is aware of all available alternatives and the factors (outcomes) associated with each. (Ch. 7)

Chain Simplest of communication networks. Although it can be used for a horizontal communication network, it is more often used vertically. (Ch. 15)

Channel appropriateness Determination whether the communication channel(s) under consideration are appropriate to the message. (Ch. 15)

Channel capacity Amount of information that a communication channel can transmit without significant distortion. (Ch. 15)

Channel duplication The use of communication subchannels to repeat or elaborate on a message. (Ch. 15)

Channel feedback Feedback, or bilateral (two-way) communication, within channels of communication. (Ch. 15)

Channel modifiability Degree to which a transmission can be changed within a communication channel while in progress. (Ch. 15)

Channel speed Speed at which a message can be sent through a communication channel. (Ch. 15)

Charisma Leadership trait involving a personal magnetic charm or appeal that arouses loyalty and enthusiasm. (Ch. 16)

Choice making Narrow set of activities associated with choosing one option

from a set of already identified alternatives. (Ch. 7)

Circle communication Network that allows each member to communicate directly with two other members. (Ch. 15)

Classical approach Task approach wherein labor is divided into jobs made up of a small number of simple, repetitive, standardized tasks. (Ch. 10)

Classical authority theory Authority is the institutional right of organizations to act, to decide, and to exercise influence. (Ch. 11)

Classical organization theory Concentrates on the management of an entire organization. Deals with the structure of an organization and with designing processes that improve its operations. (Ch. 5)

Classical school Includes the scientific-management movement and classical organization theory. It emphasized the economic rationality of decisions made by organizations and their members and the role of economic incentives as primary motivators. (Ch. 5)

Closed recruiting systems Internal recruiting systems that let managers select the types of people (and, sometimes, even the specific individuals) who will be considered for a vacancy. (Ch. 17)

Closed system Organization that operates as though it were in a world by itself. It blocks out ideas, information, and external environmental forces. (Ch. 2)

Cluster network Communication pattern that represents a careful and systematic selection of individuals to whom information will be transferred. (Ch. 15)

Coaching Training and development tool that occurs as a supervisor guides subordinates through the day-to-day activities of a job. (Ch. 17)

Coalescing Merging or joining into a venture with a member of the task environment. (Ch. 2)

Coercive power Power a person has because people believe that he or she can punish them by inflicting pain or by withholding or taking away something that they value. (Chs. 11, 15)

Cognition Psychological perspective of motivation that says that people behave rationally based on what they think the future will bring. (Ch. 14)

Cognitive component Part of an attitude that includes what people think they know about a person, task, or the like and is generally descriptive. (Ch. 14)

Cohesion (Stage 3) Third stage of group development wherein group members work through personal differences, develop a set of norms, and agree on their roles. (Ch. 13)

Collaborating conflict Conflict style that involves attempts by the participants to satisfy both (or all) of their interests. (Ch. 15)

Communicating Process of transmitting information. (Ch. 3)

Communication Process of transferring information from one person or group (sender) to another (receiver). Five components are: ideation, message encoding, channels/networks, message decoding, and received message. (Ch. 15)

Communication channels Media through which messages are sent. Any medium capable of transmitting a message is a communication channel, including mail systems, phone lines, and computers. (Ch. 15)

Communication failure Communication-related problem in which no meaningful information is exchanged. (Ch. 15)

Communication network Series of interconnected linkages. Together these linkages connect individuals or groups for communication purposes. (Ch. 15)

Comparative appraisal method Subjective appraisal method in which supervisors compare the perceived performance of each employee to the perceived performance of co-workers. (Ch. 17)

Compensation administration Administers direct compensation, such as wages and salaries. (Ch. 3)

Competing conflict Conflict style marked by high levels of assertiveness but little cooperation. (Ch. 15)

Competing values perspective Approach to assessing organizational effectiveness that attempts to integrate ideas from the four systematic approaches when none of them is an ideal solution. (Ch. 18)

Competitive advantage An organization's unique position compared to other organizations in its task environment. (Chs. 9, 21)

Competitors Because the supply of resources in the external environment is limited, organizations must compete for their share of the supply. Competitors are a significant component of the task environment. (Ch. 2)

Complexity Number of specialized job types or subsystems within an organization, the number of levels in the organizational hierarchy, and the number of geographical locations from which the organization operates. (Ch. 12)

Compromise decision-making approach Approach wherein individuals or groups who disagree about preferred outcomes bargain. (Ch. 7)

Compromising conflict style Conflict style that produces a mutually acceptable but less than optimal solution for both parties. (Ch. 15)

Compulsory staff consultation Action that forces line personnel and staff personnel to discuss issues before taking action. (Ch. 11)

Computational decision-making approach A rational, mechanical process calling for agreement on the desired outcomes and the existence of a well-developed body of knowledge that instructs an organization on how to proceed. (Ch. 7)

Computer-aided design (CAD) systems Systems designed through computers to help engineers design and draft products. (Ch. 3)

Computer-aided manufacturing (CAM) systems Systems in which computers monitor and steer products through various stages of the production process. (Ch. 3)

Computer-integrated operations Operations based on the ability to control manufacturing and service processes by computer. (Ch. 21)

Conceptual skills Skills that allow people to see, to diagnose, and to understand concepts at an abstract level (Ch. 1)

Concern for people Leadership classification that involves promoting friendships, helping subordinates with work, and paying attention to issues of importance to employees. (Ch. 16)

Concern for production Leadership classification (Blake and Mouton) that involves an emphasis on output, cost effectiveness, and (in for-profit organizations) a concern for profits. (Ch. 16)

Concurrent control Control device used by managers to make certain that deviation from a planned course of action does not occur while work is in progress. Two common forms of concurrent control are steering controls and screening controls. (Ch. 19)

Concurring authority Authority whereby a designated staff member can formally approve or disapprove an action to be taken. (Ch. 11)

Configuration Shape of an organization's structure, including the number of hierarchical levels; spans of control; and ratios of managers to technical employees, support to operating personnel, and the like. (Ch. 12)

Conflict Situation that exists when two or more people have incompatible goals and one or both believe that the behavior of the other will prevent his or her own goal attainment. (Chs. 13, 15)

Consideration Relationship-oriented behavior of a leader. (Ch. 16)

Contemporary school of management School that draws from the best of earlier theories. Contemporary management theories propose that there is no one best way to practice management. (Ch. 5)

Content theories (need theories) of motivation Theories based on the premise that all people have needs. Needs are both innate and acquired. (Ch. 14)

Contingency approach Managers organize work and design jobs to fit the characteristics of workers who will perform the jobs, the organization's technology, and other design characteristics of the organization. (Ch. 10)

Contingency management Techniques appropriate for a manager to use are contingent on the situation. (Ch. 5)

Contingency plans Plans created to deal with events that might come to pass if certain assumptions turn out to be wrong. (Ch. 6)

Contingency theory of leadership Leadership theory (Fiedler) that classified leaders according to an underlying trait, described situations that leaders face, and identified optimal matches between leaders and situations. (Ch. 16)

Continuous process Operating system that is a higher-flow version of a repetitive line. (Ch. 21)

Continuous schedules of reinforcement Reinforcing or punishing every time a behavior is shown. It is the most effective for shaping behavior. (Ch. 14)

Contracting Agreement between an organization and a member of its task environment representing a cooperative strategy. (Ch. 2)

Controlling Monitoring and evaluating organizational effectiveness and initiating the actions needed to maintain or improve effectiveness. (Chs. 1, 19)

Control prescriptions Set of recommendations to correct problems, to maintain strengths, and to provide feedback to improve organizational effectiveness. (Ch. 19)

Conventional career pattern Individuals move from an initial job to a trial job to stable employment. (Ch. 25)

Co-opting Process of absorbing part of the task environment into an organization. (Ch. 2)

Coordinating Linking two or more organizational units so that they work harmoniously together. (Ch. 10)

Corporate strategy Strategy that defines the domain of an organization and lets organization members know which priorities have been set. (Ch. 9)

Cost leadership Generic strategy wherein managers find a market niche by selling their organization's products or services more cheaply than its competitor does. (Ch. 9)

Countertrade Trade that involves simultaneous importing and exporting. (Ch. 23)

Craft approach Task approach wherein a single skilled worker designs and builds products one at a time from beginning to end. (Ch. 10)

Creative imitation "Drucker" strategy based on improving someone else's innovation. (Ch. 24)

Creative/self-actualizing model Decision-making model that assumes that individuals pursue total development of their inner selves rather than look for an external goal, such as profit seeking. (Ch. 7)

Creativity/entrepreneurship anchor Need to create, to develop, or to invent something in one's career. (Ch. 25)

Critical incidents Job analysis technique that is a variation of the direct observation method, which examines only those job behaviors leading to successful or unsuccessful performance. (Ch. 17)

Cultural values Values within a group influenced by group members striving for approval and status in the eyes of other group members. (Ch. 7)

Culture Complex whole that includes knowledge, belief, art, morals, law, customs, and any other capabilities and habits acquired by people as members of society. (Ch. 23)

Customer/client departmentalization Job design strategy that organizes activities around the type of customer or customer needs served by an organization. (Ch. 10)

Customers/markets The part of the environment that wants (or can be made to want) a particular product or service. An organization's customers may be individuals or other organizations. (Ch. 2)

Custom solutions Solutions developed specifically for a current situation. (Ch. 7)

Cybernetic control Control system based on self-regulating procedures that automatically detect and correct deviations from planned activities and effectiveness levels. (Ch. 19)

Data Representations of facts (represented by symbols, such as numerals or letters of the alphabet) pertaining to people, things, ideas, and events. (Ch. 21)

Database An organization's set of computer data files that are structured and stored so they can be easily processed and used by those who need information about the organization. (Ch. 21)

Decentralization Extent to which, by design, authority is spread throughout an organization and, thus, characterizes the organization's structure. (Ch. 11)

Decentralization of authority Degree to which decision-making authority is spread throughout an organization as opposed to being concentrated (centralized) at the top. (Ch. 12)

Decisional, or strategy-making, roles Managerial roles in which a manager functions as entrepreneur, disturbance handler, resource allocator, or negotiator. (Ch. 1)

Decision making Process of identifying a set of feasible alternatives and, from these, choosing a course of action. (Chs. 3, 7)

Decisions Judgments that directly affect a course of action. (Ch. 7)

Decision-support system (DSS) Data, information, and reports of the TPS and information-reporting system. (Ch. 21)

Decision tree Tool that helps a manager decide the extent to which subordinates should be involved in making decisions for particular situations. (Ch. 8)

Decline stage Period in Super's life-span model in which an individual moves out of an organization. (Ch. 25)

Decoding Fourth step of the communication process; a receiver interprets a message to derive meaning from it. (Ch. 15)

Defender organizations Organizations in which managers develop strategies that they hope will create and maintain a stable niche in the market for their organization's products or services. (Ch. 9)

Defense philosophies Philosophies that address social issues in order to avoid being compelled to by outside forces. (Ch. 4)

Delphi technique Qualitative tool that is a group process designed to bring information and the judgments of people together to facilitate planning and decision making. (Ch. 8)

Delegation Process managers use to transfer formal authority from one position to another within an organization and to put the authority system they have designed into place. (Ch. 11)

Delusion (Stage 4) Fourth stage of group development wherein members believe that significant problems no longer exist. (Ch. 13)

Departmentalization Process of grouping jobs into organizational units and those units into larger units. (Ch. 10)

Design and development Managers must make sure that products are designed to meet the specifications determined to satisfy market demand. (Ch. 3)

Design stage Stage of decision making process in which the decision maker and others outline alternative sets of action that can be taken to address a problem or opportunity, given the conditions identified during the intelligence stage. (Ch. 21)

Determining a course of action There are three stages to the determination of a course of action: (1) determining alternatives, (2) evaluating alternatives, (3) selecting a course of action. (Ch. 6)

Development Preparation that extends beyond a job, such as the instruction an employee will need if the design of the current job changes or if the employee changes jobs through transfer or promotion. (Ch. 17)

Diagonal communication Communication that occurs as information flows across both vertical and horizontal components. (Ch. 15)

Differential wage rate system Part of economic model of motivation wherein if a worker produced nothing during the day, no wage would be earned; the more the worker produced, the more the worker would earn. (Ch. 14)

Differentiation strategy Generic strategy to help an organization establish itself as different from the competition. (Ch. 9)

Direct exporting Direct selling of goods overseas without intermediaries. (Ch. 23)

Directing The process through which employees are led and motivated to make effective and efficient contributions to the realization of organizational goals. (Chs. 1, 13)

Directive autocrat leader Leader who retains power, making unilateral decisions and directing the activities of subordinates with close supervision. (Ch. 16)

Directive behavior Degree to which a leader lets employees execute decisions once they have been made. (Ch. 16)

Directive democrat leader Leader who shares power through participative decision making but retains the power to direct employees in the execution of their roles. (Ch. 16)

Directive leadership Effective leaders set goals and performance expectations, let subordinates know what is expected, provide guidance, establish rules and procedures to guide work, and schedule and coordinate the activities of employees. (Ch. 16)

Direct observation Job analysis technique that involves watching workers during a continuous observation period to identify every relevant job activity. (Ch. 17)

Discretionary responsibilities Voluntary acts done even if failing to do so would not be judged unethical. (Ch. 4)

Disillusion (Stage 5) Fifth stage of group development wherein members are shocked into awareness of the problems that still confront the group. (Ch. 13)

Distribution systems Systems by which an organization's inventory is transported to its customers. (Ch. 21)

Distributive justice George Homans held that distributive justice is a question of fairness; does a person believe that fair exchange has occurred between himself or herself and the organization? (Ch. 14)

Disturbance handler Manager who reacts to and attempts to resolve day-to-day crises. (Ch. 1)

Divestiture strategy Within portfolio matrix, managers get rid of an SBU that is financially unsuccessful and unlikely to respond to the retrenchment/turnaround strategy. (Ch. 9)

Divisional-level plans Plans that focus on the competitive position of a division in its market and on the ways in which the division can complement other divisions. (Ch. 6)

Divisional superstructure Organizational superstructure designed according to nonfunctional factors, such as territories, products, customer base, process, or projects. (Ch. 12)

Dogmatism Theory in which a person has a rigid belief system and sees the world from a narrow perspective. (Ch. 13)

Dogs SBUs within portfolio matrix with a small portion of a low-growth market. (Ch. 9)

Domain commitments Commitments by managers in strategic planning that create groups with vested interests, allocate resources, and exert other influences on decisions about the future. (Ch. 9)

Domain/directional planning Development of a course of action that moves an organization toward one identified domain and, therefore, away from other domains. (Ch. 6)

Drive theory Psychological perspective on motivation that states that people learn how to behave through personal experiences, and this learning drives their subsequent behavior. (Ch. 14)

Dual authority system System that allows all units to benefit from dual authorities, and some employees (usually managers in the upper hierarchical levels) to be accountable to two bosses at the same time. (Ch. 12)

Economic domain Resources (land, labor, and capital) that an organization needs to fulfill its goals. (Ch. 2)

Economic exposure Long-term effects on cash flows resulting from international exchange rates. (Ch. 23)

Economic model Model of motivation assumes that people are rational and economically motivated. (Ch. 14)

Economic order quantity Mathematical model for identifying the amount of inventory to order when managers know their inventory use, product cost, cost of procuring inventory, and annual inventory carrying costs. (Ch. 8)

Economic responsibilities Obligations to produce goods and services to be sold at a profit. (Ch. 4)

Employee-centered behaviors Leader behaviors that include consideration and support for subordinates. (Ch. 16)

Encoding Second step of the communication process; converting an intended message into a transmittable form. (Ch. 15)

Ends decisions Decisions that are oriented specifically toward achieving a goal. (Ch. 7)

Ends goals Specified goals in goal attainment approach to assessing organizations' effectiveness. (Ch. 18)

Entrepreneur Decisional role in which managers identify opportunities for and threats to an organization and initiate changes to capitalize on them. (Ch. 1)

Entrepreneurial judo Strategy that capitalizes on the weaknesses of an organization that holds a leadership position. (Ch. 24)

Entrepreneurship Involves the development of a product or service idea and the creation of an organization to further its growth. (Ch. 24)

Environmental change Change that reflects the degree to which an organization's task environment is stable or shifting. (Ch. 2)

Environmental segmentation Similarities and differences among components of the task environment and the demands that they place on an organization. (Ch. 2)

Environmental uncertainty Managers and their organizations interact with the external environment; under most circumstances, managers can neither control nor predict everything that will happen in this interaction. (Ch. 2)

Equity theory As proposed by J. Stacy Adams, suggests that people compare their own distributive justice ratio to the ratio they perceive for other people (an individual, a group, one's self in another situation, or one's idealized self). (Ch. 14)

ERG theory Hierarchy of needs developed by Clayton Alderfer (existence, relatedness, and growth). (Ch. 14)

Establishment stage Period in Super's life-span model in which an appropriate field is found and effort is put forth to make a permanent place in it. (Ch. 25)

Ethical responsibilities Responsibilities to meet society's expectations for conscientious and proper behavior, even when these expectations are not reflected in the letter of laws and regulations. (Ch. 4)

Ethics Set of standards and code of conduct that define what is right, wrong, and just in human actions. (Ch. 4)

Ethnocentric staffing International staffing wherein the staffing of subsidiaries is based on putting home-country personnel in place. (Ch. 23)

Existing solutions Alternatives that have been used (or at least considered) by other decision makers in similar situations. (Ch. 7)

Expectancy perceptions Part of expectancy theory, which holds that it is likely that a given alternative will lead to a particular performance level. (Ch. 14)

Expectancy theory Theory that holds that individuals make their decisions by thinking through the implications of each alternative and choosing the one that is most attractive. (Ch. 14)

Expected role Image of behavior within a group that exists in the minds of others in the organization. (Ch. 13)

Expert power Power that exists when an individual is perceived as having greater knowledge or ability than those around him or her. (Chs. 11, 15)

Expert systems Computer programs that store representations of human knowledge about a specific subject and process it in various ways to draw conclusions. (Ch. 21)

Exploratory stage Period in Super's life-span model in which the self-concept is emerging and being tested against reality. (Ch. 25)

Exporting Selling goods to buyers in another country. (Ch. 23)

External environment Conditions, circumstances, and influences that surround and affect the functioning of an organization. (Chs. 2, 17)

External recruiting Human resource managers' attempting to find a qualified pool of candidates from outside of an organization. (Ch. 17)

External staffing Identifying and bringing new employees into an organization. (Ch. 3)

Extinction Part of operant learning model; occurs if a consequence makes a response less likely. (Ch. 14)

Extrinsic motivators Motivators within organizational behavior modification program that are based on rewards provided by someone other than the person being motivated. (Ch. 14)

Financial and budgetary control Managers who oversee financial, operating, and nonmonetary budgets control activities at a number of different levels within an organization. (Ch. 19)

Financial management Staff function that applies the management process to an organization's financial assets. (Ch. 3)

Financing Acquiring and distributing the financial resources that an organization needs to obtain goods and services. (Ch. 3)

First-level managers Lowest level of managers, involved primarily with managing an organization's technical core. (Ch. 1)

Fixed-ratio reinforcement/punishment schedule Reinforces or punishes every "nth" behavior. (Ch. 14)

Focus Generic strategy in which organizations focus on a specific segment of a total market and concentrate their resources on competing within that segment. (Ch. 9)

Force Part of expectancy theory that refers to the overall attractiveness of an alternative, which drives a person to choose that alternative. (Ch. 14)

Forced distribution Comparative appraisal method by which supervisors create categories (such as average, above average, and superior) and place a certain number of employees into each category. (Ch. 17)

Formal/designated leader Individual appointed by an organization to serve in a formal capacity as an agent of the organization. (Ch. 16)

Formal groups Groups consciously created within organizations to serve organizational objectives. (Ch. 13)

Formalization Extent to which the norms of an organization are set forth in written records, documents, and procedure manuals. (Ch. 12)

Formal organization Organization that exists as a result of the official structures and systems designed by managers through the organizing activity. Usually contains a structured communication and command system that helps people pool their time, energy, and talents to reach common objectives. (Ch. 10)

Formal rewards Rewards, such as increases in pay or receipt of a promotion, that are stipulated by an organization to help its managers develop power. (Ch. 15)

Formulation Planning within the strategic management process that leads to the development of organizational goals and specific action statements. (Ch. 9)

Frame test Evaluates whether the strategy focuses managerial efforts and organizational resources on the issues or problems that have been identified as crucial. (Ch. 9)

Franchise Licensing of an entire business system as well as industrial property by an independent person. (Ch. 23)

Free-rein leader (laissez-faire leader) Leader who avoids power and responsibility and exists primarily as a contact person or consultant. (Ch. 16)

Frequency-of-use plans Repetitiveness plans. (Ch. 6)

Functional authority Right to direct or control specific activities that are under the span of control of other managers. (Ch. 11)

Functional departments Departments in which activities are grouped according to the nature of the work performed. (Ch. 10)

Functional group Either formal or informal group that focuses on a general and continuing area of responsibility. (Ch. 13)

Functional managers Managers classified according to their area of specialized activity (also known as organizational function served). (Ch. 1)

Functional strategy Comprehensive plan for each major functional area (such as marketing, finance, and production) within a business unit. Functional strategy should support and conform to the strategy of the business unit. (Ch. 9)

Functional superstructure Superstructure in which upper-level managers are organized around the basic organizational functions similar to the departmentalization-by-function approach adopted at lower levels. (Ch. 12)

Gantt chart Chart that summarizes work activities and identifies those that should be performed simultaneously or sequentially. (Ch. 5)

Gap analysis Step in strategic planning process that identifies the expected gaps between where managers want their organization to go and where it will go if they maintain the current strategy. (Ch. 9)

General environment Overall environment within which an organization operates, including its social and cultural context, the economic system surrounding the organization, the legal and political atmosphere, the technology from which knowledge and tools for reaching goals are derived, and the international climate. (Ch. 2)

Generic strategies Three strategies—cost leadership, differentiation, and focus—that are pursued by managers. (Ch. 9)

Global enterprises Multinational corporations that respond to world markets through a unified strategy. (Ch. 23)

Goal acceptance Degree to which one accepts a goal as one's own ("I agree that this report must be finished by 5 P.M."). (Ch. 14)

Goal attainment approach Method by which managers evaluate organizational effectiveness by assessing the degree to which one or more specified goals are met. (Ch. 18)

Goal commitment Level of attachment to or determination to reach a goal. (Ch. 14)

Goal consistency test Test that measures whether proposed strategy has goals, objectives, and policies that are consistent with one another. (Ch. 9)

Goal formulation Step in strategic planning process that requires managers to verify and affirm their organization's reasons for existence, to define its mission, and to establish strategic objectives. (Ch. 9)

Goal hierarchy Illustration of the complexities posed by many interrelated systems of goals and major plans. (Ch. 6)

Goal planning Setting specific goals and creating action statements. (Ch. 6)

Goals End states (targets) that managers hope to attain. They emerge from forces in both internal and external environments of an organization. (Ch. 6)

Goal theory Theory that specifies that particular kinds of goals motivate organization members most effectively. (Ch. 14)

Gossip network Communication pattern often used when one person believes that he or she has some "very interesting" information to pass on. This individual seeks out a number of individuals and passes on the information to each. (Ch. 15)

Great person approach Leadership approach that states that some people are born with the necessary attributes to be great leaders. (Ch. 16)

Grievance Complaint filed if a union member feels that part of a contract has been violated. (Ch. 17)

Group Two or more people who interact, who perceive themselves to be a group, and who have a common purpose or work toward the accomplishment of a common goal. (Ch. 13)

Group development stages Stages of development of groups within organizations: orientation (Stage 1), conflict (Stage 2), cohesion (Stage 3), delusion (Stage 4), disillusion (Stage 5), acceptance (Stage 6). (Ch. 13)

Group norms Stipulations of the limits of expected and acceptable behavior for group members. (Ch. 13)

Group polarization effect Process whereby group members hope to gain approval from the group by being on the leading edge of the group's values. (Ch. 7)

Group role Set of expectations for a group member's behavior. (Ch. 13)

Groupthink A group drive to reach consensus at almost any cost. (Chs. 7, 13)

Growth stage Period in Super's life-span model in which the self-concept begins to form through identification with key figures in family and school. (Ch. 25)

Growth strategy Strategy within portfolio matrix that is required for stars and for question marks that an organization hopes to transform into stars. (Ch. 9)

Halo effect Perception distortion that occurs when a specific stimulus influences a person's overall impression. (Ch. 13)

Hawthorne studies Studies that provided a transition from classical to behavioral management theories, which emphasized the human side of organizations and the importance of personal and social factors as motivators. (Ch. 5)

Hedonism Principle that says that people are motivated to do things that are pleasurable and to avoid things that are unpleasant. (Ch. 14)

Heterogeneous groups Groups whose members are dissimilar in such characteristics as education, work experience, aptitudes, and attitudes. (Ch. 7)

Heterogeneous task environment Highly segmented or differentiated task environment. (Ch. 2)

Hierarchical plans Plans drawn from hierarchical perspectives: institutional, managerial, and the technical core. (Ch. 6)

Hierarchy Set of managerial levels of authority and responsibility within an organization. (Ch. 1)

Homogeneous groups Groups whose members are similar in such characteristics as education, work experience, aptitudes, and attitudes. (Ch. 7)

Homogeneous task environment Task environment characterized by very little segmentation. (Ch. 2)

Horizontal communication Flow of information between individuals or groups who occupy positions at the same hierarchical level. (Ch. 15)

Horizontal coordination Coordination within a single hierarchical level. (Ch. 10)

Horizontal specialization Job design that creates many low-skill-level, repetitive jobs. (Ch. 10)

Host-country staffing/geocentric staffing International staffing process wherein host countries, particularly developing countries, insist that managers be locals. (Ch. 23)

Human interpersonal skills An individual's ability to work with and understand others, to lead, to motivate, to manage conflict, and to build group effort. (Ch. 1)

Human relations model Model of assessing organizational effectiveness characterizing an organization that values the well-being of its members over the development and promotion of the organization itself. (Ch. 18)

Human relations movement Movement focused on employees in the belief that satisfied workers are productive workers. (Ch. 5)

Human resource control Control of activities involving individuals, groups, and the nature of people-to-people and people-to-work interactions. (Ch. 19)

Human resource management Managerial function that tries to match an organization's needs and the skills and abilities of its employees. (Ch. 3)

Hybrid approach departmentalization Simultaneous use of two or more departmentalization strategies. (Ch. 10)

Hybrid control system Control system used by most managers to integrate precontrol, concurrent, and postaction control systems. (Ch. 19)

Hybrid planning Planning that moves from domain planning to goal planning. Planners begin with more general domain planning and establish their commitment to move in a particular direction. (Ch. 6)

Hybrid superstructure Superstructure that combines the characteristics of two or more structural approaches. (Ch. 12)

Hygiene needs Needs, classified by Herzberg, that are not directly related to work itself. Instead they relate to the context of a job and consist of such factors as pay, working conditions, coworkers, supervision, and security. (Ch. 14)

Ideation First step of the communication process; involves the decision to communicate and the development of the nature and content of the intended message based on the reasons for communicating. (Ch. 15)

Impersonal mode Method of integration in which managers assign rules, policies, and standard operating procedures to the individuals and activities that need to be integrated. (Ch. 3)

Implementation Design and use of organizational subsystems and resources to operate strategic plans. (Ch. 9)

Importing Buying goods from sellers in another country. (Ch. 23)

Incentive systems Systems used for jobs in which it is possible to measure performance objectively. (Ch. 17)

Independent contributor stage Stage in Dalton and Thompson's career model in which individuals develop in areas of expertise and work independently. (Ch. 25)

Indirect exporting Making goods within one's own country but using an intermediary to sell them abroad. (Ch. 23)

Individual pay Amount a manager decides to pay an individual within an established pay range. (Ch. 17)

Influence Ability to produce results and to bring about a change in the environment. (Ch. 11)

Informal communication networks Networks created by employees and often referred to as *the grapevine*. (Ch. 15)

Informal groups Groups that arise spontaneously and whose activity may or may not be helpful in reaching organizational objectives. (Ch. 13)

Informal leader A leader created because group members choose him or her as their natural leader. (Ch. 16)

Informal organization Two or more people who interact for a purpose or in a manner beyond that specified by managers. Often, informal organizations evolve in a natural, unplanned manner. (Ch. 10)

Informal rewards Rewards provided from a leader's own resources. (Ch. 15)

Information Meaningful data. (Ch. 21)

Informational (environmental) scan A step in the strategic planning process by which an organization collects information from the external environment about factors that can influence the organization. (Ch. 9)

Informational roles Roles in which managers collect and disperse knowledge, thus becoming an important nerve center for an organization. (Ch. 1)

Information presentation Training and development tool by which employees are presented with information via written material, films, videotapes, lectures, or computer. (Ch. 17)

Information-processing techniques Training and development tools that allow employees to manipulate information rather than merely learn facts. (Ch. 17)

Information-reporting system System that retrieves, sorts, pools, and manipulates transaction data in other ways to produce summary or management reports. (Ch. 21)

Initial work period Time in Miller and Form's life-span model characterized by part-time employment. (Ch. 25)

Initiating structure Structure that involves "task-oriented" leader behaviors and is instrumental in the efficient use of resources to attain organizational goals. (Ch. 16)

Innate needs Inborn needs, such as the needs for food and water. (Ch. 14)

Innovation Phenomenon that occurs when an organization is the first or early user of an idea among its set of similar organizations. (Ch. 20)

Inspirational decision-making approach Approach characterized by extremely high levels of uncertainty because there is no agreement on either goals or methods. (Ch. 7)

Instincts Psychological perspective on motivation that holds that people have automatic predispositions to behave in a certain fashion. (Ch. 14)

Institutional zone Zone of responsibility in which managers are primarily responsible for two aspects of an organization's external environment. (Ch. 1)

Instrumentality perception Perceived likelihood that a given performance level will lead to one or more outcomes. (Ch. 14)

Intelligence Stage of decision-making process whose basic purpose is to gather information to determine as accurately as possible what is going on internally and in the general external environment of the sociocultural, economic, technological, legal/political, or international domains. (Ch. 21)

Intensity Characteristic of stimuli wherein people are more likely to notice a loud voice or a bright light than a quiet sound or soft light. (Ch. 13)

Interdependence A natural part of doing business as managers develop a variety of exchange relationships with others (suppliers, customers, and allies). (Ch. 2)

Interdependence approach Approach that groups highly interdependent activities so they are coordinated from a common point in the organizational hierarchy. (Ch. 10)

Intermittent schedules of reinforcement Schedules that provide a consequence following some (but not all) responses. (Ch. 14)

Internal environment Wide range of factors within an organization's formal boundaries. (Ch. 3)

Internal forces Forces emanating from within an organization that encourage change. (Ch. 20)

Internal processes approach Approach that defines organizational effectiveness as the degree to which members are integrated with organizational production and management systems to function smoothly with a minimum of internal strain. (Ch. 18)

Internal processes model Model of assessing organizational effectiveness that values the well-being of organization members. (Ch. 18)

Internal recruiting Human resource program of finding employees already inside an organization who are qualified for job openings. (Ch. 17)

Internal staffing and development Process of identifying and moving current employees to different jobs or units within an organization; also expels employees from the organization into the external environment. (Ch. 3)

International domain Organizations and cultures of other countries. (Ch. 2)

International financial management Management of financial activities of a firm dealing in international business. (Ch. 23)

International joint venture Company formed by two or more parent firms from different countries. (Ch. 23)

International management Process of carrying out the managerial functions of planning, organizing, directing, and controlling in a business that operates in more than one country. (Ch. 23)

Interpersonal power Power that enables individual organization members to exert influence over others and over their organization. (Chs. 11, 15)

Interpersonal roles Roles managers must fill because of their position in an organization. (Ch. 1)

Interrole conflict Conflict that occurs when one person occupies different roles with conflicting expectations. (Ch. 13)

Interviewing Discussions between a job incumbent or supervisor and a human resource manager to identify important aspects of a job that are not obvious through direct observation. (Ch. 17)

Intraperson role conflict Conflict that occurs when role demands contradict personal values, beliefs, or preferences. (Ch. 13)

Intrapreneurship Process that takes place when individuals who identify the need for (often innovative) change in an organization create an environment in which the change can succeed and champion the implementation of the change. (Ch. 24)

Intrarole conflict Conflict that occurs when role occupants receive mixed signals about their role. (Ch. 13)

Intrinsic motivators Motivators within an organizational behavior modification program that arise from within an individual. (Ch. 14)

Inventory A measure of physical goods that are produced and not yet sold. (Ch. 21)

Irrational person model Decision-making model that suggests that many decisions stem from a variety of fears, anxieties, and drives. (Ch. 7)

Job Collection of tasks that can be performed by one person. (Ch. 17)

Job analysis Process of documenting job tasks and their associated responsibilities and requirements. (Ch. 17)

Job-centered behaviors Leader behaviors devoted to supervisory functions, such as planning, scheduling, coordinating work activities, and providing the resources needed for task performance. (Ch. 16)

Job Characteristics Model (JCM) Model that specifies the critical job components that lead to positive results for both an organization and its workers. (Ch. 10)

Job description List of the duties and responsibilities that managers expect the holder of a job to accomplish, the procedures that the job holder should follow in carrying them out, and the qualifications that a person needs to accomplish these duties and responsibilities. (Ch. 17)

Job design Method of dividing work into tasks and then assembling these tasks into jobs. (Ch. 3)

Job enlargement Job design strategy that adds breadth to a job by increasing the number and variety of activities performed by an employee. (Ch. 10)

Job enrichment Job design strategy that adds depth to a job by adding "managerial" activities (planning, organizing, directing, and controlling) to an employee's responsibilities. (Ch. 10)

Job evaluation Process of determining the relative value of jobs, based on the job requirements identified in a job analysis. (Ch. 17)

Job involvement An employee's psychological involvement with a job. (Ch. 13)

Job rotation Training and development tool that systematically moves a subordinate through a series of relatively brief job assignments. These changes are not promotions but an opportunity for the employee to broaden his or her abilities, skills, and knowledge about the organization. (Ch. 17)

Job satisfaction Affective component of people's attitudes toward their work. (Ch. 13)

Job shop Type of operation in which work centers are arranged around particular types of equipment or functions. (Ch. 21)

Judgmental decision-making approach Approach used when managers agree on their goals but have no knowledge to guide them on how to achieve these goals. (Ch. 7)

Just-in-time (JIT) Inventory control method based on the principle that inventory is a fundamental liability that must be reduced. (Ch. 21)

Labor market The number and types of people in the workforce. (Ch. 17)

Labor relations Dealing with unions through contract negotiation, contract administration, and grievance resolution. (Ch. 3)

Layout Arrangement that locates a facility's processing equipment or functions in sequence as they are needed in production. (Ch. 21)

Leadership Interpersonal process involving the exercise of influence within a social system, such as a group, family, community, or work organization. (Ch. 16)

Leadership in a new market or industry Process that involves creating and then dominating a new product or service area. (Ch. 24)

Leadership process Complex and dynamic exchange consisting of four components: leaders, followers, the context within which a process takes place, and resulting by-products. (Ch. 16)

Least preferred co-worker (LPC) Person with whom leaders least wanted to work along a number of dimensions, such as pleasant/unpleasant, friendly/unfriendly; cold/warm; open/closed, untrustworthy/trustworthy. (Ch. 16)

Legal/political domain System that allocates power among various groups in society and settles disputes as they arise. The system also develops, administers, and enforces the law. (Ch. 2)

Legal responsibilities Responsibilities to obey society's laws and regulations while fulfilling economic responsibilities. (Ch. 4)

Legitimate power Power that exists when one person believes that another person has the right to influence him or her. (Chs. 11, 15)

Letter of credit (LC) Financial instrument used between a buyer and a seller in an export transaction. (Ch. 23)

Licensing agreement Agreement in which a licensor gives a licensee the right to use a patent, trademark, copyright, technology, or other asset in return for a royalty or fee. (Ch. 23)

Life cycle Stages of an organization's development: (1) entrepreneurial, (2) collectivity, (3) formalization, (4) elaboration of structure. (Ch. 18)

Life-span models Descriptive frameworks of careers built around the biological life cycle. (Ch. 25)

Linear programming (LP) Quantitative model by which managers not only can control inventory but can also identify the appropriate quantity of product to manufacture. (Ch. 8)

Line authority Command authority that gives a manager the organizational right to make decisions and to commit the organization to action. (Ch. 11)

Line functions Four marketing activities directly involved in preparing or delivering a product (purchasing, selling, transportation, storage). (Ch. 3)

Line managers Managers with a direct responsibility for producing the service or product line of an organization. (Ch. 1)

Linkage Communication between two people or groups. (Ch. 15)

Linking pin roles Roles resulting from managers' participation in and connecting function with multiple groups. (Ch. 12)

Lockout Process in which management closes down operations and refuses to offer work to union members until an agreement is reached. (Ch. 17)

Long-range plans Plans that generally encompass a period of more than five years. (Ch. 6)

McKinsey 7-S framework Seven interdependent factors in organizations that must be managed harmoniously, because a change in one necessitates adjustments in the other six. (Ch. 5)

Maintenance stage Period in Super's life-span model in which individuals strive to hold on to their places in work by continuing along existing lines of performance. (Ch. 25)

Management Process of planning, organizing, directing, and controlling organizational resources in the pursuit of organizational goals. (Ch. 1)

Management by Objectives (MBO) Process through which an organization's goals, plans, and control systems are defined through collaboration between managers and their subordinates. (Ch. 6)

Management control Process by which managers assure that resources are obtained and used effectively and efficiently in the accomplishment of an organization's objectives. (Ch. 21)

Management information system System that provides managers with information that enables them to make better decisions and improve their job performance. (Ch. 21)

Managerial competence anchor Need to be competent in the set of activities that comprise management. (Ch. 25)

Managerial grid(R) Leadership classification tool (Blake and Mouton) that produces five distinct styles of leadership: (1) country club, (2) impoverished, (3) organization person management, (4) authority-obedience, and (5) team. (Ch. 16)

Managerial (or tactical) decisions Decisions that specify how an organization intends to integrate its institutional level with its technical core and how it will coordinate work systems within the technical core. (Ch. 7)

Managerial zone Zone of responsibility in which managers create and manage systems to coordinate and integrate various parts of the technical core. (Ch. 1)

Managers Organization members who are assigned the primary responsibility of carrying out the management process. (Ch. 1)

Market information Information that enables managers to learn about the market for a good or service by using the knowledge derived from research about the market. (Ch. 3)

Marketing Activity that identifies consumer wants and needs so an organization can convert them into tangible products and services and deliver them to consumers. (Ch. 3)

Marketing control Process by which managers in charge of an organization's marketing function control activities that place its goods and services into the market. (Ch. 19)

Marketing management Applies the management process to satisfying the needs and wants of an organization's customers through its goods and services. (Ch. 3)

Maslow's need hierarchy theory According to Maslow, people have a set of five innate needs that they try to satisfy in a particular order. (Ch. 14)

Materials management Planning and controlling the purchases that affect an organization's input inventories, which consist of the raw materials, subcomponents, and semifinished goods that will enter the organization's operating system. (Ch. 3)

Matrix boss Person who manages one of an organization's overlapping systems. (Ch. 12)

Matrix superstructure Superstructure that uses two or more integrated, coexisting structures simultaneously. (Ch. 12)

Means decisions Decisions that concern procedures or actions undertaken to achieve particular goals—in other words, how a goal is to be reached. (Ch. 7)

Means goals Specified goals that are directly tied to a systems approach. (Ch. 18)

Mechanistic system System characterized by clear definition and relative stability of tasks and responsibility. (Ch. 2)

Mediator Impartial third party who works with bargainers to identify a mutually acceptable agreement. (Ch. 17)

Mentor An experienced member of an organization who coaches, guides, and counsels newer members. (Ch. 25)

Mentoring stage Stage in Dalton and Thompson's career model in which individuals coach, teach, and guide people in Stage I. (Ch. 25)

Miscommunication Problem in which a message received is different from the one intended. (Ch. 15)

Mission statement Statement that encapsulates managers' visions for their organization based on its internal and external environments, its capabilities, and the nature of its customers or clients. (Ch. 9)

Motivation Stimulus that energizes, directs, and sustains human behavior. (Ch. 14)

Motivator needs Needs classified by Herzberg as achievement, recognition, responsibility, and advancement (like Alderfer's growth needs). (Ch. 14)

Multinational corporations (MNCs)/ multinational enterprises (MNEs) Companies that have a variety of overseas linkages, of which a significant number are wholly owned subsidiaries. (Ch. 23)

Multinational functional structure Multinational organizational structure patterned after the functional form of departmentalization. (Ch. 23)

Multinational geographic structure Multinational organizational structure that involves a territorial form of departmentalization. (Ch. 23)

Multinational matrix structure Multinational organizational structure that simultaneously employs a product and a geographic structure. (Ch. 23)

Multinational product structure
Multinational organizational structure that involves a large world headquarters that functions much like the headquarters in a multinational geographic structure. (Ch. 23)

Multiple trial pattern Situation in which an individual never stays in one field long enough to achieve stability, moving from one trial job to another. (Ch. 25)

Murray's manifest need theory People have many very specific needs. They need among other things, to succeed, to socialize, and to be loved. (Ch. 13)

Nature of work model of motivation
Model that holds that work can be interesting for organization members and that it is a manager's job to motivate employees by making the work interesting. (Ch. 14)

Need for achievement Desire to accomplish difficult and challenging objectives. (Ch. 14)

Need for affiliation Desire for warm and friendly relationships with others. (Ch. 14)

Need for power Desire to control others and to influence their behavior. (Ch. 14)

Negative reinforcement Method of making a desired response more likely when a behavior causes something undesired to be taken away. (Ch. 14)

Networking Process by which individuals in organizations gain social support from many directions. (Ch. 25)

Network of organizational plans
Requires that managers in each subsystem of their organization engage in the planning process. (Ch. 6)

Nominal group technique (NGT)
Qualitative tool that is a group decision-making process designed to generate a large number of creative potential solutions to a problem, to evaluate these solutions, and to rank them from best to worst. (Ch. 8)

Noncybernetic control Control system operated completely independently from the work system itself. (Ch. 19)

Nonprogrammed decisions Decisions generally made in unique or novel situations, when no prior routine or practice exists to guide the decision-making process. (Ch. 7)

Nonreinforcement Method of making desired responses less likely. Subordinate is permitted to engage in an undesired behavior but no consequence at all, positive or negative, follows that response. (Ch. 14)

Nonroutine decisions Decisions that usually involve the use of intuition, common sense, trial-and-error, and heuristic approaches. (Ch. 21)

Nonroutine technology Technology marked by flexible workflow patterns, low levels of automation, more customized product, great variation in the nature and character of the materials worked on, and a developing body of knowledge to guide the transformation of raw materials. (Ch. 3)

Objective measures Measures that quantify management information and specify in numeric terms a picture of reality and treat information more objectively than intuition alone can do. (Ch. 8)

Objective rationality Situation wherein managers know all possible alternatives and their probable consequences and rationally select the "one best" alternative. (Ch. 7)

Official goals An organization's general aims as expressed in public statements, in its annual report, and in its organizational charter. (Ch. 6)

Off-the-job training Training and development tool that allows employees to receive information away from the actual job site. (Ch. 17)

On-the-job training Training and development tool that consists mostly of coaching, special assignments, and job rotation. (Ch. 17)

Open system Organizational system that interacts with and depends on other systems. (Ch. 2)

Open systems Internal recruiting systems that publicize job openings so that any employee who meets specified minimum requirements can apply. (Ch. 17)

Open-systems model Model of assessing organizational effectiveness that values the need for flexibility over the need for control, as do managers using the human relations model. (Ch. 18)

Operating decisions Decisions that deal with the day-to-day operations of an organization. (Ch. 7)

Operating plans Plans that cover the day-to-day operations of an organization. (Ch. 6)

Operating systems Processes and activities needed to transform inputs, such as information and raw materials, into goods and services for delivery to consumers in the task environment. (Ch. 3)

Operational control Managerial activity of lower-level or operating managers involving the process of assuring that specific tasks are carried out effectively and efficiently. (Ch. 21)

Operational goals Goals that reflect managers' specific intentions; the concrete goals that organization members are to pursue. (Ch. 6)

Operational strategies Specific actions that are to be taken in order to accomplish strategic objectives. (Ch. 9)

Operations control Process by which managers in charge of an organization's operations function control the activities necessary to transform resources into goods and services. (Ch. 19)

Operations management Application of planning, organizing, directing, and controlling activities to that part of an organization in charge of making its product. (Ch. 3)

Optimize Find the best possible decision. (Ch. 7)

Organic organization Organization that is fluid and dynamic and capable of evolution, redesign, and adaptation to both internal and external environments. (Ch. 12)

Organic system System characterized by a flexible structure that can change, loosely defined tasks to be performed by employees, consultative-type organizational communication, and authority that flows more from knowledge centers. (Ch. 2)

Organization System of consciously coordinated activities of two or more persons. (Ch. 1)

Organizational behavior modification (OBM) Systematic application of operant learning principles to manage behavior within organizations. (Ch. 14)

Organizational change Process within an organization that takes place when the forces encouraging change become more powerful than those resisting change. (Ch. 20)

Organizational chart Schematic drawing of the positions within an organization. (Ch. 1)

Organizational climate Climate composed of such factors as structure, processes, and culture. (Ch. 3)

Organizational commitment Active association between individuals and organizations such that committed employees are willing to give something of themselves in order to contribute to the organization's well-being. (Ch. 13)

Organizational context Circumstances and conditions within which an organization operates. (Ch. 12)

Organizational culture Pattern of basic assumptions invented, discovered, or developed by a group as it learns to cope with its problems of external adaptation and internal integration. (Ch. 3)

Organizational design An organization's structure and the systems that help the organization operate. (Ch. 12)

Organizational development (OD)
Process of diagnosing organizational problems by looking for incongruencies between environment, structures, processes, and people. (Ch. 20)

Organizational development process
Series of planned actions designed to improve the effectiveness of an organiza-

tion and/or the well-being of its members. (Ch. 20)

Organizational effectiveness Degree to which organizational goals are being met. (Ch. 18)

Organizational mission Statement that specifies an organization's reason for being. (Ch. 9)

Organizational politics The management of influence to obtain ends not sanctioned by an organization or to obtain sanctioned ends through non-sanctioned influence means. (Ch. 15)

Organizational scan Step in strategic planning process that identifies an organization's present strengths and weaknesses by examining its internal resources. (Ch. 9)

Organizational structure Structure that identifies and distinguishes the individual parts of an organization and ties these pieces together to define an integrated whole. (Ch. 12)

Organizing Process by which managers design, structure, and arrange the components of an organization's internal environment to facilitate attainment of organizational goals. (Chs. 1, 10)

Orientation (Stage 1) First stage of group development wherein members exchange information, ask questions about other group members, and attempt to define the nature of the group. (Ch. 13)

Parity of authority and responsibility Principle of delegation that suggests that authority and responsibility should be equally balanced. (Ch. 11)

Participative leadership Effective leaders consult with subordinates about job-related activities and consider their opinions and suggestions when making decisions. (Ch. 16)

Path-goal theory of leadership Leadership theory (House and Evans) that suggests that an effective leader provides subordinates with a path to a valued goal. (Ch. 16)

Pay level Relationship between an organization's rate of cash compensation and the general level for comparable jobs in the labor market. (Ch. 17)

Pay structure Relative values and pay ranges for each job in an organization. (Ch. 17)

Perceived role One's definition of one's role as he or she understands it. (Ch. 13)

Perception Process by which a person gains information from the environment, organizes it, and derives its meaning. (Ch. 13)

Perceptual defense Tendency to defend existing perceptions against contradictory information. (Ch. 13)

Perceptual readiness Perception distortion that occurs when a person experiences new events according to their anticipated, rather than actual, characteristics. (Ch. 13)

Performance appraisal Evaluation of how effectively employees are fulfilling their job responsibilities and contributing to the accomplishment of organizational goals. (Ch. 17)

Permissive autocrat leader Leader who mixes his or her use of power, retaining decision-making power but permitting subordinates to exercise discretion in the execution of decisions. (Ch. 16)

Permissive behavior Degree to which a leader lets employees carry out role assignments as they see fit, including the making of decisions as well as their execution. (Ch. 16)

Permissive democrat leader Leader who shares power with group members, soliciting involvement in both decision making and decision execution. (Ch. 16)

Personality Combination of the psychological characteristics and traits that make up each person's unique style of behavior. (Ch. 13)

Personalized power seeking Dominating others for the sake of domination. (Ch. 14)

Personal specialization Level of formal education, training, and experience needed by the occupants of various organizational roles. (Chs. 11, 12)

Placement Process of putting individuals into specific jobs within an organization. (Ch. 13)

Place utility Value that a good or service has because it is available where a consumer wants it. (Ch. 3)

Planned shortage model Inventory model that reduces inventory costs in situations in which periodic stock shortages are acceptable (although back ordering is sometimes necessary). (Ch. 8)

Planning Process by which managers establish goals and define the methods by which these goals are to be attained. (Chs. 1, 6)

Planning specialists Professional planners who work singly or in groups to develop organizational plans and to help managers plan. (Ch. 6)

Point method Most widely used job evaluation tool that identifies a group of compensable factors—which typically parallel factors in job analyses—and that assigns points to each job according to level of responsibility for each factor. (Ch. 17)

Policies Broad-based statements of understanding or general statements of intent; provide limits within which decisions are to be made. (Ch. 6)

Politics The art or science concerned with guiding or influencing policy, with winning and holding control, and with competition between competing interest groups or individuals for power and leadership. (Ch. 15)

Polycentric staffing International staffing with executives from any country if they are the best people available. (Ch. 23)

Pooled interdependence Employees or departments basically act independently, each doing their own work within an organization and depending only minimally on others. (Ch. 10)

Portfolio matrix Phase of business portfolio approach that categorizes an SBU according to its relative market growth and market share. (Ch. 9)

Position analysis questionnaire (PAQ) Probably the best-known structured job analysis questionnaire; developed at Purdue University, the PAQ assesses a variety of job behaviors found in a wide range of jobs. (Ch. 17)

Positive reinforcement Method of making a desired response more likely; occurs whenever a positively valued consequence follows a response to a stimulus. (Ch. 14)

Possession utility Value derived from owning something. (Ch. 3)

Postaction controls Controls exercised after an entire set of work activities has been completed to produce a product or service. (Ch. 19)

Precontrols Control activities that occur before inputs enter the system or prior to the beginning of an activity. (Ch. 19)

Premising Forecasting what is likely to happen inside and outside of an organization. (Ch. 6)

Preparatory work period Time in Miller and Form's life-span model characterized by socialization of a child at home and at school. (Ch. 25)

Primacy effect Perception distortion that is created if a perceiver gives disproportionate weight to first pieces of information received about a person, event, or object. (Ch. 13)

Principle of charity Principle that shapes corporate social responsibility; suggests that those who have plenty should give to those who do not. (Ch. 4)

Principle of stewardship Principle that asserts that organizations have an obligation to see that the public's interests are served by corporate actions and by the way in which profits are spent. (Ch. 4)

Proaction philosophies Philosophies that call for organizations to anticipate and address social issues before society in general recognizes the issues as important. (Ch. 4)

Proactive change Type of change that occurs when an organization's managers conclude that a change would be desirable (as opposed to necessary). (Ch. 20)

Probability chain network Communication pattern that represents an almost random transfer of information. (Ch. 15)

Problem avoiders People who have a very low tolerance for ambiguity. (Ch. 7)

Problem seekers People who have a high tolerance for ambiguity and who are so comfortable with novelty and uncertainty that they actually seek challenges of this type and derive great satisfaction from conquering uncertainty. (Ch. 7)

Problem solvers Individuals who anticipate difficulties and deal with them as they arise. (Ch. 7)

Problem solving Finding and implementing a course of action to correct an unsatisfactory situation. (Chs. 3, 7)

Procedures Standing plans that guide action rather than thinking; procedures establish customary ways for handling certain activities. (Ch. 6)

Process/equipment departmentalization Strategy whereby tasks are assigned according to equipment specifically needed to perform each task. (Ch. 10)

Process layout Layout of a facility that groups processing equipment according to the functions it serves. (Ch. 21)

Process (or activity) perspective View that focuses on the actions taken by managers. (Ch. 1)

Process theories Theories that focus on the reasons people choose to behave in certain ways and the reasons they react as they do to organizational events. (Ch. 14)

Production planning Identifying the demand characteristics that are associated with various product designs. (Ch. 3)

Production-run model Inventory model useful for situations in which work is done in batches through production runs. (Ch. 8)

Product/service departmentalization Job design strategy whereby activities related to the development and delivery of a single product (or closely related group of products) are grouped together. (Ch. 10)

Profit-maximizing management Process in which business managers pursue, almost single-mindedly, the objective of maximizing profits. (Ch. 4)

Program evaluation and review technique (PERT) Time/activity technique used for project planning and control. (Ch. 8)

Programmed decisions Decisions that deal with frequently occurring situations, such as requests for vacations by employees. (Ch. 7)

Programs Single-use plans consisting of a complex set of policies, rules, procedures, and other elements necessary to carry out a course of action. (Ch. 6)

Project department Department created to address specific, often unique, organizational goals. (Ch. 10)

Projection Perception distortion in which someone "projects" his or her own characteristics onto another individual. (Ch. 13)

Projects Projects have the same characteristics as programs but are generally narrower in scope, less complex, and frequently created to support or complement programs. (Ch. 6)

Prospector organizations Innovative organizations in which managers move rapidly from one domain to another in search of new opportunities. (Ch. 9)

Punishment Method of making desired responses less likely because the undesired behavior is followed by a distinctly undesirable consequence. (Ch. 14)

Purchasing Working with vendors to supply the best product at the lowest cost. (Ch. 21)

Purchasing and acquisitions management Process by which purchasing managers oversee the acquisition of the raw materials, services, equipment, semifinished goods, and subcomponents necessary to produce and deliver an organization's goods and services. (Ch. 3)

Qualitative tools Tools designed for collecting and processing ideas, opinions, and judgments; thought-processing procedures. (Ch. 8)

Quality assurance and control Method of assuring that products or services meet customer expectations. (Ch. 21)

Quality circles Groups of workers (from the same and/or different departments) who meet regularly to work on production-quality issues; a way of building an emphasis on quality at each stage of the manufacturing (service) process through the joint involvement of management and workers in planning and controlling activities. (Ch. 6)

Quality control Process of monitoring the quality of a product, which determines its value to consumers and how well it performs the function for which it was designed. (Ch. 3)

Quality-of-life management Process in which managers behave in socially responsible ways and do more than achieve narrow economic goals. (Ch. 4)

Quantitative tools Tools that provide a way to examine, to measure, and to express information in numbers. (Ch. 8)

Quantity-discount model Inventory model that is useful if suppliers offer discounts for purchases above a certain quantity. (Ch. 8)

Question marks SBUs within portfolio matrix that possess a relatively small share of a rapidly growing market. (Ch. 9)

Queuing models Models that help managers identify the best number of waiting lines. (Ch. 8)

Ratification vote Process occurring if two parties agree on terms; a renegotiated contract is presented to union members for their approval. (Ch. 17)

Rational goals model Model of assessing organizational effectiveness that is concerned with organizational development and promotion; values control, consistency, and maintenance of the status quo. (Ch. 18)

Rationing Establishing a set of priorities for using an organization's resources. (Ch. 2)

Reaction philosophies Philosophies that call for an organization to address social issues because it is compelled to do so by outside forces, such as legal, regulatory, or social pressures. (Ch. 4)

Reactive change Type of change that occurs when the forces driving change provide so much pressure that an organization must change. (Ch. 20)

Reactor organizations Organizations that react to environmental events before they analyze the meaning and possible consequences of such events. (Ch. 9)

Reality testing Comparing one's perceptions to reality, identifying likely inaccuracies, and staying alert to the need to reconsider those perceptions. (Ch. 13)

Reciprocal interdependence Process in which an object being worked on is passed back and forth among workers before the process is completed. (Ch. 10)

Referent power Ability of managers to influence a person because he or she wants to be associated or affiliated with the power holder. (Chs. 11, 15)

Regression analysis Process in which a mathematical model (equation) describes the relationship of one or more causal variables to a dependent variable. (Ch. 8)

Regulation Form of control by regulatory agencies, often affecting the interdependence of organizations and the level of uncertainty. (Ch. 2)

Regulatory and influence groups Components in the task environment that influence the policies and practices of management. (Ch. 2)

Reinforcement Process that occurs when a consequence makes it more likely that a response will be repeated in the future. (Ch. 14)

Reinforcement theories Theories wherein a person repeats behaviors that result in desirable consequences and avoids behaviors that produce undesirable consequences. (Ch. 14)

Repetition Characteristic of stimuli which influences selection; a stimulus that is encountered frequently is more likely to be selected than a stimulus encountered only once. (Ch. 13)

Repetitive process Operating process in which functions are arranged in a sequence in accordance to the specifications of a product. (Ch. 21)

Resource allocator Manager who schedules his or her own time; programs the work of subordinates; and controls decisions involving the allocation of other resources, money, supplies, and equipment. (Ch. 1)

Resource deployment Internal distribution of an organization's resources, including how much money it will spend in pursuit of its goals. (Ch. 9)

Resource power Power a person has because others believe that he or she has and is willing to share resources that they need. (Chs. 11, 15)

Retrenchment, or turnaround, strategy Within portfolio matrix managers can try to stimulate markets by finding new uses for existing products, by attempting to change the image of a product, or by modifying a product in a search for a market niche. (Ch. 9)

Reward power Power a person has because people believe that he or she can bestow rewards or outcomes—such as money or recognition—that others desire. (Chs. 11, 15)

Risk persuaders High risk takers within a group who tend to dominate the group and effectively convince others to take greater risk. (Ch. 7)

Risky shift Tendency of groups to make decisions that are more prone toward risk than an average individual's decisions. (Ch. 7)

Role ambiguity Uncertainty about the requirements of a role. (Ch. 13)

Role conflict Conflict that occurs when people occupy several roles whose expectations contradict one another or when demands of their roles conflict with their personal preferences. (Ch. 13)

Role overload Form of role conflict that prevents people from meeting all of the expectations that their roles raise and that can result in psychological and even physical discomfort. (Ch. 13)

Routine decisions Decisions in which the factors involved and the outcomes can be clearly defined, and the timelines involved are usually short; such decisions are based on clear logic, are repetitive, and are made at low levels in an organization. (Ch. 21)

Routine technology Technology characterized by standard operating procedure (SOP), rigid workflow patterns, high levels of automation, standardized production, little variability in the nature and character of the raw materials, and a well-developed body of knowledge to direct the transformation process. (Ch. 3)

Rules Standing plans that guide employee actions. (Ch. 6)

Satisfice To find the first satisfactory solution. (Ch. 7)

Scabs Nonunion members hired by an organization to work in place of striking union members. (Ch. 17)

Scalar principle Principle of delegation wherein lines of authority must be clear as they run from the top of the organization to its lowest levels. (Ch. 11)

Scheduling Determining which employee will work when and at which machine or in which department and determining the work itself. (Ch. 21)

Scientific management movement Management that conducts a business of affairs by standards established by facts or truths gained through systematic observation, experiment, or reasoning. (Ch. 5)

Scope An organization's present and planned interactions with its environment; also identifies the organization's domain, such as the markets in which it expects to compete, and the nature and character of these interactions, such as methods of competition. (Ch. 9)

Screening controls Forms of concurrent control by which managers often try to identify critical "go, no-go" stages of organizational activity. (Ch. 19)

Security anchor Need for stability in one's career, either by remaining with the same company or by staying in a particular geographic area. (Ch. 25)

Selection Process of evaluating candidates, making predictions of the probable levels of job performance by each, and choosing a candidate for the job. (Chs. 13, 17)

Selective recruitment Tactic of hiring knowledgeable individuals from key organizations in the external environment to reduce uncertainty. (Ch. 2)

Self-designing organization Organization that continuously experiments and tries new ways to respond to environmental demands. (Ch. 12)

Self-managing work group approach Job design strategy whereby groups of workers collaborate in performing and managing their work. (Chs. 6, 10)

Sensation Stage of perception that is the physiological reaction of the body to an environmental stimulus. (Ch. 13)

Sequential, or serial, interdependence Object being worked on is passed from one worker or department to the next. (Ch. 10)

Service functions Functions that support the line functions managers use to create primary utilities. (Ch. 3)

Short-range plans Plans that cover activities that unfold relatively quickly, in most organizations, from the next several hours to the next several months. (Ch. 6)

Simulation techniques Training and development tools that give trainees a chance to encounter important aspects of a job in a safe environment, where they are free to perform inexpertly or to make mistakes. (Ch. 17)

Simultaneous production and consumption Employees in an organization's technical core generally interact with customers while a product is being delivered. (Ch. 3)

Single-use plans Plans developed for unique situations or problems that are usually replaced after one use. (Ch. 6)

Situational factor Degree to which a leader has control and influence and, therefore, feels that he or she can determine the outcomes of a group interaction. (Ch. 16)

Situational view of authority View that ultimate authority resides in the will and consent of the people who perform a particular task. (Ch. 11)

Smoothing Attempting to influence the behavior of the environment. (Ch. 2)

Social audit Detailed examination and evaluation of an organization's social performance. (Ch. 4)

Social-cultural domain Values, customs, mores, and demographic characteristics of the people within an organization. (Ch. 2)

Social effect Impact of a proposed action on society. (Ch. 4)

Social facilitation Process whereby decision making is enhanced by the presence of others. (Ch. 7)

Social impairment Impairment of decision making by the presence of others. (Ch. 7)

Socialization Process through which people develop beliefs about what is right, wrong, and just. (Ch. 4)

Socialized power seeking Acquiring power in order to benefit a group. (Ch. 14)

Social learning Part of organizational behavior modification in which people watch others and see which consequences follow their behavior. (Ch. 14)

Socially responsive organization Organization in which managers communicate and interact with external groups to anticipate social issues and to prevent problems as well as to correct problems after the fact. (Ch. 4)

Social model of motivation Model that holds that the work experience is socially pleasant. If this can be done, proponents argue, workers will be both satisfied and motivated to perform their jobs effectively, because people are social and need acceptance and recognition. (Ch. 14)

Social obligation Situation wherein managers confine their responses to social issues to those mandated by prevailing laws and the operation of the economic system. (Ch. 4)

Social responsibility An organization's obligation to engage in activities that protect and contribute to the welfare of society. (Ch. 4)

Sociological perspective Perspective that defines management as the group of organization members that occupies the social position responsible for making sure that an organization achieves its mission. (Ch. 1)

Sociotechnical changes Changes involving changes in people and the technology. (Ch. 20)

Sociotechnical systems theory Theory that balances the technical and social-psychological sides of an organization. (Chs. 5, 12)

Span of control Number of subordinates and activities that a manager oversees. (Ch. 10)

Specificity of evaluation Degree to which workflow activity can be measured using precise, quantitative means. (Ch. 3)

Sponsor stage Stage in Dalton and Thompson's career model in which individuals determine the direction and future of organizations. (Ch. 25)

Stable career pattern Individuals go directly from schooling into work, with which they stay. (Ch. 25)

Stable growth, or hold, strategy Strategy within portfolio matrix appropriate for most cash cows and some dogs. (Ch. 9)

Stable work period Time in Miller and Form's life-span model defined as a permanent job situation. (Ch. 25)

Staff authority Authority in the form of counsel, advice, and recommendation. (Ch. 11)

Staffing Finding the person to do a job well. (Ch. 17)

Staff managers Managers who support line managers but who are not directly involved in the production of goods or services. (Ch. 1)

Stakeholder groups Groups directly affected by an organization's actions— for example, owners, creditors, suppliers, and government agencies. (Ch. 3)

Standardization Extent to which work activities are described in detail and performed uniformly throughout an organization. (Ch. 12)

Standardization and grading Activities that facilitate an organization's marketing function by providing consumers with uniform criteria by which to evaluate products. (Ch. 3)

Standard operating procedure (SOP) Procedure invoked under a standing plan when an issue is faced repeatedly. (Ch. 6)

Standing plans Plans designed to be used to cover the many issues that managers face repeatedly. (Ch. 6)

Star communication Network that allows any member to communicate directly with any other member; tends to produce the highest-quality decisions and usually has relatively little distortion. (Ch. 15)

Stars SBUs within portfolio matrix with a relatively large portion of a high-growth market—for example, compact disk SBU of SONY. (Ch. 9)

Steering controls Forms of concurrent control that occur after work has begun but before the activity is completed. (Ch. 19)

Stereotype effect Perception distortion that occurs when a perceiver feels that a person, object, or event possesses the same properties as the group to which it belongs. (Ch. 13)

Steward Employee designated to represent union members. (Ch. 17)

Straight ranking Comparative appraisal method by which supervisors simply list employees from best to worst. (Ch. 17)

Strand Communication pattern that is the same as a chain and is the least complex and least accurate at passing on information. (Ch. 15)

Strategic business unit (SBU) Segment of an organization with a distinct mission, an external market, and a strategy (or potential strategy) for dealing with that market. (Ch. 9)

Strategic constituencies approach Newest approach to assessing an organization's effectiveness by evaluating the degree to which the needs of the organization's constituents (stakeholders) have been satisfied. (Ch. 18)

Strategic-contingency model of power Model wherein those people and organizational units most capable of coping with an organization's critical problems and uncertainties acquire power. (Ch. 11)

Strategic decisions Decisions that reflect management's strategies for positioning an organization in its external environment. (Ch. 7)

Strategic management That part of the management process concerned with achieving an overall integration of an organization's internal divisions, while simultaneously integrating the organization with its external environment. (Ch. 9)

Strategic objectives Statements of definable and measurable accomplishments that, when realized, fulfill an organization's mission statement. (Ch. 9)

Strategic planning Top managers' active, conscious attempts to design a scheme to position an organization in its external environment. (Chs. 9, 21)

Strategic plans Plans that define an organization's long-term vision and the organization's intent to make its vision a reality. (Ch. 6)

Strategy The art and science of combining the many resources available to achieve the best match between an organization and its environment. (Ch. 9)

Stratification Degree of difference in status among individuals and groups within an organization. (Ch. 12)

Strike Primary tool of unions involving work stoppage. (Ch. 17)

Structured questionnaires Standardized forms that elicit answers about a job. (Ch. 17)

Subsidiary Company that is legally separate from the parent company and is organized under the laws of the country in which it is located. (Ch. 23)

Superstructure Division of activities at the top of the organizational hierarchy; provides the primary structural form of the organization. (Ch. 12)

Supportive leadership Effective leaders demonstrate concern for the well-being and personal needs of subordinates. (Ch. 16)

Synectic technique Qualitative tool designed to develop creative ideas: problem statement and background information stage, goal-wishing stage, excursion stage, forced-fit stage, itemized response stage. (Ch. 8)

Synergy Combination of scope, resource deployment, and competitive advantages that produces positive results. (Ch. 9)

System Set of related parts that work together in an organized way to achieve a stated purpose. (Chs. 5, 21)

System 4 organization Organizational design that emphasizes openness. (Ch. 12)

Systems approach Approach to assessing organizational effectiveness in which managers care mostly about how things are accomplished. (Ch. 18)

Systems theory Theory that views organizations as complex networks of interrelated parts that exist interdependently with the external environment. (Ch. 5)

Tactical plans Plans that focus on subsets of an organization's overall programs, activities, and systems. (Ch. 6)

Task environment Means through which the general environment exercises its most immediate influences on an organization's management. (Ch. 2)

Task specialization Degree to which organizational work is divided into narrow tasks with extensive division of labor. (Ch. 12)

Team interdependence Relationship formed when workers interact simultaneously with one another and the object or person on which they are working. (Ch. 10)

Technical core Zone in which managers have direct responsibility for producing and delivering an organization's goods and/or services. (Ch. 1)

Technical/functional competence anchor Need to be expert in a technical field or functional area. (Ch. 25)

Technical skills Managerial skills that enable a manager to understand and use the tools, procedures, and techniques needed to perform a given task. (Ch. 1)

Technological domain The knowledge, processes, means, systems, hardware, and software available to an organization to convert its inputs (raw materials, unfinished goods, energy) into outputs (products or services). (Ch. 2)

Technology Processes that transform organizational resources into a product or service. (Ch. 3)

Technostructural changes Changes involving concurrent changes in the technology and structure of an organization. (Ch. 20)

Territorial (geographical) departmentalization Job design strategy often used when organizations have widely dispersed operations or offices. (Ch. 10)

Theory of justice Ethical standard that emphasizes engaging in acts that are fair and impartial. (Ch. 4)

Theory X Leadership theory that assumes an average individual dislikes work and is incapable of exercising adequate self-direction and self-control. (Chs. 5, 16)

Theory Y Leadership theory that assumes people have a creative capacity and both the ability and desire to exercise self-direction and self-control. (Chs. 5, 16)

Theory Z Less a major theory of management than a set of organizational and management style characteristics that emphasizes terms of employment, decision making, evaluation and promotion, control, career paths, and concern for employees. (Ch. 5)

Time-frame plans Plans classified by time frame: short-range, medium-range, long-range. (Ch. 6)

Time series analysis Quantitative model that examines past data for trends and forecasts events; assumes the past will predict the future without considering why past events occurred. (Ch. 8)

Time utility Value consumers assign a product because it is available when they want it. (Ch. 3)

Top leader Person who heads the multiple command system of a matrix organization. (Ch. 12)

Total quality control (TQC) Belief that any errors should be caught and corrected at the source—that is, where the work is performed and within the production process. (Chs. 3, 21)

Training Improving employees' levels of ability. (Chs. 13, 17)

Trait approach Leadership approach that attempts to identify physiological, psychological, attitudinal, and ability traits associated with effective leaders. (Ch. 16)

Transactional leadership Interaction between a leader and follower in which both give and receive something that is valued. (Ch. 16)

Transaction exposure Potential gain or loss on the future settlement of obligations in international markets. (Ch. 23)

Transaction processing systems (TPS) Systems wherein an organization records, processes, and manages the data related to these everyday business activities. (Ch. 21)

Transformational leadership Process that relies on leaders' charisma and deeply held personal value systems, which include such values as justice and integrity. (Ch. 16)

Transformation process Process in which resources are transformed into products and services for customers. (Ch. 21)

Translation exposure Changes in the accounting or balance sheet of a firm involved in international markets. (Ch. 23)

Translation stage of perception Stage that gives meaning to the various stimuli previously sensed, selected, and organized. (Ch. 13)

Transmitted role Written or verbal description of a role given to the person expected to fill it. (Ch. 13)

Transportation Process that creates both time and place utility by moving products when they are needed to the place where they are needed. (Ch. 3)

Trial work period Time in Miller and Form's life-span model characterized by a person's first full-time job. (Ch. 25)

Trusteeship management Managers who maintain an equitable balance among the competing interests of all groups with a stake in an organization. (Ch. 4)

Two-boss manager Person who is at the point of intersection of two or more of an organization's multiple structures and, thus, is directly responsible to more than one matrix boss. (Ch. 12)

Type A personality Personality of a person who works intensely, impatiently, and well with pressure. (Ch. 13)

Type B personality In contrast to Type A, personality of someone who has a less-pressured style and tends to be more easy-going and relaxed. (Ch. 13)

Uncertainty Situation in which a decision maker is not aware of all possible courses of action, even though he or she may be aware of several. (Ch. 7)

Undermatching Situation in which an employee does not possess the abilities that his or her job demands. (Ch. 13)

Unfreezing Systematic upsetting of equilibrium between the forces driving change and those discouraging change. (Ch. 20)

Unit functional-level plans Plans focused on the day-to-day operations of lower-level organizational units. (Ch. 6)

Unity of command Principle of delegation wherein each subordinate is accountable to only one superior. (Ch. 11)

Unstable career pattern Situation in which an individual never becomes established in one area. (Ch. 25)

Utilitarian theories Ethical standards by which managers evaluate an anticipated course of action by concentrating on the social consequences the act is likely to produce. (Ch. 4)

Utilities Reasons for consumers to want a product. (Ch. 3)

Valence perceptions Values attached to an outcome. (Ch. 14)

Variable ratio reinforcement/punishment schedule Schedule in which managers reinforce or punish on average one out of "nth" responses. (Ch. 14)

Vertical communication Communication that can flow downward, upward, or in both directions. (Ch. 15)

Vertical coordination Linkage of organizational units that are separated by hierarchical level. (Ch. 15)

Vertical loading Job design strategy designed to reverse the effects of vertical specialization. (Ch. 10)

Vertical specialization Job design that removes planning and controlling activities from production employees. (Ch. 10)

Vestibule training Training and development tool involving simulations that construct a work experience identical to the real job but that call for no actual output. (Ch. 17)

Wage surveys Surveys that contain summarized information on prevailing pay practices collected from organizations within a given labor market. (Ch. 17)

Wheel communication Network having the greatest amount of centralization; communication flows outward from the person in the center of the wheel, who can communicate directly with all other network members. (Ch. 15)

Whistleblowing A member's disclosing that someone within an organization has engaged in an illegal, immoral, unethical, or illegitimate act. (Ch. 4)

Wholly owned subsidiary Subsidiary in which the parent company owns 100 percent of the voting stock, but its liability is generally limited to the assets of that subsidiary. (Ch. 23)

Workability test Evaluation of whether a chosen strategy appears as though it will work. (Ch. 9)

Work environment Function of human resource management that copes with a variety of issues related to the working environment that affect the human side of an organization. (Ch. 3)

Workflow layout Placement of people, machines, and tools to achieve orderly and efficient production. (Ch. 3)

Workflow rigidity Degree to which the knowledge, skills, and equipment used in the transformation process are adaptable from one task to another. (Ch. 3)

Work involvement An employee's devotion to or alienation from work in general. (Ch. 13)

Work methods Methods by which goods and services are developed. (Ch. 3)

Work motivation Set of energetic forces that originate both within as well as beyond an individual's being to initiate work-related behavior and to determine its form, direction, intensity, and duration. (Ch. 14)

Work-related motivation Internal force that makes an organization member put forth effort to accomplish something. (Ch. 13)

Work sampling Job analysis technique that is a variation of the direct observation approach in which a human resource manager periodically samples workers' behavior on jobs that have relatively long cycles, that have irregular patterns of activity, or that require many different tasks. (Ch. 17)

Work unit design Method of grouping jobs into structures usually consisting of

a relatively small number of employees. (Ch. 3)

World-class manufacturing (WCM) Producing a product or service that can compete successfully anywhere in the world. (Ch. 21)

Yield ratios Human resource management tool used to estimate how many applicants are likely to qualify for a job opening and accept the job if it is offered. (Ch. 17)

Zero-base budgeting Budget system based on the premise that an item approved in a prior budget does not guarantee that it will be included in a new budget. (Ch. 19)

Zone of acceptance Specific conditions that must exist before an individual will accept another's authority. (Ch. 11)

Zones of responsibility Levels (layers) of responsibility within organizations (institutional zone, managerial zone, technical core). (Ch. 1)

Name Index

Organization Index

UAW. *See* United Auto Workers (UAW)

UFCW. *See* United Food and Commercial Workers (UFCW)

Union Carbide, 819

Unisys, 835

United Airlines, 170, 171, 198, 287, 718, 719, 723

United Auto Workers (UAW), 44, 157

United Food and Commercial Workers (UFCW), 496

United Parcel Service (UPS), 309, 429

United States Air Force (USAF), 50

United States Armed Forces, 454

United States Army (USA), 367

United States Bureau of Alcohol, Tobacco, and Firearms (BAFT), 47

United States Bureau of Labor Statistics (BLS), 22, 596, 618

United States Bureau of National Affairs (BNA), 630

United States Bureau of the Census, 596

United States Chamber of Commerce Research Association, 620

United States Defense Nuclear Agency (DNA), 50

United States Department of Commerce (DOC), 43

United States Department of Defense (DOD), 233, 771

United States Department of Energy (DOE), 50

United States Department of Labor (DOL), 596

United States Environmental Protection Agency (EPA), 6, 43, 122

United States Federal Aviation Administration (FAA), 207

United States Federal Commerce Commission, 43

United States Federal Communications Commission (FCC), 301

United States Federal Mediation and Conciliation Service, 623, 624

United States Federal Trade Commission (FTC), 315

United States Food and Drug Administration (FDA), 43, 115

United States Internal Revenue Service (IRS), 68

United States Marine Corps (USMC), 415, 416, 570, 571

United States Navy (USN), 250, 468

United States Occupational Safety and Health Agency (OSHA), 43, 386, 416–17, 598

United States Postal Service, 429

United States Post Office, 416

United States Social Security Administration, 771

United States Steel, 813

United Way, 6, 105

University of Akron, 396

University of California at Berkeley, 149, 382, 563

University of Chicago, 109

University of Cincinnati, 521

University of Detroit, 276

University of Idaho, 131

University of Illinois, 382

University of Michigan, 19, 149, 419, 565, 567, 569, 659

University of Minnesota, 18, 70, 186, 270

University of Minnesota-Duluth, 183, 558

University of Pennsylvania, 642

University of South Dakota, 162, 204

University of Southern California, 125, 581

University of South Florida, 518

University of Toronto, 576

University of Washington, 571

University of Wisconsin, 52, 138, 227, 542, 750

University of Wisconsin-La Crosse, 362, 636

University of Wisconsin-Whitewater, 94, 676

Upjohn Pharmaceutical, 400

UPS. *See* United Parcel Service (UPS)

USA. *See* United States Army (USA)

USAF. *See* United States Air Force (USAF)

USN. *See* United States Navy (USN)

Vanderbilt University, 150

Volvo, 65–66, 198, 335

Wallace Barnes Steel Company, 44

Wall Street Journal, 82, 291, 546, 717, 823

WalMart, 377

Wang Laboratories, 316, 834

Western Electric Company, 144, 145

Western Union, 302, 303

Weyerhaeuser Company, 110, 652

White Consolidated, 810

Wilson Sporting Goods, 53

Wine Institute, 115

Wisconsin Tissue Mills, 261, 262, 269, 270, 271

W. L. Gore and Associates, 422

Xerox Corporation, 54, 125, 315–17, 440, 441, 835, 845, 846

Xerox Credit Corporation, 317

Yale University, 233, 467, 486

Zilog, Inc., 77

Zimbrick, 334

Subject Index

Certainty, 210–12
Chain communication network, 534
Challenger
    and decision making, 207, 228, 233
    and ethics, 116
    and isolation, 228
Change
    and innovation, 719
    organizational, 714–51
    and organizational development. *See*
      Organizational development (OD)
    and planning and managing, 742–45
    reactions to, 723–30
    sociotechnical, 723
    support for, 730–36
    and technology, 719–21
    technostructural, 723
    types of, 718–23
Channel, communication, 529, 530–33
Channel appropriateness, 533
Channel capacity, 532
Channel duplication, 532
Channel feedback, 532
Channel modifiability, 532
Channel speed, 532
Charisma, and leadership, 580–84
Charity, principle of, 98
Cheaper by the Dozen, 138
Choice, and MIS, 765–66
Choice making, 208
Circle communication network, 534
Civil Rights Act, 598
Classical approach, 328–29
Classical authority theory, 367–68
Classical decision-making model, 220
Classical organization theory, 138–42
Classical school, 133–43
Client departmentalization, 340
Climate, organizational, 76
Closed recruiting systems, 606
Closed systems, 56–58
CLOUT, 768
Cluster network, 536
Coalescing, 49
CODAP. *See* Comprehensive Occupational
    Data Analysis Program (CODAP)
Coercion, 734–36
Coercive power, 366, 523–24
Cognition, 483
Cognitive attributes, and decision making,
    221
Cognitive component, 452
Cohesion, 471–73
    and groups, 466
Collaborating conflict style, 541–42
Collective bargaining, 623–24
Command authority, 372
Command systems, multiple, 355, 356

Command, unity of, 140, 384
Commercial activities, 139
Commitment
    goal, 507
    organizational, 457–58
    social, 104–5
Commonwealth organizations, 43
Communication
    and change, 730–31
    components of, 529–30
    diagonal, 534
    horizontal, 534
    and internal environment, 70–72
    organizational, 527–38
    process, 528
    vertical, 533
Communication channels, 529, 530–33
Communication network, 533–36
Compact disk (CD), 715–16
Compensation, 89
    and benefits, 617–22
    cash, 617–20
Competence, 466
Competence anchors, 856–58
Competence test, 294
Competing conflict style, 541
Competitive advantages, 281, 782–86
Competitors, 40, 45
Complexity, 400
Compliance, 371–72
Comprehensive Occupational Data Analysis
    Program (CODAP), 602, 603
Compromise decision-making approach,
    217
Compulsory staff consultation, 375
Computational decision-making approach,
    216
Computer, and human resources, 630
Computer-aided design (CAD) systems, 82
Computer–aided manufacturing (CAM)
    systems, 82
Computer-based information, 771–72
Computer-integrated operations, 795–96
Conceptualization, of conflict, 540–41
Conceptual skills, 20
Concurrent control, 695–96
Concurring authority, 375
Configuration, 400
Conflict, 471
    and conceptualization, 540–41
    interpersonal, 538–44
    nature and causes, 539
    process, 539–43
    role, 469–70
    and strategy, 543–44
    styles, 541–42
Consequence, 497

Consideration, 565
Consistency, 296
Consultation, compulsory staff, 375
Consumption, and production, 79–80
Contact, direct, 353
Content theories, 485–95
Context, 460
    organizational, 401–2
Contingency approach, 216, 331–33
Contingency perspective, 151–53
Contingency plans, 188
Contingency theory of leadership, 571
Continuous process, 788–89
Continuous schedules of reinforcement,
    500–501
Contract, union, 599
Contracting, 49
Control, 661
    and assessment, 687–91
    and behavior, 681, 692
    budgeting, 683
    concurrent, 695–96
    cybernetic and noncybernetic, 691–93
    and ends and means, 684–86
    evading, 699
    financial, 683
    hybrid system, 696–97
    integrated model, 686–87
    and international management, 803–4
    locus of, 449–50
    management, 769
    marketing, 683
    methods and effects, 678–713
    need for, 680–81
    operational, 770
    operations, 682–83
    and organization members, 702–7
    and planning, 180–81
    postaction, 696
    pre-, 695
    and prescriptions, 690–91
    process, 679–86
    quality, 83–84
    quality assurance, 792
    screening, 695–96
    span of, 346–50
    steering, 695
    systems, 691–701
    total quality (TQC). *See* Total quality
      control (TQC)
    traditional model, 681–82
Controlling, 679
Controlling function, 10
Co-optation, 733–34
Co-opting, 49
Coordinating, and organizing work,
    322–63
Coordinating process, 69–70

Coordination, horizontal and vertical, 351, 352–55
Corporate board, and social responsibility, 114–16
Corporate culture, 71
Corporate strategy, 284
Corporations
　and goals, 188–96
　multinational (MNC), 815
　and social responsibility, 111–13
　and strategy, 283–84
Cost leadership, 304–5
Countertrade, 816–17
CPM. *See* Critical path method (CPM)
Craft approach, 327
Creative imitation, 843–44
Creative/self-actualizing model, 219–22
Creativity/entrepreneurship anchor, 857, 858
Credit, letter of. *See* Letter of credit (LC)
Crisis Management: Planning for the Inevitable, 187
Critical path method (CPM), 250–51
Cultural values, 229
Culture
　corporate, 71
　and design, 425–26
　and international environment, 800–802
　and organizations, 71, 73–76
Curves
　bell, 446
　learning, 448
Customer/client departmentalization, 340
Customers/markets, 40, 42
Custom solutions, 214–15
Cybernetic control, 691–93

Dalton and Thompson's career stages model, 860–71
Database, and MIS, 759
Davis-Bacon Act, 598
Decentralization
　authority, and delegation, 364–97
　and external environment, 388–89
　nature and importance, 384–88
　and organizations, 389
Decisional roles, 24–27
Decision making
　and *Challenger*, 207, 228, 233
　compromise, 217
　computational, 216
　defined, 207–9
　and groups, 222–30
　individual, 219–22
　inspirational, 217

and internal environment, 70
judgmental, 216–17
and management, 206–41
and MIS, 763–66
nature of, 207–12
process, 212–19
tools for, 242–77
See also Decisions
Decisions
　defined, 207
　levels, 210
　means vs. ends, 209
　programmed vs. nonprogrammed, 210
　routine and nonroutine, 766–68
　types of, 209–12
　See also Decision making
Decision-support system (DSS), 773–74
Decision trees, 260–62
Decline stage, of Super's model, 855
Decoding, 529
Defender organizations, 298, 301
Defense, perceptual, 462
Defense philosophies, 107–8
Delegation
　authority, and decentralization, 364–97
　classical principles of, 383–84
Delphi technique, 266–68
Delusion, 473
Demand reports, 773
Democrat, directive and permissive, 560
Departmentalization, 334–50
　customer/client, 340
　functional, 337–38
　and hybrid approach, 343–44
　and interdependence approach, 344–46
　process/equipment, 340–41
　product/service, 338–39
　project, 341–43
　territorial (geographical), 339–40
Dependability, 781
Design
　approaches, 413–23
　and culture, 425–26
　and development, 82–84
　and external environment, 424–25
　and goals, 428
　and MIS, 764–76
　organizational. *See* Organizational design
　and size, 428–30
　of strategy, 293–95
　and technology, 426–27
Designated leader, 557
Desire, 445
Detail, and sophistication, 775
Development
　career, 608–9, 610
　and design, 82–84
　group, 470–74

and internal staffing, 89
organizational (OD). *See* Organizational development (OD)
resource, 280–81
and training, 609–13
Diagonal communication, 534
Differential wage rate system, 484
Differentiation strategy, 305
Difficulty, goal, 507
Diffusion of responsibility, 227
Direct contact, 353
Direct exporting, 811
Directing, and multinational structures, 806
Direction, unity of, 140
Directional planning, 174, 176
Directive autocrat, 559
Directive democrat, 560
Directive leadership, 577, 578
Direct supervision, 351
Discipline, 140
Disconnected-line process, 788
DISCOVER card, 284, 295, 297
Disillusion, 473–74
Disseminator, 23, 24
Distribution
　bell curve, 446
　international physical, 822–23
　systems, 793
Distributive justice, 122, 504
Disturbance handler, 23, 26
Divestiture strategy, 304
Divisional-level plans, 186
Divisional superstructure, 404–7
Division of labor, 11, 140
Dogmatism, 450–51
Dogs, 303
Domain planning, 173–76
Domains, 34–38
Drive theory, 483
DSS. *See* Decision-support system (DSS)
Dual authority system, 409
Duplication, channel, 532

Economic approach, and motivation, 483–84
Economic domain, 35–36
Economic exposure, 824–25
Economic factors, and human resource management, 594–95
Economic order quantity (EOQ), 245
Economic person model, 219–22
Education
　and change, 730–31
　and MIS, 761
Effectiveness, organizational. *See* Organizational effectiveness
Election, representation, 623

Embargo, Arab oil, 657
EMC. *See* Export management company (EMC)
Emotional support, 732–33
Employee-centered behaviors, 567
Employee Retirement Income Security Act (ERISA), 598
Employees, nonmanagerial, 73
Enacted role, 469
Encoding, 529
Enculturation process, 801
Ends, 661
   and control, 684–86, 689–90
Ends decisions, 209
Ends goals, 649–51
   assessment, 687–88
Engineering problem, 297
Enterprises, global, 816
Entrepreneur, 23, 24, 26
Entrepreneurial judo, 844
Entrepreneurial problem, 296
Entrepreneurial style, 285
Entrepreneurship, and intrapreneurship, 832–49
Entrepreneurship anchor, 857, 858
Environments
   and control, 681
   external. *See* External environment
   general, 33, 34–38
   internal. *See* Internal environment
   international, 800–803
   and management theory, 56–58
   and organization, 50–58
   and organization power relationship, 45–50
   shifting and heterogeneous, 54
   shifting and homogeneous, 53–54
   stability and segmentation, 51–54
   stable and heterogeneous, 53
   stable and homogeneous, 52
   studies, 54–56
   task, 33, 38–45
   work, 89
Environmental change, 51
Environmental scans, 290–91
Environmental segmentation, 51–52
EOQ. *See* Economic order quantity (EOQ)
Equal Pay Act, 598
Equipment
   automation, 80
   departmentalization, 340–41
Equity, 140
Equity theory, 504, 505–6
ERG. *See* Existence, relatedness, and growth theory (ERG)
ERISA. *See* Employee Retirement Income Security Act (ERISA)
Esprit de corps, 140
Establishment stage, of Super's model, 855
Eternal law, 122

Ethics
   and behavior, 119–26
   and *Challenger*, 116
   management. *See* Management systems, 122
Ethnocentric staffing, 818
Evaluation
   and change, 745
   specificity of, 80–81
Exception reports, 773
Excursion stage, 264–66
Existence, relatedness, and growth theory (ERG), 486–87
Existing solutions, 214
Expectancy perceptions, 510
Expectancy theory, 509–12
Expected role, 469
Expert power, 366, 524
Exploratory stage, of Super's model, 855
Export, and management, 7
Exporting
   direct and indirect, 811
   and financing, 825–27
   and importing, 811–12
Export management company (EMC), 811
Exposure, transaction, economic, translation, 824–25
External environment
   and decentralization, 388–89
   defined, 33–45
   and design, 424–25
   and human resource management, 594–99
   and management, 32–63
   See also Environments *and* Internal environment
External forces, and change, 715–18
External locus of control, 449–50
External recruiting, 603–6
External staffing, 89
Extinction, 497
Extrinsic motivators, 501

Facilitation
   group, 470–74
   social, 226–27
Facilitative support, 732
Familiarization, 227
Fayol's gangplank principle, 353
Federal Unemployment Tax Act, 598
Feedback
   and change, 745
   channel, 532
   loop, 779
Fiedler's contingency model, 571

Figurehead, 23
Financial activities, 139
Financial control, 683
Financial management, 88
   international, 823–27
Financial protection, 598
Financing, 87
   and importing and exporting, 825–27
First-level managers, 15–16
Flexibility, 661, 781
Focus strategy, 306
Force, and change, internal and external, 715–18
Forced-fit stage, 264–66
Force scores, 509, 511–12
Forecasting, 251–58
Foreign exchange, 823–25
Formal communication networks, 533–36
Formal groups, 463
Formalization, 391, 399–400
Formal leader, 557
Formal organization, 325, 326
Fortune, 42, 119, 177, 218, 385
Fourth-generation language (4GL), 765
Frame test, 294
Franchises, 815
Free-rein leader, 558
Frequency-of-use plans, 182–84
Frustration, 487, 540
Functional areas, 16
Functional authority, 375–76
Functional competence anchor, 856–57
Functional departmentalization, 337–38
Functional groups, 463
Functional-level plans, 187
Functional strategy, 284
Functional structure, multinational, 805
Functional superstructure, 402–4
Future of American Business, 757

Gangplank principle, Fayol's, 353
Gantt chart, 138, 139
Gap
   analysis, 292–93
   authority, 383
General environment, 33, 34–38
Generic strategies, 304–6
Geocentric staffing, 818–19
Geographical departmentalization, 339–40
Global enterprises, 816
Goal, 169–70, 188–96
   and design, 428
   ends, 687–88
   and motivation, 506–9
   multiple, 190–94
   official, 188
   operational, 188

and organizational effectiveness, 649–51
    superordinate, 154
Goal acceptance, 507
Goal attainment approach, 649–51, 658
Goal commitment, 507
Goal consistency test, 294
Goal difficulty, 506
Goal hierarchy, 190–94
Goal planning, 173–76
Goal specificity, 506
Goal statements, 352
Goal theory, 506
Goal-wishing stage, 264–66
Gossip network, 536
Government, 43
Grading, and standardization, 87
Great person approach, 561
Grievance, 624
Group, and size, 466
Group norms, 465–66
Group polarization effect, 229
Groups
    and decision making, 222–30
    development and facilitation, 470–74
    formation and cohesion, 464–65
    hierarchy of, 421
    nature of, 463–70
    and NGT. *See* Nominal group technique
        (NGT)
    and organizations, 442–79
    regulatory and influence, 40, 42–45
    types of, 463–64
    work, 198, 333–34, 335
Group shift, 227–29
Groupthink, 229, 467, 468
Growth stage, of Super's model, 855
Growth strategy, 303
GURU, 768

Habits, bad, 845–46
Halo effect, 461
Hawthorne studies, 144–46
Hedonism, 482
Herzberg's motivation/hygiene theory,
    492–95
Heterogeneous task environment, 52
Hierarchical plans, 181
Hierarchy, 8
    and distinctions, 15–16
    goal, 190–94
    of groups, 421
    need theory, 147–48, 485–86
Hierarchy of needs, Maslow's, 147–48,
    485–86
Hold strategy, 304
Homogeneous task environment, 52
Horizontal communication, 534

Horizontal coordination, 352–55
Horizontal loading, 330
Horizontal specialization, 329
Hospitals, 42
Hours, 597–98
Human relations model, and organizational
    effectiveness, 663–64
Human relations movement, 146–47
Human resource management, 88–89,
    592–639
    international, 817–27
Human resources, 41–42
    and computers, 630
Human resource strategic matrix, 631
Human resource strategic planning,
    625–32
"Human Side of Enterprise," 148
Human skills, 20
Hybrid approach, 343–44
Hybrid control system, 696–97
Hybrid planning, 175, 176
Hybrid superstructure, 407–8
Hygiene needs, 492–93

Ideation, 529
IFPS. *See* Interactive financial planning
    system (IFPS)
Imitation, creative, 843–44
Impairment, social, 226–27
Impersonal mode, of integration, 69
Implementation, and change, 743–45
Implementation process, and strategic
    planning, 288–96
Import, and management, 7
Importing
    and exporting, 811–12
    and financing, 825–27
Incentives, 620, 733
Independence anchor, 857, 858–59
Indirect exporting, 811
Individual pay, 620
Individuals
    nature of, 443–58
    and organizations, 442–79
Industry, service, 784–85
Influence, managerial, 365–72
Influence groups, 40, 42–45
Informal groups, 463
Informal information, 770–71
Informal leader, 557
Informal organization, 325
Information, 42
    computer-based, 771–72
    informal, 770–71
    and managers, 762–70
    market, 86–87
    and MIS, 758–59

Informational roles, 24
Informational scans, 290–91
Information-reporting system, 772–73
Information systems, types of, 770–74
Initial work period, 853–54
Initiating structure, 565
Initiative, 140
Innate needs, 485–88
Innovation, and change, 719
Inputs, 504
In Search of Excellence, 74
Inspirational decision-making approach,
    217
Instincts, 482
Institutional zone, 13–14
Instrumentality perceptions, 510
Intangibility, 80
Integrated approach, and organizational
    effectiveness, 658–72
Integrated control model, 686–87
Integration
    and modes, 69–70
    of organizational functions, 89–90
Integrators, 354
INTELLECT, 768
Intensity, 460
Interactionist model, of ethics, 124
Interactive financial planning system
    (IFPS), 765
Interdependence, 46–50
    approach, and departmentalization,
        344–46
    pooled, 344
    reciprocal, sequential or serial, team,
        345
Interdependent contributor stage, 864–66
Interest groups, 45
Intermediate plans, 184–85
Intermittent schedules of reinforcement,
    500–501
Internal environment
    components of, 65–77
    defined, 65
    and management, 64–95
    and personal beliefs, 72–76
    See also External environment *and*
        Environments
Internal forces, and change, 715–18
Internal locus of control, 449–50
Internal processes model, and
    organizational effectiveness, 668–69
Internal processing approach, and
    organizational effectiveness, 654–56,
    658
Internal recruiting, 606
Internal staffing, 89
International domain, 38
International environment, 800–803
International financial management,
    823–27

Revenues, 251
Reward power, 366, 523
Rights, 121
Rigidity, workflow, 80
Risk, 210–12, 296
Risk persuaders, 228
Risky shifts, 227
Role ambiguity, 469
Role conflict, 469–70
Role overload, 470
Roles, 469–70
  boundary, 50–51
  linking, 355
  linking pin, 421
  managerial, 21–27
Routine decisions, 766–68
Routine technology, 68
Rules, 183

Safety, 598
Satisfaction, job, 453–56, 457
Satisfaction progression, 486
Satisfice, 216
SBU. *See* Strategic business unit (SBU)
Scalar chain, 140
Scalar principle, 383
Scans, informational, environmental, organizational, 290–92
Schedules of reinforcement, 500–501
Scheduling, 792
  and sequencing, 249–51
Schein's career anchors model, 856–60
Scientific management, 134–38
Scope, 280, 281
Scorekeeping, 87–88
Screening, 605
Screening controls, 695–96
Searching, 605
Security activities, 139
Security anchor, 857, 858
Segmentation, and environments, 51–54
Selection, 459–60, 606
Selection device, 606
Selective recruitment, 49
Self-actualization, 147–48
Self-actualizing model, 219–22
Self-designing organization, 423
Self-managed work group approach, 198, 333–34, 335
Sensation, 459
Separations, 597
Sequencing, and scheduling, 249–51
Sequential interdependence, 345
Serial interdependence, 345
Service departmentalization, 338–39
Service functions, 86–87
Service industries, 784–85

Shifts, group, 227–29
Shop, job, 788
Short-range plans, 184–85
Single-strand network, 536
Single-use plans, 183
Situational approaches, to leadership, 570–78
Situational view of authority, 369
Size
  and design, 428–30
  and groups, 466
Skills, 19–21, 154
Small organizations, 307
Smoothing, 48
Social approach, and motivation, 484
Social audit, 103
Social commitment, levels and types, 104–5
Social facilitation, 226–27
Social impairment, 226–27
Socialization, 117
Socialized power seeking, 491
Social responsibility
  for and against, 108–11
  and corporate board, 114–16
  and corporations, 111–13
  defined, 97
  economic, legal, ethical, discretionary, 106–7
  integration of, 105–8
  and legality, 113–16
  and managerial ethics, 96–131
  nature of, 97–108
  and organizational stakeholders, 100–103
  views of, 108–13
  and wine industry, 115
Social responsiveness, 105
Social Security Act, 598
Social values, and management, 99–103
Sociocultural domain, 34–35
Sociological perspective, 8–9
Sociotechnical change, 723
Sociotechnical system (STS), 77
  theory, 151, 418–19
Solutions, 214–15
SOP. *See* Standard operating procedure (SOP)
Sophistication, and detail, 775
Spanners, boundary, 50–51
Span of control, 346–50
Span of management, 346–50
Span of supervision, 346–50
Specialists, planning, 198–99
Specializations
  personal, 391, 399–400
  task, 399–400
  vertical and horizontal, 329

Specificity, goal, 507
Speed, and channels, 532
Spinoff, 103
Spokesperson, 23, 24
Sponsor stage, 868–70
Stability, and environments, 51–54
Stability of tenure, 140
Stable career pattern, 854
Stable growth strategy, 304
Stable work period, 853–54
Staff, 153
Staff authority, 372–75
Staffing, 89, 602–9
  ethnocentric, geocentric, polycentric, 818–19
Staff managers, 15
Stakeholders, 88
  and social responsibility, 100–103
Standardization, 351–52, 399–400
  and grading, 87
Standard operating procedure (SOP), 182
Standards, 681
Standing project participant pool, 342
Star communication network, 535
Stars, 302
Star Wars program, 341
Steering controls, 695
Stereotype, 461
Steward, 624
Stewardship, principle of, 98
Stimuli, 460, 497
Strategic advantage, 782–86
Strategic business unit (SBU), 302
Strategic constituencies approach, and organizational effectiveness, 656–58
Strategic-contingency model of power, 367
Strategic decisions, 210
Strategic Defense Initiative program, 341
Strategic management, 278–317
  advantages and disadvantages, 286–88
  concept of, 279–88
  perspectives on, 296–306
  styles, 285–86
Strategic matrix, human resource, 631
Strategic objectives, 280, 281
Strategic plan, 279, 281
Strategic planning, 279–84, 769
  human resource, 625–32
  and implementation process, 288–96
Strategic plans, 181
Strategy, 153
  approaches, 298
  business unit, 284
  and conflict, 543–44
  corporate, 284
  designing, 293–95
  differentiation, 305
  divestiture, 304

entrepreneurial and intrapreneurial, 842–46
focus, 306
functional, 284
generic, 304–6
growth, 303
hold, 304
levels of, 283–84
operational, 280, 281
retrenchment, 304, 306
stable growth, 304
turnaround, 304, 306
Strategy-making roles, 24–27
Stratification, 400
Strike, 624
Structures, 153
  initiating, 565
  and internal environment, 65–68
  multinational geographic, 804–5
  organizational, 66–68
  and organizational design, 399–400
  pay, 618–20
STS. *See* Sociotechnical system (STS)
Style, 154
Subordination, of individual interest, 140
Subsidiary, 815–16
Substitutes, for leadership, 579–80
Success, and groups, 466
Superordinate goals, 154
Super's model, 854–56
Superstructures
  divisional, 404–7
  functional, 402–4
  hybrid, 407–8
  matrix, 408–13
  organizational, 402–13
  traditional, 402–8
Supervision
  direct, 351
  span of, 346–50
Suppliers, 40, 41–42
Supportive leadership, 577–78
Synectic technique, 264–66
Synergy, 281–82
System 4 leadership, 567–68
Systems, 153
  closed, 56–58
  control, 691–701
  defined, 151
  distribution, 793
  dual authority, 409
  and MIS, 759–61
  multiple command, 355, 356
  open, 57, 58
  organic and mechanistic, 55
  types of, 770–74
Systems approach, and organizational effectiveness, 651–54, 658
Systems perspective, 151
Systems theory, defined, 151

Tactical decisions, 210
Tactical plans, 187
Tannenbaum and Schmidt leadership continuum, 557–59
Task environment, 33, 38–45
Task force, 353
Task groups, 463
Task specialization, 399–400
Task team, 354
Team interdependence, 345
Technical activities, 139
Technical core, 14
Technical/functional competence anchor, 856–57
Technical skills, 20
Technological domain, 36
Technology
  and change, 719–21
  and design, 426–27
  and internal environment, 68
  routine and nonroutine, 68
Technostructural changes, 723
Tenure, stability of, 140
Terminations, 597
Territorial departmentalization, 339–40
Testing, reality, 462
Tests, 608
Theory A, 157
Theory J, 157
Theory of justice, 122
Theory X, 148–49, 562–63
Theory Y, 148–49, 562–63
Theory Z, 154–56
Think tanks, 68
Time
  and allocations, 185
  and managers, 23–27
Time-frame plans, 184–86
Time perspectives, 17–19
Time series analysis, 255–56
Tolerance for ambiguity, 222
Tools
  for planning and decision making, 242–77
  qualitative, 243
  quantitative, 243–59
Top leader, 412
Total quality control (TQC), 84, 794–95
TPS. *See* Transaction-processing system (TPS)
TQC. *See* Total quality control (TQC)
Trade, counter-, 816–17
Training, 447
  and development, 609–13
  vestibule, 613
Trait approach, and leadership, 561–64
Transactional leadership, 556
Transaction exposure, 824–25
Transaction-processing system (TPS), 772
Transformational leadership, 583–84

Transformation process, 779–82
Translation, 459, 461–62
Translation exposure, 824–25
Transmitted role, 469
Transportation, 86
Trees, decision, 260–62
Trial work period, 853–54
Trusteeship management, 99, 101
Turnaround strategy, 304, 306
Two-boss manager, 413
Tylenol, 844
Type A personality, 451–52
Type B personality, 451–52

Uncertainty, 46–50, 210–12
Undermatching, 447
Unfreezing component, 745
Union contract, 599
Unions, 43, 44
  formation, 622–23
  labor, 599
Unit/functional-level plans, 187
Unity of command, 140, 384
Unity of direction, 140
Universalist theory, 122
Unstable career pattern, 854
Utilitarian theories, 121
Utilities, 85
  place, 86

Valence, 510
Values
  cultural, 229
  managerial, 101
  and organizational effectiveness, 658–63
Ventures, joint, 812–13
Vertical communication, 533
Vertical coordination, 351
Vertical loading, 330
Vertical specialization, 329
Vestibule training, 613
Vroom-Yetton decision tree, 260–62

Wages, 598
Wage surveys, 617
Wall Street Journal, 42, 120, 291, 338
Walsh-Healy Act, 598
WCM. *See* World-class manufacturing (WCM)
Wealth of Nations, 328
What a Way to Go, 833
Wheel communication network, 535
Whistleblowing, 119
Wholly owned subsidiary, 815–16
Wine industry, and social responsibility, 115

Literary Credits

Chapter 3

page 74 Excerpt from *A Business and Its Beliefs: The Ideas That Helped Build IBM* by Thomas J. Watson, Jr. Copyright © 1963 by Trustees of Columbia University in the City of New York. Reprinted by permission of McGraw-Hill Book Company, Inc.

page 80 From *Organization Theory and Design* 2nd. ed. by Richard L. Daft. Copyright © 1983, 1986 by West Publishing Company. All rights reserved. Reprinted by permission.

page 85 From *Marketing Management: Concepts, Practice and Cases* by Robert W. Haas and Thomas R. Wotruba. Copyright © 1983 by Business Publications, Inc. Reprinted by permission of Richard D. Irwin, Inc.

Chapter 4

page 101 From "Social Responsibilities of Business Managers" by Robert Hay and Ed Gray, *Academy of Management Review*, 1974. Copyright © 1974 by The Academy of Management. Reprinted by permission.

page 106 From "A Three-Dimensional Conceptual Model of Corporate Performance" by Archie B. Carroll, *Academy of Management Review*, 1979. Copyright © 1979 by the Academy of Management. Reprinted by permission.

pages 107, 112, 113 From "Perceptions of Socially Responsible Activities & Attitudes" by Robert Ford and Frank McLaughlin, *Academy of Management Journal*, September 1984. Copyright © 1984 the Academy

of Management. Reprinted by permission.

page 123 From "A Janus-Headed Model of Ethical Theory: Looking Two Ways at Business/Society Issues" by F. Neil Brady, *Academy of Management Review*, 1985. Copyright © 1985 the Academy of Management. Reprinted by permission.

page 124 From "Ethical Decision Making in Organizations: A Person Situation" by Linda Klebe Trevino, *Academy of Management Review*, 1986. Copyright © 1986 by the Academy of Management. Reprinted by permission.

Chapter 5

page 139 From *Operations Management: Theory and Problems* by Joseph G. Monks. Copyright © 1977 by McGraw-Hill, Inc. Reprinted by permission.

page 154 From *In Search of Excellence* by Thomas J. Peters and Robert H. Waterman, Jr. Copyright © 1982 by Thomas J. Peters and Robert H. Waterman, Jr. Reprinted by permission of Harper & Row, Publishers, Inc.

page 155 Adapted from *Theory Z* by William G. Ouchi. Copyright © 1981 Addison-Wesley Publishing Co., Inc., Reading, Massachusetts. Reprinted with permission.

Chapter 6

page 186 From *Top Management Planning* by George A. Steiner. Copyright © 1969 by The Trustees of Columbia University

in the City of New York. Reprinted with permission of The Free Press, a Division of Macmillan, Inc.

page 190 From *Organizational Effectiveness: A Behavioral View* by Richard M. Steers. Copyright © 1977 Scott, Foresman and Company.

page 193 From *Organizational Goal Structures* by Max D. Richards. Copyright © 1978 by West Publishing Company. All rights reserved. Reprinted by permission.

Chapter 7

page 209 From *Managerial Decision Making* by George P. Huber. Copyright © 1980 Scott, Foresman and Company.

Chapter 8

page 261 Adapted from *Leadership and Decision-Making* by Victor H. Vroom and Philip W. Yetton by permission of the University of Pittsburgh Press. Copyright © 1973 by University of Pittsburgh Press.

Chapter 11

page 388 From *Organization Theory: The Structure & Design of Organizations* by Stephen P. Robbins, pp. 39, 88. Copyright © 1983 by Prentice-Hall, Inc. Reprinted by permission of Prentice-Hall, Inc., Englewood Cliffs, New Jersey.

Chapter 13

page 456 From *JSAS Catalog of Selected Documents in Psychology*, 1976. Reprinted by permission of Frank J. Smith.

Chapter 14

page 509 Adapted from "The Determinants of Goal Commitment" by Edwin A. Locke, Gary P. Latham, and Miriam Erez, *Academy of Management Review*, 1988. Copyright © 1988 by the Academy of Management. Reprinted by permission.

Chapter 15

page 545 Adapted from "Toward Multi-Dimensional Values in Teaching: The Example of Conflict Behaviors" by Kenneth W. Thomas, *Academy of Management Review*, 1977. Copyright © 1977 by the Academy of Management. Reprinted by permission.

Chapter 16

page 558 Reprinted by permission of the *Harvard Business Review*. An exhibit from "How to Choose a Leadership Pattern" by Robert Tannenbaum and Warren H. Schmidt (May/June 1973). Copyright © 1973 by the President and Fellows of Harvard College; all rights reserved.

page 560 From "The Case for Directive Leadership" by Jan Muczyk and Bernard Reimann, "Executive" vol. 1, no. 4, November 1987. Copyright © 1987 the Academy of Management. Reprinted by permission.

page 563 Excerpts from *The Human Side of Enterprise* by Douglas McGregor. Copyright © 1960 by the McGraw-Hill Book

Company, Inc. Reprinted by permission.

page 570 The Managerial Grid® figure from *The Managerial Grid III: The Key to Leadership Excellence* by Robert R. Blake and Jane Srygley Mouton. Houston: Gulf Publishing Company, Copyright © 1985, page 12. Reproduced by permission.

page 572 From *A Theory of Leadership Effectiveness* by F. E. Fiedler, 1967. Reprinted by permission of the author.

page 574 From Fiedler, F. E., "The Effects of Leadership Training and Experience: A Contingency Model Interpretation," *Administrative Science Quarterly* 17 (1972b): 453–75 and "The Situational Favorableness Dimension" from *Leadership and Effective Management* by Fred E. Fiedler and Martin M. Chemers. Copyright © 1974 by Scott, Foresman and Company.

Chapter 17

page 615 From "Managing Two Fits of Strategic Human Resource Management" by Lloyd Baird and Ilan Meshoulam, *Academy of Management Review*, 1987. Copyright © 1987 the Academy of Management. Reprinted by permission.

page 616 From "The Development and Evaluation of Behaviorally Based Rating Scales" by John P. Campbell et al. from *Journal of Applied Psychology*, February 1973. Copyright © 1973 by the American Psychological Association, Inc. Reprinted by permission of the author.

Chapter 18

page 647 Adapted from John P. Campbell, "On the Nature of Organizational Effectiveness," in P. S. Goodman, J. M. Pennings and Associates, ed. *New Perspectives on Organizational Effectiveness* (San Francisco: Jossey-Bass, 1977). Reprinted by permission.

page 664 From *Organization Theory: The Structure & Design of Organizations* by Stephen P. Robbins, pp. 39, 88. Copyright © 1983 by Prentice-Hall, Inc. Reprinted by permission of Prentice-Hall, Inc., Englewood Cliffs, New Jersey.

pages 662, 663 From "Organizational Life Cycles and Shifting Criteria of Effectiveness: Some Preliminary Evidence," by Robert E. Quinn and Kim S. Cameron, *Management Science*, January; and "A Spatial Model of Effectiveness Criteria: Towards a Competing Values Approach to Organizational Analysis" by Robert E. Quinn and John Rohrbaugh, *Management Science*, March. Reprinted by permission of Robert E. Quinn.

Chapter 19

page 712 "The Two Edges of Control" adapted by permission from *Case Problems in Management* 3rd. ed. by Schuler and Dalton. Copyright © 1986 by West Publishing Company. All rights reserved.

Chapter 20

page 721 From *Organizational Behavior: People and Processes in Management* by Randall B. Dunham. Copyright © 1984 by Richard D. Irwin, Inc. Reprinted by permission of Richard D. Irwin, Inc.

Chapter 21

page 760 Adapted from Niv Ahituv and Seev Neumann, *Principles of Information Systems for Management* 2nd. Copyright © 1986 Wm. C. Brown Publishers, Dubuque, Iowa. All Rights Reserved. Reprinted by permission.

Chapter 22

page 787 Adapted from "Link manufacturing process and product life cycles" by W. Hayes and S. Wheelwright,

Harvard Business Review, January-February 1979, p. 137. Copyright © 1979 by the President and Fellows of Harvard College; all rights reserved. Reprinted by permission.

Chapter 25

page 854 From *Managing Careers in Organizations* by Daniel C. Feldman. Copyright © 1988 by Scott, Foresman and Company.

pages 861, 862, 863, 865, 869, 870 From *Novations: Strategies for Career Management* by Gene W. Dalton and Paul H. Thompson. Copyright © 1986 by Gene W. Dalton and Paul H. Thompson. Published by Scott, Foresman and Company.

Interviews of corporate officials contained in this text represent the ideas and beliefs of the persons interviewed and not necessarily those of the corporation.

The following cases were presented at workshops conducted by the Midwest Society for Case Research (MSCR). The authors acknowledge the assistance of the MSCR in the development of these cases: Hammond General Hospital, Frank Pearson and the Allied Research Corporation, AgBanCorporation, Harvey Industries, Xerox Corporation, Growing Pains, The Open Door, The River City Library.

Photo Credits

All photos not credited are the property of Scott, Foresman and Company. Position of photographs is shown in abbreviated form as follows: top (t), bottom (b), center (c), left (l), right (r).

Artwork by Candace Haught, Becky Cutler, and PC&F Incorporated